Logarithmic Functions

Rule 9.   If $y = \log_a u$, where $u = f(x)$,

$$\frac{dy}{dx} = \frac{\log_a e}{u} \frac{du}{dx}$$

Special Case: If $a = e$, then $y = \ln u$ and $\frac{dy}{dx} = \frac{1}{u} \frac{du}{dx}$.

Exponential Functions

Rule 10.   If $y = a^u$, where $u = f(x)$,

$$\frac{dy}{dx} = a^u \ln a \frac{du}{dx}$$

Special Case: If $a = e$, then $y = e^u$ and $\frac{dy}{dx} = e^u \frac{du}{dx}$.

Rule 11.   If $y = u^v$, where $u = f(x)$ and $v = g(x)$,

$$\frac{dy}{dx} = vu^{v-1} \frac{du}{dx} + u^v \ln u \frac{dv}{dx}$$

Note that Rule 10 is a special case of Rule 11.

Trigonometric Functions

Rule 12.   If $y = \sin u$, where $u = f(x)$,

$$\frac{dy}{dx} = \cos u \frac{du}{dx}$$

Rule 13.   If $y = \cos u$, where $u = f(x)$,

$$\frac{dy}{dx} = -\sin u \frac{du}{dx}$$

Rule 14.   If $y = \tan u$, where $u = f(x)$,

$$\frac{dy}{dx} = \sec^2 u \frac{du}{dx}$$

Inverse Functions

Rule 15.   If $y = f(x)$ and $x = g(y)$ are inverse functions,

$$\frac{dy}{dx} = \frac{1}{\dfrac{dx}{dy}}$$

MATHEMATICAL
ANALYSIS

MATHEMATICAL ANALYSIS
Business and Economic Applications
FOURTH EDITION

JEAN E. WEBER

University of Arizona

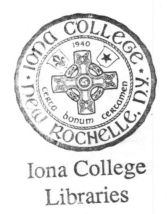

Iona College
Libraries

HARPER & ROW, PUBLISHERS, New York
Cambridge, Philadelphia, San Francisco,
London, Mexico City, São Paulo, Sydney

1817

Sponsoring Editor: Bonnie K. Binkert and Arthur P. Sotak
Project Editor: Eleanor Castellano
Production Manager: Willie Lane
Compositor: Santype International Limited
Printer and Binder: Halliday Lithograph Corporation
Art Studio: J & R Art Services, Inc. and Vantage Art, Inc.
Cover Design: Stanley Brill

MATHEMATIC ANALYSIS: Business and Economic Applications, Fourth Edition

Copyright © 1982 by Harper & Row, Publishers, Inc.

Library of Congress Cataloging in Publication Data

Weber, Jean E.
  Mathematical analysis.

  Bibliography: p.
  Includes index.
  1. Business mathematics.   2.   Mathematical analysis.
3.   Economics, Mathematical.   I.   Title.

HF5691.W38   1982   510'.2433   81-7006
ISBN 0-06-046977-3   AACR2

HARPER INTERNATIONAL EDITION
35-07464

Contents

Preface

First published in 1967, this text has been used by a broad range of students and faculty members. Their comments and recommendations over the past 14 years have strengthened each subsequent edition in terms of its coverage, presentation, and useful applications.

The book's thrust and greatest strength, as pointed out by its users, is its focus on applications in business and economics. This orientation has been maintained in the fourth edition in order to continue to provide a sense of purpose to students studying mathematical analysis. Like the previous editions, the fourth edition's objective is to offer students an understanding of quantitative techniques both in their mathematical contexts and as they are applied to business and economics.

Substantial practice in problem solving is essential to the study of mathematical analysis. Therefore, more than 1500 problems are provided. In addition, business and economics students will discover an abundance of applications to finance, accounting, banking, sales management, transportation, production, and numerous other functional areas. A list of key formulas is presented on the text's inside cover.

Although the general outline of previous editions has been retained, a number of sections have been added and others have been rearranged. Additional mathematical steps and verbal explanation have been included in many of the examples.

Several substantial additions have been incorporated in the revision. The calculus material has been rewritten in order to increase the material's applications. There are new sections concerning characteristic roots and vectors and the geometric derivation of indifference curves and their applications in risk and rate of return. The dual of the linear programming problem is discussed in the context of imputed values, sensitivity analysis, and applications in resource allocation. Additional material concerning implicit and inverse functions is included. Discussions of present value and the accuracy of approximations using Taylor's expansion, Simpson's rule, and the trapezoidal rule have been added. Examples of linear regression analysis have been included.

The order of presentation of rules of differentiation has been changed in an effort to make the composite function rule more easily understood. Two appendixes, following Chapter 1, have been added. One is an algebra review and consists of entirely new material; the other is a trigonometry review and consists primarily of material that was formerly included in the text. Many new problems have also been added. A revised solutions manual, including complete solutions to all problems, is available to instructors.

Many of the changes and additions were suggested by survey respondents, adopters, and reviewers. Therefore, thanks must go to the following individuals: David Ashley, University of Missouri at Kansas City; K. Boyer, Michigan State University; Patrick L. Brockett, University of Texas at Austin; Rochid Elias, University of Maine; S. Gupta, Northeastern University; Martha Hollis, University of California at Irvine; Joseph P. Hughes, Rutgers College; Gerald M. Lage, Oklahoma State University; Norman D. Lane, McMaster University; Robert Moreland, Texas Tech; James G. Morris, University of Wisconsin at Madison; Alfred N. Page, University of Washington; Michael J. Panik, University of Hartford; Gary Reeves, University of South Carolina.

The publisher and author have made every effort to avoid errors in the text and solutions manual. The author accepts responsibility for any errors in the text and solutions manual.

JEAN E. WEBER

Mathematical
Analysis

Introduction

From the beginning of recorded history, cultural and scientific advances have depended on the use of symbols. The history of civilization can be viewed as the history of man's increasingly sophisticated use of symbols. As thinking in any area develops, the symbols used become more abstract.

When the concepts to which symbols refer are essentially nonquantitative in nature, the symbols and their relationships can be studied in the general framework of logic and there is no need for mathematics as such. It is when symbols represent essentially quantitative concepts that mathematics is useful and, in fact, essential for analyzing their relationships. Mathematics is a branch of logic, the branch of logic that provides a systematic framework within which quantitative relationships can be studied. In pure mathematics definitions or axioms and assumptions are precisely stated symbolically, and the analysis proceeds by deduction to obtain conclusions. Applied mathematics differs from pure mathematics in a very important respect—in pure mathematics symbols represent abstract concepts whose properties are assigned by definition, while in applied mathematics many symbols represent variables observed in the real world; the properties of these variables must be determined by observation, not by abstract definition, and then stated mathematically. In addition, the empirical accuracy of the deductions of applied mathematics can be determined. Applied mathematical analysis thus is based on empirically determined definitions and assumptions from which empirically verifiable conclusions are obtained by deduction. Pure and applied mathematical analysis differ only with respect to the empirical aspect of the definitions, assumptions, and conclusions, not with respect to the methods of deduction.

Because economics is concerned with concepts that are essentially quantitative in nature—for example, price, cost, wage rates, investment, income, and profit—much of economic analysis is inescapably mathematical in nature. Mathematics provides a logical, systematic framework within which quantitative relations can be studied. When economic variables are represented by symbols and their properties stated mathematically, mathematics provides the techniques for analyzing relations among the symbols and thus among the variables they represent. Much of economic analysis is therefore applied mathematical analysis.

In economic analysis, as in applied mathematics in general, deductions obtained by mathematical analysis are interpreted and evaluated empirically. It should be noted in this regard that if the deductions following from a set of definitions and assumptions are not correct with respect to empirical observation, mathematical analysis (if correctly performed) is not responsible and the difficulty is to be found in the definitions or assumptions. Mathematics enables the economist to be precise in defining relevant variables, to state clearly the assumptions made, to be logical in developing the analysis, and to consider a larger number of variables than might be feasible verbally. However, it does not and cannot prevent the omission or the empirically incorrect definition of relevant variables nor can it prevent empirically inaccurate or incomplete statements of assumptions. Mathematical analysis takes definitions and assumptions as given and obtains the conclusions that follow logically from them. Mathematical analysis is thus by nature logical, not empirical, and can be held responsible for conclusions only with respect to their logical validity given the definitions and assumptions on which they are based and not with respect to their empirical accuracy.

Thus if mathematical analysis is correctly performed, but its conclusions are empirically incorrect, the definitions and assumptions must be examined for accuracy and completeness. By providing a systematic framework for the deduction of empirically verifiable conclusions, mathematical analysis helps the economist determine the accuracy of his definitions and assumptions—if the conclusions are untenable, the definitions and assumptions must be examined and revised.

The purpose of this book is to help the student understand, appreciate, and perform applied mathematical analysis. Mathematical proofs are minimized except when they can be made heuristic. The book is organized so that a type of analysis is discussed first with respect to its mathematical (logical) procedure and then with respect to its applications in economics and business. The assumptions required for each type of analysis are emphasized and its applications are discussed in terms of these assumptions.

The subsequent sections of this chapter review some of the basic mathematical concepts and definitions used in later chapters.

Sets

A *set* is a collection of distinguishable well-defined objects or entities. The objects or entities belonging to a set are said to be *elements* of the set. A set is determined either by a list of its elements or by specifying a rule that determines whether a given object or entity belongs to the set. Such a rule is referred to as a *defining relation*. Braces are used to denote a set; either the elements of the set or its defining relation is written inside the braces.

EXAMPLE

$A = \{a, b, c\}$ means that the set A consists of the elements a, b, and c, which are the first three letters in the English alphabet.

$B = \{x : x$ is an odd integer$\}$ means that the set B consists of the odd integers.

$C = \{1, 2, 3, 4, 5, 6\}$ means that the set C consists of the numbers 1, 2, 3, 4, 5, and 6.

$D = \{y : y$ is an integer$\}$ means that the set D consists of the integers.

The notation $x \in S$ means that the entity or object x is an element of the set S. The notation $x \notin S$ means that x is not an element of the set S.

A defining relation that is satisfied by no element is said to define the *empty set*, denoted by $\varnothing$.

EXAMPLE

Referring to the preceding example,

$a \in A$
$b \notin B$
$4 \notin B$
$4 \in C$
$4 \in D$
$7 \notin C$
$7 \in B$
$7 \in D$
$d \notin A$
$d \notin D$

EXAMPLE

$S = \{x : x$ is an odd number ending in 2$\} = \varnothing$
$P = \{y : y$ is an odd number that is the square of an even number$\} = \varnothing$.

If every element of a set S is also an element of a set T, then S is said to be a *subset* of T. If there is at least one element in T that is not also in S, then S is a *proper subset* of T. The notation $S \subset T$ means that S is a subset of T; the notation $S \not\subset T$ means that S is not a subset of T. Note that the empty set is a subset of every set. If $S \subset T$ and $T \subset S$, then every element in S is also in T and vice versa and S and T are the same set. This is denoted by $S = T$.

EXAMPLE

Referring to the preceding examples,

$A \not\subset B$
$B \subset D$
$B \not\subset C$
$C \subset D$

The *union* of two sets S and T is the set consisting of the elements of S and the elements of T. The union of S and T, denoted by $S \cup T$, is described by

$$S \cup T = \{x : x \in S \text{ and/or } x \in T\}$$

The *intersection* of two sets S and T is the set consisting of the elements that are common to S and T. The intersection of S and T is denoted by $S \cap T$ and is described by

$$S \cap T = \{x : x \in S \text{ and } x \in T\}$$

The *set difference* of two sets S and T is the set consisting of the elements of S that are not elements of T. The set difference of S and T is denoted by $S - T$ and is described by

$$S - T = \{x : x \in S \text{ and } x \notin T\}$$

A *universal set* or *universe* is a specified set that contains all the elements of interest for a particular discussion. If two sets have the property that their union is the universal set and their intersection is the null set, one set is said to be the *complement* of the other with respect to the universe. If U denotes the universal set, the complement of a given set S is denoted by S' and is described by

$$S' = U - S$$

A statement of complementation must be qualified unless the universal set is clearly understood. For example, if the complement of S is taken with respect to U and also with respect to V, the notation S'_U and S'_V is used.

EXAMPLE

Referring to the preceding example,

$B \cup D = D$
$A \cup C = \{a, b, c, 1, 2, 3, 4, 5, 6\}$
$A \cap D = \varnothing$
$B \cap D = B$
$B \cap C = \{1, 3, 5\}$
$C \cap D = C$
$C - D = \varnothing$
$C - B = \{2, 4, 6\}$
$D - A = D$
$D - B = \{x : x \text{ is an even integer}\}$

If $U = \{x : x \text{ is an integer}\}$, then

$B'_U = \{x : x \text{ is an even integer}\}$
$D'_U = \varnothing$

If $V = \{1, 2, 3, 4, 5, 6, 7, 8, 9, 10\}$, then

$C'_V = \{7, 8, 9, 10\}$

If $W = \{x : x \text{ is a lowercase letter in the English alphabet}\}$, then

$A'_W = \{d, e, f, g, h, i, j, k, l, m, n, o, p, q, r, s, t, u, v, w, x, y, z\}$

Sets formed by unions, intersections, and complements can be shown diagrammatically; in each of the following diagrams, the shaded area is the set indicated below the diagram. This type of representation of sets is called a *Venn diagram*.

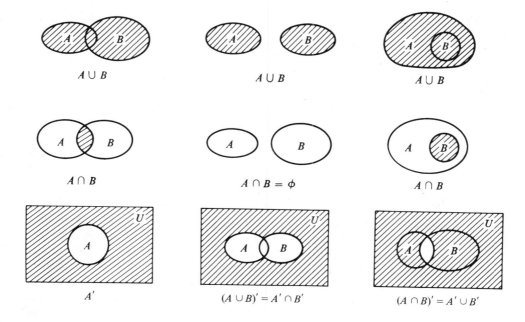

$A \cup B$ $A \cup B$ $A \cup B$

$A \cap B$ $A \cap B = \phi$ $A \cap B$

A' $(A \cup B)' = A' \cap B'$ $(A \cap B)' = A' \cup B'$

PROBLEMS

1. If A, B, and C are sets such that $A \subset B \subset C$, what is the relationship between $C - B$ and $C - A$?
2. Show that, in general, $(A \cap B)' = A' \cup B'$.
3. Show that, in general, $A \cap (B \cup C) = (A \cap B) \cup (A \cap C)$.
4. Show that $(S \cap T') \cup (S \cap T) = S \cap (S \cup T) = S \cup (S \cap T) = S$.
5. Show that $K \cup (L \cap M) = (K \cup L) \cap (K \cup M)$.
6. If $A \cap B = \varnothing$ and $A \cap C = \varnothing$, is it necessarily true that $B \cap C = \varnothing$?
7. If $A \neq B$ and $B \neq C$, is it necessarily true that $A \neq C$?
8. If $A \not\subset B$ and $B \not\subset C$, is it necessarily true that $A \not\subset C$?
9. If $A \subset C$ and $B \subset D$, is it necessarily true that $A \cup B \subset C \cup D$?
10. If $A \subset C$ and $B \subset D$, is it necessarily true that $A \cap B \subset C \cap D$?
11. If $S \cup T = \{1, 2, 3, 4\}$, $S \cap T = \{1, 3\}$, and $S - T = \{2\}$, find S and T.
12. If $A \cap B \neq \varnothing$, $A \cap C \neq \varnothing$, and $B \cap C \neq \varnothing$, is it necessarily true that $A \cap B \cap C \neq \varnothing$?
13. If U is a universal set, determine which of the following statements are incorrect and correct them by changing the right-hand side of the equation.
   a. $B \cup \varnothing = B$ h. $C \cup C = C$
   b. $C \cap U = C$ i. $(D')' = U$
   c. $A \cup A' = U$ j. $(A - C) \cup C = A - C$
   d. $B \cup U = U$ k. $B \cap (B - D) = B \cup D$
   e. $D \cap \varnothing = \varnothing$ l. If $A = B'$, then $B = A'$
   f. $A \cap A' = A$ m. $(C - D)' = C' - D'$
   g. $B \cap B = \varnothing$ n. $(A \cup D) - D = A - D$
14. If $A = \{e, f, g\}$ and $B = \{e, h\}$, find
   a. $A - B$ c. $A \cap B$
   b. $B - A$ d. $A \cup B$
15. If $R = \{w, x, y\}$, $S = \{u, v, w\}$, and $T = \{u, v, w, x\}$, and the universal set is $U = \{u, v, w, x, y, z\}$, find
   a. $R' \cap T' \cap S'$ e. $(S \cup T) - T'$
   b. $(R - S) \cap T$ f. $(R - T) - (S - R)$
   c. $(R' - T') \cup S$ g. $(S - R) - [(T - R) \cup (T - S)]$
   d. $(R' \cup S')'$ h. $(T - R) \cup S$
16. If $A \cap B = \varnothing$ and $A' = C$, is it necessarily true that $B \subset C$?

Answers to Odd-Numbered Problems

1. $C - B \subset C - A$
7. No
9. Yes
11. $S = \{1, 2, 3\}$
    $T = \{1, 3, 4\}$
13. f. $A \cap A' = \varnothing$ j. $(A - C) \cup C = A \cup C$
    g. $B \cap B = B$ k. $B \cap (B - D) = B - D$
    i. $(D')' = D$ m. $(C - D)' = C' \cup D$
15. a. $\{z\}$ c. S e. T g. $\varnothing$
    b. $\{x\}$ d. $\{w\}$ f. $\{y\}$ h. S

Variables

In mathematics there are two types of quantities, constants and variables. A *constant* is a quantity whose value remains unchanged throughout a particular problem. An *absolute* or *numerical constant* has the same value in all problems; an *arbitrary* or *parametric constant* (or a *parameter*) has the same value throughout any particular problem but may assume different values in different problems. The *absolute* or *numerical value* of a constant a is denoted by $|a|$ and means the magnitude of a regardless of its algebraic sign. Thus, $|a| = a$ if $a > 0$, $|a| = -a$ if $a < 0$, and $|a| = 0$ if $a = 0$.

A *variable* is a quantity that assumes various values in a particular problem; the set of values which a variable assumes is its *range*. A variable may be either continuous or discrete. A *continuous variable* is one that may assume any value within a specified interval of real numbers (possibly all real numbers); successive values of a continuous variable thus may differ by infinitesimal amounts. A *discrete variable* is one that may assume only values specified in a countable range. Note that the number of points or values in any specified real interval, say between 5 and 10, is uncountable and no rule can be given for obtaining all possible such values. However, the number of integers or integer values in any specified interval is countable and is finite unless the interval is $(-\infty, b)$, (a, ∞), or $(-\infty, \infty)$. The number of points on the real line (or on any part of the real line) is said to be a noncountable or nondenumerable infinity. The number of integers on the real line is a countable or denumerable infinity and any set obtained from the integers by a specified rule is also countable or denumerable.

Thus in any problem there may be

1. Absolute constants that always have the same value; such quantities are either numbers or symbols denoting numbers.
2. Parametric constants that have the same value throughout any given problem but may have different values for different problems; such quantities depend on the particular situation represented in the problem.
3. Variables that assume all values meaningful for the problem; such quantities may vary discretely or continuously and may be restricted, for example, to positive values.

EXAMPLE

In the equation of a straight line,

$$\frac{x}{a} + \frac{y}{b} = 1$$

1 is a numerical constant, a and b are parameters, and x and y are variables.

EXAMPLE

In the equation for the area of a circle,

$A = \pi r^2$

π is a numerical constant (approximately equal to 3.1416) and A and r are variables.

EXAMPLE

In the equation for revenue as a function of quantity,

$R = 10x$

10 is a numerical constant, and R and x are variables.

EXAMPLE

In the equation for total cost as a function of fixed and variable costs and quantity,

$c = \alpha + \beta x$

α and β are parameters, and c and x are variables.

In pure mathematics, usually the letters at the beginning of the alphabet are used to represent parameters and the letters at the end of the alphabet are used to represent variables. However, in applied mathematics there are many exceptions to this convention, and a variable is frequently represented by the first letter of its name—for example, p for price, q for quantity, c for cost, s for savings, and so forth.

The only values of either constants or variables considered subsequently are *real numbers*. The set of all real numbers consists of rational numbers and irrational numbers. A *rational number* is any number that can be expressed as a/b where a and b are integers and $b \neq 0$; for example, $\frac{1}{2}, \frac{3}{4}, -\frac{5}{6}, 0.8$, and -0.01 are rational numbers. An *irrational number* cannot be expressed as a fraction; for example $\sqrt{2}, \pi, e, \sqrt[3]{5}$, and $\sqrt[4]{8}$ are irrational numbers. Every real number is either negative, zero, or positive. The set of all real numbers is denoted by $\mathcal{R}$. Numbers that are not real are either imaginary or complex. An even root of a negative number is an *imaginary number*; for example, $\sqrt{-2}, \sqrt{-4}$, and $\sqrt[4]{-10}$ are imaginary numbers. A number that has both a real and an imaginary part is a *complex number*; for example, $5 + \sqrt{-2}$, $-8 - \sqrt{-4}$, and $9 - \sqrt[4]{-10}$ are complex numbers.

EXAMPLE

The equation $x^2 + 6 = 0$ has no real solution since $\sqrt{-6}$ is an imaginary number.

EXAMPLE

The equation $x^5 + 32 = 0$ has the real solution $x = -2$ (it also has four complex solutions not of interest for the present discussion).

The quotient a/b of two numbers a and b is a number x such that $a = bx$. Division by zero is not permissible as a result of this definition. Note that if $b = 0$, $a = 0 \cdot x$, which is true only if $a = 0$, in which case x can be any number. Thus the expressions

$$\frac{a}{0} \quad \text{and} \quad \frac{0}{0}$$

are meaningless. To distinguish between $a/0$ and $0/0$, $a/0$ is sometimes said to be "undefined" and $0/0$ is sometimes said to be "indeterminate." Note that $0/b = 0$ for $b \ne 0$, since $0/b$ is the value of x for which $b \cdot x = 0$ and must be zero for $b \ne 0$.

Relationships involving inequalities between or among real numbers are expressed as follows:

The notation $<$ indicates "less than"
The notation $>$ indicates "greater than"
The notation $\le$ indicates "less than or equal to"
The notation $\ge$ indicates "greater than or equal to"

Inequalities have the following properties:

If $a \le b$, then $-a \ge -b$

If $a \le b$ and $x \ge 0$, then $x \cdot a \le x \cdot b$

If $a \le b$ and $x \le 0$, then $x \cdot a \ge x \cdot b$

If $a \le b$ and $c \le d$, then $a \pm c \le b \pm d$

EXAMPLE

If $a = 7$ and $b = 8$, then $a < b$ and

$\quad -a = -7 \quad > \quad -b = -8$

If $a = 6$, $b = 9$, and $x = 3$, then $a < b$, $x > 0$, and

$\quad x \cdot a = 18 \quad < \quad x \cdot b = 27$

If $a = 6$, $b = 9$, and $x = -3$, then $a < b$, $x < 0$, and

$\quad x \cdot a = -18 \quad > \quad x \cdot b = -27$

If $a = 3$, $b = 5$, $c = 4$, and $d = 6$, then $a < b$, $c < d$, and

$\quad a + b = 8 < c + d = 10$

Corresponding properties can be stated for the case $a \ge b$, as follows:

If $a \ge b$, then $-a \le -b$

If $a \ge b$ and $x \ge 0$, then $x \cdot a \ge x \cdot b$

If $a \ge b$ and $x \le 0$, then $x \cdot a \le x \cdot b$

If $a \ge b$ and $c \ge d$, then $a \pm c \ge b \pm d$

Relations and Functions

Many problems in mathematics involve sets of ordered pairs of numbers. For example, representation of an object moving in a straight line involves pairs of numbers specifying distance of the object from the origin and the corresponding time in motion. Representation of demand for a given commodity involves pairs of numbers specifying quantity demanded and the corresponding price.

A set of ordered pairs of real numbers is referred to as a *binary relation*. The set of first elements of a binary relation is called the *domain* of the relation; the set of second elements is called the *range* of the relation. For a given set $\{(x, y)\}$, x and y are referred to as *variables*. The set of values variable x takes on is the domain and x is usually called the *independent variable*; the set of values variable y takes on is the range and y is usually called the *dependent variable*. When the number of variables is clear from the context, a binary relation may be referred to simply as a relation.

EXAMPLE

$S_1 = \{(1, 2), (2, 8), (2, 3)\}$ is a binary relation whose domain is $\{1, 2\}$ and whose range is $\{2, 3, 8\}$.

$S_2 = \{(x, y) : x, y \text{ real numbers}, x \leq y\}$ is a binary relation some of whose members are $(2, 2)$, $(3, 4)$, $(5, 5)$, and $(8, 20)$. Note that $(2, 1)$, $(3, 2)$, and $(25, 20)$, for example, are not members of S_2.

$S_3 = \{(x, y) : y = x^2, x \in \mathscr{R}\}$ is a binary relation. The domain of S_3 is $\mathscr{R}$ and the range is the set of all nonnegative real numbers.

$S_4 = \{(x, y) : y = x^2 \text{ if } 0 \leq x \leq 2, y = 3 - x \text{ if } 2 < x < 3, \text{ and } y = 3 \text{ if } x = 3\}$ is a binary relation whose domain is the set $x : 0 \leq x \leq 3$ and whose range is the set $\{y : 0 \leq y \leq 4\}$.

If a relation is such that to each element of the domain there corresponds one and only one element of the range, the relation is said to be a *function*. Functions constitute a subset of relations—all functions are relations, but not all relations are functions. Note that the relations S_3 and S_4 of the above example are functions, but the relations S_1 and S_2 are not functions. A special notation is used for functions to denote the element of the range corresponding to an element of the domain. If f denotes a function $\{(x, y)\}$, then the number y associated with a given x is denoted by $f(x)$, read "f of x." With this notation, the set of pairs defining f may be written as $\{(x, f(x))\}$ where $y = f(x)$.

EXAMPLE

Referring to the preceding example, S_3 and S_4 can be written, respectively, as

$S_3 = \{(x, f(x)) : f(x) = x^2, x \in \mathscr{R}\}$

$S_4 = \{(x, f(x)) : f(x) = x^2 \text{ if } 0 \leq x \leq 2, f(x) = 3 - x \text{ if } 2 < x < 3, \text{ and } f(x) = 3 \text{ if } x = 3\}$

Other letters, for example, g, F, G, ϕ, and Γ, are also frequently used to indicate a function. An equation such as $g(x) = x^2 + (1/x)$ provides a rule for finding the second member of a pair whose first member is x. Such an equation or formula is said to define the function, although the function is not the formula but is the set of ordered pairs $\{(x, g(x))\}$ or $\{(x, y)\}$. When a value of x is substituted in the formula for a function, the result is said to be the *function value* or the *value of the function* for that value of x.

In the case of a function involving two variables, whenever the value of the independent variable is specified the value of the dependent variable is determined. It is the independent variable whose value is thought of as being assigned arbitrarily (except for nonpermissible values), thus determining also the value of the dependent variable. It is conventional in applied mathematics to represent the independent variable by x and the dependent variable by y.

For most problems in analytic geometry and other branches of pure mathematics, the choice of independent and dependent variables is a matter of convenience and the conventional designation of x and y is concerned only with graphical representation, as discussed below. For example, in considering the equation

$$x - 4y^2 + 2y + 6 = 0$$

it is clearly more convenient to find pairs of points by regarding y as the independent variable and x as the dependent variable as follows:

$$x = 4y^2 - 2y - 6$$

When the variables are purely mathematical and do not represent quantities in a particular context, there is no basis other than convenience for making the choice of independent and dependent variables. However, when the variables do represent quantities in the context of a particular subject matter, the logic of the situation usually determines the choice of independent and dependent variables. For example, quantity produced is thought of as a primary determinant of total cost rather than vice versa. There are exceptions even in these types of problems; for example, price may be thought of as determining quantity demanded, or quantity demanded may be thought of as determining price.

It should be noted that some equations of the form $f(x, y) = 0$ cannot (or cannot conveniently) be solved explicitly for either x or y. For example, the equation

$$f(x, y) = x^2 - xy^2 + xy - 4y - 6 = 0$$

can be solved for either x or y, but it is not convenient to do so; the equation

$$f(x, y) = x^2 + e^x - y^2 - e^y = 0$$

cannot be solved explicitly for either x or y.

When an equation is written in the form $f(x, y) = 0$, it is said to determine y as an *implicit function* of x or x as an implicit function of y, providing the uniqueness condition required by the definition of a function is met. Although most economic relationships can be written as explicit functions, it is frequently convenient to express them in implicit form.

EXAMPLE

If $f(x) = x^2 - x + 2$, then

$$f(z) = z^2 - z + 2$$
$$f(2) = 4 - 2 + 2 = 4$$

$$f(-3) = 9 + 3 + 2 = 14$$
$$f(0) = 0 - 0 + 2 = 2$$
$$f(a) = a^2 - a + 2$$
$$f(x + 2) = (x + 2)^2 - (x + 2) + 2$$
$$= (x^2 + 4x + 4) - (x + 2) + 2$$
$$= x^2 + 3x + 4$$
$$f(x + h) - f(x) = (x + h)^2 - (x + h) + 2 - (x^2 - x + 2)$$
$$= x^2 + 2xh + h^2 - x - h + 2 - x^2 + x - 2$$
$$= 2hx + h^2 - h$$

EXAMPLE

If $y = f(x) = (x + 1)/x$, then

$$f(1) = \frac{1 + 1}{1} = 2$$

$$f(-1) = \frac{-1 + 1}{-1} = 0$$

$$f(0) = \frac{1}{0} \quad \text{(undefined)}$$

$$f(a + h) - f(a) = \frac{a + h + 1}{a + h} - \frac{a + 1}{a}$$

$$= \frac{a^2 + ah + a - a^2 - ah - a - h}{a(a + h)}$$

$$= -\frac{h}{a(a + h)}$$

A functional form can be obtained by the substitution of one form into another. If $y = f(x)$ and $u = g(y)$ and if $u = g[f(x)] = h(x)$, then h is called the g composite of f.

EXAMPLE

If $f(x) = x^2 - x - 1$ and $g(x) = x - 1$, then

$$f[g(x)] = [g(x)]^2 - [g(x)] - 1 = (x - 1)^2 - (x - 1) - 1 = x^2 - 3x + 1$$

and

$$g[f(x)] = [f(x)] - 1 = (x^2 - x - 1) - 1 = x^2 - x - 2$$

The above example illustrates the fact that, in general, $f[g(x)] \neq g[f(x)]$. Note the procedure used in the example. Given $f(x)$ and $g(x)$, to obtain the f composite of g, substitute $g(x)$ for x in the formula for $f(x)$ and then replace $g(x)$ by its formula; similarly, to obtain the g composite of f, substitute $f(x)$ for x in the formula for $g(x)$ and then replace $f(x)$ by its formula.

EXAMPLE

If $g(x) = x^2 + 2$, then

$$g[g(x)] = [g(x)]^2 + 2 = (x^2 + 2)^2 + 2 = x^4 + 4x^2 + 6$$

EXAMPLE

If $f(x) = 10^x$ and $\phi(x) = \log_{10} x$, show that $f[\phi(x)] = \phi[f(x)] = x$.

$$f[\phi(x)] = 10^{\phi(x)} = 10^{\log_{10} x} = x$$

$$\phi[f(x)] = \log_{10} f(x) = \log_{10} 10^x = x$$

PROBLEMS

1. For each of the following relations, state the domain and range and indicate whether the relation is a function.
   a. $S = \{(1, 3), (2, 3), (2, 4), (3, 2), (4, 1), (5, 5)\}$
   b. $A = \{(1, 3), (2, 3), (3, 3), (4, 3)\}$
   c. $T = \{(x, y): y = 4x + 1 \text{ if } 0 \le x \le 2, y = 10 - x^2 \text{ if } 2 < x \le 3\}$
   d. $B = \{(x, y): y^2 = x, y \text{ is an integer and } |y| \le 8\}$
2. For each of the following, determine if the set $\{(x, y)\}$ of pairs of real numbers formed according to the given rule is a function.

   a. $y^2 = x$
   b. $y^3 = x$
   c. $y^4 = x$
   d. $x^2 + y = 1$
   e. $x + y^2 = 1$
   f. $x^2 + y^2 = 1$
   g. $y = x^2 + 4$
   h. $xy = 1$
   i. $y = \dfrac{x^2 + 4}{x - 2}$
   j. $y = \dfrac{1}{x^2 - 6}$
   k. $x = \dfrac{1}{y^2 - y + 2}$
   l. $\dfrac{1}{y^2 + 2} = x$

3. If $f(x) = x^3 - x^2 + 6$, find a. $f(0)$; b. $f(-2)$; c. $f(a)$; and d. $f(y^2)$.

4. If $f(x) = \dfrac{3x^2 - 8}{x - 1}$, find a. $f(3)$; b. $f(-1)$; c. $f(x - 2)$; and d. $f(a - b)$.

5. If $f(y) = \sqrt{\dfrac{y^2 - 4}{y}}$, find a. $f(-1)$; b. $f(4)$; c. $f(a^2)$; and d. $f(x + 2)$.

6. If $f(y) = 2^y + y$, find a. $f(0)$; b. $f(-1)$; c. $f(5)$; and d. $f(y + b)$.

7. If $f(x) = 3x - x^2$, find a. $f(1)$; b. $f(-2)$; c. $f(a)$; and d. $f(1/h)$.

8. If $g(x) = \dfrac{x}{x - 3}$, find a. $g(0)$; b. $g(3)$; c. $g(1/x)$; and d. $g(x + b)$.

9. If $h(x) = 4x - x^2$, find a. $h(2) - h(4)$; b. $h(\frac{1}{2}) \cdot h(2)$; c. $h(a + b) - h(c)$;

   and d. $\dfrac{1}{h(a)} + [h(a)]^2$.

10. Give the domain and range of each of the following relations; determine whether each relation is a function and, if not, explain why.

a. $y = x^2 + 6$

b. $y = 10x - 5$

c. $y = \pm\sqrt{4 - 2x^2}$

d. $y = -\sqrt{4 - 2x^2}$

e. $y = \sqrt{4 - 2x^2}$

f. $y = \dfrac{9}{10x - 5}$

g. $y = \dfrac{25}{x^2}$

h. $y = \dfrac{x^2 + 16}{x + 4}$

i. $y^2 = x$

j. $2x + y = 3$

k. $3x^2 + 2y = 4$

l. $4x^2 + 6y^2 = 10$

11. If $f(x) = \dfrac{x^2}{3} - x$ and $g(t) = \dfrac{t^2 + 4}{3t}$, find

a. $f(7) - g(3)$ and   b. $\dfrac{f(3)}{g(2) + 1}$.

12. If $q(x) = p(x) + g(x)$ and $p(x) = \dfrac{x^2 - 7}{3}$, $g(x) = \dfrac{7}{x^2}$, find $q(2)$.

13. If $h(x) = x^{3/2}$ and $Q(x) = (x^2 + 1)^{-1}$, find $Q[h(x)]$.

14. If $h(y) = e^y$ and $Q(x) = x^2 + 4$, find $Q[h(y)]$.

15. If $h(x) = x^3 + 3x + 6$ and $g(y) = \dfrac{y}{1 + y}$, find $g[h(2)]$.

16. If $f(x) = \dfrac{8}{x^3}$, $g(x) = x^2$ and $Q(x) = x^3 - 10$, find $Q[f(-2) + g(2)]$.

17. If $g(t) = t^2 + 3$ and $Q(t) = t^{-1}$, find $Q[g(t)]$.

18. If $f(t) = t^3 + a$ and $g(x) = x^{-3}$, find $g[f(t)]$.

19. If $f(t) = e^{t + a}$, $h(t) = e^{b^2 t}$ and $g(y) = y^{b^2}$, find $\dfrac{g[f(t)]}{h(t)}$.

20. If $h(x) = \tfrac{4}{5} \ln x$ and $g(x) = e^{2x}$, find $h[g(10)]$.

Answers to Odd-Numbered Problems

1. a. domain: $\{1, 2, 3, 4, 5\}$
      range: $\{1, 2, 3, 4, 5\}$
      not a function
   b. domain: $\{1, 2, 3, 4\}$
      range: $\{3\}$
      a function
   c. domain: $\{x : 0 \le x \le 3\}$
      range: $\{y : 1 \le y \le 9\}$
      a function
   d. domain: $\{0, 1, 4, 9, 16, 25, 36, 49, 64\}$
      range: $\{0, \pm 1, \pm 2, \pm 3, \pm 4, \pm 5, \pm 6, \pm 7, \pm 8\}$
      not a function

3. a. 6   c. $a^3 - a^2 + 6$
   b. -6 d. $y^6 - y^4 + 6$

5. a. $\sqrt{3}$

   b. $\sqrt{3}$

   c. $\dfrac{\sqrt{a^4 - 4}}{a}$

   d. $\sqrt{\dfrac{x^2 + 4x}{x + 2}}$

7. a. 2

   b. -10

   c. $3a - a^2$

   d. $\dfrac{3h - 1}{h^2}$

9. a. 4

   b. 7

   c. $4(a + b - c) - a^2 - b^2 + c^2 - 2ab$

   d. $\dfrac{1 + (4a - a^2)^3}{4a - a^2}$

11. a. $\frac{71}{9}$,   b. 0

13. $(x^3 + 1)^{-1}$

15. $\frac{20}{21}$

17. $(t^2 + 3)^{-1}$

19. $e^{\alpha b^2}$

INVERSE FUNCTIONS

The domain and range of any relation may be interchanged to form a new relation. Each pair in the new relation is obtained by interchanging the elements of a corresponding pair in the original relation. Two such sets of pairs are said to be *inverse relations*; each relation is said to be the *inverse* of the other. If both relations are functions, they are called *inverse functions*. The inverse relation is a function if and only if the original function is such that to each element of its range there corresponds one and only one element of its domain. The inverse of a function f is denoted by the symbol f^{-1}. In this notation -1 is not an exponent; it means only that f^{-1} is the inverse of f. If f^{-1} is the inverse function of f, then

$$f[f^{-1}(x)] = x \text{ for all } x \text{ in the domain of } f^{-1}$$

and

$$f^{-1}[f(x)] = x \text{ for all } x \text{ in the domain of } f$$

Providing the algebra can be done, the relation $f^{-1}(x)$ can be found by solving $f[f^{-1}(x)] = x$ as though $f^{-1}(x)$ were a variable in the equation. When a domain is not specified, it is assumed to be the set of all real numbers.

A function and its inverse can be represented diagrammatically in terms of sets as follows.

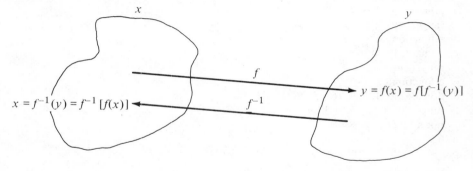

The geometric relationship between inverse functions is discussed and illustrated in Section 1.5.

EXAMPLE

Let $g = \{(x, y) : y = 2x - 1\}$. Find the inverse relation and determine whether it is a function.

$$y = 2x - 1$$

$$x = \tfrac{1}{2}(y + 1)$$

which is a function; thus the inverse function is

$$g^{-1} = \{(x, y) : y = \tfrac{1}{2}(x + 1)\}$$

Since the letters used to indicate the values of the domain and the range are arbitrary, x and y are used in their customary order.

EXAMPLE

Find the inverse of $f = \{(x, y) : y = x^2, x \geq 0\}$ and determine whether it is a function.

$$y = x^2$$

$$x = \sqrt{y}$$

which is a function; thus the inverse function is

$$f^{-1} = \{(x, y) : y = \sqrt{x}\}$$

Note that if f had as its domain the set of all real numbers in the above example, f^{-1} would not be a function since its domain would be the set of all nonnegative real numbers and its range would be the set of all real numbers; that is, the inverse would be $y = \pm\sqrt{x}$, which is not a function.

EXAMPLE

If $y = f(x) = (1 - x)/(1 + x)$, find $x = g(y)$. Solving for x,

$$y = \frac{1 - x}{1 + x}$$

$$y(1 + x) = 1 - x$$

$$y + xy = 1 - x$$

$$y + xy + x - 1 = 0$$

$$x + xy = 1 - y$$

$$x(1 + y) = 1 - y$$

$$x = \frac{1 - y}{1 + y} = g(y)$$

Note that $f(x) = g(x)$ and thus $f(x) = f^{-1}(x)$.

In summary, $y = f(x)$ is a function if y is uniquely determined for every x, that is, if there is one and only one value of y associated with each value of x. If one and only one value of x is associated with each value of y, then there is an inverse function $x = g(y)$; $y = f(x)$ and $x = g(y)$ are inverse functions if and only if $f[g(y)] = y$ and $g[f(x)] = x$. The inverse function of $f(x)$ is frequently denoted $f^{-1}(x)$; then $f[f^{-1}(x)] = f^{-1}[f(x)] = x$. Note that the choice of letter to represent the independent variable in a function is arbitrary; for example, $f(x)$ and $f(y)$ denote the same function. Because it is customary to denote the independent variable by x and the dependent variable by y, if $g(y)$ is the inverse function of $f(x)$, it is frequently denoted by $f^{-1}(x)$.

PROBLEMS

1. Determine for each of the following whether the inverse relation is a function; if it is not, alter the range of the given function so that its inverse is a function.
   a. $\{(x, y) : y = x^2 + 1\}$
   c. $\{(w, z) : z = \sqrt{1 - w^2}\}$
   b. $\{(x, y) : y = 4 - x^2\}$
   d. $\{(u, v) : v = |u|\}$

2. For each of the following functions, find the inverse function $f^{-1}(x)$ and show that $f[f^{-1}(x)] = f^{-1}[f(x)] = x$.
   a. $f(x) = 3x + 2$
   c. $f(x) = (x - 2)/(x + 2)$
   b. $f(x) = x/(x - 4)$
   d. $f(x) = (x + 3)/x$

3. Find $f[g(x)]$ and $g[f(x)]$ for each of the following.
   a. $f(x) = 1/(x - 1)$ and $g(x) = x^2/(x^2 - 1)$
   b. $f(x) = x/(4 - x)$ and $g(x) = x/(x - 4)$
   c. $f(x) = g(x) = (x + 1)/(x - 1)$
   d. $f(x) = \sqrt{x - 1}$ and $g(x) = 1/(x + 1)$

4. If $f(x) = (ax + 1)/(bx - 1)$, find values of a and b such that f is its own inverse—that is, $f[f(x)] = x$.

5. If $g(h) = he^{1/h}$ and $F\left(\dfrac{1}{y}\right) = \dfrac{y^2}{y^2 + 1}$, find

   a. $g[F(t)]$ and b. $F[g(t)]$.

6. If $f(x) = x(x + 1)$, show that $f(x + h) - f(x) = h(2x + 1 + h)$.

7. If $f(x) = \dfrac{1}{x}$, show that $f(x + h) - f(x) = \dfrac{-h}{x^2 + hx}$.

8. If $g(y) = \dfrac{y}{1 - y}$, show that $\frac{1}{2}[g(y) + g(-y)] = g(y^2)$.

9. If $F(z) = \log z$, show that $F(xy) = F(x) + F(y)$.

10. If $\phi(R) = 2^R$, show that $\phi(R + 1) = 2\phi(R)$.

11. If $P(x) = \sqrt{x}$, show that $P(x + h) - P(x) = \dfrac{h}{\sqrt{x + h} + \sqrt{x}}$.

12. If $f(x) = x^2 - 1$ and $g(x) = 2x + 1$, show that $f[g(x)] = 4x(x + 1)$.

13. If $f(x) = \dfrac{x}{1 + x}$, show that $f(x) + f(-x) = 2f(-x^2)$.

14. If $g(y) = y^2$ and $h(y) = \dfrac{y}{1 - y}$, show that $h(y^2) = \dfrac{g(y)}{1 - g(y)}$.

15. If $Q(x) = 2 \ln x$ and $f(x) = x^{3/2}$, show that $Q[f(x)] = \frac{3}{2}Q(x)$.

16. If $f(x) = x^2$, show that $f(x - h) - f(x) = f(h) - 2hx$.

17. If $h(x) = x^{1/3}$, $g(x) = (x^9 + x^6)^{1/2}$, and $Q(x) = x(x + 1)^{1/2}$, show that $g[h(x)] = Q(x)$.

18. If $f(y) = \dfrac{y}{1-y}$ and $g(y) = \dfrac{y}{1+y}$, show that $f(y) - g(y) = 2f(y^2)$.

19. If $f(y) = \dfrac{1}{1+y^2}$ and $g(y) = \dfrac{y^2}{1+y^2}$, show that $f(y) + g(y) + \dfrac{g(y)}{f(y)} = \dfrac{1}{f(y)}$.

20. If $f(x) = \dfrac{x+2}{x-2}$, $g(x) = \dfrac{1+x^2}{x}$, and $h(x) = \dfrac{1-x}{1+x}$, show that $f[g(x)] = \dfrac{1}{[h(x)]^2}$.

21. If $f(x) = x - 1$ and $g(x) = \dfrac{1}{x+1}$, show that $f(x^2)g(x) = f(x)$.

22. If $f(y) = \dfrac{2y}{1+y}$ and $g(y) = \dfrac{-y}{1-y}$, show that $f(y)g(y) = f(-y^2)$.

Answers to Odd-Numbered Problems

1. a. inverse a function
   b. inverse a function if $y \le 0$ or $y \ge 0$
   c. inverse a function
   d. inverse a function
3. a. $f[g(x)] = x^2 - 1$; $g[f(x)] = 1/x(2-x)$
   b. $f[g(x)] = x/(3x - 16)$; $g[f(x)] = x/(5x - 16)$
   c. $f[g(x)] = g[f(x)] = x$
   d. $f[g(x)] = \sqrt{-x/(x+1)}$; $g[f(x)] = (\sqrt{x-1} - 1)/(x-2)$
5. a. $\dfrac{1}{1+t^2} e^{1+t^2}$ b. $\dfrac{1}{1+t^2 e^{2/t}}$

Graphical Representation

1

1.1 Introduction

The French philosopher, Rene Descartes (1596–1650), developed a form of graphic analysis in which algebraic equations are plotted in terms of geometric curves. Thus it is possible to *see* relationships among such variables as price and quantity; direct, indirect, and total cost; savings, investment, and consumption. In addition, much of the theory of calculus can be presented in geometrical terms.

In order to relate algebra and geometry, and thus make possible this dual representation, use is made of a coordinate system which provides a means for locating specific points in a plane or in space. This correspondence may be established in many ways, but the system most commonly used is rectangular coordinates.

In this chapter, graphical representation using rectangular coordinates is discussed for straight lines and for quadratic, exponential, trigonometric, and logarithmic curves. General methods of graphing and special methods of graphing particular types of curves are considered. Applications of each type of curve in business and economics are also discussed.

1.2 Rectangular Coordinates

For rectangular coordinates, two straight lines intersecting at right angles are used as lines of reference and a point is located in the plane of these lines by giving its directed perpendicular distance from each of them. These two distances with signs indicating their directions are the *coordinates* of the point. The lines from which the distances are measured are *coordinate axes* or, briefly, *axes*. The point of intersection of the axes is the *origin of coordinates* or, briefly, the *origin*. The coordinate axes divide the plane into four areas or regions called *quadrants*, numbered counterclockwise for reference as shown in Figure 1.1.

Generally the horizontal line is called the *x-axis* and the vertical line is called the *y-axis*. The choice of positive directions is a matter of convenience and may be changed to simplify particular problems. However, it is customary to consider distances measured to the right of the *y*-axis as positive and those measured to the left as

Figure 1.1 The rectangular coordinate system.

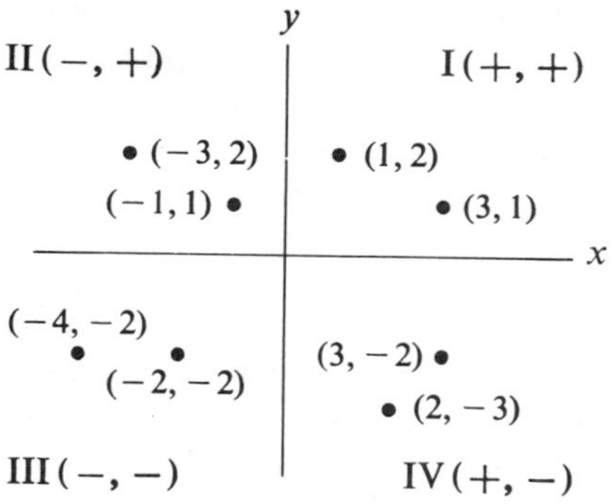

negative; similarly, it is customary to consider distances measured upward from the x-axis as positive and those measured downward as negative.

If x and y represent variables having the same physical or geometrical character-istics, or if they are given abstractly as numbers with no physical interpretation, as is frequently the case in analytic geometry, the same unit of measurement or scale is used on both axes whenever convenient. If the variables are measured in different units (for example, if x is quantity and y is total cost), the units of measurement appropriate for the particular problem are used.

The *x-coordinate*, or *abscissa*, of a point is that coordinate which indicates the direction and distance of the point to the right or left of the y-axis; the *y-coordinate*, or *ordinate*, of a point is that coordinate which indicates the direction and distance of the point above or below the x-axis. The position of a point is indicated by writing its coordinates in parentheses in x, y order: (abscissa, ordinate). Locating a point when its coordinates are given is called *plotting* the point.

Fundamental Principle

There is a one-to-one correspondence between number pairs and points in the plane in which they are represented—that is, to each pair of numbers (coordinates) there corresponds one and only one point in the plane and, conversely, to each point in the plane there corresponds one and only one pair of numbers. The terms *point* and *coordinates of a point* are generally used interchangeably. Thus a geometric problem involving a set of points can be approached by analyzing the corresponding set of pairs of numbers (x, y) algebraically. Conversely, an algebraic relation between x and y can be graphed.

1.3 Straight Lines

In this section graphical representation of straight lines is considered. The slope of a straight line is defined and four forms of the equation for a straight line are discussed. The relationships among parallel, perpendicular, and intersecting lines are con-sidered and the interpretation of the intersection of two straight lines as the simultan-eous solution of the two corresponding equations is discussed. The concept of a family of lines is defined and illustrated.

The rectangular coordinate system can be used to represent any geometric figure that corresponds to an equation in two variables (for example, an equation in x and y). The geometric figure corresponding to an equation consists of all the points, and only those points, whose coordinates satisfy the equation; in particular, for every straight line in the coordinate plane there is a corresponding linear equation in two variables, and conversely.

An equation of the form

$$Ax + By + C = 0 \qquad\qquad (1)$$

where A, B, and C are constants and at least one of A and B is nonzero, is said to be *linear in x and y* because such an equation has a straight line as its geometrical representation. Equation (1) is also referred to as the *general equation of the first degree in two variables.*

The *degree of a variable* is the value of the positive integral power to which the variable is raised. The *degree of a term* of an equation in x and y is the sum of its degrees in x and y; that is, the sum of the powers to which x and y appear in the term. The *degree of an equation* is the degree of its term of greatest degree. For example, $x^3 + y^4 + 6 + y - 12 = 0$ is a fourth-degree equation; $4x^2 + y^4 + 2x^3y^3 - 21 = 0$ is a sixth-degree equation.

There are two aspects of the problem of correspondence between a straight line and a linear equation: (1) given a linear equation, to graph the corresponding line, and (2) given (conditions determining) the line, to find the corresponding linear equation.

The coordinates x and y of every point (x, y) on a given line satisfy the equation corresponding to the line; conversely, the straight line that passes through all the points, and *only* through those points, whose coordinates satisfy the equation is called the *graph* or *locus* of the equation. However, since there are an infinite number of points on any given line or curve, establishing correspondence between algebraic equations and their geometrical representations point by point is clearly not feasible; it is the purpose of analytic geometry to develop methods that use a minimum number of points for establishing this correspondence. In general, the more simple the algebraic equation (and thus its corresponding graph), the fewer points necessary for establishing meaningful correspondence.

One easy way to graph a straight line is to compute its intercepts. The *intercepts* of a line are the points where the line crosses the axes. Thus the *y-intercept* is the point determined by setting $x = 0$ in the equation of the line; similarly, the *x-intercept* is the point determined by setting $y = 0$ in the equation of the line.

EXAMPLE

Graph the line $4x + 5y - 20 = 0$.

y-intercept	*x-intercept*
if $x = 0$,	if $y = 0$,
$5y - 20 = 0$	$4x - 20 = 0$
$5y = 20$	$4x = 20$
$y = 4$	$x = 5$
Intercept $(0, 4)$	Intercept $(5, 0)$

Figure 1.2

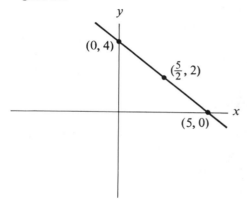

The intercepts may then be plotted and the line drawn through them, as shown in Figure 1.2. Although any two points which satisfy its equation determine a straight line, as a check for accuracy, a third point is sometimes plotted as well. For example, let $y = 2$ in the example above. Then

$$4x + 5(2) - 20 = 0$$

$$4x - 10 = 0$$

$$x = \tfrac{10}{4} = \tfrac{5}{2}$$

The third point is then $(\tfrac{5}{2}, 2)$.

SLOPE OF A STRAIGHT LINE

The direction of a straight line is indicated by its slope, which is defined in terms of the angle between the line and the x-axis. When a straight line intersects the x-axis, its inclination is the angle θ, shown in Figure 1.3, which is measured counterclockwise from the positive direction of the x-axis to the line and thus is always between 0 and 180°. If a line is parallel to the x-axis, its angle of inclination θ is defined to be 0°.

The *slope* of a line is the tangent of its angle of inclination and is usually denoted by m. The definition of the slope of a line is equivalent to the definition of the tangent of its angle of inclination. The tangent is one of the six trigonometric functions of an angle, which are defined in terms of a right triangle formed by the angle and a perpendicular to its adjacent side.

Figure 1.3

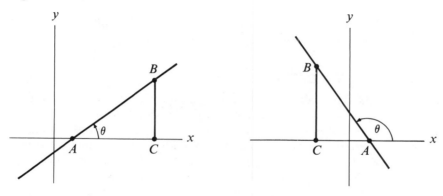

Suppose $0° < \theta < 180°$, and let a line having angle of inclination θ intersect the x-axis at A. From any other point on the line drop a perpendicular cutting the x-axis at C, as in Figure 1.3. Now the tangent of θ, denoted tan θ, is defined by tan $\theta = CB/AC$, where CB and AC are directed distances.

Equivalently, if (x_1, y_1) and (x_2, y_2) are any two distinct points on a straight line, then the slope of the line is

$$m = \tan \theta = \frac{y_2 - y_1}{x_2 - x_1} = \frac{\Delta y}{\Delta x}$$

Note, by considering similar triangles, that slope is independent of which two distinct points are used. It is customary, especially in calculus, to use the notation Δy, read delta y, to represent the difference $y_2 - y_1$. This symbol Δy denotes the change in y or the difference between two values of y. Do not think of Δy as delta times y. Similarly, Δx denotes $x_2 - x_1$.

It can be shown, by an argument based on properties of similar triangles, that the slope of a straight line is the same regardless of the two distinct points chosen for calculating it; correspondingly, the tangent of an angle is the same regardless of the point at which the perpendicular intersects the adjacent side, provided the point is not the intersection of the line and the x-axis.

Since

$$\frac{y_2 - y_1}{x_2 - x_1} = \frac{y_1 - y_2}{x_1 - x_2}$$

the slope of a line may be interpreted as the ratio of the directed change in vertical distance to the corresponding directed change in horizontal distance as a point moves along the line in either direction. In some problems (particularly in physics and engineering), $\Delta y = y_2 - y_1$ is called the *rise* and $\Delta x = x_2 - x_1$ is called the *run*; then the slope is defined as the rise per unit of run, that is, slope = rise/run = $\Delta y/\Delta x$.

If $y_1 = y_2$ and $x_1 \neq x_2$, the line through (x_1, y_1) and (x_2, y_2) is parallel to the x-axis, its angle of inclination θ is zero, and tan $\theta = \Delta y/\Delta x = 0$.

If $x_1 = x_2$ and $y_1 \neq y_2$, the line through (x_1, y_1) and (x_2, y_2) is parallel to the y-axis, its angle of inclination θ is 90°, and tan $\theta = \Delta y/\Delta x$ is undefined (see Figure 1.4). (Remember that an expression which involves division by zero is said to be *undefined* or *indeterminate* and no numerical value can meaningfully be assigned to it.)

SUMMARY: SLOPE

The slope of the x-axis is zero.

The slope of the y-axis is undefined.

If a line slopes upward to the right, Δx and Δy have the same sign and tan $\theta = \Delta y/\Delta x > 0$; in this case $0 < \theta < 90°$.

If a line slopes downward to the right, Δx and Δy have opposite signs and tan $\theta = \Delta y/\Delta x < 0$; in this case $90° < \theta < 180°$.

EQUATIONS FOR STRAIGHT LINES

A straight line, the simplest geometric curve, may be specified uniquely by either of the following: two points which lie on the line or the slope of the line and one point which lies on the line. There are several formulas for obtaining the equation of a straight line; the conditions that are given for obtaining the line determine which formula is most convenient for a particular problem. The two-point form and the intercept form determine a straight line by two points that lie on it; the point-slope form and the slope-intercept form determine a straight line by one point that

Figure 1.4

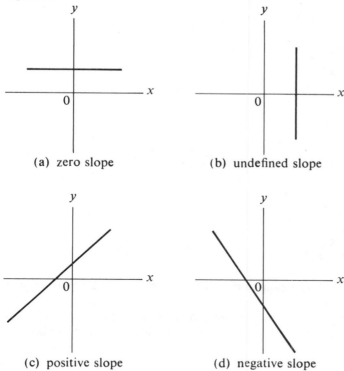

(a) zero slope

(b) undefined slope

(c) positive slope

(d) negative slope

lies on it and its slope. These formulas are all equivalent to the general equation for a straight line,

$$Ax + By + C = 0$$

and are generally easily transformed into it and into each other.

Two-Point Form

One of the fundamental properties of a straight line is its constant slope; the slope can be determined using any two distinct points on a straight line. These two facts can be used to develop a formula for obtaining the equation of a nonvertical straight line when the coordinates of two points on the line are known.

If (x_1, y_1) and (x_2, y_2) are two distinct points on a nonvertical straight line, then the slope m of the line is given by

$$m = \frac{y_2 - y_1}{x_2 - x_1}$$

If (x, y) is any other point (that is, a general point) on the straight line, then it and the point (x_1, y_1) can also be used to determine the slope m of the line

$$m = \frac{y - y_1}{x - x_1}$$

and, since the slope is constant,

$$\frac{y - y_1}{x - x_1} = \frac{y_2 - y_1}{x_2 - x_1}$$

Figure 1.5

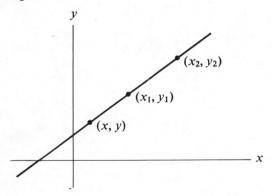

or

$$y - y_1 = \left(\frac{y_2 - y_1}{x_2 - x_1}\right)(x - x_1) \tag{1a}$$

See Figure 1.5, noting that the labeling of the points is arbitrary and may be chosen for convenience.

Equation (1a), referred to as the *two-point form* for a straight line, is generally most convenient for determining the equation of a straight line when two of its points are given.

EXAMPLE

Find the equation of the line passing through the points $(3, 4)$ and $(-5, 2)$.

$(x_1, y_1) = (3, 4) \qquad (x_2, y_2) = (-5, 2)$

$$y - y_1 = \frac{y_2 - y_1}{x_2 - x_1}(x - x_1)$$

$$y - 4 = \left(\frac{2 - 4}{-5 - 3}\right)(x - 3)$$

$$y - 4 = \tfrac{1}{4}(x - 3)$$

$$x - 4y + 13 = 0$$

Check: Insert $(3, 4)$ in $x - 4y + 13 = 0$:

$$3 - 4(4) + 13 = 0$$
$$0 = 0$$

Insert $(-5, 2)$ in $x - 4y + 13 = 0$:

$$-5 - 4(2) + 13 = 0$$
$$0 = 0$$

Intercept Form

For the special case when the point (x_1, y_1) is the y-intercept, denoted by $(0, b)$, where $b \neq 0$, and the point (x_2, y_2) is the x-intercept, denoted by $(a, 0)$, where $a \neq 0$, then equation (1a) can be written

$$y - b = \frac{-b}{a}(x - 0)$$

$$\frac{y}{b} - 1 = -\frac{x}{a}$$

$$\frac{x}{a} + \frac{y}{b} = 1 \qquad\qquad (1b)$$

Equation (1b), referred to as the *intercept form* for a straight line, is generally most convenient for determining the equation of a straight line when its two intercepts are given.

EXAMPLE

Find the equation of the line having intercepts $(0, -6)$ and $(4, 0)$.

$$b = -6 \qquad a = 4$$

$$\frac{x}{a} + \frac{y}{b} = 1$$

$$\frac{x}{4} + \frac{y}{-6} = 1$$

Multiplying by the lowest common denominator 12,

$$3x - 2y = 12$$

$$3x - 2y - 12 = 0$$

Check: Insert $(0, -6)$ in $3x - 2y - 12 = 0$:

$$3(0) - 2(-6) - 12 = 0$$

$$0 = 0$$

Insert $(4, 0)$ in $3x - 2y - 12 = 0$:

$$3(4) - 2(0) - 12 = 0$$

$$0 = 0$$

Point-Slope Form

Since the slope of a nonvertical line is $m = (y_2 - y_1)/(x_2 - x_1)$, Equation (1a) can be written

$$y - y_1 = m(x - x_1) \qquad\qquad (1c)$$

Equation (1c), referred to as the *point-slope form* for a straight line, is generally most convenient for determining the equation of a straight line when one of the points on a line and its slope are given.

EXAMPLE

Find the equation of the line passing through the point $(-1, 2)$ and having slope -4.

$$(x_1, y_1) = (-1, 2) \qquad m = -4$$
$$y - y_1 = m(x - x_1)$$
$$y - 2 = -4(x + 1)$$
$$4x + y + 2 = 0$$

Check: $m = -4$ in $4x + y + 2 = 0$. Insert $(-1, 2)$ in $4x + y + 2 = 0$:

$$4(-1) + 2 + 2 = 0$$
$$0 = 0$$

Slope-Intercept Form

For the special case when the point (x_1, y_1) is the y-intercept, denoted by $(0, b)$, equation (1a) can be written

$$y = mx + b \tag{1d}$$

Equation (1d), referred to as the *slope-intercept form* for a straight line, is generally most convenient for determining the equation of a straight line when its y-intercept and slope are given.

EXAMPLE

Find the equation of the line having y-intercept $(0, 5)$ and slope 3.

$$b = 5 \qquad m = 3$$
$$y = mx + b$$
$$= 3x + 5$$
$$3x - y + 5 = 0$$

Check: $m = 3$ in $3x - y + 5 = 0$. Insert $(0, 5)$ in $3x - y + 5 = 0$:

$$3(0) - 5 + 5 = 0$$
$$0 = 0$$

Vertical Lines

Since the slope of a vertical line is undefined, the above formulas are not appropriate for obtaining the equations of vertical lines. A vertical line passing through the point (x_1, y_1) has the equation $x = x_1$.

EXAMPLE

Find the equation of the vertical line passing through the point $(5, -4)$.

$$x = x_1 = 5$$
$$x = 5$$

Horizontal Lines

Since a horizontal line has zero slope, its equation may be obtained from the two-point, point-slope, or slope-intercept forms. A horizontal line passing through the point (x_1, y_1) has the equation $y = y_1$.

EXAMPLE

Find the equation of the horizontal line passing through the point $(-3, -2)$.

$$y = y_1 = -2$$
$$y = -2$$

SUMMARY: STRAIGHT LINES

General form: $Ax + By + C = 0$

Two-point form: $y - y_1 = \dfrac{y_2 - y_1}{x_2 - x_1}(x - x_1)$

Intercept form: $\dfrac{x}{a} + \dfrac{y}{b} = 1$

Point-slope form: $y - y_1 = m(x - x_1)$

Slope-intercept form: $y = mx + b$

Vertical lines: $x = x_1$

Horizontal lines: $y = y_1$

PROBLEMS

1. a. Which of the following points lie on the line $3x + 4y - 10 = 0$?
    i. $(1, 2)$ iv. $(-25, 21)$
    ii. $(-2, 4)$ v. $(0, 0)$
    iii. $(10, -5)$ vi. $(\frac{22}{9}, \frac{2}{3})$
  b. Graph the line indicating points above which lie on it.
2. For each of the following equations,
    i. Graph using intercepts.
    ii. Put into slope-intercept form.
    iii. Put into intercept form—this form is inappropriate for one of the equations; which one and why?
    a. $4y - 3x = 12$ c. $2y + 3x + 2 = 0$
    b. $5x - y = 10$ d. $x - 3y = 0$
3. a. Which of the following points lie on the line $x - 5y + 4 = 0$?
    i. $(0, 0)$ iv. $(3, 2)$
    ii. $(4, 0)$ v. $(0, \frac{4}{5})$
    iii. $(1, 1)$ vi. $(-1, 5)$
  b. Graph the line, indicating the points above which lie on it.
4. For each of the following pairs of points,
    i. Find the slope of the line through the two points.
    ii. Find the equation of the line using the slope.
    iii. Find the equation of the line without using the slope.
    iv. Graph the line.
    a. $(0, 0)$ and $(6, 3)$ d. $(3, -2)$ and $(3, 5)$
    b. $(\frac{10}{3}, 0)$ and $(0, \frac{5}{2})$ e. $(-1, -2)$ and $(4, 1)$
    c. $(-7, 4)$ and $(8, 4)$ f. $(-2, -3)$ and $(-5, -6)$

5. Find the equation of the line through the point $(3, -2)$ and perpendicular to the line through the points $(-1, -3)$ and $(3, 7)$.
6. Find the equation of the line through the point $(4, 3)$ and parallel to the line through the points $(0, -3)$ and $(6, 1)$.
7. Find the equation of the line through the point $(5, 15)$ and parallel to the line $y = x + 25$. What relation (parallel, perpendicular, coincident, or intersecting) does this line have to the line through the two points $(6, 0)$ and $(-2, 8)$?
8. Find the equation of the line which has intercept $(0, -3)$ and is perpendicular to the line through the points $(-2, -1)$ and $(2, 5)$.
9. Find the equation of the line which is parallel to the line through the points $(5, 6)$ and $(7, 8)$ and also passes through the intersection of the line having slope -2 through the point $(-4, -6)$ and the line having slope 3 through the point $(2, 2)$.
10. Find the equation of the line passing through the point $(-1, 1)$ and perpendicular to the line having slope $-\frac{1}{4}$ and passing through the point $(5, 2)$.

Answers to Odd-Numbered Problems

1. ii, iii, vi
3. a. $(1, 1)$, $(0, \frac{4}{3})$
5. $2x + 5y + 4 = 0$
7. $x - y + 10 = 0$
   perpendicular
9. $x - y - 8 = 0$

PARALLEL, PERPENDICULAR, AND INTERSECTING LINES

Any two lines in a plane are either parallel or intersecting; lines that intersect at right angles are *perpendicular*. Two lines that are *parallel* have equal angles of inclination and therefore have equal slopes, and conversely. Two lines that are perpendicular have slopes which are the negative reciprocals of each other, and conversely.

Note that two lines that are parallel (or perpendicular) to the coordinate axes, respectively, are perpendicular to each other; the slope of one line is zero, and the slope of the other line is undefined.

EXAMPLE

The line $2x + 6y - 4 = 0$ has the indicated relationship to each of the following lines (note that $2x + 6y - 4 = 0$ can be written in the form $y = -\frac{1}{3}x + \frac{2}{3}$):

(a) $4x + 12y - 8 = 0$

$$12y = -4x + 8$$

$$y = -\frac{1}{3}x + \frac{2}{3} \qquad \text{coincident with } y = -\frac{1}{3}x + \frac{2}{3}$$

(b) $-3x + y - 4 = 0$

$$y = 3x + 4 \qquad \text{perpendicular to } y = -\frac{1}{3}x + \frac{2}{3}$$

(c) $x + 3y - 9 = 0$

$$3y = -x + 9$$

$$y = -\frac{1}{3}x + 3 \qquad \text{parallel to } y = -\frac{1}{3}x + \frac{2}{3}$$

(d) $2x + y - 4 = 0$

$$y = -2x + 4 \qquad \text{intersecting } y = -\frac{1}{3}x + \frac{2}{3}$$

The conditions for two lines to be parallel or perpendicular can also be stated as follows. The lines

$$A_1 x + B_1 y + C_1 = 0 \quad \text{and} \quad A_2 x + B_2 y + C_2 = 0$$

are parallel if

$$A_1 B_2 - A_2 B_1 = 0$$

and perpendicular if

$$A_1 A_2 + B_1 B_2 = 0$$

EXAMPLE

Consider the preceding example. For the line $2x + 6y - 4 = 0$, $A_1 = 2$, $B_1 = 6$, and $C_1 = -4$.

(a) $4x + 12y - 8 = 0$

$A_2 = 4$, $B_2 = 12$, $C_2 = -8$

$A_1 B_2 - A_2 B_1 = (2)(12) - (4)(6) = 0$

Thus the lines are parallel.

$\left(\text{Actually the lines are coincident because } \dfrac{A_1}{A_2} = \dfrac{B_1}{B_2} = \dfrac{C_1}{C_2} \right).$

(b) $-3x + y - 4 = 0$

$A_2 = -3$, $B_2 = 1$, $C_2 = -4$

$A_1 B_2 - A_2 B_1 = (2)(1) - (-3)(6) = 20 \neq 0$

Thus the lines are not parallel.

$A_1 A_2 + B_1 B_2 = (2)(-3) + (6)(1) = 0$

Thus the lines are perpendicular.

(c) $x + 3y - 9 = 0$

$A_2 = 1$, $B_2 = 3$, $C_2 = -9$

$A_1 B_2 - A_2 B_1 = (2)(3) - (1)(6) = 0$

Thus the lines are parallel.

(d) $2x + y - 4 = 0$

$A_2 = 2$, $B_2 = 1$, $C_2 = -4$

$A_1 B_2 - A_2 B_1 = (2)(1) - (2)(6) = -10 \neq 0$

Thus the lines are not parallel.

$A_1 A_2 + B_1 B_2 = (2)(2) + (6)(1) = 10 \neq 0$

Thus the lines are not perpendicular; they are intersecting.

INTERSECTION OF TWO STRAIGHT LINES

The coordinates of the point of intersection of two straight lines must satisfy the equations of both lines. Therefore, the point of intersection of two nonparallel lines can be found by solving their equations simultaneously. The geometric property that two lines intersect corresponds to the algebraic condition that their equations are *independent* and *consistent*, and therefore have a *simultaneous solution*.

Consider two linear equations written in the form

$$A_1 x + B_1 y + C_1 = 0 \qquad A_2 x + B_2 y + C_2 = 0$$

where A_1, A_2, B_1, B_2, C_1, and C_2 are positive or negative constants.

Independent Equations

These equations are *independent* if one cannot be obtained from the other by multiplication by a nonzero constant—that is, they are independent if the equality $A_1/A_2 = B_1/B_2 = C_1/C_2$ does not hold. If the equality does hold, the equations are *dependent*.

NOTE: Two equations that are dependent are equivalent—that is, they represent the same line and have the same graph, since any point that lies on one of the equations lies on the other also.

EXAMPLE

The equations

$$3x + 5y + 10 = 0 \qquad 6x + 10y + 20 = 0$$

are dependent or equivalent, since the second equation is obtained by multiplying the first equation by 2; they have the same straight line as their graph.

Consistent Equations

Two equations are said to be *consistent* if they hold simultaneously—that is, they are consistent if

$$\frac{A_1}{A_2} = \frac{B_1}{B_2} = \frac{C_1}{C_2} \qquad \text{or if} \qquad \frac{A_1}{A_2} \neq \frac{B_1}{B_2}$$

If $A_1/A_2 = B_1/B_2 = C_1/C_2$, the lines coincide and the equations are both consistent and dependent. If $A_1/A_2 \neq B_1/B_2$, the lines have different slopes and thus intersect at just one point; such lines are consistent and independent. Two linear equations that are *inconsistent*—that is, not consistent—have parallel lines as their graphs. In this case,

$$\frac{A_1}{A_2} = \frac{B_1}{B_2} \neq \frac{C_1}{C_2}$$

EXAMPLE

The equations

$$3x + 5y + 10 = 0 \qquad 6x + 10y + 15 = 0$$

are inconsistent (since $\frac{3}{6} = \frac{5}{10} \neq \frac{10}{15}$) and cannot both hold simultaneously; they have parallel lines as their graphs.

Note that the equations $A_1 x + B_1 y + C_1 = 0$ and $A_2 x + B_2 y + C_2 = 0$ can be written

$$y = -\left(\frac{A_1}{B_1}\right)x + \left(-\frac{C_1}{B_1}\right) \qquad \text{if } B_1 \neq 0$$

$$y = -\frac{C_1}{A_1} \qquad \text{if } B_1 = 0$$

and

$$y = -\left(\frac{A_2}{B_2}\right)x + \left(-\frac{C_2}{B_2}\right) \qquad \text{if } B_2 \neq 0$$

$$y = -\frac{C_2}{A_2} \qquad \text{if } B_2 = 0$$

Thus if $A_1/A_2 = B_1/B_2$, the lines have the same slope. If $B_1/B_2 = C_1/C_2$, the lines have the same intercept. If $A_1/A_2 = B_1/B_2 = C_1/C_2$, the lines have the same slope and the same intercept and are identical.

A point is said to be a *simultaneous solution* of two equations if its coordinates satisfy both equations; geometrically, two lines intersect (or coincide) at a point which is their simultaneous solution. Two straight lines have a unique simultaneous solution if they are intersecting (consistent and independent), no simultaneous solution if they are parallel (inconsistent), and infinitely many simultaneous solutions if they are coincident (consistent and dependent). These cases are illustrated in Figure 1.6.

Figure 1.6

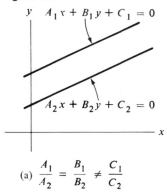

(a) $\dfrac{A_1}{A_2} = \dfrac{B_1}{B_2} \neq \dfrac{C_1}{C_2}$

lines inconsistent and independent

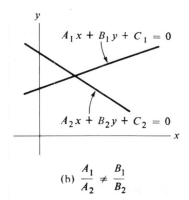

(b) $\dfrac{A_1}{A_2} \neq \dfrac{B_1}{B_2}$

lines consistent and independent

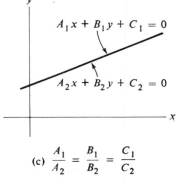

(c) $\dfrac{A_1}{A_2} = \dfrac{B_1}{B_2} = \dfrac{C_1}{C_2}$

lines consistent and dependent

Usually two linear equations can quite easily be solved simultaneously by elimination or substitution; in some cases the method of determinants (to be discussed in detail later) provides the solution more readily. To solve the equations

$$A_1 x + B_1 y + C_1 = 0 \qquad A_2 x + B_2 y + C_2 = 0$$

by *elimination*, multiply the first equation by A_2 and the second equation by A_1, subtract to eliminate x, solve for y, and obtain x by substitution in either equation. (Alternatively, multiply the equations by B_2 and B_1, respectively, and eliminate y.)

To solve by *substitution*, obtain x in terms of y (or, alternatively, y in terms of x) from one equation, substitute in the other equation, and solve.

By either of these methods or, more directly, by the *method of determinants*, the solutions for x and y are

$$x = \frac{B_1 C_2 - B_2 C_1}{A_1 B_2 - A_2 B_1} \qquad y = \frac{A_2 C_1 - A_1 C_2}{A_1 B_2 - A_2 B_1}$$

provided $A_1 B_2 - A_2 B_1 \neq 0$.

For example, following the procedure for solution by elimination outlined above, multiply the first equation by A_2 and the second equation by A_1:

$$A_1 A_2 x + A_2 B_1 y + A_2 C_1 = 0 \qquad A_1 A_2 x + A_1 B_2 y + A_1 C_2 = 0$$

subtract to eliminate x,

$$(A_2 B_1 - A_1 B_2)y + A_2 C_1 - A_1 C_2 = 0$$

solve for y,

$$y = \frac{A_2 C_1 - A_1 C_2}{A_1 B_2 - A_2 B_1}$$

and obtain x by substitution in the first equation

$$A_1 x + B_1 \left(\frac{A_2 C_1 - A_1 C_2}{A_1 B_2 - A_2 B_1} \right) + C_1 = 0$$

$$x = \frac{-B_1}{A_1} \left(\frac{A_2 C_1 - A_1 C_2}{A_1 B_2 - A_2 B_1} \right) - \frac{C_1}{A_1}$$

$$= \frac{-A_2 B_1 C_1 + A_1 B_1 C_2 - A_1 B_2 C_1 + A_2 B_1 C_1}{A_1(A_1 B_2 - A_2 B_1)}$$

$$= \frac{B_1 C_2 - B_2 C_1}{A_1 B_2 - A_2 B_1}$$

In many cases it is easier to obtain the simultaneous solution for a particular pair of linear equations directly by elimination or substitution rather than by these formulas.

EXAMPLE

Find the point of intersection of the lines represented by the equations

$$3x - 4y + 6 = 0 \qquad x - 2y - 3 = 0$$

(see Figure 1.7)

Eliminating the x-term by multiplying the second equation by -3 and adding it to the first equation,

$$3x - 4y + 6 = 0$$
$$-3x + 6y + 9 = 0$$
$$2y + 15 = 0$$
$$2y = -15$$
$$y = -\tfrac{15}{2}$$

Substituting $y = -\tfrac{15}{2}$ in the first equation,

$$3x - 4(-\tfrac{15}{2}) + 6 = 0$$
$$3x + 30 + 6 = 0$$
$$3x = -36$$
$$x = -12$$

Answer: $(-12, -\tfrac{15}{2})$.

Check: Equation 1: $3(-12) - 4(-\tfrac{15}{2}) + 6 = 0$
$$-36 + 30 + 6 = 0$$
$$0 = 0$$

Equation 2: $-12 - 2(-\tfrac{15}{2}) - 3 = 0$
$$-12 + 15 - 3 = 0$$
$$0 = 0$$

Figure 1.7

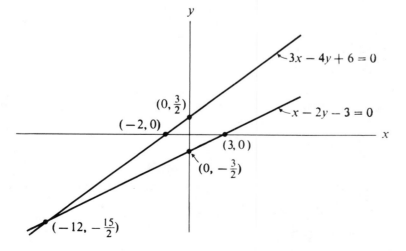

Alternatively, substituting for x obtained from the second equation in the first equation:

$$x = 2y + 3$$
$$3(2y + 3) - 4y + 6 = 0$$
$$6y + 9 - 4y + 6 = 0$$
$$2y + 15 = 0$$
$$2y = -15$$
$$y = -\tfrac{15}{2}$$

Substituting for y obtained from the second equation in the first equation:

$$y = \frac{x - 3}{2}$$

$$3x - 4\left(\frac{x - 3}{2}\right) + 6 = 0$$
$$3x - 2x + 6 + 6 = 0$$
$$x + 12 = 0$$
$$x = -12$$

Answer: $(-12, -\tfrac{15}{2})$, as above.

Using the formulas

$$x = \frac{B_1 C_2 - B_2 C_1}{A_1 B_2 - A_2 B_1} \qquad y = \frac{A_2 C_1 - A_1 C_2}{A_1 B_2 - A_2 B_1}$$

$$A_1 = 3 \quad B_1 = -4 \quad C_1 = 6 \qquad A_2 = 1 \quad B_2 = -2 \quad C_2 = -3$$

$$x = \frac{(-4)(-3) - (-2)(6)}{(3)(-2) - (1)(-4)}$$

$$= \frac{12 + 12}{-6 + 4} = \frac{24}{-2} = -12$$

$$y = \frac{(1)(6) - (3)(-3)}{(3)(-2) - (1)(-4)}$$

$$= \frac{6 + 9}{-6 + 4} = \frac{15}{-2}$$

Answer: $(-12, -\tfrac{15}{2})$, as above.

These equations are consistent and independent and have a unique simultaneous solution, the point $(-12, -\tfrac{15}{2})$.

EXAMPLE

Find the point of intersection of the lines represented by the equations

$$2x - 3y + 3 = 0 \qquad 4x - 6y + 12 = 0$$

Figure 1.8

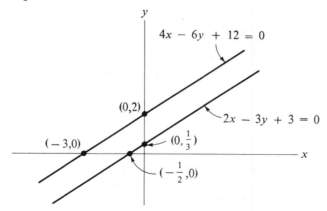

Multiplying the first equation by 2 and rewriting the second equation,

$$4x - 6y + 6 = 0 \qquad 4x - 6y + 12 = 0$$

(see Figure 1.8). These equations are inconsistent and do not have a simultaneous solution; they are represented by parallel lines.

EXAMPLE

Find the point of intersection of the lines represented by the equations

$$2x - 3y + 1 = 0 \qquad 4x - 6y + 2 = 0$$

Multiplying the first equation by 2 and rewriting the second equation,

$$4x - 6y + 2 = 0 \qquad 4x - 6y + 2 = 0$$

(see Figure 1.9). These equations are dependent and therefore equivalent and have infinitely many simultaneous solutions; they are represented by the same straight line, every point of which is a simultaneous solution of the equations.

Figure 1.9

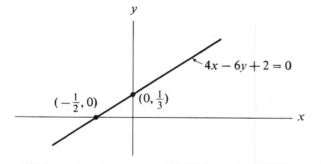

FAMILIES OF LINES

An important concept in both theoretical and applied mathematics is that of a family of straight lines or curves. The members of a family possess some geometric property (such as passing through a given point) in common, but differ in at least one other geometric property (such as having different slopes). Algebraically, this corresponds to the fact that some of the parameters in a general equation are specified and at least one is not. Remember that an arbitrary (that is, unspecified) constant is called a *parameter*.

The general equation for a straight line

$$Ax + By + C = 0$$

has two parameters, since if any one of the parameters A, B, or C is not zero, it may be used as a divisor to reduce the equation to a form involving only two parameters. The slope-intercept and intercept are two such forms.

The two essential parameters in the equation of a straight line correspond to the two geometric conditions that may be imposed on the line. For each of these geometric conditions there is an algebraic equation showing the corresponding relation between the parameters. Since any given number of variables is determined by that same number of independent linear equations involving the variables, it follows that the number of independent geometric conditions that can be put on a line is the same as the number of essential parameters in the equation of a line, that is, two.

The general equation $Ax + By + C = 0$ with two essential parameters represents all lines in the plane. When one of the two constants is specified and the other is unspecified (that is, remains a parameter) a family of lines—such as all lines of a given slope, or all lines passing through a particular point—is represented by the equation. When both constants are specified, one particular line is represented by the equation.

Every line passing through the intersection of the two lines

$$A_1 x + B_1 y + C_1 = 0 \quad \text{and} \quad A_2 x + B_2 y + C_2 = 0$$

has an equation of the form

$$\lambda_1(A_1 x + B_1 y + C_1) + \lambda_2(A_2 x + B_2 y + C_2) = 0$$

that is, it can be represented as a linear combination of the two lines. Specifying the values of λ_1 and λ_2 specifies a particular line.

EXAMPLE

Consider the point-slope form of the equation for a straight line

$$y - y_1 = m(x - x_1)$$

The two essential parameters are expressed in this form of the equation as the slope m and the point (x_1, y_1). Suppose the condition that the line is to have slope 2 is imposed. This geometric condition corresponds to the algebraic equation

$$y - y_1 = 2(x - x_1)$$

The family of lines represented by this equation consists of an infinite number of lines parallel to each other and all having slope 2. (See Figure 1.10.)

One further condition can be imposed on the line. Geometrically, a point through which the line is to pass can be specified (as a special case, this point could be either the x-intercept or the y-intercept); algebraically, a pair of constant values can be assigned to the coordinates

Figure 1.10

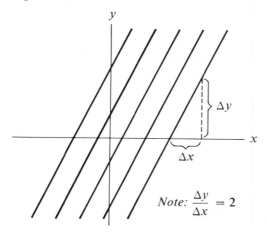

Note: $\dfrac{\Delta y}{\Delta x} = 2$

Figure 1.11

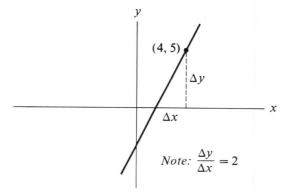

Note: $\dfrac{\Delta y}{\Delta x} = 2$

(x_1, y_1). Suppose it is specified that the line is to pass through the point $(4, 5)$, that is, $(x_1, y_1) = (4, 5)$. (See Figure 1.11.) Now a particular line is determined by the equation

$$y - 5 = 2(x - 4) \quad \text{or} \quad 2x - y - 3 = 0$$

which is obtained from the equations

$$m = 2 \quad \text{and} \quad (x_1, y_1) = (4, 5)$$

corresponding to the imposed geometric conditions; this line has slope 2 and passes through the point $(4, 5)$.

EXAMPLE

Consider the intercept form of the equation for a straight line,

$$\frac{x}{a} + \frac{y}{b} = 1$$

The two essential constants are expressed in this form of the equation as the x-intercept $(a, 0)$ and the y-intercept $(0, b)$. Suppose the condition that the line is to have the x-intercept $(3, 0)$ is imposed. This geometric condition corresponds to the algebraic equation

$$\frac{x}{3} + \frac{y}{b} = 1$$

Figure 1.12

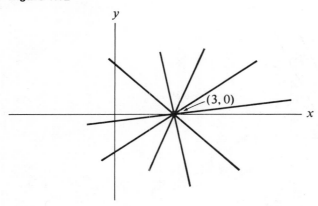

The family of lines represented by this equation consists of an infinite number of members, each having a different y-intercept (and thus a different slope) but all passing through the point $(3, 0)$. (See Figure 1.12.)

One further condition can be imposed on the line. Geometrically, the y-intercept can be specified; algebraically, a constant value can be assigned to b.

Suppose that it is specified that the y-intercept of the line is to be $(0, -1)$, that is, $b = -1$. (See Figure 1.13.) Now a particular line is specified by the equation

$$\frac{x}{3} + \frac{y}{-1} = 1$$

Figure 1.13

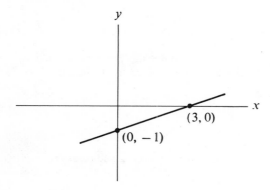

or

$$x - 3y = 3$$
$$x - 3y - 3 = 0$$

which is obtained from the two equations

$$a = 3 \qquad b = -1$$

corresponding to the imposed geometric conditions; this line has the x-intercept 3 and the y-intercept -1.

EXAMPLE

Find the line that passes through the intersection of the lines $x + y - 1 = 0$ and $2x - y + 1 = 0$ and is perpendicular to the line $x + 3y - 2 = 0$.

A line passing through the intersection of $x + y - 1 = 0$ and $2x - y + 1 = 0$ is of the form

$$\lambda_1(x + y - 1) + \lambda_2(2x - y + 1) = 0$$

or

$$x(\lambda_1 + 2\lambda_2) + y(\lambda_1 - \lambda_2) - \lambda_1 + \lambda_2 = 0$$

and is perpendicular to $x + 3y - 2 = 0$ if

$$(\lambda_1 + 2\lambda_2) \cdot 1 + 3 \cdot (\lambda_1 - \lambda_2) = 0$$

$$4\lambda_1 - \lambda_2 = 0$$

Take $\lambda_1 = 1$, $\lambda_2 = 4$. Then, the required line is

$$(x + y - 1) + 4(2x - y + 1) = 0$$

$$9x - 3y + 3 = 0$$

$$3x - y + 1 = 0$$

The idea of a general equation representing a large (frequently infinite) class of straight lines or curves and the specification of subclasses of this general class (that is, families) by imposing certain geometric (and therefore corresponding algebraic) conditions on the lines or curves is very useful in both theoretical and applied mathematics.

PROBLEMS

1. What relation (parallel, perpendicular, coincident, or intersecting) does the line $y - 2x - 4 = 0$ have to the following lines?
   a. $y - x - 2 = 0$ d. $y - 3x - 4 = 0$
   b. $4y - 8x - 16 = 0$ e. $2y + x - 6 = 0$
   c. $5y - 10x - 4 = 0$

2. What relation (parallel, perpendicular, coincident, or intersecting) does the line $2x - 5y + 6 = 0$ have to each of the following lines?
   a. $15x + 6y + 9 = 0$ d. $4x - 8y + 3 = 0$
   b. $10x + 4y - 5 = 0$ e. $6x - 15y + 8 = 0$
   c. $4x - 10y + 12 = 0$ f. $2x - 5y + 2 = 0$

3. What relation (parallel, perpendicular, coincident, or intersecting) does the line $3x + 4y - 2 = 0$ have to each of the following lines?
   a. $15x + 20y - 10 = 0$ d. $3x + y - 4 = 0$
   b. $8x - 6y + 5 = 0$ e. $12x - 9y + 2 = 0$
   c. $9x + 12y + 7 = 0$ f. $2x + y - 6 = 0$

4. Determine whether each of the following pairs of equations are a. independent or dependent and b. consistent or inconsistent.
   i. $2x - 6y + 5 = 0$ and $3x - 8y + 3 = 0$
   ii. $x + 5y - 2 = 0$ and $x + 5y - 5 = 0$
   iii. $3x - 9y + 12 = 0$ and $x - 3y + 4 = 0$
   iv. $5x - 4y - 6 = 0$ and $4x - 5y + 6 = 0$

5. Referring to the pairs of equations in Problem 4, a. determine which pairs of equations have simultaneous solutions and obtain those solutions and b. graph the pairs of equations.

6. If a pair of equations are consistent and independent, do they necessarily have a unique simultaneous solution?

7. If a pair of equations are consistent and dependent, do they necessarily have a simultaneous solution? If so, is it unique?
8. Can a pair of equations be inconsistent and dependent?
9. If a pair of equations represent perpendicular lines, are the equations consistent? Are they independent?
10. Graph the family of straight lines parallel to the x-axis and give the equation corresponding to this specification. Graph the member of this family that passes through the point $(10, -6)$.
11. Graph the family of straight lines passing through the point $(-1, 6)$ and give the equation corresponding to this specification. Graph the member of this family which is parallel to the line $y + 6x - 5 = 0$ and write the equation for this line.
12. Graph the family of straight lines perpendicular to the line $2x - 5y - 10 = 0$ and give the equation corresponding to this specification. Graph the member of this family which passes through the point $(4, -1)$ and write the equation for this line.

Answers to Odd-Numbered Problems

1. a. intersecting   d. intersecting
   b. coincident   e. perpendicular
   c. parallel
3. a. coincident   d. intersecting
   b. perpendicular   e. perpendicular
   c. parallel   f. intersecting
5. a. i. $(11, \frac{9}{2})$
      iii. all points on the line $x - 3y + 4 = 0$
      iv. $(6, 6)$
7. yes; no
9. yes; yes
11. $y = mx + m + 6$; $y = -6x$

1.4 Applications of Straight Lines in Business and Economics

In this section several applications of straight lines in business and economics are discussed. These applications include linear supply and demand curves and the corresponding market equilibria, break-even analysis, and the consumption function.

LINEAR DEMAND AND SUPPLY CURVES

Quantity demanded and quantity supplied of a given commodity are functions of a number of variables, including price of the commodity, prices of substitutes and complements, disposable income, wealth, tastes, habits, and so forth. However, in more elementary economic analysis, demand and supply are usually considered to be functions of only the most important variable, the price of the commodity being considered.

In practice, some demand and supply equations are approximately linear for the relevant range; others are not linear. Even in the latter cases, linear equations may provide reasonably accurate representations of supply and demand for a limited range. In this section linear demand and supply equations are used in illustrating certain types of analyses. Nonlinear equations are discussed in subsequent sections.

Figure 1.14(a) shows a more general representation of supply and demand curves. Figure 1.14(b) represents supply and demand as linear functions. It should be noted, as indicated by the dashed lines in Figure 1.14, that only the segments of the equations which fall in the first quadrant are pertinent to economic analysis. This is

Figure 1.14

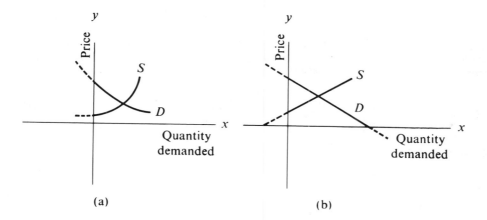

because supply, price, and quantity are, in general, either zero or positive. For example, in simpler forms of economic analysis:

Negative supply implies that goods are not available in the market either because they are not produced or because they are withheld until a satisfactory price is offered.

Negative price implies that prices are paid to buyers for the removal of goods from the market.

Negative demand implies that price is so high as to preclude market activity until quantities are offered at a satisfactory price.

These cases can occur, but their incidence is infrequent and is considered only in more advanced economic analysis.

It is very important to realize that the straight line, mathematically, is perfectly general; the formulas for a straight line do not indicate the range of values of x and y which are to be considered. When it is specified, as it is for the present purpose, that only zero or positive values of x and y are of interest—and conversely, that negative prices or quantities are not meaningful—the range of values for x and y is restricted, usually to nonnegative values. These restrictions are based on the interpretation and meaning of the equation for a *particular application*; they are *not* based on its inherent mathematical properties. This must be kept in mind to avoid misinterpretations, particularly when more complicated equations are considered.

Figure 1.15

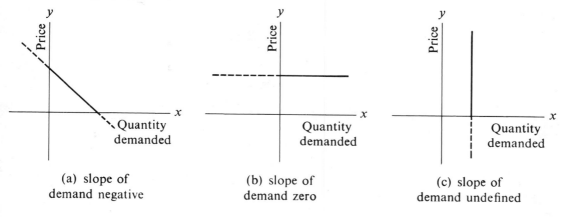

Linear Demand Curves

In the usual case, the slope of a demand curve is negative—that is, as price increases, quantity demanded decreases, and as price decreases, quantity demanded increases. In certain cases the slope of a demand curve may be zero—constant price regardless of demand. In other cases the slope of a demand curve may be undefined—constant demand regardless of price. Figure 1.15 illustrates these three cases.

Depending on the information available, various formulas for straight lines may be most convenient for obtaining the demand function.

EXAMPLE

Ten watches are sold when the price is $80; 20 watches are sold when the price is $60. What is the demand equation?

$$y - y_1 = \frac{y_2 - y_1}{x_2 - x_1}(x - x_1)$$

$$x_1 = 10 \qquad y_1 = 80$$

$$x_2 = 20 \qquad y_2 = 60$$

$$y - 80 = \left(\frac{60 - 80}{20 - 10}\right)(x - 10)$$

$$= -2(x - 10)$$

$$2x + y - 100 = 0$$

(See Figure 1.16.)

Figure 1.16

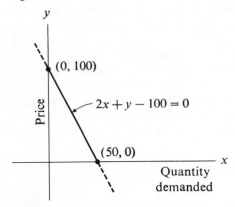

EXAMPLE

When the price is $100, no watches are sold; when watches are free, 50 are demanded. What is the demand equation?

$$\frac{x}{a} + \frac{y}{b} = 1$$

$$a = 50 \qquad b = 100$$

$$\frac{x}{50} + \frac{y}{100} = 1$$

$$2x + y = 100$$

$$2x + y - 100 = 0$$

(See Figure 1.17.)

Figure 1.17

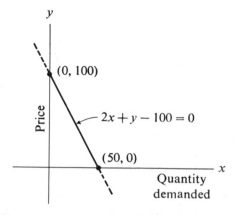

EXAMPLE

Because they are considered necessary for national security, 50 heavy-duty generators are bought every year, regardless of price. What is the demand equation?

$$x = x_1 = 50$$

(See Figure 1.18.)

Figure 1.18

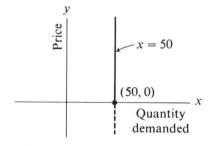

Linear Supply Curves

In the usual case, the slope of the supply curve is positive—that is, as the price increases, quantity supplied increases and as price decreases, quantity supplied decreases. In certain cases, the slope of a supply curve may be zero—constant price regardless of supply. In other cases, the slope of a supply curve may be undefined—constant supply regardless of price (see Figure 1.19).

As in the discussion of demand curves, y represents the price, in appropriate units, and x represents the quantity supplied, in appropriate units. Only positive values of x

Figure 1.19

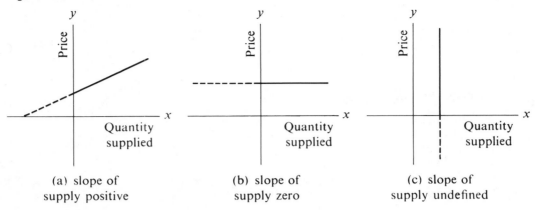

(a) slope of supply positive   (b) slope of supply zero   (c) slope of supply undefined

and y are of interest, as previously stated. Note that for the supply curve in case (a) the y-coordinate of the y-intercept may be positive, negative, or zero.

The x-coordinate of the x-intercept may be negative and, therefore, outside the range of values of interest. This is reasonable since producers usually cease to supply a commodity before the price reaches zero.

As for demand functions, various formulas for straight lines may be convenient for obtaining the supply function, depending on the information available.

EXAMPLE

When the price is \$50, 50 cameras of a fixed type are available for sale; when the price is \$75, 100 of the cameras are available. What is the supply equation?

$$y - y_1 = \frac{y_2 - y_1}{x_2 - x_1}(x - x_1)$$

$$x_1 = 50 \qquad y_1 = 50$$

$$x_2 = 100 \qquad y_2 = 75$$

$$y - 50 = \left(\frac{75 - 50}{100 - 50}\right)(x - 50)$$

$$= \tfrac{1}{2}(x - 50)$$

$$x - 2y + 50 = 0$$

(See Figure 1.20.)

Figure 1.20

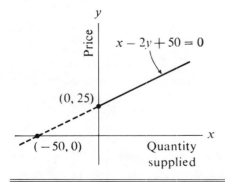

EXAMPLE

When the price is $25, no cameras of a fixed type are available for sale; for every $10 increase in price, 20 more cameras are available. What is the supply equation?

$$y = mx + b \qquad m = \tfrac{1}{2} \qquad b = 25$$
$$y = \tfrac{1}{2}x + 25$$
$$x - 2y + 50 = 0$$

(See Figure 1.21.)

Figure 1.21

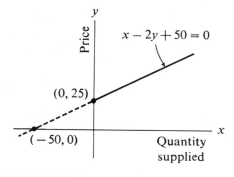

EXAMPLE

According to the terms of the contract between Company A and the telephone company, Company A pays the telephone company $500 per month for long-distance calls of unlimited number and length of time. What is the supply equation?

$$y = y_1 = 500$$

(See Figure 1.22.)

Figure 1.22

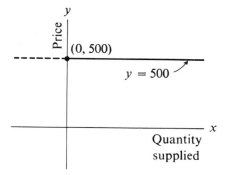

Figure 1.23

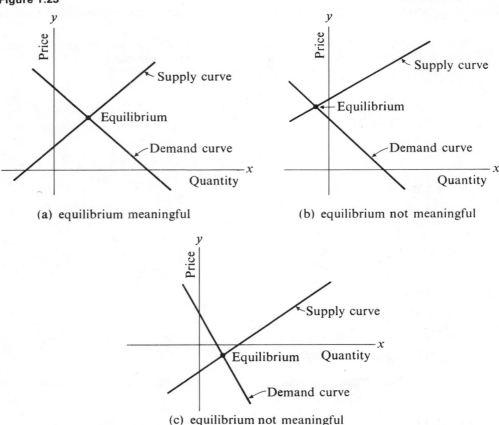

(a) equilibrium meaningful

(b) equilibrium not meaningful

(c) equilibrium not meaningful

Market Equilibrium

Market equilibrium is said to occur at that point (price) at which the quantity of a commodity demanded is equal to the quantity supplied, as shown in Figure 1.23. Thus, provided the same units for x and y are used in both equations, the equilibrium amount and the equilibrium price correspond to the coordinates of the point of intersection of the demand and supply curves. Algebraically, the equilibrium quantity and price are found by solving the supply and demand equations simultaneously (again, provided the same units for x and y are used in both equations).

In general, for an equilibrium to be meaningful, the values of both x and y must be positive or zero—that is, the demand and supply curves must intersect in the first quadrant. This occurs if and only if the y-coordinate of the y-intercept of the demand curve is greater than or equal to the y-coordinate of the y-intercept of the supply curve and the x-coordinate of the x-intercept of the demand curve is greater than or equal to the x-coordinate of the x-intercept of the supply curve. This can be seen geometrically in Figure 1.23; the proof is given in Technical Note I.

EXAMPLE

Find the point of equilibrium for the following demand and supply equations.

$$y = 10 - 2x$$

$$y = \tfrac{3}{2}x + 1$$

Solving the equations simultaneously by substitution,

$$10 - 2x = \tfrac{3}{2}x + 1$$

$$\tfrac{7}{2}x = 9$$

$$x = \tfrac{18}{7}$$

$$y = 10 - 2(\tfrac{18}{7})$$

$$= \tfrac{34}{7}$$

Answer: $(\tfrac{18}{7}, \tfrac{34}{7})$.

Thus, at equilibrium, $2\tfrac{4}{7}$ units are sold at a price of $4\tfrac{6}{7}$. (See Figure 1.24.)

Figure 1.24

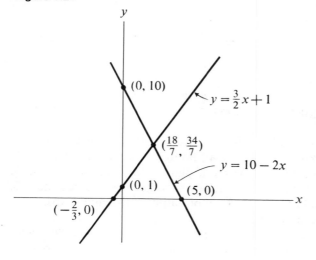

EXAMPLE

Find the point of equilibrium for the following demand and supply equations.

$$y = 5 - 3x$$

$$y = 4x + 12$$

Solving the equations simultaneously by substitution,

$$5 - 3x = 4x + 12$$

$$7x = -7$$

$$x = -1$$

$$y = 5 - 3(-1)$$

$$= 8$$

Answer: $(-1, 8)$ is not a meaningful equilibrium—note that $b_D = 5 < b_S = 12$.

(See Figure 1.25.)

Figure 1.25

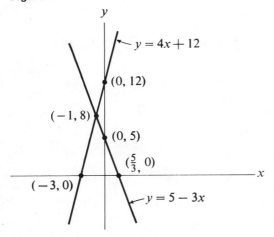

BREAK-EVEN ANALYSIS

Break-even graphs are frequently used in business and economics to analyze the implications of various pricing and production decisions. A break-even graph, in simplified form, is shown in Figure 1.26.

In this particular case, costs have been divided into two general categories: fixed and variable. Fixed costs remain constant at all levels of output and commonly include such items as rent, depreciation, interest, plant, and equipment; variable costs are those which vary with output and include such items as labor, materials, and promotional expense. Total cost at any level of output is the sum of fixed cost and the variable cost at that level of output.

In Figure 1.26 the straight line *FC* represents fixed cost. It is the straight line with the *y*-intercept equal to the constant fixed cost (that is, cost when output is zero) and slope zero.

The line *TC* represents total cost; its *y*-intercept is equal to fixed cost and its slope is equal to the increase in variable cost per unit increase in output. Note the assumption that variable cost is proportional to output over the relevant range.

Figure 1.26

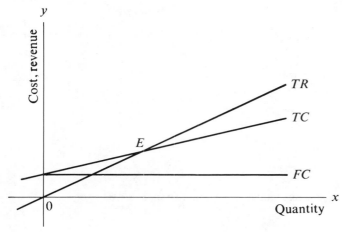

The line TR represents total revenue to the firm for different quantities sold; its intercept is at the origin and its slope is equal to the price per unit, assuming that this price is constant for all quantities sold.

The break-even point E is that point at which the lines TR and TC intersect. It represents the quantity at which the producer just breaks even—that is, the quantity for which there is just sufficient revenue to cover costs. Break-even analysis is used more frequently in practice to demonstrate probable effects of changes in production than to determine what those changes should be.

EXAMPLE

In Figure 1.27, suppose the firm decides that it could sell the same quantity of product, denoted by point Q, if the price per unit were increased so that total revenue would be raised from TR to TR'. TC remains the same, and the break-even point changes from E to E'.

At the original price, profit to the firm is represented by AB; at the higher price, it is represented by $A'B'$.

If, on the other hand, the firm assumes that the increase in price resulting in TR' would reduce the quantity sold to that denoted by point Q', the following would be indicated:

Total cost reduced from that denoted by A to A'
Total revenue reduced from that of point C to C'
Total profit changed from AB to $A'B'$.

Figure 1.27

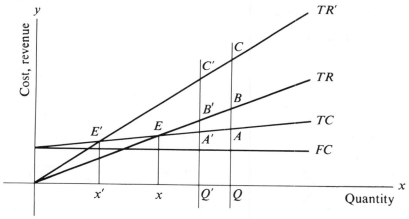

Since the profit area $E'A'C'$ is greater than the profit area EAB resulting from the larger quantity sold at the original price, the company might decide to increase the price even though sales would be expected to drop.

Break-even analysis may be used to study possible results of many combinations of factors involved in a particular problem.

EXAMPLE

Suppose the fixed cost of production for a commodity is $5000; the variable cost is $7.50 per unit and the commodity sells for $10 per unit. What is the break-even quantity?

Cost of production is given by

$$y = 5000 + 7.5x$$

and revenue is given by

$$y = 10x$$

Solving for x,

$$5000 = (10 - 7.50)x$$

$$5000 = 2.5x$$

$$x = 2000$$

The break-even quantity is 2000 units; that is, if 2000 units are produced and sold, revenue equals cost.

THE CONSUMPTION FUNCTION

National income analysis provides an interesting example of the use of linear functions, since the consumption function is frequently assumed to be linear over relatively short ranges or "in the short run." The analysis, in one of its simplest forms, is based on the following assumptions:

1. There is some absolute amount of consumption necessary to maintain life, even though there may be no money income.
2. Consumption is related to disposable income, that is, $c = f(y_d)$.
3. When disposable income increases, consumption will also increase, but by a smaller amount. Stated mathematically, if

   Δy_d represents an increase in disposable income

   and

   Δc represents the resulting change in consumption

   then

   $\dfrac{\Delta c}{\Delta y_d}$ will be positive but less than one, that is, $0 < \dfrac{\Delta c}{\Delta y_d} < 1$

4. The proportion of an increment in disposable income which will be consumed is constant. This proportion is referred to as the "marginal propensity to consume."

   These assumptions can be translated into the point-slope form of the equation for a straight line

   $$c = a + by_d$$

where c represents consumption; a is fixed, basic consumption regardless of income; b is the marginal propensity to consume; and y_d is disposable income.

EXAMPLE

When national disposable income is 0, national consumption is 5 (in billions of dollars). For the economy as a whole consumption is linearly related to national disposable income as follows: At each level of disposable income, consumption equals 5 (in billions of dollars) plus 80 percent of disposable income.

What is the equation that expresses this relationship?

$$c = 5 + 0.8y_d$$

Figure 1.28

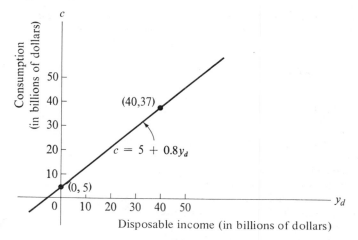

What is aggregate consumption when disposable income is 40 (in billions of dollars)?

$$c = 5 + 0.8(40) = 37$$

that is, consumption is 37 billion dollars when disposable income is 40 billion dollars.

Graph the line representing aggregate consumption as a function of national disposable income. (See Figure 1.28.)

EXAMPLE

Suppose that the consumption function is given by

$$c = 10 + 0.55y_d$$

where c is aggregate consumption and y_d is disposable income (in billions of dollars). What is aggregate consumption when disposable income is 10 billion dollars? When disposable income is 5 billion dollars, what proportion of it is consumed? When disposable income is 5 billion dollars, what proportion of aggregate consumption is consumption of disposable income?

If $y_d = 10$,

$$c = 10 + (0.55)(10)$$

$$= 15.5$$

Thus aggregate consumption is 15.5 billion dollars when disposable income is 10 billion dollars.

The proportion of disposable income that is consumed is 0.55 for any level of disposable income.

If $y_d = 5$,

$$c = 10 + (0.55)(5)$$

$$= 12.75$$

Thus, if disposable income is 10 billion dollars, consumption of disposable income is 2.75 billion dollars, which is $\frac{11}{51}$ or approximately 0.22 of aggregate consumption.

PROBLEMS

1. Which of the following equations represent demand curves, which represent supply curves, and which represent neither demand nor supply curves? (Assume y represents price and x represents quantity.)

   a. $x - 2y = 0$ f. $2x + 5y + 4 = 0$
   b. $3x + 4y - 10 = 0$ g. $3x + 4y - 12 = 0$
   c. $y - 4 = 0$ h. $5x - y - 10 = 0$
   d. $x - 3 = 0$ i. $2y + 3x + 2 = 0$
   e. $2x - 3y + 1 = 0$ j. $x - 3y = 0$

2. The demand curve for a commodity is $x = 10 - y/4$. (Assume y represents price and x represents quantity demanded.)
   a. Find the quantity demanded if the price is i. 4, ii. 16, iii. 25.
   b. Find the price if the quantity demanded is i. 9, ii. 7, iii. 2.
   c. What is the highest price that would be paid for this commodity?
   d. What quantity would be demanded if the commodity were free?
   e. Graph the curve.

3. The supply curve of a commodity is $x = 1.1y - 0.1$. (Assume y represents price and x represents quantity supplied.)
   a. Find the price if the quantity supplied is i. 1, ii. 0.8, iii. 0.5.
   b. Find the quantity supplied if the price is i. 8, ii. 6, iii. 4.1.
   c. What is the lowest price at which this commodity would be supplied?
   d. Graph the curve.

4. The demand equation of a commodity is $x = A - By$, where A and B are positive constants, y represents price, and x represents quantity demanded.
   a. Find the price if the quantity demanded is $A/3$.
   b. Find the quantity demanded if the price is $A/2B$.
   c. Find the quantity demanded if the commodity is free.
   d. What is the highest price that would be paid for this commodity?

5. The supply equation of a commodity is $x = ay - b$, where a and b are positive constants, y represents price, and x represents quantity supplied.
   a. Find the price if the quantity supplied is i. $5a - b$, ii. $a + 2b$.
   b. Find the quantity supplied if the price is i. $3b/a$, ii. $5b/a$.
   c. What is the lowest price at which this commodity would be supplied?

6. For each of the following pairs of straight lines,
   i. Determine which is the demand and which is the supply curve.
   ii. Graph the curves and estimate the market equilibrium price and quantity.
   iii. Solve the equations algebraically and verify the estimates for market equilibrium price and quantity.

   a. $y = 10 - 2x$ and $y = \frac{3}{2}x + 1$ c. $x = 15 - 3y$ and $x = 2y - 3$
   b. $y = 6$ and $x = 3y - 3$ d. $2y + 3x = 10$ and $x = 4y - 6$

7. A manufacturer sells his product at $5 per unit.
   a. What is the total revenue for sales of 5000 units of product? What is the equation for this revenue function? Graph the function.
   b. Fixed costs are constant at $3000 regardless of the number of units of product involved. Superimpose the graph of this function on graph a. above.
   c. Total cost is equal to the sum of fixed costs and variable costs. In this company, variable costs are estimated at 40 percent of total revenue. What is the total cost when 5000 units of product are sold? Graph the function superimposed on graph a.
   d. What is the break-even point? Indicate this point on the graph, and solve for the corresponding amount sold. Indicate on the graph the quantity at which the manufacturer will cover his fixed costs.

8. At a price of $5 per unit, a firm will supply 5000 plastic battery lanterns every month; at $3.50 per unit it will supply 2000 units. Determine the equation of the supply function for this product. Graph the equation.

9. For the economy as a whole, consumption is linearly related to national disposable income as follows: at each level of disposable income, consumption equals 3.5 (in billions of dollars) plus 75 percent of disposable income. a. What is the equation that expresses this relationship? b. What is aggregate consumption when disposable income is 50 (in billions of dollars)?

10. A firm has analyzed its sales and found that its customers will buy 20 percent more units of its products with each $2 reduction in the unit price. When the price is $12, the firm sells 500 units. What is the equation of the demand function for this product? Graph the equation.

11. a. Assume that water is in unlimited supply in a municipality. The consumer pays $5.00 per month for water regardless of the amount used. Graph the demand and supply equations.

    b. There is only one genuine painting by Rembrandt titled "The Night Watch." Assign arbitrary values to the painting and graph the demand and supply equations.

12. A bus company has learned that when the price of a short excursion trip is $5.00, 30 people will buy tickets; when the price is $8.00, only 10 tickets will be sold. Obtain the point-slope form of the equation for the demand function and graph the equation.

13. Identify which of the following equations represents a demand curve and which represents a supply curve; determine the equilibrium point and graph the curves.

    a. $x + y = 5$

    b. $2x - y = 5.5$

14. Change equation b. in Problem 13 to $2x - y = 6$. Graph the equation and identify it as supply or demand. Has the equilibrium quantity involved increased or decreased relative to that in Problem 13?

15. Suppose the fixed cost of production for a commodity is $45,000. The variable cost is 60 percent of the selling price of $15 per unit. What is the break-even quantity?

16. If profit is $100 per unit and the fixed cost of production is $225,000, what is the break-even quantity?

17. Aggregate national consumption is given (in billions of dollars) by the equation

$$c = 4.5 + 0.9y_d$$

where y_d is disposable income. If disposable income is 15 (in billions of dollars), a. What is aggregate consumption? b. What proportion of aggregate consumption is consumption of disposable income?

18. Aggregate national income (in billions of dollars) is 4.8 plus 80 percent of disposable income. a. What is the equation of the consumption function? b. What proportion of disposable income is consumed? c. When disposable income is 60, what proportion of aggregate consumption is consumption of disposable income?

Answers to Odd-Numbered Problems

1. a. supply
   b. demand
   c. supply or demand
   d. supply or demand
   e. supply
   f. neither
   g. demand
   h. supply
   i. neither
   j. supply

3. a. i. 1, ii. 0.818, iii. 0.545   c. 0.091 (cannot be attained)
   b. i. 8.7, ii. 6.5, iii. 4.41

5. a. i. 5, ii. $\dfrac{a + 3b}{a}$ c. b/a (cannot be attained)
   b. i. $2b$, ii. $4b$

7. a. $25,000   d. break-even point at $x = 1000$;
      $TR = 5x$ recovery of fixed costs at
   c. $13,000 $x = 600$

9. a. $c = 3.5 + 0.75y_d$ b. 41 billion dollars

13. equation a. is demand,
    equation b. is supply
    (3.5, 1.5)

15. 5000

17. a. 18 billion dollars b. 0.75

1.5 General Methods of Graphing Nonlinear Curves

Any equation whose graph is not a straight line is referred to as *nonlinear*. There are several types of nonlinear curves, all of which can be classified as either algebraic or transcendental.

A *polynomial* in x and y is the sum of a finite number of terms of the type $kx^r y^s$, where k is a constant and each of the exponents r and s is either a positive integer or zero. The *degree of a term* is $r + s$ and the *degree of the polynomial* is the degree of the term or terms of highest degree. Equations of the form $f(x, y) = 0$, where $f(x, y)$ is a polynomial in x and y, are referred to as *algebraic*; the graphical representation of an algebraic equation is an *algebraic curve*. Note that a straight line is an algebraic curve of degree one.

Any equation in x and y which is not algebraic is referred to as *transcendental*; the graphical representation of a transcendental equation is a *transcendental curve*. Included among the transcendental curves are the graphs of trigonometric, logarithmic, and exponential functions. Curves represented by algebraic equations of degree greater than two in x and y or by transcendental equations are referred to as *higher plane curves*.

The general methods of graphing discussed below can be used for any type of algebraic or transcendental curve. However, for many types of curves, special methods of graphing, which are more efficient than the general methods, are available. The general methods are discussed first. Then methods of identifying and graphing specific types of quadratic curves (circles, ellipses, parabolas, and hyperbolas) and exponential and logarithmic curves are discussed.

Graphing a straight line from its equation is a relatively simple problem, since any two distinct points uniquely determine a straight line. However, graphing more complicated equations is less straightforward. The graph representing any equation can be drawn fairly accurately if a sufficient number of points are plotted, but frequently so many points are required that this method is very laborious. Furthermore, plotting points in itself provides little or no information regarding the important properties of a curve.

From examining an equation, certain properties of the corresponding curve can be determined which will facilitate drawing the curve with a minimum of point plotting. Some of these properties are discussed below and their usefulness in graphing is illustrated. The properties discussed include intercepts, symmetry, extent, asymptotes, factorization, and real, point, and imaginary loci.

INTERCEPTS

The intercepts of a curve are the points at which it crosses the axes. The x-intercepts are obtained by setting $y = 0$ in the equation of the curve and solving for x; the y-intercepts are obtained by setting $x = 0$ in the equation of the curve and solving for y.

SYMMETRY

Two points are *symmetric with respect to a line* if that line is the perpendicular bisector of the line segment joining the two points. Two points are symmetric with respect to a third point if that third point is the midpoint of the line segment joining the first two points. From these definitions it follows that the point (x, y) is symmetric to the point

$(x, -y)$ with respect to the x-axis

$(-x, y)$ with respect to the y-axis

$(-x, -y)$ with respect to the origin

as shown in Figure 1.29.

A curve may also be symmetric with respect to the x-axis, the y-axis or the origin, as shown in Figure 1.30. Refer to parts (a), (b), and (c) of that figure.

(a) A curve is symmetric to the x-axis if for each point (x, y) on the curve the symmetric point $(x, -y)$ is also on the curve—that is, if substitution of $-y$ for y gives an equivalent equation of the curve. For example, a curve is symmetric to the x-axis if it is represented by an algebraic equation in which y occurs only to even powers. Note, however, that there are algebraic curves symmetric to the x-axis whose equations contain odd powers of y. See the example which follows.

Figure 1.29 Symmetry with respect to (a) the x-axis, (b) the y-axis, and (c) the origin.

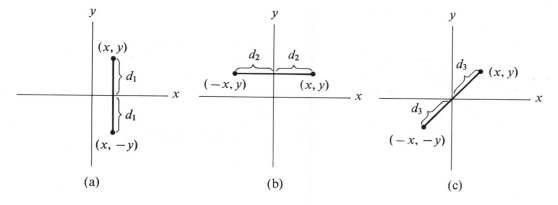

Figure 1.30 Symmetry with respect to (a) the x-axis, (b) the y-axis, and (c) the origin.

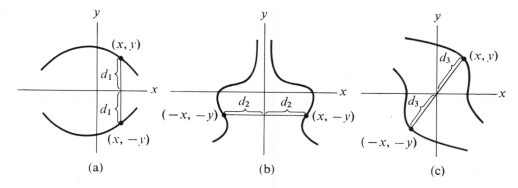

(b) A curve is symmetric to the y-axis if for each point (x, y) on the curve the symmetric point $(-x, y)$ is also on the curve—that is, if substitution of $-x$ for x gives an equivalent equation of the curve. For example, a curve is symmetric to the y-axis if it is represented by an algebraic equation in which x occurs only to even powers.

(c) A curve is symmetric to the origin if for each point (x, y) on the curve, the symmetric point $(-x, -y)$ is also on the curve—that is, if substitution of $-x$ for x and $-y$ for y gives an equivalent equation of the curve. For example, a curve is symmetric to the origin if it is represented by an algebraic equation each of whose terms is of even degree or each of whose terms is of odd degree.

In summary, the graph of an equation $f(x, y) = 0$ is symmetric with respect to

the x-axis if $f(x, y) = f(x, -y) = 0$

the y-axis if $f(x, y) = f(x, y) = 0$

the origin if $f(x, y) = f(-x, -y) = 0$

Note that symmetry with respect to both the x- and y-axes implies symmetry about the origin, but symmetry about the origin does not imply symmetry about either axis. More generally, symmetry with respect to any two of the three (x-axis, y-axis, and origin) implies symmetry with respect to the third. Thus symmetry can occur with respect to none, one, or three of the x-axis, y-axis, and origin but never with respect to just two of them. This can be seen from the definitions above:

Substitution of $-y$ for y
gives an equivalent equation
(x-axis symmetry)
and
substitution of $-x$ for x
gives an equivalent equation
(y-axis symmetry)
$\Rightarrow$
$\not\Leftarrow$
Substitution of $-x$ for x and
$-y$ for y gives an equivalent equation
(symmetry to origin)

and similarly for the other two cases. (The symbol $\Rightarrow$ means "implies," the symbol $\not\Rightarrow$ means "does not imply," the symbol $\Leftarrow$ means "is implied by," the symbol $\not\Leftarrow$ means "is not implied by.")

EXAMPLE

The curve represented by the equation

$3x^2y + y + x^3 = 0$

is symmetric to the origin but not to either axis (see Figure 1.31).

$f(x, -y) = -3x^2y - y + x^3$, so $f(x, -y) = 0$ is not equivalent to $f(x, y) = 0$ and $f(x, y) = 0$ is not symmetric to the x-axis.

$f(-x, y) = 3x^2y + y - x^3$, so $f(-x, y) = 0$ is not equivalent to $f(x, y) = 0$ and $f(x, y) = 0$ is not symmetric to the y-axis.

$f(-x, -y) = -3x^2y - y - x^3$, so $f(-x, -y) = 0$ is the same equation as $f(x, y) = 0$ and $f(x, y) = 0$ is symmetric to the origin.

Figure 1.31

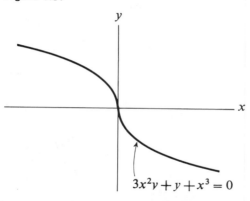

$$3x^2y + y + x^3 = 0$$

EXAMPLE

The curve represented by the equation

$$2x^4 + x^2y + y + 6 = 0$$

is symmetric to the y-axis but not to either the x-axis or the origin (see Figure 1.32).

$f(x, -y) = 2x^4 - x^2y - y + 6$, so $f(x, -y) = 0$ is not equivalent to $f(x, y) = 0$ and $f(x, y) = 0$ is not symmetric to the x-axis.

$f(-x, y) = 2x^4 + x^2y + y + 6$, so $f(-x, y) = 0$ is equivalent to $f(x, y) = 0$ and $f(x, y) = 0$ is symmetric to the y-axis.

$f(-x, -y) = 2x^4 - x^2y - y + 6$, so $f(-x - y) = 0$ is not equivalent to $f(x, y) = 0$ and $f(x, y) = 0$ is not symmetric to the origin.

Figure 1.32

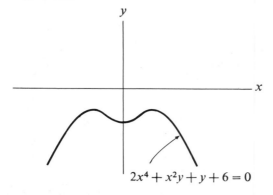

$$2x^4 + x^2y + y + 6 = 0$$

EXAMPLE

The curve represented by the equation

$$5x - y + 6x^2 = 0$$

is not symmetric to the x-axis, the y-axis, or the origin (see Figure 1.33).

$f(x, -y) = 5x + y + 6x^2$, so $f(x, -y) = 0$ is not equivalent to $f(x, y) = 0$ and $f(x, y) = 0$ is not symmetric to the x-axis.

Figure 1.33

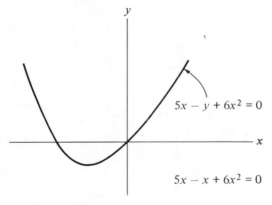

$5x - y + 6x^2 = 0$

$5x - x + 6x^2 = 0$

$f(-x, y) = 5x + y - 6x^2$, so $f(-x, y) = 0$ is not equivalent to $f(x, y) = 0$ and $f(x, y) = 0$ is not symmetric to the y-axis.

$f(-x, -y) = 5x - y - 6x^2$, so $f(-x, -y) = 0$ is not equivalent to $f(x, y) = 0$ and $f(x, y) = 0$ is not symmetric to the origin.

EXAMPLE

The curve represented by the equation

$$x^2 + y^2 - 7 = 0$$

is symmetric to the x-axis, the y-axis, and the origin (see Figure 1.34).

Figure 1.34

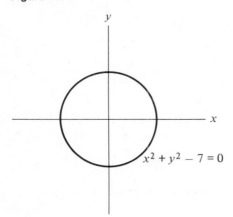

$x^2 + y^2 - 7 = 0$

$f(x, -y) = -x^3y - 3xy$, so $f(x, -y) = 0$ is equivalent to $f(x, y) = 0$ and $f(x, y) = 0$ is symmetric to the x-axis.

$f(-x, y) = -x^3y - 3xy$, so $f(-x, y) = 0$ is equivalent to $f(x, y) = 0$ and $f(x, y) = 0$ is symmetric to the y-axis.

$f(-x, -y) = x^3y + 3xy$, so $f(-x, -y) = 0$ is equivalent to $f(x, y) = 0$ and $f(x, y) = 0$ is symmetric to the origin.

Figure 1.35 Symmetry with respect to (a) the line $x = h$, (b) the line $y = k$, and (c) the point (h, k).

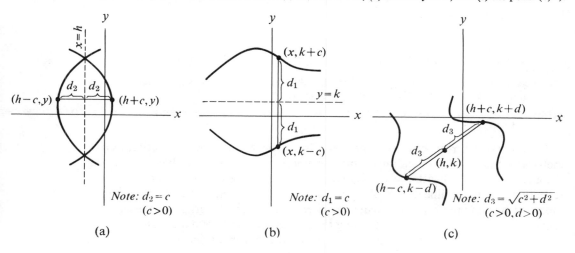

In graphing an equation it is seldom practical to consider symmetry with respect to lines other than the coordinate axes or points other than the origin; exceptions to this are curves whose equations are of a particular form from which lines or points of symmetry are readily identified. Examples of such equations are given in later sections.

Occasionally it is desired to construct an equation whose curve is symmetric with respect to certain lines or points. In these problems the following rules, of which the above are special cases, are useful (see Figure 1.35): The graph of the equation $f(x, y) = 0$ is symmetric with respect to

the line $x = h$ if $f(h + c, y) = f(h - c, y) = 0$ for all c and y

the line $y = k$ if $f(x, k + c) = f(x, k - c) = 0$ for all c and x

the point (h, k) if $f(h + c, k + d) = f(h - c, k - d) = 0$ for all c and d

Symmetry of the curve $f(x, y) = 0$ with respect to the line $Ax + By + C = 0$ can be determined as follows.

If $f(x, y) = 0 \Rightarrow f(x - 2\alpha\delta, y - 2\beta\delta) = 0$

where $\alpha = \dfrac{A}{A^2 + B^2}$, $\beta = \dfrac{B}{A^2 + B^2}$, $\delta = Ax + By + C$

then $f(x, y) = 0$ is symmetric with respect to the line $Ax + By + C = 0$.

EXAMPLE

For the line $x - h = 0$, $A = 1$, $B = 0$, and $C = -h$. Thus

$\alpha = 1$, $\beta = 0$, and $\delta = x - h$

$x - 2\alpha\delta = x - 2(x - h) = 2h - x$

$y - 2\beta\delta = y - 0 - y$

and the symmetry condition is $f(x, y) = 0 \Rightarrow f(2h - x, y) = 0$. Take $x = h + c$; then $2h - x = h - c$, and $f(h + c, y) = 0 \Rightarrow f(h - c, y) = 0$, as above.

Similarly, for the line $y - k = 0$, $A = 0$, $B = 1$, and $C = -k$. Thus

$\alpha = 0$, $\beta = 1$, and $\delta = y - k$

$x - 2\alpha\delta = x - 0 = x$

$y - 2\beta\delta = y - 2(y - k) = 2k - y$

and the symmetry condition is $f(x, y) = 0 \Rightarrow f(x, 2k - y) = 0$. Take $y = k + c$; then $2k - y = k - c$, and $f(x, k + c) = 0 \Rightarrow f(x, k - c) = 0$, as above.

Symmetry with respect to the line $y = x$ is a property of inverse functions. Geometrically, the problem of finding the inverse function of $f(x)$ is the problem of viewing the graph of $y = f(x)$ with the x-axis and y-axis interchanged, which is equivalent to reflection about the line $y = x$. Thus the graph of the inverse of a function can be obtained by drawing a perpendicular from each point on the graph of the original function to the line $y = x$ and extending the perpendicular an equal distance beyond the line $y = x$. The points thus obtained are the graph of the inverse function $y = f^{-1}(x)$. (See Figure 1.36.)

Figure 1.36 Symmetry with respect to the line $y = x$.

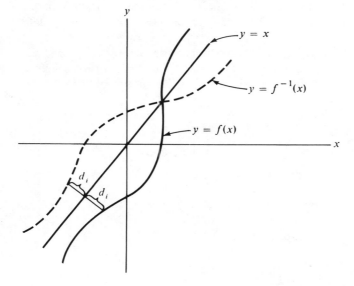

EXTENT

The rectangular coordinate system defined represents only those points (x, y) whose coordinates are real numbers; thus values of x for which y is imaginary and values of y for which x is imaginary must be excluded. When even powers of a variable appear in an equation, the solution for that variable may involve square roots (or other even roots) and the extent of the curve may then be limited, since negative numbers do not have real square roots (or other even roots). When possible, an equation should be solved explicitly for each variable to see whether the range of any variable is limited and the curve is correspondingly limited in extent. Note that any limitation on the extent of one variable may implicitly limit the extent of the other variable. Such limitations are purely mathematical, unlike those required by some applications, for example, nonnegative variables.

EXAMPLE

Determine whether there is any limitation on the extent of the curve represented by the equation

$$x^2 + y^2 = 9$$

Solving for x,

$$x = \pm\sqrt{9 - y^2}$$

the quantity under the radical sign $9 - y^2$ is negative if $|y| > 3$; the extent of the curve in the y-direction is therefore limited to the interval $-3 \le y \le 3$.

Solving for y,

$$y = \pm\sqrt{9 - x^2}$$

and the extent of the curve in the x-direction is therefore similarly limited to the interval $-3 \le x \le 3$.

EXAMPLE

Determine whether there is any limitation on the extent of the curve represented by the equation

$$x^2 - y^2 = 4$$

Solving for x,

$$x = \pm\sqrt{4 + y^2}$$

the quantity under the radical sign $4 + y^2$ is always positive and the extent of the curve in the y-direction is therefore not limited.

Solving for y,

$$y = \pm\sqrt{x^2 - 4}$$

the quantity under the radical sign $x^2 - 4$ is negative if $|x| < 2$; the extent of the curve in the x-direction is therefore limited to the values $x \le -2$ or $x \ge 2$.

PROBLEMS

For each of the following equations, determine a. the intercepts; b. whether the curve represented is symmetric to the x-axis, the y-axis, or the origin; and c. whether there is any limitation on extent.

1. $x^3 - y^2 - 9 = 0$
2. $x^2 + y^2 - 18 = 0$
3. $y^2 - 2x + 5 = 0$

4. $xy + 5x - 15 = 0$
5. $x^2 + y^4 - 6 = 0$
6. $x^2 y^2 - 25 = 0$

Answers to Odd-Numbered Problems

1. a. intercepts: $(\sqrt[3]{9}, 0)$
   b. symmetry: about the x-axis
   c. extent: $x^3 \ge 9$, y not limited
3. a. intercepts: $(\frac{5}{2}, 0)$
   b. symmetry: about the x-axis
   c. extent: $x \ge \frac{5}{2}$, y not limited

5. a. intercepts: $(0, \sqrt[4]{6})$, $(\sqrt{6}, 0)$
   b. symmetry: about the x-axis, y-axis, and origin
   c. extent: $x^2 \le 6$, $y^4 \le 6$

ASYMPTOTES

A curve may have the property that a point can move along it so that the distance from the origin to the point increases without limit. If, as the distance (in some direction) of a point from the origin increases without limit, the distance between the point and a fixed straight line approaches zero through values of the same sign, that is, the curve approaches the line from one side of it, the line is called an *asymptote* of the curve.

To show that a particular line is an asymptote of a particular curve it is necessary to show that the curve approaches arbitrarily close to the line as the distance from the origin increases without bound. This property involves the concept of limits, which will be discussed in succeeding sections.

In general, then, the line $y = mx + b$ is an asymptote of the curve $y = f(x)$ if $f(x)$ is only less than or only greater than $mx + b$ and becomes arbitrarily close to $mx + b$ as x and y increase without bound. This may be written $f(x) \to mx + b$ as $x, y \to \infty$. (See Figure 1.37.)

Asymptotes that are parallel to or coincident with one of the coordinate axes are frequently of particular interest. These vertical and horizontal asymptotes are defined as follows (see Figure 1.38).

The line $x = h$ is a *vertical asymptote* of the curve $y = f(x)$ if $x \to h$ as $y \to \infty$ and either $x < h$ or $x > h$ for all x.

The line $y = k$ is a *horizontal asymptote* of the curve $y = f(x)$ if $y \to k$ as $x \to \infty$ and either $y < k$ or $y > k$ for all y.

For purposes of graphing, it is helpful to determine the behavior of a curve with respect to each of its asymptotes, in addition to determining the existence of the asymptotes. Thus the equation should be examined as x and y in turn increase without bound $(x \to +\infty, y \to +\infty)$ and as x and y in turn decrease without bound $(x \to -\infty, y \to -\infty)$; the value of the variable which is not increasing or decreasing without bound should also be noted, in order to determine whether the curve is approaching its asymptote from the left or the right (vertical asymptotes) or from above or below (horizontal asymptotes). When investigating asymptotes, it is usually helpful to solve an equation explicitly first for one variable and then for the other

Figure 1.37| $f(x) \to mx + b$ as $x, y \to \infty$; (a) from above, (b) from below.

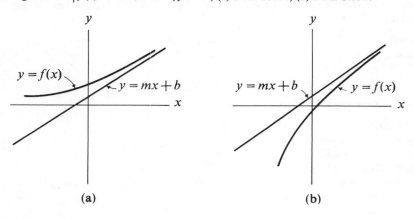

(a)   (b)

Figure 1.38

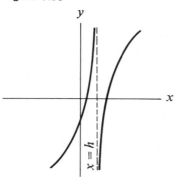 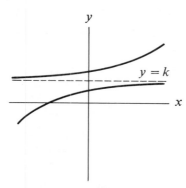

(a) vertical asymptote: $x = h$ (b) horizontal asymptote: $y = k$

variable, if possible. As noted above, this procedure is also useful in determining possible limitations on extent; since such limitations may prevent the variable involved from increasing or decreasing without bound, they are important in considering asymptotes.

EXAMPLE

Determine whether the curve represented by the following equation has vertical and/or horizontal asymptotes:

$$xy + x - 3y - 2 = 0$$

(see Figure 1.39).
Solving for x,

$$x = \frac{3y + 2}{y + 1}$$

Figure 1.39

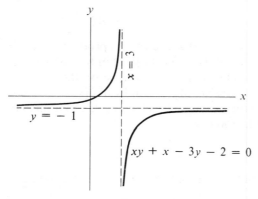

as $y \to +\infty$, $x \to 3$, and $x < 3$; as $y \to -\infty$, $x \to 3$, and $x > 3$; thus $x = 3$ is an asymptote of the curve and is approached from left and right.
Solving for y,

$$y = \frac{x - 2}{3 - x}$$

as $x \to +\infty$, $y \to -1$, and $y < -1$; as $x \to -\infty$, $y \to -1$, and $y > -1$; thus $y = -1$ is an asymptote of the curve and is approached from above and below.

EXAMPLE

Determine whether the curve represented by the following equation has vertical and/or horizontal asymptotes:

$$x^2 - y - 1 = 0$$

(see Figure 1.40).
   Solving for x,

$$x = \pm\sqrt{y + 1}$$

as $y \to +\infty$, $x \to \pm\infty$; $y > -1$, so y cannot approach $-\infty$; thus the curve does not have a vertical asymptote.
   Solving for y,

$$y = x^2 - 1$$

as $x \to +\infty$, $y \to +\infty$; as $x \to -\infty$, $y \to +\infty$ (as above); thus the curve does not have a horizontal asymptote.

Figure 1.40

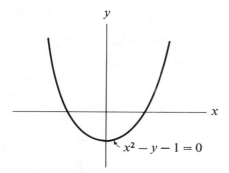

$$x^2 - y - 1 = 0$$

FACTORIZATION

If the left member of the equation $f(x, y) = 0$ can be written as the product of two or more factors, for example, if $f(x, y) = g(x, y) \cdot h(x, y) = 0$, then only those points (x, y) whose coordinates satisfy either $g(x, y) = 0$ or $h(x, y) = 0$ lie on the graph of $f(x, y) = 0$. Thus the graph of $f(x, y) = 0$ consists of the graphs of $g(x, y) = 0$ and $h(x, y) = 0$. It is important to check for factorization, since a factorable equation may be difficult to graph correctly if it is not factored.

EXAMPLE

Graph the equation

$$x^2 y - xy^2 - x + y = 0$$

(see Figure 1.41).
   Factoring,

$$xy(x - y) - x + y = 0$$
$$xy(x - y) - (x - y) = 0$$
$$(xy - 1)(x - y) = 0$$

Figure 1.41

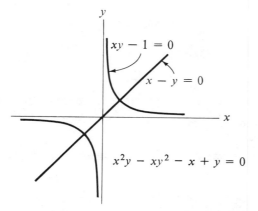

Thus the graph of $x^2y - xy^2 - x + y = 0$ consists of the graphs of the curve $xy - 1 = 0$ and the straight line $x - y = 0$.

EXAMPLE

Graph the equation

$$2x^2 - 3xy - 2y^2 = 0$$

(see Figure 1.42).

Figure 1.42

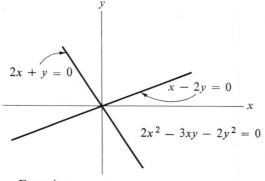

Factoring,

$$(2x + y)(x - 2y) = 0$$

Thus the graph of $2x^2 - 3xy - 2y^2 = 0$ consists of the graphs of the straight lines $2x + y = 0$ and $x - 2y = 0$.

REAL CURVE, POINT LOCUS, OR IMAGINARY LOCUS

Some equations are satisfied by the coordinates of only one point or of a finite number of points; the graphs of such equations are called *point loci*. Other equations are satisfied by the coordinates of no real point; since such equations have no graphical representation in a system of real axes, they are said to represent *imaginary loci*.

EXAMPLE

The equation $x^2 + y^2 = 0$ is satisfied only by the point $(0, 0)$, and its graph is thus a point locus.

EXAMPLE

The equation $(x^2 - 4)^2 + (y^2 - 4)^2 = 0$ is satisfied only by the points $(2, 2)$, $(2, -2)$, $(-2, 2)$, and $(-2, -2)$, and its graph is thus a point locus.

EXAMPLE

The equation $x^2 + y^2 = -5$ is satisfied by no pair of real numbers x and y and its locus is thus imaginary.

PROBLEMS

For each of the following equations, determine a. the asymptotes; b. whether the equation can be factored; and c. whether the equation represents a real curve, point locus, or imaginary curve.

1. $2xy - x + y + 5 = 0$
2. $3x^2 + 2xy - y^2 = 0$
3. $2x^2 + 3y^2 + 6 = 0$
4. $3x^2 + 3xy - 2x - 2y = 0$
5. $3x^2 + 6y^2 + x^2y^2 = 0$
6. $3x^2 - 4y^2 - 9 = 0$

Answers to Odd-Numbered Problems

1. a. asymptotes: $y \to \infty$, $x \to -\frac{1}{2}$; $x \to \infty$, $y \to \frac{1}{2}$
   b. cannot be factored
   c. real curve
3. a. asymptotes: none
   b. cannot be factored
   c. imaginary curve
5. a. asymptotes: none
   b. cannot be factored
   c. point locus

SUMMARY: GENERAL METHODS OF GRAPHING NONLINEAR CURVES

In the preceding sections properties of curves that are helpful in graphing are discussed. These properties include:

1. Intercepts
2. Symmetry
3. Extent
4. Asymptotes
5. Factorization
6. Real curve, point locus, or imaginary locus

The following examples illustrate the use of these six properties in graphing a given equation. Although factorization occurs near the end of the list (because in practice factorable equations occur relatively infrequently), it should be checked first, as it may make investigation of some of the other properties unnecessary. The emphasis here is on determining properties of the curves from their equations; greater accuracy in graphing can be attained by plotting more points and, particularly, by methods of differential calculus to be discussed subsequently.

EXAMPLE

Graph the equation

$$y = (x + 2)(x - 3)^2$$

(see Figure 1.43).

Figure 1.43

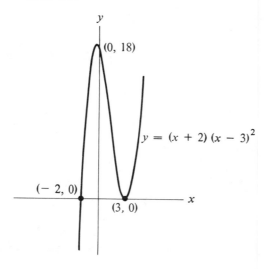

Intercepts: If $y = 0$, $x = -2, 3$; if $x = 0$, $y = 18$.
Symmetry: Not symmetric with respect to either axis or the origin.
Extent: No apparent limits.
Asymptotes: No horizontal or vertical asymptotes (as $x \to +\infty$, $y \to +\infty$ and as $x \to -\infty$, $y \to -\infty$).
Factorization: Not factorable. [Note that factorability refers to the equation $f(x, y) = (x + 2)(x - 3)^2 - y = 0$, which is not factorable, although $y = f(x) = (x + 2)(x - 3)^2$ is, in fact, factored.]
Real, point, or imaginary locus: Real curve.

EXAMPLE

Graph the equation

$$x^2 - 4x + y - 12 = 0$$

(see Figure 1.44).
Intercepts: If $y = 0$, $x = -2, 6$; if $x = 0$, $y = 12$.
Symmetry: Not symmetric with respect to either axis or the origin.
Extent: No apparent limits.

Figure 1.44

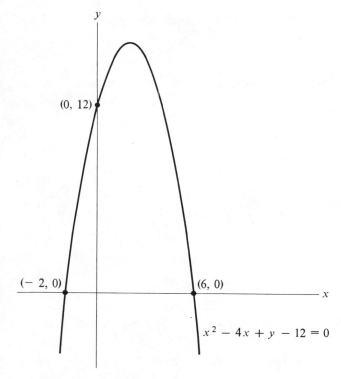

Asymptotes: None (as $x \to +\infty$, $y \to -\infty$ and $x \to -\infty$, $y \to -\infty$).
Factorization: Not factorable.
Real, point, or imaginary locus: Real curve.

EXAMPLE

Graph the equation

$$xy - y - x - 2 = 0$$

(see Figure 1.45).

Intercepts: If $y = 0$, $x = -2$; if $x = 0$, $y = -2$.
Symmetry: Not symmetric with respect to either axis or the origin.
Extent: Solving for x,

$$x = \frac{y + 2}{y - 1}$$

So no limitation on the extent of y, except x is not defined for $y = 1$. Solving for y,

$$y = \frac{x + 2}{x - 1}$$

So no limitation on the extent of x except y is not defined for $x = 1$.

Asymptotes: $x = (y + 2)/(y - 1)$. As $y \to +\infty$, $x \to 1$ and $x > 1$; as $y \to -\infty$, $x \to 1$ and $x < 1$; so $x = 1$ is an asymptote. $y = (x + 2)/(x - 1)$. As $x \to +\infty$, $y \to 1$ and $y > 1$; as $x \to -\infty$, $y \to 1$ and $y < 1$; so $y = 1$ is an asymptote.
Factorization: Not factorable.
Real, point, or imaginary locus: Real curve.

Figure 1.45

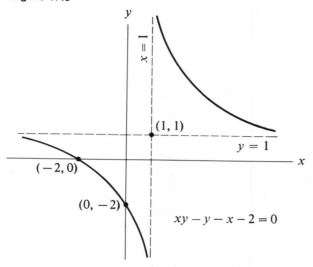

$xy - y - x - 2 = 0$

EXAMPLE

Graph the equation

$$xy + x^2 = 0$$

(see Figure 1.46).

Figure 1.46

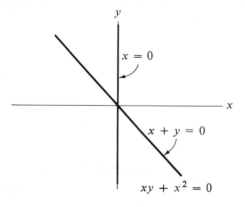

$xy + x^2 = x(y + x) = 0$, so the graph consists of the two straight lines $x = 0$ and $x + y = 0$. The line $x = 0$ is the y-axis. The line $x + y = 0$ has intercept $(0, 0)$ and slope -1.

EXAMPLE

Graph the equation

$$y^3 + xy^2 - xy - x^2 = 0$$

(see Figure 1.47).

Figure 1.47

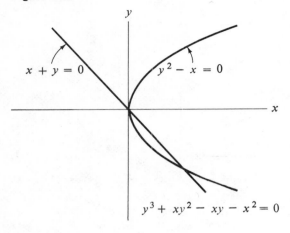

$x + y = 0$

$y^2 - x = 0$

x

$y^3 + xy^2 - xy - x^2 = 0$

$y^3 + xy^2 - xy - x^2 = y^2(y + x) - x(y + x) = (y^2 - x)(y + x) = 0$, so the graph consists of the straight line $x + y = 0$ and the curve $y^2 - x = 0$. The line $x + y = 0$ has intercept $(0, 0)$ and slope -1. Graphing the equation $y^2 - x = 0$,

Intercepts: If $y = 0$, $x = 0$; if $x = 0$, $y = 0$.

Symmetry: Symmetric with respect to the x-axis.

Extent: Solving for x, $x = y^2$, so there is no limitation on the extent of y; solving for y, $y = \pm\sqrt{x}$, so x is limited to $x \geq 0$.

Asymptotes: None (as $x \to +\infty$, $y \to \pm\infty$).

EXAMPLE

Graph the equation

$$x^4 + x^2 - y^2 - y = 0$$

(see Figure 1.48).

$$x^4 + x^2 - y^2 - y = (x^2 + y)(x^2 - y) + (x^2 - y)$$
$$= (x^2 - y)(x^2 + y + 1) = 0$$

so the graph consists of the curves $x^2 - y = 0$ and $x^2 + y + 1 = 0$. Graphing the equation $x^2 - y = 0$,

Intercepts: If $y = 0$, $x = 0$; if $x = 0$, $y = 0$.

Symmetry: Symmetric with respect to the y-axis.

Extent: Solving for x, $x = \pm\sqrt{y}$, so y is limited to $y \geq 0$. Solving for y, $y = x^2$, so there is no limitation on the extent of x.

Asymptotes: No horizontal or vertical asymptotes (as $x \to +\infty$, $y \to +\infty$; as $x \to -\infty$, $y \to +\infty$).

Graphing the equation $x^2 + y + 1 = 0$,

Intercepts: If $y = 0$, $x = \sqrt{-1}$ (imaginary); if $x = 0$, $y = -1$.

Symmetry: Symmetric with respect to the y-axis.

Extent: Solving for x, $x = \pm\sqrt{-y - 1}$, so y is limited to $y \leq -1$. Solving for y, $y = -1 - x^2$, so there is no limitation on the extent of x.

Asymptotes: None (as $x \to +\infty$, $y \to +\infty$; as $x \to -\infty$, $y \to +\infty$).

Figure 1.48

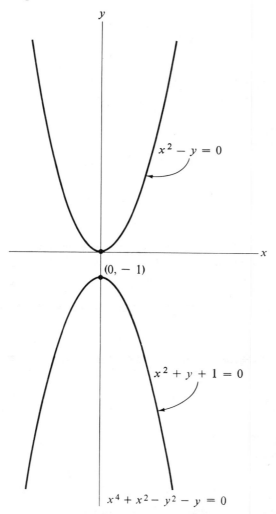

EXAMPLE

Graph the equation

$$x^2 y - x^2 - 4y = 0$$

(see Figure 1.49).

Intercepts: If $y = 0$, $x = 0$; if $x = 0$, $y = 0$.

Symmetry: Symmetric with respect to the y-axis.

Extent: Solving for x,

$$x = \pm \sqrt{\frac{4y}{y-1}} = \pm 2\sqrt{\frac{y}{y-1}}$$

$y/(y-1)$ is negative if $0 < y < 1$ and is undefined if $y = 1$, so y is limited to the intervals $y \le 0$ and $y > 1$. Solving for y, $y = x^2/(x^2 - 4)$, so there is no limitation on the extent of x except y is not defined for $x = \pm 2$.

Asymptotes: $x = \pm 2\sqrt{y/(y-1)}$. As $y \to +\infty$, $x \to \pm 2$ and $x > |2|$; as $y \to -\infty$, $x \to \pm 2$

Figure 1.49

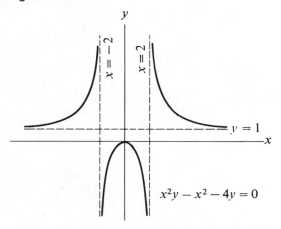

and $x < |2|$; so $x = \pm 2$ are asymptotes. $y = x^2/(x^2 - 4)$. As $x \to +\infty$, $y \to 1$ and $y > 1$; as $x \to -\infty$, $y \to 1$ and $y > 1$, so $y = 1$ is an asymptote.

Factorization: Not factorable.

Real, point, or imaginary locus: Real curve.

EXAMPLE

Graph the equation

$$x^2y - x^2 + 4y = 0$$

(see Figure 1.50).

Intercepts: If $x = 0$, $y = 0$; if $y = 0$, $x = 0$.

Symmetry: Symmetric with respect to the y-axis.

Extent: Solving for x,

$$x = \pm \sqrt{\frac{4y}{1-y}} = \pm 2\sqrt{\frac{y}{1-y}}$$

$y/(1 - y)$ is negative if $y < 0$ or $y > 1$ and is undefined if $y = 1$, so y is limited to the interval $0 \le y < 1$. Solving for y, $y = x^2/(x^2 + 4)$, so there is no limitation on the extent of x.

Figure 1.50

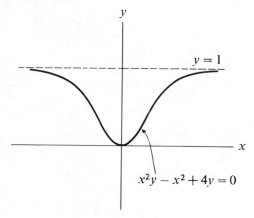

$$x^2y - x^2 + 4y = 0$$

Asymptotes: $x = \pm 2\sqrt{y/(1-y)}$. y is limited in extent and cannot become large or small without bound. $y = x^2/(x^2+4)$. As $x \to +\infty$, $y \to 1$ and $y < 1$; as $x \to -\infty$, $y \to 1$ and $y < 1$, so $y = 1$ is an asymptote.

Factorization: Not factorable.

Real, point, or imaginary locus: Real curve.

EXAMPLE

Graph the equation

$$y^2 - 4xy^2 - 1 = 0$$

(see Figure 1.51).

Intercepts: If $y = 0$, x is not defined; if $x = 0$, $y = \pm 1$.

Symmetry: Symmetric with respect to the x-axis.

Extent: Solving for x,

$$x = \frac{y^2 - 1}{4y^2}$$

so there is no limitation on the extent of y, except that x is not defined for $y = 0$. Solving for y,

$$y = \pm \sqrt{\frac{1}{1 - 4x}}$$

so x is limited to $x < \frac{1}{4}$.

Asymptotes: $x = (y^2 - 1)/4y^2$. As $y \to \pm\infty$, $x \to \frac{1}{4}$, so $x = \frac{1}{4}$ is an asymptote.

$$y = \pm \sqrt{\frac{1}{1 - 4x}}.$$

Figure 1.51

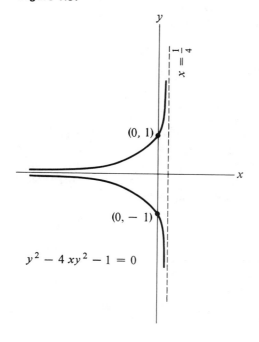

$$y^2 - 4xy^2 - 1 = 0$$

x is limited in extent and cannot become large without bound. As $x \to -\infty$, $y \to 0$, so $y = 0$ is an asymptote.

Factorization: Not factorable.

Real, point, or imaginary locus: Real curve.

PROBLEMS

Sketch the curves represented by the following equations; give intercepts, extent, symmetry, and asymptotes, as relevant.

1. $x^2 y = 10$
2. $xy^2 = -10$
3. $y = x(x - 3)(x + 4)$
4. $y = x^2(x^2 - 4x + 4)$
5. $y = x^4 - x^2$
6. $y = (x^2 - 1)(x^2 - 4)$
7. $y = x^3 - 4x$
8. $y = x^3(x - 1)(x + 6)$
9. $4y = x^3$
10. $y = x^2(x - 3)^2$
11. $y = x\sqrt{9 - x^2}$
12. $y = x^2\sqrt{9 - x^2}$
13. $y = (x - 3)(x^2 - 4x - 5)$
14. $y = x^2(x - 6)(x^2 - x - 6)$

Answers to Odd-Numbered Problems

1. intercepts: none
   extent: $y > 0$, x not limited
   symmetry: about y-axis
   asymptotes: $x = 0$, $y = 0$
3. intercepts: $(0, 0)$, $(3, 0)$, $(-4, 0)$
   extent: not limited
   symmetry: none
   asymptotes: none
5. intercepts: $(0, 0)$, $(\pm 1, 0)$
   extent: not limited
   symmetry: about y-axis
   asymptotes: none
7. intercepts: $(0, 0)$, $(\pm 2, 0)$
   extent: not limited
   symmetry: about origin
   asymptotes: none

9. intercepts: $(0, 0)$
   extent: not limited
   symmetry: about origin
   asymptotes: none
11. intercepts: $(0, 0)$, $(\pm 3, 0)$
    extent: $-3 \le x \le 3$, y not limited
       except by range of x
    symmetry: about origin
    asymptotes: none
13. intercepts: $(0, 15)$, $(3, 0)$, $(5, 0)$,
       $(-1, 0)$
    extent: not limited
    symmetry: none
    asymptotes: none

1.6 Quadratic Curves

A quadratic equation may represent a circle, an ellipse, a parabola, a hyperbola, or various degenerate or imaginary cases of these curves. The identification of a quadratic equation as representing one of these types of curves is discussed in this section; the standard form for each type of equation is then considered for purposes of graphical representation. Families of quadratic curves are also discussed.

An equation of the form

$$Ax^2 + Bxy + Cy^2 + Dx + Ey + F = 0 \tag{2}$$

where A, B, C, D, E, and F are constants and at least one of A, B, and C is nonzero, is said to be a *second-degree* or *quadratic equation*. An equation is said to be quadratic in a variable if that variable occurs to the second and no higher power. Note that if $A = C = 0$ and $B \ne 0$, then Equation (2) is of second degree in x and y combined. Equation (2) is the general equation of second degree in two variables.

Figure 1.52 Conic sections.

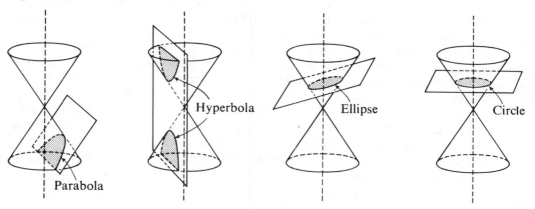

Since it is possible to remove the xy-term from any second-degree equation, making B zero, by rotating the original axes about the origin, the general quadratic equation actually can be written

$$Ax^2 + Cy^2 + Dx + Ey + F = 0$$

relative to the new axes obtained. This procedure will not be discussed in detail, because it is seldom necessary to use it in practice.

Essentially, absence of the xy-term in a second-degree equation indicates that the corresponding curve is symmetric to a line or lines (axes of the curve) parallel to one or both of the coordinate axes. A circle, by definition, always has this type of symmetry and B is always zero for a circle.

The curves represented by Equation (2) can be obtained by cutting a (double) cone with a plane and thus are known as *conic sections*. The four special forms of a conic section are the circle, the ellipse, the parabola, and the hyperbola (see Figure 1.52). In addition to these curves, Equation (2) may represent various types of *degenerate conics* (actually special cases of conic sections). Degenerate conics may be represented by two intersecting straight lines, two parallel straight lines, two coincident straight lines (that is, one straight line), a point, or no points at all.

Any conic section can be defined as the locus of a point that moves in such a way that the ratio of its distance from a fixed point (called its *focus*) to its distance from a fixed line (called its *directrix*) is a constant e (called its *eccentricity*). Conic sections can be classified into the four basic types according to the value of their eccentricity. (For a circle, $e = 0$; for an ellipse, $0 < e < 1$; for a parabola, $e = 1$; for a hyperbola, $e > 1$.)

There are many interesting scientific applications of conic sections. For example, the planets move in elliptic orbits about the sun with the sun at a focus; whispering galleries usually have elliptical ceilings arranged so that a person standing at one focus can hear a slight noise made at the other focus while someone standing between the two foci hears nothing; elliptic arches are frequently used in architecture. The cable of a suspension bridge hangs in the form of an arc of a parabola; a reflecting surface made by rotating a parabola about its axis will send the light out in parallel rays if the source of light is at the focus; the larger reflector in a reflecting telescope is usually parabolic; the path of a projectile, neglecting air resistance, is a parabola. The small reflector of a reflecting telescope is often a hyperbolic mirror (used to reflect the image to the eyepiece); the hyperbola can be used to locate an invisible source of sound, such as an enemy's guns, by considering two listening posts as the foci of a hyperbola and performing certain computations on the difference in time of arrival of the sound of the gun at the listening posts.

In economics and business, certain types of parabolic and hyperbolic curves are appropriate for representing demand and supply functions, production functions, and many other relationships. Applications of circular and elliptic curves are less common but occur, for example, in representing product transformation functions.

The type of curve represented by a second-degree equation can be identified from an examination of its coefficients, whether or not the equation includes an xy-term. However, only if the equation has no xy-term can it readily be put into an appropriate standard form from which properties useful for graphing and for other purposes can be obtained and from which degenerate cases can be identified.

Identification of a Quadratic Equation

The general quadratic equation

$$Ax^2 + Bxy + Cy^2 + Dx + Ey + F = 0$$

with at least one of A and C nonzero can be identified as a circle, ellipse, parabola, or hyperbola as follows:

If $B = 0$ and $A = C \neq 0$, the curve is a circle
If $B^2 - 4AC < 0$, the curve is an ellipse
If $B^2 - 4AC = 0$, the curve is a parabola
If $B^2 - 4AC > 0$, the curve is a hyperbola

Direct identification of degenerate and imaginary loci is discussed in Technical Note II.

For the special case $B = 0$, with at least one of A and C nonzero, the above identification procedure can be reduced to the following:

If $A = C \neq 0$, the curve is a circle
If $A \neq C$, but A and C have the same sign, the curve is an ellipse
If $A = 0$ or $C = 0$ but not both, the curve is a parabola
If A and C have opposite signs, the curve is a hyperbola

The standard forms for each of the four types of curves and their geometrical representations and properties are discussed in the following sections. The algebraic procedure known as "completing the square," which is used to put equations into these standard forms, is discussed in detail in Technical Note III.

THE CIRCLE

Geometrically, a circle is the locus of points in a plane which are a fixed distance from a given point called the *center*. The distance of the points from the center is the *radius* of the circle. The general equation of a circle can be written

$$Ax^2 + Ay^2 + Dx + Ey + F = 0$$

(since $A = C \neq 0$ and $B = 0$ in the general quadratic equation). As shown in Technical Note III, any equation that represents a circle can be written in the standard form

$$(x - h)^2 + (y - k)^2 = r^2$$

where (h, k) is the center of the circle and r is its radius, as shown in Figure 1.53.

Figure 1.53

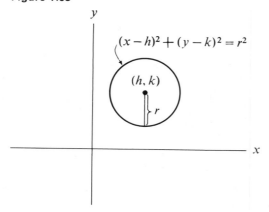

When an attempt is made to put an equation in the standard form for a circle, degenerate or imaginary loci can be detected from the indicated value of r^2:

If $r^2 < 0$, there is no real locus (imaginary radius)
If $r^2 = 0$, the locus is a point (zero radius)
If $r^2 > 0$, the locus is a circle

EXAMPLE

Put the following equations into the appropriate standard form for a circle, check for degenerate or imaginary loci, and graph.

(a) $x^2 + y^2 - 4x - 6y + 19 = 0$.
(b) $2x^2 + 2y^2 + 16x - 4y + 17 = 0$.
(c) $x^2 + y^2 - 10x + 4y + 29 = 0$.

Standard form for a circle:

$$(x - h)^2 + (y - k)^2 = r^2$$

(a) $(x^2 - 4x + 4) + (y^2 - 6y + 9) = -19 + 4 + 9$

$$(x - 2)^2 + (y - 3)^2 = -6$$

$r^2 < 0$, so no real locus.

(b) $2(x^2 + 8x + 16) + 2(y^2 - 2y + 1) = -17 + 32 + 2$

$$(x + 4)^2 + (y - 1)^2 = \tfrac{17}{2}$$

Circle: center $(-4, 1)$, radius $\sqrt{\tfrac{17}{2}}$. See Figure 1.54.

Figure 1.54

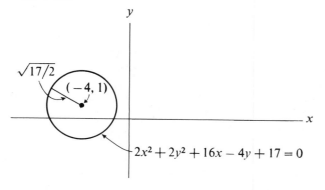

$\sqrt{17/2}$

$(-4, 1)$

$2x^2 + 2y^2 + 16x - 4y + 17 = 0$

Figure 1.55

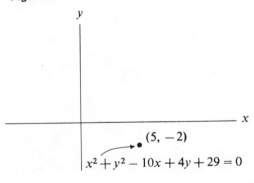

$$x^2 + y^2 - 10x + 4y + 29 = 0$$

(5, −2)

(c) $(x^2 - 10x + 25) + (y^2 + 4y + 4) = -29 + 25 + 4$

$$(x - 5)^2 + (y + 2)^2 = 0$$

Point: $(5, -2)$. See Figure 1.55.

THE ELLIPSE

Geometrically, an ellipse is the locus of points in a plane the sum of whose distances from two fixed points (called *foci*) is constant. An ellipse has two (perpendicular) axes of symmetry; the longer of these is the *major axis*, the shorter is the *minor axis*; the point at which the axes intersect is the *center* of the ellipse (see Figure 1.56).

The general equation of an ellipse can be written

$$Ax^2 + Cy^2 + Dx + Ey + F = 0$$

(where $A \neq C$ and A and C are of the same sign). As shown in Technical Note III, any equation that represents an ellipse can be written in the standard form

$$\frac{(x - h)^2}{a^2} + \frac{(y - k)^2}{b^2} = 1$$

where (h, k) is the center of the ellipse and the major axis is parallel to the x-axis if $a > b$ and to the y-axis if $a < b$. (See Figure 1.57.)

The length of the axis parallel to the x-axis is $2a$ and the length of the axis parallel

Figure 1.56

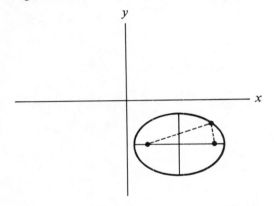

Figure 1.57

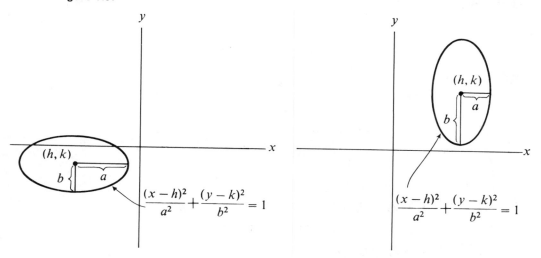

(a) ellipse with major axis
parallel to x-axis $(a > b)$

(b) ellipse with major axis
parallel to y-axis $(a < b)$

to the y-axis is $2b$. a and b are referred to as semiaxes. When $a = b$, the ellipse becomes a circle with radius $r = a = b$.

When an equation is in the standard form for an ellipse, the locus is an ellipse. However,

If $\dfrac{(x - h)^2}{a^2} + \dfrac{(y - k)^2}{b^2} = C$, where $C < 0$, there is no real locus

If $\dfrac{(x - h)^2}{a^2} + \dfrac{(y - k)^2}{b^2} = 0$, the locus is the point (h, k)

EXAMPLE

Put the following equations into the appropriate standard form for an ellipse, check for degenerate or imaginary loci, and graph.

(a) $6x^2 + 4y^2 - 36x + 16y + 70 = 0$.
(b) $9x^2 + 2y^2 + 36x + 4y + 20 = 0$.
(c) $2x^2 + y^2 - 16x - 12y + 80 = 0$.

Standard form for an ellipse:

$$\frac{(x - h)^2}{a^2} + \frac{(y - k)^2}{b^2} = 1$$

(a) $6(x^2 - 6x + 9) + 4(y^2 + 4y + 4) = -70 + 54 + 16$

$$6(x - 3)^2 + 4(y + 2)^2 = 0$$

$$\frac{(x - 3)^2}{2^2} + \frac{(y + 2)^2}{(\sqrt{6})^2} = 0$$

Point: $(3, -2)$. See Figure 1.58.

Figure 1.58

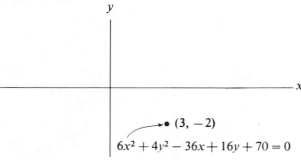

$$6x^2 + 4y^2 - 36x + 16y + 70 = 0$$

(3, −2)

(b) $9x^2 + 2y^2 + 36x + 4y + 20 = 0$

$$9(x^2 + 4x + 4) + 2(y^2 + 2y + 1) = -20 + 36 + 2$$

$$9(x + 2)^2 + 2(y + 1)^2 = 18$$

$$\frac{(x + 2)^2}{2} + \frac{(y + 1)^2}{9} = 1$$

$$\frac{(x + 2)^2}{(\sqrt{2})^2} + \frac{(y + 1)^2}{3^2} = 1$$

Ellipse: Center $(-2, -1)$, $a = \sqrt{2}$, $b = 3$.
   Major axis 6.
   Minor axis $2\sqrt{2}$.
   Major axis parallel to y-axis.
   See Figure 1.59.

(c) $2x^2 + y^2 - 16x - 12y + 80 = 0$

$$2(x^2 - 8x + 16) + (y^2 - 12y + 36) = -80 + 32 + 36$$

$$2(x - 4)^2 + (y - 6)^2 = -12$$

$$\frac{(x - 4)^2}{6} + \frac{(y - 6)^2}{12} = -1$$

$$\frac{(x - h)^2}{a^2} + \frac{(y - k)^2}{b^2} < 0,$$

so there is no real locus.

Figure 1.59

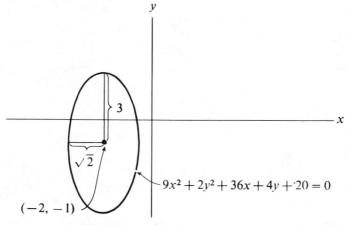

3

$\sqrt{2}$

$9x^2 + 2y^2 + 36x + 4y + 20 = 0$

$(-2, -1)$

PROBLEMS

Determine whether each of the following equations represents a circle or an ellipse, put the equation into the appropriate standard form, check for degenerate or imaginary loci, and graph.

1. $x^2 + y^2 + 2x - 4y + 1 = 0$
2. $9x^2 + 4y^2 - 24y = 0$
3. $x^2 + 4y^2 - 6x + 16y + 45 = 0$

4. $x^2 + y^2 - 8x - 4y + 18 = 0$
5. $x^2 + y^2 - 10x + 25 = 0$
6. $x^2 + y^2 - 2x + 4y + 11 = 0$

Answers to Odd-Numbered Problems

1. circle: $(x + 1)^2 + (y - 2)^2 = 2^2$
   center $(-1, 2)$
   radius 2

5. circle: $(x - 5)^2 + (y - 0)^2 = 0$
   degenerate locus: point $(5, 0)$

3. ellipse: $\dfrac{(x - 3)^2}{4} + \dfrac{(y + 2)^2}{1} = -5$
   so there is no real locus

THE PARABOLA

Geometrically, a parabola is the locus of points in a plane which are equidistant from a fixed point (called the *focus*) and a fixed straight line (called the *directrix*). A parabola is symmetric about a line, called its *axis*; the point of intersection of the parabola and its axis is the *vertex* of the parabola (see Figure 1.60).

The general equation of a parabola can be written

$$Ax^2 + Dx + Ey + F = 0$$

if the axis is parallel to the y-axis and

$$Cy^2 + Dx + Ey + F = 0$$

if the axis is parallel to the x-axis. As shown in Technical Note III, any equation that represents a parabola can be written in the standard form

$$(x - h)^2 = 4p(y - k)$$

Figure 1.60

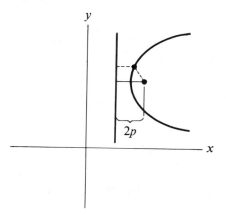

Figure 1.61

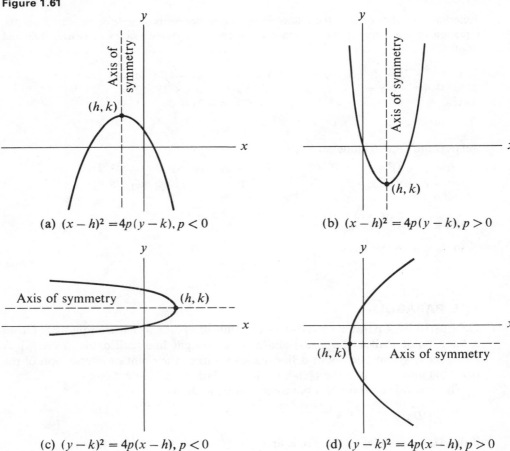

(a) $(x - h)^2 = 4p(y - k), p < 0$

(b) $(x - h)^2 = 4p(y - k), p > 0$

(c) $(y - k)^2 = 4p(x - h), p < 0$

(d) $(y - k)^2 = 4p(x - h), p > 0$

where (h, k) is the vertex of the parabola and the axis is parallel to the y-axis, or in the standard form

$$(y - k)^2 = 4p(x - h)$$

where (h, k) is the vertex of the parabola and the axis is parallel to the x-axis. The orientation and curvature of a parabola are determined by the sign and magnitude of p as follows:

For a parabola with axis parallel to the y-axis:

If $p < 0$, the parabola opens downward
If $p > 0$, the parabola opens upward

For a parabola with axis parallel to the x-axis:

If $p < 0$, the parabola opens to the left
If $p > 0$, the parabola opens to the right

(see Figure 1.61). The distance between the point (focus) and the line (directrix) defining a parabola is $2p$ (distance from a point to a line is measured along the perpendicular); as shown in Figure 1.62, the larger the value of p, the faster the parabola opens.

Figure 1.62

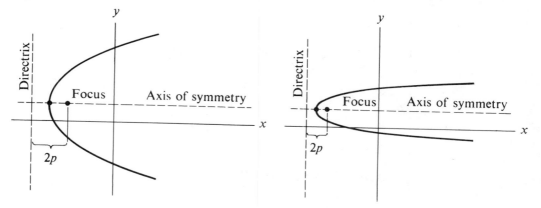

When an equation is in either standard form for a parabola, the locus is a parabola. However,

If $(x - h)^2 = C$, where $C < 0$, there is no real locus
If $(x - h)^2 = 0$, the locus is two coincident straight lines
  (that is, geometrically, one straight line)
If $(x - h)(x - k) = 0$, the locus is two parallel lines

(and similarly for a parabola with axis parallel to the x-axis).

EXAMPLE

Put the following equations into the appropriate standard form for a parabola, check for degenerate or imaginary loci, and graph.

(a) $y^2 - 8y + 17 = 0$.
(b) $x^2 - 4x + y + 14 = 0$.
(c) $x^2 - 7x + 12 = 0$.
(d) $y^2 - 10y + 25 = 0$.
(e) $y^2 - 2y - 6x + 19 = 0$.

Standard form for a parabola:

$$(y - k)^2 = 4p(x - h) \quad \text{or} \quad (x - h)^2 = 4p(y - k)$$

(a) $y^2 - 8y + 17 = 0$

$$(y^2 - 8y + 16) = -17 + 16$$

$$(y - 4)^2 = -1$$

$(y - k)^2 < 0$, so there is no real locus. Note that the x-term is missing in this example.

(b) $x^2 - 4x + y + 14 = 0$

$$x^2 - 4x + 4 = -y - 14 + 4$$

$$(x - 2)^2 = -(y + 10)$$

Parabola: Vertex $(2, -10)$, axis parallel to the y-axis, parabola opens downward.
    See Figure 1.63. (Note that $4p = -1$.)

Note the distinction between example (a), where the locus is imaginary, and example (b), where the locus is real. In (a), the square of a number is said to be a negative constant, which is

Figure 1.63

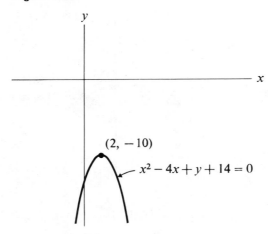

not possible for a real number. In (b), the square of a number is said to be the negative of a quantity involving a variable, which implies that the quantity $(y + 10)$ must be negative or zero; $y + 10$ is negative or zero if y is limited in extent to the interval $y \leq -10$, as shown in Figure 1.63.

(c) $x^2 - 7x + 12 = 0$

$$x^2 - 7x + \tfrac{49}{4} = -12 + \tfrac{49}{4}$$

$$(x - \tfrac{7}{2})^2 = \tfrac{1}{4}$$

$$x - \tfrac{7}{2} = \pm\sqrt{\tfrac{1}{4}}$$

$$x - \tfrac{7}{2} = \pm\tfrac{1}{2}$$

$$x = \tfrac{8}{2} \quad \text{or} \quad x - 4 = 0$$

and

$$x = \tfrac{6}{2} \quad \text{or} \quad x - 3 = 0$$

The locus is two parallel straight lines, parallel to the y-axis (see Figure 1.64). Note that the y-term is missing in this example and the equation could have been factored $(x - 4) \times (x - 3) = 0$ without completing the square.

(d) $y^2 - 10y + 25 = 0$

$$(y - 5)^2 = 0$$

Figure 1.64

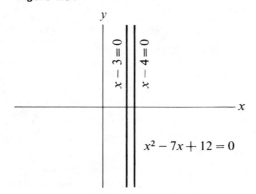

Figure 1.65

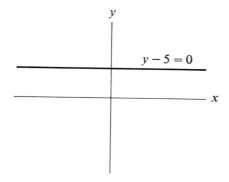

The locus is two coincident straight lines (see Figure 1.65). Note again that the x-term is missing.

(e) $y^2 - 2y - 6x + 19 = 0$

$$(y^2 - 2y + 1) = 6x - 19 + 1$$

$$(y - 1)^2 = 6x - 18$$

$$(y - 1)^2 = 6(x - 3)$$

Figure 1.66

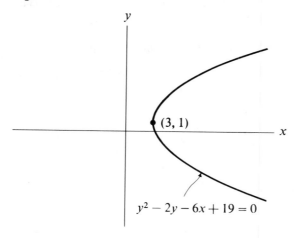

Parabola: Vertex $(3, 1)$, axis parallel to the x-axis, parabola opens to the right (see Figure 1.66).

THE HYPERBOLA

Geometrically, a hyperbola is the locus of points in a plane the difference of whose distances from two fixed points (called *foci*) is a constant. A hyperbola has two (perpendicular) axes of symmetry; the axis that intersects the hyperbola is its *transverse axis*; the point at which the axes intersect is the *center* of the hyperbola. A hyperbola always has two branches.

The general equation of a hyperbola can be written

$$Ax^2 + Cy^2 + Dx + Ey + F = 0$$

(where A and C are opposite in sign.) As shown in Technical Note III, any equation that represents a hyperbola can be written in the standard form

$$\frac{(x-h)^2}{a^2} - \frac{(y-k)^2}{b^2} = 1$$

where (h, k) is the center of the hyperbola and the transverse axis is parallel to the x-axis, or in the standard form

$$\frac{(y-k)^2}{b^2} - \frac{(x-h)^2}{a^2} = 1$$

where (h, k) is the center of the hyperbola and the transverse axis is parallel to the y-axis. (See Figure 1.67.)

Every hyperbola has a pair of intersecting straight lines as asymptotes; these asymptotes are given by the equations

$$\frac{x-h}{a} = \pm \frac{y-k}{b}$$

Note that the equations for these asymptotes can be obtained from the standard form by replacing 1 by 0, transposing the negative term, and taking square roots.

If $a = b$, the asymptotes of the hyperbola are perpendicular and the hyperbola is a *rectangular* or *equilateral hyperbola*. Equilateral hyperbolas are discussed in more detail below.

When an equation is in the standard form for a hyperbola, the locus is a hyperbola. However,

Figure 1.67

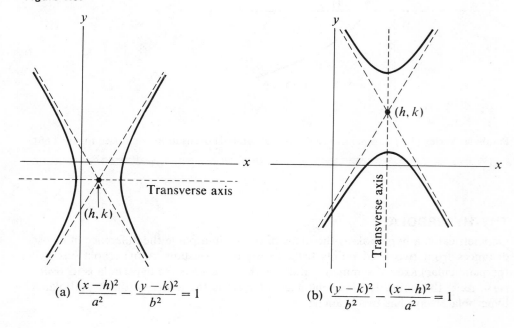

(a) $\dfrac{(x-h)^2}{a^2} - \dfrac{(y-k)^2}{b^2} = 1$

(b) $\dfrac{(y-k)^2}{b^2} - \dfrac{(x-h)^2}{a^2} = 1$

if $\dfrac{(x-h)^2}{a^2} - \dfrac{(y-k)^2}{b^2} = 0$, the locus is two intersecting straight lines,

$$\frac{x-h}{a} = \pm\frac{y-k}{b}$$

Note that these are also the equations for the asymptotes of the hyperbola.

There is no possibility of an imaginary locus in the case of a hyperbola. If, for example,

$$\frac{(x-h)^2}{a^2} - \frac{(y-k)^2}{b^2} = C \qquad \text{where } C < 0$$

then

$$\frac{(y-k)^2}{b^2} - \frac{(x-h)^2}{a^2} = C \qquad \text{where } C > 0$$

EXAMPLE

Put the following equations into the appropriate standard form for a hyperbola, check for degenerate loci, and graph.

(a) $6x^2 - 12x - 4y^2 - 16y - 34 = 0$.
(b) $2y^2 - 12y - x^2 + 6x + 7 = 0$.
(c) $5x^2 + 20x - 3y^2 - 24y - 28 = 0$.

Standard form for a hyperbola:

$$\frac{(x-h)^2}{a^2} - \frac{(y-k)^2}{b^2} = 1 \qquad \text{or} \qquad \frac{(y-k)^2}{b^2} - \frac{(x-h)^2}{a^2} = 1$$

(a) $\qquad 6x^2 - 12x - 4y^2 - 16y - 34 = 0$

$$(6x^2 - 12x) - (4y^2 + 16y) = 34$$

$$6(x^2 - 2x + 1) - 4(y^2 + 4y + 4) = 34 + 6 - 16$$

$$6(x-1)^2 - 4(y+2)^2 = 24$$

$$\frac{(x-1)^2}{4} - \frac{(y+2)^2}{6} = 1$$

$$\frac{(x-1)^2}{2^2} - \frac{(y+2)^2}{(\sqrt{6})^2} = 1$$

Hyperbola: Center $(1, -2)$, $a = 2$, $b = \sqrt{6}$, transverse axis parallel to the x-axis.

Asymptotes: $\dfrac{x-1}{2} = \pm\dfrac{y+2}{\sqrt{6}}$

$$y + 2 = \pm\frac{\sqrt{6}}{2}(x-1)$$

Plotting the asymptotes:

$y \approx 1.23(x-1) - 2 \qquad y \approx -1.23(x-1) - 2$

If $x = 0$, $y \approx -3.23$ $\qquad$ If $x = 0$, $y \approx -0.77$

If $y = 0$, $x \approx 2.63$ $\qquad$ If $y = 0$, $x \approx -0.63$

(see Figure 1.68).

Figure 1.68

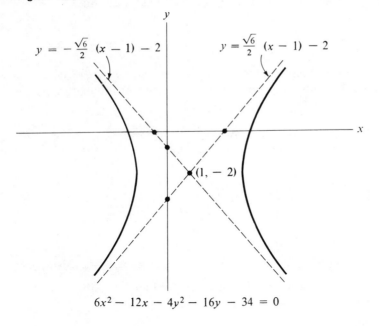

$$y = -\frac{\sqrt{6}}{2}(x-1) - 2 \qquad\qquad y = \frac{\sqrt{6}}{2}(x-1) - 2$$

$(1, -2)$

$$6x^2 - 12x - 4y^2 - 16y - 34 = 0$$

NOTE: The symbol $\approx$ means "approximately equal to" and is used because of the approximation of $\sqrt{6}$.

(b) $2y^2 - 12y - x^2 + 6x + 7 = 0$

$$2(y^2 - 6y + 9) - (x^2 - 6x + 9) = -7 + 18 - 9$$

$$2(y - 3)^2 - (x - 3)^2 = 2$$

$$\frac{(y-3)^2}{1} - \frac{(x-3)^2}{2} = 1$$

$$\frac{(y-3)^2}{1^2} - \frac{(x-3)^2}{(\sqrt{2})^2} = 1$$

Hyperbola: Center $(3, 3)$; $a = \sqrt{2}$, $b = 1$, transverse axis parallel to the y-axis.

Asymptotes: $y - 3 = \pm \dfrac{1}{\sqrt{2}}(x - 3)$

Plotting the asymptotes:

$y \approx 0.71(x - 3) + 3 \qquad y \approx -0.71(x - 3) + 3$

If $x = 0$, $y \approx 0.87$ If $x = 0$, $y \approx 5.13$

If $y = 0$, $x \approx -1.23$ If $y = 0$, $x \approx 7.23$

See Figure 1.69.

(c) $5x^2 + 20x - 3y^2 - 24y - 28 = 0$

$$5(x^2 + 4x + 4) - 3(y^2 + 8y + 16) = 28 + 20 - 48$$

$$5(x + 2)^2 + 3(y + 4)^2 = 0$$

$$\frac{(x+2)^2}{3} - \frac{(y+4)^2}{5} = 0$$

Figure 1.69

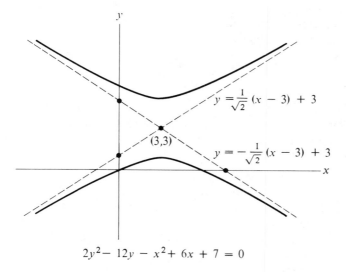

$$2y^2 - 12y - x^2 + 6x + 7 = 0$$

The locus is two straight lines,

$y = \pm\sqrt{\tfrac{5}{3}}(x + 2) - 4$

$y \approx 1.29(x + 2) - 4$ $y \approx -1.29(x + 2) - 4$

If $x = 0$, $y \approx -1.42$ If $x = 0$, $y \approx -6.58$

If $y = 0$, $x \approx 1.10$ If $y = 0$, $x \approx -5.10$

See Figure 1.70.

Figure 1.70

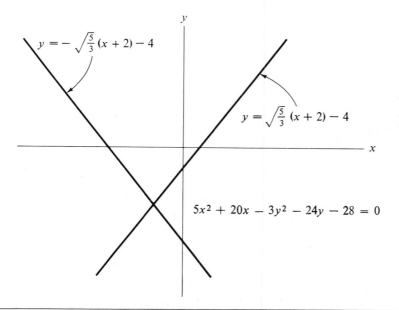

Special Cases of the Equilateral Hyperbola

In the preceding discussion of the hyperbola, an equilateral hyperbola was defined as a hyperbola whose asymptotes are perprpendicular to each other. A hyperbola whose equation can be written in the standard form

$$\frac{(x - h)^2}{a^2} - \frac{(y - k)^2}{b^2} = 1 \qquad \text{or} \qquad \frac{(y - k)^2}{b^2} - \frac{(x - h)^2}{a^2} = 1$$

is an equilateral hyperbola if and only if $a = b$.

The equation of an equilateral hyperbola whose asymptotes are parallel, respectively, to the coordinate axes can be written in the standard form

$$(x - h)(y - k) = c$$

where (h, k) is the center of the hyperbola, about which it is symmetric, and $x = h$ and $y = k$ are the asymptotes. (Note that this is the special case $A = C = 0$, $B \neq 0$, of the general second-degree equation $Ax^2 + Bxy + Cy^2 + Dx + Ey + F = 0$.) If the asymptotes are considered as coordinate axes, the hyperbola has its two branches in the first and third quadrants if $c > 0$ and in the second and fourth quadrants if $c < 0$, as shown in Figure 1.71. The intercepts of the hyperbola are the points $(h - (c/k), 0)$ and $(0, k - (c/h))$, where $h - (c/k)$ and $k - (c/h)$ may be positive or negative according to the values of h, k, and c. Note that this type of hyperbola has no more than one x-intercept and one y-intercept; for a hyperbola to have two x-intercepts, its equation must include an x^2-term, and for a hyperbola to have two y-intercepts, its equation must include a y^2-term. Similarly, for a hyperbola to have one y-intercept, its equation must include an x-term and for a hyperbola to have one y-intercept, its equation must include a y-term.

The equation of an equilateral hyperbola whose asymptotes are the coordinate axes can be written in the standard form

$$xy = c$$

[Note that this is the special case $h = k = 0$ of the equation $(x - h)(y - k) = c$.]

Figure 1.71

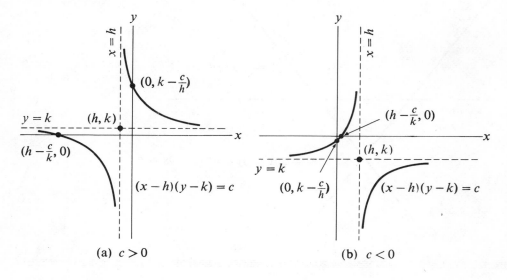

(a) $c > 0$ (b) $c < 0$

Figure 1.72

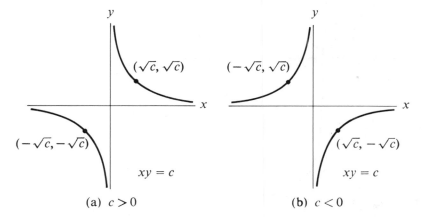

(a) $c > 0$ (b) $c < 0$

This type of hyperbola has its center at the origin, about which it is symmetric; its branches occur in the first and third quadrants if $c > 0$ and in the second and fourth quadrants if $c < 0$. Since it is asymptotic to both coordinate axes, the hyperbola has no intercepts (see Figure 1.72).

The equation $xy = c$ expresses an inversely proportional relationship between x and y—that is, as one variable increases, the other variable decreases proportionally. The variable y is said to be *inversely proportional* to the variable x, if there is a constant c such that

$$y = \frac{c}{x} \qquad \text{or} \qquad xy = c$$

By a generalization of this definition, the variable y is inversely proportional to a positive power n of a variable x, if there is a constant c such that

$$y = \frac{c}{x^n} \qquad \text{or} \qquad x^n y = c$$

The curve corresponding to such an equation or to the analogous equation $xy^m = c$ is a *generalized equilateral hyperbola*, or *hyperbola of Fermat*. Its center is at the origin; its asymptotes are the coordinate axes.

If n or m is odd, the branches of the equilateral hyperbola are symmetric to the origin and are in the first and third quadrants if $c > 0$ and are in the second and fourth quadrants if $c < 0$. If $x^n y = c$ and n is even, the branches of the equilateral hyperbola are symmetric to the y-axis and are in the first and second quadrants if $c > 0$ and are in the third and fourth quadrants if $c < 0$. If $xy^m = c$ and m is even, the branches of the equilateral hyperbola are symmetric to the x-axis and are in the first and fourth quadrants if $c > 0$ and are in the second and third quadrants if $c < 0$.

EXAMPLE

Graph the equation

$$(x - 4)(y + 12) = 2$$

(see Figure 1.73).

Figure 1.73

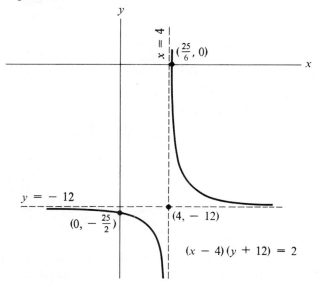

Equilateral hyperbola: Center: $(4, -12)$.

Asymptotes: $x = 4$, $y = -12$.

Lies in the first and third quadrants of its asymptotes.

EXAMPLE

Graph the equation

$$(x - 2)y = -4$$

(see Figure 1.74).

Equilateral hyperbola: Center: $(2, 0)$.

Asymptotes: $x = 2$, $y = 0$.

Lies in the second and fourth quadrants of its asymptotes.

Figure 1.74

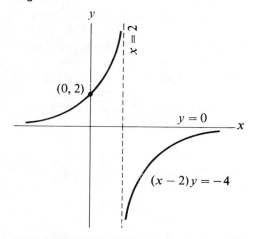

EXAMPLE

Graph the equation

$x^3y = 16$

(see Figure 1.75).

Generalized equilateral hyperbola, asymptotic to coordinate axes, symmetric to origin.

Points to aid graphing: $(2, 2)$, $(1, 16)$, $(\sqrt[3]{16}, 1)$, $(-2, -2)$, $(-1, -16)$, $(-\sqrt[3]{16}, -1)$ (note that $\sqrt[3]{16} \approx \frac{5}{2}$).

Figure 1.75

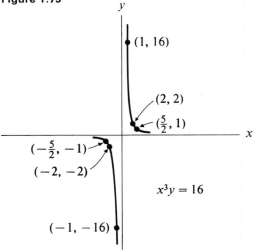

EXAMPLE

Graph the equation

$xy^2 = 25$ (See Figure 1.76.)

Figure 1.76

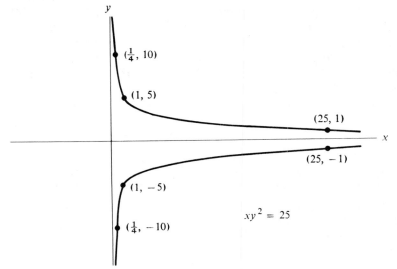

Generalized equilateral hyperbola, asymptotic to coordinate axes, symmetric to x-axis.

Points to aid graphing: $(1, 5)$, $(25, 1)$, $(\frac{1}{4}, 10)$, $(1, -5)$, $(25, -1)$, $(\frac{1}{4}, -10)$.

PROBLEMS

Determine whether each of the following equations represents a parabola or a hyperbola, put the equation into the appropriate standard form, check for degenerate or imaginary loci, and graph.

1. $y^2 - 2y - 2x + 9 = 0$
2. $x^2 - 3y^2 - 4x + 12y - 11 = 0$
3. $3x^2 - 2y^2 - 6x - 4y + 1 = 0$

4. $y^2 - 8y + 24 = 0$
5. $xy - 4x - 5y + 5 = 0$
6. $xy + 5x - y - 5 = 0$

Answers to Odd-Numbered Problems

1. parabola: $(y - 1)^2 = 2(x - 4)$
   vertex $(4, 1)$
   axis parallel to x-axis, opens to right
3. degenerate hyperbola: two intersecting
   lines $\dfrac{x - 1}{\sqrt{2}} = \pm \dfrac{y + 1}{\sqrt{3}}$

5. equilateral hyperbola: $(x - 5)(y - 4) = 15$
   center $(5, 4)$
   asymptotes $x = 5$, $y = 4$
   first and third axes quadrants

FAMILIES OF QUADRATIC CURVES

The general equation of the second degree

$$Ax^2 + Bxy + Cy^2 + Dx + Ey + F = 0$$

has five arbitrary constants, since if any of the constants A, B, C, D, E, and F is not zero, it may be used as a divisor to reduce the equation to a form involving only five arbitrary constants; after the values of five constants are set arbitrarily, the value of the other constant must be set so that the sum of the terms is zero. These five arbitrary constants in the equation of a second-degree curve permit five geometric conditions to be imposed on the curve.

As discussed above, various conditions on the constants A, B, and C determine the general form of the second-degree curve; complete specification of the constants determines a particular curve. Families of various types of curves are represented by an equation in which one (or more) of the constants is specified and the others are unspecified (that is, remain parameters). For example, a family of circles may have the same center (that is, be concentric) but have different radii, or a family of parabolas may have the same vertex but have different degrees of curvature. Such families of curves will be discussed in more detail in later sections.

PROBLEMS

For each of the following equations, identify the curve represented, put the equation into the appropriate standard form and identify the parameters and properties thus obtained, and sketch the curve.

1. $x^2 + y^2 - 6x - 2y - 6 = 0$
2. $y^2 - 6y + 9 = 0$
3. $3x^2 + 3y^2 - 6x + 4y = 1$

4. $y^2 - 10y = 0$
5. $xy - 4y = -4$
6. $x^2 - y^2 + 4x - 2y + 1 = 0$

7. $2x^2 + y^2 = 50$
8. $x^2 + y^2 - 4x - 2y + 5 = 0$
9. $4x^2 + 9y^2 - 16x - 18y + 133 = 0$
10. $xy + 3y = x + 6$
11. $3x^2 - y^2 - 12x - 6y = 0$
12. $x^2 - y^2 - 16 = 0$
13. $y = 3 + 2x - x^2$
14. $9x^2 + 25y^2 + 18x + 150y + 9 = 0$
15. $x^2 + 9y^2 - 8x + 7 = 0$
16. $16x^2 + y^2 - 32x - 6y + 25 = 0$

17. $y^2 - 3x^2 = 27$
18. $2x = 5y - y^2$
19. $5x^2 + 4y = 12$
20. $xy + 15y + 3x = 15$
21. $y^2 - 2y - 8x + 25 = 0$
22. $x^2 + y^2 - 4x - 2y + 6 = 0$
23. $y^2 - 4x^2 - 4y + 4 = 0$
24. $y^2 - 12y + 46 = 0$
25. $3y^2 + 2x = 0$
26. $xy - 6x + 2 = 0$

Answers to Odd-Numbered Problems

1. circle: $(x - 3)^2 + (y - 1)^2 = 4^2$
   center $(3, 1)$
   radius 4

3. circle: $(x - 1)^2 + (y + \frac{2}{3})^2 = (\frac{4}{3})^2$
   center $(1, -\frac{2}{3})$
   radius $\frac{4}{3}$

5. equilateral hyperbola: $y(x - 4) = -4$
   center $(4, 0)$
   asymptotes $x = 4$; $y = 0$
   second and fourth axes quadrants

7. ellipse: $\dfrac{(x - 0)^2}{5^2} + \dfrac{(y - 0)^2}{(5\sqrt{2})^2} = 1$

   center $(0, 0)$
   semiaxes $5\sqrt{2}, 5$
   major axis parallel to y-axis

9. ellipse with no real locus: $\dfrac{(x - 2)^2}{3^2} + \dfrac{(y - 1)^2}{2^2} = -3$

11. hyperbola: $\dfrac{(x - 2)^2}{1^2} - \dfrac{(y + 3)^2}{(\sqrt{3})^2} = 1$

    center $(2, -3)$
    asymptotes $y = \sqrt{3}x - 2\sqrt{3} - 3$ and $y = -\sqrt{3}x + 2\sqrt{3} - 3$
    transverse axis parallel to x-axis

13. parabola: $(x - 1)^2 = -(y - 4)$
    vertex $(1, 4)$
    axis parallel to y-axis, opens downward

15. ellipse: $\dfrac{(x - 4)^2}{3^2} + \dfrac{(y - 0)^2}{1^2} = 1$

    center $(4, 0)$
    semiaxes 3, 1
    major axis parallel to x-axis

17. hyperbola: $\dfrac{(y - 0)^2}{(3\sqrt{3})^2} - \dfrac{(x - 0)^2}{3^2} = 1$

    center $(0, 0)$
    asymptotes $y = \sqrt{3}x$ and $y = -\sqrt{3}x$
    transverse axis parallel to y-axis

19. parabola: $(x - 0)^2 = -\frac{4}{3}(y - 3)$
    vertex $(0, 3)$
    axis parallel to y-axis, opens downward

21. parabola: $(y - 1)^2 = 8(x - 3)$
    vertex $(3, 1)$
    axis parallel to x-axis, opens to right

23. degenerate hyperbola: two intersecting lines: $y = 2x + 2$ and
    $y = -2x + 2$

25. parabola: $(y - 0)^2 = -\frac{2}{3}(x - 0)$
    vertex $(0, 0)$
    axis parallel to x-axis, opens to left

1.7 Applications of Quadratic Curves in Business and Economics

In this section several applications of quadratic curves in business and economics are discussed. These applications include quadratic demand and supply curves and the associated market equilibria and product transformation curves. Pareto's law of the distribution of incomes, which is represented by an equilateral hyperbola, is also discussed.

DEMAND AND SUPPLY CURVES

The first quadrant parts of various types of parabolas frequently are appropriate for representing demand and supply functions, as illustrated in Figures 1.77 and 1.78. The first quadrant part of an equilateral hyperbola is frequently used to represent a demand function, as illustrated in Figure 1.79.

Note that each curve in Figures 1.77, 1.78, and 1.79 is only one of a family of curves appropriate for representing the functions discussed. For example, the vertex of the parabola in Figure 1.77(a) can lie anywhere in the second quadrant or on the

Figure 1.77 Examples of parabolic demand functions.

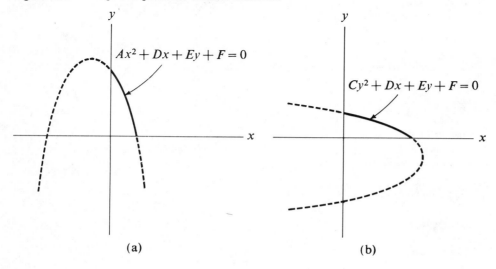

(a) (b)

Figure 1.78 Examples of parabolic supply functions.

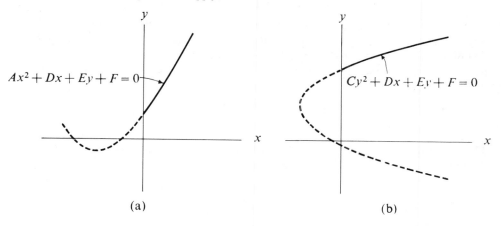

(a)   (b)

positive y-axis, provided the parabola has positive x- and y-intercepts. The conditions on the coefficients of the equation which specify the family of curves appropriate for representing a particular type of economic function can be determined using the corresponding standard form of the equation (see the problems).

Figure 1.79 Example of a hyperbolic demand function.

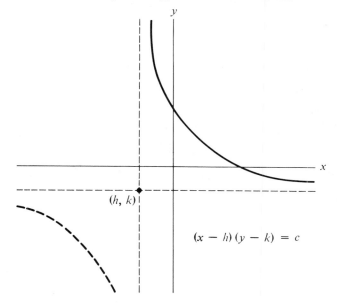

Market Equilibrium

Market equilibrium price and quantity are the price and quantity represented by the coordinates of the point of intersection of the demand and supply curves. An approximate solution for these coordinates can be obtained geometrically for any supply and demand curves. However, algebraic simultaneous solution, even for second-degree demand and supply functions, may involve solution of a third- or fourth-degree equation.

Since general methods for solution of equations of degree greater than two are not discussed here, the examples and problems are limited to cases involving solution of a quadratic equation. For example, if one equation is linear and the other equation is parabolic or hyperbolic, their simultaneous solution involves solution of a quadratic equation; similarly, simultaneous solution of two parabolic equations which are quadratic with respect to the same variable involves solution of a quadratic equation.

Unless a quadratic equation can be factored, its solution is most readily obtained by using the quadratic formula: The root(s) of a quadratic equation $ax^2 + bx + c = 0$ are given by

$$x = \frac{-b \pm \sqrt{b^2 - 4ac}}{2a}$$

This formula is obtained by the process of completing the square, as shown in Technical Note IV. Note that the number of real roots an equation has is determined by the value of $b^2 - 4ac$:

If $b^2 - 4ac < 0$, no real roots
If $b^2 - 4ac = 0$, one real root
If $b^2 - 4ac > 0$, two real roots

EXAMPLE

Find the equilibrium price and quantity for the following demand and supply equations (where x represents quantity and y represents price):

$$2x + y - 10 = 0$$

$$y^2 - 8x - 4 = 0$$

Solving the equations simultaneously,

$2x = -y + 10$ from the first equation

$8x = y^2 - 4$ from the second equation

so

$$y^2 - 4 = -4y + 40$$

$$y^2 + 4y - 44 = 0$$

and, using the quadratic formula,

$$y = \frac{-4 \pm \sqrt{16 - (4)(-44)}}{2}$$

$$= \frac{-4 \pm 8\sqrt{3}}{2}$$

$$= -2 \pm 4\sqrt{3}$$

$$x = \tfrac{1}{2}(-y + 10)$$

$$= 6 \pm 2\sqrt{3}$$

$\sqrt{3} \approx 1.732$, so the approximate solutions are $(2.5, 4.9)$ and $(9.5, -8.9)$ and the approximate equilibrium point is $(2.5, 4.9)$.

Plotting the curves to verify the result geometrically (see Figure 1.80),

$2x + y - 10 = 0$ $y^2 - 8x - 4 = 0$

If $x = 0$, $y = 10$ $y^2 = 8x + 4$

If $y = 0$, $x = 5$ $y^2 = 8(x + \tfrac{1}{2})$

Figure 1.80

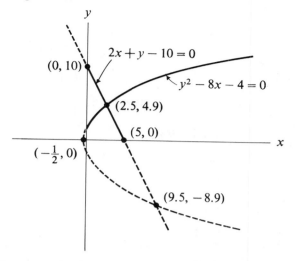

EXAMPLE

Find the equilibrium price and quantity for the following demand and supply equations (where x represents quantity and y represents price):

$$x^2 + 5x - y + 1 = 0$$
$$2x^2 + y - 9 = 0$$

Solving the equations simultaneously,

$$y = x^2 + 5x + 1$$
$$y = -2x^2 + 9$$

so

$$x^2 + 5x + 1 = -2x^2 + 9$$
$$3x^2 + 5x - 8 = 0$$
$$(3x + 8)(x - 1) = 0$$
$$x = -\tfrac{8}{3}, 1$$
$$y = -2x^2 + 9$$
$$y = -\tfrac{47}{9}, 7$$

The solutions are $(-\tfrac{8}{3}, -\tfrac{47}{9})$ and $(1, 7)$ and the equilibrium point is $(1, 7)$.
Plotting the curves to verify the result geometrically (see Figure 1.81),

$$x^2 + 5x - y + 1 = 0 \qquad\qquad 2x^2 + y - 9 = 0$$
$$(x^2 + 5x + \tfrac{25}{4}) = y - 1 + \tfrac{25}{4} \qquad 2x^2 = -(y - 9)$$
$$(x + \tfrac{5}{2})^2 = y + \tfrac{21}{4} \qquad\qquad x^2 = -\tfrac{1}{2}(y - 9)$$

Figure 1.81

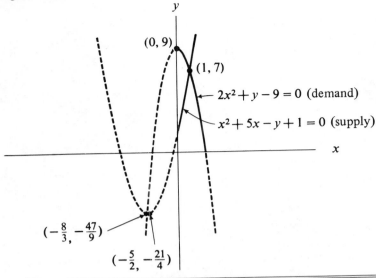

EXAMPLE

Find the equilibrium price and quantity for the following demand and supply equations (where x represents quantity and y represents price):

$$y^2 + y + x - 20 = 0$$

$$2y^2 - x - 3y - 4 = 0$$

Solving the equations simultaneously,

$$x = -y^2 - y + 20$$

$$x = 2y^2 - 3y - 4$$

so

$$-y^2 - y + 20 = 2y^2 - 3y - 4$$

$$3y^2 - 2y - 24 = 0$$

and, using the quadratic formula,

$$y = \frac{2 \pm \sqrt{4 - 4(3)(-24)}}{6}$$

$$= \frac{2 \pm 2\sqrt{73}}{6}$$

$$= \frac{1 \pm \sqrt{73}}{3}$$

$$x = -y^2 - y + 20$$

$$= -\frac{1 \pm 2\sqrt{73} + 73}{9} - \frac{1 \pm \sqrt{73}}{3} + 20$$

$$= -\frac{77 \pm 5\sqrt{73}}{9} + 20$$

Figure 1.82

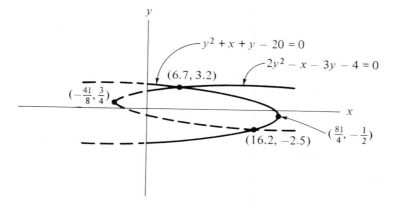

$\sqrt{73} \approx 8.544$, so the approximate solutions are $(6.7, 3.2)$ and $(16.2, -2.5)$, and the approximate equilibrium point is $(6.7, 3.2)$.

Plotting the curves to verify the result geometrically (see Figure 1.82),

$$y^2 + y + x - 20 = 0 \qquad\qquad 2y^2 - x - 3y - 4 = 0$$

$$y^2 + y + \tfrac{1}{4} = -x + 20 + \tfrac{1}{4} \qquad 2(y^2 - \tfrac{3}{2}y + \tfrac{9}{16}) = x + 4 + \tfrac{9}{8}$$

$$(y + \tfrac{1}{2})^2 = -(x - \tfrac{81}{4}) \qquad (y - \tfrac{3}{4})^2 = \tfrac{1}{2}(x + \tfrac{41}{8})$$

EXAMPLE

Find the market equilibrium price and quantity for the following demand and supply equations (where x represents quantity and y represents price):

$$(x + 12)(y + 6) = 169$$

$$x - y + 6 = 0$$

Solving the equations simultaneously,

$$y = x + 6 \qquad \text{from the second equation}$$

Substituting in the first equation,

$$(x + 12)(x + 12) = 169$$

$$x + 12 = \pm 13$$

$$x = 1, -25$$

$$y = x + 6$$

$$y = 7, -19$$

The solutions are $(1, 7)$ and $(-25, -19)$ and the equilibrium point is $(1, 7)$.

Plotting the curves to verify the result geometrically (see Figure 1.83),

$$x - y + 6 = 0 \qquad\qquad (x + 12)(y + 6) = 169$$

If $x = 0$, $y = 6$ asymptotes $x = -12$, $y = -6$

If $y = 0$, $x = -6$ If $x = 0$, $y = \tfrac{97}{12}$

                     If $y = 0$, $x = \tfrac{97}{6}$

Figure 1.83

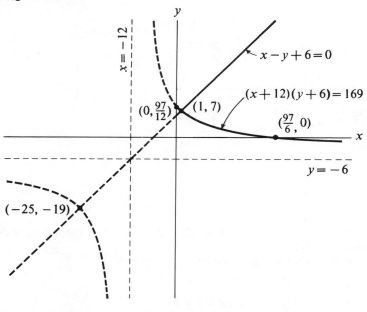

PRODUCT TRANSFORMATION CURVES

Some production processes can yield more than one output. Sheep raising is a classic example of such a process: two outputs, wool and mutton, can be produced in varying proportions by a single production process. Many industrial production processes can also yield more than one output, for example, commodities that are similar but of different type or quality. A production or product transformation curve expresses the relationship between the quantities of two different commodities (joint products) produced by the same firm using common supplies of labor and raw materials. Note that the case of joint products is distinguished on a technical, not an organizational basis; the quantities of two or more joint products are technically or technologically interdependent. Cases in which a firm produces two or more technically independent products are inappropriate for analysis by product transformation curves.

A *product transformation curve* is defined as the locus of output quantity combinations which can be obtained from a given input. If the two output quantities produced are x and y, the product transformation curve relating them must be such that as one quantity increases the other quantity decreases. In addition, in order to fulfill certain reasonable economic assumptions, which need not be discussed here, product transformation curves are usually concave from below, as in Figure 1.84.

A product transformation curve is usually one of a family of possible product transformation curves, where the curves of the family correspond to various inputs. For example, Figure 1.84 shows product transformation curves represented by the first-quadrant parts of four of a family of concentric circles; the farther a curve lies from the origin, the greater the input to which it corresponds. Suitably located and oriented elliptic, parabolic, and hyperbolic curves are also appropriate in some cases for representing product transformation curves, as illustrated in Figures 1.85, 1.86,

Figure 1.84 Members of a family of circular product transformation curves.

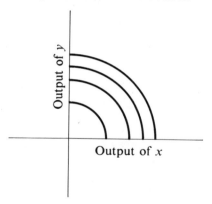

Figure 1.85 Example of an elliptic product transformation curve.

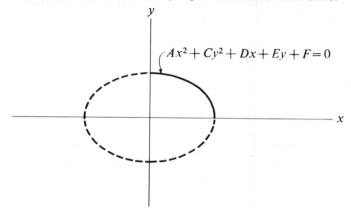

$$Ax^2 + Cy^2 + Dx + Ey + F = 0$$

Figure 1.86 Examples of parabolic product transformation curves.

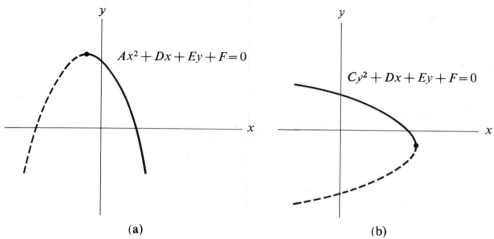

$$Ax^2 + Dx + Ey + F = 0$$

$$Cy^2 + Dx + Ey + F = 0$$

(a)

(b)

Figure 1.87 Example of a hyperbolic product transformations curve.

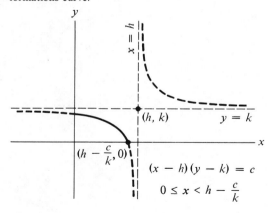

and 1.87. Note that for circular, elliptic, and parabolic product transformation curves, the entire first-quadrant part of the curve is appropriate. However, for hyperbolic product transformation curves, the range is limited to the lower branch of the hyperbola; this limitation is usually stated as a restriction on the range of x:

$$0 \le x \le h - \frac{c}{k}$$

where $(h - (c/k), 0)$ is the x-intercept.

EXAMPLE

A company produces amounts x and y of two different grades of steel using the same production process. The product transformation curve for the input used is given by

$$y^2 + x + 4y - 20 = 0$$

(see Figure 1.88).

(a) What are the largest amounts x and y that can be produced?
(b) What amounts x and y should be produced in order to have $x = 4y$?

Figure 1.88

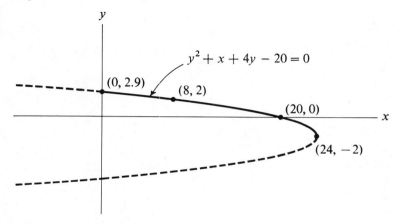

(a) x is as large as possible if $y = 0$, so the largest amount x is 20. y is as large as possible if $x = 0$, so the largest amount y is

$$y = \frac{-4 \pm \sqrt{16 - (4)(-20)}}{2}$$

$$= \frac{-4 \pm 4\sqrt{6}}{2}$$

$$= -2 \pm 2\sqrt{6}$$

$\sqrt{6} \approx 2.449$, so $y \approx 2.9$, -6.9 and the largest amount y is (approximately) 2.9.

(b) Substituting $x = 4y$ in $y^2 + x + 4y - 20 = 0$,

$$y^2 + 4y + 4y - 20 = 0$$

$$y^2 + 8y - 20 = 0$$

$$(y + 10)(y - 2) = 0$$

$$y = -10, 2$$

So the amounts produced are $x = 8$, $y = 2$.

EXAMPLE

A company produces amounts x and y of two different kinds of candy using the same production process. The product transformation curve for the input used is given by

$$5x^2 + 2y^2 = 98$$

(see Figure 1.89).

(a) What are the largest amounts x and y that can be produced?
(b) What amounts x and y should be produced in order to have $y = \frac{3}{4}x$?

(a) If $y = 0$,

$$5x^2 = 98$$

$$x^2 = \frac{98}{5}$$

$$x = \pm\sqrt{\frac{98}{5}} = \pm 7\sqrt{\frac{2}{5}} = \pm\frac{7}{5}\sqrt{10}$$

Figure 1.89

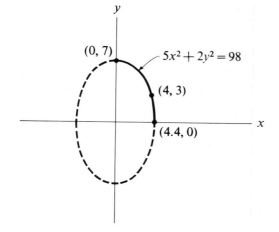

(0, 7)

$5x^2 + 2y^2 = 98$

(4, 3)

(4.4, 0)

$\sqrt{10} \approx 3.162$, so $x \approx \pm 4.4$ and the largest amount x is (approximately) 4.4. If $x = 0$,

$$2y^2 = 98$$

$$y^2 = 49$$

$$y = \pm 7$$

So the largest amount y is 7.

(b) Substituting $y = \frac{3}{4}x$ in $5x^2 + 2y^2 = 98$,

$$5x^2 + 2(\tfrac{9}{16})x^2 = 98$$

$$\tfrac{49}{8}x^2 = 98$$

$$x^2 = 16$$

$$x = \pm 4, \; y = \pm 3$$

So the amounts produced are $x = 4$, $y = 3$.

EXAMPLE

A company produces amounts x and y of two petrochemicals using the same production process. The product transformation curve for the input used is given by

$$(x - 24)(y - 36) = 240 \qquad x < \tfrac{52}{3}$$

(see Figure 1.90).

(a) What are the largest amounts x and y that can be produced?

(b) What amounts x and y should be produced to have $x = \frac{2}{3}y$?

(a) If $y = 0$,

$$x = -\tfrac{20}{3} + 24 = \tfrac{52}{3}$$

Figure 1.90

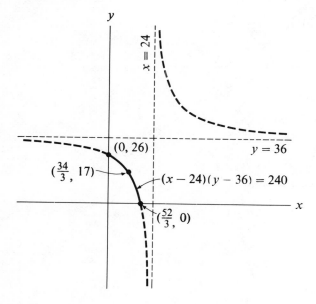

So the largest amount x is $\frac{52}{3}$. If $x = 0$,

$$y = -10 + 36 = 26$$

So the largest amount y is 26.

(b) Substituting $x = \frac{2}{3}y$ in $(x - 24)(y - 36) = 240$,

$$\left(\frac{2y}{3} - 24\right)(y - 36) = 240$$

$$(y - 36)(y - 36) = 360$$

$$y - 36 = \pm\sqrt{360}$$

$$y = 36 \pm 6\sqrt{10}$$

$$y \approx 36 \pm 19.0$$

$$y \approx 55, \ 17$$

So the amounts produced are (approximately) $x = \frac{34}{3}$, $y = 17$. (Note that the solution $x = \frac{110}{3}$, $y = 55$ violates the restriction $x \le \frac{52}{3}$ and is on the upper branch of the hyperbola.)

EXAMPLE

A company produces amounts x and y of two different textiles using the same production process. The product transformation curve for the input used is given by

$$y = 20 - \frac{x^2}{5}$$

(see Figure 1.91).

(a) What are the largest amounts x and y that can be produced?
(b) What amounts x and y should be produced to have $x = y$?

(a) If $y = 0$,

$$x^2 = 100$$

$$x = \pm 10$$

So the largest amount x is 10. If $x = 0$, $y = 20$, so the largest amount y is 20.

Figure 1.91

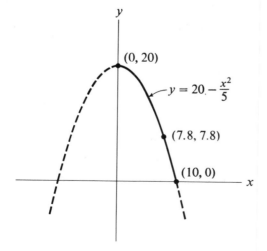

(b) Substituting $x = y$ in $y = 20 - \dfrac{x^2}{5}$,

$$5y = 100 - y^2$$

$$y^2 + 5y - 100 = 0$$

$$y = \frac{-5 \pm \sqrt{25 - (4)(-100)}}{2}$$

$$= \frac{-5 \pm 5\sqrt{17}}{2}$$

$$y \approx \frac{-5 \pm 5(4.123)}{2}$$

$$y \approx 7.8, \ -12.8$$

So the amounts produced are (approximately) $x = y = 7.8$.

PROBLEMS

For each of the following pairs of equations, i. determine which equation represents a demand curve and which equation represents a supply curve, ii. determine the market equilibrium quantity and price algebraically, and iii. check geometrically the algebraically determined equilibrium points.

1. a. $x = 16 - 2y$

   b. $4x = 4y + y^2$

2. a. $x = 130 - 4y$

   b. $y = 10 + \dfrac{x}{5} + \dfrac{x^2}{100}$

3. a. $y = 2 + \dfrac{x}{5} + \dfrac{x^2}{20}$

   b. $y = \dfrac{30 - x}{4}$

4. a. $y = 16 - x^2$

   b. $y = 4 + x$

5. a. $x = 32 - 4y - y^2$

   b. $y = \dfrac{x}{20} + 1$

6. a. $y = 9x + 12$

   b. $y = 39 - 3x^2$

7. a. $y = 6 + \dfrac{x^2}{4}$

   b. $x = \sqrt{36 - y}$

8. a. $y = (x + 2)^2$

   b. $y = 39 - 3x^2$

9. a. $y = 48 - 3x^2$

   b. $y = x^2 + 4x + 16$

10. a. $x = 84 - y^2$

   b. $x = y + 4y^2$

11. a. $x = 10y + 5y^2$

   b. $x = 64 - 8y - 2y^2$

12. a. $x = 10y + 4y^2$

   b. $x = 96 - 8y - 2y^2$

13. a. $(x + 16)(y + 12) = 480$

   b. $y = 2x + 4$

14. a. $x = 2y^2 - 2y - 6$

   b. $x = -y^2 - y + 18$

15. a. $y = 10 - 3x^2$

   b. $y = 4 + x^2 + 2x$

16. a. $xy = 30$

   b. $3y - x = 9$

17. a. $xy = 15$

   b. $y = x + 2$

18. a. $(x + 10)(y + 20) = 300$

   b. $x = 2y - 8$

19. a. $(x + 6)(y + 12) = 144$

   b. $y = 2 + \dfrac{x}{2}$

20. a. $(x + 12)(y + 6) = 169$

    b. $x - y + 6 = 0$

21. a. $(x + 5)(y + 6) = 80$

    b. $y = \dfrac{x}{3} + 3$

22. a. $(x + 1)y = 5$

    b. $y = \dfrac{x}{4}$

23. a. $x(y + 6) = 24$

    b. $y - 2x + 4 = 0$

24. a. $y(x + 3) = 18$

    b. $y - 3x + 6 = 0$

25. a. $(x + 4)(y + 2) = 24$

    b. $y = 1 + \dfrac{x}{2}$

26. a. $y = x^2 + 5x + 1$

    b. $y + 2x^2 - 9 = 0$

27. a. $x = 3y^2 - 3y - 2$

    b. $x = 10 - y^2 - y$

28. a. $(x + 10)(y + 5) = 225$

    b. $x - y + 5 = 0$

Each of the following equations represents a product transformation curve for the amounts x and y, respectively, of two related commodities; find the largest amounts x and y that can be produced.

29. $x = 36 - 6y^2$
30. $y = 65 - 12x - 5x^2$
31. $y = 45 - 9x^2$
32. $x = 16 - 4y - 2y^2$

33. The production manager has decided that the marketing department can sell 126 units of product daily, and he wants to produce that much. If he assumes that all factors other than the number of employees and the resultant output remain constant within the range of this total production, the production function can be expressed by the equation

$$2x^2 + 4x - y = 0$$

with x representing the number of employees and y representing the units of production. The production manager claims that he will need 7 men to produce the 126 units. a. Assuming that the equation is appropriate, is the production manager correct in his statement concerning the number of men needed? b. What type of curve does the equation represent? Graph the curve. c. Draw up a schedule of units of production output per man employed in the range 1 through 7 employees. Indicate the change in the number of units produced through this range as each employee is added.

34. A company's operations research director believes that the short-run average cost of production can be expressed by the equation

$$x^2 - 16x - y + 68 = 0$$

with x representing the number of units produced and y representing the average cost per unit. He says that the average cost will be lowest when eight units are produced. a. Is his statement correct? b. What type of curve is represented? Graph the curve. c. Draw up a schedule of values of y for the range $x = 4$ through $x = 12$ and indicate the amount of change in y for each change in x.

35. In national income analysis, the demand for a stock of money to be held, or the "liquidity preference," as Keynes calls it, is often considered to be dependent on three motives: the transactions motive, the precautionary motive, and the speculative motive. Assume that, at a given level of national income, the effects of the transactions and precautionary motives are constant. The speculative motive is considered to be a function of the interest rate as expressed by the equation $(x - 1)y = 4$, where x is the rate of interest (%) and y is the demand for money to hold expressed in billions of dollars. a. What type of curve does the equation express? Graph the curve. b. Draw up a schedule of values for y, the amount of money demanded to be held (in billions of dollars) for the values of x from 2% through

7%. What is the value of y when $x = 100$ (in billions of dollars)? c. Note and describe the segment of the curve which represents the "liquidity trap"—that segment in which the interest rate seems to lose its force as an effective factor in influencing the demand for money to hold.

36. According to convention, in the economic analysis discussed in Problem 35, the dependent variable (the demand for money to be held) is often assigned to the x-axis rather than the y-axis. An equation used to express Keynesian ideas concerning the relationship between the rate of interest and the money demanded to be hld is then $x(y - 1) = 4$. a. What type of curve does this equation represent? Graph the curve. b. Draw up a schedule of values for the interest rate y for the values of x from 1 through 7 (in billions of dollars). What is the value of y when $x = 100$ (in billions of dollars)? c. Note and describe the segment of the curve that represents the "liquidity trap."

37. Consider the parabola $y = \frac{1}{4}x^2 - x + 4$ and the equilateral hyperbola $(x + 2)(y - 2) = 4$. a. Show that for $x = 0$ and $x = 2$ both equations have the same value of y, but for $x = 4$ and $x = -2$ they have different values of y. b. Show that the two equations have the same value of y only for $x = 0$ and $x = 2$. c. Sketch the two curves on the same set of axes.

38. A company produces x and y amounts of steel of two different grades, using the same resources; the product transformation curve is

$$y = 20 - \frac{300}{30 - x} \qquad (x < 30)$$

a. Sketch the curve. b. Determine the largest amounts of x and y that can be produced. c. If the demand for grade x steel is twice that for grade y steel, determine the amounts the company should produce.

39. A company manufactures two grades of candy from the same resources. If x and y represent the quantities produced, the product transformation curve is

$$(x - 24)(y - 36) = 240 \qquad (x < 24)$$

a. Sketch the curve. b. Determine the largest amounts of x and y that can be produced. c. If the demand for grade x candy is two-thirds that for grade y, determine the amounts the company should produce.

40. A company manufactures two grades of paper from the same resources; if x and y represent the quantities produced, the product transformation curve is

$$(x - 30)(y - 15) = 150 \qquad (x < 30)$$

a. Sketch the curve. b. If the demand for grade x paper is three times that for grade y paper, determine the amounts of paper the company should produce. c. If the demand for grade y paper exceeds that for grade x paper by four units, determine the amounts the company should produce.

Answers to Odd-Numbered Problems

1. a. demand
   b supply
   (8, 4)
3. a. supply
   b. demand
   (6.91, 5.77)
5. a. demand
   b. supply
   (20, 2)
7. a. supply
   b. demand
   (4.90, 12)
9. a. demand
   b. supply
   (2.37, 31.15)

11. a. supply
    b. demand
    (40, 2)
13. a. demand
    b. supply
    (4, 12)
15. a. demand
    b. supply
    (1, 7)
17. a. demand
    b. supply
    (3, 5)
19. a. demand
    b. supply
    (3.22, 3.61)

21. a. demand
    b. supply
    (3, 4)
23. a. demand
    b. supply
    (3, 2)
25. a. demand
    b. supply
    (2, 2)
33. a. yes
    b. parabola, vertex $(-1, -2)$, axis parallel to y-axis

27. a. supply
    b. demand
    (4, 2)
29. $x_{max} = 36$
    $y_{max} = \sqrt{6}$
31. $x_{max} = \sqrt{5}$
    $y_{max} = 45$

c.

Number of employees x	Total units produced y	Δy
1	6	
2	16	10
3	30	14
4	48	18
5	70	22
6	96	26
7	126	30

35. a. equilateral hyperbola, transverse axis parallel to y-axis
    center $(1, 0)$
    lies in first and third quadrants of its asymptotes
    asymptotes: $x = 1$, $y = 0$
    intercept: $(0, -4)$

b.

Interest rate x	Amount of money demanded to be held y
2	4
3	2
4	$\frac{4}{3}$
5	1
6	$\frac{4}{5}$
7	$\frac{2}{3}$
100	$\frac{4}{99}$

c. segment for which $x > 2$
39. b. $x_{max} = 17\frac{1}{3}$, $y_{max} = 26$
    c. $x = 11.36$, $y = 17.04$

PARETO'S LAW OF DISTRIBUTION OF INCOME

The economist Vilfredo Pareto proposed the following law of distribution of income:
The number of individuals N from a given population of size a whose income exceeds x is

$$N = \frac{a}{x^b}$$

Figure 1.92

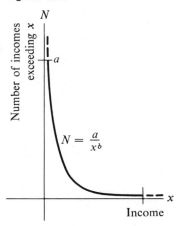

where b is a population parameter, usually approximately 1.5. This equation represents a generalized equilateral hyperbola and is appropriate only for the range $0 < N \leq a$ and $0 < x <$ maximum income in the population (see Figure 1.92).

Note that Pareto's equation implies that both N and x are continuous; in fact, although x might be considered approximately continuous, N is by definition discrete. For convenience, relationships involving discrete variables are frequently represented as continuous; the discrepancy between the discrete nature of a variable and its continuous representation must be considered in interpeting analyses based on such representations.

For above-subsistence incomes, data indicate that Pareto's law is generally fairly accurate. Pareto suggested that the value of b is approximately 1.5; data indicate that this varies from population to population, but 1.5 is usually a good approximation.

As discussed in Appendix A, it is frequently convenient to express numbers that are very large (or very small) in absolute value in terms of a constant multiplied by an exponent of 10. This scientific notation is used in the following examples. Note, however, that the convention concerning decimal points that is used in scientific notation is violated for computational convenience.

EXAMPLE

Pareto's law for the distribution of incomes for a particular group is

$$N = \frac{216 \times 10^{10}}{x^{3/2}}$$

(a) How many people are millionaires?
(b) How many people have incomes between \$3600 and \$10,000?
(c) What is the lowest income of the 80 people with the highest incomes?

(a) $N = \dfrac{216 \times 10^{10}}{(10^6)^{3/2}} = 2160$ millionaires

(b) The number with incomes exceeding \$3600 is

$$N = \frac{216 \times 10^{10}}{(3600)^{3/2}} = \frac{216 \times 10^{10}}{6^3 \times 10^3} = 10^7$$

The number with incomes exceeding \$10,000 is

$$N = \frac{216 \times 10^{10}}{(10^4)^{3/2}} = 216 \times 10^4$$

so the number with incomes between \$3600 and \$10,000 is $10^7 - 216 \times 10^4 = (1000 - 216) \times 10^4 = 784 \times 10^4$ or 7,840,000.

(c) $\quad 80 = \dfrac{216 \times 10^{10}}{x^{3/2}}$

$$x^{3/2} = \dfrac{216 \times 10^{10}}{80} = 27 \times 10^9$$

$$x = (27 \times 10^9)^{2/3} = 9 \times 10^6$$

or \$9,000,000 is the lowest income of the 80 people with the highest incomes.

EXAMPLE

Pareto's law for the distribution of incomes for a given population is

$$N = \dfrac{16 \times 10^{12}}{x^{5/3}}$$

(a) How many people have incomes below \$8000?
(b) How many people have incomes over \$125,000 but less than \$1,000,000?
(c) What is the lowest income of the 50 people with the highest incomes?

(a) $N = \dfrac{16 \times 10^{12}}{(8 \times 10^3)^{5/3}} = \dfrac{16 \times 10^{12}}{2^5 \times 10^5} = 5 \times 10^6$

so 5×10^6 people have incomes above \$8000 and $16 \times 10^{12} - (5 \times 10^6) = (16 \times 10^6 - 5) \times 10^6$ or 15,999,995,000,000 have incomes below \$8000.

(b) The number with incomes over \$125,000 is

$$N = \dfrac{16 \times 10^{12}}{(5^3 \times 10^3)^{5/3}} = \dfrac{16 \times 10^{12}}{5^5 \times 10^5} = \dfrac{16 \times 10^7}{5^5}$$

$$= 16 \times 2^5 \times 10^2 = 512 \times 10^2 \text{ or } 51,200$$

The number with incomes over \$1,000,000 is

$$N = \dfrac{16 \times 10^{12}}{(10^6)^{5/3}} = 16 \times 10^2 \text{ or } 1600$$

So the number with incomes over \$125,000 but less than \$1,000,000 is $51,200 - 1600 = 49,600$.

(c) $\quad 50 = \dfrac{16 \times 10^{12}}{x^{5/3}}$

$$x^{5/3} = \dfrac{16 \times 10^{12}}{50} = 32 \times 10^{10}$$

$$x = (32 \times 10^{10})^{3/5} = 8 \times 10^6$$

or \$8,000,000 is the lowest income of the 50 people with the highest incomes.

PROBLEMS

1. Pareto's law for the distribution of incomes for a particular group is

$$N = \dfrac{8 \times 10^8}{x^{3/2}}$$

a. How many have incomes exceeding \$1600?
b. How many have incomes between \$1600 and \$3600?
c. What is the lowest income of the 800 who have the highest incomes?

2. Pareto's law for the distribution of incomes for a particular group is

$$N = \frac{1.9 \times 10^{12}}{x^{1.70}}$$

a. How many have incomes exceeding $50,000?
b. How many have incomes between $25,000 and $50,000?
c. What is the lowest income of the million who have the highest incomes?

3. Pareto's law for the distribution of incomes for a particular group is

$$N = \frac{100,000}{x^2}$$

a. How many have incomes exceeding $15?
b. How many have incomes between $50 and $75?
c. What is the lowest income of the 5 who have the highest incomes?

4. Pareto's law for the distribution of incomes for a particular group is

$$N = \frac{32 \times 10^{10}}{x^{4/3}}$$

a. How many have incomes between $125,000 and $1,000,000?
b. What is the lowest income of the 200 who have the highest incomes?

5. Pareto's law for the distribution of incomes for a particular group is

$$N = \frac{625 \times 10^9}{x^{3/2}}$$

a. How many have incomes between $2500 and $10,000?
b. What is the lowest income of the 5000 who have the highest incomes?

6. Pareto's law for the distribution of incomes for a particular group is

$$N = \frac{6 \times 10^9}{x^{3/2}}$$

a. How many have incomes exceeding $2500?
b. How many have incomes between $2500 and $10,000?
c. What is the lowest income of the 6 who have the highest incomes?

7. Pareto's law for the distribution of incomes is

$$N = \frac{a}{x^b}$$

a. How many have incomes exceeding k?
b. How many have incomes exceeding $100,000?
c. What is the lowest income of the 10 who have the highest incomes?
d. How many have incomes between s and t?
e. How many have incomes between $500,000 and $1,500,000?

8. If the demand function is

$$y = \frac{17.6}{x^{1.43}}$$

(where x is quantity demanded and y is price):
a. Find the price if the quantity demanded is 2.
b. Find the quantity demanded if the price is $5.

9. If the demand function is

$$x = \frac{12.03}{y^{0.21}}$$

(where x is quantity demanded and y is price):
Find the price if the quantity demanded is a. 6, b. 3.3.
Find the quantity demanded if the price is c. $100, d. $67.

10. If the demand function is

$$x = \frac{a}{y^b}$$

(where x is quantity demanded and y is price):
Find the price if the quantity demanded is a. $5a$, b. 1.
Find the quantity demanded if the price is c. \$1, d. a.

Answers to Odd-Numbered Problems

1. a. 12,500

   b. 8796

   c. \$10,000

   c. $\left(\dfrac{a}{10}\right)^{1/b}$

   d. $\dfrac{a(t^b - s^b)}{s^b t^b}$

3. a. 444

   b. 22

   e. $\dfrac{a(3^b - 1)}{(15 \times 10^5)^b}$

   c. \$141

9. a. \$27.455

5. a. 4,375,000

   b. \$473.21

   b. \$250,000

   c. 4.574

7. a. $\dfrac{a}{k^b}$

   d. 4.975

   b. $\dfrac{a}{10^{5b}}$

1.8 Exponential and Logarithmic Curves

Exponential and logarithmic curves are closely related. Graphical representations of exponential and logarithmic functions are discussed in this section.

EXPONENTIAL FUNCTIONS

A function having a variable base and a constant exponent is a *power function*. For example, $y = x^a$ is a power function, where x is the base and a is the exponent. Note that the quadratic equations and equilateral hyperbolas discussed in previous sections contain power functions. A function having a constant base and a variable exponent is an *exponential function*. For example, $y = a^x$ is an exponential function, where a is the base and x is the exponent.

The properties of exponents reviewed in Appendix A are applicable to both power functions and exponential functions. For convenience, these properties are stated below in notation conventionally used for exponential functions. If a and b are positive real numbers and x and y assume rational values,

$$a^x \cdot a^y = a^{x+y}$$

$$\frac{a^x}{a^y} = a^{x-y}$$

$$(a^x)^y = a^{xy}$$

$$(ab)^x = a^x b^x$$

$$\left(\frac{a}{b}\right)^x = \frac{a^x}{b^x} \qquad b \neq 0$$

$$a^{-x} = \frac{1}{a^x}$$

$$a^{x/y} = \sqrt[y]{a^x} \qquad x, y \text{ integers, } x > 0$$

NOTE: By definition, if $x \neq 0$, $x^0 = 1$; that is, any base to the zero power is 1.

The simplest exponential functions are of the form $y = b^x$, $b > 0$. The curve representing the function $y = b^x$ lies entirely in the first two quadrants; it is monotonically decreasing if $0 < b < 1$ and monotonically increasing if $b > 1$; in both cases the curve is asymptotic to the x-axis and has y-intercept (0, 1). The parameter b determines the curvature of the function (see Figure 1.93). Note that if $b = 1$, $y = b^x$ becomes $y = 1$, a straight line parallel to the x-axis.

Figure 1.93

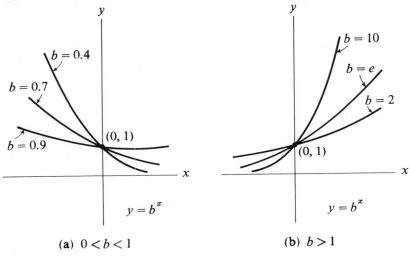

(a) $0 < b < 1$ \qquad (b) $b > 1$

The most frequently used exponential function is $y = e^x$, where e is the base of the natural logarithms, approximately 2.718. Almost all the exponential functions used in economic theory have the base e. The precise definition of this base and its advantages are discussed in connection with logarithms in the following sections.

A more general form for exponential functions is

$$y = ae^{kx} + c$$

The curve representing the function $y = ae^{kx} + c$ is asymptotic to the line $y = c$; it approaches its asymptote from above if $a > 0$ and from below if $a < 0$. The curve is monotonically increasing if a and k are of the same sign and monotonically decreasing if a and k are of opposite signs. The curve has y-intercept $(0, a + c)$ and, if $c < 0$, x-intercept $((1/k) \ln |c/a|, 0)$; see Figure 1.94. (The x-intercept is obtained in Technical Note V.)

LOGARITHMIC FUNCTIONS

In 1614, John Napier wrote the first treatise on logarithms. He based his discussion on the comparison of two sets of numbers—one in arithmetic progression, that is, one having terms such that the difference between the nth and $(n-1)$st terms is

Figure 1.94

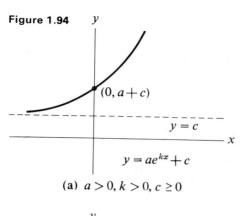

(a) $a > 0, k > 0, c \geq 0$

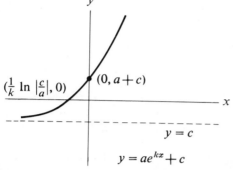

(b) $a > 0, k < 0, c \geq 0$

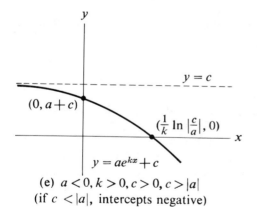

(c) $a > 0, k > 0, c \leq 0, |c| < a$
(if $|c| > a$, intercepts negative)

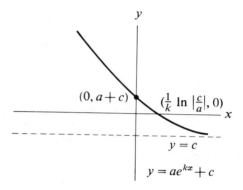

(d) $a > 0, k < 0, c \leq 0, |c| < a$
(if $|c| > a$, intercepts negative)

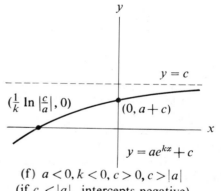

(e) $a < 0, k > 0, c > 0, c > |a|$
(if $c < |a|$, intercepts negative)

(f) $a < 0, k < 0, c > 0, c > |a|$
(if $c < |a|$, intercepts negative)

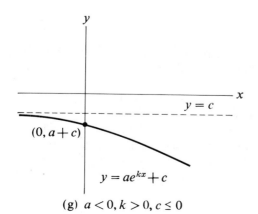

(g) $a < 0, k > 0, c \leq 0$

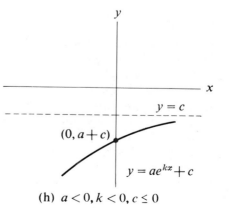

(h) $a < 0, k < 0, c \leq 0$

constant, and one in geometric progression, that is, one having terms such that the ratio of the nth and $(n - 1)$st terms is constant. For example, consider the following two progressions:

Arithmetic: 0   1   2   3   4   5   6 ...
Geometric: 1   3   9   27   81   243   729 ...

If the numbers of the arithmetic progression are considered as exponents (powers) of 3, the corresponding numbers of the geometric progression result from raising 3 to the indicated power. Thus

$$3^0 = 1$$

$$3^1 = 3$$

$$3^2 = 9$$

$$3^3 = 27$$

and so forth. Furthermore, the two progressions indicate that in order to multiply, it is necessary only to add exponents: $3^2 \times 3^3 = 3^{2+3} = 3^5$. And to divide, it is necessary only to subtract exponents: $3^5 \div 3^2 = 3^{5-2} = 3^3$. This idea is the basis for the computational short cuts possible using logarithms.

By definition, the *logarithm* of a positive number y to a positive base b, other than 1, is the exponent x to which the base must be raised to obtain the number. Thus, if $b > 0$, $b \neq 1$, and b, x, and y are related by the equation

$$y = b^x \tag{3}$$

then x, the exponent of b, is the logarithm of y to the base b. This relationship may also be expressed by the equation

$$x = \log_b y \tag{4}$$

Equations (3) and (4) express inverse relationships between b, x, and y in exponential and logarithmic forms, respectively, and are inverse functions—that is, if y is an exponential function of x, then x is a logarithmic function of y.

Although the base of a logarithm can be any positive number other than 1, in practice the base is almost always either 10 (common or Briggsian logarithms) or $e \approx 2.718$ (natural or Naperian logarithms). The base e is defined in terms of limits as follows:

$$e = \lim_{n \to \infty} \left(1 + \frac{1}{n}\right)^n$$

The concept of limits is discussed in detail later; for present purposes it is sufficient to note that e can be approximated as accurately as desired by increasing n in the expression $(1 + 1/n)^n$.

In some cases, common logarithms are more convenient for computational work; natural logarithms are more convenient for theoretical work because of calculus considerations. By convention, $\log x$ denotes the common logarithm of x, and $\ln x$ denotes the natural logarithm of x. If any other base is used, it is specified.

The use of logarithms can save considerable work in computations involving numbers that are very large or very small in absolute value. The essential properties of logarithms are summarized in the following rules:

If x and y are positive real numbers,

Rule

1. $\log_b(xy) = \log_b x + \log_b y$

2. $\log_b\left(\dfrac{x}{y}\right) = \log_b x - \log_b y$

3. $\log_b x^r = r\log_b x$

4. $\log_a x = \log_a b(\log_b x)$

$$= \left(\dfrac{1}{\log_b a}\right)\log_b x$$

The simplest logarithmic functions, mentioned above, are of the form

$$y = \log_b x, \qquad b > 0 \text{ and } b \neq 1$$

The curve representing the function $y = \log_b x$ lies entirely in the first and fourth quadrants; it is monotonically decreasing if $0 < b < 1$ and monotonically increasing if $b > 1$; in both cases the curve is asymptotic to the y-axis and has x-intercept $(1, 0)$. The parameter b determines the curvature of the function (see Figures 1.93 and 1.95).

Since $y = b^x$ and $y = \log_b x$ are inverse functions, the graph of either one of these families of curves (or of one particular curve for some specified value of b) can be obtained from the graph of the other geometrically by reflection about the line $y = x$. (Recall that reflection of a curve about a line consists of obtaining the curve that is symmetric to the given curve with respect to the line; see Figure 1.96.)

A more general form for logarithmic functions is

$$y = A \ln(1 + x) + B \qquad x > -1$$

The curve representing the function $y = A \ln(1 + x) + B$ lies to the right of and is asymptotic to the line $x = -1$; the curve is monotonically increasing if $A > 0$ and monotonically decreasing if $A < 0$. It has x-intercept $(e^{-B/A} - 1, 0)$ and y-intercept $(0, B)$; see Figure 1.97. (The x-intercept is obtained in Technical Note V.)

Figure 1.95

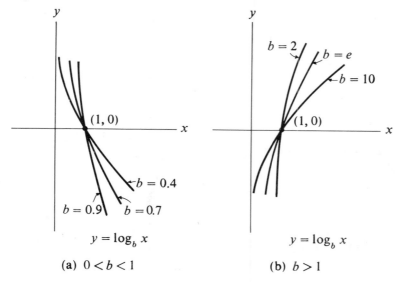

$$y = \log_b x$$

(a) $0 < b < 1$

$$y = \log_b x$$

(b) $b > 1$

Figure 1.96

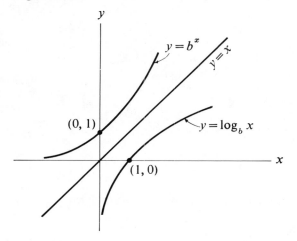

Figure 1.97

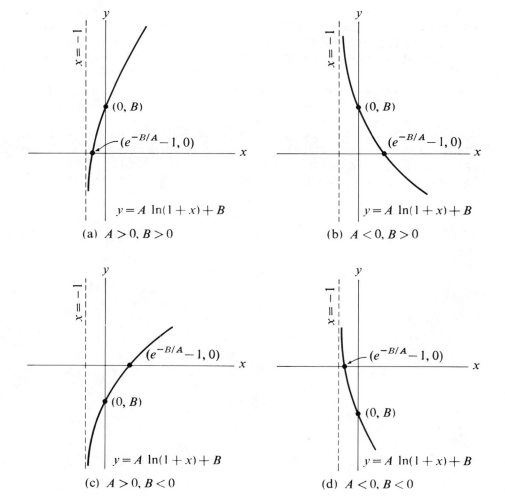

$y = A \ln(1 + x) + B$

(a) $A > 0, B > 0$

$y = A \ln(1 + x) + B$

(b) $A < 0, B > 0$

$y = A \ln(1 + x) + B$

(c) $A > 0, B < 0$

$y = A \ln(1 + x) + B$

(d) $A < 0, B < 0$

PROBLEMS

1. For what ranges of x are the following curves defined?
   a. $y = \ln(x + 1)$ c. $y = \ln(x^3 + 27)$
   b. $y = \ln(x - 4)$ d. $y = \ln(x^4 - 16)$

2. Sketch on the same set of axes the curves represented by the equations
   a. $y = 2^x$ c. $y = 2^{x/2}$
   b. $y = 2^{-x}$ d. $y = 2^{2x}$

3. Sketch on the same set of axes the curves represented by $y = a^x$ for $a = 2$, e, 3, and 10.

4. Sketch on the same set of axes the curves represented by $y = \log_a x$ for $a = 2$, e, 3, and 10.

5. Sketch on the same set of axes the curves represented by the equations
   a. $y = 3^x$ b. $y = \log_3 x$

6. For what ranges of x are the following curves defined?
   a. $y = \frac{1}{2}\ln(1 - x^2)$ d. $y = -3 - 6\ln(x - 2)$
   b. $y = \ln(36 - x^2)$ e. $y = \ln(x - 27)$
   c. $y = \ln(x^2 - 36)$

Answers to Odd-Numbered Problems

1. a. $x > -1$ c. $x > -3$
   b. $x > 4$ d. $x < -2$ and $x > 2$

1.9 Applications of Exponential and Logarithmic Curves in Business and Economics

As can be noted in Figures 1.94 and 1.97, several types of exponential and logarithmic functions are appropriate for representing demand or supply curves. Exponential cost functions, representing total cost as an exponential function of number of units produced, are also frequently used. Many examples of exponential and logarithmic demand, supply, and cost curves appear in later sections. The applications discussed in this section are compound interest and various types of growth functions, problems for which exponential and logarithmic functions are uniquely appropriate. A table of exponential functions and a table of logarithms are provided at the end of the book.

COMPOUND INTEREST

If the interest rate is $100i$ percent per year payable (that is, compounded) k times per year, after n years an amount of money x (the principal) becomes

$$y = x\left(1 + \frac{i}{k}\right)^{nk}$$

(when k is large, $y \approx xe^{in}$, where $e \approx 2.718$ is the base of the natural logarithms).

This formula can be developed as follows: If the interest at rate $100i$ percent is payable yearly, then the amount (principal plus interest) y_1 at the end of the first year is

$$y_1 = x + ix = x(1 + i)$$

The amount y_2 after 2 years is

$$y_2 = [x(1 + i)][1 + i] = x(1 + i)^2$$

The amount y_3 after 3 years is

$$y_3 = [x(1 + i)^2][1 + i] = x(1 + i)^3$$

$$\vdots$$

The amount y_n after n years is

$$y_n = x(1 + i)^n$$

If interest is payable k times per year, then the rate of interest in any one period is $100(i/k)$ percent and the number of periods is nk. Thus the amount after n years is

$$y = x\left(1 + \frac{i}{k}\right)^{nk}$$

EXAMPLE

A man deposits $5000 at 4% interest. How much has he (principal plus interest) after 10 years (a) if interest is payable yearly, and (b) if interest is payable quarterly?

(a) $y = x(1 + i)^n$

$\qquad = 5000(1 + 0.04)^{10}$

$\log y = \log 5000 + 10 \log 1.04$

$\qquad = 3.6990 + (10)(0.0170)$

$\qquad = 3.8690$

$\quad y = \$7396.67$

(b) $y = x\left(1 + \dfrac{i}{k}\right)^{nk}$

$\qquad = 5000\left(1 + \dfrac{0.04}{4}\right)^{40}$

$\log y = \log 5000 + 40 \log 1.01$

$\qquad = 3.6990 + 40(0.0043)$

$\qquad = 3.8710$

$\quad y = \$7430.00$

Thus, after 10 years, he has $7396.67 if interest is paid yearly and $7430.00 if interest is paid quarterly.

The equation for compound interest

$$y = x\left(1 + \frac{i}{k}\right)^{nk}$$

has five variables, y, the amount accumulated; x, the amount originally deposited; i, the yearly interest rate; n, the number of years for which interest is paid; and k, the number of times per year the interest is compounded. If the values of any four of these variables are known, the value of the fifth can be determined.

In particular, if a specified amount y is to be available after interest at rate i is compounded k times a year for n years, the amount required for the initial deposit, x, can be determined. An amount that can be deposited today to yield a specified amount in the future is the *present value* of this specified amount. Thus, in the preceding formula, x is the present value of y.

EXAMPLE

Mr. Education wishes to have $10,000 available in 10 years when his twins graduate from high school. What amount must he deposit now at 10% interest compounded annually to obtain the desired amount?

$$y = x\left(1 + \frac{i}{k}\right)^{nk}$$

$$10{,}000 = x(1 + 0.10)^{10}$$

$$\log 10{,}000 = \log x + 10 \log 1.10$$

$$4 = \log x + (10)(0.0414)$$

$$\log x = 4 - 0.414$$

$$= 3.5860$$

$$x = \$3854.55$$

Note that tables for computing compound interest, present value, and interest rates are available in standard books of tables and in many finance and accounting texts. Their use is not discussed here, but is straightforward and is recommended for solving practical problems. A calculator with a power function can also be used and has the advantage of not being limited to the interest rates included in a table.

GROWTH FUNCTIONS

There are many relationships in business and economics which are appropriately represented by curves referred to as growth functions. For example, number of employees as a function of annual sales of a company, amount of finished stock as a function of days after beginning a production run, sales as a function of advertising expenditure, maintenance cost as a function of number of hours a machine is run, and sales as a function of length of time a product has been on the market, can be represented by growth functions.

The basic property of the various curves referred to as growth functions is that they are monotonically increasing. Growth functions may or may not have an upper asymptote (although usually for business and economic applications absence of an upper asymptote is reasonable only when relatively short periods of time are considered) and they may be of various shapes. Three particular types of growth functions are discussed below: (1) very simple functions, which were originally developed to describe certain types of biological growth and are appropriate only for growth that does not have an upper asymptote, (2) Gompertz functions, which are used to describe growth that starts rather slowly and approaches an upper asymptote, and

(3) learning functions, which were originally used by psychologists to describe human learning and are appropriate for growth that begins rapidly, levels off, and approaches an asymptote.

Biological Growth Curves

Many laws of biological growth can be represented by the equation

$$N = N_0 R^t$$

where N is the number of individuals in the population at time t, N_0 is the initial number of individuals in the population (at time zero), and $R > 0$ is the rate of growth (see Figure 1.98). This equation is based on the model of a population each of whose members produces $R - 1$ additional members in each unit of time and none of whose members die. (This situation is approximated for certain laboratory cultures, at least for limited periods of time.) The equation can be developed as follows:

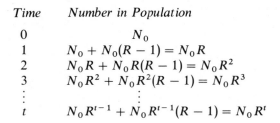

Time	Number in Population
0	N_0
1	$N_0 + N_0(R - 1) = N_0 R$
2	$N_0 R + N_0 R(R - 1) = N_0 R^2$
3	$N_0 R^2 + N_0 R^2(R - 1) = N_0 R^3$
$\vdots$	$\vdots$
t	$N_0 R^{t-1} + N_0 R^{t-1}(R - 1) = N_0 R^t$

Figure 1.98

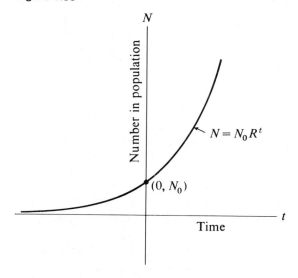

Organization theorists have claimed that the function $N = N_0 R^t$ is appropriate for describing the early growth of a rapidly developing company. Because it has no upper asymptote, the function is inappropriate for describing biological or organizational growth for an indefinite period of time. In addition, the behavior of the curve, as illustrated in the example below, indicates that it should be used with extreme caution in theoretical analyses.

EXAMPLE

The National Aerospace Research Organization is beginning its operations with a staff of 5 men. At the end of each year of its operation, each employee will hire 3 assistants. How many employees will National Aerospace Research Organization have after 10 years of operation?

$$N = N_0 R^t$$

$$= (5)(4^{10})$$

$$= 1,048,576 \text{ employees after 10 years}$$

Gompertz Curves

Gompertz curves, named for their originator, are represented by the equation

$$N = ca^{R^t}$$

where N is the number of individuals in the population at time t, R $(0 < R < 1)$ is the rate of growth, a is the proportion of initial growth, and c is the growth at maturity (that is, the upper asymptote). Note that when $t = 0$, $N = ca$, which corresponds to N_0 of the biological growth function.

The two basic types of Gompertz curves are characterized as follows and are illustrated in Figure 1.99:

Type I: $0 < a < \dfrac{1}{e}$

Type II: $\dfrac{1}{e} \le a < 1$

Curves of Type I are positively accelerated for small positive values of t and negatively accelerated for large positive values of t; curves of Type II are negatively accelerated for all positive values of t. The mathematical definitions of positive and negative acceleration are discussed later; essentially, a positively accelerated function is increasing at an increasing rate and a negatively accelerated function is increasing at a decreasing rate.

Figure 1.99

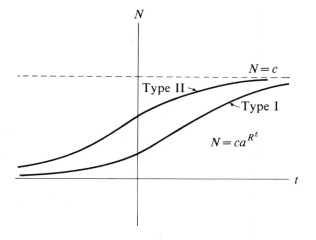

Gompertz curves have been used extensively by psychologists to describe various aspects of human growth and development, including some types of learning. Organization theorists have found Gompertz curves appropriate for describing the growth of many types of organizations. These curves are also appropriate for many other functions in business and economics, for example, total revenue and production.

EXAMPLE

On the basis of expected sales and data for similar companies, the Personnel Director of National Industries predicts that the number of employees can be described by the equation

$$N = 200(0.04)^{0.5^t}$$

where N is the number of employees after t years. Assuming he is correct, how many employees will National Industries have after 3 years? How many employees did the company employ initially? How many will it employ when it reaches its maximum size?

The company employs $(200)(0.04) = 8$ people initially and 200 at maximum size. After 3 years it employs

$$N = (200)(0.04)^{0.5^3}$$

$$\log N = \log 200 + 0.5^3 \log 0.04$$

$$= 2.3010 + (0.125)(-1.3979)$$

$$= 2.1263$$

$$N = 133.75 \quad \text{or approximately 134 people}$$

Learning Curves

Because of their extensive use by psychologists to describe learning, exponential curves of the form

$$y = c - ae^{-kx}$$

where c, a, and k are positive, are frequently referred to as learning curves. [Note that this is case (f) of the general form $y = ae^{kx} + c$ discussed previously.] In his reinforcement theory of learning, Clark Hull uses the special case $c = a$ of this function as one of the basic equations for describing the relationship between strength of learning, y, and number of reinforcements, x.

Figure 1.100

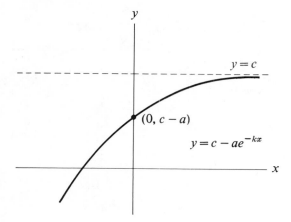

The function $y = c - ae^{-kx}$ rises rapidly at first, flattens out, and then approaches its asymptote $y = c$ (see Figure 1.100). These curves have been found to be appropriate for representing various cost and production functions.

EXAMPLE

If the number of items y manufactured per day x days after the beginning of a production run is given by

$$y = 200(1 - e^{-0.1x})$$

how many items are manufactured per day 10 days after beginning the run and what per cent of the maximum is this?

$$y = 200(1 - e^{-1})$$

$$= 200(1 - 0.368)$$

$$= 200(0.632)$$

$$= 126.4 \quad \text{or approximately 126 items, } 63.2\% \text{ of the maximum of 200 items.}$$

EXAMPLE

If the yearly maintenance cost y of a computer is related to its average monthly use x (in hundreds of hours) by the equation

$$y = 35,000 - 25,000e^{-0.02x}$$

what is the yearly maintenance cost for 200 hours average monthly use?

$$y = 35,000 - 25,000e^{-0.04}$$

$$= 35,000 - 25,000(0.135)$$

$$= 35,000 - 3375$$

$$= \$31,625 \text{ yearly maintenance}$$

PROBLEMS

1. Chem Corporation has $10,000 to deposit and expects to leave the deposit for 20 years. Two options are available: 5% interest payable semiannually and $4\frac{1}{2}\%$ interest payable quarterly. Which option should Chem Corporation choose?
2. In order to have $20,000 after 20 years at 6% interest payable yearly, how much must be deposited?
3. The National Professional Society has been formed with 10 original members. The rules state that each member may invite 2 people to join at the beginning of each year. If each member always takes advantage of this rule, how many members will the society have after 15 years?
4. Monthly total revenue (in dollars) for a particular firm can be described by the equation

$$R = 1000(0.10)^{0.8p}$$

where p is the amount spent for promotion and advertising. What is total revenue when nothing is spent for promotion and advertising? What is the maximum attainable total revenue? What is total revenue if $20 is spent for promotion and advertising?

5. Production costs (in hundreds of dollars) for a firm are described by the equation

$$C = 100 - 70e^{-0.02x}$$

where x is the number of units of output. What are the firm's fixed costs? When output is 100 units, what proportion of the production costs are fixed?

6. One job on a production line consists of screwing a small screw into a metal plate. For a typical employee, the number of plates completed per hour is described by the equation

$$y = 50 - 40e^{-0.30x}$$

where x is number of hours the employee has worked on the production line. a. How many plates can an employee complete the first hour? b. How many the sixth hour?

7. The number of firms in a particular industry is described by the equation

$$N = 6(0.5)^{0.75^t}$$

where t is the number of years since the industry began. How many firms were there in the industry after 5 years? How many firms were in the industry originally? How many firms will there be when the industry reaches maximum size?

8. In order to have $10,000 after $6,000 has been deposited for 25 years with interest payable yearly, what interest rate must be paid?

9. For a 10-year deposit, what interest rate payable annually is equivalent to 5% interest payable quarterly?

10. For a 25-year deposit, what interest payable semiannually is equivalent to 4% payable quarterly?

Answers to Odd-Numbered Problems

1. 5% payable semiannually ($26,841) rather than $4\frac{1}{2}$% payable quarterly ($24,480)
3. 143,489,070
5. $3000 fixed costs
   33.14% of production costs are fixed for 100 units output
7. 5 firms after 5 years
   3 firms originally
   6 firms at maximum size
9. 5.1%

Technical Note I Conditions for Equilibrium

Two linear equations of the form

$$A_1 x + B_1 y + C_1 = 0 \qquad A_2 x + B_2 y + C_2 = 0$$

have the simultaneous solution (x, y), where

$$x = \frac{B_1 C_2 - B_2 C_1}{A_1 B_2 - A_2 B_1} \qquad y = \frac{A_2 C_1 - A_1 C_2}{A_1 B_2 - A_2 B_1}$$

provided $A_1 B_2 - A_2 B_1 \neq 0$.

Thus if the nonvertical demand and supply curves

$$y = m_D x + b_D \qquad y = m_S x + b_S$$

(where the subscripts D and S distinguish demand and supply curves) are written

$$m_D x - y + b_D = 0 \qquad m_S x - y + b_S = 0$$

then the equilibrium quantity and price are

$$x = \frac{b_D - b_S}{m_S - m_D} \qquad y = \frac{b_D m_S - b_S m_D}{m_S - m_D}$$

since $m_S - m_D \neq 0$. Since $m_D < 0$, $m_S > 0$, $y_D > 0$, and y_S is unrestricted, $m_S - m_D > 0$ and $x \geq 0$ if $b_D - b_S \geq 0$, that is, if $b_D \geq b_S$, which is the first condition stated for equilibrium in the first quadrant; $y \geq 0$ if

$$b_D m_S - b_S m_D \geq 0$$

or

$$b_D m_S \geq b_S m_D$$

$$\frac{b_D}{m_D} \leq \frac{b_S}{m_S} \quad (\text{since } m_D < 0)$$

$$\frac{-b_D}{m_D} \geq \frac{-b_S}{m_S}$$

which is the second condition stated for equilibrium in the first quadrant, since the x-coordinate of the x-intercept of the line $y = mx + b$ is $-(b/m)$.

Technical Note II Identification of Degenerate and Imaginary Loci

The type of conic section represented by a second-degree equation, $Ax^2 + Bxy + Cy^2 + Dx + Ey + F = 0$, can be determined from certain conditions on the coefficients as summarized in Table 1.1.

Table 1.1

Case	Conditions on the coefficients	Type of conic
Proper conic, $\bar{D} \neq 0$	$\bar{C} > 0$; I, $\bar{D}$ opposite in sign, $A = C$, $B = 0$ (no xy-term)	Circle
	$\bar{C} > 0$; I, $\bar{D}$ opposite in sign	Ellipse
	$\bar{C} < 0$	Hyperbola
	$\bar{C} = 0$	Parabola
	$\bar{C} > 0$, I, $\bar{D}$ same in sign	No real locus
Degenerate conic, $\bar{D} = 0$	$\bar{C} < 0$	Two intersecting lines
	$\bar{C} = 0$, $J < 0$	Two parallel lines
	$\bar{C} = 0$, $J = 0$	Two coincident lines
	$\bar{C} > 0$	A point
	$\bar{C} = 0$, $J > 0$	No real locus

In this table,

$$I = A + C$$

$$\bar{C} = AC - \frac{B^2}{4}$$

$$J = AC + CF + AF - \frac{E^2}{4} - \frac{D^2}{4} - \frac{B^2}{4}$$

$$\bar{D} = ACF + \frac{BED}{4} - \frac{CD^2}{4} - \frac{AE^2}{4} - \frac{FB^2}{4}$$

In many cases it can be assumed (owing to the nature of the application) that the given equation represents a proper conic (that is, $\bar{D} \neq 0$) and a real locus (that is, I and $\bar{D}$ opposite in sign if $\bar{C} > 0$). In such cases it is necessary only to compute $\bar{C}$ and note the coefficients A, C, and B in order to determine which type of conic section is represented by the equation.

The results given in this technical note are obtained using the procedure discussed in Technical Note III.

Technical Note III Completing the Square

In many problems it is convenient to have an equation written so that variables which occur in terms of second degree occur only as terms of a perfect square; this is accomplished by putting the terms of the perfect square(s) on one side and all other terms on the other side of the equation and adding the appropriate constant terms to both sides of the equation.

The process of completing the square is based on the formula $(x + a)^2 = x^2 + 2ax + a^2$. Thus, given $x^2 + cx$, take half the coefficient of x and square it to complete the square: $x^2 + cx + (c/2)^2$. Any constant term added to one side of an equation must, of course, be added also to the other side in order to preserve the equality. Completing the square is the essential step in putting a second-degree equation into the appropriate standard form.

If $ax^2 + bx + cy + d = 0$, then the terms to be included in the perfect square are ax^2 and bx; thus

$$a\left(x^2 + \frac{b}{a}x\right) = -cy - d$$

$$a\left(x^2 + \frac{b}{a}x + \frac{b^2}{4a^2}\right) = -cy - d + \frac{b^2}{4a}$$

$$\left(x + \frac{b}{2a}\right)^2 = -\frac{c}{a}\left(y + \frac{d}{c} - \frac{b^2}{4ac}\right)$$

EXAMPLE

Complete the square for the equation

$$3x^2 + 4x + 2y - 4 = 0$$

$$3(x^2 + \tfrac{4}{3}x + \tfrac{4}{9}) = -2y + 4 + \tfrac{4}{3}$$

$$(x + \tfrac{2}{3})^2 = -\tfrac{2}{3}(y - \tfrac{8}{3})$$

If $ax^2 + by^2 + cx + dy + e = 0$, then the terms to be included in the perfect squares are ax^2, cx, by^2, and dy; thus

$$a\left(x^2 + \frac{c}{a}x\right) + b\left(y^2 + \frac{d}{b}y\right) = -e$$

$$a\left(x^2 + \frac{c}{a}x + \frac{c^2}{4a^2}\right) + b\left(y^2 + \frac{d}{b}y + \frac{d^2}{4b^2}\right) = -e + \frac{c^2}{4a} + \frac{d^2}{4b}$$

$$\frac{\left(x + \frac{c}{2a}\right)^2}{b} + \frac{\left(y + \frac{d}{2b}\right)^2}{a} = \frac{1}{ab}\left(\frac{c^2}{4a} + \frac{d^2}{4b} - e\right) = \frac{c^2}{4a^2b} + \frac{d^2}{4ab^2} - \frac{e}{ab}$$

EXAMPLE

Complete the squares for the equation

$$3x^2 + 4y^2 - 6x + 7y - 10 = 0$$

$$3(x^2 - 2x) + 4(y^2 + \tfrac{7}{4}y) = 10$$

$$3(x^2 - 2x + 1) + 4(y^2 + \tfrac{7}{4}y + \tfrac{49}{64}) = 10 + 3 + \tfrac{49}{16}$$

$$\frac{(x-1)^2}{4} + \frac{(y + \tfrac{7}{8})^2}{3} = \tfrac{1}{12}(13 + \tfrac{49}{16}) = \tfrac{257}{192}$$

The essential aspect of the process of completing the square is the addition of the appropriate constant terms so that groups of terms form perfect squares; the most convenient form of writing the constant coefficients depends on the particular problem.

A second-degree equation can be put into the appropriate standard form for the type of conic it represents by the process of completing the square.

The circle:

$$Ax^2 + Ay^2 + Dx + Ey + F = 0$$

$$A\left(x^2 + \frac{D}{A}x + \frac{D^2}{4A^2}\right) + A\left(y^2 + \frac{E}{A}y + \frac{E^2}{4A^2}\right) = \frac{D^2}{4A} + \frac{E^2}{4A} - F$$

$$\left(x + \frac{D}{2A}\right)^2 + \left(y + \frac{E}{2A}\right)^2 = \frac{D^2}{4A^2} + \frac{E^2}{4A^2} - \frac{F}{A}$$

which is of the form $(x - h)^2 + (y - k)^2 = r^2$, where

$$h = -\frac{D}{2A} \qquad k = -\frac{E}{2A} \qquad r^2 = \frac{D^2}{4A^2} + \frac{E^2}{4A^2} - \frac{F}{A}$$

The ellipse: $Ax^2 + Cy^2 + Dx + Ey + F = 0$, A and C same sign

$$A\left(x^2 + \frac{D}{A}x + \frac{D^2}{4A^2}\right) + C\left(y^2 + \frac{E}{C}y + \frac{E^2}{4C^2}\right) = \frac{D^2}{4A} + \frac{E^2}{4C} - F$$

Denoting $\dfrac{D^2}{4A} + \dfrac{E^2}{4C} - F$ by k,

$$\frac{\left(x + \dfrac{D}{2A}\right)^2}{\dfrac{k}{A}} + \frac{\left(y + \dfrac{E}{2C}\right)^2}{\dfrac{k}{C}} = 1$$

which is of the form

$$\frac{(x-h)^2}{a^2} + \frac{(y-k)^2}{b^2} = 1$$

where

$$h = -\frac{D}{2A} \qquad k = -\frac{E}{2C}$$

The parabola: $Ax^2 + Dx + Ey + F = 0$

$$A\left(x^2 + \frac{D}{A}x + \frac{D^2}{4A^2}\right) = -E\left(y + \frac{F}{E} - \frac{D^2}{4AE}\right)$$

$$\left(x + \frac{D}{2A}\right)^2 = -\frac{E}{A}\left(y - \frac{D^2 - 4AF}{4AE}\right)$$

which is of the form $(x - h)^2 = 4p(y - k)$, where

$$h = -\frac{D}{2A} \qquad k = \frac{D^2 - 4AF}{4AE} \qquad 4p = -\frac{E}{A}$$

(and similarly for the parabola $Cy^2 + Dx + Ey + F = 0$).

The hyperbola: $Ax^2 + Cy^2 + Dx + Ey + F = 0$, A and C opposite in sign

$$A\left(x^2 + \frac{D}{A}x + \frac{D^2}{4A^2}\right) + C\left(y^2 + \frac{E}{C}y + \frac{E^2}{4C^2}\right) = \frac{D^2}{4A} + \frac{E^2}{4C} - F$$

Denoting $\dfrac{D^2}{4A} + \dfrac{E^2}{4C} - F$ by k,

$$\frac{\left(x + \dfrac{D}{2A}\right)^2}{\dfrac{k}{A}} + \frac{\left(y + \dfrac{E}{2C}\right)^2}{\dfrac{k}{C}} = 1$$

which is of the form

$$\frac{(x - h)^2}{a^2} - \frac{(y - k)^2}{b^2} = 1$$

or

$$\frac{(y - k)^2}{b^2} - \frac{(x - h)^2}{a^2} = 1$$

since A and C are opposite in sign, where

$$h = -\frac{D}{2A} \qquad k = -\frac{E}{2C}$$

The various properties of particular second-degree curves can be obtained by identifying the type of conic section represented and then substituting appropriate numerical values in the corresponding formulas given above, rather than by putting each equation into standard form.

Technical Note IV Formula for Roots of a Quadratic Equation

The formula for the roots of a quadratic equation is obtained by completing the square as follows:

$$ax^2 + bx + c = 0$$

$$a\left(x^2 + \frac{bx}{a} + \frac{b^2}{4a^2}\right) = -c + \frac{b^2}{4a}$$

$$\left(x + \frac{b}{2a}\right)^2 = \frac{b^2 - 4ac}{4a^2}$$

$$x + \frac{b}{2a} = \pm \sqrt{\frac{b^2 - 4ac}{4a^2}}$$

$$x = \frac{-b \pm \sqrt{b^2 - 4ac}}{2a}$$

Technical Note V ***x-intercepts of*** $y = ae^{kx} + c$ ***and*** $y = A \ln (1 + x) + B$

To obtain the x-intercept for the curve $y = ae^{kx} + c$: Let $y = 0$; then

$$ae^{kx} = -c$$

$$e^{kx} = -\frac{c}{a}$$

$$\ln \left(-\frac{c}{a} \right) = kx$$

$$x = \frac{1}{k} \ln \left(-\frac{c}{a} \right)$$

In order for $\ln \left(-\frac{c}{a} \right)$ to be defined,

$$c \le 0, a > 0 \qquad \text{[cases (c) and (d)]}$$

or

$$c > 0, a < 0 \qquad \text{[cases (e) and (f)]}$$

Note in Figure 1.94 that only cases (c), (d), (e), and (f) have x-intercepts and that

$$\frac{1}{k} \ln \left(-\frac{c}{a} \right) > 0 \text{ if } a > 0, c \le 0, k < 0, a > |c| \qquad \text{[case (d)]}$$

$$\text{or}$$

$$a < 0, c > 0, k > 0, c > |a| \qquad \text{[case (e)]}$$

$$\frac{1}{k} \ln \left(-\frac{c}{a} \right) < 0 \text{ if } a > 0, c \le 0, k > 0, a > |c| \qquad \text{[case (c)]}$$

$$\text{or}$$

$$a < 0, c > 0, k < 0, c > |a| \qquad \text{[case (f)]}$$

To obtain the x-intercept for the curve $y = A \ln (1 + x) + B$: Let $y = 0$; then

$$A \ln (1 + x) = -B$$

$$\ln (1 + x) = -\frac{B}{A}$$

$$e^{-(B/A)} = 1 + x$$

$$x = e^{-(B/A)} - 1$$

and

$$e^{-(B/A)} - 1 > 0 \qquad \text{if } \frac{B}{A} < 0$$

$$e^{-(B/A)} - 1 = 0 \qquad \text{if } \frac{B}{A} = 0 \qquad \text{that is, if } B = 0$$

$$e^{-(B/A)} - 1 < 0 \qquad \text{if } \frac{B}{A} > 0$$

Thus

$$e^{-(B/A)} - 1 > 0$$

if

$\quad A > 0, B > 0 \qquad$ [case (a)]

$\quad A < 0, B < 0 \qquad$ [case (d)]

and

$$e^{-(B/A)} - 1 < 0$$

if

$\quad A > 0, B < 0 \qquad$ [case (c)]

$\quad A < 0, B > 0 \qquad$ [case (b)]

Appendix A
Algebra Review

EXPONENTS

In the expression b^n (read "b to the nth power " or " the nth power of b "), b is the *base* and n is the *exponent*. If n is a positive integer, then

$$b^n = b \cdot b \cdots b$$

where b is a factor n times.

EXAMPLE

(a) $3^2 = 3 \cdot 3 = 9$

(b) $4^1 = 4$

(c) $\left(\frac{3}{2}\right)^3 = \left(\frac{3}{2}\right)\left(\frac{3}{2}\right)\left(\frac{3}{2}\right) = \frac{27}{8}$

By definition, if $n = 0$ and $b \neq 0$, $b^n = b^0 = 1$. Thus, if b is any nonzero real number,

$$b^0 = 1$$

Note that this definition is based on the fact that, for example,

$$\frac{b^m}{b^m} = b^{m-m} = b^0 = 1$$

EXAMPLE

(a) $5^0 = 1$

(b) $(-2)^0 = 1$

(c) $-7^0 = -1$

If n is a positive integer and $b \neq 0$, then

$$b^{-n} = \frac{1}{b^n}$$

Note that this definition is based on the fact that, for example,

$$b^{-n} = b^{0-n} = \frac{b^0}{b^n} = \frac{1}{b^n}$$

EXAMPLE

(a) $2^{-4} = \dfrac{1}{2^4} = \dfrac{1}{16}$

(b) $7^{-1} = \dfrac{1}{7}$

(c) $(\frac{3}{8})^{-1} = \dfrac{1}{\frac{3}{8}} = \dfrac{8}{3}$

(d) $(\frac{4}{5})^{-2} = \dfrac{1}{(\frac{4}{5})^2} = \dfrac{1}{(\frac{4}{5})(\frac{4}{5})} = \dfrac{25}{16}$

Properties of Exponents

For any integers m and n and any real numbers a and b for which the following expressions are defined,

(1) $b^m \cdot b^n = b^{m+n}$

(2) $\dfrac{b^m}{b^n} = b^{m-n}$

(3) $(b^m)^n = b^{mn}$

(4) $(ab)^m = a^m \cdot b^m$

(5) $\left(\dfrac{a}{b}\right)^m = \dfrac{a^m}{b^m}$ $b \neq 0$

EXAMPLE

(a) $5^4 \cdot 5^3 = 5^7$ Property 1

(b) $\dfrac{4^6}{4^3} = 4^{6-3} = 4^3$ Property 2

(c) $\dfrac{7^8}{7^{15}} = 7^{8-15} = 7^{-7}$ Property 2

(d) $(9^2)^3 = 9^{2 \cdot 3} = 9^6$ Property 3

(e) $(3 \cdot 7)^2 = 3^2 \cdot 7^2$ Property 4

(f) $(4x)^3 = 4^3 \cdot x^3$ Property 4

(g) $\left(\dfrac{4}{5}\right)^6 = \dfrac{4^6}{5^6}$ Property 5

(h) $\left(\dfrac{x}{2}\right)^7 = \dfrac{x^7}{2^7}$ Property 5

PROBLEMS

Simplify each of the following expressions.

1. $3^3 \cdot 3^{-2}$

2. $(5^3)^0$

3. $(7y)^2$

4. $(3 \cdot 9)^2$

5. $\left(\dfrac{x}{4}\right)^{-2}$

6. $(6y)^{-3}$

7. $(\tfrac{3}{2})^{-5}$

8. $\dfrac{4^4}{4^3}$

9. $(10^3)^2$

10. $\left(\dfrac{z}{2}\right)^{-1}$

11. $(5^{-1})^2$

12. $\left(\dfrac{z^3}{3}\right)^2$

13. $\left(\dfrac{3x}{2y}\right)^{-2}$

14. $\left(\dfrac{3}{2}\right)\left(\dfrac{x}{y}\right)^{-2}$

15. $(3x)^{-1}(2y)$

16. $(3x^{-1})(2y)$

17. $2^{-3} + 4^{-1}$

18. $x^3 \cdot y^{-3}$

19. $\dfrac{x^{-2}}{y^{-2}}$

20. $3^2 + 5^0$

Solutions of Problems

1. $3^3 \cdot 3^{-2} = 3^{3-2} = 3^1 = 3$

2. $(5^3)^0 = 1$

3. $(7y)^2 = 7^2 \cdot y^2 = 49y^2$

4. $(3 \cdot 9)^2 = 3^2 \cdot 9^2 = 9 \cdot 81 = 729$

5. $\left(\dfrac{x}{4}\right)^{-2} = \dfrac{1}{(x/4)^2} = \dfrac{1}{(x/4)(x/4)} = \dfrac{16}{x^2} = 16x^{-2}$

6. $(6y)^{-3} = \dfrac{1}{(6y)^3} = \dfrac{1}{6^2 \cdot y^3} = \dfrac{1}{36y^3} = \dfrac{1}{36}y^{-3}$

7. $(\tfrac{3}{2})^{-5} = (\tfrac{2}{3})^5 = \dfrac{2^5}{3^5} = \dfrac{32}{243}$

8. $\dfrac{4^4}{4^3} = 4^{4-3} = 4^1 = 4$

9. $(10^3)^2 = 10^{3 \cdot 2} = 10^6$

10. $\left(\dfrac{z}{2}\right)^{-1} = \dfrac{2}{z} = 2z^{-1}$

11. $(5^{-1})^2 = 5^{-1 \cdot 2} = 5^{-2} = \tfrac{1}{25}$

12. $\left(\dfrac{z^3}{3}\right)^2 = \dfrac{z^{3 \cdot 2}}{3^2} = \dfrac{z^6}{9}$

13. $\left(\dfrac{3x}{2y}\right)^{-2} = \left(\dfrac{2y}{3x}\right)^2 = \dfrac{4y^2}{9x^2}$

14. $\left(\dfrac{3}{2}\right)\left(\dfrac{x}{y}\right)^{-2} = \left(\dfrac{3}{2}\right)\left(\dfrac{y}{x}\right)^2 = \dfrac{3y^2}{2x^2}$

15. $(3x)^{-1}(2y) = \left(\dfrac{1}{3x}\right)(2y) = \dfrac{2y}{3x}$

16. $(3x^{-1})(2y) = \left(\dfrac{3}{x}\right)(2y) = \dfrac{6y}{x}$

17. $2^{-3} + 4^{-1} = \dfrac{1}{2^3} + \dfrac{1}{4} = \dfrac{1}{8} + \dfrac{1}{4} = \dfrac{3}{8}$

18. $x^3 \cdot y^{-3} = \dfrac{x^3}{y^3} = \left(\dfrac{x}{y}\right)^3$

19. $\dfrac{x^{-2}}{y^{-2}} = \dfrac{y^2}{x^2} = \left(\dfrac{y}{x}\right)^2$

20. $3^2 + 5^0 = 9 + 1 = 10$

Fractional Exponents

The properties of exponentials of the form b^n previously stated hold for all nonzero real numbers b and all integer values of n, both positive and negative. With appropriate definition of b^n, these properties hold for any rational value of n. (Recall that a rational number is any number of the form p/q, where p and q are integers and $q \neq 0$.)

Extension of the properties of exponentials to fractional (that is, rational) exponents requires that expressions of the form $b^{p/q}$ be defined in a manner consistent with these properties. For example, consider the exponential expression $b^{1/n}$. If the property $(b^m)^n = b^{mn}$ is to hold for $m = 1/n$, then

$$(b^{1/n})^n = b^{(1/n)(n)} = b^1 = b$$

Thus, the nth power of $b^{1/n}$ must be b. For this reason, $b^{1/n}$ is called the nth *root* of b. For example, $b^{1/2}$ denotes the second root or *square root* of b; $b^{1/3}$ denotes the third root or *cube root* of b; $b^{1/4}$ denotes the fourth root of b, and so forth. In cases where there is both a positive and a negative nth root, $b^{1/n}$ denotes the positive root. Thus $25^{1/2} = 5$, although $5^2 = 25$ and $(-5)^2 = 25$. Similarly, $16^{1/4} = 2$, although $(2)^4 = 16$ and $(-2)^4 = 16$.

Note that any even power of a real number is positive. Thus, if n is an even integer and $b < 0$, then $b^{1/n}$ is not a real number. Also note that if n is an odd integer and b is any real number, positive or negative, then there is only one real number equal to $b^{1/n}$.

EXAMPLE

(a) $64^{1/3} = 4$
(b) $64^{1/2} = 8$
(c) $(-125)^{1/2}$ not a real number
(d) $125^{1/3} = 5$
(e) $(-125)^{1/3} = -5$
(f) $(-10000)^{1/4}$ not a real number

The definition of $b^{1/n}$, where n is a positive integer, can be extended to include all rational values of n as follows. For all real numbers b and any rational number m/n,

$$b^{m/n} = (b^{1/n})^m$$

whenever the roots exist, that is, are real.

EXAMPLE

(a) $125^{2/3} = (125^{1/3})^2 = 5^2 = 25$
(b) $32^{6/5} = (32^{1/5})^6 = 2^6 = 64$
(c) $(-8)^{4/3} = [(-8)^{1/3}]^4 = (-2)^4 = 16$
(d) $(-64)^{3/2}$ not a real number
(e) $1000^{4/3} = (1000^{1/3})^4 = 10^4 = 10000$
(f) $(-243)^{3/5} = [(-243)^{1/5}]^3 = (-3)^3 = -27$

It is customary to express $b^{1/2}$ as $\sqrt{b}$, where $\sqrt{}$ is the *radical sign*. Similarly, if n is an integer greater than 1, $b^{1/n}$ can be written $\sqrt[n]{b}$. More generally, the expression $b^{m/n}$ can be written using radical signs as follows

$$b^{m/n} = (\sqrt[n]{b})^m = \sqrt[n]{b^m}$$

whenever these roots exist. Using this equality, expressions can be changed from exponential to radical form, and vice versa.

EXAMPLE

(a) $15^{7/2} = (\sqrt{15})^7 = \sqrt{15^7}$
(b) $3x^{2/3} = 3(\sqrt[3]{x})^2 = 3\sqrt[3]{x^2}$

(c) $(\sqrt[3]{14})^2 = 14^{2/3}$

(d) $9^{-2/3} = \dfrac{1}{9^{2/3}} = \dfrac{1}{(\sqrt[3]{9})^2} = \dfrac{1}{\sqrt[3]{9^2}}$

(e) $2(\sqrt{y})^5 = 2y^{5/2}$

(f) $\dfrac{3}{\sqrt[4]{x}} = 3x^{-1/4}$

PROBLEMS

Simplify the following expressions.

1. $(-1000)^{1/3}$
2. $(-1000)^{2/3}$
3. $25^{1/2}$
4. $625^{1/4}$
5. $125^{-1/3}$
6. $16^{3/4}$
7. $32^{-2/5}$
8. $16^{-1/4}$
9. $(-125)^{1/3}$
10. $(-125)^{-1/3}$
11. $8^{-2/3}$
12. $(-27)^{4/3}$
13. $9^{-3/2}$
14. $(-9)^{-3/2}$
15. $(-16)^{1/4}$
16. $25^{-3/2}$

Change the form of each of the following expressions from radical to exponential form or from exponential to radical form.

17. $(\sqrt{13})^3$

18. $4(\sqrt[4]{5})^5$

19. $3(\sqrt[3]{y})^6$

20. $\dfrac{6}{\sqrt[5]{y}}$

21. $3y^{2/3}$

22. $(3y)^{2/3}$

23. $4x^{-1/5}$

24. $5x^{-5}$

Solutions of Problems

1. $(-1000)^{1/3} = -10$

2. $(-1000)^{2/3} = (-10)^2 = 100$

3. $25^{1/2} = 5$

4. $625^{1/4} = 5$

5. $125^{-1/3} = \dfrac{1}{125^{1/3}} = \dfrac{1}{5}$

6. $16^{3/4} = 2^3 = 8$

7. $32^{-2/5} = \dfrac{1}{32^{2/5}} = \dfrac{1}{2^2} = \dfrac{1}{4}$

8. $16^{-1/4} = \dfrac{1}{16^{1/4}} = \dfrac{1}{2}$

9. $(-125)^{1/3} = -5$

10. $(-125)^{-1/3} = \dfrac{1}{(-125)^{1/3}} = -\dfrac{1}{5}$

11. $8^{-2/3} = \dfrac{1}{8^{2/3}} = \dfrac{1}{2^2} = \dfrac{1}{4}$

12. $(-27)^{4/3} = (-3)^4 = 81$

13. $9^{-3/2} = \dfrac{1}{9^{3/2}} = \dfrac{1}{3^3} = \dfrac{1}{27}$

14. $(-9)^{-3/2} = \dfrac{1}{(-9)^{3/2}}$ not a real number

15. $(-16)^{1/4}$ not a real number

16. $25^{-3/2} = \dfrac{1}{25^{3/2}} = \dfrac{1}{5^3} = \dfrac{1}{125}$

17. $(\sqrt{13})^3 = 13^{3/2}$

18. $4(\sqrt[4]{5})^5 = 4 \cdot 5^{5/4}$

19. $3(\sqrt[3]{y})^6 = 3y^{6/3} = 3y^2$

20. $\dfrac{6}{\sqrt[5]{y}} = \dfrac{6}{y^{1/5}} = 6y^{-1/5}$

21. $3y^{2/3} = 3(\sqrt[3]{y})^2 = 3\sqrt[3]{y^2}$

22. $(3y)^{2/3} = (\sqrt[3]{3y})^2 = \sqrt[3]{9y^2}$

23. $4x^{-1/5} = \dfrac{4}{x^{1/5}} = \dfrac{4}{\sqrt[5]{x}}$

24. $5x^{-5} = \dfrac{5}{x^5} = \dfrac{5}{\sqrt[5]{x}}$

Scientific Notation

One very convenient method of representing numbers that are very large or very small in absolute value is to express them as a constant between 1 and 10 (but less than 10) multiplied by an exponent of 10. For example, 80,000 can be written 8×10^4; 5,000,000 can be written 5×10^6. Similarly, the fraction 0.002 can be written 2×10^{-3}; the fraction 0.00000000096 can be written 9.6×10^{-10}. This representation of numbers is referred to as *scientific notation*; the significant digits in the number are conventionally expressed with one digit to the left of the decimal point.

LOGARITHMS

A *logarithm* is an exponent. By definition, a logarithm indicates the power to which a base must be raised to equal a given number. In the notation used previously, if $y = b^n$, $b > 0$ and $b \neq 1$, then n is the logarithm of y to the base b, which is written $n = \log_b y$.

EXAMPLE

(a) $2^4 = 16 \Leftrightarrow 4 = \log_2 16$
(b) $10^3 = 1000 \Leftrightarrow 3 = \log_{10} 1000$
(c) $10^{-3} = 0.001 \Leftrightarrow -3 = \log_{10} 0.001$
(d) $\log_{1/3} 9 = -2 \Leftrightarrow \left(\frac{1}{3}\right)^{-2} = 9$
(e) $\log_4 64 = 3 \Leftrightarrow 4^3 = 64$
(f) $\log_5 1 = 0 \Leftrightarrow 5^0 = 1$

Properties of Logarithms

For any positive real numbers x and y, any real number r, and any positive real number $b \neq 1$,

(1) $\log_b xy = \log_b x + \log_b y$

(2) $\log_b \left(\dfrac{x}{y}\right) = \log_b x - \log_b y$

(3) $\log_b x^r = r \log_b x$

(4) $\log_a x = (\log_a b)(\log_b x)$

(5) $\log_b b = 1$

(6) $\log_b 1 = 0$

As discussed in Section 1.8, the most commonly used bases for logarithms are 10 (common logarithms) and $e \approx 2.718$ (natural or Naperian logarithms).

EXAMPLE

(a) $\log_3 (9 \cdot 27) = \log_3 9 + \log_3 27 = 2 + 3 = 5$ Property 1

(b) $\log_{10} \left(\dfrac{1000}{100}\right) = \log_{10} 1000 - \log_{10} 100 = 3 - 2 = 1$ Property 2

(c) $\log_5 25^2 = 2 \log_5 25 = (2)(2) = 4$ Property 3

(d) $\log_6 36^{-3} = -3 \log_6 36 = (-3)(2) = -6$ Property 3

(e) Changing from base 9 to base 3, $\log_3 729 = (\log_3 9) \times (\log_9 729) = 2 \cdot 3 = 6$ (Note that $3^6 = 729$, so $\log_3 729 = 6$.)

(f) Changing from base 2 to base 4, $\log_4 16 = (\log_4 2)(\log_2 16) = \frac{1}{2} \cdot 4 = 2$ (Note that $4^2 = 16$, so $\log_4 16 = 2$.)

(g) $\log_7 7 = 1$ Property 5

(h) $\log_8 1 = 0$ Property 6

PROBLEMS

Write the following in logarithmic form.

1. $3^{-2} = \frac{1}{9}$
2. $10^4 = 10000$
3. $2^5 = 32$
4. $6^0 = 1$
5. $(\frac{1}{4})^2 = \frac{1}{16}$

Write the following in exponential form.

6. $\log_2 \frac{1}{16} = -4$
7. $\log_{1/5} 25 = -2$
8. $\log_9 9 = 1$
9. $\log_6 1 = 0$
10. $\log_4 64 = 3$

Simplify the following expressions.

11. $\log_4 (4 \cdot 16)$
12. $\log_5 (\frac{25}{125})$
13. $\log_3 27^{10}$
14. $\log_8 8$
15. $\log_7 (\frac{343}{49})$
16. $\log_{1/5} 25$
17. $\log_3 1$
18. $\log_8 64^{-3}$
19. $\log_{10} (\frac{10}{1000})$
20. $\log_2 (4 \cdot 32)$
21. $\log_{1/8} (\frac{1}{8})$
22. $\log_{1/4} (\frac{1}{256})$
23. $\log_9 1$
24. $\log_3 (\frac{1}{27})$

Change bases as indicated.

25. $\log_{25} 625$ in terms of $\log_5 625$
26. $\log_{49} 343$ in terms of $\log_7 343$
27. $\log_{16} 2$ in terms of $\log_4 2$
28. $\log_{64} 4$ in terms of $\log_2 4$
29. $\log_9 81$ in terms of $\log_3 81$
30. $\log_{216} 36$ in terms of $\log_6 36$
31. $\log_9 243$ in terms of $\log_3 243$
32. $\log_8 16$ in terms of $\log_2 16$

Solutions of Problems

1. $3^{-2} = \frac{1}{9} \Leftrightarrow \log_3 \frac{1}{9} = -2$
2. $10^4 = 10000 \Leftrightarrow \log_{10} 10000 = 4$
3. $2^5 = 32 \Leftrightarrow \log_2 32 = 5$
4. $6^0 = 1 \Leftrightarrow \log_6 1 = 0$
5. $(\frac{1}{4})^2 = \frac{1}{16} \Leftrightarrow \log_{1/4} \frac{1}{16} = 2$ or $\log_4 (\frac{1}{16}) = -2$
6. $\log_2 (\frac{1}{16}) = -4 \Leftrightarrow 2^{-4} = \frac{1}{16}$
7. $\log_{1/5} 25 = -2 \Leftrightarrow (\frac{1}{5})^{-2} = 25$
8. $\log_9 9 = 1 \Leftrightarrow 9^1 = 9$
9. $\log_6 1 = 0 \Leftrightarrow 6^0 = 1$
10. $\log_4 64 = 3 \Leftrightarrow 4^3 = 64$
11. $\log_4 (4 \cdot 16) = \log_4 4 + \log_4 16 = 1 + 2 = 3$
12. $\log_5 (\frac{25}{125}) = \log_5 25 - \log_5 125 = 2 - 3 = -1$

13. $\log_3 27^{10} = 10 \log_3 27 = 10 \cdot 3 = 30$
14. $\log_8 8 = 1$
15. $\log_7 \left(\frac{343}{49}\right) = \log_7 343 - \log_7 49 = 3 - 2 = 1$
16. $\log_{1/5} 25 = -2$
17. $\log_3 1 = 0$
18. $\log_8 64^{-3} = -3 \log_8 64 = -3 \cdot 2 = -6$
19. $\log_{10} \left(\frac{10}{1000}\right) = \log_{10} 10 - \log_{10} 1000 = 1 - 3 = -2$
20. $\log_2 (4 \cdot 32) = \log_2 4 + \log_2 32 = 2 + 5 = 7$
21. $\log_{1/8} \left(\frac{1}{8}\right) = 1$
22. $\log_{1/4} \left(\frac{1}{256}\right) = 4$
23. $\log_9 1 = 0$
24. $\log_3 \left(\frac{1}{27}\right) = -3$
25. $\log_{25} 625 = (\log_{25} 5)(\log_5 625) = \frac{1}{2} \cdot 4 = 2$ (Note that $25^2 = 625$.)
26. $\log_{49} 343 = (\log_{49} 7)(\log_7 343) = \frac{1}{2} \cdot 3 = \frac{3}{2}$ (Note that $49^{3/2} = 343$.)
27. $\log_{16} 2 = (\log_{16} 4)(\log_4 2) = \frac{1}{2} \cdot \frac{1}{2} = \frac{1}{4}$ (Note that $16^{1/4} = 2$.)
28. $\log_{64} 4 = (\log_{64} 2)(\log_2 4) = \frac{1}{6} \cdot 2 = \frac{1}{3}$ (Note that $64^{1/3} = 4$.)
29. $\log_9 81 = (\log_9 3)(\log_3 81) = \frac{1}{2} \cdot 4 = 2$ (Note that $9^2 = 81$.)
30. $\log_{216} 36 = (\log_{216} 6)(\log_6 36) = \frac{1}{3} \cdot 2 = \frac{2}{3}$ (Note that $216^{2/3} = 36$.)
31. $\log_9 243 = (\log_9 3)(\log_3 243) = \frac{1}{2} \cdot 5 = \frac{5}{2}$ (Note that $9^{5/2} = 243$.)
32. $\log_8 16 = (\log_8 2)(\log_2 16) = \frac{1}{3} \cdot 4 = \frac{4}{3}$ (Note that $8^{4/3} = 16$.)

Appendix B
Trigonometry Review

DEGREE AND RADIAN MEASURE

An angle may be measured in either degrees or radians. Although measurement of angles in degrees is probably more familiar, measurement in radians is more convenient for stating formulas and solving problems in calculus.

A positive angle is measured in the counterclockwise direction. The measurement of an angle in degrees is based on the arbitrary assumption that a circle contains 360°; thus a straight line contains 180° and a right angle contains 90°.

The radian or circular measure of an angle whose vertex is at the center of a circle is defined as the ratio of the length of the intercepted arc to the radius of the circle (see Figure B.1). The unit angle, referred to as a *radian*, is the angle which, when placed with its vertex at the center of a circle, intercepts an arc equal in length to the radius of the circle (see Figure B.2). Since the circumference of a circle is $2\pi r$, there are 2π radians in a circle, π radians in a straight angle, and $\pi/2$ radians in a right angle.

The relationship between radian measure and degree measure may be expressed by

$$\pi \text{ radians} = 180°$$

Thus

$$1 \text{ radian} = \left(\frac{180}{\pi}\right)° \approx 57.296°$$

$$1° = \left(\frac{\pi}{180}\right) \text{ radians} \approx 0.01745 \text{ radians}$$

Figure B.1

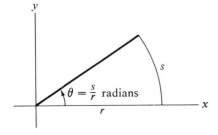

Figure B.2

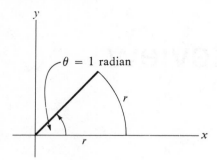

EXAMPLE

$$200° = \frac{200\pi}{180} \text{ radians} = \frac{10\pi}{9} \text{ radians}$$

$$-35° = -\frac{35\pi}{180} \text{ radians} = -\frac{7\pi}{36} \text{ radians}$$

$$300° = \frac{300\pi}{180} \text{ radians} = \frac{5\pi}{3} \text{ radians}$$

PROBLEMS

Find the number of radians in each of the following angles given in degrees.

1. $\theta = -240°$
2. $\theta = 70°$
3. $\theta = 120°$
4. $\theta = -40°$
5. $\theta = -100°$
6. $\theta = 315°$

Solutions of Problems

1. $s = -\dfrac{4\pi}{3}$

2. $s = \dfrac{7\pi}{18}$

3. $s = \dfrac{2\pi}{3}$

4. $s = -\dfrac{2\pi}{9}$

5. $s = -\dfrac{5\pi}{9}$

6. $s = \dfrac{7\pi}{4}$

TRIGONOMETRIC FUNCTIONS

The trigonometric functions of an angle θ are the sine of θ (sin θ), the cosine of θ (cos θ), the tangent of θ (tan θ), the cosecant of θ (csc θ), the secant of θ (sec θ), and the cotangent of θ (cot θ). When the angle θ is at the center of a circle of radius r and is measured counterclockwise, as in Figure B.3, the trigonometric functions of θ are defined by the equations

$$\sin \theta = \frac{a}{r} \qquad \cos \theta = \frac{b}{r} \qquad \tan \theta = \frac{a}{b}$$

$$\csc \theta = \frac{r}{a} \qquad \sec \theta = \frac{r}{b} \qquad \cot \theta = \frac{b}{a}$$

Note that

$$\csc \theta = \frac{1}{\sin \theta} \qquad \sec \theta = \frac{1}{\cos \theta} \qquad \cot \theta = \frac{1}{\tan \theta}$$

$$\tan \theta = \frac{\sin \theta}{\cos \theta} \qquad \cot \theta = \frac{\cos \theta}{\sin \theta}$$

The signs of the trigonometric functions in the four quadrants can be summarized as follows:

+	+
−	−

sin, csc

−	+
−	+

cos, sec

−	+
+	−

tan, cot

The values of the trigonometric functions can be obtained geometrically for some commonly used angles. For example, if $\theta = 45° = \pi/4$ radians, $b = a$ and, using the

Figure B.3

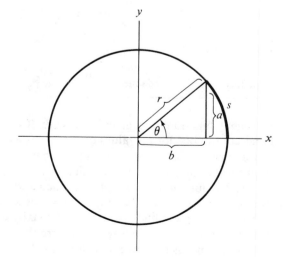

Pythagorean theorem, $r^2 = a^2 + b^2$ and $r = a\sqrt{2}$, as shown below.

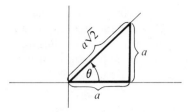

Thus

$$\sin \theta = \frac{a}{a\sqrt{2}} = \frac{\sqrt{2}}{2} \qquad \cos \theta = \frac{a}{a\sqrt{2}} = \frac{\sqrt{2}}{2} \qquad \tan \theta = \frac{a}{a} = 1$$

Similarly, if $\theta = 90° = \pi/2$ radians, $r = a$ and $b = 0$, as shown below.

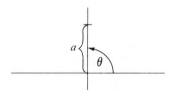

Thus

$$\sin \theta = \frac{a}{a} = 1 \qquad \cos \theta = \frac{0}{a} = 0 \qquad \tan \theta = \frac{a}{0} \quad \text{not defined}$$

Values of the sine, cosine and tangent are given for some commonly used angles in the table below. These values can all be obtained geometrically.

Degrees	0	30	45	60	90	180	270	360
Radians	0	$\frac{\pi}{6}$	$\frac{\pi}{4}$	$\frac{\pi}{3}$	$\frac{\pi}{2}$	π	$\frac{3\pi}{2}$	2π
Sine	0	$\frac{1}{2}$	$\frac{\sqrt{2}}{2}$	$\frac{\sqrt{3}}{2}$	1	0	-1	0
Cosine	1	$\frac{\sqrt{3}}{2}$	$\frac{\sqrt{2}}{2}$	$\frac{1}{2}$	0	-1	0	1
Tangent	0	$\frac{\sqrt{3}}{3}$	1	$\sqrt{3}$	not defined	0	not defined	0

The graphs of the sine, cosine, and tangent functions are given in Figure B.4. Note that the function $\sin x$ is defined and continuous for all values of x. Sin x is a periodic function with the period 2π, since $\sin (x + 2\pi) = \sin x$ for any x; that is, when the value of x is increased by 2π, the value of y is unchanged and 2π is the smallest positive number with this property. The function $\cos x$ is also defined and continuous for all values of x and is periodic with period 2π. The graph of $y = \cos x$ can be obtained from the graph of $y = \sin x$ by taking the line $x = \pi/2$ as the y-axis; that is, the graph of $y = \cos x$ is the same as the graph of $y = \sin x$ when that graph is shifted to the right by $\pi/2$ radians. The function $\tan x$ is discontinuous for all values

Figure B.4

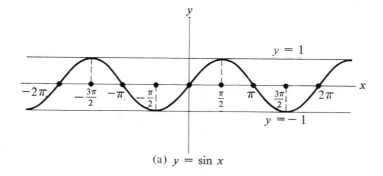

(a) $y = \sin x$

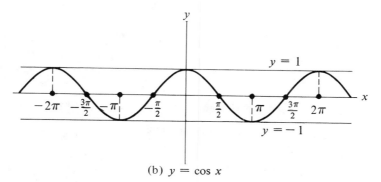

(b) $y = \cos x$

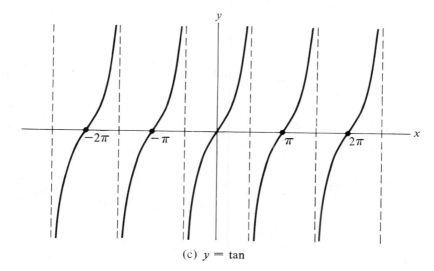

(c) $y = \tan$

of x such that $x = (n + \frac{1}{2})\pi$, where n is any positive or negative integer; $\tan x$ is periodic with period π.

The symmetry and periodicity of the sine, cosine, and tangent functions make it possible to obtain a trigonometric function of any angle, $0 \le \theta \le 2\pi$, from the trigonometric function of an angle θ such that $0 \le \theta \le \pi/2$. Thus trigonometric functions are tabled only for angles between 0 and $\pi/2$. The formulas for reducing angles are given below. Note, for example, that $\sin(-\theta) = -\sin\theta$, $\cos(-\theta) = \cos\theta$, $\tan(-\theta) = -\tan\theta$, and so forth.

Angle	sin	cos	tan	cot	sec	csc
$-\theta$	$-\sin\theta$	$\cos\theta$	$-\tan\theta$	$-\cot\theta$	$\sec\theta$	$-\csc\theta$
$\dfrac{\pi}{2}-\theta$	$\cos\theta$	$\sin\theta$	$\cot\theta$	$\tan\theta$	$\csc\theta$	$\sec\theta$
$\dfrac{\pi}{2}+\theta$	$\cos\theta$	$-\sin\theta$	$-\cot\theta$	$-\tan\theta$	$-\csc\theta$	$\sec\theta$
$\pi-\theta$	$\sin\theta$	$-\cos\theta$	$-\tan\theta$	$-\cot\theta$	$-\sec\theta$	$\csc\theta$
$\pi+\theta$	$-\sin\theta$	$-\cos\theta$	$\tan\theta$	$\cot\theta$	$-\sec\theta$	$-\csc\theta$
$\dfrac{3\pi}{2}-\theta$	$-\cos\theta$	$-\sin\theta$	$\cot\theta$	$\tan\theta$	$-\csc\theta$	$-\sec\theta$
$\dfrac{3\pi}{2}+\theta$	$-\cos\theta$	$\sin\theta$	$-\cot\theta$	$-\tan\theta$	$\csc\theta$	$-\sec\theta$
$2\pi-\theta$	$-\sin\theta$	$\cos\theta$	$-\tan\theta$	$-\cot\theta$	$\sec\theta$	$-\csc\theta$

EXAMPLE

Find the value of each of the following trigonometric functions: $\cos 3\pi/4$, $\tan 5\pi/6$, $\sin 5\pi/3$, $\sec 7\pi/6$, $\csc 2\pi/3$, $\cot(-\pi/4)$.

$$\cos\frac{3\pi}{4} = \cos\left(\frac{\pi}{2}+\frac{\pi}{4}\right) = -\sin\frac{\pi}{4} = -\frac{\sqrt{2}}{2}$$

$$\tan\frac{5\pi}{6} = \tan\left(\pi-\frac{\pi}{6}\right) = -\tan\frac{\pi}{6} = -\frac{\sqrt{3}}{3}$$

$$\sin\frac{5\pi}{3} = \sin\left(2\pi-\frac{\pi}{3}\right) = -\sin\frac{\pi}{3} = -\frac{\sqrt{3}}{2}$$

$$\sec\frac{7\pi}{6} = \sec\left(\pi+\frac{\pi}{6}\right) = -\sec\frac{\pi}{6} = -\frac{1}{\cos\dfrac{\pi}{6}} = -\frac{2\sqrt{3}}{3}$$

$$\csc\frac{2\pi}{3} = \csc\left(\pi-\frac{\pi}{3}\right) = \csc\frac{\pi}{3} = \frac{1}{\sin\dfrac{\pi}{3}} = \frac{2\sqrt{3}}{3}$$

$$\cot\left(-\frac{\pi}{4}\right) = -\cot\frac{\pi}{4} = -\frac{1}{\tan\dfrac{\pi}{4}} = -1$$

PROBLEMS

Find the value of the following trigonometric functions.

1. $\sin\dfrac{7\pi}{6}$ 3. $\tan\dfrac{5\pi}{4}$

2. $\csc\dfrac{4\pi}{3}$ 4. $\cos\dfrac{5\pi}{3}$

Answers to Problems

1. $\sin \dfrac{7\pi}{6} = \sin\left(\pi + \dfrac{\pi}{6}\right) = -\sin\dfrac{\pi}{6} = -\dfrac{1}{2}$

2. $\csc \dfrac{4\pi}{3} = \csc\left(\pi + \dfrac{\pi}{3}\right) = -\csc\dfrac{\pi}{3} = -\dfrac{2\sqrt{3}}{3}$

3. $\tan \dfrac{5\pi}{4} = \tan\left(\pi + \dfrac{\pi}{4}\right) = \tan\dfrac{\pi}{4} = 1$

4. $\cos \dfrac{5\pi}{3} = \cos\left(2\pi - \dfrac{\pi}{3}\right) = \cos\dfrac{\pi}{3} = \dfrac{1}{2}$

TRIGONOMETRIC IDENTITIES

There are a number of trigonometric identities which are useful in simplifying results involving trigonometric functions. Some of the more commonly used identities are given below without proof; additional identities and proofs can be found in any trigonometry book.

$$\sin^2 \theta + \cos^2 \theta = 1 \qquad \sec^2 \theta - \tan^2 \theta = 1 \qquad \csc^2 \theta - \cot^2 \theta = 1$$

$$\sin (x + y) = \sin x \cos y + \cos x \sin y$$

$$\sin (x - y) = \sin x \cos y - \cos x \sin y$$

$$\cos (x + y) = \cos x \cos y - \sin x \sin y$$

$$\cos (x - y) = \cos x \cos y + \sin x \sin y$$

$$\tan (x + y) = \frac{\tan x + \tan y}{1 - \tan x \tan y} \qquad \tan (x - y) = \frac{\tan x - \tan y}{1 + \tan x \tan y}$$

$$\sin 2x = 2 \sin x \cos x \qquad \cos 2x = \cos^2 x - \sin^2 x \qquad \tan 2x = \frac{2 \tan x}{1 - \tan^2 x}$$

$$\sin \frac{x}{2} = \pm\sqrt{\frac{1 - \cos x}{2}} \qquad \cos \frac{x}{2} = \pm\sqrt{\frac{1 + \cos x}{2}}$$

$$\tan \frac{x}{2} = \pm\sqrt{\frac{1 - \cos x}{1 + \cos x}} = \frac{\sin x}{1 + \cos x} = \frac{1 - \cos x}{\sin x}$$

$$\sin^2 x = \tfrac{1}{2} - \tfrac{1}{2} \cos 2x \qquad \cos^2 x = \tfrac{1}{2} + \tfrac{1}{2} \cos 2x$$

POLAR COORDINATES

It is frequently more convenient to describe a point by its polar coordinates rather than by its rectangular coordinates. If a point is described by the rectangular coordinates (x, y), then it can also be described by the *polar coordinates* (r, θ) as follows. Consider a line drawn between the point and a given origin; the angle θ which this line makes with the horizontal axis and the distance r between the point and the origin determine the point, as shown in Figure B.5.

Figure B.5

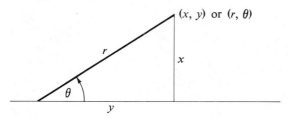

Note that the polar coordinates of a point are not unique. For example, the polar coordinates (r, θ), $(r, \theta + 2\pi)$, and $(r, \theta - 2\pi)$ all represent the same point. In practice, the polar coordinates of a point are usually written using the angle between 0 and 2π.

The rectangular coordinates (x, y) and the polar coordinates (r, θ) of a point are related as follows:

$$x = r \cos \theta \qquad\qquad y = r \sin \theta \qquad\qquad r = \sqrt{x^2 + y^2}$$

$$\sin \theta = \frac{y}{\sqrt{x^2 + y^2}} \qquad \cos \theta = \frac{x}{\sqrt{x^2 + y^2}} \qquad \tan \theta = \frac{y}{x}$$

These relations are used to change from one system of coordinates to the other.

EXAMPLE

Find polar coordinates for the following points given in rectangular coordinates,

(a) $(0, \sqrt{2})$
(b) $(1, 1)$

(a) $(x, y) = (0, \sqrt{2})$

$$r = \sqrt{x^2 + y^2} = \sqrt{0 + 2} = \sqrt{2}$$

$$\cos \theta = 0 \qquad \text{and} \qquad \sin \theta = 1$$

so

$$\theta = \frac{\pi}{2}$$

Polar coordinates $(r, \theta) = \left(\sqrt{2}, \dfrac{\pi}{2}\right)$.

(b) $(x, y) = (1, 1)$

$$r = \sqrt{x^2 + y^2} = \sqrt{1 + 1} = \sqrt{2}$$

$$\cos \theta = \frac{1}{\sqrt{2}} = \frac{\sqrt{2}}{2} \qquad \text{and} \qquad \sin \theta = \frac{1}{\sqrt{2}} = \frac{\sqrt{2}}{2}$$

so

$$\theta = \frac{\pi}{4}$$

Polar coordinates $(r, \theta) = \left(\sqrt{2}, \dfrac{\pi}{4}\right)$.

EXAMPLE

Find rectangular coordinates for the following points given in polar coordinates.

(a) $\left(3, \dfrac{\pi}{2}\right)$

(b) $\left(\sqrt{2}, \dfrac{\pi}{6}\right)$

(a) $(r, \theta) = \left(3, \dfrac{\pi}{2}\right)$

$\quad r \cos \theta = (3)(0) = 0$

$\quad r \sin \theta = (3)(1) = 3$

$\quad (x, y) = (0, 3)$

(b) $(r, \theta) = \left(\sqrt{2}, \dfrac{\pi}{6}\right)$

$\quad r \cos \theta = (\sqrt{2})\left(\dfrac{\sqrt{3}}{2}\right) = \dfrac{\sqrt{6}}{2}$

$\quad r \sin \theta = (\sqrt{2})\left(\dfrac{1}{2}\right) = \dfrac{\sqrt{2}}{2}$

$\quad (x, y) = \left(\dfrac{\sqrt{6}}{2}, \dfrac{\sqrt{2}}{2}\right)$

EXAMPLE

Find the equation in rectangular coordinates of the curve whose equation in polar coordinates is $r = 4/(1 + 2 \cos \theta)$.

$$\sqrt{x^2 + y^2} = \dfrac{4}{1 + \dfrac{2x}{\sqrt{x^2 + y^2}}}$$

$$\sqrt{x^2 + y^2} + 2x = 4$$

$$\sqrt{x^2 + y^2} = 4 - 2x$$

$$x^2 + y^2 = 16 - 16x + 4x^2$$

$$3x^2 - y^2 - 16x + 16 = 0 \qquad\qquad \text{(hyperbola)}$$

EXAMPLE

Find the equation in polar coordinates of the curve whose equation in rectangular coordinates is $Ax + By + C = 0$.

$$Ar \cos \theta + Br \sin \theta + C = 0$$

$$r(A \cos \theta + B \sin \theta) + C = 0$$

PROBLEMS

1. Obtain polar coordinates for the following points given in rectangular coordinates.
   a. $(1, \sqrt{3})$ c. $(3, 3\sqrt{3})$
   b. $(-1, -1)$ d. $(-1, 0)$

2. Obtain rectangular coordinates for the following points given in polar coordinates.

   a. $\left(4, \dfrac{\pi}{3}\right)$ c. $\left(3, \dfrac{\pi}{6}\right)$

   b. $(-2, \pi)$ d. $\left(-1, \dfrac{\pi}{2}\right)$

   Obtain the equation in rectangular coordinates that corresponds to each of the following equations given in polar coordinates.

   3. $r = 5$ 10. $r = a \sec \theta$

   4. $r = \sin \theta + \cos \theta$ 11. $r^2 = a^2 \cot \theta$

   5. $r = \dfrac{2}{2 - \cos \theta}$ 12. $r = \tan \theta \sec \theta$

                                                 13. $r^3 = a^3 \csc \theta$

   6. $r = 1 + \cos \theta$ 14. $r = a \tan^2 \theta$

   7. $r = a \cos \theta$ 15. $r^2 = \theta$

   8. $r = a \sin \theta$

   9. $r = \theta$ 16. $\theta = \dfrac{\pi}{2}$

   Obtain the equation in polar coordinates that corresponds to each of the following equations given in rectangular coordinates.

   17. $y^2 = 4ax$ 22. $(x^2 + y^2)^2 = a^2(x^2 - y^2)$
   18. $x^2 + y^2 = a^2$ 23. $2xy = a^2$
   19. $x^2 + y^2 = x + y$ 24. $y = x^2$
   20. $y = x$ 25. $xy^2 = a$
   21. $y^3 = ax^2$ 26. $x + y = a$

Solutions of Problems

1. (a) $r = 2$, $\cos \theta = \dfrac{1}{2}$, $\sin \theta = \dfrac{\sqrt{3}}{2}$, $\theta = \dfrac{\pi}{6}$ $\left(2, \dfrac{\pi}{6}\right)$

   (b) $r = \sqrt{2}$, $\cos = \dfrac{-\sqrt{2}}{2}$, $\theta = \dfrac{5}{4}\pi$ $\left(\sqrt{2}, \dfrac{5}{4}\pi\right)$

   (c) $r = 6$, $\cos \theta = \dfrac{1}{2}$, $\sin \theta = \dfrac{\sqrt{3}}{2}$, $\theta = \dfrac{\pi}{3}$ $\left(6, \dfrac{\pi}{3}\right)$

   (d) $r = 1$, $\cos \theta = -1$, $\sin \theta = 0$, $\theta = \pi$ $(1, \pi)$

2. (a) $x = 4\left(\dfrac{1}{2}\right) = 2$, $y = 4\left(\dfrac{\sqrt{3}}{2}\right) = 2\sqrt{3}$ $(2, 2\sqrt{3})$

   (b) $x = -2(-1) = 2$, $y = -2(0) = 0$ $(2, 0)$

   (c) $x = 3\left(\dfrac{\sqrt{3}}{2}\right) = \dfrac{3\sqrt{3}}{2}$, $y = 3\left(\dfrac{1}{2}\right) = \dfrac{3}{2}$ $\left(\dfrac{3\sqrt{3}}{2}, \dfrac{3}{2}\right)$

   (d) $x = (-1)(0) = 0$, $y = (-1)(1) = -1$ $(0, -1)$

3. $r^2 = 25$
   $x^2 + y^2 = 25$

4. $r^2 = r \sin \theta + r \cos \theta$
   $x^2 + y^2 - x - y = 0$

5. $2r - r \cos \theta = 2$
   $3x^2 + 4y^2 - 4x - 4 = 0$

6. $r = 1 + \cos \theta$
   $x^4 + y^4 - 2x^3 + 2x^2 y^2 - 2xy^2 - y^2 = 0$

7. $r = a \cos \theta$
   $x^2 + y^2 - ax = 0$

8. $r = a \sin \theta$
   $x^2 + y^2 - ay = 0$

9. $\tan r = \tan \theta$
   $y = x \tan \left(\sqrt{x^2 + y^2} \right)$

10. $r = a \sec \theta$
    $x = a$

11. $r^2 = a^2 \cot \theta$
    $y^3 + x^2 y - a^2 x = 0$

12. $r = \tan \theta \sec \theta$
    $y = x^2$

13. $r^3 = a^3 \csc \theta$
    $x^2 y + y^3 = a^3$

14. $r = a \tan^2 \theta$
    $x^2 \sqrt{x^2 + y^2} - ay^2 = 0$

15. $\tan r^2 = \tan \theta$
    $y = x \tan (x^2 + y^2)$

16. $\sin \theta = \sin \dfrac{\pi}{2}$
    $x = 0$

17. $r^2 \sin^2 \theta = 4a(r \cos \theta)$
    $r = 4a \cot \theta \csc \theta$

18. $r^2 = a^2$
    $r = \pm a$

19. $r^2 = r \cos \theta + r \sin \theta$
    $r = \cos \theta + \sin \theta$

20. $r \sin \theta = r \cos \theta$
    $\theta = \dfrac{\pi}{4}$

21. $r^3 \sin^3 \theta = ar^2 \cos^2 \theta$
    $r = a \cot^2 \theta \csc \theta$

22. $r^4 = a^2 (r^2 \cos^2 \theta - r^2 \sin^2 \theta)$
    $r^2 = a^2 (\cos^2 \theta - \sin^2 \theta)$

23. $2r^2 \cos \theta \sin \theta = a^2$
    $r^2 = \frac{1}{2} a^2 \sec \theta \csc \theta$

24. $r \sin \theta = r^2 \cos^2 \theta$
    $r = \tan \theta \sec \theta$

25. $r^3 \cos \theta \sin^2 \theta = a$
    $r^3 = a \sec \theta \csc^2 \theta$

26. $r(\cos \theta + \sin \theta) = a$
    $r = \dfrac{a}{\cos \theta + \sin \theta}$

Note that many economic phenomena can be described in part by sine or cosine functions. In the study of business cycles, seasonal or other cyclic variations are described by sine or cosine functions. In spectral analysis, the method most frequently used currently to analyze periodicity or cyclic variation in time series, the detrended series is analyzed in terms of cosine functions. Spectral analysis, and even less complicated types of analysis of cyclic variation, involve statistical problems beyond the scope of the present discussion. However, these analyses are an application of trigonometric curves, and the logic on which they are based is intuitively reasonable: A series is described in terms of components representing trends and cyclic variations.

Differential Calculus: Functions of One Variable

2.1 Introduction

Calculus is concerned with the mathematical analysis of change or movement. Because everything in the world changes, calculus has applications in virtually all areas of scientific inquiry. It is nearly impossible to exaggerate the importance of calculus, particularly differential calculus, as a basis for mathematical analysis.

As a distinctly new mathematical method, calculus was developed in the seventeenth century by Sir Isaac Newton and Gottfried Leibnitz, working independently. For Newton, calculus originated in attempts to solve certain problems connected with his work in physics and astronomy: finding the velocity of a moving body, the work done by force, the center of mass of a body. For Leibnitz, calculus originated in attempts to solve certain problems in geometry: finding the tangent to a curve, the length of a portion of a curve, the area bounded by one or more curves, the volume of a solid.

The basic operations of calculus are differentiation and integration; these operations are the inverses of each other, as are addition and subtraction, and multiplication and division. Differentiation is concerned essentially with determining the rate of change of a given function. Integration is concerned essentially with the inverse problem of finding a function when its rate of change is given.

The analogy of a moving-picture film is frequently used in discussing the processes of differentiation and integration. A moving-picture film is a series of (static) pictures, each at least slightly different from the others; each frame depicts the subjects in given positions at a particular instant of time. When the film is run through a projector at proper speed, the pictures are summed up and the illusion of motion is created. Similarly, differentiation essentially breaks up a function into many infinitesimally small (static) pieces and thus analyzes it at a particular point of time or for a particular value of the independent variable; integration, on the other hand, sums up the infinitesimally small pieces to obtain the function.

When relations among variables are stated in equations, calculus can be used to analyze these relations. Calculus has been used by physicists, astronomers, chemists, and engineers almost since its development; more recently, calculus has also been used by biologists, anthropologists, ecologists, sociologists, psychologists, and economists.

Since analysis in business and economics is frequently concerned with change, calculus is an extremely valuable tool for solving problems in these areas. Marginal analysis is perhaps the most direct application of calculus in business and economics; marginal rate of change or variation on the margin is expressed analytically as the first derivative of the relevant function. Differential calculus is also the method by which maxima or minima of functions are obtained. Thus problems of maximizing profit or minimizing cost under various assumptions can be solved using calculus. Mathematical programming, which is concerned with maximizing or minimizing a function subject to constraints, is applied increasingly in business and economics; the methods used in mathematical programming are based on differential calculus.

The concept of rate of change of a function, which is the basis of differential calculus, is discussed in the following paragraphs. The applications of this concept to marginal analysis and to various problems of maximization and minimization are discussed in some detail in following chapters.

The simplest type of functional relationship between two variables is represented by a straight line and corresponds to a *constant*, or *uniform*, rate of change in the dependent variable with respect to change in the independent variable. A *variable* rate of change in the dependent variable with respect to change in the independent variable is represented by a curvilinear (or nonlinear) function. The *average variable* rate of change is the average value over an interval of the variable rate of change.

For many analyses the most important concept is that of *instantaneous* rate of change, that is, the variable rate of change at a particular instant of time or for a particular value of the independent variable. Instantaneous rate of change is obtained by differentiation and is the first derivative of the function evaluated at the point of interest. The concept of instantaneous change is the basis of marginal analysis in economics; marginal analysis considers the effect on the dependent variable of small changes in the independent variable, that is, variation on the margin.

The mathematical definition and derivation of instantaneous or marginal rate of change are discussed in detail later; the concept can perhaps best be understood intuitively in terms of an example of physical movement. If a car is driven from city A to city B at a constant speed, then the rate of change in its distance from city A is constant with respect to change in time since leaving city A; the car is traveling at a constant or uniform rate. However, if the car occasionally slows down for curves, towns, traffic, and so forth, it travels at a variable rate. Suppose the trip from city A to city B takes 5 hours; the number of miles traveled each hour could be averaged to obtain the average variable rate of travel per hour. There is clearly another rate of travel of interest to both drivers and traffic policemen—the rate of travel at a particular instant of time. It is this instantaneous rate that is obtained by differential calculus.

Although rate of change is perhaps most readily understood in terms of physical motion, it can be generalized to any type of functional relationship. For example, total cost is a function of the quantity produced and usually changes at a variable rate as the quantity produced changes. The rate of change of total cost as quantity produced changes is the marginal cost and is the first derivative of total cost; marginal cost is a function of the quantity produced and can be evaluated for any quantity of interest.

The first derivative, that is, the rate of change of a function, can be used to determine its maximum and minimum points, if any. A function may increase (positive rate of change) until it reaches a maximum and then decrease (negative rate of change); similarly, a function may decrease until it reaches a minimum and then increase. This basic method for determining the maxima and minima of a function by differentiation has been developed and generalized for use in problems of varying complexity; as noted above, it is the basis of the methods of mathematical programming.

Calculus is concerned with infinitesimally small changes in the independent and dependent variables. Mathematically, such changes are defined using the concepts of limits and continuity. Thus the first sections of this chapter concern the mathematical concepts of limits and continuity, which provide the foundation for the theory of calculus.

The first derivative of a function is then defined and some of its applications in business and economics are considered. Rules for differentiating various types of functions, differentials and their use in approximating functions, higher-order derivatives, implicit differentiation, and differentiability and continuity are discussed. The use of first and second derivatives in graphing functions and a number of applications of derivatives in business and economics are considered. Indeterminate forms are defined and discussed. Convergence of sequences and series is considered and the use of Taylor's theorem for approximating functions is illustrated.

2.2 Limits

The concept of a limit seems to be one of the most troublesome in mathematics. Apparently, the idea of approaching a point or value arbitrarily closely and still never reaching it is not intuitively appealing. Actually, limit-type concepts are used frequently in nonmathematical thinking and conversation. For example, the theoretical maximum production of a machine is a limit, that is, the ideal (or limiting) performance which is never attained in practice but which can be approached arbitrarily closely. This same idea applies to the performance of any mechanical or electronic device for which engineers can calculate an ideal (or limiting) performance; it applies also, for example, to profits under ideal conditions, gas mileage under ideal conditions and operation, and so forth. Similarly, there are lower limits of cost, waste, spoilage, and so forth.

The mathematical concept of a limit is fundamental in understanding differential calculus and is discussed in some detail below. Properties of limits are also considered; these properties are used in later sections concerning series and indeterminate forms.

DEFINITION OF A LIMIT

Consider a function $f(x)$ and let the independent variable x assume values near a given constant a; then the function $f(x)$ assumes a corresponding set of values. Suppose that when x is close to a, the corresponding values of $f(x)$ are close to some constant A. Moreover, suppose that the values of $f(x)$ can be made to differ arbitrarily little from A by taking values of x that are sufficiently close to a, but not equal to a and that this is true for all such values of x. Then $f(x)$ is said to approach the *limit A* as x approaches a. More concisely, the definitions of the limit of a variable and the limit of a function are as follows.

A variable x is said to approach a constant a as a limit when x varies in such a way that the absolute difference $|x - a|$ becomes and remains less than any preassigned positive number, however small this number is chosen. This is indicated by the notation

$$\lim x = a \qquad \text{or} \qquad x \to a$$

EXAMPLE

If x assumes the sequence of values

$$\frac{1}{2}, \frac{3}{4}, \frac{7}{8}, \frac{15}{16}, \ldots, \frac{2^n - 1}{2^n}, \ldots$$

then $x \to 1$. But if x assumes the sequence of values

$$\frac{1}{2}, -\frac{3}{4}, \frac{7}{8}, -\frac{15}{16}, \ldots, (-1)^{n-1}\frac{2^n - 1}{2^n}, \ldots$$

then x does not approach a limit, since the positive terms approach $+1$ and the negative terms approach -1.

If the function $f(x)$ approaches a constant A when x approaches a in whatever manner without assuming the value a, A is said to be the limit of $f(x)$ as x approaches a. This is indicated by the notation

$$\lim_{x \to a} f(x) = A \qquad \text{or} \qquad f(x) \to A \text{ as } x \to a$$

EXAMPLE

If $f(x) = 2x + 5$, $\lim_{x \to 0} f(x) = 5$; for example,

$f(1) = 7$	$f(-1) = 3$
$f(\frac{1}{2}) = 6$	$f(-\frac{1}{2}) = 4$
$f(\frac{1}{4}) = 5\frac{1}{2}$	$f(-\frac{1}{4}) = 4\frac{1}{2}$
$f(\frac{1}{100}) = 5\frac{1}{50}$	$f(-\frac{1}{100}) = 4\frac{49}{50}$
$f(\frac{1}{1000}) = 5\frac{1}{500}$	$f(-\frac{1}{1000}) = 4\frac{499}{500}$
etc.	etc.

The following two statements of the definition of the limit of a function are equivalent to the definition given above.

A function $f(x)$ is said to approach a limit A as x approaches a if the absolute difference between $f(x)$ and A is less than an arbitrarily small positive number for all values of x that are sufficiently close to a and for which $x \neq a$.

A function $f(x)$ approaches a limit A as x approaches a if, and only if, for each $\varepsilon > 0$ there exists a δ such that whenever $0 < |x - a| < \delta$, $|f(x) - A| < \varepsilon$.

In the above discussion of limits it is implied that both x and $f(x)$ approach finite constants (a and A, respectively) as limits. It is also possible, however, for either one or both of x and $f(x)$ to become arbitrarily large or arbitrarily small. These types of limiting behavior are defined as follows:

If the difference between a function $f(x)$ and a constant A is less in absolute value than an arbitrarily small positive number for all positive values of x that are sufficiently large, then $f(x)$ is said to approach A as a limit when x becomes positively infinite, that is, increases without limit. This is indicated by the notation

$$\lim_{x \to \infty} f(x) = A \qquad \text{or} \qquad f(x) \to A \text{ as } x \to \infty$$

NOTE: The notation $\lim_{x \to +\infty} f(x) = A$ or $f(x) \to A$ as $x \to +\infty$ is sometimes used. However, ∞ is understood to mean $+\infty$, as would be the case if it were a number, and the plus sign is usually omitted for convenience.

EXAMPLE

If $f(x) = 1 - (1/x)$, $\lim_{x \to \infty} f(x) = 1$; for example,

$$f(1) = 0$$
$$f(5) = \tfrac{4}{5}$$
$$f(20) = \tfrac{19}{20}$$
$$f(100) = \tfrac{99}{100}$$
$$f(1000) = \tfrac{999}{1000}$$
$$f(10,000) = \tfrac{9999}{10000}$$
$$\text{etc.}$$

Similarly, the limit of $f(x)$ may be defined when x becomes negatively infinite, that is, decreases without limit. This is indicated by the notation

$$\lim_{x \to -\infty} f(x) = A' \qquad \text{or} \qquad f(x) \to A' \text{ as } x \to -\infty$$

EXAMPLE

If $f(x) = 1 - (1/x)$, then

$$\lim_{x \to -\infty} f(x) = 1$$

If a function $f(x)$ is greater than an arbitrarily large positive number for all values of x that are sufficiently near a constant a and for which $x \neq a$, then $f(x)$ is said to become positively infinite (that is, increases without limit) as x approaches a. This is indicated by the notation

$$\lim_{x \to a} f(x) = \infty \qquad \text{or} \qquad f(x) \to \infty \text{ as } x \to a$$

Similarly, $f(x)$ becomes negatively infinite (that is, decreases without limit) when it assumes numerically large negative values as x approaches a. This is indicated by the notation

$$\lim_{x \to a} f(x) = -\infty \qquad \text{or} \qquad f(x) \to -\infty \text{ as } x \to a$$

EXAMPLE

If $f(x) = 1/(x - 2)^2$, then

$$\lim_{x \to 2} f(x) = \infty$$

If a function $f(x)$ is greater than an arbitrarily large positive number for all positive values of x that are sufficiently large, then $f(x)$ is said to become positively infinite (that is, increases without limit) as x becomes positively infinite (that is, increases without limit). This is indicated by the notation

$$\lim_{x \to \infty} f(x) = \infty \qquad \text{or} \qquad f(x) \to \infty \text{ as } x \to \infty$$

The cases indicated by the following notation are defined similarly:

$$\lim_{x \to \infty} f(x) = -\infty \qquad \text{or} \qquad f(x) \to -\infty \text{ as } x \to \infty$$

$$\lim_{x \to -\infty} f(x) = \infty \qquad \text{or} \qquad f(x) \to \infty \text{ as } x \to -\infty$$

$$\lim_{x \to -\infty} f(x) = -\infty \qquad \text{or} \qquad f(x) \to -\infty \text{ as } x \to -\infty$$

EXAMPLE

If $f(x) = x^4 - 4$, then

$$\lim_{x \to \infty} f(x) = \infty \qquad \text{and} \qquad \lim_{x \to -\infty} f(x) = \infty$$

EXAMPLE

If $f(x) = x^3 - 8$, then

$$\lim_{x \to \infty} f(x) = \infty \qquad \text{and} \qquad \lim_{x \to -\infty} f(x) = -\infty$$

In some cases a function may approach either of two different limits, depending on whether the variable approaches its limit through values larger or smaller than that limit; in such a case, the limit is not defined (does not exist) but the right-hand and left-hand limits exist.

The *right-hand limit* of a function is the value the function approaches when the variable approaches its limit through decreasing values (that is, from the right); this type of limiting behavior is indicated by the notation

$$\lim_{x \to a^+} f(x) = A^+ \qquad \text{or} \qquad f(x) \to A^+ \text{ as } x \to a^+$$

The *left-hand limit* of a function is the value the function approaches when the variable approaches its limit through increasing values (that is, from the left); this is indicated by the notation

$$\lim_{x \to a^-} f(x) = A^- \qquad \text{or} \qquad f(x) \to A^- \text{ as } x \to a^-$$

Thus the limit of a function exists if and only if its right-hand and left-hand limits exist and are identical; in that case

$$\lim_{x \to a^+} f(x) = \lim_{x \to a^-} f(x) = \lim_{x \to a} f(x)$$

EXAMPLE

If $f(t) = [t]$ = largest integer in t, then

$$\lim_{t \to 3^+} f(t) = 3 \quad \text{and} \quad \lim_{t \to 3^-} f(t) = 2$$

Thus $\lim_{t \to 3} f(x)$ is not defined.

It might seem that the limit of this function $f(t)$ as $t \to 3$ should be 3. However, when t is arbitrarily close to 3, some of the values of $[t]$ are 2 (when $t < 3$), others are 3 (when $t > 3$). Thus the values of t are not close to any one value A when t is arbitrarily close to 3 and $\lim_{t \to 3} [t]$ does not exist, although the right-hand and left-hand limits do exist. This is indicated in Figure 2.1 by the unbroken horizontal lines between successive integer values of t. That is, $f(t)$ approaches 2 as t approaches 3 from the left; $f(t)$ approaches 3 as t approaches 3 from the right. Clearly there is nothing unique about the integer 3; in fact, $f(t)$ does not have a limit (although it has right-hand and left-hand limits) as t approaches any integer value; $f(t)$ does, however, have the limit $[t]$ as t approaches any noninteger value.

Figure 2.1

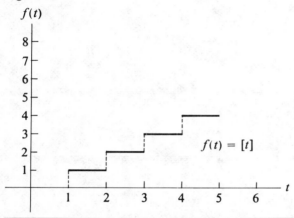

$$f(t) = [t]$$

EXAMPLE

If $f(t) = 1/t$, then

$$\lim_{t \to 0^+} f(t) = \infty \quad \text{and} \quad \lim_{t \to 0^-} f(t) = -\infty$$

(see Figure 2.2).

Figure 2.2

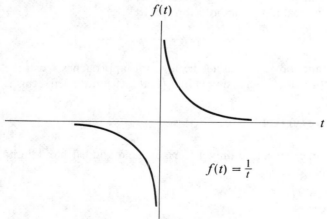

$$f(t) = \frac{1}{t}$$

Thus $\lim_{t \to 0} f(t)$ is not defined; as t approaches 0 from above, $f(t)$ becomes positively infinite; as t approaches 0 from below, $f(t)$ becomes negatively infinite.

PROPERTIES OF LIMITS

Limits can be shown to have several properties that are useful in evaluating the limit of a function.

If $\lim_{x \to a} f(x) = b$, $\lim_{x \to a} g(x) = c$, and K is a constant, the following properties or rules can be shown to follow from the definition of a limit.

1. $\lim_{x \to a} K = K$.

That is, the limit of a constant is equal to that constant. For purposes of interpreting the following properties of limits, a constant may be thought of as a special type of function—that is, a function that assumes only one value. Thus the following statements are valid (as special cases) if some or all of the functions are constants.

2. $\lim_{x \to a} [f(x) \pm g(x)] = \lim_{x \to a} f(x) \pm \lim_{x \to a} g(x) = b \pm c$.

That is, the limit of the sum (or difference) of two functions is equal to the sum (or difference) of their limits.

NOTE: This rule applies to the sum or difference of any finite number of functions, that is, if $\lim_{x \to a} f_i(x) = a_i$ for $i = 1, 2, \ldots, n$, then

$$\lim_{x \to a} \left(\sum_{i=1}^{n} f_i(x) \right) = \sum_{i=1}^{n} \lim_{x \to a} f_i(x) = \sum_{i=1}^{n} a_i$$

3. $\lim_{x \to a} [f(x) \cdot g(x)] = \left[\lim_{x \to a} f(x) \right] \left[\lim_{x \to a} g(x) \right] = bc$.

That is, the limit of the product of two functions is equal to the product of their limits.

NOTE: This rule applies to the product of any finite number of functions, that is, if $\lim_{x \to a} f_i(x) = a_i$ for $i = 1, 2, \ldots, n$, then

$$\lim_{x \to a} \left(\prod_{i=1}^{n} f_i(x) \right) = \prod_{i=1}^{n} \lim_{x \to a} f_i(x) = \prod_{i=1}^{n} a_i$$

4. $\lim_{x \to a} \dfrac{f(x)}{g(x)} = \dfrac{\lim_{x \to a} f(x)}{\lim_{x \to a} g(x)} = \dfrac{b}{c}$ if $c \neq 0$.

That is, the limit of the quotient of two functions is equal to the quotient of their limits, provided the limit of the divisor is not zero.

5. $\lim_{x \to a} [f(x)]^n = \left[\lim_{x \to a} f(x) \right]^n = b^n$.

That is, the limit of the nth power of any function is equal to the nth power of the limit of the function. (This follows from rule 3 applied to the product of n equal factors.)

6. $\lim_{x \to a} (\sqrt[n]{f(x)}) = \sqrt[n]{\lim_{x \to a} f(x)} = \sqrt[n]{b}$.

That is, the limit of the principal nth root of a positive function is equal to the principal nth root of the limit of that function. (This follows from rule 5.)

EXAMPLE

$$\lim_{x \to 2} (3x + 5) = \lim_{x \to 2} 3x + \lim_{x \to 2} 5 \qquad \text{(rule 2)}$$

$$= 6 + 5 \qquad \text{(rules 3, 1)}$$

$$= 11$$

EXAMPLE

$$\lim_{x \to -1} \left(\frac{x^2}{x^2 + a} \right) = \frac{\lim_{x \to -1} x^2}{\lim_{x \to -1} (x^2 + a)} \qquad \text{(rule 4)}$$

$$= \frac{\left(\lim_{x \to -1} x \right)^2}{\left(\lim_{x \to -1} x \right)^2 + \left(\lim_{x \to -1} a \right)} \qquad \text{(rules 5, 2)}$$

$$= \frac{1}{1 + a} \qquad \text{if } a \neq -1 \qquad \text{(rule 1)}$$

EXAMPLE

$$\lim_{x \to 5} (10 \sqrt[3]{x^2 + 2}) = \left(\lim_{x \to 5} 10 \right) \left[\lim_{x \to 5} (x^2 + 2) \right]^{1/3} \qquad \text{(rules 3, 6)}$$

$$= 10(27)^{1/3} \qquad \text{(rules 1, 2, 5)}$$

$$= 30$$

EXAMPLE

$$\lim_{x \to 0} \left(\frac{x^2 + a}{x^2 + b} \right) = \frac{\lim_{x \to 0} (x^2 + a)}{\lim_{x \to 0} (x^2 + b)} \cdot \qquad \text{(rule 4)}$$

$$= \frac{a}{b} \qquad \text{if } b \neq 0 \qquad \text{(rules 2, 1, 5)}$$

EXAMPLE

$$\lim_{x \to \infty} \left(\frac{a}{1 + \dfrac{1}{x}} \right) = \frac{\lim_{x \to \infty} a}{\lim_{x \to \infty} 1 + \dfrac{\lim_{x \to \infty} 1}{\lim_{x \to \infty} x}} \qquad \text{(rules 4, 2, 4)}$$

$$= \frac{a}{1 + 0} \qquad \text{(rule 1)}$$

$$= a$$

EXAMPLE

$$\lim_{x \to -\infty} \left(b - \frac{2}{3x + 10} \right) = \lim_{x \to -\infty} b - \frac{\displaystyle\lim_{x \to -\infty} 2}{\displaystyle\lim_{x \to -\infty} (3x + 10)} \qquad \text{(rules 2, 4)}$$

$$= b - 0$$
$$= b \qquad \text{(rules 1, 2, 3)}$$

In applying rule 4 concerning the limit of a quotient, it may happen that the quotient of the limits takes the form 0/0. This is one of the indeterminate forms discussed in some detail in a later section; however, it is frequently possible to obtain a determinate limit for the original quotient using a very simple procedure. This procedure consists of dividing both the numerator and denominator by an expression which in the limit is equal to zero, thereby obtaining an expression that has a limit.

EXAMPLE

If $f(x) = (x^2 - 4)/(x - 2)$, then $\lim_{x \to 2} f(x)$ is the indeterminate form 0/0. But if $x \neq 2$, both numerator and denominator can be divided by $x - 2$. Then $f(x) = (x^2 - 4)/(x - 2) = x + 2$ and $\lim_{x \to 2} f(x) = 4$.

Recall that in evaluating $\lim_{x \to 2} f(x)$, it is not the value of $f(x)$ at $x = 2$ but only the values of $f(x)$ for x close to 2 which are of interest. It is assumed that x becomes arbitrarily close to 2, but does not equal 2. For $x \neq 2$, $f(x) = x + 2$ and $\lim_{x \to 2} f(x) = \lim_{x \to 2} (x + 2) = 4$. Thus, even though $f(x)$ is undefined at $x = 2$, it has the limit 4 as $x \to 2$.

EXAMPLE

If $F(h) = [(2 + h)^2 - 4]/h$, then $\lim_{h \to 0} F(h)$ is the indeterminate form 0/0. However, for $h \neq 0$, $F(h) = (4 + 4h + h^2 - 4)/h = (4h + h^2)/h = 4 + h$ and thus $\lim_{h \to 0} F(h) = 4$.

A second type of indeterminate form, ∞/∞, can arise as a result of applying rule 4. This is another of the indeterminate forms discussed in later sections; in this case it is frequently possible to obtain a determinate limit for the original quotient if both the numerator and denominator are divided by the highest power of the variable which appears in the denominator.

EXAMPLE

If $f(x) = (2x^3 + x^2 - 3)/(x^3 + x + 2)$, then $\lim_{x \to \infty} f(x)$ is the indeterminate form ∞/∞. However, if both the numerator and denominator are divided by x^3, then

$$f(x) = \frac{2x^3 + x^2 - 3}{x^3 + x + 2} = \frac{2 + \dfrac{1}{x} - \dfrac{3}{x^3}}{1 + \dfrac{1}{x^2} + \dfrac{2}{x^3}}$$

and thus $\lim_{x \to \infty} f(x) = 2$, since $\dfrac{1}{x} \to 0$, $\dfrac{3}{x^3} \to 0$, $\dfrac{1}{x^2} \to 0$, and $\dfrac{2}{x^3} \to 0$ as $x \to \infty$.

EXAMPLE

If $f(x) = [x + (1/x)]/(2x - (1/x)]$, then $\lim_{x \to \infty} f(x)$ is the indeterminate form ∞/∞. However, if both the numerator and denominator are divided by x, then

$$f(x) = \frac{x + \dfrac{1}{x}}{2x - \dfrac{1}{x}} = \frac{1 + \dfrac{1}{x^2}}{2 - \dfrac{1}{x^2}}$$

and thus $\lim_{x \to \infty} f(x) = \frac{1}{2}$, since $1/x^2 \to 0$ as $x \to \infty$.

Several of the foregoing examples could also be solved using the rule for finding the limit of a rational function $f(x)$ as $x \to \infty$. When $f(x)$ is a rational function, that is, when

$$f(x) = \frac{P(x)}{Q(x)} = \frac{\sum_{i=0}^{m} a_i x^i}{\sum_{j=0}^{n} b_j x^j}$$

where $P(x)$ is a polynomial of degree m and $Q(x)$ is a polynomial of degree n, then

$$\lim_{x \to \infty} f(x) = \begin{cases} 0 & \text{if } m < n \\ \dfrac{a_m}{b_n} & \text{if } m = n \\ \infty & \text{if } m > n \end{cases}$$

For the case $m > n$, the limit is $+\infty$ if $a_m > 0$ and $-\infty$ if $a_m < 0$. If the limit is taken as $x \to -\infty$, then for the case $m > n$, the limit is $+\infty$ if $a_m > 0$ and m is even or if $a_m < 0$ and m is odd; the limit is $-\infty$ if $a_m > 0$ and m is odd or if $a_m < 0$ and m is even.

CAUTION: This rule applies only if $f(x)$ is a rational function and the limit is taken as $x \to \infty$.

EXAMPLE

$f(x) = \dfrac{2x^3 + x^2 - 3}{x^3 + x - 2}$ is a rational function; $a_m = 2$, $b_n = 1$, and $m = n$. Thus

$$\lim_{x \to \infty} f(x) = \frac{a_m}{b_n} = 2$$

as above.

EXAMPLE

$f(x) = \dfrac{x + 1/x}{2x - 1/x} = \dfrac{x^2 + 1}{2x^2 - 1}$ is a rational function; $a_m = 1$, $b_n = 2$, and $m = n$. Thus

$$\lim_{x \to \infty} f(x) = \frac{a_m}{b_n} = \frac{1}{2}$$

as above.

EXAMPLE

$f(x) = \dfrac{x^2 + 3x - 1}{2x^3 + 5x + 4}$ is a rational function; $a_m = 1$, $b_n = 2$, and $m < n$. Thus

$$\lim_{x \to \infty} f(x) = 0$$

Using the above procedure and dividing by x^3, $f(x) = \dfrac{1/x + 3/x^2 - 1/x^3}{2 + 5/x^2 + 4/x^3}$ and

$$\lim_{x \to \infty} f(x) = \dfrac{0 + 0 + 0}{2 + 0 + 0} = 0$$

EXAMPLE

$f(x) = \dfrac{1/x^2 - 3/x}{1/x^3 - 1/x^2} = \dfrac{x - 3x^2}{1 - x}$ is a rational function; $a_m = -3$, $b_n = -1$, and $m > n$; $a_m < 0$

and m is even. Thus

$$\lim_{x \to \infty} f(x) = -\infty$$

Using the above procedure and dividing by x, $f(x) = \dfrac{1 - 3x}{1/x - 1}$ and

$$\lim_{x \to \infty} f(x) = \dfrac{\infty}{-1} = -\infty$$

PROBLEMS

Evaluate the following limits.

1. $\lim_{t \to 2} (t^2 + 6t + 5)$

2. $\lim_{x \to 0} (x^2 + 6x + 3)$

3. $\lim_{y \to 5} \left(\dfrac{3y - 5}{y - 2} \right)$

4. $\lim_{y \to -2} (y - 3)^2$

5. $\lim_{x \to 2} (x^3 - 3x + 5)$

6. $\lim_{x \to 2} \left(\dfrac{x^2 \sqrt{x + 2}}{x^2 + 1} \right)$

7. $\lim_{x \to \infty} \left(\dfrac{2}{x^2 + 1} \right)$

8. $\lim_{x \to 0} \left(1 + \dfrac{1}{x^2} \right)$

9. $\lim_{x \to -1} \left(\dfrac{x^2 + 1}{x^2 + x + 1} \right)$

10. $\lim_{x \to \infty} \left(4 - \dfrac{2}{x + 1} \right)$

11. $\lim_{t \to 0} \left(\dfrac{3t - 5}{t + 2} \right)$

12. $\lim_{t \to \infty} \left(\dfrac{3t^2 - 5t + 4}{t^2 + 2} \right)$

13. $\lim_{h \to 0} a^{x+h}$

14. $\lim_{h \to 0} 2^{-h}$

15. $\lim_{x \to 2} x^{-4}$

16. $\lim_{x \to -2} x^4$

17. $\lim_{x \to -\infty} 2^x$

18. $\lim_{x \to \infty} 2^{-x}$

19. $\lim_{t \to \infty} e^{-t}$

20. $\lim_{t \to 0} \left(\dfrac{e^t + e^{-t}}{2} \right)$

21. $\lim_{x \to 0} \left(\dfrac{x - y}{x + y} \right)$

22. $\lim\limits_{x \to 0} \left(\dfrac{2^x - 2^{-x}}{2^x + 2^{-x}} \right)$

23. $\lim\limits_{y \to 0} \left(\dfrac{x - y}{x + y} \right)$

24. $\lim\limits_{x \to \infty} \left(\dfrac{x^3 - 2x + 5}{2x^3 - 7} \right)$

25. $\lim\limits_{x \to \infty} \left(\dfrac{x^2 + a^2}{x^3 + a^3} \right)$

26. $\lim\limits_{x \to 0} \left(\dfrac{x^3 - 5x + 6}{x^2 - 2x + 3} \right)$

27. $\lim\limits_{x \to \infty} \left(\dfrac{1}{1 + 2^{1/x}} \right)$

28. $\lim\limits_{x \to -\infty} \left(\dfrac{1}{1 + 2^{1/x}} \right)$

29. $\lim\limits_{x \to 0^+} \left(\dfrac{1}{1 + 2^{1/x}} \right)$

30. $\lim\limits_{x \to 0^-} \left(\dfrac{1}{1 + 2^{1/x}} \right)$

31. $\lim\limits_{x \to -2} x^3$

32. $\lim\limits_{x \to 2} x^{-3}$

33. $\lim\limits_{x \to a} \left(\dfrac{ax + 10}{x} \right)$

34. $\lim\limits_{x \to \infty} \left(\dfrac{1}{1 + e^{1/x}} \right)$

35. $\lim\limits_{x \to 0^-} \left(\dfrac{1}{1 + e^{1/x}} \right)$

36. $\lim\limits_{x \to 0^+} \left(\dfrac{1}{1 + e^{1/x}} \right)$

37. $\lim\limits_{x \to 0} \left(\dfrac{x + e^{x^2 + 3} + x^2}{e^3 + x} \right)$

38. $\lim\limits_{x \to 0} \left(\dfrac{x}{1 + e^x} \right)$

39. $\lim\limits_{h \to 1} \left(\dfrac{e^{-h}}{h^3 + 4h + 5} \right)$

40. $\lim\limits_{t \to 2} \left[\dfrac{t^2 + 4}{(t + 2)(t + 3)} \right]$

41. $\lim\limits_{t \to \infty} (e^{1/t} + 5)$

42. $\lim\limits_{t \to 0} \left(\dfrac{e^t - e^{-2t} - e^{3t^2}}{10} \right)$

43. $\lim\limits_{x \to 4} \left[\dfrac{x^2 - 16}{(x - 4)^2} \right]$

44. $\lim\limits_{x \to -4} \left[\dfrac{x^2 - 16}{(x - 4)^2} \right]$

45. $\lim\limits_{x \to 4} \left[\dfrac{x^2 - 16}{(x + 4)^2} \right]$

46. $\lim\limits_{x \to 0} \left(\dfrac{h^{-x} + h^x}{x} \right)$

47. $\lim\limits_{t \to 2} e^{-t + 2}$

48. $\lim\limits_{h \to 0} \left(\dfrac{e^{-h} - e^{2h}}{3} \right)$

49. $\lim\limits_{x \to \infty} (1 + 3^{1/x})$

50. $\lim\limits_{y \to 0} \left(\dfrac{x - y + 3}{x + y - 6} \right)$

51. $\lim\limits_{x \to 3} \left(\dfrac{x^3 - 3x^2 + 2x - 6}{x + 4} \right)$

52. $\lim\limits_{h \to 0} \left[\dfrac{(h + 1)e^{-h}}{h^2 + 1} \right]$

53. $\lim\limits_{x \to \infty} e^{1/x}$

54. $\lim\limits_{y \to 0} \left(\dfrac{x^2 - y^2 + 2}{x^3 - y} \right)$

55. $\lim\limits_{x \to 2} \left(\dfrac{x^4 - 6x - 4}{x + 1} \right)$

56. $\lim\limits_{t \to \infty} \left(\dfrac{t^3 + 4t^2 + 10}{5t^2 + 12t} \right)$

57. $\lim\limits_{h \to \infty} \left(\dfrac{1 + e^{1/h}}{e^h} \right)$

58. $\lim\limits_{h \to -\infty} \left(\dfrac{1 + e^{1/h}}{e^h} \right)$

59. $\lim\limits_{h \to 2} \left(\dfrac{x - h}{x + h} \right)$

60. $\lim\limits_{t \to 2} \left(\dfrac{t^2 - 6t + 8}{t^2 - 5t + 6} \right)$

61. $\lim\limits_{h \to \infty} \left(\dfrac{h^4 + 5h^5}{3h + 2h^6} \right)$

62. $\lim\limits_{t \to 0} \left(\dfrac{e^{-t}}{1 + e^{1/t}} \right)$

63. $\lim\limits_{t \to -3} \left(\dfrac{t^2 - t - 12}{t^2 + 4t + 3} \right)$

64. $\lim\limits_{x \to 0} \left(\dfrac{x^2 + 2ax + a^2}{a^3} \right)$

65. $\lim\limits_{x \to 0^+} \left(\dfrac{2 - e^x}{e^{1/x}} \right)$

66. $\lim\limits_{x \to 0^-} \left(\dfrac{2 - e^x}{e^{1/x}} \right)$

Answers to Odd-Numbered Problems

1. 21
3. $\frac{10}{3}$
5. 7
7. 0
9. 2
11. $-\frac{5}{2}$
13. a^x
15. $\frac{1}{16}$
17. 0
19. 0
21. -1
23. 1
25. 0
27. $\frac{1}{2}$
29. 0
31. -8
33. $\dfrac{a^2 + 10}{a}$
35. 1

37. 1
39. $\dfrac{1}{10e}$
41. 6
43. ∞
45. 0
47. 1
49. 2
51. 0
53. 1
55. 0
57. 0
59. $\dfrac{x - 2}{x + 2}$
61. 0
63. $\frac{7}{2}$
65. 0

2.3 Continuity

In this section continuity of a function is defined. Types of discontinuities are discussed and properties of continuous functions are given.

Essentially, a function is continuous if its graph consists of an unbroken curve. The mathematical definition of continuity involves properties of limits. In the definition of $\lim_{x \to a} f(x)$ the value of $f(x)$ for $x = a$ is not specified; that is, this limit depends only on the values of $f(x)$ in the neighborhood of (i.e., close to) $x = a$ but not on the value of $f(x)$ at $x = a$. Thus $\lim_{x \to a} f(x)$ may or may not be equal to $f(a)$. If $\lim_{x \to a} f(x)$ exists and the value $f(a)$ exists and is equal to $\lim_{x \to a} f(x)$, then $f(x)$ is continuous at $x = a$. That is, a function $f(x)$ is said to be *continuous at* $x = a$ if

1. $f(a)$ is defined.
2. $\lim_{x \to a} f(x)$ exists.
3. $\lim_{x \to a} f(x) = f(a)$.

NOTE: When a limit is said to exist, this should be understood to mean that the limit exists finitely. Possible confusion arises because, for example, the expression $\lim_{x \to a} A = \infty$ is written; however, this does not mean that A approaches a number designated by ∞, but only that A becomes arbitrarily large as x approaches a. It should be remembered that ∞ is *not* a number and should not be thought of as a number, even though for convenience it is used as a number in some expressions.

A function $f(x)$ is said to be *continuous in* (or on) *an interval* $b \le x \le c$ (or $b < x < c$) if it is continuous at every point of the interval.

A function that is not continuous at a point $x = a$ is said to be *discontinuous at* $x = a$.

From the definition of continuity, it follows that the graph of a function that is continuous on an interval consists of an unbroken curve (that is, a curve that can be drawn without raising the pen from the paper) over that interval. Continuity was tacitly assumed for the curves discussed in the preceding sections concerning graphical representation. In subsequent sections this assumption, which makes it possible to sketch a curve by plotting relatively few points and drawing an unbroken curve through them, will be justified for several (large) classes of curves.

TYPES OF DISCONTINUITIES

The three conditions that must be satisfied for a function to be continuous can be violated in various ways, resulting in different types of discontinuities. In general, three types of discontinuities occur.

1. A function $f(x)$ is said to have an *infinite discontinuity* at $x = a$ if $f(x)$ becomes infinite (positively or negatively) as $x \to a$. That is, even if $f(a)$ is defined and $\lim_{x \to a} f(x)$ does not exist.
2. A function $f(x)$ is said to have a *finite* or *step discontinuity* at $x = a$ if $f(x)$ remains finite but changes abruptly at $x = a$. That is, $f(a)$ is defined but $\lim_{x \to a} f(x)$ does not exist [although, in general, the right-hand and left-hand limits exist and $f(a)$ is equal to one of them].
3. A function $f(x)$ is said to have a *missing-point discontinuity* at $x = a$ if $f(a)$ is not defined but $\lim_{x \to a} f(x)$ exists.

It should be noted that a *discrete function* is defined for only a finite number of values of x in any interval and is thus discontinuous at all (infinitely many) values of x in the interval. Since x assumes only a finite number of values, the concept of a limit is not appropriate for discrete functions.

Geometrically, the curves representing functions having different types of discontinuities are quite different in appearance. The curve representing a function having an infinite discontinuity at $x = a$ approaches $x = a$ as an asymptote. The curve representing a function having a finite discontinuity at $x = a$ has an abrupt jump or step at $x = a$. The curve representing a function having a missing-point discontinuity at $x = a$ appears to be continuous, but the single point at $x = a$ is missing.

A missing-point discontinuity at $x = a$ occurs because $f(a)$ is not defined; this type of discontinuity may be removed by defining

$$f(a) = \lim_{x \to a} f(x)$$

since all three conditions of the definition of a continuous function at $x = a$ are then satisfied. It is possible for a function to have more than one missing-point discontinuity; as long as the number of these discontinuities is finite, they may be removed by the procedure described. Note that there is also the logical possibility (although a practical example is difficult to find) that there is a discontinuity at $x = a$ because $f(a)$, although defined, is not equal to $\lim_{x \to a} f(x)$. Such a discontinuity is not removable, since $f(a)$ is already defined and cannot therefore be defined as equal to $\lim_{x \to a} f(x)$.

Although missing-point discontinuities are removable, finite and infinite discontinuities are not removable. This is the case because the definition of a function is an arbitrary set of rules; adding another rule to this set, provided it is compatible with the others, is perfectly permissible, and this is all that is required to remove a missing-point discontinuity. On the other hand, finite and infinite discontinuities occur because the function in question does not approach a limit under the specified conditions. A limit either exists or does not exist as a mathematical fact associated with the nature of the function in question and cannot be defined into existence; thus there is no way to remove a discontinuity resulting from the nonexistence of a limit.

EXAMPLE

The function $f(x) = 1/(x - 2)^2$ has an infinite discontinuity at $x = 2$, since $f(x) \to \infty$ as $x \to 2$ and $f(2)$ is undefined. This function is continuous at all values of x other than $x = 2$ (see Figure 2.3).

Figure 2.3

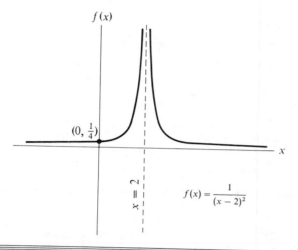

EXAMPLE

The function $f(x) = 4x/(4 - x^2)$ has infinite discontinuities at $x = \pm 2$, since $f(x) \to \infty$ as $x \to 2^-$, $f(x) \to -\infty$ as $x \to 2^+$, $f(x) \to \infty$ as $x \to -2^-$, and $f(x) \to -\infty$ as $x \to -2^+$, and $f(+2)$ and $f(-2)$ are undefined. This function is continuous for all values of x other than $x = \pm 2$ (see Figure 2.4).

Figure 2.4

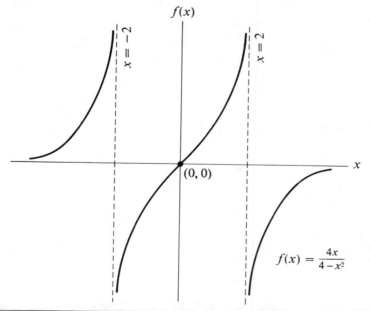

EXAMPLE

The function $f(x) = 1/(1 + 2^{1/x})$ has a finite discontinuity (that is, a "jump") at $x = 0$, since $\lim_{x \to 0} f(x)$ is undefined. This function is continuous at all values of x other than $x = 0$ (see Figure 2.5).

Figure 2.5

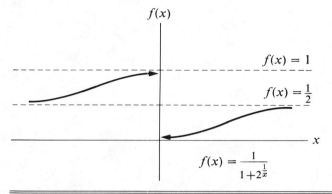

EXAMPLE

The function $f(x) = (x^3 - 2x^2 - 3x + 6)/(x - 2)$ is undefined and is thus discontinuous for $x = 2$. However, for $x \neq 2$,

$$f(x) = \frac{x^3 - 2x^2 - 3x + 6}{x - 2} = \frac{(x^2 - 3)(x - 2)}{x - 2} = x^2 - 3$$

and $\lim_{x \to 2} f(x) = 1$. Thus if, by definition,

$$f(2) = \lim_{x \to 2} f(x) = 1$$

then $f(x)$ is continuous for all x and its graph is the parabola

$$y = x^2 - 3$$

(see Figure 2.6).

Figure 2.6

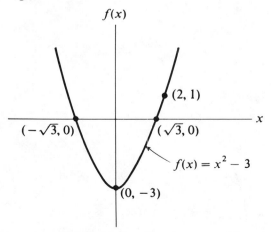

EXAMPLE

The function $f(x) = (x^2 - 9)/(x + 3)$ is undefined and is thus discontinuous for $x = -3$. However, for $x \neq -3$,

$$f(x) = \frac{x^2 - 9}{x + 3} = x - 3$$

and $\lim\limits_{x \to -3} f(x) = -6$. Thus if, by definition,

$$f(-3) = \lim_{x \to -3} f(x) = -6$$

then $f(x)$ is continuous for all x and its graph is the straight line

$$y = x - 3$$

(see Figure 2.7).

Figure 2.7

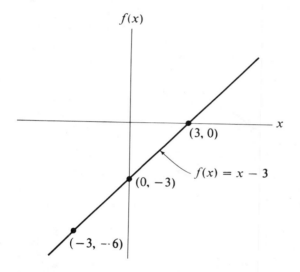

Many functions in business and economics are discrete or have finite discontinuities of the step-function type. For example, price and cost functions are frequently discrete because of the nature of the commodity involved or have discontinuities because cost and price per unit decrease (or increase) abruptly for particular quantities. Supply and demand and many other economic functions are also frequently discrete because of the nature of the commodity involved. It should be noted that functions which are, in fact, discrete are frequently represented as continuous for convenience; this applies, for example, to the supply and demand functions for commodities sold in units—such as refrigerators, eggs, light bulbs, chairs, lawn mowers, cars, and so forth. Representation of a function as continuous when it is by nature discrete makes possible the use of many tools of analysis not otherwise applicable. However, in interpreting the results of such analyses, the inherent discreteness should not be forgotten—for example, it is inappropriate to discuss the price of 1.632 refrigerators or the wages of 29.2 workers.

EXAMPLE

A wholesale grocer sells number 2 size cans of mixed vegetables in case lots according to the following price schedule:

$6.50 per case for 20 cases or less
$6.00 per case for orders of more than 20 cases and not more than 50 cases
$5.75 per case for orders of more than 50 cases and not more than 100 cases
$5.50 per case for orders of more than 100 cases

If y is total price and x is quantity in cases, the price function can be represented algebraically as follows.

$$y = \begin{cases} 6.50x & 0 \le x \le 20 \\ 6.00x & 20 < x \le 50 \\ 5.75x & 50 < x \le 100 \\ 5.50x & x > 100 \end{cases}$$

and geometrically as shown in Figure 2.8.

Figure 2.8

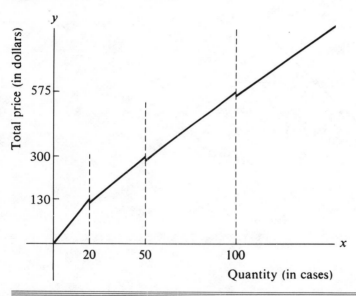

Note that, for this price function, total price is not a monotonic function of quantity ordered. This makes certain orders unlikely. For example, the price of 20 cases is $130, while the price of 21 cases is only $126; thus an order of 20 cases probably would be unlikely.

EXAMPLE

A company sells printed business stationery only in boxes of 200 sheets at $2.25 per box. If y is total price and x is number of boxes, the price function can be represented algebraically by the equation

$$y = 2.25x \quad \text{for} \quad x = 1, 2, 3, \dots$$

Figure 2.9

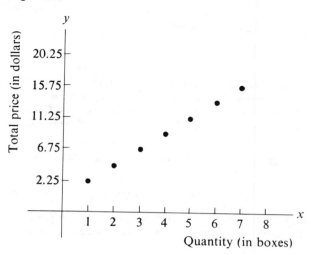

and geometrically by the graph in Figure 2.9. This function is discrete, since it is defined only for integer values of x.

EXAMPLE

An oil refinery has 5 distillation towers and operates as many of them as needed to process the raw materials available. The overhead cost of operating each distillation tower (operator, maintenance, and so forth) is \$500 per week; in addition, the cost of raw materials is \$5.50 per

Figure 2.10

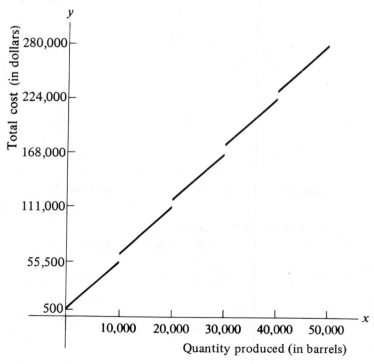

barrel of oil refined. Each distillation tower can process raw materials yielding 10,000 barrels of oil refined per week. If y is the total cost of operation and x is the quantity of oil refined (in barrels), the cost function can be represented by the equation

$$f(x) = 500\left(\left[\frac{x}{10,000}\right] + 1\right) + 5.50x$$

where $[x/10,000]$ denotes the largest integer part of $x/10,000$. Note that 1 is added to $[x/10,000]$ because $[x/10,000]$ distillation towers produce a maximum of $10,000x$ gallons. Thus for any additional production, another distillation tower must be operated. The graph of the function is shown in Figure 2.10. This function has finite discontinuities at $x = 10,000, 20,000, 30,000,$ and 40,000.

EXAMPLE

A stationery store sells Christmas cards for 30 cents each or \$3.00 for a dozen. If y is price and x is number of cards sold, the price function for a customer can be represented by the equation

$$y = 3\left[\frac{x}{12}\right] + 0.30\left(x - 12\left[\frac{x}{12}\right]\right) \qquad \text{for } x = 1, 2, 3, \ldots$$

where $[x/12]$ denotes the largest integer part of $x/12$. This function is discrete since it is defined only for integer values of x; it is also nonmonotonic, as a result of discounting for larger quantities purchased. (See Figure 2.11.)

Figure 2.11

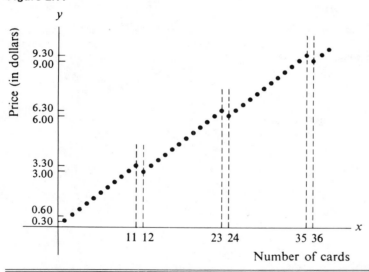

Number of cards

PROPERTIES OF CONTINUOUS FUNCTIONS

The following properties of continuous functions follow from the definition of a continuous function and the properties of limits.

If $f(x)$ and $g(x)$ are two functions that are continuous at $x = a$, then

$$F(x) = f(x) + g(x)$$

$$G(x) = f(x) - g(x)$$

$$H(x) = f(x) \cdot g(x)$$

are also continuous at $x = a$. If $g(a) \neq 0$, then

$$I(x) = \frac{f(x)}{g(x)}$$

is also continuous at $x = a$. [Note that if $g(a) = 0$, then $I(a)$ is undefined.]

The following properties can also be proved (but by more advanced arguments):
If a function $f(x)$ is continuous on a closed interval $a \leq x \leq b$, then

1. $f(x)$ has a greatest value (maximum) and a least value (minimum) in the interval.
2. If k is a number between a and b, then there is at least one point c between a and b such that $f(c) = k$.
3. If $f(a)$ and $f(b)$ are opposite in sign, then there exists at least one point d in the interval such that $f(d) = 0$.

PROBLEMS

For each of the following functions, determine the values of x for which the function is discontinuous, identify the types of discontinuities, and give appropriate definitions for removing any removable discontinuities.

1. $f(x) = \dfrac{3x + 5}{x^2 + 4x + 4}$

2. $f(x) = \dfrac{x - 2}{x + 1}$

3. $f(x) = \dfrac{x^2 - 1}{x - 1}$

4. $f(x) = \dfrac{x^2 + 4}{x^2 - x - 2}$

5. $f(x) = \log(2x - 5)$

6. $f(x) = \dfrac{1}{2^x - 1}$

7. $f(x) = \dfrac{1}{x(x - 2)}$

8. $f(x) = \sqrt{\dfrac{x + 1}{x - 1}}$

9. $f(x) = \dfrac{(x - 1)^2}{(x - 1)(x^2 - 4x + 5)}$

10. $f(x) = \log\left(\dfrac{x - 2}{x}\right)$

11. $f(x) = \dfrac{x^2 + 5x + 6}{x + 2}$

12. $f(x) = \dfrac{x^2 - 3}{x^2 - 4}$

13. $f(x) = \dfrac{x^2 - 2x}{x^3 - x^2 + x}$

14. $f(x) = \dfrac{x^2 - 5x + 6}{x - 2}$

15. $f(x) = \dfrac{x^2 + 1}{x^3 - 4x}$

16. $f(x) = \dfrac{4x}{4 - x^2}$

17. $f(x) = \dfrac{1}{4x^2 - 16}$

18. $f(x) = \dfrac{x - 2}{(x - 2)(x^2 + 2x + 10)}$

19. $f(x) = \dfrac{1}{e^{4x} - 1}$

20. $f(x) = \dfrac{x - 2}{(x - 2)(x^2 + 2x - 3)}$

21. $f(x) = \dfrac{e^x + 2x^2}{2e^{3x} - 2}$

22. $f(x) = \dfrac{x^2 - 5x + 6}{(x - 2)(x^2 - 3x + 5)}$

23. $f(x) = \dfrac{1}{e^x - 1}$

24. $f(x) = \dfrac{x^2 - 3}{x^2 - 16}$

25. $f(x) = \dfrac{(x - 3)^3}{(x - 3)(x^2 - 2x + 6)}$

26. $f(x) = \dfrac{x^2 + 2x - 8}{x + 4}$

27. $f(x) = \dfrac{1}{3e^{3x} - 3}$

28. $f(x) = \dfrac{(x + 5)^2(x + 3)}{(x + 5)(x^2 - 4x + 8)}$

29. $f(x) = \dfrac{x^2 + 5x + 6}{x + 2}$

30. $f(x) = \dfrac{x^2 + 3x + 6}{x^2 - 1}$

31. $f(x) = \dfrac{10}{e^{6x} - 1}$

32. $f(x) = \dfrac{x^2 + x - 2}{x^2 + 27x + 50}$

33. $f(x) = \dfrac{x^2 + 10x + 1}{x^2 - 9}$

34. $f(x) = \dfrac{x^2 - 5x + 4}{x - 4}$

35. $f(x) = \ln(x^2 - 6)$

36. $f(x) = \dfrac{x^2 - 5x + 6}{(x - 2)(x^2 - 2x - 3)}$

37. $f(x) = \dfrac{2x^2 + 3x}{x^3 - 9x}$

38. $f(x) = \dfrac{1}{3e^x - 3}$

39. $f(x) = \dfrac{e^x + 4x}{3e^{4x} - 3}$

40. $f(x) = \dfrac{x^2 + 5x + 4}{(x + 4)(x^2 - 6x + 10)}$

41. $f(x) = \dfrac{x^2 - 1}{x + 1} \quad$ for $x \neq -1$

$\qquad = -2 \qquad$ for $x = -1$

Is $f(x)$ continuous at $x = -1$?

42. $f(x) = \dfrac{x^2 + 3x - 10}{x - 2} \qquad$ for $x \neq 2$.

What value should be assigned to $f(2)$ to make $f(x)$ continuous at $x = 2$?

43. $f(x) = \sqrt[3]{x}$. Is $f(x)$ continuous at $x = 0$?

44. $f(x) = \dfrac{x^2 - 7x + 12}{x - 3} \qquad$ for $x \neq 3$

$\qquad = 1 \qquad$ for $x = 3$

Is $f(x)$ continuous at $x = 3$?

Answers to Odd-Numbered Problems

1. $x = -2$
3. $x = 1, f(1) = 2$
5. $x \leq \frac{5}{2}$
7. $x = 0, x = 2$
9. $x = 1, f(1) = 0$
11. $x = -2, f(-2) = 1$
13. $x = 0, f(0) = -2$
15. $x = 0, x = \pm 2$
17. $x = \pm 2$
19. $x = 0$
21. $x = 0$

23. $x = 0$
25. $x = 3, f(3) = 0$
27. $x = 0$
29. $x = -2, f(-2) = 1$
31. $x = 0$
33. $x = \pm 3$
35. $x = \pm \sqrt{6}$
37. $x = \pm 3, x = 0, f(0) = -\frac{1}{3}$
39. $x = 0$
41. $x = -1, f(-1) = -2$
43. continuous

2.4 Definition of the First Derivative

In this section the first derivative of a function is defined and several of its interpretations are considered. The first derivative of a function at a point is the slope of the function at that point. This concept is defined precisely as follows:

The slope m of a straight line is defined as the tangent of its angle of inclination or, equivalently, as the ratio of the change in vertical distance (rise) to the change in horizontal distance (run) as a point moves along the line in either direction (see Figure 2.12).

$$m = \tan \theta = \frac{y_2 - y_1}{x_2 - x_1} = \frac{\Delta y}{\Delta x}$$

Figure 2.12

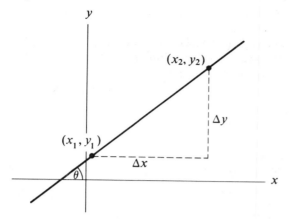

The slope of any given straight line is a constant—that is, the rate of change of y as x changes is constant over the length of the line. However, for other curves the slope is not constant and must be determined for each particular point of interest.

Suppose that (x_1, y_1) and (x_2, y_2) are any two points on the curve $y = f(x)$. Then the slope of the line (called a secant) joining (x_1, y_1) and (x_2, y_2) is

$$m_{sec} = \frac{y_2 - y_1}{x_2 - x_1} = \frac{\Delta y}{\Delta x}$$

[See Figure 2.13.]

Suppose now that the point (x_1, y_1) is held fixed while the point (x_2, y_2) is moved along the curve $y = f(x)$ toward the point (x_1, y_1); as the point (x_2, y_2) is moved along the curve $f(x)$, the slope of the line joining (x_1, y_1) and (x_2, y_2) will, in general, vary. However, it may happen, and does happen for most curves encountered in practice, that as the point (x_2, y_2) moves closer and closer to the point (x_1, y_1), the slope of the secant line varies by smaller and smaller amounts and, in fact,

Figure 2.13

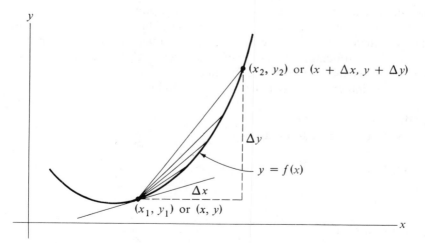

approaches a constant limiting value. When this occurs, the limiting value is said to be the slope of the tangent to the curve at (x_1, y_1) or the slope of the curve at (x_1, y_1) [see Figure 2.13].

More concisely, if, as the point (x_2, y_2) approaches the point (x_1, y_1) along the curve $y = f(x)$, the slope of the secant line approaches a constant limiting value, then this limiting value is said to be the slope of the tangent to the curve at (x_1, y_1) or, briefly, the slope of the curve at (x_1, y_1) or the slope of $f(x)$ at (x_1, y_1). That is,

$$\lim_{\Delta x \to 0} m_{\text{sec}} = \lim_{\Delta x \to 0} \frac{\Delta y}{\Delta x} = \text{slope of } f(x) \text{ at } (x_1, y_1)$$

The slope of a function at a given point is the *first derivative* of the function at the given point.

It is customary in defining the first derivative to use the notation (x, y) for the stationary point (x_1, y_1) and the notation $(x + \Delta x, y + \Delta y)$ for the moving point (x_2, y_2). Then

$$\frac{dy}{dx} = \lim_{\Delta x \to 0} \frac{\Delta y}{\Delta x} = \lim_{\Delta x \to 0} \frac{f(x + \Delta x) - f(x)}{\Delta x}$$

is the first derivative with respect to x of the function $y = f(x)$. This limit may exist for some values of x and fail to exist for other values of x. At each point (x, y) where this limit does exist, the function $y = f(x)$ is said to have a derivative or to be *differentiable* and $\dfrac{dy}{dx}$ is said to be the *first derivative* or the derivative of $y = f(x)$. The process of obtaining the first derivative of a function is referred to as *differentiation*. Various types of notation, in addition to $\dfrac{dy}{dx}$, are used to denote the first derivative of $y = f(x)$ with respect to x. The most common of these are

$$f'(x) \qquad y' \qquad \frac{d}{dx}(y) \qquad D_x y \qquad D_x(y)$$

It should be noted that the first derivative of a function with respect to x is, in general, another function of x which must be evaluated for particular values of interest. This corresponds to the statement above that, except for straight lines, curves do not in general have the same slope at different points.

From the definition of a derivative and the properties of limits, rules for obtaining the derivatives of various types of functions can be obtained. These are given in a later section. For illustration, the derivatives of several relatively simple functions are obtained directly rather than by using the formulas.

The steps for obtaining a derivative directly are as follows:

1. Consider the function $y = f(x)$.
2. Give increments to x and y to obtain

$$y + \Delta y = f(x + \Delta x)$$

3. Subtract to obtain

$$\Delta y = f(x + \Delta x) - f(x)$$

4. Divide by Δx to obtain

$$\frac{\Delta y}{\Delta x} = \frac{f(x + \Delta x) - f(x)}{\Delta x}$$

5. Take the limit to obtain

$$\frac{dy}{dx} = \lim_{\Delta x \to 0} \frac{\Delta y}{\Delta x} = \lim_{\Delta x \to 0} \frac{f(x + \Delta x) - f(x)}{\Delta x}$$

EXAMPLE

Find the first derivative of $y = 4x + 1$.

$$\frac{dy}{dx} = \lim_{\Delta x \to 0} \frac{f(x + \Delta x) - f(x)}{\Delta x}$$

$$= \lim_{\Delta x \to 0} \frac{4(x + \Delta x) + 1 - (4x + 1)}{\Delta x}$$

$$= \lim_{\Delta x \to 0} \frac{4\Delta x}{\Delta x}$$

$$= \lim_{\Delta x \to 0} 4 = 4$$

Note that $y = 4x + 1$ represents a straight line and thus $\dfrac{dy}{dx}$ is a constant.

EXAMPLE

Find the first derivative of $y = x^3 - 12x + 13$.

$$\frac{dy}{dx} = \lim_{\Delta x \to 0} \frac{f(x + \Delta x) - f(x)}{\Delta x}$$

$$= \lim_{\Delta x \to 0} \frac{(x + \Delta x)^3 - 12(x + \Delta x) + 13 - (x^3 - 12x + 13)}{\Delta x}$$

$$= \lim_{\Delta x \to 0} \frac{x^3 + 3x(\Delta x)^2 + 3x^2(\Delta x) + (\Delta x)^3 - 12(x + \Delta x) + 13 - x^3 + 12x - 13}{\Delta x}$$

[NOTE: $(a + b)^3 = a^3 + 3a^2b + 3ab^2 + b^3$]

$$= \lim_{\Delta x \to 0} \frac{3x^2(\Delta x) + 3x(\Delta x)^2 + (\Delta x)^3 - 12(\Delta x)}{\Delta x}$$

$$= \lim_{\Delta x \to 0} [3x^2 + 3x(\Delta x) + (\Delta x)^2 - 12]$$

$$= 3x^2 - 12$$

Note that $\dfrac{dy}{dx}$ is a function of x and can be evaluated for any value of x.

EXAMPLE

Find the first derivative of $y = x^2 + (1/x)$ for $x \neq 0$.

$$\frac{dy}{dx} = \lim_{\Delta x \to 0} \frac{f(x + \Delta x) - f(x)}{\Delta x}$$

$$= \lim_{\Delta x \to 0} \frac{(x + \Delta x)^2 + \dfrac{1}{x + \Delta x} - \left(x^2 + \dfrac{1}{x}\right)}{\Delta x}$$

$$= \lim_{\Delta x \to 0} \frac{x^2 + 2x(\Delta x) + (\Delta x)^2 + \dfrac{1}{x + \Delta x} - x^2 - \dfrac{1}{x}}{\Delta x}$$

$$= \lim_{\Delta x \to 0} \frac{2x(\Delta x) + (\Delta x)^2 + \left(\dfrac{1}{x + \Delta x} - \dfrac{1}{x}\right)}{\Delta x}$$

$$= \lim_{\Delta x \to 0} \frac{2x(\Delta x) + (\Delta x)^2 + \dfrac{x - x - \Delta x}{x(x + \Delta x)}}{\Delta x}$$

$$= \lim_{\Delta x \to 0} \left[2x + \Delta x - \frac{1}{x(x + \Delta x)}\right]$$

$$= 2x - \frac{1}{x^2} \qquad \text{for } x \neq 0$$

Note that again $\dfrac{dy}{dx}$ is a function of x and can be evaluated for any value of $x \neq 0$.

PROBLEMS

For each of the following functions $f(x)$, find the first derivative $\dfrac{dy}{dx}$ using the definition

$$\frac{dy}{dx} = \lim_{\Delta x \to 0} \frac{f(x + \Delta x) - f(x)}{\Delta x}$$

1. $f(x) = x^2 - x + 1$

2. $f(x) = \dfrac{1}{x^2}$

3. $f(x) = \sqrt{2x}$

4. $f(x) = x - \dfrac{1}{x}$

5. $f(x) = 6 - 2x^3$

6. $f(x) = 5x^4 - 2$

Answers to Odd-Numbered Problems

1. $2x - 1$

3. $\dfrac{1}{\sqrt{2x}}$

5. $-6x^2$

INTERPRETATION OF THE FIRST DERIVATIVE

Although the geometrical interpretation of the first derivative has historical significance and is perhaps the most intuitive, other interpretations are equally valid and sometimes are more useful in applications.

Two of the classical interpretations of a derivative are in terms of the velocity of a moving body and the rate of change of a function. Although both of these interpretations originated in the study of various problems in physics and mathematics, they have since been applied in many fields. For example, marginal analysis in economics can be discussed in terms of the rate of change of a function.

Velocity of a Moving Body

Consider a body (or a particle) moving along a straight-line path. Let t denote the time measured from some fixed instant and let s denote the distance of the particle from some fixed origin on the line, where s is positive or negative according to the direction of displacement from the origin. Suppose distance from the origin is given in terms of time by a function $s = f(t)$, called the *law of motion*. [For example, think of the body or particle as being a car that is driven along a straight road in such a way that its distance from the starting point is given as a function of t by $s = f(t)$.]

At a certain time t_1, let the particle be at a distance s_1 from the origin 0, and suppose that during the following time interval Δt it moves a distance Δs farther from the origin (see Figure 2.14).

If the ratio $\dfrac{\Delta s}{\Delta t}$ is constant, so that equal distances are always traversed in equal intervals of time, the motion is said to be *uniform* and the ratio $\dfrac{\Delta s}{\Delta t}$ is called the *velocity* at any instant. The term *speed* is used frequently to mean the magnitude— that is, absolute value—of the velocity.

If, however, the motion is not uniform, the ratio $\dfrac{\Delta s}{\Delta t}$ varies as Δt varies and is no longer the velocity of the particle at any instant. It is instead the *average velocity* of the particle during the particular time interval Δt:

$$\text{average velocity during interval } \Delta t = \frac{\Delta s}{\Delta t}$$

As the time interval Δt approaches zero, this average velocity $\dfrac{\Delta s}{\Delta t}$ may approach a limit. If so, this limit is said to be the *instantaneous velocity* at time t_1:

$$\text{instantaneous velocity at time } t_1 = \lim_{\Delta t \to 0} \frac{\Delta s}{\Delta t}$$

But, by definition, $\lim_{\Delta t \to 0} \dfrac{\Delta s}{\Delta t}$ is the first derivative of $f(t)$ at the point $t = t_1$. Thus, at an instant t_1, the velocity of a particle moving in a straight line according to the law of motion $s = f(t)$, where s is the directed distance from a fixed origin and t is the time, is given by the value of the derivative of s with respect to t for $t = t_1$.

Figure 2.14

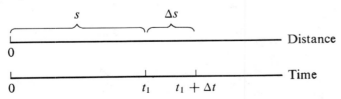

EXAMPLE

The distance of a train from its starting point when it is traveling along a straight track is given by the equation

$$s = 16t^2 + 2t$$

where s is distance in miles and t is time in hours. Find the distance traveled and the velocity after 2 hours.

$$s = 16t^2 + 2t$$

So after 2 hours, $s = 64 + 4 = 68$ miles traveled.

$$\frac{ds}{dt} = \lim_{\Delta t \to 0} \frac{f(t + \Delta t) - f(t)}{\Delta t}$$

$$= \lim_{\Delta t \to 0} \frac{16(t + \Delta t)^2 + 2(t + \Delta t) - (16t^2 + 2t)}{\Delta t}$$

$$= \lim_{\Delta t \to 0} \frac{16t^2 + 32t(\Delta t) + 16(\Delta t)^2 + 2t + 2\Delta t - 16t^2 - 2t}{\Delta t}$$

$$= \lim_{\Delta t \to 0} \frac{32t(\Delta t) + 16(\Delta t)^2 + 2(\Delta t)}{\Delta t}$$

$$= \lim_{\Delta t \to 0} [32t + 16(\Delta t) + 2]$$

$$= \lim_{\Delta t \to 0} (32t + 2)$$

and the velocity after 2 hours is

$$\left. \frac{ds}{dt} \right|_{t=2} = 64 + 2 = 66 \text{ miles per hour}$$

(The notation $\left. \dfrac{ds}{dt} \right|_{t=2}$ indicates that is the function $\dfrac{ds}{dt}$ is evaluated for $t = 2$.)

EXAMPLE

One of the attractions at a carnival is a "prove your strength" bell, which rings if a lever is hit with sufficient strength to propel an iron ball up a vertical shaft to hit the bell. When the lever is hit with a force of 50 lb, the distance of the ball from the bottom of the shaft is given by

$$s = 40t - 32t^2$$

Figure 2.15

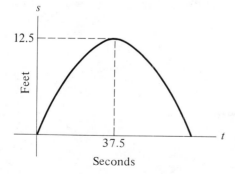

where s is distance in feet and t is time in minutes since the lever was hit.

(a) If the bell is at the top of a 15-ft shaft, is a force of 50 lb sufficient to ring it?

(b) How far from the bottom of the shaft is the ball after 30 seconds, 45 seconds, 1 minute, and 75 seconds, respectively?

(a) Velocity $\dfrac{ds}{dt}$ is zero when the ball is at the top of the shaft, so solving the equation $\dfrac{ds}{dt} = 0$ provides the time the ball travels up the shaft before coming back down.

$$\frac{ds}{dt} = \lim_{\Delta t \to 0} \frac{f(t + \Delta t) - f(t)}{\Delta t}$$

$$= \lim_{\Delta t \to 0} \frac{40(t + \Delta t) - 32(t + \Delta t)^2 - (40t - 32t^2)}{\Delta t}$$

$$= \lim_{\Delta t \to 0} \frac{40t + 40(\Delta t) - 32t^2 - 64t(\Delta t) - 32(\Delta t)^2 - 40t + 32t^2}{\Delta t}$$

$$= \lim_{\Delta t \to 0} \frac{40(\Delta t) - 64t(\Delta t) - 32(\Delta t)^2}{\Delta t}$$

$$= \lim_{\Delta t \to 0} [40 - 64t - 32(\Delta t)]$$

$$= 40 - 64t$$

If $\dfrac{ds}{dt} = 0$, $t = \frac{40}{64} = \frac{5}{8}$ minutes (or 37.5 seconds) and $s = 40(\frac{5}{8}) - 32(\frac{25}{64}) = 12.5$ feet, so the force is not sufficient to ring the bell 15 ft up the shaft. (See Figure 2.15.)

(b) If $t = 30$ seconds $= \frac{1}{2}$, $s = 40(\frac{1}{2}) - 32(\frac{1}{4}) = 12$ ft (on the way up)

If $t = 45$ seconds $= \frac{3}{4}$, $s = 40(\frac{3}{4}) - 32(\frac{9}{16}) = 12$ ft (on the way down)

If $t = 1$, $s = 40 - 32 = 8$ ft (on the way down)

If $t = 75$ seconds $= \frac{5}{4}$, $s = 40(\frac{5}{4}) - 32(\frac{25}{16}) = 0$ (back down)

Rate of Change of a Function

Let p and q denote the measures of two related variables and regard q as a function of p—that is, $q = f(p)$. If the ratio $\dfrac{\Delta q}{\Delta p}$ of corresponding changes in the two quantities has the same value for all values of Δp, it is called the *rate of change* of q with respect to p and q is said to change uniformly with respect to p. But if the ratio $\dfrac{\Delta q}{\Delta p}$ is not constant as Δp changes, q does not change uniformly, and $\dfrac{\Delta q}{\Delta p}$ is then called the *average rate of change* of q with respect to p over the interval Δp.

If the ratio $\dfrac{\Delta q}{\Delta p}$ approaches a limit when Δp approaches zero, then this limit is said to be the *instantaneous rate of change* of q with respect to p.

From the definition of the derivative, it follows that the instantaneous rate of change of a variable quantity q with respect to a related variable quantity p is given by the derivative of q with respect to p, that is, $\dfrac{dq}{dp}$.

It is customary to use the expression "rate of change of a function" as equivalent to the derivative of the function.

If the variable q can be expressed as a function of the variable time t, then the derivative $\dfrac{dq}{dt}$ of q with respect to t gives the *time rate of change* of q. Thus the velocity of a particle is the time rate of change of its directed distance from the origin.

The interpretation of a derivative in terms of the rate of change of a function is frequently applicable in economics, as discussed below.

2.5 Applications of the First Derivative in Business and Economics

In this section several applications of the first derivative in business and economics are discussed. These applications include marginal cost, marginal revenue, elasticity, and marginal propensity to save and to consume.

It is customary in economics to describe the variation of one quantity y with respect to another quantity x in terms of two concepts, *average* and *marginal*. The average concept expresses the variation of y over a range of values of x, usually the range from zero to a certain selected value. The marginal concept, on the other hand, concerns the variation of y " on the margin "—that is, for very small variations of x from a given value. The marginal concept is thus precise only when it is considered in the limiting sense, as the variation in x approaches zero.

The economic concepts of average and marginal variation correspond to the more general concepts of the average rate of change of a function over an interval and the instantaneous rate of change (that is, the derivative) of a function.

Average and marginal variations in quantities are essential considerations in the development of both microeconomic and macroeconomic theory. Examples of the application of the derivative in both microeconomic theory (cost, revenue, elasticity) and macroeconomic theory (income, consumption, savings) are discussed below; additional examples are given in later sections.

COST

Suppose the total cost y of producing and marketing x units of a commodity is given by the function

$$y = f(x)$$

Then the *average cost* per unit is

$$\frac{y}{x} = \frac{f(x)}{x}$$

If output is increased by an amount Δx from a certain level x and if the corresponding increase in cost is Δy, then the average increase in cost per unit increase in output is $\dfrac{\Delta y}{\Delta x}$ and marginal cost is defined as

$$\lim_{\Delta x \to 0} \frac{\Delta y}{\Delta x} = \frac{dy}{dx} = f'(x)$$

That is, marginal cost is the derivative $f'(x)$ of the total cost function $y = f(x)$ with respect to x and is the rate of increase in total cost with increase in output.

EXAMPLE

Consider the total cost function

$$y = 20 + 2x + 0.5x^2$$

where y denotes total cost and x denotes quantity produced. Average cost is

$$\bar{y} = \frac{y}{x} = \frac{20}{x} + 2 + 0.5x$$

and marginal cost is

$$\frac{dy}{dx} = 2 + x$$

Thus total cost increases as output increases; average cost per unit decreases and then increases as output increases; and marginal cost (rate of increase in total cost) increases as output increases (see Figure 2.16).

Figure 2.16

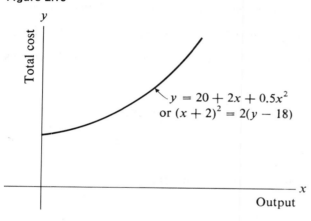

$$y = 20 + 2x + 0.5x^2$$
$$\text{or } (x + 2)^2 = 2(y - 18)$$

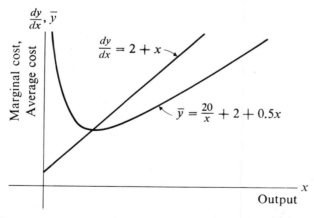

$$\frac{dy}{dx} = 2 + x$$

$$\bar{y} = \frac{20}{x} + 2 + 0.5x$$

NOTE: Derivatives are given in these examples without any explanation of how they were obtained. The method of the preceding section or the rules given in the next section can be used for verification.

REVENUE

For any given demand function

$$y = f(x)$$

where y is the price per unit and x is the number of units, *total revenue* R is the product of x and y—that is,

$$R = xy = x \cdot f(x)$$

Marginal revenue with respect to demand is the derivative with respect to x of total revenue,

$$\frac{dR}{dx} = R'(x)$$

and is thus the rate of change in revenue with change in demand.

Note that *average revenue*, or revenue per unit, also represents the price per unit, y—that is, the average revenue curve and the demand curve are identical.

Since x and y are nonnegative within our previously stated analytical framework, R is also nonnegative. However, $\frac{dR}{dx}$ may be positive or negative—that is, although total revenue is always nonnegative, it may increase or decrease as demand increases.

EXAMPLE

Consider the demand function

$$3x + 4y = 10$$

where y is the price per unit and x is the number of units. Then

$$y = \frac{5}{2} - \frac{3}{4}x$$

Total revenue is

$$R = x \cdot y = \frac{5}{2}x - \frac{3}{4}x^2$$

Figure 2.17

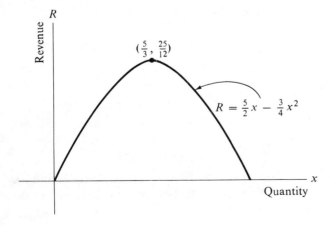

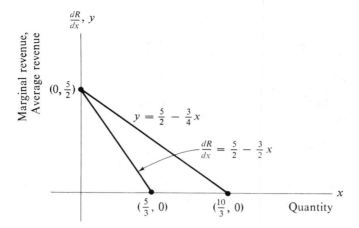

and marginal revenue is

$$\frac{dR}{dx} = \frac{5}{2} - \frac{3}{2}x$$

(see Figure 2.17).

For the example above, note the following properties, which hold for all linear demand functions. Total revenue increases and then decreases as quantity increases; both average revenue and marginal revenue decrease (linearly) as quantity increases. The average and marginal revenue curves have the same y-intercept and, apart from this common point, the marginal revenue curve lies below the average revenue curve. The marginal revenue curve intersects the x-axis at the output for which total revenue is greatest and the average revenue curve intersects the x-axis at twice that output. The slope of the average revenue curve is one-half the slope of the marginal revenue curve.

ELASTICITY

The *point elasticity* of the function $y = f(x)$ at the point x is the proportional rate of change in y per unit change in x:

$$\frac{Ey}{Ex} = \frac{\dfrac{dy}{y}}{\dfrac{dx}{x}} = \frac{x}{y} \cdot \frac{dy}{dx}$$

Note that the elasticity of a function is independent of the units in which the variables are measured, since elasticity is defined in terms of proportional changes, which are necessarily independent of units of measurement.

Point elasticity is an important concept in economic theory and is applied in studying, for example, demand, supply, cost, and productivity. Detailed examples of these and other applications of derivatives are discussed in later sections, following the discussion of rules for differentiation.

NATIONAL INCOME, CONSUMPTION, AND SAVINGS

The relationship between total national disposable income and total national consumption is often referred to as the *consumption function*. In simple forms of theoretical analysis of the consumption function, it is assumed that as income increases (or decreases) consumption increases (or decreases), but by less than the increase (or decrease) in income; that is, the marginal propensity to consume is greater than zero but less than 1, where marginal propensity to consume is the rate of change in consumption as disposable income changes.

If the consumption function is given by

$$c = f(x)$$

where c is total national consumption and x is total national income (and c and x are in the same units), then the marginal propensity to consume is

$$\frac{dc}{dx} = f'(x)$$

In elementary theoretical analyses of national income, the assumption is often made that disposable income equals consumption plus savings. This is expressed as

$$x = c + s$$

Then the *marginal propensity to consume* is

$$\frac{dc}{dx} = f'(x)$$

and *the marginal propensity to save* is

$$\frac{ds}{dx} = 1 - \frac{dc}{dx}$$

In national income analysis, investment is considered as capital formation and represents an increase in real capital as typified by equipment, buildings, inventories, and so forth. Investment and consumption are assumed to be related in such a way that an initial investment expenditure may result in an increase in income of several times that amount. A precise numerical expression for this relationship is given by the multiplier. The multiplier is the ratio of the ultimate increase in income to the increase in investment that gave rise to it.

The *multiplier k* is related to the marginal propensity to save or to consume and is given by

$$k = \frac{1}{1 - \dfrac{dc}{dx}} = \frac{1}{\dfrac{ds}{dx}}$$

Note that if $\dfrac{dc}{dx} = 0$, then $k = 1$; that is, if none of the additional income is spent, the total increase in income is equal to the initial expenditure; if $\dfrac{dc}{dx} \to 1$, $k \to \infty$; that is, if all the additional income is spent, the total increase in income becomes infinitely large.

EXAMPLE

Suppose the consumption function is

$$c = 10 + 0.8x + 0.5\sqrt{x}$$

Figure 2.18

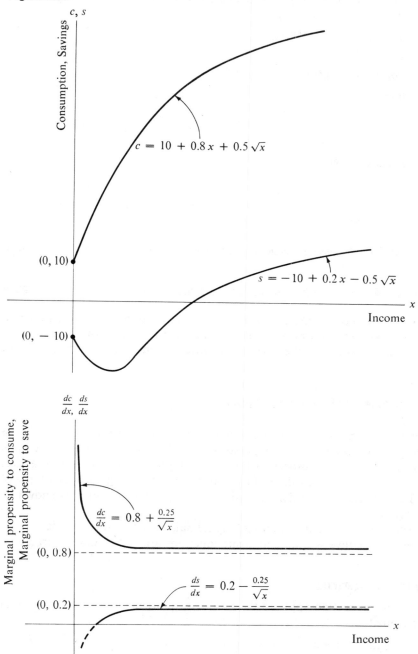

where c is total consumption and x is total disposable income. Then the amount saved is

$$s = x - c$$

$$= x - (10 + 0.8x + 0.5\sqrt{x})$$

$$= -10 + 0.2x - 0.5\sqrt{x}$$

Note that c is positive for all positive values of x; s is negative for small positive values of x and positive for larger values of x; for every value of x, $c + s = x$. Note also that c is an increasing function of x; s is at first a decreasing and then an increasing function of x. (See Figure 2.18.)

The marginal propensity to consume is

$$\frac{dc}{dx} = 0.8 + \frac{0.25}{\sqrt{x}}$$

The marginal propensity to save is

$$\frac{ds}{dx} = 0.2 - \frac{0.25}{\sqrt{x}}$$

and

$$\frac{dc}{dx} + \frac{ds}{dx} = 1.$$ The multiplier is

$$k = \frac{1}{0.2 - \dfrac{0.25}{\sqrt{x}}}$$

Note that $\dfrac{dc}{dx}$ and k are decreasing functions of x and $\dfrac{ds}{dx}$ is an increasing function of x. (See Figure 2.18.)

NOTE: For certain economic analyses, it is more appropriate to consider income as a function of consumption rather than consumption as a function of income. In this case, income is plotted on the y-axis and consumption is plotted on the x-axis.

2.6 Rules for Differentiation

The procedure for obtaining derivatives directly was illustrated for several simple functions in previous sections. Although straightforward, this procedure is tedious and likely to result in errors, especially for more complicated functions. In practice, derivatives are obtained using rules or formulas for differentiating particular types of functions. These rules can be derived using the general procedure, as shown in Technical Note I.

In this section, rules for differentiating polynomial, algebraic, logarithmic, exponential, trigonometric, inverse, and composite functions are stated and illustrated.

ALGEBRAIC FUNCTIONS

The formulas in this section apply to the products, quotients, powers, and roots of differentiable functions.

Rule 1.   The derivative of a constant is zero: If $y = c$,

$$\frac{dy}{dx} = 0$$

EXAMPLE

If $y = 6$, $\dfrac{dy}{dx} = 0$.

EXAMPLE

If $y = a$, $\dfrac{dy}{dx} = 0$.

Rule 2. The derivative of the nth power of a variable is the product of n and the $(n-1)$st power of the variable: If $y = x^n$,

$$\frac{dy}{dx} = nx^{n-1}$$

EXAMPLE

If $y = x^2$, $\dfrac{dy}{dx} = 2x$.

EXAMPLE

If $y = x^{1/4}$, $\dfrac{dy}{dx} = \frac{1}{4}x^{-3/4}$.

EXAMPLE

If $y = x^{-4}$, $\dfrac{dy}{dx} = -4x^{-5} = -\dfrac{4}{x^5}$.

EXAMPLE

If $y = x^{-5/3}$, $\dfrac{dy}{dx} = -\dfrac{5}{3}x^{-8/3} = -\dfrac{5}{3x^{8/3}}$.

Rule 3. The derivative of the product of a constant and a differentiable function is the product of the constant and the derivative of the function: If $y = cu$, where $u = f(x)$ is a differentiable function of x,

$$\frac{dy}{dx} = c\frac{du}{dx}$$

EXAMPLE

If $y = 10x$, $\dfrac{dy}{dx} = 10$.

EXAMPLE

If $y = 3x^2$, $\dfrac{dy}{dx} = (3)(2x) = 6x$

EXAMPLE

If $y = -2x^{4/3}$, $\dfrac{dy}{dx} = (-2)(\tfrac{4}{3})x^{1/3} = -\tfrac{8}{3}x^{1/3}$

EXAMPLE

If $y = -3x^{-1}$, $\dfrac{dy}{dx} = (-3)(-1)x^{-2} = 3x^{-2} = \dfrac{3}{x^2}$

Rule 4.   The derivative of the sum of a finite number of differentiable functions is the sum of their derivatives: If $y = u + v$, where $u = f(x)$ and $v = g(x)$ are differentiable functions of x,

$$\frac{dy}{dx} = \frac{du}{dx} + \frac{dv}{dx}$$

In general, if $y = \sum_{i=1}^{n} u_i$, where $u_i = f_i(x)$ are differentiable functions of x for $i = 1$, $2, \ldots, n$, then

$$\frac{dy}{dx} = \sum_{i=1}^{n} \frac{du_i}{dx}$$

EXAMPLE

If $y = 3x^2 + 4x + 2$, $\dfrac{dy}{dx} = 3\dfrac{d}{dx}(x^2) + 4\dfrac{d}{dx}(x) + \dfrac{d}{dx}(2) = (3)(2x) + (4)(1) + 0 = 6x + 4$

EXAMPLE

If $y = 5x^{1/2} + 3x^{1/4} + 7$, $\dfrac{dy}{dx} = 5\dfrac{d}{dx}(x^{1/2}) + 3\dfrac{d}{dx}(x^{1/4}) + \dfrac{d}{dx}(7) = \tfrac{5}{2}x^{-1/2} + \tfrac{3}{4}x^{-3/4}$

EXAMPLE

If $y = 10 - 6x^{-1/2}$, $\dfrac{dy}{dx} = \dfrac{d}{dx}(10) - 6\dfrac{d}{dx}(x^{-1/2}) = -(-\tfrac{1}{2})(6)x^{-3/2} = 3x^{-3/2}$

EXAMPLE

If $y = 6x^5 + x^4 + 2x^{3/2} + 5$, $\dfrac{dy}{dx} = 6\dfrac{d}{dx}(x^5) + \dfrac{d}{dx}(x^4) + 2\dfrac{d}{dx}(x^{3/2}) = 30x^4 + 4x^3 + 3x^{1/2}$

Rule for Differentiation of Polynomial Functions

These four rules for differentiation can be summarized and generalized as the rule for differentiation of polynomial functions. A single term of the form cx^n, where c is a constant and n is zero or a positive integer, is called a *monomial* in x. A function that is the sum of a finite number of such monomial terms is called a *polynomial* or a *polynomial function* in x.

The derivative of a monomial in x is

$$\frac{d}{dx}(cx^n) = cnx^{n-1}$$

and the derivative of the sum of a finite number of such terms (that is, the derivative of a polynomial) is the sum of the derivatives of the terms:

$$\frac{d}{dx}\left(\sum_{i=1}^{n} c_i x^{n_i}\right) = \sum_{i=1}^{n} c_i n_i x^{n_i - 1}$$

PROBLEMS

Find the first derivative with respect to x for each of the following functions $y = f(x)$.

1. $y = 6x + 2$
2. $y = x^3 + x$
3. $y = 4x^2 + 2x$
4. $y = x^{1/2} + 4$
5. $y = 3x^2 - x^{1/3} + 2$
6. $y = 5x^{-1/3} + 5$

7. $y = 5x^{3/5} + 6x$
8. $y = 7x^2 + 8x^{-1/2} + 2$
9. $y = 9x^3 + 5x^{-1/4}$
10. $y = 10x^4 + 2x^{5/4}$
11. $y = 12x^{3/2} + 6x^{1/2} + 2$
12. $y = x^5 + 3x^{-7/3} + 5$

Answers to Odd-Numbered Problems

1. 6
3. $8x + 2$
5. $6x - \frac{1}{3}x^{-2/3}$

7. $3x^{-2/5} + 6$
9. $27x^2 - \frac{5}{4}x^{-5/4}$
11. $18x^{1/2} + 3x^{-1/2}$

Rule 5. The derivative of the product of two differentiable functions is equal to the first function times the derivative of the second function plus the second function times the derivative of the first function. Similarly, the product of more than two differentiable functions is the sum of the products of the derivative of each function and the other functions. If $y = uv$, where $u = f(x)$ and $v = g(x)$ are differentiable functions of x,

$$\frac{dy}{dx} = u\frac{dv}{dx} + v\frac{du}{dx}$$

In general, if $y = \prod_{i=1}^{n} u_i$, where $u_i = f_i(x)$ are differentiable functions of x for $i = 1$, 2, ..., n, then

$$\frac{d}{dx}\left(\prod_{i=1}^{n} u_i\right) = \sum_{i=1}^{n} \left[f_i'(x) \prod_{\substack{j=1 \\ j \neq i}}^{n} u_j \right]$$

EXAMPLE

If $y = (x^3 + 4)(x + 3)$, let $u = x^3 + 4$ and $v = x + 3$; then $y = u \cdot v$ and

$$\frac{dy}{dx}(uv) = u\frac{dv}{dx} + v\frac{du}{dx}$$

$$\frac{du}{dx} = 3x^2$$

$$\frac{dv}{dx} = 1(x^{1-1}) = 1$$

$$\frac{dy}{dx} = (x^3 + 4)(1) + (x + 3)(3x^2)$$

$$= x^3 + 4 + 3x^3 + 9x^2$$

$$= 4x^3 + 9x^2 + 4$$

EXAMPLE

If $y = (\sqrt{x} + 3)(x^2 + 6)$, let $u = \sqrt{x} + 3$ and $v = x^2 + 6$; then $y = u \cdot v$ and

$$\frac{dy}{dx}(uv) = u\frac{dv}{dx} + v\frac{du}{dx}$$

$$\frac{du}{dx} = \tfrac{1}{2}x^{-1/2}$$

$$\frac{dv}{dx} = 2x$$

$$\frac{dy}{dx} = (\sqrt{x} + 3)(2x) + (x^2 + 6)(\tfrac{1}{2}x^{-1/2})$$

$$= 2x^{3/2} + 6x + \tfrac{1}{2}x^{3/2} + 3x^{-1/2}$$

$$= \tfrac{5}{2}x^{3/2} + 6x + 3x^{-1/2}$$

EXAMPLE

If $y = (3x + 7)(x^{-2} + 8)$,

$$\frac{d}{dx}(3x + 1) = 3$$

$$\frac{d}{dx}(x^{-2} + 8) = -2x^{-3}$$

and

$$\frac{dy}{dx} = (3x + 7)(-2x^{-3}) + (x^{-2} + 8)(3)$$

$$= -6x^{-2} - 14x^{-3} + 3x^{-2} + 24$$

$$= -3x^{-2} - 14x^{-3} + 24$$

EXAMPLE

If $y = (x + 3)(2x + 3)(x^2 + 1)$,

$$\frac{d}{dx}(x + 3) = 1$$

$$\frac{d}{dx}(2x + 3) = 2$$

$$\frac{d}{dx}(x^2 + 1) = 2x$$

and

$$\frac{dy}{dx} = (1)(2x + 3)(x^2 + 1) + (2)(x + 3)(x^2 + 1) + (2x)(x + 3)(2x + 3)$$

$$= (4x + 9)(x^2 + 1) + 2x(2x^2 + 9x + 9)$$

$$= 4x^3 + 9x^2 + 4x + 9 + 4x^3 + 18x^2 + 18x$$

$$= 8x^3 + 27x^2 + 22x + 9$$

Rule 6. The derivative of the quotient of two differentiable functions is the quotient of the product of the denominator and the derivative of the numerator minus the product of the numerator and the derivative of the denominator divided by the square of the denominator: If $y = u/v$, where $u = f(x)$ and $v = g(x)$ are differentiable functions of x,

$$\frac{dy}{dx} = \frac{v\dfrac{du}{dx} - u\dfrac{dv}{dx}}{v^2}$$

EXAMPLE

If $y = \dfrac{x^2 - 4x + 1}{x - 6}$,

$$u = x^2 - 4x + 1 \qquad v = x - 6$$

$$\frac{du}{dx} = 2x - 4 \qquad \frac{dv}{dx} = 1$$

and

$$\frac{dy}{dx} = \frac{(x-6)(2x-4) - (x^2 - 4x + 1)(1)}{(x-6)^2}$$

$$= \frac{2x^2 - 16x + 24 - x^2 + 4x - 1}{(x-6)^2}$$

$$= \frac{x^2 - 12x + 23}{(x-6)^2}$$

EXAMPLE

If $y = \dfrac{4}{x^6}$,

$$u = 4 \qquad v = x^6$$

$$\frac{du}{dx} = 0 \qquad \frac{dv}{dx} = 6x^5$$

and

$$\frac{dy}{dx} = \frac{(x^6)(0) - 4(6x^5)}{(x^6)^2}$$

$$= \frac{-24x^5}{x^{12}}$$

$$= \frac{-24}{x^7}$$

NOTE: This example could be solved quickly using Rule 2, as follows:

$$y = 4x^{-6}$$

$$\frac{dy}{dx} = -24x^{-7}$$

$$= \frac{-24}{x^7}$$

EXAMPLE

If $y = \dfrac{x^3 + 16}{x^2}$,

$$\frac{d}{dx}(x^3 + 16) = 3x^2$$

$$\frac{d}{dx}(x^2) = 2x$$

and

$$\frac{dy}{dx} = \frac{(x^2)(3x^2) - (x^3 + 16)(2x)}{x^4}$$

$$= \frac{3x^4 - 2x^4 - 32x}{x^4}$$

$$= \frac{x^4 - 32x}{x^4}$$

$$= \frac{x^3 - 32}{x^3}$$

NOTE: This example could also be solved more quickly using Rule 2, as follows:

$$y = x + 16x^{-2}$$

$$\frac{dy}{dx} = 1 - 32x^{-3}$$

$$= 1 - \frac{32}{x^3}$$

$$= \frac{x^3 - 32}{x^3}$$

As illustrated in the preceding examples, there are frequently several ways of obtaining the derivative of a function, and they may differ considerably in convenience. With practice, it is usually possible to identify the most convenient method of differentiating a function of a particular form.

EXAMPLE

If $y = \dfrac{x^3 + 3x + 15}{x^2 + 2x + 2}$,

$$\frac{d}{dx}(x^3 + 3x + 15) = 3x^2 + 3$$

$$\frac{d}{dx}(x^2 + 2x + 2) = 2x + 2$$

and

$$\frac{dy}{dx} = \frac{(x^2 + 2x + 2)(3x^2 + 3) - (x^3 + 3x + 15)(2x + 2)}{(x^2 + 2x + 2)^2}$$

$$= \frac{3x^4 + 6x^3 + 6x^2 + 3x^2 + 6x + 6 - 2x^4 - 6x^2 - 30x - 2x^3 - 6x - 30}{(x^2 + 2x + 2)^2}$$

$$= \frac{x^4 + 4x^3 + 3x^2 - 30x - 24}{(x^2 + 2x + 2)^2}$$

COMPOSITE FUNCTIONS

If y is a function of u and u is a function of x, then y is a function of a function or a *composite function*; the derivative of y with respect to x is the product of the derivative of y with respect to u and the derivative of u with respect to x.

Rule 7.　If $y = g(u)$ and $u = h(x)$, that is, $y = g[h(x)] = f(x)$,

$$\frac{dy}{dx} = \frac{dy}{du} \cdot \frac{du}{dx}$$

(This is sometimes called the *chain rule of differentiation*.)

Note that Rules 8, 9, 10, 11, 12, 13, and 14 are special cases of Rule 7.

EXAMPLE

If $y = (x^2 + 1)^{2/3}$, find $\dfrac{dy}{dx}$.

Let $u = x^2 + 1$; then $y = u^{2/3}$

$$\frac{dy}{dx} = \frac{dy}{du} \cdot \frac{du}{dx}$$

$$\frac{dy}{du} = \tfrac{2}{3}u^{-1/3}$$

$$\frac{du}{dx} = 2x$$

$$\frac{dy}{dx} = (\tfrac{2}{3}u^{-1/3})(2x) = \tfrac{2}{3}(x^2 + 1)^{-1/3}(2x)$$

$$= \frac{4x}{3(x^2 + 1)^{1/3}}$$

EXAMPLE

If $y = \dfrac{z^2}{z^2 + 1}$ and $z = \sqrt{2u + 1}$, find $\dfrac{dy}{du}$.

$$\frac{dy}{du} = \frac{dy}{dz} \cdot \frac{dz}{du}$$

$$\frac{dy}{dz} = \frac{2z(z^2 + 1) - z^2(2z)}{(z^2 + 1)^2}$$

$$= \frac{2z}{(z^2 + 1)^2}$$

$$= \frac{2\sqrt{2u + 1}}{(2u + 2)^2}$$

$$= \frac{\sqrt{2u + 1}}{2(u + 1)^2}$$

$$\frac{dz}{du} = \tfrac{1}{2}(2u + 1)^{-1/2}(2)$$

$$= \frac{1}{\sqrt{2u + 1}}$$

$$\frac{dy}{du} = \frac{dy}{dz} \cdot \frac{dz}{du} = \frac{1}{2(u + 1)^2}$$

Alternatively,

$$y = \frac{z^2}{z^2 + 1} = \frac{2u + 1}{2u + 2}$$

$$\frac{dy}{dx} = \frac{2(2u + 2) - (2u + 1)(2)}{(2u + 2)^2}$$

$$= \frac{2}{(2u + 2)^2}$$

$$= \frac{1}{2(u + 1)^2}$$

EXAMPLE

If $y = \dfrac{x}{x + 1}$ and $x = 3u^2$, find $\dfrac{dy}{du}$.

$$\frac{dy}{dx} = \frac{(x + 1) - x}{(x + 1)^2} = \frac{1}{(x + 1)^2}$$

$$= \frac{1}{(3u^2 + 1)^2}$$

$$\frac{dx}{du} = 6u$$

$$\frac{dy}{du} = \frac{dy}{dx} \cdot \frac{dx}{du} = \frac{6u}{(3u^2 + 1)^2}$$

Alternatively,

$$y = \frac{x}{x + 1} = \frac{3u^2}{3u^2 + 1}$$

$$\frac{dy}{du} = \frac{6u(3u^2 + 1) - 3u^2(6u)}{(3u^2 + 1)^2}$$

$$= \frac{6u}{(3u^2 + 1)^2}$$

Rule 8.   The derivative of the nth power of a differentiable function is the product of n, the $(n - 1)$st power of the function, and the derivative of the function: If $y = u^n$, where $u = f(x)$ is a differentiable function of x and n is any real number (positive or negative, integer or noninteger),

$$\frac{dy}{dx} = nu^{n-1} \frac{du}{dx}$$

Special Case: If $u = f(x) = x$, then $u^n = x^n$ and

$$\frac{dy}{dx} = nu^{n-1} = nx^{n-1}$$

which is Rule 2.

EXAMPLE

If $y = (x^2 + 3)^3$,

$$\frac{d}{dx}(u^n) = nu^{n-1} \frac{du}{dx}$$

$$u = (x^2 + 3)$$

$$n = 3$$

$$\frac{du}{dx} = 2x$$

and

$$\frac{dy}{dx} = 3(x^2 + 3)^2(2x)$$

$$= 6x(x^2 + 3)^2$$

EXAMPLE

If $y = (x + 3)^{-1/3}$,

$$\frac{d}{dx}(u^n) = nu^{n-1}\frac{du}{dx}$$

$$u = (x + 3)$$

$$n = -\tfrac{1}{3}$$

$$\frac{du}{dx} = 1$$

and

$$\frac{dy}{dx} = (-\tfrac{1}{3})(x + 3)^{-4/3}(1)$$

$$= \frac{-1}{3(x + 3)^{4/3}}$$

EXAMPLE

If $y = [(x + 1)/(x - 1)]^2$,

$$\frac{dy}{dx}(u^n) = nu^{n-1}\frac{du}{dx}$$

but note that $u = (x + 1)/(x - 1)$ is a fraction and thus Rule 6 gives $\frac{du}{dx}$.

$$\frac{du}{dx} = \frac{(x - 1)(1) - (x + 1)(1)}{(x - 1)^2}$$

$$= \frac{-2}{(x - 1)^2}$$

and

$$\frac{dy}{dx} = 2\left(\frac{x + 1}{x - 1}\right)\left(\frac{-2}{(x - 1)^2}\right)$$

$$= \frac{-4(x + 1)}{(x - 1)^3}$$

EXAMPLE

If $y = (x + 1)^2(x^2 + 1)^{-3}$,

$$\frac{dy}{dx}(uv) = u\frac{dv}{dx} + v\frac{du}{dx}$$

note that $u = (x + 1)^2$ and $v = (x^2 + 1)^{-3}$ and thus Rule 8 must be used to obtain $\frac{du}{dx}$ and $\frac{dv}{dx}$.

$$\frac{d}{dx}(x + 1)^2 = 2(x + 1)$$

$$\frac{d}{dx}(x^2 + 1)^{-3} = -3(x^2 + 1)^{-4}(2x)$$

$$= -6x(x^2 + 1)^{-4}$$

and

$$\frac{dy}{dx} = (x + 1)^2(-6x)(x^2 + 1)^{-4} + (x^2 + 1)^{-3}(2)(x + 1)$$

$$= (x + 1)(x^2 + 1)^{-4}[-6x(x + 1) + 2(x^2 + 1)]$$

$$= (x + 1)(x^2 + 1)^{-4}(-4x^2 - 6x + 2)$$

$$= -2(x + 1)(2x^2 + 3x - 1)(x^2 + 1)^{-4}$$

$$= \frac{-2(x + 1)(2x^2 + 3x - 1)}{(x^2 + 1)^4}$$

EXAMPLE

If $y = (x^2 - x)^{-2}$,

$$\frac{dy}{dx} = -2(x^2 - x)^{-3}(2x - 1)$$

$$= -\frac{2(2x - 1)}{(x^2 - x)^3}$$

$$= \frac{2(1 - 2x)}{x^3(x - 1)^3}$$

EXAMPLE

If $y = x^2(x + 1)^{-1}$,

$$\frac{dy}{dx} = 2x(x + 1)^{-1} + x^2(-1)(x + 1)^{-2}$$

$$= (x + 1)^{-2}[2x(x + 1) - x^2]$$

$$= (x + 1)^{-2}(2x^2 + 2x - x^2)$$

$$= (x + 1)^{-2}(x^2 + 2x)$$

$$= \frac{x(x + 2)}{(x + 1)^2}$$

EXAMPLE

If $y = (x + x^{-1})^2$,

$$\frac{dy}{dx} = 2(x + x^{-1})(1 - x^{-2})$$

$$= 2(x - x^{-1} + x^{-1} - x^{-3})$$

$$= 2(x - x^{-3})$$

$$= 2x^{-3}(x^4 - 1)$$

$$= \frac{2(x^4 - 1)}{x^3}$$

EXAMPLE

If $y = 2x(3x^2 + 1)^{-1}$,

$$\frac{dy}{dx} = 2(3x^2 + 1)^{-1} + 2x(-1)(3x^2 + 1)^{-2}(6x)$$

$$= 2(3x^2 + 1)^{-2}(3x^2 + 1 - 6x^2)$$

$$= 2(3x^2 + 1)^{-2}(1 - 3x^2)$$

$$= \frac{2(1 - 3x^2)}{(3x^2 + 1)^2}$$

PROBLEMS

Find the first derivative with respect to x for each of the following functions $y = f(x)$.

1. $y = 2x^3 + 4x^2 - 5x + 8$

2. $y = -5 + 3x - \frac{3}{2}x^2 - 7x^3$

3. $y = (2x^2 + 4x - 5)^6$

4. $y = \frac{1}{5}x^{5/2} + \frac{1}{3}x^{3/2}$

5. $y = (1 - x^2)^{1/2}$

6. $y = \frac{6}{x} + \frac{4}{x^2} - \frac{3}{x^3}$

7. $y = (x^3 - 3x)^4$

8. $y = (x + x^{-1})^2$

9. $y = (x - 1)^3(x + 2)^4$

10. $y = (x + 2)^2(2 - x)^3$

11. $y = (x + 1)^2(x^2 + 1)^{-3}$

12. $y = \frac{2x + 1}{x^2 - 1}$

13. $y = \frac{x}{x^2 + 1}$

14. $y = \left(\frac{x + 1}{x - 1}\right)^2$

15. $y = (x^2 - x)^{-2}$

16. $y = x^2(x + 1)^{-1}$

17. $y = \frac{1}{(x^2 - 9)^{1/2}}$

18. $y = \frac{1}{(16 - x^2)^{1/2}}$

19. $y = \frac{x}{(x + 1)^{1/2}}$

20. $y = \frac{(x^2 + 2)^{1/2}}{x}$

21. $y = \frac{2x}{(x^5 + 10)^{1/8}}$

22. $y = (x + 2)^3(x^2 + 1)^{-1}$

23. $y = \left(\frac{x^2 + 10}{x}\right)^{10}$

24. $y = \dfrac{3}{(x^3 - 4)^{2/3}}$

25. $y = \dfrac{(x^2 + 1)^{1/2}}{(2x + 4)^{1/4}}$

26. $y = (x + 2)^{-3/2}(3x^2 + 1)$

27. $y = x^3(x^2 + 3)^{-1}$

28. $y = x^6 + x^{4/3} + 6x^{1/2}$

29. If $u = x^2$ and $x = \dfrac{y}{(y + 1)^2}$, find $\dfrac{du}{dy}$.

30. If $y = \dfrac{x}{x + 2}$ and $x = u^3 - 5$, find $\dfrac{dy}{du}$.

31. If $v = y^{-3}$ and $y = x^2 + 2x$, find $\dfrac{dv}{dx}$.

32. If $x = y^3 + 2y - 1$ and $y = v^{-1/2}$, find $\dfrac{dx}{dv}$.

33. If $y = v^{-1/2}$ and $v = x^2 + 5$, find $\dfrac{dy}{dx}$.

34. If $x = \dfrac{3y - 1}{y + 7}$ and $y = u^2 - 5u$, find $\dfrac{dx}{du}$.

Answers to Odd-Numbered Problems

1. $6x^2 + 8x - 5$

3. $24(x + 1)(2x^2 + 4x - 5)^5$

5. $-x(1 - x^2)^{-1/2}$

7. $12x^3(x^2 - 1)(x^2 - 3)^3$

9. $(x - 1)^2(x + 2)^3(7x + 2)$

11. $-2(x + 1)(x^2 + 1)^{-4}(2x^2 + 3x - 1)$

13. $\dfrac{1 - x^2}{(x^2 + 1)^2}$

15. $-2x^{-3}(x - 1)^{-3}(2x - 1)$

17. $-x(x^2 - 9)^{-3/2}$

19. $\dfrac{x + 2}{2(x + 1)^{3/2}}$

21. $(x^5 + 10)^{-9/8}(\tfrac{3}{4}x^5 + 20)$

23. $10\left(\dfrac{x^2 - 10}{x^2}\right)\left(\dfrac{x^2 + 10}{x}\right)^9$

25. $\tfrac{1}{2}(x^2 + 1)^{-1/2}(2x + 4)^{-5/4}(3x^2 + 8x - 1)$

27. $x^2(x^2 + 9)(x^2 + 3)^{-2}$

29. $\dfrac{2y(1 - y)}{(y + 1)^5}$

31. $-\dfrac{6(x + 1)}{x^2(x + 2)^2}$

33. $-x(x^2 + 5)^{-3/2}$

LOGARITHMIC FUNCTIONS

The notation "log" denotes common logarithm (base 10). The notation "ln" denotes natural logarithm; the base of the natural logarithms is defined by $e = \lim_{n \to \infty}(1 + (1/n))^n$, and is approximately 2.718. If any other base is meant, it is specified.

Rule 9. If $y = \log_a u$, where $u = f(x)$ is a differentiable function of x,

$$\frac{dy}{dx} = \frac{\log_a e}{u}\frac{du}{dx}$$

EXAMPLE

If $y = \log\left(\dfrac{x}{x + 1}\right)$,

$$\frac{d}{dx}\left(\frac{x}{x + 1}\right) = \frac{(x + 1) - x}{(x + 1)^2} \qquad \text{(Rule 6)}$$

$$= \frac{1}{(x + 1)^2}$$

and

$$\frac{dy}{dx} = \frac{\log e}{\left(\dfrac{x}{x+1}\right)} \left(\frac{1}{(x+1)^2}\right)$$

$$= \frac{\log e}{x(x+1)}$$

EXAMPLE

If $y = \sqrt{\log x}$,

$$\frac{dy}{dx} = \frac{1}{2}(\log x)^{-1/2}\left(\frac{\log e}{x}\right)$$

$$= \frac{\log e}{2x\sqrt{\log x}}$$

EXAMPLE

If $y = (\log x^2)^3$,

$$\frac{dy}{dx} = 3(\log x^2)^2 \left(\frac{\log e}{x^2}\right)(2x)$$

$$= \frac{6(\log x^2)^2 \log e}{x}$$

SPECIAL CASE: If $y = \ln u$, where $u = f(x)$ is a differential function of x,

$$\frac{dy}{dx} = \frac{1}{u}\frac{du}{dx}$$

since $\ln e = 1$.

EXAMPLE

If $y = \frac{1}{2} \ln (x^2 + 1)$,

$$\frac{d}{dx}(x^2 - 1)^{1/2} = \frac{1}{2}(x^2 - 1)^{-1/2}(2x)$$

$$= x(x^2 - 1)^{-1/2}$$

and

$$\frac{dy}{dx} = (x^2 - 1)^{-1/2}(\tfrac{1}{2})(x^2 - 1)^{-1/2}(2x)$$

$$= \frac{x}{x^2 - 1}$$

EXAMPLE

If $y = \dfrac{\ln x}{x}$,

$$\frac{d}{dx}(\ln x) = \frac{1}{x}$$

and

$$\frac{dy}{dx} = \frac{\left(\dfrac{1}{x}\right)x - \ln x}{x^2}$$

(Rule 6)

$$= \frac{1 - \ln x}{x^2}$$

EXAMPLE

If $y = \ln\left(x + \sqrt{x^2 + 4}\right)$,

$$\frac{d}{dx}\left(x + \sqrt{x^2 + 4}\right) = 1 + \tfrac{1}{2}(x^2 + 4)^{-1/2}(2x)$$

$$= 1 + x(x^2 + 4)^{-1/2}$$

and

$$\frac{dy}{dx} = \frac{1}{x + \sqrt{x^2 + 4}}\left[1 + x(x^2 + 4)^{-1/2}\right]$$

$$= \frac{1 + \dfrac{x}{\sqrt{x^2 + 4}}}{x + \sqrt{x^2 + 4}}$$

$$= \frac{\dfrac{x + \sqrt{x^2 + 4}}{\sqrt{x^2 + 4}}}{x + \sqrt{x^2 + 4}}$$

$$= \frac{1}{\sqrt{x^2 + 4}}$$

EXPONENTIAL FUNCTIONS

Rule 10.   If $y = a^u$, where $u = f(x)$ is a differentiable function of x,

$$\frac{dy}{dx} = a^u \ln a \, \frac{du}{dx}$$

EXAMPLE

If $y = 2^{-x}$,

$$\frac{dy}{dx} = 2^{-x}(\ln 2)(-1)$$

$$= -2^{-x}\ln 2$$

EXAMPLE

If $y = 10^{x^2-x}$,

$$\frac{dy}{dx} = 10^{x^2-x}(\ln 10)(2x - 1)$$

$$= (2x - 1)10^{x^2-x} \ln 10$$

EXAMPLE

If $y = a^x x^a$,

$$\frac{dy}{dx} = a^x(\ln a)x^a + a^x(ax^{a-1})$$

$$= a^x x^{a-1}(a + x \ln a)$$

SPECIAL CASE. If $y = e^u$, where $u = f(x)$ is a differentiable function of x,

$$\frac{dy}{dx} = e^u \frac{du}{dx}$$

since $\ln e = 1$

EXAMPLE

If $y = \dfrac{e^x}{x}$,

$$\frac{dy}{dx} = \frac{xe^x - e^x}{x^2}$$

$$= \frac{e^x(x - 1)}{x^2}$$

EXAMPLE

If $y = 10e^{x^2+4}$,

$$\frac{dy}{dx} = 10e^{x^2+4}(2x)$$

$$= 20xe^{x^2+4}$$

EXAMPLE

If $y = \dfrac{e^x - e^{-x}}{e^x + e^{-x}}$,

$$\frac{d}{dx}(e^x - e^{-x}) = e^x + e^{-x}$$

$$\frac{d}{dx}(e^x + e^{-x}) = e^x - e^{-x}$$

and

$$\frac{dy}{dx} = \frac{(e^x + e^{-x})^2 - (e^x - e^{-x})^2}{(e^x + e^{-x})^2}$$

$$= \frac{e^{2x} + 2 + e^{-2x} - e^{2x} + 2 - e^{-2x}}{(e^x + e^{-x})^2} = \frac{4}{(e^x + e^{-x})^2}$$

Rule 11. If $y = u^v$, where $u = f(x)$ and $v = g(x)$ are differentiable functions of x, differentiate $\ln y = v \ln u$ to obtain

$$\frac{dy}{dx} = vu^{v-1} \frac{du}{dx} + u^v \ln u \frac{dv}{dx}$$

Rule 11 can be obtained by noting that $u = e^{\ln u} \Rightarrow u^v = e^{v \ln u}$ and using the special case of Rule 9. If $y = u^v = e^{v \ln u}$, then

$$\frac{du}{dx} = \frac{d}{dx} (e^{v \ln u}) = e^{v \ln u} \left(\ln u \frac{dv}{dx} + \frac{v}{u} \frac{du}{dx} \right)$$

$$= u^v \left(\ln u \frac{dv}{dx} + \frac{v}{u} \frac{du}{dx} \right)$$

$$= vu^{v-1} \frac{du}{dx} + u^v \ln u \frac{dv}{dx}$$

Note that Rule 10 is a special case of Rule 11, where $u = a$. Some algebraic functions are also easier to differentiate if the logarithm of each side is differentiated and the resulting equation is solved for the derivative of the function. (See the fourth example below.)

EXAMPLE

If $y = x^{x^2}$,

$$\ln y = x^2 \ln x$$

$$\frac{1}{y} \frac{dy}{dx} = 2x \ln x + x^2 \left(\frac{1}{x}\right)$$

$$= x(2 \ln x + 1)$$

$$\frac{dy}{dx} = x^{x^2+1}(1 + 2 \ln x)$$

EXAMPLE

If $y = x^{e^x}$,

$$\ln y = e^x \ln x$$

$$\frac{1}{y} \frac{dy}{dx} = e^x \ln x + e^x \left(\frac{1}{x}\right)$$

$$= e^x \left(\ln x + \frac{1}{x} \right)$$

$$\frac{dy}{dx} = x^{e^x} e^x \left(\frac{1}{x} + \ln x \right)$$

EXAMPLE

If $y = (x^4 + 5)^{x^2}$,

$\ln y = x^2 \ln (x^4 + 5)$

$\dfrac{1}{y}\dfrac{dy}{dx} = 2x \ln (x^4 + 5) + x^2\left(\dfrac{4x^3}{x^4 + 5}\right)$

$\qquad = 2x\left[\ln (x^4 + 5) + \dfrac{2x^4}{x^4 + 5}\right]$

$\qquad = (x^4 + 5)^{x^2}(2x)\left[\ln (x^4 + 5) + \dfrac{2x^4}{x^4 + 5}\right]$

$\dfrac{dy}{dx} = 2x(x^4 + 5)^{x^2-1}[(x^4 + 5) \ln (x^4 + 5) + 2x^4]$

EXAMPLE

If $y = \sqrt[3]{\dfrac{x + 1}{x - 1}}$,

$\ln y = \tfrac{1}{3} \ln (x + 1) - \tfrac{1}{3} \ln (x - 1)$

$\dfrac{1}{y}\dfrac{dy}{dx} = \dfrac{1}{3(x + 1)} - \dfrac{1}{3(x - 1)}$

$\qquad = \dfrac{x - 1 - (x + 1)}{3(x^2 - 1)}$

$\qquad = \dfrac{-2}{3(x^2 - 1)}$

$\dfrac{dy}{dx} = \dfrac{-2}{3(x^2 - 1)}\left(\dfrac{x + 1}{x - 1}\right)^{1/3}$

PROBLEMS

Find the first derivative of each of the following functions.

1. $y = \log(1 - 2t)$

2. $y = \ln \left(\dfrac{1 - 4x}{1 + 4x}\right)$

3. $R = \log_a (a^2 - x^2)^3$

4. $t = 6^{-2u}$

5. $y = e^x \ln x$

6. $y = \dfrac{\sqrt{x + 1}}{\sqrt[3]{x + 2}}$

7. $t = e^{\ln x}$

8. $y = a^x e^x$

9. $y = \log (x^3 - 3x)^{1/3}$

10. $y = t^2 \ln t$

11. $y = 2 \ln \left(\sqrt{\dfrac{1 - t^2}{t}}\right)$

12. $y = 25^{3x^3 - 6}$

13. $y = e^{-1/x}$

14. $y = x^{x^3}$

15. $y = x^{e^{x^2 + 1}}$

16. $y = \dfrac{(x + 1)^6}{(x^2 + 2x + 2)^3}$

17. $y = 2x^2 e^{x^2 + 3}$

18. $y = \log_5 (x^3 + x^2)^6$

19. $y = x^{2x^4 + x}$

20. $y = \log_b (b - x^3)^2$

21. $y = \left(\dfrac{x + 3}{x - 1}\right)^2$

22. $y = e^{\ln x^2}$

23. $y = 16^{x^2 - 2x}$

24. $y = x^{x^4}$

25. $y = e^{x^2 + 4x + 3}$

26. $y = e^{\ln(x + 3)}$

27. $y = \log_8 (6 - x^2)^4$

28. $y = x^{x^3 + 2}$

29. $y = 2 \ln (x^3 + 4x^2)^{1/4}$

30. $y = (x^2 + 4)^2 e^{x^2 + 1}$

31. $y = \frac{1}{3} e^{3 \ln x}$

32. $y = x e^{\ln (x^2 + 5)}$

33. $y = x^2 e^{x^2 + 4x + 2}$

34. $y = e^{\ln (x^4 + 3x^2 + 10)}$

35. $y = (x + 1)^x$

36. $y = (x + 1)^{x^3 + 1}$

Answers to Odd-Numbered Problems

1. $\dfrac{-2 \log e}{1 - 2t}$

3. $\dfrac{6x \log_a e}{x^2 - a^2}$

5. $\dfrac{e^x}{x}(1 + x \ln x)$

7. 1

9. $\dfrac{(x^2 - 1) \log e}{x(x^2 - 3)}$

11. $\dfrac{t^2 + 1}{t(t^2 - 1)}$

13. $\dfrac{1}{x^2} e^{-1/x}$

15. $x^{e^{x^2 + 1}}(e^{x^2 + 1})\left(\dfrac{1}{x} + 2x \ln x\right)$

17. $4x(x^2 + 1)e^{x^2 + 3}$

19. $x^{2x^4 + x}[2x^3 + 1 + (8x^3 + 1) \ln x]$

21. $\dfrac{-8(x + 3)}{(x - 1)^3}$

23. $2(x - 1)16^{x^2 - 2x} \ln 16$

25. $(2x + 4)e^{x^2 + 4x + 3}$

27. $\dfrac{-8x \log_8 e}{6 - x^2}$

29. $\dfrac{3x + 8}{2(x^2 + 4x)}$

31. x^2

33. $2x(x + 1)^2 e^{x^2 + 4x + 2}$

35. $(x + 1)^{x - 1}[x + (x + 1) \ln (x + 1)]$

TRIGONOMETRIC FUNCTIONS

Note that the rules in this section apply when angles are measured in radians.
Rule 12.   If $y = \sin u$, where $u = f(x)$ is a differentiable function of x,

$$\frac{dy}{dx} = \cos u \, \frac{du}{dx}$$

EXAMPLE

If $y = \sin (x^2 + \theta)$,

$$\frac{dy}{dx} = 2x \cos (x^2 + \theta)$$

EXAMPLE

If $y = \sin^2 3x$, using both the chain rule and Rule 12,

$$\frac{dy}{dx} = 2(\sin 3x)(\cos 3x)(3)$$

$$= 6 \sin 3x \cos 3x$$

Rule 13. If $y = \cos u$, where $u = f(x)$ is a differentiable function of x,

$$\frac{dy}{dx} = -\sin u \frac{du}{dx}$$

Rule 14. If $y = \tan u$, where $u = f(x)$ is a differentiable function of x,

$$\frac{dy}{dx} = \sec^2 u \frac{du}{dx}$$

Similarly,

$$y = \csc u = \frac{1}{\sin u}$$

$$y = \sec u = \frac{1}{\cos u}$$

$$y = \cot u = \frac{1}{\tan u}$$

can be differentiated to obtain the derivatives of the cosecant, secant, and cotangent functions.

$$\frac{d}{dx}(\csc u) = -\csc u \cot u \frac{du}{dx}$$

$$\frac{d}{dx}(\sec u) = \sec u \tan u \frac{du}{dx}$$

$$\frac{d}{dx}(\cot u) = -\csc^2 u \frac{du}{dx}$$

EXAMPLE

If $y = \cos x + \sec x$,

$$\frac{dy}{dx} = -\sin x + \sec x \tan x$$

$$= -\sin x + \sin x \sec^2 x$$

$$= \sin x(\sec^2 x - 1)$$

$$= \sin x \tan^2 x$$

EXAMPLE

If $y = (1 + \cot x)^2$,

$$\frac{dy}{dx} = 2(1 + \cot x)(-\csc^2 x)$$

$$= -2 \csc^2 x(1 + \cot x)$$

EXAMPLE

If $y = \tan^2 (x + 3) + \sec^2 (x + 3)$,

$$\frac{dy}{dx} = 2 \tan (x + 3) \sec^2 (x + 3) + 2 \sec^2 (x + 3) \tan (x + 3)$$

$$= 4 \tan (x + 3) \sec^2 (x + 3)$$

EXAMPLE

If $y = (\sin x + \cos x)^2$,

$$\frac{dy}{dx} = 2(\sin x + \cos x)(\cos x - \sin x)$$

$$= 2(\cos^2 x - \sin^2 x)$$

$$= 2 \cos 2x$$

Alternatively,

$$y = \sin^2 x + \cos^2 x + 2 \sin x \cos x$$

$$= 1 + \sin 2x$$

$$\frac{dy}{dx} = 2 \cos 2x$$

EXAMPLE

If $y = \dfrac{\cot (x^2 + 2)}{\sec (x^2 + 2)}$,

$$\frac{dy}{dx} = \frac{-2x \csc^2 (x + 2) \sec (x^2 + 2) - 2x \cot (x^2 + 2) \sec (x^2 + 2) \tan (x^2 + 2)}{\sec^2 (x^2 + 2)}$$

$$= \frac{-2x \csc^2 (x + 2) - 2x}{\sec (x^2 + 2)}$$

$$= \frac{-2x[\csc^2 (x + 2) + 1]}{\sec (x^2 + 2)}$$

EXAMPLE

If $y = \tan (x^3 + 2x + 3) \sin (x^3 + 2x + 3)$,

$$\frac{dy}{dx} = (3x^2 + 2) \sec^2 (x^3 + 2x + 3) \sin (x^3 + 2x + 3)$$

$$+ (3x^2 + 2) \tan (x^3 + 2x + 3) \cos (x^3 + 2x + 3)$$

$$= (3x^2 + 2) \sin (x^3 + 2x + 3)[\sec^2 (x^3 + 2x + 3) + 1]$$

PROBLEMS

Find the first derivative of each of the following functions.

1. $y = \dfrac{\csc x}{x}$

2. $y = \dfrac{\sin x - \cos x}{x}$

3. $y = x^2 \cot x$

4. $y = \tan x \csc x$

5. $y = \sin 3x \tan 3x$

6. $y = \cot (x^2 + 1)$

7. $y = x + \cot x$

8. $y = \dfrac{x + \sin x}{x}$

9. $y = \cos^2 2x$

10. $y = \sin x \cos x$

11. $y = \sin^2 x + \cos^2 x$

12. $y = x \sin x$

13. $y = \dfrac{\sin x}{x}$

14. $y = x^2 - \cos x$

15. $y = \dfrac{\tan x}{(1 + x)^2}$

16. $y = \sin x^2$

17. $y = \tan 3x$

18. $y = \tan x + \sec 2x$

19. $y = \dfrac{\sin x}{\sec x}$

20. $y = \cos x \csc x$

21. $y = \sec^2 3x$

22. $y = \dfrac{x}{\sec x}$

23. $y = \dfrac{1}{1 + \cot x}$

24. $y = \dfrac{\cot x}{1 + x^2}$

Answers to Odd-Numbered Problems

1. $\dfrac{-\csc x(1 + x \cot x)}{x^2}$

3. $2x \cot x - x^2 \csc^2 x$

5. $3 \sin 3x(1 + \sec^2 3x)$

7. $1 - \csc^2 x$

9. $-4 \cos 2x \sin 2x$

11. 0

13. $\dfrac{x \cos x - \sin x}{x^2}$

15. $\dfrac{(1 + x) \sec^2 x - 2 \tan x}{(1 + x)^3}$

17. $3 \sec^2 3x$

19. $\cos^2 x - \sin^2 x$

21. $6 \sec^2 3x \tan 3x$

23. $\dfrac{1}{(\sin x + \cos x)^2}$

INVERSE FUNCTIONS

Rule 15. The derivative of the inverse of a function is equal to the reciprocal of the derivative of the function. If $y = f(x)$ and $x = g(y)$ are inverse differentiable functions,

$$\frac{dy}{dx} = \frac{1}{\dfrac{dx}{dy}}$$

or

$$\frac{df(x)}{dx} = \frac{1}{\dfrac{dg(y)}{dy}}$$

EXAMPLE

If $x = y^2 + 6$, find $\dfrac{dy}{dx}$.

$$\frac{dx}{dy} = 2y$$

$$\frac{dy}{dx} = \frac{1}{\dfrac{dx}{dy}} = \tfrac{1}{2}y^{-1}$$

EXAMPLE

If $x = y + \tfrac{1}{3}y^3 + \tfrac{1}{5}y^5$, find $\dfrac{dy}{dx}$.

$$\frac{dx}{dy} = 1 + y^2 + y^4$$

$$\frac{dy}{dx} = \frac{1}{\dfrac{dx}{dy}} = \frac{1}{1 + y^2 + y^4}$$

EXAMPLE

If $x = \ln(y^4 + 3y^2)$,

$$\frac{dx}{dy} = \frac{4y^3 + 6y}{y^4 + 3y^2}$$

$$= \frac{4y^2 + 6}{y^3 + 3y^2}$$

$$\frac{dy}{dx} = \frac{1}{\dfrac{dx}{dy}} = \frac{y^3 + 3y^2}{4y^2 + 6}$$

EXAMPLE

If $x = e^{-y^2 + 4y + 2}$,

$$\frac{dx}{dy} = (-2y + 4)e^{-y^2 + 4y + 2}$$

$$\frac{dy}{dx} = \frac{1}{\dfrac{dx}{dy}} = \frac{e^{y^2 - 4y - 2}}{4 - 2y}$$

EXAMPLE

If $x = \tan^2 (y^3 + a)$,

$$\frac{dx}{dy} = 6y^2 \tan (y^3 + a) \sec^2 (y^3 + a)$$

$$\frac{dy}{dx} = \frac{1}{\dfrac{dx}{dy}} = \frac{1}{6y^2} \cot (y^3 + a) \cos^2 (y^3 + a)$$

PROBLEMS

Find the first derivative with respect to x of each of the following functions $x = f(y)$.

1. $x = y^2 + 3y + 2$
2. $x = y^3 - 2y^{3/2} + 6y$
3. $x = 5y^4 - e^y$

4. $x = \ln (y^5 - 6)$
5. $x = \cos^2 y + \sin y$
6. $x = y \sec y$

Find the first derivative with respect to y of each of the following functions $y = f(x)$.

7. $y = e^{-x} - 6$

8. $y = \ln \left(\dfrac{x^3}{x + 2}\right)$

9. $y = \tan x \sin x$

10. $y = \dfrac{x}{\cos x}$

Answers to Odd-Numbered Problems

1. $\dfrac{1}{2y + 3}$

3. $\dfrac{1}{20y^3 - e^y}$

5. $\dfrac{\sec y}{1 - 2 \sin y}$

7. $-e^x$

9. $\dfrac{\csc x}{1 + \sec^2 x}$

Summary of Procedure for Differentiation

1. Determine whether the entire function to be differentiated is a sum or difference of functions; a product or quotient of functions; a logarithmic, exponential, or trigonometric function of a function; a power of a function; a composite function; or some combination of these.
2. Differentiate using the appropriate rule for the entire function and the appropriate rules for the different parts of the function.

EXAMPLE

Find the first derivative of $y = x^2 + \ln x^3$.

The entire function is the sum of two functions

$$y = u(x) + v(x) \qquad \text{where } u(x) = x^2$$

$$v(x) = \ln x^3$$

Thus $\dfrac{dy}{dx} = \dfrac{du}{dx} + \dfrac{dv}{dx}$ (Rule 4).

$u = x^2$ is differentiated using Rule 2, and $v = \ln x^3$ is differentiated using Rules 2 and 9.

$$\frac{du}{dx} = 2x \qquad \text{and} \qquad \frac{dv}{dx} = \frac{3}{x}$$

Thus

$$\frac{dy}{dx} = 2x + \frac{3}{x}$$

EXAMPLE

Find the first derivative of $y = e^{x^2 + 2}(x + 1)^2$.

The entire function is the product of two functions

$$y = u(x) \cdot v(x) \qquad \text{where } u(x) = e^{x^2 + 2}$$

$$v(x) = (x + 1)^2$$

Thus $\dfrac{dy}{dx} = u\dfrac{dv}{dx} + v\dfrac{du}{dx}$ (Rule 5).

$u = e^{x^2 + 2}$ is differentiated using Rules 1, 2, 4, and 10, and $v = (x + 1)^2$ is differentiated using Rules 1, 2, 4, and 8.

$$\frac{du}{dx} = 2xe^{x^2 + 2}$$

$$\frac{dv}{dx} = 2(x + 1)$$

Thus

$$\frac{dy}{dx} = 2e^{x^2 + 2}(x + 1) + 2x(x + 1)^2 e^{x^2 + 2}$$

$$= 2(x + 1)e^{x^2 + 2}[1 + x(x + 1)]$$

$$= 2(x + 1)(x^2 + x + 1)e^{x^2 + 2}$$

EXAMPLE

Find the first derivative of $y = x^{\tan x}$.

The entire function is a function raised to a functional power

$$y = u(x)^{v(x)} \qquad \text{where } u(x) = x$$

$$v(x) = \tan x$$

Thus $\dfrac{dv}{dx} = vu^{v-1}\dfrac{du}{dx} + (\ln u)u^v\dfrac{dv}{dx}$ (Rule 11)

$u = x$ is differentiated using Rule 2 and $v = \tan x$ is differentiated using Rule 14.

$$\frac{du}{dx} = 1 \quad \text{and} \quad \frac{dv}{dx} = \sec^2 x$$

Thus

$$\frac{dy}{dx} = (\tan x)x^{(\tan x)-1} + (\ln x)x^{\tan x}(\sec^2 x)$$

$$= x^{\tan x}\left(\frac{\tan x}{x} + \sec^2 x \ln x\right)$$

PROBLEMS

Obtain the first derivative of each of the following functions.

1. $y = \dfrac{2}{x+1}$

2. $s = \dfrac{\theta+4}{\theta}$

3. $y = \ln(x + \sqrt{1+x^2})$

4. $y = \dfrac{2}{e^x}$

5. $y = \dfrac{x^3+1}{x}$

6. $y = \dfrac{3}{x^2+2}$

7. $s = \dfrac{1}{1-2t}$

8. $y = \dfrac{x^2}{4-x^2}$

9. $y = e^{ax}\sin bx$

10. $y = \dfrac{x}{x^2+1}$

11. $y = \dfrac{ax+b}{bx+d}$

12. $y = \ln\left(\tan\dfrac{x}{2}\right)$

13. $y = \ln^3 x$

14. $y = \log\left(\dfrac{2}{x}\right)$

15. $y = 10^{nx}$

16. $y = \ln(ax^2+b)$

17. $s = e^{-t}\cos 2t$

18. $y = \tfrac{1}{3}\tan^3\theta - \tan\theta + \theta$

19. $s = \dfrac{a+bt+ct^2}{\sqrt{t}}$

20. $z = \dfrac{a+bx+cx^2}{x}$

21. $z = a^{2y}$

22. $y = e^{x^2}$

23. $y = x^x$

24. $y = x^n(a+bx)^m$

25. $y = x^{\sin x}$

26. $y = x^{\sqrt{x}}$

27. $s = \left(\dfrac{a}{t}\right)^t$

28. $y = (\cos x)^x$

Determine $\dfrac{dy}{dx}$ for each of the following functions.

29. $x = \sqrt{1-2y}$

30. $x = \sqrt[3]{4-9y}$

31. $x = (2-3y^2)^3$

32. $x = \left(a - \dfrac{b}{y}\right)^2$

33. $x = y\sqrt{a^2+y^2}$

34. $x = \dfrac{a - y}{a + y}$

35. $x = y\sqrt{a + by}$

36. $x = \dfrac{b}{a}\sqrt{a^2 - y^2}$

37. $x = \ln{(ay^2 + b)}$

38. $x = \dfrac{e^y - e^{-y}}{e^y + e^{-y}}$

39. $x = \dfrac{2}{e^y}$

40. $x = \dfrac{\ln y}{y}$

41. $x = y^2 e^{-y}$

42. $x = \ln{(y^2 e^y)}$

43. $x = \ln{(\sqrt{\cos 2y})}$

44. $x = \dfrac{4}{\sqrt{\sec y}}$

45. $x = \ln{\left(\dfrac{1 + \sin y}{1 - \sin y}\right)^{1/2}}$

46. $x = (\sin 2y)^{1/2}$

47. $y = u^6; u = 1 + 2\sqrt{x}$

48. $y = u \sin u; u = \ln x$

49. $y = u^2 \cos u; u = ax^2$

50. $y = \dfrac{a - u}{a + u}; u = \dfrac{b - x}{b + x}$

51. If $y = x^4 + 5$ and $x = \log z$, find $\dfrac{dy}{dz}$.

52. If $y = e^{3u}$ and $u = 2x^2 - 3x$, find $\dfrac{dy}{dx}$.

53. If $u = \ln{(y + 4)}$ and $y = x^2$, find $\dfrac{du}{dx}$.

54. If $x = \dfrac{4y + 2}{y + 6}$ and $y = u^3 + 10u$, find $\dfrac{dx}{du}$.

55. If $y = e^t + 6$ and $t = \ln{(x^2 + 6x)}$, find $\dfrac{dy}{dx}$.

56. If $y = \dfrac{4t - 8}{t + 4}$ and $t = x^2 - 4$, find $\dfrac{dy}{dx}$.

Answers to Odd-Numbered Problems

1. $-\dfrac{2}{(x + 1)^2}$

3. $\dfrac{1}{\sqrt{1 + x^2}}$

5. $\dfrac{2x^3 - 1}{x^2}$

7. $\dfrac{2}{(1 - 2t)^2}$

9. $e^{ax}(a \sin bx + b \cos bx)$

11. $\dfrac{ad - bc}{(cx + d)^2}$

13. $\dfrac{3 \ln^2 x}{x}$

15. $10^{nx} n \ln 10$

17. $-e^{-t}(\cos 2t + 2 \sin 2t)$

19. $-\tfrac{1}{2}at^{-3/2} + \tfrac{1}{2}bt^{-1/2} + \tfrac{3}{2}ct^{1/2}$

21. $2a^{2y} \ln a$

23. $x^x(1 + \ln x)$

25. $x^{\sin x}\left(\dfrac{\sin x}{x} + \cos x \ln x\right)$

27. $\left(\dfrac{a}{t}\right)^t\left(\ln{\left(\dfrac{a}{t}\right)} - 1\right)$

29. $|-x$

31. $-\dfrac{1}{18y(2 - 3y^2)^2}$

33. $\dfrac{(a^2 + y^2)^{1/2}}{a^2 + 2y^2}$

35. $\dfrac{2(a + by)^{1/2}}{2a + 3by}$

37. $\dfrac{ay^2 + b}{2ay}$

39. $-\frac{1}{2}e^y$

41. $\dfrac{e^y}{y(2-y)}$

43. $-\cot 2y$

45. $\cos y$

47. $\dfrac{6(1+2\sqrt{x})^5}{\sqrt{x}}$

49. $2a^2x^3(2\cos ax^2 - ax^2\sin ax^2)$

51. $\dfrac{4(\log z)^3}{z}\log e$

53. $\dfrac{2x}{x^2+4}$

55. $2x+6$

SUMMARY OF RULES FOR DIFFERENTIATION

Algebraic Functions

Rule 1. If $y = c$, $\dfrac{dy}{dx} = 0$.

Rule 2. If $y = x^n$, $\dfrac{dy}{dx} = nx^{n-1}$.

Rule 3. If $y = cu$, where $u = f(x)$, $\dfrac{dy}{dx} = c\dfrac{du}{dx}$.

Rule 4. If $y = u + v$, where $u = f(x)$ and $v = g(x)$,

$$\frac{dy}{dx} = \frac{du}{dx} + \frac{dv}{dx}$$

Rule 5. If $y = uv$, where $u = f(x)$ and $v = g(x)$,

$$\frac{dy}{dx} = u\frac{dv}{dx} + v\frac{du}{dx}$$

Rule 6. If $y = \dfrac{u}{v}$, where $u = f(x)$ and $v = g(x)$,

$$\frac{dy}{dx} = \frac{v\dfrac{du}{dx} - u\dfrac{dv}{dx}}{v^2}$$

Composite Functions

Rule 7. If $y = g(u)$ and $u = h(x)$,

$$\frac{dy}{dx} = \frac{dy}{du} \cdot \frac{du}{dx}$$

Note that Rules 8, 9, 10, 11, 12, 13, and 14 are special cases of Rule 7.

Rule 8. If $y = u^n$, where $u = f(x)$,

$$\frac{dy}{dx} = nu^{n-1}\frac{du}{dx}$$

Special Case: If $u = f(x) = x$, then $u^n = x^n$ and $\dfrac{dy}{dx} = nu^{n-1} = nx^{n-1}$ (Rule 3).

Logarithmic Functions

Rule 9.   If $y = \log_a u$, where $u = f(x)$,

$$\frac{dy}{dx} = \frac{\log_a e}{u} \frac{du}{dx}$$

Special Case: If $a = e$, then $y = \ln u$ and $\dfrac{dy}{dx} = \dfrac{1}{u} \dfrac{du}{dx}$.

Exponential Functions

Rule 10.   If $y = a^u$, where $u = f(x)$,

$$\frac{dy}{dx} = a^u \ln a \frac{du}{dx}$$

Special Case: If $a = e$, then $y = e^u$ and $\dfrac{dy}{dx} = e^u \dfrac{du}{dx}$.

Rule 11.   If $y = u^v$, where $u = f(x)$ and $v = g(x)$,

$$\frac{dy}{dx} = vu^{v-1} \frac{du}{dx} + u^v \ln u \frac{dv}{dx}$$

Note that Rule 10 is a special case of Rule 11.

Trigonometric Functions

Rule 12.   If $y = \sin u$, where $u = f(x)$,

$$\frac{dy}{dx} = \cos v \frac{du}{dx}$$

Rule 13.   If $y = \cos u$, where $u = f(x)$,

$$\frac{dy}{dx} = -\sin u \frac{du}{dx}$$

Rule 14.   If $y = \tan u$, where $u = f(x)$,

$$\frac{dy}{dx} = \sec^2 u \frac{du}{dx}$$

Inverse Functions

Rule 15.   If $y = f(x)$ and $x = g(y)$ are inverse functions,

$$\frac{dy}{dx} = \frac{1}{\dfrac{dx}{dy}}$$

2.7 Differentials

In the preceding discussion of derivatives, $\dfrac{dy}{dx}$ is considered not as a fraction with numerator dy and denominator dx, but as a symbol denoting the limit of $\dfrac{\Delta y}{\Delta x}$ as Δx

approaches zero as a limit. In some problems it is useful to interpret dy and dx separately. In this context, dy is referred to as the *differential of y* and dx is referred to as the *differential of x*. Differentials are useful, for example, in applications of integral calculus and in approximating changes in the dependent variable associated with small changes in the independent variable. Approximation of the value of a function using differentials is discussed in this section.

If $f'(x)$ is the derivative of $y = f(x)$ for a particular value of x and Δx is an arbitrarily chosen increment of x, then the differential of y, denoted by $df(x)$ or dy, is

$$dy = df(x) = f'(x)\,\Delta x = \frac{dy}{dx}\,\Delta x$$

and the differential of x, denoted by dx, is

$$dx = \Delta x$$

Thus the differential of a function is defined as its derivative multiplied by an increment of the independent variable. Note that if the function $f(x)$ is taken to be x, then $f'(x) = 1$ and it follows that the differential dx of x is Δx.

Geometrically, consider the curve $y = f(x)$ (see Figure 2.19) and let $f'(x)$ be the value of the derivative at P. Then $\Delta x = PQ$ and

$$dy = f'(x)\,dx = (\tan \theta)(PQ) = \frac{QT}{PQ}\,PQ = QT$$

Therefore, dy is the increment (equal to QT) of the ordinate of the tangent corresponding to dx.

This geometrical argument provides the following interpretation of the derivative as a fraction. If an arbitrarily chosen increment of the independent variable x for a point $P(x, y)$ on the curve $y = f(x)$ is denoted by dx, then in the derivative

$$\frac{dy}{dx} = f'(x) = \tan \theta$$

dy denotes the corresponding increment of the ordinate of the tangent at P.

Figure 2.19

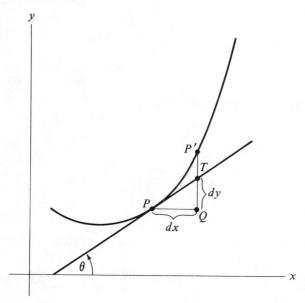

Note that the differential dy and the increment Δy of the function corresponding to the same value of $dx = \Delta x$ are not in general equal. In Figure 2.20, $dy = QT$ but $\Delta y = QP'$.

Approximations

It can be seen in Figure 2.19 that $\Delta y = QP'$ and $dy = QT$ are approximately equal when $\Delta x = PQ$ is small. In fact, the differential of a function can be made arbitrarily close to the increment of the function for sufficiently small changes in the independent variable. The value of the corresponding differential thus can be used as an approximation for the change in a function when the independent variable changes by a small amount.

EXAMPLE

If $y = x^4 - 2x^3 + 9x + 7$, use differentials to find an approximate value of y when $x = 1.997$.

Consider 1.997 to be the result of applying an increment $\Delta x = -0.003$ to an original value of $x = 2$. Then

$$dy = (4x^3 - 6x^2 + 9)\, \Delta x$$

$$= (32 - 24 + 9)(-0.003)$$

$$= -0.051$$

Since $y = 25$ when $x = 2$ and -0.051 is the approximate change in y when x changes from 2 to 1.997,

$$y + dy = 25 - 0.051$$

$$= 24.949$$

and y is approximately 24.949 when $x = 1.997$.

To obtain an estimate of the accuracy of this approximation, compute the error of the approximation, which is given by $\Delta y - dy$.

$$\Delta y = f(x + \Delta x) - f(x)$$

$$= (x + \Delta x)^4 - 2(x + \Delta x)^3 + 9(x + \Delta x) + 7 - x^4 + 2x^3 - 9x - 7$$

$$= x^4 - 2x^3 + 9x + 7 + 4x^3(\Delta x) + 6x^2(\Delta x)^2$$

$$+ 4x(\Delta x)^3 + (\Delta x)^4 - 6x^2(\Delta x) - 6x(\Delta x)^2$$

$$- 2(\Delta x)^3 + 9(\Delta x) - x^4 + 2x^3 - 9x - 7$$

$$= 4x^3(\Delta x) + 6x^2(\Delta x)^2 + 4x(\Delta x)^3 + (\Delta x)^4 - 6x^2(\Delta x)$$

$$- 6x(\Delta x)^2 - 2(\Delta x)^3 + 9(\Delta x)$$

and

$$dy = (4x^3 - 6x^2 + 9)(\Delta x)$$

$$= 4x^3(\Delta x) - 6x^2(\Delta x) + 9(\Delta x)$$

Thus

$$dy - \Delta y = 6x^2(\Delta x)^2 + 4x(\Delta x)^3 + (\Delta x)^4 - 6x(\Delta x)^2 - 2(\Delta x)^3$$

And, for $x = 2$,

$$dy - \Delta y = (24 - 12)(-0.003)^2 + (8 - 2)(-0.003)^3 + (-0.003)^4$$

$$= 0.000107838081$$

Thus $y + \Delta y = y + dy + (\Delta y - dy) = 24.949107838081$ and the approximation $y = 24.949$ is accurate to three decimal places.

EXAMPLE

Using differentials, find an approximate value of $\sqrt{98}$.

The number 98 is close to the number 100, which is a perfect square. Thus the change in $y = \sqrt{x}$ corresponding to a change in x from 100 to 98 can be added to $y = \sqrt{100} = 10$ to obtain an approximate value for $\sqrt{98}$. When x changes to $x + dx$, y changes to $y + dy$, approximately.

For $x = 100$ and $\Delta x = -2$,

$$dy = \frac{dx}{2\sqrt{x}}$$

$$= \frac{-2}{2\sqrt{100}}$$

$$= -0.1$$

and thus $\sqrt{98} = \sqrt{100} - 0.1 = 9.9$ approximately.

EXAMPLE

Using differentials, find an approximate value for $\tan 46°$ given $\tan 45° = 1$, $\sec 45° = \sqrt{2}$, and $1° = 0.0175$ radians.

If $y = \tan x$, $dy = \sec^2 x \, dx$. When x changes to dx, y changes to $y + dy$, approximately. Converting to radians so that the rules for differentiating trigonometric functions apply,

$$x = 45° = \frac{\pi}{4} \text{ radians}$$

$$\Delta x = 1° = 0.0175 \text{ radians}$$

$$dy = \sec^2 x \, dx$$

$$= (\sqrt{2})^2 (0.0175)$$

$$= 0.0350$$

Since $y = \tan 45° = 1$, $y + dy = 1.0350$, and $\tan 46° = 1.0350$ approximately.

Differentials can also be used to estimate small errors in calculation of a function which arise from lack of precision in the measurement of the independent variable or from other causes.

EXAMPLE

Suppose $C = 5 + 0.6x + 0.2\sqrt{x}$, where C is total consumption (billions of dollars) and x is total disposable income (billions of dollars). If $x = 25$ with a maximum error of 0.3, find the approximate maximum error in consumption.

$$dC = 0.6 + \frac{0.1}{\sqrt{x}} \, dx$$

$$= \left(0.6 + \frac{0.1}{\sqrt{25}} \right) (0.3)$$

$$= \left(0.6 + \frac{0.1}{5} \right) (0.3)$$

$$= (0.62)(0.3)$$

$$= 0.186$$

If du is the error in u, then

$\dfrac{du}{u}$ is the relative error in u

and

$100\,\dfrac{du}{u}$ is the percentage error in u

For this example, the approximate maximum relative error is

$$\frac{dC}{C} = \frac{0.186}{25} = 0.00744$$

and the percentage error is 0.744.

It is frequently convenient to find the relative error by logarithmic differentiation, since if $y = \ln x$, $dy = dx/x$.

EXAMPLE

For the demand function

$$x = \frac{16}{y^4}$$

where x is number of units demanded and y is price in dollars, assume y is 200 with a maximum error of 10 and determine the approximate maximum relative error in x.

$\ln x = \ln 16 - 4 \ln y$

$$\frac{dx}{x} = -4\frac{dy}{y}$$

and, for $y = 200$ and $dy = 10$, the relative error in x is

$$\frac{dx}{x} = -\frac{40}{200} = -\frac{1}{5}$$

and the percentage error is -20. The negative sign of the error indicates that the errors in estimating x and y are opposite in sign.

PROBLEMS

Use differentials to find the approximate value of each of the following.

1. $\sqrt[3]{1010}$ 3. $\sqrt{66}$

2. $\sqrt[4]{15}$ 4. $\sqrt[5]{34}$

Find dy and Δy for each of the following.

5. $y = x^4 - x^2/2$ for $x = 2$, $\Delta x = 0.1$ 7. $y = (x + 1)^3$ for $x = -3$, $\Delta x = -0.003$

6. $y = 12.8/x$ for $x = 10$, $\Delta x = 0.24$ 8. $y = \sqrt{x}$ for $x = 4$, $\Delta x = 0.04$

9. A container is made in the form of a 10-cm cube to hold 1 liter (1000 cm³). How accurately must the inner edge be made so that the volume will be correct to within 3 cm³?

10. Using differentials, find the allowable percentage error in the diameter of a circle if the area is to be correct to within 4 percent.

11. Show that the relative error in the nth power of a measurement is approximately n times the relative error in the measurement.
12. Show that the relative error in the nth root of a measurement is approximately $1/n$ times the relative error in the measurement.

Answers to Odd-Numbered Problems

1. 10.033
3. 8.125
5. $dy = 3$; $\Delta y = 3.2431$

7. $dy = -0.036$; $\Delta y = -0.036054$
9. error must not exceed 0.01 cm

2.8 Higher-Order Derivatives

In some problems it is useful to differentiate a function more than once. The result of two or more successive differentiations of a function is a higher-order derivative.

The derivative of $y = f(x)$ with respect to x is, in general, a function of x and may be differentiated with respect to x. The derivative of the first derivative is the *second derivative*; its derivative is the *third derivative*, and so on.

In general, the nth derivative of a function $y = f(x)$ is obtained by differentiating n times. The result of this differentiation—that is, the nth derivative—is denoted by

$$\frac{d^n y}{dx^n} \qquad f^{(n)}(x) \qquad y^{(n)} \qquad \frac{d^n}{dx}(y) \qquad D_x^n y \qquad D_x^n(y)$$

EXAMPLE

If $y = x^3 - 3x^2 + 2$,

$$\frac{dy}{dx} = 3x^2 - 6x$$

$$\frac{d^2 y}{dx^2} = 6x - 6$$

$$\frac{d^3 y}{dx^3} = 6$$

$$\frac{d^4 y}{dx^4} = 0$$

and higher-order derivatives are also zero.

EXAMPLE

If $x = \sqrt{t^2 + 1}$,

$$\frac{dx}{dt} = \tfrac{1}{2}(t^2 + 1)^{-1/2}(2t)$$

$$= t(t^2 + 1)^{-1/2}$$

$$\frac{d^2 x}{dt^2} = (t^2 + 1)^{-1/2} + (-\tfrac{1}{2})t(t^2 + 1)^{-3/2}(2t)$$

$$= (t^2 + 1)^{-3/2}[(t^2 + 1) - t^2]$$

$$= (t^2 + 1)^{-3/2}$$

$$\frac{d^3x}{dt^3} = -\tfrac{3}{2}(t^2 + 1)^{-5/2}(2t)$$

$$= -3t(t^2 + 1)^{-5/2}$$

$$\frac{d^4x}{dt^4} = -3(t^2 + 1)^{-5/2} - \tfrac{5}{2}(-3t)(t^2 + 1)^{-7/2}(2t)$$

$$= (t^2 + 1)^{-7/2} - 3(t^2 + 1) + 15t^2$$

$$= 3(4t^2 - 1)(t^2 + 1)^{-7/2}$$

and so forth for higher-order derivatives.

EXAMPLE

If $y = \sin x$,

$$\frac{dy}{dx} = \cos x$$

$$\frac{d^2y}{dx^2} = -\sin x$$

$$\frac{d^3y}{dx^3} = -\cos x$$

$$\frac{d^4y}{dx^4} = \sin x$$

and so forth for higher-order derivatives.

Just as the derivative of the function $y = f(x)$ with respect to x represents the rate of change in y as x changes, the second derivative of $y = f(x)$ with respect to x represents the rate of change in the first derivative $y' = f'(x)$ as x changes.

In general, the nth derivative with respect to x of a function $y = f(x)$ represents the rate of change in the $(n - 1)$st derivative of $y = f(x)$ as x changes.

Higher-order derivatives are very important for certain theoretical problems in mathematics and statistics; however, in most applied work, derivatives of order higher than the second are not encountered frequently.

Second-order derivatives are useful in graphical representation of functions, as discussed in later sections, and are also useful whenever the rate of change of the quantity represented by the first derivative is of interest. For example, the rate of change of velocity is acceleration and the rate of change of marginal cost indicates whether marginal cost is increasing, decreasing, or constant under varying conditions of production.

EXAMPLE

If the position of a moving body at time t is represented by

$$s = (2t + 3)^2$$

find its velocity, $v = \dfrac{ds}{dt}$, and its acceleration, $a = \dfrac{dv}{dt} = \dfrac{d^2s}{dt^2}$.

$$v = \frac{ds}{dt} = 2(2t + 3)(2)$$

$$= 8t + 12$$

$$a = \frac{dv}{dt} = 8$$

EXAMPLE

An object projected vertically upward with a speed of 160 feet/second reaches an elevation of

$$s = 160t - 16t^2$$

at the end of t seconds.

(a) How high does it rise?
(b) How fast is it traveling when it reaches an elevation of 256 feet going up and again when it reaches this elevation coming down?
(c) What is its acceleration?

(a) Velocity is zero when the object is at the highest point, that is, when $v = \frac{ds}{dt} = 0$, because

v goes from positive (object rising) to negative (object falling). $v = \frac{ds}{dt} = 160 - 32t$ and $v = 0$

when $t = 5$. Thus its maximum height is

$$s = 160(5) - 16(5^2)$$

$$= 800 - 400$$

$$= 400 \text{ ft}$$

(b) If $s = 256$,

$$256 = 160t - 16t^2$$

$$t^2 - 10t + 16 = 0$$

$$(t - 8)(t - 2) = 0$$

$$t = 8, 2$$

The object is thus at an elevation of 256 feet going up after 2 seconds and coming down after 8 seconds.

If $t = 2$, $v = \frac{ds}{dt} = 160 - 32t = 160 - 64 = 96$ ft/sec

If $t = 8$, $v = \frac{ds}{dt} = 160 - 32t = 160 - 256 = -96$ ft/sec

(c) $a = \frac{dv}{dt} = -32$ ft/sec^2

EXAMPLE

Total cost is represented by

$$y = 50 + 60x - 12x^2 + x^3$$

(see Figure 2.20).

Figure 2.20

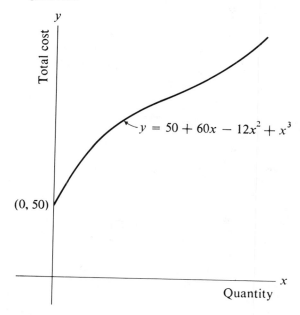

$$y = 50 + 60x - 12x^2 + x^3$$

(0, 50)

Total cost

x

Quantity

where y is total cost and x is output. Average cost is $y/x = (50/x) + 60 - 12x + x^2$ and marginal cost is $\dfrac{dy}{dx} = 60 - 24x + 3x^2$ (see Figure 2.21).

$$\frac{d^2y}{dx^2} = -24 + 6x$$

$$= 0 \quad \text{when } x = 4$$
$$< 0 \quad \text{when } x < 4$$
$$> 0 \quad \text{when } x > 4$$

Thus marginal cost decreases for $x < 4$, increases for $x > 4$, and is constant for $x = 4$.

Figure 2.21

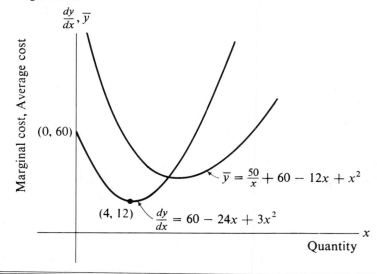

$\dfrac{dy}{dx}, \bar{y}$

Marginal cost, Average cost

(0, 60)

$$\bar{y} = \frac{50}{x} + 60 - 12x + x^2$$

(4, 12) $\dfrac{dy}{dx} = 60 - 24x + 3x^2$

x

Quantity

EXAMPLE

Total cost is represented by

$$y = 200 + 1000x - 24x^2 + 4x^3 + x^4$$

(see Figure 2.22).

where y is total cost and x is output. Average cost is

$$\frac{y}{x} = \frac{200}{x} + 1000 - 24x + 4x^2 + x^3$$

and marginal cost is

$$\frac{dy}{dx} = 1000 - 48x + 12x^2 + 4x^3$$

(see Figure 2.23).

$$\frac{d^2y}{dx^2} = -48 + 24x + 12x^2$$

$$= 0 \quad \text{when } x^2 + 2x - 4 = 0$$

$$x = \frac{-2 \pm \sqrt{4 + 16}}{2}$$

$$= \frac{-2 \pm \sqrt{20}}{2} = -1 \pm \sqrt{5}$$

Appropriate value is $x = -1 + \sqrt{5}$ (approximately $x = 1.236$).

$$\frac{d^2y}{dx^2} = 0 \quad \text{when } x = -1 + \sqrt{5}$$

$$< 0 \quad \text{when } x < -1 + \sqrt{5}$$

$$> 0 \quad \text{when } x > -1 + \sqrt{5}$$

Thus marginal cost decreases for $x < 1.236$, increases for $x > 1.236$, and is constant for $x = 1.236$.

Figure 2.22

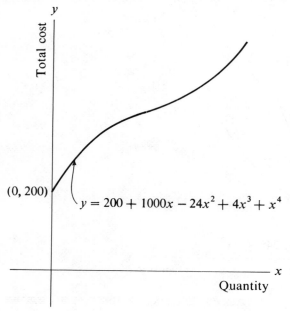

$$y = 200 + 1000x - 24x^2 + 4x^3 + x^4$$

Figure 2.23

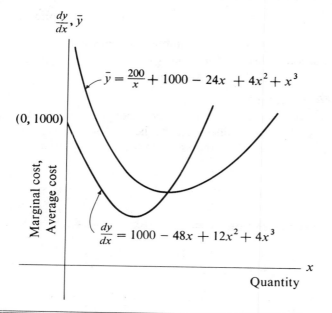

$$\frac{dy}{dx}, \bar{y}$$

$$\bar{y} = \frac{200}{x} + 1000 - 24x + 4x^2 + x^3$$

(0, 1000)

Marginal cost,
Average cost

$$\frac{dy}{dx} = 1000 - 48x + 12x^2 + 4x^3$$

x

Quantity

PROBLEMS

Find the first and second derivatives of each of the following functions.

1. $y = e^{3x}$

2. $y = x \ln x$

3. $y = \log \left(\frac{3}{x} \right)$

4. $y = x^2 e^x$

5. $y = e^{\ln (x^3 - 3)}$

6. $y = \left(\frac{x - 5}{x + 1} \right)^{-1}$

Answers to Odd-Numbered Problems

1. $3e^{3x}, 9e^{3x}$

3. $-\frac{1}{x} \log e, \frac{1}{x^2} \log e$

5. $3x^2, 6x$

2.9 Implicit Differentiation

Functions of the form $y = f(x)$ express y explicitly in terms of x and can be differentiated according to the rules for the types of functions involved. However, as noted in preceding sections, some equations involving x and y, of the form $f(x, y) = 0$, do not give y explicitly in terms of x and cannot conveniently be written so that they do. Such equations define y as a function of x in the sense that for each value of x there is a corresponding value of y which satisfies the equation; the equation is said to determine y as an *implicit function* of x. It is possible to calculate $\frac{dy}{dx}$ from such an equation by the method of *implicit differentiation*. In this method, y is treated as an unknown but differentiable function of x and the rules for finding derivatives are applied. In general, this method gives an expression for $\dfrac{dy}{dx}$ in terms of both x and y. Higher-order derivatives can also be obtained by implicit differentiation. The procedure for implicit differentiation is discussed and illustrated below.

Procedure for Implicit Differentiation

When y is defined as an implicit function of x by an equation $f(x, y) = 0$, the derivative of y with respect to x is obtained by differentiating the equation $f(x, y) = 0$ term by term, regarding y as a function of x, and then solving the resulting equation for the derivative $\dfrac{dy}{dx}$.

EXAMPLE

Find $\dfrac{dy}{dx}$ for the equation $xy^2 - x^2 + y = 0$. Differentiating with respect to x,

$$2xy\frac{dy}{dx} + y^2 - 2x + \frac{dy}{dx} = 0$$

$$(2xy + 1)\frac{dy}{dx} = 2x - y^2$$

$$\frac{dy}{dx} = \frac{2x - y^2}{2xy + 1}$$

NOTE: In this example, xy^2 is the product of two functions of x, x and y^2, and is differentiated using the product rule

$$\frac{d}{dx}(uv) = u\frac{dv}{dx} + v\frac{du}{dx}$$

where $u = x$, $v = y^2$, $\dfrac{du}{dx} = \dfrac{dx}{dx} = 1$, and $\dfrac{dv}{dx} = 2y\dfrac{dy}{dx}$. Thus $\dfrac{d}{dx}(xy^2) = 2xy\dfrac{dy}{dx} + y^2$. The derivative of $-x^2$ is $-2x$, as in differentiation of explicit functions $\left(\text{note again that } \dfrac{dx}{dx} = 1\right)$. The derivative of y is $\dfrac{dy}{dx}$, again as in differentiation of explicit functions.

EXAMPLE

Find $\dfrac{dy}{dx}$ for the equation $x^3 + y^3 - 3axy = 0$. Differentiating with respect to x,

$$3x^2 + 3y^2\frac{dy}{dx} - 3ax\frac{dy}{dx} - 3ay = 0$$

$$(y^2 - ax)\frac{dy}{dx} = ay - x^2$$

$$\frac{dy}{dx} = \frac{ay - x^2}{y^2 - ax}$$

EXAMPLE

Find $\dfrac{dy}{dx}$ for the equation $\sin x \cos y - \tan y = 0$. Differentiating with respect to x,

$$\cos x \cos y - \sin x \sin y \frac{dy}{dx} - \sec^2 y \frac{dy}{dx} = 0$$

$$\frac{dy}{dx} = \frac{\cos x \cos y}{\sin x \sin y + \sec^2 y}$$

EXAMPLE

Find $\dfrac{dy}{dx}$ and $\dfrac{d^2y}{dx^2}$ for the equation $x^2 - y^2 = 1$. Differentiating with respect to x,

$$2x - 2y \frac{dy}{dx} = 0$$

$$\frac{dy}{dx} = \frac{x}{y}$$

Differentiating $\dfrac{dy}{dx}$ with respect to x,

$$\frac{d^2y}{dx^2} = \frac{y - x\dfrac{dy}{dx}}{y^2}$$

Substituting $\dfrac{dy}{dx} = \dfrac{x}{y}$,

$$\frac{d^2y}{dx^2} = \frac{y - x\dfrac{x}{y}}{y^2}$$

$$= \frac{y^2 - x^2}{y^3}$$

or, since $y^2 - x^2 = -1$,

$$\frac{d^2y}{dx^2} = -\frac{1}{y^3}$$

EXAMPLE

Find $\dfrac{dy}{dx}$ and $\dfrac{d^2y}{dx^2}$ for the equation $e^y - xe^x = 0$. Differentiating with respect to x,

$$e^y \frac{dy}{dx} - e^x - xe^x = 0$$

$$\frac{dy}{dx} = \frac{e^x(x + 1)}{e^y}$$

or, since $e^y = xe^x$,

$$\frac{dy}{dx} = \frac{x+1}{x}$$

and

$$\frac{d^2y}{dx^2} = \frac{x - (x+1)}{x^2}$$

$$= -\frac{1}{x^2}$$

EXAMPLE

Find $\dfrac{dy}{dx}$ and $\dfrac{d^2y}{dx^2}$ for the equation $x^{1/2} + y^{1/2} = a^{1/2}$. Differentiating with respect to x,

$$\tfrac{1}{2}x^{-1/2} + \tfrac{1}{2}y^{-1/2}\frac{dy}{dx} = 0$$

$$\frac{dy}{dx} = -\frac{y^{1/2}}{x^{1/2}}$$

Differentiating $\dfrac{dy}{dx}$ with respect to x,

$$\frac{d^2y}{dx^2} = -\frac{\left(\tfrac{1}{2}y^{-1/2}\dfrac{dy}{dx}\right)x^{1/2} - y^{1/2}\left(\tfrac{1}{2}x^{-1/2}\right)}{x}$$

Substituting $\dfrac{dy}{dx} = -\dfrac{y^{1/2}}{x^{1/2}}$,

$$\frac{d^2y}{dx^2} = \frac{\tfrac{1}{2} + \tfrac{1}{2}x^{-1/2}y^{1/2}}{x}$$

$$= \tfrac{1}{2}x^{-1} + \tfrac{1}{2}x^{-3/2}y^{1/2}$$

$$= \tfrac{1}{2}x^{-3/2}(x^{1/2} + y^{1/2})$$

or, since $x^{1/2} + y^{1/2} = a^{1/2}$,

$$\frac{d^2y}{dx^2} = \tfrac{1}{2}a^{1/2}x^{-3/2}$$

PROBLEMS

Find a. $\dfrac{dy}{dx}$ and b. $\dfrac{d^2y}{dx^2}$ for each of the following functions by the method of implicit differentiation.

1. $x^2 + y^2 = 1$
2. $x^3 + y^3 = 1$
3. $x^{2/3} + y^{2/3} = 1$
4. $xy + y^2 = 1$
5. $y^2 = x^3$
6. $xy = a$
7. $x^2y^2 = b$
8. $x^2y^3 = c$
9. $x + y - xy = 2$

10. $x^2y^2 + xy = 1$
11. $x^3y^3 + x^2y^2 = a$
12. $x + y + xy + y^2 = b$
13. $x^3y^2 = a$
14. $x^2 + xy = a^2$
15. $xy^2 + y^2 = a$
16. $xy + y^3 = b$
17. $(x + y)^2 + (x + y)^3 = a^2$
18. $x^2 + y^2 = ab$

Find $\dfrac{dy}{dx}$ for each of the following functions by the method of implicit differentiation.

19. $y^2 = \dfrac{x-1}{x+1}$

20. $x^3 - xy + y^3 = 1$

21. $x^2 = \dfrac{x-y}{x+y}$

22. $y = x(x^2 + 1)^{-1/2}$

23. $y = x^{1/2} + x^{1/3} + x^{1/4}$

24. $y^2 = \dfrac{x^2 - 1}{x^2 + 1}$

25. $(x + y)^3 + (x - y)^3 = x^4 + y^4$

26. $y = (x + 5)^4(x^2 - 2)^3$

27. $\dfrac{1}{y} + \dfrac{1}{x} = 1$

28. $y = (x^2 + 3)^{1/3}x^{-1}$

29. $\cos^2 x + \tan y \sin y = 0$

30. $\csc x - \sec y + \tan y + \cot x = 0$

31. $xye^x + e^y = 0$

32. $ye^x = 10 + ye^y$

33. $x^5 + 4xy^3 - 3y^5 = 2$

34. $x^2 + xy + y^2 = 1$

Answers to Odd-Numbered Problems

1. a. $-\dfrac{x}{y}$ b. $-\dfrac{1}{y^3}$

3. a. $-x^{-1/3}y^{1/3}$ b. $\tfrac{1}{3}x^{-4/3}y^{-1/3}$

5. a. $\dfrac{3x^2}{2y}$ b. $\dfrac{3x}{4y}$

7. a. $-\dfrac{y}{x}$ b. $\dfrac{2y}{x^2}$

9. a. $\dfrac{y-1}{1-x}$ b. $\dfrac{2(y-1)}{(1-x)^2}$

11. a. $-\dfrac{y}{x}$ b. $\dfrac{2y}{x^2}$

13. a. $-\dfrac{3y}{2x}$ b. $\dfrac{15y}{4x^2}$

15. a. $\dfrac{-y}{2(x+1)}$ b. $\dfrac{3y}{4(x+1)^2}$

17. a. -1 b. 0

19. $\dfrac{1}{y(x+1)^2}$

21. $\dfrac{y}{x} - (x+y)^2$

23. $\tfrac{1}{2}x^{-1/2} + \tfrac{1}{3}x^{-2/3} + \tfrac{1}{4}x^{-3/4}$

25. $\dfrac{2x^3 - 3x^2 - 3y^2}{6xy - 2y^3}$

27. $-\dfrac{y^2}{x^2}$

29. $\dfrac{2 \sin x \cos x}{\sin y(1 + \sec^2 y)}$

31. $-\dfrac{y(1+x)}{x(1-y)}$

33. $\dfrac{5x^4 + 4y^3}{15y^4 - 12xy^2}$

2.10 Differentiability and Continuity

The relationships between differentiability and continuity are discussed in this section and smooth functions are defined and illustrated.

It can be shown that if the function $y = f(x)$ has a finite derivative

$$f'(c) = \lim_{\Delta x \to 0} \frac{f(c + \Delta x) - f(c)}{\Delta x}$$

at $x = c$, then $f(x)$ is continuous at $x = c$.

Continuity at a point does not, however, imply the existence of a derivative at that point. Thus

Differentiability $\Rightarrow$ Continuity

Continuity $\not\Rightarrow$ Differentiability

as in the following examples.

EXAMPLE

$f(x) = |x| = \begin{cases} x & \text{for } x \geq 0 \\ -x & \text{for } x < 0 \end{cases}$ is continuous at $x = 0$, but does *not* have a derivative at $x = 0$,

since

$f'(x) = 1 \quad \text{for } x > 0$

$\quad\quad = -1 \quad \text{for } x < 0$

(see Figure 2.24).

Figure 2.24

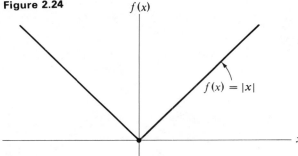

EXAMPLE

$f(x) = x^{1/3}$ is continuous at $x = 0$, but does *not* have a derivative at $x = 0$, since $f'(x) = \frac{1}{3}x^{-2/3}$ is not defined for $x = 0$ (see Figure 2.25).

Figure 2.25

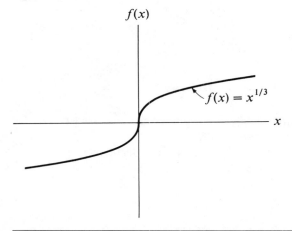

Smooth Functions

A function $f(x)$ is said to be a *smooth function* if both $f(x)$ and its first derivative are continuous. The graph of a smooth function is said to be a smooth curve; such a curve is not only continuous and unbroken but also has a continuously turning tangent. As shown in the following sections, a smooth function has some useful properties not possessed by a continuous curve whose first derivative is discontinuous at one or more points.

EXAMPLE

$y = 1 - x^2$ is a smooth function, since y and its derivative $\dfrac{dy}{dx} = -2x$ are everywhere continuous. Note that $y = 1 - x^2$ has a continuously turning tangent. (See Figure 2.26.)

Figure 2.26

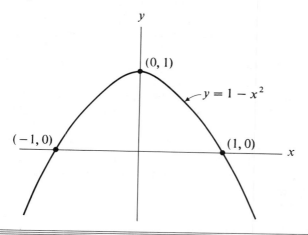

EXAMPLE

Figure 2.27

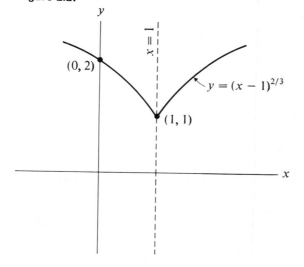

$y = (x - 1)^{2/3} + 1$ is *not* a smooth function at $x = 1$, since its derivative

$$\frac{dy}{dx} = \frac{2}{3\sqrt[3]{x-1}}$$

is discontinuous (becomes infinite) at $x = 1$. Note that $y = (x - 1)^{2/3}$ does not have a continuously turning tangent at $x = 1$. (See Figure 2.27.)

2.11 Applications of Derivatives

In this section the information which can be obtained from the first and second derivatives of a function is discussed. Such information is useful not only for graphing the function but also for determining its appropriateness for representing various relationships in business, economics, and the behavioral sciences.

THE FIRST DERIVATIVE

The first derivative of a function can be used to determine where the function is increasing and where it is decreasing. The first derivative can also be used to locate maximum and minimum values of the function (stationary points), if there are any.

Increasing and Decreasing Functions

Consider the function $y = f(x)$ at the point $x = a$. The first derivative of y with respect to x, $y' = f'(x)$ is the slope at the point x of the curve representing the function $y = f(x)$; in particular, $f'(a)$ is the slope of the curve $y = f(x)$ at the point $x = a$.

If the first derivative $f'(a)$ is positive, $y = f(x)$ is an *increasing function* of x at $x = a$; that is, $y = f(x)$ increases as x increases past $x = a$; if the first derivative $f'(a)$ is negative, $y = f(x)$ is a *decreasing function* of x at $x = a$; that is, $y = f(x)$ decreases as x increases past $x = a$. See Figure 2.28.

Figure 2.28

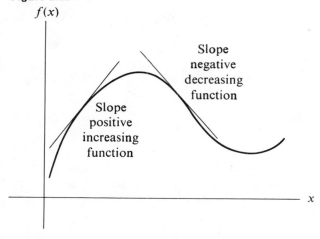

EXAMPLE

$f(x) = 2x^2 + 10$, $f'(x) = 4x$. Since $f'(x) > 0$ for $x > 0$ and $f'(x) < 0$ for $x < 0$, $f(x)$ is an increasing function of x for positive x and a decreasing function of x for negative x. Note that $f'(x) = 0$ for $x = 0$. (See Figure 2.29.)

Figure 2.29

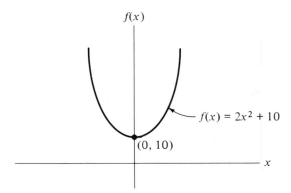

$f(x) = 2x^2 + 10$

$(0, 10)$

EXAMPLE

$f(x) = 3x^3$, $f'(x) = 9x^2$. Since $f'(x)$ is nonnegative for all values of x, $f(x)$ is an increasing function of x for all values of x. (See Figure 2.30.)

Figure 2.30

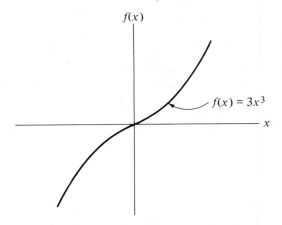

$f(x) = 3x^3$

EXAMPLE

$f(x) = x^3 + 6x^2 + 15$, $f'(x) = 3x^2 + 12x = 3x(x + 4)$. Since $f'(x) > 0$ for $x > 0$ or $x < -4$ and $f'(x) < 0$ for $-4 < x < 0$, $f(x)$ is a decreasing function of x for the interval $-4 < x < 0$ and an increasing function of x for $x < -4$ and $x > 0$. Note that $f'(x) = 0$ for $x = 0$ or $x = 4$. (See Figure 2.31.)

Figure 2.31

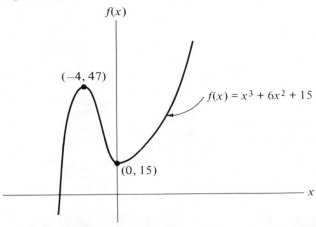

In the examples above, the values of x for which $f'(x) = 0$ are not discussed; such values are of particular interest, as discussed below.

Relative (Local) Maxima and Minima

A function $y = f(x)$ is said to have a *relative maximum* or *local maximum* at $x = a$ if $f(a)$ is greater than any other value of $f(x)$ for x in an interval around a; a function $y = f(x)$ is said to have a *relative minimum* or *local minimum* at $x = a$ if $f(a)$ is smaller than any other value of $f(x)$ for x in an interval around a. Note that a relative maximum or minimum of a function is its maximum or minimum for a given interval; the (absolute) maximum or minimum of the function over a larger interval can occur at an end point of the interval, rather than at any relative maximum or minimum. Also note that it is possible for a relative maximum value of a function to be less than a relative minimum value of the function (see Figure 2.32).

If a function $f(x)$ has a relative maximum or minimum at a value $x = a$ for which its first derivative is continuous, then $f'(a) = 0$. Values of x for which $f'(x)$ is discontinuous must be considered separately, as discussed below.

Figure 2.32

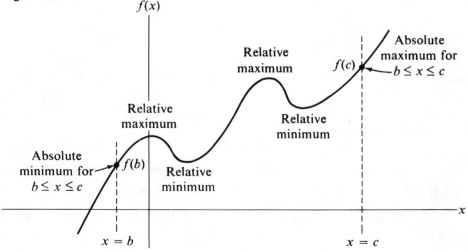

CAUTIONS

1. A relative maximum or minimum at $x = a$ implies $f'(a) = 0$ only if $f(x)$ and $f'(x)$ are continuous at $x = a$.
2. $f'(a) = 0$ does *not* imply a relative maximum or minimum at $x = a$ even if $f(x)$ and $f'(x)$ are continuous at $x = a$; that is, if $f(x)$ and $f'(x)$ are continuous at $x = a$, $f'(a) = 0$ is a necessary but not a sufficient condition for a relative maximum or minimum at $x = a$.

EXAMPLE (CAUTION 1)

Figure 2.33

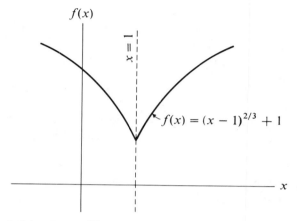

If $f(x) = (x - 1)^{2/3} + 1$, then

$$f'(x) = \frac{2}{3(x - 1)^{1/3}}$$

and $f'(x)$ is (infinitely) discontinuous at $x = 1$. Thus, although the function has a relative minimum at $x = 1$, $f'(1) \neq 0$ (see Figure 2.33).

EXAMPLE (CAUTION 2)

Figure 2.34

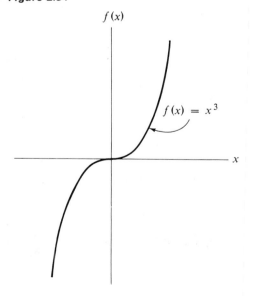

If $f(x) = x^3$, then

$$f'(x) = 3x^2$$

and $f'(x) = 0$ for $x = 0$. However, the function $f(x) = x^3$ does not have a relative maximum or minimum at $x = 0$ (see Figure 2.34).

Consider a function $f(x)$ at a value $x = a$ for which $f(x)$ and $f'(x)$ are continuous. It is evident geometrically that if $f(a)$ is a relative maximum of $f(x)$, then the slope $f'(x)$ of $f(x)$ changes from positive to negative as x passes through the point $x = a$; similarly, if $f(a)$ is a relative minimum of $f(x)$, then the slope $f'(x)$ of $f(x)$ changes from negative to positive as x passes through the point $x = a$ (see Figure 2.35). The corresponding algebraic argument is based on the fact that an increasing function has a positive slope and a decreasing function has a negative slope.

Thus, in order to determine the relative maximum and minimum values, if any, of a function $y = f(x)$,
1. Solve the equation $f'(x) = 0$ to obtain its roots (sometimes called critical values).
2. For each root a, determine whether $f'(x)$ changes sign as x increases through a:

Figure 2.35

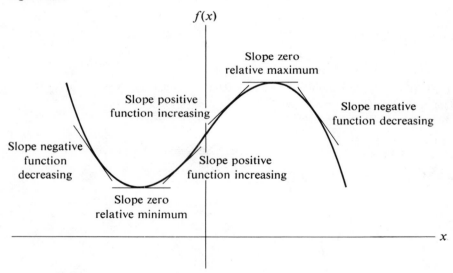

$f'(x)$ changes from $+$ to $-$ at $x = a \Rightarrow$ relative maximum at $x = a$

$f'(x)$ changes from $-$ to $+$ at $x = a \Rightarrow$ relative minimum at $x = a$

$f'(x)$ does not change sign at $x = a \Rightarrow$ no relative maximum or
minimum at $x = a$

NOTE: The above procedure locates all relative maxima and minima that occur at values of x for which $f(x)$ and $f'(x)$ are continuous. Relative maxima and minima which occur at values of x for which $f'(x)$ is discontinuous are discussed below.

EXAMPLE

Find the relative maxima and minima (if any) of the function $y = 2x^3 - 3x^2 - 12x + 13$.

$$\frac{dy}{dx} = 6x^2 - 6x - 12$$

$$= 0 \quad \text{if } x^2 - x - 2 = 0$$

$$(x - 2)(x + 1) = 0$$

$$x = 2, -1$$

If $-1 < x < 2$, $\frac{dy}{dx} < 0$
so minimum at $x = 2$
If $x > 2$, $\frac{dy}{dx} > 0$

If $x < -1$, $\frac{dy}{dx} > 0$
so maximum at $x = -1$
If $-1 < x < 2$, $\frac{dy}{dx} < 0$

See Figure 2.36.

Figure 2.36

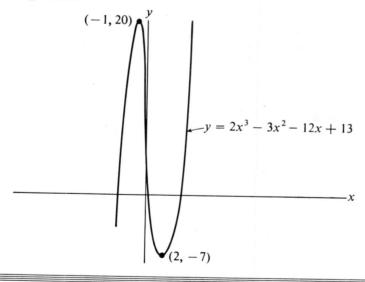

$(-1, 20)$

$y = 2x^3 - 3x^2 - 12x + 13$

$(2, -7)$

EXAMPLE

Find the relative maxima and minima (if any) of the function $y = 3x^4 - 4x^3$.

$$\frac{dy}{dx} = 12x^3 - 12x^2$$

$$= 0 \quad \text{if } x^3 - x^2 = 0$$

$$x^2(x - 1) = 0$$

$$x = 0, 1$$

Figure 2.37

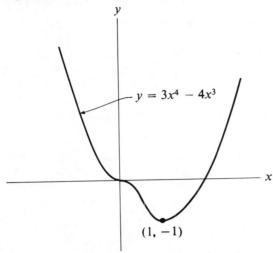

$y = 3x^4 - 4x^3$

$(1, -1)$

If $x < 0$, $\dfrac{dy}{dx} < 0$

If $0 < x < 1$, $\dfrac{dy}{dx} < 0$ $\left.\right\}$ so no maximum or minimum at $x = 0$

If $0 < x < 1$, $\dfrac{dy}{dx} < 0$

If $x > 1$, $\dfrac{dy}{dx} > 0$ $\left.\right\}$ so minimum at $x = 1$

See Figure 2.37.

EXAMPLE

Figure 2.38

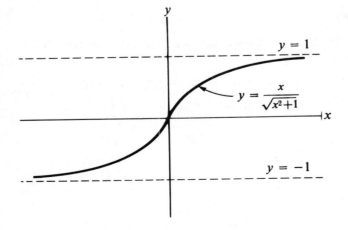

$y = 1$

$y = \dfrac{x}{\sqrt{x^2+1}}$

$y = -1$

Find the relative maxima and minima (if any) of the function $y = x/\sqrt{x^2 + 1}$.

$$\frac{dy}{dx} = \frac{(x^2 + 1)^{1/2} - \frac{1}{2}x(x^2 + 1)^{-1/2}(2x)}{(x^2 + 1)}$$

$$= \frac{(x^2 + 1)^{-1/2}(x^2 + 1 - x^2)}{(x^2 + 1)}$$

$$= \frac{1}{(x^2 + 1)^{3/2}}$$

$f'(x) \neq 0$ for all values of x, so $f(x)$ has no maximum or minimum (see Figure 2.38).

In each of the examples above, the first derivative is continuous for all values of x. Thus relative maxima and minima can occur only for values $x = a$ for which $f'(a) = 0$. As noted above, relative maxima or minima can also occur for values $x = a$ for which $f'(a)$ is discontinuous. That is, if $f(x)$ is continuous at $x = a$ but its first derivative is discontinuous at $x = a$, then $f(a)$ may be a relative maximum or minimum even though $f'(a) \neq 0$. Again, a change in the sign of the first derivative as x passes through a is necessary for the existence of a relative maximum or minimum at $x = a$.

Thus, in order to determine relative maximum and minimum values (if any) of a function $y = f(x)$ at points where $f(x)$ is continuous but $f'(x)$ is discontinuous,
1. Determine the values of x for which $f'(x)$ is discontinuous and $f(x)$ is continuous.
2. For each value a such that $f(x)$ is continuous at $x = a$ and $f'(x)$ is discontinuous at $x = a$, determine whether $f'(x)$ changes sign as x increases through a:

$f'(x)$ changes from $+$ to $-$ at $x = a \Rightarrow$ relative maximum at $x = a$

$f'(x)$ changes from $-$ to $+$ at $x = a \Rightarrow$ relative minimum at $x = a$

$f'(x)$ does not change sign at $x = a \Rightarrow$ no relative maximum or
minimum at $x = a$

EXAMPLE

Find the relative maxima and minima (if any) of the function $y = x^{2/3}$.

$$\frac{dy}{dx} = \frac{2}{3}x^{-1/3}$$

$$\frac{dy}{dx} \neq 0 \qquad \text{for all values of } x$$

$$\frac{dy}{dx} \to -\infty \text{ as } x \to 0^- \qquad \text{and} \qquad \frac{dy}{dx} \to \infty \text{ as } x \to 0^+$$

so $\dfrac{dy}{dx}$ has an infinite discontinuity at $x = 0$.

If $x < 0$, $\dfrac{dy}{dx} < 0$
If $x > 0$, $\dfrac{dy}{dx} > 0$ $\left.\right\}$ so minimum at $x = 0$

See Figure 2.39.

Figure 2.39

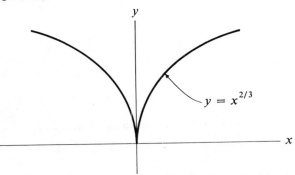

$y = x^{2/3}$

EXAMPLE

Find the relative maxima and minima (if any) of the function $y = (1 - x)^{2/3}(2 + x)^{1/3}$.

$$\frac{dy}{dx} = -\tfrac{2}{3}(1 - x)^{-1/3}(2 + x)^{1/3} + (1 - x)^{2/3}(\tfrac{1}{3})(2 + x)^{-2/3}$$

$$= \tfrac{1}{3}(1 - x)^{-1/3}(2 + x)^{-2/3}[-2(2 + x) + (1 - x)]$$

$$= \frac{-3 - 3x}{3(1 - x)^{1/3}(2 + x)^{2/3}}$$

$$= \frac{-(x + 1)}{(1 - x)^{1/3}(2 + x)^{2/3}}$$

$$= 0 \qquad \text{if } x = -1$$

$$\frac{dy}{dx} \to -\infty \text{ as } x \to 1^{-} \qquad \text{and} \qquad \frac{dy}{dx} \to \infty \text{ as } x \to 1^{+}$$

so $\dfrac{dy}{dx}$ has an infinite discontinuity at $x = 1$.

$$\frac{dy}{dx} \to -\infty \text{ as } x \to -2 \qquad \text{and} \qquad \frac{dy}{dx} \to \infty \text{ as } x \to -2$$

so $\dfrac{dy}{dx}$ has an infinite discontinuity at $x = -2$.

Figure 2.40

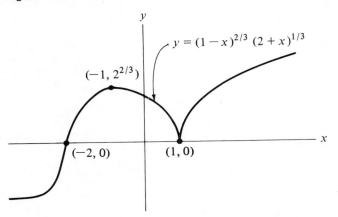

$y = (1 - x)^{2/3}(2 + x)^{1/3}$

$(-1, 2^{2/3})$

$(-2, 0)$

$(1, 0)$

If $-2 < x < -1$, $\dfrac{dy}{dx} > 0$

If $-1 < x < 1$, $\dfrac{dy}{dx} < 0$ } so maximum at $x = -1$

If $-1 < x < 1$, $\dfrac{dy}{dx} < 0$

If $x > 1$, $\dfrac{dy}{dx} > 0$ } so minimum at $x = 1$

If $x < -2$, $\dfrac{dy}{dx} > 0$

If $-2 < x < -1$, $\dfrac{dy}{dx} > 0$ } so no maximum or minimum at $x = -2$

See Figure 2.40.

EXAMPLE

Find the relative maxima and minima (if any) of the function $y = -(4 - x)^{1/2} - 2$.

$$\frac{dy}{dx} = \tfrac{1}{2}(4 - x)^{-1/2}$$

$$= \frac{1}{2(4 - x)^{1/2}}$$

$\dfrac{dy}{dx} \to \infty$ if $x \to 4^-$, so $\dfrac{dy}{dx}$ has an infinite discontinuity at $x = 4$. Note that y and $\dfrac{dy}{dx}$ are undefined if $x > 4$. Thus $y = -(4 - x)^{1/2} - 2$ has no relative maximum or minimum (see Figure 2.41).

Figure 2.41

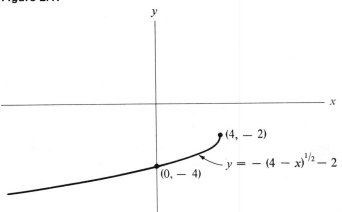

$(4, -2)$

$y = -(4 - x)^{1/2} - 2$

$(0, -4)$

As illustrated above and below, the least (or greatest) value of a function in an interval—that is, its absolute minimum or maximum in an interval—may occur at an end point of the interval rather than at a relative minimum or maximum value.

EXAMPLE

Find the maximum and minimum values of the function $y = x^2 - 2x$ in the interval $2 \leq x \leq 4$.

$$\frac{dy}{dx} = 2x - 2$$

$$= 0 \qquad \text{if } x = 1$$

$\left. \begin{array}{ll} < 0 & \text{if } x < 1 \\ > 0 & \text{if } x > 1 \end{array} \right\}$ so minimum at $x = 1$

But $x = 1$ is outside the interval $2 \leq x \leq 4$.

If $x = 2$, $y = 0$

If $x = 4$, $y = 8$

Thus in the interval $2 \leq x \leq 4$, the least value of y occurs at the end point $x = 2$, and the greatest value occurs at the end point $x = 4$; at neither of these points is $\frac{dy}{dx}$ equal to zero (see Figure 2.42).

Figure 2.42

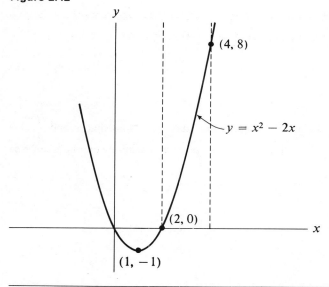

y

(4, 8)

$y = x^2 - 2x$

(2, 0)

x

(1, −1)

EXAMPLE

The total cost curve of a commodity is $y = 15x - 8x^2 + 2x^3$, where y represents total cost and x represents quantity. Suppose market conditions indicate that between 3 and 10 units should be produced (that is, $3 \leq x \leq 10$). Determine the quantity in this interval for which average cost is a minimum.

Average cost $= y/x = \bar{y} = 15 - 8x + 2x^2$.

$$\frac{d\bar{y}}{dx} = -8 + 4x$$

$$= 0 \qquad \text{if } x = 2$$

$\left. \begin{array}{ll} < 0 & \text{if } x < 2 \\ > 0 & \text{if } x > 2 \end{array} \right\}$ so minimum at $x = 2$

Figure 2.43

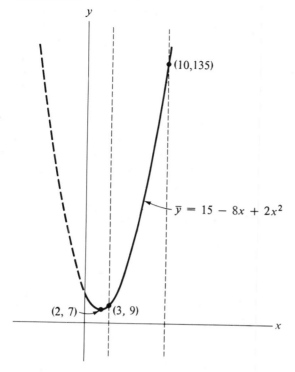

$$\bar{y} = 15 - 8x + 2x^2$$

But $x = 2$ is outside the interval $3 \leq x \leq 10$.

If $x = 3$, $\bar{y} = 9$

If $x = 10$, $\bar{y} = 135$

Thus in the interval $3 \leq x \leq 10$, the least value of $\bar{y}$ occurs at $x = 3$ and the greatest value occurs at $x = 10$; at neither of these points is $\dfrac{d\bar{y}}{dx}$ equal to zero. Thus, for between 3 and 10 units, average cost is minimum for 3 units (see Figure 2.43).

SUMMARY OF THE INFORMATION THAT CAN BE OBTAINED FROM THE FIRST DERIVATIVE

Consider the function $y = f(x)$ at the point $x = a$

$f'(a) > 0 \Rightarrow f(x)$ is an increasing function of x at $x = a$

$f'(a) < 0 \Rightarrow f(x)$ is a decreasing function of x at $x = a$

If
$\begin{cases} f(x) \text{ is continuous at } x = a \\ \quad \text{and either} \\ f'(a) = 0 \\ \quad \text{or} \\ f'(x) \text{ is discontinuous at} \\ \quad x = a \end{cases}$
then
$\begin{cases} f'(x) \text{ changes sign from } + \text{ to } - \text{ at} \\ x = a \Rightarrow \text{relative maximum at } x = a \\ f'(x) \text{ changes sign from } - \text{ to } + \text{ at} \\ x = a \Rightarrow \text{relative minimum at } x = a \\ f'(x) \text{ does not change sign at} \\ x = a \Rightarrow \text{no relative maximum} \\ \quad \text{or minimum at } x = a \end{cases}$

Note that the least or greatest value of a function in an interval, that is, its absolute minimum or maximum in an interval, may occur at an end point of the interval rather than at a relative minimum or maximum value.

PROBLEMS

For each of the following functions, determine maxima and minima; sketch the curve representing each function.

1. $y = 12 - 12x + x^3$

2. $y = \dfrac{x}{x + 1}$

3. $y = \dfrac{x^3}{3} - \dfrac{x^2}{2} - 6x$

4. $y = x^4 - 32x + 48$

5. $y = \dfrac{x}{\sqrt{x^2 + 7}}$

6. $y = \dfrac{2x}{\sqrt{x^2 - 1}}$

7. $y = x^2 - 4x + 3$

8. $y = x\sqrt{1 - x^2}$

9. $y = x^3 - 3x^2 + 2$

10. $y = \dfrac{1}{x^2 + 4}$

11. $y = \dfrac{x^2}{\sqrt{x^2 - 8}}$

12. $y = x^4 - 4x^3 + 12$

13. $y = \dfrac{3x^2}{\sqrt{x^2 + 3}}$

14. $y = \dfrac{1}{16 - x^2}$

15. $y = \tfrac{2}{3}x^3 - 4x^2 + 6x + 2$

16. $y = \dfrac{8x}{x^2 + 4}$

17. $y = \dfrac{x + 3}{x^2}$

18. $y = x^5 + 6$

19. $y = (x - 1)^{1/3}(x + 1)^{2/3}$

20. $y = \tfrac{1}{6}(x^3 - 6x^2 + 9x + 6)$

Answers to Odd-Numbered Problems

1. max $(-2, 28)$
   min $(2, -4)$
3. max $(-2, \frac{22}{3})$
   min $(3, -\frac{27}{2})$
5. no max
   no min
7. no max
   min $(2, -1)$
9. max $(0, 2)$
   min $(2, -2)$
11. no max

   min $(\pm 4, 4\sqrt{2})$
13. no max
   min $(0, 0)$
15. max $(1, \frac{14}{3})$
   min $(3, 2)$
17. no max
   min $(-6, -\frac{1}{12})$
19. max $(-1, 0)$
   min $\left(\dfrac{1}{3}, -\dfrac{2^{5/3}}{3}\right)$

THE SECOND DERIVATIVE

The second derivative of a function can be used to determine where the function is convex and where it is concave. The second derivative can also be used to locate the points of inflection of a function, if there are any.

Concavity

Consider the function $y = f(x)$ at the point $x = a$. The second derivative of y with respect to x, $y'' = f''(x)$, is the slope at the point x of the curve representing the first derivative $y' = f'(x)$ of the function $f(x)$; in particular, $f''(a)$ is the slope of the curve $y' = f'(x)$ at the point $x = a$.

If the second derivative $f''(a)$ of a function $y = f(x)$ is positive, $y' = f'(x)$ is an increasing function of x at $x = a$; the curve representing $y = f(x)$ is said to be *convex* where $f''(x)$ is positive. If the second derivative $f''(a)$ of a function $y = f(x)$ is negative, $y' = f'(x)$ is a decreasing function of x at $x = a$; the curve representing $y = f(x)$ is said to be *concave* where $f''(x)$ is negative (see Figure 2.44).

Consider a function $f(x)$ at a value $x = a$ for which $f(x)$ and $f'(x)$ are continuous. It is evident geometrically that if $f'(a) = 0$ and $f(x)$ is concave at $x = a$, then $f(x)$ has a maximum at a; similarly, if $f'(a) = 0$ and $f(x)$ is convex at $x = a$, then $f(x)$ has a minimum at a. The corresponding algebraic argument is based on the fact that a positive second derivative indicates an increasing slope and a negative second derivative indicates a decreasing slope.

CAUTION: The second derivative test is only sufficient, not necessary, for a relative maximum or minimum, since $f(x)$ may be convex or concave at $x = a$ if $f''(a) = 0$. That is, if $f'(a) = 0$, then

$$f''(a) > 0 \gneqq \text{convex}$$

$$f''(a) < 0 \gneqq \text{concave}$$

From this follows a very convenient, although not always applicable, test for relative maximum and minimum values:

If
$$\begin{cases} f(x) \text{ and } f'(x) \text{ are continuous} \\ \quad \text{at } x = a \\ \\ \quad \text{and} \\ \\ f'(a) = 0 \end{cases}$$
then
$$\begin{cases} f''(a) > 0 \Rightarrow \text{relative minimum} \\ \quad \text{at } x = a \\ f''(a) < 0 \Rightarrow \text{relative maximum} \\ \quad \text{at } x = a \\ f''(a) = 0 \Rightarrow \text{test does not apply} \end{cases}$$

Figure 2.44

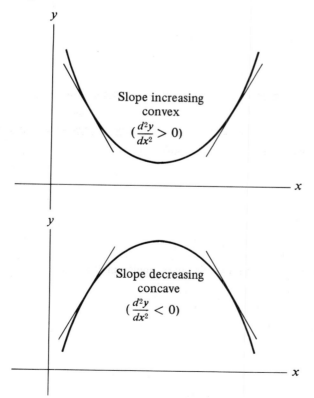

EXAMPLE

Find the relative maxima and minima (if any) of the function $y = \frac{1}{3}x^3 - 2x^2 + 3x + 1$.

$$\frac{dy}{dx} = x^2 - 4x + 3$$

$$= 0 \qquad \text{if } x^2 - 4x + 3 = 0$$

$$(x - 3)(x - 1) = 0$$

$$x = 3, 1$$

$$\frac{dy^2}{dx^2} = 2x - 4$$

If $x = 1$, $\frac{d^2y}{dx^2} < 0$, so maximum at $x = 1$

If $x = 3$, $\frac{d^2y}{dx^2} > 0$, so minimum at $x = 3$

See Figure 2.45.

Figure 2.45

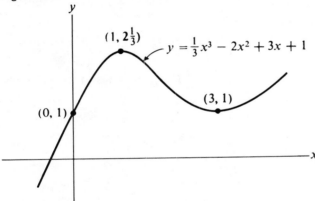

EXAMPLE

Find the relative maxima and minima (if any) of the function $y = x^4$.

$$\frac{dy}{dx} = 4x^3$$

$$= 0 \qquad \text{if } x = 0$$

$$\frac{d^2y}{dx^2} = 12x^2$$

If $x = 0$, $\frac{d^2y}{dx^2}\bigg| = 0$, so there may or may not be a maximum or minimum at $x = 0$

If $x < 0$, $\dfrac{dy}{dx} < 0$ ⎫
⎬ so minimum at $x = 0$
If $x > 0$, $\dfrac{dy}{dx} > 0$ ⎭

See Figure 2.46.

Figure 2.46

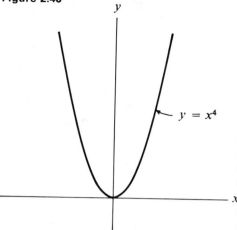

$y = x^4$

EXAMPLE

Find the relative maxima and minima (if any) of the function $y = x^3$.

$$\frac{dy}{dx} = 3x^2$$

$$= 0 \qquad \text{if } x = 0$$

$$\frac{d^2y}{dx^2} = 6x$$

If $x = 0$, $\dfrac{d^2y}{dx^2} = 0$, so there may or may not be a maximum or minimum at $x = 0$

If $x < 0$, $\dfrac{dy}{dx} > 0$

If $x > 0$, $\dfrac{dy}{dx} > 0$ } so no maximum or minimum at $x = 0$

See Figure 2.47.

Figure 2.47

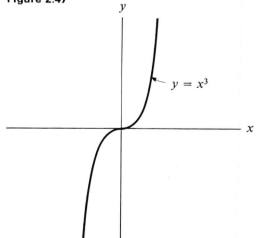

$y = x^3$

In the examples above, when $f''(a) = 0$—that is, when the second derivative test for a maximum or minimum does not apply—the first derivative is examined for change of sign as x passes through a. There is, however, an alternative procedure, involving derivatives of higher order, which is more convenient in some cases.

If $\left\{ \begin{array}{l} f'(a) = f''(a) = \cdots = f^{(n-1)}(a) = 0 \\[2ex] \text{and} \\[2ex] f^{(n)}(a) \neq 0 \end{array} \right.$ then $\left\{ \begin{array}{l} \text{for } n \text{ even } \left\{ \begin{array}{l} f^{(n)}(a) < 0 \Rightarrow \text{relative} \\ \quad \text{maximum at } x = a \\[1ex] f^{(n)}(a) > 0 \Rightarrow \text{relative} \\ \quad \text{minimum at } x = a \end{array} \right. \\[4ex] \text{for } n \text{ odd, } f(a) \text{ is neither a} \\ \text{relative maximum or minimum} \end{array} \right.$

EXAMPLE

Find the relative maxima and minima (if any) of the function $y = 3x^4 - x^3 + 2$.

$$\frac{dy}{dx} = 12x^3 - 3x^2$$

$$= 0 \qquad \text{if } 12x^3 - 3x^2 = 0$$

$$3x^2(4x - 1) = 0$$

$$x = 0, \tfrac{1}{4}$$

$$\frac{d^2y}{dx^2} = 36x^2 - 6x$$

$$= 6x(6x - 1)$$

If $x = \tfrac{1}{4}$, $\dfrac{d^2y}{dx^2} > 0$, so minimum at $x = \tfrac{1}{4}$

If $x = 0$, $\dfrac{d^2y}{dx^2} = 0$, so there may or may not be a maximum or minimum at $x = 0$

$$\frac{d^3y}{dx^3} = 72x - 6$$

$$= 6(12x - 1)$$

If $x = 0$, $\dfrac{d^3y}{dx^3} \neq 0$, so no maximum or minimum at $x = 0$

Alternative procedure using change of sign of the first derivative:

If $x < 0$, $\dfrac{dy}{dx} < 0$ $\left.\begin{array}{l} \\ \\ \end{array}\right\}$ so no maximum or minimum at $x = 0$

If $0 < x < \tfrac{1}{4}$, $\dfrac{dy}{dx} < 0$

If $0 < x < \tfrac{1}{4}$, $\dfrac{dy}{dx} < 0$ $\left.\begin{array}{l} \\ \\ \end{array}\right\}$ so minimum at $x = \tfrac{1}{4}$

If $x > \tfrac{1}{4}$, $\dfrac{dy}{dx} > 0$

See Figure 2.48.

Figure 2.48

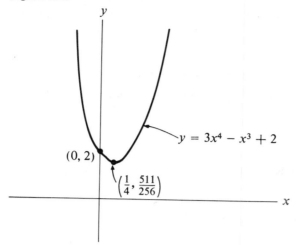

$y = 3x^4 - x^3 + 2$

$(0, 2)$

$\left(\dfrac{1}{4}, \dfrac{511}{256}\right)$

Points of Inflection

A function $y = f(x)$ is said to have a *point of inflection* at a point where the concavity or convexity of the curve changes. Geometrically, at a point of inflection the tangent crosses the curve. Since the sign of the second derivative indicates the concavity or convexity of a curve, it follows that a change in the sign of the second derivative implies a change in concavity or convexity (and thus a point of inflection).

If a function $f(x)$ has a point of inflection at a value $x = a$ for which its second derivative is continuous, then $f''(a) = 0$. Values of x for which $f''(x)$ is discontinuous must be considered separately, as discussed below.

CAUTIONS

1. A point of inflection at $x = a$ implies $f''(a) = 0$ only if $f(x)$ and $f''(x)$ are continuous at $x = a$.
2. $f''(a) = 0$ does *not* imply a point of inflection at $x = a$ even if $f(x)$ and $f''(x)$ are continuous at $x = a$; that is, if $f(x)$ and $f''(x)$ are continuous at $x = a$, $f''(a) = 0$ is a necessary but not a sufficient condition for a point of inflection at $x = a$.

Consider a function $f(x)$ at a value $x = a$ for which $f(x)$ and $f''(x)$ are continuous. If $f''(x)$ changes sign as x passes through the point $x = a$, then the curve representing $f(x)$ has a point of inflection at $x = a$. In this case $f''(a) = 0$.

A point of inflection may also occur at a value $x = a$ for which $f(x)$ is continuous but $f''(x)$ is discontinuous. Again, change in the sign of the second derivative as x passes through a is sufficient for the existence of a point of inflection at $x = a$.

Thus, in order to determine the points of inflection (if any) of a function $y = f(x)$,
1. Determine the values of x for which $f''(x)$ is either zero or discontinuous and $f(x)$ is continuous.
2. For each value a such that $f(x)$ is continuous at $x = a$ and $f''(x)$ is either zero or discontinuous at $x = a$, determine whether $f''(x)$ changes sign as x increases through a:

$f''(x)$ changes sign at $x = a \Rightarrow$ point of inflection at $x = a$

$f''(x)$ does not change sign at $x = a \Rightarrow$ no point of inflection at $x = a$

NOTE: If $f(x)$ and $f''(x)$ are continuous at $x = a$ and $f''(a) = 0$, then $f'''(a) \neq 0$ implies a point of inflection at $x = a$; this may be used as an alternative to checking for change of sign of the second derivative at $x = a$. This is analogous to using higher-derivative tests as an alternative to change of sign of the first derivative in checking for maxima and minima.

EXAMPLE

Find the relative maxima and minima and the points of inflection (if any) of the function $y = x^{1/3}$.

$$\frac{dy}{dx} = \tfrac{1}{3}x^{-2/3}$$

$\neq 0$ for all x and is discontinuous at $x = 0$

If $x < 0$, $\dfrac{dy}{dx} > 0$ ⎫
⎬ so no maximum or minimum at $x = 0$
If $x > 0$, $\dfrac{dy}{dx} > 0$ ⎭

$$\frac{d^2 y}{dx^2} = -\tfrac{2}{9}x^{-5/3}$$

$\neq 0$ for all x and is discontinuous at $x = 0$

If $x < 0$, $\dfrac{d^2 y}{dx^2} > 0$ ⎫
⎬ so point of inflection at $x = 0$
If $x > 0$, $\dfrac{d^2 y}{dx^2} < 0$ ⎭

See Figure 2.49.

Figure 2.49

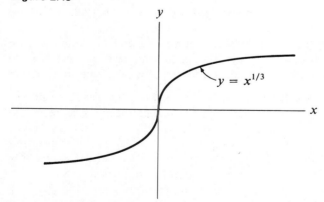

$y = x^{1/3}$

EXAMPLE

Find the relative maxima and minima and the points of inflection (if any) of the function $y = x/\sqrt{1 - x^2}$.

$$\frac{dy}{dx} = -\tfrac{1}{2}x(1 - x^2)^{-3/2}(-2x) + (1 - x^2)^{-1/2}$$

$$= (1 - x^2)^{-3/2}[x^2 + (1 - x^2)]$$

$$= (1 - x^2)^{-3/2}$$

$\dfrac{dy}{dx} \to \infty$ as $x \to \pm 1$, so infinite discontinuities at $x = \pm 1$

$\dfrac{dy}{dx} \geq 0$ for all x, $-1 \leq x \leq 1$, so no maximum or minimum

(Note that $y = x/\sqrt{1 - x^2}$ is defined only for $-1 \leq x \leq 1$.)

$$\dfrac{d^2y}{dx^2} = -\tfrac{3}{2}(1 - x^2)^{-5/2}(-2x)$$

$$= 3x(1 - x^2)^{-5/2}$$

$$= 0 \quad \text{if} \quad x = 0$$

If $-1 < x < 0$, $\dfrac{d^2y}{dx^2} < 0$

If $0 < x < 1$, $\dfrac{d^2y}{dx^2} > 0$ $\Bigg\}$ so point of inflection at $x = 0$

See Figure 2.50.

Figure 2.50

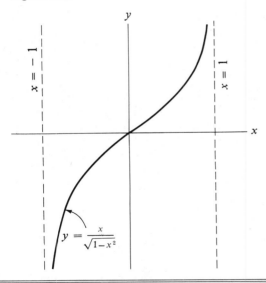

EXAMPLE

Find the relative maxima and minima and the points of inflection (if any) of the function $y = x + (1/x)$.

$$\dfrac{dy}{dx} = 1 - \dfrac{1}{x^2}$$

$$= \dfrac{x^2 - 1}{x^2}$$

$$= 0 \quad \text{if } x = \pm 1 \text{ and is discontinuous at } x = 0$$

If $x < -1$, $\dfrac{dy}{dx} > 0$

If $-1 < x < 0$, $\dfrac{dy}{dx} < 0$ $\Bigg\}$ so maximum at $x = -1$

If $0 < x < 1$, $\dfrac{dy}{dx} < 0$ ⎫

If $x > 1$, $\dfrac{dy}{dx} > 0$ ⎭ so minimum at $x = 1$

If $-1 < x < 0$, $\dfrac{dy}{dx} < 0$ ⎫

If $0 < x < 1$, $\dfrac{dy}{dx} < 0$ ⎭ so no maximum or minimum at $x = 0$

$$\frac{d^2y}{dx^2} = \frac{2}{x^3}$$

$$\neq 0 \qquad \text{for all } x$$

$\dfrac{d^2y}{dx^2}$ is discontinuous at $x = 0$ but y is also discontinuous at $x = 0$, so no point of inflection at $x = 0$

See Figure 2.51.

Figure 2.51

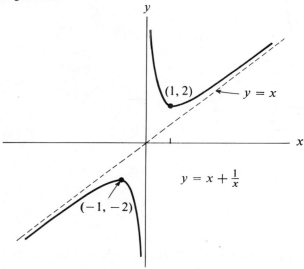

$$(1, 2) \quad \leftarrow y = x$$

$$y = x + \frac{1}{x}$$

$$(-1, -2)$$

SUMMARY OF THE INFORMATION THAT CAN BE OBTAINED FROM THE SECOND DERIVATIVE

Consider the function $y = f(x)$ at the point $x = a$:

$f''(a) > 0 \Rightarrow f(x)$ convex at $x = a$

$f''(a) < 0 \Rightarrow f(x)$ concave at $x = a$

If $\begin{cases} f(x) \text{ and } f'(x) \text{ are continuous} \\ \quad \text{at } x = a \\ \text{and} \\ f'(a) = 0 \end{cases}$ then $\begin{cases} f''(a) > 0 \Rightarrow \text{relative minimum at} \\ \quad x = a \\ f''(a) < 0 \Rightarrow \text{relative maximum at} \\ \quad x = a \\ f''(a) = 0 \Rightarrow \text{test does not apply} \end{cases}$

$$\text{If} \begin{cases} f(x) \text{ is continuous at } x = a \\ \quad \text{and either} \\ f''(a) = 0 \\ \quad \text{or} \\ f''(x) \text{ is discontinuous at } x = a \end{cases} \quad \text{then} \begin{cases} f''(x) \text{ changes sign at } x = a \\ \Rightarrow \text{point of inflection at } x = a \\[1em] f''(x) \text{ does not change sign at } x = a \\ \Rightarrow \text{no point of inflection at } x = a \end{cases}$$

SUMMARY OF THE PROCEDURE FOR SKETCHING THE GRAPH OF $y=f(x)$ USING INFORMATION PROVIDED BY FIRST AND SECOND DERIVATIVES

1. Obtain $\dfrac{dy}{dx}$ and $\dfrac{d^2y}{dx^2}$.

2. Determine the ranges of values of x for which $\dfrac{dy}{dx}$ is positive and for which it is negative.

3. Check points where $\dfrac{dy}{dx} = 0$ for possible maxima or minima.

4. Check points where $\dfrac{dy}{dx}$ is discontinuous for possible maxima or minima.

5. Determine the ranges of values of x for which $\dfrac{d^2y}{dx^2}$ is positive and for which it is negative.

6. Check points where $\dfrac{d^2y}{dx^2} = 0$ for possible points of inflection.

7. Check points where $\dfrac{d^2y}{dx^2}$ is discontinuous for possible points of inflection.

8. Determine the intercepts.

9. Note the nature of the curve for very small and very large values of x.

10. Sketch the curve as indicated by the signs of $\dfrac{dy}{dx}$ (increasing or decreasing) and of $\dfrac{d^2y}{dx^2}$ (convex or concave), the intercepts, asymptotic properties, and discontinuities.

EXAMPLE

Sketch the curve represented by the function $y = 4 + 3x - x^3$.

$$\frac{dy}{dx} = 3 - 3x^2$$

$$\frac{d^2y}{dx^2} = -6x$$

$$\frac{dy}{dx} = 0 \qquad \text{if } x = \pm 1$$

If $x < -1$, $\dfrac{dy}{dx} < 0$ (decreasing)

If $-1 < x < 1$, $\dfrac{dy}{dx} > 0$ (increasing)

If $x > 1$, $\dfrac{dy}{dx} < 0$ (decreasing)

so minimum at $(-1, 2)$ and maximum at $(1, 6)$. $\left(\text{As a check, if } x = -1, \dfrac{d^2y}{dx^2} = 6, \text{ and if } x = 1,\right.$

$\left.\dfrac{d^2y}{dx^2} = -6.\right)$

$\dfrac{d^2y}{dx^2} = 0$ if $x = 0$

       > 0 if $x < 0$ (convex)

       < 0 if $x > 0$ (concave)

so there is a point of inflection at $(0, 4)$. If $x = 0$, $y = 4$. As $x \to \infty$, $y \to -\infty$, and as $x \to -\infty$, $y \to \infty$. See Figure 2.52.

Figure 2.52

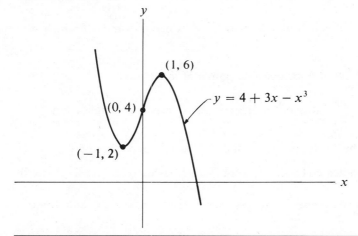

$y = 4 + 3x - x^3$

(1, 6)

(0, 4)

(−1, 2)

EXAMPLE

Sketch the curve represented by the function $y = \dfrac{x}{x + 4}$.

$\dfrac{dy}{dx} = \dfrac{(x + 4) - x}{(x + 4)^2} = \dfrac{4}{(x + 4)^2}$

$\dfrac{d^2y}{dx^2} = \dfrac{-(4)(2)(x + 4)}{(x + 4)^4} = \dfrac{-8}{(x + 4)^3}$

$\dfrac{dy}{dx} \neq 0$ for all x and is discontinuous at $x = -4$

If $x < -4$, $\dfrac{dy}{dx} > 0$ (increasing)

If $x > -4$, $\dfrac{dy}{dx} > 0$ (increasing)

so no minimum or maximum.

$\dfrac{d^2y}{dx^2} \neq 0$ for all x and is discontinuous at $x = -4$, but $\dfrac{dy}{dx}$ is also discontinuous at $x = -4$, so there is no point of inflection at $x = -4$.

If $x < -4$, $\dfrac{d^2y}{dx^2} > 0$ (convex)

If $x > -4$, $\dfrac{d^2y}{dx^2} < 0$ (concave)

If $x = 0$, $y = 0$. As $x \to \infty$, $y \to 1$, and as $x \to -\infty$, $y \to 1$. See Figure 2.53.

Figure 2.53

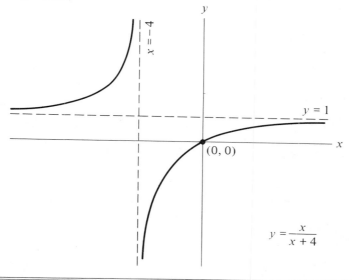

EXAMPLE

Find the points at which the curve represented by $x - y^4 + 2y^2 - 2 = 0$ has vertical tangents and sketch the curve.

$$1 - 4y^3 \frac{dy}{dx} + 4y \frac{dy}{dx} = 0$$

$$\frac{dy}{dx} = \frac{1}{4y(y^2 - 1)}$$

so $\dfrac{dy}{dx} \neq 0$ for all x. Vertical tangents occur when $\dfrac{dy}{dx}$ is undefined, so there are vertical tangents at $(2, 0)$, $(1, -1)$, and $(1, 1)$. (Note that $x = y^4 - 2y^2 + 2$.)

$$\frac{d^2y}{dx^2} = \frac{-(12y^2 - 4)\frac{dy}{dx}}{[4y(y^2 - 1)]^2} = \frac{-4(3y^2 - 1)}{[4y(y^2 - 1)]^3}$$

$\dfrac{d^2y}{dx^2} = 0$ if $y = \pm\sqrt{\tfrac{1}{3}}$ and is discontinuous at $y = 0$ and $y = \pm 1$

If $y < -1$, $\dfrac{d^2y}{dx^2} > 0$ (convex)

If $-1 < y < -\sqrt{\tfrac{1}{3}}$, $\dfrac{d^2y}{dx^2} < 0$ (concave)

so there is an inflection point at $y = -1$.

If $-\sqrt{\tfrac{1}{3}} < y < 0$, $\dfrac{d^2y}{dx^2} > 0$ (convex)

so there is an inflection point at $y = -\sqrt{\tfrac{1}{3}}$.

If $0 < y < \sqrt{\tfrac{1}{3}}$, $\dfrac{d^2y}{dx^2} < 0$ (concave)

so there is an inflection point at $y = 0$.

If $\sqrt{\tfrac{1}{3}} < y < 1$, $\dfrac{d^2y}{dx^2} > 0$ (convex)

Figure 2.54

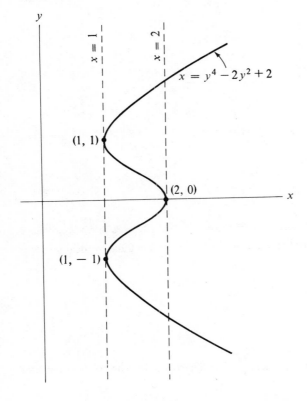

$x = y^4 - 2y^2 + 2$

so there is an inflection point at $y = \sqrt{\frac{1}{3}}$.

If $y > 1$, $\dfrac{d^2 y}{dx^2} < 0$ (concave)

so there is an inflection point at $y = 1$. If $y = 0$, $x = 2$. As $y \to \infty$, $x \to \infty$, and as $y \to -\infty$, $x \to \infty$. See Figure 2.54.

PROBLEMS

For each of the following functions, determine any maxima, minima, and points of inflection; sketch the curve representing each function. (Refer to problems on page 250 for maxima and minima.)

1. $y = 12 - 12x + x^3$

2. $y = \dfrac{x}{x + 1}$

3. $y = \dfrac{x^3}{3} - \dfrac{x^2}{2} - 6x$

4. $y = x^4 - 32x + 48$

5. $y = \dfrac{x}{\sqrt{x^2 + 7}}$

6. $y = \dfrac{2x}{\sqrt{x^2 - 1}}$

7. $y = x^2 - 4x + 3$

8. $y = x\sqrt{1 - x^2}$

9. $y = x^3 - 3x^2 + 2$

10. $y = \dfrac{1}{x^2 + 4}$

11. $y = \dfrac{x^2}{\sqrt{x^2 - 8}}$

12. $y = x^4 - 4x^3 + 12$

13. $y = \dfrac{3x^2}{\sqrt{x^2 + 3}}$

14. $y = \dfrac{1}{16 - x^2}$

15. $y = \frac{2}{3}x^3 - 4x^2 + 6x + 2$

16. $y = \dfrac{8x}{x^2 + 4}$

17. $y = \dfrac{x + 3}{x^2}$

18. $y = x^5 + 6$

19. $y = (x - 1)^{1/3}(x + 1)^{2/3}$

20. $y = \frac{1}{6}(x^3 - 6x^2 + 9x + 6)$

21. Sketch a smooth curve $y = f(x)$ having all the following properties:
   a. $f(1) = 0$
      $f'(x) < 0$ for $x < 1$
      $f'(x) > 0$ for $x > 1$
   b. $f(1) = 0$
      $f''(x) < 0$ for $x < 1$
      $f''(x) > 0$ for $x > 1$

22. Sketch a smooth curve $y = f(x)$ having all the following properties:
   $f(0) = 10$ $f'(6) = 0$ $f''(x) < 0$ for $x < 9$
   $f(6) = 15$ $f'(10) = 0$ $f''(9) = 0$
   $f(10) = 0$ $f''(x) > 0$ for $x > 9$

23. Sketch a continuous curve $y = f(x)$ having all of the following properties:
   $f(-2) = 8$ $f'(x) > 0$ for $|x| > 2$ $f''(x) < 0$ for $x < 0$
   $f(0) = 4$ $f'(2) = f'(-2) = 0$ $f''(x) > 0$ for $x > 0$
   $f(2) = 0$

24. Sketch a continuous curve $y = f(x)$ having the properties $f'(x) > 0$ for $x < 2$ and $f'(x) < 0$ for $x > 2$:
   a. If $f'(x)$ is continuous at $x = 2$
   b. If $f'(x) \to 1$ as $x \to 2^-$ and $f'(x) \to -1$ as $x \to 2^+$
   c. If $f'(x) = 1$ for $x < 2$ and $f'(x) = -1$ for $x > 2$

25. Sketch a continuous curve $y = f(x)$ having the following properties:
   a. $f(2) = f'(2) = 0$
      $f(0) = 2$
      $f''(x) < 0$ for $x < 1$ and $x > 3$
      $f''(x) > 0$ for $1 < x < 3$
   b. $f(2) = f'(2) = 0$
      $f(0) = 2$
      $f''(x) > 0$ for all x

26. Sketch a continuous curve $y = f(x)$ having all of the following properties:

    $f(0) = 10 \qquad f'(x) > 0$ for $x < 0 \qquad f''(x) > 0$ for $x < 0$

    $f(-3) = 0 \qquad f'(x) < 0$ for $x > 0 \qquad f''(x) > 0$ for $x > 0$

    $f(3) = 0$

27. Show that a cubic curve whose equation is of the form

    $$y = ax^3 + bx^2 + cx + d \qquad a, b, c, d \neq 0$$

    has one (and only one) point of inflection.

28. Sketch a continuous curve $y = f(x)$ for $x > 0$ if $f(1) = 0$ and $f'(x) = \dfrac{1}{x}$ for $x > 0$. Is such a curve necessarily convex or concave?

The curves representing the functions discussed on pages 241–249 were sketched without discussion of points of inflection; investigate points of inflection and sketch the curves accurately.

Answers to Odd-Numbered Problems

1. max $(-2, 28)$
   min $(2, -4)$
   pt. inf. $(0, 12)$
3. max $(-2, \frac{22}{3})$
   min $(3, -\frac{27}{2})$
   pt. inf. $(\frac{1}{2}, -\frac{37}{12})$
5. no max
   no min
   pt. inf. $(0, 0)$
7. no max
   min $(2, -1)$
   no pt. inf.
9. max $(0, 2)$
   min $(2, -2)$
   pt. inf. $(1, 0)$
11. no max
    min $(\pm 4, 4\sqrt{2})$
    no pt. inf.

13. no max
    min $(0, 0)$
    pt. inf. $(\pm\sqrt{6}, 6)$
15. max $(1, \frac{14}{3})$
    min $(3, 2)$
    pt. inf. $(2, \frac{10}{3})$
17. no max
    min $(-6, -\frac{1}{12})$
    pt. inf. $(-9, -\frac{2}{27})$
19. max $(-1, 0)$
    min $\left(\frac{1}{3}, -\dfrac{2^{5/3}}{3}\right)$

    pt. inf. $(1, 0)$
27. pt. inf. at $x = -\dfrac{b}{3a}$

2.12 Applications of Derivatives in Business and Economics

In this section several applications of derivatives in business and economics are discussed. Marginal cost, elasticity and marginal revenue are considered in much more detail than in previous sections. In addition, revenue from taxation, profit under monopoly, the effect of taxation on monopoly and inventory models are discussed.

COST, AVERAGE COST, AND MARGINAL COST

If the total cost y of producing and marketing x units of a commodity is assumed to be a function of x only, then the total cost function can be represented by $y = f(x)$.

Functions of various types are used to represent total cost curves; in general, cost curves have the following properties:

1. When no units are produced, total cost is zero or positive—that is, $f(0) \geq 0$. If $f(0) > 0$, then $f(0)$ is the amount of overhead or the fixed cost of production.

2. Total cost increases as x increases, so $f'(x)$ is always positive.
3. The total cost of producing an extremely large quantity of any commodity usually reaches a point at which it increases at an increasing rate. Thus usually the total cost curve eventually is concave upward, that is, $f''(x) > 0$; however, in a limited range the total cost curve is frequently concave downward, corresponding to decreasing marginal cost.

If the total cost function is

$$y = f(x)$$

then the average or per unit cost is

$$\bar{y} = \frac{y}{x} = \frac{f(x)}{x}$$

and the marginal cost is

$$\frac{dy}{dx} = f'(x)$$

The first derivative of average cost (the marginal average cost) is

$$\frac{d\bar{y}}{dx} = \frac{xf'(x) - f(x)}{x^2}$$

$$= 0 \qquad \text{if and only if } xf'(x) - f(x) = 0$$

$$\text{that is, } f(x) = xf'(x),$$

$$\frac{f(x)}{x} = f'(x)$$

Thus average cost is minimum at the value of x for which average cost equals marginal cost; that is, the average and marginal cost curves intersect at the point of minimum average cost. Note that the value of x (if any) for which $\frac{d\bar{y}}{dx} = 0$ is assumed to be a minimum because of the third property of cost curves mentioned above; for a particular total cost curve the existence of this minimum can be checked in the usual way.

EXAMPLE

Linear cost functions:

Total cost: $y = ax + b$, where $a > 0$, $b \geq 0$

Average cost: $\bar{y} = y/x = a + (b/x)$

Marginal cost: $\frac{dy}{dx} = a$

Marginal average cost: $\frac{d\bar{y}}{dx} = -\frac{b}{x^2}$

Total cost and marginal cost are represented by straight lines and average cost is represented by the first quadrant branch of an equilateral hyperbola with horizontal asymptote $\bar{y} = a$. Average cost is thus a decreasing function of the number of units produced; it has no minimum value but approaches a, the marginal cost, as the number of units increases (see Figure 2.55).

Figure 2.55

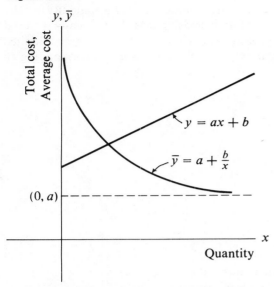

EXAMPLE

Quadratic cost functions:

Total cost: $y = ax^2 + bx + c$, where $a > 0$, $b \geq 0$, $c \geq 0$

Average cost: $\bar{y} = y/x = ax + b + (c/x)$

Marginal cost: $\dfrac{dy}{dx} = 2ax + b$

Marginal average cost: $\dfrac{d\bar{y}}{dx} = a - \dfrac{c}{x^2}$

Total cost is represented by the first quadrant part of a parabola, average cost is represented by the first quadrant branch of a hyperbola, and marginal cost is represented by a straight line (see Figure 2.56).

$$\frac{d\bar{y}}{dx} = 0 \qquad \text{if } ax^2 = c$$

$$x = \pm\sqrt{\frac{c}{a}}, \text{ but only } x = \sqrt{\frac{c}{a}} \text{ is of interest}$$

$$\frac{d\bar{y}^2}{dx^2} = -\frac{-2cx}{x^4} = \frac{2c}{x^3} > 0 \text{ for } x > 0, \text{ so minimum at } x = \sqrt{\frac{c}{a}}$$

Note that average and marginal cost are equal if $x = \sqrt{c/a}$, since

$$\bar{y} = a\sqrt{\frac{c}{a}} + b + c\sqrt{\frac{a}{c}}$$

$$= 2\sqrt{ac} + b$$

and

$$\frac{dy}{dx} = 2a\sqrt{\frac{c}{a}} + b$$

$$= 2\sqrt{ac} + b$$

Figure 2.56

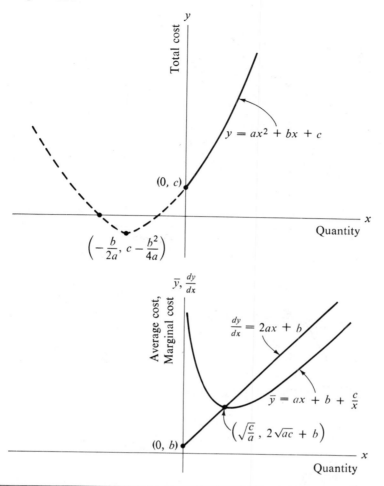

EXAMPLE

Cubic cost functions:

Total cost: $y = ax^3 + bx^2 + cx + d$, where $a > 0$, $b \le 0$, $c \ge 0$, $d \ge 0$, $b^2 \le 3ac$

Average cost: $\bar{y} = \dfrac{y}{x} = ax^2 + bx + c + \dfrac{d}{x}$

Marginal cost: $\dfrac{dy}{dx} = 3ax^2 + 2bx + c$

Marginal average cost: $\dfrac{d\bar{y}}{dx} = 2ax + b - \dfrac{d}{x^2}$

Total cost is represented by the first quadrant part of a cubic curve, average cost is represented by the first quadrant branch of a hyperbola, and marginal cost is represented by the first quadrant part of a parabola (see Figure 2.57).

Figure 2.57

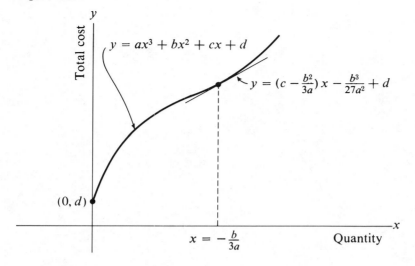

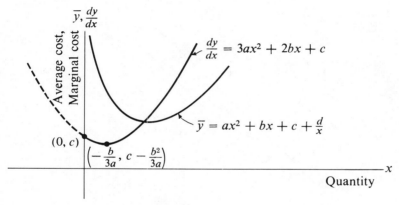

Cubic cost functions are frequently appropriate when the concavity of the cost function changes in a specified interval; however, such a function must have no relative maximum or minimum in the first quadrant:

$$\frac{dy}{dx} = 3ax^2 + 2bx + c$$

$$= 0 \qquad \text{if } 3ax^2 + 2bx + c = 0$$

$$x = \frac{-2b \pm \sqrt{4b^2 - 12ac}}{6a} = \frac{-b \pm \sqrt{b^2 - 3ac}}{3a}$$

If $b^2 - 3ac < 0$, $y = ax^3 + bx^2 + cx + d$ has no relative maximum or minimum.
If $b^2 - 3ac = 0$, $x = -b/3a$ and

$$y = a\left(\frac{-b^3}{27a^3}\right) + b\left(\frac{b^2}{9a^2}\right) + c\left(\frac{-b}{3a}\right) + d$$

$$= \frac{2b^3}{27a^2} - \frac{bc}{3a} + d$$

$$= \frac{b(2b^2 - 9ac)}{27a^2} + d$$

$2b^2 - 9ac < 0$, since $b^2 - 3ac < 0$ and thus, since $a > 0$ and $b \leq 0$, $b(2b^2 - 9ac)/27a^2 \geq 0$ and $\{-b/3a, [b(2b^2 - 9ac)/27a^2] + d\}$ lies in the first quadrant.

$$\frac{d^2y}{dx^2} = 6ax + 2b$$

$$\left.\frac{d^2y}{dx^2}\right|_{x = -b/3a} = 0$$

$$\frac{d^3y}{dx^3} = 6a \neq 0$$

So there is no relative maximum or minimum at $x = -b/3a$, but there is a point of inflection at $x = -b/3a$. Thus, if $b^2 - 3ac \leq 0$, then $y = ax^3 + bx^2 + cx + d$ has no relative maximum or minimum in the first quadrant; a point of inflection occurs at

$$x = -\frac{b}{3a}, \qquad y = \frac{b(2b^2 - 9ac)}{27a^2} + d$$

Note that $b^2 - 3ac \leq 0$ is a sufficient but not a necessary condition for $y = ax^3 + bx^2 + cx + d$ to have no relative maximum or minimum in the first quadrant. Other cases are discussed in Technical Note II.

Frequently the tangent at the point of inflection provides a good linear approximation of a cubic cost function for a limited range. The tangent at the point of inflection $x = -b/3a$ has slope

$$\frac{dy}{dx} = 3ax^2 + 2bx + c$$

$$\left.\frac{dy}{dx}\right|_{x = -b/3a} = \frac{b^2}{3a} - \frac{2b^2}{3a} + c$$

$$= c - \frac{b^2}{3a} \qquad \text{which is } \geq 0, \text{ since } b^2 \leq 3ac$$

If $x = -b/3a$,

$$y = a\left(-\frac{b^3}{27a^3}\right) + b\left(\frac{b^2}{9a^2}\right) + c\left(-\frac{b}{3a}\right) + d$$

$$= \frac{2b^3}{27a^2} - \frac{bc}{3a} + d$$

The line through the point $(-b/3a, \; 2b^3/27a^2 - (bc/3a) + d)$ and having slope $c - (b^2/3a)$ is given by

$$y - y_1 = m(x - x_1)$$

$$y - \left(\frac{2b^3}{27a^2} - \frac{bc}{3a} + d\right) = \left(c - \frac{b^2}{3a}\right)\left(x + \frac{b}{3a}\right)$$

$$y = \left(c - \frac{b^2}{3a}\right)x + \frac{bc}{3a} - \frac{b^3}{9a^2} + \frac{2b^3}{27a^2} - \frac{bc}{3a} + d$$

$$= \left(c - \frac{b^2}{3a}\right)x - \frac{b^3}{27a^2} + d$$

EXAMPLE

Higher-order polynomial cost functions:

Total cost: $y = ax^b + c$, where $a > 0$, $b > 1$, $c \geq 0$

Average cost: $\bar{y} = \dfrac{y}{x} = ax^{b-1} + \dfrac{c}{x}$

Marginal cost: $\dfrac{dy}{dx} = abx^{b-1}$

Marginal average cost: $\dfrac{d\bar{y}}{dx} = a(b-1)x^{b-2} - \dfrac{c}{x^2}$

Total cost is represented by the first quadrant part of an algebraic curve, average cost is represented by the first quadrant branch of a hyperbola, and marginal cost is represented by the first quadrant part of an algebraic curve (see Figure 2.58).

Figure 2.58

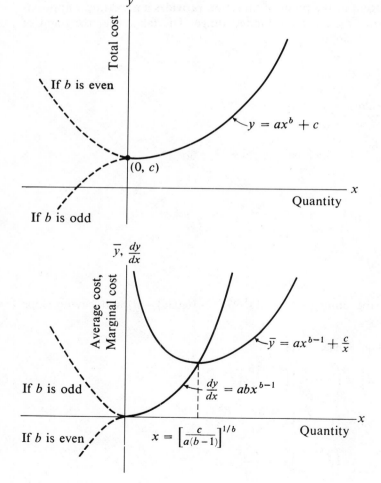

This type of simple polynomial curve is always concave upward for $x \geq 0$ and thus in practice is usually appropriate only for limited ranges of x.

$$\frac{d\bar{y}}{dx} = 0 \qquad \text{if } a(b-1)x^b = c$$

$$x = \left[\frac{c}{a(b-1)}\right]^{1/b}$$

$$\frac{d\bar{y}^2}{dx^2} = a(b-1)(b-2)x^{b-3} + \frac{2c}{x^3}$$

$$= x^{-3}[a(b-1)(b-2)x^b + 2c]$$

If $x = \left[\dfrac{c}{a(b-1)}\right]^{1/b}$, then

$$\frac{d\bar{y}^2}{dx^2} = \left[\frac{c}{a(b-1)}\right]^{-3/b}\left[a(b-1)(b-2)\frac{c}{a(b-1)} + 2c\right]$$

$$= \left[\frac{c}{a(b-1)}\right]^{-3/b}[bc]$$

$$> 0$$

so minimum at $x = \left[\dfrac{c}{a(b-1)}\right]^{1/b}$

Note that average cost and marginal cost are equal if $x = (c/a(b-1))^{1/b}$, since

$$\bar{y} = a\left(\frac{c}{a(b-1)}\right)^{(b-1)/b} + c\left(\frac{c}{a(b-1)}\right)^{-1/b}$$

$$= \left(\frac{c}{a(b-1)}\right)^{(b-1)/b}\left[a + c\left(\frac{c}{a(b-1)}\right)^{-1}\right]$$

$$= \left(\frac{c}{a(b-1)}\right)^{(b-1)/b}[a + a(b-1)]$$

$$= ab\left(\frac{c}{a(b-1)}\right)^{(b-1)/b}$$

and

$$\frac{dy}{dx} = ab\left(\frac{c}{a(b-1)}\right)^{(b-1)/b}$$

EXAMPLE

Exponential cost functions:

Total cost: $y = ae^{bx}$, where $a > 0, b > 0$

Average cost: $\bar{y} = \dfrac{y}{x} = \dfrac{ae^{bx}}{x}$

Marginal cost: $\dfrac{dy}{dx} = abe^{bx}$

Marginal average cost: $\dfrac{d\bar{y}}{dx} = \dfrac{abxe^{bx} - ae^{bx}}{x^2} = \dfrac{ae^{bx}(bx-1)}{x^2}$

Figure 2.59

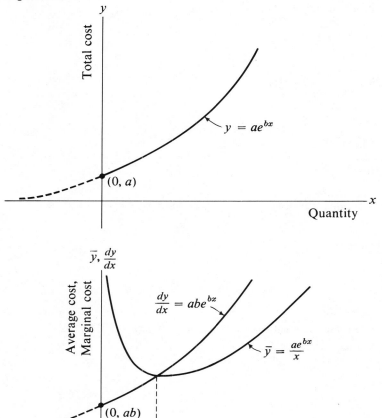

Total cost is represented by the first quadrant part of an exponential curve, average cost is represented by the first quadrant branch of an exponential hyperbola, and marginal cost is represented by the first quadrant part of an exponential curve (see Figure 2.59).

Exponential and logarithmic curves are either concave upward or concave downward for all $x \geq 0$ and thus in practice are usually appropriate only for limited ranges of x.

$$\frac{d\bar{y}}{dx} = 0 \qquad \text{if } ae^{bx}(bx - 1) = 0$$

$$x = \frac{1}{b}$$

$$\frac{d\bar{y}^2}{dx^2} = \frac{(abe^{bx} + ab^2xe^{bx} - abe^{bx})x^2 - (abxe^{bx} - ae^{bx})(2x)}{x^4}$$

$$= \frac{axe^{bx}(b^2x^2 - 2bx + 2)}{x^4}$$

If $x = 1/b$, then

$$\frac{d\bar{y}^2}{dx^2} = \frac{\frac{a}{b}e(1 - 2 + 2)}{\frac{1}{b^4}}$$

$$= ab^3e > 0$$

so minimum at $x = 1/b$. Note that average cost and marginal cost are equal if $x = 1/b$, since

$$\bar{y} = abe$$

and

$$\frac{dy}{dx} = abe$$

PROBLEMS

1. For each of the following average cost functions, find the minimum average cost and show that at the minimum average cost, marginal cost and average cost are equal.

   a. $\bar{y} = 25 - 8x + x^2$ e. $\bar{y} = 2x + 5 + \dfrac{18}{x}$

   b. $\bar{y} = 2 + x \ln x$ f. $\bar{y} = 20 + 2x^2 + 4x^4$

   c. $\bar{y} = 2e^x + e^{-x}$ g. $\bar{y} = 10 - 4x^3 + 3x^4$

   d. $\bar{y} = 3x + 5 + \dfrac{6}{x}$ h. $\bar{y} = 6x + 7 + \dfrac{36}{x}$

2. For each of the following total cost functions, find marginal cost and determine the nature of marginal cost (increasing, decreasing).
   a. $y = 1000x - 180x^2 + 3x^3$ b. $y = 220 + 55x - 2x^3 + x^4$

3. Determine the nature of the marginal and average cost functions (increasing, decreasing) for each of the following total cost functions.
   a. $y = \sqrt{x + 25}, \ 0 \leq x \leq 10$ b. $y = 9x + 5xe^{-2x}$

4. For the following total cost function, find the equation of the tangent at the point of inflection as an approximation of the function near that point.

   $$y = x^3 - 6x^2 + 14x + 6$$

5. The Precision Machine Tool Manufacturing Company has a total cost function represented by the equation $y = 2x^3 - 3x^2 - 12x$, where y represents cost and x represents quantity.

   a. What equation represents the marginal cost function?

   b. What is the equation for the average cost function? At what point is average cost at its minimum?

   c. Is this a set of equations one might realistically expect to find in practice? Why?

6. The Minute Man Colonial Furniture Company's total revenue function is expressed by the equation $R = 24x - 3x^2$, where R represents revenue and x represents quantity.

   a. What is the maximum revenue the company can expect, assuming this equation is valid?

   b. What equation represents the average revenue function?

   c. What equation represents the marginal revenue function?

   d. On one graph, plot the total, average, and marginal revenue functions.

7. Arto Company manufactures cabinets for TV sets; the total cost of producing a certain model is given by $y = 4x - x^2 + 2x^3$, where y represents total cost and x represents quantity, in thousands of units. The sales department has indicated that between 2 and 6 units (in thousands) should be produced. At what quantity is marginal cost a minimum? Explain your answer, and graph the marginal cost curve.

8. If the general formula for the total cost function is

   $$TC = f(x) = ax^3 + bx^2 + cx + d$$

   a. What is the corresponding equation for the marginal cost function?

   b. What is the corresponding equation for the average cost function?

9. An important generalization is often made about the relationships between the total revenue (TR), average revenue (AR), and marginal revenue (MR) functions:

When $MR = 0$, TR is at a maximum point
When $MR > AR$, AR is increasing
When $MR < AR$, AR is decreasing
When $MR = AR$, AR is unchanging

a. Illustrate this with an example from your reading or an example from the text.
b. Work out the analogous relationships for the total cost (TC), average cost (AC), and marginal cost (MC) functions.

10. Henderson and Quandt in their book *Microeconomic Theory* state the following*:

"A monopolist is free to select any price-quantity combination which lies on his negatively sloped demand curve. Since an expansion of his output results in a reduction of his price, his MR is less than his price. His first-order condition for profit maximization requires the equality of MR and MC. His second-order condition requires that MC be increasing more rapidly than MR." (Note that increasing more rapidly is logically equivalent to decreasing less rapidly.)

Which, if any, of the three diagrams in Figure 2.60 satisfies both conditions?

Figure 2.60

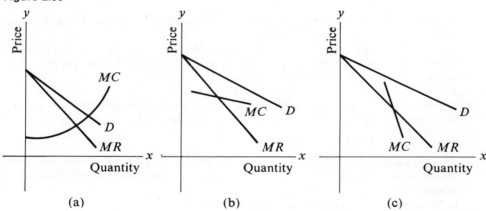

(a)   (b)   (c)

Answers to Odd-Numbered Problems

1. a. $\bar{y}_{\min} = 9$

b. $\bar{y}_{\min} = 2 - \dfrac{1}{e}$

c. $\bar{y}_{\min} = 2^{3/2}$
d. $\bar{y}_{\min} = 5 + 6\sqrt{2}$
e. $\bar{y}_{\min} = 17$
f. $\bar{y}_{\min} = 20$
g. $\bar{y}_{\min} = 9$
h. $\bar{y}_{\min} = 7 + 12\sqrt{6}$

3. a. for $0 \leq x \leq 10$, marginal and average cost always decreasing
b. marginal cost decreasing for $x < 1$ and increasing for $x > 1$; average cost always decreasing; $\bar{y}_c \to 9$ as $x \to \infty$

---

* J. M. Henderson and R. E. Quandt, *Microeconomic Theory, a Mathematical Approach*, McGraw-Hill, New York, 1958, p. 198.

5. a. $MC = 6x^2 - 6x - 12$

  b. $AC = 2x^2 - 3x - 12$, min at $x = \frac{3}{4}$

  c. no, TC not in first quadrant for $x < \dfrac{3 + \sqrt{105}}{4}$

7. in interval $2 \leq x \leq 6$, MC is minimum for $x = 2$

9. b. when $MC = 0$, TC is maximum
  when $MC > AC$, AC is increasing
  when $MC < AC$, AC is decreasing
  when $MC = AC$, AC is unchanging

ELASTICITY

It is frequently of interest to consider the relative change in the dependent variable which results from a small change in the independent variable. The ratio of the relative change in the dependent variable, y, to the relative change in the independent variable, x, is referred to as the *elasticity* of y with respect to x. The elasticity of y with respect to x measures the responsiveness of y to changes in x. Because relative changes are used in the definition of elasticity, the elasticity of a function is dimensionless. That is, elasticity is independent of the units in which the variables are measured.

There are two types of measurement of elasticity, arc elasticity and point elasticity. *Arc elasticity* measures the elasticity of a function between two points, that is, over an arc. Unfortunately, the definition of arc elasticity is somewhat ambiguous, as discussed below. However, for a continuous function of a continuous variable, *point elasticity*, the elasticity of a function at a specific point, can be defined unambiguously.

If $y = f(x)$, the elasticity of y with respect to x is defined by

$$\frac{Ey}{Ex} = \frac{\Delta y}{y} \bigg/ \frac{\Delta x}{x} = \frac{x}{y} \cdot \frac{\Delta y}{\Delta x}$$

where, as $\Delta x \to 0$, $\dfrac{\Delta y}{\Delta x} \to \dfrac{dy}{dx}$. Elasticity is frequently denoted by η.

In general, the elasticity of a function varies over its range. For example, in Figure 2.61, elasticity of the function over the two arcs noted is not the same; although $\dfrac{\Delta y}{\Delta x} = \dfrac{\Delta y'}{\Delta x'}$, $\dfrac{x}{y} \neq \dfrac{x'}{y'}$ and thus $\dfrac{Ey}{Ex} \neq \dfrac{Ey'}{Ex'}$. Figure 2.61 also illustrates the ambiguity in defining arc elasticity since, for example, it is not clear whether x_1/y_1 or x_2/y_2 should be used for x/y.

Arc Elasticity

The following formulas are frequently used for measuring arc elasticity between the points (x_1, y_1) and (x_2, y_2).

$$\frac{Ey}{Ex} = \frac{x_1}{y_1} \cdot \frac{y_2 - y_1}{x_2 - x_1} = \frac{x_1}{y_1} \cdot \frac{\Delta y}{\Delta x}$$

$$\frac{Ey}{Ex} = \frac{x_2}{y_2} \cdot \frac{y_2 - y_1}{x_2 - x_1} = \frac{x_2}{y_2} \cdot \frac{\Delta y}{\Delta x}$$

$$\frac{Ey}{Ex} = \frac{x_1 + x_2}{y_1 + y_2} \cdot \frac{y_2 - y_1}{x_2 - x_1} = \frac{x_1 + x_2}{y_1 + y_2} \cdot \frac{\Delta y}{\Delta x}$$

Figure 2.61

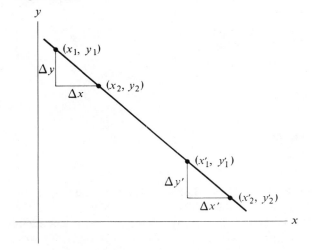

The first formula gives an approximation of the point elasticity at (x_1, y_1). The second formula gives an approximation of the point elasticity at (x_2, y_2). The third formula gives an average of the elasticity between the points (x_1, y_1) and (x_2, y_2) and is probably the most commonly used.

Point Elasticity

For point elasticity, this ambiguity does not arise. The point elasticity of $y = f(x)$ at (x_1, y_1) is

$$\frac{Ey}{Ex} = \frac{x_1}{y_1} \cdot \frac{dy}{dx}\bigg|_{x_1,\, y_1}$$

and, in general, the point elasticity of y with respect to x is given by

$$\eta = \frac{Ey}{Ex} = \frac{\dfrac{dy}{y}}{\dfrac{dx}{x}} = \frac{x}{y} \cdot \frac{dy}{dx}$$

NOTE: the ratio of the derivative of a function to the function itself is called the *logarithmic derivative* of the function; that is, if $y = f(x)$, then

$$\frac{f'(x)}{f(x)} = \frac{\dfrac{dy}{dx}}{y} = \frac{1}{y}\frac{dy}{dx} = \frac{d}{dx}\ln y$$

is the logarithmic derivative of $f(x)$. The elasticity of the function $y = f(x)$ at the point x is the ratio of the logarithmic derivative of y to the logarithmic derivative of x:

$$\frac{Ey}{Ex} = \frac{\dfrac{d}{dx}\ln y}{\dfrac{d}{dx}\ln x} = \frac{\dfrac{1}{y}\dfrac{dy}{dx}}{\dfrac{1}{x}\dfrac{dx}{dx}} = \frac{x}{y} \cdot \frac{dy}{dx}$$

Elasticity of Demand

Elasticity is defined as a property of any differentiable function; however, in economic theory elasticity is most frequently considered for demand, supply, price, cost, and revenue functions. Elasticity is used, for example, as a measure of the responsiveness of demand or supply to changes in price or income, and the responsiveness of price, total cost, or total revenue to changes in quantity. Probably the most frequent use of elasticity in economics involves analyses of price elasticity of demand as a measure of the effect of a change in price on total revenue; this type of analysis is discussed below.

The classical use of the concept of elasticity is in analyzing the responsiveness of demand for a commodity to changes in its price. Because the slope of a demand curve is negative, its first derivative is negative, and thus $\eta \leq 0$. Since elasticity is dimensionless, the responsiveness of different commodity demands to price changes can be compared. For this purpose, demand is frequently classified in general categories as perfectly elastic ($\eta = -\infty$), relatively elastic ($\eta < -1$), unit elastic ($\eta = -1$), relatively inelastic ($-1 < \eta < 0$), and perfectly inelastic ($\eta = 0$). Thus, demand is elastic if $|\eta| > 1$, unit elastic if $|\eta| = 1$, and inelastic if $|\eta| < 1$. Demand curves having differing elasticities are shown in Figure 2.62. Note that elasticity is not generally constant over the range of a function; note also that slope is only one aspect of elasticity and should not be equated with elasticity.

The price elasticity of demand for a commodity is of interest to a firm; for example, if demand is price elastic at a given price, a price decrease raises quantity demanded proportionately more than the price decreases, so that total revenue, which is the product of price and quantity, increases. Similarly, when demand is unit elastic, total revenue is unchanged by a decrease in price; when demand is inelastic, total revenue is decreased by an increase in price.

Figure 2.62

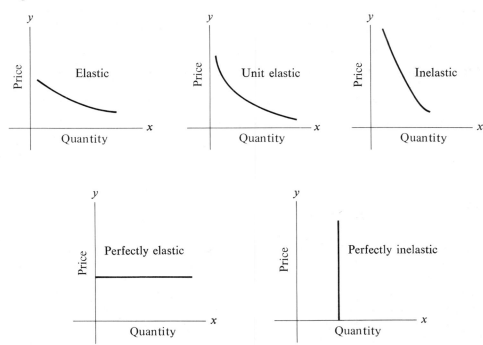

Cross Elasticity

The concept of *cross elasticity* is useful as a measure of the relationship between the demands for two or more commodities. Cross elasticity measures the responsiveness of demand for one commodity to changes in the price of another commodity. The elasticity of demand for A with respect to price of B is defined as

$$\frac{Ex_A}{Ey_B} = \frac{\dfrac{dx_A}{x_A}}{\dfrac{dy_B}{y_B}} = \frac{y_B}{x_A} \cdot \frac{dx_A}{dy_B}$$

and *arc cross elasticity* as y_B changes from y_{B_1} to y_{B_2} and x_A changes from x_{A_1} to x_{A_2} is given by

$$\frac{Ex_A}{Ey_B} = \frac{y_{B_1} + y_{B_2}}{x_{A_1} + x_{A_2}} \cdot \frac{x_{A_2} - x_{A_1}}{y_{B_2} - y_{B_1}}$$

where the x_A's are the quantities of A, the y_B's are the prices of B, and the price of A is assumed to be constant. The elasticity of demand for B with respect to price of A is similarly defined.

When commodities are substitutes for each other, their cross elasticities are positive. For example, when the price of butter increases, the consumption of margarine also increases, assuming that the price of magarine and other relevant factors remain constant. When commodities are complementary to each other, their cross elasticities are negative. For example, when the price of lettuce increases, the consumption of salad dressing decreases, assuming that other relevant factors remain constant.

NOTE: Demand functions are customarily written with price as the dependent variable and quantity demanded as the independent variable and are graphed in a corresponding manner. However, in analyses involving price elasticity of demand, demand is logically considered to be the dependent variable and price the independent variable. In the examples below, the demand function is given in one form in some cases and in the other form in other cases and is represented graphically in both forms. When a demand function is given in the form $y = f(x)$ and it is not convenient to solve for x, $\dfrac{dx}{dy}$ can be obtained by implicit differentiation.

Because demand functions are conventionally written $y = f(x)$, where y is price and x is quantity demanded, and the elasticity of demand involves the derivative $\dfrac{dx}{dy}$, equations and graphs must be read carefully to avoid misinterpretation.

EXAMPLE

The demand function for a particular commodity is given by $y = \sqrt{(20 - x)/2}$ for $0 \leq x \leq 20$, where y is price per unit and x is number of units demanded. Consider the point $x = 12$, $y = 2$. If the price decreases by 6%, determine the corresponding increase in demand and an approximation to the elasticity of demand at the point $x = 12$, $y = 2$. Compare this with the exact elasticity of demand at the point $x = 12$, $y = 2$. Then compute an approximation to the elasticity of demand and the exact elasticity of demand at the point representing the changed price and quantity; also compute the arc elasticity based on average price and quantity (see Figure 2.63).

Figure 2.63

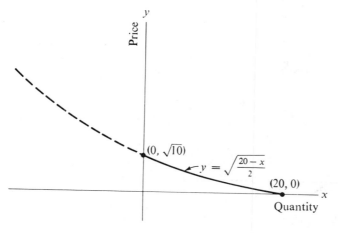

Solving the demand equation for x,

$$y = \sqrt{\frac{20 - x}{2}}$$

$$y^2 = \tfrac{1}{2}(20 - x)$$

$$x = 20 - 2y^2$$

See Figure 2.64.

$y_1 = 2$	$y_2 = 2 - (0.06)(2) = 1.88$	$\Delta y = -0.12$
$x_1 = 12$	$x_2 = 20 - 2(1.88)^2 = 12.93$	$\Delta x = 0.93$

Arc elasticity of demand at $y = 2$, $x = 12$, is

$$\frac{Ex}{Ey} = \frac{y_1}{x_1} \cdot \frac{\Delta x}{\Delta y}$$

$$= \frac{2}{12}\left(-\frac{0.93}{0.12}\right)$$

$$= -1.29$$

Figure 2.64

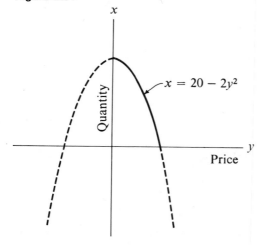

Figure 2.65

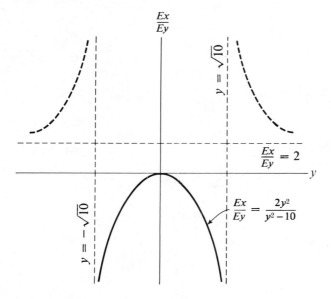

Point elasticity of demand at $y = 2$, $x = 12$, is

$$\frac{Ex}{Ey} = \frac{y}{x} \cdot \frac{dx}{dy}$$

$$= \frac{y}{20 - 2y^2}(-4y)$$

$$= \frac{2y^2}{y^2 - 10}$$

See Figure 2.65.

$$\left.\frac{Ex}{Ey}\right|_{y=2} = -\frac{8}{6} = -1.33$$

Arc elasticity of demand at $y_2 = 1.88$, $x_2 = 12.93$, is

$$\frac{Ex}{Ey} = \frac{y_2}{x_2} \cdot \frac{\Delta x}{\Delta y}$$

$$= \frac{1.88}{12.93}\left(-\frac{0.93}{0.12}\right)$$

$$= -1.13$$

Point elasticity of demand at $y_2 = 1.88$, $x_2 = 12.93$, is

$$\frac{Ex}{Ey} = \frac{2y^2}{y^2 - 10}$$

$$\left.\frac{Ex}{Ey}\right|_{y=1.88} = -1.09$$

Arc elasticity based on average price and quantity is

$$\frac{Ex}{Ey} = \frac{y_1 + y_2}{x_1 + x_2} \cdot \frac{x_2 - x_1}{y_2 - y_1} = \frac{3.88}{24.93}\left(-\frac{0.93}{0.12}\right)$$

$$= -1.21$$

EXAMPLE

Figure 2.66

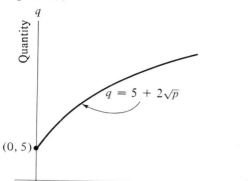

$q = 5 + 2\sqrt{p}$

The demand for margarine is related to the price of butter as follows:

$$q = 5 + 2\sqrt{p}$$

where q is the demand for margarine (hundreds of pounds) and p is the price of butter (dollars per pound). Find the equation for cross elasticity of demand for margarine with respect to price of butter. What is the demand for margarine when butter is \$0.81 per pound? What is the demand for margarine when butter is \$1.00 per pound? What is the cross elasticity of demand for margarine as butter goes from \$0.81 to \$1.00 per pound? (See Figure 2.66).

Solving the demand equation for p,

$$q = 5 + 2\sqrt{p}$$
$$\sqrt{p} = \tfrac{1}{2}(q - 5)$$
$$p = \tfrac{1}{4}(q^2 - 10q + 25)$$

See Figure 2.67.

The elasticity of demand for margarine with respect to price of butter is

$$\frac{Eq}{Ep} = \frac{dq}{dp} \cdot \frac{p}{q} = \frac{1}{\sqrt{p}} \cdot \frac{p}{5 + 2\sqrt{p}}$$

$$= \frac{\sqrt{p}}{5 + 2\sqrt{p}}$$

Figure 2.67

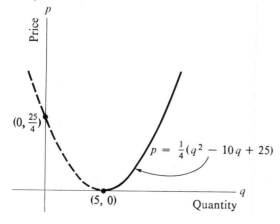

$p = \tfrac{1}{4}(q^2 - 10q + 25)$

Figure 2.68

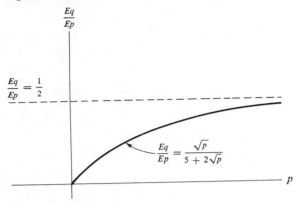

See Figure 2.68.

When $p = 0.81$, $q = 5 + 2\sqrt{.81}$ or 680 pounds.

When $p = 1.00$, $q = 5 + 2\sqrt{1.00}$ or 700 pounds.

Cross elasticity is

$$\frac{Eq}{Ep} = \frac{\sqrt{p}}{5 + 2\sqrt{p}}$$

For $p = 0.81$,

$$\left.\frac{Eq}{Ep}\right|_{p=0.81} = \frac{0.9}{5 + 2(0.9)} = \frac{0.9}{6.8} = 0.13$$

For $p = 1.00$,

$$\left.\frac{Eq}{Ep}\right|_{p=1.00} = \frac{1}{5 + 2} = \frac{1}{7} = 0.14$$

Constant Elasticity of Demand

As noted previously, the elasticity of a function is not, in general, constant over the range of the function. However, one type of function, the equilateral hyperbola, has constant elasticity over its range. In many theoretical analyses, the demand function is represented by an equilateral hyperbola, because it is convenient to have constant elasticity of demand over the range of the function.

If the demand function is given by the generalized equilateral hyperbola

$$x = \frac{a}{y^m}$$

then

$$\frac{dx}{dy} = -amy^{-m-1}$$

$$\frac{Ex}{Ey} = \frac{y}{x} \cdot \frac{dx}{dy}$$

$$= y\left(\frac{y^m}{a}\right)(-amy^{-m-1})$$

$$= -m$$

That is, elasticity of demand is the constant $-m$. In terms of approximate changes in price and quantity demanded, an increase of 1 percent in price results in a decrease of m percent in demand at any level of price and quantity. Only an equilateral hyperbola has constant elasticity over its range. For any other type of function, elasticity varies for different points on the curve. (See previous examples.)

EXAMPLE

The demand function is given by

$$x = \frac{25}{y^4} \qquad \text{for } 1 \le y \le 5$$

Determine the elasticity of demand. Consider the point $y = 2$, $x = \frac{25}{16}$; if the price increases by 5 percent, determine arc elasticity at the point $y = 2$, $x = \frac{25}{16}$, and at the point representing the changed price and quantity (see Figure 2.69).
  Solving the demand equation for y,

$$x = \frac{25}{y^4}$$

$$y = \left(\frac{25}{x}\right)^{1/4}$$

See Figure 2.70.
(Note that if $1 \le y \le 5$, then $\frac{1}{25} \le x \le 25$.)

$$\frac{dx}{dy} = \frac{-100}{y^5}$$

$$\frac{Ex}{Ey} = \frac{y}{x} \cdot \frac{dx}{dy}$$

$$= \frac{y}{\dfrac{25}{y^4}} \left(\frac{-100}{y^5}\right)$$

$$= -4$$

Figure 2.69

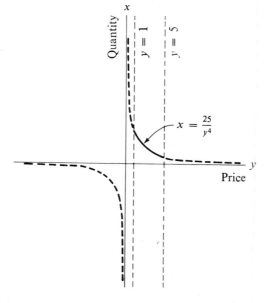

Figure 2.70

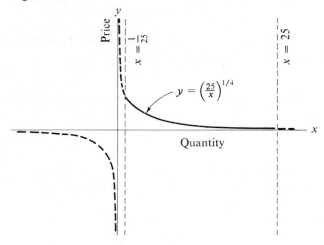

as could be obtained by applying the derivation for the general case given above. See Figure 2.71.

$$y_1 = 2 \qquad y_2 = 2 + (0.05)(2) = 2.1 \qquad \Delta y = 0.1$$

$$x_1 = 1.56 \qquad x_2 = \frac{25}{(2.1)^4} = 1.29 \qquad \Delta x = -0.27$$

For the point $y_1 = 2$, $x_1 = 1.56$, arc elasticity of demand is

$$\frac{Ex}{Ey} = \frac{y_1}{x_1} \cdot \frac{\Delta x}{\Delta y}$$

$$= \frac{2}{1.56}\left(\frac{-0.27}{0.1}\right)$$

$$= -3.46$$

For the point $y_2 = 2.1$, $x_2 = 1.29$, arc elasticity of demand is

$$\frac{Ex}{Ey} = \frac{y_2}{x_2} \cdot \frac{\Delta x}{\Delta y}$$

$$= \frac{2.1}{1.29}\left(\frac{-0.27}{0.1}\right)$$

$$= -4.40$$

Figure 2.71

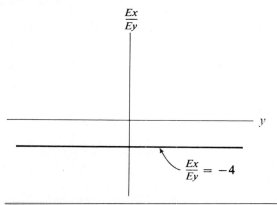

PROBLEMS

1. For each of the following demand functions, i. determine arc elasticity at the point specified, ii. determine arc elasticity at the point corresponding to the specified change in price or demand, iii. determine point elasticity at the two points, iv. determine arc elasticity based on average quantities and prices, and v. show that $\frac{dy}{dx}$ and $\frac{dx}{dy}$ are reciprocals of each other.

   a. $x = 60 - 2y^2$; $x = 10$, $y = 5$; price decrease 8%
   b. $x + 2y = 15$; $x = 7$, $y = 4$; price increase 5%
   c. $x = 25 - 5y^2$; $x = 5$, $y = 2$; price increase 5%
   d. $x = 10 - 5y^2$; $x = 5$, $y = 1$; price increase 10%
   e. $y = (x - 10)^2$; $0 \le x \le 10$; $x = 8$, $y = 4$; demand decrease 5%
   f. $x = 19 - 4y^2$; $x = 3$, $y = 2$; price decrease 5%
   g. $x = 36 - 4y^2$; $x = 20$, $y = 2$; price increase 5%
   h. $y = (x - 4)^2$; $x = 1$, $y = 9$; demand increase 30%

2. Find elasticity of demand, y, with respect to price, x, for each of the following functions.

   a. $y = \dfrac{3}{1 + 2x^2}$

   b. $y = (x - 8)^2$, $0 \le x \le 8$

   c. $y = ae^{-kx}$

   d. $y = 13e^{-(5/4)x}$

   e. $x = \dfrac{10}{y^{5/4}}$

   f. $y = 100 - 15x^2$

Answers to Odd-Numbered Problems

1. a. -9.6, -5.00, -10, -4.79, -6.66
   b. -1.14, -1.27, -1.14, -1.27, -1.21
   c. -8.2, -14.59, -8, -14.95, -10.57
   d. -2.1, -2.92, -2, -3.06, -2.46
   e. -0.11, -0.17, -0.13, -0.16, -0.14
   f. -10.4, -6.5, -10.67, -6.33, -8.05
   g. -1.64, -1.88, -1.6, -1.92, -1.75
   h. -1.58, $-.98$, -1.50, -1.04, -1.24

REVENUE, MARGINAL REVENUE, AND ELASTICITY OF DEMAND

For any given demand function $y = f(x)$, the total revenue R, is the product of x, the number of units demanded, and y, the price per unit quantity demanded,

$$R = xy = x \cdot f(x)$$

and the marginal revenue with respect to demand is

$$\frac{dR}{dx} = x\frac{dy}{dx} + y$$

Elasticity of demand with respect to price is

$$\frac{Ex}{Ey} = \frac{y}{x} \cdot \frac{dx}{dy}$$

and, since $\dfrac{dx}{dy} = \dfrac{1}{\frac{dy}{dx}}$,

$$\frac{Ex}{Ey} = \frac{y}{x}\left(\frac{1}{\frac{dy}{dx}}\right)$$

$$\frac{dy}{dx} = \frac{y}{x\left(\frac{Ex}{Ey}\right)}$$

Thus

$$\frac{dR}{dx} = \frac{y}{\dfrac{Ex}{Ey}} + y$$

$$= y\left(1 + \frac{1}{\dfrac{Ex}{Ey}}\right)$$

Alternatively,

$$\frac{dR}{dx} = x\frac{dy}{dx} + y$$

$$= y\left(\frac{x}{y}\frac{dy}{dx} + 1\right)$$

$$= y\left(1 + \frac{Ey}{Ex}\right)$$

$$= y\left(1 + \frac{1}{\dfrac{Ex}{Ey}}\right)$$

That is, marginal revenue is the product of the price per unit quantity demanded and one plus the reciprocal of the elasticity of demand.

Since both x and y are either zero or positive, the total revenue, $R = xy$, is also either zero or positive; however, the marginal revenue may be either positive or negative.

NOTE: Logically, R could also be considered a function of price

$$R = xy = y \cdot g(y) = G(y)$$

and marginal revenue with respect to price defined as

$$\frac{dR}{dy} = y\frac{dx}{dy} + x$$

This would perhaps be simpler for cases when the demand function is in the form $x = g(y)$ and it is not easy to solve for y in terms of x. However, to keep the geometrical representation consistent (that is, to use x as the independent variable), it is preferable to use implicit differentiation and the chain rule to obtain $\dfrac{dR}{dx}$ and $\dfrac{d^2R}{dx^2}$ when the demand function is in the form $x = g(y)$.

EXAMPLE

The demand for a particular commodity is given by

$$y = (12 - x)^{1/2} \qquad \text{for } 0 \le x \le 12$$

where x is quantity demanded and y is price per unit.

Determine the price and quantity for which revenue is maximum. Show for this demand function that the relationship between marginal revenue and elasticity of demand holds.

Demand: $\quad y = (12 - x)^{1/2} \qquad \text{for } 0 \le x \le 12$

Revenue: $R = x(12 - x)^{1/2}$

$$\frac{dR}{dx} = (12 - x)^{1/2} - \tfrac{1}{2}x(12 - x)^{-1/2}$$

$$= (12 - x)^{-1/2}[(12 - x) - \tfrac{1}{2}x]$$

$$= \frac{3(8 - x)}{2(12 - x)^{1/2}}$$

$$= 0 \qquad \text{if } x = 8, R = 16$$

$$\frac{d^2R}{dx^2} = \frac{3}{2}\left[\frac{-(12 - x)^{1/2} - (8 - x)(-\tfrac{1}{2})(12 - x)^{-1/2}}{12 - x}\right]$$

$$= \frac{3}{2}\left[\frac{(12 - x)^{-1/2}[-(12 - x) + \tfrac{1}{2}(8 - x)]}{12 - x}\right]$$

$$= \frac{3}{4}\left[\frac{x - 16}{(12 - x)^{3/2}}\right]$$

$$< 0 \qquad \text{if } x = 8, \text{ so maximum at } x = 8, y = 16$$

$$< 0 \qquad \text{for } 0 \le x < 12, \text{ so no point of inflection}$$

Figure 2.72

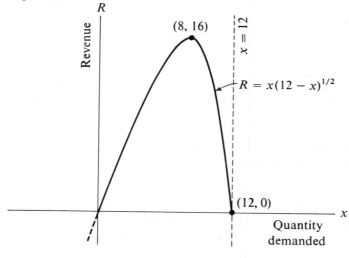

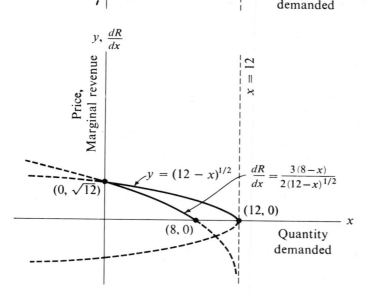

Thus $R = x(12 - x)^{1/2}$ is concave for $0 \leq x \leq 12$. See Figure 2.72.

$$\frac{Ex}{Ey} = \frac{y}{x} \cdot \frac{dx}{dy}$$

$$= \frac{y}{x} \left(\frac{1}{\dfrac{dy}{dx}} \right)$$

$$= \frac{(12 - x)^{1/2}}{x} \left[\frac{1}{-\frac{1}{2}(12 - x)^{-1/2}} \right]$$

$$= \frac{-2(12 - x)}{x}$$

$$\frac{dR}{dx} = y \left(1 + \frac{1}{\dfrac{Ex}{Ey}} \right)$$

$$= (12 - x)^{1/2} \left[1 - \frac{x}{2(12 - x)} \right]$$

$$= \frac{(12 - x)^{1/2}(24 - 3x)}{2(12 - x)}$$

$$= \frac{3(8 - x)}{2(12 - x)^{1/2}} \qquad \text{(as above)}$$

EXAMPLE

The demand for a particular commodity is given by

$$y = 15e^{-x/3} \qquad \text{for } 0 \leq x \leq 8$$

where x is quantity demanded and y is price per unit.

Determine the price and quantity for which revenue is maximum. Show for this demand function that the relationship between marginal revenue and elasticity of demand stated on page 285 holds.

Demand: $\quad y = 15e^{-x/3} \qquad \text{for } 0 \leq x \leq 8$

Revenue: $\quad R = 15xe^{-x/3}$

$$\frac{dR}{dx} = -5xe^{-x/3} + 15e^{-x/3}$$

$$= 5e^{-x/3}(3 - x)$$

$$= 0 \qquad \text{if } x = 3, \ R = \frac{45}{e}$$

$$\frac{d^2R}{dx^2} = -\tfrac{5}{3}e^{-x/3}(3 - x) - 5e^{-x/3}$$

$$= 5e^{-x/3}(\tfrac{1}{3}x - 2)$$

$$< 0 \qquad \text{if } x = 3, \text{ so maximum at } x = 3, \ R = \frac{45}{e} \approx 16.6$$

$$= 0 \qquad \text{if } x = 6$$

$$\frac{d^3R}{dx^3} = -\tfrac{5}{3}e^{-x/3}(\tfrac{1}{3}x - 2) + \tfrac{5}{3}e^{-x/3}$$

$$= 5e^{-x/3}(1 - \tfrac{1}{9}x) > 0 \qquad \text{if } x = 6$$

so point of inflection at $x = 6$, $R = \dfrac{90}{e^2} \approx 12.2$. See Figure 2.73.

$$\frac{Ex}{Ey} = \frac{y}{x} \cdot \frac{dx}{dy}$$

$$= \frac{y}{x}\left(\frac{1}{\dfrac{dy}{dx}}\right)$$

$$= \frac{15e^{-x/3}}{x}\left(\frac{1}{-5e^{-x/3}}\right)$$

$$= -\frac{3}{x}$$

Figure 2.73

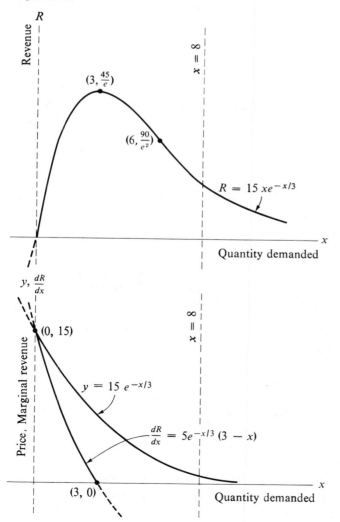

$$\frac{dR}{dx} = y\left(1 + \frac{1}{\dfrac{Ex}{Ey}}\right)$$

$$= 15e^{-x/3}\left(1 - \frac{x}{3}\right)$$

$$= 5e^{-x/3}(3 - x) \qquad \text{(as above)}$$

PROBLEMS

1. When Mr. Smythe's income was \$300 per month he bought 20 qt of milk per month. When his income increased to \$350 per month he bought 24 qt of milk per month. Assuming no change in the price of milk or other relevant factors, what was Mr. Smythe's income elasticity of demand for milk?

2. When the price of A was \$5.00, 100 units of B were sold. When the price of A fell to \$4.00, 120 units of B were sold. What is the cross elasticity of demand for B in terms of the price of A? Are A and B substitutes or complements?

3. What is the relation between the slope (positive or negative) of the average cost curve and the elasticity of total cost?

4. Demonstrate algebraically that the elasticity of total cost is equal to

$$E_{TC} = \frac{MC}{AC}$$

where MC is marginal cost and AC is average cost.

5. For each of the following demand functions demonstrate the relationship between marginal revenue and elasticity of demand given by

$$\frac{dR}{dx} = y\left(1 + \frac{1}{\dfrac{Ex}{Ey}}\right)$$

a. $y = 550 - 3x - 6x^2$ d. $y = 86 - 25x$

b. $y = \dfrac{3250}{x^3}$ e. $y = 100 - 6x^2$

c. $y = 17 - 6x$

6. Show that if demand is linear and negatively sloped, the elasticity of total revenue is always less than 1, but to the left of its maximum value the elasticity of total revenue is positive and to the right of the maximum value the elasticity of total revenue is negative.

Answers to Odd-Numbered Problems

1. $\frac{13}{11}$
3. when slope of AC is negative, E_{TC} is less than 1
   when slope of AC is zero, E_{TC} is equal to 1
   when slope of AC is positive, E_{TC} is greater than 1

REVENUE FROM TAXATION

If the government imposes a tax on a given commodity, it is assumed that the price to the consumer will increase and correspondingly the quantity demanded will decrease. The discussion in this section concerns the effect of taxation on market

Figure 2.74

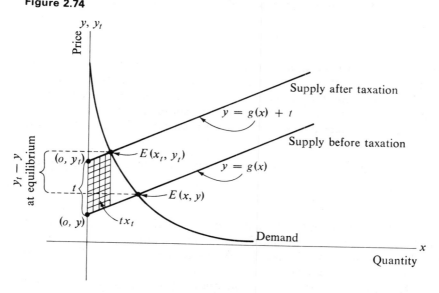

equilibrium under the following conditions: there is pure competition in which the consumers' demand depends only on price, the demand function does not change, the producers adjust the supply curve to the new price which includes the tax, and a tax of t monetary units is imposed on each unit of quantity produced.

The supply function can be represented by

$$y = g(x)$$

where x is the number of units of the commodity supplied and y is the price per unit. If a tax of t per unit quantity is imposed, the supply function after taxation is

$$y_t = g(x) + t$$

If the demand function is

$$y = f(x)$$

then the equilibrium point before taxation, $E(x, y)$, is the solution of the equations

Demand: $y = f(x)$

Supply: $y = g(x)$

and the equilibrium point after taxation, $E(x_t, y_t)$, is the solution of the equations

Demand: $y = f(x)$

Supply: $y_t = g(x) + t$

See Figure 2.74.

NOTE: If the supply function before taxation is in the form

$$x = G(y)$$

it may be possible to solve for y in a convenient form. If not, the supply function after taxation,

$$y_t - t = g(x)$$

shows that the quantity supplied is

$$x = G(y_t - t)$$

and equilibrium after taxation occurs at the solution of the equations

Demand: $y = f(x)$

Supply: $x = G(y_t - t)$

Geometrically, this is equivalent to moving the original supply curve upward t units. Except for the case of constant price, where price does not depend on quantity produced, the increase in equilibrium price is less than the amount of the tax. Note that a subsidy may be considered a negative tax. The supply curve is moved downward the amount of the subsidy, price to the consumer decreases, and demand increases.

The total tax revenue T received by the government from a tax of t per unit quantity is

$$T = tx_t$$

where x_t is the equilibrium quantity after taxation. This total may be represented by the area of a rectangle of dimensions t and x_t, which, if the supply function is linear, is equivalent to the parallelogram in Figure 2.74. As this diagram indicates, the tax may be large enough to reduce demand to the vanishing point. If the government is interested in taxation for revenue purposes, the question is what amount of tax will maximize revenue—if the tax t is considered as a variable, then there is no revenue if $t = 0$ and there is also no revenue if t is large enough so that demand is zero; for some intermediate value of t the tax revenue $T = tx_t$ is maximum. Since T may be considered a function of either t or x, maximum revenue possible from taxation can be determined by considering marginal tax revenue with respect to either t or x. It is usually more convenient to consider T as a function of x, since t occurs linearly in the relation between t and x.

EXAMPLE

The demand and supply functions for a particular commodity are

Demand: $2y + x = 14$

Supply: $y = \dfrac{3}{4} + \dfrac{x}{3}$

Determine the maximum possible revenue from taxation which can be obtained from a tax of t per unit quantity and the corresponding tax rate.

The supply function after taxation is $y = \frac{3}{4} + (x/3) + t$. Thus, after taxation, at equilibrium,

$$y = 7 - \frac{x}{2} = \frac{3}{4} + \frac{x}{3} + t$$

$$t = \tfrac{25}{4} - \tfrac{5}{6}x$$

$$T = tx = \tfrac{25}{4}x - \tfrac{5}{6}x^2$$

$$\frac{dT}{dx} = \tfrac{25}{4} - \tfrac{5}{3}x$$

$$= 0 \quad \text{if } x = \tfrac{15}{4}$$

$$\frac{d^2T}{dx^2} = -\tfrac{5}{3} < 0, \text{ so maximum at } x = \tfrac{15}{4}$$

If $x = \tfrac{15}{4}$, $t = \tfrac{25}{4} - \tfrac{5}{6}(\tfrac{15}{4}) = \tfrac{25}{8}$, and $T_{max} = \tfrac{375}{32}$. So the maximum possible revenue from taxation is $T_{max} = \tfrac{375}{32}$ obtained from a tax of $t = \tfrac{25}{8}$ per unit quantity. (See Figure 2.75.)

Figure 2.75

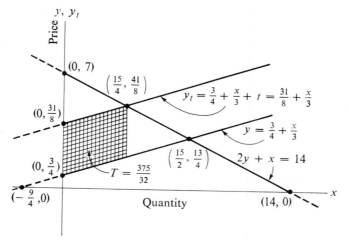

Alternatively,

$$x = \tfrac{15}{2} - \tfrac{6}{5}t$$

$$T = \tfrac{15}{2}t - \tfrac{6}{5}t^2$$

$$\frac{dT}{dt} = \tfrac{15}{2} - \tfrac{12}{5}t$$

$$= 0 \quad \text{if } t = \tfrac{25}{8}$$

$$\frac{d^2T}{dt^2} = -\tfrac{12}{5} < 0, \text{ so maximum at } t = \tfrac{25}{8}$$

$$T_{\max} = (\tfrac{15}{2})(\tfrac{25}{8}) - \tfrac{6}{5}(\tfrac{25}{8})^2 = \tfrac{375}{32}$$

EXAMPLE

The demand and supply functions for a particular commodity are

Demand: $y = 30 - 2x^2$

Supply: $y = 3 + x^2$

Determine the maximum possible revenue from taxation which can be obtained from a tax of t per unit quantity and the corresponding tax rate.

The supply function after taxation is $y = 3 + x^2 + t$. Thus, after taxation, at equilibrium,

$$y = 30 - 2x^2 = 3 + x^2 + t$$

$$t = 27 - 3x^2$$

$$T = tx = 27x - 3x^3$$

$$\frac{dT}{dx} = 27 - 9x^2$$

$$= 0 \quad \text{if } x = \sqrt{3}$$

$$\frac{d^2T}{dx^2} = -18x < 0 \quad \text{if } x = \sqrt{3}, \text{ so maximum at } x = \sqrt{3}$$

If $x = \sqrt{3}$, $t = 27 - 9 = 18$, and $T_{\max} = 18\sqrt{3}$. Thus the maximum possible revenue from taxation is $T_{\max} = 18\sqrt{3}$, obtained from a tax of $t = 18$ per unit quantity. (See Figure 2.76.)

Figure 2.76

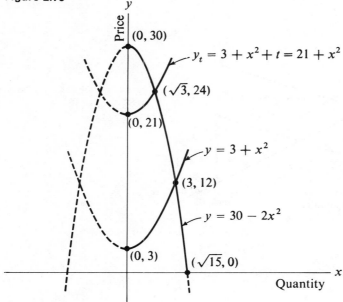

Alternatively,

$$x = \sqrt{\frac{27 - t}{3}}$$

$$T = t\left(\frac{27 - t}{3}\right)^{1/2} = \left(\frac{27t^2 - t^3}{3}\right)^{1/2}$$

$$\frac{dT}{dt} = \frac{1}{2}\left(\frac{27t^2 - t^3}{3}\right)^{-1/2}\left(\frac{54t - 3t^2}{3}\right)$$

$$= \frac{1}{2}\left(\frac{27t^2 - t^3}{3}\right)^{-1/2}(18t - t^2)$$

$$= \frac{1}{2}\left(\frac{27 - t}{3}\right)^{-1/2}(18 - t)$$

$$= 0 \quad \text{if } t = 18$$

$$\frac{d^2T}{dt^2} = \left(-\frac{1}{2}\right)\left(\frac{1}{2}\right)\left(\frac{27 - t}{3}\right)^{-3/2}(-1)(18 - t) - \frac{1}{2}\left(\frac{27 - t}{3}\right)^{-1/2}$$

$$= \left(\frac{27 - t}{3}\right)^{-3/2}\left[\tfrac{1}{4}(18 - t) - \frac{1}{2}\left(\frac{27 - t}{3}\right)\right]$$

$$= -\frac{t}{12}\left(\frac{27 - t}{3}\right)^{-3/2} < 0 \quad \text{if } t = 18, \text{ so maximum at } t = 18$$

$$T_{\max} = 18\left(\frac{27 - 18}{3}\right)^{1/2} = 18\sqrt{3}$$

PROFIT UNDER MONOPOLY

In the usual forms of imperfect competition, it is assumed that the demand function $y = f(x)$ is known and that the price the consumer must pay depends only on the quantity demanded. In a monopolistic situation, the monopolist controls the price by regulating the supply of the commodity—when supply is limited, price is relatively high, and when supply increases, price decreases.

If $\bar{y}_c$ is the average cost of producing a unit of commodity (as a function of the quantity produced), then the total cost y_c of producing x units is

$$y_c = x\bar{y}_c$$

(Note that in previous sections y has been used to denote price in some contexts and cost in others; the subscript c is used here to differentiate cost from price.)

Presumably the monopolist will control the supply x and thus the price y (determined by the demand function) so as to maximize his profit. The total revenue he receives is

$$R = xy$$

where $y = f(x)$; the total profit P is the difference between total revenue and total cost

$$P = R - y_c = xy - x\bar{y}_c$$

P has a relative maximum if and only if

$$\frac{dP}{dx} = 0 \qquad \text{that is} \qquad \frac{dR}{dx} = \frac{dy_c}{dx}$$

and

$$\frac{d^2P}{dx^2} < 0 \qquad \text{that is} \qquad \frac{d^2R}{dx^2} < \frac{d^2y_c}{dx^2}$$

In order to be meaningful this maximum must occur in the interval for which the cost and demand functions have economic significance.

NOTE: If the demand function is in the form

$$x = F(y)$$

and it is not possible or convenient to solve for y in terms of x, profit may be expressed as a function of y and the problem solved with y as the independent variable.

EXAMPLE

The demand function for a particular commodity is

$$y = 26 - 2x - 4x^2$$

and the average cost to the monopolist of producing and marketing the commodity is

$$\bar{y}_c = x + 8$$

Determine the maximum profit obtainable by the monopolist.

Revenue: $R = xy = 26x - 2x^2 - 4x^3$

Total cost: $y_c = x\bar{y}_c = x^2 + 8x$

Profit: $P = 26x - 2x^2 - 4x^3 - x^2 - 8x$

$\qquad = 18x - 3x^2 - 4x^3$

$$\frac{dP}{dx} = 18 - 6x - 12x^2$$

$$= 0 \quad \text{if } 2x^2 + x - 3 = 0$$

$$(2x + 3)(x - 1) = 0$$

$$x = 1$$

$\left(x = -\frac{3}{2}\right.$ is not meaningful for this problem.$\left.\right)$

$$\frac{d^2P}{dx^2} = -6 - 24x$$

$$< 0 \quad \text{if } x = 1, \text{ so maximum at } x = 1$$

$$P_{\max} = 11$$

Alternatively,

$$\frac{dR}{dx} = 26 - 4x - 12x^2$$

$$\frac{dy_c}{dx} = 2x + 8$$

$$\frac{dR}{dx} = \frac{dy_c}{dx} \quad \text{if } 26 - 4x - 12x^2 = 2x + 8$$

$$2x^2 + x - 3 = 0$$

$$(2x + 3)(x - 1) = 0$$

$$x = 1$$

$$\left.\begin{matrix} \dfrac{d^2R}{dx^2} = -4 - 24x \\[2mm] \dfrac{d^2y_c}{dx^2} = 2 \end{matrix}\right\} \quad \frac{d^2R}{dx^2} < \frac{d^2y_c}{dx^2} \quad \text{if } x = 1, \text{ so maximum at } x = 1$$

$$P_{\max} = 11$$

EXAMPLE

The demand function for a particular commodity is

$$y = 28 - 5x$$

and the total cost to the monopolist of producing and marketing the commodity is

$$y_c = x^2 + 4x$$

Determine the maximum profit obtainable by the monopolist.

Revenue: $R = xy = 28x - 5x^2$

Total cost: $y_c = x\bar{y}_c = x^2 + 4x$

Profit: $P = 28x - 5x^2 - x^2 - 4x$

$$= 24x - 6x^2$$

$$\frac{dP}{dx} = 24 - 12x$$

$$\frac{dP}{dx} = 0 \qquad \text{if } 2 - x = 0$$

$$x = 2$$

$$\frac{d^2P}{dx^2} = -12 < 0, \text{ so maximum at } x = 2$$

$$P_{max} = 24$$

Alternatively,

$$\frac{dR}{dx} = 28 - 10x$$

$$\frac{dy_c}{dx} = 2x + 4$$

$$\frac{dR}{dx} = \frac{dy_c}{dx} \qquad \text{if } 28 - 10x = 2x + 4$$

$$x = 2$$

$$\left.\begin{array}{l} \dfrac{d^2R}{dx^2} = -10 \\[2mm] \dfrac{d^2y_c}{dx^2} = 2 \end{array}\right| \quad \frac{d^2R}{dx^2} < \frac{d^2y_c}{dx^2}, \text{ so maximum at } x = 2$$

$$P_{max} = 24$$

or alternatively,

$$x = \tfrac{1}{5}(28 - y)$$

$$R = \tfrac{1}{5}y(28 - y)$$

$$y_c = \tfrac{1}{25}(28 - y)^2 + \tfrac{4}{5}(28 - y)$$

$$= \tfrac{1}{25}(28 - y)[(28 - y) + 20]$$

$$= \tfrac{1}{25}(28 - y)(48 - y)$$

$$\frac{dR}{dy} = \tfrac{28}{5} - \tfrac{2}{5}y$$

$$\frac{dy_c}{dy} = -\tfrac{1}{25}(48 - y) - \tfrac{1}{25}(28 - y)$$

$$= \tfrac{2}{25}y - \tfrac{76}{25}$$

$$\frac{dR}{dy} = \frac{dy_c}{dy} \qquad \text{if } \tfrac{28}{5} - \tfrac{2}{5}y = \tfrac{2}{25}y - \tfrac{76}{25}$$

$$y = 18$$

$$\left.\begin{array}{l} \dfrac{d^2R}{dy^2} = -\tfrac{2}{5} \\[2mm] \dfrac{d^2y_c}{dy^2} = \tfrac{2}{25} \end{array}\right| \quad \frac{d^2R}{dy^2} < \frac{d^2y_c}{dy^2}, \text{ so maximum at } y = 18$$

$$P_{max} = R - y_c = 36 - 12 = 24$$

The following two geometric representations of profit under monopoly illustrate the economic relationships involved and also provide a method for determining

Figure 2.77

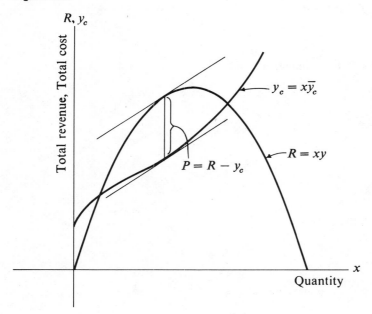

approximate maximum profit in cases for which algebraic solution is difficult or impossible.

If the revenue and total cost curves are drawn on the same diagram, the vertical distance between them at any given value of x measures the profit corresponding to production of x units of the commodity. The maximum vertical distance corresponds to maximum profit and this occurs for the value of x where the slopes of the curves are equal, that is, where $\dfrac{dR}{dx} = \dfrac{dy_c}{dx}$ (see Figure 2.77).

Figure 2.78

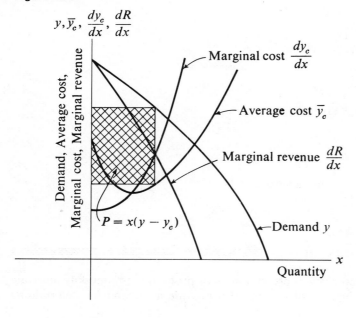

If the marginal revenue and marginal cost curves are drawn on the same diagram, they intersect at a point which gives the value of x corresponding to maximum profit. If the demand curve $y = f(x)$ and the average cost curve $\bar{y}_c = g(x)$ are also drawn on the diagram, the vertical distance between them is $y - \bar{y}_c$. For any given value of x, the area of the rectangle of height $y - \bar{y}_c$ and width x represents profit; this area is greatest for the value of x where the marginal revenue and marginal cost curves intersect (see Figure 2.78).

EFFECT OF TAXATION ON MONOPOLY

The imposition of a tax t per unit quantity on a commodity produced by a monopolist increases the average cost by t and the total cost by tx. The equilibrium price and quantity for which the monopolist's profit is maximum after taxation are thus obtained by maximizing profit using the cost function after taxation,

$$y_{c_t} = y_c + tx$$

Profit after taxation is

$$P = R - y_{c_t} = R - y_c - tx$$

P has a relative maximum if and only if

$$\frac{dP}{dx} = 0 \qquad \text{that is} \qquad \frac{dR}{dx} = \frac{dy_{c_t}}{dx}$$

and

$$\frac{d^2P}{dx^2} < 0 \qquad \text{that is} \qquad \frac{d^2R}{dx^2} < \frac{d^2y_{c_t}}{dx^2}$$

Since the marginal cost curve after taxation is the marginal cost curve before taxation translated upward a distance t, the amount produced for maximum profit will be decreased and the price increased after taxation. (See Figure 2.79).

Figure 2.79

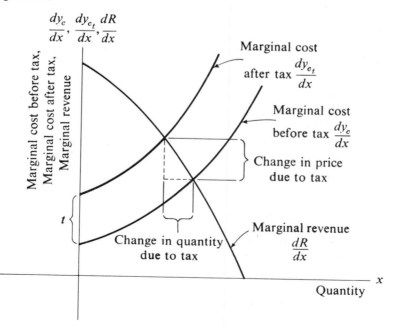

The total revenue received by the government is

$$T = tx$$

where x is the amount produced after the tax is imposed. T is again a function of t and is zero if t is either zero or large enough to tax the product out of the market. Thus T has a maximum value obtainable in the usual way. As before, a subsidy may be considered a negative tax and the general analysis is unchanged.

EXAMPLE

The demand function for a particular commodity is

$$y = 20 - 4x$$

and the average cost to the monopolist is

$$\bar{y}_c = 2$$

(a) If a tax of t per unit quantity is imposed on the monopolist, determine his maximum possible profit and the value of t for which tax revenue is maximized.
(b) Determine the monopolist's maximum possible profit if a $33\frac{1}{3}\%$ sales tax is imposed.

Demand: $y = 20 - 4x$

Revenue: $R = xy = x(20 - 4x)$

Average cost: $\bar{y}_c = 2$

Total cost: $y_c = 2x$

Total cost after tax: $y_{c_t} = 2x + tx$

(a) Profit: $P = R - y_{c_t} = 20x - 4x^2 - 2x - tx$

$$= (18 - t)x - 4x^2$$

$$\frac{dP}{dx} = 18 - t - 8x$$

$$\frac{dP}{dx} = 0 \quad \text{if } x = \frac{18 - t}{8}, \, y = \frac{22 + t}{2}$$

$$\frac{d^2P}{dx^2} = -8, \text{ so maximum if } x = \frac{18 - t}{8}$$

$$P_{\max} = \frac{(18 - t)^2}{8} - 4\left(\frac{18 - t}{8}\right)^2$$

$$= \frac{(18 - t)^2}{16}$$

Tax revenue: $T = tx = \frac{t(18 - t)}{8}$

$$\frac{dT}{dt} = \frac{18 - 2t}{8} = \frac{9 - t}{4}$$

$$= 0 \quad \text{if } t = 9$$

$$\frac{d^2T}{dt^2} = -\frac{1}{4} < 0, \text{ so maximum if } t = 9$$

Figure 2.80

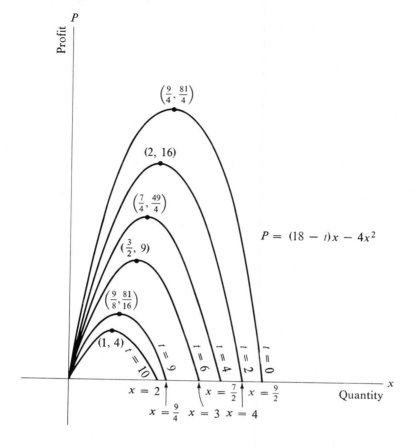

$P = (18 - t)x - 4x^2$

If $t = 9$,

$$P_{max} = \tfrac{81}{16}$$

$$T_{max} = \tfrac{81}{8}$$

See Figure 2.80.

(b) Demand function: $y = 20 - 4x$. So the price paid the monopolist after allowing for $33\tfrac{1}{3}\%$ sales tax is

$$y_t = \tfrac{3}{4}(20 - 4x)$$

Profit: $\quad P = R - y_c = \tfrac{3}{4}x(20 - 4x) - 2x$

$$= 13x - 3x^2$$

$$\frac{dP}{dx} = 13 - 6x$$

$$= 0 \qquad \text{if } x = \tfrac{13}{6}$$

$$\frac{d^2P}{dx^2} = -6, \text{ so maximum if } x = \tfrac{13}{6}$$

$$P_{max} = \tfrac{169}{12}$$

EXAMPLE

The demand function for a particular commodity is

$$y = 14 - 3x$$

and the total cost to the monopolist is

$$y_c = x^2 + 5x$$

(a) If a tax of t per unit quantity is imposed on the monopolist, determine his maximum possible profit, the change in price, and the tax revenue received by the government as a function of t.

(b) Determine the maximum tax revenue obtainable by the government.

Demand: $y = 14 - 3x$

Revenue: $R = xy = 14x - 3x^2$

Total cost: $y_c = x^2 + 5x$

Total cost after tax: $y_{c_t} = x^2 + 5x + tx$

(a) Profit: $P = R - y_{c_t} = 14x - 3x^2 - x^2 - 5x - tx$

$$= (9 - t)x - 4x^2$$

$$\frac{dP}{dx} = 9 - t - 8x$$

$$= 0 \quad \text{if } x = \frac{9 - t}{8}, y = \frac{85}{8} + \frac{3}{8}t$$

Figure 2.79

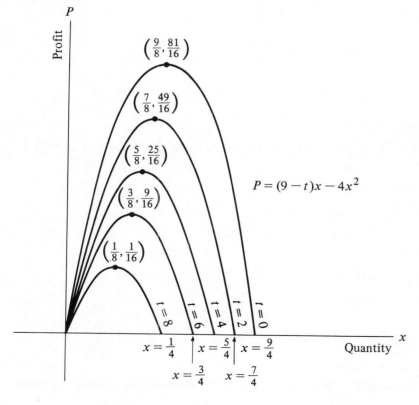

$$\frac{d^2 P}{dx^2} = -8, \text{ so maximum if } x = \frac{9-t}{8}$$

$$P_{\max} = \frac{(9-t)^2}{8} - 4\left(\frac{9-t}{8}\right)^2$$

$$= \frac{(9-t)^2}{16}$$

If $x = (9-t)/8$, $y = \frac{85}{8} + \frac{3}{8}t$, so there is a change in price of $\frac{3}{8}t$; and tax revenue is $T = \frac{t(9-t)}{8}$ (see Figure 2.81).

(b) Tax revenue: $\quad T = tx = \frac{t(9-t)}{8}$

$$\frac{dT}{dt} = \frac{9}{8} - \frac{t}{4}$$

$$= 0 \qquad \text{if } t = \frac{9}{2}$$

$$\frac{d^2 T}{dt^2} = -\frac{1}{4}, \text{ so maximum if } t = \frac{9}{2}$$

$$T_{\max} = \frac{\frac{9}{2}\left(9 - \frac{9}{2}\right)}{8} = \frac{81}{32}$$

PROBLEMS

1. Plot the demand curve $y = 120 - x$ and the supply curve $y = x + 10$, where x is quantity demanded and y is price per unit, and indicate the equilibrium price and quantity. a. Assume that a tax of $15 per unit is imposed on the seller; draw the new supply curve and indicate the new equilibrium. b. Assume that instead of a tax, a subsidy of $10 is paid to the producers; draw the appropriate supply curve and indicate the corresponding equilibrium.

2. For each of the following pairs of demand and supply functions find the maximum revenue that can be obtained by imposing a tax of t per unit and illustrate graphically (by sketching the demand curve, the supply curves before and after taxation, and the revenue curve).
   a. Demand: $y = 14 - 3x$ d. Demand: $y = 28 - x^2$
       Supply: $y = 4 + 2x$ Supply: $y = 4 + x^2$
   b. Demand: $y = 25 - 2x^2$ e. Demand: $y = 45 - x^2$
       Supply: $y = 5 + x$ Supply: $y = 6 + 2x$
   c. Demand: $y = 50 - 4x^2$ f. Demand: $y = 30 - 2x^2$
       Supply: $y = 5 + x^2$ Supply: $y = 3 + x^2$

3. For each of the following pairs of demand and (average or total) cost functions find the maximum profit obtainable by a monopolist.
   a. $y = 24 - 7x$ d. $y = 12 - 5x$
       $\bar{y}_c = 6 - x$ $\bar{y}_c = 4x + 6$
   b. $y = 26 - 3x^2$ e. $y = 26 - 2x - 4x^2$
       $y_c = 3x^2 + 2x + 14$ $\bar{y}_c = x + 8$
   c. $y = 12 - 4x$
       $y_c = 8x - x^2$

4. For each of the following pairs of demand and cost functions find i. change in price, maximum profit, and maximum revenue from taxation as functions of t if an additive tax of t per unit is imposed on a monopolist and determine the maximum revenue that can be obtained by such taxation, and ii. find the maximum revenue that can be obtained by the specified sales tax.
   a. $y = 50 - 6x$ d. $y = 33 - 5x^2$
       $y_c = x^2 + 9x$ $\bar{y}_c = 3x^2$
       Sales tax 20%   Sales tax 10%

b. $y = 25 - 2x^2$
   $y_c = 3x$
   Sales tax 25%

c. $y = 12 - 4x$
   $\bar{y}_c = 2x$
   Sales tax $33\frac{1}{3}\%$

e. $y = 20 - 4x$
   $\bar{y}_c = 2$
   Sales tax $33\frac{1}{3}\%$

f. $y = 72 - 7x^2$
   $\bar{y}_c = x^2$
   Sales tax 40%

Answers to Odd-Numbered Problems

3. a. $P_{max} = \frac{27}{2}$
   b. $P_{max} = \frac{50}{9}$
   c. $P_{max} = \frac{4}{3}$
   d. $P_{max} = 1$
   e. $P_{max} = 11$

INVENTORY MODELS

The objective of inventory control is to minimize total inventory cost. Inventory costs are of three types: (1) cost of placing an order or starting a production run (setup cost); (2) cost of holding inventory, including cost of capital or interest and storage cost (carrying cost); and (3) cost of going short, including loss of goodwill (shortage cost). Inventory control attempts to balance the economies of large orders or large production runs against the cost of holding inventory and, in some models, takes into account the cost of going short.

In practice, various situations occur with respect to the nature of demand, the procedures involved in ordering or production, the ease of storage, the seriousness of shortages, and so forth. All the inventory models discussed in this book (including two in this section and one in Chapter 3) assume that demand is known and uniform. This assumption may be appropriate, at least as an approximation, in many situations involving demand for an input of production; however, it is entirely unrealistic in many situations involving retail demand. For these latter situations a model assuming probabilistic demand is more appropriate.

The models in this book also assume that the setup cost, the per unit carrying cost, and the per unit shortage cost do not depend on the number of items involved. Neither of the two models discussed in this section permits shortages; each of them can be derived as a special case of a model that does permit shortages by letting the shortage cost become very large. The first model assumes that items enter inventory in batches; the second model assumes that items enter inventory continuously during the period of ordering or production.

Figure 2.82

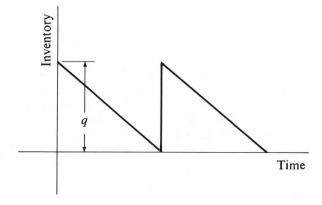

Model A: uniform demand, no shortages, batch arrival

D = demand per period
c_1 = setup cost
c_2 = carrying cost per item per period
q = number of items placed in inventory at one time

(See Figure 2.82.)

There are D/q batches per period for which the total setup cost is $(c_1 D)/q$. The average inventory is $q/2$ and the carrying cost per period is $(c_2 q)/2$. The total cost of inventory per period is thus

$$C = \frac{c_2 q}{2} + \frac{c_1 D}{q}$$

$$\frac{dC}{dq} = \frac{c_2}{2} - \frac{c_1 D}{q^2}$$

If $\dfrac{dC}{dq} = 0$, $q = \sqrt{\dfrac{2c_1 D}{c_2}}$.

$$\frac{d^2 C}{dq^2} = \frac{2c_1 D}{q^3}$$

$$> 0$$

so C is minimum if $q = \sqrt{(2c_1 D)/c_2}$. Thus $\sqrt{(2c_1 D)/c_2}$ items should be placed in inventory D/q times per period.

Model B: uniform demand, no shortages, continuous arrival

D = demand per period
k = rate of arrival of items (number per period)
c_1 = setup cost
c_2 = carrying cost per item per period
q = number of items placed in inventory during buildup of inventory
t_1 = time during which items are placed in inventory
t_2 = time during which items are not placed in inventory
$t = t_1 + t_2$ = time required for one inventory cycle

(See Figure 2.83).

Figure 2.83

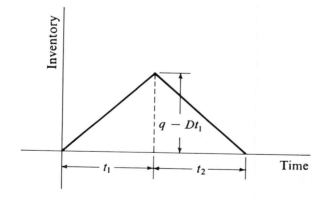

Note that $t_1 = q/k$ and $t = D/q$. The carrying cost per period is

$$\frac{c_2(q - Dt_1)}{2} = \frac{c_2 q\left(1 - \dfrac{D}{k}\right)}{2}$$

and the setup cost is $c_1(D/q)$. So the total inventory cost per period is

$$C = \tfrac{1}{2}c_2 q\left(1 - \frac{D}{k}\right) + \frac{c_1 D}{q}$$

$$\frac{dC}{dq} = \tfrac{1}{2}c_2\left(1 - \frac{D}{k}\right) - \frac{c_1 D}{q^2}$$

$$= 0 \quad \text{if } q = \sqrt{\frac{2c_1 D}{c_2\left(1 - \dfrac{D}{k}\right)}}$$

$$\frac{d^2 C}{dq^2} = \frac{2c_1 D}{q^3} > 0$$

So C is minimum if $q = \sqrt{(2c_1 D)/c_2[1 - (D/k)]}$. Thus $\sqrt{(2c_1 D)/c_2[1 - (D/k)]}$ items should be produced D/q times per period.

EXAMPLE

Alicor needs 2500 widgets per quarter. It costs \$3.00 a month to store a widget. The cost of ordering a supply of widgets (any number of widgets not exceeding 2500) is \$0.50. Alicor has two alternatives: (1) purchase the widgets periodically in lots and allow no shortages to occur and (2) purchase the widgets periodically from a supplier who sends them continuously at the rate of 1500 per month until an order is filled and allow no shortages to occur. Determine the quarterly cost of the optimal policy for each of these alternatives. In order to minimize total quarterly cost of inventory, what policy should Alicor adopt?

Considering demand and costs on a quarterly basis,

$D = 2500$

$c_1 = 0.50$

$c_2 = 9.00$

$k = 4500$

The optimal order quantity for alternative 1 is given by

$$q = \sqrt{\frac{2c_1 D}{c_2}} = \sqrt{\frac{(2)(0.50)(2500)}{9}} = \frac{50}{3}$$

and the associated quarterly cost is

$$C = \frac{c_2 q}{2} + \frac{c_1 D}{q} = \frac{9\left(\frac{50}{3}\right)}{2} + \frac{\left(\frac{1}{2}\right)(2500)}{\frac{50}{3}} = 150$$

The optimal order quantity for alternative 2 is given by

$$q = \sqrt{\frac{2c_1 D}{c_2\left(1 - \dfrac{D}{k}\right)}} = \sqrt{\frac{(2)(0.50)(2500)}{9\left(1 - \frac{2500}{4500}\right)}} = 25$$

and the associated quarterly cost is

$$C = \tfrac{1}{2}c_2 q\left(1 - \frac{D}{k}\right) + \frac{c_1 D}{q} = \tfrac{1}{2}(9)(25)\left(1 - \tfrac{5}{9}\right) + \frac{\tfrac{1}{2}(2500)}{25} = 100$$

Alternative 2 is preferable. As can be observed by comparing the cost equations, this is always the case if the costs of ordering and carrying are the same for the two models.

For this problem, demand, supply and costs could be considered on a monthly basis. Since demand and supply are assumed to be uniform, any convenient common time base can be used for computation.

PROBLEMS

1. The Ace Manufacturing Company has a contract to supply 4000 refrigerators a year at a uniform monthly rate. The annual storage cost per refrigerator is $50 and the setup cost for a production run is $160. If production is instantaneous and shortages are not permitted, determine the number of refrigerators which should be produced in each run in order to minimize the total annual cost of inventory.

2. The Harvest Company has a contract to supply 500 tractors a month at a uniform daily rate. The monthly storage cost per tractor is $10 and the setup cost for a production run is $200. Production is at a constant rate of 1000 tractors per month. If shortages are not permitted, determine the number of tractors which should be produced in each run to minimize the total monthly inventory cost.

3. Profitco Electronics requires 25 transistors per month to make color TV sets. The monthly storage cost is $2.00 per transistor and every time an order is placed it costs Profitco $4.00.
   a. If orders are filled immediately and no shortages are permitted, how many orders of what size should be placed every month? What is the monthly total cost of this inventory policy?
   b. Suppose Profitco can order so that delivery is at the rate of 45 per month (in a uniform flow, not a block) and that no shortages are permitted. How much inventory should be accumulated before stopping the flow and how many times per month will the flow be stopped? What is the total monthly cost of this inventory policy?

4. Fabric Corporation owns a machine which can produce 25 bolts of a particular type of cloth per day and another machine which can make 10 bolts of this cloth into slipcovers per day. It costs $1.50 to hold a bolt of cloth in inventory for a day and it costs $2.00 every time the machine producing the cloth must be stopped. a. What amount of inventory should be built up before the machine producing the cloth is stopped in order to minimize total inventory cost? b. How many times will the machine be shut down in a period of 90 days? c. What is the total amount of cloth that will be produced in a period of 90 days? d. If the demand and cost conditions remain the same, except that the cost of stopping the machine is interpreted as the cost of ordering, and the cloth must be ordered in batches from another company, how many orders of what size will be placed in 90 days (assume no shortages)?

5. The yearly demand for a large cable bolt produced by Lanier Corporation is 9000. It costs Lanier $1000 to put the production line for this cable into operation. The monthly cost of carrying this item in inventory is $6.00. Assuming that Lanier does not permit shortages to occur, how many cable bolts should be produced per production run and how frequently should production be stopped?

6. Bookworms Cooperative stocks a very popular gourmet cookbook for which there is a demand of 1500 copies per month. The publisher pays postage, but the cooperative pays $2.50 for each order in secretarial and administrative costs. Carrying cost is $0.50 per copy per month. In order to minimize total inventory cost, how many books should be ordered at one time? How frequently should orders be placed?

Answers to Odd-Numbered Problems

1. 160
3. a. 10 transistors $2\frac{1}{2}$ times per month
      cost $20
   b. accumulate $\frac{20}{3}$ transistors and stop $\frac{5}{3}$ times per month
      cost $\approx$ $13.33
5. 500 cable bolts and stop 18 times per year

2.13 Indeterminate Forms

For some particular types of functions $f(x)$, the evaluation of

$$\lim_{x \to a} f(x) \qquad \text{when } f(a) = \frac{0}{0} \text{ or } \frac{\infty}{\infty}$$

is discussed on page 165. In this section more general procedures for evaluating these and other indeterminate forms are discussed. These procedures are based on *L'Hospital's rule*:

$$\text{If} \begin{cases} f(a) = g(a) = 0 \\ \qquad \text{or} \\ f(a) = g(a) = \infty \qquad \text{then } \lim_{x \to a} \frac{f(x)}{g(x)} = \lim_{x \to a} \frac{f'(x)}{g'(x)} \\ \qquad \text{and} \\ \lim_{x \to a} \frac{f'(x)}{g'(x)} \text{ exists} \end{cases}$$

(this rule holds for finite or infinite a). If $\lim_{x \to a} \dfrac{f'(x)}{g'(x)}$ is itself an indeterminate form $\dfrac{0}{0}$ or $\dfrac{\infty}{\infty}$, then L'Hospital's rule is applied again and $\lim_{x \to a} \dfrac{f'(x)}{g'(x)} = \lim_{x \to a} \dfrac{f''(x)}{g''(x)}$, and so forth.

CAUTIONS

1. $\lim_{x \to a} \dfrac{f'(x)}{g'(x)} \neq \lim_{x \to a} \dfrac{d}{dx}\left(\dfrac{f(x)}{g(x)}\right)$, that is, the quotient of the derivatives of the two functions is *not* in general equal to the derivative of the quotient of the two functions.

2. $\lim_{x \to a} \dfrac{f'(x)}{g'(x)} = \lim_{x \to a} \dfrac{f''(x)}{g''(x)}$ if and *only if* $\lim_{x \to a} \dfrac{f'(x)}{g'(x)}$ is the indeterminate form $\dfrac{0}{0}$ or $\dfrac{\infty}{\infty}$, that is, L'Hospital's rule applies only to indeterminate forms; thus when the rule is applied successively, the first determinate answer is correct and, in general, further applications give incorrect answers.

EXAMPLE

Evaluate $\lim\limits_{h \to 0} \dfrac{\sqrt{4 + h} - 2}{h}$.

type $\dfrac{0}{0}$, so $\lim\limits_{h \to 0} \dfrac{\sqrt{4 + h} - 2}{h} = \lim\limits_{h \to 0} \dfrac{\frac{1}{2}(4 + h)^{-1/2}}{1} = \dfrac{1}{4}$

EXAMPLE

Evaluate $\lim\limits_{x \to 0} \dfrac{e^x - (1 + x)}{x^2}$.

type $\dfrac{0}{0}$, so $\lim\limits_{x \to 0} \dfrac{e^x - (1 + x)}{x^2} = \lim\limits_{x \to 0} \dfrac{e^x - 1}{2x} \qquad \left(\text{also type } \dfrac{0}{0}\right)$

$$= \lim\limits_{x \to 0} \dfrac{e^x}{2} = \dfrac{1}{2}$$

EXAMPLE

Evaluate $\lim\limits_{x\to\infty} \dfrac{\ln x}{x}$.

type $\dfrac{\infty}{\infty}$, so $\lim\limits_{x\to\infty} \dfrac{\ln x}{x} = \lim\limits_{x\to\infty} \dfrac{1/x}{1} = 0$

EXAMPLE

Evaluate $\lim\limits_{x\to\infty} \dfrac{x^n}{e^x}$.

type $\dfrac{\infty}{\infty}$, so $\lim\limits_{x\to\infty} \dfrac{x^n}{e^x} = \lim\limits_{x\to\infty} \dfrac{nx^{n-1}}{e^x}$ $\left(\text{also type } \dfrac{\infty}{\infty}\right)$

$\qquad\qquad = \lim\limits_{x\to\infty} \dfrac{n(n-1)x^{n-2}}{e^x}$ $\left(\text{also type } \dfrac{\infty}{\infty}\right)$

$\qquad\qquad = \cdots = \lim\limits_{x\to\infty} \dfrac{n!}{e^x} = 0$

PROBLEMS

Evaluate the following limits.

1. $\lim\limits_{y\to\infty} \dfrac{e^y}{y^2}$

2. $\lim\limits_{x\to\infty} \dfrac{x}{e^x}$

3. $\lim\limits_{x\to\infty} \dfrac{\ln x}{x^k}$ $(k > 0)$

4. $\lim\limits_{x\to0} \dfrac{e^x - e^{-x}}{\sin x}$

5. $\lim\limits_{x\to0} \dfrac{e^x - \ln(x+1) - 1}{x^2}$

6. $\lim\limits_{x\to\pi/2} \dfrac{\sec x + 1}{\tan x}$

7. $\lim\limits_{x\to\infty} \dfrac{x^2 + x - 1}{e^x + e^{-x}}$

8. $\lim\limits_{x\to0} \dfrac{e^x + e^{-x} - 2}{x^2}$

9. $\lim\limits_{x\to\infty} \dfrac{x^k}{e^x}$ $(k > 0)$

10. $\lim\limits_{x\to1} \dfrac{\ln x}{x^2 - 1}$

11. $\lim\limits_{x\to1} \dfrac{\ln(1 - x)}{\cot \pi x}$

12. $\lim\limits_{x\to0} \dfrac{\sin^2 x}{x}$

13. $\lim\limits_{x\to0} \dfrac{\sin x - x}{x^3}$

14. $\lim\limits_{x\to\infty} \dfrac{x^k}{\ln x}$

15. $\lim\limits_{x\to\infty} \dfrac{e^x}{x^k}$

16. $\lim\limits_{x\to0} \dfrac{e^x - e^{-x} - 2\sin x}{3x^3}$

17. $\lim\limits_{x\to0} \dfrac{e^{2x} - 1}{x^2 - \sin x}$

18. $\lim\limits_{x\to0} \dfrac{2 - 3e^{-x} + e^{-2x}}{2x^2}$

19. $\lim\limits_{x\to\infty} \dfrac{e^x}{x^3}$

20. $\lim\limits_{x\to2} \dfrac{x^4 - 4x^3 + 16}{x^3 - 8}$

21. $\lim\limits_{x\to0} \dfrac{4 - 3e^x - e^{-3x}}{4x^2}$

22. $\lim\limits_{x\to2} \dfrac{x^3 - 4x}{x^2 - 2x}$

23. $\lim\limits_{t\to 0} \dfrac{1 - \cos t - \frac{1}{2}t^2}{t^4}$

24. $\lim\limits_{x\to\infty} \dfrac{x^3}{e^x + x^2 - 2}$

25. $\lim\limits_{h\to 0} \dfrac{(\sin h)/h - \cos h}{h^2}$

26. $\lim\limits_{x\to\infty} \dfrac{4x^2 + 3x - 6}{8x + 2}$

27. $\lim\limits_{y\to 0} \dfrac{4y^3 + 6y}{3y^3 + 2y}$

28. $\lim\limits_{x\to\infty} \dfrac{e^x}{x}$

29. $\lim\limits_{z\to 0} \dfrac{\sin z^2 - \sin^2 z}{z^4}$

30. $\lim\limits_{x\to\pi/4} \dfrac{1 - \sin 2x}{(\pi/4) - x}$

31. $\lim\limits_{x\to\pi} \dfrac{1 + \cos x}{(\pi - x)^2}$

32. $\lim\limits_{\theta\to 0} \dfrac{\tan\theta - \sin\theta}{\theta^2}$

33. $\lim\limits_{x\to 0} \dfrac{e^x - 1}{x^2 - x}$

34. $\lim\limits_{x\to -3} \dfrac{x^3 + 27}{x + 3}$

35. $\lim\limits_{x\to\infty} \dfrac{x^2}{e^x - 1}$

36. $\lim\limits_{x\to 0} \dfrac{\cot x}{\cot 2x}$

37. $\lim\limits_{x\to 0} \dfrac{\tan x - x}{x - \sin x}$

38. $\lim\limits_{x\to\pi/2} \dfrac{\ln \sin x}{(\pi - 2x)^2}$

39. $\lim\limits_{x\to\phi} \dfrac{\sin x - \sin\phi}{x - \phi}$

40. $\lim\limits_{y\to 0} \dfrac{e^y + \sin y - 1}{\ln(1 + y)}$

41. $\lim\limits_{x\to 0} \dfrac{\cot x}{\ln x}$

42. $\lim\limits_{x\to 0} \dfrac{\ln \sin 2x}{\ln \sin x}$

Answers to Odd-Numbered Problems

1. ∞
3. 0
5. 1
7. 0
9. 0
11. 0
13. $-\frac{1}{6}$

15. ∞
17. -2
19. ∞
21. $-\frac{3}{2}$
23. $-\frac{1}{24}$
25. $\frac{1}{3}$
27. 3

29. $\frac{1}{3}$
31. $\frac{1}{2}$
33. -1
35. 0
37. 2
39. $\cos\phi$
41. $-\infty$

L'Hospital's rule is also applicable to other types of indeterminate forms, if they are first put into the form 0/0 or ∞/∞, as follows.

Type $\infty \cdot 0$:

If $\lim\limits_{x\to a} f(x)g(x) = \infty \cdot 0$, where $\lim\limits_{x\to a} f(x) = \infty$, $\lim\limits_{x\to a} g(x) = 0$, then

$\lim\limits_{x\to a} \dfrac{f(x)}{\dfrac{1}{g(x)}}$ is of type ∞/∞ or, alternatively, $\dfrac{g(x)}{\dfrac{1}{f(x)}}$ is of type 0/0

Type 1^∞:

If $\lim\limits_{x\to a} f(x)^{g(x)} = 1^\infty$, where $\lim\limits_{x\to a} f(x) = 1$, $\lim\limits_{x\to a} g(x) = \infty$, then

$\lim\limits_{x\to a} \left(\dfrac{g(x)}{\dfrac{1}{\ln f(x)}} \right)$ is of type $\dfrac{\infty}{\infty}$ or, alternatively, $\lim\limits_{x\to a} \left(\dfrac{\ln f(x)}{\dfrac{1}{g(x)}} \right)$ is of type 0/0 and, if

one of the above limits is b, the limit of the original function is e^b.

EXAMPLE

Evaluate $\lim_{x \to \infty} x(e^{1/x} - 1)$.

type $\infty \cdot 0$, so $\quad \lim_{x \to \infty} x(e^{1/x} - 1) = \lim_{x \to \infty} \dfrac{e^{1/x} - 1}{\dfrac{1}{x}}$

$$= \lim_{x \to \infty} \dfrac{-\dfrac{e^{1/x}}{x^2}}{-\dfrac{1}{x^2}} = 1$$

EXAMPLE

Evaluate $\lim_{x \to 1} (1 - x) \tan \frac{1}{2}\pi x$.

type $0 \cdot \infty$, so $\quad \lim_{x \to 1} (1 - x) \tan \frac{1}{2}\pi x = \lim_{x \to 1} \dfrac{1 - x}{\cot \frac{1}{2}\pi x}$

$$= \lim_{x \to 1} \dfrac{-1}{-\frac{1}{2}\pi \csc^2 \frac{1}{2}\pi x}$$

$$= \dfrac{1}{\pi/2} = \dfrac{2}{\pi}$$

EXAMPLE

Evaluate $\lim_{x \to 0} (1 - 2x)^{3/x}$.

type 1^∞, so $\quad \lim_{x \to 0} (1 - 2x)^{3/x} = \lim_{x \to 0} \exp \dfrac{\ln (1 - 2x)}{\dfrac{x}{3}}$

$$\lim_{x \to 0} \dfrac{\ln (1 - 2x)}{\dfrac{x}{3}} = \lim_{x \to 0} \dfrac{\dfrac{-2}{1 - 2x}}{\dfrac{1}{3}} = -6$$

$$\lim_{x \to 0} (1 - 2x)^{3/x} = e^{-6}$$

NOTE: Notation exp $f(x)$ means $e^{f(x)}$.

EXAMPLE

Evaluate $\lim_{x \to 0} (\sin x + \cos x)^{1/x}$.

type 1^{∞}, so $\quad \lim_{x \to 0} (\sin x + \cos x)^{1/x} = \exp \lim_{x \to 0} \dfrac{\ln (\sin x + \cos x)}{x}$

$$\lim_{x \to 0} \dfrac{\ln (\sin x + \cos x)}{x} = \lim_{x \to 0} \dfrac{\dfrac{\cos x - \sin x}{\sin x + \cos x}}{1} = \dfrac{1}{1} = 1$$

$$\lim_{x \to 0} (\sin x + \cos x)^{1/x} = e^1 = e$$

Type 0^0:

If $\lim_{x \to a} f(x)^{g(x)} = 0^0$, where $\lim_{x \to a} f(x) = 0$ and $\lim_{x \to a} g(x) = 0$, then

$$\lim_{x \to a} \left(\dfrac{g(x)}{\dfrac{1}{\ln f(x)}} \right) \text{ is of type } \dfrac{0}{0}$$

or

$$\lim_{x \to a} \left(\dfrac{\ln f(x)}{\dfrac{1}{g(x)}} \right) \text{ is of type } \dfrac{\infty}{\infty}$$

and, if one of the above limits is b, the limit of the original functions is e^b.

Type ∞^0:

If $\lim_{x \to a} f(x)^{g(x)} = \infty^0$, where $\lim_{x \to a} f(x) = \infty$ and $\lim_{x \to a} g(x) = 0$, then

$$\lim_{x \to a} \left(\dfrac{g(x)}{\dfrac{1}{\ln f(x)}} \right) \text{ is of type } \dfrac{0}{0}$$

or

$$\lim_{x \to a} \left(\dfrac{\ln f(x)}{\dfrac{1}{g(x)}} \right) \text{ is of type } \dfrac{\infty}{\infty}$$

and, if one of the above limits is b, the limit of the original function is e^b.

EXAMPLE

Evaluate $\lim_{x \to 0^+} x^x$.

type 0^0, so $\quad \lim_{x \to 0^+} x^x = \exp \lim_{x \to 0^+} \dfrac{\ln x}{\dfrac{1}{x}}$

$$\lim_{x \to 0^+} \dfrac{\ln x}{\dfrac{1}{x}} = \lim_{x \to 0^+} \dfrac{\dfrac{1}{x}}{-\dfrac{1}{x^2}} = \lim_{x \to 0^+} (-x) = 0$$

$$\lim_{x \to 0^+} x^x = e^0 = 1$$

EXAMPLE

Evaluate $\lim_{x \to 1} (1 - x)^{\tan \pi x}$.

type 0^0, so $\quad \lim_{x \to 1} (1 - x)^{\tan \pi x} = \exp \lim_{x \to 1} \dfrac{\ln (1 - x)}{\cot \pi x}$

$$\lim_{x \to 1} \frac{\ln (1 - x)}{\cot \pi x} = \lim_{x \to 1} \frac{\dfrac{-1}{1 - x}}{\csc^2 \pi x}$$

$$= \lim_{x \to 1} \frac{\sin^2 \pi x}{1 - x}$$

$$= \lim_{x \to 1} (2\pi \sin \pi x \cos \pi x)$$

$$= 0$$

$$\lim_{x \to 1} (1 - x)^{\tan \pi x} = e^0 = 1$$

EXAMPLE

Evaluate $\lim_{x \to \infty} x^{1/x}$.

type ∞^0, so $\quad \lim_{x \to \infty} x^{1/x} = \exp \lim_{x \to \infty} \dfrac{\ln x}{x}$

$$\lim_{x \to \infty} \frac{\ln x}{x} = \lim_{x \to \infty} \frac{1/x}{1} = 0$$

$$\lim_{x \to \infty} x^{1/x} = e^0 = 1$$

EXAMPLE

Evaluate $\lim_{x \to \infty} (x + e^x)^{2/x}$

type ∞^0, so $\quad \lim_{x \to \infty} (x + e^x)^{2/x} = \exp \lim_{x \to \infty} \dfrac{\ln (x + e^x)}{\dfrac{x}{2}}$

$$\lim_{x \to \infty} \frac{\ln (x + e^x)}{\dfrac{x}{2}} = \lim_{x \to \infty} \frac{\dfrac{1 + e^x}{x + e^x}}{\dfrac{1}{2}}$$

$$= \lim_{x \to \infty} \frac{2(1 + e^x)}{x + e^x}$$

$$= \lim_{x \to \infty} \frac{2e^x}{1 + e^x}$$

$$= \lim_{x \to \infty} \frac{2e^x}{e^x} = 2$$

$$\lim_{x \to \infty} (x + e^x)^{2/x} = e^2$$

Type $\infty - \infty$:

If $\lim_{x \to a} [f(x) - g(x)] = \infty - \infty$, where $\lim_{x \to a} f(x) = \infty$, $\lim_{x \to a} g(x) = \infty$, then

$$\lim_{x \to a} \left(\frac{1}{\frac{1}{f(x)}} - \frac{1}{\frac{1}{g(x)}} \right) = \lim_{x \to a} \left(\frac{\frac{1}{g(x)} - \frac{1}{f(x)}}{\frac{1}{g(x)} \cdot \frac{1}{f(x)}} \right) \text{ is of type } \frac{0}{0}$$

EXAMPLE

Evaluate $\lim_{x \to 0} \left(\cot x - \frac{1}{x} \right)$.

type $\infty - \infty$, so $\lim_{x \to 0} \left(\cot x - \frac{1}{x} \right) = \lim_{x \to 0} \frac{x - \tan x}{x \tan x}$

$$= \lim_{x \to 0} \frac{1 - \sec^2 x}{\tan x + x \sec^2 x}$$

$$= \lim_{x \to 0} \frac{-2 \sec^2 x \tan x}{\sec^2 x + \sec^2 x + 2x \sec^2 x \tan x}$$

$$= \lim_{x \to 0} \frac{-2 \tan x}{2(1 + x \tan x)}$$

$$= \frac{0}{2} = 0$$

EXAMPLE

Evaluate $\lim_{x \to 0} \left(\frac{1}{x} - \frac{1}{e^x - 1} \right)$.

type $\infty - \infty$, so $\lim_{x \to 0} \left(\frac{1}{x} - \frac{1}{e^x - 1} \right) = \lim_{x \to 0} \frac{e^x - 1 - x}{x(e^x - 1)}$

$$= \lim_{x \to 0} \frac{e^x - 1}{e^x + xe^x - 1}$$

$$= \lim_{x \to 0} \frac{e^x}{e^x + e^x + xe^x} = \frac{1}{2}$$

The types of indeterminate forms which can be evaluated using L'Hospital's rule are summarized in Table 2.1.

Table 2.1 Summary of Application of L'Hospital's Rule

Type of indeterminate form	Apply L'Hospital's rule to
1. $\lim \dfrac{f(x)}{g(x)} = \dfrac{0}{0}$	$\lim \dfrac{f(x)}{g(x)}$
2. $\lim \dfrac{f(x)}{g(x)} = \dfrac{\infty}{\infty}$	$\lim \dfrac{f(x)}{g(x)}$
3. $\lim f(x)g(x) = \infty \cdot 0$	$\lim \left(\dfrac{g(x)}{\frac{1}{f(x)}}\right)$ or to $\lim \left(\dfrac{f(x)}{\frac{1}{g(x)}}\right)$
4. $\lim f(x)^{g(x)} = 1^\infty$	$\lim \left(\dfrac{\ln f(x)}{\frac{1}{g(x)}}\right)$ or to $\lim \left(\dfrac{g(x)}{\frac{1}{\ln f(x)}}\right)$
5. $\lim f(x)^{g(x)} = 0^0$	$\lim \left(\dfrac{g(x)}{\frac{1}{\ln f(x)}}\right)$ or to $\lim \left(\dfrac{\ln f(x)}{\frac{1}{g(x)}}\right)$
6. $\lim f(x)^{g(x)} = \infty^0$	$\lim \left(\dfrac{g(x)}{\frac{1}{\ln f(x)}}\right)$ or to $\lim \left(\dfrac{\ln f(x)}{\frac{1}{g(x)}}\right)$
7. $\lim [f(x) - g(x)] = \infty - \infty$	$\lim \left(\dfrac{\frac{1}{g(x)} - \frac{1}{f(x)}}{\frac{1}{g(x)} \cdot \frac{1}{f(x)}}\right)$

If L'Hospital's rule applied to one of these gives a constant b for the limit, then the original limit is e^b.

PROBLEMS

Evaluate the following limits.

1. $\lim\limits_{x \to 1^+} x^{1/(1 - x^2)}$

2. $\lim\limits_{x \to 0} x \cot x$

3. $\lim\limits_{x \to 0} x \ln \sin x$

4. $\lim\limits_{z \to \infty} z^{1/z}$

5. $\lim\limits_{x \to \pi/2} \tan x \ln \sin x$

6. $\lim\limits_{x \to 0} (1 + x^2)^{1/x^2}$

7. $\lim\limits_{x \to 0} x^2 \csc x \cot x$

8. $\lim\limits_{x \to 0} x \ln x$

9. $\lim\limits_{x \to 0} (1 + \sin x)^{\cot x}$

10. $\lim\limits_{x \to \infty} \left(1 + \dfrac{2}{x}\right)^x$

11. $\lim\limits_{x \to \infty} xe^{-x}$

12. $\lim\limits_{x \to \pi/2} (\sec x - \tan x)$

13. $\lim\limits_{x \to \infty} (1 + x)^{1/x}$

14. $\lim\limits_{x \to 0} x^n \ln x \quad (n > 0)$

15. $\lim\limits_{x \to 0} (e^x + x)^{1/x}$

16. $\lim\limits_{x \to \infty} (1 + ax)^{b/x}$

17. $\lim\limits_{x \to 1^+} \left(\dfrac{1}{x - 1} - \dfrac{1}{\sqrt{x - 1}}\right)$

18. $\lim\limits_{x \to 1} \left(\dfrac{1}{\ln x} - \dfrac{x}{\ln x}\right)$

19. $\lim\limits_{x \to 1} \left(\dfrac{1}{\ln x} - \dfrac{x}{x - 1}\right)$

20. $\lim\limits_{x \to \infty} (x - 1)e^{-x^2}$

21. $\lim\limits_{x\to-\infty} x^2 e^x$

22. $\lim\limits_{x\to\pi/2} \sin x^{\tan x}$

23. $\lim\limits_{x\to 0^+} (x + \sin x)^{\tan x}$

24. $\lim\limits_{x\to\infty} (1 + e^{-x})^{e^x}$

25. $\lim\limits_{x\to 0^+} xe^{1/x}$

26. $\lim\limits_{x\to\infty} (x - \sqrt{x^2 + x})$

27. $\lim\limits_{x\to 0} (e^x + 2x)^{1/x}$

28. $\lim\limits_{x\to 1^-} x^{1/(1-x^2)}$

29. $\lim\limits_{x\to 0} \dfrac{\sqrt{1-x} - \sqrt{1+x}}{x}$

30. $\lim\limits_{x\to 0} \dfrac{1 - \sqrt{x+1}}{x}$

31. $\lim\limits_{x\to 1} \csc \pi x \log x$

32. $\lim\limits_{x\to\infty} (x - 2)e^{-x^2}$

33. $\lim\limits_{x\to\infty} x^2 e^{-3x}$

34. $\lim\limits_{x\to 0^+} \sin x \ln x$

35. $\lim\limits_{\theta\to(\pi/2)^-} e^{-\tan\theta} \sec^2\theta$

36. $\lim\limits_{x\to 4} (x - 4)^{x^2 - 16}$

37. $\lim\limits_{x\to 1} x^{\cot \pi x}$

38. $\lim\limits_{x\to 0^+} (x + 1)^{\cot x}$

39. $\lim\limits_{x\to\infty} (x^2 + a)^{1/x}$

40. $\lim\limits_{x\to(\pi/2)^-} \tan x^{\cos x}$

41. $\lim\limits_{\alpha\to(\pi/2)^-} \sin \alpha^{\tan \alpha}$

42. $\lim\limits_{x\to\infty} x^2 e^{-x}$

43. $\lim\limits_{t\to 0} (1 + ct^2)^{c/t}$

44. $\lim\limits_{\alpha\to 0^+} \sin \alpha^{\tan \alpha}$

45. $\lim\limits_{x\to 1} x^{(1/x^2)-1}$

46. $\lim\limits_{y\to\infty} (e^y - 1)^{1/y}$

47. $\lim\limits_{x\to 0^+} \csc x^{\sin x}$

48. $\lim\limits_{x\to 0} x^2 \csc x$

49. $\lim\limits_{\phi\to 0} \dfrac{\pi}{\phi} \tan \dfrac{\pi\phi}{2}$

50. $\lim\limits_{x\to\infty} (1 + x^2)^{1/x}$

51. $\lim\limits_{x\to\infty} x \sin \dfrac{a}{x}$

52. $\lim\limits_{x\to(\pi/2)} (\pi - 2x) \tan x$

53. $\lim\limits_{x\to 0} x^2 \ln x$

54. $\lim\limits_{\theta\to(\pi/4)} (1 - \tan\theta) \sec 2\theta$

55. $\lim\limits_{x\to 1^+} \left(\dfrac{1}{\ln x} - \dfrac{1}{x-1}\right)$

56. $\lim\limits_{x\to 1^-} (\sqrt{2 - x^2} - 1)^{x-1}$

Answers to Odd-Numbered Problems

1. $e^{-1/2}$

3. 0

5. 0

7. 1

9. e

11. 0

13. 1

15. e^2

17. ∞

19. $-\frac{1}{2}$

21. 0

23. 0

25. 0

27. e^3

29. -1

31. $-\dfrac{\log e}{\pi}$

33. 0

35. 0

37. $e^{1/\pi}$

39. 1

41. 1

43. 1

45. $e^{1/2}$

47. 1

49. $\dfrac{\pi^2}{2}$

51. a

53. 0

55. $\frac{1}{2}$

2.14 Sequences and Series

In this section, infinite sequences and series are defined and tests for determining convergence or divergence of an infinite series are considered. Power series are defined and the representation of a function by a Taylor's series is discussed.

A *sequence* is a succession of terms, $u_1, u_2, \ldots$, formed according to some fixed rule; a *series* is the indicated sum $u_1 + u_2 + \cdots$ of the terms of a sequence. A finite sequence or a finite series has a specified (finite) number of terms; an infinite sequence or an infinite series has an unspecified (infinite) number of terms. The general term, or nth term, of a sequence or series indicates the rule or formula for obtaining the terms.

For example, $1, \frac{1}{2}, \frac{1}{3}, \frac{1}{4}, \frac{1}{5}$ is a finite sequence, and $1 + \frac{1}{2} + \frac{1}{3} + \frac{1}{4} + \frac{1}{5}$ is a finite series. The nth or general term is $1/n$. However, if continued indefinitely, $1, \frac{1}{2}, \frac{1}{3}, \frac{1}{4}, \frac{1}{5}, \frac{1}{6}, \frac{1}{7}, \frac{1}{8}, \ldots$ is an infinite sequence and $1 + \frac{1}{2} + \frac{1}{3} + \frac{1}{4} + \frac{1}{5} + \frac{1}{6} + \frac{1}{7} + \frac{1}{8} + \cdots = \sum_{n=1}^{\infty} 1/n$ is an infinite series, still with the general term $1/n$.

Another method of specifying the terms of a sequence or series is by a *recursion formula* which gives the $(n + 1)$st term as a function of the preceding term or terms. For example, the infinite sequence $1, 2, 6, 24, 120, \ldots$ may be specified by the general term $u_n = n!$ or by the recursion formula $u_{n+1} = nu_n$, where u_n is the nth term and u_{n+1} is the $(n + 1)$st term. Many sequences are more conveniently specified by a recursion formula than by a general term; other sequences, including the examples above, are as conveniently specified by a general term, but additional terms are more easily obtained by recursion. In order to specify a sequence completely by a recursion formula, the first term must be specified separately. Thus the sum of the sequence above is given by $\sum_{n=1}^{\infty} u_n = \sum_{n=1}^{\infty} n!$ or by $\sum_{n=1}^{\infty} u_n = 1 + \sum_{n=2}^{\infty} nu_{n-1}$. There are some sequences for which it is necessary to specify the first term or terms separately, even if the general term is specified.

Although a finite sequence must have a finite sum, the sum of an infinite sequence, as defined below, may be finite or infinite.

Let S_n represent the sum of the first n terms of an infinite sequence $u_1, u_2, \ldots, u_n, \ldots$,

$$S_n = u_1 + u_2 + \cdots + u_n = \sum_{i=1}^{n} u_i$$

and let S represent the limit of S_n as $n \to \infty$,

$$S = \lim_{n \to \infty} S_n = \sum_{i=1}^{\infty} u_i$$

If the limit S exists finitely, the infinite series is *convergent* and is said to converge to the value S; if the limit does not exist finitely, the infinite series is *divergent*. Divergence may occur because S_n becomes infinite as $n \to \infty$ or because S_n oscillates without approaching a limit as $n \to \infty$.

Infinite series are essential in evaluating many functions and are also used to define a number of useful functions. There are two problems generally associated with infinite series: determining whether the limit of an infinite series exists and determining the value of the limit, if it exists.

Establishing convergence or divergence of a series is discussed first. Determining the limit of a series, if it exists, is then discussed in connection with representing functions using infinite series. If an expression for S_n can be obtained, the limit of a series can be determined using the rules discussed in previous sections and is relatively straightforward.

EXAMPLE

For the geometric series of n terms,

$$S_n = a + ar + ar^2 + \cdots + ar^{n-1}$$

it can be shown that

$$S_n = \frac{a(1 - r^n)}{1 - r} = \frac{a(r^n - 1)}{r - 1}$$

The first form is generally used if $|r| < 1$; the second form is generally used if $|r| > 1$.

If $|r| < 1$, $\lim_{n \to \infty} r^n = 0$ and $\lim_{n \to \infty} S_n = \dfrac{a}{1 - r}$ and the series is convergent.

If $|r| \geq 1$, $\lim_{n \to \infty} r^n = \infty$ and $\lim_{n \to \infty} S_n = \infty$ and the series is divergent.

NOTE: If $r = -1$, the geometric series is

$$a - a + a - a + a - a + \cdots$$

when n is odd, $S_n = a$; when n is even, $S_n = 0$. Such a series has no limit and is thus divergent; it is referred to as an *oscillating series*.

Establishing convergence or divergence of a series is clearly more difficult if an expression for S_n cannot be obtained. In such cases, the following tests are used.

1. *Necessary condition for convergence.* If an infinite series $\sum_{n=1}^{\infty} u_n$ is convergent, then $\lim_{n \to \infty} u_n = 0$. That is, if the nth term of a series does not approach 0 as n becomes infinite, the series is divergent. Note that $\lim_{n \to \infty} u_n = 0$ is a necessary but *not* a sufficient condition for convergence.
2. *Alternating-series test.* An alternating series is a series whose terms are alternately positive and negative. Such a series is convergent if $\lim_{n \to \infty} u_n = 0$ and each term is less in absolute value than the term which precedes it, that is, if $|u_{n+1}| < |u_n|$ for all $n = 1, 2, \ldots$.

   NOTE: It can be shown that the error involved in breaking a convergent alternating series at any term does not exceed in absolute value the first of the terms discarded. That is, if $u_1 - u_2 + u_3 - u_4 + \cdots$ is a convergent alternating series, then for any k,

   $$\left| \sum_{n=k+1}^{\infty} u_n \right| \leq |u_k|.$$

3. *Absolute convergence.* A series of some positive and some negative terms is said to be *absolutely convergent* if the series formed from it by making all of its terms positive is convergent. Other convergent series of some positive and some negative terms are said to be *conditionally convergent*. If a series of some positive and some negative terms is absolutely convergent, it is conditionally convergent, but the converse is not necessarily true.
4. *Cauchy's ratio test.* Let

   $$u_1 + u_2 + u_3 + \cdots + u_{n+1} + \cdots$$

   be an infinite series of positive terms. Using consecutive general terms u_n and u_{n+1}, form the ratio

   $$\frac{u_{n+1}}{u_n}$$

and let

$$\rho = \lim_{n \to \infty} \frac{u_{n+1}}{u_n}$$

Then

If $\rho < 1$, the series is convergent

If $\rho > 1$, the series is divergent

If $\rho = 1$, the test fails

5. *Comparison tests.* In many cases it is possible to determine whether a given series is convergent or divergent by comparing it term by term with a series known to be convergent or divergent. A series of positive terms is convergent if each of its terms is less than or equal to the corresponding term of a known convergent series. A series of positive terms is divergent if each of its terms is greater than or equal to the corresponding term of a known divergent series. The geometric series discussed above and the "*p*-series" are frequently useful in applying the comparison test. The "*p*-series" is given by

$$1 + \frac{1}{2^p} + \frac{1}{3^p} + \cdots + \frac{1}{n^p} + \cdots$$

This series is convergent if $p > 1$ and divergent if $p \leq 1$. If $p = 1$, the *p*-series is the harmonic series.

NOTE: Since convergence or divergence of a series cannot be affected by the omission of a finite number of terms, comparison tests may be applied to the terms $u_k, u_{k+1}, u_{k+2}, \ldots$ rather than to the terms $u_1, u_2, u_3, \ldots$.

SUMMARY OF PROCEDURE FOR TESTING CONVERGENCE OR DIVERGENCE OF AN INFINITE SERIES

In determining convergence or divergence of an infinite series, the tests should generally be applied in the order in which they are given above; thus the procedure is:

1. Determine whether $\lim_{n \to \infty} u_n$ is zero.

   If $\lim_{n \to \infty} u_n \neq 0$, the series is divergent

   If $\lim_{n \to \infty} u_n = 0$, further testing is necessary

   Assuming $\lim_{n \to \infty} u_n = 0$,

2. Apply the alternating-series test (if appropriate): An alternating series whose terms decrease in numerical value and for which $\lim_{n \to \infty} u_n = 0$ is convergent.

3. Apply the ratio test: If $\lim_{n \to \infty} \frac{u_{n+1}}{u_n} = \rho$, then

   $|\rho| > 1 \Rightarrow$ series divergent

   $|\rho| < 1 \Rightarrow$ series convergent (absolutely)

   $|\rho| = 1 \Rightarrow$ test fails

4. Apply the comparison test: Compare the series with a series known to be convergent or divergent, such as the geometric series or the *p*-series.

Geometric series: $a + ar + ar^2 + \cdots + ar^{n-1} + \cdots$
Convergent if $|r| < 1$
Divergent if $|r| \geq 1$

p-series: $1 + \dfrac{1}{2^p} + \dfrac{1}{3^p} + \cdots + \dfrac{1}{n^p} + \cdots$
Convergent if $p > 1$
Divergent if $p \leq 1$

EXAMPLE

Determine the convergence or divergence of the infinite series

$$\frac{1}{2} - \frac{3}{2^2} + \frac{5}{2^3} - \frac{7}{2^4} + \cdots$$

General term:

$$u_n = (-1)^{n+1} \frac{2n-1}{2^n}$$

Note that the numerators of the terms are 1, 3, 5, 7, ..., which is an arithmetic series with first term 1 and common difference 2; the nth term of this series is $2n - 1$.

$$\lim_{n \to \infty} u_n = 0$$

and $|u_{n+1}| < |u_n|$ for all n, so the alternating series is convergent. Testing for absolute convergence,

$$\rho = \lim_{n \to \infty} \frac{u_{n+1}}{u_n} = \lim_{n \to \infty} \left(-\frac{\dfrac{2(n+1)-1}{2^{n+1}}}{\dfrac{2n-1}{2^n}} \right)$$

$$= \lim_{n \to \infty} \left(-\frac{2n+1}{2(2n-1)} \right) = \lim_{n \to \infty} \left(-\tfrac{2}{4} \right) = -\tfrac{1}{2}$$

$$|\rho| = |-\tfrac{1}{2}| < 1$$

so the series is absolutely convergent.

EXAMPLE

Determine the convergence or divergence of the infinite series

$$\tfrac{2}{3} - \tfrac{3}{5} + \tfrac{4}{7} - \tfrac{5}{9} + \cdots$$

General term:

$$u_n = (-1)^{n+1} \frac{n+1}{2n+1}$$

$$\lim_{n \to \infty} u_n = \tfrac{1}{2}$$

so the series is divergent.

EXAMPLE

Determine the convergence or divergence of the infinite series

$$1 - \frac{1}{\sqrt{3}} + \frac{1}{\sqrt{5}} - \frac{1}{\sqrt{7}} + \cdots$$

General term:

$$u_n = (-1)^{n+1} \frac{1}{\sqrt{2n-1}}$$

$$\lim_{n \to \infty} u_n = 0$$

and $|u_{n+1}| < |u_n|$ for all n, so the alternating series is convergent. Testing for absolute convergence,

$$\rho = \lim_{n \to \infty} \frac{u_{n+1}}{u_n} = \lim_{n \to \infty} \left(-\frac{\dfrac{1}{\sqrt{2(n+1)-1}}}{\dfrac{1}{\sqrt{2n-1}}} \right)$$

$$= \lim_{n \to \infty} \left(-\frac{(2n-1)^{1/2}}{(2n+1)^{1/2}} \right) = -1$$

$$|\rho| = 1$$

so the ratio test for absolute convergence fails.

$1/(2n-1)^{1/2} > (1/n)$ (p-series, p = 1), so the series is divergent as a positive series. Thus the alternating series is conditionally convergent but not absolutely convergent.

EXAMPLE

Determine the convergence or divergence of the infinite series

$$\frac{1}{9} + \frac{2!}{9^2} + \frac{3!}{9^3} + \frac{4!}{9^4} + \cdots$$

General term:

$$u_n = \frac{n!}{9^n}$$

$$\lim_{n \to \infty} u_n = \infty$$

so the series is divergent.

EXAMPLE

Determine the convergence or divergence of the infinite series

$$\tfrac{3}{4} + 2(\tfrac{3}{4})^2 + 3(\tfrac{3}{4})^3 + 4(\tfrac{3}{4})^4 + \cdots$$

General term:

$$u_n = n(\tfrac{3}{4})^n$$

$$\lim_{n \to \infty} u_n = 0$$

$$\rho = \lim_{n \to \infty} \frac{u_{n+1}}{u_n} = \lim_{n \to \infty} \left(\frac{(n+1)(\frac{3}{4})^{n+1}}{n(\frac{3}{4})^n} \right)$$

$$= \lim_{n \to \infty} \frac{3}{4} \left(\frac{n+1}{n} \right) = \frac{3}{4}$$

$$|\rho| = |\tfrac{3}{4}| < 1$$

so the series is convergent.

EXAMPLE

Determine the convergence or divergence of the infinite series

$$5 + \frac{5^2}{2!} + \frac{5^3}{3!} + \frac{5^4}{4!} + \cdots$$

General term:

$$u_n = \frac{5^n}{n!}$$

$$\lim_{n \to \infty} u_n = 0$$

$$\rho = \lim_{n \to \infty} \left(\frac{\dfrac{5^{n+1}}{(n+1)!}}{\dfrac{5^n}{n!}} \right) = \lim_{n \to \infty} \frac{5}{n+1} = 0$$

$$|\rho| = 0 < 1$$

so the series is convergent.

PROBLEMS

For each of the following series, write out the first few terms and determine whether the series is divergent or convergent (conditionally or absolutely for alternating series).

1. $\displaystyle\sum_{n=1}^{\infty} (-1)^{n+1} \frac{1}{n^2+1}$

2. $\displaystyle\sum_{n=1}^{\infty} \frac{\sqrt{n}}{n^2+1}$

3. $\displaystyle\sum_{n=1}^{\infty} \frac{n}{n+2}$

4. $\displaystyle\sum_{n=1}^{\infty} \frac{1}{1+\ln n}$

5. $\displaystyle\sum_{n=0}^{\infty} (-1)^{n+1} \frac{1}{(2n+1)!}$

6. $\displaystyle\sum_{n=1}^{\infty} \frac{(n+1)(n+2)}{n!}$

7. $\displaystyle\sum_{n=1}^{\infty} (-1)^{n+1} \frac{n^2}{2^n}$

8. $\displaystyle\sum_{n=0}^{\infty} \frac{(n+3)!}{3!\, n!\, 3^n}$

9. $\displaystyle\sum_{n=1}^{\infty} (-1)^{n+1} \frac{2^n}{n^3+1}$

10. $\displaystyle\sum_{n=1}^{\infty} \frac{10^n}{n!}$

11. $\displaystyle\sum_{n=1}^{\infty} \frac{n!}{9^n}$

12. $\displaystyle\sum_{n=1}^{\infty} \frac{n^2}{10(2n-1)}$

13. $\displaystyle\sum_{n=1}^{\infty} e^{1/n}$

14. $\displaystyle\sum_{n=1}^{\infty} (-1)^{n+1} \frac{3^n}{n2^n}$

15. $\displaystyle\sum_{n=0}^{\infty} (-1)^{n+1} \frac{3n-1}{4^n}$

16. $\displaystyle\sum_{n=0}^{\infty} (-1)^{n+1} \frac{3n^{2/3}-1}{4^n}$

17. $\displaystyle\sum_{n=0}^{\infty} (-1)^{n+1} \frac{10}{(5n-2)^{1/4}}$

18. $\displaystyle\sum_{n=0}^{\infty} (-1)^{n+1} \frac{(n+3)!}{3^{n-1}}$

19. $\displaystyle\sum_{n=1}^{\infty} (-1)^{n+1} \frac{n+2}{n+1}$

20. $\displaystyle\sum_{n=1}^{\infty} \frac{n^3}{n!}$

21. $\displaystyle\sum_{n=1}^{\infty} \frac{3^{2n-1}}{n^2+1}$

22. $\displaystyle\sum_{n=1}^{\infty} (-1)^{n+1} \frac{1}{\sqrt{n}}$

Answers to Odd-Numbered Problems

1. absolutely convergent
3. divergent
5. absolutely convergent
7. absolutely convergent
9. divergent
11. divergent

13. divergent
15. absolutely convergent
17. conditionally convergent
19. divergent
21. divergent

POWER SERIES

An infinite series of the form

$$a_0 + a_1 x + a_2 x^2 + \cdots + a_n x^n + \cdots = \sum_{n=0}^{\infty} a_n x^n$$

where the coefficients $a_0, a_1, a_2, \ldots$ are independent of x, is called a *power series in x*. More generally, an infinite series of the form

$$b_0 + b_1(x-a) + b_2(x-a)^2 + \cdots + b_n(x-a)^n + \cdots = \sum_{n=0}^{\infty} b_n(x-a)^n$$

where the coefficients $b_0, b_1, b_2, \ldots$ are independent of x, is called a *power series in x − a*.

A power series in x (or in $x - a$) may converge for all values of x, or for no values of x other than $x = 0$ (or $x = a$); or it may converge for some values of x and diverge for others. If a power series converges for values of x in the interval $-R < x < R$, then $-R < x < R$ is the *interval of convergence* of the power series and R is the *radius of convergence*. The interval of convergence is determined by the following procedure, derived from the Cauchy ratio test.

Power series in x:

If $\displaystyle\lim_{n \to \infty} \frac{a_{n+1}}{a_n} = L$, then
$\begin{cases} L = 0 \Rightarrow \text{series converges for all } x \\ L \neq 0 \Rightarrow \text{series converges for the interval} \\ -1/|L| < x < 1/|L| \text{ and diverges outside this interval; the end points of the interval of convergence must be examined separately. Note that } L = 1/R. \end{cases}$

Power series in x − a:

If $\displaystyle\lim_{n \to \infty} \frac{b_{n+1}}{b_n} = M$, then
$\begin{cases} M = 0 \Rightarrow \text{series converges for all } x \\ M \neq 0 \Rightarrow \text{series converges for the interval} \\ a - (1/|M|) < x < a + (1/|M|) \text{ and diverges outside this interval; the end points of the interval of convergence must be examined separately. Note that } M = 1/R. \end{cases}$

EXAMPLE

Find the interval of convergence for the power series

$$1 + 2x + 3x^2 + 4x^3 + \cdots$$

General term:

$$u_n = nx^{n-1}$$

$$L = \lim_{n \to \infty} \frac{n+1}{n} = 1,$$

so the interval of convergence is $-1 < x < 1$ and the end points must be tested.

If $x = -1$, the series is $1 - 2 + 3 - 4 + \cdots$

$$u_n = (-1)^{n-1}n$$

$$\lim_{n \to \infty} u_n \neq 0$$

so the series is divergent.

If $x = 1$, the series is $1 + 2 + 3 + 4 + \cdots$

$$u_n = n$$

$$\lim_{n \to \infty} u_n \neq 0$$

so the series is divergent.

Thus the original power series converges for $-1 < x < 1$.

EXAMPLE

Find the interval of convergence for the power series

$$1 - \frac{x}{2} + \frac{x^2}{3 \cdot 2^2} - \frac{x^3}{5 \cdot 2^3} + \frac{x^4}{7 \cdot 2^4} - \cdots$$

General term:

$$u_n = \frac{(-1)^{n+1}x^{n-1}}{(2n-3)2^{n-1}}$$

$$L = \lim_{n \to \infty} \left(-\frac{(2n-3)2^{n-1}}{[2(n+1)-3]2^n} \right) = \lim_{n \to \infty} \left(-\frac{2n-3}{4n-2} \right) = -\tfrac{1}{2}$$

so the interval of convergence is $-2 < x < 2$ and the end points must be tested.

If $x = -2$, the series is

$$1 + \frac{2}{2} + \frac{2^2}{3 \cdot 2^2} + \frac{2^3}{5 \cdot 2^3} + \frac{2^4}{7 \cdot 2^4} + \cdots$$

or

$$1 + 1 + \tfrac{1}{3} + \tfrac{1}{5} + \tfrac{1}{7} + \cdots$$

$$u_n = \frac{1}{2n-1} \qquad \text{(omitting the first term)}$$

$$\lim_{n \to \infty} u_n = 0$$

$$\lim_{n \to \infty} \frac{u_{n+1}}{u_n} = \lim_{n \to \infty} \frac{\dfrac{1}{2(n+1)-1}}{\dfrac{1}{2n-1}} = \lim_{n \to \infty} \frac{2n-1}{2n+1} = 1$$

so the ratio test fails.

$$u_n = \frac{1}{2n-1} > \frac{1}{2n} \qquad (p\text{-series}, \ p = 1)$$

so the series is divergent.

NOTE: Multiplying a series by a constant does *not* affect convergence.

If $x = 2$, the series is

$$1 - \frac{2}{2} + \frac{2^2}{3 \cdot 2^2} - \frac{2^3}{5 \cdot 2^3} + \frac{2^4}{7 \cdot 2^4} - \cdots$$

or

$$1 - 1 + \tfrac{1}{3} - \tfrac{1}{5} + \tfrac{1}{7} - \cdots$$

$$u_n = (-1)^n \frac{1}{2n-1} \qquad \text{(omitting first term)}$$

$$\lim_{n \to \infty} u_n = 0$$

$$|u_{n+1}| < |u_n|$$

so the alternating series is convergent.

Thus the original power series converges for $-2 < x \leq 2$.

EXAMPLE

Find the interval of convergence for the power series

$$1 + x + 2!\,x^2 + 3!\,x^3 + \cdots$$

General term:

$$u_n = (n-1)!\,x^{n-1}$$

$$L = \lim_{n \to \infty} \frac{n!}{(n-1)!} = \lim_{n \to \infty} n = \infty$$

Thus the power series converges only for $x = 0$, that is, the series is divergent for all $x \neq 0$.

EXAMPLE

Find the interval of convergence for the power series

$$(x-1) - \tfrac{1}{2}(x-1)^2 + \tfrac{1}{3}(x-1)^3 - \tfrac{1}{4}(x-1)^4 + \cdots$$

General term:

$$u_n = (-1)^{n+1} \frac{(x-1)^n}{n}$$

$$M = \lim_{n \to \infty} \left(-\frac{n}{n+1} \right) = -1$$

so the interval of convergence is $0 < x < 2$ and the end points must be tested.

If $x = 0$, the series is $-1 - \frac{1}{2} - \frac{1}{3} - \frac{1}{4} - \cdots$.

$$u_n = -\frac{1}{n}$$

$$\lim_{n \to \infty} u_n = 0$$

$$\lim_{n \to \infty} \frac{u_{n+1}}{u_n} = 1$$

so the ratio test fails.

$$u_n = \frac{1}{n} \quad (p\text{-series, } p = 1)$$

so the series is divergent.

If $x = 2$, the series is $1 - \frac{1}{2} + \frac{1}{3} - \frac{1}{4} + \cdots$.

$$u_n = (-1)^{n+1} \frac{1}{n}$$

$$\lim_{n \to \infty} u_n = 0$$

$$|u_{n+1}| < |u_n|$$

so the alternating series is convergent.

Thus the original power series converges for $0 < x \leq 2$.

EXAMPLE

Find the interval of convergence for the power series

$$(x - 1) - \tfrac{1}{4}(x - 1)^2 + \tfrac{1}{9}(x - 1)^3 - \tfrac{1}{16}(x - 1)^4 + \cdots$$

General term:

$$u_n = (-1)^{n+1} \frac{(x - 1)^n}{n^2}$$

$$M = \lim_{n \to \infty} \left(-\frac{n^2}{(n + 1)^2} \right) = -1$$

so the interval of convergence is $0 < x < 2$ and the end points must be tested.

If $x = 0$, the series is $-1 - \frac{1}{4} - \frac{1}{9} - \frac{1}{16} - \cdots$.

$$u_n = -\frac{1}{n^2}$$

$$\lim_{n \to \infty} u_n = 0$$

$$\lim_{n \to \infty} \frac{u_{n+1}}{u_n} = 1$$

so the ratio test fails.

$$|u_n| = \frac{1}{n^2} \quad (p\text{-series, } p = 2)$$

so the series is convergent.

If $x = 2$, the series is $1 - \frac{1}{4} + \frac{1}{9} - \frac{1}{16} + \cdots$.

$$u_n = (-1)^{n+1} \frac{1}{n^2}$$

so the series is absolutely convergent (as shown above).

Thus the original power series converges for $0 \le x \le 2$.

EXAMPLE

Find the interval of convergence for the power series

$$2(x - 2) + \frac{3(x - 2)^2}{2!} + \frac{4(x - 2)^3}{3!} + \frac{5(x - 2)^4}{4!} + \cdots.$$

General term:

$$u_n = \frac{(n + 1)(x - 2)^n}{n!}$$

$$M = \lim_{n \to \infty} \left(\frac{\frac{n + 2}{(n + 1)!}}{\frac{n + 1}{n!}} \right) = \lim_{n \to \infty} \frac{n + 2}{(n + 1)^2} = 0$$

Thus the power series converges for all x.

TAYLOR'S THEOREM

For either theoretical or computational purposes, it is frequently convenient to represent a function of x by a power series. Taylor's theorem provides appropriate power series for representing many functions.

TAYLOR'S THEOREM: The infinite series

$$\sum_{k=0}^{\infty} \frac{f^{(k)}(a)}{k!} (x - a)^k = f(a) + f'(a) \frac{x - a}{1!} + f''(a) \frac{(x - a)^2}{2!} + \cdots$$

$$+ f^{(n-1)}(a) \frac{(x - a)^{n-1}}{(n - 1)!} + R_n$$

converges and represents the function $f(x)$ for those values of x for which all the derivatives of $f(x)$ exist and for which $R_n \to 0$ as $n \to \infty$. In this case $f(x)$ is said to be expanded in a *Taylor's series about* $x = a$. For the special case $a = 0$, the expansion is a *Maclaurin's series*.

R_n is called the *remainder after n terms* and it can be shown that

$$R_n = f^{(n)}(\xi) \frac{(x - a)^n}{n!} \qquad \text{where } a \le \xi \le x$$

This formula can be used to determine a bound for the error involved in using only the first n terms of the series if $\max_{a \le \xi \le x} R_n$ is obtained.

NOTE: There are some functions for which a Taylor's series converges for values of x for which the remainder does not approach 0 as $n \to \infty$; for such values of x, the series does not represent the function. However, in most cases the interval of convergence of the series is the same as the interval for which $R_n \to 0$ as $n \to \infty$, as is the case for the examples considered below.

A Taylor's series about $x = a$ is useful for evaluating the function it represents for values of x near a. Similarly, a Maclaurin series is useful for evaluating the function it represents for values of x near zero.

A rigorous proof of Taylor's theorem is beyond the scope of this discussion and is not given. However, the result can be made plausible by the argument presented in Technical Note III.

It should be noted that any differentiable function can be expanded in a Taylor's series. A function that can be differentiated only a finite number of times can be expanded in a series having a finite number of terms; a function that can be differentiated indefinitely can be expanded in an infinite series. However, to be a valid representation of a function, a series must converge for values of x in the range of interest; in addition, to be useful for computational purposes, the series must converge fairly rapidly, so a reasonably accurate approximation can be obtained using relatively few terms. Before using a Taylor's series expansion to represent a function, its convergence properties should be investigated.

EXAMPLE

Expand the function $f(x) = x^{-1/3}$ in powers of $(x - 1)$ and determine the interval of convergence of the series.

$$f(x) = x^{-1/3}$$

$$f'(x) = -\tfrac{1}{3}x^{-4/3}$$

$$f''(x) = \frac{1 \cdot 4}{3^2} x^{-7/3}$$

$$f'''(x) = -\frac{1 \cdot 4 \cdot 7}{3^3} x^{-10/3}$$

$$f^{(IV)}(x) = \frac{1 \cdot 4 \cdot 7 \cdot 10}{3^4} x^{-13/3}$$

$$f^{(V)}(x) = -\frac{1 \cdot 4 \cdot 7 \cdot 10 \cdot 13}{3^5} x^{-16/3}$$

$$\vdots$$

$$f^n(x) = (-1)^n \frac{(3n - 2)(3n - 5) \cdots 1}{3^n} x^{-(3n+1)/3}$$

$$f(x) = f(a) + \frac{f'(a)}{1!}(x - a) + \frac{f''(a)}{2!}(x - a)^2 + \cdots + \frac{f^{(n)}(a)}{n!}(x - a)^n + \cdots$$

$$= 1 - \frac{1}{3 \cdot 1!}(x - 1) + \frac{1 \cdot 4}{3^2 \cdot 2!}(x - 1)^2 - \frac{1 \cdot 4 \cdot 7}{3^3 \cdot 3!}(x - 1)^3 + \cdots$$

$$+ (-1)^n \frac{(3n - 2)(3n - 5) \cdots 1}{3^n \cdot n!}(x - 1)^n + \cdots$$

$$\frac{b_{n+1}}{b_n} = -\frac{\dfrac{(3n + 1)(3n - 2) \cdots 1}{3^{n+1}(n + 1)!}}{\dfrac{(3n - 2)(3n - 5) \cdots 1}{3^n n!}} = -\frac{3n + 1}{3(n + 1)}$$

$\lim_{n \to \infty} b_{n+1}/b_n = -1$, so the interval of convergence is $0 < x < 2$ and the end points must be tested.

If $x = 0$,

$$u_n = \frac{(3n - 2)(3n - 5) \cdots 1}{3^n \cdot n!}$$

$$\lim_{n \to \infty} u_n = 1 \neq 0$$

so the series is divergent.

NOTE: For notational consistency, the general term is denoted u_n; actually it is the term involving the nth derivative and is the $(n + 1)$st term of the series.

If $x = 2$,

$$u_n = (-1)^n \frac{(3n - 2)(3n - 5) \cdots 1}{3^n n!}$$

$$\lim_{n \to \infty} u_n = 1 \neq 0$$

so the series is divergent.

Thus the Taylor series expansion of $f(x) = x^{-1/3}$ about $x = 1$ converges for $0 < x < 2$.

EXAMPLE

Expand the function $f(x) = 1/(1 + x)^2$ in powers of $(x - 2)$ and determine the interval of convergence of the series.

$$f(x) = (1 + x)^{-2}$$

$$f'(x) = -2(1 + x)^{-3}$$

$$f''(x) = 2 \cdot 3(1 + x)^{-4}$$

$$f'''(x) = -2 \cdot 3 \cdot 4(1 + x)^{-5}$$

$$f^{(IV)}(x) = 2 \cdot 3 \cdot 4 \cdot 5(1 + x)^{-6}$$

$$f^{(V)}(x) = -2 \cdot 3 \cdot 4 \cdot 5 \cdot 6(1 + x)^{-7}$$

$$\vdots$$

$$f^n(x) = (-1)^n(n + 1)! \, (1 + x)^{-(n + 2)}$$

$$f(x) = f(a) + \frac{f'(a)}{1!}(x - a) + \frac{f''(a)}{2!}(x - a)^2 + \cdots + \frac{f^{(n)}(a)}{n!}(x - a)^n + \cdots$$

$$= \frac{1}{3^2} - \frac{2}{3^3}(x - 2) + \frac{3}{3^4}(x - 2)^2 - \frac{4}{3^5}(x - 2)^3 + \cdots + (-1)^n \frac{n + 1}{3^{n+2}}(x - 2)^n + \cdots$$

$$\frac{b_{n+1}}{b_n} = -\frac{\dfrac{n + 2}{3^{n+3}}}{\dfrac{n + 1}{3^{n+2}}} = -\frac{n + 2}{3(n + 1)}$$

$\lim_{n \to \infty} b_{n+1}/b_n = -\frac{1}{3}$ so the interval of convergence is $-1 < x < 5$ and the end points must be tested.

If $x = -1$, $u_n = (n + 1)/3^2$.

$$\lim_{n \to \infty} u_n = \infty \neq 0,$$

so the series is divergent. Note that $f(-1)$ is not defined, so the series will not converge for $x = 1$.

If $x = 5$, $u_n = (-1)^n(n+1)/3^2$.

$$\lim_{n \to \infty} u_n = \infty \neq 0,$$

so the series is divergent.

Thus the Taylor series expansion of $f(x) = (1+x)^{-2}$ about $x = 2$ converges for $-1 < x < 5$.

EXAMPLE

Expand the function $f(x) = (1+x)^m$, where m is any real number, in powers of x and determine the interval of convergence of the series. This series is known as the *binomial expansion*.

$$f(x) = (1+x)^m$$

$$f'(x) = m(1+x)^{m-1}$$

$$f''(x) = m(m-1)(1+x)^{m-2}$$

$$f'''(x) = m(m-1)(m-2)(1+x)^{m-3}$$

$$f^{(IV)}(x) = m(m-1)(m-2)(m-3)(1+x)^{m-4}$$

$$f^{(V)}(x) = m(m-1)(m-2)(m-3)(m-4)(1+x)^{m-5}$$

$$\vdots$$

$$f^n(x) = \frac{m!}{(m-n)!}(1+x)^{m-n}$$

$$f(x) = f(a) + \frac{f'(a)}{1!}x + \frac{f''(a)}{2!}x^2 + \cdots + \frac{f^{(n)}(a)}{n!}x^n + \cdots$$

$$= 1 + \frac{m}{1!}x + \frac{m(m-1)}{2!}x^2 + \frac{m(m-1)(m-2)}{3!}x^3 + \cdots$$

$$+ \frac{m(m-1)(m-2)\cdots(m-n+1)}{n!}x^n + \cdots$$

$$\frac{b_{n+1}}{b_n} = \frac{\dfrac{m(m-1)(m-2)\cdots(m-n)}{(n+1)!}}{\dfrac{m(m-1)(m-2)\cdots(m-n+1)}{n!}} = \frac{m-n}{n+1}$$

$\lim_{n \to \infty} b_{n+1}/b_n = -1$, so the interval of convergence is $-1 < x < 1$ and the end points must be tested.

If $x = -1$, $u_n = (-1)^n \dfrac{m(m-1)(m-2)\cdots(m-n+1)}{n!}$.

$$\lim_{n \to \infty} u_n = 0$$

If $x = 1$, $u_n = \dfrac{m(m-1)(m-2)\cdots(m-n+1)}{n!}$.

$$\lim_{n \to \infty} u_n = 0$$

If $x = \pm 1$, $|u_{n+1}/u_n| = |(m-n)/(n+1)|$, so $|u_{n+1}| < |u_n|$ does not hold for unrestricted m.

Thus the Taylor series expansion of $f(x) = (1+x)^m$ about $x = 0$ converges for $-1 < x < 1$.

EXAMPLE

Expand the function $f(x) = \ln x$ in a Taylor's series about $x = 1$ and determine the interval of convergence; use this series to evaluate $\ln 1.04$ correct to five decimal places.

$$f(x) = \ln x$$

$$f'(x) = \frac{1}{x}$$

$$f''(x) = -\frac{1}{x^2}$$

$$f'''(x) = \frac{2}{x^3}$$

$$f^{(IV)}(x) = -\frac{6}{x^4}$$

$$f^{(V)}(x) = \frac{24}{x^5}$$

$$\vdots$$

$$f^n(x) = (-1)^{n+1}\frac{(n-1)!}{x^n}$$

$$\ln x = f(a) + \frac{f'(a)}{1!}(x-a) + \frac{f''(a)}{2!}(x-a)^2 + \cdots + \frac{f^{(n-1)}(a)}{(n-1)!}(x-a)^{n-1} + R_n$$

$$= 0 + (x-1) - \tfrac{1}{2}(x-1)^2 + \tfrac{1}{3}(x-1)^3 - \cdots + (-1)^n\left(\frac{1}{n-1}\right)(x-1)^{n-1} + R_n$$

$$\frac{b_{n+1}}{b_n} = -\frac{\frac{1}{n}}{\frac{1}{n-1}} = -\frac{n-1}{n}$$

$\lim_{n\to\infty} b_{n+1}/b_n = -1$, so the interval of convergence is $0 < x < 2$ and the end points must be tested.

If $x = 0$, $u_n = -\frac{1}{n-1}$

$$\lim_{n\to\infty} u_n = 0$$

$$\lim_{n\to\infty} \frac{u_{n+1}}{u_n} = \lim_{n\to\infty} \frac{\frac{1}{n}}{\frac{1}{n-1}} = \lim_{n\to\infty} \frac{n-1}{n} = 1$$

so the ratio test fails. But

$$u_n = -\frac{1}{n-1} \qquad (p\text{-series}, p = 1),$$

so the series is divergent.

NOTE: Omitting a finite number of terms from a series does not affect convergence, nor does multiplying the series by a positive or negative constant.

If $x = 2$, $u_n = (-1)^n(1/n - 1)$.

$$\lim_{n \to \infty} u_n = 0$$

$$|u_{n+1}| < |u_n|$$

so the series is conditionally convergent.
Thus the Taylor series expansion of $f(x) = \ln x$ about $x = 1$ converges for $0 < x \le 2$.

$$\ln (1.04) = 0 + 0.04 - \tfrac{1}{2}(0.04)^2 + \tfrac{1}{3}(0.04)^3 + R_4$$

$$= 0.04 - 0.0008 + 0.000021 + R_4$$

$$= 0.039221 + R_4$$

$$R_n = f^n(\xi) \frac{(x-a)^n}{n!} \qquad a \le \xi \le x$$

$$R_4 = (-1)^5 \frac{3!}{\xi^4} \frac{(0.04)^4}{4!} \qquad 1 \le \xi \le 1.04$$

$$= (-1)^5 \frac{(0.04)^4}{4\xi^4}$$

$$|R_4| \le \tfrac{1}{4}(0.04)^4 = 0.00000064$$

so $\ln 1.04 = 0.03922$, correct to five decimal places.

NOTE: Since the series is alternating, the error in truncating is less in absolute value than the next term, which for this example gives the same bound on the error as above.

EXAMPLE

Expand the function $f(x) = e^x$ in a Maclaurin's series about $x = 0$ and determine the interval of convergence; use this series to evaluate $e^{1/2}$ correct to four decimal places.

$$f(x) = e^x$$

$$f'(x) = e^x$$

$$f''(x) = e^x$$

$$\vdots$$

$$f^n(x) = e^x$$

$$e^x = f(a) + \frac{f'(a)}{1!} x + \frac{f''(a)}{2!} x^2 + \cdots + \frac{f^{(n-1)}(a)}{(n-1)!} x^{n-1} + R_n$$

$$= 1 + x + \frac{x^2}{2!} + \frac{x^3}{3!} + \cdots + \frac{x^{n-1}}{(n-1)!} + R_n$$

$$\frac{b_{n+1}}{b_n} = \frac{\dfrac{1}{n!}}{\dfrac{1}{(n-1)!}} = \frac{(n-1)!}{n!} = \frac{1}{n}$$

$$\lim_{n \to \infty} \frac{b_{n+1}}{b_n} = 0$$

Thus the power series expansion converges for all x.

$$e^{1/2} = 1 + \tfrac{1}{2} + \frac{(\tfrac{1}{2})^2}{2!} + \frac{(\tfrac{1}{2})^3}{3!} + \frac{(\tfrac{1}{2})^4}{4!} + \frac{(\tfrac{1}{2})^5}{5!} + R_6$$

$$= 1 + 0.5 + 0.125 + 0.02083333 + 0.00260417 + 0.000260417 + R_6$$

$$= 1.648697917 + R_6$$

$$R_n = f^n(\xi)\frac{(x-a)^n}{n!} \qquad a \leq \xi \leq x$$

$$R_6 = e^{\xi}\frac{(\tfrac{1}{2})^6}{6!} \qquad 0 \leq \xi \leq \tfrac{1}{2}$$

$$|R_6| \leq \frac{(\tfrac{1}{2})^6}{6!}e^{1/2}$$

and, since $e^{1/2} < 2$, $|R^6| < 0.000043$, so $e^{1/2} = 1.6487$, correct to four decimal places.

EXAMPLE

Expand the function $f(x) = (1 + x)^{1/2}$ in a Maclaurin's series about $x = 0$ and determine the interval of convergence; use this series to evaluate $\sqrt{1.10}$ correct to six decimal places.

$$f(x) = (1 + x)^{1/2}$$

$$f'(x) = \tfrac{1}{2}(1 + x)^{-1/2}$$

$$f''(x) = -\frac{1}{2^2}(1 + x)^{-3/2}$$

$$f'''(x) = \frac{1 \cdot 3}{2^3}(1 + x)^{-5/2}$$

$$f^{(\mathrm{IV})}(x) = -\frac{1 \cdot 3 \cdot 5}{2^4}(1 + x)^{-7/2}$$

$$f^{(\mathrm{V})}(x) = \frac{1 \cdot 3 \cdot 5 \cdot 7}{2^5}(1 + x)^{-9/2}$$

$$\vdots$$

$$f^n(x) = (-1)^{n+1}\frac{(2n-3)(2n-5)\cdots 1}{2^n}(1 + x)^{-(2n-1)/2}$$

$$(1 + x)^{1/2} = f(a) + \frac{f'(a)}{1!}x - \frac{f''(a)}{2!}x^2 + \cdots + \frac{f^{(n-1)}(a)}{(n-1)!}x^{n-1} + R_n$$

$$= 1 + \frac{1}{2 \cdot 1!}x - \frac{1}{2^2 \cdot 2!}x^2 + \frac{3 \cdot 1}{2^3 \cdot 3!}x^3 - \cdots$$

$$+ (-1)^n\frac{(2n-5)(2n-7)\cdots 1}{2^{n-1}(n-1)!}x^{n-1} + R_n$$

$$\frac{b_{n+1}}{b_n} = -\frac{\dfrac{(2n-3)(2n-5)(2n-7)\cdots 1}{2^n n!}}{\dfrac{(2n-5)(2n-7)\cdots 1}{2^{n-1}(n-1)!}} = -\frac{2n-3}{2n}$$

$\lim_{n \to \infty} b_{n+1}/b_n = -1$, so the interval of convergence is $-1 < x < 1$ and the end points must be tested.

If $x = -1$, $f(x) = 0$, so expansion is unnecessary.

If $x = 1$, $u_n = (-1)^n \dfrac{(2n-5)(2n-7) \cdots 1}{2^{n-1}(n-1)!}$.

$$\lim_{n \to \infty} u_n = 0$$

$$\left| \frac{u_{n+1}}{u_n} \right| = \frac{2n-3}{2n} < 1$$

so the alternating series is conditionally convergent.

Thus the Taylor series expansion of $f(x) = (1+x)^{1/2}$ about $x = 0$ converges for $-1 < x \le 1$.

$$(1.10)^{1/2} = 1 + \frac{1}{2 \cdot 1!}\left(\tfrac{1}{10}\right) - \frac{1}{2^2 \cdot 2!}\left(\tfrac{1}{10}\right)^2 + \frac{3 \cdot 1}{2^3 \cdot 3!}\left(\tfrac{1}{10}\right)^3 - \frac{5 \cdot 3 \cdot 1}{2^4 \cdot 4!}\left(\tfrac{1}{10}\right)^4$$

$$+ \frac{7 \cdot 5 \cdot 3 \cdot 1}{2^5 \cdot 5!}\left(\tfrac{1}{10}\right)^5 + R_6$$

$$= 1 + 0.05 - 0.00125 + 0.0000625 - 0.000003906 + 0.000000273 + R_6$$

$$= 1.048808867 + R_6$$

Alternating series, so the error is less than the absolute value of next term,

$$\frac{9 \cdot 7 \cdot 5 \cdot 3 \cdot 1}{2^6 \cdot 6!}\left(\tfrac{1}{10}\right)^6 = 0.0000000205$$

so correct to six decimal places, $(1.10)^{1/2} = 1.048809$.

NOTE: Alternatively, a bound on the error can be obtained using R_6:

$$R_n = f^n(\xi)\frac{(x-a)^n}{n!} \qquad a \le \xi \le x$$

$$R_6 = -\frac{9 \cdot 7 \cdot 5 \cdot 3 \cdot 1}{2^6 \cdot 6!}(1+\xi)^{-11/2}\left(\tfrac{1}{10}\right)^6 \qquad 0 \le \xi \le \tfrac{1}{10}$$

$$|R_6| \le \frac{9 \cdot 7 \cdot 5 \cdot 3 \cdot 1}{2^6 \cdot 6!}\left(\tfrac{1}{10}\right)^6$$

$$|R_6| \le 0.0000000205$$

Note that the accuracy of the approximation obtained from a power series expansion increases with the number of terms used in the calculation. Fewer terms are required for a specified accuracy if the series converges more rapidly. The number of terms required for a given accuracy must be determined for each power series approximation by considering the remainder term or, for an alternating series, by considering the next term. Note that the remainder after n terms

$$R_n = f^{(n)}(\xi)\frac{(x-a)^n}{n!} \qquad a \le \xi \le x$$

is equal in absolute value to the next term of an alternating series if $\xi = a$. Thus, for an alternating series, the bound on the error determined by obtaining $\max_{a \le \xi \le x} R_n$ is equal to the bound determined by obtaining the absolute value of the next term of the alternating series, if $\max_{a \le \xi \le x} R_n$ occurs for $\xi = a$.

PROBLEMS

For each of the following power series, determine the general term and the interval of convergence.

1. $x - \dfrac{x^3}{3!} + \dfrac{x^5}{5!} - \dfrac{x^7}{7!} + \cdots$

2. $2x + 4x^2 + 8x^3 + 16x^4 + \cdots$

3. $1 + \dfrac{x}{\sqrt{2}} + \dfrac{x^2}{\sqrt{3}} + \dfrac{x^3}{\sqrt{4}} + \cdots$

4. $\dfrac{x}{1 \cdot 2} + \dfrac{x^2}{2^2 \cdot 2^2} + \dfrac{x^3}{3^2 \cdot 2^3} + \dfrac{x^4}{4^2 \cdot 2^4} + \cdots$

5. $1 - \dfrac{3x}{2} + \dfrac{5x^2}{4} - \dfrac{7x^3}{8} + \dfrac{9x^4}{16} - \cdots$

6. $1 + \dfrac{(x + 3)}{2^2} + \dfrac{(x + 3)^2}{3^2} + \dfrac{(x + 3)^3}{4^2} + \cdots$

7. $\dfrac{1}{2!} x + \dfrac{2}{3!} x^3 + \dfrac{3}{4!} x^5 + \dfrac{4}{5!} x^7 + \cdots$

8. $\dfrac{x + 4}{\sqrt[3]{2}} - \dfrac{(x + 4)^2}{\sqrt[3]{3}} + \dfrac{(x + 4)^3}{\sqrt[3]{4}} - \dfrac{(x + 4)^4}{\sqrt[3]{5}} + \cdots$

9. $\dfrac{1}{2} x - \dfrac{2^2}{5} x^2 + \dfrac{3^2}{8} x^3 - \dfrac{4^2}{11} x^4 + \dfrac{5^2}{14} x^5 + \cdots$

10. $\dfrac{6}{2} (x - 5) + \dfrac{6^2}{5} (x - 5)^2 + \dfrac{6^3}{10} (x - 5)^3 + \dfrac{6^4}{17} (x - 5)^4 + \dfrac{6^5}{26} (x - 5)^5 + \cdots$

Expand the following functions in power series, determine the interval of convergence, and choose some appropriate value of x for which to estimate the function.

11. $f(x) = x^{1/2}$ in powers of $(x - 1)$

12. $f(x) = \dfrac{1}{1 + x^2}$ in powers of x

13. $f(x) = e^{-(1/2)x}$ in powers of $(x - 2)$

14. $f(x) = \frac{1}{2}(e^x + e^{-x})$ in powers of x

15. $f(x) = \ln (a - x)$ in powers of x

16. $f(x) = \ln (a + x)$ in powers of x

17. $f(x) = \sin x$ in powers of x

18. $f(x) = \cos x$ in powers of x

19. $f(x) = \tan x$ in powers of x

20. $f(x) = \cot x$ in powers of x

21. $f(x) = \sec x$ in powers of x

22. $f(x) = \csc x$ in powers of x

Answers to Odd-Numbered Problems

1. $(-1)^{n+1} \dfrac{x^{2n-1}}{(2n - 1)!}$, conv. all x

3. $\dfrac{x^{n-1}}{\sqrt{n}}$, conv. $-1 \leq x < 1$

5. $(-1)^{n-1} \dfrac{(2n - 1)x^{n-1}}{2^{n-1}}$, conv. $-2 < x < 2$

7. $\dfrac{n}{(n + 1)!} x^{2n-1}$, conv. all x

9. $(-1)^{n+1} \dfrac{n^2}{3n - 1} x^n$, conv. $-1 < x < 1$

11. $f(x) = 1 + \dfrac{1}{2 \cdot 1!}(x-1) - \dfrac{1}{2^2 \cdot 2!}(x-1)^2 + \dfrac{1 \cdot 3}{2^3 \cdot 3!}(x-1)^3$

$$- \dfrac{1 \cdot 3 \cdot 5}{2^4 \cdot 4!}(x-1)^4 + \dfrac{1 \cdot 3 \cdot 5 \cdot 7}{2^5 \cdot 5!}(x-1)^5 + \cdots$$

$$+ (-1)^{n+1}\dfrac{(2n-3)(2n-5)\cdots 1}{2^n \cdot n!}(x-1)^n + \cdots, \qquad \text{conv. } 0 < x \le 2$$

13. $f(x) = e^{-1} - \dfrac{e^{-1}}{2 \cdot 1!}(x-2) + \dfrac{e^{-1}}{2^2 \cdot 2!}(x-2)^2 - \dfrac{e^{-1}}{2^3 \cdot 3!}(x-2)^3$

$$+ \dfrac{e^{-1}}{2^4 \cdot 4!}(x-2)^4 - \dfrac{e^{-1}}{2^5 \cdot 5!}(x-2)^5 + \cdots$$

$$+ (-1)^n \dfrac{e^{-1}}{2^n \cdot n!}(x-2)^n + \cdots, \text{ conv. all } x$$

15. $f(x) = \ln a - \dfrac{1}{a}x - \dfrac{1}{2a^2}x^2 - \dfrac{1}{3a^3}x^3 - \dfrac{1}{4a^4}x^4 - \cdots - \dfrac{1}{na^n}x^n - \cdots, \qquad \text{conv. } -a \le x < a$

17. $f(x) = x - \dfrac{x^3}{3!} + \dfrac{x^5}{5!} - \dfrac{x^7}{7!} + \cdots + (-1)^{n+1}\dfrac{x^{2n-1}}{(2n-1)!} + \cdots, \qquad \text{conv. all } x$

19. $f(x) = x + \dfrac{x^3}{3} + \dfrac{2x^5}{15} + \dfrac{17x^7}{315} + \cdots, \qquad \text{conv. } |x| < \dfrac{\pi}{2}$

21. $f(x) = 1 + \dfrac{x^2}{2} + \dfrac{5x^4}{24} + \dfrac{61x^6}{720} + \cdots, \qquad \text{conv. } |x| < \dfrac{\pi}{2}$

Technical Note I   Derivation of Rules for Differentiation

NOTE: For mathematical convenience, the rules for differentiation are not derived in the same order that they are given in the text.

Algebraic Functions

Rule 1.   If $y = c$,

$$\Delta y = 0$$

$$\dfrac{\Delta y}{\Delta x} = 0$$

$$\dfrac{dy}{dx} = \lim_{\Delta x \to 0} \dfrac{\Delta y}{\Delta x} = 0$$

Rule 3.   If $y = cu$, where $u = f(x)$ is a differentiable function of x,

$$y + \Delta y = c(u + \Delta u)$$

$$\Delta y = c\,\Delta u$$

$$\dfrac{\Delta y}{\Delta x} = c\dfrac{\Delta u}{\Delta x}$$

$$\dfrac{dy}{dx} = \lim_{\Delta x \to 0} \dfrac{\Delta y}{\Delta x} = c\dfrac{du}{dx}$$

Rule 2. If $y = x^n$, where n is a positive integer,

$$y + \Delta y = (x + \Delta x)^n$$

$$= x^n + nx^{n-1} \Delta x + \frac{n(n-1)}{2!} x^{n-2}(\Delta x)^2 + \cdots + (\Delta x)^n$$

$$\Delta y = nx^{n-1} \Delta x + \frac{n(n-1)}{2!} x^{n-2}(\Delta x)^2 + \cdots + (\Delta x)^n$$

$$\frac{\Delta y}{\Delta x} = nx^{n-1} + \frac{n(n-1)}{2!} x^{n-2}(\Delta x) + \cdots + (\Delta x)^{n-1}$$

$$\frac{dy}{dx} = \lim_{\Delta x \to 0} \frac{\Delta y}{\Delta x} = nx^{n-1}$$

Rule 4. If $y = u + v$, where $u = f(x)$ and $v = g(x)$ are differentiable functions of x,

$$y + \Delta y = u + \Delta u + v + \Delta v$$

$$\Delta y = \Delta u + \Delta v$$

$$\frac{\Delta y}{\Delta x} = \frac{\Delta u}{\Delta x} + \frac{\Delta v}{\Delta x}$$

$$\frac{dy}{dx} = \lim_{\Delta x \to 0} \frac{\Delta y}{\Delta x} = \frac{du}{dx} + \frac{dv}{dx}$$

Rule 5. If $y = uv$, where $u = f(x)$ and $v = g(x)$ are differentiable functions of x,

$$y + \Delta y = (u + \Delta u)(v + \Delta v)$$

$$= uv + u(\Delta v) + v(\Delta u) + (\Delta u)(\Delta v)$$

$$\Delta y = u(\Delta v) + v(\Delta u) + (\Delta u)(\Delta v)$$

$$\frac{\Delta y}{\Delta x} = u \frac{\Delta v}{\Delta x} + v \frac{\Delta u}{\Delta x} + \frac{(\Delta u)(\Delta v)}{\Delta x}$$

$$\frac{dy}{dx} = \lim_{\Delta x \to 0} \frac{\Delta y}{\Delta x} = u \frac{dv}{dx} + v \frac{du}{dx}$$

Rule 6. If $y = u/v$, where $u = f(x)$ and $v = g(x)$ are differentiable functions of x,

$$y + \Delta y = \frac{u + \Delta u}{v + \Delta v}$$

$$\Delta y = \frac{v(u + \Delta u) - u(v + \Delta v)}{v(v + \Delta v)}$$

$$= \frac{v(\Delta u) - u(\Delta v)}{v(v + \Delta v)}$$

$$\frac{\Delta y}{\Delta x} = \frac{v \dfrac{\Delta u}{\Delta x} - u \dfrac{\Delta v}{\Delta x}}{v(v + \Delta v)}$$

$$\frac{dy}{dx} = \lim_{\Delta x \to 0} \frac{\Delta y}{\Delta x} = \frac{v \dfrac{du}{dx} - u \dfrac{dv}{dx}}{v^2}$$

Logarithmic Functions

Rule 9. If $y = \log_a u$, where $u = f(x)$ is a differentiable function of x,

$$y + \Delta y = \log_a (u + \Delta u)$$

$$\Delta y = \log_a (u + \Delta u) - \log_a u$$

$$= \log_a \left(\frac{u + \Delta u}{u} \right)$$

$$= \log_a \left(1 + \frac{\Delta u}{u} \right)$$

$$\frac{\Delta y}{\Delta u} = \frac{1}{\Delta u} \log_a \left(1 + \frac{\Delta u}{u} \right)$$

$$= \frac{1}{u} \cdot \frac{u}{\Delta u} \log_a \left(1 + \frac{\Delta u}{u} \right)$$

$$= \frac{1}{u} \log_a \left(1 + \frac{\Delta u}{u} \right)^{u/\Delta u}$$

Let $\Delta u / u = h$; then $u/\Delta u = 1/h$ and $h \to 0$ as $\Delta u \to 0$. Thus $\Delta y / \Delta u = (1/u) \log_a (1 + h)^{1/h}$ and, since (by definition) $(1 + h)^{1/h} \to e$ as $h \to 0$,

$$\lim_{\Delta u \to 0} \frac{\Delta y}{\Delta u} = \frac{1}{u} \log_a \left[\lim_{h \to 0} (1 + h)^{1/h} \right]$$

$$\frac{dy}{du} = \frac{1}{u} \log_a e$$

If $u = f(x)$,

$$\frac{dy}{dx} = \frac{1}{u} \log_a e \frac{du}{dx}$$

Exponential Functions

Rule 10. If $y = a^u$, where $u = f(x)$ is a differentiable function of x,

$$\ln y = \ln a^u$$

$$= u \ln a$$

$$\frac{1}{y} \frac{dy}{dx} = \frac{du}{dx} \ln a$$

$$\frac{dy}{dx} = y \frac{du}{dx} \ln a$$

$$= a^u \ln a \frac{du}{dx}$$

Rule 11. If $y = u^v$, where $u = f(x)$ and $v = g(x)$ are differentiable functions of x,

$$\ln y = v \ln u$$

$$\frac{1}{y} \frac{dy}{dx} = v \frac{1}{u} \frac{du}{dx} + \ln u \frac{dv}{dx}$$

$$\frac{dy}{dx} = vu^{v-1} \frac{du}{dx} + u^v \ln u \frac{dv}{dx}$$

Rule 8. If $y = u^n$, where $u = f(x)$ is a differentiable function of x and n is any real number,

$$\ln y = n \ln u$$

$$\frac{1}{y}\frac{dy}{dx} = n\frac{1}{u}\frac{du}{dx}$$

$$\frac{dy}{dx} = nu^{n-1}\frac{du}{dx}$$

Trigonometric Functions

Rule 12. If $y = \sin u$, where $u = f(x)$ is a differentiable function of x,

$$y + \Delta y = \sin(u + \Delta u)$$

$$\Delta y = \sin(u + \Delta u) - \sin u$$

$$= 2\cos\left(u + \frac{\Delta u}{2}\right)\sin\frac{\Delta u}{2}$$

since $\sin x - \sin y = 2\cos\frac{1}{2}(x + y)\sin\frac{1}{2}(x - y)$

$$\frac{\Delta y}{\Delta u} = 2\cos\left(u + \frac{\Delta u}{2}\right)\frac{\sin(\Delta u/2)}{\Delta u}$$

$$= \cos\left(u + \frac{\Delta u}{2}\right)\frac{\sin(\Delta u/2)}{\Delta u/2}$$

$$\frac{dy}{du} = \lim_{\Delta u \to 0}\frac{\Delta y}{\Delta u} = \lim_{\Delta u \to 0}\cos\left(u + \frac{\Delta u}{2}\right)\frac{\sin(\Delta u/2)}{\Delta u/2}$$

$$= \cos u \qquad \text{since } \lim_{\Delta u \to 0}\frac{\sin(\Delta u/2)}{\Delta u/2} = 1$$

If $u = f(x)$,

$$\frac{dy}{dx} = \cos u\,\frac{du}{dx}$$

Rule 13. If $y = \cos u$, where $u = f(x)$ is a differentiable function of x,

$$y = \sin\left(\frac{\pi}{2} - u\right)$$

and

$$\frac{dy}{dx} = \cos\left(\frac{\pi}{2} - u\right)\left(-\frac{du}{dx}\right)$$

$$= -\sin u\,\frac{du}{dx}$$

Rule 14. If $y = \tan u$, where $u = f(x)$

$$y = \frac{\sin u}{\cos u}$$

and

$$\frac{dy}{dx} = \frac{\cos^2 u \dfrac{du}{dx} + \sin^2 u \dfrac{du}{dx}}{\cos^2 u}$$

but $\cos^2 u + \sin^2 u = 1$, so

$$\frac{dy}{dx} = \frac{\dfrac{du}{dx}}{\cos^2 u} = \sec^2 u \frac{du}{dx}$$

Inverse Functions

Rule 15. If $y = f(x)$ and $x = g(y)$ are inverse differentiable functions,

$$\frac{g(y + \Delta y) - g(y)}{\Delta y} = \frac{h}{\Delta y} \qquad \begin{aligned} &\text{where } x = g(y) \\ &\qquad x + h = g(y + \Delta y) \end{aligned}$$

$$y + \Delta y = f(x + h) \qquad \text{since } f[g(x)] = x$$

and thus

$$\Delta y = f(x + h) - f(x)$$

$$\frac{g(y + \Delta y) - g(y)}{\Delta y} = \frac{\Delta x}{f(x + h) - f(x)}$$

As $\Delta y \to 0$, $\Delta x \to 0$ and

$$\lim_{\Delta y \to 0} \frac{g(y + \Delta y) - g(y)}{\Delta y} = g'(y) = \lim_{\Delta x \to 0} \frac{\Delta x}{f(x + h) - f(x)} = \frac{1}{f'(x)}$$

That is,

$$\frac{dx}{dy} = \frac{1}{\dfrac{dy}{dx}}$$

Composite Functions

Rule 7. If $y = g(u)$ and $u = h(x)$

$$\frac{\Delta y}{\Delta x} = \frac{\Delta y}{\Delta u} \cdot \frac{\Delta u}{\Delta x}$$

$$\lim_{\Delta x \to 0} \frac{\Delta y}{\Delta x} = \frac{dy}{du} \cdot \frac{du}{dx}$$

Technical Note II Conditions for a Cubic Cost Function

$b^2 - 3ac \le 0$ is a sufficient but not a necessary condition for the function

$$y = ax^3 + bx^2 + cx + d \qquad a > 0,\ b \le 0,\ c \ge 0,\ d \ge 0$$

to have no relative maximum or minimum in the first quadrant. If $b^2 - 3ac > 0$, then $\frac{dy}{dx} = 0$ if $x = (-b \pm \sqrt{b^2 - 3ac})/3a$.

$$x = \frac{-b \pm \sqrt{b^2 - 3ac}}{3a} > 0 \quad \text{since } a > 0, b < 0, c \geq 0 \quad \text{and} \quad |b^2 - 3ac| < |b|$$

(note that $b^2 - 3ac > 0 \Rightarrow b \neq 0$).

$$y = a\left(\frac{-b \pm \sqrt{b^2 - 3ac}}{3a}\right)^3 + b\left(\frac{-b \pm \sqrt{b^2 - 3ac}}{3a}\right)^2 + c\left(\frac{-b \pm \sqrt{b^2 - 3ac}}{3a}\right) + d$$

Since $a > 0$, $b < 0$, $c \geq 0$, $d \geq 0$ and $(-b \pm \sqrt{b^2 - 3ac})/3a > 0$, the first term in the expression for y is positive, the second term is negative, and the third and fourth terms are positive or zero. Thus y may be positive or negative depending on the relative value of the coefficients a, b, c, and d, and (x, y) may lie in either the first or second quadrant. Since

$$\left.\frac{d^2y}{dx^2}\right|_{x=[-b \pm \sqrt{b^2 - 3ac}]/3a} = 2(-b \pm \sqrt{b^2 - 3ac} + b) = \pm 2\sqrt{b^2 - 3ac}$$

and $b^2 - 3ac > 0$,

$$\left.\frac{d^2y}{dx^2}\right|_{x=[-b \pm \sqrt{b^2 - 3ac}]/3a} \neq 0$$

and $y = ax^3 + bx^2 + cx + d$ has a relative maximum or minimum at the point for which $\frac{dy}{dx} = 0$. Thus, if $b^2 - 3ac > 0$, $y = ax^3 + bx^2 + cx + d$ has a relative maximum or minimum in the first quadrant only for certain values of the coefficients. For simplicity, only equations for which $b^2 - 3ac \leq 0$ are considered in the text.

Technical Note III Taylor's Theorem

Assume that the function $f(x)$ has a power series expansion and that the power series can be differentiated term by term.

$$f(x) = a_0 + a_1(x - a) + a_2(x - a)^2 + \cdots + a_n(x - a)^n + \cdots$$

If $x = a$, $f(a) = a_0$.

$$f'(x) = a_1 + 2a_2(x - a) + \cdots + na_n(x - a)^{n-1} + \cdots$$

If $x = a$, $f'(a) = a_1$.

$$f''(x) = 2a_2 + 3 \cdot 2a_3(x - a) + \cdots + n(n - 1)a_n(x - a)^{n-2} + \cdots$$

If $x = a$, $f''(a) = 2a_2$.

$$f'''(x) = 3 \cdot 2a_3 + 4 \cdot 3 \cdot 2a_4(x - a) + \cdots + n(n - 1)(n - 2)a_n(x - a)^{n-3} + \cdots$$

If $x = a$, $f'''(a) = 3 \cdot 2a_3$.

$$\vdots$$

$$f^k(x) = k(k - 1)a_k + (k + 1)(k)(k - 1)a_{k+1}(x - a) + \cdots$$
$$+ n(n - 1) \cdots (n - k + 1)a_n(x - a)^{n-k} + \cdots$$

If $x = a$, $f^k(a) = k! \, a_k$.

Thus

$$a_n = \frac{f^n(a)}{n!} \qquad \text{for } n = 1, 2, \ldots; a_0 = f(a)$$

$$f(x) = f(a) + \frac{f'(a)}{1!}(x-a) + \frac{f''(a)}{2!}(x-a)^2 + \cdots + \frac{f^n(a)}{n!}(x-a)^n + \cdots$$

Differential Calculus: Functions of More Than One Variable

3

3.1 Introduction

The discussion and examples in previous sections concern functions of one variable, that is, functions of the explicit form $y = f(x)$ or the implicit form $f(x, y) = 0$. Such functions express a relationship between two variables, x and y, and implicitly assume that the processes being studied can be represented adequately in terms of only these two variables. Although in many cases this type of representation provides a reasonably accurate first approximation to reality, there are many cases in which such a representation is so inadequate as to be virtually useless. In these cases the relationship must be expressed in terms of several variables, or one variable must be expressed as a function of more than one other variable. For example, in economic theory supply and demand of a commodity frequently depend not only on its price but also on the prices of related commodities, on income level, on time, and on various other factors. Profit depends not just on the output of one commodity, but on the output levels for several commodities and on the combination of several inputs.

Relations and functions of several variables can be defined by appropriate extensions of the corresponding definitions for two variables. Geometric representation is not possible for functions involving more than three variables, but, with this exception, the following discussion and definitions are appropriate for any finite number of variables. Partial differentiation is defined and several applications of partial derivatives in business and economics are discussed. Constrained and unconstrained maxima and minima of functions of two variables are considered, and constrained utility maximization is discussed as an example of the application of these concepts in business and economics.

FUNCTIONS OF MORE THAN ONE VARIABLE

Just as a point in two-dimensional space is represented by an ordered pair of real numbers, a point in three-dimensional space is represented by an ordered triple of real numbers and a point in n-dimensional space is represented by an ordered n-tuple of real numbers $(x_1, x_2, \ldots, x_n)$. Thus a point in n-dimensional space is represented by an ordered arrangement of n real numbers. The set of all points in n-dimensional space is denoted by U_n. For convenience, a point in n-dimensional space is sometimes denoted by a single letter, say X.

A set of ordered pairs $\{(X, z)\}$, where $X \in U_n$, is a relation. If $(X_1, z_1) \in F$ and $(X_1, z_2) \in F$ implies that $z_1 = z_2$, then $\{(X, z)\}$ is a function of n variables. The domain of the function is the set of points $\{X\}$ in the space U_n and the range is the set of values $\{z\}$ appearing in the set of pairs in F. Note that the set of ordered pairs is a relation and, if to each point of the domain there corresponds only one point of the range, the relation is a function.

When $X \in U_2$, the pair (X, z) is an ordered triple, say (x, y, z), which may be interpreted as a point in three-dimensional space. Note again that functions whose domain is U_k, where $k > 2$, cannot be represented geometrically.

A function of several variables is frequently described by an equation expressing the correspondence between the coordinates of the point X and the function value z. For this purpose, the notation $y = f(x)$ can be extended for functions defined on U_n. For example, if $X \in U_n$, $z = F(X)$ indicates that F is a function of n variables. If the domain is in U_2,

$$z = F(x, y) \qquad \text{or} \qquad z = F(X)$$

and z is a function of two variables. In general, if $X \in U_n$,

$$z = F(x_1, x_2, \ldots, x_n) \qquad \text{or} \qquad z = F(X)$$

and z is a function of n variables. The coordinates of X are called *independent variables* and z is called the *dependent variable*. Implicit functions of several variables can be written, for example, as $f(x, y, z) = 0$ or, more generally, as $f(x_1, x_2, \ldots, x_n, z) = 0$.

The definition of a function is extended to the case of n independent variables in the above discussion. Most of the definitions and formulas given subsequently for functions involving more than two variables are stated explicitly for functions involving three or, in some cases, four variables. This is for convenience. These definitions and formulas can also be extended to the general case of n variables, but additional notation is required to write the corresponding statements concisely. Several results concerning maxima and minima of functions of n variables, which are not obtained easily as generalizations of the corresponding results for two variables, are stated in matrix notation, after that notation is defined in Chapter 7.

Continuity

A function $f(x, y)$ is said to be *continuous at* $x = a$, $y = b$, if the following three conditions are satisfied:

1. $f(a, b)$ exists.
2. $\lim_{x \to a, y \to b} f(x, y)$ exists.
3. $\lim_{x \to a, y \to b} f(x, y) = f(a, b)$, no matter in what manner $x \to a$ and $y \to b$.

A function of x and y is said to be *continuous in a region* of the xy-plane if it is continuous at every point of the region. Analogous definitions are appropriate for functions of n variables.

3.2 Partial Differentiation

In this section partial differentiation of explicit and implicit functions, the total differential, and the total derivative are defined and illustrated.

Consider a function z of two independent variables x and y.

$$z = f(x, y)$$

If y is held constant, z is a function only of x and the derivative of z with respect to x can be computed. The derivative obtained in this way is the *partial derivative* of z with respect to x and is denoted by

$$\frac{\partial z}{\partial x} \qquad \frac{\partial f}{\partial x} \qquad \frac{\partial}{\partial x} f(x, y) \qquad f_x(x, y) \qquad f_x \qquad z_x$$

Similarly, if x is held constant, the partial derivative with respect to y can be computed and is denoted by

$$\frac{\partial z}{\partial y} \qquad \frac{\partial f}{\partial y} \qquad \frac{\partial}{\partial y} f(x, y) \qquad f_y(x, y) \qquad f_y \qquad z_y$$

The partial derivative of z with respect to x is defined as

$$\frac{\partial z}{\partial x} = \lim_{\Delta x \to 0} \frac{\Delta z}{\Delta x} = \lim_{\Delta x \to 0} \frac{f(x + \Delta x, y) - f(x, y)}{\Delta x}$$

and the partial derivative of z with respect to y is defined as

$$\frac{\partial z}{\partial y} = \lim_{y \to 0} \frac{\Delta z}{\Delta y} = \lim_{\Delta y \to 0} \frac{f(x, y + \Delta y) - f(x, y)}{\Delta y}$$

NOTE: In general, a function of any number of variables may have a partial derivative with respect to each of its variables.

EXAMPLE

If $z = 2x^2 + 3xy - 6y^2$,

$$\frac{\partial z}{\partial x} = 4x + 3y$$

$$\frac{\partial z}{\partial y} = 3x - 12y$$

EXAMPLE

If $z = xy + \ln x$,

$$\frac{\partial z}{\partial x} = y + \frac{1}{x}$$

$$\frac{\partial z}{\partial y} = x$$

EXAMPLE

If $z = (x + y) \sin (3x - y)$,

$$\frac{\partial z}{\partial x} = \sin (3x - y) + 3(x + y) \cos (3x - y)$$

$$\frac{\partial z}{\partial y} = \sin (3x - y) - 3(x + y) \cos (3x - y)$$

EXAMPLE

If $z = \dfrac{x^3 - y^3}{xy}$, show that $x\dfrac{\partial z}{\partial x} + y\dfrac{\partial z}{\partial y} = z$.

Multiplying numerator and denominator by $x^{-1}y^{-1}$,

$$z = x^2y^{-1} - x^{-1}y^2$$

$$\frac{\partial z}{\partial x} = 2xy^{-1} + x^{-2}y^2$$

$$\frac{\partial z}{\partial y} = -x^2y^{-2} - 2x^{-1}y$$

$$x\frac{\partial z}{\partial x} + y\frac{\partial z}{\partial y} = 2x^2y^{-1} + x^{-1}y^2 - x^2y^{-1} - 2x^{-1}y^2$$

$$= x^2y^{-1} - x^{-1}y^2 = z$$

Just as a function of one variable can be represented by a curve in a plane, a function of two variables can be represented by a surface in space. Consider the surface represented by $z = f(x, y)$ in Figure 3.1. If a plane is passed through any point of P of the surface parallel to the xz-plane, it cuts the surface in the curve APB, along which y remains constant; the slope of the tangent line to APB at P represents the rate at which z changes with respect to x at the point P. Similar statements hold for a plane parallel to the yz-plane. Thus the partial derivatives have the following geometrical significance:

$$\frac{\partial z}{\partial x} = \frac{\partial z}{\partial x}\bigg|_P = \tan \alpha = \text{slope of } APB \text{ at } P$$

$$\frac{\partial z}{\partial y} = \frac{\partial z}{\partial y}\bigg|_P = \tan \beta = \text{slope of } CPD \text{ at } P$$

That is, if $z = f(x, y)$, the partial derivatives $\dfrac{\partial z}{\partial x}$ and $\dfrac{\partial z}{\partial y}$ are interpreted geometrically as the slopes of the curves of intersection of the surface $z = f(x, y)$ and the planes $y = $ constant and $x = $ constant, respectively.

Since, in general, the partial derivatives of a function $z = f(x, y)$ are functions of x

Figure 3.1

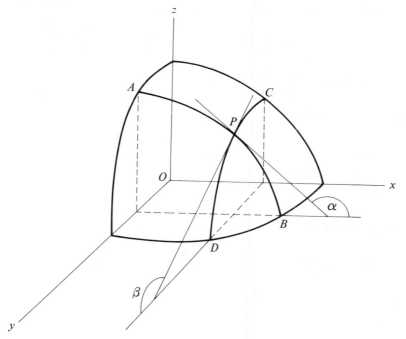

and y, they may be differentiated with respect to either x or y; these derivatives, if they exist, are called the *second-order partial derivatives* of z and are denoted, respectively, by

$$\frac{\partial}{\partial x}\left(\frac{\partial z}{\partial x}\right) = \frac{\partial^2 z}{\partial x^2} = z_{xx} = \frac{\partial^2 f}{\partial x^2} = f_{xx}$$

$$\frac{\partial}{\partial x}\left(\frac{\partial z}{\partial y}\right) = \frac{\partial^2 z}{\partial x \, \partial y} = z_{xy} = \frac{\partial^2 f}{\partial x \, \partial y} = f_{xy}$$

$$\frac{\partial}{\partial y}\left(\frac{\partial z}{\partial x}\right) = \frac{\partial^2 z}{\partial y \, \partial x} = z_{yx} = \frac{\partial^2 f}{\partial y \, \partial x} = f_{yx}$$

$$\frac{\partial}{\partial y}\left(\frac{\partial z}{\partial y}\right) = \frac{\partial^2 z}{\partial y^2} = z_{yy} = \frac{\partial^2 f}{\partial y^2} = f_{yy}$$

A second- or higher-order partial derivative which is obtained by differentiating with respect to more than one variable is referred to as a *mixed partial derivative*. Thus f_{xy} and f_{yx} are mixed partial derivatives. Of the four derivatives above, only three are generally distinct, since $f_{xy} = f_{yx}$ for all values of x and y for which f_{xy} and f_{yx} are continuous. From this property, it follows that a mixed partial derivative of second (or higher) order can be obtained by differentiating with respect to the variables in any order, provided only that the derivatives are continuous.

Similar definitions and equalities hold for higher-order partial derivatives of functions of two variables and for partial derivatives of functions of more than two variables.

EXAMPLE

If $u = Ax^4 + Bx^3y + Cx^2y^2 + Dxy^3 + Ey^4$, find $\dfrac{\partial^3 u}{\partial x^3}$, $\dfrac{\partial^3 u}{\partial x\,\partial y^2}$, $\dfrac{\partial^3 u}{\partial x^2\,\partial y}$, and $\dfrac{\partial^3 u}{\partial y^3}$.

$$\frac{\partial u}{\partial x} = 4Ax^3 + 3Bx^2y + 2Cxy^2 + Dy^3$$

$$\frac{\partial^2 u}{\partial x^2} = 12Ax^2 + 6Bxy + 2Cy^2$$

$$\frac{\partial^3 u}{\partial x^3} = 24Ax + 6By$$

$$\frac{\partial^3 u}{\partial x^2\,\partial y} = 6Bx + 4Cy$$

$$\frac{\partial u}{\partial y} = Bx^3 + 2Cx^2y + 3Dxy^2 + 4Ey^3$$

$$\frac{\partial^2 u}{\partial y^2} = 2Cx^2 + 6Dxy + 12Ey^2$$

$$\frac{\partial^3 u}{\partial y^2\,\partial x} = 4Cx + 6Dy$$

$$\frac{\partial^3 u}{\partial y^3} = 6Dx + 24Ey$$

EXAMPLE

If $z = (x^2 + y^2)^{3/2}$,

$$\frac{\partial z}{\partial x} = \tfrac{3}{2}(x^2 + y^2)^{1/2}(2x)$$

$$= 3x(x^2 + y^2)^{1/2}$$

$$\frac{\partial^2 z}{\partial y\,\partial x} = \tfrac{3}{2}x(x^2 + y^2)^{-1/2}(2y)$$

$$= 3xy(x^2 + y^2)^{-1/2}$$

$$\frac{\partial z}{\partial y} = \tfrac{3}{2}(x^2 + y^2)^{1/2}(2y)$$

$$= 3y(x^2 + y^2)^{1/2}$$

$$\frac{\partial^2 z}{\partial x\,\partial y} = \tfrac{3}{2}y(x^2 + y^2)^{-1/2}(2x)$$

$$= 3xy(x^2 + y^2)^{-1/2}$$

Note that $\dfrac{\partial^2 z}{\partial y\,\partial x} = \dfrac{\partial^2 z}{\partial x\,\partial y}$ except at $(0, 0)$.

PROBLEMS

1. If $u = xy - \ln xy$, find u_x and u_y.

2. If $z = (x - y)/(x + y)$, find z_x and z_y.

3. If $z = ye^{x/y}$, find z_x and z_y.

4. If $z = \ln\left(\dfrac{x^2 - y^2}{x^2 + y^2}\right)$, find z_x and z_y.

5. If $u = \sin xy$, find u_x and u_y.

6. If $z = \sqrt{xy}$, find z_x and z_y.

7. If $z = e^{au + bv2 + cw3}$, find z_u, z_v, and z_w.

8. If $u = x^2y + y^2z + z^2x$, show that $u_x + u_y + u_z = (x + y + z)^2$.

9. If $z = x^2 \sin (y/x) + y^2 \cos (y/x)$, find $xz_x + yz_y$.

10. If $a = \cos xu \sin yu$, find z_x, z_y, and z_u.

11. If $z = xy + y \ln xy$, show that $x\dfrac{\partial^2 z}{\partial x^2} + y\dfrac{\partial^2 z}{\partial x \, \partial y} = y^2 \dfrac{\partial^2 z}{\partial y^2}$.

12. If $u = \sqrt{x - y^2}$, show that $\dfrac{\partial u}{\partial x} \cdot \dfrac{\partial^2 u}{\partial x \, \partial y} = \dfrac{\partial u}{\partial y} \cdot \dfrac{\partial^2 u}{\partial x^2}$.

13. If $z = xy + xe^{1/y}$, show that $\dfrac{\partial^2 z}{\partial x \, \partial y} = \dfrac{\partial^2 z}{\partial y \, \partial x}$.

14. If $v = \dfrac{x + y}{x - y}$, show that $\dfrac{\partial^2 v}{\partial x \, \partial y} = \dfrac{\partial^2 v}{\partial y \, \partial x}$.

15. If $z = 2x^2 - 2y^2 - 3x - 4xy^2$, show that $\dfrac{\partial^2 z}{\partial x \, \partial y} = \dfrac{\partial^2 z}{\partial y \, \partial x}$.

16. If $z = \ln (x^2 + y^2)$, show that $\dfrac{\partial^2 z}{\partial x^2} + \dfrac{\partial^2 z}{\partial y^2} = 0$.

17. If $f(x, y) = x^3 e^{x^2 + y}$, find f_x, f_y, and f_{xy}.

18. If $f(x, y) = Ax + By + Ce^{xy}$, find f_{xx}, f_{yy}, and f_{xy}.

19. If $f(x, y) = x^2 \cos y + y^2 \sin x$, find f_{xx}, f_{yy}, and f_{xy}.

20. If $f(x, y) = x^3 + 3x^2y + 6xy^2 - y^3$, find $f_{xx}(2, 3), f_{yy}(2, 3)$, and $f_{xy}(2, 3)$.

21. If $f(x, y) = x^4 - 4x^3y + 8xy^3 - y^4$, find $f_{xx}(0, 1), f_{yy}(0, 1)$, and $f_{xy}(0, 1)$.

22. If $f(x, y) = 2x^2 - 3xy + 4y^2$, find $f_x(1, -1)$ and $f_y(1, -1)$.

23. If $f(x, y) = \dfrac{2x}{x - y}$, find $f_x(3, 1)$ and $f_y(3, 1)$.

24. If $f(x, y) = e^{-x} \sin (x + 2y)$, find $f_x\left(0, \dfrac{\pi}{4}\right)$ and $f_y\left(0, \dfrac{\pi}{4}\right)$.

25. If $u = \dfrac{x^2 y^2}{x + y}$, show that $xu_x + yu_y = 3u$.

26. If $u = \ln (x + y + z)$, show that $\ln u_x + \ln u_y + \ln u_z = -3u$.

27. If $u = \dfrac{Ax^n + By^n}{Cx^2 + Dy^2}$, show that $xu_x + yu_y = (n - 2)u$.

28. If $u = f(x, y)$, $v = g(x, y)$, $u_x = v_y$, and $u_y = -v_x$, show that if $x = r \cos \theta$

and $y = r \sin \theta$, then $u_r = \frac{1}{r} v_\theta$ and $v_r = \frac{1}{r} u_\theta$.

29. If $u = f(x, y)$, $x = r \cos \theta$, and $y = r \sin \theta$, find $u_r^2 + \frac{1}{r} u_\theta^2$ in terms of x and y.

30. If $z = f(x, y)$, $x = g(u, v)$, and $y = h(u, v)$, find z_{uu}.

31. If $u = \ln \sqrt{x^2 + y^2}$, show that $u_{xx} = -u_{yy}$.

32. If $u = \frac{1}{r}$ and $r = \sqrt{x^2 + y^2 + z^2}$, show that $u_x^2 + u_y^2 + u_z^2 = \frac{1}{r^4}$.

Answers to Odd-Numbered Problems

1. $u_x = y - \frac{1}{x}$; $u_y = x - \frac{1}{y}$

3. $z_x = e^{x/y}$; $z_y = e^{x/y}\left(1 - \frac{x}{y}\right)$

5. $u_x = y \cos xy$; $u_y = x \cos xy$

7. $z_u = ae^{au + bv2 + cw3}$; $z_v = 2bve^{au + bv2 + cw3}$; $z_w = 3cw^2 e^{au + bv2 + cw3}$

9. $2z$

17. $f_x = x^2(3 + 2x^2)e^{x^2 + y}$; $f_y = x^3 e^{x^2 + y}$; $f_{xy} = x^2(3 + 2x^2)e^{x^2 + y}$

19. $f_{xx} = 2 \cos y - y^2 \sin x$; $f_{yy} = -x^2 \cos y + 2 \sin x$;

   $f_{xy} = -2x \sin y + 2y \cos x$

21. $f_{xx}(0, 1) = 0$; $f_{yy}(0, 1) = -12$; $f_{xy}(0, 1) = 24$

23. $f_x(3, 1) = -\frac{1}{2}$; $f_y(3, 1) = \frac{3}{2}$

29. $u_x^2 + u_y^2$

THE TOTAL DIFFERENTIAL

The total differential of a function

$$w = f(x, y, z)$$

is defined by

$$dw = \frac{\partial w}{\partial x} dx + \frac{\partial w}{\partial y} dy + \frac{\partial w}{\partial z} dz$$

The separate terms $\frac{\partial w}{\partial x}$, $\frac{\partial w}{\partial y}$ and $\frac{\partial w}{\partial z}$ are sometimes called partial differentials of w with respect to x, y, and z, respectively. The sum of the partial differentials of a function is its *total differential*.

In general, the total differential of a function

$$w = f(x_1, x_2, \ldots, x_n)$$

is the sum of all its partial differentials

$$dw = \sum_{i=1}^{n} \frac{\partial f}{\partial x_i} dx_i$$

If the x's are differentiable functions of another variable, say t, then

$$dx_i = \frac{dx_i}{dt}\, dt$$

and if the x's are differentiable functions of two variables, say r and s, then

$$dx_i = \frac{\partial x_i}{\partial r}\, dr + \frac{\partial x_i}{\partial s}\, ds$$

EXAMPLE

If $z = 2x^3 - 4xy^2 + 3y^3$,

$$dz = 6x^2\, dx - 4y^2\, dx - 8xy\, dy + 9y^2\, dy$$
$$= (6x^2 - 4y^2)\, dx + (9y^2 - 8xy)\, dy$$

EXAMPLE

If $w = x^2 + y^2 + z^2$, where $x = r \cos t$, $y = r \sin t$, and $z = r$, then

$$dw = \frac{\partial w}{\partial x}\, dx + \frac{\partial w}{\partial y}\, dy + \frac{\partial w}{\partial z}\, dz$$
$$= 2x\, dx + 2y\, dy + 2z\, dz$$

But

$$dx = \cos t\, dr - r \sin t\, dt$$
$$dy = \sin t\, dr + r \cos t\, dt$$
$$dz = dr$$

and thus

$$dw = 2x(\cos t\, dr - r \sin t\, dt) + 2y(\sin t\, dr + r \cos t\, dt) + 2z\, dr$$

Substituting for x, y, and z,

$$dw = 2r \cos t\, (\cos t\, dr - r \sin t\, dt)$$
$$+ 2r \sin t\, (\sin t\, dr + r \cos t\, dt) + 2r\, dr$$
$$= 2r\, (\cos^2 t\, dr + \sin^2 t\, dr + dr)$$
$$= 2(r + r)\, dr$$
$$= 4r\, dr$$

Alternatively,

$$w = r^2 \cos^2 t + r^2 \sin^2 t + r^2$$
$$= 2r^2$$
$$dw = 4r\, dr$$

EXAMPLE

If $u = (x + y)(x - y)^{1/2}$, compute du when $x = 6$, $y = 2$, $dx = \frac{1}{2}$, and $dy = -1$.

$$du = \frac{\partial u}{\partial x} dx + \frac{\partial u}{\partial y} dy$$

$$= [(x - y)^{1/2} + (x + y)(\tfrac{1}{2})(x - y)^{-1/2}] dx$$
$$\quad + [(x - y)^{1/2} + (x + y)(-\tfrac{1}{2})(x - y)^{-1/2}] dy$$
$$= (x - y)^{-1/2}[(x - y) + \tfrac{1}{2}(x + y)] dx$$
$$\quad + (x - y)^{-1/2}[(x - y) - \tfrac{1}{2}(x + y)] dy$$
$$= (x - y)^{-1/2}[\tfrac{3}{2}x - \tfrac{1}{2}y] dx + (x - y)^{-1/2}[\tfrac{1}{2}x - \tfrac{3}{2}y] dy$$
$$= \tfrac{1}{2}(x - y)^{-1/2}[(3x - y) dx + (x - 3y) dy]$$

Substituting the given values,

$$du = (\tfrac{1}{2})(\tfrac{1}{2})[(16)(\tfrac{1}{2}) + 0]$$
$$= 2$$

THE TOTAL DERIVATIVE

If $w = f(x, y, z)$ has continuous partial derivatives $\dfrac{\partial w}{\partial x}, \dfrac{\partial w}{\partial y}$, and $\dfrac{\partial w}{\partial z}$ in some region and x, y, and z are functions of another variable t, then

$$\frac{dw}{dt} = \frac{\partial w}{\partial x}\frac{dx}{dt} + \frac{\partial w}{\partial y}\frac{dy}{dt} + \frac{\partial w}{\partial z}\frac{dz}{dt}$$

and $\dfrac{dw}{dt}$ is said to be the *total derivative* of w with respect to t. Thus $\dfrac{dw}{dt}$ represents the rate of change in w as t changes and actually is a function only of t. The total derivative can be obtained by dividing the total differential by Δt and letting Δt approach zero as a limit.

EXAMPLE

If $w = x^2 + y^2 + z^2$, where $x = e^t \cos t$, $y = e^t \sin t$, and $z = e^t$, find $\dfrac{dw}{dt}$.

$$\frac{dw}{dt} = \frac{\partial w}{\partial x}\frac{dx}{dt} + \frac{\partial w}{\partial y}\frac{dy}{dt} + \frac{\partial w}{\partial z}\frac{dz}{dt}$$

$$\frac{dw}{dt} = 2x(e^t \cos t - e^t \sin t) + 2y(e^t \sin t + e^t \cos t) + 2ze^t$$

Substituting for x, y, and z in terms of t,

$$\frac{dw}{dt} = 2[e^{2t} \cos^2 t - e^{2t} \sin t \cos t + e^{2t} \sin^2 t + e^{2t} \sin t \cos t + e^{2t}]$$

$$= 2[e^{2t}(\cos^2 t + \sin^2 t)] + 2e^{2t}$$

$$= 4e^{2t}$$

Alternatively,

$$w = e^{2t} \cos^2 t + e^{2t} \sin^2 t + e^{2t}$$

$$\frac{dw}{dt} = 2e^{2t} \cos^2 t - 2e^{2t} \sin t \cos t + 2e^{2t} \sin^2 t + 2e^{2t} \sin t \cos t + 2e^{2t}$$

$$= 2e^{2t}(\cos^2 t + \sin^2 t) + 2e^{2t}$$

$$= 4e^{2t}$$

EXAMPLE

If $u = \dfrac{x}{y} + \dfrac{y}{z}$, where $x = 2t$, $y = \dfrac{1}{t}$, and $z = t^2$,

$$\frac{du}{dt} = \frac{\partial u}{\partial x} \cdot \frac{dx}{dt} + \frac{\partial u}{\partial y} \cdot \frac{dy}{dt} + \frac{\partial u}{\partial z} \cdot \frac{dz}{dt}$$

$$= \left(\frac{1}{y}\right)(2) + \left(-\frac{x}{y^2} + \frac{1}{z}\right)\left(-\frac{1}{t^2}\right) + \left(-\frac{y}{z^2}\right)(2t)$$

$$= \frac{2}{y} + \frac{x}{y^2 t^2} - \frac{1}{zt^2} - \frac{2yt}{z^2}$$

Substituting for x, y, and z,

$$\frac{du}{dt} = 2t + 2t - \frac{1}{t^4} - \frac{2}{t^4}$$

$$= 4t - \frac{3}{t^4}$$

Alternatively, using direct substitution,

$$u = 2t^2 + \frac{1}{t^3}$$

$$\frac{du}{dt} = 4t - \frac{3}{t^4}$$

Similarly, if $w = f(x, y, z)$ and x, y, and z are differentiable functions of r and s, then $\dfrac{\partial w}{\partial r}$ and $\dfrac{\partial w}{\partial s}$ can be obtained as follows:

$$\frac{\partial w}{\partial r} = \frac{\partial w}{\partial x}\frac{\partial x}{\partial r} + \frac{\partial w}{\partial y}\frac{\partial y}{\partial r} + \frac{\partial w}{\partial z}\frac{\partial z}{\partial r}$$

$$\frac{\partial w}{\partial s} = \frac{\partial w}{\partial x}\frac{\partial x}{\partial s} + \frac{\partial w}{\partial y}\frac{\partial y}{\partial s} + \frac{\partial w}{\partial z}\frac{\partial z}{\partial s}$$

In general, if w is a differentiable function of x_1, x_2, ..., x_n and the x's are differentiable functions of a second set of variables u_1, u_2, ..., u_m, then the partial derivative of w with respect to a variable in the second set, say u_j, is given by

$$\frac{\partial w}{\partial u_j} = \frac{\partial w}{\partial x_1}\frac{\partial x_1}{\partial u_j} + \frac{\partial w}{\partial x_2}\frac{\partial x_2}{\partial u_j} + \cdots + \frac{\partial w}{\partial x_n}\frac{\partial x_n}{\partial u_j}$$

EXAMPLE

If $u = x^2 - xy + y^2$, where $x = rs$ and $y = r^2 + s^2$,

$$\frac{\partial u}{\partial r} = \frac{\partial u}{\partial x} \cdot \frac{\partial x}{\partial r} + \frac{\partial u}{\partial y} \cdot \frac{\partial y}{\partial r}$$

$$= (2x - y)s + 2(2y - x)r$$

Substituting for x and y,

$$\frac{\partial u}{\partial r} = (2rs - r^2 - s^2)s + 2(2r^2 + 2s^2 - rs)r$$

$$= 2rs^2 - r^2s - s^3 + 4r^3 + 4s^2r - 2r^2s$$

$$= 4r^3 - 3r^2s + 6rs^2 - s^3$$

$$\frac{\partial u}{\partial s} = \frac{\partial u}{\partial x} \cdot \frac{\partial x}{\partial s} + \frac{\partial u}{\partial y} \cdot \frac{\partial y}{\partial s}$$

$$= (2x - y)r + 2(2y - x)s$$

Substituting for x and y,

$$\frac{\partial u}{\partial s} = (2rs - r^2 - s^2)r + 2(2r^2 + 2s^2 - rs)s$$

$$= 2r^2s - r^3 - rs^2 + 4r^2s + 4s^3 - 2rs^2$$

$$= 4s^3 - 3rs^2 + 6r^2s - r^3$$

EXAMPLE

If $w = \ln (x^2 + y^2 + 2z)$, where $x = r + s$, $y = r - s$, and $z = 2rs$,

$$\frac{\partial w}{\partial r} = \frac{\partial w}{\partial x}\frac{\partial x}{\partial r} + \frac{\partial w}{\partial y}\frac{\partial y}{\partial r} + \frac{\partial w}{\partial z}\frac{\partial z}{\partial r}$$

$$= \left(\frac{2x}{x^2 + y^2 + 2z}\right)(1) + \left(\frac{2y}{x^2 + y^2 + 2z}\right)(1) + \left(\frac{2}{x^2 + y^2 + 2z}\right)(2s)$$

$$= \frac{2(x + y + 2s)}{x^2 + y^2 + 2z}$$

$$= \frac{2(r + s + r - s + 2s)}{r^2 + 2rs + s^2 + r^2 - 2rs + s^2 + 4rs}$$

$$= \frac{4(r + s)}{2(r + s)^2}$$

$$= \frac{2}{r + s}$$

and

$$\frac{\partial w}{\partial s} = \frac{\partial w}{\partial x}\frac{\partial x}{\partial s} + \frac{\partial w}{\partial y}\frac{\partial y}{\partial s} + \frac{\partial w}{\partial z}\frac{\partial z}{\partial s}$$

$$= \left(\frac{2x}{x^2 + y^2 + 2z}\right)(1) + \left(\frac{2y}{x^2 + y^2 + 2z}\right)(-1) + \left(\frac{2}{x^2 + y^2 + 2z}\right)(2r)$$

$$= \frac{2(x - y + 2r)}{x^2 + y^2 + 2z}$$

$$= \frac{2(r + s - r + s + 2r)}{r^2 + 2rs + s^2 + r^2 - 2rs + s^2 + 4rs}$$

$$= \frac{4(r + s)}{2(r + s)^2}$$

$$= \frac{2}{r + s}$$

The composite function or chain rule is valid for partial derivatives, and can be used to obtain the total derivatives of functions whose independent variables are related in various ways.

For example, if $u = f(x, y, z)$, where $x = t$, $y = y(t)$, and $z = z(t)$, then

$$\frac{du}{dt} = \frac{\partial u}{\partial x}\frac{dx}{dt} + \frac{\partial u}{\partial y}\frac{dy}{dt} + \frac{\partial u}{\partial z}\frac{dz}{dt}$$

$$= \frac{\partial u}{\partial x} + \frac{\partial u}{\partial y}\frac{dy}{dt} + \frac{\partial u}{\partial z}\frac{dz}{dt}$$

since $\dfrac{dx}{dt} = 1$.

If $u = f(x, y, z)$, where $x = x(t)$, $y = y(x)$, and $z = z(t)$, then

$$\frac{du}{dt} = \frac{\partial u}{\partial x}\frac{dx}{dt} + \frac{\partial u}{\partial y}\frac{dy}{dx}\frac{dx}{dt} + \frac{\partial u}{\partial z}\frac{dz}{dt}$$

since $\dfrac{dy}{dt} = \dfrac{\partial y}{\partial x}\dfrac{dx}{dt}$.

If $u = f(x, y, z)$, where $x = x(r, s)$, $y = y(r)$, and $z = z(y)$, then

$$\frac{\partial u}{\partial r} = \frac{\partial u}{\partial x}\frac{\partial x}{\partial r} + \frac{\partial u}{\partial y}\frac{dy}{dr} + \frac{\partial u}{\partial z}\frac{dz}{dy}\frac{dy}{dr}$$

and

$$\frac{\partial u}{\partial s} = \frac{\partial u}{\partial x}\frac{\partial x}{\partial s}$$

since $\dfrac{\partial y}{\partial s} = 0$.

If $u = f(x, y, z)$, where $x = x(t)$, $y = y(x)$, and $z = z(y)$, then

$$\frac{du}{dt} = \frac{\partial u}{\partial x}\frac{dx}{dt} + \frac{\partial u}{\partial y}\frac{dy}{dx}\frac{dx}{dt} + \frac{\partial u}{\partial z}\frac{dz}{dy}\frac{dy}{dx}\frac{dx}{dt}$$

DIFFERENTIATION OF IMPLICIT FUNCTIONS

The process of implicit differentiation discussed in previous sections can be formalized using partial derivatives and then generalized to provide formulas for obtaining partial derivatives of implicit functions of several variables.

In most cases, the equation $f(x, y) = 0$ defines x and y as implicit functions of each other. For purposes of notation, let

$$u = f(x, y) = 0$$

Then

$$\frac{\partial u}{\partial x} = \frac{\partial f}{\partial x} + \frac{\partial f}{\partial y}\frac{dy}{dx}$$

But if $f(x, y) = 0$, then $u = 0$, $\dfrac{\partial u}{\partial x} = 0$ and

$$\frac{\partial f}{\partial x} + \frac{\partial f}{\partial y}\frac{dy}{dx} = 0$$

Thus

$$\frac{dy}{dx} = -\frac{\dfrac{\partial f}{\partial x}}{\dfrac{\partial f}{\partial y}} \qquad \text{for } \frac{\partial f}{\partial y} \neq 0$$

and, similarly, $\dfrac{dx}{dy}$ is the reciprocal of $\dfrac{dy}{dx}$ and is defined for $\dfrac{\partial f}{\partial x} \neq 0$.

Note that the equation $\dfrac{\partial f}{\partial x} + \dfrac{\partial f}{\partial y} \cdot \dfrac{dy}{dx} = 0$ is obtained by implicit differentiation.

EXAMPLE

If $e^x \sin y + e^y \cos x = 1$, find $\dfrac{dy}{dx}$ and $\dfrac{dx}{dy}$.

$$f(x, y) = e^x \sin y + e^y \cos x - 1 = 0$$

$$\frac{dy}{dx} = -\frac{\dfrac{\partial f}{\partial x}}{\dfrac{\partial f}{\partial y}}$$

$$= -\frac{e^x \sin v - e^y \sin x}{e^x \cos y + e^y \cos x}$$

Implicit differentiation can also be used directly to obtain $\dfrac{dy}{dx}$, as follows:

$$e^x \sin y + e^x \cos y \, \frac{dy}{dx} + e^y \cos x \, \frac{dy}{dx} - e^y \sin x = 0$$

$$\frac{dy}{dx} = \frac{e^y \sin x - e^x \sin y}{e^x \cos y + e^y \cos x}$$

$\dfrac{dx}{dy}$ can be obtained by either of the methods above or, more easily, as the reciprocal of $\dfrac{dy}{dx}$.

$$\frac{dx}{dy} = \frac{1}{\dfrac{dy}{dx}} \qquad \text{for } \frac{dy}{dx} \neq 0$$

$$= \frac{e^x \cos y + e^y \cos x}{e^y \sin x - e^x \sin y}$$

EXAMPLE

If $f(x, y) = x^3 + y^3 - 3axy = 0$, find $\dfrac{dy}{dx}$ and $\dfrac{dx}{dy}$.

$$\frac{dy}{dx} = -\frac{\dfrac{\partial f}{\partial x}}{\dfrac{\partial f}{\partial y}}$$

$$= -\frac{3x^2 - 3ay}{3y^2 - 3ax}$$

$$= \frac{ay - x^2}{y^2 - ax}$$

$$\frac{dx}{dy} = \frac{1}{\dfrac{dy}{dx}} \qquad \text{for } \frac{dy}{dx} \neq 0$$

$$= \frac{y^2 - ax}{ay - x^2}$$

Note that $\dfrac{dy}{dx}$ and $\dfrac{dx}{dy}$ can also be obtained using the usual procedure of implicit differentiation.

Similar formulas are appropriate for obtaining the partial derivatives of implicit functions of any finite number of variables; these formulas can be obtained using the same method of derivation shown above.

If z is defined as an implicit function of x and y by the equation $F(x, y, z) = 0$, then

$$\frac{\partial z}{\partial x} = -\frac{\dfrac{\partial F}{\partial x}}{\dfrac{\partial F}{\partial z}} \qquad \text{for } \frac{\partial F}{\partial z} \neq 0$$

$$\frac{\partial z}{\partial y} = -\frac{\dfrac{\partial F}{\partial y}}{\dfrac{\partial F}{\partial z}} \qquad \text{for } \frac{\partial F}{\partial z} \neq 0$$

The choice of z as the dependent variable is arbitrary; other partial derivatives can also be obtained. For example,

$$\frac{\partial y}{\partial x} = -\frac{\dfrac{\partial F}{\partial x}}{\dfrac{\partial F}{\partial y}} \qquad \text{for } \frac{\partial F}{\partial y} \neq 0$$

Similarly, $\dfrac{\partial x}{\partial z}$, $\dfrac{\partial y}{\partial z}$, and $\dfrac{\partial x}{\partial y}$ can be obtained directly or as reciprocals.

More generally, if z is defined as an implicit function of $x_1, x_2, \ldots, x_n$ by the equation $F(x_1, x_2, \ldots, x_n, z) = 0$, then

$$\frac{\partial z}{\partial x_i} = -\frac{\dfrac{\partial F}{\partial x_i}}{\dfrac{\partial F}{\partial z}} \qquad \text{for } i = 1, 2, \ldots, n \qquad \text{and} \qquad \frac{\partial F}{\partial z} \neq 0$$

Again, choice of z as the dependent variable is arbitrary; $\dfrac{\partial x_i}{\partial x_j}$ can also be obtained as follows

$$\frac{\partial x_i}{\partial x_j} = -\frac{\dfrac{\partial F}{\partial x_j}}{\dfrac{\partial F}{\partial x_i}} \qquad \text{for } i = 1, 2, \ldots, n, \, i \neq j \qquad \text{and} \qquad \frac{\partial F}{\partial x_i} \neq 0$$

EXAMPLE

Find $\dfrac{\partial z}{\partial x}$ and $\dfrac{\partial z}{\partial y}$ for the function $ze^x + e^y - ye^z = 0$.

Let $F = ze^x + e^y - ye^z = 0$

$$\frac{\partial F}{\partial x} = ze^x = -e^y + ye^z$$

$$\frac{\partial F}{\partial y} = e^y - e^z$$

$$\frac{\partial F}{\partial z} = e^x - ye^z$$

$$\frac{\partial z}{\partial x} = -\frac{\dfrac{\partial F}{\partial x}}{\dfrac{\partial F}{\partial z}} = \frac{e^y - ye^z}{e^x - ye^z}$$

$$\frac{\partial z}{\partial y} = -\frac{\dfrac{\partial F}{\partial y}}{\dfrac{\partial F}{\partial z}} = \frac{e^z - e^y}{e^x - ye^z}$$

EXAMPLE

Find $\dfrac{\partial z}{\partial x}$ and $\dfrac{\partial y}{\partial x}$ for the function $z \sin x + z^2 + x \sin y + xyz = 0$.

$$\frac{\partial z}{\partial x} = -\frac{\dfrac{\partial F}{\partial x}}{\dfrac{\partial F}{\partial z}} = -\frac{z \cos x + \sin y + yz}{\sin x + 2z + xy}$$

$$\frac{\partial y}{\partial x} = -\frac{\dfrac{\partial F}{\partial x}}{\dfrac{\partial F}{\partial y}} = -\frac{z \cos x + \sin y + yz}{x \cos y + xz}$$

PROBLEMS

1. If $z = x^3 + x^2y - y^3$, find dz.

2. If $u = \ln (x^2 + y^2 + z^2)^{1/2}$, find du.

3. If $u = e^{xyz}$, find du.

4. If $u = e^z \sin [(x - y)z]$, find du.

5. If $z = 2x^3 - 4xy^2 + 3y^3$, find dz.

6. If $u = xy^2z^3$, find du.

7. If $x^2 + y^2 + z^2 = a^2$, find dz.

8. If $u = x + 4x^{1/2}y^{1/2} - 3y$, $x = t^3$, and $y = \dfrac{1}{t}$, find $\dfrac{du}{dt}$.

9. If $x^3 + y^3 - 3bxy = 0$, find $\dfrac{dy}{dx}$.

10. If $x^2 + 2xy + 2y = 15$, find $\dfrac{dy}{dx}$ if $x = 2$, $y = 3$.

11. If $x^3 - y^3 - 4xy = -\frac{1}{2}$, find $\dfrac{dy}{dx}$ if $x = 2$, $y = -2$.

12. If $Ax + By + Ce^{xy} = D$, find $\dfrac{dy}{dx}$ if $x = y = 0$.

13. If $Ax^2 + By^2 + Cz^2 = D$, find z_x and z_y.

14. If $xy + yz + zx = 9xyz$, find z_x and z_y.

15. If $xz = \cos yz + a$, find z_x and z_y.

16. If $e^x + e^y + e^z = axyz$, find y_x.

17. If $F(x, y, z) = 0$, show that $x_y y_z z_x = -1$.

18. If $u = x^3 - 3xy + y^3$, $x = r^2 + s$, and $y = rs^2$, find $\dfrac{\partial u}{\partial r}$.

19. If $u = xy + yz$, $x = \dfrac{e^t}{t}$, $y = \dfrac{e^{-t}}{t}$, and $z = t^2$, find $\dfrac{du}{dt}$.

20. If $z = x \ln y + y \ln x$, $x = e^{u+v}$, and $y = e^{u-v}$, find $\dfrac{\partial z}{\partial u}$ and $\dfrac{\partial z}{\partial v}$.

21. If $z = \ln (x^2 + y^2) + \sqrt{x^2 + y^2}$, $x = e^u \cos v$, and $y = e^u \sin v$, find $\dfrac{\partial z}{\partial u}$.

22. If $u = xy + yz + zx$, $x = r^s$, $y = sr$, and $z = r + s$, find u_r.

23. If $x \ln yz - y \ln xz = 0$, find z_x and z_y.

24. If $e^{xyz} = e^x + e^y + e^z$, find z_x and z_y.

25. If $e^x + e^y + e^z = e^{x+y+z}$, find z_x and z_y.

26. If $u \ln \dfrac{v}{w} - w \ln uv = 0$, find u_v and u_w.

Answers to Odd-Numbered Problems

1. $dz = (3x^2 + 2xy)\, dx + (x^2 - 3y^2)\, dy$

3. $du = e^{xyz}(yz\, dx + xz\, dy + xy\, dz)$

5. $dz = (6x^2 - 4y^2)\, dx + (9y^2 - 8xy)\, dy$

7. $dz = -(x\, dx + y\, dy)/z$

9. $\dfrac{dy}{dx} = \dfrac{by - x^2}{y^2 - bx}$

11. $\dfrac{dy}{dx} = 1$

13. $z_x = -\dfrac{Ax}{Cz}$; $z_y = -\dfrac{By}{Cz}$

15. $z_x = -z/(x + y \sin yz)$; $z_y = -(z \sin yz)/(x + y \sin yz)$

19. $\dfrac{du}{dt} = e^{-t}(1 - t) - \dfrac{2}{t^3}$

21. $\dfrac{\partial z}{\partial u} = 2 + e^u$

23. $z_x = \dfrac{yz(1 - \ln xz)}{x(x - y)}$

$z_y = \dfrac{xz(1 - \ln yz)}{y(y - x)}$

25. $z_x = -\dfrac{e^y + e^z}{e^x + e^y}$

$z_y = -\dfrac{e^x + e^z}{e^x + e^y}$

3.3 Applications of Partial Derivatives in Business and Economics

In this section several applications of partial derivatives in business and economics are discussed. These applications include marginal cost, demand surfaces, production functions, Euler's theorem, constant product curves, returns to scale, and utility functions.

MARGINAL COST

If the joint-cost function for producing the quantities x and y of two commodities is given by

$$C = Q(x, y)$$

then the partial derivatives of C are the *marginal cost functions*:

$\dfrac{\partial C}{\partial x}$ is the marginal cost with respect to x

$\dfrac{\partial C}{\partial y}$ is the marginal cost with respect to y

In most cases in practice marginal costs are positive.

EXAMPLE

If the joint-cost function of producing quantities x and y of two commodities is

$$C = x \ln (5 + y)$$

then

$\dfrac{\partial C}{dx} = \ln (5 + y)$ is the marginal cost with respect to x

and

$\dfrac{\partial C}{\partial y} = \dfrac{x}{5 + y}$ is the marginal cost with respect to y

EXAMPLE

If the joint-cost function for producing quantities x and y of two commodities is

$$C = 15 + 2x^2 + xy + 5y^2$$

then

$\dfrac{\partial C}{\partial x} = 4x + y$ is the marginal cost with respect to x

and

$\dfrac{\partial C}{\partial y} = x + 10y$ is the marginal cost with respect to y

If $x = 3$ and $y = 6$, $\dfrac{\partial C}{\partial x} = 18$ and $\dfrac{\partial C}{\partial y} = 63$. Thus, if y is kept constant at 6, producing an additional unit of x adds \$18 to the total cost; if x is kept constant at 3, producing an additional unit of y adds \$63 to the total cost.

DEMAND SURFACES

If there are two related commodities for which the quantities demanded are x and y and the respective prices are p and q, then the demand functions can be represented by

$$x = f(p, q) \qquad \text{and} \qquad y = g(p, q)$$

assuming that the quantities demanded, x and y, depend only on the respective prices, p and q, of the two commodities. If a demand function for two independent variables is continuous, it can be represented by a surface, referred to as a *demand surface*.

NOTE: The notation p_x and p_y is frequently used for the prices of the two commodities. It is not used in this section to avoid possible confusion with the subscript notation for partial derivatives.

In the usual economic situations, the demand functions $x = f(p, q)$ and $y = g(p, q)$ have the following properties:

1. All the variables, x, y, p, and q, are zero or positive.
2. If q is constant, x is a monotonically decreasing function of p, that is, as p increases, x decreases; similarly, if p is constant, y is a monotonically decreasing function of q.
3. The functions $f(p, q)$ and $g(p, q)$ and the region for which they are defined are such that it is possible to obtain their inverse functions $p = F(x, y)$ and $q = G(x, y)$.

For a constant price p, as q increases, y decreases, but x may either increase or decrease; if x increases, the two commodities are said to be *competitive*, since a decrease in the demand for one corresponds to an increase in the demand for the other. For a constant price p, as q decreases, y increases; if x also increases, the commodities are said to be *complementary*, since an increase in the demand for one corresponds to an increase in the demand for the other. Corresponding relationships hold for changes in p for a constant q.

Usually, it is assumed that related commodities which are either competitive or complementary at one set of prices have the same relationship at other prices; however, in some cases the relationship between commodities may differ for different prices and thus must be specified for a particular set of prices.

Marginal Demand

If the demand functions for two related commodities are

$$x = f(p, q) \qquad \text{and} \qquad y = g(p, q)$$

then the partial derivatives of x and y are the *marginal demand functions*:

$\dfrac{\partial x}{\partial p}$ is the marginal demand of x with respect to p

$\dfrac{\partial x}{\partial q}$ is the marginal demand of x with respect to q

$\dfrac{\partial y}{\partial p}$ is the marginal demand of y with respect to p

$\dfrac{\partial y}{\partial q}$ is the marginal demand of y with respect to q

For the usual demand functions, x increases if its corresponding price p decreases and y increases if its corresponding price q decreases, so $\dfrac{\partial x}{\partial p}$ and $\dfrac{\partial y}{\partial q}$ are negative for all economically meaningful values of p and q.

If $\dfrac{\partial x}{\partial q}$ and $\dfrac{\partial y}{\partial p}$ are both negative for given (p, q), the commodities are complementary, because a decrease in either price corresponds to increases in both demands. If $\dfrac{\partial x}{\partial q}$ and $\dfrac{\partial y}{\partial p}$ are both positive for given (p, q), the goods are competitive, because a decrease in either price corresponds to an increase in one demand and a decrease in the other. If $\dfrac{\partial x}{\partial q}$ and $\dfrac{\partial y}{\partial p}$ have opposite signs, the commodities are neither complementary nor competitive; in this case, a decrease in the price of one of the commodities corresponds to increases in both demands while a decrease in the price of the other commodity corresponds to an increase in one demand and a decrease in the other. Such a situation is unusual but might occur, for example, if two different grades of a material could be used and the better grade could be obtained only by processing the lower grade.

NOTE: Complementary and competitive commodities are defined in terms of the signs of their cross elasticities in Chapter 2. Those definitions and the definitions above are equivalent, since the signs of the cross elasticities are the same as the signs of the appropriate partial derivatives representing marginal demand.

EXAMPLE

If the demand surfaces are linear functions of p and q,

$$x = a_1 + b_1 p + c_1 q \qquad y = a_2 + b_2 p + c_2 q$$

then the marginal demand functions are

$$\frac{\partial x}{\partial p} = b_1 \qquad \frac{\partial y}{\partial p} = b_2$$

$$\frac{\partial x}{\partial q} = c_1 \qquad \frac{\partial y}{\partial q} = c_2$$

Thus for the usual economic situations, $b_1 < 0$ and $c_2 < 0$. If c_1 and b_2 are both positive, the commodities are competitive; if c_1 and b_2 are both negative, the commodities are complementary.

EXAMPLE

If the demand functions for two related commodities are given by

$$x = \frac{a}{p^2 q} \qquad y = \frac{a}{pq} \qquad a > 0$$

then the marginal demand functions are

$$\frac{\partial x}{\partial p} = -\frac{2a}{p^3 q} \qquad \frac{\partial y}{\partial p} = -\frac{a}{p^2 q}$$

$$\frac{\partial x}{\partial q} = -\frac{a}{p^2 q^2} \qquad \frac{\partial y}{\partial q} = -\frac{a}{pq^2}$$

Since $\dfrac{\partial x}{\partial q} < 0$ and $\dfrac{\partial y}{\partial q} < 0$, the commodities are complementary.

EXAMPLE

If the demand functions for two related commodities are given by

$$x = ae^{q-p} \qquad y = be^{p-q} \qquad a > 0, b > 0$$

then the marginal demand functions are

$$\frac{\partial x}{\partial p} = -ae^{q-p} \qquad \frac{\partial y}{\partial p} = be^{p-q}$$

$$\frac{\partial x}{\partial q} = ae^{q-p} \qquad \frac{\partial y}{\partial q} = -be^{p-q}$$

Since $\dfrac{\partial x}{\partial q} > 0$ and $\dfrac{\partial y}{\partial p} > 0$, the commodities are competitive.

EXAMPLE

If the demand functions for two related commodities are given by

$$x = a_1 q^2 - b_1 pq \qquad y = a_2 p^2 - b_2 pq \qquad a_1 > 0, a_2 > 0, b_1 > 0, b_2 > 0$$

then the marginal demand functions are

$$\frac{\partial x}{\partial p} = -b_1 q \qquad\qquad \frac{\partial y}{\partial p} = 2a_2 p - b_2 q$$

$$\frac{\partial x}{\partial q} = 2a_1 q - b_1 p \qquad \frac{\partial y}{\partial q} = -b_2 p$$

$$\frac{\partial x}{\partial q} > 0 \text{ if } \frac{q}{p} > \frac{b_1}{2a_1} \qquad \frac{\partial y}{\partial p} > 0 \text{ if } \frac{q}{p} < \frac{2a_2}{b_2}$$

$$\frac{\partial x}{\partial q} < 0 \text{ if } \frac{q}{p} < \frac{b_1}{2a_1} \qquad \frac{\partial y}{\partial p} < 0 \text{ if } \frac{q}{p} > \frac{2a_2}{b_2}$$

$$x > 0 \text{ if } \frac{q}{p} > \frac{b_1}{a_1} \qquad\qquad y > 0 \text{ if } \frac{q}{p} < \frac{a_2}{b_2}$$

Thus the demand functions are appropriate for values of p and q such that

$$\frac{b_1}{a_1} < \frac{q}{p} < \frac{a_2}{b_2}$$

and the commodities are competitive for values of p and q such that the demand functions are appropriate (since $b_1/a_1 < q/p < a_2/b_2 \Rightarrow b_1/2a_1 < q/p < 2a_2/b_2$).

EXAMPLE

If the demand functions for two related commodities are given by

$$x = ae^{-pq} \qquad y = be^{p-q} \qquad a > 0, b > 0$$

then the marginal demand functions are

$$\frac{\partial x}{\partial p} = -aqe^{-pq} \qquad \frac{\partial y}{\partial p} = be^{p-q}$$

$$\frac{\partial x}{\partial q} = -ape^{-pq} \qquad \frac{\partial y}{\partial q} = -be^{p-q}$$

Since $\dfrac{\partial x}{\partial q} < 0$ and $\dfrac{\partial y}{\partial p} > 0$, the commodities are neither competitive nor complementary.

Partial Elasticities of Demand

If the demand functions for two related commodities are

$$x = f(p, q) \qquad \text{and} \qquad y = g(p, q)$$

then the partial elasticities of demand are given by

$$\left. \frac{Ex}{Ep} \right|_{q=c_1} = \frac{p}{x} \cdot \frac{\partial x}{\partial p} = \frac{\dfrac{\partial}{\partial x} \ln x}{\dfrac{\partial}{\partial x} \ln p}$$
the partial elasticity of demand x with respect to price p, for a constant price $q = c_1$

$$\left. \frac{Ex}{Eq} \right|_{p=c_2} = \frac{q}{x} \cdot \frac{\partial x}{\partial q} = \frac{\dfrac{\partial}{\partial x} \ln x}{\dfrac{\partial}{\partial x} \ln q}$$
the partial elasticity of demand x with respect to price q, for a constant price $p = c_2$

$$\left. \frac{Ey}{Ep} \right|_{q=c_3} = \frac{p}{y} \cdot \frac{\partial y}{\partial p} = \frac{\dfrac{\partial}{\partial y} \ln y}{\dfrac{\partial}{\partial y} \ln p}$$
the partial elasticity of demand y with respect to price p, for a constant price $q = c_3$

$$\left. \frac{Ey}{Eq} \right|_{p=c_4} = \frac{q}{y} \cdot \frac{\partial y}{\partial q} = \frac{\dfrac{\partial}{\partial y} \ln y}{\dfrac{\partial}{\partial y} \ln q}$$
the partial elasticity of demand y with respect to price q, for a constant price $p = c_4$

Note that Ex/Eq and Ey/Ep are cross partial elasticities of demand; their signs, which are the same as the signs of the corresponding marginal demands, can be used to determine whether commodities are competitive or complementary.

EXAMPLE

If the demand functions for two related commodities are given by

$$x = ae^{q-p} \qquad y = be^{p-q}$$

then the partial elasticities of demand are

$$\frac{Ex}{Ep} = \frac{p}{x} \cdot \frac{\partial x}{\partial p} = \frac{p}{ae^{q-p}}(-ae^{q-p}) = -p \qquad \frac{Ey}{Ep} = \frac{p}{y} \cdot \frac{\partial y}{\partial p} = \frac{p}{be^{p-q}}(be^{p-q}) = p$$

$$\frac{Ex}{Eq} = \frac{q}{x} \cdot \frac{\partial x}{\partial q} = \frac{q}{ae^{q-p}}(ae^{q-p}) = q \qquad \frac{Ey}{Eq} = \frac{q}{y} \cdot \frac{\partial y}{\partial q} = \frac{q}{be^{p-q}}(-be^{p-q}) = -q$$

and, since $Ex/Eq > 0$ and $Ey/Ep > 0$, x and y are competitive commodities (as above).

EXAMPLE

If the demand functions for two related commodities are given by

$$x = a_1 q^2 - b_1 pq \qquad y = a_2 p^2 - b_2 pq \qquad a_1 > 0,\ a_2 > 0,\ b_1 > 0,\ b_2 > 0$$

then the partial elasticities of demand are

$$\frac{Ex}{Ep} = \frac{p}{x} \cdot \frac{\partial x}{\partial p} = \frac{p}{a_1 q^2 - b_1 pq}(-b_1 q) = -\frac{b_1 p}{a_1 q - b_1 p}$$

$$\frac{Ex}{Eq} = \frac{q}{x} \cdot \frac{\partial x}{\partial q} = \frac{q}{a_1 q^2 - b_1 pq}(2a_1 q - b_1 p) = \frac{2a_1 q - b_1 p}{a_1 q - b_1 p}$$

$$\frac{Ey}{Ep} = \frac{p}{y} \cdot \frac{\partial y}{\partial p} = \frac{p}{a_2 p^2 - b_2 pq}(2a_2 p - b_2 q) = \frac{2a_2 p - b_2 q}{a_2 p - b_2 q}$$

$$\frac{Ey}{Eq} = \frac{q}{y} \cdot \frac{\partial y}{\partial q} = \frac{q}{a_2 p^2 - b_2 pq}(-b_2 p) = -\frac{b_2 q}{a_2 p - b_2 q}$$

$Ex/Eq > 0$ since $x > 0$, and thus both numerator and denominator of Ex/Eq are greater than zero. $Ey/Ep > 0$ since $y > 0$, and thus both numerator and denominator of Ey/Ep are greater than zero. Thus x and y are competitive commodities (as above).

PROBLEMS

1. For the following joint-cost functions, determine the marginal cost with respect to x and the marginal cost with respect to y.
   a. $C = x^2 \ln(y + 10)$
   b. $C = x^3 + 2y^2 - xy + 20$
   c. $C = e^x + e^y + xy + 5$
   d. $C = x^2 y^2 - 3xy + y + 8$

2. For each of the following pairs of demand functions, determine the four marginal demands, the nature of the relationship between the two commodities, and the four partial elasticities of demand. Quantities are denoted by x and y and the corresponding prices are denoted by p and q, respectively.

   a. $x = 20 - 2p - q$
   $\quad y = 9 - p - 2q$

   b. $x = 15 - 2p + q$
   $\quad y = 16 + p - q$

   c. $x = 5 - 2p + q$
   $\quad y = 8 - 2p - 3q$

   d. $x = \dfrac{q}{p}$
   $\quad y = \dfrac{p^2}{q}$

   e. $x = \dfrac{4}{p^2 q}$
   $\quad y = \dfrac{16}{pq^2}$

   f. $x = \dfrac{4}{pq}$
   $\quad y = \dfrac{16}{pq}$

Answers to Odd-Numbered Problems

1. a. $\dfrac{\partial C}{\partial x} = 2x \ln (y + 10)$ c. $\dfrac{\partial C}{\partial x} = e^x + y$

$\dfrac{\partial C}{\partial y} = \dfrac{x^2}{y + 10}$ $\dfrac{\partial C}{\partial y} = e^y + x$

   b. $\dfrac{\partial C}{\partial x} = 3x^2 - y$ d. $\dfrac{\partial C}{\partial x} = 2xy^2 - 3y$

$\dfrac{\partial C}{\partial y} = 4y - x$ $\dfrac{\partial C}{\partial y} = 2x^2y - 3x + 1$

PRODUCTION FUNCTIONS

The production of most commodities requires the use of at least two factors of production, for example, labor, land, capital, materials, or machines. If the quantity z of a commodity is produced using the amounts x and y, respectively, of two factors of production, then the *production function*

$$z = f(x, y)$$

gives the amount of *output* z when the amounts x and y, respectively, of the *inputs* are used simultaneously. For such a representation to be economically meaningful, it is assumed that the amounts of the inputs can be varied without restriction, at least in the range of interest, and that the production function is continuous.

Marginal Productivity

If the production function is given by $z = f(x, y)$, then the partial derivative $\dfrac{\partial z}{\partial x}$ of z with respect to x (with y held constant) is the *marginal productivity of x* or the *marginal product of x*; the partial derivative $\dfrac{\partial z}{\partial y}$ of z with respect to y (with x held constant) is the *marginal productivity of y* or the *marginal product of y*. Note that the marginal productivity of either input is the rate of increase of the total product as that input is increased, assuming that the amount of the other input remains constant.

Marginal productivity with respect to either factor usually is positive for a considerable range, that is, as the amount of one input increases, with the amount of the other input held constant, the output also increases. However, as one input is increased with the other held constant, output usually increases at a decreasing rate until the point is reached at which there is no further increase in output and, in fact, a decrease in output occurs with additional inputs of the factor. This characteristic behavior of production functions is known as the *law of eventually diminishing marginal productivity*.

EXAMPLE

If the production function is given by

$$z = 4x^{3/4}y^{1/4}$$

then the marginal productivity of x is

$$\frac{\partial z}{\partial x} = 3x^{-1/4}y^{1/4}$$

and the marginal productivity of y is

$$\frac{\partial z}{\partial y} = x^{3/4} y^{-3/4}$$

Note that $\frac{\partial z}{\partial x}$ is always positive, but decreases as x increases; similarly, $\frac{\partial z}{\partial y}$ is always positive, but decreases as y increases.

EXAMPLE

If the production function is given by

$$z = 4xy - x^2 - 3y^2$$

then the marginal productivity of x is

$$\frac{\partial z}{\partial x} = 4y - 2x$$

and the marginal productivity of y is

$$\frac{\partial z}{\partial y} = 4x - 6y$$

Note that $\frac{\partial z}{\partial x} > 0$ for $x < 2y$, $\frac{\partial z}{\partial x} = 0$ for $x = 2y$, and $\frac{\partial z}{\partial x} < 0$ for $x > 2y$; similarly, $\frac{\partial z}{\partial y} > 0$ for $y < \frac{2}{3}x$, $\frac{\partial z}{\partial y} = 0$ for $y = \frac{2}{3}x$, and $\frac{\partial z}{\partial y} < 0$ for $y > \frac{2}{3}x$. Thus, for either x or y, the marginal productivity at first increases and then decreases as input increases.

EXAMPLE

If a production function is given by

$$z^2 + 4x^2 + 5y^2 - 12xy = 0$$

where z is the amount of output and x and y are the amounts of the inputs, then, using implicit differentiation,

$$\frac{\partial F}{\partial x} = 8x - 12y$$

$$\frac{\partial F}{\partial y} = 10y - 12x$$

$$\frac{\partial F}{\partial z} = 2z$$

The marginal productivity of x is

$$\frac{\partial z}{\partial x} = -\frac{\dfrac{\partial F}{\partial x}}{\dfrac{\partial F}{\partial z}} = -\frac{8x - 12y}{2z} = \frac{6y - 4x}{z}$$

and the marginal productivity of y is

$$\frac{\partial z}{\partial y} = -\frac{\dfrac{\partial F}{\partial y}}{\dfrac{\partial F}{\partial z}} = -\frac{10y - 12x}{2z} = \frac{6x - 5y}{z}$$

Since z is positive for any economically meaningful region of the production function, $\dfrac{\partial z}{\partial x}$ is positive for $x < \frac{3}{2}y$, zero for $x = \frac{3}{2}y$, and negative for $x > \frac{3}{2}y$; $\dfrac{\partial z}{\partial y}$ is positive for $y < \frac{2}{3}x$, zero for $y = \frac{2}{3}y$, and negative for $y > \frac{2}{3}x$.

For any analysis involving production functions, it is assumed that output is a homogeneous function of inputs. If the function $z = f(x, y)$ has the property that, for any constant λ,

$$f(\lambda x, \lambda y) = \lambda^n f(x, y)$$

then z is said to be *homogeneous of degree n*. If $n > 0$, the function is said to be *positively homogeneous*; if $n = 1$, the function is said to be *linear homogeneous*.

If $z = f(x, y)$ is positively homogeneous of degree n and the first-order partial derivatives exist, then it can be shown that

$$x\frac{\partial z}{\partial x} + y\frac{\partial z}{\partial y} = nf(x, y)$$

This relationship is known as *Euler's theorem*.

EXAMPLE

The function $z = f(x, y) = 3x^4 + 2x^2y^2 + 7y^4$ is homogeneous of degree 4, since

$$f(\lambda x, \lambda y) = 3\lambda^4 x^4 + 2\lambda^4 x^2 y^2 + 7\lambda^4 y^4$$
$$= \lambda^4 f(x, y)$$

Thus, according to Euler's theorem,

$$x\frac{\partial z}{\partial x} + y\frac{\partial z}{\partial y} = 4f(x, y)$$

which can be verified as follows:

$$x\frac{\partial z}{\partial x} + y\frac{\partial z}{\partial y} = x(12x^3 + 4xy^2) + y(4x^2y + 28y^3)$$
$$= 12x^4 + 8x^2y^2 + 28y^4$$
$$= 4f(x, y)$$

EXAMPLE

The function $z = f(x, y) = \dfrac{xy}{x^2 + y^2}$ is homogeneous of degree zero, since

$$f(\lambda x, \lambda y) = \frac{\lambda^2 xy}{\lambda^2(x^2 + y^2)}$$
$$= \lambda^0 f(x, y) = f(x, y)$$

Thus, according to Euler's theorem,

$$x\frac{\partial z}{\partial x} + y\frac{\partial z}{\partial y} = 0$$

which can be verified as follows:

$$x\frac{\partial z}{\partial x} + y\frac{\partial z}{\partial y} = x\frac{y(x^2 + y^2) - xy(2x)}{(x^2 + y^2)^2} + y\frac{x(x^2 + y^2) - xy(2y)}{(x^2 + y^2)^2}$$

$$= \frac{2xy(x^2 + y^2) - 2x^3y - 2xy^3}{(x^2 + y^2)^2}$$

$$= 0$$

Homogeneous Production Functions

In economic theory, production functions are frequently assumed to be linear homogeneous, because such functions have convenient properties. If a production function $z = f(x, y)$ is linear homogeneous, then according to Euler's theorem,

$$\underbrace{x\frac{\partial z}{\partial x}}_{\substack{\text{total due} \\ \text{to} \\ \text{factor } x}} + \underbrace{y\frac{\partial z}{\partial y}}_{\substack{\text{total due} \\ \text{to} \\ \text{factor } y}} = f(x, y)$$

That is, total production or output is equal to the product of the amount of one input and its marginal productivity plus the product of the amount of the other input and its marginal productivity. Thus the total product can be allocated to the two factors on the basis of their marginal productivities.

Euler's theorem plays an important part in the marginal-productivity theory of distribution. The basic assumptions of this theory are that each input is paid the value of its marginal productivity and that total output is just exhausted. As shown by Euler's theorem, these conditions are satisfied by linear homogeneous production functions; thus production functions are generally assumed to be linear homogeneous in analyses based on the marginal productivity theory of distribution. Note that if the production function is homogeneous of degree n and each input is allocated or paid the value of its marginal productivity, then total output exceeds payments for $n > 1$ and is less than payments for $n < 1$.

Constant Product Curves

The production function $z = f(x, y)$ is frequently studied by considering the family of curves

$$f(x, y) = \text{constant}$$

in the xy-plane. These curves, no two of which intersect, are called *constant product curves*, *equal product curves*, or *isoquants*. Each curve shows the combinations of factors x and y which result in a specified output. As discussed below, constant product curves are such that a decrease in the input of one factor is compensated for by an increase in the input of the other factor. The slope $\frac{dy}{dx}$ of the tangent at a point on an isoquant is the rate at which x must be substituted for y to maintain the level of output. The negative of this derivative $-\frac{dy}{dx}$ is defined as the *rate of technical substitution*.

Figure 3.2

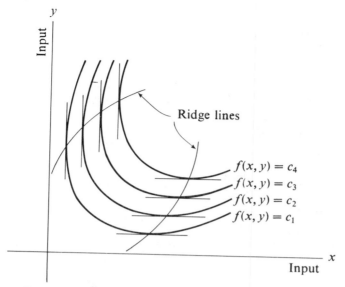

Equal product curves are of various shapes, depending on the nature of the production function, but in general they have negative slopes and are convex to the origin in the area of economic interest. However, there are some situations in which portions of the equal product curves have positive slopes, that is, there are some situations in which marginal productivity is diminishing and additional amounts of a factor of input result in decreased production. For example, if the two factors of production are land and labor, so many men might be employed (for a fixed amount of land) that they would interfere with each other and production would decrease. However, assuming the objective of profit maximization, portions of equal product curves having positive slopes would not be used in practice, since the given output could be obtained at less cost by a factor combination on a portion of the curve having negative slope. Thus, as shown in Figure 3.2, only the portions of the equal product curves lying between their respective vertical and horizontal tangents are economically relevant; the lines through these points of tangency are known as *ridge lines*. The firm would never operate above the upper ridge line or to the right of the lower ridge line, since this would require more input than necessary to produce a specified output.

The assumption that equal product curves are convex to the origin implies that the marginal significance of one factor with respect to the other factor decreases along an equal product curve—that is, as the amount of factor x that is used increases, the amount of factor y that can be given up in exchange for a further unit of factor x decreases, if the product remains constant; similarly, as the amount of factor y that is used increases, the amount of factor x that can be given up in exchange for a further unit of factor y decreases, if the product remains constant. If the marginal significance of a factor increased as the amount used increased, as would be the case for a concave equal product curve, then only that one factor should be used, since each unit of the factor would be progressively more worth purchasing. Thus, in practice, any portions of equal product curves for which marginal significance of the factors is increasing are not relevant.

If factors x and y are purchased in a perfectly competitive market at constant unit prices, then the total cost of production is given by

$$C = p_x x + p_y y + b$$

Figure 3.3

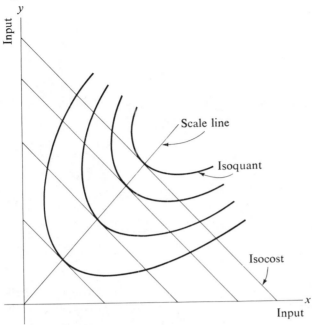

where p_x and p_y are the respective unit prices of x and y and b is the cost of the fixed inputs. *Isocost curves* give the combinations of input factors that can be purchased for a specified total cost; for the cost function given above, the isocost curves are represented by the family of lines

$$p_x x + p_y y + b = \text{constant}$$

The slopes of the isocost lines are equal to the negative of the input price ratio, since

$$y = -\frac{p_x}{p_y} x - \frac{b}{p_y} + \frac{\text{constant}}{p_y}$$

The greatest total output which can be produced for a specified total cost is given by the point of tangency of the corresponding isocost curve and an isoquant. Similarly, the lowest possible cost of producing a specified output is given by the point of tangency of the corresponding isoquant and an isocost curve. The curve connecting the points of tangency of the isocost curves and isoquants is known as the *expansion path* or *scale line*. This line gives the lowest-cost combinations of factors as output increases; the firm will thus always produce at some point on the scale line (see Figure 3.3). The expansion path, at all points of which the rate of technical substitution equals the fixed input-price ratio, is a straight line if the production function is homogeneous of any degree. A straight-line expansion path does not, however, imply a homogeneous production function.

Returns to Scale

Returns to scale describes the change in output with a proportionate increase in all inputs. If output increases by the same proportion as the inputs increase, then returns to scale are constant; if output increases by a greater proportion than inputs, returns to scale are increasing; if output increases by a smaller proportion than inputs,

Figure 3.4

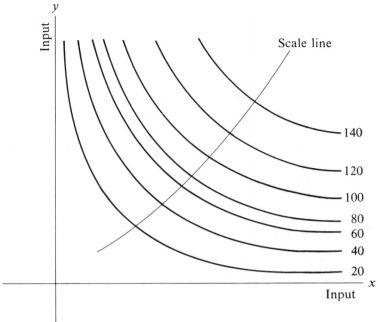

returns to scale are decreasing. Very frequently, there are increasing returns to scale for relatively small inputs (economies of scale), returns to scale are then constant for a range of inputs, and finally there are decreasing returns to scale for large inputs (diseconomies of scale).

Returns to scale are easily determined for homogeneous production functions. If a production function is homogeneous of degree n, returns to scale are increasing if $n > 1$, constant if $n = 1$, and decreasing if $n < 1$. In practice, a degree of homogeneity other than 1 is seldom assumed for a production function. If a set of equal product curves (not necessarily homogeneous) represent successive increases in production of a given amount, then returns to scale increase as output increases if the distance along the scale line between successive curves decreases; similarly, returns to scale decrease as output increases if the distance along the scale line between successive curves increases. Thus, in Figure 3.4, returns to scale increase from 20 to 80 units of production and decrease from 80 to 140 units of production.

Note that if the proportions of the amounts of the two factors of production vary, it is necessary to refer to *returns to outlay* rather than returns to scale, since the factors are not increased by the same scale.

UTILITY FUNCTIONS

In the theory of consumer behavior, the consumer is assumed to choose among the alternatives available to him in such a way that the satisfaction derived from consuming or using commodities is maximized. This implies that the consumer is aware of his alternatives and is capable of evaluating them. All relevant information concerning the satisfaction a consumer derives from various quantities of commodities is contained in his utility function.

The concept of utility is based not on some type of psychological satisfaction on the part of the consumer, but on his choice behavior. The assertion that a consumer derives more satisfaction or utility from A than from B means that he would choose A rather than B if A and B were presented as alternatives. In addition, the consumer is assumed to make consistent choices so that if A is preferred to B and B is preferred to C, then A is preferred to C.

Modern utility theory assumes only an ordinal utility scale; that is, for all pairs or alternatives A and B, the consumer is assumed to know whether he prefers A to B, prefers B to A, or is indifferent between them; he is not assumed capable of assigning numbers representing amounts of utility to alternatives.

A consumer's ranking (preference order) of commodities is expressed mathematically by his utility function. The utility function associates certain numbers (utilities) with various quantities of commodities consumed, but these numbers represent only a ranking or ordering of preferences. Thus if the utility of alternative A is 20 and the utility of alternative B is 5, then A is preferred to B but it is incorrect to say that A is preferred 4 times as strongly as B.

Consider the simple case in which the consumer's purchases are limited to two commodities and the utility function is

$$U = f(q_1, q_2)$$

where q_1 and q_2 are the quantities of the two commodities Q_1 and Q_2 which are consumed. It is assumed that $f(q_1, q_2)$ is continuous and has continuous first-order and second-order partial derivatives.

The utility function is with respect to consumption during a specified period of time, a period long enough for the desire for variety to be satisfied but not so long that tastes change. Utility is assumed to be derived from the consumption of commodities. By definition, a commodity is something of which the consumer would rather have more than less; otherwise a discommodity is involved. In reality, a commodity consumed in sufficiently large amounts may become a discommodity (for example, too much candy); the following discussion assumes that such a point of satiation has not been reached. Thus the partial derivatives of U with respect to q_1 and q_2, denoted f_1 and f_2, are positive.

Since the utility function is continuous, a given level of utility can be derived from an infinite number of combinations of q_1 and q_2. The locus of all combinations of quantities of commodities from which the consumer derives the same utility is an *indifference curve*. A collection of indifference curves corresponding to different levels of utility is an *indifference map*. (See Figure 3.5.) One and only one indifference curve passes through every point of the first quadrant; indifference curves corresponding to increasing levels of utility are farther from the origin. Note that indifference curves cannot intersect because this would imply that the same combination of q_1 and q_2 has different utilities.

Note that $U = f(q_1, q_2)$ can be represented by a utility surface in three dimensions. Each indifference curve represents the intersection of that surface and a plane parallel to the $q_1 q_2$-plane at a certain value of U. Note that the points on an indifference curve represent the various combinations of quantities of the commodities that have the same utility for the consumer and among which, therefore, he is indifferent.

The total differential of the utility function $U = f(q_1, q_2)$ is

$$dU = f_1 \, dq_1 + f_2 \, dq_2$$

where f_1 and f_2 are the partial derivatives of U with respect to q_1 and q_2, respectively. Since the change in utility along any indifference curve is zero by definition, $dU = 0$ and

$$f_1 \, dq_1 + f_2 \, dq_2 = 0$$

$$-\frac{dq_2}{dq_1} = \frac{f_1}{f_2}$$

Figure 3.5

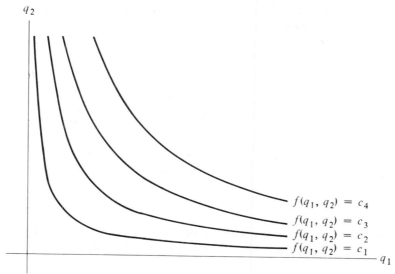

$f(q_1, q_2) = c_4$
$f(q_1, q_2) = c_3$
$f(q_1, q_2) = c_2$
$f(q_1, q_2) = c_1$

The slope of an indifference curve dq_2/dq_1 is the rate at which a consumer would be willing to substitute Q_1 for Q_2 or Q_2 for Q_1 to maintain a given level of utility. The negative of the slope—dq_2/dq_1 is the *rate of commodity substitution or marginal rate of substitution* of Q_1 for Q_2 or Q_2 for Q_1 and equals the ratio of the partial derivatives of the utility function. Note that the rate of commodity substitution at a point on an indifference curve is the same for movements in either direction, so the verbal definition can be in terms of substituting Q_1 for Q_2 or Q_2 for Q_1.

The partial derivatives f_1 and f_2 are said to be marginal utilities of the commodities Q_1 and Q_2. The magnitudes of the marginal utilities have no meaning when the utility function is ordinal, but their signs and ratios are meaningful. Note that if the marginal utilities are positive, an increase in the quantity consumed of one commodity with no change in the quantity consumed of the other commodity will move the consumer to a higher indifference curve.

Note that $U = f(q_1, q_2)$ can be represented by a utility surface in three dimensions. Each indifference curve represents the intersection of that surface and a plane parallel to the $q_1 q_2$-plane at a certain level of U. A consumer's indifference curves are thus actually contour lines (iso-utility lines) of his utility surface. Indifference curves are the loci of commodity combinations of equal utility, just as the contour lines on an ordinary geographic map are loci of combinations of latitude and longitude of equal height above sea level.

However, note that there is one important difference. A contour line on a map is labeled by a number indicating the height of its points above sea level. No similar designation can be made for an indifference curve, because indifference curves indicate preferences among choices but not numerical magnitudes of utility. This property has the following geometric implications:

1. Indifference curves can be inferred from a consumer's utility surface, but an indifference map does not provide sufficient information to draw the utility surface.
2. Above any utility curve the utility surface is level. The surface is higher for higher indifference curves, but the actual height of the utility surface above any indifference curve is not specified.

3. Thus, in general, any of an infinite number of utility surfaces is consistent with a given indifference map; that is, all of the surfaces in an infinite set give the same indifference map.

Indifference Curves for Risk and Rate of Return

Indifference curves are useful, for example, for representing trade-offs between risk and rate of return in choosing among alternative investments. A rational, risk-averse, wealth-seeking investor selects investments that minimize risk at any given level of expected return and is willing to accept some increase in risk to obtain higher expected returns. Examples of indifference curves for such an investor are shown in Figure 3.6. The investor's utility is equal all along each curve. For example, the investor obtains equal expected utility from the investments A, B, and D, which are all on the same indifference curve, although their expected returns and risks differ considerably.

An infinite number of indifference curves could be drawn for this risk-averse investor; they would all be similar in shape and would have the following characteristics:

1. Higher indifference curves represent more investor satisfaction; that is, $U_6 > U_5 > U_4 > U_3 > U_2 > U_1$, because the investor likes higher expected return and dislikes higher risk.
2. All indifference curves slope upward, because the investor requires higher expected returns as an inducement to assume larger risks, as exemplified by his indifference among investments A, B, and D. Note that investment A, which involves no risk, is referred to as the *certainty equivalent* of investments B and D.
3. The indifference curves grow steeper at higher levels of risk, which reflects the investor's diminishing willingness to assume risk as returns become higher.

Figure 3.6

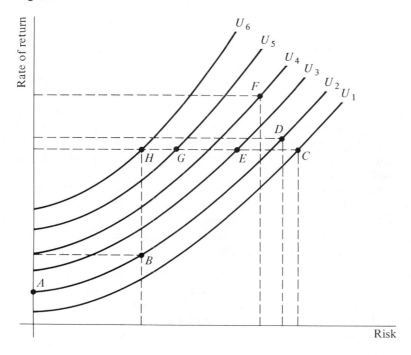

Note that Figure 3.6 implies that the investor has the following preferences:
$$U(H) > U(G) > U(F) > U(E) > U(A) = U(B) = U(D) > U(C).$$

PROBLEMS

1. For each of the following production functions, find the marginal productivities. Output is denoted by z and the inputs are denoted by x and y.

a. $z = 25 - \dfrac{1}{x} - \dfrac{1}{y}$ at $x = 1$, $y = 1$

b. $z = 5xy - 2x^2 - 2y^2$ at $x = 1$, $y = 1$

c. $16z^2 - z - 80 + 4(x - 5)^2 + 2(y - 4)^2 = 0$

d. $6z^3 - z^2 - 6x - 24y + x^2 + 4y^2 + 50 = 0$

2. The Cobb-Douglas production function for the economy as a whole is given by

$$z = ax^b y^c$$

where z is total product, x is quantity of labor, y is quantity of capital, and a, b, and c are constants. It is frequently assumed that $b + c = 1$. Is this function homogeneous and, if so, of what degree?

3. For each of the following production functions, determine the degree of homogeneity and the nature of the returns to scale. Output is denoted by z and the inputs are denoted by x and y, respectively.

a. $z = 3x^3 + 5xy^2 + y^3$ 　　　　c. $z = 25y^6 - x^2 y^4$

b. $z = \dfrac{14}{x} - \dfrac{20}{y}$ 　　　　d. $z = \dfrac{3}{x^2} + \dfrac{25}{xy} + \dfrac{6}{y^2}$

4. In addition to the property known as Euler's theorem, linear homogeneous functions have the following properties: If $z = f(x, y)$ is a linear homogeneous function, then

$$\begin{cases} \dfrac{z}{x} = g_1\left(\dfrac{y}{x}\right) & \text{that is, } \dfrac{z}{x} \text{ is a function of } \dfrac{y}{x} \\[2ex] \dfrac{z}{y} = g_2\left(\dfrac{x}{y}\right) & \text{that is, } \dfrac{z}{y} \text{ is a function of } \dfrac{x}{y} \\[2ex] \dfrac{\partial z}{\partial x} = h_1\left(\dfrac{y}{x}\right) & \text{that is, } \dfrac{\partial z}{\partial x} \text{ is a function of } \dfrac{y}{x} \\[2ex] \dfrac{\partial z}{\partial y} = h_2\left(\dfrac{x}{y}\right) & \text{that is, } \dfrac{\partial z}{\partial y} \text{ is a function of } \dfrac{x}{y} \\[2ex] \dfrac{\partial^2 z}{\partial x^2} = -\dfrac{y}{x} \cdot \dfrac{\partial^2 z}{\partial x \, \partial y} \\[2ex] \dfrac{\partial^2 z}{\partial y^2} = -\dfrac{x}{y} \cdot \dfrac{\partial^2 z}{\partial x \, \partial y} \end{cases}$$

Determine whether each of the following functions is homogeneous; for homogeneous functions, determine the degree and demonstrate Euler's theorem; for linear homogeneous functions, also demonstrate the other three properties given above.

a. $z = 3x^2 + 4xy + 15y^3$ 　　　　c. $z = 3e^x + 3e^y$

b. $z = 4x^3 + x^2 y - 3xy^2 - 7y^3$ 　　　　d. $z = 6 \ln 3^{-2x} - \ln 4^{-5y}$

e. $z = \dfrac{x^4 + 3x^2y^2 + xy^3 + 6y^4}{x^3}$

f. $z = 3x \ln 5^{x/y} - 9y \ln 8^{y/x}$

g. $z = \dfrac{x^2y + y^3}{x^6}$

h. $z = \dfrac{x^2 + 3xy + y^2}{y^2}$

i. $z = 4x^2e^y + 3y^2e^x$

j. $z = 3x^2 \ln a^{1/y^2} - 5y^3 \ln b^{1/y^3}$

k. $z = \dfrac{x^2 + xy}{3y}$

l. $z = 3x^2y + 4xy^2 + y^3 + 10$

m. $z = \dfrac{xy}{x + y}$

n. $z = xy - \ln xy$

5. If a consumer's utility function is given by $U = q_1 q_2^2$ and the consumer purchases 4 units of Q_1 and 5 units of Q_2, a. what quantity of Q_1 must he purchase to maintain the same level of utility if his purchase of Q_2 increases to 6 units? b. What quantity of Q_2 must he purchase to maintain the same level of utility if his purchase of Q_1 increases to 6 units? c. What quantity of Q_1 must he purchase to maintain the same level of utility if his purchase of Q_2 decreases to 4 units? d. What quantity of Q_2 must he purchase to maintain the same level of utility if his purchase of Q_1 decreases to 2 units?

6. Find the marginal utilities for each of the following utility functions. Utility is denoted by U and the amounts of the two commodities consumed are denoted by q_1 and q_2, respectively.
   a. $U = q_1^3 q_2$
   b. $U = q_1 q_2 + q_1^2$

Answers to Odd-Numbered Problems

1. a. $\dfrac{\partial z}{\partial x} = 1,\ \dfrac{\partial z}{\partial y} = 1$

   b. $\dfrac{\partial z}{\partial x} = 1,\ \dfrac{\partial z}{\partial y} = 1$

   c. $\dfrac{\partial z}{\partial x} = -\dfrac{8(x - 5)}{32z - 1}$

   $\dfrac{\partial z}{\partial y} = -\dfrac{4(y - 4)}{32z - 1}$

   d. $\dfrac{\partial z}{\partial x} = -\dfrac{x - 3}{z(9z - 1)}$

   $\dfrac{\partial z}{\partial y} = -\dfrac{4(y - 3)}{z(9z - 1)}$

3. a. degree 3, increasing returns to scale
   b. degree -1, decreasing returns to scale
   c. degree 6, increasing returns to scale
   d. degree -2, decreasing returns to scale

5. a. $q_1 = 25/9$
   b. $q_2 = \dfrac{5\sqrt{6}}{3}$
   c. $q_1 = 25/4$
   d. $q_2 = 5\sqrt{2}$

3.4 Maxima and Minima of Functions of Two Variables

As discussed in Section 2.11, the first and second derivatives of a function of one variable can be used to determine its maxima and minima; similarly, the first-order and second-order partial derivatives can be used to determine maxima and minima of a function of two variables. The discussion below concerns functions of two independent variables; maxima and minima of functions of n variables are discussed in Chapter 8. The procedure becomes more complicated as the number of variables increases, but the definitions and methods are essentially the same.

A function $f(x, y)$ of two independent variables is said to have a local maximum (or minimum) value for $x = a$, $y = b$, if $f(a, b)$ is greater (or less) than $f(x, y)$ for all values of x and y close to $x = a$, $y = b$. If $f(x, y)$ has a maximum (or minimum) value at $x = a$, $y = b$, it follows that the function $f(x, b)$ has a maximum (or minimum) at $x = a$ and the function $f(a, y)$ has a maximum (or minimum) at $y = b$. Thus, for the function $f(x, y)$ to have a maximum (or minimum) at $x = a$, $y = b$, it is necessary that

$$\frac{\partial}{\partial x} f(x, y) \bigg|_{x=a, y=b} = 0$$

$$\frac{\partial}{\partial y} f(x, y) \bigg|_{x=a, y=b} = 0$$

These two conditions are used to determine the critical points; the procedure below is then used to determine whether the critical points are in fact local maxima or minima.

If
$$\begin{cases} \dfrac{\partial}{\partial x} f(x, y) \bigg|_{x=a, y=b} = 0 \\[2em] \dfrac{\partial}{\partial y} f(x, y) \bigg|_{x=a, y=b} = 0 \end{cases}$$

and

$$\Delta = \left(\frac{\partial^2}{\partial x^2} f(x, y) \bigg|_{x=a, y=b} \right) \left(\frac{\partial^2}{\partial y^2} f(x, y) \bigg|_{x=a, y=b} \right) - \left(\frac{\partial^2}{\partial x \, \partial y} f(x, y) \bigg|_{x=a, y=b} \right)^2$$

then
$$\begin{cases} \Delta > 0 \Rightarrow \begin{cases} \text{maximum at } x = a, y = b, \text{ if } \dfrac{\partial^2}{\partial x^2} f(x, y) < 0 \text{ and } \dfrac{\partial^2}{\partial y^2} f(x, y) < 0 \\[1.5em] \text{minimum at } x = a, y = b, \text{ if } \dfrac{\partial^2}{\partial x^2} f(x, y) > 0 \text{ and } \dfrac{\partial^2}{\partial y^2} f(x, y) > 0 \end{cases} \\[3em] \Delta < 0 \Rightarrow \text{neither maximum nor minimum at } x = a, y = b, \text{ but a saddle point at} \\ \qquad x = a, y = b \\[0.5em] \Delta = 0 \Rightarrow \text{test fails; function must be investigated near } x = a, y = b \end{cases}$$

These conditions can be stated in more concise notation as follows:

necessary condition for a critical point: $\quad f_x = 0, f_y = 0$

determination of local maxima or minima:

$$f_{xx} f_{yy} - f_{xy}^2 > 0 \Rightarrow \begin{cases} \text{maximum if } f_{xx} < 0, f_{yy} < 0 \\ \text{minimum if } f_{xx} > 0, f_{yy} > 0 \end{cases}$$

$$f_{xx} f_{yy} - f_{xy}^2 < 0 \Rightarrow \text{saddle point}$$

$$f_{xx} f_{yy} - f_{xy}^2 = 0 \Rightarrow \text{test fails and the function must be investigated near the critical point}$$

where all partial derivatives are evaluated for the critical point.

Figure 3.7

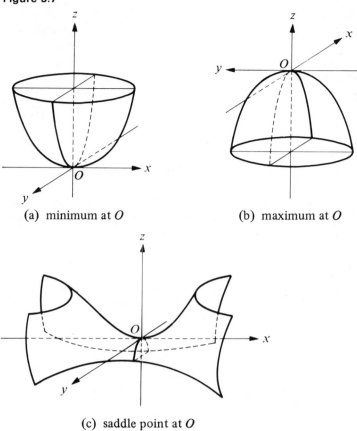

(a) minimum at O (b) maximum at O

(c) saddle point at O

Note that the above procedure is used to identify local maxima and minima. To determine global maxima or minima it is necessary not only to compare the values of the local maxima or minima, but also to determine the values of the function at the limits of its range, if its range is limited. The procedure for determining global maxima and minima for functions of two variables is thus analogous to procedure for functions of one variable.

Examples of functions having at the origin (a) a minimum, (b) a maximum, and (c) a saddle point are illustrated in Figure 3.7. Note that at a saddle point a function has a minimum with respect to one variable and a maximum with respect to the other variable. For example, in Figure 3.7(c) the origin looks like a maximum to a person traveling along the surface in the yz-plane but like a minimum to a person traveling in the xz-plane.

EXAMPLE

Examine the function

$$f(x, y) = x^2 + xy + y^2 - 3x + 2$$

for maximum and minimum values.

$$\frac{\partial f}{\partial x} = 2x + y - 3$$

$$\frac{\partial f}{\partial y} = x + 2y$$

Setting the partial derivatives equal to zero gives the linear equations

$$2x + y = 3$$
$$x + 2y = 0$$

Multiplying the second equation by 2 and then subtracting it from the first equation,

$$3y = -3$$

Thus

$$y = -1, x = 2$$

so $(2, -1)$ is a critical point and may be a maximum or minimum point.

$$\frac{\partial^2 f}{\partial x^2} = 2$$

$$\frac{\partial^2 f}{\partial y^2} = 2$$

$$\frac{\partial^2 f}{\partial x \, \partial y} = 1$$

$$\Delta = \frac{\partial^2 f}{\partial x^2} + \frac{\partial^2 f}{\partial y^2} - \left(\frac{\partial^2 f}{\partial x \, \partial y} \right)^2 = (2)(2) - 1 = 3 > 0 \qquad \text{for all } x \text{ and } y$$

and

$$\frac{\partial^2 f}{\partial x^2} = 2 > 0 \qquad \frac{\partial^2 f}{\partial y^2} = 2 > 0$$

Thus $f(x, y)$ has a minimum at $(2, -1)$.

EXAMPLE

Examine the function

$$f(x, y) = xy - \ln (x^2 + y^2)$$

for maximum and minimum values.

$$\frac{\partial f}{\partial x} = y - \frac{2x}{x^2 + y^2}$$

$$\frac{\partial f}{\partial y} = x - \frac{2y}{x^2 + y^2}$$

Set $\dfrac{\partial f}{\partial x} = 0$ and $\dfrac{\partial f}{\partial y} = 0$. Then

$$x^2 y + y^3 - 2x = 0$$
$$x^3 + xy^2 - 2y = 0$$

Multiplying the first equation by x and the second equation by y and subtracting,

$$-2x^2 + 2y^2 = 0$$

$$x^2 = y^2$$

Substituting for x^2 in the first equation and for y^2 in the second equation, $y^3 = x$ and $x^3 = y$, so $(1, 1)$ and $(-1, -1)$ may be maximum or minimum points.

$$\frac{\partial^2 f}{\partial x^2} = -\frac{2(x^2 + y^2) - 2x(2x)}{(x^2 + y^2)^2} = -\frac{2(y^2 - x^2)}{(x^2 + y^2)^2}$$

$$\frac{\partial^2 f}{\partial y^2} = -\frac{2(x^2 + y^2) - 2y(2y)}{(x^2 + y^2)^2} = -\frac{2(x^2 - y^2)}{(x^2 + y^2)^2}$$

$$\frac{\partial f}{\partial x \, \partial y} = 1 + \frac{(2x)(2y)}{(x^2 + y^2)^2} = 1 + \frac{4xy}{(x^2 + y^2)^2}$$

$$\left.\frac{\partial^2 f}{\partial x^2}\right|_{x=y=1} = \left.\frac{\partial^2 f}{\partial x^2}\right|_{x=y=-1} = 0$$

$$\left.\frac{\partial^2 f}{\partial y^2}\right|_{x=y=1} = \left.\frac{\partial^2 f}{\partial y^2}\right|_{x=y=-1} = 0$$

$$\left.\frac{\partial^2 f}{\partial x \, \partial y}\right|_{x=y=1} = \left.\frac{\partial^2 f}{\partial x \, \partial y}\right|_{x=y=-1} = 1 + 1 = 2$$

$$\Delta = (0)(0) - (2)^2 = -4 < 0 \quad \text{at each of the points}$$

Thus $f(x, y)$ has no maximum or minimum, but does have saddle points at $(1, 1)$ and $(-1, -1)$.

EXAMPLE

Examine the function

$$f(x, y) = 1 + x^2 - y^2$$

for maximum and minimum values.

$$\frac{\partial f}{\partial x} = 2x$$

$$\frac{\partial f}{\partial y} = -2y$$

Setting $\dfrac{\partial f}{\partial x} = 0$ and $\dfrac{\partial f}{\partial y} = 0$,

$$2x = 0$$
$$-2y = 0$$

so $(0, 0)$ may be a maximum or minimum point.

$$\frac{\partial^2 f}{\partial x^2} = 2$$

$$\frac{\partial^2 f}{\partial y^2} = -2$$

$$\frac{\partial^2 f}{\partial x \, \partial y} = 0$$

$$\Delta = (2)(-2) - 0 = -4 < 0$$

Thus $f(x, y)$ has neither a maximum nor a minimum at $(0, 0)$, but does have a saddle point at $(0, 0)$.

EXAMPLE

Examine the function

$$f(x, y) = \sin x + \sin y + \sin (x + y) \qquad \text{where } 0 \le x \le \pi/2 \text{ and } 0 \le y \le \pi/2$$

for maximum and minimum values.

$$\frac{\partial f}{\partial x} = \cos x + \cos (x + y)$$

$$\frac{\partial f}{\partial y} = \cos y + \cos (x + y)$$

If $\dfrac{\partial f}{\partial x} = \dfrac{\partial f}{\partial y} = 0$, $\cos x = \cos y = -\cos (x + y)$, so $(\pi/3, \pi/3)$ may be a maximum or minimum point.

$$\frac{\partial^2 f}{\partial x^2} = -\sin x - \sin (x + y)$$

$$\frac{\partial^2 f}{\partial y^2} = -\sin y - \sin (x + y)$$

$$\frac{\partial^2 f}{\partial x\, \partial y} = -\sin (x + y)$$

$$\frac{\partial^2 f}{\partial x^2}\bigg|_{x=y=\pi/3} = -\frac{\sqrt{3}}{2} - \frac{\sqrt{3}}{2} = -\sqrt{3}$$

$$\frac{\partial^2 f}{\partial y^2}\bigg|_{x=y=\pi/3} = -\frac{\sqrt{3}}{2} - \frac{\sqrt{3}}{2} = -\sqrt{3}$$

$$\frac{\partial^2 f}{\partial x\, \partial y}\bigg|_{x=y=\pi/3} = -\frac{\sqrt{3}}{2}$$

$$\Delta = (-\sqrt{3})(-\sqrt{3}) - \left(-\frac{\sqrt{3}}{2}\right)^2$$

$$= 3 - \tfrac{3}{4} = \tfrac{9}{4} > 0$$

$$\frac{\partial^2 f}{\partial x^2} < 0 \qquad \text{and} \qquad \frac{\partial^2 f}{\partial y^2} < 0$$

Thus $f(x, y)$ has a maximum for $x = y = \pi/3$.

EXAMPLE

Examine the function

$$f(x, y) = 25 + (x - y)^4 + (y - 1)^4$$

for maximum and minimum values.

Using the chain rule,

$$\frac{\partial f}{\partial x} = 4(x - y)^3$$

$$\frac{\partial f}{\partial y} = -4(x - y)^3 + 4(y - 1)^3$$

Setting $\dfrac{\partial f}{\partial x} = 0$ and $\dfrac{\partial f}{\partial y} = 0$,

$$(x - y)^3 = 0 \qquad \text{if } x = y$$
$$(x - y)^3 = (y - 1)^3 \qquad \text{if } x = y = 1$$

so $(1, 1)$ may be a maximum or minimum point.

$$\frac{\partial^2 f}{\partial x^2} = 12(x - y)^2$$

$$\frac{\partial^2 f}{\partial y^2} = 12(x - y)^2 + 12(y - 1)^2$$

$$\frac{\partial^2 f}{\partial x \, \partial y} = -12(x - y)^2$$

$$\left. \frac{\partial^2 f}{\partial x^2} \right|_{x=y=1} = 0$$

$$\left. \frac{\partial^2 f}{\partial y^2} \right|_{x=y=1} = 0$$

$$\left. \frac{\partial^2 f}{\partial x \, \partial y} \right|_{x=y=1} = 0$$

so $\Delta = 0$ and $f(x, y)$ must be examined further for maximum or minimum values. Suppose h and k are arbitrarily small numbers such that $h^2 + k^2 > 0$. Then

$$f(1 + h, 1 + k) - f(1, 1) = 25 + [(1 + h) - (1 + k)]^4 + (1 + k - 1)^4 - 25$$
$$= (h - k)^4 + k^4$$

But $(h - k)^4 + k^4 > 0$ for all nonzero h and k, so $f(1 + h, 1 + k) > f(1, 1)$ for all h and k, and thus $f(x, y)$ has a minimum at $(1, 1)$.

EXAMPLE

Examine the function

$$f(x, y) = x^2 - 6xy + 9y^2 + 3x - 10$$

for maximum and minimum values.

$$\frac{\partial f}{\partial x} = 2x - 6y + 3$$

$$\frac{\partial f}{\partial y} = -6x + 18y$$

Setting $\dfrac{\partial f}{\partial x} = 0$ and $\dfrac{\partial f}{\partial y} = 0$,

$$2x - 6y = -3$$
$$-2x + 6y = 0$$

These equations are inconsistent and have no simultaneous solution, so $f(x, y)$ has no maximum or minimum or saddle point

EXAMPLE

If the demand functions for x and y are

$$p = 36 - 3x \quad \text{and} \quad q = 40 - 5y$$

and the joint-cost function is

$$C = x^2 + 2xy + 3y^2$$

determine the quantities and prices that maximize profit for the monopolist and find the maximum profit.

$$P = px + qy - C$$
$$= 36x - 3x^2 + 40y - 5y^2 - x^2 - 2xy - 3y^2$$
$$= -4x^2 - 8y^2 - 2xy + 36x + 40y$$

$$\frac{\partial P}{\partial x} = -8x - 2y + 36$$

$$\frac{\partial P}{\partial y} = -16y - 2x + 40$$

Setting $\dfrac{\partial P}{\partial x} = 0$ and $\dfrac{\partial P}{\partial y} = 0$,

$$4x + y = 18$$
$$x + 8y = 20$$

Multiplying the second equation by 4 and subtracting the first equation from it,

$$31y = 62$$
$$y = 2$$
$$x = 4$$

so P may have a maximum or minimum at $(4, 2)$

$$\frac{\partial^2 P}{\partial x^2} = -8$$

$$\frac{\partial^2 P}{\partial y^2} = -16$$

$$\frac{\partial^2 P}{\partial x \, \partial y} = -2$$

$$\Delta = (-8)(-16) - (-2)^2 = 124 > 0$$

$$\frac{\partial^2 P}{\partial x^2} < 0 \quad \text{and} \quad \frac{\partial^2 P}{\partial y^2} < 0,$$

so P has a maximum value for $x = 4$, $y = 2$. If $x = 4$, $y = 2$, then $p = 24$, $q = 30$, and $C = 44$. Thus $P_{\text{max}} = (24)(4) + (30)(2) - 44 = 112$.

EXAMPLE

Suppose the production function is

$$16z = 65 - 2(x - 5)^2 - 4(y - 4)^2$$

the unit prices of the inputs x and y (under pure competition) are 8 and 4, respectively, and the unit price of the output is 32; determine the maximum profit.

$$P = 32z - 8x - 4y$$
$$= 130 - 4(x - 5)^2 - 8(y - 4)^2 - 8x - 4y$$

Setting $\dfrac{\partial P}{\partial x} = 0$ and $\dfrac{\partial P}{\partial y} = 0$,

$$\frac{\partial P}{\partial x} = -8(x - 5) - 8 = -8x + 32$$

$$\frac{\partial P}{\partial y} = -16(y - 4) - 4 = -16y + 60$$

$$\left. \begin{array}{c} 8x = 32 \\ x = 4 \\ 16y = 60 \\ y = \frac{15}{4} \end{array} \right\} \text{ so } P \text{ may have a maximum or minimum at } (4, \tfrac{15}{4})$$

$$\frac{\partial^2 P}{\partial x^2} = -8$$

$$\frac{\partial^2 P}{\partial y^2} = -16$$

$$\frac{\partial^2 P}{\partial x \, \partial y} = 0$$

$$\Delta = (-8)(-16) - 0 = 128 > 0$$

$$\frac{\partial^2 P}{\partial x^2} < 0 \quad \text{and} \quad \frac{\partial^2 P}{\partial y^2} < 0,$$

so P has a maximum value for $x = 4$, $y = \frac{15}{4}$ and $P_{\max} = 78\frac{1}{2}$.

EXAMPLE

In simple bivariate regression analysis, the model involves the assumption of a linear relationship between a predicted variable y and an explanatory variable x and disturbance term u. For a sample of n observations of x and y, the model is

$$y_i = \alpha + \beta x_i + u_i \qquad i = 1, 2, \ldots, n$$

and the problem is to obtain estimates of α and β. These estimates are customarily obtained using the least squares principle. Let $\hat{\alpha}$ and $\hat{\beta}$ denote estimates of α and β. Then $y_i = \hat{\alpha} + \hat{\beta}x_i + e_i$ where e_i denotes the ith residual $y_i - \hat{\alpha} - \hat{\beta}x_i$. Using least squares, the sum of the squared residuals

$$\sum_{i=1}^{n} e_i^2 = \sum_{i=1}^{n} (y_i - \hat{\alpha} - \hat{\beta}x_i)^2$$

is minimized. Differentiating this sum of squares partially with respect to $\hat{\alpha}$ and $\hat{\beta}$,

$$\frac{\partial}{\partial \hat{\alpha}} \left(\sum_{i=1}^{n} e_i^2 \right) = -2 \sum_{i=1}^{n} (y_i - \hat{\alpha} - \hat{\beta}x_i) = -2 \left[n\hat{\alpha}_i + \sum_{i=1}^{n} y_i - \hat{\beta} \sum_{i=1}^{n} x_i \right]$$

$$\frac{\partial}{\partial \hat{\beta}} \left(\sum_{i=1}^{n} e_i^2 \right) = -2 \sum_{i=1}^{n} x_i(y_i - \hat{\alpha} - \hat{\beta}x_i) = -2 \left[\sum_{i=1}^{n} x_i y_i - \hat{\alpha} \sum_{i=1}^{n} x_i - \hat{\beta} \sum_{i=1}^{n} x_i^2 \right]$$

Equating the partial derivatives to zero,

$$\sum_{i=1}^{n} y_i - n\hat{\alpha} - \hat{\beta} \sum_{i=1}^{n} x_i = 0$$

$$\sum_{i=1}^{n} x_i y_i - \hat{\alpha} \sum_{i=1}^{n} x_i - \hat{\beta} \sum_{i=1}^{n} x_i^2 = 0$$

Multiplying the first equation by $\sum_{i=1}^{n} x_i$ and the second equation by n and solving the equations simultaneously,

$$\hat{\beta} = \frac{n \sum_{i=1}^{n} x_i y_i - \left(\sum_{i=1}^{n} x_i\right)\left(\sum_{i=1}^{n} y_i\right)}{n \sum_{i=1}^{n} x_i^2 - \left(\sum_{i=1}^{n} x_i\right)^2}$$

$$\hat{\alpha} = \frac{\sum_{i=1}^{n} y_i - \hat{\beta} \sum_{i=1}^{n} x_i}{n}$$

and $\hat{\alpha}$ and $\hat{\beta}$ are the least squares extimates for the regression coefficients α and β, respectively.

To show that this solution minimizes $\sum_{i=1}^{n} e_i^2$, the second-order condition for a minimum must be checked.

$$\frac{\partial^2}{\partial \hat{\alpha}^2}\left(\sum_{i=1}^{n} e_i^2\right) = 2n$$

$$\frac{\partial^2}{\partial \hat{\beta}^2}\left(\sum_{i=1}^{n} e_i^2\right) = 2 \sum_{i=1}^{n} x_i^2$$

$$\frac{\partial^2}{\partial \hat{\alpha}\, \partial \hat{\beta}}\left(\sum_{i=1}^{n} e_i^2\right) = 2 \sum_{i=1}^{n} x_i$$

$\Delta = (2n)(2 \sum_{i=1}^{n} x_i^2) - (2 \sum_{i=1}^{n} x_i)^2 > 0$, since $n \sum_{i=1}^{n} x_i^2 - (\sum_{i=1}^{n} x_i)^2 > 0$ and

$$\frac{\partial^2}{\partial \hat{\alpha}^2}\left(\sum_{i=1}^{n} e_i^2\right) > 0 \qquad \frac{\partial^2}{\partial \hat{\beta}^2}\left(\sum_{i=1}^{n} e_i^2\right) > 0$$

Thus $\hat{\alpha}$, $\hat{\beta}$ minimize $\sum_{i=1}^{n} e_i^2$ and are the least squares estimators of α and β.

EXAMPLE

Suppose a flour processing company has discovered that its machines are giving excess fill. In planning its servicing schedule for the machines, the company is interested in the relationship between time since the last servicing and amount of excess fill. A random sample of 10 bags of flour was obtained from the stockroom, excess fill was measured, which machine had been used was determined (from a code on the bag), and the time since its last servicing was noted. The data obtained are given in Table 3.1.

Table 3.1

Excess Weight (grams)	Time Since Servicing (days)
15	2
23	6
20	5
17	4
19	3
15	2
15	1
10	0
16	8
30	9

The least squares regression of y, excess weight, on x, time since servicing, is obtained as follows:

$$\tilde{y}_i = \hat{\alpha} + \hat{\beta} x_i$$

where

$$\hat{\beta} = \frac{n \sum_{i=1}^{n} x_i y_i - (\sum_{i=1}^{n} x_i)(\sum_{i=1}^{n} y_i)}{n \sum_{i=1}^{n} x_i^2 - (\sum_{i=1}^{n} x_i)^2}$$

$$= \frac{(10)(836) - (40)(180)}{(10)(240) - (40)^2} = 1.45$$

and

$$\hat{\alpha} = \frac{\sum_{i=1}^{n} y_i - \sum_{i=1}^{n} x_i}{n}$$

$$= \frac{180 - (1.45)(40)}{10} = 12.2$$

and the least squares regression of y on x is given by

$$\tilde{y}_i = 12.2 + 1.45 x_i$$

EXAMPLE

A manufacturer has a demand of D units per time period T. The storage cost per period per unit is c_2 dollars, the shortage cost is c_3 dollars per unit short per period, and it costs c_1 dollars each time a production run is started (setup cost). Assuming that production orders are filled with no delay and that demand is at a uniform rate, determine the frequency with which production should be scheduled and the quantity which should be produced in each run in order to minimize the total per period inventory cost C. In Figure 3.8, $t = $ interval between production orders, $q = $ production quantity, $z = $ planned inventory at completion of a production run, $t_1 = $ time (during cycle) when stock is on hand, and $t_2 = $ time (during cycle) when no stock is on hand. Note that shortages are assumed to be backlogged; that is, the orders are not lost.

Figure 3.8

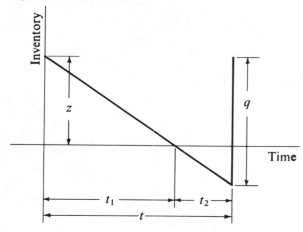

Note that $\dfrac{t_1}{t} = \dfrac{z}{q}$, $\dfrac{t_2}{t} = \dfrac{q-z}{q}$, and $\dfrac{t}{T} = \dfrac{q}{D}$.

setup cost: c_1

carrying cost per run: $\dfrac{c_2 t_1 z}{2} = \dfrac{c_2 t z^2}{2q} = \dfrac{c_2 T z^2}{2D}$

shortage cost per run: $\dfrac{c_3 t_2 (q-z)}{2} = \dfrac{c_3 t(q-z)^2}{2q} = \dfrac{c_3 T(q-z)^2}{2D}$

since the number of runs per period is $\dfrac{D}{q}$, the total inventory cost per period is

$$C = \frac{c_1 D}{q} + \frac{c_2 T z^2}{2q} + \frac{c_3 T(q-z)^2}{2q}$$

and, since C is a function of both q and z, partial derivatives must be obtained and set equal to zero to determine a minimum

$$\frac{\partial C}{\partial z} = \frac{c_2 Tz}{q} - \frac{c_3 T(q-z)}{q}$$

If $\dfrac{\partial C}{\partial z} = 0$,

$$c_2 Tz = c_3 T(q-z)$$

$$z = \frac{c_3 q}{c_2 + c_3}$$

$$\frac{\partial C}{\partial q} = \frac{4qc_3 T(q-z) - 2c_3 T(q-z)^2}{4q^2}$$

$$= \frac{c_3 T(q-z)}{q} - \frac{c_3 T(q-z)^2}{2q^2}$$

$$= -\frac{c_1 D}{q^2} - \frac{c_2 T z^2}{2q^2} + \frac{c_3 T}{2} - \frac{c_3 T z^2}{2q^2}$$

$$= -\frac{c_1 D}{q^2} - \frac{c_2 T z^2}{2q^2} + \frac{c_3 T(q^2 - z^2)}{2q^2}$$

If $\dfrac{\partial C}{\partial q} = 0$,

$$c_3 T(q^2 - z^2) = 2c_1 D + c_2 T z^2$$

$$q^2 = \frac{2c_1 D + c_2 T z^2 + c_3 T z^2}{c_3 T}$$

$$= \frac{2c_1 D}{c_3 T} + \frac{c_2 + c_3}{c_3} z^2$$

Substituting $z = \dfrac{c_3 q}{c_2 + c_3}$,

$$q^2 = \frac{2c_1 D}{c_3 T} + \frac{c_3 q^2}{c_2 + c_3}$$

thus

$$q^2 = \frac{2c_1 D}{\left(1 - \dfrac{c_3}{c_2 + c_3}\right) c_3 T}$$

$$q = \sqrt{\frac{2c_1(c_2 + c_3)D}{c_2 c_3 T}}$$

$$z = \frac{c_3 q}{c_2 + c_3} = \sqrt{\frac{2c_1 c_3 D}{c_2(c_2 + c_3)T}}$$

$$t = \frac{Tq}{D} = \sqrt{\frac{2c_1(c_2 + c_3)T}{c_2 c_3 D}}$$

Thus the manufacturer should produce q units at intervals of time t, where q and t are determined by the formulas above.

PROBLEMS

Determine the maxima, minima, and saddle points (if any) for each of the following functions.

1. $g(x, y) = 2x^2 - 2xy + y^2 + 5x - 3y$
2. $h(x, y) = 3 + 2x + 2y - 2x^2 - 2xy - y^2$
3. $z(x, y) = xy + x - y$
4. $f(x, y) = x^2 + xy + y^2 - 6x + 2$
5. $u(x, y) = 4x + 2y - x^2 + xy - y^2$
6. $v(x, y) = x^2 + y^2 - 2x + 4y + 6$
7. $z(x, y) = x^3 - 3bxy + y^3$
8. $w(x, y) = x^2 - 2xy + 2y^2 - 2x + 2y + 1$
9. $g(x, y) = x^2 - y^2 - 2x + 4y + 6$
10. $h(x, y) = x^2 + 2xy$
11. $z(x, y) = xy - 2y^2$
12. $f(x, y) = axy$

Find the quantities and prices that maximize profit and the maximum profit for each of the following sets of demand functions and joint-cost functions for two commodities. Quantities are denoted by x and y and the corresponding prices are denoted by p and q, respectively; total cost is denoted by C.

13. $x = 1 - p + 2q$
    $y = 11 + p - 3q$
    $C = 4x + y$
14. $x = 11 - 2p - 2q$
    $y = 16 - 2p - 3q$
    $C = 3x + y$
15. $p = 40 - 2x^2$
    $q = 12 - 3y$
    $C = 8 + 4x + 3y$
16. $p = 16 - x^2$
    $q = 9 - y^2$
    $C = x^2 + 3y^2$

17. $p = 26 - x$
    $q = 40 - 4y$
    $C = x^2 + 2xy + y^2$
18. $p = 35 - 2x^2$
    $q = 20 - y$
    $C = 16 - 2x^3 + xy + 30x + 12y + \frac{1}{2}x^2$
19. $p = 40 - 5x$
    $q = 30 - 3y$
    $C = x^2 + 2xy + 3y^2$
20. $p = 28 - 3x^2$
    $q = 56 - y^2$
    $C = 2x^2 + y^2$

21. Determine the maximum profit if the production function is $z = 20 - x^2 + 10x - 2y^2 + 5y$, the prices of the inputs x and y are 2 and 1, respectively, and the price of the output z is 5.

22. Determine the maximum profit if the production function is $z = 10 - 2x^2 + xy - y^2 + 5y$, the prices of the inputs x and y are each 3, and the price of the output z is 6.

23. The following data were obtained for a random sample of uranium ores; x represents purity grade of ore (expert's grading at site of mine), and y represents grams of uranium obtained per 1000 lb of ore.

x	y
85	2.3
65	1.2
73	1.5
90	1.9
82	1.8
80	2.0
68	1.3
88	2.1

Obtain the least squares regression of y on x.

24. The purity of sheet polythene (measured by a standard method) is related to the time it remains in the reactor, if temperature and pressure are held constant. The following data were obtained from one reactor; x represents number of seconds and y represents purity.

x	y
1.5	0.890
2.0	0.974
2.5	1.175
3.0	1.096
3.5	1.349
4.0	1.347
4.5	1.417
5.0	1.440
5.5	1.492
6.0	1.519
6.5	1.523
7.0	1.531
7.5	1.538
8.0	1.555
8.5	1.560

Obtain the least squares regression of y on x.

25. The Portland Company has a contract to furnish 1350 cement mixers annually. The yearly storage cost is $40 per cement mixer, the shortage cost is $50 per cement mixer short per year, and it costs $150 to start a production run. If production orders are filled without delay and demand is at a constant rate, determine the frequency with which production should be scheduled and the quantity which should be produced in each run in order to minimize the total average annual cost.

26. The Filaway Company has a contract to supply 600 filing cabinets at a uniform rate during a 9-month period. The storage cost during this period is $30 per cabinet, the shortage cost is $60 per cabinet, and it costs $20 to start a production run. If production occurs at a constant rate of 2400 cabinets per 9-month period, determine the frequency with which production should be scheduled and the quantity which should be produced in each run in order to minimize the total average annual cost.

Answers to Odd-Numbered Problems

1. minimum $(-1, \frac{1}{2})$
3. saddle point $(1, -1)$
5. maximum $(\frac{10}{3}, \frac{8}{3})$
7. minimum (b, b)

9. saddle point $(1, 2)$

11. saddle point $(0, 0)$

13. $p = 14$
    $q = 8$
    $x = 3$
    $y = 1$
    $P_{max} = 37$

15. $p = 28$
    $q = \frac{15}{2}$
    $x = \sqrt{6}$
    $y = \frac{3}{2}$
    $P_{max} = 24\sqrt{6} - \frac{5}{4}$
    (approximately 57.53)

17. $p = 21$
    $q = 28$
    $x = 5$
    $y = 3$
    $P_{max} = 125$

19. $p = 25$
    $q = 24$
    $x = 3$
    $y = 2$
    $P_{max} = 90$

21. $P_{max} = 229\frac{3}{5}$ for $x = \frac{24}{5}$ and $y = \frac{6}{5}$

23. $\tilde{y}_i = -1.21 + 0.038x_i$

25. Schedule production 10 times a year, producing 135 cement mixers each run.

3.5 Maxima and Minima Subject to Constraints

In many practical applications of maximization and minimization, the problem is to maximize or minimize a given function subject to specified side conditions or constraints on the variables involved. These constraints may be stated as equalities or inequalities.

For example, if a manufacturer produces two ouputs, he may want to minimize the joint cost, while producing a specified minimum total amount; a company may want to maximize sales resulting from the use of two advertising media, while keeping total advertising costs within a specified budget constraint; an engineer may want to minimize frequency of breakdowns, while keeping total cost of two types of preventive repairs from exceeding a specified amount; a consumer may want to maximize utility derived from the consumption of commodities, subject to his budget constraint; a chemist may want to minimize total sedimentation in a two-stage process, while keeping the temperatures in the two stages equal.

In some cases equations obtained from the constraints can be substituted into the function to be maximized or minimized, and the problem is thus reduced to unconstrained maximization or minimization, for which the methods of the preceding section are applicable. However, this procedure frequently is not feasible, particularly if the function to be maximized or minimized involves more than two variables and several constraints. The methods discussed in this section are applicable in all cases of constrained maximization and minimization of functions of two variables and can be generalized for use with any number of variables and constraints.

The method of Lagrange multipliers is used in obtaining maxima or minima of functions subject to equality constraints, and this method is easily generalized for the case of one inequality constraint. Maxima or minima subject to multiple equality and inequality constraints are obtained using the Kuhn-Tucker conditions.

LAGRANGE MULTIPLIERS

The most widely used method of obtaining maxima or minima of functions subject to equality constraints is *Lagrange multipliers*. Suppose $f(x, y)$ is to be maximized or minimized subject to the constraint $g(x, y) = 0$. Form the *objective function*

$$F(x, y, \lambda) = f(x, y) - \lambda g(x, y)$$

where the quantity λ, the Lagrange multiplier, is independent of x and y and is unknown. Differentiate $F(x, y, \lambda)$ partially with respect to x, with respect to y, and with respect to λ, and set the resulting equations equal to zero; then solve the three equations

$$\frac{\partial F}{\partial x} = \frac{\partial f}{\partial x} - \lambda \frac{\partial g}{\partial x} = 0$$

$$\frac{\partial F}{\partial y} = \frac{\partial f}{\partial y} - \lambda \frac{\partial g}{\partial y} = 0$$

$$\frac{\partial F}{\partial \lambda} = g(x, y) = 0$$

for the three unknowns x, y, and λ. Note that $\frac{\partial F}{\partial \lambda} = g(x, y) = 0$ is the constraint, so $F(x, y, \lambda)$ really need be differentiated partially only with respect to x and with respect to y. In some cases the values of the λ's (Lagrange multipliers) are not of interest and are not found; for this reason they are sometimes referred to as "undetermined multipliers." The Lagrange multiplier is sometimes preceded by a plus sign rather than by a minus sign; the only resulting change in the solution is a change in the sign of λ.

The logic involved in using Lagrange multipliers is quite straightforward. The problem is to determine possible maximum or minimum values of a function that will satisfy a constraint. If it can be assumed that the points being considered satisfy the constraint, this problem reduces to the problem of finding an unconstrained maximum or minimum. Essentially, the method of Lagrange multipliers screens the possible maximum or minimum values to obtain only those values that satisfy the constraint.

Note that, if the constraint is satisfied, $g(x, y) = 0$ and thus $\lambda g(x, y) = 0$, regardless of the value of λ. In that case, the objective function becomes the unconstrained function $f(x, y)$. By considering λ to be an additional variable and setting the partial derivative with respect to λ equal to zero, the constraint $g(x, y) = 0$ is incorporated into the problem and the possible maximum or minimum values satisfy the constraint.

Solution of the three equations above provides the critical points of the constrained function. These critical points satisfy the constraint, but must be tested as maxima or minima of the function by a procedure similar to that for unconstrained maxima or minima.

For a critical point $x = a$, $y = b$,

$$\text{If} \begin{cases} \left. \frac{\partial F}{\partial x} \right|_{x=a,\, y=b} = 0 \\[2ex] \left. \frac{\partial F}{\partial y} \right|_{x=a,\, y=b} = 0 \end{cases}$$

and

$$\Delta^* = \left(\left. \frac{\partial^2 F}{\partial x^2} \right|_{x=a,\, y=b} \right) \left(\left. \frac{\partial^2 F}{\partial y^2} \right|_{x=a,\, y=b} \right) - \left(\left. \frac{\partial^2 F}{\partial x\, \partial y} \right|_{x=a,\, y=b} \right)^2$$

$$\text{then} \begin{cases} \Delta^* > 0 \Rightarrow \begin{cases} \text{maximum at } x = a, \ y = b, \text{ if } \dfrac{\partial^2 F}{\partial x^2} < 0 \text{ and } \dfrac{\partial^2 F}{\partial y^2} < 0 \\[2mm] \text{minimum at } x = a, \ y = b, \text{ if } \dfrac{\partial^2 F}{\partial x^2} > 0 \text{ and } \dfrac{\partial^2 F}{\partial y^2} > 0 \end{cases} \\[4mm] \Delta^* \le 0 \Rightarrow \text{test fails; function must be investigated near } x = a, \ y = b \end{cases}$$

Note that for unconstrained maxima and minima, if $\Delta < 0$, the critical point is neither a maximum nor a minimum; however, for constrained maxima and minima, if $\Delta^* < 0$, the critical point may in fact be a maximum or minimum. This corresponds to the fact that a point may be a maximum or minimum of the constrained function, although it is not a maximum or minimum of the unconstrained function.

These conditions can be stated more concisely as follows.

necessary condition for a critical point: $\quad F_x = 0, \ F_y = 0$

determination of constrained maxima or minima:

$$F_{xx}F_{yy} - F_{xy}^2 > 0 \Rightarrow \begin{cases} \text{maximum if } F_{xx} < 0, \ F_{yy} < 0 \\ \text{minimum if } F_{xx} > 0, \ F_{yy} > 0 \end{cases}$$

$F_{xx}F_{yy} - F_{xy}^2 \le 0 \Rightarrow$ test fails and the function must be investigated near the critical point

where the partial derivatives are evaluated for the critical point.

NOTE: The method of Lagrange multipliers can be extended for a function of n variables, $f(x_1, x_2, \ldots, x_n)$, subject to the k constraints $g_j(x_1, x_2, \ldots, x_n) = 0, j = 1, 2, \ldots, k$, where $k \le n$. Then

$$F(x_1, \ldots, x_n; \lambda_1, \ldots, \lambda_k) = f(x_1, \ldots, x_n) - \sum_{j=1}^{k} \lambda_j g_j(x_1, \ldots, x_n)$$

and partial differentiation results in $n + k$ equations to be solved for $n + k$ unknowns. The method of testing critical points as maxima or minima can also be extended for the general case.

EXAMPLE

Find the maxima and minima (if any) of $f(x, y) = 5x^2 + 6y^2 - xy$ subject to the constraint $x + 2y = 24$.

$$F(x, y, \lambda) = 5x^2 + 6y^2 - xy - \lambda(x + 2y - 24)$$

$$\frac{\partial F}{\partial x} = 10x - y - \lambda$$

$$\frac{\partial F}{\partial y} = 12y - x - 2\lambda$$

$$\frac{\partial F}{\partial \lambda} = x + 2y - 24$$

Setting each of the partial derivatives equal to zero,

$$10x - y - \lambda = 0$$
$$12y - x - 2\lambda = 0$$
$$x + 2y - 24 = 0$$

which has the solution $x = 6, \ y = 9, \ \lambda = 51$.

$$\frac{\partial^2 F}{\partial x^2} = 10$$

$$\frac{\partial^2 F}{\partial y^2} = 12$$

$$\frac{\partial^2 F}{\partial x \, \partial y} = -1$$

$$\Delta^* = (10)(12) - (-1)^2 = 119$$

$$\frac{\partial^2 F}{\partial x^2} > 0 \quad \text{and} \quad \frac{\partial^2 F}{\partial y^2} > 0$$

so $(6, 9)$ is a constrained minimum of $f(x, y)$.

Alternative method: $f(x, y) = 5x^2 + 6y^2 - xy, \quad x + 2y = 24.$

Solving the constraint equation for x in terms of y,

$$G(y) = 5(24 - 2y)^2 + 6y^2 - y(24 - 2y)$$

$$= 2880 - 480y + 20y^2 + 6y^2 - 24y + 2y^2$$

$$= 2880 - 504y + 28y^2$$

$$\frac{dG}{dy} = -504 + 56y$$

Setting $\dfrac{\partial G}{\partial y} = 0$, $y = 9$ and $x = 6$. Then

$$\frac{d^2 G}{dy^2} = 56 > 0$$

so $(6, 9)$ is a constrained minimum of $f(x, y)$.

EXAMPLE

Find the maxima and minima (if any) of $f(x, y) = 12xy - 3y^2 - x^2$ subject to the constraint $x + y = 16$.

$$F(x, y, \lambda) = 12xy - 3y^2 - x^2 - \lambda(x + y - 16)$$

$$\frac{\partial F}{\partial x} = 12y - 2x - \lambda$$

$$\frac{\partial F}{\partial y} = 12x - 6y - \lambda$$

$$\frac{\partial F}{\partial \lambda} = -(x + y - 16)$$

Setting each of the partial derivatives equal to zero and solving simultaneously, the solution $x = 9$, $y = 7$, $\lambda = 66$ is obtained.

$$\frac{\partial^2 F}{\partial x^2} = -2$$

$$\frac{\partial^2 F}{\partial y^2} = -6$$

$$\frac{\partial^2 F}{\partial x\, \partial y} = 12$$

$$\Delta^* = (-2)(-6) - (12)^2 = -132 < 0$$

Thus $f(x, y)$ has a constrained maximum at $(9, 7)$.

Alternative method: $f(x, y) = 12xy - 3y^2 - x^2$, $x + y = 16$.

$$G(y) = 12y(16 - y) - 3y^2 - (16 - y)^2$$

$$= 192y - 12y^2 - 3y^2 - 256 + 32y - y^2$$

$$= -16y^2 + 224y - 256$$

$$\frac{dG}{dy} = -32y + 224$$

$$\frac{dG}{dy} = 0 \qquad \text{if } 32y = 224$$

$$y = 7$$

$$x = 9$$

$$\frac{d^2 G}{dy^2} = -32$$

so $(9, 7)$ is a constrained maximum of $f(x, y)$.

EXAMPLE

A factory manufactures two types of heavy-duty machines in quantities x and y. The joint-cost function is given by

$$f(x, y) = x^2 + 2y^2 - xy$$

To minimize cost, how many machines of each type should be produced if there must be a total of 8 machines?

The constraint is $x + y = 8$ and the objective function is

$$F(x, y, \lambda) = x^2 + 2y^2 - xy - \lambda(x + y - 8)$$

$$\frac{\partial F}{\partial x} = 2x - y - \lambda$$

$$\frac{\partial F}{\partial y} = 4y - x - \lambda$$

$$\frac{\partial F}{\partial \lambda} = -(x + y - 8)$$

Setting each of the partial derivatives equal to zero and solving simultaneously, the solution $x = 5$, $y = 3$, $\lambda = 7$ is obtained.

$$\frac{\partial^2 F}{\partial x^2} = 2$$

$$\frac{\partial^2 F}{\partial y^2} = 4$$

$$\frac{\partial^2 F}{\partial x\, \partial y} = -1$$

$$\Delta = (2)(4) - (-1)^2 = 7 > 0$$

$$\frac{\partial^2 F}{\partial x^2} > 0 \quad \text{and} \quad \frac{\partial^2 F}{\partial y^2} > 0$$

so (5, 3) is a constrained minimum of $f(x, y)$.

NOTE: Assuming nonnegative cost, the unconstrained minimum of the function $f(x, y) = x^2 + 2y^2 - xy$ occurs at $(0, 0)$, which corresponds to the fact that cost is zero when nothing is produced.

Alternative method: $f(x, y) = x^2 + 2y^2 - xy, \quad x + y = 8.$

$$G(x) = x^2 + 2(8 - x)^2 - x(8 - x)$$

$$= x^2 + 128 - 32x + 2x^2 - 8x + x^2$$

$$= 4x^2 - 40x + 128$$

$$\frac{dG}{dx} = 8x - 40 = 0 \quad \text{if } x = 5$$

$$y = 3$$

$$\frac{d^2 G}{dx^2} = 8 > 0$$

so (5, 3) is a constrained minimum of $f(x, y)$.

EXAMPLE

The relationship between sales S and the amounts x and y spent on two advertising media is given by

$$S = \frac{200x}{5 + x} + \frac{100y}{10 + y}$$

Net profit is $\frac{1}{5}$ of sales minus the cost of advertising. The advertising budget is 25; determine how it should be allocated between the two media in order to maximize net profit.

The constraint is $x + y = 25$ and the objective function is

$$F(x, y, \lambda) = \frac{1}{5} \left[\frac{200x}{5 + x} + \frac{100y}{10 + y} \right] - x - y - \lambda(x + y - 25)$$

$$= \frac{40x}{5 + x} + \frac{20y}{10 + y} - x - y - \lambda(x + y - 25)$$

$$\frac{\partial F}{\partial x} = \frac{40(5 + x) - 40x}{(5 + x)^2} - 1 - \lambda = \frac{200}{(5 + x)^2} - 1 - \lambda$$

$$\frac{\partial F}{\partial y} = \frac{20(10 + y) - 20y}{(10 + y)^2} - 1 - \lambda = \frac{200}{(10 + y)^2} - 1 - \lambda$$

$$\frac{\partial F}{\partial \lambda} = -(x + y - 25)$$

Setting each of the partial derivatives equal to zero and solving simultaneously, the solution $x = 15, y = 10, \lambda = -\frac{1}{2}$ is obtained.

$$\frac{\partial^2 F}{\partial x^2} = 200(-2)(5 + x)^{-3} = -\frac{400}{(5 + x)^3}$$

$$\frac{\partial^2 F}{\partial y^2} = 200(-2)(10 + y)^{-3} = -\frac{400}{(10 + y)^3}$$

$$\frac{\partial^2 F}{\partial x \, \partial y} = 0$$

since $x \geq 0$ and $y \geq 0$, $\quad \Delta = \left(\dfrac{-400}{(5 + x)^3}\right)\left(\dfrac{-400}{(10 + y)^3}\right) - 0 > 0$

$$\frac{\partial^2 F}{\partial x^2} < 0 \qquad \text{and} \qquad \frac{\partial^2 F}{\partial y^2} < 0$$

so (15, 10) is a constrained maximum of $f(x, y)$.

NOTE: The unconstrained maximum of the function

$$P(x, y) = \frac{1}{5}\left[\frac{200x}{5 + x} + \frac{100y}{10 + y}\right] - x - y \text{ occurs at } (10\sqrt{2} - 5, 10\sqrt{2} - 10).$$

Alternative method: $P(x, y) = \dfrac{40x}{5 + x} + \dfrac{20y}{10 + y} - x - y, \quad x + y = 25.$

$$Q(x) = \frac{40x}{5 + x} + \frac{500 - 20x}{35 - x} - 25$$

$$\frac{dQ}{dx} = \frac{40(5 + x) - 40x}{(5 + x)^2} + \frac{-20(35 - x) + (500 - 20x)}{(35 - x)^2}$$

$$= \frac{200}{(5 + x)^2} - \frac{200}{(35 - x)^2} = 0$$

$$\frac{200}{(5 + x)^2} = \frac{200}{(35 - x)^2}$$

$$5 + x = \pm(35 - x)$$

$$x = 15$$

$$y = 10$$

$$\frac{d^2Q}{dx^2} = 200(-2)(5 + x)^{-3} + 200(-2)(35 - x)^{-3}$$

$$= -\frac{400}{(5 + x)^3} - \frac{400}{(35 - x)^3} < 0$$

so (15, 10) is a constrained maximum of $f(x, y)$.

EXAMPLE

Maximum profit for a given production function and given prices of the inputs and output can be determined using Lagrange multipliers. Suppose the production function is

$$16z = 65 - 2(x - 5)^2 - 4(y - 4)^2$$

and the unit prices of the inputs x and y are 8 and 4, respectively, and the unit price of the output is 32. (See the example on page 385.) Profit is maximized if the net revenue function $32z - 8x - 4y$ is maximized subject to the production function constraint $16z - 65 + 2(x - 5)^2 + 4(y - 4)^2 = 0$.

$$F(x, y, z, \lambda) = 32z - 8x - 4y - \lambda[16z - 65 + 2(x - 5)^2 + 4(y - 4)^2]$$

$$\frac{\partial F}{\partial z} = 32 - 16\lambda$$

$$\frac{\partial F}{\partial x} = -8 - 4(x - 5)\lambda$$

$$\frac{\partial F}{\partial y} = -4 - 8\lambda(y - 4)$$

As shown previously, profit is maximized when $x = 4$, $y = \frac{15}{4}$. F is a function of three variables x, y, and z. The second-order conditions for maximization of functions of more than two variables, which are somewhat more complex than the conditions for functions of two variables, are discussed in Chapter 8.

PROBLEMS

Find the maxima and/or minima of each of the following functions subject to the given constraint.

1. $f(x, y) = 3x^2 + 4y^2 - xy$ if $2x + y = 21$.
2. $f(x, y) = x^2 + y^2 - 2xy$ if $x^2 + y^2 = 50$.
3. $f(x, y) = x^2 - 10y^2$ if $x - y = 18$.
4. $f(x, y) = 3xy + 4y^2$ if $x^2 + y^2 = 10$.
5. $f(x, y) = x + y$ if $x^2 + y^2 = 1$.
6. $f(x, y) = x^2 + 24xy + 8y^2$ if $x^2 + y^2 = 25$.

Answers to Odd-Numbered Problems

1. minimum $(8.5, 4)$
3. maximum $(20, 2)$
5. minimum $\left(-\sqrt{\frac{1}{2}}, -\sqrt{\frac{1}{2}}\right)$
   maximum $\left(\sqrt{\frac{1}{2}}, \sqrt{\frac{1}{2}}\right)$

KUHN-TUCKER CONDITIONS

The method of Lagrange multipliers can be modified to determine the maximum or minimum of a function of two variables subject to one inequality constraint as follows. Assume that the inequality constraint holds as an equality constraint and obtain the maximum or minimum using the method of Lagrange multipliers; if $\lambda > 0$, this maximum or minimum is also the maximum or minimum subject to the inequality constraint; if $\lambda \leq 0$, the maximum or minimum determined without regard to the constraint satisfies the constraint and is thus also the constrained maximum or minimum.

This procedure can be generalized to include multiple inequality constraints, some of which may be satisfied as equalities and others as inequalities in any particular problem. In the more general procedure, the conditions necessary for a maximum or minimum subject to inequality constraints are known as the Kuhn-Tucker conditions. These conditions are given for the general case in Chapter 8; for the case of a function of two variables subject to one inequality constraint, the Kuhn-Tucker conditions are as follows.

A point (x, y) is a local maximum of $f(x, y)$ subject to $g(x, y) \leq 0$ only if there exists a nonnegative λ such that λ and (x, y) satisfy the following conditions:

$$\frac{\partial f(x, y)}{\partial x} - \lambda \frac{\partial g(x, y)}{\partial x} = 0$$

$$\frac{\partial f(x, y)}{\partial y} - \lambda \frac{\partial g(x, y)}{\partial y} = 0$$

$$\lambda g(x, y) = 0$$

$$g(x, y) \leq 0$$

These conditions are also sufficient if $f(x, y)$ is concave and $g(x, y)$ is convex. Since a maximum point of $f(x, y)$ is a minimum point of $-f(x, y)$, this result is also applicable to minimizing a convex function over a convex set. If the constraint is of the form $g(x, y) \geq 0$, then $g(x, y)$ must be concave.

NOTE: A function $f(x, y)$ is convex in a region if a line segment drawn through any two points on the surface does not fall below the surface. A function of two variables is convex if and only if

$$f[(1 - t)x_1 + tx_2, (1 - t)y_1 + ty_2] \leq (1 - t)f(x_1, y_1) + tf(x_2, y_2)$$

$$\text{for } 0 < t < 1$$

The function is strictly convex if $\leq$ can be replaced by $<$; the function is concave if $\leq$ can be replaced by $\geq$ and strictly concave if $\leq$ can be replaced by $>$.

A second-degree polynomial of the form

$$f(x, y) = Ax^2 + Bxy + Cy^2 + Dx + Ey + F$$

is convex if $4AC - B^2 > 0$ and $A > 0$, $C > 0$; it is concave if $4AC - B^2 > 0$ and $A < 0$, $C < 0$; and it is neither convex nor concave everywhere if $4AC - B^2 < 0$. Note that this result is a reformulation of the conditions for a maximum or minimum of a function of two variables.

As shown in the following examples, the method of Lagrange multipliers modified for one inequality constraint and the Kuhn-Tucker conditions for one inequality constraint give the same solution. The advantage of the Kuhn-Tucker conditions is that they can be generalized for more than one inequality constraint. Although the method of Lagrange multipliers can be generalized for more than one equality constraint, it cannot conveniently be modified for more than one inequality constraint. If the function to be maximized or minimized is linear and the constraints are also linear, the solution may be obtained using linear programming for both equality and inequality constraints.

Note that each of the following examples is a modification of an example involving equality constraints which is discussed in the section concerning Lagrange multipliers.

EXAMPLE

Find the minimum of $f(x, y) = 5x^2 + 6y^2 - xy$ subject to the constraint $x + 2y \geq 24$.

Assuming the inequality constraint holds as an equality constraint, $\lambda = 51$ (see page 394). Since $\lambda > 0$, the minimum, $x = 6$, $y = 9$, assuming the equality constraint is also the minimum assuming the inequality constraint.

Using the Kuhn-Tucker conditions with $g(x, y) = x + 2y - 24 \geq 0$,

$$\frac{\partial f}{\partial x} - \lambda \frac{\partial g}{\partial x} = 10x - y - \lambda = 0$$

$$\frac{\partial f}{\partial y} - \lambda \frac{\partial g}{\partial y} = 12y - x - 2\lambda = 0$$

$$\lambda g = \lambda(x + 2y - 24) = 0$$

$$g = x + 2y - 24 \geq 0$$

Either $\lambda = 0$ or $x + 2y - 24 = 0$. If $\lambda = 0$, then $x = y = 0$ in order to satisfy the first two equations, but then the constraint $x + 2y \geq 24$ is not satisfied. If $x + 2y - 24 = 0$, then $x = 24 - 2y$ and, substituting in the first two equations and solving them simultaneously,

$$240 - 20y - y - \lambda = 0$$

$$12y - 24 + 2y - 2\lambda = 0$$

$$\lambda + 21y = 240$$

$$-2\lambda + 14y = 24$$

$$56y = 504$$

$$y = 9$$

$$x = 6$$

Thus, as above, $f(x, y) = 5x^2 + 6y^2 - xy$ is minimized subject to the constraint $x + 2y \geq 24$ when $x = 6$, $y = 9$.

NOTE: $f(x, y) = 5x^2 + 6y^2 - xy$ is convex, since $4AC - B^2 = (4)(5)(6) - (-1)^2 = 119 > 0$ and $A > 0$, $C > 0$.

EXAMPLE

Find the maximum of $f(x, y) = 12xy - 3y^2 - x^2$ subject to the constraint $x + y \leq 16$.

Assuming the inequality constraint to hold as an equality constraint, $\lambda = 66$ (see page 395). Since $\lambda > 0$, the maximum, $x = 9$, $y = 7$, assuming the equality constraint is also the maximum subject to the inequality constraint.

Using the Kuhn-Tucker conditions with $g(x, y) = x + y - 16 \leq 0$,

$$\frac{\partial f}{\partial x} - \lambda \frac{\partial g}{\partial x} = 12y - 2x - \lambda = 0$$

$$\frac{\partial f}{\partial y} - \lambda \frac{\partial g}{\partial y} = 12x - 6y - \lambda = 0$$

$$\lambda g = \lambda(x + y - 16) = 0$$

$$g = x + y - 16 \leq 0$$

Either $\lambda = 0$ or $x + y - 16 = 0$. If $\lambda = 0$, then $x = y = 0$ in order to satisfy the first two equations, and the constraint $x + y \leq 16$ is also satisfied. If $x + y - 16 = 0$, then $x = 16 - y$ and, substituting in the first two equations,

$$12y - 32 + 2y - \lambda = 0$$

$$192 - 12y - 6y - \lambda = 0$$

$$y = 7$$

$$x = 9$$

The solution $x = 9$, $y = 7$ satisfies the equations $12y - 2x - \lambda = 0$ and $12x - 6y - \lambda = 0$ if $\lambda = 66$. $f(9, 7) = 528$, which is larger than $f(0, 0) = 0$. Thus, as above, $f(x, y) = 12xy - 3y^2 - x^2$ is maximized subject to the constraint $x + y \leq 16$ when $x = 9$, $y = 7$.

NOTE: $f(x, y) = 12xy - 3y^2 - x^2$ is concave, since $4AC - B^2 = 4(-1)(-3) - (12)^2 = -132 < 0$ and $A < 0$, $C < 0$.

EXAMPLE

A factory manufactures two types of heavy-duty machines, x and y. The joint-cost function is given by

$$f(x, y) = x^2 + 2y^2 - xy$$

To minimize cost, how many machines of each type should be produced if there must be a total of at least 8 machines?

Assuming the inequality constraint to hold as an equality constraint, $\lambda = 7$ (see page 396). Since $\lambda > 0$, the maximum, $x = 5$, $y = 3$, assuming the equality constraint is also the maximum subject to the inequality constraint.

Using the Kuhn-Tucker conditions,

$$\frac{\partial f}{\partial x} - \lambda \frac{\partial g}{\partial x} = 2x - y - \lambda = 0$$

$$\frac{\partial f}{\partial y} - \lambda \frac{\partial g}{\partial y} = 4y - x - \lambda = 0$$

$$\lambda g = \lambda(x + y - 8) = 0$$

$$g = x + y - 8 \geq 0$$

Either $\lambda = 0$ or $x + y - 8 = 0$. If $\lambda = 0$, then $x = y = 0$ in order to satisfy the first two equations, but then the constraint $x + y \geq 8$ is not satisfied. If $x + y - 8 = 0$, then $x = 8 - y$ and, substituting in the first two equations,

$$16 - 2y - y - \lambda = 0$$

$$4y - 8 + y - \lambda = 0$$

$$y = 3$$

$$x = 5$$

Thus, as above, $f(x, y) = x^2 + 2y^2 - xy$ is minimized subject to the constraint $x + y \geq 8$ when $x = 5$, $y = 3$.

NOTE: $f(x, y) = x^2 + 2y^2 - xy$ is convex, since $4AC - B^2 = 4(1)(2) - (-1)^2 = 7 > 0$ and $A > 0$, $C > 0$.

EXAMPLE

The relationship between sales S and the amounts x and y spent on two advertising media is given by

$$S = \frac{200x}{5 + x} + \frac{100y}{10 + y}$$

Net profit is $\frac{1}{5}$ of sales minus the cost of advertising. The advertising budget has a maximum of 25; determine how it should be allocated between the two media to maximize net profit.

Assuming the inequality constraint to hold as an equality constraint, $\lambda = -\frac{1}{2}$ (see page 397). Since $\lambda < 0$, the unconstrained maximum is also the maximum subject to the inequality constraint.

$$f(x, y) = \frac{1}{5}\left[\frac{200x}{5 + x} + \frac{100y}{10 + y}\right] - x - y$$

$$\frac{\partial f}{\partial x} = \frac{40(5 + x) - 40x}{(5 + x)^2} - 1$$

$$\frac{\partial f}{\partial y} = \frac{20(10 + y) - 20y}{(10 + y)^2} - 1$$

Setting $\dfrac{\partial f}{\partial x} = 0$ and $\dfrac{\partial f}{\partial y} = 0$ and solving,

$$x = 10\sqrt{2} - 5 \quad \text{and} \quad y = 10\sqrt{2} - 10$$

$f(x, y)$ is thus maximized subject to the inequality constraint when $x = 10\sqrt{2} - 5 \approx 9.14$, $y = 10\sqrt{2} - 10 \approx 4.14$.

Using the Kuhn-Tucker conditions,

$$\frac{\partial f}{\partial x} - \lambda \frac{\partial g}{\partial x} = \frac{40(5 + x) - 40x}{(5 + x)^2} - 1 - \lambda = 0$$

$$\frac{\partial f}{\partial y} - \lambda \frac{\partial g}{\partial y} = \frac{20(10 + y) - 20y}{(10 + y)^2} - 1 - \lambda = 0$$

$$\lambda g = \lambda(x + y - 25) = 0$$

$$g(x, y) = x + y - 25 \leq 0$$

Either $\lambda = 0$ or $x + y - 25 = 0$. If $\lambda = 0$, then in order to satisfy the first two equations,

$$40(5 + x) - 40x = (5 + x)^2$$

$$x = 10\sqrt{2} - 5$$

and

$$20(10 + y) - 20y = (10 + y)^2$$

$$y = 10\sqrt{2} - 10$$

and the constraint $x + y \leq 25$ is also satisfied. If $x + y - 25 = 0$, $x = 25 - y$; setting $\dfrac{\partial F}{\partial x} = 0$ and $\dfrac{\partial F}{\partial y} = 0$ and solving, $x = 15$, $y = 10$, $\lambda = -\frac{1}{2}$ (see page 397). $f(15, 10) = 15$, which is less than $f(10\sqrt{2} - 5, 10\sqrt{2} - 10) = 75 - 40\sqrt{2}$. Thus, as above,

$$f(x, y) = \frac{1}{5}\left[\frac{200x}{5 + x} + \frac{100y}{10 + y}\right] - x - y$$

is maximized subject to the constraint $x + y \leq 25$ when $x = 10\sqrt{2} - 5$, $y = 10\sqrt{2} - 10$.

3.6 Applications of Constrained Maximization and Minimization in Business and Economics

There are many areas of application of constrained maxima and minima in business and economics, as illustrated in the examples of the preceding section. Many aspects of consumer behavior can be analyzed in the framework of constrained maximization or minimization. For example, in utility theory the consumer maximizes the utility derived from the purchase of two commodities, where the consumer's fixed income and the prices of the commodities constitute a budget constraint. The problem of constrained utility maximization is considered in this section.

CONSTRAINED UTILITY MAXIMIZATION

If his purchases are limited to two commodities Q_1 and Q_2, the rational consumer wishes to purchase that combination of Q_1 and Q_2 which will maximize his utility, subject to his budget constraint. Since his purchases are limited to the two commodities, the consumer's budget constraint can be written

$$y° = p_1 q_1 + p_2 q_2$$

where $y°$ is his fixed income and p_1, p_2, q_1, and q_2 are the prices and quantities of Q_1 and Q_2, respectively.

The budget line $y° = p_1 q_1 + p_2 q_2$ shows all possible combinations of q_1 and q_2 which the consumer can purchase, given his budget constraint. In order to maximize his utility, the consumer chooses to purchase a combination of q_1 and q_2 lying on the highest possible indifference curve. As shown in Figure 3.5, this maximizing point is the point at which the budget line is tangent to an indifference curve. Any movement from this point along the budget constraint puts the consumer on a lower indifference curve and results in diminished utility.

Mathematically, the problem can be stated in terms of obtaining a constrained maximum:

maximize $U(q_1, q_2)$

subject to $y° = p_1 q_1 + p_2 q_2$

The budget constraint can be written

$$\frac{y° - p_1 q_1}{p_2} = q_2$$

and the consumer's utility, as a function only of q_1, is

$$U = f\left(q_1, \frac{y° - p_1 q_1}{p_2}\right)$$

Note that, since q_2 is determined if q_1 is specified, it is sufficient to maximize U with respect to q_1. Differentiating U with respect to q_1,

$$\frac{dU}{dq_1} = f_1 + f_2\left(-\frac{p_1}{p_2}\right) = 0$$

and

$$\frac{f_1}{f_2} = \frac{p_1}{p_2}$$

NOTE: The utility function can be written

$$U = f(q_1, q_2) \quad \text{where } q_2 = \frac{y^\circ - p_1 q_1}{p_2} = g(q_1)$$

Then

$$\frac{dU}{dq_1} = \frac{\partial f}{\partial q_1} \cdot \frac{\partial q_1}{\partial q_1} + \frac{\partial f}{\partial q_2} \cdot \frac{\partial q_2}{\partial q_1}$$

$$= f_1 + f_2 \left(-\frac{p_1}{p_2} \right)$$

Thus, for a maximum to occur, the ratio of the marginal utilities must equal the ratio of the prices, or equivalently,

$$\frac{f_1}{p_1} = \frac{f_2}{p_2}$$

that is, marginal utility divided by price must be the same for both commodities. This condition is necessary, but not sufficient, for occurrence of a maximum. The second-order condition for a maximum requires that

$$\frac{d^2 U}{dq_1^2} < 0$$

But

$$\frac{\partial^2 U}{\partial q_1^2} = \frac{\partial}{\partial q_1} \left(\frac{dU}{dq_1} \right) \left(\frac{\partial q_1}{\partial q_1} \right) + \frac{\partial}{\partial q_2} \left(\frac{dU}{dq_2} \right) \left(\frac{\partial q_2}{\partial q_1} \right)$$

$$= \left[f_{11} + f_{12} \left(-\frac{p_1}{p_2} \right) \right] + \left[f_{12} \left(-\frac{p_1}{p_2} \right) + f_{22} \left(-\frac{p_1}{p_2} \right)^2 \right]$$

$$= f_{11} + 2f_{12} \left(-\frac{p_1}{p_2} \right) + f_{22} \left(-\frac{p_1}{p_2} \right)^2$$

The second-order condition for a maximum requires that

$$f_{11} + 2f_{12} \left(-\frac{p_1}{p_2} \right) + f_{22} \left(-\frac{p_1}{p_2} \right)^2 < 0$$

or

$$f_{11} p_2^2 - 2f_{12} p_1 p_2 + f_{22} p_1^2 < 0$$

In Technical Note I, the second-order condition for a maximum is shown to require that the utility curves are convex from below. Since $\dfrac{dq_2}{dq_1} = -\dfrac{f_1}{f_2} = -\dfrac{p_1}{p_2}$ and prices are positive, the indifference curves are negatively sloped. Thus if the utility function has a maximum, the indifference curves are of the general form shown in Figure 3.5.

EXAMPLE

If $U = q_1 q_2$, $p_1 = 15$, $p_2 = 5$, and the consumer's income for the period is 150, the budget constraint is

$$150 - 15q_1 - 5q_2 = 0$$

$$q_2 = \frac{150 - 15q_1}{5} = 30 - 3q_1$$

and

$$U = 30q_1 - 3q_1^2$$

$$\frac{dU}{dq_1} = 30 - 6q_1$$

If $\dfrac{dU}{dq_1} = 0$, then $q_1 = 5$, $q_2 = 15$, and $\dfrac{d^2U}{dq_1^2} = -6$, so the consumer maximizes utility subject to his budget constraint by purchasing 5 units of Q_1 and 15 units of Q_2. Note that

$$\frac{f_1}{f_2} = \frac{q_2}{q_1} = \frac{15}{5} = \frac{p_1}{p_2}$$

as required for a maximum.

EXAMPLE

If $U = q_1 q_2^2 - 10q_1$, $p_1 = 2$, $p_2 = 8$, and the consumer's income for the period is 116, the budget constraint is

$$116 - 2q_1 - 8q_2 = 0$$

$$q_1 = \frac{116 - 8q_2}{2} = 58 - 4q_2$$

and

$$U = (58 - 4q_2)q_2^2 - 10(58 - 4q_2)$$
$$= 58q_2^2 - 4q_2^3 - 580 + 40q_2$$

$$\frac{dU}{dq_2} = 116q_2 - 12q_2^2 + 40$$

If $\dfrac{dU}{dq_2} = 0$,

$$3q_2^2 - 29q_2 - 10 = 0$$

$$(3q_2 + 1)(q_2 - 10) = 0$$

$$q_2 = -\tfrac{1}{3}, \ 10$$

But $q_2 \geq 0$, so the solution is $q_2 = 10$, $q_1 = 18$.

$$\frac{d^2U}{dq_2^2} = 116 - 24q_2$$

$$\left. \frac{d^2U}{dq_2^2} \right|_{q_2 = 10} = 116 - 240 = -124 < 0$$

So the consumer maximizes utility subject to his budget constraint by purchasing 18 units of Q_1 and 10 units of Q_2.

Note that

$$\frac{f_1}{f_2} = \frac{q_2^2 - 10}{2q_1 q_2} = \frac{90}{360} = \frac{2}{8} = \frac{p_1}{p_2}$$

as required for a maximum.

Alternatively, the constrained maximum can be obtained using Lagrange multipliers

$$Z = f(q_1, q_2) - \lambda(y° - p_1 q_1 - p_2 q_2)$$

Taking partial derivations and setting them equal to zero,

$$\frac{\partial Z}{\partial q_1} = f_1 + \lambda p_1 = 0$$

$$\frac{\partial Z}{\partial q_2} = f_2 + \lambda p_2 = 0$$

$$\frac{\partial Z}{\partial \lambda} = y° - p_1 q_1 - p_2 q_2 = 0$$

Thus

$$\lambda = -\frac{f_1}{p_1} = -\frac{f_2}{p_2}$$

and

$$\frac{f_1}{f_2} = \frac{p_1}{p_2}$$

and so forth, as above.

PROBLEMS

1. Find the minimum of $f(x, y) = 4x^2 + 5y^2 - 6y$ if $x + 2y \geq 18$.
2. Find the maximum of $f(x, y) = 16x + 12y - 2x^2 - 3y^2$ if $x + y \leq 11$.
3. Find the minimum of $f(x, y) = 3x^2 + 3y^2$ if $x + y \geq 10$.
4. Find the minimum of $f(x, y) = 12x^2 + 4y^2 - 8xy - 32x$ if $x + y \geq 1$.
5. Find the maximum of $f(x, y) = 10xy - 5x^2 - 7y^2 + 40x$ if $x + y \leq 13$.
6. Find the maximum of $f(x, y) = 6xy - 3x^2 - 4y^2$ if $3x + y \leq 19$.
7. Production, P, as a function of two inputs x and y, is given by

$$P = x^2 + 5xy - 4y^2$$

Find the amounts of x and y which maximize production if a. $2x + 3y = 74$, b. $2x + 3y \leq 74$.

8. Sales, S, as a function of the amounts, x and y, spent on two types of promotion is given by

$$S = \frac{240x}{25 + 3x} + \frac{150y}{10 + y}$$

Net profit $= \frac{1}{10}S - x - y$. Find the allocation of x and y which will maximize net profit if $x + y = 15$.

9. Cost of production, C, as a function of the numbers produced, x and y, of two types of items is given by

$$C = 6x^2 + 3y^2$$

To minimize cost, what numbers of the two items should be produced if a. $x + y = 18$, b. $x + y \geq 18$?

10. The cost of repairs, C, as a function of the numbers, x and y, of inspections at two points in a process is given by

$$C = 2x^2 + 3y^2 + xy - 22x + 5$$

To minimize repair cost, what number of inspections should be made at each point if $x - y = 2$?

11. The number of breakdowns, N, as a function of the numbers, x and y, of replacements of two parts of a machine is given by

$$N = 3x^2 + y^2 + 2xy - 22x + 6$$

To minimize breakdowns, what numbers of replacements should be made for each part if $2x = y$?

12. The cost of repairs, C, as a function of the numbers, x and y, of inspections at two points in a process is given by

$$C = 4x^2 + 2y^2 + 5xy - 20x + 30$$

To minimize repair costs, what number of inspections should be made at each point if the total number of inspections is a. 10, b. not fewer than 10?

13. Using Lagrange multipliers, determine the maximum profit if the production function is $z = 20 - x^2 + 10x - 2y^2 + 5y$, the prices of the inputs x and y are 2 and 1, respectively, and the price of the output is 5. (See Problem 21, page 390.)

14. Using Lagrange multipliers, determine the maximum profit if the production function is $z = 10 - 2x^2 + xy - y^2 + 5y$, the prices of the inputs x and y are each 3, and the price of the output is 6. (See Problem 22, page 390.)

15. If the consumer's utility function is $U = q_1^2 q_2$, $p_1 = 4$, $p_2 = 5$, and $y^\circ = 120$, determine the quantities q_1 and q_2 which he should purchase in order to maximize his derived utility.

16. If the consumer's utility function is $U = q_1 q_2 - q_1^2$, $p_1 = 3$, $p_2 = 6$, and $y^\circ = 90$, determine the quantities q_1 and q_2 which he should purchase in order to maximize his derived utility.

17. If the consumer's utility function is $U = q_1^2 + 2q_2^2 + 5q_1 q_2$, $p_1 = 5$, $p_2 = 10$, and the consumer's income for the period is 90, determine the quantities q_1 and q_2 which he should purchase in order to maximize his derived utility.

18. If the consumer's utility function is $U = q_1 q_2 - 3q_2^2$, $p_1 = 10$, $p_2 = 15$, and the consumer's income for the period is 180, determine the quantities q_1 and q_2 which he should purchase in order to maximize his derived utility.

Answers to Odd-Numbered Problems

1. $(4, 7)$
3. $(5, 5)$
5. $(8, 5)$
7. a. $x = 31$, $y = 4$
   b. $x = 31$, $y = 4$
9. a. $x = 6$, $y = 12$
   b. $x = 6$, $y = 12$

11. $x = 1$, $y = 2$
13. $P_{\max} = 229\frac{3}{5}$, $x = \frac{24}{5}$, $y = \frac{6}{5}$
15. $q_1 = 20$, $q_2 = 8$
17. $q_1 = \frac{27}{2}$, $q_2 = \frac{9}{4}$

Technical Note I. Proof of Convexity of Utility Curves

Obtain the total derivative $\dfrac{d^2 q_2}{dq_1^2}$ by further differentiating $\dfrac{dq_2}{dq_1} = -\dfrac{f_1}{f_2}$

$$\frac{d^2 q_2}{dq_1^2} = \left[\frac{\partial}{\partial q_1}\left(\frac{dq_2}{dq_1}\right)\right]\left[\frac{\partial q_1}{\partial q_1}\right] + \left[\frac{\partial}{\partial q_2}\left(\frac{dq_2}{dq_1}\right)\right]\left[\frac{\partial q_2}{\partial q_1}\right]$$

But

$$\frac{\partial}{\partial q_1}\left(\frac{dq_2}{dq_1}\right) = \frac{\partial}{\partial q_1}\left(-\frac{f_1}{f_2}\right) = -\frac{f_{11} f_2 - f_1 f_{12}}{f_2^2}$$

$$\frac{\partial q_1}{\partial q_1} = 1$$

$$\frac{\partial}{\partial q_2}\left(\frac{dq_2}{dq_1}\right) = \frac{\partial}{\partial q_2}\left(-\frac{f_1}{f_2}\right) = -\frac{f_{12} f_2 - f_1 f_{22}}{f_2^2}$$

$$\frac{\partial q_2}{\partial q_1} = -\frac{f_1}{f_2}$$

Thus

$$\frac{d^2 q_2}{dq_1^2} = -\frac{f_{11} f_2 - f_1 f_{12} + (f_{12} f_2 - f_1 f_{22})\left(-\dfrac{f_1}{f_2}\right)}{f_2^2}$$

$$= -\frac{1}{f_2^3}(f_{11} f_2^2 - 2f_{12} f_1 f_2 + f_{22} f_1^2)$$

Substituting $f_1 = (p_1/p_2)/f_2$,

$$\frac{d^2 q_2}{dq_1^2} = -\frac{1}{f_2^3}\left(f_{11} f_2^2 - 2f_{12} f_2^2 \frac{p_1}{p_2} + f_{22} f_2^2 \frac{p_1^2}{p_2^2}\right)$$

$$= -\frac{1}{f_2 p_2^2}(f_{11} p_2^2 - 2f_{12} p_1 p_2 + f_{22} p_1^2)$$

But the second-order condition for a maximum requires that

$$f_{11} p_2^2 - 2f_{12} p_1 p_2 + f_{22} p_1^2 < 0$$

and, since $f_2 > 0$,

$$\frac{d^2 q_2}{dq_1^2} > 0$$

and the indifference curves are convex from below.

Integral
Calculus

4.1 Introduction

Integration has two distinct interpretations as a procedure that is the inverse of differentiation and as a method of determining the area under a curve. There are many important applications of integration in each of these contexts.

As mentioned earlier, integration is the inverse of differentiation; that is, if a function is differentiated and the resulting function is then integrated, the result is the original function. As discussed in detail below, this is true only if the constant of integration is specified in some way; otherwise the result may differ from the original function by a constant. In this context, integration is the process of finding a function when its derivative (or rate of change) is known. In economics, integration can be used to find a total cost function when the marginal cost function is given, to find a total revenue function when the marginal revenue function is given, and so forth.

Integration can also be defined as the process of finding the limiting value of a sum of terms when the number of terms increases infinitely and when the numerical value of each term approaches zero. It is in this context that integration is used in finding the area under a curve. In fact, integral calculus was developed for the purpose of evaluating areas by supposing them to be divided into an infinite number of infinitesimally small parts whose sum is the area required; the integral sign is the elongated S used by early writers to indicate "sum." In economics total revenue can be evaluated as the area under the marginal revenue curve, consumer's surplus and producers' surplus can be evaluated as areas under demand and supply curves, and so forth.

In either context, integration requires operationally that a function be determined when its derivative is given. Unfortunately, the techniques of integration are inherently more difficult than those of differentiation and there are functions, some of them deceptively simple in appearance, whose integrals cannot be expressed in terms of elementary functions. The simpler cases of integration are accomplished by reversing the corresponding formulas for differentiation; more complicated cases are handled by the use of tables of standard forms, by various procedures of substitution, and, if necessary, by numerical (approximation) methods.

In this chapter, the two interpretations of integration and some of their applications in business and economics are discussed first, using functions that are easily integrated by reversing the formulas for differentiation. Subsequent sections discuss special methods useful for integrating more difficult functions and several approximate methods of integration. Multiple integration, the inverse of partial differentiation, is also defined and illustrated.

4.2 Indefinite Integration

The process of determining a function whose derivative is known is called *integration* and the required function is called an *integral* or an *antiderivative* of the given function. Integration of a function is defined and illustrated in this section.

If $F(x)$ is an integral with respect to x of the function $f(x)$, the relationship between $F(x)$ and $f(x)$ is expressed as follows:

$$\int f(x)\, dx = F(x) + C$$

where the left-hand member is read "integral of f of x with respect to x." The symbol $\int$ is the *integral sign*, $f(x)$ is the *integrand*, $F(x)$ is a *particular integral*, C is the *constant of integration*, and $F(x) + C$ is the *indefinite integral*.

Note that if $F(x)$ is an integral of $f(x)$ with respect to x, then $F(x) + C$ is also such an integral, where C is any constant, since the derivative of any constant is zero—that is, if $F(x)$ is an integral of $f(x)$ with respect to x,

$$\frac{d}{dx}[F(x) + C] = \frac{dF(x)}{dx} + \frac{dC}{dx}$$

$$= \frac{dF(x)}{dx}$$

$$= f(x)$$

Thus a function whose derivative is given is not completely determined, because the integral includes an arbitrary additive constant, the constant of integration. It is for this reason that the function $\int f(x)\, dx$ is referred to as the *indefinite* integral of $f(x)$.

It can be shown that two functions which have the same derivative differ at most by a constant; that is, if $F(x)$ is an integral of $f(x)$, all integrals of $f(x)$ are included in the set $F(x) + C$, where C is any constant. In many applications of integration, certain information given in the problem, often referred to as an *initial* or *boundary condition*, uniquely determines the constant of integration.

Geometrically, $y = F(x) + C$ represents a family of curves any one of which can be obtained by shifting the curve $y = F(x)$ (corresponding to $C = 0$) through a vertical displacement C (see Figure 4.1). The curves represented by $y = F(x) + C$ are parallel to each other in the sense that the slope of the tangent to any one of them at the point having abscissa x is $f(x)$. Thus this family of curves has the property that, given any point (x_0, y_0), there is one and only one curve of the family which passes through this particular point. For the curve to pass through the point, its equation must be satisfied by the coordinates of the point, and this uniquely specifies the value of C, since then

$$C = y_0 - F(x_0)$$

With C thus determined, a definite function expressing y in terms of x is obtained, that is, the constant of integration is uniquely determined if one point is specified through which the curve representing the integral passes. This specification is

Figure 4.1

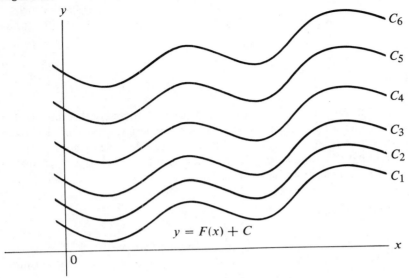

$$y = F(x) + C$$

referred to as an *initial condition*, because evaluation of the constant of integration was first done in connection with problems in mechanics where initial velocities or positions of moving bodies were specified; however, the terminology is usually appropriate for business or behavioral-science applications as well, since the point most likely to be specified in such cases is the origin or an intercept.

EXAMPLE

Figure 4.2

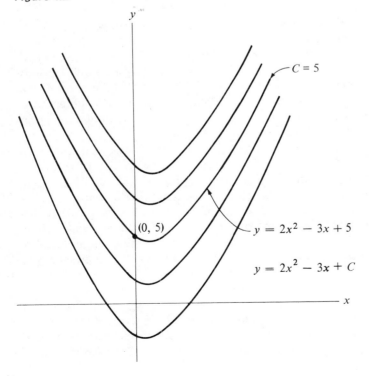

$(0, 5)$

$C = 5$

$y = 2x^2 - 3x + 5$

$y = 2x^2 - 3x + C$

The integral of $f(x) = 4x - 3$ can be obtained by reversing the appropriate formulas for differentiation:

$$\int (4x - 3)\, dx = 2x^2 - 3x + C$$

Note that $\dfrac{d}{dx}(2x^2 - 3x + C) = 4x - 3$, regardless of the vaue of C. Thus, geometrically, the integral is represented by a family of parabolas each corresponding to a different value of C. (See Figure 4.2.) Suppose it is specified, for example, that $f(x) = 5$ when $x = 0$; then

$$2x^2 - 3x + C = 5$$

$$C = 5$$

and

$$F(x) = 2x^2 - 3x + 5$$

which specifies a particular curve of the family given by $F(x) = 2x^2 - 3x + C$. (See Figure 4.2.)

The rules (or standard forms) for integration used in the preceding example are obtained directly by reversing the corresponding rules for differentiation and can be summarized as follows:

1. $\displaystyle\int dx = x + C.$

2. $\displaystyle\int K\, dx = K \int dx$, where K is any constant.

3. $\displaystyle\int (du + dv) = \int du + \int dv$, where $u = f(x)$ and $v = g(x)$ are differentiable functions of x.

4. $\displaystyle\int x^n\, dx = \frac{x^{n+1}}{n+1} + C, \qquad n \neq -1.$

5. $\displaystyle\int u^n\, du = \frac{u^{n+1}}{n+1} + C, \qquad n \neq -1,$

   where $u = f(x)$ is a differentiable function of x.

EXAMPLE

$$\int (8x^2 + 4)\, dx = \frac{8x^3}{3} + 4x + C \qquad\qquad \text{(rules 1, 2, 3, 4)}$$

$$\int x^{3/2}\, dx = \frac{2x^{5/2}}{5} + C \qquad\qquad \text{(rule 4)}$$

$$\int (3x^2 + 2)^3 x\, dx = \frac{1}{6} \int \underbrace{(3x^2 + 2)^3}_{u^3}\, \underbrace{(6x)\, dx}_{du} \qquad\qquad \text{(rule 2)}$$

$$= \left(\frac{1}{6}\right) \frac{(3x^2 + 2)^4}{4} + C \qquad\qquad \text{(rule 5)}$$

$$= \frac{(3x^2 + 2)^4}{24} + C$$

Alternatively,

$$\int (3x^2 + 2)^3 x \, dx = \int (27x^7 + 54x^5 + 36x^3 + 8x) \, dx$$

$$= \frac{27x^8}{8} + 9x^6 + 9x^4 + 4x^2 + C$$

$$= \frac{81x^8 + 216x^6 + 216x^4 + 96x^2}{24} + C$$

$$= \frac{(3x^2 + 2)^4}{24} + C$$

Note that C in the last step is not equal to C in the preceding step, since

$$(3x^2 + 2)^4 = 81x^8 + 216x^6 + 216x^4 + 96x^2 + 16$$

and the value of C in the last step is thus $\frac{16}{24}$ less than the value of C in the preceding step. It is customary to make no notational distinction when the value of a constant of integration is changed by changing the form of the equation, since C must be evaluated for particular boundary values in any case.

EXAMPLE

Evaluate the following integrals.

(a) $y = \int (x^3 + 2x^{5/2} + 5x^{3/2} + 10x) \, dx$ if $y = 0$ when $x = 0$

Integrating,

$$y = \tfrac{1}{4}x^4 + \tfrac{4}{7}x^{7/2} + 2x^{5/2} + 5x^2 + C$$

If $x = 0$, $y = 0$, then $C = 0$ and

$$y = \tfrac{1}{4}x^4 + \tfrac{4}{7}x^{7/2} + 2x^{5/2} + 5x^2$$

(b) $y = \int (x + 2)^2 \, dx$ if $y = 10$ when $x = 1$

Integrating,

$$y = \frac{(x + 2)^3}{3} + C$$

If $x = 1$, $y = 10$, then $C = 1$ and

$$y = \frac{(x + 2)^3}{3} + 1$$

(c) $y = \int (3x^2 + 2x + 6) \, dx$ if $y = 5$ when $x = 0$

Integrating,

$$y = x^3 + x^2 + 6x + C$$

If $x = 0, y = 5$, then $C = 5$ and

$$y = x^3 + x^2 + 6x + 5$$

EXAMPLE

For each of the following, find the curve having the given slope and passing through the given point.

(a) $\dfrac{dy}{dx} = \dfrac{x^2 - 4}{x^2}$, $\quad (4, 1) \quad$ for $x \neq 0$

(b) $\dfrac{dy}{dx} = x^2 \sqrt{x}$, $\quad (1, 0) \quad$ for $x > 0$

(a) $\displaystyle \int \dfrac{x^2 - 4}{x^2}\, dx = \int dx - \int \dfrac{4}{x^2}\, dx$

$$= x + \dfrac{4x^{-1}}{1} + C$$

$$= x + \dfrac{4}{x} + C$$

Thus

$$y = x + \dfrac{4}{x} + C$$

Substituting for the point $(4, 1)$,

$$1 = 4 + 1 + C$$

$$C = -4$$

so

$$y = x + \dfrac{4}{x} - 4$$

$$= \dfrac{x^2 - 4x + 4}{x}$$

$$= \dfrac{(x - 2)^2}{x} \qquad x \neq 0$$

is the required curve.

(b) $\displaystyle \int x^2 \sqrt{x}\, dx = \int x^{5/2}\, dx$

$$= \dfrac{x^{7/2}}{\frac{7}{2}} + C$$

$$= \tfrac{2}{7} x^{7/2} + C$$

Thus

$$y = \tfrac{2}{7} x^{7/2} + C$$

Substituting for the point $(1, 0)$,

$$0 = \tfrac{2}{7} + C$$

$$C = -\tfrac{2}{7}$$

so

$$y = \tfrac{2}{7} x^{7/2} - \tfrac{2}{7}$$

$$= \tfrac{2}{7}(x^{7/2} - 1)$$

$$= \tfrac{2}{7}(x^3 \sqrt{x} - 1) \qquad x > 0$$

is the required curve.

PROBLEMS

Evaluate the following integrals.

1. $\int (x^2 - \sqrt{x} + 4)\, dx$

2. $\int (2 - 7t)^{2/3}\, dt$

3. $\int \sqrt{2 + 5y}\, dy$

4. $\int \dfrac{dx}{(3x + 2)^2}$

5. $\int \dfrac{3r\, dr}{\sqrt{1 - r^2}}$

6. $\int x\sqrt{2x^2 + 1}\, dx$

7. $\int \left(\sqrt{x} + \dfrac{1}{\sqrt{x}}\right) dx$

8. $\int \dfrac{(z + 1)\, dz}{\sqrt[3]{z^2 + 2z + 2}}$

9. $\int \dfrac{(1 - 2x)^2\, dx}{\sqrt{2x}}$

10. $\int \dfrac{dx}{x\sqrt{2x}}$

11. $\int (x\sqrt{x} - 5)^2\, dx$

12. $\int \dfrac{(x^3 - 1)\, dx}{x - 1}$

13. $\int (2x + 3)\, dx$

14. $\int (x^2 - \sqrt{x})\, dx$

15. $\int (\sqrt{2 + 5y})\, dy$

16. Find the equation of the curve having slope $\dfrac{dy}{dx} = 2x - 5$ and passing through the point $(5, 4)$.

17. Find the equation of the curve having slope $\dfrac{dy}{dx} = (x + 1)(x + 2)$ and passing through the point $(-3, -\tfrac{3}{2})$.

18. If $\dfrac{dy}{dx} = 2x - 3$ and $y = 2$ if $x = 3$, find the value of y if $x = 5$.

19. If $\dfrac{dp}{dx} = \dfrac{1}{\sqrt{2ax}}$ and $p = 2a$ if $x = \tfrac{1}{2}a^3$, find the value of p if $x = 2a^3$.

20. Find the equation of the curve which has a slope of -2 at its point of inflection $(1, 3)$ and for which $y''' = 2$.

21. Find the equation of the curve which is tangent to the line $2x + y = 5$ at the point $(1, 3)$ and for which $y'' = 4/x^3$.

22. Find the equation of the curve which passes through the points $(0, 2)$ and $(-1, 3)$ and for which $y'' = 6x^2$.

23. Find the equation of the curve which passes through the point $(1, 2)$ with a slope of $\tfrac{5}{2}$ and for which $y'' = x$.

24. Find the equation of the curve which has a slope of zero at the point $(0, 2)$, has a point of inflection at $(-1, \tfrac{10}{3})$, and for which $y''' = 4$.

Answers to Odd-Numbered Problems

1. $\tfrac{1}{3}x^3 - \tfrac{2}{3}x^{3/2} + 4x + C$

3. $\tfrac{2}{15}(2 + 5y)^{3/2} + C$

5. $-3\sqrt{1 - r^2} + C$

7. $\tfrac{2}{3}x^{3/2} + 2x^{1/2} + C$

9. $\sqrt{2x}\,(1 - \tfrac{4}{3}x + \tfrac{4}{5}x^2) + C$

11. $\tfrac{1}{4}x^4 - 4x^{5/2} + 25x + C$

13. $x^2 + 3x + C$

15. $\tfrac{2}{15}(2 + 5y)^{3/2} + C$

17. $y = \frac{1}{3}x^3 + \frac{3}{2}x^2 + 2x$

19. $p(2a^3) = 3a$

21. $y = \dfrac{2}{x} + 1$

23. $y = \frac{1}{6}x^3 + 2x - \frac{1}{6}$

4.3 Applications of Indefinite Integration in Business and Economics

As mentioned previously in several contexts, in economics the variation of one quantity y with respect to another quantity x is frequently discussed in terms of two concepts—*average* variation and *marginal* variation. Just as the equation for its marginal variation can be obtained by differentiating a function, the function (apart from a constant) can be obtained by integrating the equation for its marginal variation. This application of integration is illustrated for cost, revenue, and consumption functions in this section. A similar application is illustrated for capital formation.

COST

If the total cost y of producing and marketing x units of a commodity is given by the function

$$y = f(x)$$

Then the *average cost* per unit is

$$\frac{y}{x} = \frac{f(x)}{x}$$

and the *marginal cost* is

$$y' = \frac{dy}{dx} = f'(x)$$

That is, marginal cost is the derivative with respect to x, $f'(x)$, of the total cost function $y = f(x)$. Thus total cost is the integral with respect to x of the marginal cost function; that is,

$$y = \int f'(x)\,dx = f(x) + C$$

To obtain a unique total cost function by integrating the corresponding marginal cost function, an initial condition must be specified. Frequently this specification is in terms of a fixed cost or initial overhead, that is, the cost when $x = 0$.

EXAMPLE

Marginal cost y' as a function of units produced x is given by

$$y' = 1.064 - 0.005x$$

Find the total and average cost functions if fixed cost is 16.3.

$$y = \int (1.064 - 0.005x)\,dx$$

$$= 1.064x - 0.0025x^2 + C$$

If $x = 0$, $y = 16.3$, and thus $C = 16.3$ and

$$y = 16.3 + 1.064x - 0.0025x^2 \qquad \text{(total cost)}$$

$$\frac{y}{x} = \frac{16.3}{x} + 1.064 - 0.0025x \qquad \text{(average cost)}$$

EXAMPLE

Marginal cost y' as a function of units produced x is given by

$$y' = 2 + 60x - 5x^2$$

Find the total and average cost functions if fixed cost is 65.

$$y = \int (2 + 60x - 5x^2)\, dx$$

$$= 2x + 30x^2 - \tfrac{5}{3}x^3 + C$$

If $x = 0$, $y = 65$, and thus $C = 65$ and

$$y = 65 + 2x + 30x^2 - \tfrac{5}{3}x^3 \qquad \text{(total cost)}$$

$$\frac{y}{x} = \frac{65}{x} + 2 + 30x - \tfrac{5}{3}x^2 \qquad \text{(average cost)}$$

REVENUE

For any demand function

$$y = f(x)$$

where y is the price per unit and x is the number of units, *total revenue*, R, is the product of x and y; that is,

$$R = xy = x \cdot f(x)$$

Marginal revenue with respect to demand is the derivative with respect to x of the total revenue

$$\frac{dR}{dx} = R'(x)$$

Thus the total revenue function is the integral with respect to x of the marginal revenue function; that is,

$$R = \int R'(x)\, dx$$

And, since

$$\int R'(x)\, dx = R(x) + C$$

an initial condition must be specified to obtain a unique total revenue function by integrating the corresponding marginal revenue function. The initial condition that revenue is zero if demand is zero is frequently used to evaluate the constant of integration.

Note that *average revenue* or revenue per unit is the price per unit, y, and thus the average revenue curve and the demand curve are identical.

EXAMPLE

If the marginal revenue function is

$$R'(x) = 8 - 6x - 2x^2$$

determine the total revenue and demand functions.

$$R(x) = \int (8 - 6x - 2x^2)\, dx$$

$$= 8x - 3x^2 - \tfrac{2}{3}x^3 + C$$

If $x = 0$, $R = 0$, and thus $C = 0$ and

$$R = 8x - 3x^2 - \tfrac{2}{3}x^3 \qquad \text{(total revenue function)}$$

$$y = \frac{R}{x} = 8 - 3x - \tfrac{2}{3}x^2 \qquad \text{(demand function)}$$

EXAMPLE

If the marginal revenue function is

$$R'(x) = 12 - 8x + x^2$$

determine the revenue and demand functions.

$$R(x) = \int (12 - 8x + x^2)\, dx$$

$$= 12x - 4x^2 + \tfrac{1}{3}x^3 + C$$

If $x = 0$, $R = 0$, and thus $C = 0$ and

$$R = 12x - 4x^2 + \tfrac{1}{3}x^3 \qquad \text{(total revenue function)}$$

$$y = \frac{R}{x} = 12 - 4x + \tfrac{1}{3}x^2$$

$$y = \frac{(6 - x)^2}{3} \qquad \text{(demand function)}$$

NATIONAL INCOME, CONSUMPTION, AND SAVINGS

If the consumption function is given by

$$c = f(x)$$

where c is total national consumption and x is total national income, then the *marginal propensity to consume* is the derivative with respect to x of the consumption function

$$\frac{dc}{dx} = f'(x)$$

and, assuming $x = c + s$, where s is savings, the *marginal propensity to save* is

$$\frac{ds}{dx} = 1 - \frac{dc}{dx}$$

Total national consumption is the integral with respect to x of the marginal propensity to consume,

$$c = \int f'(x)\, dx = f(x) + C$$

An initial condition must be specified to obtain a unique consumption function by integrating the corresponding function for the marginal propensity to consume.

EXAMPLE

The marginal propensity to consume (in billions of dollars) is

$$\frac{dc}{dx} = 0.7 + \frac{0.2}{\sqrt{x}}$$

When income is zero, consumption is 8 billion dollars. Find the consumption function.

$$c = \int \left(0.7 + \frac{0.2}{\sqrt{x}}\right) dx$$
$$= 0.7x + 0.4\sqrt{x} + C$$

If $x = 0$, $c = 8$, and thus $C = 8$ and

$$c = 8 + 0.7x + 0.4\sqrt{x} \quad \text{(consumption function)}$$

EXAMPLE

The marginal propensity to save is $\frac{1}{3}$. When income is zero, consumption is 11 billion dollars. Find the consumption function.

$$\frac{dc}{dx} = 1 - \frac{ds}{dx} = \frac{2}{3}$$

$$c = \int \tfrac{2}{3}\, dx$$

$$= \tfrac{2}{3}x + C$$

If $x = 0$, $c = 11$, and thus $C = 11$ and

$$c = \tfrac{2}{3}x + 11 \quad \text{(consumption function)}$$

CAPITAL FORMATION

The process of adding to a given stock of capital is referred to as *capital formation*. If this process is considered to be continuous over time, capital stock can be expressed as a function of time, $K(t)$, and the rate of capital formation is then given by $\frac{dK(t)}{dt} = K'(t)$. The rate of capital formation at time t is the same as the rate of *net investment* flow at time t, denoted by $I(t)$. Thus

$$K(t) = \int K'(t)\, dt = \int I(t)\, dt$$

and capital stock is the integral with respect to time of the rate of capital formation or, equivalently, the integral with respect to time of net investment. And, since

$$\int I(t)\, dt = K(t) + C$$

an initial condition must be specified to obtain a unique function for capital by integrating the rate of net-investment flow. For example, if the capital at time zero is a specified amount, $K(0)$, then this condition can be used to evaluate the constant of integration.

EXAMPLE

If investment flow is given by $I(t) = 5t^{3/7}$ and the initial capital stock at $t = 0$ is $K(0)$, find the function representing capital, K.

$$K = \int 5t^{3/7}\, dt$$

$$= \tfrac{7}{2} t^{10/7} + C$$

If $t = 0$, $K = C$, and thus $C = K(0)$ and

$$K = \tfrac{7}{2} t^{10/7} + K(0) \qquad \text{(capital)}$$

EXAMPLE

If investment flow is given by $I(t) = 15t^{1/4}$ and the initial capital stock at $t = 0$ is 30, find the function representing capital, K.

$$K = \int 15t^{1/4}\, dt$$

$$= 12t^{5/4} + C$$

If $t = 0$, $K = 30$, and thus $C = 30$ and

$$K = 12t^{5/4} + 30$$

PROBLEMS

1. If marginal revenue is a constant different from zero, show that price is constant.
2. If $R'(x) = 0$ and $R(0) \neq 0$, what is the nature of the demand curve?
3. If marginal cost is constant, show that the cost function is a straight line.
4. The marginal propensity to consume (in billions of dollars) is

$$\frac{dc}{dx} = 0.6 + \frac{0.5}{2x^{1/2}}$$

When income is zero, consumption is 10 billion dollars. Find the consumption function.
5. The marginal cost function for production is $y' = 10 + 24x - 3x^2$; if the (total) cost of producing 1 unit is 25, find the total cost function and the average cost function.
6. The marginal propensity to save is $\tfrac{1}{2}$. When income is zero, consumption is 6 billion dollars. Find the consumption function.
7. If marginal revenue is $R' = 15 - 9x - 3x^2$, find the revenue and demand functions.
8. If marginal revenue is $R' = \dfrac{3}{x^2} - \dfrac{2}{x}$, find the revenue and demand functions if $R(1) = 6$.

9. If marginal revenue is $R' = 10 - 5x$, find the revenue and demand functions.

10. If marginal revenue is $R' = 20 - 3x^2$, find the revenue and demand functions.

11. The marginal propensity to consume (in billions of dollars) is

$$\frac{dc}{dx} = 0.5 + \frac{1}{3x^{1/3}}$$

When income is zero, consumption is 6 billion dollars. Find the consumption function.

12. The marginal propensity to save (in billions of dollars) is

$$\frac{dc}{ds} = 1 - 0.4 - \frac{1}{6x^{2/3}}$$

When income is zero, consumption is 9 billion dollars. Find the consumption function.

13. If investment flow is given by $I(t) = 20t^{3/7}$ and the initial capital stock at $t = 0$ is 25, find the function representing capital, K.

14. If investment flow is given by $I(t) = 25t^{4/11}$ and the initial capital stock at $t = 0$ is 22, find the function representing capital, K.

Answers to Odd-Numbered Problems

5. $y = 10x + 12x^2 - x^3 + 4$

$\bar{y} = 10 + 12x - x^2 + \frac{4}{x}$

7. $R = 15x - \frac{9}{2}x^2 - x^3$

$y = 15 - \frac{9}{2}x - x^2$

9. $R = 10x - \frac{5}{2}x^2$

$y = 10 - \frac{5}{2}x$

11. $c = 0.5x + 0.5x^{2/3} + 6$

13. $K = 14t^{10/7} + 25$

4.4 Definite Integration

As noted above, finding the areas of figures of various shapes was one of the problems that led to the development of integral calculus. In elementary geometry, the area of a rectangle is shown to be equal to the product of its width and its height, and from this the areas of other figures bounded by straight-line segments are obtained by elementary geometrical methods. However, these methods are not directly applicable to figures bounded entirely or in part by curved lines. In general, to find areas of curvilinear figures, the method of limits must be used; for example, the area of a circle is obtained in geometry by considering it to be the common limit of sets of regular inscribed and circumscribed polygons as the number of their sides is indefinitely increased. This use of the method of limits leads to the interpretation of the definite integral as the area under a curve.

Consider the problem of determining the area bounded by the continuous positive curve $y = f(x)$, the x-axis, and the lines $x = a$ and $x = b$. Divide the base $[a, b]$ into n subintervals and denote the points of division by $a = x_1, x_2, \ldots, x_n, x_{n+1} = b$ and the lengths of the n subintervals by $\Delta x_i = x_{i+1} - x_i$; $i = 1, \ldots, n$. Erect ordinates at the points of division and inscribe rectangles (see Figure 4.3).

The areas of these inscribed rectangles are $f(x_1)\, \Delta x_1, f(x_2)\, \Delta x_2, \ldots, f(x_n)\, \Delta x_n$ and their sum is

$$\sum_{i=1}^{n} f(x_i)\, \Delta x_i$$

Figure 4.3

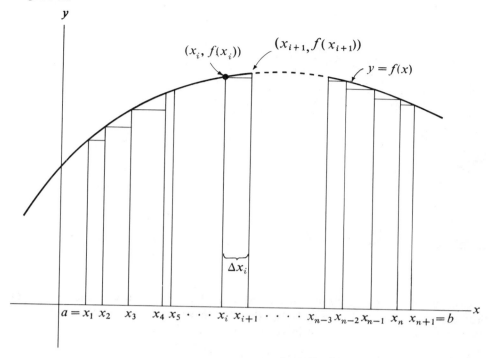

By increasing the number of inscribed rectangles, that is, by letting $n \to \infty$ and max $\Delta x_i \to 0$, the area under the curve between a and b which is not included in the rectangles is decreased and, in fact, approaches zero.

DEFINITION: The area bounded by the continuous positive function

$$y = f(x)$$

the x-axis, and two fixed ordinates $x = a$, $x = b$ is

$$A = \lim_{\substack{n \to \infty \\ \text{max } \Delta x_i \to 0}} \sum_{i=1}^{n} f(x_i)\, \Delta x_i$$

NOTE: The same limit would be obtained by circumscribing rather than inscribing the rectangles, that is,

$$\lim_{\substack{n \to \infty \\ \text{max } \Delta x_i \to 0}} \sum_{i=1}^{n} f(x_i)\, \Delta x_i = \lim_{\substack{n \to \infty \\ \text{max } \Delta x_i \to 0}} \sum_{i=1}^{n} f(x_{i+1})\, \Delta x_i$$

If $f(x)$ is nonmonotonic, the argument is modified by using, respectively, the minimum or maximum values of the function in the intervals rather than $f(x_i)$ or $f(x_{i+1})$. In fact, *any* point in an interval can be used without affecting the result.

If $f(x)$ is continuous for the interval $[a, b]$, then

$$\lim_{\substack{n \to \infty \\ \text{max } \Delta x_i \to 0}} \sum_{i=1}^{n} f(x_i)\, \Delta x_i$$

exists, $f(x)$ is said to be *integrable* over the interval $[a, b]$, and it can be shown that

$$\text{Area} = \lim_{\substack{n \to \infty \\ \text{max } \Delta x_i \to 0}} \sum_{i=1}^{n} f(x_i)\, \Delta x_i = \int_{a}^{b} f(x)\, dx$$

by the following argument.

Figure 4.4

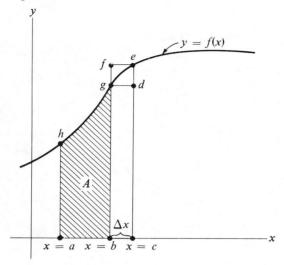

Consider the area between a fixed ordinate at $x = a$ and a variable (movable) ordinate at $x = b$ (see Figure 4.4) and denote the area $abgh$ by A. When x takes a small increment Δx, A takes an increment $\Delta A =$ area $bceg$. Note that

Area $(bcdg) <$ Area $(bceg) <$ Area $(bcef)$

$(bg)(\Delta x) < \Delta A < (ce)(\Delta x)$

$$bg < \frac{\Delta A}{\Delta x} < ce$$

Let $\Delta x \to 0$. (If it happens that the shape of $f(x)$ is such that $ce < bg$, the inequality signs can be reversed without affecting the argument.) Then, since y is a continuous function of x, ce approaches bg and

$$\frac{dA}{dx} = bg = y = f(x)$$

$$dA = f(x)\,dx$$

Integrating,

$$A = \int f(x)\,dx$$

Denote $\int f(x)\,dx$ by $F(x) + C$. Then $A = F(x) + C$. Note that $A = 0$ when $x = a$ and thus

$$0 = F(a) + C$$

$$C = -F(a)$$

and

$$A = F(x) - F(a)$$

For the area $abgh$ (Figure 4.4), $x = b$ and

$$A = F(b) - F(a)$$

which is denoted by

$$\int_a^b y\, dx \qquad \text{or} \qquad \int_a^b f(x)\, dx$$

and is read "the integral from a to b of $y\, dx$." This operation is referred to as *integration between limits*, a being the *lower limit* of integration and b being the *upper limit* of integration. In this context the word "limit" means the value of the variable at one end of its range; this should not be confused with the meaning of the word in the theory of limits. In the evaluation of $\int_a^b f(x)\, dx$, the constant of integration disappears; the integral thus has a definite value and, for this reason, is referred to as the *definite integral* of $f(x)$ from a to b. From the definition of a definite integral, it can be shown that definite integrals have the following properties.

1. $\displaystyle\int_a^b f(x)\, dx = -\int_b^a f(x)\, dx.$

2. $\displaystyle\int_a^a f(x)\, dx = 0.$

3. $\displaystyle\int_a^b f(x)\, dx = \int_a^c f(x)\, dx + \int_c^b f(x)\, dx,$ where $a \le c \le b.$

NOTE: For some problems, definite integrals occur for which one or both limits of integration are infinite. An integral of the form

$$\int_{-\infty}^b f(x)\, dx \qquad \int_a^\infty f(x)\, dx \qquad \int_{-\infty}^\infty f(x)\, dx$$

is referred to as an *improper integral* and is evaluated by taking limits as follows:

$$\int_{-\infty}^b f(x)\, dx = \lim_{a \to -\infty} \int_a^b f(x)\, dx$$

$$\int_a^\infty f(x)\, dx = \lim_{b \to \infty} \int_a^b f(x)\, dx$$

$$\int_{-\infty}^\infty f(x)\, dx = \lim_{\substack{a \to -\infty \\ b \to \infty}} \int_a^b f(x)\, dx$$

If the limit exists, the improper integral *converges*; if the limit does not exist, the improper integral *diverges*.

EXAMPLE

(First Property)

$$\int_1^3 y(y^2 - 4)^2\, dy = \frac{1}{2} \int_1^3 (2y)(y^2 - 4)^2\, dy$$

$$= \left[\frac{(y^2 - 4)^3}{6} \right]_1^3$$

$$= \tfrac{125}{6} - \left(-\tfrac{27}{6}\right)$$

$$= \tfrac{152}{6} = \tfrac{76}{3}$$

$$\int_3^1 y(y^2 - 4)^2 \, dy = \left[\frac{(y^2 - 4)^3}{6}\right]_3^1$$

$$= -\tfrac{27}{6} - \tfrac{125}{6}$$

$$= -\tfrac{152}{6} = -\tfrac{76}{3}$$

and

$$\int_1^3 y(y^2 - 4)^2 \, dy = -\int_3^1 y(y^2 - 4)^2 \, dy$$

(Second Property)

$$\int_{-1}^{-1} \sqrt{1 - z} \, dz = [-\tfrac{2}{3}(1 - z)^{3/2}]_{-1}^{-1}$$

$$= -\tfrac{2}{3}(2)^{3/2} - [-\tfrac{2}{3}(2)^{3/2}]$$

$$= 0$$

(Third Property)

$$\int_1^4 \frac{v + 1}{\sqrt{v}} \, dv = \int_1^4 (v^{1/2} + v^{-1/2}) \, dv$$

$$= [\tfrac{2}{3}v^{3/2} + 2v^{1/2}]_1^4$$

$$= \tfrac{16}{3} + 4 - \tfrac{2}{3} - 2$$

$$= \tfrac{20}{3}$$

$$\int_1^4 \frac{v + 1}{\sqrt{v}} \, dv = \int_1^2 \frac{v + 1}{\sqrt{v}} \, dv + \int_2^4 \frac{v + 1}{\sqrt{v}} \, dv$$

$$= [\tfrac{2}{3}v^{3/2} + 2v^{1/2}]_1^2 + [\tfrac{2}{3}v^{3/2} + 2v^{1/2}]_2^4$$

$$= \tfrac{2}{3}(2)^{3/2} + 2^{3/2} - \tfrac{2}{3} - 2 + \tfrac{16}{3} + 4 - \tfrac{2}{3}(2)^{3/2} - 2^{3/2}$$

$$= \tfrac{20}{3}$$

PROBLEMS

Evaluate the following integrals.

1. $\int_0^1 (x^2 - 2x + 3) \, dx$

2. $\int_{-1}^1 (v + 1)^2 \, dv$

3. $\int_0^2 (4x + 1)^{1/2} \, dx$

4. $\int_0^1 \frac{dx}{(2x + 1)^3}$

5. $\int_{-3}^{-2} t(t + 1)^2 \, dt$

6. $\int_2^5 \left(x^2 + \frac{1}{x^2}\right) dx$

7. $\int_1^3 (2\theta + 1)(3 - \theta) \, d\theta$

8. $\int_{-1}^1 (x^2 + 1)^2 \, dx$

9. $\int_a^{2a} (a + z) \, dz$

10. $\int_1^2 \frac{x^2 - 1}{x^4} \, dx$

11. $\int_1^8 (u^{1/3} - u^{-1/3}) \, du$

12. $\int_{-1}^0 (2x + x^2 - x^3) \, dx$

13. $\int_a^{2a} (a^3 + 3ax^2 + x^3) \, dx$

14. $\int_0^a (\sqrt{a} - \sqrt{x})^2 \, dx$

15. $\int_{1}^{4} (\sqrt{z} - z)^2 \, dz$ 16. $\int_{-1}^{2} (x^2 + x)(3x + 1) \, dx$

Answers to Odd-Numbered Problems

1. $\frac{7}{3}$ 9. $\frac{7}{2}a^2$
3. $\frac{13}{3}$ 11. $\frac{27}{4}$
5. $-\frac{73}{12}$ 13. $\frac{47}{4}a^4$
7. $\frac{26}{3}$ 15. $\frac{37}{10}$

AREA AS A DEFINITE INTEGRAL

The result which justifies the evaluation of area by integration is known as the *fundamental theorem of integral calculus* and can be summarized in somewhat more rigorous form as follows:

Let $f(x)$ be continuous and positive for the interval $x = a$ to $x = b$. Divide this interval into n subintervals of lengths $\Delta x_1, \Delta x_2, \ldots, \Delta x_n$ and choose points, one in each subinterval, with abscissas denoted by $x_1, x_2, \ldots, x_n$, respectively. Then

$$\lim_{\substack{n \to \infty \\ \max \Delta x_i \to 0}} \sum_{i=1}^{n} f(x_i) \, \Delta x_i = \int_{a}^{b} f(x) \, dx = F(b) - F(a)$$

This is an important theorem because it states that the limit of a sum of terms can be evaluated by integration and that this limit can be interpreted as the area under a curve. Specifically, the definite integral $\int_{a}^{b} f(x) \, dx$ can be interpreted as the area bounded by the continuous positive function $y = f(x)$, the x-axis, and the lines $x = a$ and $x = b$, where $a < b$.

EXAMPLE

Find the area bounded by the curve

$y = x^3 + 3x^2$

Figure 4.5

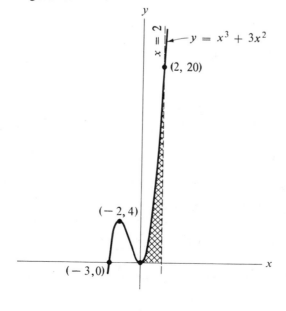

the x-axis, and the lines $x = 0$ and $x = 2$ (see Figure 4.5).

$$A = \int_0^2 (x^3 + 3x^2)\, dx = \left[\frac{x^4}{4} + x^3\right]_0^2 = (4 + 8) - 0 = 12$$

EXAMPLE

Find the area bounded by the curve

$$x^2 y = x^2 - 4$$

the x-axis, and the lines $x = 2$ and $x = 4$ (see Figure 4.6).

Figure 4.6

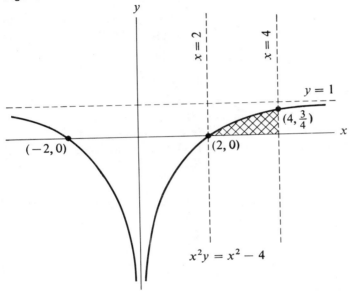

$$A = \int_2^4 \frac{x^2 - 4}{x^2}\, dx = \int_2^4 \left(1 - \frac{4}{x^2}\right) dx = [x + 4x^{-1}]_2^4$$

$$= (4 + 1) - (2 + 2)$$

$$= 1$$

EXAMPLE

Find the area in the first quadrant bounded by the x-axis and the curve

$$y = 6x + x^2 - x^3$$

(see Figure 4.7).

$$A = \int_0^3 (6x + x^2 - x^3)\, dx = \left[3x^2 + \frac{x^3}{3} - \frac{x^4}{4}\right]_0^3 = (27 + 9 - \tfrac{81}{4}) - 0 = 15\tfrac{3}{4}$$

Figure 4.7

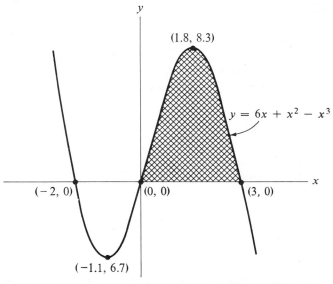

EXAMPLE

Find the total area between the parabola

$$y = x^2 - 4x$$

the x-axis, and the line $x = -2$ (see Figure 4.8).

$$A = \int_{-2}^{0} (x^2 - 4x)\, dx = \left[\frac{x^3}{3} - 2x^2\right]_{-2}^{0} = 0 - (-\tfrac{8}{3} - 8) = 10\tfrac{2}{3}$$

Figure 4.8

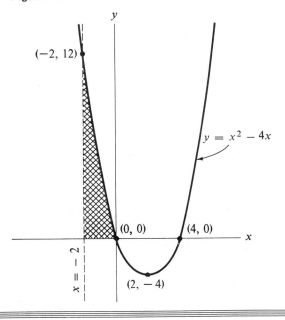

Interpretation of Negative Areas

In the definition of area given above,

$$A = \int_a^b f(x)\, dx$$

$f(x)$ is assumed to be a continuous positive function between a and b. If $f(x)$ is negative between a and b, that is, if the curve $y = f(x)$ lies below the x-axis between a and b, then the value of the integral

$$A = \int_a^b f(x)\, dx$$

is negative. Such areas below the x-axis are called *negative areas*; the total absolute area between a curve, the x-axis, and two ordinates is given by

$$\text{Total area} = \sum (\text{positive areas}) - \sum (\text{negative areas})$$

NOTE: This is equivalent to saying that area is equal to the absolute value of the integral and thus is always positive.

EXAMPLE

Find the area bounded by the curve

$$y = 2x + x^2 - x^3$$

the x-axis, and the lines $x = -1$ and $x = 1$.

The curve is sketched in Figure 4.9. Note that if $y = 0$, $x = -1$, 0, 2. Also, $f(x) < 0$ for $-1 < x < 0$, and $f(x) > 0$ for $0 < x < 1$.

$$A = \int_0^1 (2x + x^2 - x^3)\, dx - \int_{-1}^0 (2x + x^2 - x^3)\, dx$$

$$= \left[x^2 + \frac{x^3}{3} - \frac{x^4}{4} \right]_0^1 - \left[x^2 + \frac{x^3}{3} - \frac{x^4}{4} \right]_{-1}^0$$

$$= [(1 + \tfrac{1}{3} - \tfrac{1}{4}) - 0] - [0 - (1 - \tfrac{1}{3} - \tfrac{1}{4})]$$

$$= \tfrac{13}{12} - (-\tfrac{5}{12}) \text{ (positive area minus negative area)}$$

$$= \tfrac{3}{2}$$

Figure 4.9

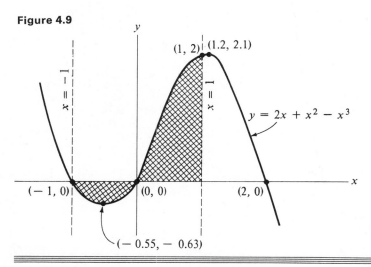

EXAMPLE

Find the area bounded by the curve

$$y = x^3 - 4x$$

and the x-axis.

The curve is sketched in Figure 4.10. Note that if $y = 0$, $x = 0$, -2, 2. Also, $f(x) > 0$ for $-2 < x < 0$ and $f(x) < 0$ for $0 < x < 2$.

Figure 4.10

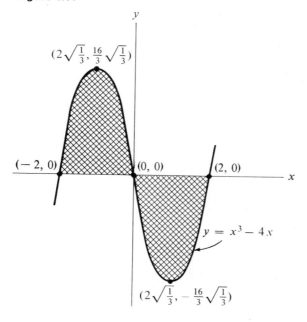

$$A = \int_{-2}^{0} (x^3 - 4x)\, dx - \int_{0}^{2} (x^3 - 4x)\, dx$$

$$= \left[\frac{x^4}{4} - 2x^2\right]_{-2}^{0} - \left[\frac{x^4}{4} - 2x^2\right]_{0}^{2}$$

$$= [0 - (4 - 8)] - [(4 - 8) - 0]$$

$$= 4 - (-4)$$

$$= 8$$

Area Between Two Curves

Suppose that the area to be evaluated is between the curves $y_1 = f(x)$ and $y_2 = g(x)$ and the lines $x = a$ and $x = b$ and that (for definiteness) $f(x) \le g(x)$ for $a \le x \le b$ (see Figure 4.11). Then

$$A = \int_{a}^{b} [g(x) - f(x)]\, dx$$

Note that this formula includes negative areas (with appropriate signs) in the total area between the curves.

Figure 4.11

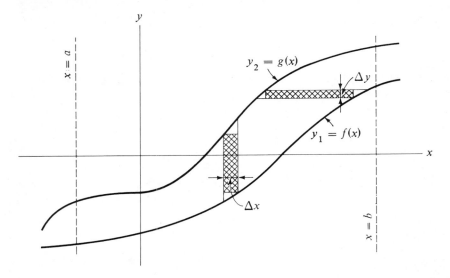

EXAMPLE

Find the area bounded by the curves

$$y = x^2 \qquad \text{and} \qquad y = x$$

Finding the points of intersection of the curves by setting $x = x^2$,

$$x = x^2$$
$$x(1 - x) = 0$$
$$x = 0, 1$$

and the points of intersection are $(0, 0)$ and $(1, 1)$. (See Figure 4.12.)

Figure 4.12

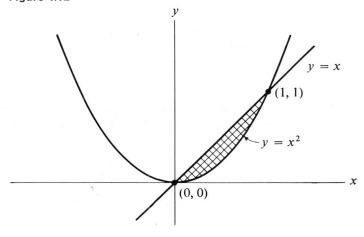

$$A = \int_0^1 (x - x^2)\, dx = \left[\frac{x^2}{2} - \frac{x^3}{3}\right]_0^1$$

$$= (\tfrac{1}{2} - \tfrac{1}{3}) - 0$$

$$= \tfrac{1}{6}$$

EXAMPLE

Find the area bounded by the curves

$$y = x^3 \qquad \text{and} \qquad y = 2x^2$$

Finding the points of intersection of the curves by setting $x^3 = 2x^2$,

$$x^3 = 2x^2$$

$$x^2(x - 2) = 0$$

$$x = 0, 2$$

And the points of intersection are $(0, 0)$ and $(2, 8)$. (See Figure 4.13.)

$$A = \int_0^2 (2x^2 - x^3)\, dx = \left[\frac{2x^3}{3} - \frac{x^4}{4}\right]_0^2$$

$$= (\tfrac{16}{3} - 4) - 0$$

$$= \tfrac{4}{3}$$

Figure 4.13

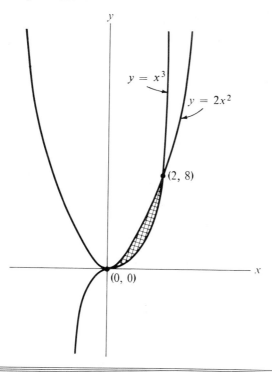

EXAMPLE

Find the area bounded by the curves

$$x + 2y = 2 \qquad y - x = 1 \qquad \text{and} \qquad 2x + y = 7$$

(see Figure 4.14).

Figure 4.14

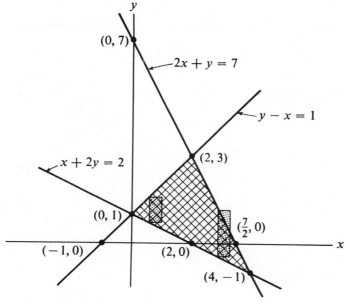

Finding the points of intersection of the straight lines,

$x + 2y = 2$	$x + 2y = 2$	$y - x = 1$
$y - x = 1$	$2x + y = 7$	$2x + y = 7$
$3y = 3$	$-3y = 3$	$3y = 9$
$y = 1$	$y = -1$	$y = 3$
$x = 0$	$x = 4$	$x = 2$

$$A = \int_0^2 \left[(1 + x) - \left(\frac{2 - x}{2} \right) \right] dx + \int_2^4 \left[(7 - 2x) - \left(\frac{2 - x}{2} \right) \right] dx$$

$$= \int_0^2 \tfrac{3}{2}x \, dx + \int_2^4 (6 - \tfrac{3}{2}x) \, dx = \left[\frac{3x^2}{4} \right]_0^2 + \left[6x - \frac{3x^2}{4} \right]_2^4$$

$$= 3 - 0 + (24 - 12) - (12 - 3)$$

$$= 6$$

EXAMPLE

Find the area bounded by the curves

$$y = x^2 \qquad y = x \qquad y = 2x$$

(see Figure 4.15).

Figure 4.15

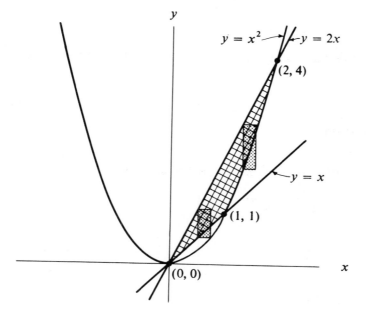

Finding the points of intersection of the curves,

$$y = x = x^2 \qquad y = 2x = x^2 \qquad y = x = 2x$$

$$x(x - 1) = 0 \qquad x(x - 2) = 0 \qquad x = 0$$

$$x = 0, 1 \qquad x = 0, 2 \qquad y = 0$$

If $x = 0$, $y = 0$ If $x = 0$, $y = 0$

If $x = 1$, $y = 1$ If $x = 2$, $y = 4$

Thus

$$A = \int_0^1 (2x - x) \, dx + \int_1^2 (2x - x^2) \, dx$$

$$= \left[\frac{x^2}{2} \right]_0^1 + \left[x^2 - \frac{x^3}{3} \right]_1^2$$

$$= \tfrac{1}{2} - 0 + (4 - \tfrac{8}{3}) - (1 - \tfrac{1}{3})$$

$$= \tfrac{7}{6}$$

NOTE: In evaluating an area it is of no theoretical importance whether horizontal or vertical elements of area are used (see Figure 4.11); the choice depends on the number and difficulty of the integrals needed to determine the particular area. In the above examples, the curves can be written easily in the form $x = g(y)$, and horizontal elements of area can then be used.

EXAMPLE

The area bounded by the curves

$$y = x^2 \qquad \text{and} \qquad y = x$$

could have been determined using horizontal elements of area as follows:

$$A = \int_0^1 (y^{1/2} - y)\, dy = \left[\frac{2y^{3/2}}{3} - \frac{y^2}{2}\right]_0^1 = (\tfrac{2}{3} - \tfrac{1}{2}) - 0 = \tfrac{1}{6}$$

EXAMPLE

The area bounded by the curves

$$y = x^3 \qquad \text{and} \qquad y = 2x^2$$

could have been determined using horizontal elements of area as follows:

$$A = \int_0^8 \left(y^{1/3} - \frac{y^{1/2}}{2^{1/2}}\right) dy = \left[\frac{3y^{4/3}}{4} - \frac{2^{1/2}y^{3/2}}{3}\right]_0^8$$

$$= (12 - \tfrac{32}{3}) - 0 = \tfrac{4}{3}$$

EXAMPLE

The area bounded by the curves

$$x + 2y = 2 \qquad y - x = 1 \qquad 2x + y = 7$$

could have been determined using horizontal elements of area as follows:

$$A = \int_{-1}^1 \left[\left(\frac{7 - y}{2}\right) - (2 - 2y)\right] dy + \int_1^3 \left[\left(\frac{7 - y}{2}\right) - (y - 1)\right] dy$$

$$= \int_{-1}^1 \tfrac{3}{2}(y + 1)\, dy + \int_1^3 \tfrac{3}{2}(3 - y)\, dy$$

$$= \left[\frac{3y^2}{4} + \frac{3y}{2}\right]_{-1}^1 + \left[\frac{9y}{2} - \frac{3y^2}{4}\right]_1^3$$

$$= (\tfrac{3}{4} + \tfrac{3}{2}) - (\tfrac{3}{4} - \tfrac{3}{2}) + (\tfrac{27}{2} - \tfrac{27}{4}) - (\tfrac{9}{2} - \tfrac{3}{4})$$

$$= 6$$

EXAMPLE

The area bounded by the curves

$$y = x^2 \qquad y = x \qquad y = 2x$$

could have been determined using horizontal elements of area as follows:

$$A = \int_0^1 \left(y - \frac{y}{2}\right) dy + \int_1^4 \left(y^{1/2} - \frac{y}{2}\right) dy$$

$$= \left[\frac{y^2}{4}\right]_0^1 + \left[\frac{2y^{3/2}}{3} - \frac{y^2}{4}\right]_1^4$$

$$= \tfrac{1}{4} - 0 + (\tfrac{16}{3} - 4) - (\tfrac{2}{3} - \tfrac{1}{4})$$

$$= \tfrac{7}{6}$$

Probability as an Area

One of the most useful applications of definite integration as a method of obtaining the area under a curve is in evaluating probabilities. The probability of an event can be obtained by determining the corresponding area under a frequency function. A *frequency function* for a continuous variable x is a function $f(x)$ having the following properties

1. $f(x) \geq 0$

2. $\displaystyle\int_{-\infty}^{\infty} f(x)\, dx = 1$

3. $\displaystyle\int_{a}^{b} f(x)\, dx = P(a < x < b)$

where a and b are any two values of x and $a < b$.

These properties state that (1) probability is always nonnegative; (2) the probability of an event that is certain to occur is one; and (3) the probability that the value of x is in the interval (a, b) is equal to the area bounded by $y = f(x)$, $y = 0$, $x = a$, and $x = b$. (See Figure 4.16).

NOTE: If $f(x)$ is continuous, $P(a < x < b) = P(a \leq x \leq b)$.

Figure 4.16

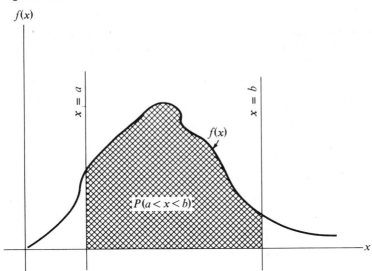

EXAMPLE

In an autoparts warehouse, the proportion of orders filled per day has a frequency function given by

$$f(x) = 20(x^3 - x^4) \qquad 0 \leq x \leq 1$$

(a) What is the probability that less than 20 percent of the orders will be filled in a day?
(b) What is the probability that between 90 and 100 percent of the orders will be filled in a day?

(a) $P(x < 0.20) = 20 \int_0^{0.2} (x^3 - x^4)\, dx$

$$= 20 \left[\frac{x^4}{4} - \frac{x^5}{5} \right]_0^{0.2}$$

$$= 20 \left[\left(\frac{0.0016}{4} \right) - \left(\frac{0.00032}{5} \right) - 0 \right]$$

$$= 0.008 - 0.00128$$

$$= 0.00672$$

(See area a in Figure 4.17.)

Thus the probability of filling less than 20 percent of the orders is 0.00672, which means that this event is quite unlikely to occur.

(b) $P(0.9 \le x \le 1) = 20 \int_{0.9}^1 (x^3 - x^4)\, dx$

$$= 20 \left[\frac{x^4}{4} - \frac{x^5}{5} \right]_{0.9}^1$$

$$= 20 \left[\left(\frac{1}{4} - \frac{1}{5} \right) - \left(\frac{0.6561}{4} - \frac{0.59049}{5} \right) \right]$$

$$= (5 - 4) - (3.2805 - 2.36196)$$

$$= 0.08146$$

(See area b in Figure 4.17.)

Thus the probability of filling between 90 and 100 percent of the orders is 0.08146.

Note that, since $f(x) = 20(x^3 - x^4)$ is defined only for $0 \le x \le 1$ and is zero elsewhere,

$$\int_{-\infty}^{\infty} f(x)\, dx = \int_0^1 f(x)\, dx = \int_0^1 20(x^3 - x^4)\, dx$$

$$= 20 \left[\frac{x^4}{4} - \frac{x^5}{5} \right]_0^1$$

$$= 1$$

Figure 4.17

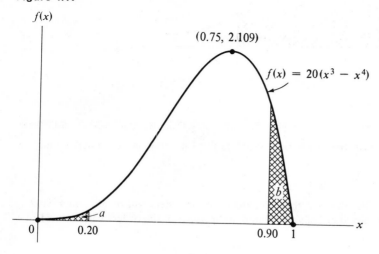

So $\int_{-\infty}^{\infty} f(x)\, dx = 1$ as required for a frequency function; note also that $f(x) \geq 0$ for $0 \leq x \leq 1$ and is zero elsewhere.

EXAMPLE

Suppose that measurements of daily temperature are recorded to the nearest tenth of a degree. Then the difference between the true and recorded temperatures, the rounding error, is between -0.05 and 0.05 degrees. If the error is uniformly distributed in this interval, its frequency function is represented by

$$f(x) = \frac{1}{0.1} = 10 \qquad -0.05 \leq x \leq 0.05$$

Note that, in general, if x is uniformly distributed on the interval $a \leq x \leq b$, then

$$f(x) = \frac{1}{b-a} \qquad a \leq x \leq b$$

and is zero elsewhere.

(a) What is the probability that the rounding error is between -0.01 and 0.01?
(b) What is the probability that the rounding error is between 0.04 and 0.05?

(a) $P(-0.01 \leq x \leq 0.01) = \int_{-0.01}^{0.01} 10\, dx$

$$= [10x]_{-0.01}^{0.01}$$

$$= 0.1 - (-0.1) = 0.2$$

(See area a in Figure 4.18.)

(b) $P(0.04 \leq x \leq 0.05) = \int_{0.04}^{0.05} 10\, dx$

$$= [10x]_{0.04}^{0.05}$$

$$= 0.5 - 0.4 = 0.1$$

(See area b in Figure 4.18.)

Figure 4.18

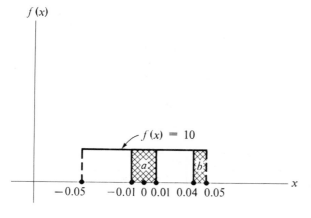

Note that

$$\int_{-\infty}^{\infty} 10 \, dx = \int_{-0.05}^{0.05} 10 \, dx = [10x]_{-0.05}^{0.05}$$

$$= 0.5 - (-0.5) = 1$$

So $\int_{-\infty}^{\infty} f(x) \, dx = 1$ as required for a frequency function; note also that $f(x) \geq 0$ for $-0.05 \leq x \leq 0.05$ and is zero elsewhere.

PROBLEMS

Sketch each of the following curves and find the area bounded by the curve, the x-axis, and the given ordinates.

1. $y = \sqrt{x}$; $x = 1$, $x = 16$
2. $y = 2x + 1$; $x = 0$, $x = 4$
3. $y = x^{99}$; $x = 0$, $x = 1$
4. $y = 3x^2$; $x = 1$, $x = 3$
5. $y = x^2 - 3x$; $x = -1$, $x = 4$
6. $y = -x^2 + 4x$ (and x-axis)
7. $f(x) = \begin{cases} x^2 & x \leq 2 \\ -x + 6 & x > 2 \end{cases}$ $x = 0$, $x = 3$
8. $f(x) = \begin{cases} 2x + 3 & x \leq 3 \\ -x + 12 & x > 3 \end{cases}$ $x = 2$, $x = 5$
9. Find the area between the curve $y = 2x^4 - x^2$, the x-axis, and the two minimum ordinates.
10. Find the area bounded by the coordinate axes and the parabolic arc $\sqrt{x} + \sqrt{y} = \sqrt{a}$.

Draw a sketch and find the area bounded by the following curves.

11. $y^2 = 2x$
    $y = x - 4$
12. $x^2 = 2ay$
    $y = 2a$
13. $y = x - x^2$
    $y = -x$
14. $y^2 = 4ax$
    $x^2 = 4ay$
15. $y^2 = x$
    $y = x^3$
16. $y = (x - 1)^3$
    $y = x^2 - x - 1$
17. $y^2 = 5a^2 - ax$
    $y^2 = 4ax$
18. $x^2y = 4$
    $y = 7 - 3x$
19. $y = x^2$
    $y = 8 - x^2$
    $y = 4x + 12$
20. $y^3 = x^2$
    $2x + y + 1 = 0$
    $x - y = 4$

21. $y = x^2$
    $y = x + 2$
    $y = -3x + 18$
22. $y = 4x - 4$
    $y = \frac{1}{3}x^2$
    $y = 6 - x$
23. $y = x^3 + 3x^2 + 2$
    $y = x^3 + 6x^2 - 25$
24. $y = 25 - x^2$
    $y = (5 - x)^2$
25. $y = x^3 - 3x^2 - 10x$
    $y = -6x$
26. $y = (x + 2)(x - 1)(x - 5)$
    $y = (x + 2)(x - 1)$
27. $y = x(x - 3)(x + 3)$
    $y = -5x$
28. $y = x^3 + 3x^2 + 6$
    $y = x^3 + 4x^2 + 5x$
29. $y = x^3 - 5x^2 - 8x + 12$
    $y = x^3 - 6x^2 + 21$

HINTS
15. $y^2 = x$ and $y = x^3$ intersect at $(0, 0)$ and $(1, 1)$
18. $x^2y = 4$ and $y = 7 - 3x$ intersect at $(1, 4)$ and $(2, 1)$
20. $y^3 = x^2$ and $2x + y + 1 = 0$ intersect at $(-1, 1)$
    $y^3 = x^2$ and $x - y = 4$ intersect at $(8, 4)$

29. $x^3 - 5x^2 - 8x + 12 = (x + 2)(x - 1)(x - 6)$

30. A computer center is open 12 hours a day and repairs, except for emergencies, are scheduled for the other 12 hours. The frequency function for the number of hours the center is actually in operation is given by

$$f(x) = \frac{1}{24} + \frac{x^2}{1152} \qquad 0 \le x \le 12$$

a. Find the probability that the center is in operation between 10 and 12 hours a day. b. Find the probability that the center is in operation less than 6 hours a day.

31. A firm has a very large number of company cars for use by its employees. Records of the time each car is out of service for repairs are kept as the basis for deciding when a car should be sold. The frequency function for the total number of days a car is out of service before it is considered too expensive to repair and is sold is given by

$$f(x) = 0.2e^{-0.2x} \qquad 0 \le x < \infty$$

a. Find the probability that a car is out of service a total of more than 30 days before being sold. b. Find the probability that a car is out of service a total of less than 5 days before being sold.

32. Determine whether each of the following is a frequency function.

a. $f(x) = x^{-2}, \qquad 1 \le x < \infty$

b. $f(x) = \frac{3}{8} - \frac{x^2}{576}, \qquad 0 \le x \le 24$

c. $f(x) = 2e^{-4x}, \qquad 0 \le x < \infty$

d. $f(x) = \frac{1}{10}, \qquad 1 \le x \le 20$

e. $f(x) = \frac{4x^3}{15}, \qquad 1 \le x \le 2$

f. $f(x) = \frac{144}{5}x - 6, \qquad \frac{1}{3} \le x \le \frac{1}{2}$

Answers to Odd-Numbered Problems

1. 42
3. 0.01
5. $\frac{49}{6}$
7. $\frac{37}{6}$
9. $\frac{7}{120}$
11. 18
13. $\frac{4}{3}$
15. $\frac{5}{12}$
17. $\frac{40}{3}a^2$

19. 64
21. $\frac{23}{6}$
23. 108
25. $96\frac{3}{4}$
27. 8
29. $166\frac{2}{3}$
31. a. 0.002
    b. 0.632

4.5 Applications of Definite Integration in Business and Economics

Definite integration has a variety of applications in business and economics. Applications involving consumers' surplus, producers' surplus, and revenue vs. cost are discussed in this section.

CONSUMERS' SURPLUS

A demand function represents the quantities of a commodity that would be purchased at various prices. If the market price is y_0 and the corresponding market demand is x_0, then those consumers who would be willing to pay more than this market price gain from the fact that the price is only y_0 (see Figure 4.19). Under certain economic assumptions, the total consumer gain is represented by the area below the demand curve and above the line $y = y_0$ and is known as *consumers'*

Figure 4.19

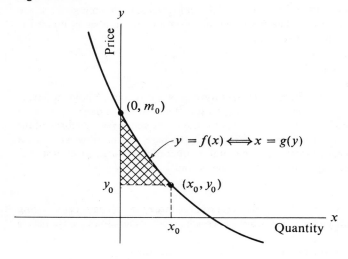

surplus. This area is evaluated as follows:

$$\text{consumers' surplus} = \int_0^{x_0} f(x)\,dx - x_0 y_0$$

where the demand function is $y = f(x)$; alternatively,

$$\text{consumers' surplus} = \int_{y_0}^{m_0} g(y)\,dy$$

where the demand function is $x = g(y)$ and m_0 is the value of y when $x = 0$, that is, m_0 is the y-intercept of the demand function. Thus

$$\text{consumers' surplus} = \int_0^{x_0} f(x)\,dx - x_0 y_0 = \int_{y_0}^{m_0} g(y)\,dy$$

Note that consumers' surplus is generally in the units used for y; for example, if y is in dollars, so is consumers' surplus.

EXAMPLE

If the demand function is $y = 32 - 4x - x^2$, find the consumers' surplus

(a) if $x_0 = 3$,
(b) if $y_0 = 27$. (See Figure 4.20.)

$$\begin{aligned}
\text{(a) consumers' surplus} &= \int_0^3 (32 - 4x - x^2)\,dx - (3)(11) \\
&= \left[32x - 2x^2 - \frac{x^3}{3} \right]_0^3 - 33 \\
&= (96 - 18 - 9) - 0 - 33 \\
&= 36
\end{aligned}$$

Figure 4.20

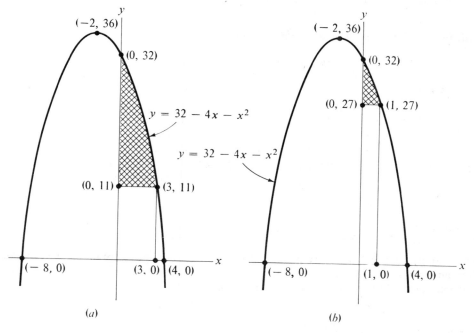

(a) (b)

(b) consumers' surplus $= \displaystyle\int_0^1 (32 - 4x - x^2)\, dx - (1)(27)$

$$= \left[32x - 2x^2 - \frac{x^3}{3} \right]_0^1 - 27$$

$$= (32 - 2 - \tfrac{1}{3}) - 0 - 27$$

$$= \tfrac{8}{3}$$

EXAMPLE

If the demand function is $y = \sqrt{9-x}$ and $x_0 = 5$, find the consumers' surplus using two different methods (see Figure 4.21).

Figure 4.21

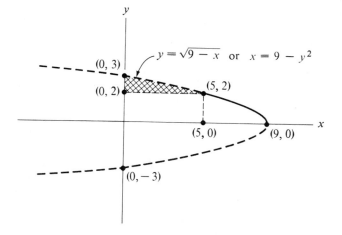

$$\text{consumers' surplus} = \int_0^5 (9-x)^{1/2}\,dx - (5)(2) = \int_2^3 (9-y^2)\,dy$$

$$\int_0^5 (9-x)^{1/2}\,dx - 10 = [-\tfrac{2}{3}(9-x)^{3/2}]_0^5 - 10$$

$$= -\tfrac{16}{3} - (-18) - 10 = \tfrac{8}{3}$$

Alternatively,

$$\int_2^3 (9-y^2)\,dy = \left[9y - \frac{y^3}{3}\right]_2^3$$

$$= (27-9) - (18 - \tfrac{8}{3}) = \tfrac{8}{3} \qquad \text{(as above)}$$

EXAMPLE

The quantity sold and the corresponding price, under a monopoly, are determined by the demand function $y = 16 - x^2$ and by the marginal cost function $y' = 6 + x$ in such a way as to maximize profit. Determine the corresponding consumers' surplus (see Figure 4.22).

$$\text{revenue} = 16x - x^3$$

$$\text{marginal revenue} = 16 - 3x^2$$

Profit is maximized when marginal revenue equals marginal cost (see page 295)—that is, when

$$16 - 3x^2 = 6 + x$$

$$3x^2 + x - 10 = 0$$

$$(3x - 5)(x + 2) = 0$$

$$x = \tfrac{5}{3}, \; -2$$

Figure 4.22

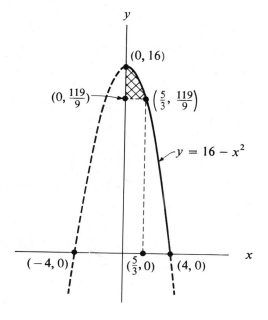

so $x_0 = \frac{5}{3}$, $y_0 = \frac{119}{9}$.

$$\text{consumers' surplus} = \int_0^{5/3} (16 - x^2)\, dx - (\tfrac{5}{3})(\tfrac{119}{9})$$

$$= \left[16x - \frac{x^3}{3} \right]_0^{5/3} - \frac{595}{27}$$

$$= (\tfrac{80}{3} - \tfrac{125}{81}) - 0 - \tfrac{595}{27}$$

$$= \tfrac{250}{81} \approx 3.09$$

PRODUCERS' SURPLUS

A supply function represents the respective quantities of a commodity that would be supplied at various prices. If the market price is y_0 and the corresponding market supply is x_0, then those producers who would be willing to supply the commodity below this market price gain from the fact that the price is y_0. Under certain economic assumptions the total producer gain is represented by the area above the supply curve and below the line $y = y_0$ and is known as *producers' surplus* (see Figure 4.23). This area is evaluated as follows:

$$\text{producers' surplus} = x_0 y_0 - \int_0^{x_0} f(x)\, dx$$

where the supply function is $y = f(x)$ and as

$$\text{producers' surplus} = \int_{M_0}^{y_0} g(y)\, dy$$

where the supply function is $x = g(y)$ and M_0 is the value of y when $x = 0$, that is, M_0 is the y-intercept of the supply function. Thus

$$\text{producers' surplus} = x_0 y_0 - \int_0^{x_0} f(x)\, dx = \int_{M_0}^{y_0} g(y)\, dy$$

As is the case for consumers' surplus, producers' surplus is generally in the units used for y.

Figure 4.23

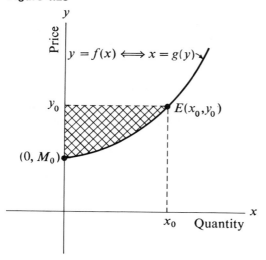

EXAMPLE

If the supply function is $y = (x + 2)^2$ and the price is $y_0 = 25$, find the producers' surplus using two different methods (see Figure 4.24).

$$\text{producers' surplus} = (3)(25) - \int_0^3 (x + 2)^2 \, dx = \int_4^{25} (y^{1/2} - 2) \, dy$$

$$75 - \int_0^3 (x + 2)^2 \, dx = 75 - \left[\frac{(x + 2)^3}{3} \right]_0^3 = 75 - \left(\tfrac{125}{3} - \tfrac{8}{3} \right) = 36$$

Figure 4.24

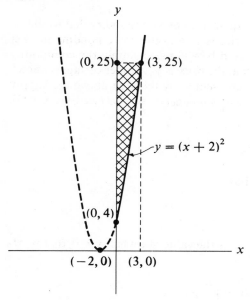

Alternatively,

$$\int_4^{25} (y^{1/2} - 2) \, dy = \left[\frac{2y^{3/2}}{3} - 2y \right]_4^{25} = \left(\tfrac{250}{3} - 50 \right) - \left(\tfrac{16}{3} - 8 \right) = 36$$

(as above).

EXAMPLE

The quantity demanded and the corresponding price, under pure competition, are determined by the demand and supply functions $y = 16 - x^2$ and $y = 4 + x$, respectively. Determine the corresponding producers' surplus (see Figure 4.25).

$$y = 16 - x^2 = 4 + x$$

$$x^2 + x - 12 = 0$$

$$(x + 4)(x - 3) = 0$$

$$x = 3, \; -4$$

$$x_0 = 3, \quad y_0 = 7$$

Figure 4.25

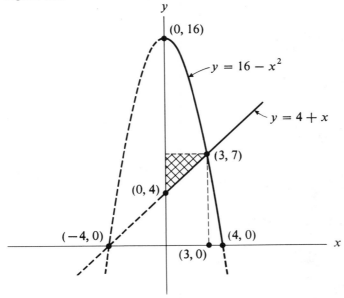

$$\text{producers' surplus} = (3)(7) - \int_0^3 (4 + x)\, dx$$

$$= 21 - \left[4x + \frac{x^2}{2}\right]_0^3$$

$$= 21 - [(12 + \tfrac{9}{2}) - 0]$$

$$= \tfrac{9}{2}$$

NOTE: The area represented by $\int_0^3 (4 + x)\, dx$ could have been evaluated also by the formula for the area of a trapezoid, $A = \frac{1}{2}a(b_1 + b_2) = \frac{3}{2}(4 + 7) = \frac{33}{2}$.

EXAMPLE

The quantity demanded and the corresponding price, under pure competition, are determined by the demand and supply functions $y = 36 - x^2$ and $y = 6 + (x^2/4)$, respectively. Determine the corresponding consumers' surplus and producers' surplus (see Figure 4.26).

$$y = 36 - x^2 = 6 + \frac{x^2}{4}$$

$$5x^2 = 120$$

$$x^2 = 24$$

$$x = \pm 2\sqrt{6}$$

$$x_0 = 2\sqrt{6}, \quad y_0 = 12$$

$$\text{consumers' surplus} = \int_0^{2\sqrt{6}} (36 - x^2)\, dx - (2\sqrt{6})(12)$$

$$= \left[36x - \frac{x^3}{3}\right]_0^{2\sqrt{6}} - 24\sqrt{6}$$

$$= (72\sqrt{6} - 16\sqrt{6}) - 0 - 24\sqrt{6}$$

$$= 32\sqrt{6} \approx 78.4$$

Figure 4.26

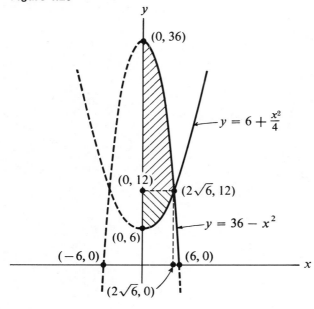

$$\text{producers' surplus} = (2\sqrt{6})(12) - \int_0^{2\sqrt{6}} \left(6 + \frac{x^2}{4}\right) dx$$

$$= 24\sqrt{6} - \left[6x + \frac{x^3}{12}\right]_0^{2\sqrt{6}}$$

$$= 24\sqrt{6} - (12\sqrt{6} + 4\sqrt{6}) - 0$$

$$= 8\sqrt{6} \approx 19.6$$

REVENUE VERSUS COST

Integration can be used to determine total profit or total net earnings in various contexts. In general, profit is maximized (assuming pure competition) when marginal revenue equals marginal cost. Total profit can be obtained as the integral of marginal revenue minus marginal cost from zero to the quantity for which profit is maximized.

EXAMPLE

Find the profit-maximizing output and the total profit at that point if the marginal revenue and marginal cost functions are given by

$$MR = 25 - 5x - 2x^2$$
$$MC = 15 - 2x - x^2$$

(see Figure 4.27).

If $MR - MC = 0$,

$$25 - 5x - 2x^2 - 15 + 2x + x^2 = 0$$
$$10 - 3x - x^2 = 0$$
$$(5 + x)(2 - x) = 0$$
$$x = -5, 2$$

Figure 4.27

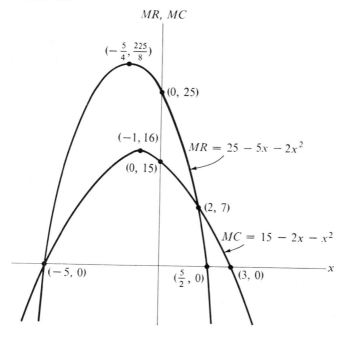

The first derivative of $MR - MC$ is the second derivative of total profit and its sign thus indicates whether profit is maximized or minimized for a particular value of x.

$$\frac{d}{dx}(MR - MC) = \frac{d^2P}{dx^2} = -3 - 2x \qquad \text{and} \qquad \frac{d^2P}{dx^2}\bigg|_{x=2} = -7$$

so profit is maximized for $x = 2$.

$$\text{total profit} = \int_0^2 [(25 - 5x - 2x^2) - (15 - 2x - x^2)]\, dx$$

$$= \int_0^2 (10 - 3x - x^2)\, dx$$

$$= \left[10x - \frac{3x^2}{2} - \frac{x^3}{3}\right]_0^2$$

$$= (20 - 6 - \tfrac{8}{3}) - 0$$

$$= \tfrac{34}{3}$$

EXAMPLE

A manufacturing company has purchased a machine that has an output representing additional earnings (additional revenue minus additional cost of labor and materials) at time t of

$$E(t) = 225 - \tfrac{1}{4}t^2$$

Figure 4.28

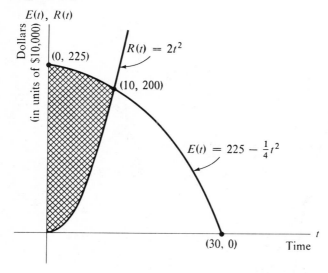

where $E(t)$ is in units of $10,000 and t is years. The additional repair and maintenance cost at time t is

$$R(t) = 2t^2$$

where $R(t)$ is in units of $10,000 and t is years. First, suppose that the machine can be disposed of at any time with no cost or salvage value. Then the machine should be disposed of at the time when additional earnings equals additional cost of repair and maintenance (see Figure 4.28).

Additional earnings equals additional cost of repair and maintenance if

$$225 - \tfrac{1}{4}t^2 = 2t^2$$
$$225 = \tfrac{9}{4}t^2$$
$$t^2 = 100$$
$$t = 10$$

Thus the machine should be disposed of after 10 years. The total net earnings (earnings minus cost of repair and maintenance) after 10 years is

$$\int_0^{10} [E(t) - R(t)] \, dt = \int_0^{10} [(225 - \tfrac{1}{4}t^2) - 2t^2] \, dt = \int_0^{10} (225 - \tfrac{9}{4}t^2) \, dt$$
$$= [225t - \tfrac{3}{4}t^3]_0^{10}$$
$$= (2250 - 750) - 0$$
$$= 1500 \quad \text{or } \$15,000,000$$

Now suppose the machine has a salvage value at time t of

$$S(t) = \frac{6480}{6 + t}$$

where $S(t)$ is in units of $10,000 and t is years. Then the company will maximize its net earnings if it disposes of the machine at time T when the net earnings after T equals the salvage value at T (see Figure 4.29).

Figure 4.29

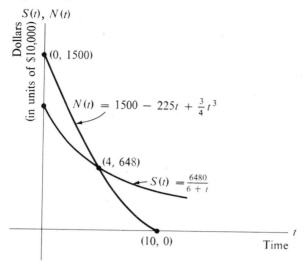

Net earnings after T is

$$N(t) = \int_{T}^{10} [E(t) - R(t)] \, dt = \int_{T}^{10} (225 - \tfrac{9}{4}t^2) \, dt$$

$$= \left[225t - \frac{3t^3}{4} \right]_{T}^{10}$$

$$= \left[(2250 - 750) - \left(225T - \frac{3T^3}{4} \right) \right]$$

$$= 1500 - 225T + \tfrac{3}{4}T^3$$

Net earnings after T equals salvage value at T if

$$\frac{6480}{6 + T} = 1500 - 225T + \tfrac{3}{4}T^3$$

$$6480 = 9000 - 1350T + \tfrac{9}{2}T^3 + 1500T - 225T^2 + \tfrac{3}{4}T^4$$

$$0 = 2520 + 150T - 225T^2 + \tfrac{9}{2}T^3 + \tfrac{3}{4}T^4$$

$$= (T - 4)(\tfrac{3}{4}T^3 + \tfrac{15}{2}T^2 - 195T - 630)$$

Thus the machine should be disposed of after 4 years.

EXAMPLE

A company is considering adding salesmen to its staff. The cost of employing additional salesmen is given by

$$5y^2 = 48x$$

where y is cost in units of $1,000 and x is number of additional salesmen employed, and the additional revenue is given by

$$(R - 2)^2 = 4(x + 10)$$

where R is revenue in units of $1,000 and x is number of additional salesmen employed. (Assume the cost and revenue functions are continuous, although actually they are meaningful

Figure 4.30

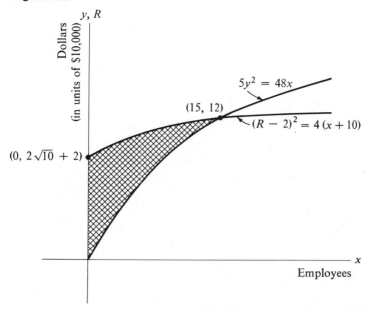

only for integer values of x.) The company should employ additional salesmen until the cost of doing so equals the additional revenue obtained (see Figure 4.30).

The cost of employing additional salesmen equals the additional revenue obtained if $R = y$. From the first equation,

$$x = \frac{5y^2}{48}$$

From the second equation,

$$x = \frac{(R - 2)^2 - 40}{4}$$

Solving simultaneously and putting $R = y$,

$$\frac{5y^2}{48} = \frac{(R - 2)^2 - 40}{4}$$

$$5y^2 = 12y^2 - 48y + 48 - 480$$

$$7y^2 - 48y - 432 = 0$$

$$(7y + 36)(y - 12) = 0$$

$$y = 12$$

$$x = 15$$

and 15 additional salesmen should be employed. The total resulting net revenue (total revenue minus cost) is

$$\int_0^{12} [\tfrac{5}{48}y^2 - (\tfrac{1}{4}(y - 2)^2 - 10)]\, dy = \int_0^{12} [y + 9 - \tfrac{7}{48}y^2]\, dy$$

$$= \left[\frac{y^2}{2} + 9y - \tfrac{7}{144}y^3\right]_0^{12}$$

$$= (72 + 108 - 84) - 0$$

$$= 96 \quad \text{or } \$96{,}000$$

PROBLEMS

1. If the demand function is $y = 39 - x^2$, find the consumers' surplus if a. $x_0 = \frac{5}{2}$ and b. the commodity is free, that is, $y_0 = 0$.

2. If the demand function is $y = 16 - x^2$ and the supply function is $y = 2x + 1$, find consumers' surplus and producers' surplus under pure competition.

3. If the supply function is $y = \sqrt{9 + x}$ and $x_0 = 7$, find the producers' surplus.

4. If the supply function is $y = 4e^{x/3}$ and $x_0 = 3$, find the producers' surplus.

5. The demand and supply functions under pure competition are $y = \frac{1}{4}(9 - x)^2$ and $y = \frac{1}{4}(1 + 3x)$, respectively. If an additive tax of 3 per unit quantity is imposed on the commodity, determine the decrease in consumers' surplus.

6. Under monopoly, the quantity sold and the corresponding price are determined by the demand function $y = \frac{1}{4}(10 - x)^2$ and the total cost function $y = (x^3/4) + 5x$ so that profit is maximized. Determine the corresponding consumers' surplus.

7. Under monopoly, the quantity sold and the corresponding price are determined by the demand function $y = 20 - 4x^2$ and the marginal cost function $y' = 2x + 6$ so that profit is maximized. Determine the corresponding consumers' surplus.

8. If the demand function is that part of the equilateral hyperbola $y = [8/(x + 1)] - 2$ in the first quadrant, and the supply curve is $y = \frac{1}{2}(x + 3)$, find the consumers' surplus and the producers' surplus under pure competition.

9. Under monopoly, the quantity sold and the corresponding price are determined by the demand function $y = 45 - x^2$ and the marginal cost function $y' = 6 + (x^2/4)$ so that profit is maximized. Determine the corresponding consumers' surplus.

10. The demand and supply functions under pure competition are, respectively, $y = 14 - x^2$ and $y = 2x^2 + 2$; find a. consumers' surplus, and b. producers' surplus.

11. The demand function is $y = 20 - 3x^2$ and the supply function is $y = 2x^2$; find the consumers' surplus and the producers' surplus under pure competition.

12. The demand and supply functions under pure competition are, respectively, $y = 32 - 2x^2$ and $y = \frac{1}{3}x^2 + 2x + 5$; find a. consumers' surplus, and b. producers' surplus.

13. Find the profit-maximizing output and the corresponding total profit, assuming pure competition, if $MR = 20 - 2x$ and $MC = 4 + (x - 4)^2$.

14. The marginal revenue function is $MR = 25 - 3x$ and the marginal cost function is $MC = 25 - 7x + x^2$. Find the profit-maximizing output and the corresponding total profit under pure competition.

15. If $MR = 44 - 9x$ and $MC = 20 - 7x + 2x^2$, find the profit-maximizing output and the corresponding total profit under pure competition.

16. Assuming pure competition, find the profit-maximizing output and the corresponding total profit if $MR = 24 - 6x - x^2$ and $MC = 4 - 2x - x^2$.

17. If $MR = 15 - 5x$ and $MC = 10 - 3x + 3x^2$, find the profit-maximizing output and the corresponding total profit assuming pure competition.

18. A manufacturing company has purchased a machine whose output represents earnings at time t given by $y^2 = 6(t + 9)$, where y is in units of $10,000 and t is years. The repair and maintenance cost at time t is given by $(y + 4)^2 = 8(t + 17)$, where y is in units of $10,000 and t is years. Assuming the machine can be disposed of at any time with no cost or salvage value, how many years should it be kept to maximize total net earnings (earnings minus cost of repair and maintenance)?

19. A company is considering purchasing additional companion units for its computer. The savings (in time and mistakes) from added units is given by $y = 3x^2 + 11$, where y is in units of $11,000 and x is number of units added. The cost of repair and maintenance is given by $y = 4x^2 + 2$, where y is in units of $1000 and x is the number of units added. To maximize total net revenue (revenue minus cost of repair and maintenance), how many units should be added and what is the associated savings? Assume the units are added in a specified order and that the savings and cost curves are continuous.

20. A company is considering adding advertising personnel. The cost of adding such personnel is given by $y = \frac{1}{2}x$, where y is in units of $5000 and x is the number of personel added. Additional revenue from adding personnel is $R^2 = 4x$, where R is in units of $5000 and x is number of personnel added. What number of advertising personnel should be added to

maximize profit (revenue minus cost) and what is the associated additional revenue? Assume continuous functions.

21. If net investment flow is $I(t) = 6t^{1/2}$, determine a. capital accumulation during the first year; b. capital accumulation during the first nine years; and c. total amount of capital after the first nine years if the initial capital is $500.

22. If net investment flow is $I(t) = 4t^{1/3}$, determine a. capital accumulation during the first year; b. capital accumulation during the first eight years; and c. total amount of capital after the first eight years if the initial capital is $500.

Answers to Odd-Numbered Problems

1. a. $31\frac{1}{4}$
   b. $26\sqrt{13}$
3. $\frac{10}{3}$
5. $\frac{121}{12}$
7. $\frac{8}{3}$
9. $16\sqrt{3}$
11. c.s. $= 16$
    p.s. $= \frac{32}{3}$

13. $x = 6$; $P_{max} = 36$
15. $x = 3$; $P_{max} = 45$
17. $x = 1$, $P_{max} = 3$
19. 18
21. a. $4.00
    b. $108.00
    c. $608.00

4.6 Special Methods of Integration

Many functions cannot be integrated by reversing the rules of differentiation. A number of special methods are available for determining the integral in such cases. The special methods considered in this section are standard forms for integration, integration by parts, integration by partial fractions, integration by rationalizing substitution, and integration by miscellaneous substitution.

STANDARD FORMS FOR INTEGRATION

In differential calculus there is a general rule for differentiation, from which other particular rules are derived. Unfortunately, there is no corresponding general rule for integration, and the integral of a given expression must be obtained through knowledge of the results of differentiation. Thus integration is inherently more difficult than differentiation. In order to expedite the process of integrating a given expression, tables of known integrals, called *standard forms*, have been compiled. The simplest of these standard forms are obtained directly by reversing the corresponding rules for differentiation; additional standard forms are derived from the results of more complicated differentiation. Note that a formula for integration can be derived from the result of any differentiation; the most frequently occurring of such formulas are given in tables of standard forms.

In the following list of standard forms, the first 14 formulas are obtained by reversing the corresponding rules for differentiation (the first 5 of these are discussed at the beginning of the chapter); the last 12 formulas are examples of standard forms obtained from the results of more complicated differentiation.

1. $\int dx = x + C$.

2. $\int K\, dx = K \int dx$, where K is any constant.

3. $\int [du + dv] = \int du + \int dv$, where $u = f(x)$ and $v = g(x)$ are differentiable functions of x.

4. $\int x^n \, dx = \dfrac{x^{n+1}}{n+1} + C, \; n \neq -1.$

5. $\int u^n \, du = \dfrac{u^{n+1}}{n+1} + C, \; n \neq -1,$ where $u = f(x)$ is a differentiable function of x.

6. $\int \dfrac{1}{u} \, du = \ln u + C,$ where $u = f(x)$ is a differentiable function of x.

7. $\int e^u \, du = e^u + C,$ where $u = f(x)$ is a differentiable function of x.

8. $\int a^u \, du = \dfrac{a^u}{\ln a} + C,$ where $u = f(x)$ is a differentiable function of x.

9. $\int \sin u \, du = -\cos u + C.$

10. $\int \cos u \, du = \sin u + C.$

11. $\int \sec^2 u \, du = \tan u + C.$

12. $\int \csc^2 u \, du = -\cot u + C.$

13. $\int \sec u \tan u \, du = \sec u + C.$

14. $\int \csc u \cot u \, du = -\csc u + C.$

15. $\int \tan u \, du = -\ln \cos u + C = \ln \sec u + C.$

16. $\int \cot u \, du = \ln \sin u + C.$

17. $\int \sec u \, du = \ln (\sec u + \tan u) + C.$

18. $\int \csc u \, du = \ln (\csc u - \cot u) + C.$

19. $\int \dfrac{du}{a^2 - u^2} = \dfrac{1}{2a} \ln \dfrac{a+u}{a-u} + C, \quad u^2 < a^2.$

20. $\int \dfrac{du}{u^2 - a^2} = \dfrac{1}{2a} \ln \dfrac{u-a}{u+a} + C, \quad u^2 > a^2.$

21. $\int \dfrac{du}{\sqrt{u^2 + a^2}} = \ln (u + \sqrt{u^2 + a^2}) + C.$

22. $\int \sqrt{u^2 + a^2} \, du = \dfrac{u}{2}\sqrt{u^2 + a^2} + \dfrac{a^2}{2} \ln (u + \sqrt{u^2 + a^2}) + C.$

23. $\int u e^u \, du = e^u(u - 1) + C.$

24. $\int \ln u \, du = u \ln u - u + C.$

25. $\int u^n \ln u \, du = u^{n+1} \left[\dfrac{\ln u}{n+1} - \dfrac{1}{(n+1)^2} \right] + C.$

26. $\int \dfrac{du}{u \ln u} = \ln (\ln u) + C.$

The first step in the procedure for integrating a given expression consists of comparing it with various standard forms. If an expression is identical with a standard form, its integral is known; if an expression is not identical with a standard form, there are various methods by which it may in some cases be reduced to a standard form. Some of these methods are discussed in later sections.

EXAMPLES

Evaluate the following integrals.

$\displaystyle\int \frac{x \, dx}{x^2 + 1} = \frac{1}{2} \int \frac{2x \, dx}{x^2 + 1}$

$\qquad\qquad = \tfrac{1}{2} \ln (x^2 + 1) + C$ (standard form 6)

$\displaystyle\int xe^{-x^2} \, dx = -\frac{1}{2} \int -2xe^{-x^2} \, dx$

$\qquad\qquad = -\tfrac{1}{2} e^{-x^2} + C$ (standard form 7)

$\displaystyle\int a^{2x-1} \, dx = \frac{1}{2} \int 2a^{2x-1} \, dx$

$\qquad\qquad = \dfrac{a^{2x-1}}{2 \ln a} + C$ (standard form 8)

$\displaystyle\int \sin 3x \cos^2 3x \, dx = -\frac{1}{3} \int (-3 \sin 3x)(\cos^2 3x) \, dx$

$\qquad\qquad = -\tfrac{1}{9} \cos^3 3x + C$ (standard form 5)

$\displaystyle\int \frac{\sin ax \, dx}{\sqrt{b + \cos ax}} = -\frac{1}{a} \int (-a \sin ax)(b + \cos ax)^{-1/2} \, dx$

$\qquad\qquad = -\dfrac{2}{a} \sqrt{b + \cos ax} + C$ (standard form 5)

$\displaystyle\int \frac{\sec^2 by \, dy}{a + c \tan by} = \frac{1}{bc} \int \frac{(bc \sec^2 by) \, dy}{a + c \tan by}$

$\qquad\qquad = \dfrac{1}{bc} \ln (a + c \tan by) + C$ (standard form 6)

$\displaystyle\int (x^2 - 1) \csc^2 (2x^3 - 6x) \, dx = -\tfrac{1}{6} \cot (2x^3 - 6x) + C$ (standard form 12)

$$\int (e^x + 2x) \tan (e^x + x^2 + 5) \, dx = -\ln \cos (e^x + x^2 + 5) + C$$

$$= \ln \sec (e^x + x^2 + 5) + C \qquad \text{(standard form 15)}$$

$$\int \sec 4\pi x \tan 4\pi x \, dx = \frac{1}{4\pi} \sec 4\pi x + C \qquad \text{(standard form 13)}$$

$$\int (\theta + x) \csc^2 (\theta + x)^2 \, dx = -\tfrac{1}{2} \cot (\theta + x) + C \qquad \text{(standard form 12)}$$

$$\int \pi \csc \theta x \, dx = \frac{\pi}{\theta} \ln (\csc \theta x - \cot \theta x) + C \qquad \text{(standard form 18)}$$

$$\int 4 \csc 4\theta \cot 4\theta \, d\theta = -\csc 4\theta + C \qquad \text{(standard form 14)}$$

$$\int y^2 \sec (\theta + y^3) \, dy = \tfrac{1}{3} \ln [\sec (\theta + y^3) + \tan (\theta + y^3)] + C \qquad \text{(standard form 17)}$$

$$\int x \cot (x^2 + \theta x) \, dx = \tfrac{1}{2} \ln \sin (x^2 + \theta x) + C \qquad \text{(standard form 19)}$$

$$\int \frac{4 + 6x}{6 - (4x + 3x^2)^2} \, dx = \frac{1}{2\sqrt{6}} \ln \left(\frac{\sqrt{6} + 4x + 3x^2}{\sqrt{6} - 4x - 3x^2} \right) + C \qquad \text{(standard form 20)}$$

$$\int 4x^3 e^{x^2} \, dx = 2e^{x^2}(x^2 - 1) + C \qquad \text{(standard form 23)}$$

$$\int \frac{x^2}{x^3 \ln x^3} \, dx = \tfrac{1}{3} \ln (\ln x^3) + C \qquad \text{(standard form 26)}$$

$$\int (2x - 3)(x^2 - 3x - 1)^4 \ln (x^2 - 3x - 1) \, dx$$

$$= (x^2 - 3x - 1)^5 \left[\frac{\ln (x^2 - 3x - 1)}{5} - \frac{1}{25} \right] + C$$

$$\text{(standard form 25)}$$

$$\int (x^2 + 2x + 6)^{1/2} \, dx = \int \sqrt{(x + 1)^2 + (\sqrt{5})^2} \, dx$$

$$= \frac{x + 1}{2} (x^2 + 2x + 6)^{1/2} + \tfrac{5}{2} \ln [(x + 1) + (x^2 + 2x + 6)^{1/2}] + C$$

$$\text{(standard form 22)}$$

$$\int (x^2 + 2x) \ln (x^3 + 3x^2 + 14) \, dx$$

$$= \tfrac{1}{3}[(x^3 + 3x^2 + 14) \ln (x^3 + 3x^2 + 14) - (x^3 + 3x^2 + 14)] + C$$

$$\text{(standard form 24)}$$

PROBLEMS

Evaluate the following integrals.

1. $\int x e^{x^2} \, dx$

2. $\int \sin^2 x \cos x \, dx$

3. $\int \sin ax \cos ax \, dx$

4. $\int \sec^2 \frac{x}{a} \tan \frac{x}{a} \, dx$

5. $\int \left(\dfrac{\sec 2x}{1 + \tan 2x} \right)^2 dx$

6. $\int (x^2 + 1)5^{x^3 + 3x} dx$

7. $\int \dfrac{\cos x \, dx}{1 + \sin x}$

8. $\int e^{\cos z} \sin z \, dz$

9. $\int \dfrac{dx}{\sin^2 ax}$

10. $\int \dfrac{du}{\cos^2 u}$

11. $\int \sec ax \, dx$

12. $\int \dfrac{dt}{1 + \cos t}$

13. $\int 2x \cos x^2 \, dx$

14. $\int \dfrac{\sin 2x}{\cos^2 2x} dx$

15. $\int (\sin x + \cos x) \, dx$

16. $\int (3x^2 + 5 \cos x) \, dx$

17. $\int (3x + e^x) \, dx$

18. $\int (e^x - e^{-x}) \, dx$

19. $\int 2x \sec x^2 \tan x^2 \, dx$

20. $\int (x^3 + 3x)(3x^2 + 3)e^{x^3 + 3x} \, dx$

Answers to Odd-Numbered Problems

1. $\frac{1}{2}e^{x^2} + C$

3. $\dfrac{\sin^2 ax}{2a} + C$

5. $-\dfrac{1}{2(1 + \tan 2x)} + C$

7. $\ln (1 + \sin x) + C$

9. $-\dfrac{1}{a} \cot ax + C$

11. $\dfrac{1}{a} \ln (\sec ax + \tan ax) + C$

13. $-\sin x^2 + C$

15. $\sin x - \cos x + C$

17. $\frac{3}{2}x^2 + e^x + C$

19. $\sec x^2 + C$

INTEGRATION BY PARTS

When an expression involving products or logarithms cannot be evaluated directly using standard forms, one of the most useful techniques for transforming it to a standard form is integration by parts. The formula for integration by parts is based on the inverse of the formula for differentiation of a product.

If u and v are both functions of x, then from the formula for the differentiation of a product,

$$\frac{d}{dx}(uv) = u\frac{dv}{dx} + v\frac{du}{dx}$$

or

$$u\frac{dv}{dx} = \frac{d}{dx}(uv) - v\frac{du}{dx}$$

and, integrating with respect to x,

$$\int u \, dv = uv - \int v \, du$$

This is the *formula for integration by parts*. The usefulness of this formula depends on the appropriate choice of u and dv, so that $\int v\, du$ and $\int dv$ can be evaluated, even though $\int u\, dv$ cannot.

Unfortunately, there is no general rule for separating a given expression into two factors u and dv so that the formula for integration by parts can be applied. However, note that

1. dx is always a part of dv.
2. dv must be integrable.
3. When the expression to be integrated is the product of two functions, it is usually advisable to choose the most complicated looking one that can be integrated as part of dv in order to make $\int v\, du$ as easily integrable as possible.

It may be necessary to apply the formula for integration by parts more than once, as in example (e) below.

EXAMPLES

Evaluate the following integrals.

(a) $\int xe^{ax}\, dx$

$$\int xe^{ax}\, dx = \frac{xe^{ax}}{a} - \int \frac{e^{ax}}{a}\, dx + C \qquad u = x \qquad dv = e^{ax}\, dx$$

$$= \frac{xe^{ax}}{a} - \frac{e^{ax}}{a^2} + C \qquad du = dx \qquad v = \frac{e^{ax}}{a}$$

$$= \frac{e^{ax}}{a}\left(x - \frac{1}{a}\right) + C$$

(Note that, alternatively, standard form 23 could be used.)

(b) $\int \ln x\, dx$

$$\int \ln x\, dx = x \ln x - \int x\left(\frac{1}{x}\right) dx + C \qquad u = \ln x \qquad dv = dx$$

$$= x \ln x - x + C \qquad du = \frac{1}{x}\, dx \qquad v = x$$

$$= x(\ln x - 1) + C$$

(Note that, alternatively, standard form 24 could be used.)

(c) $\int x \sin \frac{x}{a}\, dx$

$$\int x \sin \frac{x}{a}\, dx = -ax \cos \frac{x}{a} + \int a \cos \frac{x}{a}\, dx + C \qquad u = x \qquad dv = \sin \frac{x}{a}\, dx$$

$$= -ax \cos \frac{x}{a} + a^2 \sin \frac{x}{a} + C \qquad du = dx \qquad v = -a \cos \frac{x}{a}$$

$$= a^2 \sin \frac{x}{a} - ax \cos \frac{x}{a} + C$$

(d) $\int e^x \cos x \, dx$

$$\int e^x \cos x \, dx = e^x \sin x - \int e^x \sin x \, dx + C \qquad\qquad u = e^x \qquad dv = \cos x \, dx$$

$$= e^x \sin x - \left[-e^x \cos x + \int e^x \cos x \, dx \right] + C \qquad du = e^x \qquad v = \sin x$$

$$= e^x \sin x + e^x \cos x - \int e^x \cos x \, dx + C \qquad u = e^x \qquad dv = \sin x \, dx$$

$$\int e^x \cos x \, dx = \tfrac{1}{2} e^x (\sin x + \cos x) + C \qquad\qquad du = e^x \qquad v = -\cos x$$

(e) $\int x^2 e^{-x} \, dx$

$$\int x^2 e^{-x} \, dx = -x^2 e^{-x} + 2 \int x e^{-x} \, dx + C \qquad\qquad u = x^2 \qquad dv = e^{-x} \, dx$$

$$= -x^2 e^{-x} + 2\left[-x e^{-x} + \int e^{-x} \, dx \right] + C \qquad du = 2x \, dx \qquad v = -e^{-x}$$

$$= -x^2 e^{-x} - 2x e^{-x} - 2 e^{-x} + C \qquad\qquad u = x \qquad dv = e^{-x} \, dx$$

$$= -e^{-x}(x^2 + 2x + 2) + C \qquad\qquad du = dx \qquad v = -e^{-x}$$

(f) $\int \dfrac{\ln (x + 1) \, dx}{\sqrt{x + 1}}$

$$\int \frac{\ln (x + 1) \, dx}{\sqrt{x + 1}} = 2(x + 1)^{1/2} \ln (x + 1) - 2 \int \frac{1}{x + 1} (x + 1)^{1/2} \, dx + C$$

$$= 2(x + 1)^{1/2} \ln (x + 1) - 4(x + 1)^{1/2} + C \qquad u = \ln (x + 1) \qquad dv = (x + 1)^{-1/2} \, dx$$

$$= 2(x + 1)^{1/2}[\ln (x + 1) - 2] + C \qquad\qquad du = \frac{dx}{x + 1} \qquad v = 2(x + 1)^{1/2}$$

(Note that, alternatively, standard form 25 could be used.)

As suggested by examples (a), (b), and (f) above, the formula for integration by parts is the basis for a number of standard forms for integration.

PROBLEMS

Evaluate the following integrals.

1. $\int \dfrac{x e^x \, dx}{(1 + x)^2}$

2. $\int x e^{-x} \, dx$

3. $\int x^2 e^x \, dx$

4. $\int x e^{2x} \, dx$

5. $\int t \ln t \, dt$

6. $\int z^2 e^{-3z} \, dz$

7. $\int e^x (x + 1)^2 \, dx$

8. $\int (x^{1/2} + x^{1/4})^2 \, dx$

9. $\int \dfrac{(x + 1) \, dx}{(x + 1)^2 + (a + 1)^2}$

10. $\int (x + 1) \ln x \, dx$

11. $\int (x^2 + 3x + 4)^3 (2x + 3)\, dx$

12. $\int e^{3x^2 + 6x + 10}(x + 1)\, dx$

13. $\int (x^{1/3} + x^{2/3})^2\, dx$

14. $\int \dfrac{6x^2 + 8x + 8}{x^3 + 2x^2 + 4x}\, dx$

15. $\int \dfrac{(x^3 + x)\, dx}{\sqrt[4]{x^4 + 2x^2 + 1}}$

16. $\int \left(x^2 + \dfrac{1}{x} + 6x\right) dx$

17. $\int xe^{-3x}\, dx$

18. $\int \dfrac{x^3 + 2}{x^4 + 8x + 10}\, dx$

19. $\int \dfrac{\sin v\, dv}{1 + \cos v}$

20. $\int \dfrac{dx}{1 + \sin x}$

21. $\int u \sin u^2\, du$

22. $\int (x + \sin 2x)\, dx$

23. $\int xa^x\, dx$

24. $\int x^n \ln x\, dx$

25. $\int \dfrac{\sin x\, dx}{\sqrt{2 - \cos x}}$

26. $\int \dfrac{\sec^2 \theta\, d\theta}{\sqrt{1 + 2 \tan \theta}}$

27. $\int x \cos x\, dx$

28. $\int e^{-ax} \sin nx\, dx$

29. $\int \theta \sec^2 \theta\, d\theta$

30. $\int y^2 \sin ny\, dy$

Answers to Odd-Numbered Problems

1. $\dfrac{e^x}{1 + x} + C$

3. $e^x(x^2 - 2x + 2) + C$

5. $\frac{1}{2}t^2 \left|\ln t - \frac{1}{4}t^2 + C\right.$

7. $e^x(x^2 + 1) + C$

9. $\frac{1}{2} \ln [(x + 1)^2 + (a + 1)^2] + C$

11. $\frac{1}{4}(x^2 + 3x + 4)^4 + C$

13. $\frac{3}{5}x^{5/3} + x^2 + \frac{3}{7}x^{7/3} + C$

15. $\frac{1}{3}(x^4 + 2x^2 + 1)^{3/4} + C$

17. $-\frac{1}{9}e^{-3x}(3x + 1) + C$

19. $-\ln (1 + \cos v) + C$

21. $-\frac{1}{2} \cos u^2 + C$

23. $\dfrac{a^x}{\ln a}\left(x - \dfrac{1}{\ln a}\right) + C$

25. $2\sqrt{2 - \cos x} + C$

27. $x \sin x + \cos x + C$

29. $\theta \tan \theta + \ln \cos \theta + C$

INTEGRATION BY PARTIAL FRACTIONS

A rational algebraic function, by definition, can be expressed as the quotient of two polynomials. In theory, every rational function has an integral that can be expressed in terms of elementary functions. If a rational function cannot be integrated directly, the method of partial fractions frequently can be used to transform the rational fraction into a sum of simpler functions which can then be integrated by standard forms. The method of partial fractions is appropriate *only* for proper fractions, that is, for fractions in which the polynomial in the numerator is of lower degree than the polynomial in the denominator. Any improper fraction, that is, a fraction in which the polynomial in the numerator is of the same or higher degree than the polynomial in the denominator, can be reduced by division to the sum of a polynomial (easily integrated) and a proper fraction (integrated by the method of partial fractions). The method of integration by partial fractions consists of the following steps:

1. Express the denominator of the fraction as the product of linear factors of the form $ax + b$ and irreducible quadratic factors of the form $ax^2 + bx + c$; although this is not always easy in practice, it is always possible in theory for any polynomial in x with real coefficients.

2. Determine the form of the partial fractions; several cases arise, depending on the nature of the factors occurring in the denominator:

Factor Occurring in Denominator	*Corresponding Partial Fraction*
(a) Distinct linear factor: $ax + b$	$\dfrac{A}{ax + b}$ where A is a constant to be determined
(b) Repeated linear factor: $(ax + b)^n$	$\dfrac{A_1}{ax + b} + \dfrac{A_2}{(ax + b)^2} + \cdots + \dfrac{A_n}{(ax + b)^n}$ where $A_1 \ldots, A_n$ are constants to be determined
(c) Distinct quadratic factor: $ax^2 + bx + c$	$\dfrac{Ax + B}{ax^2 + bx + c}$ where A and B are constants to be determined
(d) Repeated quadratic factor: $(ax^2 + bx + c)^n$	$\dfrac{A_1 x + B_1}{ax^2 + bx + c} + \dfrac{A_2 x + B_2}{(ax^2 + bx + c)^2} + \cdots + \dfrac{A_n x + B_n}{(ax^2 + bx + c)^n}$ where A_i and B_i, $i = 1, 2, \ldots, n$ are constants to be determined

3. Determine the constants occurring in the numerators of the partial fractions. When a rational fraction is separated into partial fractions, the resulting equation is an identity, that is, it is true for all meaningful values of the variables. The method for evaluating the constants occurring in partial fractions, as illustrated in the example below, is based on the algebraic theorem which states that if two polynomials of the same degree are identical, the coefficients of like powers of the variable in both polynomials must be equal.

4. Integrate the partial fractions using standard forms.

EXAMPLES

Evaluate the following integrals.

(a) $\displaystyle \int \frac{(x + 3)\, dx}{x^2 + 3x + 2}$

Factoring the denominator and identifying the expression as case (a),

$$\int \frac{(x+3)\,dx}{x^2+3x+2} = \int \frac{(x+3)\,dx}{(x+1)(x+2)} = \int \left[\frac{A}{x+1}+\frac{B}{x+2}\right]dx = \int \left[\frac{A(x+2)+B(x+1)}{(x+1)(x+2)}\right]dx$$

Thus

$$x+3 = A(x+2)+B(x+1)$$
$$= (A+B)x + (2A+B)$$

equating coefficients of like powers of x,

$$A + B = 1$$
$$2A + B = 3$$
$$A = 2$$
$$B = -1$$

and

$$\int \frac{(x+3)\,dx}{(x+1)(x+2)} = \int \frac{2\,dx}{x+1} - \int \frac{dx}{x+2}$$
$$= 2\ln(x+1) - \ln(x+2) + C$$
$$= \ln\left[\frac{(x+1)^2}{x+2}\right] + C$$

(b) $\int \dfrac{(x^2-3x-8)}{x^2-2x+1}\,dx$

Writing the expression as a proper fraction and identifying it as case (b),

$$\int \frac{(x^2-3x-8)}{x^2-2x+1} = \int \left[1 - \frac{x+9}{(x-1)^2}\right]dx = x - \int \left[\frac{A}{x-1}+\frac{B}{(x-1)^2}\right]dx$$

$$= x - \int \left[\frac{A(x-1)+B}{(x-1)^2}\right]dx$$

Thus

$$x+9 = A(x-1)+B$$
$$= Ax - (A-B)$$

equating coefficients of like powers of x,

$$A = 1$$
$$A - B = -9$$
$$B = 10$$

and

$$\int \frac{(x^2-3x-8)\,dx}{x^2-2x+1} = x - \int \frac{dx}{x-1} - \int \frac{10\,dx}{(x-1)^2}$$

$$= x - \ln(x-1) + \frac{10}{x-1} + C$$

(c) $\int \dfrac{t\,dt}{t^4 + 6t^2 + 5}$

Factoring the denominator and identifying the expression as case (c),

$$\int \frac{t\,dt}{t^4 + 6t^2 + 5} = \int \frac{t\,dt}{(t^2 + 5)(t^2 + 1)} = \int \left[\frac{A_1 t + B_1}{t^2 + 5} + \frac{A_2 t + B_2}{t^2 + 1}\right] dt$$

$$= \int \left[\frac{(A_1 t + B_1)(t^2 + 1) + (A_2 t + B_2)(t^2 + 5)}{(t^2 + 5)(t^2 + 1)}\right] dt$$

Thus

$$t = (A_1 t + B_1)(t^2 + 1) + (A_2 t + B_2)(t^2 + 5)$$

$$= (A_1 + A_2)t^3 + (B_1 + B_2)t^2 + (A_1 + 5A_2)t + (B_1 + 5B_2)$$

and

$$A_1 + A_2 = 0$$

$$B_1 + B_2 = 0$$

$$A_1 + 5A_2 = 1$$

$$B_1 + 5B_2 = 0$$

From the first and third equations,

$$A_2 = \tfrac{1}{4}$$

$$A_1 = -\tfrac{1}{4}$$

From the second and fourth equations,

$$B_1 = B_2 = 0$$

and

$$\int \frac{t\,dt}{(t^2 + 5)(t^2 + 1)} = -\frac{1}{4}\int \frac{t\,dt}{t^2 + 5} + \frac{1}{4}\int \frac{t\,dt}{t^2 + 1}$$

$$= -\tfrac{1}{8}\ln(t^2 + 5) + \tfrac{1}{8}\ln(t^2 + 1) + C$$

$$= \tfrac{1}{8}\ln\left(\frac{t^2 + 1}{t^2 + 5}\right) + C$$

(d) $\int \dfrac{dz}{z(z^2 + 1)^2}$

Identifying the expression as cases (a) and (d),

$$\int \frac{dz}{z(z^2 + 1)^2} = \int \left[\frac{A_0}{z} + \frac{A_1 z + B_1}{z^2 + 1} + \frac{A_2 z + B_2}{(z^2 + 1)^2}\right] dz$$

$$= \int \left[\frac{A_0(z^2 + 1)^2 + (A_1 z + B_1)z(z^2 + 1) + (A_2 z + B_2)z}{z(z^2 + 1)^2}\right] dz$$

Thus

$$1 = A_0(z^2 + 1)^2 + (A_1 z + B_1)z(z^2 + 1) + (A_2 z + B_2)z$$

$$= A_0(z^4 + 2z^2 + 1) + A_1(z^4 + z^2) + B_1(z^3 + z) + A_2 z^2 + B_2 z$$

$$= (A_0 + A_1)z^4 + B_1 z^3 + (2A_0 + A_1 + A_2)z^2 + (B_1 + B_2)z + A_0$$

equating coefficients,

$$A_0 + A_1 = 0$$
$$B_1 = 0$$
$$2A_0 + A_1 + A_2 = 0$$
$$B_1 + B_2 = 0$$
$$A_0 = 1$$

Substituting $A_0 = 1$ and solving the other equations,

$$A_1 = -1$$
$$A_2 = -1$$
$$B_2 = 0$$

and

$$\int \frac{dz}{z(z^2 + 1)^2} = \int \frac{dz}{z} - \int \frac{z\,dz}{z^2 + 1} - \int \frac{z\,dz}{(z^2 + 1)^2}$$

$$= \ln z - \tfrac{1}{2} \ln (z^2 + 1) + \frac{1}{2(z^2 + 1)} + C$$

$$= \tfrac{1}{2} \ln \left(\frac{z^2}{z^2 + 1} \right) + \frac{1}{2(z^2 + 1)} + C$$

(e) $\int \dfrac{dx}{x^3 + 5x^2 + 4x}$

Factoring the denominator and identifying the expression as case (a),

$$\int \frac{dx}{x^3 + 5x^2 + 4x} = \int \frac{dx}{x(x + 1)(x + 4)} = \int \left[\frac{A}{x} + \frac{B}{x + 1} + \frac{C}{x + 4} \right] dx$$

$$= \int \left[\frac{A(x + 1)(x + 4) + Bx(x + 4) + Cx(x + 4)}{x(x + 1)(x + 4)} \right] dx$$

Thus

$$1 = A(x + 1)(x + 4) + Bx(x + 4) + Cx(x + 1)$$
$$= A(x^2 + 5x + 4) + B(x^2 + 4x) + C(x^2 + x)$$
$$= (A + B + C)x^2 + (5A + 4B + C)x + 4A$$

equating coefficients,

$$A + B + C = 0$$
$$5A + 4B + C = 0$$
$$4A = 1$$
$$A = \tfrac{1}{4}$$

Substituting $A = \tfrac{1}{4}$ and solving the first two equations,

$$4A + 3B = 0$$
$$B = -\tfrac{1}{3}$$
$$C = \tfrac{1}{12}$$

and

$$\int \frac{dx}{x(x+1)(x+4)} = \frac{1}{4}\int \frac{dx}{x} - \frac{1}{3}\int \frac{dx}{x+1} + \frac{1}{12}\int \frac{dx}{x+4}$$

$$= \tfrac{1}{4}\ln x - \tfrac{1}{3}\ln (x+1) + \tfrac{1}{12}\ln (x+4) + C$$

$$= \tfrac{1}{12}\ln \left[\frac{x^3(x+4)}{(x+1)^4}\right] + C$$

(f) $\int \dfrac{(x^3 - 2x)\, dx}{x^4 - 81}$

Factoring the denominator and identifying the expression as cases (a) and (c),

$$\int \frac{(x^3 - 2x)\, dx}{x^4 - 81} = \int \frac{(x^3 - 2x)\, dx}{(x-3)(x+3)(x^2+9)}$$

$$= \int \left[\frac{A}{x-3} + \frac{B}{x+3} + \frac{Cx+D}{x^2+9}\right] dx$$

$$= \int \left[\frac{A(x+3)(x^2+9) + B(x-3)(x^2+9) + (Cx+D)(x-3)(x+3)}{(x-3)(x+3)(x^2+9)}\right] dx$$

Thus

$$x^3 - 2x = A(x+3)(x^2+9) + B(x-3)(x^2+9) + (Cx+D)(x^2-9)$$

$$= A(x^3 + 3x^2 + 9x + 27) + B(x^3 - 3x^2 + 9x - 27)$$

$$+ C(x^3 - 9x) + D(x^2 - 9)$$

$$= (A + B + C)x^3 + (3A - 3B + D)x^2 + (9A + 9B - 9C)x$$

$$+ (27A - 27B - 9D)$$

so, equating coefficients,

$$A + B + C = 1$$

$$3A - 3B + D = 0$$

$$9A + 9B - 9C = -2$$

$$27A - 27B - 9D = 0$$

From the first and third equations,

$$18C = 11$$

$$C = \tfrac{11}{18}$$

From the second and fourth equations,

$$18D = 0$$

$$D = 0$$

Substituting $C = \tfrac{11}{18}$, $D = 0$, and solving the first two equations,

$$A + B = \tfrac{7}{18}$$

$$3A - 3B = 0$$

$$6A = \tfrac{21}{18}$$

$$A = \tfrac{7}{36}$$

$$B = \tfrac{7}{36}$$

and

$$\int \frac{(x^3 - 2x)\,dx}{(x-3)(x+3)(x^2+9)} = \frac{7}{36}\int \frac{dx}{x-3} + \frac{7}{36}\int \frac{dx}{x+3} + \frac{11}{18}\int \frac{x\,dx}{x^2+9}$$

$$= \tfrac{7}{36}\ln(x-3) + \tfrac{7}{36}\ln(x+3) + \tfrac{11}{36}\ln(x^2+9) + C$$

$$= \tfrac{1}{36}\ln[(x-3)^7(x+3)^7(x^2+9)^{11}] + C$$

$$= \tfrac{1}{36}\ln[(x^2-9)^7(x^2+9)^{11}] + C$$

NOTE: In this particular problem the correct solution is also obtained using the factors $(x^2 - 9)(x^2 + 9)$; however, in general, *irreducible* quadratic factors and linear factors must be used.

PROBLEMS

1-8

Evaluate each of the following integrals using partial fractions.

1. $\int \dfrac{(4x-2)\,dx}{x^3 - x^2 - 2x}$

2. $\int \dfrac{(4x^3 + 2x^2 + 1)\,dx}{4x^3 - x}$

3. $\int \dfrac{z^2\,dz}{(z-1)^3}$

4. $\int \dfrac{(y^4 - 8)\,dy}{y^3 + 2y^2}$

5. $\int \dfrac{(4x^2 + 6)\,dx}{x^3 + 3x}$

6. $\int \dfrac{(x^3 + 3x)\,dx}{(x^2 + 1)^2}$

7. $\int \dfrac{t^5\,dt}{(t^2 + 4)^2}$

8. $\int \dfrac{(2t^2 - 8t - 8)\,dt}{(t-2)(t^2+4)}$

Answers to Odd-Numbered Problems

1. $\ln\left[\dfrac{x(x-2)}{(x+1)^2}\right] + C$

3. $\ln(z-1) + \dfrac{3-4z}{2(z-1)^2} + C$

5. $\ln[x^2(x^2+3)] + C$

7. $\dfrac{t^2}{2} - 4\ln(t^2+4) - \dfrac{8}{t^2+4} + C$

INTEGRATION BY A RATIONALIZING SUBSTITUTION

As discussed in the preceding section, all rational functions are integrable in terms of elementary functions; however, only a relatively small number of algebraic functions which are not rational can be integrated in terms of elementary functions. In some cases, by substitution of a new variable, functions which are not rational can be transformed into functions which are rational. These functions are then integrable either by partial fractions or directly by standard forms. The method of integrating a function that is not rational by transforming it into a rational function by substitution of a variable is called *integration by rationalization*. This method is useful for various classes of functions; two of the most common of these are discussed in the following sections.

1. An expression involving fractional powers of x only can be transformed into a rational form by the substitution

$$x = z^n$$

where n is the least common denominator of the fractional exponents of x.

2. An expression involving fractional powers of $(a + bx)$ only can be transformed into a rational form by the substitution

$$a + bx = z^n$$

where n is the least common denominator of the fractional exponents of $(a + bx)$.

EXAMPLES

Evaluate the following integrals.

(a) $\int \dfrac{x^{1/2}\, dx}{1 + x^{3/4}}$

the integrand involves fractional powers of x whose least common denominator is 4. Substituting,

$$x = z^4$$

$$dx = 4z^3\, dz$$

$$\int \frac{x^{1/2}\, dx}{1 + x^{3/4}} = \int \frac{z^2 \cdot 4z^3\, dz}{1 + z^3}$$

$$= 4 \int \frac{z^5\, dz}{z^3 + 1}$$

$$= 4 \int \left[z^2 - \frac{z^2}{z^3 + 1} \right] dz$$

$$= \tfrac{4}{3} z^3 - \tfrac{4}{3} \ln (z^3 + 1) + C$$

Substituting to obtain a function of x,

$$\int \frac{x^{1/2}\, dx}{1 + x^{3/4}} = \tfrac{4}{3} x^{3/4} - \tfrac{4}{3} \ln (x^{3/4} + 1) + C$$

(b) $\int \dfrac{x\, dx}{(a + bx)^{3/2}}$

the integrand involves a fractional power of $a + bx$ whose least common denominator is 2. Substituting,

$$a + bx = z^2$$

$$b\, dx = 2z\, dz$$

$$dx = \frac{2}{b} z\, dz$$

$$\int \frac{x\, dx}{(a + bx)^{3/2}} = \frac{2}{b^2} \int \frac{(z^2 - a) \cdot z\, dz}{z^3}$$

$$= \frac{2}{b^2} \int \frac{(z^3 - az)\, dz}{z^3}$$

$$= \frac{2}{b^2} \int \left[1 - \frac{a}{z^2} \right] dz$$

$$= \frac{2}{b^2} \left[z + \frac{a}{z} \right] + C$$

$$= \frac{2}{b^2} \left[\frac{z^2 + a}{z} \right] + C$$

Substituting to obtain a function of x,

$$\int \frac{x \, dx}{(a + bx)^{3/2}} = \frac{2}{b^2} \left[\frac{2a + bx}{(a + bx)^{1/2}} \right] + C$$

(c) $\int \dfrac{(5x + 9) \, dx}{(x - 9)x^{3/2}}$

the integrand involves a fractional power of x whose least common denominator is 2. Substituting,

$$x = z^2$$

$$dx = 2z \, dz$$

$$\int \frac{(5x + 9) \, dx}{(x - 9)x^{3/2}} = \int \frac{(5z^2 + 9) \cdot 2z \, dz}{(z^2 - 9)z^3}$$

$$= 2 \int \frac{(5z^2 + 9) \, dz}{z^2(z - 3)(z + 3)}$$

Integrating using partial fractions,

$$\int \frac{(5z + 9) \, dz}{(z - 9)z^{3/2}} = 2 \int \left[\frac{A}{z} + \frac{B}{z^2} + \frac{C}{z - 3} + \frac{D}{z + 3} \right] dz$$

$$5z^2 + 9 = Az(z^2 - 9) + B(z^2 - 9) + Cz^2(z + 3) + Dz^2(z - 3)$$

$$= A(z^3 - 9z) + B(z^2 - 9) + C(z^3 + 3z^2) + D(z^3 - 3z^2)$$

Equating coefficients,

$$A + C + D = 0$$

$$B + 3C - 3D = 5$$

$$-9A = 0$$

$$-9B = 9$$

$$A = 0$$

$$B = -1$$

Substituting $A = 0$, $B = -1$, and solving the first two equations,

$$C + D = 0$$

$$3C - 3D = 6$$

$$6C = 6$$

$$C = 1$$

$$D = -1$$

and

$$\int \frac{(5z + 9) \, dz}{(z - 9)z^{3/2}} = 2 \left[-\int \frac{dz}{z^2} + \int \frac{dz}{z - 3} - \int \frac{dz}{z + 3} \right]$$

$$= 2 \left[\frac{1}{z} + \ln \, (z - 3) - \ln \, (z + 3) \right] + C$$

$$= 2 \left[\frac{1}{z} + \ln \, \left(\frac{z - 3}{z + 3} \right) \right] + C$$

Substituting to obtain a function of x,

$$\int \frac{(5x + 9)\, dx}{(x - 9)x^{3/2}} = 2\left[\frac{1}{x^{1/2}} + \ln\left(\frac{x^{1/2} - 3}{x^{1/2} + 3}\right)\right] + C$$

(d) $\displaystyle \int \frac{dx}{x - x^{4/3}}$

the integrand involves a fractional power of x whose least common denominator is 3. Substituting,

$$x = z^3$$

$$dx = 3z^2\, dz$$

$$\int \frac{dx}{x - x^{4/3}} = \int \frac{3z^2\, dz}{z^3 - z^4}$$

$$= 3\int \frac{dz}{z(1 - z)}$$

Integrating using partial fractions,

$$\int \frac{dz}{z - z^{4/3}} = 3\int \left[\frac{A}{z} + \frac{B}{1 - z}\right] dz$$

$$1 = A(1 - z) + Bz$$

so

$$-A + B = 0$$

$$A = 1$$

$$B = 1$$

and

$$\int \frac{dz}{z - z^{4/3}} = 3\left[\int \frac{dz}{z} + \int \frac{dz}{1 - z}\right]$$

$$= 3[\ln z - \ln (1 - z)] + C$$

$$= 3\ln\left(\frac{z}{1 - z}\right) + C$$

Substituting to obtain a function of x,

$$\int \frac{dx}{x - x^{4/3}} = 3\ln\left(\frac{x^{1/3}}{1 - x^{1/3}}\right) + C$$

(e) $\displaystyle \int y(a + y)^{1/3}\, dy$

the integrand involves a fractional power of $(a + y)$ whose least common denominator is 3. Substituting,

$$a + y = z^3$$

$$dy = 3z^2\, dz$$

$$\int y(a+y)^{1/3}\, dy = \int (z^3 - a) \cdot z \cdot 3z^2\, dz$$

$$= 3\int (z^6 - az^3)\, dz$$

$$= 3\left[\frac{z^7}{7} - \frac{az^4}{4}\right] + C$$

$$= \tfrac{3}{28}[z^4(4z^3 - 7a)] + C$$

Substituting to obtain a function of x,

$$\int y(a+y)^{1/3}\, dy = \tfrac{3}{28}[(a+y)^{4/3}(4a + 4y - 7a)] + C$$

$$= \tfrac{3}{28}[(a+y)^{4/3}(4y - 3a)] + C$$

(f) $\displaystyle \int \frac{x^2\, dx}{(4x+1)^{5/2}}$

the integrand involves a fractional power of $(4x + 1)$ whose least common denominator is 2. Substituting,

$$4x + 1 = z^2$$

$$4\, dx = 2z\, dz$$

$$dx = \tfrac{1}{2}z\, dz$$

$$\int \frac{x^2\, dx}{(4x+1)^{5/2}} = \int \frac{\tfrac{1}{16}(z^2 - 1)^2 \cdot \tfrac{1}{2}z\, dz}{z^5}$$

$$= \frac{1}{32}\int \frac{(z^4 - 2z^2 + 1)\, dz}{z^4}$$

$$= \frac{1}{32}\int \left[1 - \frac{2}{z^2} + \frac{1}{z^4}\right] dz$$

$$= \frac{1}{32}\left[z + \frac{2}{z} - \frac{1}{3z^3}\right] + C$$

$$= \frac{1}{32}\left[\frac{3z^4 + 6z^2 - 1}{3z^3}\right] + C$$

Substituting to obtain a function of x,

$$\int \frac{x^2\, dx}{(4x+1)^{5/2}} = \frac{1}{32}\left[\frac{3(4x+1)^2 + 6(4x+1) - 1}{3(4x+1)^{3/2}}\right] + C$$

$$= \frac{1}{32}\left[\frac{3(16x^2 + 8x + 1) + 6(4x+1) - 1}{3(4x+1)^{3/2}}\right] + C$$

$$= \frac{6x^2 + 6x + 1}{12(4x+1)^{3/2}} + C$$

INTEGRATION BY MISCELLANEOUS SUBSTITUTIONS

The substitutions considered in the preceding section made integration possible by rationalizing the function to be integrated. There are also a number of functions which can be integrated by means of substitutions that do not rationalize them. Unfortunately, no general rules can be given for these substitutions and they must be determined by trial and error, guided by experience. A very useful substitution of this type is the *reciprocal substitution*:

$$x = \frac{1}{z} \qquad dx = \frac{-dz}{z^2}$$

Algebraic functions which cannot be rationalized frequently can be integrated using this substitution.

EXAMPLES

Evaluate the following integrals.

(a) $\int \dfrac{(x - x^3)^{1/3}\, dx}{x^4}$

$$x = \frac{1}{z}$$

$$dx = \frac{-dz}{z^2}$$

$$\int \frac{(x - x^3)^{1/3}\, dx}{x^4} = -\int \frac{\left(\dfrac{1}{z} - \dfrac{1}{z^3}\right)^{1/3} \dfrac{dz}{z^2}}{\dfrac{1}{z^4}}$$

$$= -\int z(z^2 - 1)^{1/3}\, dz$$

$$= -\tfrac{3}{8}(z^2 - 1)^{4/3} + C$$

Substituting to obtain a function of x,

$$\int \frac{(x - x^3)^{1/3}\, dx}{x^4} = -\frac{3}{8}\left(\frac{1}{x^2} - 1\right)^{4/3} + C$$

(b) $\int \dfrac{dx}{x\sqrt{1 + x + x^2}}$

using the standard form

$$\int \frac{du}{\sqrt{a + bu + cu^2}} = \frac{1}{\sqrt{c}} \ln\left(2cu + b + 2\sqrt{c}\sqrt{a + bu + cu^2}\right) + C$$

$$x = \frac{1}{z}$$

$$dx = \frac{-dz}{z^2}$$

$$\int \frac{dx}{x\sqrt{1+x+x^2}} = -\int \frac{\dfrac{dz}{z^2}}{\dfrac{1}{z}\sqrt{1+\dfrac{1}{z}+\dfrac{1}{z^2}}}$$

$$= -\int \frac{dz}{z\sqrt{\dfrac{z^2+z+1}{z^2}}}$$

$$= -\int \frac{dz}{\sqrt{z^2+z+1}}$$

$$= -\ln\left(2z+1+2\sqrt{z^2+z+1}\right)+C$$

Substituting to obtain a function of x,

$$\int \frac{dx}{x\sqrt{1+x+x^2}} = -\ln\left(\frac{2}{x}+1+2\sqrt{\frac{1}{x^2}+\frac{1}{x}+1}\right)+C$$

$$= -\ln\left(\frac{2+x}{x}+2\sqrt{\frac{1+x+x^2}{x^2}}\right)+C$$

$$= -\ln\left(\frac{2+x+2\sqrt{1+x+x^2}}{x}\right)+C$$

$$= \ln\left(\frac{x}{2+x+2\sqrt{1+x+x^2}}\right)+C$$

PROBLEMS

Evaluate each of the following integrals by rationalization.

1. $\displaystyle\int \frac{y\,dy}{\sqrt{2+4y}}$

2. $\displaystyle\int \frac{dt}{2\sqrt{t}+\sqrt[3]{t}}$

3. $\displaystyle\int \frac{(x^{3/2}-x^{1/3})\,dx}{6x^{1/4}}$

4. $\displaystyle\int \frac{(\sqrt{x+1}+1)\,dx}{\sqrt{x+1}-1}$

5. $\displaystyle\int \frac{dx}{1+\sqrt[3]{x+a}}$

6. $\displaystyle\int \frac{dx}{1+\sqrt{x}}$

Evaluate each of the following integrals by reciprocal substitution.

7. $\displaystyle\int \frac{dx}{x^2\sqrt{x^2+a^2}}$

8. $\displaystyle\int \frac{\sqrt{x^2-a^2}\,dx}{x^4}$

9. $\displaystyle\int \frac{dx}{x\sqrt{2x-x^2}}$

10. $\displaystyle\int \frac{\sqrt{4-x^2}\,dx}{x^4}$

11. $\displaystyle\int \frac{-dx}{x\sqrt{1+4x+5x^2}}$

12. $\displaystyle\int \frac{dx}{x^2\sqrt{2x-x^2}}$

Answers to Odd-Numbered Problems

1. $\frac{1}{6}(2+4y)^{1/2}(y-1)+C$

3. $\frac{2}{27}x^{9/4}-\frac{2}{13}x^{13/12}+C$

5. $\frac{3}{2}(x+a)^{2/3}-3(x+a)^{1/3}+3\ln\left[(x+a)^{1/3}+1\right]+C$

7. $-\dfrac{\sqrt{x^2 + a^2}}{a^2 x} + C$

9. $-\left(\dfrac{2 - x}{x}\right)^{1/2} + C$

11. $\ln\left(\dfrac{1 + 2x + \sqrt{1 + 4x + 5x^2}}{x}\right) + C$

4.7 Numerical (Approximate) Methods of Integration

Approximate integration is useful in many practical problems, for example, when an integral cannot be expressed in terms of elementary functions or when an integrand is defined by an empirical table of values or by an empirical graph. Three methods of approximate integration are discussed in the following sections: the *trapezoidal rule* (linear approximation), *Simpson's rule* (quadratic approximation), and *Taylor's expansion* (series approximation). In all three of these methods, the function to be integrated is replaced by an approximation whose integral is known. The trapezoidal rule and Simpson's rule (but not Taylor's expansion) can also be used when the integrand is defined empirically by a table of values or a graph, rather than by a function.

The methods discussed in this section and various other approximation methods are used to evaluate integrals using computers. Approximate integration, even of quite difficult integrals, can be done accurately and efficiently using a computer and, in practice, a computer is used for almost all approximate integration. The main purpose of the following sections is to discuss the principles involved in such approximation. The examples involve fairly crude approximations of relatively simple functions; the amount of calculation required, even for these cases, indicates the advantage of using a computer.

THE TRAPEZOIDAL RULE

The trapezoidal rule uses a series of straight-line segments to approximate the given function $f(x)$; it is in this sense a method of linear approximation.

Suppose the problem is to evaluate $\int_a^b f(x)\,dx$. Divide the interval $[a, b]$ into n equal parts, each of length Δx, and denote the points of division by $a = x_0, x_1, \ldots, x_n = b$. Erect ordinates at the points of division and denote them by $y_0 = f(x_0)$, $y_1 = f(x_1), \ldots, y_n = f(x_n)$. Join the ends of consecutive ordinates to form trapezoids (see Figure 4.31). Then

Area of first trapezoid $= \frac{1}{2}(y_0 + y_1)\Delta x$

Area of second trapezoid $= \frac{1}{2}(y_1 + y_2)\Delta x$

$$\vdots$$

Area of nth trapezoid $= \frac{1}{2}(y_{n-1} + y_n)\Delta x$

and the total area of the n trapezoids is

$$\Delta x\left[\tfrac{1}{2}y_0 + \sum_{i=1}^{n-1} y_i + \tfrac{1}{2}y_n\right]$$

Figure 4.31

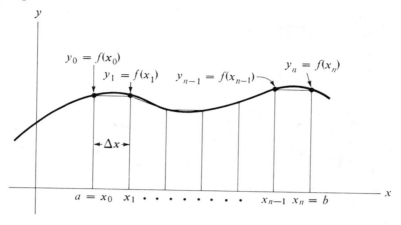

The trapezoidal rule for approximate integration is thus

$$\int_a^b f(x)\, dx \approx \Delta x \left[\tfrac{1}{2}(y_0 + y_n) + \sum_{i=1}^{n-1} y_i \right]$$

Notes Concerning the Accuracy of the Trapezoidal Rule

1. As the number of divisions n increases, the sum of the areas of the trapezoids more closely approximates the area under the curve.
2. The trapezoidal rule gives a closer approximation to the area under the curve than does the sum of the areas of the corresponding rectangles—that is,

$$\left| \int_a^b f(x)\, dx - \Delta x \left[\tfrac{1}{2}(y_0 + y_n) + \sum_{i=1}^{n-1} y_i \right] \right| < \left| \int_a^b f(x)\, dx - \Delta x \sum_{i=0}^{n-1} y_i \right|$$

and

$$\left| \int_a^b f(x)\, dx - \Delta x \left[\tfrac{1}{2}(y_0 + y_n) + \sum_{i=1}^{n-1} y_i \right] \right| < \left| \int_a^b f(x)\, dx - \Delta x \sum_{i=1}^{n} y_i \right|$$

3. The integral $\int_a^b f(x)\, dx$ is bounded by $\Delta x \sum_{i=0}^{n-1} y_i$ and $\Delta x \sum_{i=1}^{n} y_i$; depending on which bound is smaller,

$$\Delta x \sum_{i=0}^{n-1} y_i \leq \int_a^b f(x)\, dx \leq \Delta x \sum_{i=1}^{n} y_i$$

or

$$\Delta x \sum_{i=1}^{n} y_i \leq \int_a^b f(x)\, dx \leq \Delta x \sum_{i=0}^{n-1} y_i$$

The trapezoidal rule averages these two bounds.

4. A bound on the absolute error of approximation using the trapezoidal rule is given by

$$|E_T| \leq \frac{(\Delta x)^2 (b - a)\, \max_{[a,\, b]} |f^{(2)}(x)|}{12}$$

EXAMPLE

Evaluate $\int_2^4 x(16 - x^2)^{1/2}\,dx$ by the trapezoidal rule using $n = 4$. (See Figure 4.32).

Figure 4.32

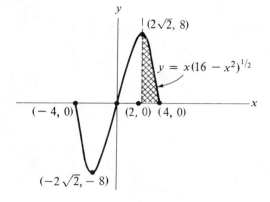

i	0	1	2	3	4
x_i	2.0	2.5	3.0	3.5	4.0
$f(x_i) = y_i$	$4\sqrt{3} \approx 6.928$	$\frac{5}{4}\sqrt{39} \approx 7.806$	$3\sqrt{7} \approx 7.937$	$\frac{7}{4}\sqrt{15} \approx 6.778$	0

$$\int_2^4 x(16 - x^2)^{1/2}\,dx \approx \Delta x\left[\tfrac{1}{2}(y_0 + y_4) + \sum_{i=1}^{3} y_i\right]$$

$$\approx 0.5[\tfrac{1}{2}(6.928) + (7.806 + 7.937 + 6.778)]$$

$$\approx 0.5[3.464 + 22.522]$$

$$\approx 12.993$$

NOTE: $\quad \Delta x\sum_{i=1}^{n} y_i \leq \int_a^b f(x)\,dx \leq \Delta x\sum_{i=0}^{n-1} y_i$

$$11.261 \leq \int_2^4 x(16 - x^2)^{1/2}\,dx \leq 14.725$$

SIMPSON'S RULE

Simpson's rule uses a series of parabolic arcs to approximate the given function $f(x)$; it is in this sense a method of quadratic approximation. Simpson's rule provides a closer approximation than the trapezoidal rule for any given number of subdivisions of the interval over which the integral is to be evaluated.

A parabola with vertical axis can be passed through any three points. The equation of this parabola can be obtained from the coordinates of the points; however, for the purpose of using Simpson's rule this is not necessary, since the area under an arc of the parabola can be evaluated without finding the equation of the parabola.

If a parabola with vertical axis is passed through three points (x_0, y_0), (x_1, y_1) and (x_2, y_2), where $x_2 - x_1 = x_1 - x_0 = \Delta x$, then the area bounded by the parabola, the

Figure 4.33

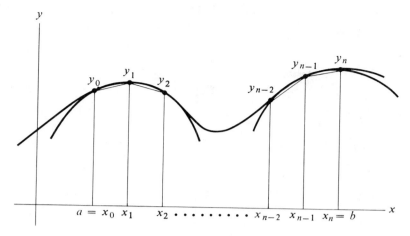

x-axis, and the ordinates at x_0 and x_2 is given by

$$A = \frac{\Delta x}{3}(y_0 + 4y_1 + y_2)$$

Again suppose the problem is to evaluate $\int_a^b f(x)\, dx$. Divide the interval $[a, b]$ into n equal parts, where n *must now be an even number*, each of length Δx, and denote the points of division by $a = x_0, x_1, \ldots, x_n = b$; the corresponding ordinates are $y_0, y_1, \ldots, y_n$; consider these ordinates in groups of three: $y_0, y_1, y_2; y_2, y_3, y_4; y_4, y_5, y_6; \ldots; y_{n-2}, y_{n-1}, y_n$, and pass a parabolic arc with vertical axis through each set of three points (see Figure 4.33). The areas under these parabolic arcs are, respectively,

$$A_1 = \frac{\Delta x}{3}(y_0 + 4y_1 + y_2)$$

$$A_2 = \frac{\Delta x}{3}(y_2 + 4y_3 + y_4)$$

$$\vdots$$

$$A_n = \frac{\Delta x}{3}(y_{n-2} + 4y_{n-1} + y_n)$$

and the sum of these areas is

$$\frac{\Delta x}{3}[y_0 + 4y_1 + 2y_2 + 4y_3 + 2y_4 + \cdots + 2y_{n-2} + 4y_{n-1} + y_n]$$

Simpson's rule for approximate integration is thus

$$\int_a^b f(x)\, dx \approx \frac{\Delta x}{3}[y_0 + 4y_1 + 2y_2 + \cdots + 2y_{n-2} + 4y_{n-1} + y_n]$$

As in the case of the trapezoidal rule, as the number of divisions, n, increases, the sum of the areas under the parabolic arcs more closely approximates the area under the curve. Again, note that Simpson's rule always provides a closer approximation than does the trapezoidal rule for a given number of subdivisions. A bound on the absolute error of approximation using Simpson's rule is given by

$$|E_S| \leq \frac{(b-a)(\Delta x)^4 \max_{[a, b]} f^{(4)}(x)}{180}$$

EXAMPLE

Evaluate $\int_2^4 x(16 - x^2)^{1/2}\, dx$ by Simpson's rule using $n = 4$. (See Figure 4.33)

i	0	1	2	3	4
x_i	2.0	2.5	3.0	3.5	4.0
$f(x_i) = y_i$	$4\sqrt{3} \approx 6.928$	$\frac{5}{4}\sqrt{39} \approx 7.806$	$3\sqrt{7} \approx 7.937$	$\frac{7}{4}\sqrt{15} \approx 6.778$	0

$$\int_2^4 x(16 - x)^{1/2}\, dx \approx \frac{\Delta x}{3}[y_0 + 4(y_1 + y_3) + 2y_2 + y_4]$$

$$\approx \frac{0.5}{3}[6.928 + 4(7.806 + 6.778) + 2(7.937) + 0]$$

$$\approx \frac{0.5}{3}[6.928 + 58.336 + 15.874]$$

$$\approx 13.523$$

NOTE:

$$\int_2^4 x(16 - x^2)^{1/2}\, dx = [-\tfrac{1}{3}(16 - x^2)^{3/2}]_2^4 = 0 + \tfrac{1}{3}(12)^{3/2} = 8\sqrt{3} \approx 13.856$$

and, as noted above, Simpson's rule gives a closer approximation than does the trapezoidal rule. Note also that the exact answer is in fact within the bounds given by the trapezoidal rule.

✗ TAYLOR'S EXPANSION

Taylor's theorem may be used to expand a function $f(x)$ in an infinite series; $\int_c^d f(x)\, dx$ may then be evaluated approximately by integrating the series term by term and evaluating as many terms as necessary to obtain the required accuracy. For this procedure to be valid, the series must converge to $f(x)$ for all values of x in the interval $[c, d]$ over which the integral is to be evaluated. The rate of convergence determines the number of terms required for specified accuracy or, equivalently, the accuracy attainable with a specified number of terms. The required accuracy usually can be obtained with fewer terms by expanding the series about a value of a such that $c \le a \le d$.

Thus, providing the convergence conditions are met,

$$\int_c^d f(x)\, dx = \int_c^d \left[f(a) + \frac{f'(a)}{1!}(x - a) + \frac{f''(a)}{2!}(x - a)^2 + \cdots \right.$$

$$\left. + \frac{f^{(n)}(a)}{n!}(x - a)^n + \cdots \right] dx$$

$$= \left[f(a)x + \frac{f'(a)}{2!}(x - a)^2 + \frac{f''(a)}{3!}(x - a)^3 + \cdots \right.$$

$$\left. + \frac{f^{(n)}(a)}{(n + 1)!}(x - a)^{n+1} + \cdots \right]_c^d$$

where, in general, $c \le a \le d$.

EXAMPLE

Evaluate $\displaystyle\int_0^{1/2} \frac{x^2\,dx}{x+1}$ using Taylor's series.

$$f(x) = \frac{x^2}{x+1} \qquad\qquad f(\tfrac{1}{4}) = \frac{\frac{1}{16}}{\frac{5}{4}} = \frac{1}{20}$$

$$f'(x) = \frac{2x(x+1) - x^2}{(x+1)^2} = \frac{x^2 + 2x}{(x+1)^2} \qquad\qquad f'(\tfrac{1}{4}) = \frac{\frac{1}{16} + \frac{1}{2}}{(\frac{5}{4})^2} = \frac{9}{25}$$

$$f''(x) = \frac{(2x+2)(x+1)^2 - (x^2+2x)(2x+2)}{(x+1)^4} \qquad\qquad f''(\tfrac{1}{4}) = \frac{2}{(\frac{5}{4})^3} = \frac{128}{125}$$

$$= \frac{2}{(x+1)^3}$$

$$f'''(x) = \frac{-6(x+1)^2}{(x+1)^6} = -\frac{6}{(x+1)^4} \qquad\qquad f'''(\tfrac{1}{4}) = -\frac{6}{(\frac{5}{4})^4} = -\frac{1536}{625}$$

$$f^{(IV)}(x) = \frac{24(x+1)^3}{(x+1)^8} = \frac{24}{(x+1)^5} \qquad\qquad f^{(IV)}(\tfrac{1}{4}) = \frac{24}{(\frac{5}{4})^5} = \frac{24576}{3125}$$

$$\vdots \qquad\qquad\qquad\qquad \vdots$$

$$f^{(n)}(x) = (-1)^n \frac{n!}{(x+1)^{n+1}} \qquad\qquad f^{(n)}(\tfrac{1}{4}) = (-1)^n \frac{n!}{(\frac{5}{4})^{n+1}}$$

$$\int_c^d f(x)\,dx = \left[f(a)x + \frac{f'(a)}{2!}(x-a)^2 + \frac{f''(a)}{3!}(x-a)^3 + \cdots \right.$$

$$\left. + \frac{f^{(n)}(a)}{(n+1)!}(x-a)^{n+1} + \cdots \right]_c^d$$

Letting $a = \tfrac{1}{4}$,

$$\int_0^{1/2} \frac{x^2\,dx}{x+1} \approx \left[\frac{1}{20}x + \frac{9}{25 \cdot 2!}(x - \tfrac{1}{4})^2 + \frac{128}{125 \cdot 3!}(x - \tfrac{1}{4})^3 \right.$$

$$\left. - \frac{1536}{625 \cdot 4!}(x - \tfrac{1}{4})^4 + \frac{24756}{3125 \cdot 5!}(x - \tfrac{1}{4})^5 \right]_0^{1/2}$$

$$\approx \left(\frac{1}{40} + \frac{9}{25 \cdot 2!}(\tfrac{1}{4})^2 + \frac{128}{125 \cdot 3!}\left(\tfrac{1}{4}\right)^3 - \frac{1536}{625 \cdot 4!}(\tfrac{1}{4})^4 + \frac{24576}{3125 \cdot 5!}\left(\tfrac{1}{4}\right)^5 \right)$$

$$- \left(0 + \frac{9}{25 \cdot 2!}(-\tfrac{1}{4})^2 + \frac{128}{125 \cdot 3!}\left(-\tfrac{1}{4}\right)^3 \right.$$

$$\left. - \frac{1536}{624 \cdot 4!}(-\tfrac{1}{4})^4 + \frac{24576}{3125 \cdot 5!}\left(-\tfrac{1}{4}\right)^5 \right)$$

$$\approx \frac{1}{40} + \frac{2}{375} + \frac{2}{15625}$$

$$\approx 0.025 + 0.0053333 + 0.000128$$

$$\approx 0.0304613$$

or 0.0305 to four decimal places.

NOTE: Using standard forms,

$$\int_0^{1/2} \frac{x^2}{x+1}\,dx = \int_0^{1/2}\left(x - 1 + \frac{1}{x+1}\right)dx = \left[\frac{x^2}{2} - x + \ln(x+1)\right]_0^{1/2}$$

$$= (\tfrac{1}{8} - \tfrac{1}{2} + \ln\tfrac{3}{2}) - (0 - 0 + 0)$$

$$= -\tfrac{3}{8} + \ln\tfrac{3}{2}$$

$$\approx -0.375 + 0.4055$$

$$\approx 0.0305 \quad \text{to four decimal places}$$

EXAMPLE

Evaluate $\int_0^1 x^3\,dx$ using (a) trapezoidal rule, (b) Simpson's rule, (c) Taylor's series, and (d) exactly.

Divide the range into 10 equal parts as summarized in the following table:

i	0	1	2	3	4	5
x_i	0	0.1	0.2	0.3	0.4	0.5
$f(x_i) = y_i$	0	0.001	0.008	0.027	0.064	0.125

i	6	7	8	9	10
x_i	0.6	0.7	0.8	0.9	1.0
$f(x_i) = y_i$	0.216	0.343	0.512	0.729	1.00

(a) trapezoidal rule: $\displaystyle\int_a^b f(x)\,dx \approx \Delta x\left[\tfrac{1}{2}(y_0 + y_n) + \sum_{i=1}^{n-1} y_i\right]$

$$\int_0^1 x^3\,dx \approx 0.1[\tfrac{1}{2}(0 + 1.000) + 2.025]$$

$$\approx 0.2525$$

(b) Simpson's rule:

$$\int_a^b f(x)\,dx \approx \frac{\Delta x}{3}[y_0 + 4y_1 + 2y_2 + 4y_3 + \cdots + 4y_{n-1} + y_n]$$

$$\int_0^1 x^3\,dx \approx \frac{0.1}{3}[(0 + 1.000) + 2(0.800) + 4(1.224)]$$

$$\approx 0.2499$$

(c) $\displaystyle\int_c^d f(x)\,dx = \left[f(a)x + \frac{f'(a)}{2!}(x-a)^2 + \frac{f''(a)}{3!}(x-a)^3 + \cdots\right]_c^d$

Letting $a = \tfrac{1}{2}$,

$$\int_0^1 x^3\,dx = \left[f(\tfrac{1}{2})x + \frac{f'(\tfrac{1}{2})}{2!}(x-\tfrac{1}{2})^2 + \frac{f''(\tfrac{1}{2})}{3!}(x-\tfrac{1}{2})^3 + \cdots\right]_0^1$$

$$f(x) = x^3 \qquad f(\tfrac{1}{2}) = \tfrac{1}{8}$$

$$f'(x) = 3x^2 \qquad f'(\tfrac{1}{2}) = \tfrac{3}{4}$$

$$f''(x) = 6x \qquad f''(\tfrac{1}{2}) = 3$$

$$f'''(x) = 6 \qquad f'''(\tfrac{1}{2}) = 6$$

$$f^{(IV)}(x) = 0 \qquad f^{(IV)}(\tfrac{1}{2}) = 0$$

$$\int_0^1 x^3 \, dx = \left[\frac{1}{8} x + \frac{\frac{3}{4}}{2!} (x - \tfrac{1}{2})^2 + \frac{3}{3!} (x - \tfrac{1}{2})^3 + \frac{6}{4!} (x - \tfrac{1}{2})^4 \right]_0^1$$

$$= \left(\frac{1}{8} + \frac{\frac{3}{4}}{2!} \left(\frac{1}{2} \right)^2 + \frac{3}{3!} \left(\frac{1}{2} \right)^3 + \frac{6}{4!} \left(\frac{1}{2} \right)^4 \right)$$

$$- \left(0 + \frac{\frac{3}{4}}{2!} \left(\frac{1}{2} \right)^2 + \frac{3}{3!} \left(-\frac{1}{2} \right)^3 + \frac{6}{4!} \left(\frac{1}{2} \right)^4 \right)$$

$$= 0.125 + 0.125$$

$$= 0.250$$

(d) $\int_0^1 x^3 \, dx = \left[\dfrac{x^4}{4} \right]_0^1 = \tfrac{1}{4} - 0 = 0.25$

NOTE: Both Simpson's rule and the Taylor's series expansion provide the exact answer for this particular problem. Because of the nature of the approximation (quadratic), Simpson's rule is exact for any quadratic or cubic function. The Taylor's series expansion is exact if all further terms are zero—that is, if n terms are used and the nth derivative of $f(x)$ is zero. Because Simpson's rule is exact, the answer could have been obtained by dividing the range into only two parts:

i	0	1	2
x_i	0	0.5	1
$f(x_i) = y_i$	0	0.125	1

$$\int_0^1 x^3 \, dx = \frac{0.5}{3} [1 + 4(0.125)] = 0.25$$

However, using $n = 2$ instead of $n = 10$ would reduce the accuracy of the trapezoidal rule:

$$\int_0^1 x^3 \, dx = 0.5[\tfrac{1}{2}(1) + 0.125] = 0.3125$$

EXAMPLE

Evaluate $\int_2^6 \dfrac{dx}{x^2 - 1}$ using (a) trapezoidal rule, (b) Simpson's rule, (c) Taylor's series, and (d) exactly.

Divide the range into four equal parts as summarized in the following table:

i	0	1	2	3	4
x_i	2	3	4	5	6
$f(x_i) = y_i$	$\frac{1}{3}$	$\frac{1}{8}$	$\frac{1}{15}$	$\frac{1}{24}$	$\frac{1}{35}$
	(0.3333)	(0.1250)	(0.0667)	(0.0417)	(0.0286)

(a) trapezoidal rule: $\int_a^b f(x)\, dx \approx \Delta x \left[\frac{1}{2}(y_0 + y_n) + \sum_{i=1}^{n-1} y_i \right]$

$\int_2^6 \dfrac{dx}{x^2 - 1} \approx 1[\frac{1}{2}(0.3333 + 0.0286) + 0.2334]$

≈ 0.4143

(b) Simpson's rule: $\int_a^b f(x)\, dx \approx \dfrac{\Delta x}{3}[y_0 + 4y_1 + 2y_2 + \cdots + 4y_{n-1} + y_n]$

$\int_2^6 \dfrac{dx}{x^2 - 1} \approx \frac{1}{3}[(0.3333 + 0.0286) + 4(0.1250 + 0.0417) + 2(0.0667)]$

≈ 0.3874

(c) $\int_c^d f(x)\, dx = \left[f(a)x + \dfrac{f'(a)}{2!}(x - a)^2 + \dfrac{f''(a)}{3!}(x - a)^3 + \cdots \right]_c^d$

Letting $a = 4$,

$\int_2^6 \dfrac{dx}{x^2 - 1} \approx \left[f(4)x + \dfrac{f'(4)}{2!}(x - 4)^2 + \dfrac{f''(4)}{3!}(x - 4)^3 + \dfrac{f'''(4)}{3!}(x - 4)^4 \right.$

$\left. + \dfrac{f^{(IV)}(4)}{5!}(x - 4)^5 \right]_2^6$

$f(x) = (x^2 - 1)^{-1}$

$f'(x) = -1(x^2 - 1)^{-2}(2x)$

$\quad = -2x(x^2 - 1)^{-2}$

$f''(x) = -2(x^2 - 1)^{-2} - 2x(-2)(x^2 - 1)^{-3}(2x)$

$\quad = (x^2 - 1)^{-3}[-2(x^2 - 1) + 8x^2]$

$\quad = 2(3x^2 + 1)(x^2 - 1)^{-3}$

$f'''(x) = 2(6x)(x^2 - 1)^{-3}$

$\quad + 2(3x^2 + 1)(-3)(x^2 - 1)^{-4}(2x)$

$\quad = 12x(x^2 - 1) - 12x(3x^2 + 1)$

$\quad = (x^2 - 1)^{-4}[12x^3 - 12x - 36x^3 - 12x]$

$\quad = -24x(x^2 + 1)(x^2 - 1)^{-4}$

$f^{(IV)}(x) = -24(3x^2 + 1)(x^2 - 1)^{-4} - 24(x^3 + x)(-4)(x^2 - 1)^{-5}(2x)$

$\quad = -24(x^2 - 1)^{-5}[(3x^2 + 1)(x^2 - 1) - 8x(x^3 + x)]$

$\quad = 24(5x^4 + 10x^2 + 1)(x^2 - 1)^{-5}$

$f(4) = \dfrac{1}{15}$

$f'(4) = \dfrac{-8}{(15)^2}$

$f''(4) = \dfrac{98}{(15)^3}$

$f'''(4) = \dfrac{-(96)(17)}{(15)^4}$

$f^{(IV)}(4) = \dfrac{(24)(1441)}{(15)^5}$

$$\int_2^6 \frac{dx}{x^2 - 1} \approx \left[\frac{1}{15} x - \frac{8}{(15)^2 \cdot 2!} (x-4)^2 + \frac{98}{(15)^3 \cdot 3!} (x-4)^3 \right.$$

$$\left. - \frac{(96)(17)}{(15)^4 \cdot 4!} (x-4)^4 + \frac{(24)(1441)}{(15)^5 \cdot 5!} (x-4)^5 \right]_2^6$$

$$\approx \left(\frac{6}{15} - \frac{8}{(15)^2 \cdot 2!}(2)^2 + \frac{98}{(15)^3 \cdot 3!}(2)^3 - \frac{(96)(17)}{(15)^4 \cdot 4!}(2)^4 + \frac{(24)(1441)}{(15)^5 \cdot 5!}(2)^5 \right)$$

$$- \left(\frac{2}{15} - \frac{8}{(15)^2 \cdot 2!}(-2)^2 + \frac{98}{(15)^3 \cdot 3!}(-2)^3 \right.$$

$$\left. - \frac{(96)(17)}{(15)^4 \cdot 4!}(-2)^4 + \frac{(24)(1441)}{(15)^5 \cdot 5!}(-2)^5 \right)$$

$$\approx 0.2667 + 0.0774 + 0.0243$$

$$\approx 0.3684$$

(d) $\displaystyle \int_2^6 \frac{dx}{x^2 - 1} = \left[\tfrac{1}{2} \ln \left(\frac{x-1}{x+1} \right) \right]_2^6 = \tfrac{1}{2}[\ln \tfrac{5}{7} - \ln \tfrac{1}{3}]$

$$= \tfrac{1}{2}[\ln 5 - \ln 7 - \ln 1 + \ln 3]$$

$$\approx \tfrac{1}{2}[1.6094 - 1.9459 - 0 + 1.0986]$$

$$\approx 0.3811$$

NOTE: $\displaystyle \int \frac{du}{u^2 - a^2} = \frac{1}{2a} \ln \left(\frac{u-a}{u+a} \right) + C.$

It should be noted that the seemingly better results using Simpson's rule are due to the truncation effects of using only 4 terms in Taylor's series. If a sufficient number of terms are computed, Taylor's series is more accurate than Simpson's rule.

Whenever an approximation is used, consideration should be given to its accuracy. The trapezoidal rule provides a linear approximation of the function to be integrated for each of the specified sub-intervals; the error in this approximation depends on the departure of the function from linearity over the various subintervals.

Similarly, Simpson's rule provides a quadratic approximation, and the error in this approximation depends on how closely the function to be integrated is fit by a quadratic function over the various subintervals. A quadratic function provides more flexibility and a better fit for approximation than does a linear function, and, thus, for specified sub-intervals, Simpson's rule is more accurate than the trapezoidal rule. It is obvious, geometrically, that some functions are more readily approximated than others. In particular, a function that has several maxima, minima, and points of inflection and whose slope is relatively large in absolute value over at least part of the range of integration is relatively difficult to approximate accurately. For such a function, more subintervals are required to attain a specified accuracy of approximation.

Although Taylor's series approximation cannot be represented geometrically in the manner used for the trapezoidal and Simpson methods, the same considerations apply. Essentially, the accuracy of approximation using Taylor's series depends on the nature of the function being approximated and the rate of convergence of the series used to approximate it. If convergence of the series is relatively rapid, fewer terms need be evaluated to attain a specified accuracy of approximation. As discussed in Section 2.14, a bound on the accuracy of a Taylor series expansion of a function can be obtained from the remainder term.

PROBLEMS

Evaluate each of the following integrals approximately using a. trapezoidal rule, b. Simpson's rule, c. Taylor's series, and d. exactly.

1. $\int_0^3 (x^4 + 3x^2)\, dx$, $n = 6$

3. $\int_{-2}^2 e^{2x}\, dx$, $n = 4$

2. $\int_3^5 \dfrac{dx}{x^2}$, $n = 4$

4. $\int_{-2}^2 e^{(1/2)x}\, dx$, $n = 4$

Evaluate each of the following integrals by expanding the function in a Taylor's series; comment on the interval of convergence and the accuracy of the evaluation.

5. $\int_0^1 (x^4 - x^3 + \tfrac{1}{2})\, dx$

7. $\int_0^2 \left(\dfrac{x^4}{4} + x^3 + 2x^2 + 1\right) dx$

6. $\int_0^2 (5x^4 + \tfrac{1}{3}x^3 + 6x)\, dx$

8. $\int_2^4 (x^3 - 6x + 3)\, dx$

Answers to Odd-Numbered Problems

1. a. 78.219, b. 75.625, c. 75.6, d. 75.6
3. a. 35.832, b. 28.904, c. 27.173, d. 27.290
5. $\tfrac{9}{20}$ (exact, no problem of interval of convergence)
7. $12\tfrac{14}{15}$ (exact, no problem of interval of convergence)

4.8 Multiple Integrals

Multiple integrals are evaluated by successive partial integration. In this section partial integration, the inverse of partial differentiation, is defined and its use in evaluating multiple integrals is illustrated. The use of double integrals in evaluating probabilities associated with joint frequency functions is also discussed and illustrated.

The definite integral $\int_a^b f(x)\, dx$ is defined with respect to the function $f(x)$ over an interval $a \le x \le b$. Similarly, the *double integral*

$$\iint_R f(x, y)\, dy\, dx$$

is defined with respect to the function $f(x, y)$ over a bounded region, R, of the xy-plane.

Just as the definite integral of $f(x)$ can be interpreted in terms of area, the definite double integral of $f(x, y)$ can be interpreted in terms of volume. (See Figure 4.34.) Note that in Figure 4.34 the function $f(x, y)$ is assumed to be positive over the region R and the volume computed is that below the surface $z = f(x, y)$ and above the region R in the xy-plane.

The evaluation of double integrals is most easily accomplished by successive *partial integration*, which is the inverse of partial differentiation. That is, to evaluate a

Figure 4.34

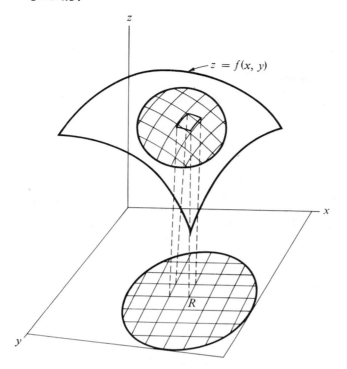

double integral, a function of two independent variables is integrated with respect to one of the variables while the other variable is considered as constant; the result of this partial integration is then integrated with respect to the other variable. For this purpose the double integral

$$\iint\limits_{R} f(x, y) \, dy \, dx \qquad \text{or} \qquad \int_{a}^{b} \int_{h(x)}^{g(x)} f(x, y) \, dy \, dx$$

where a and b are constants, can be written as the *iterated integral*

$$\int_{a}^{b} \left[\int_{h(x)}^{g(x)} f(x, y) \, dy \right] dx$$

To evaluate this expression, $f(x, y)$ is first integrated partially with respect to y and evaluated for the appropriate limits; the result is a function of x which is then integrated with respect to x and evaluated for the appropriate limits. Similarly,

$$\int_{a}^{b} \int_{h(y)}^{g(y)} f(x, y) \, dx \, dy \qquad \text{or} \qquad \int_{a}^{b} \left[\int_{h(y)}^{g(y)} f(x, y) \, dx \right] dy$$

is first integrated partially with respect to x and then with respect to y.

NOTE: If the order of integration is reversed, new limits of integration must be determined, that is,

$$\int_{a}^{b} \int_{h(x)}^{g(x)} f(x, y) \, dy \, dx \neq \int_{h(x)}^{g(x)} \int_{a}^{b} f(x, y) \, dx \, dy$$

The limits of integration must involve only variables with respect to which integration is to be performed subsequently, and the limits of integration must be rewritten in this manner. Thus

$$\int_a^b \int_{h(x)}^{g(x)} f(x, y) \, dy \, dx = \int_c^d \int_{n(y)}^{m(y)} f(x, y) \, dx \, dy$$

where the new limits of integration are determined so that, for example, if $y = g(x)$, then $x = m(y)$.

It is important to note that multiple integration is performed from the inside outward; thus the first integral sign belongs to the last differential and so forth. Note also that when an integration is performed with respect to a variable, that variable is eliminated completely from the remaining integral, including the limits of integration. The concepts and definitions used in evaluating double integrals can be generalized for functions of more than two independent variables by using multiple integrals. There are relatively few practical applications that require more than triple integration.

EXAMPLE

Evaluate the double integral $\int_0^1 \int_{x^2}^x \sqrt{\dfrac{x}{y}} \, dy \, dx$.

$$\int_0^1 \int_{x^2}^x \sqrt{\frac{x}{y}} \, dy \, dx = \int_0^1 [2x^{1/2}y^{1/2}]_{x^2}^x \, dx \qquad \text{integrating w.r.t. } y$$

$$= \int_0^1 (2x - 2x^{3/2}) \, dx \qquad \text{evaluating for the limits } y = x \text{ and } y = x^2$$

$$= \left[x^2 - \frac{4x^{5/2}}{5}\right]_0^1 \qquad \text{integrating w.r.t. } x$$

$$= (1 - \tfrac{4}{5}) - 0 = \tfrac{1}{5} \qquad \text{evaluating for the limits } x = 1 \text{ and } x = 0$$

EXAMPLE

Evaluate the double integral $\int_0^a \int_0^{\sqrt{a^2 - y^2}} x \, dx \, dy$.

$$\int_0^a \int_0^{\sqrt{a^2 - y^2}} x \, dx \, dy = \int_0^a \left[\frac{x^2}{2}\right]_0^{\sqrt{a^2 - y^2}} \, dy \qquad \text{integrating w.r.t. } x$$

$$= \int_0^a \frac{a^2 - y^2}{2} \, dy \qquad \text{evaluating for the limits } x = \sqrt{a^2 - y^2} \text{ and } x = 0$$

$$= \left[\frac{a^2 y}{2} - \frac{y^3}{6}\right]_0^a \qquad \text{integrating w.r.t. } y$$

$$= \left(\frac{a^3}{2} - \frac{a^3}{6}\right) - 0 = \frac{a^3}{3} \qquad \text{evaluating for the limits } y = a \text{ and } y = 0$$

EXAMPLE

Evaluate the double integral $\int_0^\pi \int_0^x x \sin y \, dy \, dx$.

$$\int_0^\pi \int_0^x x \sin y \, dy \, dx = \int_0^\pi [-x \cos y]_0^x \, dx \qquad \text{integrating w.r.t. } y$$

$$= \int_0^\pi (-x \cos x + x) \, dx \qquad \text{evaluating for the limits } y = x \text{ and } y = 0$$

$$= -\int_0^\pi x \cos x \, dx + \left[\frac{x^2}{2}\right]_0^\pi \qquad \text{integrating w.r.t. } x$$

Integrating $\int_0^\pi x \cos x \, dx$ by parts,

$$u = x \qquad dv = \cos x$$
$$du = dx \qquad v = \sin x$$

and

$$\int_0^\pi x \cos x = [x \sin x]_0^\pi - \int_0^\pi \sin x \, dx$$

$$= [x \sin x + \cos x]_0^\pi$$
$$= (0 - 1) - (0 + 1)$$
$$= -2$$

Thus

$$\int_0^\pi \int_0^x x \sin y \, dy \, dx = -(-2) + \frac{\pi^2}{2}$$

$$= \frac{4 + \pi^2}{2}$$

EXAMPLE

Evaluate the double integral $\int_1^2 \int_1^{e^y} \frac{1}{xy} \, dx \, dy$.

$$\int_1^2 \int_1^{e^y} \frac{1}{xy} \, dx \, dy = \int_1^2 \left[\int_1^{e^y} \frac{1}{xy} \, dx\right] dy \quad \text{integrating w.r.t. } x$$

$$= \int_1^2 \left[\frac{1}{y} \ln x\right]_1^{e^y} dy \qquad \text{evaluating for the limits } x = e^y \text{ and } x = 1$$

$$= \int_1^2 dy \qquad \text{integrating w.r.t. } y$$

$$= [y]_1^2 \qquad \text{evaluating for the limits } y = 2 \text{ and } y = 1$$

$$= 1 - (-1) = 2$$

EXAMPLE

Evaluate the triple integral $\int_1^2 y \int_y^{y^2} \int_0^{\ln x} e^z \, dz \, dx \, dy$.

$$\int_1^2 y \int_y^{y^2} \int_0^{\ln x} e^z \, dz \, dx \, dy = \int_1^2 y \int_y^{y^2} [e^z]_0^{\ln x} \, dx \, dy \qquad \text{integrating w.r.t. } z$$

$$= \int_1^2 y \int_y^{y^2} (x - 1) \, dx \, dy \qquad \begin{array}{l}\text{evaluating for the limits}\\ z = \ln x \text{ and } z = 0\end{array}$$

$$= \int_1^2 y \left[\frac{x^2}{2} - x\right]_y^{y^2} dy \qquad \text{integrating w.r.t. } x$$

$$= \int_1^2 \left(\frac{y^5}{2} - y^3 - \frac{y^3}{2} + y^2\right) dy \qquad \begin{array}{l}\text{evaluating for the limits}\\ x = y^2 \text{ and } x = y\end{array}$$

$$= \int_1^2 \left(\frac{y^5}{2} - \frac{3y^3}{2} + y^2\right) dy \qquad \text{integrating w.r.t. } y$$

$$= \left[\frac{y^6}{12} - \frac{3y^4}{8} + \frac{y^3}{3}\right]_1^2 \qquad \begin{array}{l}\text{evaluating for the limits}\\ y = 2 \text{ and } y = 1\end{array}$$

$$= (\tfrac{16}{3} - 6 + \tfrac{8}{3}) - (\tfrac{1}{12} - \tfrac{3}{8} + \tfrac{1}{3})$$

$$= \tfrac{47}{24}$$

Note that the integrand in the example above can also be written

$$\int_1^2 \int_y^{y^2} \int_0^{\ln x} y e^z \, dz \, dx \, dy$$

and y can be carried as a constant in the first two integrations. However, when an integrand includes a factor which is constant with respect to one or more integrations, that factor can be moved outside the integral(s), and usually it is more convenient to separate the integrand in this manner.

EXAMPLE

Evaluate the triple integral $\int_0^\pi \int_0^{\pi/6} \int_0^{a \sin \theta} r^2 \cos \theta \sin \phi \, dr \, d\theta \, d\phi$.

$$\int_0^\pi \int_0^{\pi/6} \int_0^{a \sin \theta} r^2 \cos \theta \sin \phi \, dr \, d\theta \, d\phi$$

$$= \int_0^\pi \sin \phi \int_0^{\pi/6} \cos \theta \int_0^{a \sin \theta} r^2 \, dr \, d\theta \, d\phi$$

$$= \int_0^\pi \sin \phi \int_0^{\pi/6} \cos \theta \left[\frac{r^3}{3}\right]_0^{a \sin \theta} d\theta \, d\phi \qquad \text{integrating w.r.t. } r$$

$$= \int_0^\pi \sin \phi \left[\int_0^{\pi/6} \frac{a^3}{3} \cos \theta \sin^3 \theta \, d\theta\right] d\phi \qquad \begin{array}{l}\text{evaluating for the limits } r = a \sin \theta \text{ and}\\ r = 0\end{array}$$

$$= \frac{a^3}{3} \int_0^\pi \sin \phi [\tfrac{1}{4} \sin^4 \theta]_0^{\pi/6} \, d\phi \qquad \text{integrating w.r.t. } \theta$$

$$= \frac{a^3}{12} \int_0^\pi \sin \phi (\tfrac{1}{16}) \, d\phi$$

evaluating for the limits $\theta = \pi/6$ and $\theta = 0$

$$= \frac{a^3}{192} \int_0^\pi \sin \phi \, d\phi$$

integrating w.r.t. ϕ

$$= \frac{a^3}{192} [-\cos \phi]_0^\pi$$

$$= \frac{a^3}{192} (1 + 1) = \frac{a^3}{96}$$

evaluating for the limits $\phi = \pi$ and $\phi = 0$

Most applications of multiple integration involve definite integrals. Any consideration of indefinite integration as the reverse process of differentiation is complicated in the case of multiple integration by the form of the constant of integration. For example, when integration is with respect to y, x is constant and, in general, the constant of integration is a function of x. Thus, since multiple integration is the reverse of successive partial differentiations with respect to different variables, the constants of integration are functions of one or more variables; determining these constants requires rather complicated initial conditions. Most problems of this type and complexity are more conveniently stated in terms of differential equations, as discussed in the next chapter.

PROBLEMS

Evaluate the following multiple integrals.

1. $\int_0^1 \int_0^2 (x + 2) \, dy \, dx$

2. $\int_0^2 \int_1^3 (x + y) \, dx \, dy$

3. $\int_0^1 \int_{y^2}^y x^{1/2} \, dx \, dy$

4. $\int_0^2 \int_1^{x^2} y \, dy \, dx$

5. $\int_0^{-1} \int_{y+1}^{2y} xy \, dx \, dy$

6. $\int_0^1 \int_0^{x^2} e^{y/x} \, dy \, dx$

7. $\int_{-b}^a \int_0^b \int_a^{2a} x^2 y^2 z \, dz \, dy \, dx$

8. $\int_0^1 \int_{y^2}^1 \int_0^{1-x} x \, dz \, dx \, dy$

9. $\int_0^1 \int_0^{1-x} \int_0^{1-y^2} z \, dz \, dy \, dx$

10. $\int_0^1 \int_0^x \int_0^{x+y} e^{x+y+z} \, dz \, dy \, dx$

11. $\int_{-1}^1 \int_y^{2y} x^2 y \, dx \, dy$

12. $\int_{-3}^0 \int_0^y y^2 e^{xy} \, dx \, dy$

13. $\int_1^2 \int_0^{x^2} (xy + 1) \, dy \, dx$

14. $\int_0^3 \int_x^{x+1} (x + y) \, dy \, dx$

15. $\int_{-1}^1 \int_{x-1}^{x+1} (x - y - 1) \, dy \, dx$

16. $\int_0^2 \int_y^{y+2} y \, dx \, dy$

17. $\int_0^1 x^2 \int_0^1 e^{xy} \, dy \, dx$

18. $\int_0^1 \int_0^x \int_0^{x+y} (x + y + z) \, dz \, dy \, dx$

Answers to Odd-Numbered Problems

1. 5
3. $\frac{1}{10}$
5. $\frac{11}{24}$
7. $\frac{1}{6}a^2 b^3 (a^3 - b^3)$
9. $\frac{11}{60}$

11. $\frac{14}{15}$
13. $\frac{91}{12}$
15. -4
17. $\frac{1}{2}$

PROBABILITY AS A DOUBLE INTEGRAL

One of the most frequent applications of double integration is concerned with determining the probability that two variables fall within specified ranges. These problems are stated in terms of the double integral of a joint frequency function, just as the probability that one variable falls within a specified range is stated in terms of the integral of a frequency function of one variable.

A joint frequency function for continuous variables x and y is a function $f(x, y)$ having the following properties:

1. $f(x, y) \geq 0$

2. $\displaystyle\int_{-\infty}^{\infty} \int_{-\infty}^{\infty} f(x, y) \, dx \, dy = 1$

3. $\displaystyle\int_{a_2}^{b_2} \int_{a_1}^{b_1} f(x, y) \, dx \, dy = P(a_1 < x < b_1, a_2 < y < b_2)$

These properties are similar to those for a frequency function of one variable and state that (1) probability is always nonnegative; (2) the probability of an event that is certain to occur is one; and (3) the probability that the value of x is in the interval (a_1, b_1) and the value of y is in the interval (a_2, b_2) is given by the corresponding integral. Geometrically, $f(x, y)$ is a surface in three dimensions and the volume under the surface lying above the rectangle determined by $a_1 < x < b_1$ and $a_2 < y < b_2$ is the probability that x and y will assume values corresponding to points in this rectangle. (See Figure 4.29.) If $f(x, y)$ is continuous, $P(a_1 < x < b_1, a_2 < y < b_2) = P(a_1 \leq x \leq b_1, a_2 \leq y \leq b_2)$.

EXAMPLE

In a study of costs for a certain type of fluorescent tube, a company has determined that the frequency function for size of order, x, and total cost for the order, y, is approximately

$$f(x, y) = \frac{1}{3.5} \quad 1 \leq x \leq 6 \quad 0.1 + 0.9x \leq y < 0.1 + 1.1x$$

where x is in thousands of fluorescent tubes and y is in thousands of dollars. If the company sets a price of $1.05 per tube, on what proportion of the orders will the company break even or make a profit?

$P(1 \leq x \leq 6, 0.1 + 0.9x \leq y \leq 1.05x)$

$\displaystyle = \int_1^6 \int_{0.1+0.9x}^{1.05x} \frac{1}{3.5} \, dy \, dx$

$\displaystyle = \frac{1}{3.5} \int_1^6 [y]_{0.1+0.9x}^{1.05x} \, dx$ integrating w.r.t. y

$\displaystyle = \frac{1}{3.5} \int_1^6 (1.05x - 0.1 - 0.9x) \, dx$ evaluating for the limits $y = 1.05x$ and $y = 0.1 + 0.9x$

$\displaystyle = \frac{1}{3.5} \int_1^6 (0.15x - 0.1) \, dx$

$\displaystyle = \frac{1}{3.5} [0.075x^2 - 0.1x]_1^6$ integrating w.r.t. x

$$= \frac{1}{3.5}[(2.7 - 0.6) - (0.075 - 0.1)] \qquad \text{evaluating for the limits } x = 6 \text{ and } x = 1$$

$$= \frac{2.125}{3.5}$$

$$= 0.6071$$

NOTE: Integrating w.r.t. x,

$$\int_1^6 \int_{0.1+0.9x}^{0.1+1.1x} \frac{1}{3.5} \, dy \, dx$$

$$= \frac{1}{3.5} \int_1^6 [y]_{0.1+0.9x}^{0.1+1.1x}$$

$$= \frac{1}{3.5} \int_1^6 [(0.1 + 1.1x) - (0.1 + 0.9x)] \, dx \qquad \begin{array}{l}\text{evaluating for the limits } y = 0.1 + 1.1x \\ \text{and } y = 0.1 + 0.9x\end{array}$$

$$= \frac{1}{3.5} \int_1^6 0.2x \, dx$$

$$= \frac{1}{3.5} [0.1x^2]_1^6 \qquad \text{integrating w.r.t. } x$$

$$= \frac{1}{3.5} [3.6 - 0.1] \qquad \text{evaluating for the limits } x = 6 \text{ and } x = 1$$

$$= 1 \qquad \text{as required for a joint frequency function}$$

EXAMPLE

The joint frequency function for the time (in microseconds) required for two switches to close is given by

$$f(x_1, x_2) = 15e^{-(3x_1 + 5x_2)} \qquad x_1 > 0, x_2 > 0$$

(a) Find the probability that the first switch requires less than 0.1 microsecond and the second switch requires more than 0.5 microsecond to close.
(b) Find the probability that the first switch requires more than 0.2 microsecond and the second switch requires more than 0.5 microsecond to close.

The given function is a frequency function since it is positive for all x_1 and x_2 and

$$\int_0^\infty \int_0^\infty 15e^{-(3x_1 + 5x_2)} \, dx_1 \, dx_2 = \int_0^\infty [-5e^{-(3x_1 + 5x_2)}]_0^\infty \, dx_2 \qquad \text{integrating w.r.t. } x_1$$

$$= \int_0^\infty 5e^{-5x_2} \, dx_2 \qquad \begin{array}{l}\text{evaluating for the limits } x_1 = \infty \\ \text{and } x_1 = 0\end{array}$$

$$= [-e^{-5x_2}]_0^\infty \qquad \text{integrating w.r.t. } x_2$$

$$= 0 - (-1) \qquad \begin{array}{l}\text{evaluating for the limits } x_2 = \infty \\ \text{and } x_2 = 0.2\end{array}$$

$$= 1 \qquad \begin{array}{l}\text{as required for a joint frequency} \\ \text{function}\end{array}$$

(a) $P(0 < x_1 < 0.1, x_2 > 0.5) = 15 \int_0^{0.1} \int_{0.5}^{\infty} e^{-(3x_1 + 5x_2)} \, dx_2 \, dx_1$

$= -3 \int_0^{0.1} [e^{-(3x_1 + 5x_2)}]_{0.5}^{\infty} \, dx_1$ integrating w.r.t. x_2

$= 3 \int_0^{0.1} e^{-(3x_1 + 2.5)} \, dx_1$ evaluating for the limits $x_2 = \infty$ and $x_2 = 0.5$

$= [-e^{-(3x_1 + 2.5)}]_0^{0.1}$ integrating w.r.t. x_1

$= -e^{-2.8} + e^{-2.5}$ evaluating for the limits $x_1 = 0.1$ and $x_1 = 0$

$= -0.061 + 0.082$

$= 0.021$

(b) $P(x_1 > 0.2, x_2 > 0.5) = 15 \int_{0.2}^{\infty} \int_{0.5}^{\infty} e^{-(3x_1 + 5x_2)} \, dx_2 \, dx_1$

$= -3 \int_{0.2}^{\infty} [e^{-(3x_1 + 5x_2)}]_{0.5}^{\infty} \, dx_1$ integrating w.r.t. x_2

$= 3 \int_{0.2}^{\infty} e^{-(3x_1 + 2.5)} \, dx_1$ evaluating for the limits $x_2 = \infty$ and $x_2 = 0.5$

$= [-e^{-(3x_1 + 2.5)}]_{0.2}^{\infty}$ integrating w.r.t. x_1

$= 0 + e^{-3.1}$ evaluating for the limits $x_1 = \infty$ and $x_1 = 0.2$

$= 0.045$

Note also that $f(x_1, x_2) = f(x_1)f(x_2) = (3e^{-3x_1})(5e^{-5x_2})$. Thus

$P(x_2 > 0.5) = 5 \int_{0.5}^{\infty} e^{-5x_2} \, dx_2 = [-e^{-5x_2}]_{0.5}^{\infty} = 0 + e^{-2.5} = 0.082$

$P(x_1 < 0.1) = 3 \int_0^{0.1} e^{-3x_1} \, dx_1 = [-e^{-3x_1}]_0^{0.1} = -e^{-0.3} + 1 = 0.259$

$P(x_1 > 0.2) = 3 \int_{0.2}^{\infty} e^{-3x_1} \, dx_1 = [-e^{-3x_1}]_{0.2}^{\infty} = 0 + e^{-0.6} = 0.549$

These probabilities are referred to as marginal probabilities, and the joint probabilities obtained above can be obtained as the products of the corresponding marginal probabilities. This is characteristic of probabilities of independent events.

EXAMPLE

Show that $f(x, y) = \lambda^2 e^{-\lambda y}$, $0 \leq x \leq y$, $\lambda > 0$ is a joint frequency function.

$f(x, y) \geq 0$ since $\lambda^2 > 0$ and $e^{\lambda y} > 0$

$\int_0^{\infty} \int_0^y \lambda^2 e^{-\lambda y} \, dx \, dy = \lambda^2 \int_0^{\infty} [xe^{-\lambda y}]_0^y \, dy$ integrating w.r.t. x

$= \lambda^2 \int_0^{\infty} ye^{-\lambda y} \, dy$ evaluating for the limits $x = \infty$ and $x = 0$

Integrating by parts,

$$u = y \qquad dv = e^{-\lambda y}$$

$$du = dy \qquad v = -\frac{1}{\lambda} e^{-\lambda y}$$

and

$$\lambda^2 \int_0^\infty y e^{-\lambda y} \, dy = \lambda^2 \left(\left[-\frac{y}{\lambda} e^{-\lambda y} \right]_0^\infty + \frac{1}{\lambda} \int_0^\infty e^{-\lambda y} \, dy \right)$$

$$= \lambda^2 \left[-\frac{y}{\lambda} e^{-\lambda y} - \frac{1}{\lambda^2} e^{-\lambda y} \right]_0^\infty$$

$$= \left[-\lambda y e^{-\lambda y} - e^{-\lambda y} \right]_0^\infty$$

$$= (0 - 0) - (0 - 1)$$

$$= 1$$

PROBLEMS

1. Show that $f(x, y) = \frac{3}{4}(x + y)^2$, $0 \le x \le 1$, $0 \le y \le 1$ is a frequency function.
2. Show that $f(x, y) = \frac{15}{4}(y - x)^{1/2}$, $0 \le x \le y \le 1$ is a frequency function.
3. Show that $f(x, y) = 8xy$, $0 \le x \le 1$, $0 \le y \le x$, is a frequency function and find a. $P(0 \le x \le 0.5, 0 \le y \le x)$ and b. $P(0.2 \le x \le 0.5, 0.1 \le y \le x)$.
4. Show that $f(x, y) = 12(y - x)^2$, $0 \le x < y \le 1$ is a frequency function and find a. $P(0.5 \le x < y \le 1)$ and b. $P(0 \le x < y < 0.5)$.
5. Determine the value of k for which

$$f(x, y) = k(x + y) \qquad 0 < x < 4, 0 < y < 6$$

is a frequency function.
6. Determine the value of c for which

$$f(x, 6y) = \frac{xy}{c} \qquad 2 \le x \le 4, 5 < y < 9$$

is a frequency function.
7. The joint frequency function for the errors in measuring two variables is given by

$$f(x, y) = \frac{1}{x} \qquad 0 < y < x < 1$$

a. Find the probability that the measurement error x is between 0 and 0.5 and the measurement error y is between 0 and $0.2x$. b. Find the probability that the measurement error x is between 0.8 and 1 and the measurement error y is between 0.8 and 1. c. Show that $f(x, y)$ is a frequency function.
8. The waste from a chemical plant consists of soluble and nonsoluble substances. The nonsoluble substances are of two types, A and B. The plant's engineers have studied data and have determined that the composition of the nonsoluble waste on one day does not depend on its composition on preceding days. The joint frequency function for the proportion of all soluble substances (A and B), denoted by x, and type B nonsoluble substances, denoted by y, is given by

$$f(x, y) = 15xy^2 \qquad 0 \le x \le 1, 0 \le y \le x$$

a. For what proportion of the days does the waste contain more than 20% of type B nonsoluble substances? b. For what proportion of the days does the waste contain less than 50% of nonsoluble substances? c. For what proportion of the days does the waste contain more than 50% nonsoluble substances and more than 20% type B substances? d. Show that $f(x, y)$ is a frequency function.

Answers to Odd-Numbered Problems

3. a. 0.0625
   b. 0.0567
5. $k = \frac{1}{120}$
7. a. 0.1
   b. 0.2

Differential Equations

5.1 Introduction

In many problems the relationships between or among variables are most appropriately stated directly in terms of rates of change. The rate of change of any variable may be expressed as a function of the rates of change or the values of other variables. For example, in physics equations involving rates of change in energy are used in the derivation of the laws of conservation of energy; in economics it is assumed that the rate at which price approaches its equilibrium value depends on the magnitude of the discrepancy between the quantities supplied and demanded.

Rates of change can be stated in either of two mathematical forms, depending on whether time (or, more generally, any variable with respect to which changes are considered) is viewed as continuous or discrete. When changes are considered to occur continuously or instantaneously, rates of change are stated as derivatives and equations involving them are differential equations. When changes are considered to occur discretely or discontinuously at certain points in time or as average changes over a period of time, rates of change are stated as differences in the values of variables at different points in time and equations involving them are difference equations. Differential equations are the limiting case of difference equations as the time period between changes or over which an average change is computed approaches zero.

Differential equations, that is, equations involving derivatives, are discussed in this chapter; difference equations, that is, equations involving differences between values of variables at different points in time or with respect to different values of another variable are discussed in Chapter 6.

The definition and classification of differential equations are discussed and types of solutions of ordinary differential equations are considered and illustrated. A classification of differential equations of first order and first degree is given and the solutions of these classes of equations are discussed. Applications of differential equations in economic models are illustrated.

5.2 Definition and Classification of Differential Equations

A *differential equation* is an equation that involves one or more derivatives. Differential equations are classified according to type, order, and degree.

If a differential equation involves one or more derivatives of a function of one independent variable, it is an *ordinary differential equation*; if it involves one or more partial derivatives of a function of two or more independent variables, it is a *partial differential equation.*

The *order* of a differential equation is the order of the highest-order derivative occurring in the equation. The *degree* of a differential equation is the power of the highest-order derivative occurring after the differential equation has been rationalized to remove fractional power derivative terms.

EXAMPLE

$$\frac{dy}{dx} = 2x$$

is an ordinary differential equation of first order and first degree

$$x \, dy - y \, dx = 0$$

is an ordinary differential equation of first order and first degree

$$\frac{d^2y}{dx^2} + \left(\frac{dy}{dx}\right)^2 + y = 0$$

is an ordinary differential equation of second order and first degree

$$\left(\frac{dy}{dx}\right)^2 = 4 - y^2$$

is an ordinary differential equation of first order and second degree

$$\frac{\partial z}{\partial x} + \frac{\partial z}{\partial y} = z$$

is a partial differential equation of first order and first degree

$$\frac{\partial^2 u}{\partial x^2} + \frac{\partial^2 u}{\partial y^2} + x + y - uz = 0$$

is a partial differential equation of second order and first degree

$$\frac{d^3z}{dx^3} + x\left(\frac{d^2z}{dx^2}\right)^2 - xz\frac{dz}{dx} + 10 = 0$$

is an ordinary differential equation of third order and first degree

$$\left(\frac{\partial^3 u}{\partial x^3}\right)^2 + u^2\left(\frac{\partial u}{\partial x}\right)^3 - x^2u - 15 = 0$$

is a partial differential equation of third order and second degree

$$\frac{d^4y}{dx^4} + x^2\frac{d^2y}{dx^2} + xy\frac{dy}{dx} - 100y = 0$$

is an ordinary differential equation of fourth order and first degree

$$\frac{\partial^3 y}{\partial x^3} + xy\frac{\partial y}{\partial u} - 3u^4 = 0$$

is a partial differential equation of third order and first degree

$$\left(\frac{dy}{dx}\right)^3 - 5xy^3 + 2 = 0$$

is an ordinary differential equation of first order and third degree

$$\left(\frac{d^4y}{dx^4}\right)^4 - 6x\left(\frac{d^2y}{dx^2}\right) - 3y\frac{dy}{dx} = 0$$

is an ordinary differential equation of fourth order and fourth degree

Many of the equations in Chapter 4 are differential equations, since any equation involving at least one derivative is a differential equation. If a differential equation can be written in the form

$$\frac{d^n y}{dx^n} = f(x)$$

its solution is obtained in a straightforward manner by (successive) integration, as in Chapter 4.

EXAMPLE

Find the general solution of the differential equation $\dfrac{dy}{dx} = \cos x + 2x$.

If $\dfrac{dy}{dx} = \cos x + 2x$,

$$y = \sin x + x^2 + C$$

where C is an arbitrary constant.

EXAMPLE

Find the general solution of the differential equation $\dfrac{d^2 y}{dx^2} = 20x^3 - \dfrac{1}{x^2}$.

If $\dfrac{d^2 y}{dx^2} = 20x^3 - \dfrac{1}{x^2}$,

$$\frac{dy}{dx} = 5x^4 + \frac{1}{x} + C_1$$

and

$$y = x^5 + \ln x + C_1 x + C_2$$

where C_1 and C_2 are arbitrary constants.

The methods discussed in this chapter are appropriate for solving several types of differential equations whose solutions cannot be obtained by straightforward integration. Five types of differential equations of first order and first degree are discussed in some detail; second-order differential equations and first-degree differential equations of higher order are discussed briefly.

5.3 Solutions of Ordinary Differential Equations

A solution of an ordinary differential equation is a function not containing derivatives or differentials, which satisfies the differential equation. Such a solution may be expressed as an explicit or implicit function and may be a general or particular solution, depending on whether the constants of integration have been specified.

The *general solution* of an nth-order differential equation is a solution containing n independent arbitrary constants of integration. For example, the general solution of an nth-order differential equation could be of the implicit form

$$f(x, y) + c_1 + c_2 + \cdots + c_n = 0$$

or the explicit form

$$f(y) = f(x) + c_1 + c_2 + \cdots + c_n$$

A *particular solution* of a differential equation is a solution that can be obtained from the general solution by giving specific values to the arbitrary constants of the general solution. Thus, in either the implicit or explicit form of the solution above, a particular solution is obtained if $c_1, c_2, \ldots, c_n$ have specific values.

Some differential equations also have *singular solutions* that cannot be obtained as particular solutions; these exceptional cases do not occur in most practical applications and are not considered here.

As in simple integration, the constants of integration of a differential equation are specified by *boundary conditions* or *initial conditions*. A condition of the form $y = y_0$ when $x = x_0$ is a boundary condition; the special case $y = y_0$ when $x = 0$ is an initial condition.

Clearly, the problem of the solution or integration of a differential equation is an extension of the problem of simple integration. As in simple integration, a particular solution of a differential equation frequently is needed in practical applications. To obtain such a particular solution it is usually necessary first to find the general solution and then to determine the arbitrary constants from the boundary conditions of the problem. A constant of integration may be written in various forms, such as C, $2C$, C^2, $\sqrt{C}$, e^C, $\ln C$; frequently solutions of differential equations may be expressed in simpler form by proper choice of the form of the constant or constants of integration. When the form of a constant of integration is changed, the constant frequently continues to be written using the same notation, with the understanding that it is a "generic constant." Until the numerical value of a constant is determined, its form has no real meaning and thus the constant is written in the simplest way possible.

In each of the following examples, a differential equation and its solution are given and the solution is shown to satisfy the differential equation. Methods for obtaining solutions of differential equations are then discussed.

EXAMPLE

Show that $y = \dfrac{x^2}{3} + \dfrac{C}{x}$ is a solution of $x\dfrac{dy}{dx} + y = x^2$, where C is an arbitrary constant.

If $y = \dfrac{x^2}{3} + \dfrac{C}{x}$,

$$\frac{dy}{dx} = \frac{2x}{3} - \frac{C}{x^2}$$

and thus

$$\underbrace{x\left(\frac{2x}{3} - \frac{C}{x^2}\right) + \left(\frac{x^2}{3} + \frac{C}{x}\right)}_{x\frac{dy}{dx} + y} = x^2$$

EXAMPLE

Show that $y = c_1 e^{kx} + c_2 e^{-kx}$ is a solution of $\dfrac{d^2y}{dx^2} - k^2 y = 0$, where C_1 and C_2 are arbitrary constants.

If $y = c_1 e^{kx} + c_2 e^{-kx}$,

$$\frac{dy}{dx} = c_1 k e^{kx} - c_2 k e^{-kx}$$

$$\frac{d^2 y}{dx^2} = c_1 k^2 e^{kx} + c_2 k^2 e^{-kx}$$

and thus

$$\underbrace{c_1 k^2 e^{kx} + c_2 k^2 e^{-kx} - k^2 (c_1 e^{kx} + c_2 e^{-kx})}_{\frac{d^2 y}{dx^2} - k^2 y} = 0$$

EXAMPLE

Show that $4y = 1/(3x) + c_1 x^5 + c_2 x$ is a solution of $x^2 \frac{d^2 y}{dx^2} - 5x \frac{dy}{dx} + 5y = \frac{1}{x}$, where C_1 and C_2 are arbitrary constants.

If $4y = 1/(3x) + c_1 x^5 + c_2 x$,

$$4\frac{dy}{dx} = -\frac{1}{3x^2} + 5c_1 x^4 + c_2$$

$$4\frac{d^2 y}{dx^2} = \frac{2}{3x^3} + 20c_1 x^3$$

and thus

$$\underbrace{\frac{1}{4}\left(\frac{2}{3x} + 20c_1 x^5\right) - \frac{5}{4}\left(-\frac{1}{3x} + 5c_1 x^5 + c_2 x\right) + \frac{5}{4}\left(\frac{1}{3x} + c_1 x^5 + c_2 x\right)}_{x^2 \frac{d^2 y}{dx^2} - 5x \frac{dy}{dx} + 5y}$$

$$= \underbrace{(\tfrac{2}{12} + \tfrac{5}{12} + \tfrac{5}{12})\frac{1}{x}}_{\frac{1}{x}} + \underbrace{(5 - \tfrac{25}{4} + \tfrac{5}{4})c_1 x^5}_{0} + \underbrace{(-\tfrac{5}{4} + \tfrac{5}{4})c_2 x}_{0} = \frac{1}{x}$$

EXAMPLE

Show that $y = c_1 e^x + c_2 e^{-2x}$ is a solution of $\frac{d^2 y}{dx^2} + \frac{dy}{dx} - 2y = 0$ for arbitrary constants C_1 and C_2 and find a particular solution that satisfies the condition $y = \frac{dy}{dx} = 1$ when $x = 0$.

If $y = c_1 e^x + c_2 e^{-2x}$,

$$\frac{dy}{dx} = c_1 e^x - 2c_2 e^{-2x}$$

$$\frac{d^2 y}{dx^2} = c_1 e^x + 4c_2 e^{-2x}$$

and thus

$$(c_1 e^x + 4c_2 e^{-2x}) + (c_1 e^x - 2c_2 e^{-2x}) - 2(c_1 e^x - c_2 e^{-2x}) = 0$$

$$\underbrace{\phantom{(c_1 e^x + 4c_2 e^{-2x}) + (c_1 e^x - 2c_2 e^{-2x}) - 2(c_1 e^x - c_2 e^{-2x})}}$$

$$\frac{d^2 y}{dx^2} + \frac{dy}{dx} - 2y$$

If $y = y' = 1$ when $x = 0$,

$$c_1 + c_2 = 1$$
$$c_1 - 2c_2 = 1$$
$$c_2 = 0$$
$$c_1 = 1$$

Thus the particular solution is $y = e^x$.

EXAMPLE

Show that $y = 2Cx^2 + C^2$ is a solution of $\left(\frac{dy}{dx}\right)^2 + 8x^3 \frac{dy}{dx} = 16x^2 y$ where C is an arbitrary constant and find a particular solution that satisfies the condition $y = -1$ when $x = 1$.

If $y = 2Cx^2 + C^2$,

$$\frac{dy}{dx} = 4Cx$$

and thus

$$\underbrace{16C^2 x^2 + 8x^3(4Cx)}_{\left(\frac{dy}{dx}\right)^2 + 8x^3\left(\frac{dy}{dx}\right)} = 16x^2(2Cx^2 + C^2) = 16x^2 y$$

If $y = -1$ when $x = 1$,

$$-1 = 2C + C^2$$
$$C^2 + 2C + 1 = 0$$
$$(C + 1)^2 = 0$$
$$C = -1,$$

and thus the particular solution is $y = 1 - 2x^2$.

EXAMPLE

Show that $(x - c_1)^2 + y^2 = c_2$ is a solution of

$$y\frac{d^2 y}{dx^2} + \left(\frac{dy}{dx}\right)^2 + 1 = 0$$

Find a particular solution that satisfies the condition $y = 3$, and $\frac{dy}{dx} = -\frac{4}{3}$ when $x = 5$ where C_1 and C_2 are arbitrary constants.

If $(x - c_1)^2 + y^2 = c_2$,

$$2y\frac{dy}{dx} = -2(x - c_1)$$

$$\frac{dy}{dx} = -\frac{x - c_1}{\sqrt{c_2 - (x - c_1)^2}}$$

$$\frac{d^2y}{dx^2} = \frac{-\sqrt{c_2 - (x - c_1)^2} + (x - c_1)(\frac{1}{2})[c_2 - (x - c_1)^2]^{-1/2}(-2)(x - c_1)}{c_2 - (x - c_1)^2}$$

$$= \frac{-1}{\sqrt{c_2 - (x - c_1)^2}} - \frac{(x - c_1)^2}{[c_2 - (x - c_1)^2]^{3/2}}$$

and thus

$$\underbrace{-1 - \frac{(x - c_1)^2}{c_2 - (x - c_1)^2}}_{y\frac{d^2y}{dx^2}} + \underbrace{\left[-\frac{x - c_1}{\sqrt{c_2 - (x - c_1)^2}}\right]^2}_{\left(\frac{dy}{dx}\right)^2} + 1 = 0$$

If $y = 3$ and $\frac{dy}{dx} = -\frac{4}{3}$ when $x = 5$,

$$3 = \sqrt{c_2 - (5 - c_1)^2}$$

$$\frac{4}{3} = \frac{5 - c_1}{\sqrt{c_2 - (5 - c_1)^2}}$$

$$5 - c_1 = 4$$

$$c_1 = 1$$

$$c_2 = 25$$

and thus the particular solution is $(x - 1)^2 + y^2 = 25$.

PROBLEMS

$1-13$ all

State the type, order, and degree of each of the following differential equations.

1. $\dfrac{d^2y}{dx^2} + 6x + y = 0$

2. $x^2\,dy = xy^2\,dx$

3. $\left(\dfrac{d^2y}{dx^2}\right)^2 + 5xy = 0$

4. $\dfrac{\partial z}{\partial x} + \dfrac{\partial z}{\partial y} = xyz$

5. $\left(\dfrac{\partial z}{\partial x}\right)^2 + \dfrac{\partial z}{\partial y} - 2x = 0$

6. $3x\left(\dfrac{dy}{dx}\right)^2 = 4xy$

7. $\dfrac{\partial^2 z}{\partial x^2} = \dfrac{\partial z}{\partial y}$

8. $\dfrac{d^2y}{dx^2} + \dfrac{dy}{dx} - 3x = 0$

9. $\left(\dfrac{d^2y}{dx^2}\right)^2 - \dfrac{dy}{dx} = 4y$

10. $\dfrac{d^3y}{dx^3} = 10y$

11. Verify that $y^2 = Cx + \frac{1}{8}C^3$ is a solution of $y = 2x\dfrac{dy}{dx} + y^2\left(\dfrac{dy}{dx}\right)^3$ and find the particular solution if $y' = 1$ when $x = 0$.

12. Verify that $(x - c_1)^2 + y^2 = c_2$ is a solution of $y\dfrac{d^2y}{dx^2} + \left(\dfrac{dy}{dx}\right)^2 + 1 = 0$ and find the particular solution if $y = 3$ and $y' = -\tfrac{4}{3}$ when $x = 5$.

13. Verify that $\ln y = c_1 e^x + c_2 e^{-x} + x^2 + 2$ is a solution of $\left(\dfrac{1}{y}\dfrac{dy}{dx}\right)^2 - \dfrac{1}{y}\dfrac{d^2y}{dx^2} = x^2 - \ln y$.

14. Verify that $x = \cos 2t + 2c_1 \cos 3t + 3c_2 \sin 3t$ is a solution of $\dfrac{d^2x}{dt^2} + 9x = 5 \cos 2t$.

15. Verify that $y = (c_1 + c_2 \ln x)\sqrt{x} + c_3$ is a solution of $4x^2\dfrac{d^3y}{dx^3} + 8x\dfrac{d^2y}{dx^2} + \dfrac{dy}{dx} = 0$.

16. Verify that $y = x^3 + c_1 x^2 + c_2$ is a solution of $\dfrac{d^2y}{dx^2} - \dfrac{1}{x}\dfrac{dy}{dx} - 3x = 0$ and find the particular solution if $y = 1$ when $x = 1$ and $y = 5$ when $x = 2$.

17. Verify that $y = c_1 \cos x + c_2 \sin x - \tfrac{1}{3}\cos 2x$ is a solution of $\dfrac{d^2y}{dx^2} + y = \cos 2x$.

18. Verify that $y = e^{-x}(x + C)$ is a solution of $\dfrac{dy}{dx} + y = e^{-x}$.

19. Verify that $y = c_1 x + \dfrac{c_2}{x} + c_3$ is a solution of $\dfrac{d^3y}{dx^3} + \dfrac{3}{x}\dfrac{d^2y}{dx^2} = 0$.

20. Verify that $y^2 = c_1 x^2 + c_2 x$ is a solution of $x^2 y\dfrac{d^2y}{dx^2} + \left(x\dfrac{dy}{dx} - y\right)^2 = 0$ and find a particular solution that satisfies the condition $y = 2$ and $\dfrac{dy}{dx} = 1$ when $x = 1$.

Answers to Odd-Numbered Problems

1. ordinary, second order, first degree
3. ordinary, second order, second degree
5. partial, first order, second degree

7. partial, second order, first degree
9. ordinary, second order, second degree
11. $y^2 = 2x + 1$

5.4 Differential Equations of First Order and First Degree

In this section methods of solution are discussed and illustrated for differential equations of first order and first degree which can be classified as separable, homogeneous, exact, linear, or linear in a function.

A differential equation of first order and first degree can be written in the form

$$\dfrac{dy}{dx} = F(x, y)$$

If $F(x, y)$ is a constant or a function only of x, that is, if $\dfrac{dy}{dx} = F(x)$, the differential equation is solved by the usual methods of integration; if $F(x, y)$ is in fact a function of both x and y, the methods discussed below are appropriate for solving the differential equation.

An alternative form, frequently more useful for classifying differential equations of first order and first degree, is

$$M(x, y)\, dx + N(x, y)\, dy = 0$$

There is one difference between these equations which should be noted. In the first equation y is the dependent variable and x is the independent variable; thus the solution expresses y as a function of x and an arbitrary constant. In the second equation the relationship is expressed implicitly and the choice of the dependent and independent variables is a matter of convenience; the solution is frequently also expressed as an implicit function.

Methods for the solution of the following types of differential equations of the first order and first degree are discussed in considerable detail; note that facility in solving a differential equation of any order and degree depends to a very considerable extent on classifying it correctly.

1. *Separable differential equations:* M is a function only of x and N is a function only of y, so the equation is of the form $M(x)\,dx + N(y)\,dy = 0$.

2. *Homogeneous differential equations:* M and N are homogeneous functions of the same degree of homogeneity.

3. *Exact differential equations:* $\dfrac{\partial}{\partial y}(M(x, y)) = \dfrac{\partial}{\partial x}(N(x, y))$ so the equation is of the form $\dfrac{\partial F}{\partial x}\,dx + \dfrac{\partial F}{\partial y}\,dy = 0$, where $F(x, y)$ is the solution of the differential equation.

4. *Linear differential equations:* The equation is of the first degree in y and $\dfrac{dy}{dx}$ or in x and $\dfrac{dx}{dy}$ and thus is of the form $\dfrac{dy}{dx} + yP(x) = Q(x)$ or $\dfrac{dx}{dy} + xP(y) = Q(y)$.

5. *Differential equations linear in a function of y or in a function of x:* The equation is of the first degree in $f(y)$ and $\dfrac{d}{dy}f(y)$ or in $f(x)$ and $\dfrac{d}{dx}f(x)$ and thus is of the form $\dfrac{d}{dy}f(y) + f(y)P(x) = Q(x)$ or $\dfrac{d}{dx}f(x) - f(x)P(y) = Q(y)$.

SEPARABLE DIFFERENTIAL EQUATIONS

If a differential equation can be written in the form

$$M(x)\,dx + N(y)\,dy = 0$$

where, as indicated, M is a function only of x and N is a function only of y, then the variables are said to be *separated* and the general solution of the differential equation is obtained by the usual methods of integration:

$$\int M(x)\,dx + \int N(y)\,dy = C$$

and

$$f(x) + g(y) = C$$

where $f(x) = \int M(x)\,dx$ and $g(y) = \int N(y)\,dy$.

EXAMPLE

Solve the equation $(1 + x^2)\dfrac{dy}{dx} + xy = 0$.

$$(1 + x^2)\, dy + xy\, dx = 0$$

$$\frac{x}{1 + x^2}\, dx + \frac{1}{y}\, dy = 0$$

The variables are separated and, integrating,

$$\tfrac{1}{2}\ln (1 + x^2) + \ln y = C$$

$$\ln (y\sqrt{1 + x^2}) = C$$

$$y\sqrt{1 + x^2} = C$$

Note that the constant in the last equation is actually e^C in terms of the preceding equations. As mentioned in the discussion of constants of integration above, until a constant is evaluated to obtain a particular solution, its form is arbitrary and the constant is thus written in the most convenient way.

EXAMPLE

Solve the equation $y^2\, dx - (1 - x)\, dy = 0$.

$$\frac{1}{x - 1}\, dx + \frac{1}{y^2}\, dy = 0$$

The variables are separated and, integrating,

$$\ln (x - 1) - \frac{1}{y} = C$$

$$y \ln (x - 1) - 1 = Cy$$

$$y \ln [C(x - 1)] = 1$$

Dividing both sides of the equation by y and then taking antilogs,

$$\ln [C(x - 1)] = \frac{1}{y}$$

$$C(x - 1) = e^{1/y}$$

EXAMPLE

If the interest rate is $100i\%$ compounded continuously and A is the amount at any time (principal plus any accumulated interest), then

$$\frac{dA}{dt} = iA$$

and, separating the variables,

$$\frac{dA}{A} = i\, dt$$

and, integrating,

$$\int \frac{dA}{A} = \int i \, dt$$

$$\ln A = it + C$$

$$A = e^{it+c}$$

or

$$A = Ce^{it}$$

If $A = A_0$ at $t = 0$, then $C = A_0$ and

$$A = A_0 e^{it}$$

NOTE: The formula for discrete compounding is given by

$$y = x\left(1 + \frac{i}{k}\right)^{nk}$$

where y is the amount after n years (principal plus any accumulated interest) and interest rate is $i\%$ per year compounded k times per year. In the notation of this section, the discrete formula can be written

$$A = A_0\left(1 + \frac{i}{k}\right)^{kt}$$

and the formula for the continuous case can be obtained by taking the limit as $k \to \infty$ of the formula for the discrete case, since

$$e = \lim_{k \to \infty} \left(1 + \frac{1}{k}\right)^k$$

EXAMPLE

The relationship between net profit P and advertising expenditure x is such that the rate of increase of net profit as advertising expenditure increases is proportional to a constant, a, minus net profit. Find the relationship between net profit and advertising expenditure if $P = P_0 < a$ when $x = 0$.

$$\frac{dP}{dx} = k(a - P)$$

$$\frac{dP}{a - P} = k \, dx$$

$$-\ln (a - P) = kx + C$$

$$\ln (a - P) = -kx + C$$

$$a - P = Ce^{-kx}$$

$$P = a - Ce^{-kx}$$

so

$$P_0 = a - C$$

$$C = a - P_0$$

and

$$P = a - (a - P_0)e^{-kx}$$

Figure 5.1

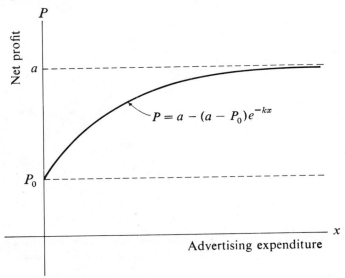

Thus net profit is P_0 with no advertising expenditure and increases, as advertising expenditure increases, toward an (asymptotic) maximum of a. (See Figure 5.1.)

HOMOGENEOUS DIFFERENTIAL EQUATIONS

A differential equation of the form

$$M(x, y)\, dx + N(x, y)\, dy = 0$$

is said to be homogeneous if $M(x, y)$ and $N(x, y)$ are homogeneous functions of the same degree in x and y. Recall that $F(x, y)$ is a homogeneous function of degree n in x and y if and only if $F(kx, ky) = k^n F(x, y)$, where k is any constant. When a differential equation is homogeneous, its variables can be separated by the substitution

$$y = vx$$

$$dy = v\, dx + x\, dv$$

or, equivalently, by the substitution

$$x = vy$$

$$dx = v\, dy + y\, dv$$

The resulting differential equations can then be written, respectively, in the form

$$M(x)\, dx + N(v)\, dv = 0$$

or in the form

$$M(v)\, dv + N(y)\, dy = 0$$

and solved by the usual methods of integration. The general solution of the original equation is then obtained by substituting, respectively,

$$v = \frac{y}{x} \quad \text{or} \quad v = \frac{x}{y}$$

in the solution of the separable differential equation.

NOTE: This procedure can be justified mathematically as follows. If $M(x, y) \, dx + N(x, y) \, dy = 0$, $M(x, y)$ and $N(x, y)$ are homogeneous of the same degree n and $N(x, y) \neq 0$, then

$$\frac{dy}{dx} = -\frac{M(x, y)}{N(x, y)}$$

But, since $M(x, y) = t^{-n}M(tx, ty)$ and $N(x, y) = t^{-n}N(tx, ty)$,

$$\frac{dy}{dx} = -\frac{M(tx, ty)}{N(tx, ty)}$$

for any value of t. If $t = 1/x$, then

$$\frac{dy}{dx} = -\frac{M\left(1, \dfrac{y}{x}\right)}{N\left(1, \dfrac{y}{x}\right)}$$

and the differential equation can be written

$$\frac{dy}{dx} = F\left(\frac{y}{x}\right)$$

Substituting $y = vx$ and $\dfrac{dy}{dx} = v + x \dfrac{dv}{dx}$, this equation can be written

$$v + x \frac{dv}{dx} = F(v)$$

$$(v - F(v)) \, dx + x \, dv = 0$$

$$\frac{dx}{x} + \frac{dv}{v - F(v)} = 0$$

and the variables x and v are separated. If $v - F(v) = 0$, then $x \, dv = 0$, $dy - v \, dx = 0$, and $M(x, y) \, dx + N(x, y) \, dy = 0$ has the simple form $y \, dx - x \, dy = 0$.

A similar argument shows that the substitution $x = vy$ also results in an equation in which the variables are separable.

EXAMPLE

Solve the equation $(y^2 - xy) \, dx + x^2 \, dy = 0$.
The equation is homogeneous (degree 2). Substituting $y = vx$, $dy = v \, dx + x \, dv$,

$$(v^2x^2 - vx^2) \, dx + x^2(v \, dx + x \, dv) = 0$$

$$v^2x^2 \, dx + x^3 \, dv = 0$$

$$\frac{1}{x} \, dx + \frac{1}{v^2} \, dv = 0$$

The variables are separated and, integrating,

$$\ln x - \frac{1}{v} = C$$

Substituting $v = y/x$,

$$\ln x - \frac{x}{y} = C$$

$$y = \frac{x}{\ln x - C}$$

EXAMPLE

Solve the equation $(x + y)\, dx + (x - y)\, dy = 0$.

The equation is homogeneous (degree 1). Substituting $x = vy$, $dx = v\, dy + y\, dv$,

$$(vy + y)(v\, dy + y\, dv) + (vy - y)\, dy = 0$$

$$(vy^2 + y^2)\, dv + (v^2 y + 2vy - y)\, dy = 0$$

$$y^2(v + 1)\, dv + y(v^2 + 2v - 1)\, dy = 0$$

$$\frac{v + 1}{v^2 + 2v - 1}\, dv + \frac{1}{y}\, dy = 0$$

The variables are separated and, integrating,

$$\tfrac{1}{2} \ln (v^2 + 2v - 1) + \ln y = C$$

$$y(v^2 + 2v - 1)^{1/2} = C$$

$$y^2(v^2 + 2v - 1) = C$$

Substituting $v = x/y$,

$$x^2 + 2xy - y^2 = C$$

EXAMPLE

The relationship between the manufacturing cost per item, M, and the number of types of items manufactured, N, is such that the rate of increase of manufacturing cost as number of types of items increases is equal to the ratio of the cost per item plus the number of types of items divided by the number of types of items. Find the relationship between manufacturing cost per item and number of types of items manufactured if $M = M_0$ when $N = 1$.

$$\frac{dM}{dN} = \frac{M + N}{N}$$

$$N\, dM = (M + N)\, dN$$

Substituting $M = vN$ and $dM = v\, dN + N\, dv$,

$$vN\, dN + N^2\, dv = vN\, dN + N\, dN$$

$$dv = \frac{dN}{N}$$

$$v = \ln N + C$$

Substituting $v = M/N$,

$$\frac{M}{N} = \ln N + C$$

$$M = N \ln N + NC$$

Figure 5.2

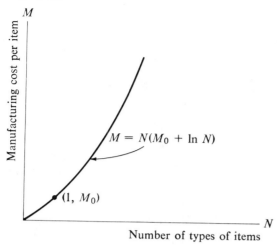

$M = N(M_0 + \ln N)$

$(1, M_0)$

Number of types of items

and, since $M = M_0$ when $N = 1$,

$$M_0 = 0 + C$$

$$C = M_0$$

and

$$M = N \ln N + N M_0$$

$$M = N(M_0 + \ln N)$$

(see Figure 5.2).

EXAMPLE

Suppose that the rate of increase in the cost of ordering and holding, y, as the size of the order, s, increases is equal to the ratio of the sum of the squares of the cost and the size divided by twice the product of the cost and the size. Find the relationship between the cost of ordering and holding and the size of the order if $y = 3$ when $s = 1$.

$$\frac{dy}{ds} = \frac{y^2 + s^2}{2sy}$$

$$2sy \, dy - (y^2 + s^2) \, ds = 0$$

Substituting $y = vs$ and $dy = v \, ds + s \, dv$,

$$2vs^2(v \, ds + s \, dv) - (v^2 s^2 + s^2) \, ds = 0$$

$$(v^2 s^2 - s^2) \, ds + 2vs^3 \, dv = 0$$

$$s^2(v - 1) \, ds + 2vs^3 \, dv = 0$$

$$\frac{ds}{s} + \frac{2v}{v^2 - 1} \, dv = 0$$

$$\ln s + \ln (v^2 - 1) = C$$

$$s(v^2 - 1) = e^c = c$$

Figure 5.3

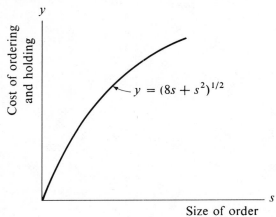

Substituting $v = y/s$,

$$s\left(\frac{y^2}{s^2} - 1\right) = c$$

$$y^2 - s^2 = cs$$

$$y = (cs + s^2)^{1/2}$$

and, using the initial condition,

$$3 = (c + 1)^{1/2}$$

and

$$c = 8$$

$$y = (8s + s^2)^{1/2}$$

(see Figure 5.3).

PROBLEMS

Find the general solution for each of the following differential equations.

1. $(x^2 + y^2)\, dx - 2xy\, dy = 0$

2. $(xy - x^2)\dfrac{dy}{dx} = y^2$

3. $y^3\, dx - x^3\, dy = 0$

4. $(y + 3)\, dx + \cot x\, dy = 0$

5. $\dfrac{dx}{dt} = 1 - \sin 2t$

6. $\dfrac{d^3 y}{dx^3} = e^{-x}$

7. $\dfrac{d^2 y}{dx^2} = \dfrac{1}{x^2}$

8. $\sec x \cos^2 y\, dx = \cos x \sin y\, dy$

9. $\sin x \cos^2 y\, dx + \cos^2 x\, dy = 0$

10. $dr + r \cos \theta\, d\theta = 0$

11. $\dfrac{dy}{dx} = \dfrac{x - y}{x + y}$

12. $(xy^2 - x)\, dx + (x^2 y + y)\, dy = 0$

13. $\dfrac{dy}{dx} = \dfrac{xy + y}{x + xy}$

14. $\dfrac{dy}{dx} = \dfrac{2x - y}{x + 4y}$

15. $dy = 2xy\, dx$

16. $\dfrac{1}{\rho}\dfrac{d\rho}{d\theta} = \dfrac{\rho^2 - 1}{\rho^2 + 1} \tan \theta$

17. $r \, d\theta + \theta \, dr = 2 \, dr$

18. $d\rho + \rho \tan \theta \, d\theta = 0$

19. $(r^2 + 1) \, d\theta + \dfrac{dr}{\sec^2 \theta} = 0$

20. $(xy - y^2) \, dx + \left(y^2 - \dfrac{x^2}{2}\right) dy = 0$

21. $\dfrac{y^2}{x} \, dx + (x - y) \, dy = 0$

22. $(xy^3 - x) \, dx + xy^2 \, dy = 0$

23. $\tan x \sin^2 y \, dx + \cos^2 x \cot y \, dy = 0$

24. $x \dfrac{dy}{dx} - y - x \sin \dfrac{y}{x} = 0$

25. $\sin x \cos y \, dx + \cos x \sin y \, dy = 0$

26. $\dfrac{dy}{dx} = -\dfrac{y}{x}$

27. $x^3 - 2y^3 + 3xy^2 \dfrac{dy}{dx} = 0$

28. $\dfrac{dy}{dx} = \dfrac{x^2}{y^3}$

29. $x \, dy - y \, dx = 0$

30. $(x^2 + 2y^2) \, dx = xy \, dy$

31. $(x^3 - y^3) \, dx + xy^2 \, dy = 0$

32. $(x + y) \, dx + x \, dy = 0$

33. $\dfrac{dy}{dx} = e^{x-y}$

34. $x(2y - 3) \, dx + (x^2 + 1) \, dy = 0$

35. $(x + y) \, dx = x \, dy$

36. $x \, dy - y \, dx = \sqrt{xy} \, dx$

Find the particular solution for each of the following differential equations under the given conditions.

37. $\dfrac{dy}{dx} = \dfrac{y}{x}$, $y = 3$ when $x = 1$

38. $xy \, dx + \sqrt{1 + x^2} \, dy = 0$, $y = 1$ when $x = 0$

39. $(x^2 + y^2) \, dx = 2xy \, dy$, $y = 0$ when $x = 1$

40. $x \, dy + 2y \, dx = 0$, $y = 1$ when $x = 2$

41. $(xe^{y/x} + y) \, dx = x \, dy$, $y = 0$ when $x = 1$

42. $y^2(y \, dx - x \, dy) + x^3 \, dx = 0$, $y = 3$ when $x = 1$

43. $x \, dx - 4y \, dy = 0$, $y = 2$ when $x = 5$

44. $x(y + 1) \, dx + y(x + 1) \, dy = 0$, $y = 1$ when $x = 0$

45. $(x - \sqrt{xy}) \, dy = y \, dx$, $y = 1$ when $x = 4$

46. $(x + 4)(2y + 6) \, dy + xy^2 \, dx = 0$, $y = 16$ when $x = 0$

47. $(xy^2 + x^2 y) \, dy - xy^2 \, dx = 0$, $y = 1$ when $x = 6$

48. $y(x^2 + 6) \, dy + x(y^2 + 1) \, dx$, $y = 3$ when $x = 0$

49. $\dfrac{1}{xy} \, dx + \dfrac{e^{y^2}}{x^3 - 1} \, dy = 0$, $y = 0$ when $x = 1$

50. $\dfrac{dy}{dx} = \dfrac{y}{x} + \tan \dfrac{y}{x}$, $y = \pi$ when $x = 6$

51. $\cot y \, dx + \cot x \, dy = 0$, $y = 0$ when $x = 0$

52. The relationship between price, p, and quantity demanded, x, is such that the rate of decrease in demand as price increases is proportional to the quantity demanded and inversely proportional to the price plus a constant. Find the demand function if $p = p_0$ when $x = 1$. Sketch the relationship obtained.

53. The rate of increase of total cost, y, as number of units manufactured, x, increases is proportional to the number of units manufactured plus a constant and inversely proportional to the total cost. Find the cost function if $y = y_0$ when $x = 0$. Sketch the relationship obtained.

54. The rate of increase in sales, s, as advertising expenditure, x, increases is equal to a constant plus advertising expenditure. Find the relationship between sales and advertising expenditure if $s = s_0$ when $x = 0$. Sketch the relationship obtained.

55. The relationship between revenue, R, and quantity demanded, x, is such that the rate of increase in revenue as quantity demanded increases is equal to twice the cube of the revenue minus the cube of the quantity demanded, all divided by three times the product of the quantity demanded and the square of the revenue. Find the relationship between revenue and quantity demanded if $R = 0$ when $x = 10$. Sketch the relationship obtained.

56. The relationship between average cost, $\bar{y}$, and number of units produced, x, is such that the change in average cost as the number of units increases is equal to the ratio of the number of units minus average cost divided by number of units. Find the relationship between average cost and the number of units produced if $\bar{y} = \frac{9}{2}$ when $x = 1$. Sketch the relationship obtained.

57. The rate of increase in cost, y, as the number of units manufactured, x, increases is equal to the ratio of twice the square of the cost minus the square of the number of units divided by the product of the cost and the number of units. Find the relationship between cost and the number of units manufactured if $y = 3$ when $x = 1$. Sketch the relationship obtained.

58. The rate of increase of sales volume, s, as price, p, decreases is proportional to sales volume and inversely proportional to price minus a constant. Find the relationship between sales volume and price if $s = s_0$ when $p = p_0$.

59. If interest is compounded continuously, a. find the amount available after 10 years if $5000 is deposited at 4%; and b. find the amount available after 20 years if $20,000 is deposited at 6%. (Compare the answers with those obtained for the example on page 122 and Problem 2 on page 127, respectively.)

60. If growth is continuous and the rate, r, is proportional to the number, N, present in the population, then

$$\frac{dN}{dt} = rN \qquad r > 0 \text{ growth}; r < 0 \text{ decay}$$

If $N = N_0$ when $t = 0$, obtain a formula for the number in the population at time t. (Compare with the discrete case on page 124.)

61. If the growth rate is continuous at the rate of 5% per year and the original number in the population is 200, what is the size of the population after 10 years?

62. A manufacturer has found that the change in the cost of distribution, D, as sales, S, increases is equal to a constant times sales plus another constant. Find the relationship between the cost of distribution and sales if $D = 0$ when $S = 0$. Sketch the relationship obtained.

63. The rent for an apartment (two-bedroom, standard furnishings) in a college town varies with the distance of the apartment from campus. Suppose this relationship is given by

$$\frac{dy}{dx} = -\left(\frac{k}{x} + a\right) \qquad 1 \le x \le 10$$

where y is monthly rent (in dollars) and x is distance (in miles) and k and a are constants. If $y = 225$ when $x = 1$, find y as a function of x and sketch the relationship obtained.

64. The relationship between the cost of operating a warehouse and the number of gallons of oil stored in the warehouse is given by

$$\frac{dy}{dx} = kx + a$$

where y is the monthly cost of operating the warehouse (in dollars) and x is the number of gallons of oil in storage. If $y = y_0$ (fixed cost) when $x = 0$, find y as a function of x and sketch the relationship obtained.

Answers to Odd-Numbered Problems

1. $x^2 - y^2 = Cx$

3. $x^2 - y^2 = Cx^2y^2$

5. $x = t + \frac{1}{2}\cos 2t + C$

7. $y = -\ln x + c_1 x + c_2$

9. $\sec x + \tan y = C$

11. $y^2 + 2xy - x^2 = C$

13. $y - x + \ln \dfrac{y}{x} = C$

15. $y = Ce^{x^2}$

17. $r(\theta - 2) = C$

19. $\tan \theta + \ln \sqrt{r^2 + 1} = C$

21. $y = Ce^{y/x}$

23. $\tan^2 x - \cot^2 y = C$

25. $\cos y = C \sec x$

27. $x^3 + y^3 = Cx^2$

29. $y = Cx$

31. $x^3 e^{y^3/x^3} = C$

33. $e^y - e^x = C$

35. $x = Ce^{y/x}$

37. $y = 3x$

39. $y^2 = x^2 - x$

41. $\ln x + e^{-y/x} = 1$

43. $x^2 - 4y^2 = 9$

45. $2\sqrt{\dfrac{x}{y}} - \ln y = 4$

47. $\ln y - \dfrac{x}{y} + 6 = 0$

49. $2x^3 - 6 \ln x + 3e^{y^2} - 5 = 0$

51. $\cos y = \sec x$

53. $y = (ax^2 + 2abx + y_0^2)^{1/2}$

55. $R = (10x^2 - x^3)^{1/3}$

57. $y = \sqrt{8x^4 + x^2}$

59. a. $\$7460$

    b. $\$66{,}402$

61. 329.8

63. $y = 225 + a - ax - k \ln x$

EXACT DIFFERENTIAL EQUATIONS

The total derivative of a function of x and y, say $F(x, y)$, is given by

$$dF(x, y) = \frac{\partial F}{\partial x}\, dx + \frac{\partial F}{\partial y}\, dy$$

Thus the differential equation

$$\frac{\partial F}{\partial x}\, dx + \frac{\partial F}{\partial y}\, dy = 0$$

has the general solution $F(x, y) = C$ and is said to be an *exact differential equation.* A differential equation of the general form

$$M(x, y)\, dx + N(x, y)\, dy = 0$$

is said to be an exact differential equation if $M(x, y)\, dx + N(x, y)\, dy$ is the total derivative of some function $F(x, y)$; $M(x, y)$ and $N(x, y)$ are then the partial derivatives of $F(x, y)$ with respect to x and y, respectively.

If the second-order mixed partial derivatives of $F(x, y)$ exist and are continuous, then

$$\frac{\partial}{\partial y}\left(\frac{\partial F}{\partial x}\right) = \frac{\partial}{\partial x}\left(\frac{\partial F}{\partial y}\right)$$

Thus if a differential equation of the form $M(x, y) dx + N(x, y) dy = 0$ is exact,

$$\frac{\partial}{\partial y} M(x, y) = \frac{\partial}{\partial x} N(x, y)$$

It can be shown that this is also a sufficient condition for exactness; that is,

$$\frac{\partial}{\partial y} M(x, y) = \frac{\partial}{\partial x} N(x, y) \Leftrightarrow M(x, y) dx + N(x, y) dy = 0 \text{ is exact}$$

If a differential equation is exact, its solution can be found by the following method.

1. Integrate $M(x, y)$ with respect to x replacing the usual constant of integration with a function $f(y)$ of y.

$$F(x, y) = \int M(x, y) dx = G(x, y) + f(y)$$

2. Differentiate $F(x, y) = G(x, y) + f(y)$ obtained from step 1 with respect to y and compare this with $N(x, y)$ from the differential equation to be solved to obtain the value of $\frac{\partial}{\partial y} f(y)$.

$$\frac{\partial G}{\partial y} + \frac{\partial}{\partial y} f(y) = \frac{\partial N}{\partial y}$$

$$\frac{\partial}{\partial y} f(y) = \frac{\partial N}{\partial y} - \frac{\partial G}{\partial y}$$

3. Integrate $\frac{\partial}{\partial y} f(y)$ with respect to y to obtain $f(y)$.

$$\int \frac{\partial}{\partial y} f(y) \, dy = f(y)$$

It is not necessary to include the usual constant of integration, since it is introduced in the final step of the solution.

4. The solution, from steps 1 and 3, is

$$F(x, y) = G(x, y) + f(y) + C = 0$$

clearly the solution may also be obtained by integrating first with respect to y.

EXAMPLE

Solve the equation $[y(2 + x^3 y)/x^3] dx = [(1 - 2x^3 y)/x^2] dy$.

$$\frac{\partial}{\partial y}\left(\frac{y(2 + x^3 y)}{x^3}\right) = \frac{2 + 2x^3 y}{x^3} = \frac{\partial}{\partial x}\left(-\frac{1 - 2x^3 y}{x^2}\right), \text{ so the equation is exact.}$$

$$\frac{\partial F}{\partial x} = \frac{y(2 + x^3 y)}{x^3}$$

Integrating w.r.t. x,

$$F(x, y) = -\frac{y}{x^2} + y^2 x + f(y) \qquad \text{(step 1)}$$

$$\frac{\partial F}{\partial y} = -\frac{1}{x^2} + 2xy + \frac{\partial}{\partial y} f(y) = -\frac{1}{x^2} + 2xy \qquad \text{(step 2)}$$

so

$$\frac{\partial}{\partial y} f(y) = 0$$

$$f(y) = C \qquad \text{(step 3)}$$

and

$$F(x, y) = -\frac{y}{x^2} + y^2 x + C = 0 \qquad \text{(step 4)}$$

Thus the solution is

$$x^3 y^2 - y = Cx^2$$

EXAMPLE

Solve the equation $(x^2 - x + y^2)\, dx - (ye^y - 2xy)\, dy = 0$.

$$\frac{\partial}{\partial y}(x^2 - x + y^2) = 2y = \frac{\partial}{\partial x}(-ye^y + 2xy), \text{ so the equation is exact.}$$

$$\frac{\partial F}{\partial x} = x^2 - x + y^2$$

Integrating w.r.t. x,

$$F(x, y) = \frac{x^3}{3} - \frac{x^2}{2} + xy^2 + f(y) \qquad \text{(step 1)}$$

$$\frac{\partial F}{\partial y} = 2xy + \frac{\partial}{\partial y} f(y) = -ye^y + 2xy \qquad \text{(step 2)}$$

so

$$\frac{\partial}{\partial y} f(y) = -ye^y$$

$$f(y) = -(y - 1)e^y \qquad \text{(step 3)}$$

and

$$F(x, y) = \frac{x^3}{3} - \frac{x^2}{2} + xy^2 - (y - 1)e^y + C = 0 \qquad \text{(step 4)}$$

Thus the solution is

$$2x^3 - 3x^2 + 6xy^2 - 6(y - 1)e^y = C$$

NOTE: Alternatively, the terms of the original equation can be considered in two sets: $x^2\, dx - x\, dx - ye^y\, dy$ is exact by inspection and can be integrated by the usual methods; $y^2\, dx + 2xy\, dy$ is $d\,(y^2 x)$ and thus is exact and can be integrated by the method above. When this approach is used, $f(y)$ is a constant, as illustrated in the following example.

EXAMPLE

Solve the equation $[(2xy - 1)/y] \, dx + [(x + 3y)/y^2] \, dy = 0$ and find the particular solution if $y = 1$ when $x = 2$.

$$\underbrace{2x \, dx + \frac{3}{y} \, dy} - \underbrace{\frac{1}{y} \, dx + \frac{x}{y^2} \, dy} = 0$$

exact, integrable $\quad \dfrac{\partial}{\partial y}\left(-\dfrac{1}{y}\right) = \dfrac{1}{y^2} = \dfrac{\partial}{\partial x}\left(\dfrac{x}{y^2}\right)$
by usual methods
to obtain $x^2 + 3 \ln y$

so the equation is exact.

$$\frac{\partial F}{\partial x} = -\frac{1}{y}$$

Integrating w.r.t. x,

$$F(x, y) = -\frac{x}{y} + f(y) \qquad \text{(step 1)}$$

$$\frac{\partial F}{\partial y} = \frac{x}{y^2} + \frac{\partial}{\partial y} f(y) = \frac{x}{y^2} \qquad \text{(step 2)}$$

so

$$\frac{\partial}{\partial y} f(y) = 0$$

$$f(y) = C \qquad \text{(step 3)}$$

and

$$F(x, y) = -\frac{x}{y} + C \qquad \text{(step 4)}$$

Thus

$$x^2 + 3 \ln y - \frac{x}{y} = C$$

and the solution is

$$x^2 y - x + 3y \ln y = Cy$$

If $y = 1$ when $x = 2$,

$$4 - 2 = C$$

$$C = 2$$

and

$$x^2 y - x - 2y + 3y \ln y = 0$$

is the particular solution for $x = 2$, $y = 1$.

EXAMPLE

The change in price, y, with change in quantity demanded, x, of a particular commodity is given by

$$\frac{dy}{dx} = -\frac{2xy + 24x}{x^2 + 16}$$

Find the relationship between price and quantity demanded if the price is 7.5 when the quantity demanded is 4.

$$(2xy + 24x)\, dx + (x^2 + 16)\, dy = 0$$

$$\frac{\partial}{\partial y}(2xy + 24x) = 2x = \frac{\partial}{\partial x}(x^2 + 16)$$

so the equation is exact.

$$\frac{\partial F}{\partial x} = 2xy + 24x$$

Integrating w.r.t. x,

$$F(x, y) = x^2y + 12x^2 + f(y) \qquad \text{(step 1)}$$

$$\frac{\partial F}{\partial y} = x^2 + \frac{\partial}{\partial y} f(y) = x^2 + 16 \qquad \text{(step 2)}$$

so

$$\frac{\partial}{\partial y} f(y) = 16$$

$$f(y) = 16y \qquad \text{(step 3)}$$

and

$$F(x, y) = x^2y + 12x^2 + 16y + C = 0 \qquad \text{(step 4)}$$

thus the solution is

$$x^2y + 12x^2 + 16y = C$$

Figure 5.4

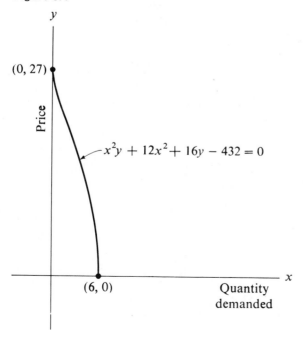

$-x^2y + 12x^2 + 16y - 432 = 0$

$(0, 27)$

Price

$(6, 0)$

Quantity demanded

If $y = 7.5$ when $x = 4$,

$$120 + 192 + 120 = C$$

$$C = 432$$

and

$$x^2y + 12x^2 + 16y - 432 = 0$$

is the particular solution for $x = 4$, $y = 7.5$. (See Figure 5.4.)

LINEAR DIFFERENTIAL EQUATIONS

In some cases a differential equation which is not exact can be made exact by multiplication by a factor; such a factor is called an *integrating factor*, since it permits the equation to be integrated. In general, determining the appropriate integrating factor for a given differential equation is not an easy matter; however, it can be shown that any linear first-order differential equation has the integrating factor $e^{\int P(x)\,dx}$.

An equation which can be written in the form

$$\frac{dy}{dx} + yP(x) = Q(x)$$

is a *linear differential equation of first order*. If this equation is multiplied by the integrating factor $e^{\int P(x)\,dx}$, the resulting equation

$$e^{\int P(x)\,dx}\frac{dy}{dx} + yP(x)e^{\int P(x)\,dx} = Q(x)e^{\int P(x)\,dx}$$

can be integrated with respect to x to obtain

$$ye^{\int P(x)\,dx} = \int e^{\int P(x)\,dx}Q(x)\,dx + C \qquad \text{where } C \text{ is an arbitrary constant}$$

since

$$\frac{d}{dx}\left(ye^{\int P(x)\,dx}\right) = e^{\int P(x)\,dx}\frac{dy}{dx} + yP(x)e^{\int P(x)\,dx}$$

Thus the equation

$$\frac{dy}{dx} + yP(x) = Q(x)$$

has as its solution

$$y = e^{-\int P(x)\,dx}\left[\int e^{\int P(x)\,dx}Q(x)\,dx + C\right]$$

Similarly, the equation

$$\frac{dx}{dy} + xP(y) = Q(y)$$

has $e^{\int P(y)\,dy}$ as an integrating factor and its solution is

$$x = e^{-\int P(y)\,dy}\left[\int e^{\int P(y)\,dy}Q(y)\,dy + C\right]$$

NOTE: Every differential equation of first order and first degree, which has a solution, can be shown to have an infinite number of integrating factors, although determining these integrating factors may not be easy. As discussed in the following section, first-order differential equations which are linear in a function of a variable can also be integrated using integrating factors.

EXAMPLE

Solve the equation $x^2\, dy + (y - 2xy - 2x^2)\, dx = 0$.

Writing the equation in the form $\dfrac{dy}{dx} + yP(x) = Q(x)$,

$$\frac{dy}{dx} + y\left(\frac{1 - 2x}{x^2}\right) = 2$$

The integrating factor is $e^{\int P(x)\, dx}$, that is,

$$e^{\int [(1 - 2x)/x^2]\, dx} = e^{-(1/x) - \ln x^2} = \frac{e^{-1/x}}{x^2}$$

and $ye^{\int P(x)\, dx} = \displaystyle\int e^{\int P(x)\, dx}\, Q(x) + C$, that is,

$$\frac{ye^{-1/x}}{x^2} = \int \frac{2e^{-1/x}}{x^2}\, dx$$

$$= 2e^{-1/x} + C$$

$$y = 2x^2 + Cx^2 e^{1/x}$$

$$= x^2(2 + Ce^{1/x})$$

where C is an arbitrary constant.

EXAMPLE

Solve the equation $y\dfrac{dx}{dy} = 2ye^{3y} + x(3y + 2)$.

Writing the equation in the form $\dfrac{dx}{dy} + xP(y) = Q(y)$,

$$\frac{dx}{dy} - x\left(\frac{3y + 2}{y}\right) = 2e^{3y}$$

The integrating factor is $e^{\int P(y)\, dy}$, that is,

$$e^{\int -[(3y + 2)/y]\, dy} = e^{-3y - 2\ln y} = \frac{e^{-3y}}{y^2}$$

and $xe^{\int P(y)\, dy} = \displaystyle\int e^{\int P(y)\, dy}\, Q(y) + e$, that is,

$$\frac{xe^{-3y}}{y^2} = \int \frac{2}{y^2}\, dy$$

$$= -\frac{2}{y} + C$$

$$x = -2ye^{3y} + Cy^2 e^{3y}$$

$$= ye^{3y}(Cy - 2)$$

EXAMPLE

Solve the equation $2y\,dx = (y^4 + x)\,dy$ and find the particular solution if $y = 1$ when $x = 0$.

Writing the equation in the form $\dfrac{dx}{dy} + xP(y) = Q(y)$,

$$\frac{dx}{dy} - x\left(\frac{1}{2y}\right) = \frac{y^3}{2}$$

The integrating factor is $e^{\int P(y)\,dy}$, that is,

$$e^{\int -dy/2y} = e^{-(1/2)\ln y} = y^{-1/2}$$

and $xe^{\int P(y)\,dy} = \displaystyle\int e^{\int P(y)\,dy}\,Q(y) + C$, that is,

$$xy^{-1/2} = \frac{1}{2}\int y^{5/2}\,dy$$

$$= \tfrac{1}{7}y^{7/2} + C$$

$$x = \tfrac{1}{7}y^4 + Cy^{1/2}$$

$$7x = y^4 + Cy^{1/2}$$

If $y = 1$ when $x = 0$,

$$0 = 1 + C$$

$$C = -1$$

and

$$7x = y^4 - y^{1/2}$$

is the particular solution for $x = 0$, $y = 1$.

EXAMPLE

A manufacturing company has found that the cost, c, of operating and maintaining its equipment is related to the length, x, of the interval between overhauls by the equation

$$\frac{dc}{dx} - \frac{b-1}{x}c = -\frac{ba}{x^2}$$

where a and b are constants. Find c as a function of x if $c = c_0$ when $x = x_0$.

Writing the equation in the form $\dfrac{dc}{dx} + cP(X) = Q(x)$,

$$\frac{dc}{dx} + c\left(-\frac{(b-1)}{x}\right) = -\frac{ba}{x^2}$$

The integrating factor is $e^{\int P(x)\,dx}$, that is,

$$e^{\int -[(b-1)/x]\,dx} = e^{-(b-1)\ln x} = x^{-(b-1)}$$

and $ce^{\int P(x)\,dx} = \displaystyle\int e^{\int P(x)\,dx}\,Q(x) + C$, that is,

$$cx^{-(b-1)} = -ba\int x^{-b-1}$$

$$= ax^{-b} + C$$

$$c = \frac{a}{x} + Cx^{b-1}$$

Figure 5.5

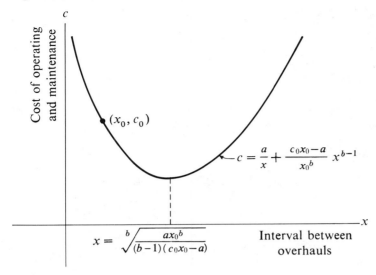

If $c = c_0$ when $x = x_0$,

$$c_0 = \frac{a}{x_0} + Cx_0^{b-1}$$

so

$$C = \frac{c_0 x_0 - a}{x_0^b}$$

and

$$c = \frac{a}{x} + \frac{c_0 x_0 - a}{x_0^b} x^{b-1}$$

(See Figure 5.5.)

DIFFERENTIAL EQUATIONS LINEAR IN A FUNCTION OF y OR IN A FUNCTION OF x

An equation which can be written in the form

$$\frac{d}{dx} f(y) + f(y)P(x) = Q(x)$$

is a linear differential equation in the variable $f(y)$; that is, it is of the first degree in $f(y)$ and $\dfrac{d}{dy} f(y)$. Its solution is thus given by

$$f(y) = e^{-\int P(x)\,dx} \left[\int e^{\int P(x)\,dx} Q(x)\,dx + C \right]$$

Similarly, an equation which can be written in the form

$$\frac{d}{dy} f(x) + f(x)P(y) = Q(y)$$

is a linear differential equation in the variable $f(x)$; that is, it is of the first degree in $f(x)$ and $\dfrac{d}{dx} f(x)$. Its solution is thus given by

$$f(x) = e^{-\int P(y)\,dy}\left[\int e^{\int P(y)\,dy}Q(y)\,dy + C\right]$$

EXAMPLE

Solve the equation $y\,dx + x(1 - x^2y^4)\,dy = 0$.

Writing the equation in the form $\dfrac{d}{dy} f(x) + f(x)P(y) = Q(y)$,

$$\frac{dx}{dy} + \frac{x}{y} = x^3y^3$$

$$x^{-3}\frac{dx}{dy} + x^{-2}\left(\frac{1}{y}\right) = y^3$$

$$-2x^{-3}\frac{dx}{dy} + x^{-2}\left(-\frac{2}{y}\right) = -2y^3$$

$$\frac{d}{dy}(x^{-2}) + x^{-2}\left(-\frac{2}{y}\right) = -2y^3$$

The integrating factor is $e^{\int P(y)\,dy}$, that is,

$$e^{\int -(2/y)\,dy} = e^{-2\ln y} = y^{-2}$$

and $f(x) = e^{-\int P(y)\,dy}[e^{\int P(y)\,dy}\,Q(y)\,dy + C]$, that is,

$$x^{-2} = y^2\left[-2\int y^{-2}y^3\,dy + C\right]$$

$$= y^2\left[-2\int y\,dy + C\right]$$

$$= y^2[-y^2 + C]$$

$$1 = -x^2y^4 + Cx^2y^2$$

$$1 + x^2y^4 = Cx^2y^2$$

EXAMPLE

Solve the equation $\dfrac{dy}{dx} + xy \ln y = xye^{-x^2}$ and find the particular solution if $y = 1$ when $x = 0$.

Writing the equation in the form $\dfrac{d}{dx} f(y) + f(y)P(x) = Q(x)$,

$$\frac{1}{y}\frac{dy}{dx} + (\ln y)(x) = xe^{-x^2}$$

$$\frac{d}{dx}(\ln y) + (\ln y)(x) = xe^{-x^2}$$

The integrating factor is $e^{\int P(x)\,dx}$, that is,

$$e^{\int x\,dx} = e^{x^2/2}$$

and $f(y) = e^{-\int P(x)\,dx}[e^{\int P(x)\,dx}\, Q(x)\,dx + C]$

$$\ln y = e^{-x^2/2}\left[\int xe^{x^2/2}e^{-x^2}\,dx + C\right]$$

$$= e^{-x^2/2}\left[\int xe^{-x^2/2}\,dx + C\right]$$

$$= e^{-x^2/2}[-e^{-x^2/2} + C]$$

$$= -e^{-x^2} + Ce^{-x^2/2}$$

If $y = 1$ when $x = 0$,

$$0 = -1 + C$$

$$C = 1$$

and

$$\ln y = -e^{-x^2} + e^{-x^2/2}$$

$$= e^{-x^2/2}(1 - e^{-x^2/2})$$

is the particular solution for $x = 0$, $y = 1$.

EXAMPLE

The cost control unit of a large public accounting firm has found, as the company has increased in size, that the average monthly cost, y, of office supplies is related to the number, x, of employees (in addition to the unit director) by the equation

$$\frac{dy}{dx} + 2y = y^2e^{-x}$$

Find y as a function of x if $y = 3$ when $x = 0$.

Writing the equation in the form $\dfrac{d}{dx} f(y) + f(y)P(x) = Q(x)$,

$$y^{-2}\frac{dy}{dx} + 2y^{-1} = e^{-x}$$

$$-y^{-2}\frac{dy}{dx} - 2y^{-1} = -e^{-x}$$

$$\frac{d}{dx}(y^{-1}) - 2y^{-1} = -e^{-x}$$

The integrating factor is $e^{\int P(x)\,dx}$, that is,

$$e^{\int -2\,dx} = e^{-2x}$$

Figure 5.6

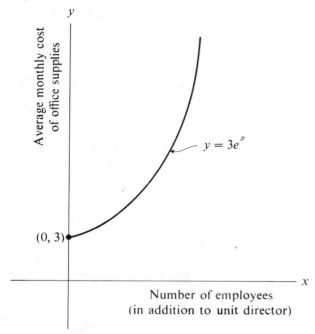

and $f(y) = e^{-\int P(x)\,dx}[e^{\int P(x)\,dx}\,Q(x)\,dx + C]$, that is,

$$y^{-1} = e^{2x}\left[\int -e^{-2x}e^{-x}\,dx + C\right]$$

$$= e^{2x}\left[-\int e^{-3x}\,dx + C\right]$$

$$= e^{2x}\left[\frac{e^{-3x}}{3} + C\right]$$

$$= \frac{e^{-x}}{3} + Ce^{2x}$$

$$3e^x = y + Cye^{3x}$$

If $y = 3$ when $x = 0$,

$$3 = 3 + 3C$$

$$C = 0$$

and

$$y = 3e^x$$

is the particular solution for $x = 0$, $y = 3$. (See Figure 5.6.)

NOTE: In general, there is no rule for determining the function $f(y)$ or $f(x)$ in terms of which a differential equation is, or can be made, linear. The equation must be put in the form $g(y)\dfrac{dy}{dx} + f(y)P(x) = Q(x)$ or the form $g(x)\dfrac{dx}{dy} + f(x)P(y) = Q(y)$ so that it can be determined by inspection whether the differential equation can be made linear in $f(y)$ or $f(x)$. However, there is one class of differential equations for which the appropriate function is known. An equation of the form

$$\frac{dy}{dx} + yP(x) = y^n Q(x)$$

or

$$\frac{dx}{dy} + xP(y) = x^n Q(y)$$

can be made linear in y^{n-1} or x^{n-1} by multiplication by $(1 - n)y^{-n}$ or $(1 - n)x^{-n}$, respectively. Equations of this type are known as *Bernoulli equations*. The first and last examples of this section involve Bernoulli equations.

5.5 Differential Equations of Higher Order and/or Higher Degree

Except for special cases, methods of solution of differential equations of the second order or degree are somewhat complicated and, in general, solution becomes more difficult as the order or degree of the differential equation increases. In many cases, methods for obtaining an exact solution are not known and numerical methods for obtaining approximate solutions must be used. It should be noted that there are, in fact, some types of differential equations of first order and first degree for which exact solutions are not known. With electronic computers, highly accurate approximate solutions can be obtained; these methods of solution may sometimes be preferred, for reasons of convenience, even though methods for exact solution are known.

PROBLEMS

Find the general solution for each of the following differential equations.

1. $x\,dy - 3y\,dx = x^2\,dx$

2. $\dfrac{dy}{dx} + 2xy - 2xe^{-x^2} = 0$

3. $y\dfrac{dx}{dy} + (1 + y)x - e^y = 0$

4. $y\dfrac{dx}{dy} + 2x - 3y = 0$

5. $x(6xy + 5)\,dx + (2x^3 + 3y)\,dy = 0$

6. $(a_1 x + b_1 y + c_1)\,dx + (b_1 x + b_2 y + c_2)\,dy = 0$

7. $y\,dx + 3x^2 e^x\,dx = dy$

8. $(ye^{xy} + 2xy)\,dx + (xe^{xy} + x^2)\,dy = 0$

9. $(x + 1)\dfrac{dy}{dx} + 2y = e^x(x + 1)^{-1}$

10. $(y\cos x - 2\sin y)\,dx = (2x\cos y - \sin x)\,dy$

11. $(3x^2 y + xy^2 + e^x)\,dx + (x^3 + x^2 y + \sin y)\,dy = 0$

12. $2y\sin xy\,dx + (2x\sin xy + y^3)\,dy = 0$

13. $(3y\sin x - \cos y)\,dx + (x\sin y - 3\cos x)\,dy = 0$

14. $(y^2 \csc^2 x + 6xy - 2) \, dx = (2y \cot x - 3x^2) \, dy$

15. $\cos y \, dx - (x \sin y - y^2) \, dy = 0$

16. $2\left(\dfrac{y}{x^3} + \dfrac{x}{y^2}\right) dx = \left(\dfrac{1}{x^2} + \dfrac{2x^2}{y^3}\right) dy$

17. $\dfrac{dy}{dx} + 2y - x = 0$

23. $y^3 \dfrac{dy}{dx} + xy^4 = xe^{-x^2}$

18. $x\dfrac{dy}{dx} = x^3 + y$

24. $xy \, dy = (x^2 - y^2) \, dx$

25. $(x + y) \, dx + (x - 2y) \, dy = 0$

19. $3\dfrac{dy}{dx} + \dfrac{2y}{x+1} = \dfrac{x}{y^2}$

26. $\dfrac{dy}{dx} + \left(y - \dfrac{1}{y}\right)x = 0$

20. $\dfrac{dx}{dy} + x = e^{-y}$

27. $\dfrac{ds}{dt} - s \cot t = 1 - (t + 2) \cot t$

21. $\dfrac{dy}{dx} - xy = y^{1/2}xe^{x^2}$

28. $\dfrac{ds}{dt} + \dfrac{s}{t} = \cos t + \dfrac{\sin t}{t}$

22. $\dfrac{dy}{dx} - xy = \dfrac{x}{y}$

29. $\dfrac{dy}{dx} + y = \cos x - \sin x$

30. $(2x \cos y - e^x) \, dx - x^2 \sin y \, dy = 0$

31. $(y \sin x + xy \cos x) \, dx + (x \sin x + \sin y + e^y) \, dy = 0$

32. $\dfrac{dy}{dx} - xy = e^{(1/2)x^2} \cos x$

33. $\cos \theta \dfrac{dr}{d\theta} = 2 + 2r \sin \theta$

34. $\cos x \sec y \, dx + \sin x \sin y \sec^2 y \, dy = 0$

35. $\dfrac{ds}{dt} + s \tan t = 2t + t^2 \tan t$

36. $\cos y \, dy + (\sin y - 1) \cos x \, dx = 0$

37. $x \tan^2 y \, dy + x \, dy = (2x^2 + \tan y) \, dx$

38. $3y^2 \dfrac{dy}{dx} - xy^3 = e^{(1/2)x^2} \cos x$

39. $(\ln y + y^3 + ye^{xy}) \, dx + \left(\dfrac{x}{y} + 3xy^2 + xe^{xy}\right) dy = 0$

40. $dx + (2xy - 4xy^3 - 2y^3 e^{y^4}) \, dy = 0$

41. $\left(y^2 + \dfrac{1}{y} + ye^y\right) dx + \left(2xy - \dfrac{x}{y^2} + xe^y + xye^y\right) dy = 0$

42. $y^2 \dfrac{dx}{dy} + (y^2 + 2y)x - 1 = 0$

47. $x^2 \dfrac{dy}{dx} + y^2 = xy$

43. $x \, dy = (5y + x + 1) \, dx$

48. $\sin \theta \, d\theta + \cos \theta \, dt = te^t \, dt$

44. $\dfrac{xy + 1}{y} \, dx + \dfrac{2y - x}{y^2} \, dy = 0$

49. $\csc y \cot y \, dy = (\csc y + e^x) \, dx$

50. $x\dfrac{dy}{dx} + y = y^2 x^2 \cos x$

45. $\dfrac{dx}{dy} = x + e^y$

51. $\dfrac{dx}{dy} - x \cot y = e^y(1 - \cot y)$

46. $x\dfrac{dy}{dx} + 2y = 3x^3 y^{4/3}$

Find the particular solution for each of the following differential equations under the given conditions.

52. $\dfrac{dy}{dx} + y \tan x = \sec x$, $y = -1$ when $x = 0$

53. $dy + (y \cot x - \sec x) \, dx = 0$, $y = 1$ when $x = 0$

54. $(y^2 + 1)\dfrac{dx}{dy} + 2xy = y^2$, $y = -1$ when $x = 0$

55. $dy = x(1 - e^{2y-x^2}) \, dx$, $y = 0$ when $x = 0$

56. $\left(x^2 + \dfrac{1}{x} + ye^{xy}\right) dx + (e^y + 3y^2 + xe^{xy}) \, dy = 0$, $y = 0$ when $x = 1$

57. $(1 - x^2)\dfrac{dy}{dx} + xy = x(1 - x^2)y^{1/2}$, $y = 1$ when $x = 0$

58. $\dfrac{dy}{dx} + y = y^2 e^{-x}$, $y = 2$ when $x = 0$

59. $y \, dx + 2(x - 2y^2) \, dy = 0$, $y = -1$ when $x = 2$

60. $(y + y^3) \, dx + 4(xy^2 - 1) \, dy = 0$, $y = 1$ when $x = 0$

61. $2y \, dx = (x^2 y^4 + x) \, dy$, $y = 1$ when $x = 1$

62. $(x^2 - 1)\dfrac{dy}{dx} + (x^2 - 1)^2 + 4y = 0$, $y = -6$ when $x = 0$

63. $(ye^x - 2x) \, dx + e^x \, dy = 0$, $y = 6$ when $x = 0$

64. $\left(\dfrac{2}{y} - \dfrac{y}{x^2}\right) dx + \left(\dfrac{1}{x} - \dfrac{2x}{y^2}\right) dy = 0$, $y = 2$ when $x = 1$

65. $(2y - xy - 3) \, dx + x \, dy = 0$, $y = 1$ when $x = 1$

66. $(ye^y + 2x + y) \, dx + (xe^y + xye^y + 3y^2 + x) \, dy = 0$, $y = 0$ when $x = 2$

67. $\left(3x^2 y - \dfrac{2y}{x} - 6x^4\right) dx + dy = 0$, $y = 0$ when $x = -1$

68. $dr = (1 + 2r \cot \theta) \, d\theta$, $r = 3$ when $\theta = \pi/2$

69. The change in net profit, P, as advertising expenditure, x, changes is given by the equation

$$\dfrac{dP}{dx} = k - a(P + x)$$

where a and k are constants. Find P as a function of x if $P = P_0$ when $x = 0$.

70. The change in the cost of ordering and holding, C, as quantity, x, changes is given by the equation

$$\dfrac{dC}{dx} = a - \dfrac{C}{x}$$

where a is a constant. Find C as a function of x if $C = C_0$ when $x = x_0$.

71. Manufacturing and marketing costs, C, are related to the number of items, x, by the equation

$$\dfrac{dC}{dx} + aC = b + kx$$

where a, b, and k are constants. Find C as a function of x if $C = 0$ when $x = 0$.

72. The change in consumption, c, of a particular commodity as income, I, changes is given by the equation

$$\frac{dc}{dI} = c + ke^I$$

where k is a constant. Find c as a function of I if $c = c_0$ when $I = 0$.

Answers to Odd-Numbered Problems

1. $y = -x^2 + Cx^3$

3. $2xye^y - e^{2y} = C$

5. $4x^3y + 5x^2 + 3y^2 = C$

7. $y = x^3e^x + Ce^x$

9. $y(x + 1)^2 = e^x + C$

11. $2x^3y + x^2y^2 + 2e^x - 2 \cos y = C$

13. $3y \cos x + x \cos y = C$

15. $y^3 + 3x \cos y = C$

17. $y = \frac{1}{2}x - \frac{1}{4} + Ce^{-2x}$

19. $12(x + 1)^2y^3 = 3x^4 + 8x^3 + 6x^2 + C$

21. $3y^{1/2} = e^{x^2} + Ce^{x^2/4}$

23. $e^{2x^2}y^4 = 2e^{x^2} + C$

25. $x^2 + 2xy - 2y^2 = C$

27. $s = t + 2 + C \sin t$

29. $y = \cos x + Ce^{-x}$

31. $xy \sin x - \cos y + e^y = C$

33. $r \cos^2 \theta = 2 \sin \theta + C$

35. $s = t^2 + C \cos t$

37. $\tan y = 2x^2 + Cx$

39. $x \ln y + xy^3 + e^{xy} = C$

41. $x\left(y^2 + \frac{1}{y} + ye^y\right) = C$

43. $20y + 5x + 4 = Cx^5$

45. $x = ye^y + Ce^y$

47. $x = y \ln Cx$

49. $2e^x \csc y + e^{2x} = C$

51. $x = e^y + C \sin y$

53. $y \sin x + \ln \cos x = 0$

55. $x^2 + 1 = e^{x^2 - 2y}$

57. $3y^{1/2} + 1 - x^2 = 4(1 - x^2)^{1/4}$

59. $y^2(x - y^2) = 1$

61. $10x = (9 + xy^4)y^{1/2}$

63. $ye^x - x^2 = 6$

65. $x^2y + 3(x + 1) = 7e^{x-1}$

67. $y = 2x^2 - 2x^2e^{-x^3-1}$

69. $P = \frac{k + 1}{a} - x + \left(P_0 - \frac{k + 1}{a}\right)e^{-ax}$

71. $C = \frac{ab - k}{a^2}(1 - e^{-ax}) + \frac{k}{a}x$

5.6 Applications of Differential Equations in Economic Models

Economic models are of two general types, *static* and *dynamic*. Static models concern equilibrium situations, that is, situations which if attained will be maintained. Dynamic models concern situations which change over time. In dynamic models, time enters either explicitly as a variable or implicitly in the form of lagged variables. The models discussed in this chapter are very simple dynamic economic models expressed in terms of differential equations.

There are two general classes of variables in economic models, referred to as *endogenous* and *exogenous* variables. Endogenous variables are those variables whose values or levels are to be predicted or explained; exogenous variables are assumed to be determined and known in advance and can be regarded as constant in the model. Endogenous and exogenous come from Greek words meaning "generated from inside" and "generated from outside," respectively. Endogenous variables are predicted from the model; exogenous variables are determined outside the model.

Usually a model is first written in terms of *structural equations* which express relationships among endogenous and exogenous variables. This set of structural equations is then solved, if possible, for what are called *reduced form* equations, each of which expresses an endogenous variable as a function of exogenous variables and parameters. A model is solved by obtaining a reduced form equation for each endogenous variable in the model. Solution of economic models is illustrated in this section for the Domar macro model, two Domar debt models, the Evans price adjustment model, and an income-consumption-investment model.

DOMAR MACRO MODEL

The following very simple macro model was proposed by E. D. Domar.

$$S(t) = \alpha y(t)$$

$$I(t) = \beta \frac{dy}{dt}$$

$$S(t) = I(t)$$

$$y(0) = y_0$$

$$\alpha > 0 \qquad \beta > 0$$

where S is saving, I is investment, y is income, and each of these endogenous variables is a function of time.

The first equation states that saving is a fixed proportion of income; the second equation states that investment is proportional to the rate of change of income over time; the third equation states that saving equals investment; the fourth equation states the initial condition. From these relationships, specific functions expressing variations in the variables over time can be obtained.

Since $S(t) = I(t)$,

$$\alpha y(t) = \beta \frac{dy}{dt}$$

and the differential equation

$$\frac{dy}{dt} - \frac{\alpha}{\beta} y = 0$$

is obtained for solution. Separating the variables and integrating,

$$\frac{1}{y} \frac{dy}{dt} = \frac{\alpha}{\beta}$$

$$\ln y = \frac{\alpha}{\beta} t + C$$

$$y = C e^{(\alpha/\beta)t}$$

If $y = y_0$ at $t = 0$, then

$$y_0 = C$$

and the particular solution is

$$y = y_0 e^{(\alpha/\beta)t}$$

Note that this solution gives income, y, as a function of time, t. Since $\alpha > 0$, $\beta > 0$, the function has an increasing positive slope, the rate of increase depending on α/β. Solutions for the remaining variables of the model, I and S, are as follows:

$$I = S = \alpha y = \alpha y_0 e^{(\alpha/\beta)t}$$

DOMAR DEBT MODEL

Domar uses a set of models similar to the macro model above to express relationships between national income and national debt. Consider the model

$$\frac{dD}{dt} = \alpha y(t)$$

$$\frac{dy}{dt} = \beta$$

$$y(0) = y_0$$

$$D(0) = D_0$$

$$\alpha > 0 \qquad \beta > 0$$

where D is national debt and y is national income (both endogenous). In this model, national income increases at a constant rate β over time and the rate of increase of national debt is a fixed proportion of national income. The third and fourth equations state the initial conditions. Integrating the second equation,

$$y = \beta t + C$$

Since $y = y_0$ when $t = 0$, $C = y_0$ and

$$y = \beta t + y_0$$

Substituting in the first equation of the model,

$$\frac{dD}{dt} = \alpha \beta t + \alpha y_0$$

$$D = \tfrac{1}{2}\alpha \beta t^2 + \alpha y_0 t + C$$

Since $D = D_0$ when $t = 0$, $C = D_0$ and

$$D = \tfrac{1}{2}\alpha \beta t^2 + \alpha y_0 t + D_0$$

The solution of the model is thus

$$D(t) = \tfrac{1}{2}\alpha \beta t^2 + \alpha y_0 t + D_0$$

$$y(t) = \beta t + y_0$$

Domar was interested in the ratio of national debt to national income

$$\frac{D(t)}{y(t)} = \frac{\tfrac{1}{2}\alpha \beta t^2 + \alpha y_0 t + D_0}{\beta t + y_0}$$

or

$$\frac{D(t)}{y(t)} = \frac{D_0}{\beta t + y_0} + \frac{\alpha y_0 t}{\beta t + y_0} + \frac{\tfrac{1}{2}\alpha \beta t^2}{\beta t + y_0}$$

As $t \to \infty$,

$$\frac{D_0}{\beta t + y_0} \to 0$$

$$\frac{\alpha y_0 t}{\beta t + y_0} \to \frac{\alpha y_0}{\beta} \quad \text{(a constant)}$$

$$\frac{\frac{1}{2}\alpha \beta t^2}{\beta t + y_0} \to \infty$$

Thus, as $t \to \infty$, $D(t)/y(t) \to \infty$ and, for this model, the ratio of national debt to national income increases over time without limit.

A SECOND DOMAR DEBT MODEL

A second version of the Domar debt model is obtained by modifying the second equation in the above model, so that income increases by a constant proportion of income, and leaving the other equations unchanged.

$$\frac{dD}{dt} = \alpha y(t)$$

$$\frac{dy}{dt} = \beta y(t)$$

$$y(0) = y_0$$

$$D(0) = D_0$$

$$\alpha > 0 \qquad \beta > 0$$

Integrating the second equation,

$$\frac{1}{y}\frac{dy}{dt} = \beta$$

$$\ln y = \beta t + C$$

$$y = Ce^{\beta t}$$

Since $y = y_0$ when $t = 0$, $C = y_0$ and

$$y = y_0 e^{\beta t}$$

Substituting in the first equation of the model and integrating,

$$\frac{dD}{dt} = \alpha y_0 e^{\beta t}$$

$$D = \frac{\alpha}{\beta} y_0 e^{\beta t} + C$$

Since $D = D_0$ when $t = 0$, $C = D_0 - \frac{\alpha}{\beta} y_0$ and

$$D = D_0 - \frac{\alpha}{\beta} y_0 + \frac{\alpha}{\beta} y_0 e^{\beta t}$$

or

$$D = D_0 + \frac{\alpha}{\beta} y_0 (e^{\beta t} - 1)$$

The solution of the model is thus

$$D(t) = D_0 + \frac{\alpha}{\beta} y_0 (e^{\beta t} - 1)$$

$$y(t) = y_0 e^{\beta t}$$

The ratio of national debt to national income is

$$\frac{D(t)}{y(t)} = \frac{D_0}{y_0 e^{\beta t}} + \frac{\alpha}{\beta}\left(1 - \frac{1}{e^{\beta t}}\right)$$

As $t \to \infty$,

$$\frac{D_0}{y_0 e^{\beta t}} \to 0$$

$$\frac{\alpha}{\beta}\left(1 - \frac{1}{e^{\beta t}}\right) \to \frac{\alpha}{\beta}$$

Thus, as $t \to \infty$, $D(t)/y(t) \to \alpha/\beta$, a (finite) constant.

EVANS PRICE ADJUSTMENT MODEL

A model of a particular market for a commodity was proposed by G. C. Evans. The demand and supply equations are the same as those for the usual simple linear model and can be solved for the equilibrium price in the usual way. In addition, there is an equation stating that the rate of change of price over time is proportional to the excess demand $(d - s)$. This factor of proportionality is positive, implying that a positive excess demand causes a rise in price and a negative excess demand causes a fall in price.

$$d(t) = \alpha_0 + \alpha_1 p(t)$$

$$s(t) = \beta_0 + \beta_1 p(t)$$

$$\frac{dp}{dt} = \gamma(d - s)$$

$$\alpha_1 < 0 \qquad \beta_1 > 0 \qquad \gamma > 0$$

where d is demand, s is supply, and p is price. Substituting the first two equations into the third equation,

$$\frac{dp}{dt} = \gamma[\alpha_0 - \beta_0 + (\alpha_1 - \beta_1)p]$$

$$= \gamma(\alpha_1 - \beta_1)(p - p_e)$$

where $p_e = (\alpha_0 - \beta_0)/(\beta_1 - \alpha_1)$ is the equilibrium price in the model obtained in the usual way by solving $d(t) = s(t)$ for $p(t)$, the equilibrium price. Letting $\lambda = \gamma(\alpha_1 - \beta_1)$,

$$\frac{dp}{dt} = \lambda(p - p_e)$$

$$\frac{1}{p - p_e}\frac{dp}{dt} = \lambda$$

$$\ln (p - p_e) = \lambda t + C$$

$$p - p_e = Ce^{\lambda t}$$

$$p = p_e + Ce^{\lambda t}$$

Since $p = p_0$ when $t = 0$, $C = p_0 - p_e$ and

$$p = p_e + (p_0 - p_e)e^{\lambda t}$$

where, as above, $p_e = (\alpha_0 - \beta_0)/(\beta_1 - \alpha_1)$ and $\lambda = \gamma(\alpha_1 - \beta_1)$. Since $\lambda < 0$, $p \to p_e$ as $t \to \infty$.

INCOME-CONSUMPTION-INVESTMENT MODEL

Consider a differential-equations form of the income-consumption-investment model where current consumption and investment are linear functions of current income and income changes at a rate that is proportional to excess demand, that is, to consumption plus investment minus income.

$$C_\delta(t) = \alpha Y_\delta(t)$$

$$I_\delta(t) = \gamma Y_\delta(t)$$

$$\frac{dY_\delta}{dt} = \lambda(C_\delta + I_\delta - Y_\delta)$$

$$Y_\delta(0) = Y_0 - Y_e$$

$$0 < \alpha < 1 \qquad 0 < \gamma < 1 \qquad 0 < \lambda < 1$$

where C_δ, I_δ, and Y_δ are deviations of consumption, investment, and income, respectively, from their equilibrium values C_e, I_e, and Y_e. Substituting the first two equations into the third equation,

$$\frac{dY_\delta}{dt} = \lambda(\alpha + \gamma - 1)Y_\delta$$

$$\frac{dY_\delta}{Y_\delta} = \lambda(\alpha + \gamma - 1) \, dt$$

$$\ln Y_\delta = \lambda(\alpha + \gamma - 1)t + C$$

$$Y_\delta = Ce^{\lambda(\alpha + \gamma - 1)t}$$

Since $Y_\delta = Y_0 - Y_e$ when $t = 0$, $C = Y_0 - Y_e$ and

$$Y_\delta = (Y_0 - Y_e)e^{\lambda(\alpha + \gamma - 1)t}$$

That is,

$$Y = Y_e + (Y_0 - Y_e)e^{\lambda(\alpha + \gamma - 1)t}$$

And, if $\alpha + \gamma < 1$, $e^{\lambda(\alpha + \gamma - 1)t} \to 0$ and $Y \to Y_e$ as $t \to \infty$.

PROBLEMS

1. Demand, x, and supply, y, of a product are given as a function of unit price, p, by the following equations:

$$x = ap + b \qquad y = cp + d$$

Suppose that price changes in such a way that the excess of demand over supply is decreased at a rate proportional to the excess. Show that

a. $\dfrac{d}{dt}(x - y) = -k(x - y)$

b. $\dfrac{dp}{dt} + k(p - \bar{p}) = 0$, where $\bar{p} = \dfrac{b - d}{c - a}$

c. The unit price tends to an equilibrium value $\bar{p}$ and

$$p = \bar{p} + (p_0 - \bar{p})e^{-kt}$$

where p_0 is the initial price at $t = 0$.

2. Consider the model

$$\frac{dD}{dt} = \alpha y(t) + \beta$$

$$\frac{dy}{dt} = \gamma y(t)$$

$$y(0) = y_0$$

$$D(0) = D_0$$

$$\alpha > 0 \qquad \beta > 0 \qquad \gamma > 0$$

where D is national debt and y is national income.
a. Solve the model.
b. Determine the limit as $t \to \infty$ of the ratio of national debt to national income.

3. Consider the model

$$\frac{dR}{dt} = \frac{\alpha}{S(t)}$$

$$\frac{dS}{dt} = -\lambda S(t)$$

$$R(0) = 0$$

$$S(0) = S_0 \text{ (original cost)}$$

$$\alpha > 0 \qquad \lambda > 0$$

where R is running cost of a car and S is resale value. Solve the model.

4. The increase in the number of new products tested, y, as amount, x, allocated to research and development increases equals a constant times the product of the number of new products tested and the amount allocated to research and development plus another constant times the ratio of the amount allocated to research and development divided by the number of new products tested. Find the relationship between the number of new products tested and the amount allocated to research and development if $y = y_0$ when $x = 0$.

5. Consider the model

$$\frac{dR}{dt} = \frac{\alpha}{S(t)} + \beta$$

$$\frac{dS}{dt} = -\lambda S(t)$$

$$R(0) = R_0$$

$$S(0) = S_0$$

$$\alpha > 0 \qquad \beta \geq 0 \qquad \lambda > 0$$

where R is the cost of repairing and operating a machine and S is salvage value of the machine. Find R and S as functions of time, t.

6. Consider the model

$$\frac{dw}{dt} = \frac{1}{\alpha y(t)} + ke^{\beta t}$$

$$\frac{dy}{dt} = \beta y(t)$$

$$w(0) = w_0$$

$$y(0) = y_0$$

$$\beta > 0 \qquad \alpha > \frac{k}{\beta y_0}$$

where w is per capita consumption of wheat products and y is per capita income. Find w and y as functions of time and determine the limit as $t \to \infty$ of the ratio of per capita consumption of wheat to per capita income.

Answers to Odd-Numbered Problems

3. $S(t) = S_0 e^{-\lambda t}$

$$R(t) = \frac{\alpha}{\lambda S_0} (e^{\lambda t} - 1)$$

5. $S = S_0 e^{-\lambda t}$

$$R = R_0 + \beta t + \frac{\alpha}{\lambda S_0} (e^{\lambda t} - 1)$$

Difference Equations

6.1 Introduction

When variables are considered to change discretely or discontinuously rather than continuously or instantaneously, difference equations rather than differential equations are appropriate for expressing relationships among the changes. Difference equations are frequently useful in business and economic analyses, since many economic data are recorded for uniformly spaced periods of time, for example, gross national product may be given for a year; net profit for a quarter; quantities produced, bought, or sold for a month.

In many economic analyses, time is the independent variable, and changes in other variables over time are studied. Studies of variables over discrete sets of time values are referred to as *period analyses*, and difference equations provide the basis for such analyses. Recall that when the time periods (or, more generally, the changes in the independent variable) are made smaller and smaller, difference equations approach differential equations as a limiting case.

For generality, the following discussion of the classification and solution of difference equations is in terms of an independent variable x. In many economic and business analyses, including the models discussed later, the independent variable time is denoted by t.

After the definition and classification of difference equations are discussed, the solution of a difference equation is defined. The method of solution and the behavior of the solution sequence are considered for linear first-order difference equations with constant coefficients and applications of these difference equations in economic models are illustrated. Methods of solution, behavior of the solution sequence, and applications in economic models are then discussed for second-order difference equations.

536

6.2 Definition and Classification of Difference Equations

In this section, a difference equation is defined and the classification of difference equations by order and degree is discussed. Since most difference equations used in applications are linear, particular attention is given to the definition and classification of linear difference equations.

Suppose that y is a function of x, $y = f(x)$, where y is defined for integer values of x, $x = 0, 1, 2, 3, \ldots$. In the context of difference equations, the functional relationship $y = f(x)$ is frequently indicated by y_x. The change in y as x changes from x to $x + 1$ is the *first difference* of y_x and is written

$$\Delta y_x = y_{x+1} - y_x \qquad \text{(read ``delta'' } y_x)$$

Note that Δy_x is also a function of x; Δ is an *operator* and provides the rule for computing Δy_x from the sequence $y_0, y_1, y_2, \ldots$. Similarly, higher-order differences are obtained as differences of differences by applying the operator Δ:

the second difference of y_x is $\Delta^2 y_x = \Delta(\Delta y_x) = \Delta y_{x+1} - \Delta y_x$

$$= (y_{x+2} - y_{x+1}) - (y_{x+1} - y_x)$$

$$= y_{x+2} - 2y_{x+1} + y_x$$

the third difference of y_x is $\Delta^3 y_x = \Delta(\Delta^2 y_x) = \Delta y_{x+2} - 2\Delta y_{x+1} + \Delta y_x$

$$= (y_{x+3} - y_{x+2}) - 2(y_{x+2} - y_{x+1})$$

$$+ (y_{x+1} - y_x)$$

$$= y_{x+3} - 3y_{x+2} + 3y_{x+1} - y_x$$

$$\vdots$$

the kth difference of y_x is $\Delta^k y_x = \Delta(\Delta^{k-1} y_x) = \sum_{i=0}^{k} \frac{k!}{(k-i)! \, i!} (-1)^i y_{x+k-i}$

EXAMPLE

If $y = 2x^2 - 3$,

$$\Delta^2 y = \Delta y_{x+1} - \Delta y_x$$

$$= [2(x+2)^2 - 3] - [2(x+1)^2 - 3] - \{[2(x+1)^2 - 3] - [2x^2 - 3]\}$$

$$= 4$$

Alternatively,

$$\Delta^2 y_x = y_{x+2} - 2y_{x+1} + y_x = [2(x+2)^2 - 3] - 2[2(x+1)^2 - 3] + [2x^2 - 3]$$

$$= 4$$

EXAMPLE

If $y = 3x + 5$,

$$\Delta^3 y_x = \Delta y_{x+2} - 2\Delta y_{x+1} + \Delta y_x$$

$$= [3(x+3)+5] - [3(x+2)+5] - 2\{[3(x+2)+5] - [3(x+1)+5]\}$$
$$+ [3(x+1)+5] - [3x+5]$$

$$= 0$$

Alternatively,

$$\Delta^3 y_x = y_{x+3} - 3y_{x+2} + 3y_{x+1} - y_x$$

$$= [3(x+3)+5] - 3[3(x+2)+5] + 3[3(x+1)+5] - [3x+5]$$

$$= 0$$

A difference equation states a relationship involving differences or, equivalently, a relationship involving the values of a dependent variable for a discrete set of (lagged) values of the independent variable. In the following discussion, the values of the independent variable are assumed to be equally spaced; for convenience, the independent variable is redefined, if necessary, so that its values are successive positive integers.

LINEAR DIFFERENCE EQUATIONS

A difference equation is said to be *linear* if the dependent variable occurs only in expressions of the first degree, that is, if the dependent variable does not occur raised to a power higher than one and does not occur in cross-product terms. Thus a difference equation is linear if it can be written in the form

$$a_0(x)y_{x+n} + a_1(x)y_{x+n-1} + \cdots + a_{n-1}(x)y_{x+1} + a_n(x)y_x = g(x)$$

where $a_0, a_1, \ldots, a_{n-1}, a_n$ and g are functions of x (but not of y_x) defined for $x = 0, 1, 2, \ldots$.

A linear difference equation is of *order n* if, when written in this form, both a_0 and a_n are unequal to zero for all values of x under consideration; that is, a linear difference equation is of order n if it involves values of y corresponding to values of x differing by n but by not more than n. Nonlinear difference equations are, in general, very difficult to solve and are seldom used. The following discussion is confined to linear difference equations.

EXAMPLE

Each of the following difference equations is linear and of the order indicated.

$y_{x+2} - 7y_{x+1} + 5y_x = 3x$	order 2
$3y_{x+2} + 4y_{x+1} = 2x$	order 1
$18y_{x+2} - 6y_x = 5x$	order 2
$8^x y_{x+3} - 3^x y_{x+2} + 9^x y_{x+1} + 2y_x = 3$	order 3

An *n*th-order difference equation can be written as an implicit function of the values of the variable y at n different values of x, that is, n *lagged* values of y,

$$f[y_{x+n}, y_{x+n-1}, \ldots, y_x] = 0$$

Alternatively, since knowledge of $n + 1$ adjacent values of y permits calculation of the value of y and its first n differences, an nth-order difference equation can also be written as a function of y and its first n differences,

$$F[\Delta^n y_x, \Delta^{n-1} y_x, \ldots, \Delta y_x, y_x] = 0$$

EXAMPLE

$\Delta y_x = 0$ can be written

$$y_{x+1} - y_x = 0 \tag{order 1}$$

$\Delta y_x - 2y_x = 5$ can be written

$$y_{x+1} - y_x - 2y_x = 5$$

$$y_{x+1} - 3y_x - 5 = 0 \tag{order 1}$$

$\Delta^2 y_x - 3\Delta y_x - 3y_x = x$ can be written

$$\Delta(y_{x+1} - y_x) - 3(y_{x+1} - y_x) - 3y_x = x$$

$$y_{x+2} - y_{x+1} - y_{x+1} + y_x - 3y_{x+1} + 3y_x - 3y_x = x$$

$$y_{x+2} - 5y_{x+1} + y_x - x = 0 \tag{order 2}$$

$\Delta^3 y_x + \Delta^2 y_x + \Delta y_x + y_x = 0$ can be written

$$\Delta^2(y_{x+1} - y_x) + \Delta(y_{x+1} - y_x) + y_{x+1} - y_x + y_x = 0$$

$$\Delta(y_{x+2} - y_{x+1} - y_{x+1} + y_x) + y_{x+2} - y_{x+1} - y_{x+1} + y_x + y_{x+1} = 0$$

$$y_{x+3} - y_{x+2} - 2y_{x+2} + 2y_{x+1} + y_{x+1} - y_x + y_{x+2} - y_{x+1} + y_x = 0$$

$$y_{x+3} - 2y_{x+2} + 2y_{x+1} = 0 \tag{order 2}$$

6.3 Solutions of Difference Equations

A *solution* of a difference equation is a functional relation, not involving differences, which is defined for all nonnegative integers and which satisfies the difference equation.

The *general solution* of an nth-order difference equation is a solution containing n arbitrary constants. It can be shown that the general solution of a difference equation is unique.

A *particular solution* of a difference equation is a solution that can be obtained from the general solution by giving specific values to the arbitrary constants of the general solution. As in the case of differential equations, the arbitrary constants of a difference equation are specified by *boundary conditions* or *initial conditions*. The general solution of an nth-order difference equation includes n arbitrary constants, and a particular solution thus requires the specification of n boundary conditions.

In each of the following examples a proposed solution is shown to satisfy a given difference equation and a particular solution is determined for the specified boundary condition(s). Methods for obtaining solutions of linear first- and second-order difference equations with constant coefficients are then discussed. Similar methods of solution are appropriate for higher-order linear difference equations.

EXAMPLE

Show that $y_x = x + c$ is a solution of $y_{x+1} - y_x = 1$ and find a particular solution if $y_0 = 1$.

If $y_x = x + c$,

$$y_{x+1} - y_x = (x + 1 + c) - (x + c) = 1$$

so $y_x = x + c$ is a solution of $y_{x+1} - y_x = 1$. Obtaining the particular solution,

If $y_0 = 1$,

$$1 = 0 + c$$

$$c = 1$$

and

$$y_x = x + 1$$

is the particular solution when $y_0 = 1$.

EXAMPLE

Show that $y_x = [x(x - 1)/2] + c$ is a solution of $y_{x+1} - y_x = x$ and find a particular solution if $y_0 = 2$.

If $y_x = x(x - 1)/2$,

$$y_{x+1} - y_x = \frac{(x + 1)x}{2} + c - \left(\frac{x(x - 1)}{2} + c \right)$$

$$= \frac{x(x + 1 - x + 1)}{2}$$

$$= x$$

$$\frac{2x}{2} = x$$

so

$$y_x = \frac{x(x - 1)}{2} + c$$

is a solution of $y_{x+1} - y_x = x$. Obtaining the particular solution,

If $y_0 = 2$,

$$2 = 0 + c$$

$$c = 2$$

and

$$y_x = \frac{x(x - 1)}{2} + 2$$

is the particular solution when $y_0 = 2$.

EXAMPLE

Show that $y_x = c_1 + c_2(-1)^x$ is a solution of $y_{x+2} - y_x = 0$ and find a particular solution if $y_0 = 2$, $y_1 = 5$.

If $y_x = c_1 + c_2(-1)^x$,

$$y_{x+2} - y_x = c_1 + c_2(-1)^{x+2} - [c_1 + c_2(-1)^x]$$
$$= c_2[(-1)^{x+2} - (-1)^x]$$
$$= 0$$

so $y_x = c_1 + c_2(-1)^x$ is a solution of $y_{x+2} - y_x = 0$. Obtaining the particular solution,
If $y_0 = 2$, $y_1 = 5$,

$$2 = c_1 + c_2$$
$$5 = c_1 - c_2$$
$$2c_1 = 7$$
$$c_1 = \tfrac{7}{2}$$
$$c_2 = -\tfrac{3}{2}$$

and

$$y_x = \tfrac{7}{2} - \tfrac{3}{2}(-1)^x$$

is the particular solution for $y_0 = 2$, $y_1 = 5$.

Similarities Between Difference Equations and Differential Equations

There are many similarities in the classification and solution of difference and differential equations; these similarities occur because the derivative of a function is defined as a limit of a difference quotient

$$\frac{dy}{dx} = \lim_{\Delta x \to 0} \frac{\Delta y_x}{\Delta x} = \lim_{\Delta x \to 0} \frac{y_{x+\Delta x} - y_x}{\Delta x}$$

and, as $\Delta x \to 0$, the discrete case (difference equations) approaches as a limit the continuous case (differential equations).

PROBLEMS

1. Determine the order of each of the following linear difference equations.
   a. $3y_{x+2} - 3y_{x+1} = 3x$ c. $7y_{x+1} - 5y_x = 3$
   b. $8y_{x+3} - y_x = 4$ d. $6y_{x+2} - 7y_x = 5x$
2. If $y = x^2 + 2x$, find $\Delta^2 y_x$.
3. If $y = e^x$, find $\Delta^2 y_x$.
4. If $y = x^3 + 3$, find $\Delta^2 y_x$ and $\Delta^3 y_x$.
5. Show that $y_x = \dfrac{c}{1 + cx}$ is a solution of $y_{x+1} = \dfrac{y_x}{1 + y_x}$ and find a particular solution if $y_0 = -4$.
6. Show that $y_x = c_1 + c_2 2^x$ is a solution of $y_{x+2} - 3y_{x+1} + 2y_x = 0$ and find a particular solution if $y_0 = 1$, $y_1 = 2$.

7. Show that $y_x = c_1 + c_2 2^x - x$ is a solution of $y_{x+2} - 3y_{x+1} + 2y_x = 1$ and find a particular solution if $y_0 = 0$, $y_1 = 3$.

8. Show that $y_x = c_1 + c_2 2^x + c_3 3^x$ is a solution of $y_{x+3} - 6y_{x+2} + 11y_{x+1} - 6y_x = 0$ and find a particular solution if $y_0 = 1$, $y_1 = 1$, $y_2 = -1$.

9. Show that $y_x = c_1 + c_2 x + c_3 x^2 + c_4 x^3$ is a solution of $y_{x+4} - 4y_{x+3} + 6y_{x+2} - 4y_{x+1} + y_x = 0$ and find a particular solution if $y_0 = 1$, $y_1 = 5$, $y_2 = 9$, $y_3 = 7$.

10. Write each of the following difference equations in terms of lagged values of y.
    a. $\Delta y_x = 10$
    b. $\Delta^2 y_x - 3\Delta y_x - 5 = 0$
    c. $\Delta^2 y_x - 4y_x = 2$
    d. $\Delta^3 y_x + 5\Delta y_x = y_x$

Answers to Odd-Numbered Problems

1. a. order 1
   b. order 3
   c. order 1
   d. order 2

3. $e^x(e-1)^2$

5. $y_x = \dfrac{4}{4x - 1}$

7. $y_x = 4(2^x - 1) - x$

9. $y_x = 1 + 2x + 3x^2 - x^3$

6.4 Linear First-Order Difference Equations with Constant Coefficients

In this section, the method of solution for linear first-order difference equations with constant coefficients is discussed. The behavior of the solution sequence is considered and equilibrium and stability are defined.

A linear first-order difference equation can be written in the form

$$a_0(x)y_{x+1} + a_1(x)y_x = g(x) \qquad x = 0, 1, 2, \ldots$$

where $a_0(x) \neq 0$ and $a_1(x) \neq 0$ or, alternatively, as

$$y_{x+1} = -\frac{a_1(x)}{a_0(x)} y_x + \frac{g(x)}{a_0(x)}$$

If $a_0(x)$, $a_1(x)$, and $g(x)$ are constants, that is, are not in fact functions of x, then

$$y_{x+1} = Ay_x + B$$

where A and B are constants and $A \neq 0$. ($B = 0$ if and only if $g = 0$ in the original equation.) The difference equation $y_{x+1} = Ay_x + B$ is the general linear first-order difference equation with constant coefficients.

The solution of this equation can be obtained by induction as follows:

$$y_1 = Ay_0 + B$$
$$y_2 = Ay_1 = A(Ay_0 + B) + B$$
$$= A^2 y_0 + AB + B$$
$$y_3 = Ay_2 = A(A^2 y_0 + AB + B) + B$$
$$= A^3 y_0 + A^2 B + AB + B$$

$$y_4 = Ay_3 = A(A^3 y_0 + A^2 B + AB + B) + B$$
$$= A^4 y_0 + A^3 B + A^2 B + AB + B$$

$$\vdots$$

$$y_x = A^x y_0 + B(1 + A + A^2 + A^3 + \cdots + A^{x-1})$$

and thus, noting that $1 + A + A^2 + A^3 + \cdots + A^{x-1}$ is a geometric series with sum $(1 - A^x)/(1 - A)$, the solution of $y_{x+1} = Ay_x + B$ is

$$y_x = A^x y_0 + B \frac{1 - A^x}{1 - A} \qquad \text{for } A \neq 1 \qquad x = 0, 1, 2, \ldots$$

$$y_x = y_0 + Bx \qquad\qquad\qquad \text{for } A = 1 \qquad x = 0, 1, 2, \ldots$$

This solution, obtained by induction, does in fact satisfy the equation $y_{x+1} = Ay_x + B$, since

For $A \neq 1$,

$$y_{x+1} = Ay_x + B$$

$$= A\left(A^x y_0 + B \frac{1 - A^x}{1 - A}\right) + B$$

$$= A^{x+1} y_0 + B\left(\frac{A - A^{x+1} + 1 - A}{1 - A}\right)$$

$$= A^{x+1} y_0 + B \frac{1 - A^{x+1}}{1 - A}$$

For $A = 1$,

$$y_{x+1} = y_x + B$$

$$= (y_0 + Bx) + B$$

$$= y_0 + B(x + 1)$$

There are three special cases of the difference equation $y_{x+1} = Ay_x + B$ which occur frequently in analyses of business and economic data.

1. First-order difference a constant:

$$y_{x+1} - y_x = B \text{ (special case: } A = 1)$$

Solution: $y_x = y_0 + Bx$

2. First-order difference proportional to the variable:

$$y_{x+1} - y_x = \alpha y_{x+1}\left(\text{special case: } A = \frac{1}{1 - \alpha}, B = 0\right)$$

Solution: $y_x = \left(\frac{1}{1 - \alpha}\right)^x y_0$

3. First-order difference a linear function of the variable:

$$y_{x+1} - y_x = \alpha y_{x+1} + \beta\left(\text{special case: } A = \frac{1}{1 - \alpha}, B = \frac{1}{1 - \alpha}\right)$$

Solution: $y_x = \left(\frac{1}{1 - \alpha}\right)^x y_0 + \frac{\beta}{\alpha}\left[\left(\frac{1}{1 - \alpha}\right)^x - 1\right]$

Examples of solutions of linear first-order difference equations with constant coefficients and of economic models in which they occur are given in the following sections.

EXAMPLE

Solve the equation $2y_{x+1} = 4y_x + 3$ and find the particular solution if $y_0 = \frac{1}{2}$.

$$2y_{x+1} = 4y_x + 3$$

$$y_{x+1} = 2y_x + \tfrac{3}{2}$$

$$y_x = 2^x y_0 + \frac{3}{2}\left(\frac{1 - 2^x}{-1}\right)$$

$$y_x = 2^x y_0 - \tfrac{3}{2}(1 - 2^x)$$

$$y_x = (y_0 + \tfrac{3}{2})2^x - \tfrac{3}{2}$$

If $y_0 = \frac{1}{2}$,

$$y_x = 2^{x+1} - \tfrac{3}{2}$$

EXAMPLE

Solve the equation $3y_{x+1} = 3y_x - 7$ and find the particular solution if $y_0 = 3$.

$$3y_{x+1} = 3y_x - 7$$

$$y_{x+1} = y_x - \tfrac{7}{3}x$$

$$y_x = y_0 - \tfrac{7}{3}x$$

If $y_0 = 3$,

$$y_x = 3 - \tfrac{7}{3}x$$

EXAMPLE

Solve the equation $6y_{x+1} + 2y_x = 0$ and find the particular solution if $y_0 = 2$.

$$6y_{x+1} + 2y_x = 0$$

$$y_{x+1} = -\tfrac{1}{3}y_x$$

$$y_x = (-\tfrac{1}{3})^x y_0$$

If $y_0 = 2$,

$$y_x = 2(-\tfrac{1}{3})^x$$

EXAMPLE

Solve the equation $3y_{x+1} - 9y_x + 8 = 0$ and find the particular solution if $y_0 = \frac{1}{3}$.

$$3y_{x+1} - 9y_x + 8 = 0$$

$$y_{x+1} = 3y_x - \tfrac{8}{3}$$

$$y_x = 3^x y_0 - \frac{8}{3}\left(\frac{1 - 3^x}{-2}\right)$$

$$y_x = 3^x y_0 + \tfrac{4}{3}(1 - 3^x)$$

$$y_x = (y_0 - \tfrac{4}{3})3^x + \tfrac{4}{3}$$

If $y_0 = \tfrac{4}{3}$,

$$y_x = \tfrac{4}{3} - 3^x$$

BEHAVIOR OF THE SOLUTION SEQUENCE

A sequence is a succession of terms formed according to some rule or, equivalently, a sequence is a function defined for positive integer values of the independent variable. The solution of a difference equation is a sequence. When the independent variable is time, this sequence is sometimes referred to as the time path of the dependent variable. For a linear first-order difference equation, the specification of y_0 determines or generates the solution sequence $y_0, y_1, y_2, y_3, \ldots$; each term is found from the difference equation

$$y_{x+1} = Ay_x + B \qquad x = 0, 1, 2, \ldots$$

or, equivalently, from its solution,

$$y_x = A^x y_0 + B\frac{1 - A^x}{1 - A} \qquad \text{for } A \neq 1 \qquad x = 0, 1, 2, \ldots$$

$$y_x = y_0 + Bx \qquad \text{for } A = 1 \qquad x = 0, 1, 2, \ldots$$

When A and B are given, specification of y_0 thus determines a solution sequence of real numbers.

The behavior of the solution sequence of a difference equation is of interest for many applications; this behavior depends on the values of y_0, A, and B, as shown in Table 6.1. A sketch typical of each type of behavior is given in Figure 6.1, labeled to match the corresponding case in the table.

Figure 6.1

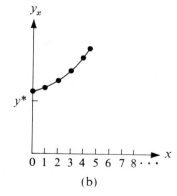

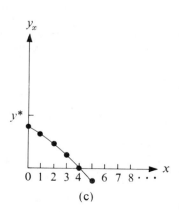

(a)   (b)   (c)

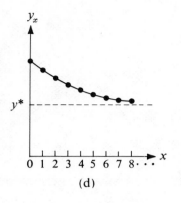

(d)

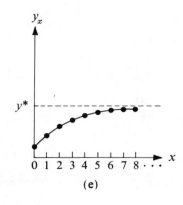

(e)

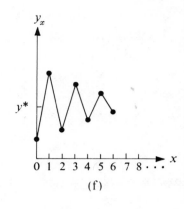

(f)

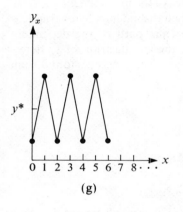

(g)

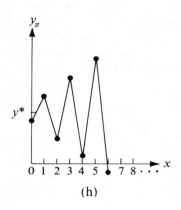

(h)

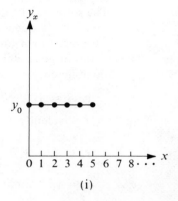

(i)

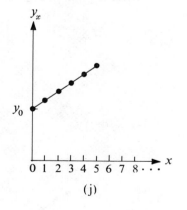

(j)

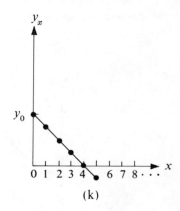

(k)

Table 6.1 Behavior of the Solution Sequence for $y_{x+1} = Ay_x + B$

Case	A	B	y_0	y_x, $x = 1, 2, \ldots$	Behavior of the solution sequence
(a)	$A \neq 1$		$y_0 = y^*$	$y_x = y^*$	Constant: $y_x = y^*$
(b)	$A > 1$		$y_0 > y^*$	$y_x > y^*$	Diverges to $+\infty$ (monotone increasing)
(c)	$A > 1$		$y_0 < y^*$	$y_x < y^*$	Diverges to $-\infty$ (monotone decreasing)
(d)	$0 < A < 1$		$y_0 > y^*$	$y_x > y^*$	Converges to y^* (monotone decreasing)
(e)	$0 < A < 1$		$y_0 < y^*$	$y_x < y^*$	Converges to y^* (monotone increasing)
(f)	$-1 < A < 0$		$y_0 \neq y^*$		Converges to y^* (damped oscillatory)
(g)	$A = -1$		$y_0 \neq y^*$		Diverges (oscillates finitely)
(h)	$A < -1$		$y_0 \neq y^*$		Diverges (oscillates infinitely)
(i)	$A = 1$	$B = 0$		$y_x = y_0$	Constant: $y_x = y_0$
(j)	$A = 1$	$B > 0$		$y_x > y_0$	Diverges to $+\infty$ (monotone increasing)
(k)	$A = 1$	$B < 0$		$y_x < y_0$	Diverges to $-\infty$ (monotone decreasing)

The results given in the table can be summarized in the following theorem.

THEOREM: The linear first-order difference equation

$$y_{x+1} = Ay_x + B \qquad x = 0, 1, 2, \ldots$$

has the solution

$$y_x = A^x(y_0 - y^*) + y^* \qquad \text{if } A \neq 1 \quad x = 0, 1, 2, \ldots$$

$$y_x = y_0 + Bx \qquad \text{if } A = 1 \quad x = 0, 1, 2, \ldots$$

where $y^* = B/(1 - A)$. If $-1 < A < 1$, the solution sequence converges to y^*; otherwise it diverges, unless $y_x = y_0$.

EXAMPLE

Solve each of the following difference equations, determine the behavior of the solution sequence, and calculate the first few values of the solution sequence.

(a) $6y_{x+1} + 2y_x - 3 = 0$, $y_0 = 1$.

$$y_{x+1} = -\tfrac{1}{3}y_x + \tfrac{1}{2}$$

$$y_x = \left(-\tfrac{1}{3}\right)^x y_0 + \frac{1}{2}\left(\frac{1 - \left(-\tfrac{1}{3}\right)^x}{1 - \left(-\tfrac{1}{3}\right)}\right)$$

$$= \left(-\tfrac{1}{3}\right)^x y_0 + \tfrac{3}{8}\left(1 - \left(-\tfrac{1}{3}\right)^x\right)$$

$$= \left(-\tfrac{1}{3}\right)^x \left(y_0 - \tfrac{3}{8}\right) + \tfrac{3}{8}$$

If $y_0 = 1$,

$$y_x = \tfrac{5}{8}\left(-\tfrac{1}{3}\right)^x + \tfrac{3}{8}$$

$A = -\frac{1}{3}$, $B = \frac{1}{2}$, $y^* = \frac{3}{8}$; case (f), so y_x converges to y^*, damped oscillatory. $y_0 = 1$, $y_1 = \frac{1}{6}$, $y_2 = \frac{4}{9}$, $y_3 = \frac{19}{54}$, $y_4 = \frac{31}{81}$, and so forth.

(b) $5y_{x+1} - 4y_x - 15 = 0$, $y_0 = 10$.

$$y_{x+1} = \frac{4}{5}y_x + 3$$

$$y_x = \left(\frac{4}{5}\right)^x y_0 + 3\left(\frac{1 - \left(\frac{4}{5}\right)^x}{1 - \frac{4}{5}}\right)$$

$$= \left(\frac{4}{5}\right)^x y_0 + 15\left(1 - \left(\frac{4}{5}\right)^x\right)$$

$$= \left(\frac{4}{5}\right)^x (y_0 - 15) + 15$$

If $y_0 = 10$,

$$y_x = 15 - 5\left(\frac{4}{5}\right)^x$$

$A = \frac{4}{5}$, $B = 3$, $y^* = 15$; case (e), so y_x converges to y^*, monotone increasing. $y_0 = 10$, $y_1 = 11$, $y_2 = 11\frac{4}{5}$, $y_3 = 12\frac{11}{25}$, $y_4 = 12\frac{119}{125}$, and so forth.

(c) $5y_{x+1} - 25y_x - 1 = 0$, $y_0 = 0$.

$$y_{x+1} = 5y_x + \frac{1}{5}$$

$$y_x = 5^x y_0 + \frac{1}{5}\left(\frac{1 - 5^x}{1 - 5}\right)$$

$$= 5^x y_0 - \frac{1}{20}(1 - 5^x)$$

$$= 5^x\left(y_0 + \frac{1}{20}\right) - \frac{1}{20}$$

If $y_0 = 0$,

$$y_x = \frac{1}{20}(5^x - 1)$$

$A = 5$, $B = \frac{1}{5}$, $y^* = -\frac{1}{20}$; case (b), so y_x diverges to $+\infty$, monotone increasing. $y_0 = 0$, $y_1 = \frac{1}{5}$, $y_2 = \frac{6}{5}$, $y_3 = \frac{31}{5}$, $y_4 = \frac{156}{5}$, and so forth.

EXAMPLE

If funds earn simple interest, the amount on deposit at any interest date is equal to the amount on deposit one period (usually a year) previously plus the interest earned in that period on the initial principal invested. If S_0 is the initial deposit, S_t is the amount on deposit after t periods, and r is the interest rate per period, then

$$S_{t+1} = S_t + rS_0 \qquad t = 0, 1, 2, \ldots$$

which has the solution

$$S_t = S_0(1 + tr) \qquad t = 0, 1, 2, \ldots$$

When the initial amount accumulates at compound interest, the interest earned during any period is computed on the total sum on deposit at the beginning of that period, rather than on the initial deposit, and

$$S_{t+1} = S_t + iS_t = (1 + i)S_t \qquad t = 0, 1, 2, \ldots$$

where i is the interest rate per conversion period; thus

$$S_t = (1 + i)^t S_0 \qquad t = 0, 1, 2, \ldots$$

The amount on deposit diverges to $+\infty$ linearly for simple interest [case (j)] and nonlinearly (more rapidly) for compound interest [case (b)].

EQUILIBRIUM AND STABILITY

If a difference equation has a constant function $y_x = y^*$ as its solution, then the value y^* of this function is called an *equilibrium* or *stationary* value of y_x. An equilibrium value y^*, or the corresponding difference equation, is said to be *stable* if every solution of the difference equation converges to y^*, independent of the initial conditions. This is the type of stability referred to in economic literature as "perfect stability of the first kind."

A displacement from the equilibrium value is equivalent to a new solution with different initial conditions, and thus a stable equilibrium can be defined as one for which *any* displacement from equilibrium is followed by a sequence of values of y which again converge to equilibrium.

THEOREM: For the difference equation

$$y_{x+1} = Ay_x + B$$

an equilibrium value of y is given by

$$y^* = \frac{B}{1 - A} \qquad \text{if } A \neq 1$$

and y^* is stable if and only if $-1 < A < 1$, unless y_x is constant.

Note that this theorem is closely related to the preceding theorem, which states that the solution sequence converges to y^* if $-1 < A < 1$ and diverges otherwise, unless $y_x = y_0$. Stable equilibrium occurs only for cases (a), (d), (e), (f), and (i) of Table 6.1.

PROBLEMS

Solve each of the following difference equations.

1. $3y_{x+1} = 2y_x + 3$
2. $2y_{x+1} + y_x - 3 = 0$
3. $y_{x+1} + 3y_x = 0$
4. $y_{x+1} + y_x - 2 = 0$

Solve each of the following difference equations, determine the behavior of the solution sequence, and calculate the first few values of the solution sequence.

5. $y_{x+1} - y_x - 10 = 0$, $y_0 = 2$
6. $y_{x+1} = 7y_x + 6$, $y_0 = 1$
7. $8y_{x+1} + 4y_x - 3 = 0$, $y_0 = \frac{1}{2}$
8. $16y_{x+1} - 6y_x = 1$, $y_0 = \frac{1}{10}$
9. $3y_{x+1} - 2y_x - 3 = 0$, $y_0 = 5$
10. $3y_{x+1} - y_x = \frac{6}{5}$, $y_0 = \frac{2}{3}$
11. $y_{x+1} = 3y_x - 1$, $y_0 = \frac{1}{2}$
12. $y_{x+1} + 3y_x + 1 = 0$, $y_0 = 1$
13. $2y_{x+1} - y_x = 2$, $y_0 = 4$
14. $y_{x+1} = y_x - 1$, $y_0 = 5$
15. $7y_{x+1} + 2y_x - 7 = 0$, $y_0 = 1$
16. $y_{x+1} + y_x + 2 = 0$, $y_0 = 3$
17. $15y_{x+1} - 10y_x - 3 = 0$, $y_0 = 1$
18. $5y_{x+1} - y_x - 60 = 0$, $y_0 = 15$
19. $y_{x+1} + 4y_x + 12 = 0$, $y_0 = 6$
20. $8y_{x+1} + y_x - 4 = 0$, $y_0 = \frac{1}{3}$
21. $4y_{x+1} - y_x - 3 = 0$, $y_0 = \frac{1}{2}$
22. $4y_{x+1} + 3y_x - 4 = 0$, $y_0 = 1$
23. $3y_{x+1} - 2y_x - 6 = 0$, $y_0 = 4$
24. $9y_{x+1} + 5y_x - 18 = 0$, $y_0 = 1$

Answers to Odd-Numbered Problems

1. $y_x = (\frac{2}{3})^x(y_0 - 3) + 3$
3. $y_x = (-3)^x y_0$
5. $y_x = 2 + 10x$; monotone increasing, diverges to $+\infty$; $y_0 = 2$, $y_1 = 12$, $y_2 = 22$, $y_3 = 32$, $y_4 = 42$, $y_5 = 52$
7. $y_x = \frac{1}{4}(-\frac{1}{2})^x + \frac{1}{4}$; damped oscillatory, converges to $y^* = \frac{1}{4}$; $y_0 = \frac{1}{2}$, $y_1 = \frac{1}{8}$, $y_2 = \frac{5}{16}$, $y_3 = \frac{7}{32}$, $y_4 = \frac{17}{64}$, $y_5 = \frac{31}{128}$
9. $y_x = 2(\frac{2}{3})^x + 3$; monotone decreasing, converges to $y^* = 3$; $y_0 = 5$, $y_1 = 4\frac{1}{3}$, $y_2 = 3\frac{8}{9}$, $y_3 = 3\frac{16}{27}$, $y_4 = 3\frac{32}{81}$, $y_5 = 3\frac{64}{243}$

11. $y_x = \frac{1}{2}$; constant
13. $y_x = 2(\frac{1}{2})^x + 2$; monotone decreasing, converges to $y^* = 2$; $y_0 = 4$, $y_1 = 3$, $y_2 = \frac{5}{2}$, $y_3 = \frac{9}{4}$, $y_4 = \frac{17}{8}$, $y_5 = \frac{33}{16}$
15. $y_x = \frac{2}{9}(-\frac{7}{7})^x + \frac{7}{9}$; damped oscillatory, converges to $y^* = \frac{7}{9}$; $y_0 = 1$, $y_1 = \frac{5}{7}$, $y_2 = \frac{39}{49}$, $y_3 = \frac{265}{343}$, $y_4 = \frac{1871}{2401}$, $y_5 = \frac{13065}{16807}$
17. $y_x = \frac{2}{3}(\frac{2}{3})^x + \frac{1}{3}$; monotone decreasing, converges to $y^* = \frac{1}{3}$; $y_0 = 1$, $y_1 = \frac{13}{15}$, $y_2 = \frac{7}{9}$, $y_3 = \frac{97}{135}$, $y_4 = \frac{55}{81}$, $y_5 = \frac{29}{45}$
19. $y_x = \frac{42}{5}(-4)^x - \frac{12}{5}$; divergent, oscillates infinitely; $y_0 = 6$, $y_1 = -36$, $y_2 = 132$, $y_3 = -540$, $y_4 = 2148$, $y_5 = -8604$
21. $y_x = -(\frac{1}{2})(\frac{1}{4})^x + 1$; monotone increasing, converges to $y^* = 1$; $y_0 = \frac{1}{2}$, $y_1 = \frac{7}{8}$, $y_2 = \frac{31}{32}$, $y_3 = \frac{127}{128}$, $y_4 = \frac{511}{512}$, $y_5 = \frac{2047}{2048}$
23. $y_x = -2(\frac{2}{3})^x + 6$; monotone increasing, converges to $y^* = 6$; $y_0 = 4$, $y_1 = \frac{14}{3}$, $y_2 = \frac{46}{9}$, $y_3 = \frac{146}{27}$, $y_4 = \frac{454}{81}$, $y_5 = \frac{1394}{243}$

6.5 Applications of Difference Equations in Economic Models

The following very simple economic models are examples of the use of first-difference equations to express the dependence of the value of a variable on its value in the preceding period. The Harrod model, the general cobweb model, a consumption model, and an income-consumption-investment model are discussed.

THE HARROD MODEL
The following model for national income analysis was proposed by R. F. Harrod.

$$S_t = \alpha Y_t$$

$$I_t = \beta(Y_t - Y_{t-1})$$

$$S_t = I_t$$

$$Y_0 = Y_0 \text{ (known value at } t = 0)$$

$$\alpha > 0 \qquad \beta > 0$$

where S is saving, I is investment, Y is income, and each of these variables is a function of time t.

From the first three equations of the model, the difference equation

$$\alpha Y_t = \beta(Y_t - Y_{t-1})$$

is obtained for solution and

$$Y_t = \left(\frac{\beta}{\beta - \alpha}\right) Y_{t-1}$$

$$Y_t = \left(\frac{\beta}{\beta - \alpha}\right)^t Y_0$$

$$I_t = S_t = \alpha\left(\frac{\beta}{\beta - \alpha}\right)^t Y_0$$

Assuming $Y_0 > 0$, the behavior of the solution sequence depends on the value of the constant $\beta/(\beta - \alpha)$. Since Y represents income and is assumed to be nonnegative,

$$\frac{\beta}{\beta - \alpha} \geq 0$$

and from the model, $\alpha > 0$, $\beta > 0$, and thus

$$\frac{\beta}{\beta - \alpha} > 1$$

Since $Y^* = 0$, the sequence $\{Y_t\}$ is monotone increasing, diverging to $+\infty$ [case (b)]. Since $\alpha > 0$, the sequences $\{I_t\}$ and $\{S_t\}$ are also monotone increasing, diverging to $+\infty$. None of the variables of this model have equilibrium values.

NOTE: The Harrod model discussed above is one of the classical models used to study the growth of national income in an expanding economy; models for which the solution sequences do not diverge have also been considered.

THE GENERAL COBWEB MODEL

The adjustment of supply and demand can be studied using the following model.

Supply: $\quad q_t = \alpha + \beta p_{t-1}$

Demand: $\quad p_t = \gamma + \delta q_t$

$\quad\quad q_0 = q_0 \quad$ (known value at $t = 0$)

$\quad\quad \beta > 0, \delta < 0$

where p is price, q is quantity, and both are functions of time t. Substituting the second equation into the first equation,

$$q_t = \alpha + \beta\gamma + \beta\delta q_{t-1}$$

and, substituting the first equation into the second equation,

$$p_t = \gamma + \alpha\delta + \beta\delta p_{t-1}$$

These difference equations can be solved in the usual way; however, it is the behavior of the solution sequence that is of interest. Since $\beta > 0$, $\delta < 0$, their product $\beta\delta < 0$, and the solution sequence are thus always oscillatory. The equilibrium point is

$$(p^*, q^*) = \left(\frac{\gamma + \alpha\delta}{1 - \beta\delta}, \frac{\alpha + \beta\gamma}{1 - \beta\delta} \right)$$

If $-1 < \beta\delta < 0$, the sequences $\{p_t\}$ and $\{q_t\}$ are damped and converge to (p^*, q^*); if $\beta\delta = -1$, the sequences oscillate finitely; if $\beta\delta < -1$, the sequences oscillate infinitely. Thus the equilibrium is stable only if $-1 < \beta\delta < 0$.

NOTE: If the supply curve is written so that its slope is with respect to the quantity variable, the slope is $1/\beta$. Thus the equilibrium is stable if and only if the slope of the demand curve is less (in numerical value) than the slope of the supply curve.

CONSUMPTION MODEL

The following simple model for consumption has been proposed.

$$C_t + S_t = Y_t$$

$$Y_t = \alpha S_{t-1}$$

$$C_t = \gamma Y_t$$

$$Y_0 = Y_0 \quad \text{(known value at } t = 0)$$

$$\alpha > 0 \quad\quad 0 < \gamma < 1$$

where C is consumption, S is saving, Y is income, and each of these variables is a function of time, t, and γ is the marginal propensity to consume.

Substituting the second and third equations in the first equation of the model, the difference equation

$$Y_{t+1} = \alpha(1 - \gamma)Y_t$$

is obtained for solution and

$$Y_t = (\alpha - \alpha\gamma)^t Y_0$$
$$C_t = \gamma Y_t$$

so

$$C_t = \gamma(\alpha - \alpha\gamma)^t Y_0$$

and, since $C_0 = \gamma Y_0$,

$$C_t = (\alpha - \alpha\gamma)^t C_0$$
$$S_t = Y_t - C_t$$

so

$$S_t = (1 - \gamma)(\alpha - \alpha\gamma)^t Y_0$$

and, since $S_0 = Y_0 - C_0 = (1 - \gamma)Y_0$,

$$S_t = (\alpha - \alpha\gamma)^t S_0$$

Since $0 < \gamma < 1$, $\alpha - \alpha\gamma > 0$; the sequences $\{Y_t\}$, $\{C_t\}$, and $\{S_t\}$ are monotone increasing and diverge to $+\infty$ if $\alpha(1 - \gamma) > 1$, monotone decreasing and converge to $y^* = 0$ if $\alpha(1 - \gamma) < 1$, and constant at $Y^* = 0$ if $\alpha(1 - \gamma) = 1$.

INCOME-CONSUMPTION-INVESTMENT MODEL

When changes over time are considered to occur periodically rather than continuously, the income-consumption-investment model stated in terms of differential equations in Chapter 5 can be stated in terms of difference equations, as follows.

$$C_t = \alpha Y_t + \beta$$
$$I_t = \gamma Y_t + g$$
$$\Delta Y_{t-1} = \theta[C_{t-1} + I_{t-1} - Y_{t-1}]$$
$$Y_0 = Y_0$$
$$0 < \alpha < 1 \qquad 0 < \gamma < 1 \qquad 0 < \theta < 1$$

Rewriting the third equation and substituting the first and second equations into it,

$$\begin{aligned}
Y_t - Y_{t-1} &= \theta[C_{t-1} + I_{t-1} - Y_{t-1}] \\
Y_t &= \theta[C_{t-1} + I_{t-1}] + (1 - \theta)Y_{t-1} \\
&= \theta[\alpha Y_{t-1} + \beta + \gamma Y_{t-1} + g] + (1 - \theta)Y_{t-1} \\
&= [\theta(\alpha + \gamma) + (1 - \theta)]Y_{t-1} + \theta(\beta + g) \\
&= [\theta(\alpha + \gamma) + (1 - \theta)]^t Y_0 + \theta(\beta + g)\frac{1 - [\theta(\alpha + \gamma) + (1 - \theta)]^t}{1 - [\theta(\alpha + \gamma) + (1 - \theta)]}
\end{aligned}$$

The solution is stable if

$$-1 < \theta(\alpha + \gamma) + (1 - \theta) < 1$$

$$-\frac{1}{\theta} < \alpha + \gamma + \frac{1}{\theta} - 1 < \frac{1}{\theta}$$

$$1 - \frac{2}{\theta} < \alpha + \gamma < 1$$

Since $0 < \theta < 1$ and $\alpha + \gamma > 0$, the left-hand part of the inequality $1 - (2/\theta) < \alpha + \gamma$ is satisfied. Thus the stability condition is $\alpha + \gamma < 1$, as for the differential equations form of the model.

PROBLEMS

1. In the Cobweb model, if the supply curve has negative slope, state the conditions for stable equilibrium.
2. Derive the solution of the Kahn model:

   $$C_t = \alpha Y_{t-1} + \beta$$

   $$Y_t = C_t + I_t$$

   where C is consumption, Y is income, and I is investment.
3. Solve the following model, determine the behavior of the solution sequences, and state any additional "logical" restrictions on the parameters.

   $$S_t = \alpha Y_t + \beta$$

   $$I_t = \gamma(Y_t - Y_{t-1})$$

   $$S_t = \delta I_t$$

   $$Y_0 = Y_0$$

   $$\alpha > 0 \qquad \beta > 0 \qquad \gamma > 0 \qquad \delta > 0$$

   where S is savings, Y is income, and I is investment.
4. Solve the following simplified Metzler inventory model:

   $$y_t = u_t + v_0$$

   $$u_t = \beta y_{t-1}$$

   $$y_0 = y_0$$

   $$0 < \beta < 1$$

   where y is income produced, u is the number of units produced for sale, with units of measurement appropriately chosen, v_0 is the constant noninduced investment, and β is the marginal propensity to consume of one year's consumption with respect to the previous year's income.
5. Consider the model

   $$p_t = 2 - q_t$$

   $$q_{t+1} = p_{t+1}^* + 1$$

   $$p_{t+1}^* = \alpha \rho_{t+1} + (1 - \alpha)p_t$$

   $$p_0 = p_0$$

   $$0 \le \alpha \le 1$$

   where q is the quantity supplied, p is the actual price, p^* is the supplier's estimated price for the next period, and ρ is a public forecast for the price. Note that $\alpha = 1$ implies that the suppliers have perfect confidence in the public forecast; $\alpha = 0$ implies they have no confidence in the public forecast. Defining Δ_{t+1} by the equation

$$\Delta_{t+1} = p^*_{t+1} - p_{t+1}$$

show that $\Delta_t = 1 - 2p_t$.

6. Solve the following model of the growth of national income in an expanding economy:

$$Y_t = C_t + I_t$$

$$C_t = \alpha + \beta Y_t$$

$$Y_{t+1} - Y_t = \gamma I_t$$

$$Y_0 = Y_0 \qquad C_0 = C_0 \qquad I_0 = I_0$$

$$\alpha \geq 0 \qquad 0 < \beta < 1 \qquad \gamma > 0$$

where Y is income, C is consumption, and I is investment.

7. Consider the following model of a market:

$$Q_{dt} = \alpha - \beta P_t \qquad \text{(demand)}$$

$$Q_{st} = -\gamma + \delta P^*_t \qquad \text{(supply)}$$

$$Q_{dt} = Q_{st}$$

$$\alpha > 0 \qquad \beta > 0 \qquad \gamma > 0 \qquad \delta > 0$$

where P^*_t denotes the expected price in period t and sellers have an "adaptive" price expectation so that

$$P^*_t = P^*_{t-1} + \eta(P_{t-1} - P^*_{t-1}) \qquad 0 < \eta < 1$$

a. Show that the model can be represented by the first-order difference equation

$$P_{t+1} - \left(1 - \eta - \frac{\eta\delta}{\beta}\right)P_t = \frac{\eta(\alpha + \gamma)}{\beta}$$

Hint: Solve the supply equation for P^*_t and note that $Q_{st} = Q_{dt} = \alpha - \beta P_t$.

b. Determine the nature of the solution sequence.

c. Show that the solution sequence, if oscillatory, converges only if $1 - \frac{2}{\eta} < -\frac{\delta}{\beta}$.

8. In the Harrod model, graph $\{Y_t\}$ for each of the following cases and comment on the plausibility of each.

Case	α	β	Y_0
(a)	$\frac{1}{5}$	2	100
(b)	$-\frac{1}{5}$	2	100
(c)	-4	2	100
(d)	$\frac{1}{5}$	2	-100

Answers to Odd-Numbered Problems

1. If $\delta < 0$ and $\beta < 0$, the approach to equilibrium will not be oscillatory and $|\delta\beta| < 1$ (the stability condition) indicates that the demand curve must be flatter than the supply curve.

3. $Y_t = \left(\dfrac{\delta\gamma}{\delta\gamma - \alpha}\right)^t \left(Y_0 + \dfrac{\beta}{\alpha}\right) - \dfrac{\beta}{\alpha}$ approaches $+\infty$

$S_t = \left(\dfrac{\delta\gamma}{\delta\gamma - \alpha}\right)^t (\alpha Y_0 + \beta)$ approaches $+\infty$

$I_t = \left(\dfrac{\delta\gamma}{\delta\gamma - \alpha}\right)^t \left(\dfrac{\alpha}{\delta} Y_0 + \dfrac{\beta}{\delta}\right)$ approaches $+\infty$

$\delta\gamma > \alpha$

7. b. $0 < 1 - \eta - \dfrac{\eta\delta}{\beta} < 1$ converges (nonoscillatory)

$-1 < 1 - \eta - \dfrac{\eta\delta}{\beta} < 0$ converges (oscillatory)

$1 - \eta - \dfrac{\eta\delta}{\beta} < -1$ diverges (oscillatory)

$1 - \eta - \dfrac{\eta\delta}{\beta} = -1$ diverges (oscillatory)

6.6 Linear Second-Order Difference Equations with Constant Coefficients

The method of solution for linear second-order difference equations with constant coefficients and the behavior of the solution sequence are discussed in this section. Special methods of solution are required when second-order difference equations are nonhomogeneous; these methods are considered and equilibrium and stability are defined.

The general second-order difference equation with constant coefficients can be written in the form

$$y_{x+2} + A_1 y_{x+1} + A_2 y_x = g(x)$$

Consider first the special case $g(x) = 0$:

$$y_{x+2} + A_1 y_{x+1} + A_2 y_x = 0$$

An equation whose constant term is zero is sometimes said to be *homogeneous*. Thus $y_{x+2} + A_1 y_{x+1} + A_2 y_x = 0$ is the general homogeneous second-order linear difference equation with constant coefficients. The definition of a homogeneous equation should not be confused with the definition of a homogeneous function; the two uses of the word homogeneous are not related.

In order to obtain the solution of

$$y_{x+2} + A_1 y_{x+1} + A_2 y_x = 0$$

form the auxiliary equation

$$m^2 + A_1 m + A_2 = 0$$

and solve for its roots, using the quadratic formula (if necessary):

$$m_1 = \dfrac{-A_1 + \sqrt{A_1^2 - 4A_2}}{2}$$

$$m_2 = \dfrac{-A_1 - \sqrt{A_1^2 - 4A_2}}{2}$$

These roots m_1 and m_2 may be real and unequal, real and equal, or complex (involving the square root of a negative number). The form of the solution of the equation $y_{x+2} + A_1 y_{x+1} + A_2 y_x = 0$ depends on the nature of the roots m_1 and m_2, as summarized below. The general solution of a second-order difference equation includes two arbitrary constants and a particular solution is specified by two boundary conditions, that is, by two consecutive values of y.

Case 1. m_1 and m_2 are real and unequal ($m_1 \neq m_2$)
    solution: $y_x = C_1 m_1^x + C_2 m_2^x$

Case 2. m_1 and m_2 are real and equal ($m_1 = m_2 = m$)
    solution: $y_x = C_1 m^x + C_2 x m^x$

Case 3. m_1 and m_2 are complex ($m_1 = a + bi$, $m_2 = a - bi$ where $i = \sqrt{-1}$)
    solution: $y_x = r^x(C_1 \cos \theta x + C_2 \sin \theta x)$, where $r = \sqrt{a^2 + b^2}$ and θ is the angle having $\tan = a/b$; alternatively, θ is the angle having $\sin \theta = a/r$, $\cos \theta = b/r$.

Note that a and b can be interchanged in these definitions, since the trigonometric functions are periodic. For convenience, the solution is usually written for θ in the first quadrant.

EXAMPLE

Obtain the general solution for the difference equation

$$y_{x+2} - 5y_{x+1} + 6y_x = 0$$

and the particular solution if $y_0 = 2$, $y_1 = 5$.
    The auxiliary equation is

$$m^2 - 5m + 6 = 0$$

and

$$m_1 = \frac{5 + \sqrt{25 - 24}}{2} = 3$$

$$m_2 = \frac{5 - \sqrt{25 - 24}}{2} = 2$$

Thus the general solution is

$$y_x = C_1 3^x + C_2 2^x$$

If $y_0 = 2$, $y_1 = 5$,

$$2 = C_1 + C_2$$

$$5 = 3C_1 + 2C_2$$

$$C_2 = 1$$

$$C_1 = 1$$

and the particular solution is

$$y_x = 3^x + 2^x$$

EXAMPLE

Obtain the general solution for the difference equation

$$y_{x+2} - 4y_{x+1} + 4y_x = 0$$

and the particular solution if $y_0 = 1$, $y_1 = 6$.
The auxiliary equation is

$$m^2 - 4m + 4 = 0$$

and

$$m_1 = \frac{4 + \sqrt{16 - 16}}{2} = 2$$

$$m_2 = \frac{4 - \sqrt{16 - 16}}{2} = 2$$

Thus the general solution is

$$y_x = C_1 2^x + C_2 x 2^x$$

If $y_0 = 1$, $y_1 = 6$,

$$1 = C_1 + 0$$

$$6 = 2C_1 + 2C_2$$

$$C_1 = 1$$

$$C_2 = 2$$

and the particular solution is

$$y_x = 2^x + x2^{x+1}$$

EXAMPLE

Obtain the general solution for the difference equation

$$y_{x+2} - y_{x+1} + \tfrac{1}{2}y_x = 0$$

and the particular solution if $y_0 = 3$, $y_1 = \tfrac{1}{2}$.
The auxiliary equation is

$$m^2 - m + \tfrac{1}{2} = 0$$

and

$$m_1 = \frac{1 + \sqrt{1 - 2}}{2} = \tfrac{1}{2} + \tfrac{1}{2}i$$

$$m_2 = \frac{1 - \sqrt{1 - 2}}{2} = \tfrac{1}{2} - \tfrac{1}{2}i$$

$$r = \sqrt{(\tfrac{1}{2})^2 + (\tfrac{1}{2})^2} = \frac{\sqrt{2}}{2}$$

$$\tan \theta = 1$$

$$\theta = \tfrac{1}{4}\pi$$

Thus the general solution is

$$y_x = \left(\frac{\sqrt{2}}{2}\right)^x (C_1 \cos \tfrac{1}{4}\pi x + C_2 \sin \tfrac{1}{4}\pi x)$$

If $y_0 = 3$, $y_1 = \tfrac{5}{2}$,

$$3 = (1)[(C_1)(1) + (C_2)(0)]$$

$$C_1 = 3$$

$$\frac{5}{2} = \frac{\sqrt{2}}{2}\left[3\left(\frac{\sqrt{2}}{2}\right) + C_2\left(\frac{\sqrt{2}}{2}\right)\right]$$

$$\tfrac{5}{2} = \tfrac{3}{2} + \tfrac{1}{2}C_2$$

$$C_2 = 2$$

and the particular solution is

$$y_x = \left(\frac{\sqrt{2}}{2}\right)^x (3 \cos \tfrac{1}{4}\pi x + 2 \sin \tfrac{1}{4}\pi x)$$

BEHAVIOR OF THE SOLUTION SEQUENCE

The behavior of the solution sequence depends on both the difference equation and the initial conditions; the roots of the auxiliary equation indicate the limiting behavior of the solution sequence as follows.

Case 1. Real roots, $m_1 \neq m_2$

If m_1 is the root with the greater absolute value, that is, $|m_1| > |m_2|$, then the limiting behavior of the solution sequence $\{C_1 m_1^x + C_2 m_2^x\}$ is the same as that of $\{C_1 m_1^x\}$, provided $C_1 \neq 0$.

This can be shown by writing

$$C_1 m_1^x + C_2 m_2^x = m_1^x [C_1 + C_2(m_2/m_1)^x]$$

Since $-1 < m_2/m_1 < 1$, $(m_2/m_1)^x \to 0$ as $x \to \infty$ and

$$\frac{C_1 m_1^x}{C_1 m_1^x + C_2 m_2^x} = \frac{C_1}{C_1 + C_2(m_2/m_1)^x} \to \frac{C_1}{C_1} = 1 \qquad \text{as } x \to \infty$$

Thus the limiting behavior of $\{C_1 m_1^x + C_2 m_2^x\}$ is the same as the limiting behavior of $\{C_1 m_1^x\}$ if $|m_1| > |m_2|$. The limiting behavior of $\{C_1 m_1^x\}$ is discussed in the preceding sections concerning solution sequences of first-order difference equations. This limiting behavior can be summarized in the notation of the present section as follows.

If $|m_1| \leq 1$, the sequence converges
If $|m_1| > 1$, the sequence diverges
If $-1 < m_1 < 0$, the sequence is damped oscillatory
If $m < -1$, the sequence oscillates infinitely

If $C_1 = 0$, the solution sequence is $\{C_2 m_2^x\}$ and similar statements apply to this sequence. Note that if $C_1 = 0$, $y_0 = C_2$ and $y_1 = C_2 m_2$. Thus $C_1 = 0$ implies boundary conditions which specify a particular solution.

Case 2. Real roots, $m_1 = m_2 = m$

The solution sequence is $\{(C_1 + C_2 x)m^x\}$, which diverges if $|m| > 1$ unless $C_1 = C_2 = 0$ and also diverges if $|m| = 1$ unless $C_2 = 0$. If $|m| < 1$, the sequence $\{xm^x\}$ converges to zero and $\{(C_1 + C_2 x)m^x\}$ also converges to zero. If m is negative, the sequence is oscillatory.

Case 3. Complex roots, $m_1 = a + bi$, $m_2 = a - bi$

The solution sequence is oscillatory; it converges to zero if $0 < \sqrt{a^2 + b^2} < 1$ and diverges if $\sqrt{a^2 + b^2} > 1$.

A complete classification of the solution sequences of the second-order linear homogeneous difference equation $y_{x+2} + A_1 y_{x+1} + A_2 y_x = 0$ is somewhat involved, since for exceptional initial values C_1 or C_2 or both are zero. There is one case in which the solution sequence for a homogeneous second-order linear difference equation converges to zero for every possible pair of initial values, as summarized in the following theorem.

THEOREM: If $\rho = \max\left(|m_1|, |m_2|\right)$, where m_1 and m_2 are the roots of the auxiliary equation of the homogeneous second-order difference equation,

$$y_{x+2} + A_1 y_{x+1} + A_2 y_x = 0$$

then $\rho < 1$ is a necessary and sufficient condition for the solution sequence $\{y_x\}$ to converge with limit 0 for all initial values y_0 and y_1.

More specifically, the definition of ρ is as follows.

Case 1. m_1 and m_2 real and unequal

$$\rho = \max\left(|m_1|, |m_2|\right)$$

Case 2. m_1 and m_2 real and equal, $m_1 = m_2 = m$

$$\rho = |m|$$

Case 3. m_1 and m_2 complex, $m_1 = a + bi$, $m_2 = a - bi$

$$\rho = \sqrt{a^2 + b^2}$$

EXAMPLE

In the preceding example the general solution for the difference equation $y_{x+2} - 5y_{x+1} + 6y_x = 0$ is found to be

$$y_x = C_1 3^x + C_2 2^x$$

and, since $m_1 = 3$ and $m_2 = 2$, $\rho > 1$ and the solution sequence diverges, as can be seen from the first few values of the particular solution $y_x = 3^x + 2^x$: $y_0 = 2$, $y_1 = 5$, $y_2 = 13$, $y_3 = 35$, $y_4 = 97$, $y_5 = 275$, and so forth.

In another previous example, the general solution for the difference equation $y_{x+2} - 4y_{x+1} + 4y_x = 0$ is found to be

$$y_x = C_1 2^x + C_2 x 2^x$$

and, since $m_1 = m_2 = 2$, $\rho > 1$ and the solution sequence diverges, as can be seen from the first few values of the particular solution $y_x = 2^x + x2^{x+1}$: $y_0 = 1$, $y_1 = 6$, $y_2 = 20$, $y_3 = 56$, $y_4 = 144$, $y_5 = 352$, and so forth.

In another previous example, the general solution for the difference equation $y_{x+2} - y_{x+1} + \frac{1}{2}y_x = 0$ is found to be

$$y_x = \left(\frac{\sqrt{2}}{2}\right)^x (C_1 \cos \tfrac{1}{4}\pi x + C_2 \sin \tfrac{1}{4}\pi x)$$

and $\rho = \sqrt{2}/2 < 1$, so the solution sequence is oscillatory and converges to zero, as can be seen from the first few values of the particular solution

$$y_x = \left(\frac{\sqrt{2}}{2}\right)^x (3 \cos \tfrac{1}{4}\pi x + 2 \sin \tfrac{1}{4}\pi x)$$

$y_0 = 3$, $y_1 = \frac{5}{2}$, $y_2 = 1$, $y_3 = -\frac{1}{4}$, $y_4 = -\frac{3}{4}$, $y_5 = -\frac{5}{8}$, and so forth.

NONHOMOGENEOUS SECOND-ORDER DIFFERENCE EQUATIONS

If the second-order linear homogeneous difference equation

$$y_{x+2} + A_1 y_{x+1} + A_2 y_x = 0$$

has the general solution y_x, then the second-order linear nonhomogeneous difference equation

$$y_{x+2} + A_1 y_{x+1} + A_2 y_x = g(x)$$

has the general solution $y_x + y_p$, where y_p is any particular solution of the nonhomogeneous equation.

Unfortunately, there is no general rule for determining y_p. The form of y_p depends on the form of $g(x)$; for simpler forms, y_p is similar to $g(x)$, but there are many special cases.

When $g(x)$ is a constant, y_p can be determined quite easily. Suppose $g(x)$ is a constant, K, that is,

$$y_{x+2} + A_1 y_{x+1} + A_2 y_x = K$$

First try a solution of the form: y_p equals a constant; say, $y_p = k$. If the solution $y_p = k$ satisfies the difference equation, then

$$k + A_1 k + A_2 k = K$$

and

$$k = \frac{K}{1 + A_1 + A_2}$$

Thus $y_p = K/(1 + A_1 + A_2)$ is a particular solution of the difference equation $y_{x+2} + A_1 y_{x+1} + A_2 y_x = K$, unless $1 + A_1 + A_2 = 0$.

If $1 + A_1 + A_2 = 0$, try a solution of the form $y_p = kx$. Then

$$k(x + 2) + A_1 k(x + 1) + A_2 kx = K$$

$$k(1 + A_1 + A_2)x + k(2 + A_1) = K$$

But $1 + A_1 + A_2 = 0$, and thus

$$k = \frac{K}{A_1 + 2}$$

and $y_p = K/(A_1 + 2)$, unless $1 + A_1 + A_2 = 0$ and $A_1 + 2 = 0$.

If both $1 + A_1 + A_2 = 0$ and $A_1 = -2$, that is, if $A_1 = -2$ and $A_2 = 1$, then try a solution of the form $y_p = kx^2$. It can be verified that, in this case, $y_p = (K/2)x^2$. Note that this solution is appropriate only for the difference equation $y_{x+2} - 2y_{x+1} + y_x = K$. Except for this one case, if $g(x)$ is a constant, the difference equation $y_{x+2} + A_1 y_{x+1} + A_2 y_x = g(x)$ has a particular solution, y_p, which is a constant.

In summary, when $g(x)$ is constant, the difference equation $y_{x+2} + A_1 y_{x+1} + A_2 y_x = g(x)$ has a particular solution as follows:

$$y_p = \frac{K}{1 + A_1 + A_2} \qquad \text{if } 1 + A_1 + A_2 \neq 0$$

$$y_p = \frac{K}{A_1 + 2} \qquad \begin{array}{l} \text{if } 1 + A_1 + A_2 = 0 \\ A_1 + 2 \neq 0 \end{array}$$

$$y_p = \frac{K}{2} x^2 \qquad \begin{array}{l} \text{if } 1 + A_1 + A_2 = 0 \\ A_1 + 2 = 0 \\ \text{(that is, if } A_1 = -2, A_2 = 1) \end{array}$$

EXAMPLE

Find the general solution of the equation

$$y_{x+2} - 6y_{x+1} + 8 = 9$$

and a particular solution if $y_0 = 10$, $y_1 = 25$.

The auxiliary equation of the homogeneous equation is

$$m^2 - 6m + 8 = 0$$

$$(m - 4)(m - 2) = 0$$

$$m_1 = 4$$

$$m_2 = 2$$

The general solution of the homogeneous equation is thus

$$y_x = C_1 4^x + C_2 2^x$$

and the general solution of the nonhomogeneous equation is

$$y_x = C_1 4^x + C_2 2^x + y_p$$

where $y_p = K/(1 + A_1 + A_2) = 9/(1 - 6 + 8) = 3$ and thus

$$y_x = C_1 4^x + C_2 2^x + 3$$

If $y_0 = 10$, $y_1 = 25$,

$$C_1 + C_2 = 10 - 3 = 7$$

$$4C_1 + 2C_2 = 25 - 3 = 22$$

$$2C_1 = 8$$

$$C_1 = 4$$

$$C_2 = 3$$

and the particular solution is

$$y_x = 4^{x+1} + (3)2^x + 3$$

EXAMPLE

Find the general solution of the equation

$$y_{x+2} + 3y_{x+1} - 4 = 10$$

and a particular solution if $y_0 = 5$, $y_1 = 20$.

The auxiliary equation of the homogeneous equation is

$$m^2 + 3m - 4 = 0$$

$$(m + 4)(m - 1) = 0$$

$$m_1 = -4$$

$$m_2 = 1$$

The general solution of the homogeneous equation is thus

$$y_x = C_1(-4)^x + C_2(1)^x$$

and the general solution of the nonhomogeneous equation is

$$y_x = C_1(-4)^x + C_2 + y_p$$

where $y_p = K/(A_1 + 2) = 10/5 = 2$, since $1 + A_1 + A_2 = 1 + 3 - 4 = 0$. Thus

$$y_x = C_1(-4)^x + C_2 + 2$$

If $y_0 = 5$, $y_1 = 20$,

$$C_1 + C_2 = 5 - 2 = 3$$

$$-4C_1 + C_2 = 20 - 2 = 18$$

$$-5C_1 = 15$$

$$C_1 = -3$$

$$C_2 = 6$$

and the particular solution is

$$y_x = -3(-4)^x + 8$$

Particular solutions of nonhomogeneous difference equations for which $g(x)$ is not constant, but is in fact a function of x, can be obtained similarly by examining trial solutions. However, this procedure may be quite tedious when $g(x)$ is not constant; these cases are not discussed here.

EQUILIBRIUM AND STABILITY

If a nonhomogeneous difference equation is of the form $y_{x+2} + A_1 y_{x+1} + A_2 y_x = K$, it can be shown that the solution sequence, of the corresponding homogeneous equation converges to zero if and only if $2 \pm A_1 > 1 - A_2 > 0$, which implies that $1 + A_1 + A_2 \neq 0$. Thus the solution sequence of the homogeneous equation converges to zero only when the nonhomogeneous equation has a particular solution $y_p = K/(1 + A_1 + A_2)$.

If the solution sequence of the corresponding homogeneous equation converges to zero, the solution of the nonhomogeneous equation $y_{x+2} + A_1 y_{x+1} + A_2 y_x = K$ converges to $K/(1 + A_1 + A_2)$; if the solution of the corresponding homogeneous equation diverges, the solution of the nonhomogeneous equation also diverges.

If the equation $y_{x+2} + A_1 y_{x+1} + A_2 y_x = K$ has a particular solution $y_p = K/(1 + A_1 + A_2)$, then y_p is an *equilibrium or stationary value of y*, denoted y^*.

An equilibrium value has the property that if two consecutive values of a solution of the equation $y_{x+2} + A_1 y_{x+1} + A_2 y_x = K$ are equal to y^*, then all succeeding values are equal to y^*. Substituting $y_x = y_{x+1} = y^* = K/(1 + A_1 + A_2)$ into $y_{x+2} + A_1 y_{x+1} + A_2 y_x = K$,

$$y_{x+2} + A_1 y^* + A_2 y^* = K$$

$$y_{x+2} = K - (A_1 + A_2)y^*$$

$$= K - \frac{K(A_1 + A_2)}{1 + A_1 + A_2}$$

$$= \frac{K}{1 + A_1 + A_2} = y^*$$

The equilibrium value is said to be *stable* or the difference equation $y_{x+2} + A_1 y_{x+1} + A_2 y_x = K$ is said to be *stable* if every solution of the difference equation converges to y^* for every possible set of initial conditions y_0 and y_1, that is, if

$$\lim y_x = y^* \qquad \text{for all } y_0 \text{ and } y_1$$

It can be shown that a necessary and sufficient condition for the equilibrium value $y^* = K/(1 + A_1 + A_2)$ to be stable is $\rho < 1$, where, as above, $\rho = \max\ (|m_1|, |m_2|)$ and m_1 and m_2 are the roots of the auxiliary equation $m^2 + A_1 m + A_2 = 0$.

It can be shown that $\rho < 1$ if and only if $2 \pm A_1 > 1 - A_2 > 0$. Thus these inequalities are necessary and sufficient for stability of the equilibrium value y^* and $y^* = K/(1 + A_1 + A_2)$ is a stable equilibrium for the difference equation $y_{x+2} + A_1 y_{x+1} + A_2 y_x = K$ if and only if $2 \pm A_1 > 1 - A_2 > 0$.

PROBLEMS

Obtain the general solution for each of the following difference equations.

1. $y_{x+2} + 2y_{x+1} + y_x = 0$
2. $y_{x+2} - y_x = 0$
3. $2y_{x+2} - 5y_{x+1} + 2y_x = 0$
4. $3y_{x+2} - 6y_{x+1} + 4y_x = 0$
5. Find the general solution for the difference equation $y_{x+2} + 2y_x = 0$ and the particular solution if $y_0 = 1$, $y_1 = \sqrt{2}$.
6. Find the general solution for the difference equation $y_{x+2} + 3y_{x+1} + 3y_x = 0$ and the particular solution if $y_0 = 3$, $y_1 = 0$.

For each of the following difference equations, obtain the general solution and the particular solution for the specified initial values.

7. $y_{x+2} + 4y_{x+1} + 8y_x = 26$, $y_0 = 6$, $y_1 = 3$
8. $y_{x+2} + 8y_{x+1} + 16y_x = 25$, $y_0 = 0$, $y_1 = 4$
9. $y_{x+2} - 8y_{x+1} - 9y_x = 24$, $y_0 = 2$, $y_1 = 0$
10. $3y_{x+2} - 10y_{x+1} + 3y_x = 8$, $y_0 = 5$, $y_1 = 3$

Solve each of the following difference equations, determine the behavior of the solution sequence, and calculate the first few values of the solution sequence.

11. $y_{x+2} - 3y_{x+1} + 3y_x = 5$, $y_0 = 5$, $y_1 = 8$
12. $9y_{x+2} - 6y_{x+1} + y_x = 16$, $y_0 = 0$, $y_1 = 3$
13. $6y_{x+2} + 5y_{x+1} - y_x = 20$, $y_0 = 3$, $y_1 = 8$
14. $4y_{x+2} - y_x = 15$, $y_0 = 15$, $y_1 = 10$
15. $8y_{x+2} - 6y_{x+1} + y_x = 9$, $y_0 = 10$, $y_1 = 5$
16. $y_{x+2} - 4y_{x+1} + 4y_x = 1$, $y_0 = 0$, $y_1 = 1$
17. $y_{x+2} - 5y_{x+1} + 6y_x = 4$, $y_0 = 0$, $y_1 = 1$
18. $y_{x+2} - 7y_{x+1} + 12y_x = 2$, $y_0 = 0$, $y_1 = 1$
19. $y_{x+2} - 2y_{x+1} + 2y_x = 3$, $y_0 = 5$, $y_1 = 6$
20. $y_{x+2} - 4y_x = 9$, $y_0 = 0$, $y_1 = 1$
21. $12y_{x+2} - 7y_{x+1} + y_x = 18$, $y_0 = 0$, $y_1 = 3$
22. $3y_{x+2} + 5y_{x+1} + 2y_x = 4$, $y_0 = 0$, $y_1 = 1$

Answers to Odd-Numbered Problems

1. $y_x = (-1)^x\ (C_1 + C_2 x)$
3. $y_x = C_1(\tfrac{1}{2})^x + C_2(2)^x$
5. $y_x = (\sqrt{2})^x(\cos \tfrac{1}{2}\pi x + \sin \tfrac{1}{2}\pi x)$
7. $y_x = (2\sqrt{2})^x(4 \cos \tfrac{1}{4}\pi x - \tfrac{7}{2} \sin \tfrac{1}{4}\pi x) + 2$
9. $y_x = 3(-1)^x + \tfrac{1}{2}(9)^x - \tfrac{3}{2}$
11. $y_x = 2(\sqrt{3})^x(\sin \tfrac{1}{3}\pi x) + 5$, divergent (oscillatory), $y_0 = 5$, $y_1 = 8$, $y_2 = 5 + 3\sqrt{3}$, $y_3 = 5$, $y_4 = 5 - 9\sqrt{3}$, $y_5 = -22$
13. $y_x = -5(-1)^x + (\tfrac{1}{6})^{x-1} + 2$, divergent (oscillatory), $y_0 = 3$, $y_1 = 8$, $y_2 = -2\tfrac{5}{6}$, $y_3 = 7\tfrac{1}{36}$, $y_4 = -2\tfrac{215}{216}$, $y_5 = 7\tfrac{1}{1296}$
15. $y_x = 6(\tfrac{1}{4})^x + (\tfrac{1}{2})^x + 3$, convergent, $y_0 = 10$, $y_1 = 5$, $y_2 = 3\tfrac{5}{8}$, $y_3 = 3\tfrac{7}{32}$, $y_4 = 3\tfrac{11}{128}$, $y_5 = 3\tfrac{19}{512}$

17. $y_x = 3^{x+1} - 5(2)^x + + 2$, divergent, $y_0 = 0$, $y_1 = 1$, $y_2 = 9$, $y_3 = 43$, $y_4 = 165$, $y_5 = 571$

19. $y_x = (\sqrt{2})^x (2 \cos \frac{1}{4}\pi x + \sin \frac{1}{4}\pi x) + 3$, divergent (oscillatory), $y_0 = 5$, $y_1 = 6$, $y_2 = 5$, $y_3 = 1$, $y_4 = -5$, $y_5 = -9$

21. $y_x = -12(\frac{1}{4})^x + 9(\frac{1}{3})^x + 3$, convergent, $y_0 = 0$, $y_1 = 3$, $y_2 = 3\frac{1}{4}$, $y_3 = 3\frac{7}{48}$, $y_4 = 3\frac{37}{576}$, $y_5 = 3\frac{175}{6912}$

6.7 Applications of Second-Order Difference Equations in Economic Models

Second-order difference equations are used in many economic models to indicate the dependence of the value of a variable on its value for two preceding periods. Second-order difference equations may be associated with various types of relationships among variables in the model; some of these relationships are illustrated in Samuelson's interaction model and Metzler's inventory model, which are discussed in this section.

SAMUELSON'S INTERACTION MODEL

The following model was proposed by P. A. Samuelson for national income analysis.

$$Y_t = C_t + I_t + G_t$$

$$C_t = \alpha Y_{t-1}$$

$$I_t = \beta[C_t - C_{t-1}]$$

$$Y_0 = Y_0$$

$$Y_1 = Y_1$$

$$\alpha > 0 \qquad \beta > 0$$

where Y is national income, C is consumption, I is investment, and G is government expenditure. G is assumed constant (exogenous) from period to period and, for convenience, the units are assumed to be such that $G = 1$. Note that investment in any period is equal to a constant times the increase in consumption of that period over the preceding period; this is referred to as the acceleration principle.

Substituting the second and third equations into the first equation,

$$Y_t = \alpha Y_{t-1} + \beta(\alpha Y_{t-1} - \alpha Y_{t-2}) + 1$$

$$Y_t - \alpha(1 + \beta)Y_{t-1} + \alpha\beta Y_{t-2} - 1 = 0$$

The three types of general solution of the homogeneous equation, depending on the nature of the roots of the auxiliary equation, are as follows:

(a) $Y_t = C_1 m_1^t + C_2 m_2^t$, where

$$m_1 = \frac{\alpha(1 + \beta) + \sqrt{\alpha^2(1 + \beta)^2 - 4\alpha\beta}}{2}$$

$$m_2 = \frac{\alpha(1 + \beta) - \sqrt{\alpha^2(1 + \beta)^2 - 4\alpha\beta}}{2}$$

(b) $Y_t = C_1 m^t + C_2 tm^t$, where

$$m = \frac{\alpha}{2}(1 + \beta)$$

(c) $Y_t = r^t(C_1 \cos \theta t + C_2 \sin \theta t)$, where

$$r = \sqrt{\frac{\alpha^2(1 + \beta^2)}{4} + \frac{4\alpha\beta - \alpha^2(1 + \beta^2)}{4}} = \sqrt{\alpha\beta}$$

$$\sin \theta = \frac{\alpha(1 + \beta)}{2\sqrt{\alpha\beta}}$$

$$\cos \theta = \sqrt{\frac{4\alpha\beta - \alpha^2(1 + \beta^2)}{4\alpha\beta}} = \sqrt{1 - \frac{\alpha(1 + \beta)}{4\beta}}$$

A particular solution of the nonhomogeneous equation

$$Y_t - \alpha(1 + \beta)Y_{t-1} + \alpha\beta Y_{t-2} - 1 = 0$$

is given by

$$y_p = \frac{1}{1 - \alpha(1 + \beta) + \alpha\beta}$$

$$= \frac{1}{1 - \alpha}$$

assuming that $1 - \alpha \neq 0$. Since α is the marginal propensity to consume, $\alpha < 1$ and $1 - \alpha \neq 0$.

Thus the solution of the nonhomogeneous equation has the form

(a) $Y_t = C_1 m_1^t + C_2 m_2^t + \dfrac{1}{1 - \alpha}$

(b) $Y_t = C_1 m^t + C_2 tm^t + \dfrac{1}{1 - \alpha}$

(c) $Y_t = r^t(C_1 \cos \theta t + C_2 \sin \theta t) + \dfrac{1}{1 - \alpha}$

where m_1, m_2, m, r, and θ are defined as above and the arbitrary constants can be determined from the initial conditions Y_0 and Y_1. Whenever the sum of the first two terms of the solution (in any of the three possible forms) tends to zero, $y^* = y_p = 1/(1 - \alpha)$ is an equilibrium solution.

The stability conditions $1 + A_1 + A_2 > 0$, $1 - A_1 + A_2 > 0$ and $1 - A_2 > 0$ become

$1 - \alpha(1 + \beta) + \alpha\beta > 0$ or $1 - \alpha > 0$

$1 + \alpha(1 + \beta) + \alpha\beta > 0$ or $1 + \alpha + 2\alpha\beta > 0$

$1 - \alpha\beta > 0$

Since $\alpha > 0$, $\beta > 0$, the second condition is satisfied and the necessary and sufficient conditions for y^* to be a stable equilibrium value are

$\alpha < 1$

$\alpha\beta < 1$

That is, both the marginal propensity to consume (one year's consumption with respect to the previous year's income) and its product with the accelerator parameter must be less than 1 for the sequence of income values to converge to y^* for all possible initial conditions. The convergence to y^* is oscillatory if the roots of the auxiliary equation are complex numbers. This is the case if $A_1^2 - 4A_2$ is negative, that is, if $\alpha^2(1 + \beta)^2 - 4\alpha\beta < 0$.

METZLER'S INVENTORY MODEL

The following model was proposed by L. A. Metzler for analyzing inventory cycles.

$$y_t = u_t + s_t + v_0$$

$$u_t = \beta y_{t-1}$$

$$s_t = \beta(y_{t-1} - y_{t-2})$$

$$0 < \beta < 1$$

where y_t is total income produced in period t, u_t is consumers' goods produced for sale in period t, s_t is consumers' goods produced for inventories in period t, and v_0 is the constant noninduced net investment in each period.

The total income produced in any period is equal to the total production of consumers' goods plus net investment. Sales in any period are a constant proportion of the income in the preceding period. Production for inventory is equal to the difference between actual and anticipated sales of the preceding period; that is, there is an attempt to keep inventory at a constant level. It is assumed that inventories are sufficient to meet differences between production and consumer demand.

Substituting the second and third equations into the first equation,

$$y_t = \beta y_{t-1} + \beta(y_{t-1} - y_{t-2}) + v_0$$

$$y_t - 2\beta y_{t-1} + \beta y_{t-2} = v_0$$

equivalently, so the t-values can begin at $t = 0$,

$$y_{t+2} - 2\beta y_{t+1} + \beta y_t = v_0$$

The auxiliary equation of the homogeneous difference equation corresponding to the equation $y_{t+2} - 2\beta y_{t+1} + \beta y_t = v_0$ is

$$m^2 - 2\beta m + \beta = 0$$

$$m = \frac{2\beta \pm \sqrt{4\beta^2 - 4\beta}}{2} = \beta \pm \sqrt{\beta^2 - \beta}$$

Since $0 < \beta < 1$, $\beta^2 - \beta < 0$ and the roots are complex numbers

$$m = \beta \pm i\sqrt{\beta(1 - \beta)}$$

Thus

$$r = \sqrt{\beta^2 + \beta(1 - \beta)} = \sqrt{\beta}$$

$$\cos \theta = \frac{\beta}{\sqrt{\beta}} = \sqrt{\beta}$$

$$\sin \theta = \frac{\sqrt{\beta(1 - \beta)}}{\sqrt{\beta}} = \sqrt{1 - \beta}$$

The general solution of the homogeneous equation

$$y_{t+2} - 2\beta y_{t+1} + \beta y_t = 0$$

is thus given by

$$y_t = (\sqrt{\beta})^t(C_1 \cos \theta t + C_2 \sin \theta t)$$

A particular solution of the nonhomogeneous equation

$$y_{t+2} - 2\beta y_{t+1} + \beta y_t = v_0$$

is given by

$$y_p = \frac{v_0}{1 - \beta}$$

since $0 < \beta < 1$ and thus $1 - \beta \neq 0$. The general solution of the nonhomogeneous equation thus has the form

$$y_t = (\sqrt{\beta})^t(C_1 \cos \theta t + C_2 \sin \theta t) + \frac{v_0}{1 - \beta}$$

The term involving sines and cosines oscillates between positive and negative values and results in cyclical fluctuations. These fluctuations are damped by the factor $(\sqrt{\beta})^t$ since $0 < \beta < 1$. Thus

$$(\sqrt{\beta})^t(C_1 \cos \theta t + C_2 \sin \theta t) \to 0 \qquad \text{as } t \to \infty$$

and

$$y_t \to \frac{v_0}{1 - \beta} \qquad \text{as } t \to \infty$$

as an equilibrium value.

PROBLEMS

1. For the Samuelson model, verify the expressions for m_1, m_2, m, r, and θ given in the text.
2. For the Samuelson model, show that the roots of the auxiliary equation are complex if and only if

$$\alpha^2(1 + \beta)^2 - 4\alpha\beta < 0.$$

3. For the Samuelson model, obtain the solution and determine the behavior of the solution sequence if a. $\alpha = 0.8$, $\beta = 3$ and b. $\alpha = 0.5$, $\beta = 1$.
4. For the price-adjustment equation

$$p_{t+2} = \beta r_0 + \beta\alpha(p_{t+1} - p_t)$$

where p is price and β, α, and r_0 are positive constants, determine the limiting behavior of the solution if a. $\beta\alpha = 1$, b. $\beta\alpha = \frac{1}{2}$, c. $\beta\alpha = 2$, d. $\beta\alpha = \frac{3}{4}$.
5. Consider the following difference equation discussed by Baumol:

$$Y_{t+2} - \frac{C}{s} Y_{t+1} + \frac{C}{s} Y_t = 0$$

where Y is warranted income and C and s are positive constants. Show that for $C \geq 4s$ this equation gives an explosive (divergent) solution for warranted income, but for $C < 4s$ warranted income is cyclic.
6. For the Metzler model, note that (total) inventory, denoted by i, is given by

$$i_t = i_{t-i} + s_t + u_t - \beta y_t$$

Obtain an expression for change in inventory, $i_t - i_{t-1}$, in terms of y_t and determine the behavior of this solution sequence.

Answers to Odd-Numbered Problems

3. a. $y_t = C_1(2)^t + C_2(\frac{6}{5})^t + 5$, divergent
   b. $y_t = (\frac{1}{2}\sqrt{2})^t(C_1 \cos \frac{1}{4}\pi t + C_2 \sin \frac{1}{4}\pi t) + 2$, convergent (oscillatory) to 2

Matrix Algebra

7.1 Introduction

In many analyses, variables are assumed to be related by sets of linear equations. Matrix algebra provides a clear and concise notation for the formulation and solution of such problems, many of which would be almost impossibly complicated in conventional algebraic notation.

In this chapter, vectors, matrices, and operations involving them are defined. Special types of matrices, the transpose of a matrix, partitioned matrices, and the determinant of a matrix are considered. Linear dependence of a set of vectors and the rank and inverse of a matrix are also discussed and are applied to the solution of simultaneous equations. Vector differentiation is defined and illustrated. In Chapter 8 further applications of matrix algebra are considered.

7.2 Definition of a Matrix

A *matrix* is a rectangular array of numbers written in the form

$$\mathbf{A} = \begin{pmatrix} a_{11} & a_{12} & \cdots & a_{1n} \\ a_{21} & a_{22} & \cdots & a_{2n} \\ \vdots & \vdots & & \vdots \\ a_{m1} & a_{m2} & \cdots & a_{mn} \end{pmatrix} \quad \text{or} \quad \mathbf{A} = \begin{bmatrix} a_{11} & a_{12} & \cdots & a_{1n} \\ a_{21} & a_{22} & \cdots & a_{2n} \\ \vdots & \vdots & & \vdots \\ a_{m1} & a_{m2} & \cdots & a_{mn} \end{bmatrix}$$

The a_{ij}'s stand for real numbers, the *elements* of the matrix. Note that a_{ij} is the element in the ith row and the jth column of the matrix $\mathbf{A}$; the matrix $\mathbf{A}$ is sometimes denoted by (a_{ij}) or by $\{a_{ij}\}$. A matrix that has m rows and n columns is said to be an $m \times n$ (read "m by n") matrix or a matrix of *order* $m \times n$. If $m = n$, the matrix is said to be *square*. Especially when various operations are being performed on them, the order of matrices is frequently denoted by subscripts, for example, $\mathbf{A}_{m \times n}$ or $(a_{ij})_{m \times n}$.

EXAMPLE

$$\begin{bmatrix} 1 & 0 & -2 & 6 \\ 4 & 8 & 3 & -9 \end{bmatrix} \quad \text{is a } 2 \times 4 \text{ matrix}$$

$$\begin{bmatrix} 6 & 6 & 3 \\ 3 & 8 & -2 \\ -1 & 0 & 0 \end{bmatrix} \quad \text{is a } 3 \times 3 \text{ (square) matrix}$$

$$\begin{bmatrix} 5 & -8 & -2 \\ 12 & 10 & -1 \\ 13 & 9 & -3 \\ 2 & 7 & 6 \\ 6 & 4 & 10 \end{bmatrix} \quad \text{is a } 5 \times 3 \text{ matrix}$$

$$\begin{bmatrix} 1 & -1 \\ -1 & 1 \end{bmatrix} \quad \text{is a } 2 \times 2 \text{ (square) matrix}$$

Two matrices of the same order are said to be *equal* if and only if all the corresponding elements are equal, that is, if the matrices are identical. Note that, by definition, matrices that are of different order can not be equal.

EXAMPLE

If

$$A = \begin{bmatrix} 2 & -2 \\ -2 & 2 \end{bmatrix}$$

$$B = \begin{bmatrix} 2 & -2 & 2 \\ -2 & 2 & -2 \end{bmatrix}$$

$$C = \begin{bmatrix} -2 & 2 \\ 2 & -2 \end{bmatrix}$$

$$D = \begin{bmatrix} 2 & -2 \\ -2 & 2 \end{bmatrix}$$

$A = D$, but $A \neq B$, $A \neq C$, $B \neq C$, $B \neq D$, and $C \neq D$.

DEFINITION OF A VECTOR

A matrix that consists of a single column, that is, an $m \times 1$ matrix, is said to be a *column vector* and is written

$$\mathbf{u} = \begin{pmatrix} u_1 \\ u_2 \\ \vdots \\ u_m \end{pmatrix} \quad \text{or} \quad \mathbf{u} = \begin{bmatrix} u_1 \\ u_2 \\ \vdots \\ u_m \end{bmatrix}$$

The letters u_i stand for real numbers, the *components* of the vector; u_i is the ith component of the vector $\mathbf{u}$. A column vector that has m rows is said to be an *m-component* or an *m-dimensional* vector.

Similarly, a matrix that contains only a single row, that is, a $1 \times n$ matrix, is said to be a *row vector* and is written

$$\mathbf{v} = (v_1, v_2, \ldots, v_n) \qquad \text{or} \qquad v = [v_1, v_2, \ldots, v_n]$$

The letters v_j stand for real numbers, the *components* of the vector; v_j is the jth component of the vector $\mathbf{v}$. A row vector that has n columns is said to be an *n-component* or an *n-dimensional vector*.

EXAMPLE

$\begin{bmatrix} -1 \\ -1 \end{bmatrix}$ is a 2×1 matrix, a 2-dimensional column vector

$\begin{bmatrix} 0 \\ 0 \\ 3 \\ 0 \\ 2 \end{bmatrix}$ is a 5×1 matrix, a 5-dimensional column vector

$[0, 3, 0]$ is a 1×3 matrix, a 3-dimensional row vector

$[-1, -1, 5, -1]$ is a 1×4 matrix, a 4-dimensional row vector

Two row vectors having the same number of rows or two column vectors having the same number of columns are said to be *equal* if and only if all the corresponding elements are equal, that is, if the vectors are identical.

EXAMPLE

$\mathbf{u} = [1, 3]$

$\mathbf{v} = \begin{bmatrix} 1 \\ 3 \end{bmatrix}$

$\mathbf{w} = [1, 3]$

$\mathbf{x} = [3, 1]$

$\mathbf{u} = \mathbf{w}$, but $\mathbf{u} \neq \mathbf{v}$, $\mathbf{u} \neq \mathbf{x}$, and $\mathbf{v} \neq \mathbf{w}$, $\mathbf{v} \neq \mathbf{x}$, and $\mathbf{w} \neq \mathbf{x}$.

NOTE: Frequently it is useful to regard a matrix as being composed of a series of row or column vectors; for example, the matrix

$$\begin{bmatrix} 1 & -6 \\ 2 & 2 \\ -3 & 4 \end{bmatrix}$$

can be regarded as consisting of the two column vectors

$\begin{bmatrix} 1 \\ 2 \\ -3 \end{bmatrix}$ and $\begin{bmatrix} -6 \\ 2 \\ 4 \end{bmatrix}$

or, alternatively, of the three row vectors

$[1, -6] \qquad [2, 2] \qquad$ and $\qquad [-3, 4]$.

7.3 Matrix Operations

Operations analogous to the operations of addition, subtraction, multiplication, and division of real numbers can be defined for matrices. Since a matrix is an array of numbers, rather than a single number, some of the properties of operations for real numbers do not hold for the analogous matrix operations; specific examples are noted in following sections. In this section addition and subtraction of matrices, multiplication of a matrix by a scalar, and multiplication of matrices by each other are defined and illustrated.

ADDITION AND SUBTRACTION OF MATRICES

Matrices can be added or subtracted if and only if they are of the same order. The sum or difference of two $m \times n$ matrices is another $m \times n$ matrix whose elements are the sums or differences of the corresponding elements in the original matrices; thus, if

$$\mathbf{A} = \begin{bmatrix} a_{11} & \cdots & a_{1n} \\ \vdots & & \vdots \\ a_{m1} & \cdots & a_{mn} \end{bmatrix}$$

$$\mathbf{B} = \begin{bmatrix} b_{11} & \cdots & b_{1n} \\ \vdots & & \vdots \\ b_{m1} & \cdots & b_{mn} \end{bmatrix}$$

then

$$\mathbf{A} \pm \mathbf{B} = \mathbf{C}$$

where

$$\mathbf{C} = \begin{bmatrix} a_{11} \pm b_{11} & \cdots & a_{1n} \pm b_{1n} \\ \vdots & & \vdots \\ a_{m1} \pm b_{m1} & \cdots & a_{mn} \pm b_{mn} \end{bmatrix} = \begin{bmatrix} c_{11} & \cdots & c_{1n} \\ \vdots & & \vdots \\ c_{m1} & \cdots & c_{mn} \end{bmatrix}$$

that is, $(a_{ij}) + (b_{ij}) = (c_{ij})$, where $c_{ij} = a_{ij} + b_{ij}$ for all i and j.

EXAMPLE

(a) $\begin{bmatrix} 3 & 2 & -4 \\ 5 & 6 & 8 \\ 3 & 0 & 0 \end{bmatrix} + \begin{bmatrix} 0 & 3 & 8 \\ -5 & -6 & 2 \\ 0 & 0 & -4 \end{bmatrix} = \begin{bmatrix} 3 & 5 & 4 \\ 0 & 0 & 10 \\ 3 & 0 & -4 \end{bmatrix}$

(b) $\begin{bmatrix} 3 & -10 \\ -11 & 25 \end{bmatrix} - \begin{bmatrix} -6 & -4 \\ 22 & -21 \end{bmatrix} = \begin{bmatrix} 9 & -6 \\ -33 & 46 \end{bmatrix}$

(c) $[4, 6, 12] + [-3, 2, -12] = [1, 8, 0]$

(d) $\begin{bmatrix} 1 \\ 1 \\ 2 \\ 4 \\ 1 \end{bmatrix} - \begin{bmatrix} 1 \\ 1 \\ 2 \\ 4 \\ 1 \end{bmatrix} = \begin{bmatrix} 0 \\ 0 \\ 0 \\ 0 \\ 0 \end{bmatrix}$

(e) $\begin{bmatrix} 2 & 3 \\ 6 & 4 \end{bmatrix} + \begin{bmatrix} 1 & 1 \\ -1 & 2 \end{bmatrix} - \begin{bmatrix} 0 & 0 \\ 6 & 4 \end{bmatrix} = \begin{bmatrix} 3 & 4 \\ -1 & 2 \end{bmatrix}$

(f) $\begin{bmatrix} 1 \\ 1 \\ 1 \end{bmatrix} + \begin{bmatrix} 3 \\ 2 \\ 4 \end{bmatrix} - \begin{bmatrix} 6 \\ 8 \\ 10 \end{bmatrix} + \begin{bmatrix} 0 \\ 1 \\ 0 \end{bmatrix} = \begin{bmatrix} -2 \\ -4 \\ -5 \end{bmatrix}$

(g) $[2, 1] + [3, 4] + [6, 7] - [11, 12] = [0, 0]$

(h) $\begin{bmatrix} 1 & 4 \\ 2 & 6 \\ 3 & 8 \end{bmatrix} - \begin{bmatrix} 0 & 5 \\ 7 & 9 \\ 11 & 12 \end{bmatrix} - \begin{bmatrix} 10 & 13 \\ 20 & 0 \\ 1 & 0 \end{bmatrix} = \begin{bmatrix} -9 & -14 \\ -25 & -3 \\ -9 & -4 \end{bmatrix}$

PROBLEMS

Obtain the matrix resulting from each of the following operations.

1. $\begin{bmatrix} 2 & -3 & 6 \\ 5 & 4 & 5 \\ 0 & -1 & -9 \end{bmatrix} - \begin{bmatrix} 1 & -3 & 4 \\ 0 & -2 & 5 \\ 1 & 0 & -1 \end{bmatrix}$

2. $\begin{bmatrix} 6 & -1 & 0 \\ 4 & 2 & 1 \end{bmatrix} + \begin{bmatrix} 5 & 0 & 2 \\ 0 & -1 & 3 \end{bmatrix} + \begin{bmatrix} -2 & -1 & -3 \\ -4 & 1 & -1 \end{bmatrix}$

3. $\begin{bmatrix} 1 \\ 3 \\ 4 \end{bmatrix} - \begin{bmatrix} 2 \\ 0 \\ 2 \end{bmatrix} + \begin{bmatrix} 3 \\ 1 \\ -2 \end{bmatrix}$

4. $\begin{bmatrix} 2 & 1 \\ 1 & 2 \end{bmatrix} + \begin{bmatrix} -1 & 0 \\ 0 & -1 \end{bmatrix} - \begin{bmatrix} 2 & 2 \\ 2 & 2 \end{bmatrix}$

5. $[1, 3, -1, 2] - [0, 1, -2, 3]$

6. $[-1, 2] - [3, 4] + [1, -2] - [6, 5]$

Answers to Odd-Numbered Problems

1. $\begin{bmatrix} 1 & 0 & 2 \\ 5 & 6 & 0 \\ -1 & -1 & -8 \end{bmatrix}$ 3. $\begin{bmatrix} 2 \\ 4 \\ 0 \end{bmatrix}$

5. $[1, 2, 1, -1]$

MULTIPLICATION OF A MATRIX BY A SCALAR

A real number (which is a 1×1 matrix) is referred to as a *scalar* when it occurs in operations involving matrices. When a matrix is multiplied by scalar, every element in the matrix is multiplied by that scalar (constant); thus, if

$$A = \begin{bmatrix} a_{11} & \cdots & a_{1n} \\ \vdots & & \vdots \\ a_{m1} & \cdots & a_{mn} \end{bmatrix} \quad \text{and } k \text{ is any scalar (constant)}$$

then

$$k \times A_{m \times n} = kA_{m \times n} = \begin{bmatrix} ka_{11} & \cdots & ka_{1n} \\ \vdots & & \vdots \\ ka_{m1} & \cdots & ka_{mn} \end{bmatrix} = k(a_{ij})_{m \times n} = (ka_{ij})_{m \times n}$$

EXAMPLE

(a) $3 \begin{bmatrix} 4 & -3 \\ 8 & -2 \\ -1 & 0 \end{bmatrix} = \begin{bmatrix} 12 & -9 \\ 24 & -6 \\ -3 & 0 \end{bmatrix}$

(b) $5 \begin{bmatrix} 0 \\ -1 \\ 0 \end{bmatrix} = \begin{bmatrix} 0 \\ -5 \\ 0 \end{bmatrix}$

(c) $-1[6, -2, -3] = [-6, 2, 3]$

(d) $a \begin{bmatrix} 5 & 6 & 2 & 4 \\ -3 & -1 & 0 & -6 \end{bmatrix} = \begin{bmatrix} 5a & 6a & 2a & 4a \\ -3a & -a & 0 & -6a \end{bmatrix}$

(e) $-b \begin{bmatrix} 0 \\ -2 \\ 3 \\ -1 \\ 5 \end{bmatrix} = \begin{bmatrix} 0 \\ 2b \\ -3b \\ b \\ -5b \end{bmatrix}$

(f) $c[0, 0, 0, 0, 16] = [0, 0, 0, 0, 16c]$

MULTIPLICATION OF MATRICES

Two matrices can be multiplied if and only if the number of columns in one matrix is equal to the number of rows in the other matrix. In particular, the matrix product **AB** is defined if and only if the number of columns in **A** is the same as the number of rows in **B**, in this case the matrices **A** and **B** are said to be *conformable* for multiplication and the product matrix has the same number of rows as **A** and the same number of columns as **B**. Thus an $m \times n$ matrix may be multiplied times an $n \times p$ matrix to obtain an $m \times p$ matrix.

DEFINITION: When a $1 \times n$ row vector multiplies an $n \times 1$ column vector, the result is a scalar, the *inner product* of the two vectors; the value of the inner product is the sum of products of the components of the vectors. Thus if

$$\mathbf{u} = [u_1, \ldots, u_n] \qquad \text{and} \qquad \mathbf{v} = \begin{bmatrix} v_1 \\ \vdots \\ v_n \end{bmatrix}$$

then $\mathbf{u}_{1 \times n} \mathbf{v}_{n \times 1} = w$ (a scalar), where $w = u_1 v_1 + u_2 v_2 + \cdots + u_n v_n = \sum_{i=1}^{n} u_i v_i$.

When two matrices are multiplied, the element in the ith row and jth column of the product matrix is the inner product of the ith row vector of the first matrix with the jth column vector of the second matrix. Thus the product of two matrices may be written as a matrix of their inner products: If $\mathbf{A} = (a_{ij})_{m \times n}$ and $\mathbf{B} = (b_{jk})_{n \times p}$, then $\mathbf{AB} = \mathbf{C}$, where

$$\mathbf{C} = (c_{ik})_{m \times p} = \begin{bmatrix} \sum_{j=1}^{n} a_{1j} b_{j1} & \cdots & \sum_{j=1}^{n} a_{1j} b_{jm} \\ \vdots & & \vdots \\ \sum_{j=1}^{n} a_{mj} b_{j1} & \cdots & \sum_{j=1}^{n} a_{mj} b_{jn} \end{bmatrix}$$

that is, $c_{ik} = \sum_{j=1}^{n} a_{ij} b_{jk}$.

EXAMPLE

(a) $\begin{bmatrix} 1 & 3 & -1 \\ 2 & 0 & 0 \\ 0 & -1 & 6 \end{bmatrix}_{3 \times 3} \begin{bmatrix} 1 & 0 \\ -1 & 2 \\ 1 & 3 \end{bmatrix}_{3 \times 2} = \begin{bmatrix} -3 & 3 \\ 2 & 0 \\ 7 & 16 \end{bmatrix}_{3 \times 2}$

where

$$(1)(1) + (3)(-1) + (-1)(1) = -3$$
$$(2)(1) + (0)(-1) + (0)(1) = 2$$
$$(0)(1) + (-1)(-1) + (6)(1) = 7$$
$$(1)(0) + (3)(2) + (-1)(3) = 3$$
$$(2)(0) + (0)(2) + (0)(3) = 0$$
$$(0)(0) + (-1)(2) + (6)(3) = 16$$

(b) $[-1, 0, 6, 3, 2]_{1 \times 5} \begin{bmatrix} 3 & 0 \\ 4 & 0 \\ -2 & 3 \\ 1 & 8 \\ 0 & -2 \end{bmatrix}_{5 \times 2} = [-12, 38]_{1 \times 2}$

where

$$(-1)(3) + (0)(4) + (6)(-2) + (3)(1) + (2)(0) = -12$$
$$(-1)(0) + (0)(0) + (6)(3) + (3)(8) + (2)(-2) = 38$$

In matrix multiplication, the sequence in which multiplication is performed is very important. If **A** is $m \times n$ and **B** is $n \times m$, then it is possible to obtain both of the product matrices **AB** and **BA**; however, in general, $AB \neq BA$. In the matrix product **AB**, **A** is said to *premultiply* **B** or, alternatively, **B** is said to *postmultiply* **A**. Since, in general, premultiplication and postmultiplication give different results, even when both are defined, care must be taken to preserve the appropriate sequence in all matrix multiplications. Note that this precaution is not necessary in the multiplication of numbers.

EXAMPLE

(a) If

$$\mathbf{A} = \begin{bmatrix} 4 & 6 & -1 & 3 \\ 0 & -1 & 2 & 1 \end{bmatrix} \quad \text{and} \quad \mathbf{B} = \begin{bmatrix} 1 & 2 \\ -1 & 1 \\ 1 & 6 \\ 2 & 3 \end{bmatrix}$$

then

$$\mathbf{AB} = \begin{bmatrix} 4 & 6 & -1 & 3 \\ 0 & -1 & 2 & 1 \end{bmatrix}_{2 \times 4} \begin{bmatrix} 1 & 2 \\ -1 & 1 \\ 1 & 6 \\ 2 & 3 \end{bmatrix}_{4 \times 2} = \begin{bmatrix} 3 & 17 \\ 5 & 14 \end{bmatrix}_{2 \times 2}$$

$$\mathbf{BA} = \begin{bmatrix} 1 & 2 \\ -1 & 1 \\ 1 & 6 \\ 2 & 3 \end{bmatrix}_{4 \times 2} \begin{bmatrix} 4 & 6 & -1 & 3 \\ 0 & -1 & 2 & 1 \end{bmatrix}_{2 \times 4} = \begin{bmatrix} 4 & 4 & 3 & 5 \\ -4 & -7 & 3 & -2 \\ 4 & 0 & 11 & 9 \\ 8 & 9 & 4 & 9 \end{bmatrix}_{4 \times 4}$$

(b) If

$$\mathbf{A} = \begin{bmatrix} 5 & -6 \\ -1 & 0 \\ 0 & 3 \end{bmatrix} \quad \text{and} \quad \mathbf{B} = \begin{bmatrix} -1 & 8 & -3 \\ 0 & 10 & -4 \end{bmatrix}$$

then

$$AB = \begin{bmatrix} 5 & -6 \\ -1 & 0 \\ 0 & 3 \end{bmatrix}_{3 \times 2} \begin{bmatrix} -1 & 8 & -3 \\ 0 & 10 & -4 \end{bmatrix}_{2 \times 3} = \begin{bmatrix} -5 & -20 & 9 \\ 1 & -8 & 3 \\ 0 & 30 & -12 \end{bmatrix}_{3 \times 3}$$

$$BA = \begin{bmatrix} -1 & 8 & -3 \\ 0 & 10 & -4 \end{bmatrix}_{2 \times 3} \begin{bmatrix} 5 & -6 \\ -1 & 0 \\ 0 & 3 \end{bmatrix}_{3 \times 2} = \begin{bmatrix} -13 & -3 \\ -10 & -12 \end{bmatrix}_{2 \times 2}$$

(c) If

$$A = \begin{bmatrix} -1 & 3 & 1 \\ 2 & 0 & -2 \\ 0 & 4 & 5 \end{bmatrix} \quad \text{and} \quad B = \begin{bmatrix} 0 & 2 & 3 \\ 8 & -1 & 9 \\ -2 & 0 & 5 \end{bmatrix}$$

then

$$AB = \begin{bmatrix} -1 & 3 & 1 \\ 2 & 0 & -2 \\ 0 & 4 & 5 \end{bmatrix}_{3 \times 3} \begin{bmatrix} 0 & 2 & 3 \\ 8 & -1 & 9 \\ -2 & 0 & 5 \end{bmatrix}_{3 \times 3} = \begin{bmatrix} 22 & -5 & 29 \\ 4 & 4 & -4 \\ 22 & -4 & 61 \end{bmatrix}_{3 \times 3}$$

$$BA = \begin{bmatrix} 0 & 2 & 3 \\ 8 & -1 & 9 \\ -2 & 0 & 5 \end{bmatrix}_{3 \times 3} \begin{bmatrix} -1 & 3 & 1 \\ 2 & 0 & -2 \\ 0 & 4 & 5 \end{bmatrix}_{3 \times 3} = \begin{bmatrix} 4 & 12 & 11 \\ -10 & 60 & 55 \\ 2 & 14 & 23 \end{bmatrix}_{3 \times 3}$$

NOTE: When a row vector premultiplies a column vector, the result is their inner product, a scalar whose value is the sum of the products of the elements of the two vectors. When an $n \times 1$ column vector premultiplies a $1 \times n$ row vector, the result is an $n \times n$ square matrix whose elements are the products of the elements of the vectors; thus if

$$\mathbf{u} = [u_1, \ldots, u_n] \quad \text{and} \quad \mathbf{v} = \begin{bmatrix} v_1 \\ \vdots \\ v_n \end{bmatrix}$$

then, as above, $\mathbf{u}_{1 \times n} \mathbf{v}_{n \times 1} = w$ (a scalar) where $w = \sum_{i=1}^{n} u_i v_i$, and $\mathbf{v}_{n \times 1} \mathbf{u}_{1 \times n} = \mathbf{X}_{n \times n}$ (a square matrix), where $x_{ij} = v_i u_j$.

EXAMPLE

(a) $[1, 3, 6] \begin{bmatrix} -2 \\ 4 \\ -1 \end{bmatrix} = -2 + 12 - 6 = 4$

$$\begin{bmatrix} -2 \\ 4 \\ -1 \end{bmatrix} [1, 3, 6] = \begin{bmatrix} -2 & -6 & 12 \\ 4 & 12 & 24 \\ -1 & -3 & -6 \end{bmatrix}$$

(b) $[1, 0, 0, 2, -3] \begin{bmatrix} 0 \\ -1 \\ -4 \\ -3 \\ -2 \end{bmatrix} = 0 + 0 + 0 - 6 + 6 = 0$

$$\begin{bmatrix} 0 \\ -1 \\ -4 \\ -3 \\ -2 \end{bmatrix} [1, 0, 0, 2, -3] = \begin{bmatrix} 0 & 0 & 0 & 0 & 0 \\ -1 & 0 & 0 & -2 & 3 \\ -4 & 0 & 0 & -8 & 12 \\ -3 & 0 & 0 & -6 & 9 \\ -2 & 0 & 0 & -4 & 6 \end{bmatrix}$$

Although the sequence in which two matrices are multiplied affects the result, the order in which three or more matrices are multiplied does not affect the result, provided the sequence is preserved. That is,

$$\mathbf{A}_{m \times n}\, \mathbf{B}_{n \times p}\, \mathbf{C}_{p \times q} = \mathbf{A}_{m \times n}(\mathbf{B}_{n \times p}\, \mathbf{C}_{p \times q}) = (\mathbf{A}_{m \times n}\, \mathbf{B}_{n \times p})\mathbf{C}_{p \times q}$$

A corresponding property holds for multiplication of numbers. In summary, addition of matrices is commutative, that is, $\mathbf{A} + \mathbf{B} = \mathbf{B} + \mathbf{A}$ and both addition and subtraction are associative, that is, $\mathbf{A} \pm \mathbf{B} \pm \mathbf{C} = \mathbf{A} \pm (\mathbf{B} \pm \mathbf{C}) = (\mathbf{A} \pm \mathbf{B}) \pm \mathbf{C}$; multiplication of matrices is *not* commutative, that is, $\mathbf{AB} \neq \mathbf{BA}$, but is associative, that is, $\mathbf{ABC} = \mathbf{A(BC)} = \mathbf{(AB)C}$. For numbers, addition, subtraction, and multiplication are both associative and commutative.

EXAMPLE

$$
\underset{\mathbf{A}}{\begin{bmatrix} 1 & -1 & 0 \\ 2 & -3 & 4 \\ 0 & 0 & 1 \end{bmatrix}_{3 \times 3}}
\underset{\mathbf{B}}{\begin{bmatrix} 3 \\ 1 \\ -1 \end{bmatrix}_{3 \times 1}}
\underset{\mathbf{C}}{[0,\, 2,\, -1]_{1 \times 3}}
=
\underset{\mathbf{A}}{\begin{bmatrix} 1 & -1 & 0 \\ 2 & -3 & 4 \\ 0 & 0 & 1 \end{bmatrix}_{3 \times 3}}
\underset{\mathbf{BC}}{\begin{bmatrix} 0 & 6 & -3 \\ 0 & 2 & -1 \\ 0 & -2 & 1 \end{bmatrix}_{3 \times 3}}
$$

$$
= \underset{\mathbf{ABC}}{}
$$

$$
= \begin{bmatrix} 0 & 4 & -2 \\ 0 & -2 & 1 \\ 0 & -2 & 1 \end{bmatrix}_{3 \times 3}
$$

Alternatively, by associativity,

$$
\underset{\mathbf{A}}{\begin{bmatrix} 1 & -1 & 0 \\ 2 & -3 & 4 \\ 0 & 0 & 1 \end{bmatrix}_{3 \times 3}}
\underset{\mathbf{B}}{\begin{bmatrix} 3 \\ 1 \\ -1 \end{bmatrix}_{3 \times 1}}
\underset{\mathbf{C}}{[0,\, 2,\, -1]_{1 \times 3}}
=
\underset{\mathbf{A\,B}}{\begin{bmatrix} 2 \\ -1 \\ -1 \end{bmatrix}_{3 \times 1}}
\underset{\mathbf{C}}{[0,\, 2,\, -1]_{1 \times 3}}
$$

$$
= \underset{\mathbf{ABC}}{}
$$

$$
= \begin{bmatrix} 0 & 4 & -2 \\ 0 & -2 & 1 \\ 0 & -2 & 1 \end{bmatrix}_{3 \times 3}
$$

EXAMPLE

$$
\underset{\mathbf{A}}{\begin{bmatrix} 1 & -1 \\ 6 & 10 \end{bmatrix}_{2 \times 2}}
\underset{\mathbf{B}}{\begin{bmatrix} 5 & -2 & 3 \\ -8 & 0 & 6 \end{bmatrix}_{2 \times 3}}
\underset{\mathbf{C}}{\begin{bmatrix} -1 \\ 0 \\ -4 \end{bmatrix}_{3 \times 1}}
=
\underset{\mathbf{A}}{\begin{bmatrix} 1 & -1 \\ 6 & 10 \end{bmatrix}_{2 \times 2}}
\underset{\mathbf{BC}}{\begin{bmatrix} -17 \\ -16 \end{bmatrix}_{2 \times 1}}
$$

$$
= \underset{\mathbf{ABC}}{}
$$

$$
= \begin{bmatrix} -1 \\ -262 \end{bmatrix}_{2 \times 1}
$$

Alternatively, by associativity,

$$
\underset{\mathbf{A}}{\begin{bmatrix} 1 & -1 \\ 6 & 10 \end{bmatrix}_{2\times2}} \underset{\mathbf{B}}{\begin{bmatrix} 5 & -2 & 3 \\ -8 & 0 & 6 \end{bmatrix}_{2\times3}} \underset{\mathbf{C}}{\begin{bmatrix} -1 \\ 0 \\ -4 \end{bmatrix}_{3\times1}} = \underset{\mathbf{A\,B}}{\begin{bmatrix} 13 & -2 & -3 \\ -50 & -12 & 78 \end{bmatrix}_{2\times3}} \underset{\mathbf{C}}{\begin{bmatrix} -1 \\ 0 \\ -4 \end{bmatrix}_{3\times1}}
$$

$$= \mathbf{A\,B\,C}$$

$$= \begin{bmatrix} -1 \\ -262 \end{bmatrix}_{2\times1}$$

EXAMPLE

$$
\underset{\mathbf{A}}{\begin{bmatrix} 3 & 4 \\ 4 & 3 \end{bmatrix}_{2\times2}} \underset{\mathbf{B}}{\begin{bmatrix} 0 & 1 \\ -1 & 0 \end{bmatrix}_{2\times2}} \underset{\mathbf{C}}{\begin{bmatrix} -6 & -8 & 10 \\ -5 & 5 & 4 \end{bmatrix}_{2\times3}} = \underset{\mathbf{A}}{\begin{bmatrix} 3 & 4 \\ 4 & 3 \end{bmatrix}_{2\times2}} \underset{\mathbf{B\,C}}{\begin{bmatrix} -5 & 5 & 4 \\ 6 & 8 & -10 \end{bmatrix}_{2\times3}}
$$

$$= \mathbf{A\,B\,C}$$

$$= \begin{bmatrix} 9 & 47 & -28 \\ -2 & 44 & -14 \end{bmatrix}_{2\times3}$$

Alternatively, by associativity,

$$
\underset{\mathbf{A}}{\begin{bmatrix} 3 & 4 \\ 4 & 3 \end{bmatrix}_{2\times2}} \underset{\mathbf{B}}{\begin{bmatrix} 0 & 1 \\ -1 & 0 \end{bmatrix}_{2\times2}} \underset{\mathbf{C}}{\begin{bmatrix} -6 & -8 & 10 \\ -5 & 5 & 4 \end{bmatrix}_{2\times3}} = \underset{\mathbf{A\,B}}{\begin{bmatrix} -4 & 3 \\ -3 & 4 \end{bmatrix}_{2\times2}} \underset{\mathbf{C}}{\begin{bmatrix} -6 & -8 & 10 \\ -5 & 5 & 4 \end{bmatrix}_{2\times3}}
$$

$$= \mathbf{A\,B\,C}$$

$$= \begin{bmatrix} 9 & 47 & -28 \\ -2 & 44 & -14 \end{bmatrix}_{2\times3}$$

EXAMPLE

$$
\underset{\mathbf{A}}{[1, -1, 4, 2]_{1\times4}} \underset{\mathbf{B}}{\begin{bmatrix} 0 \\ 2 \\ -1 \\ 0 \end{bmatrix}_{4\times1}} \underset{\mathbf{C}}{[-1, 0, 6]_{1\times3}} = \underset{\mathbf{A}}{[1, -1, 4, 2]_{1\times4}} \underset{\mathbf{B\,C}}{\begin{bmatrix} 0 & 0 & 0 \\ -2 & 0 & 12 \\ 1 & 0 & -6 \\ 0 & 0 & 0 \end{bmatrix}_{4\times3}}
$$

$$= \mathbf{A\,B\,C}$$

$$= [6, 0, -36]_{1\times3}$$

Alternatively, by associativity,

$$
\underset{\mathbf{A}}{[1, -1, 4, 2]_{1\times4}} \underset{\mathbf{B}}{\begin{bmatrix} 0 \\ 2 \\ -1 \\ 0 \end{bmatrix}_{4\times1}} \underset{\mathbf{C}}{[-1, 0, 6]_{1\times3}} = \underset{\mathbf{A\,B}}{} \underset{\mathbf{C}}{} \; -6 \times [-1, 0, 6]_{1\times3}
$$

$$= \mathbf{A\,B\,C}$$

$$= [6, 0, -36]_{1\times3}$$

PROBLEMS

Obtain the matrix resulting from each of the following operations.

1. $3 \begin{bmatrix} -1 & 2 & 3 & 4 \\ 0 & -1 & -1 & 2 \\ 1 & 2 & 0 & 3 \end{bmatrix}$

2. $\begin{bmatrix} 2 & -1 \\ 1 & 0 \\ 3 & -3 \end{bmatrix} \begin{bmatrix} 2 & 1 \\ 1 & 0 \end{bmatrix}$

3. $[1, -1, 0, 2] \begin{bmatrix} 2 & 1 \\ 1 & 3 \\ -1 & 0 \\ 0 & 2 \end{bmatrix}$

4. $[1, -2, 0] \begin{bmatrix} 1 & -1 \\ 3 & 0 \\ -2 & 1 \end{bmatrix} \begin{bmatrix} 2 \\ 1 \end{bmatrix}$

5. $\begin{bmatrix} -1 & 1 \\ 1 & -1 \end{bmatrix} \begin{bmatrix} 2 & 0 \\ 0 & 2 \end{bmatrix} \begin{bmatrix} 1 & 1 & 1 \\ 1 & 1 & 1 \end{bmatrix}$

6. $[1, -1, 1] \begin{bmatrix} 2 & 0 \\ 0 & 2 \\ 2 & 2 \end{bmatrix} \begin{bmatrix} 1 & 0 \\ 0 & 1 \end{bmatrix}$

Answers to Odd-Numbered Problems

1. $\begin{bmatrix} -3 & 6 & 9 & 12 \\ 0 & -3 & -3 & 6 \\ 3 & 6 & 0 & 9 \end{bmatrix}$

3. $[1, 2]$

5. $\begin{bmatrix} 0 & 0 & 0 \\ 0 & 0 & 0 \end{bmatrix}$

7.4 Special Types of Matrices

In this section three special types of matrices are discussed. These are diagonal matrices, identity matrices, and null matrices.

DIAGONAL MATRICES

A *diagonal matrix* is a square matrix that has zeros everywhere except on the main diagonal, that is, the diagonal running from upper left to lower right; thus

$$\mathbf{A} = \begin{bmatrix} a_{11} & \cdots & a_{1n} \\ \vdots & & \vdots \\ a_{n1} & \cdots & a_{nn} \end{bmatrix} = (a_{ij})_{n \times n}$$

is a diagonal matrix if and only if

$a_{ij} = 0$ for $i \neq j$

$a_{ij} \neq 0$ for at least one $i = j$ (if all the elements of a matrix are zero, it is a *null matrix* discussed below)

An $n \times n$ diagonal matrix may be indicated by the notation

$$\mathbf{A} = \begin{bmatrix} a_{11} & & 0 \\ & \ddots & \\ 0 & & a_{nn} \end{bmatrix} \quad \text{or} \quad \begin{bmatrix} a_1 & & 0 \\ & \ddots & \\ 0 & & a_n \end{bmatrix}$$

or by

$$\mathbf{D}_n = \begin{bmatrix} d_1 & & 0 \\ & \ddots & \\ 0 & & d_n \end{bmatrix}$$

EXAMPLE

$$\begin{bmatrix} 1 & 0 & 0 \\ 0 & -3 & 0 \\ 0 & 0 & 10 \end{bmatrix} \quad \text{and} \quad \begin{bmatrix} -1 & 0 & 0 & 0 \\ 0 & 0 & 0 & 0 \\ 0 & 0 & 0 & 0 \\ 0 & 0 & 0 & 7 \end{bmatrix}$$

are diagonal matrices.

IDENTITY MATRICES

An *identity matrix* is a diagonal matrix each of whose diagonal elements is postive one; thus

$$\mathbf{A} = \begin{bmatrix} a_{11} & \cdots & a_{1n} \\ \vdots & & \vdots \\ a_{n1} & \cdots & a_{nn} \end{bmatrix} = (a_{ij})_{n \times n}$$

is an identity matrix if and only if

$$a_{ij} = 0 \qquad \text{for } i \neq j$$
$$a_{ij} = 1 \qquad \text{for } i = j$$

or equivalently, a diagonal matrix $\mathbf{D}_n$ is an identity matrix if and only if

$$d_i = 1 \qquad \text{for } i = 1, 2, \ldots, n$$

An $n \times n$ identity matrix is denoted by $\mathbf{I}_n$.

EXAMPLE

$$\mathbf{I}_3 = \begin{bmatrix} 1 & 0 & 0 \\ 0 & 1 & 0 \\ 0 & 0 & 1 \end{bmatrix} \quad \text{and} \quad \mathbf{I}_6 = \begin{bmatrix} 1 & 0 & 0 & 0 & 0 & 0 \\ 0 & 1 & 0 & 0 & 0 & 0 \\ 0 & 0 & 1 & 0 & 0 & 0 \\ 0 & 0 & 0 & 1 & 0 & 0 \\ 0 & 0 & 0 & 0 & 1 & 0 \\ 0 & 0 & 0 & 0 & 0 & 1 \end{bmatrix}$$

are the 3×3 and 6×6 identity matrices.

Note that premultiplying or postmultiplying a matrix by the appropriately sized identity matrix leaves it unchanged—that is,

$$\mathbf{A}_{m \times n} = \mathbf{I}_m \mathbf{A}_{m \times n} = \mathbf{A}_{m \times n} \mathbf{I}_n = \mathbf{A}_{m \times n}$$

EXAMPLE

$$\overset{\mathbf{A}_{2\times 4}}{\begin{bmatrix} 2 & -3 & -6 & 4 \\ -1 & -1 & 0 & 3 \end{bmatrix}_{2\times 4}} = \overset{\mathbf{I}_2}{\begin{bmatrix} 1 & 0 \\ 0 & 1 \end{bmatrix}_{2\times 2}} \overset{\mathbf{A}_{2\times 4}}{\begin{bmatrix} 2 & -3 & -6 & 4 \\ -1 & -1 & 0 & 3 \end{bmatrix}_{2\times 4}}$$

$$= \overset{\mathbf{A}_{2\times 4}}{\begin{bmatrix} 2 & -3 & -6 & 4 \\ -1 & -1 & 0 & 3 \end{bmatrix}_{2\times 4}} \overset{\mathbf{I}_4}{\begin{bmatrix} 1 & 0 & 0 & 0 \\ 0 & 1 & 0 & 0 \\ 0 & 0 & 1 & 0 \\ 0 & 0 & 0 & 1 \end{bmatrix}_{4\times 4}}$$

$$= \overset{\mathbf{A}_{2\times 4}}{\begin{bmatrix} 2 & -3 & -6 & 4 \\ -1 & -1 & 0 & 3 \end{bmatrix}_{2\times 4}}$$

EXAMPLE

$$\overset{\mathbf{A}_{3\times 3}}{\begin{bmatrix} 3 & 0 & 0 \\ 0 & -2 & 0 \\ 0 & 0 & 6 \end{bmatrix}_{3\times 3}} = \overset{\mathbf{I}_3}{\begin{bmatrix} 1 & 0 & 0 \\ 0 & 1 & 0 \\ 0 & 0 & 1 \end{bmatrix}_{3\times 3}} \overset{\mathbf{A}_{3\times 3}}{\begin{bmatrix} 3 & 0 & 0 \\ 0 & -2 & 0 \\ 0 & 0 & 6 \end{bmatrix}_{3\times 3}}$$

$$= \overset{\mathbf{A}_{3\times 3}}{\begin{bmatrix} 3 & 0 & 0 \\ 0 & -2 & 0 \\ 0 & 0 & 6 \end{bmatrix}_{3\times 3}} \overset{\mathbf{I}_3}{\begin{bmatrix} 1 & 0 & 0 \\ 0 & 1 & 0 \\ 0 & 0 & 1 \end{bmatrix}_{3\times 3}}$$

$$= \overset{\mathbf{A}_{3\times 3}}{\begin{bmatrix} 3 & 0 & 0 \\ 0 & -2 & 0 \\ 0 & 0 & 6 \end{bmatrix}_{3\times 3}}$$

NULL MATRICES

A *null matrix* is an $m \times n$ matrix all of whose elements are zeros; it is denoted by $\mathbf{O}$. When the appropriately sized null matrix is added to or subtracted from another matrix that matrix is unchanged, that is,

$$\mathbf{A}_{m\times n} \pm \mathbf{O}_{m\times n} = \mathbf{A}_{m\times n}$$

Premultiplying or postmultiplying a matrix by the appropriately sized null matrix results in another null matrix—that is,

$$\mathbf{O}_{k\times m}\,\mathbf{A}_{m\times n} = \mathbf{O}_{k\times n} \qquad \text{and} \qquad \mathbf{A}_{m\times n}\,\mathbf{O}_{n\times 1} = \mathbf{O}_{m\times 1}$$

EXAMPLE

$$\overset{\mathbf{A}_{2\times 3}}{\begin{bmatrix} 0 & 1 & 0 \\ 10 & 0 & -3 \end{bmatrix}_{2\times 3}} \pm \overset{\mathbf{O}_{2\times 3}}{\begin{bmatrix} 0 & 0 & 0 \\ 0 & 0 & 0 \end{bmatrix}_{2\times 3}} = \overset{\mathbf{A}_{2\times 3}}{\begin{bmatrix} 0 & 1 & 0 \\ 10 & 0 & -3 \end{bmatrix}_{2\times 3}}$$

EXAMPLE

$$\underset{3 \times 2}{\mathbf{O}_{3 \times 2}} \qquad\qquad \underset{}{\mathbf{A}_{2 \times 4}} \qquad\qquad\qquad \mathbf{O}_{3 \times 4}$$

$$\begin{bmatrix} 0 & 0 \\ 0 & 0 \\ 0 & 0 \end{bmatrix}_{3 \times 2} \begin{bmatrix} 1 & 6 & 4 & -10 \\ -1 & 20 & -13 & 11 \end{bmatrix}_{2 \times 4} = \begin{bmatrix} 0 & 0 & 0 & 0 \\ 0 & 0 & 0 & 0 \\ 0 & 0 & 0 & 0 \end{bmatrix}_{3 \times 4}$$

$$\mathbf{A}_{2 \times 4} \qquad\qquad \mathbf{O}_{4 \times 1} \qquad \mathbf{O}_{2 \times 1}$$

$$\begin{bmatrix} 1 & 6 & 4 & -10 \\ -1 & 20 & -13 & 11 \end{bmatrix}_{2 \times 4} \begin{bmatrix} 0 \\ 0 \\ 0 \\ 0 \end{bmatrix}_{4 \times 1} = \begin{bmatrix} 0 \\ 0 \end{bmatrix}_{2 \times 1}$$

7.5 The Transpose of a Matrix

For many matrix analyses it is convenient to use the transpose of a matrix. In this section the transpose of matrix is defined and the transpose of a sum or difference of matrices and the transpose of a product of matrices are discussed.

The *transpose* of an $m \times n$ matrix $\mathbf{A}$ is an $n \times m$ matrix, denoted by $\mathbf{A}'$, whose rows are the columns of $\mathbf{A}$ and whose columns are the rows of $\mathbf{A}$. Thus if

$$\mathbf{A}_{m \times n} = \begin{bmatrix} a_{11} & \cdots & a_{1n} \\ \vdots & & \vdots \\ a_{m1} & \cdots & a_{mn} \end{bmatrix} = (a_{ij})_{m \times n}$$

then the transpose of $\mathbf{A}$ is

$$\mathbf{A}'_{n \times m} = \begin{bmatrix} a_{11} & \cdots & a_{1n} \\ \vdots & & \vdots \\ a_{m1} & \cdots & a_{mn} \end{bmatrix}' = \begin{bmatrix} a_{11} & \cdots & a_{m1} \\ \vdots & & \vdots \\ a_{1n} & \cdots & a_{mn} \end{bmatrix} = (a_{ji})_{n \times m} = (a_{ij})'_{m \times n}$$

Note that the transpose of an n-dimensional row vector is an n-dimensional column vector and, similarly, the transpose of an n-dimensional column vector is an n-dimensional row vector. The transpose of a diagonal matrix is that same diagonal matrix.

EXAMPLES

If $\mathbf{A} = \begin{bmatrix} 3 & 2 & 0 \\ -6 & 0 & -1 \end{bmatrix}_{2 \times 3}$, then $\mathbf{A}' = \begin{bmatrix} 3 & -6 \\ 2 & 0 \\ 0 & -1 \end{bmatrix}_{3 \times 2}$

If $\mathbf{A} = [6, 2, -1, 0, -5]_{1 \times 5}$, then $\mathbf{A}' = \begin{bmatrix} 6 \\ 2 \\ -1 \\ 0 \\ -5 \end{bmatrix}_{5 \times 1}$

If $\mathbf{A} = \begin{bmatrix} 6 & -8 & -10 \\ -2 & 0 & 7 \\ 30 & 40 & 0 \end{bmatrix}_{3 \times 3}$, then $\mathbf{A}' = \begin{bmatrix} 6 & -2 & 30 \\ -8 & 0 & 40 \\ -10 & 7 & 0 \end{bmatrix}_{3 \times 3}$

If $A = \begin{bmatrix} 3 \\ 0 \\ -1 \\ 4 \end{bmatrix}_{4 \times 1}$, then $A' = [3, 0, -1, 4]_{1 \times 4}$

If $A = \begin{bmatrix} -1 & 5 & -3 \\ 5 & 0 & 4 \\ -3 & 4 & 9 \end{bmatrix}_{3 \times 3}$, then $A' = \begin{bmatrix} -1 & 5 & -3 \\ 5 & 0 & 4 \\ -3 & 4 & 9 \end{bmatrix}_{3 \times 3}$

If $A = \begin{bmatrix} 6 & 0 & 0 & 0 \\ 0 & -2 & 0 & 0 \\ 0 & 0 & 3 & 0 \\ 0 & 0 & 0 & 5 \end{bmatrix}_{4 \times 4}$, then $A' = \begin{bmatrix} 6 & 0 & 0 & 0 \\ 0 & -2 & 0 & 0 \\ 0 & 0 & 3 & 0 \\ 0 & 0 & 0 & 5 \end{bmatrix}_{4 \times 4}$

If a (square) matrix and its transpose are equal, that is, if $a_{ij} = a_{ji}$ for all i and j, then the matrix is said to be *symmetric* (about its main diagonal). In the last two examples above, the matrices are symmetric.

A symmetric matrix that reproduces itself when it is multiplied by itself is said to be *idempotent*. Thus A is idempotent if and only if

$$A' = A$$

and

$$A A = A$$

EXAMPLE

The identity matrix (of any size) is idempotent, since

$$I'_n = I_n$$

and

$$I_n I_n = I_n$$

EXAMPLE

The matrix

$$\begin{bmatrix} \frac{1}{5} & \frac{2}{5} \\ \frac{2}{5} & \frac{4}{5} \end{bmatrix}$$

is idempotent, since

$$\begin{bmatrix} \frac{1}{5} & \frac{2}{5} \\ \frac{2}{5} & \frac{4}{5} \end{bmatrix}' = \begin{bmatrix} \frac{1}{5} & \frac{2}{5} \\ \frac{2}{5} & \frac{4}{5} \end{bmatrix}$$

and

$$\begin{bmatrix} \frac{1}{5} & \frac{2}{5} \\ \frac{2}{5} & \frac{4}{5} \end{bmatrix}\begin{bmatrix} \frac{1}{5} & \frac{2}{5} \\ \frac{2}{5} & \frac{4}{5} \end{bmatrix} = \begin{bmatrix} \frac{1}{5} & \frac{2}{5} \\ \frac{2}{5} & \frac{4}{5} \end{bmatrix}$$

TRANSPOSE OF A SUM OR DIFFERENCE OF MATRICES

The transpose of a sum or difference of matrices is equal to the sum or difference of the transposes of the matrices; thus

$$(\mathbf{A}_{m \times n} \pm \mathbf{B}_{m \times n} \pm \mathbf{C}_{m \times n})' = \mathbf{A}'_{n \times m} \pm \mathbf{B}'_{n \times m} \pm \mathbf{C}'_{n \times m}$$

that is,

$$(d_{ij})'_{m \times n} = (d_{ji})_{n \times m}$$

where $d_{ij} = a_{ij} \pm b_{ij} \pm c_{ij}$ and $d_{ji} = a_{ji} \pm b_{ji} \pm c_{ji}$.

EXAMPLE

If

$$\mathbf{A} = \begin{bmatrix} 3 & 0 & 2 \\ -6 & 8 & -1 \end{bmatrix} \quad \mathbf{B} = \begin{bmatrix} -1 & 6 & -2 \\ 3 & -2 & 1 \end{bmatrix} \quad \mathbf{C} = \begin{bmatrix} 0 & 0 & 6 \\ -2 & 5 & 25 \end{bmatrix}$$

then

$$[\mathbf{A} + \mathbf{B} + \mathbf{C}]' = \begin{bmatrix} 2 & 6 & 6 \\ -5 & 11 & 25 \end{bmatrix}' = \begin{bmatrix} 2 & -5 \\ 6 & 11 \\ 6 & 25 \end{bmatrix}$$

or, alternatively,

$$\mathbf{A}' + \mathbf{B}' + \mathbf{C}' = \begin{bmatrix} 3 & -6 \\ 0 & 8 \\ 2 & -1 \end{bmatrix} + \begin{bmatrix} -1 & 3 \\ 6 & -2 \\ -2 & 1 \end{bmatrix} + \begin{bmatrix} 0 & -2 \\ 0 & 5 \\ 6 & 25 \end{bmatrix} = \begin{bmatrix} 2 & -5 \\ 6 & 11 \\ 6 & 25 \end{bmatrix}$$

EXAMPLE

If

$$\mathbf{A} = \begin{bmatrix} 2 & -1 \\ 0 & -1 \end{bmatrix} \quad \mathbf{B} = \begin{bmatrix} 6 & 8 \\ 10 & -12 \end{bmatrix} \quad \mathbf{C} = \begin{bmatrix} 0 & -1 \\ 0 & 0 \end{bmatrix}$$

then

$$[\mathbf{A} - \mathbf{B} + \mathbf{C}]' = \begin{bmatrix} -4 & -10 \\ -10 & 11 \end{bmatrix}' = \begin{bmatrix} -4 & -10 \\ -10 & 11 \end{bmatrix}$$

or, alternatively,

$$\mathbf{A}' - \mathbf{B}' + \mathbf{C}' = \begin{bmatrix} 2 & 0 \\ -1 & -1 \end{bmatrix} - \begin{bmatrix} 6 & 10 \\ 8 & -12 \end{bmatrix} + \begin{bmatrix} 0 & 0 \\ -1 & 0 \end{bmatrix} = \begin{bmatrix} -4 & -10 \\ -10 & 11 \end{bmatrix}$$

TRANSPOSE OF A PRODUCT OF MATRICES

The transpose of a product of matrices is equal to the product of the transposes of the matrices in reverse sequence; thus

$$[\mathbf{A}_{m \times n} \mathbf{B}_{n \times p} \mathbf{C}_{p \times q}]' = \mathbf{C}'_{q \times p} \mathbf{B}'_{p \times n} \mathbf{A}'_{n \times m}$$

EXAMPLE

If

$$A = \begin{bmatrix} 3 & 0 \\ -4 & -1 \end{bmatrix} \qquad B = \begin{bmatrix} 3 & 5 & -7 \\ 0 & -1 & 8 \end{bmatrix} \qquad C = \begin{bmatrix} 6 \\ -1 \\ 0 \end{bmatrix}$$

then

$$ABC = \begin{bmatrix} 9 & 15 & -21 \\ -12 & -19 & 20 \end{bmatrix} \begin{bmatrix} 6 \\ -1 \\ 0 \end{bmatrix} = \begin{bmatrix} 39 \\ -53 \end{bmatrix}$$

$$[ABC]' = \begin{bmatrix} 39 \\ -53 \end{bmatrix}'$$

$$= [39, -53]$$

or, alternatively,

$$[ABC]' = C'B'A' = [6, -1, 0] \begin{bmatrix} 3 & 0 \\ 5 & -1 \\ -7 & 8 \end{bmatrix} \begin{bmatrix} 3 & -4 \\ 0 & -1 \end{bmatrix}$$

$$= [13 \quad 1] \begin{bmatrix} 3 & -4 \\ 0 & -1 \end{bmatrix}$$

$$= [39, -53]$$

EXAMPLE

If

$$A = [3, -1, 0] \qquad B = \begin{bmatrix} 6 & 0 \\ -7 & 2 \\ 0 & 3 \end{bmatrix} \qquad C = \begin{bmatrix} 0 \\ 1 \end{bmatrix}$$

then $ABC = [26 \quad -2] \begin{bmatrix} 0 \\ 1 \end{bmatrix} = -2$ and $[ABC]' = -2$ (the transpose of a scalar is that scalar)

or, alternatively,

$$[ABC]' = C'B'A' = [0, 1] \begin{bmatrix} 6 & -7 & 0 \\ 0 & 2 & 3 \end{bmatrix} \begin{bmatrix} 3 \\ -1 \\ 0 \end{bmatrix} = [0 \quad 2 \quad 3] \begin{bmatrix} 3 \\ -1 \\ 0 \end{bmatrix} = -2$$

PROBLEMS

Obtain the transpose of each of the following matrices.

1. $\begin{bmatrix} 2 & 6 \\ 5 & -3 \end{bmatrix}$

2. $\begin{bmatrix} -3 \\ 6 \\ 5 \\ -2 \end{bmatrix}$

3. $\begin{bmatrix} -7 & -5 & 6 \\ 8 & 10 & -3 \end{bmatrix}$

4. $\begin{bmatrix} 1 & -6 & 3 \\ -1 & 4 & -8 \\ 0 & 5 & 7 \end{bmatrix}$

5. $[3, -2, 4, -9]$

6. $\begin{bmatrix} -1 & 3 \\ 2 & 1 \\ -4 & 2 \end{bmatrix}$

7. If $\mathbf{A} = \begin{bmatrix} 1 & 2 \\ 2 & 1 \end{bmatrix}$, $\mathbf{B} = \begin{bmatrix} -2 & 3 \\ 4 & 0 \end{bmatrix}$, $\mathbf{C} = \begin{bmatrix} 0 & -1 \\ 2 & 3 \end{bmatrix}$; find:

   a. $[\mathbf{A} + \mathbf{B}]'$
   b. $[\mathbf{B} + \mathbf{C}]'$
   c. $[\mathbf{AB}]'$
   d. $[\mathbf{ABC}]'$

8. If $\mathbf{A} = \begin{bmatrix} 2 & -1 \\ 1 & 2 \\ 0 & 1 \end{bmatrix}_{3 \times 2}$, $\mathbf{B} = \begin{bmatrix} 3 \\ -1 \end{bmatrix}_{2 \times 1}$, $\mathbf{C} = \begin{bmatrix} 3 & 0 & 2 \\ -1 & 2 & -4 \end{bmatrix}_{2 \times 3}$,

   and $\mathbf{D} = \begin{bmatrix} -3 & 0 & -2 \\ 1 & -2 & 4 \end{bmatrix}_{2 \times 3}$, find:

   a. $[\mathbf{AB}]'$
   b. $[\mathbf{C} + \mathbf{D}]'$
   c. $[\mathbf{D}'\mathbf{C}]'$
   d. $\mathbf{A} + \mathbf{D}' + \mathbf{C}'$

Answers to Odd-Numbered Problems

1. $\begin{bmatrix} 2 & 5 \\ 6 & -3 \end{bmatrix}$

3. $\begin{bmatrix} -7 & 8 \\ -5 & 10 \\ 6 & -3 \end{bmatrix}$

5. $\begin{bmatrix} 3 \\ -2 \\ 4 \\ -9 \end{bmatrix}$

7. a. $\begin{bmatrix} -1 & 6 \\ 5 & 1 \end{bmatrix}$

   b. $\begin{bmatrix} -2 & 6 \\ 2 & 3 \end{bmatrix}$

   c. $\begin{bmatrix} 6 & 0 \\ 3 & 6 \end{bmatrix}$

   d. $\begin{bmatrix} 6 & 12 \\ 3 & 18 \end{bmatrix}$

7.6 Partitioned Matrices

It is frequently convenient to partition a matrix into submatrices. These submatrices can then be treated as scalars in performing operations on the original matrix. Partitioning of a matrix is indicated by horizontal and vertical lines between rows and columns.

The $m \times n$ matrix $\mathbf{A}$ may be partitioned, for example, as follows

$$\mathbf{A} = (\mathbf{A}_1 \vdots \mathbf{A}_2)$$

where $\mathbf{A}_1$ is $m \times n_1$, $\mathbf{A}_2$ is $m \times n_2$, and $n_1 + n_2 = n$. The transpose of a partitioned matrix can be written in terms of the transposes of its submatrices; thus

$$\mathbf{A}' = \begin{bmatrix} \mathbf{A}'_1 \\ \hline \mathbf{A}'_2 \end{bmatrix}$$

EXAMPLE

If

$$\mathbf{A} = [\mathbf{A}_1 \vdots \mathbf{A}_2] = \begin{bmatrix} 4 & -3 & \vdots & 5 & 0 \\ 2 & -1 & \vdots & 1 & 6 \\ 8 & -2 & \vdots & 3 & -7 \end{bmatrix}$$

then

$$\mathbf{A}' = \begin{bmatrix} \mathbf{A}'_1 \\ \hline \mathbf{A}'_2 \end{bmatrix} \begin{bmatrix} 4 & 2 & 8 \\ -3 & -1 & -2 \\ \hline 5 & 1 & 3 \\ 0 & 6 & -7 \end{bmatrix}$$

If they are partitioned conformably, partitioned matrices can be added, subtracted, or multiplied. If an $m \times n$ matrix $\mathbf{A}$ is partitioned $\mathbf{A} = [\mathbf{A}_1 \vdots \mathbf{A}_2]$, where $\mathbf{A}_1$ is $m \times n_1$, $\mathbf{A}_2$ is $m \times n_2$, and $n_1 + n_2 = n$, and an $m \times n$ matrix $\mathbf{B}$ is partitioned $\mathbf{B} = [\mathbf{B}_1 \vdots \mathbf{B}_2]$, where $\mathbf{B}_1$ is $m \times n_1$, $\mathbf{B}_2$ is $m \times n_2$, and $n_1 + n_2 = n$, then

$$\mathbf{A} \pm \mathbf{B} = [\mathbf{A}_1 \pm \mathbf{B}_1 \vdots \mathbf{A}_2 \pm \mathbf{B}_2]$$

Similarly, if

$$\mathbf{A} = \begin{bmatrix} \mathbf{A}_1 \\ \hline \mathbf{A}_2 \end{bmatrix}$$

where $\mathbf{A}$ is $m \times n$, $\mathbf{A}_1$ is $m_1 \times n$, $\mathbf{A}_2$ is $m_2 \times n$, and $m_1 + m_2 = m$, and

$$\mathbf{B} = \begin{bmatrix} \mathbf{B}_1 \\ \hline \mathbf{B}_2 \end{bmatrix}$$

where $\mathbf{B}$ is $m \times n$, $\mathbf{B}_1$ is $m_1 \times n$, $\mathbf{B}_2$ is $m_2 \times n$, and $m_1 + m_2 = m$, then

$$\mathbf{A} \pm \mathbf{B} = \begin{bmatrix} \mathbf{A}_1 \pm \mathbf{B}_1 \\ \hline \mathbf{A}_2 \pm \mathbf{B}_2 \end{bmatrix}$$

EXAMPLE

If

$$\mathbf{A} = \begin{bmatrix} 3 & 4 & -2 & 0 \\ -1 & 0 & 5 & 6 \\ 7 & 3 & 3 & 2 \end{bmatrix} \quad \text{and} \quad \mathbf{B} = \begin{bmatrix} -3 & 0 & 2 & 4 \\ -1 & -1 & -2 & 5 \\ 5 & 4 & 3 & 1 \end{bmatrix}$$

then

$$A + B = (A_1 \mid A_2) + (B_1 \mid B_2)$$

$$= \begin{bmatrix} 3 & 4 & -2 & 0 \\ -1 & 0 & 5 & 6 \\ 7 & 3 & 3 & 2 \end{bmatrix} + \begin{bmatrix} -3 & 0 & 2 & 4 \\ -1 & -1 & -2 & 5 \\ 5 & 4 & 3 & 1 \end{bmatrix}$$

$$= \begin{bmatrix} 0 & 4 & 0 & 4 \\ -2 & -1 & 3 & 11 \\ 12 & 7 & 6 & 3 \end{bmatrix} = [A_1 + B_1 \mid A_2 + B_2]$$

or

$$A + B = \begin{bmatrix} A_1 \\ \hline A_2 \end{bmatrix} + \begin{bmatrix} B_1 \\ \hline B_2 \end{bmatrix}$$

$$= \begin{bmatrix} 3 & 4 & -2 & 0 \\ -1 & 0 & 5 & 6 \\ \hline 7 & 3 & 3 & 2 \end{bmatrix} + \begin{bmatrix} -3 & 0 & 2 & 4 \\ -1 & -1 & -2 & 5 \\ \hline 5 & 4 & 3 & 1 \end{bmatrix}$$

$$= \begin{bmatrix} 0 & 4 & 0 & 4 \\ -2 & -1 & 3 & 11 \\ \hline 12 & 7 & 6 & 3 \end{bmatrix} = \begin{bmatrix} A_1 + B_1 \\ \hline A_2 + B_2 \end{bmatrix}$$

Many other partitionings are possible and will give the same result.

Partitioning is frequently conceptually convenient when matrices are to be added or subtracted, but the computational advantages of matrix partitioning are associated primarily with multiplication and other more complex operations. Partitioned matrices must be partitioned conformably for multiplication. If an $m \times n$ matrix A is partitioned $A = [A_1 \mid A_2]$, where A_1 is $m \times n_1$, A_2 is $m \times n_2$, and $n_1 + n_2 = n$, and an $n \times p$ matrix B is partitioned

$$B = \begin{bmatrix} B_1 \\ \hline B_2 \end{bmatrix}$$

where B_1 is $n_1 \times p$ and B_2 is $n_2 \times p$, then

$$AB = [A_1 \mid A_2] \begin{bmatrix} B_1 \\ \hline B_2 \end{bmatrix} = A_1 B_1 + A_2 B_2$$

EXAMPLE

If

$$A = \begin{bmatrix} 3 & 0 & -1 \\ -2 & 4 & 1 \\ 1 & -1 & 2 \end{bmatrix} \quad \text{and} \quad B = \begin{bmatrix} 2 & 1 \\ 1 & 3 \\ -1 & 1 \end{bmatrix}$$

then

$$AB = \begin{bmatrix} 3 & 0 & -1 \\ -2 & 4 & 1 \\ 1 & -1 & 2 \end{bmatrix} \begin{bmatrix} 2 & 1 \\ 1 & 3 \\ -1 & 1 \end{bmatrix}$$

$$= \begin{bmatrix} 3 & 0 \\ -2 & 4 \\ 1 & -1 \end{bmatrix} \begin{bmatrix} 2 & 1 \\ 1 & 3 \end{bmatrix} + \begin{bmatrix} -1 \\ 1 \\ 2 \end{bmatrix} [-1, 1]$$

$$= \begin{bmatrix} 6 & 3 \\ 0 & 10 \\ 1 & -2 \end{bmatrix} + \begin{bmatrix} 1 & -1 \\ -1 & 1 \\ -2 & 2 \end{bmatrix}$$

$$= \begin{bmatrix} 7 & 2 \\ -1 & 11 \\ -1 & 0 \end{bmatrix}$$

which can be verified by direct matrix multiplication.

Matrices can be partitioned into more than two submatrices. In fact, it is possible to partition an $m \times n$ matrix into a maximum of mn submatrices; note that maximum partitioning is equivalent to no partitioning, since each element is treated as a scalar matrix. Unless there is a logical partitioning in terms of the variables in a problem, matrices should be partitioned for ease of computation; this involves some reasonable compromise between minimizing the number of submatrices and minimizing their maximum size.

Frequently matrices are partitioned once horizontally and once vertically. Thus the $m \times n$ matrix $\mathbf{A}$ may be partitioned

$$\mathbf{A} = \begin{bmatrix} \mathbf{A}_{11} & \vdots & \mathbf{A}_{12} \\ \cdots & \cdots & \cdots \\ \mathbf{A}_{21} & \vdots & \mathbf{A}_{22} \end{bmatrix}$$

where $\mathbf{A}_{11}$ is $m_1 \times n_1$, $\mathbf{A}_{12}$ is $m_1 \times n_2$, $\mathbf{A}_{21}$ is $m_2 \times n_1$, $\mathbf{A}_{22}$ is $m_2 \times n_2$, and $m_1 + m_2 = m$, $n_1 + n_2 = n$. Then

$$\mathbf{A}' = \begin{bmatrix} \mathbf{A}_{11} & \vdots & \mathbf{A}_{12} \\ \cdots & \cdots & \cdots \\ \mathbf{A}_{21} & \vdots & \mathbf{A}_{22} \end{bmatrix}' = \begin{bmatrix} \mathbf{A}'_{11} & \vdots & \mathbf{A}'_{12} \\ \cdots & \cdots & \cdots \\ \mathbf{A}'_{21} & \vdots & \mathbf{A}'_{22} \end{bmatrix}$$

If the $n \times p$ matrix $\mathbf{B}$ is partitioned

$$\mathbf{B} = \begin{bmatrix} \mathbf{B}_{11} & \vdots & \mathbf{B}_{12} \\ \cdots & \cdots & \cdots \\ \mathbf{B}_{21} & \vdots & \mathbf{B}_{22} \end{bmatrix}$$

where $\mathbf{B}_{11}$ is $n_1 \times p_1$, $\mathbf{B}_{12}$ is $n_1 \times p_2$, $\mathbf{B}_{21}$ is $n_2 \times p_1$, $\mathbf{B}_{22}$ is $n_2 \times p_2$, and $n_1 + n_2 = n$, $p_1 + p_2 = p$, then $\mathbf{A}$ and $\mathbf{B}$ are partitioned conformably for multiplication and

$$\mathbf{AB} = \begin{bmatrix} \mathbf{A}_{11} & \vdots & \mathbf{A}_{12} \\ \cdots & \cdots & \cdots \\ \mathbf{A}_{21} & \vdots & \mathbf{A}_{22} \end{bmatrix} \begin{bmatrix} \mathbf{B}_{11} & \vdots & \mathbf{B}_{12} \\ \cdots & \cdots & \cdots \\ \mathbf{B}_{21} & \vdots & \mathbf{B}_{22} \end{bmatrix}$$

$$= \begin{bmatrix} \mathbf{A}_{11}\mathbf{B}_{11} + \mathbf{A}_{12}\mathbf{B}_{21} & \vdots & \mathbf{A}_{11}\mathbf{B}_{12} + \mathbf{A}_{12}\mathbf{B}_{22} \\ \cdots & \cdots & \cdots \\ \mathbf{A}_{21}\mathbf{B}_{11} + \mathbf{A}_{22}\mathbf{B}_{21} & \vdots & \mathbf{A}_{21}\mathbf{B}_{12} + \mathbf{A}_{22}\mathbf{B}_{22} \end{bmatrix}$$

EXAMPLE

If

$$\mathbf{A} = \begin{bmatrix} 1 & 3 & 1 \\ -1 & 0 & 1 \\ 2 & -1 & 4 \\ 0 & 2 & -3 \end{bmatrix} \quad \text{and} \quad \mathbf{B} = \begin{bmatrix} 3 & -2 & 1 & 0 & -1 \\ 5 & -1 & 4 & -3 & 2 \\ 3 & -2 & 0 & 1 & -1 \end{bmatrix}$$

then

$$\mathbf{AB} = \begin{bmatrix} \mathbf{A}_{11} & \vdots & \mathbf{A}_{12} \\ \hline \mathbf{A}_{21} & \vdots & \mathbf{A}_{22} \end{bmatrix} \begin{bmatrix} \mathbf{B}_{11} & \vdots & \mathbf{B}_{12} \\ \hline \mathbf{B}_{21} & \vdots & \mathbf{B}_{22} \end{bmatrix}$$

$$= \begin{bmatrix} 1 & 3 & \vdots & 1 \\ -1 & 0 & \vdots & 1 \\ 2 & -1 & \vdots & 4 \\ \hline 0 & 2 & \vdots & -3 \end{bmatrix} \begin{bmatrix} 3 & -2 & \vdots & 1 & 0 & -1 \\ 5 & -1 & \vdots & 4 & -3 & 2 \\ \hline 3 & -2 & \vdots & 0 & 1 & -1 \end{bmatrix}$$

and

$$\mathbf{A}_{11} \mathbf{B}_{11} + \mathbf{A}_{12} \mathbf{B}_{21} = \begin{bmatrix} 1 & 3 \\ -1 & 0 \\ 2 & -1 \end{bmatrix} \begin{bmatrix} 3 & -2 \\ 5 & -1 \end{bmatrix} + \begin{bmatrix} 1 \\ 1 \\ 4 \end{bmatrix} [3, -2]$$

$$= \begin{bmatrix} 18 & -5 \\ -3 & 2 \\ 1 & -3 \end{bmatrix} + \begin{bmatrix} 3 & -2 \\ 3 & -2 \\ 12 & -8 \end{bmatrix}$$

$$= \begin{bmatrix} 21 & -7 \\ 0 & 0 \\ 13 & -11 \end{bmatrix}$$

$$\mathbf{A}_{11} \mathbf{B}_{12} + \mathbf{A}_{12} \mathbf{B}_{22} = \begin{bmatrix} 1 & 3 \\ -1 & 0 \\ 2 & -1 \end{bmatrix} \begin{bmatrix} 1 & 0 & -1 \\ 4 & -3 & 2 \end{bmatrix} + \begin{bmatrix} 1 \\ 1 \\ 4 \end{bmatrix} [0, 1, -1]$$

$$= \begin{bmatrix} 13 & -9 & 5 \\ -1 & 0 & 1 \\ -2 & 3 & -4 \end{bmatrix} + \begin{bmatrix} 0 & 1 & -1 \\ 0 & 1 & -1 \\ 0 & 4 & -4 \end{bmatrix}$$

$$= \begin{bmatrix} 13 & -8 & 4 \\ -1 & 1 & 0 \\ -2 & 7 & -8 \end{bmatrix}$$

$$\mathbf{A}_{21} \mathbf{B}_{11} + \mathbf{A}_{22} \mathbf{B}_{21} = [0, 2] \begin{bmatrix} 3 & -2 \\ 5 & -1 \end{bmatrix} + [-3][3, -2]$$

$$= [10, -2] + [-9, 6]$$

$$= [1, 4]$$

$$\mathbf{A}_{21} \mathbf{B}_{12} + \mathbf{A}_{22} \mathbf{B}_{22} = [0, 2] \begin{bmatrix} 1 & 0 & -1 \\ 4 & -3 & 2 \end{bmatrix} + [-3][0, 1, -1]$$

$$= [8, -6, 4] + [0, -3, 3]$$

$$= [8, -9, 7]$$

Thus

$$\mathbf{AB} = \begin{bmatrix} \mathbf{A}_{11} \mathbf{B}_{11} + \mathbf{A}_{12} \mathbf{B}_{21} & \vdots & \mathbf{A}_{11} \mathbf{B}_{12} + \mathbf{A}_{12} \mathbf{B}_{12} \\ \hline \mathbf{A}_{21} \mathbf{B}_{11} + \mathbf{A}_{22} \mathbf{B}_{21} & \vdots & \mathbf{A}_{21} \mathbf{B}_{12} + \mathbf{A}_{22} \mathbf{B}_{22} \end{bmatrix}$$

$$= \begin{bmatrix} 21 & -7 & \vdots & 13 & -8 & 4 \\ 0 & 0 & \vdots & -1 & 1 & 0 \\ 13 & -11 & \vdots & -2 & 7 & -8 \\ \hline 1 & 4 & \vdots & 8 & -9 & 7 \end{bmatrix}$$

which can be verified by direct matrix multiplication.

PROBLEMS

1. Compute the following.

a. $2 \begin{bmatrix} 6 & 1 \\ 0 & -3 \\ -1 & 2 \end{bmatrix} - 3 \begin{bmatrix} 4 & 2 \\ 0 & 1 \\ -5 & -1 \end{bmatrix}$

b. $\begin{bmatrix} 6 & 0 & -1 \\ 1 & -3 & 2 \end{bmatrix} \begin{bmatrix} 4 & 2 \\ 0 & 1 \\ -5 & -1 \end{bmatrix}$

Use partitioned matrices to check the results.

2. If $U = [1, -1, 4]$, $X = [0, 1, 2]$, $V = \begin{bmatrix} 5 \\ 0 \\ 1 \end{bmatrix}$, and $Y = \begin{bmatrix} -1 \\ -1 \\ 2 \end{bmatrix}$, find

a. $UV + XY$
b. $5UV + 10[X(2V - Y)]$

3. If A is 2×3, B is 4×3, C is 3×3, and D is 3×2, determine the shape of
   a. AC d. BC
   b. DA e. DAC
   c. AD f. $BCDA$

4. If

$$A = \begin{bmatrix} 1 & 2 & 3 \\ 0 & -1 & 1 \\ 2 & 3 & 0 \end{bmatrix} \qquad B = \begin{bmatrix} 3 & 1 & 0 \\ 1 & -1 & 2 \\ 0 & 2 & 1 \end{bmatrix}$$

find $2(AB - BA)$ and use partitioned matrices to check the result.

5. If

$$A = \begin{bmatrix} -1 & -2 & -2 \\ 1 & 2 & 1 \\ -1 & -1 & 0 \end{bmatrix} \qquad B = \begin{bmatrix} -3 & -6 & 2 \\ 2 & 4 & -1 \\ 2 & 3 & 0 \end{bmatrix} \qquad C = \begin{bmatrix} -5 & -8 & 0 \\ 3 & 5 & 0 \\ 1 & 2 & -1 \end{bmatrix}$$

show that
a. $A^2 = B^2 = C^2 = I$ c. $BC = CB = A$
b. $AB = BA = C$ d. $AC = CA = B$
Use partitioned matrices to check the results.

6. If

$$A = \begin{bmatrix} 5 & 4 & -2 \\ 4 & 5 & -2 \\ -2 & -2 & 2 \end{bmatrix}$$

show that $A^2 - 11A + 10I = O$. Use partitioned matrices to check the result.

7. If

$$A = \begin{bmatrix} 1 & 0 \\ 1 & 0 \end{bmatrix} \qquad B = \begin{bmatrix} 0 & 0 \\ 1 & 1 \end{bmatrix} \qquad C = \begin{bmatrix} 2 & 2 \\ 2 & 2 \end{bmatrix} \qquad D = \begin{bmatrix} 2 & 3 \\ 4 & 5 \end{bmatrix}$$

find a. $AB - 2CD$
      b. A^2
      c. $(BC)^2$

8. If

$$U = [1, 0, 1] \quad V = \begin{bmatrix} 1 \\ 2 \\ 3 \end{bmatrix} \quad X = \begin{bmatrix} 4 & 2 & -1 \\ -1 & 3 & 0 \\ 0 & 1 & 1 \end{bmatrix} \quad Y = \begin{bmatrix} 1 & 0 & 0 \\ 0 & 1 & 0 \\ 0 & 0 & 1 \end{bmatrix}$$

find a. **UV**
    b. **VU + X**
    c. **XY**
Use partitioned matrices to check the results.

9. If

$$U = \begin{bmatrix} 2 & -2 & -4 \\ -1 & 3 & 4 \\ 1 & -2 & -3 \end{bmatrix} \quad V = \begin{bmatrix} -1 & 2 & 4 \\ 1 & -2 & -4 \\ -1 & 2 & 4 \end{bmatrix}$$

show that
a. $U^2 = U$ and $V^2 = V$
b. $UV = VU = O$
c. $U + V = I$
Use partitioned matrices to check the results.

10. If

$$X = \begin{bmatrix} 1 & 2 & 3 \\ 1 & 2 & 3 \\ -1 & -2 & -3 \end{bmatrix}$$

show that $X^2 = O$. Use partitioned matrices to check the result.

11. If

$$A = \begin{bmatrix} 1 & -2 & 1 \\ 2 & 1 & -3 \\ -5 & 2 & 3 \end{bmatrix} \quad X = \begin{bmatrix} 2 & 5 & -1 & -7 \\ -2 & 1 & 3 & 4 \\ 3 & 2 & 1 & 2 \end{bmatrix}$$

$$Y = \begin{bmatrix} 3 & 6 & 0 & -6 \\ -1 & 2 & 4 & 5 \\ 4 & 3 & 2 & 3 \end{bmatrix}$$

show that $AX = AY$ (although $X \neq Y$) and use partitioned matrices to check the result.

12. If

$$A = \begin{bmatrix} 1 & -2 \\ 0 & 3 \\ 2 & -1 \end{bmatrix} \quad B = \begin{bmatrix} 0 & -2 & 3 \\ 0 & 1 & 3 \end{bmatrix} \quad C = \begin{bmatrix} -2 \\ 3 \\ -3 \end{bmatrix} \quad D = \begin{bmatrix} -1 \\ 1 \\ 2 \end{bmatrix}$$

find $AB - CD'$.

Answers to Odd-Numbered Problems

1. a. $\begin{bmatrix} 0 & -4 \\ 0 & -9 \\ 13 & 7 \end{bmatrix}$

  b. $\begin{bmatrix} 29 & 13 \\ -6 & -3 \end{bmatrix}$

3. a. 2×3
  b. 3×3
  c. 2×2
  d. 4×3
  e. 3×3
  f. 4×3

7. a. $\begin{bmatrix} -24 & -32 \\ -24 & -32 \end{bmatrix}$

b. $\begin{bmatrix} 1 & 0 \\ 1 & 0 \end{bmatrix}$

c. $\begin{bmatrix} 0 & 0 \\ 16 & 16 \end{bmatrix}$

7.7 The Determinant of a Matrix

The determinant of a matrix is a scalar (number), obtained from the elements of a matrix by specified operations, which is characteristic of the matrix. Determinants are defined only for square matrices. Methods for obtaining determinants and properties of determinants are discussed in this section.

The determinant of a 2×2 matrix

$$\mathbf{A} = \begin{bmatrix} a_{11} & a_{12} \\ a_{21} & a_{22} \end{bmatrix}$$

is given by

$$\det \mathbf{A} = |\mathbf{A}| = a_{11}a_{22} - a_{12}a_{21}$$

EXAMPLE

If $\mathbf{A} = \begin{bmatrix} 3 & -6 \\ 4 & 1 \end{bmatrix}$ then $|\mathbf{A}| = \begin{vmatrix} 3 & -6 \\ 4 & 1 \end{vmatrix} = 3 - (-24) = 27$

If $\mathbf{A} = \begin{bmatrix} -1 & 0 \\ 6 & 10 \end{bmatrix}$ then $|\mathbf{A}| = \begin{vmatrix} -1 & 0 \\ 6 & 10 \end{vmatrix} = -10 - 0 = -10$

Similarly, the determinant of a 3×3 matrix,

$$\mathbf{A} = \begin{bmatrix} a_{11} & a_{12} & a_{13} \\ a_{21} & a_{22} & a_{23} \\ a_{31} & a_{32} & a_{33} \end{bmatrix}$$

is given by

$$|\mathbf{A}| = a_{11}a_{22}a_{33} + a_{12}a_{23}a_{31} + a_{13}a_{32}a_{21} - a_{13}a_{22}a_{31} - a_{23}a_{32}a_{11}$$
$$- a_{33}a_{21}a_{12}$$

The terms can be obtained by the rule illustrated in Figure 7.1, where positive product terms are formed of elements connected by solid lines and negative product terms are formed of elements connected by dashed lines. Note that similar rules are *not* valid for higher-order matrices.

By definition, a determinant of order n, $|\mathbf{A}| = |a_{ij}|$ with $i, j = 1, 2, \ldots, n$, is the algebraic sum of $n!$ terms, each representing the product of n elements selected one from each row and one from each column in all possible and distinct combinations, having either a positive or negative sign depending on whether the number of inversions in the order of j (after the i in the product term have been arranged in increasing order) is even or odd.

Figure 7.1

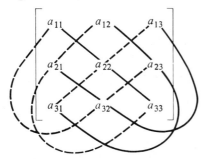

Using this rule to obtain the determinant of a matrix larger than, say, 3×3 is tedious. For example, the determinant of a 4×4 matrix is the algebraic sum of $4! = 24$ terms, each of which is the product of four elements; the determinant of a 5×5 matrix is the algebraic sum of $5! = 120$ terms, each of which is the product of five elements.

Determinants of matrices larger than 3×3 are frequently computed by a procedure known as *expansion by cofactors*. For example, the determinant of the 3×3 matrix above can be written

$$|\mathbf{A}| = a_{11}(a_{22}a_{33} - a_{23}a_{32}) - a_{12}(a_{21}a_{33} - a_{23}a_{31}) + a_{13}(a_{21}a_{32} - a_{22}a_{31})$$

$$= a_{11} \begin{vmatrix} a_{22} & a_{23} \\ a_{32} & a_{33} \end{vmatrix} - a_{12} \begin{vmatrix} a_{21} & a_{23} \\ a_{31} & a_{33} \end{vmatrix} + a_{13} \begin{vmatrix} a_{21} & a_{22} \\ a_{31} & a_{32} \end{vmatrix}$$

Note that each determinant in the sum is the determinant of a submatrix of $\mathbf{A}$ obtained by deleting a row and column of $\mathbf{A}$. These determinants are called *minors*.

DEFINITION: Let $\mathbf{M}_{ij}$ denote the $(n-1) \times (n-1)$ matrix obtained by deleting the ith row and the jth column of $\mathbf{A}_{n \times n}$. The determinant

$$|\mathbf{M}_{ij}|$$

is a *minor* of the matrix $\mathbf{A}$. The scalar

$$C_{ij} = (-1)^{i+j} |\mathbf{M}_{ij}|$$

is referred to as the *cofactor* or *signed minor* of the element a_{ij} of the matrix $\mathbf{A}$. The $n \times n$ matrix

$$(C_{ij})'$$

is referred to as the *adjoint* of $\mathbf{A}$ and is denoted by adj $\mathbf{A}$.

As noted above, the determinant of a matrix can be obtained by a procedure known as *expansion by cofactors*. The determinant of $\mathbf{A}$ can be expanded in terms of row i by the formula

$$|\mathbf{A}| = \sum_{j=1}^{n} a_{ij} C_{ij} \qquad \text{for any row } i = 1, 2, \ldots, n$$

and in terms of column j by the formula

$$|\mathbf{A}| = \sum_{i=1}^{n} a_{ij} C_{ij} \qquad \text{for any column } j = 1, 2, \ldots, n$$

Thus the determinant of $\mathbf{A}_{3 \times 3}$ given above as

$$|\mathbf{A}| = a_{11} \begin{vmatrix} a_{22} & a_{23} \\ a_{32} & a_{33} \end{vmatrix} - a_{12} \begin{vmatrix} a_{21} & a_{23} \\ a_{31} & a_{33} \end{vmatrix} + a_{13} \begin{vmatrix} a_{21} & a_{22} \\ a_{31} & a_{32} \end{vmatrix}$$

can be written

$$|\mathbf{A}| = a_{11}C_{11} + a_{12}C_{12} + a_{13}C_{13} = \sum_{j=1}^{3} a_{1j}C_{1j}$$

EXAMPLE

Find the determinant of the matrix

$$\mathbf{A} = \begin{bmatrix} 3 & 0 & -2 \\ 6 & -8 & 1 \\ 0 & 3 & 4 \end{bmatrix}$$

$$|\mathbf{A}| = -96 + 0 - 36 - (0 + 9 + 0)$$

$$= -141$$

Alternatively, expanding in terms of the first row,

$$|\mathbf{A}| = 3 \begin{vmatrix} -8 & 1 \\ 3 & 4 \end{vmatrix} + 0 - 2 \begin{vmatrix} 6 & -8 \\ 0 & 3 \end{vmatrix}$$

$$= 3(-32 - 3) - 2(18 - 0)$$

$$= -105 - 36 = -141$$

Alternatively, expanding in terms of the second column,

$$|\mathbf{A}| = 0 - 8 \begin{vmatrix} 3 & -2 \\ 0 & 4 \end{vmatrix} - 3 \begin{vmatrix} 3 & -2 \\ 6 & 1 \end{vmatrix}$$

$$= 0 - 8(12 - 0) - 3(3 + 12)$$

$$= -96 - 45 = -141$$

Note that cofactors are essentially determinants and can be evaluated by further expansion in terms of determinants of lower order. By repeated expansion, an nth-order determinant can be written in terms of second- or third-order determinants which can be evaluated easily. To simplify computation, a determinant should be expanded in terms of the row or column having the largest number of zero elements.

PROPERTIES OF DETERMINANTS

The following properties of determinants are frequently useful in their evaluation:

1. Interchanging the corresponding rows and columns of a determinant does not change its value, that is, $|\mathbf{A}| = |\mathbf{A}'|$.
2. If every element of a row (or of a column) of a determinant is zero, the value of the determinant is zero.
3. If every element of a row (or of a column) of a determinant is multiplied by the same constant, the value of the determinant is multiplied by that constant.

4. If two rows (or two columns) of a determinant are interchanged, the sign of the determinant is changed, but its absolute value is unchanged.
5. If two rows (or two columns) of a determinant are identical, the value of the determinant is zero.
6. The value of a determinant is not changed if each element of any row (or of any column), or each element multiplied by the same constant, is added to or subtracted from the corresponding element of any other row (or column).
7. The determinant of the product of two matrices is equal to the product of the determinants of the two matrices, that is, $|\mathbf{AB}| = |\mathbf{A}||\mathbf{B}|$.
8. The determinant of a diagonal matrix is equal to the product of its diagonal elements.

EXAMPLES

If $\mathbf{A} = \begin{bmatrix} 1 & 3 & -3 \\ 2 & 0 & 1 \\ -1 & 4 & -2 \end{bmatrix}$,

(Property 1)

$$|\mathbf{A}| = \begin{vmatrix} 1 & 3 & -3 \\ 2 & 0 & 1 \\ -1 & 4 & -2 \end{vmatrix}$$

$$= 0 - 3 - 24 - (0 + 4 - 12)$$

$$= -19$$

$$|\mathbf{A}'| = \begin{vmatrix} 1 & 2 & -1 \\ 3 & 0 & 4 \\ -3 & 1 & -2 \end{vmatrix}$$

$$= 0 - 24 - 3 - (0 + 4 - 12)$$

$$= -19$$

(Property 3)

$$|A^*| = \begin{vmatrix} 3 & 3 & -3 \\ 6 & 0 & 1 \\ -3 & 4 & -2 \end{vmatrix}$$

$$= 0 - 9 - 72 - (0 + 12 - 36)$$

$$= -57 \qquad -$$

$$= 3|\mathbf{A}|$$

(Note: First column of A is multiplied by 3 to form A^*.)

(Property 4)

$$|\mathbf{B}| = \begin{bmatrix} 1 & 3 & -3 \\ -1 & 4 & -2 \\ 2 & 0 & 1 \end{bmatrix} = 4 - 12 + 0 - (-24 + 0 - 3)$$

$$= 19$$

$$= -|\mathbf{A}|$$

(Note: Second and third rows of $\mathbf{A}$ are interchanged to form $\mathbf{B}$)

(Property 6)

$$|\mathbf{C}| = \begin{vmatrix} 1 & 3 & -3 \\ 3 & 4 & 0 \\ 2 & 0 & 1 \end{vmatrix} = 4 + 0 + 0 - (-24 + 0 + 9)$$

$$= 19$$

$$= |B|$$

(Note: Second row of $\mathbf{C}$ is equal to second row of B plus two times the third row of B.)

(Property 2)

$$\text{If } \mathbf{A} = \begin{bmatrix} 1 & 3 & -3 \\ 0 & 0 & 0 \\ -1 & 4 & -2 \end{bmatrix}, \text{ then}$$

$$|\mathbf{A}| = \begin{vmatrix} 1 & 3 & -3 \\ 0 & 0 & 0 \\ -1 & 4 & 2 \end{vmatrix}$$

$$= 0 + 0 + 0 - (0 + 0 + 0)$$

$$= 0$$

(Property 5)

$$\text{If } \mathbf{A} = \begin{bmatrix} 1 & 1 & -3 \\ 2 & 2 & 1 \\ -1 & -1 & -2 \end{bmatrix} \text{ then}$$

$$|\mathbf{A}| = \begin{vmatrix} 1 & 1 & -3 \\ 2 & 2 & 1 \\ -1 & -1 & -2 \end{vmatrix}$$

$$= -4 - 1 + 6 - (6 - 1 - 4)$$

$$= 0$$

(Property 7)

$$\text{If } \mathbf{A} = \begin{bmatrix} 1 & 3 & -3 \\ 2 & 0 & 1 \\ -1 & 4 & -2 \end{bmatrix} \quad \text{and} \quad \mathbf{B} = \begin{bmatrix} -1 & 0 & 2 \\ 3 & -2 & -2 \\ 1 & 0 & -1 \end{bmatrix}, \text{ then}$$

$$|\mathbf{AB}| = \begin{vmatrix} 5 & -6 & -1 \\ -1 & 0 & 3 \\ 11 & -8 & -8 \end{vmatrix}$$

$$= 0 - 198 - 8 - (0 - 120 - 48)$$

$$= -38$$

$$|\mathbf{A}| = \begin{vmatrix} 1 & 3 & -3 \\ 2 & 0 & 1 \\ -1 & 4 & -2 \end{vmatrix} = -19$$

$$|\mathbf{B}| = \begin{vmatrix} -1 & 0 & 2 \\ 3 & -2 & -2 \\ 1 & 0 & -1 \end{vmatrix}$$

$$= -2 + 0 + 0 - (-4 + 0 + 0)$$

$$= 2$$

and $|\mathbf{AB}| = |\mathbf{A}|\,|\mathbf{B}| = (-19)(2) = -38$

(Property 8)

If $\mathbf{A} = \begin{bmatrix} 3 & 0 & 0 \\ 0 & -2 & 0 \\ 0 & 0 & 1 \end{bmatrix}$, then

$$|\mathbf{A}| = \begin{vmatrix} 3 & 0 & 0 \\ 0 & -2 & 0 \\ 0 & 0 & 1 \end{vmatrix}$$

$$= -6 + 0 + 0 - (0 + 0 + 0)$$

$$= -6$$

7.8 The Inverse of a Matrix

The inverse of a matrix is used in solving simultaneous linear equations and in other analyses. The inverse of a matrix is defined and several methods of inversion are discussed in this section; these methods include inversion by Gaussian elimination, inversion using adjoints and determinants, and inversion of partitioned matrices. Properties of inverses are also considered.

If for an $n \times n$ (square) matrix $\mathbf{A}$ there is another $n \times n$ (square) matrix $\mathbf{B}$ such that their product is the identity matrix of size n, that is, if

$$\mathbf{A}_{n \times n} \mathbf{B}_{n \times n} = \mathbf{I}_n = \mathbf{B}_{n \times n} \mathbf{A}_{n \times n}$$

then $\mathbf{B}$ is said to be the *reciprocal* or *inverse* of $\mathbf{A}$ and is written

$$\mathbf{B} = \mathbf{A}^{-1} = (a_{ij})^{-1} = (a^{ij}) = (b_{ij})$$

(it can be shown that $\mathbf{AB} = \mathbf{I} \Leftrightarrow \mathbf{BA} = \mathbf{I}$).

NOTE: In ordinary algebra, division of a quantity x by a quantity y is equivalent to multiplication of x by the reciprocal of y—that is,

$$\frac{x}{y} = x\left(\frac{1}{y}\right) = xy^{-1}$$

Finding the reciprocal or inverse of a matrix is an operation analogous to division in ordinary algebra; however, although every nonzero number has a reciprocal, there are square matrices, in addition to the null matrix, which do not have inverses. A matrix that has an inverse is said to be *nonsingular*; a matrix that has no inverse is said to be *singular*.

A matrix which is not square may have a left or right inverse. An $n \times s$ matrix $\mathbf{A}$ is said to have $\mathbf{B}$ as a *left inverse* if $\mathbf{BA} = \mathbf{I}$; in this case $\mathbf{I}$ must be $s \times s$ and $\mathbf{B}$ must be $s \times n$. Similarly, if $\mathbf{AC} = \mathbf{I}$, $\mathbf{C}$ is said to be a *right inverse* of $\mathbf{A}$; in this case $\mathbf{I}$ must be $n \times n$ and $\mathbf{C}$ must be $s \times n$. It can be shown that if $\mathbf{A}$ has both a left inverse $\mathbf{B}$ and a right inverse $\mathbf{C}$, then $\mathbf{B} = \mathbf{C} = \mathbf{A}^{-1}$ and $\mathbf{A}$ is square (and nonsingular).

Obtaining the inverse of a matrix, referred to as *matrix inversion*, is essential for the matrix solution of sets of simultaneous linear equations; such equations arise, for example, in the solution of economic models and in linear programming problems.

Any set of simultaneous linear equations can be written in matrix notation; for example,

$$a_{11}x_1 + a_{12}x_2 + a_{13}x_3 + \cdots + a_{1n}x_n = c_1$$
$$a_{21}x_1 + a_{22}x_2 + a_{23}x_3 + \cdots + a_{2n}x_n = c_2$$
$$\vdots$$
$$a_{m1}x_1 + a_{m2}x_2 + a_{m3}x_3 + \cdots + a_{mn}x_n = c_m$$

can be written

$$\mathbf{A}_{m \times n}\, \mathbf{x}_{n \times 1} = \mathbf{c}_{m \times 1}$$

If $m = n$ and $\mathbf{A}$ has an inverse, that is, if $\mathbf{A}$ is square and nonsingular, then the set of simultaneous linear equations represented by

$$\mathbf{A}_{n \times n}\, \mathbf{x}_{n \times 1} = \mathbf{c}_{n \times 1}$$

has the solution

$$\mathbf{x}_{n \times 1} = \mathbf{A}_{n \times n}^{-1}\, \mathbf{c}_{n \times 1}$$

Solution of simultaneous linear equations is considered in detail in section 7.9.

INVERSION OF 2×2 MATRICES

If $n = 2$, that is, if the set of simultaneous equations consists of two equations in two unknowns,

$$a_{11}x_1 + a_{12}x_2 = c_1$$
$$a_{21}x_1 + a_{22}x_2 = c_2$$

or, in matrix notation,

$$\mathbf{A}_{2 \times 2}\, \mathbf{x}_{2 \times 1} = \mathbf{c}_{2 \times 1}$$

then $\mathbf{A}_{2 \times 2}^{-1}$ can be obtained directly from its definition, as follows. If

$$\mathbf{A} = \begin{bmatrix} a_{11} & a_{12} \\ a_{21} & a_{22} \end{bmatrix}$$

and $\mathbf{A}^{-1}$ is denoted by

$$\mathbf{B} = \begin{bmatrix} b_{11} & b_{12} \\ b_{21} & b_{22} \end{bmatrix}$$

then, be definition, $\mathbf{AB} = \mathbf{I}$, that is,

$$\begin{bmatrix} a_{11} & a_{12} \\ a_{21} & a_{22} \end{bmatrix} \begin{bmatrix} b_{11} & b_{12} \\ b_{21} & b_{22} \end{bmatrix} = \begin{bmatrix} 1 & 0 \\ 0 & 1 \end{bmatrix}$$

and thus

$$\begin{bmatrix} a_{11}b_{11} + a_{12}b_{21} & a_{11}b_{12} + a_{12}b_{22} \\ a_{21}b_{11} + a_{22}b_{21} & a_{21}b_{12} + a_{22}b_{22} \end{bmatrix} = \begin{bmatrix} 1 & 0 \\ 0 & 1 \end{bmatrix}$$

and

$$a_{11}b_{11} + a_{12}b_{21} = 1$$
$$a_{11}b_{12} + a_{12}b_{22} = 0$$
$$a_{21}b_{11} + a_{22}b_{21} = 0$$
$$a_{21}b_{12} + a_{22}b_{22} = 1$$

Solving these four equations for the four b_{ij}'s,

$$b_{11} = \frac{a_{22}}{a_{11}a_{22} - a_{21}a_{12}}$$

$$b_{12} = \frac{-a_{12}}{a_{11}a_{22} - a_{21}a_{12}}$$

$$b_{21} = \frac{-a_{21}}{a_{11}a_{22} - a_{21}a_{12}}$$

$$b_{22} = \frac{a_{11}}{a_{11}a_{22} - a_{21}a_{12}}$$

Note that the denominator of each of these expressions is the *determinant* of **A**

$$\det \mathbf{A} = \begin{vmatrix} a_{11} & a_{12} \\ a_{21} & a_{22} \end{vmatrix} = a_{11}a_{22} - a_{21}a_{12}$$

If $\det \mathbf{A} = 0$, the b_{ij}'s are not defined and $\mathbf{A}^{-1}$ cannot be obtained. It can be shown that a square matrix of any size has an inverse if and only if its determinant is nonzero.

EXAMPLE

Determine, if it exists, the inverse of the matrix

$$\begin{bmatrix} -1 & 6 \\ 4 & 3 \end{bmatrix}$$

$$\begin{vmatrix} -1 & 6 \\ 4 & 3 \end{vmatrix} = -3 - 24 = -27, \text{ so the inverse exists.}$$

$$b_{11} = \frac{3}{-27} = -\frac{1}{9}$$

$$b_{12} = \frac{-6}{-27} = \frac{2}{9}$$

$$b_{21} = \frac{-4}{-27} = \frac{4}{27}$$

$$b_{22} = \frac{-1}{-27} = \frac{1}{27}$$

and thus

$$\begin{bmatrix} -1 & 6 \\ 4 & 3 \end{bmatrix}^{-1} = \begin{bmatrix} -\frac{1}{9} & \frac{2}{9} \\ \frac{4}{27} & \frac{1}{27} \end{bmatrix}$$

Note that

$$\begin{bmatrix} -1 & 6 \\ 4 & 3 \end{bmatrix}\begin{bmatrix} -\frac{1}{9} & \frac{2}{9} \\ \frac{4}{27} & \frac{1}{27} \end{bmatrix} = \begin{bmatrix} 1 & 0 \\ 0 & 1 \end{bmatrix}$$

EXAMPLE

Determine, if it exists, the inverse of the matrix

$$\begin{bmatrix} -3 & 15 \\ 1 & -5 \end{bmatrix}$$

$\begin{vmatrix} -3 & 15 \\ 1 & -5 \end{vmatrix} = 15 - 15 = 0$, so the inverse does not exist, that is, the matrix is singular.

PROBLEMS

For each of the following matrices, evaluate the determinant and find the inverse, if it exists. Use partitioned matrices to check the results.

1. $\begin{bmatrix} 1 & 6 \\ 0 & 1 \end{bmatrix}$

2. $\begin{bmatrix} 1 & 0 \\ 0 & 1 \end{bmatrix}$

3. $\begin{bmatrix} 0 & 1 \\ 1 & 0 \end{bmatrix}$

4. $\begin{bmatrix} 0 & 1 \\ 1 & 6 \end{bmatrix}$

5. $\begin{bmatrix} 2 & -3 \\ 4 & -6 \end{bmatrix}$

6. $\begin{bmatrix} 2 & 2 \\ -4 & -4 \end{bmatrix}$

7. $\begin{bmatrix} -1 & 3 \\ 2 & 7 \end{bmatrix}$

8. $\begin{bmatrix} -1 & -1 \\ -1 & -1 \end{bmatrix}$

Answers to Odd-Numbered Problems

1. $\det = 1, \begin{bmatrix} 1 & -6 \\ 0 & 1 \end{bmatrix}$

3. $\det = -1, \begin{bmatrix} 0 & 1 \\ 1 & 0 \end{bmatrix}$

5. $\det = 0$, so no inverse

7. $\det = -13, \begin{bmatrix} -\frac{7}{13} & \frac{3}{13} \\ \frac{2}{13} & \frac{1}{13} \end{bmatrix}$

INVERSION OF LARGER MATRICES

In principle, the inverse of any nonsingular matrix can be obtained from its definition in the same way the inverse of a 2×2 matrix is obtained above. That is, if

$$\mathbf{A} = \begin{bmatrix} a_{11} & a_{12} & \cdots & a_{1n} \\ a_{21} & a_{22} & \cdots & a_{2n} \\ \vdots & \vdots & & \vdots \\ a_{n1} & a_{n2} & \cdots & a_{nn} \end{bmatrix}$$

and $\mathbf{B} = \mathbf{A}^{-1}$, then $\mathbf{AB} = \mathbf{I}$.

$$
\begin{bmatrix} a_{11} & a_{12} & \cdots & a_{1n} \\ a_{21} & a_{22} & \cdots & a_{2n} \\ \vdots & \vdots & & \vdots \\ a_{n1} & a_{n2} & \cdots & a_{nn} \end{bmatrix}
\begin{bmatrix} b_{11} & b_{12} & \cdots & b_{1n} \\ b_{21} & b_{22} & \cdots & b_{2n} \\ \vdots & \vdots & & \vdots \\ b_{n1} & b_{n2} & \cdots & b_{nn} \end{bmatrix}
=
\begin{bmatrix} c_{11} & c_{12} & \cdots & c_{1n} \\ c_{21} & c_{22} & \cdots & c_{2n} \\ \vdots & \vdots & & \vdots \\ c_{n1} & c_{n2} & \cdots & c_{nn} \end{bmatrix}
$$

$$
=
\begin{bmatrix} 1 & & & 0 \\ & 1 & & \\ & & \ddots & \\ 0 & & & 1 \end{bmatrix}
= \mathbf{I}_n
$$

where $c_{ik} = \sum_{j=1}^{n} a_{ij} b_{jk}$ and the n^2 elements of the inverse matrix (b_{jk}) can be obtained by solution of the n^2 equations

$$\sum_{j=1}^{n} a_{ij} b_{jk} = 1 \qquad \text{if } i = k$$

$$\sum_{j=1}^{n} a_{ij} b_{jk} = 0 \qquad \text{if } i \neq k$$

where $i = 1, 2, \ldots, n$ and $k = 1, 2, \ldots, n$.

For a matrix of size 3×3 or larger, this method of inversion is tedious. Fortunately, numerous alternative computational procedures are available and inversion is also a standard program for most computers. Two methods of inversion are discussed in following sections; both of these are feasible unless the matrix is quite large or its elements consist of several digits.

INVERSION USING ROW OR COLUMN OPERATIONS

To solve a system of simultaneous linear equations, certain simple operations are commonly used to convert the original system to an equivalent system—that is, to a system having the same solution as the original system—which is easier to solve. An equivalent system is obtained if (1) two equations are interchanged, (2) an equation is multiplied by any nonzero constant, or (3) the ith equation is replaced by the sum of the ith equation and k times the jth equation, where k is any nonzero constant.

Similarly, three *elementary row operations* on matrices are defined by (1) interchange of two rows, (2) multiplication of a row by any nonzero scalar, and (3) replacement of the ith row by the sum of the ith row and k times the jth row, where k is any nonzero scalar.

The corresponding operations on the columns of a matrix are *elementary column operations*. Elementary row or column operations can be used to obtain the inverse of a matrix, as stated in the following theorem.

THEOREM: If a matrix $\mathbf{A}$ is converted to the identity matrix by a series of row operations or by a series of column operations, then the same series of operations performed on the identity matrix will convert it to $\mathbf{A}^{-1}$.

There is a standard method, invariably appropriate, for converting a nonsingular matrix to the identity matrix or for establishing the singularity of a matrix which cannot be converted to the identity matrix. This standard method is outlined and illustrated below. The generality of the method, which is appropriate for any matrix and which can be programmed for machine computation, makes it especially useful, although for particular cases shorter methods are available.

Steps in Converting a Square Matrix to the Identity Matrix (Gaussian Elimination)

1. Divide the first row of the matrix by the element in its first column; use the resulting row to obtain zeros in the first column of each of the other rows.
2. Divide the second row by the element in its second column; use the resulting row to obtain zeros in the second column of each of the other rows.

$$\vdots \qquad \vdots \qquad \vdots$$

n. Divide the nth row by the element in its nth column; use the resulting row to obtain zeros in the nth column of each of the other rows.

NOTE: In the above procedure, if at the kth step the element in the kth column is zero, interchange that row with a subsequent row having a nonzero element in the kth column. Then proceed with the kth step.

To find the inverse of a matrix $\mathbf{A}$, it is customary to work with a tableau of the form

$$[\mathbf{A}\,|\,\mathbf{I}]$$

and change it by the standard procedure given above to the tableau

$$[\mathbf{I}\,|\,\mathbf{B}]$$

Then, by the theorem stated above, $\mathbf{B}$ is $\mathbf{A}^{-1}$.

Even if $\mathbf{A}$ has no inverse, this procedure can be started. At some point a tableau will be obtained which is not of the appropriate form and which cannot be changed in the manner outlined above. It can be shown that if the above procedure cannot be completed to obtain $[\mathbf{I}\,|\,\mathbf{B}]$ from $[\mathbf{A}\,|\,\mathbf{I}]$, then $\mathbf{A}$ does not have an inverse.

EXAMPLE

Find the inverse, if it exists, of the matrix

$$\begin{bmatrix} 0 & -2 & -3 \\ 1 & 3 & 3 \\ -1 & -2 & -2 \end{bmatrix}$$

Following the standard procedure outlined above,

$$\left[\begin{array}{ccc|ccc} 0 & -2 & -3 & 1 & 0 & 0 \\ 1 & 3 & 3 & 0 & 1 & 0 \\ -1 & -2 & -2 & 0 & 0 & 1 \end{array}\right]$$

$$\left[\begin{array}{ccc|ccc} 1 & 3 & 3 & 0 & 1 & 0 \\ 0 & -2 & -3 & 1 & 0 & 0 \\ -1 & -2 & -2 & 0 & 0 & 1 \end{array}\right] \qquad \text{interchanging first and second rows}$$

$$\left[\begin{array}{ccc|ccc} 1 & 3 & 3 & 0 & 1 & 0 \\ 0 & -2 & -3 & 1 & 0 & 0 \\ 0 & 1 & 1 & 0 & 1 & 1 \end{array}\right] \qquad \text{Step 1}$$

$$\left[\begin{array}{ccc|ccc} 1 & 3 & 3 & 0 & 1 & 0 \\ 0 & 1 & \frac{3}{2} & -\frac{1}{2} & 0 & 0 \\ 0 & 1 & 1 & 0 & 1 & 1 \end{array}\right]$$

$$\left[\begin{array}{ccc|ccc} 1 & 0 & -\frac{3}{2} & \frac{3}{2} & 1 & 0 \\ 0 & 1 & \frac{3}{2} & -\frac{1}{2} & 0 & 0 \\ 0 & 0 & -\frac{1}{2} & \frac{1}{2} & 1 & 1 \end{array}\right] \qquad \text{Step 2}$$

$$\left[\begin{array}{ccc|ccc} 1 & 0 & -\frac{3}{2} & \frac{3}{2} & 1 & 0 \\ 0 & 1 & \frac{3}{2} & -\frac{1}{2} & 0 & 0 \\ 0 & 0 & 1 & -1 & -2 & -2 \end{array}\right]$$

$$\left[\begin{array}{ccc|ccc} 1 & 0 & 0 & 0 & -2 & -3 \\ 0 & 1 & 0 & 1 & 3 & 3 \\ 0 & 0 & 1 & -1 & -2 & -2 \end{array}\right]$$

Step 3

Thus

$$\left[\begin{array}{ccc} 0 & -2 & -3 \\ 1 & 3 & 3 \\ -1 & -2 & -2 \end{array}\right]^{-1} = \left[\begin{array}{ccc} 0 & -2 & -3 \\ 1 & 3 & 3 \\ -1 & -2 & -2 \end{array}\right]$$

and this matrix is equal to its inverse. Note that

$$\left[\begin{array}{ccc} 0 & -2 & -3 \\ 1 & 3 & 3 \\ -1 & -2 & -2 \end{array}\right] \left[\begin{array}{ccc} 0 & -2 & -3 \\ 1 & 3 & 3 \\ -1 & -2 & -2 \end{array}\right] = \left[\begin{array}{ccc} 1 & 0 & 0 \\ 0 & 1 & 0 \\ 0 & 0 & 1 \end{array}\right]$$

EXAMPLE

Find the inverse, if it exists, of the matrix

$$\left[\begin{array}{ccc} 1 & 2 & 3 \\ -1 & 0 & 4 \\ 0 & 2 & 2 \end{array}\right]$$

$$\left[\begin{array}{ccc|ccc} 1 & 2 & 3 & 1 & 0 & 0 \\ -1 & 0 & 4 & 0 & 1 & 0 \\ 0 & 2 & 2 & 0 & 0 & 1 \end{array}\right]$$

$$\left[\begin{array}{ccc|ccc} 1 & 2 & 3 & 1 & 0 & 0 \\ 0 & 2 & 7 & 1 & 1 & 0 \\ 0 & 2 & 2 & 0 & 0 & 1 \end{array}\right]$$

Step 1

$$\left[\begin{array}{ccc|ccc} 1 & 2 & 3 & 1 & 0 & 0 \\ 0 & 1 & \frac{7}{2} & \frac{1}{2} & \frac{1}{2} & 0 \\ 0 & 2 & 2 & 0 & 0 & 1 \end{array}\right]$$

$$\left[\begin{array}{ccc|ccc} 1 & 0 & -4 & 0 & -1 & 0 \\ 0 & 1 & \frac{7}{2} & \frac{1}{2} & \frac{1}{2} & 0 \\ 0 & 0 & -5 & -1 & -1 & 1 \end{array}\right]$$

Step 2

$$\left[\begin{array}{ccc|ccc} 1 & 0 & -4 & 0 & -1 & 0 \\ 0 & 1 & \frac{7}{2} & \frac{1}{2} & \frac{1}{2} & 0 \\ 0 & 0 & 1 & \frac{1}{5} & \frac{1}{5} & -\frac{1}{5} \end{array}\right]$$

$$\left[\begin{array}{ccc|ccc} 1 & 0 & 0 & \frac{4}{5} & -\frac{1}{5} & -\frac{4}{5} \\ 0 & 1 & 0 & -\frac{1}{5} & -\frac{1}{5} & \frac{7}{10} \\ 0 & 0 & 1 & \frac{1}{5} & \frac{1}{5} & -\frac{1}{5} \end{array}\right]$$

Step 3

Thus

$$\left[\begin{array}{ccc} 1 & 2 & 3 \\ -1 & 0 & 4 \\ 0 & 2 & 2 \end{array}\right]^{-1} = \left[\begin{array}{ccc} \frac{4}{5} & -\frac{1}{5} & -\frac{4}{5} \\ -\frac{1}{5} & -\frac{1}{5} & \frac{7}{10} \\ \frac{1}{5} & \frac{1}{5} & -\frac{1}{5} \end{array}\right]$$

Note that

$$\begin{bmatrix} 1 & 2 & 3 \\ -1 & 0 & 4 \\ 0 & 2 & 2 \end{bmatrix} \begin{bmatrix} \frac{4}{5} & -\frac{1}{5} & -\frac{4}{5} \\ -\frac{1}{5} & -\frac{1}{5} & \frac{7}{10} \\ \frac{1}{5} & \frac{1}{5} & -\frac{1}{5} \end{bmatrix} = \begin{bmatrix} 1 & 0 & 0 \\ 0 & 1 & 0 \\ 0 & 0 & 1 \end{bmatrix}$$

and

$$\begin{bmatrix} \frac{4}{5} & -\frac{1}{5} & -\frac{4}{5} \\ -\frac{1}{5} & -\frac{1}{5} & \frac{7}{10} \\ \frac{1}{5} & \frac{1}{5} & -\frac{1}{5} \end{bmatrix} \begin{bmatrix} 1 & 2 & 3 \\ -1 & 0 & 4 \\ 0 & 2 & 2 \end{bmatrix} = \begin{bmatrix} 1 & 0 & 0 \\ 0 & 1 & 0 \\ 0 & 0 & 1 \end{bmatrix}$$

EXAMPLE

Find the inverse, if it exists, of the matrix

$$\begin{bmatrix} 1 & 2 & -1 \\ -3 & 4 & 5 \\ -4 & 2 & 6 \end{bmatrix}$$

Following the standard procedure outlined above,

$$\begin{bmatrix} 1 & 2 & -1 & | & 1 & 0 & 0 \\ -3 & 4 & 5 & | & 0 & 1 & 0 \\ -4 & 2 & 6 & | & 0 & 0 & 1 \end{bmatrix}$$

$$\begin{bmatrix} 1 & 2 & -1 & | & 1 & 0 & 0 \\ 0 & 10 & 2 & | & 3 & 1 & 0 \\ 0 & 10 & 2 & | & 4 & 0 & 1 \end{bmatrix} \qquad \text{Step 1}$$

$$\begin{bmatrix} 1 & 2 & -1 & | & 1 & 0 & 0 \\ 0 & 1 & \frac{1}{5} & | & \frac{3}{10} & \frac{1}{10} & 0 \\ 0 & 10 & 2 & | & 4 & 0 & 1 \end{bmatrix}$$

$$\begin{bmatrix} 1 & 0 & -\frac{7}{5} & | & \frac{2}{5} & -\frac{1}{5} & 0 \\ 0 & 1 & \frac{1}{5} & | & \frac{3}{10} & \frac{1}{10} & 0 \\ 0 & 0 & 0 & | & 1 & -1 & 1 \end{bmatrix}$$

$$\left.\begin{matrix} \\ \\ \\ \\ \\ \end{matrix}\right\} \text{Step 2}$$

The procedure cannot be continued and thus the matrix has no inverse. Note that the procedure can be discontinued at the end of Step 1; at the end of Step 1 the left-hand matrix has two identical rows and thus the determinant of the matrix is zero (Property 5) and it has no inverse. The determinant of the original matrix is also zero (Property 6) and it has no inverse.

INVERSION USING ADJOINTS AND DETERMINANTS

An alternative method of matrix inversion involves obtaining the adjoint and determinant of the matrix to be inverted. If **A** is nonsingular, that is, if $|\mathbf{A}| \neq 0$, then

$$\mathbf{A}^{-1} = \frac{1}{|\mathbf{A}|} \text{ adj } \mathbf{A}$$

EXAMPLE

Find the inverse, if it exists, of the matrix

$$A = \begin{bmatrix} 0 & -2 & -3 \\ 1 & 3 & 3 \\ -1 & -2 & -2 \end{bmatrix}$$

$$|A| = 0 + 6 + 6 - (9 + 0 + 4) = -1$$

Alternatively, expanding by elements of the first row,

$$|A| = 0 + (-2)(-1)^{1+2} \begin{vmatrix} 1 & 3 \\ -1 & -2 \end{vmatrix} + (-3)(-1)^{1+3} \begin{vmatrix} 1 & 3 \\ -1 & -2 \end{vmatrix}$$

$$= 0 + 2(-2 + 3) + (-3)(-2 + 3) = -1$$

or, expanding by elements of the second column,

$$|A| = (-2)(-1)^{1+2} \begin{vmatrix} 1 & 3 \\ -1 & -2 \end{vmatrix} + (3)(-1)^{2+2} \begin{vmatrix} 0 & -3 \\ -1 & -2 \end{vmatrix} + (-2)(-1)^{3+2} \begin{vmatrix} 0 & -3 \\ 1 & 3 \end{vmatrix}$$

$$= 2(-2 + 3) + 3(0 - 3) + 2(0 + 3) = -1$$

Obtaining the adjoint,

$$C_{11} = (-1)^{1+1} \begin{vmatrix} 3 & 3 \\ -2 & -2 \end{vmatrix} = -6 + 6 = 0$$

$$C_{12} = (-1)^{1+2} \begin{vmatrix} 1 & 3 \\ -1 & -2 \end{vmatrix} = -(-2 + 3) = -1$$

$$C_{13} = (-1)^{1+3} \begin{vmatrix} 1 & 3 \\ -1 & -2 \end{vmatrix} = -2 + 3 = 1$$

$$C_{21} = (-1)^{2+1} \begin{vmatrix} -2 & -3 \\ -2 & -2 \end{vmatrix} = -(4 - 6) = 2$$

$$C_{22} = (-1)^{2+2} \begin{vmatrix} 0 & -3 \\ -1 & -2 \end{vmatrix} = 0 - 3 = -3$$

$$C_{23} = (-1)^{2+3} \begin{vmatrix} 0 & -2 \\ -1 & -2 \end{vmatrix} = -(0 - 2) = 2$$

$$C_{31} = (-1)^{3+1} \begin{vmatrix} -2 & -3 \\ 3 & 3 \end{vmatrix} = -6 + 9 = 3$$

$$C_{32} = (-1)^{3+2} \begin{vmatrix} 0 & -3 \\ 1 & 3 \end{vmatrix} = -(0 + 3) = -3$$

$$C_{33} = (-1)^{3+3} \begin{vmatrix} 0 & -2 \\ 1 & 3 \end{vmatrix} = 0 + 2 = 2$$

Thus

$$\text{adj } A = (C_{ij})' = \begin{bmatrix} 0 & 2 & 3 \\ -1 & -3 & -3 \\ 1 & 2 & 2 \end{bmatrix}$$

$$A^{-1} = \frac{1}{|A|} \text{adj } A = \begin{bmatrix} 0 & -2 & -3 \\ 1 & 3 & 3 \\ -1 & -2 & -2 \end{bmatrix}$$

(as obtained in the example above by the standard procedure for row operations).

EXAMPLE

Find the inverse, if it exists, of the matrix

$$A = \begin{bmatrix} 1 & 2 & 3 \\ -1 & 0 & 4 \\ 0 & 2 & 2 \end{bmatrix}$$

$$|A| = 0 + 0 - 6 - (0 + 8 - 4) = -10$$

Alternatively, expanding by elements of the first column,

$$|A| = (-1)^{1+1} \begin{vmatrix} 0 & 4 \\ 2 & 2 \end{vmatrix} - (-1)^{2+1} \begin{vmatrix} 2 & 3 \\ 2 & 2 \end{vmatrix} + 0$$

$$= (0 - 8) + (4 - 6) = -10$$

or, expanding by elements of the second row,

$$|A| = (-1)(-1)^{2+1} \begin{vmatrix} 2 & 3 \\ 2 & 2 \end{vmatrix} + 0 + 4(-1)^{2+3} \begin{vmatrix} 1 & 2 \\ 0 & 2 \end{vmatrix}$$

$$= (4 - 6) + 0 + (-4)(2 - 0) = -10$$

Obtaining the adjoint,

$$C_{11} = (-1)^{1+1} \begin{vmatrix} 0 & 4 \\ 2 & 2 \end{vmatrix} = 0 - 8 = -8$$

$$C_{12} = (-1)^{1+2} \begin{vmatrix} -1 & 4 \\ 0 & 2 \end{vmatrix} = -(-2 + 0) = 2$$

$$C_{13} = (-1)^{1+3} \begin{vmatrix} -1 & 0 \\ 0 & 2 \end{vmatrix} = -2 + 0 = -2$$

$$C_{21} = (-1)^{2+1} \begin{vmatrix} 2 & 3 \\ 2 & 2 \end{vmatrix} = -(4 - 6) = 2$$

$$C_{22} = (-1)^{2+2} \begin{vmatrix} 1 & 3 \\ 0 & 2 \end{vmatrix} = 2 + 0 = 2$$

$$C_{23} = (-1)^{2+3} \begin{vmatrix} 1 & 2 \\ 0 & 2 \end{vmatrix} = -(2 + 0) = -2$$

$$C_{31} = (-1)^{3+1} \begin{vmatrix} 2 & 3 \\ 0 & 4 \end{vmatrix} = 8 + 0 = 8$$

$$C_{32} = (-1)^{3+2} \begin{vmatrix} 1 & 3 \\ -1 & 4 \end{vmatrix} = -(4 + 3) = -7$$

$$C_{33} = (-1)^{3+3} \begin{vmatrix} 1 & 2 \\ -1 & 0 \end{vmatrix} = 0 + 2 = 2$$

Thus

$$\text{adj } A = (C_{ij})' = \begin{bmatrix} -8 & 2 & 8 \\ 2 & 2 & -7 \\ -2 & -2 & 2 \end{bmatrix}$$

$$A^{-1} = \frac{1}{|A|} \text{adj } A = \begin{bmatrix} \frac{4}{5} & -\frac{1}{5} & -\frac{4}{5} \\ -\frac{1}{5} & -\frac{1}{5} & \frac{7}{10} \\ \frac{1}{5} & \frac{1}{5} & -\frac{1}{5} \end{bmatrix}$$

(as obtained in the example above by the standard procedure for row operations).

EXAMPLE

Find the inverse, if it exists, of the matrix

$$A = \begin{bmatrix} 1 & 2 & -1 \\ -3 & 4 & 5 \\ -4 & 2 & 6 \end{bmatrix}$$

$$|A| = 24 + 6 - 40 - (16 + 10 - 36) = 0$$

Thus A is singular, that is, A has no inverse.

In general, inversion by row or column operations is less laborious if the elements of a matrix are small whole numbers; inversion by determinant and adjoint is less laborious if the elements of a matrix are large numbers or fractions. For large matrices both of these methods are tedious, and computers should be used, if available.

Unless there is good reason to believe that a matrix is nonsingular, as in some practical applications, it is advisable first to find its determinant, even if inversion by row or column operations is intended. A number of row or column operations may be necessary before the singularity of a matrix becomes apparent using this method of inversion, and much useless computation is thus avoided by establishing the existence of an inverse before attempting (by any method) to compute it.

INVERSION OF PARTITIONED MATRICES

It is sometimes convenient to obtain the inverse of a matrix in partitioned form. If an $n \times n$ matrix A is partitioned

$$A = \left[\begin{array}{c|c} A_{11} & A_{12} \\ \hline A_{21} & A_{22} \end{array} \right]$$

where A_{11} is $n_1 \times n_1$, A_{12} is $n_1 \times n_2$, A_{21} is $n_2 \times n_1$, A_{22} is $n_2 \times n_2$, and $n_1 + n_2 = n$, then

$$A^{-1} = \begin{bmatrix} A_{11}^{-1}[I + A_{12} B^{-1}A_{21} A_{11}^{-1}] & -A_{11}^{-1}A_{12} B^{-1} \\ -B^{-1}A_{21} A_{11}^{-1} & B^{-1} \end{bmatrix}$$

where $B = A_{22} - A_{21} A_{11}^{-1}A_{12}$ and A_{11} and B are nonsingular. This result can be verified by multiplication:

$$\begin{bmatrix} A_{11} & A_{12} \\ A_{21} & A_{22} \end{bmatrix}\begin{bmatrix} A_{11}^{-1}[I + A_{12} B^{-1}A_{21} A_{11}^{-1}] & -A_{11}^{-1}A_{12} B^{-1} \\ -B^{-1}A_{21} A_{11}^{-1} & B^{-1} \end{bmatrix} = \begin{bmatrix} I & 0 \\ 0 & I \end{bmatrix}$$

since

$$A_{11} A_{11}^{-1}[I + A_{12} B^{-1}A_{21} A_{11}^{-1}] - A_{12} B^{-1}A_{21} A_{11}^{-1} = I$$

$$-A_{11} A_{11}^{-1}A_{12} B^{-1} + A_{12} B^{-1} = 0$$

$$\mathbf{A}_{21}\,\mathbf{A}_{11}^{-1}[\mathbf{I} + \mathbf{A}_{12}\,\mathbf{B}^{-1}\mathbf{A}_{21}\,\mathbf{A}_{11}^{-1}] - \mathbf{A}_{22}\,\mathbf{B}^{-1}\mathbf{A}_{21}\,\mathbf{A}_{11}^{-1}$$

$$= [\mathbf{I} + \underbrace{\mathbf{A}_{21}\,\mathbf{A}_{11}^{-1}\mathbf{A}_{12}\,\mathbf{B}^{-1} - \mathbf{A}_{22}\,\mathbf{B}^{-1}}_{[\mathbf{A}_{21}\,\mathbf{A}_{11}^{-1}\mathbf{A}_{12} - \mathbf{A}_{22}]\mathbf{B}^{-1}}]\mathbf{A}_{21}\,\mathbf{A}_{11}^{-1}$$

$$= [\mathbf{I} - \mathbf{B}\mathbf{B}^{-1}]\mathbf{A}_{21}\,\mathbf{A}_{11}^{-1}$$

$$= 0$$

$$-\mathbf{A}_{21}\,\mathbf{A}_{11}^{-1}\mathbf{A}_{12}\,\mathbf{B}^{-1} + \mathbf{A}_{22}\,\mathbf{B}^{-1} = [-\mathbf{A}_{21}\,\mathbf{A}_{11}^{-1}\mathbf{A}_{12} + \mathbf{A}_{22}]\mathbf{B}^{-1}$$

$$= \mathbf{B}\mathbf{B}^{-1}$$

$$= \mathbf{I}$$

EXAMPLE

Find the inverse, if it exists, of the matrix

$$\begin{bmatrix} 0 & -2 & -3 \\ 1 & 3 & 3 \\ -1 & -2 & -2 \end{bmatrix}$$

Partitioning the matrix,

$$\begin{bmatrix} 0 & -2 & \vdots & -3 \\ 1 & 3 & \vdots & 3 \\ \cdots & \cdots & & \cdots \\ -1 & -2 & \vdots & -2 \end{bmatrix} = \begin{bmatrix} \mathbf{A}_{11} & \vdots & \mathbf{A}_{12} \\ \cdots & & \cdots \\ \mathbf{A}_{21} & \vdots & \mathbf{A}_{22} \end{bmatrix}$$

and

$$\mathbf{A}_{11}^{-1}[\mathbf{I} + \mathbf{A}_{12}\,\mathbf{B}^{-1}\mathbf{A}_{21}\,\mathbf{A}_{11}^{-1}] = \begin{bmatrix} \frac{3}{2} & 1 \\ -\frac{1}{2} & 0 \end{bmatrix} \left(\begin{bmatrix} 1 & 0 \\ 0 & 1 \end{bmatrix} + \begin{bmatrix} -3 \\ 3 \end{bmatrix}[-2][-1,\ -2]\begin{bmatrix} \frac{3}{2} & 1 \\ -\frac{1}{2} & 0 \end{bmatrix} \right)$$

$$= \begin{bmatrix} \frac{3}{2} & 1 \\ -\frac{1}{2} & 0 \end{bmatrix} \left(\begin{bmatrix} 1 & 0 \\ 0 & 1 \end{bmatrix} + \begin{bmatrix} -6 & -12 \\ 6 & 12 \end{bmatrix}\begin{bmatrix} \frac{3}{2} & 1 \\ -\frac{1}{2} & 0 \end{bmatrix} \right)$$

$$= \begin{bmatrix} \frac{3}{2} & 1 \\ -\frac{1}{2} & 0 \end{bmatrix} \left(\begin{bmatrix} 1 & 0 \\ 0 & 1 \end{bmatrix} + \begin{bmatrix} -3 & -6 \\ 3 & 6 \end{bmatrix} \right)$$

$$= \begin{bmatrix} \frac{3}{2} & 1 \\ -\frac{1}{2} & 0 \end{bmatrix}\begin{bmatrix} -2 & -6 \\ 3 & 7 \end{bmatrix}$$

$$= \begin{bmatrix} 0 & -2 \\ 1 & 3 \end{bmatrix}$$

where

$$\mathbf{B} = \mathbf{A}_{22} - \mathbf{A}_{21}\,\mathbf{A}_{11}^{-1}\mathbf{A}_{12} = [-2] - [-1,\ -2]\begin{bmatrix} \frac{3}{2} & 1 \\ -\frac{1}{2} & 0 \end{bmatrix}\begin{bmatrix} -3 \\ 3 \end{bmatrix}$$

$$= [-2] - [-\tfrac{1}{2},\ -1]\begin{bmatrix} -3 \\ 3 \end{bmatrix}$$

$$= -2 - (-\tfrac{3}{2})$$

$$= -\tfrac{1}{2}$$

and

$$\mathbf{B}^{-1} = [-2]$$

$$\mathbf{A}_{11}^{-1}\mathbf{A}_{12}\mathbf{B}^{-1} = \begin{bmatrix} \frac{3}{2} & 1 \\ -\frac{1}{2} & 0 \end{bmatrix}\begin{bmatrix} -3 \\ 3 \end{bmatrix}[-2]$$

$$= \begin{bmatrix} \frac{3}{2} & 1 \\ -\frac{1}{2} & 0 \end{bmatrix}\begin{bmatrix} 6 \\ -6 \end{bmatrix}$$

$$= \begin{bmatrix} 3 \\ -3 \end{bmatrix}$$

$$\mathbf{B}^{-1}\mathbf{A}_{21}\mathbf{A}_{11}^{-1} = [2][-1, -2]\begin{bmatrix} \frac{3}{2} & 1 \\ -\frac{1}{2} & 0 \end{bmatrix}$$

$$= [-2, -4]\begin{bmatrix} \frac{3}{2} & 1 \\ -\frac{1}{2} & 0 \end{bmatrix}$$

$$= [-1, -2]$$

Thus

$$\begin{bmatrix} 0 & -2 & -3 \\ 1 & 3 & 3 \\ -1 & -2 & -2 \end{bmatrix}^{-1} = \begin{bmatrix} 0 & -2 & -3 \\ 1 & 3 & 3 \\ -1 & -2 & -2 \end{bmatrix}$$

as above.

EXAMPLE

Find the inverse, if it exists, of the matrix

$$\begin{bmatrix} 1 & 2 & 3 \\ -1 & 0 & 4 \\ 0 & 2 & 2 \end{bmatrix}$$

Partitioning the matrix,

$$\begin{bmatrix} 1 & 2 & 3 \\ -1 & 0 & 4 \\ 0 & 2 & 2 \end{bmatrix} = \begin{bmatrix} \mathbf{A}_{11} & \mathbf{A}_{12} \\ \mathbf{A}_{21} & \mathbf{A}_{22} \end{bmatrix}$$

and

$$\mathbf{A}_{11}^{-1}[\mathbf{I} + \mathbf{A}_{12}\mathbf{B}^{-1}\mathbf{A}_{21}\mathbf{A}_{11}^{-1}] = [1]\left([1] + [2, 3]\begin{bmatrix} -\frac{1}{5} & \frac{7}{10} \\ \frac{1}{5} & -\frac{1}{5} \end{bmatrix}\begin{bmatrix} -1 \\ 0 \end{bmatrix}[1]\right)$$

$$= [1]\left([1] + [\frac{1}{5}, \frac{4}{5}]\begin{bmatrix} -1 \\ 0 \end{bmatrix}\right)$$

$$= 1(1 - \frac{1}{5})$$

$$= \frac{4}{5}$$

where

$$\mathbf{B} = \mathbf{A}_{22} - \mathbf{A}_{21}\mathbf{A}_{11}^{-1}\mathbf{A}_{12} = \begin{bmatrix} 0 & 4 \\ 2 & 2 \end{bmatrix} - \begin{bmatrix} -1 \\ 0 \end{bmatrix}[1][2, 3]$$

$$= \begin{bmatrix} 0 & 4 \\ 2 & 2 \end{bmatrix} - \begin{bmatrix} -2 & -3 \\ 0 & 0 \end{bmatrix}$$

$$= \begin{bmatrix} 2 & 7 \\ 2 & 2 \end{bmatrix}$$

and

$$\mathbf{B}^{-1} = \begin{bmatrix} -\frac{1}{5} & \frac{7}{10} \\ \frac{1}{5} & -\frac{1}{5} \end{bmatrix}$$

$$-\mathbf{A}_{11}^{-1}\mathbf{A}_{12}\,\mathbf{B}^{-1} = [-1][2,\,3]\begin{bmatrix} -\frac{1}{5} & \frac{7}{10} \\ \frac{1}{5} & -\frac{1}{5} \end{bmatrix}$$

$$= [-\tfrac{1}{5},\, -\tfrac{4}{5}]$$

$$-\mathbf{B}^{-1}\mathbf{A}_{21}\,\mathbf{A}_{11}^{-1} = \begin{bmatrix} \frac{1}{5} & -\frac{7}{10} \\ -\frac{1}{5} & \frac{1}{5} \end{bmatrix}\begin{bmatrix} -1 \\ 0 \end{bmatrix}[1]$$

$$= \begin{bmatrix} -\frac{1}{5} \\ \frac{1}{5} \end{bmatrix}$$

Thus

$$\begin{bmatrix} 1 & 2 & 3 \\ -1 & 0 & 4 \\ 0 & 2 & 2 \end{bmatrix}^{-1} = \begin{bmatrix} \frac{4}{5} & -\frac{1}{5} & -\frac{4}{5} \\ -\frac{1}{5} & -\frac{1}{5} & \frac{7}{10} \\ \frac{1}{5} & \frac{1}{5} & -\frac{1}{5} \end{bmatrix}$$

as above.

PROPERTIES OF INVERSES

The following properties of inverses are frequently useful in their evaluation.

1. The inverse of the inverse of a matrix is the original matrix; that is, $[\mathbf{A}^{-1}]^{-1} = \mathbf{A}$.
2. The determinant of the inverse of a matrix is equal to the reciprocal of the determinant of the matrix; that is, $|\mathbf{A}^{-1}| = 1/|\mathbf{A}|$.
3. The inverse of the transpose of a matrix is equal to the transpose of the inverse of the matrix; that is, $[\mathbf{A}']^{-1} = [\mathbf{A}^{-1}]'$.
4. The inverse of the product of two matrices is equal to the product of their inverses in reverse order; that is, $[\mathbf{AB}]^{-1} = \mathbf{B}^{-1}\mathbf{A}^{-1}$.

EXAMPLES

If $\mathbf{A} = \begin{bmatrix} 1 & 2 & 3 \\ -1 & 0 & 4 \\ 0 & 2 & 2 \end{bmatrix}$, then $\mathbf{A}^{-1} = \begin{bmatrix} \frac{4}{5} & -\frac{1}{5} & -\frac{4}{5} \\ -\frac{1}{5} & -\frac{1}{5} & \frac{7}{10} \\ \frac{1}{5} & \frac{1}{5} & -\frac{1}{5} \end{bmatrix}$ (see previous example).

(Property 1)

$$[\mathbf{A}^{-1}]^{-1} = \begin{bmatrix} \frac{4}{5} & -\frac{1}{5} & -\frac{4}{5} \\ -\frac{1}{5} & -\frac{1}{5} & \frac{7}{10} \\ \frac{1}{5} & \frac{1}{5} & -\frac{1}{5} \end{bmatrix}^{-1}$$

$$= \begin{bmatrix} 1 & 2 & 3 \\ -1 & 0 & 4 \\ 0 & 2 & 2 \end{bmatrix}$$

$$= \mathbf{A}$$

that is, $[\mathbf{A}^{-1}]^{-1} = \mathbf{A}$.

(Property 2)

$$|\mathbf{A}| = \begin{vmatrix} 1 & 2 & 3 \\ -1 & 0 & 4 \\ 0 & 2 & 2 \end{vmatrix}$$

$$= 0 + 0 - 6 - (0 + 8 - 4)$$

$$= -10$$

$$|\mathbf{A}^{-1}| = \begin{vmatrix} \frac{4}{5} & -\frac{1}{5} & -\frac{4}{5} \\ -\frac{1}{5} & -\frac{1}{5} & \frac{7}{10} \\ \frac{1}{5} & \frac{1}{5} & -\frac{1}{5} \end{vmatrix}$$

$$= \tfrac{1}{125}[4 - \tfrac{7}{2} + 4 - (4 + 14 - 1)]$$

$$= (\tfrac{1}{125})(-\tfrac{25}{2})$$

$$= -\tfrac{1}{10}$$

that is, $|\mathbf{A}^{-1}| = \dfrac{1}{|\mathbf{A}|}$.

(Property 3)

$$(\mathbf{A}')^{-1} = \begin{bmatrix} 1 & -1 & 0 \\ 2 & 0 & 2 \\ 3 & 4 & 2 \end{bmatrix}^{-1}$$

$$= \begin{bmatrix} \frac{4}{5} & -\frac{1}{5} & \frac{1}{5} \\ -\frac{1}{5} & -\frac{1}{5} & \frac{1}{5} \\ -\frac{4}{5} & \frac{7}{10} & -\frac{1}{5} \end{bmatrix}$$

$$[\mathbf{A}^{-1}]' = \begin{bmatrix} \frac{4}{5} & -\frac{1}{5} & -\frac{4}{5} \\ -\frac{1}{5} & -\frac{1}{5} & \frac{7}{10} \\ \frac{1}{5} & \frac{1}{5} & -\frac{1}{5} \end{bmatrix}'$$

$$= \begin{bmatrix} \frac{4}{5} & -\frac{1}{5} & \frac{1}{5} \\ -\frac{1}{5} & -\frac{1}{5} & \frac{1}{5} \\ -\frac{4}{5} & \frac{7}{10} & -\frac{1}{5} \end{bmatrix}$$

Thus $[\mathbf{A}']^{-1} = [\mathbf{A}^{-1}]'$.

(Property 4)

If $\mathbf{B} = \begin{bmatrix} -1 & 3 & 1 \\ 0 & 2 & 0 \\ -2 & 0 & 4 \end{bmatrix}$, then $\mathbf{B}^{-1} = \begin{bmatrix} -2 & 3 & \frac{1}{2} \\ 0 & \frac{1}{2} & 0 \\ -1 & \frac{3}{2} & \frac{1}{2} \end{bmatrix}$

$$\mathbf{AB} = \begin{bmatrix} 1 & 2 & 3 \\ -1 & 0 & 4 \\ 0 & 2 & 2 \end{bmatrix} \begin{bmatrix} -1 & 3 & 1 \\ 0 & 2 & 0 \\ -2 & 0 & 4 \end{bmatrix}$$

$$= \begin{bmatrix} -7 & 7 & 13 \\ -7 & -3 & 15 \\ -4 & 4 & 8 \end{bmatrix}$$

$$[AB]^{-1} = \begin{bmatrix} -7 & 7 & 13 \\ -7 & -3 & 15 \\ -4 & 4 & 8 \end{bmatrix}^{-1}$$

$$= \begin{bmatrix} -\frac{21}{10} & -\frac{1}{10} & \frac{18}{5} \\ -\frac{1}{10} & -\frac{1}{10} & \frac{7}{20} \\ -1 & 0 & \frac{7}{4} \end{bmatrix}$$

$$\mathbf{B}^{-1}\mathbf{A}^{-1} = \begin{bmatrix} -2 & 3 & \frac{1}{2} \\ 0 & \frac{1}{2} & 0 \\ -1 & \frac{3}{2} & \frac{1}{2} \end{bmatrix} \begin{bmatrix} \frac{4}{5} & -\frac{1}{5} & -\frac{4}{5} \\ -\frac{1}{5} & -\frac{1}{5} & \frac{7}{10} \\ \frac{1}{5} & \frac{1}{5} & -\frac{1}{5} \end{bmatrix}$$

$$= \begin{bmatrix} -\frac{21}{10} & -\frac{1}{10} & \frac{18}{5} \\ -\frac{1}{10} & -\frac{1}{10} & \frac{7}{20} \\ -1 & 0 & \frac{7}{4} \end{bmatrix}$$

Thus $[AB]^{-1} = \mathbf{B}^{-1}\mathbf{A}^{-1}$.

PROBLEMS

For each of the following matrices, evaluate the determinant and find the inverse, if it exists. Use partitioned matrices to check the results.

1. $\begin{bmatrix} 0 & -2 & -1 \\ 1 & -3 & 4 \\ -1 & -1 & -1 \end{bmatrix}$

4. $\begin{bmatrix} 1 & 2 & -1 \\ 0 & -3 & 2 \\ 4 & 1 & 0 \end{bmatrix}$

2. $\begin{bmatrix} 3 & 1 & 3 \\ 3 & 3 & 1 \\ 2 & 0 & 3 \end{bmatrix}$

5. $\begin{bmatrix} 2 & 4 & 6 \\ -1 & 2 & 3 \\ 1 & 4 & 9 \end{bmatrix}$

3. $\begin{bmatrix} 3 & 2 & -1 \\ 4 & 3 & -1 \\ -1 & 2 & 4 \end{bmatrix}$

6. $\begin{bmatrix} 2 & 3 & 4 \\ 4 & 3 & 1 \\ 1 & 2 & 4 \end{bmatrix}$

7. If

$$\mathbf{A} = \begin{bmatrix} 3 & 2 & -2 \\ 0 & 1 & 4 \\ -1 & 0 & 5 \end{bmatrix} \quad \mathbf{B} = \begin{bmatrix} 1 & 0 \\ 0 & 1 \\ 0 & 1 \end{bmatrix} \quad \mathbf{C} = \begin{bmatrix} 1 & 1 & 1 \\ 1 & 1 & 1 \end{bmatrix} \quad \mathbf{D} = \begin{bmatrix} 3 & -2 \\ 2 & 3 \end{bmatrix}$$

find a. det $[[\mathbf{AB}]'\mathbf{C}' - \mathbf{D}]$
b. $[\mathbf{BC}]^{-1}$
c. $[\mathbf{D}^2]^{-1}$

8. If

$$\mathbf{A} = \begin{bmatrix} 3 & -1 \\ -4 & 0 \\ 2 & 1 \end{bmatrix} \quad \mathbf{B} = \begin{bmatrix} 2 & 1 \\ -1 & -2 \\ 1 & 1 \end{bmatrix} \quad \mathbf{C} = \begin{bmatrix} 3 & 4 \\ 2 & 2 \end{bmatrix}$$

find a. $[\mathbf{A} - \mathbf{BC}]'$
b. $[\mathbf{A}'\mathbf{B}]^{-1}$

9. If

$$\mathbf{A} = \begin{bmatrix} 2 & 1 \\ 1 & 2 \end{bmatrix} \quad \mathbf{B} = \begin{bmatrix} 1 & 0 \\ 0 & 1 \end{bmatrix} \quad \mathbf{C} = \begin{bmatrix} 1 & 2 \\ 3 & 4 \\ 1 & 2 \end{bmatrix} \quad \mathbf{D} = \begin{bmatrix} 0 & 1 & 0 \\ 1 & 1 & 1 \end{bmatrix}$$

find a. $\mathbf{A} + \mathbf{B} - 2\mathbf{DC}$
b. $\mathbf{A}^{-1}\mathbf{B}^{-1}$
c. $\mathbf{C}[\mathbf{A} + \mathbf{B}]\mathbf{B}^{-1}$
d. $\mathbf{CA}^{-1}\mathbf{B}^{-1}\mathbf{D}$

10. If

$$\mathbf{A} = \begin{bmatrix} 0 & 1 & -1 \\ 3 & -2 & 3 \\ 2 & -2 & 3 \end{bmatrix} \qquad \mathbf{B} = \begin{bmatrix} 4 & -3 & 3 \\ 2 & -1 & 2 \\ -3 & 3 & -2 \end{bmatrix}$$

show that a. $\mathbf{A}^2 = \mathbf{B}^2 = [\frac{1}{2}[\mathbf{A} + \mathbf{B}]]^2 = \mathbf{I}$
   b. $[\mathbf{A} - \mathbf{B}]^2 = \mathbf{O}$

Answers to Odd-Numbered Problems

1. det $= 10$, $\begin{bmatrix} \frac{7}{10} & -\frac{1}{10} & -\frac{11}{10} \\ -\frac{3}{10} & -\frac{1}{10} & -\frac{1}{10} \\ -\frac{2}{5} & \frac{1}{5} & \frac{1}{5} \end{bmatrix}$

3. det $= 1$, $\begin{bmatrix} 14 & -10 & 1 \\ -15 & 11 & -1 \\ 11 & -8 & 1 \end{bmatrix}$

5. det $= 24$, $\begin{bmatrix} \frac{1}{4} & -\frac{1}{2} & 0 \\ \frac{1}{2} & \frac{1}{2} & -\frac{1}{2} \\ -\frac{1}{4} & -\frac{1}{6} & \frac{1}{3} \end{bmatrix}$

7. a. -39
   b. inverse does not exist
   c. $\begin{bmatrix} \frac{5}{169} & \frac{12}{169} \\ -\frac{12}{169} & \frac{5}{169} \end{bmatrix}$

9. a. $\begin{bmatrix} -3 & -7 \\ -9 & -13 \end{bmatrix}$ c. $\begin{bmatrix} 5 & 7 \\ 13 & 15 \\ 5 & 7 \end{bmatrix}$
   b. $\begin{bmatrix} \frac{2}{3} & -\frac{1}{3} \\ -\frac{1}{3} & \frac{2}{3} \end{bmatrix}$
      d. $\begin{bmatrix} 1 & 1 & 1 \\ \frac{5}{3} & \frac{7}{3} & \frac{5}{3} \\ 1 & 1 & 1 \end{bmatrix}$

7.9 Simultaneous Linear Equations

Many analyses of economic models and other linear systems involve solution of sets of simultaneous linear equations. The concepts and operations of matrix algebra are extremely useful in determining the existence and nature of solutions of sets of simultaneous linear equations and in obtaining those solutions when they exist. In this section, linear dependence of a set of vectors and the related concept of rank of a matrix are defined and then used in determining whether a set of simultaneous linear equations has a unique solution. Methods of obtaining the solution of a set of simultaneous linear equations are also discussed.

LINEAR DEPENDENCE AND RANK

A set of m vectors $\mathbf{a}_1, \mathbf{a}_2, \ldots, \mathbf{a}_m$ each with n elements is said to be *linearly dependent* if there is a nontrivial linear combination of the vectors that is equal to the zero vector with n elements. That is, if there is a set of numbers $\lambda_1, \lambda_2, \ldots, \lambda_m$ (not all zero) such that

$$\lambda_1 \mathbf{a}_1 + \lambda_2 \mathbf{a}_2 + \cdots + \lambda_m \mathbf{a}_m = \sum_{i=1}^{m} \lambda_i \mathbf{a}_i = \mathbf{0}$$

then the set of vectors $a_1, a_2, \ldots, a_m$ is said to be *linearly dependent*. If there is no set of λ's (except all zeros) such that $\sum_{i=1}^{m} \lambda_i a_i = 0$, the set of vectors is said to be *linearly independent*.

A matrix can be thought of as a set of row vectors or a set of column vectors. It can be shown that, for any matrix, the number of linearly independent rows is equal to the number of linearly independent columns; this number is the *rank* of the matrix. Thus if a matrix is $m \times n$ and its rank is denoted by r, then $r \leq \min(m, n)$.

EXAMPLE

Determine the rank of the matrix

$$\begin{bmatrix} 1 & 4 \\ 5 & 10 \\ 3 & 2 \end{bmatrix}$$

Min $(m, n) = 2$, so $r \leq 2$.

Each pair of two rows are linearly independent; the two columns are also linearly independent. Thus the rank of the matrix is 2.

EXAMPLE

Determine the rank of the matrix

$$\begin{bmatrix} 3 & 6 \\ 1 & 2 \\ 2 & 4 \end{bmatrix}$$

Min $(m, n) = 2$, so $r \leq 2$.

Each pair of two rows are linearly dependent, since

(first row) $-$ 3(second row) $= 0$

2(first row) $-$ 3(third row) $= 0$

2(second row) $-$ (third row) $= 0$

Note that the two columns are also linearly dependent, since

2(first column) $-$ (second column) $= 0$

Thus the rank of the matrix is 1.

The following very useful result provides a systematic method of testing for linear dependence: Consider all the square submatrices of A whose determinants are non-zero. The rank of A is the order of the determinant of largest order. Thus one method of computing the rank of a matrix is to look for the largest nonzero determinant; the order of this determinant is the rank of the matrix.

The following properties are useful in determining the rank of a matrix:

1. Since the determinant of a diagonal matrix is equal to the product of its diagonal elements, if A is a diagonal matrix, then $r(A)$ is the number of nonzero diagonal elements in A. In particular, $r(I_n) = n$.
2. Since any submatrix of A' is the transpose of a submatrix of A and since $|B| = |B'|$, $r(A') = r(A)$.

3. The rank of the product of two matrices cannot exceed the smaller rank of the two matrices; that is, $r(\mathbf{AB}) \le \min\{r(\mathbf{A}), r(\mathbf{B})\}$.
4. If $\mathbf{A}$ is an $n \times n$ (square) matrix, then $r(\mathbf{A}) = n$ if and only if $\mathbf{A}$ is nonsingular; $r(\mathbf{A}) < n$ if and only if $\mathbf{A}$ is singular. Thus if a square matrix is singular, its rows (and also its columns) are linearly dependent; if a square matrix is nonsingular, its rows (and also its columns) are linearly independent.

Consider the solution of a general system of n linear equations in n variables x_1, $x_2, \ldots, x_n$,

$$\mathbf{y} = \mathbf{Ax}$$

where $\mathbf{y}$ is $n \times 1$, $\mathbf{A}$ is $n \times n$, and $\mathbf{x}$ is $n \times 1$. If $\mathbf{A}$ is nonsingular, the unique solution is

$$\mathbf{x} = \mathbf{A}^{-1}\mathbf{y}$$

and, conversely, if $\mathbf{y} = \mathbf{Ax}$ has a unique solution, $\mathbf{A}$ is nonsingular.

More generally, if $\mathbf{y} = \mathbf{Ax}$, then the whole set of equations is consistent and has at least one solution if $r(\mathbf{A}) = r(\mathbf{A} \vdots \mathbf{y})$. The solution is unique if and only if $r(\mathbf{A}) = r(\mathbf{A} \vdots \mathbf{y}) = n$, that is, if and only if $\mathbf{A}$ is nonsingular.

In the special (homogeneous) case $\mathbf{y} = \mathbf{0}$, if $\mathbf{A}$ is nonsingular, the unique solution is $\mathbf{x} = \mathbf{0}$ and there cannot be a nonzero solution. Thus, when the set of equations $\mathbf{Ax} = \mathbf{0}$ has a nonzero solution, $\mathbf{A}$ must be singular.

Suppose that $\mathbf{y} = \mathbf{Ax}$ and $\mathbf{A}$ is $m \times n$ (not square), that is, there are m equations in n variables where m may be less than, equal to, or greater than n; then $r(\mathbf{A}) \le \min(m, n)$.

The following summary concerning solution of simultaneous linear equations applies to the general case of m equations in n variables and also to the special case of n equations in n variables.

If $r(\mathbf{A} \vdots \mathbf{y}) = r(\mathbf{A})$, the equations in the set are logically consistent and there is at least one solution

If $r(\mathbf{A} \vdots \mathbf{y}) = r(\mathbf{A}) = n$, there is a unique solution

If $r(\mathbf{A} \vdots \mathbf{y}) = r(\mathbf{A}) < n$, there are infinitely many solutions and the rows (and columns) of $\mathbf{A}$ are linearly dependent

If $r(\mathbf{A} \vdots \mathbf{y}) \ne r(\mathbf{A})$, the equations in the set are not logically consistent and there is no solution

EXAMPLE

Consider the following set of simultaneous linear equations

$$x + 2y - \ z = 10$$
$$2x + 4y - 2z = 5$$
$$x + \ y + \ z = 6$$

The determinant of the coefficient matrix $\mathbf{A}$ is zero

$$\begin{vmatrix} 1 & 2 & -1 \\ 2 & 4 & -2 \\ 1 & 1 & 1 \end{vmatrix} = 4 - 4 - 2 - (-4 - 2 + 4) = 0$$

so the rank of the matrix is not 3; the rank is 2 since, for example,

$$\begin{vmatrix} 2 & 4 \\ 1 & 1 \end{vmatrix} = 2 - 4 = -2 \neq 0$$

The augmented coefficient matrix $[\mathbf{A} \vdots \mathbf{Y}]$

$$\begin{bmatrix} 1 & 2 & -1 & 10 \\ 2 & 4 & -2 & 5 \\ 1 & 1 & 1 & 6 \end{bmatrix}$$

has rank 3 since, for example,

$$\begin{vmatrix} 2 & -1 & 10 \\ 4 & -2 & 5 \\ 1 & 1 & 6 \end{vmatrix} = -24 - 5 + 40 - (-20 + 10 - 24) = 45 \neq 0$$

Thus $r(\mathbf{A}) \neq r(\mathbf{A} \vdots \mathbf{y})$ and the set of equations has no solution since they are not all consistent. Note, for example, that the first and second equations are clearly inconsistent.

EXAMPLE

Consider the following set of simultaneous linear equations

$$x + 2y - z = 10$$
$$2x + 4y - 2z = 20$$
$$x + y + z = 6$$

The coefficient matrix is the same as that for the preceding example and its rank is 2. The augmented coefficient matrix $(\mathbf{A} \vdots \mathbf{y})$

$$\begin{bmatrix} 1 & 2 & -1 & 10 \\ 2 & 4 & -2 & 20 \\ 1 & 1 & 1 & 6 \end{bmatrix}$$

is also rank 2, since

$$\begin{vmatrix} 1 & 2 & 10 \\ 2 & 4 & 20 \\ 1 & 1 & 6 \end{vmatrix} = \begin{vmatrix} 1 & -1 & 10 \\ 2 & -2 & 20 \\ 1 & 1 & 6 \end{vmatrix} = \begin{vmatrix} 2 & -1 & 10 \\ 4 & -2 & 20 \\ 1 & 1 & 6 \end{vmatrix} = 0$$

Thus $r(\mathbf{A}) = r(\mathbf{A} \vdots \mathbf{y}) = 2 \neq n = 3$, and the set of equations has infinitely many solutions; the rows (and columns) of the coefficient matrix are linearly dependent. Note, for example, that the first and second equations are linearly dependent.

EXAMPLE

Consider the following set of simultaneous linear equations

$$x + 2y - z = 10$$
$$2x - 4y - 2z = 5$$
$$x + y + z = 6$$

The determinant of the coefficient matrix $\mathbf{A}$ is nonzero

$$\begin{vmatrix} 1 & 2 & -1 \\ 2 & -4 & -2 \\ 1 & 1 & 1 \end{vmatrix} = -4 - 4 - 2 - (4 - 2 + 4) = -16$$

and the rank of the matrix is 3; the rank of the augmented coefficient matrix is also 3. Thus $r(\mathbf{A}) = r(\mathbf{A} \vdots \mathbf{y}) = 3 = n$ and the set of equations has a unique solution.

PROBLEMS

Determine the rank of each of the following matrices.

1. $\begin{bmatrix} 1 & 2 \\ 0 & 1 \end{bmatrix}$

2. $\begin{bmatrix} 1 & 2 & 3 \\ -1 & 0 & 1 \\ 0 & 4 & 8 \end{bmatrix}$

3. $\begin{bmatrix} 1 & -1 & 0 \\ -1 & 2 & 3 \\ 0 & 1 & 2 \end{bmatrix}$

4. $\begin{bmatrix} 1 & -1 & 0 \\ -1 & 1 & 0 \\ 2 & -2 & 0 \end{bmatrix}$

5. $\begin{bmatrix} 1 & 3 \\ 2 & 6 \end{bmatrix}$

6. $\begin{bmatrix} -2 & 1 & 4 \\ 0 & -1 & 5 \\ -2 & 0 & -9 \end{bmatrix}$

7. $\begin{bmatrix} 3 & 1 & -2 \\ 2 & 5 & 4 \\ -4 & 3 & 1 \end{bmatrix}$

8. $\begin{bmatrix} -1 & 2 & -3 \\ 2 & -3 & 1 \\ 0 & 1 & -5 \end{bmatrix}$

9. $\begin{bmatrix} 3 & -1 & 0 & 2 \\ -2 & 1 & 5 & -2 \\ 0 & -4 & 6 & -3 \\ -3 & 5 & -6 & 1 \end{bmatrix}$

10. $\begin{bmatrix} 2 & -1 & 3 & 0 \\ -3 & 3 & 4 & 2 \\ 4 & -5 & -11 & -4 \\ -1 & 2 & 7 & 2 \end{bmatrix}$

Answers to Odd-Numbered Problems

1. rank 2
3. rank 3
5. rank 1

7. rank 3
9. rank 3

SOLUTION OF SIMULTANEOUS LINEAR EQUATIONS

There are various methods for obtaining the solution of a set of simultaneous linear equations which have a unique solution. Several of these methods are discussed in this section. If one of the methods is applied to a set of linear equations that does not have a unique solution, the method cannot be completed, thus indicating that there is no unique solution.

As noted above, a set of n simultaneous linear equations in n unknowns can be written in matrix notation as

$$\mathbf{A}_{n \times n} \, \mathbf{x}_{n \times 1} = \mathbf{c}_{n \times 1}$$

and the solution obtained by inversion of $\mathbf{A}$ can be denoted by

$$\mathbf{x}_{n \times 1} = \mathbf{A}_{n \times n}^{-1} \, \mathbf{c}_{n \times 1}$$

Alternatively, the standard procedure described previously can be used to change the tableau

$$(\mathbf{A} \,|\, \mathbf{I} \,|\, \mathbf{c})$$

into the tableau

$$(\mathbf{I} \,|\, \mathbf{A}^{-1} \,|\, \mathbf{x})$$

from which the solution can be read directly.

A third matrix method for the solution of simultaneous linear equations is given by *Cramer's rule*: The solution of

$$\mathbf{A}_{n \times n} \mathbf{x}_{n \times 1} = \mathbf{c}_{n \times 1}$$

can be obtained as the ratios of determinants

$$x_1 = \frac{\begin{vmatrix} c_1 & a_{12} & \cdots & a_{1n} \\ c_2 & a_{22} & \cdots & a_{2n} \\ \vdots & \vdots & & \vdots \\ c_n & a_{n2} & \cdots & a_{nn} \end{vmatrix}}{|\mathbf{A}|}$$

$$x_2 = \frac{\begin{vmatrix} a_{11} & c_1 & \cdots & a_{1n} \\ a_{21} & c_2 & \cdots & a_{2n} \\ \vdots & \vdots & & \vdots \\ a_{n1} & c_n & \cdots & a_{nn} \end{vmatrix}}{|\mathbf{A}|}$$

$$\vdots$$

$$x_n = \frac{\begin{vmatrix} a_{11} & a_{12} & \cdots & c_1 \\ a_{21} & a_{22} & \cdots & c_2 \\ \vdots & \vdots & & \vdots \\ a_{n1} & a_{n2} & \cdots & c_n \end{vmatrix}}{|\mathbf{A}|}$$

For each x_i, $i = 1, 2, \ldots, n$, the denominator is the determinant of the coefficient matrix and the numerator is the determinant of the coefficient matrix with the ith column replaced by the column of constant terms from the right-hand side of the equations. If there is no unique solution for a set of linear equations, $|\mathbf{A}| = 0$ and these quotients are not defined.

EXAMPLE

Solve the set of simultaneous linear equations

$$3x_1 + x_2 - x_3 = 2$$
$$x_1 - 2x_2 + x_3 = -9$$
$$4x_1 + 3x_2 + 2x_3 = 1$$

Apply the standard procedure to the tableau

$$(\mathbf{A} \,|\, \mathbf{I} \,|\, \mathbf{c})$$

to obtain the tableau

$$(\mathbf{I} \,|\, \mathbf{A}^{-1} \,|\, \mathbf{x})$$

Then the solution can be read directly from the tableau

$(\mathbf{I}\,|\,\mathbf{x})$

or obtained as

$\mathbf{x} = \mathbf{A}^{-1}\mathbf{c}$

$$\left[\begin{array}{rrr|rrr|r} 3 & 1 & -1 & 1 & 0 & 0 & 2 \\ 1 & -2 & 1 & 0 & 1 & 0 & -9 \\ 4 & 3 & 2 & 0 & 0 & 1 & 1 \end{array}\right]$$

$$\left[\begin{array}{rrr|rrr|r} 1 & -2 & 1 & 0 & 1 & 0 & -9 \\ 3 & 1 & -1 & 1 & 0 & 0 & 2 \\ 4 & 3 & 2 & 0 & 0 & 1 & 1 \end{array}\right]$$

$$\left[\begin{array}{rrr|rrr|r} 1 & -2 & 1 & 0 & 1 & 0 & -9 \\ 0 & 7 & -4 & 1 & -3 & 0 & 29 \\ 0 & 11 & -2 & 0 & -4 & 1 & 37 \end{array}\right]$$

$$\left[\begin{array}{rrr|rrr|r} 1 & 0 & -\frac{1}{7} & \frac{2}{7} & \frac{1}{7} & 0 & -\frac{5}{7} \\ 0 & 1 & -\frac{4}{7} & \frac{1}{7} & -\frac{3}{7} & 0 & \frac{29}{7} \\ 0 & 0 & \frac{30}{7} & -\frac{11}{7} & \frac{5}{7} & 1 & -\frac{60}{7} \end{array}\right]$$

$$\left[\begin{array}{rrr|rrr|r} 1 & 0 & 0 & \frac{7}{30} & \frac{1}{6} & \frac{1}{30} & -1 \\ 0 & 1 & 0 & -\frac{1}{15} & -\frac{1}{3} & \frac{2}{15} & 3 \\ 0 & 0 & 1 & -\frac{11}{30} & \frac{1}{6} & \frac{7}{30} & -2 \end{array}\right]$$

Thus, reading directly from the tableau,

$$\begin{bmatrix} x_1 \\ x_2 \\ x_3 \end{bmatrix} = \begin{bmatrix} -1 \\ 3 \\ -2 \end{bmatrix}$$

or, using the inverse matrix, $\mathbf{x} = \mathbf{A}^{-1}\mathbf{c}$,

$$\begin{bmatrix} x_1 \\ x_2 \\ x_3 \end{bmatrix} = \begin{bmatrix} \frac{7}{30} & \frac{1}{6} & \frac{1}{30} \\ -\frac{1}{15} & -\frac{1}{3} & \frac{2}{15} \\ -\frac{11}{30} & \frac{1}{6} & \frac{7}{30} \end{bmatrix} \begin{bmatrix} 2 \\ -9 \\ 1 \end{bmatrix} = \begin{bmatrix} -1 \\ 3 \\ -2 \end{bmatrix}$$

In practice, the solution would be obtained from $\mathbf{x} = \mathbf{A}^{-1}\mathbf{c}$ only if $\mathbf{A}^{-1}$ had been obtained without obtaining the tableau $(\mathbf{I}\,|\,\mathbf{A}^{-1}\,|\,\mathbf{x})$.

Using Cramer's rule,

$$|\mathbf{A}| = \begin{vmatrix} 3 & 1 & -1 \\ 1 & -2 & 1 \\ 4 & 3 & 2 \end{vmatrix} = -12 + 4 - 3 - (8 + 9 + 2) = -30$$

$$x_1 = \frac{\begin{vmatrix} 2 & 1 & -1 \\ -9 & -2 & 1 \\ 1 & 3 & 2 \end{vmatrix}}{-30} = \frac{-8 + 1 + 27 - (2 + 6 - 18)}{-30} = \frac{30}{-30} = -1$$

$$x_2 = \frac{\begin{vmatrix} 3 & 2 & -1 \\ 1 & -9 & 1 \\ 4 & 1 & 2 \end{vmatrix}}{-30} = \frac{-54 + 8 - 1 - (36 + 3 + 4)}{-30} = \frac{-90}{-30} = 3$$

$$x_3 = \frac{\begin{vmatrix} 3 & 1 & 2 \\ 1 & -2 & -9 \\ 4 & 3 & 1 \end{vmatrix}}{-30} = \frac{-6 - 36 + 6 - (-16 - 81 + 1)}{-30} = \frac{60}{-30} = -2$$

EXAMPLE

Solve the set of simultaneous linear equations

$$x_1 + x_2 - x_3 = 6$$
$$3x_1 - 4x_2 + 2x_3 = -2$$
$$2x_1 + 5x_2 + x_3 = 0$$

Apply the standard procedure to the tableau

$$(\mathbf{A}\,|\,\mathbf{I}\,|\,\mathbf{c})$$

to obtain the tableau

$$(\mathbf{I}\,|\,\mathbf{A}^{-1}\,|\,\mathbf{x})$$

$$\begin{bmatrix} 1 & 1 & -1 & | & 1 & 0 & 0 & | & 6 \\ 3 & -4 & 2 & | & 0 & 1 & 0 & | & -2 \\ 2 & 5 & 1 & | & 0 & 0 & 1 & | & 0 \end{bmatrix}$$

$$\begin{bmatrix} 1 & 1 & -1 & | & 1 & 0 & 0 & | & 6 \\ 0 & -7 & 5 & | & -3 & 1 & 0 & | & -20 \\ 0 & 3 & 3 & | & -2 & 0 & 1 & | & -12 \end{bmatrix}$$

$$\begin{bmatrix} 1 & 0 & -\frac{2}{7} & | & \frac{4}{7} & \frac{1}{7} & 0 & | & \frac{22}{7} \\ 0 & 1 & -\frac{5}{7} & | & \frac{3}{7} & -\frac{1}{7} & 0 & | & \frac{20}{7} \\ 0 & 0 & \frac{36}{7} & | & -\frac{23}{7} & \frac{3}{7} & 1 & | & -\frac{144}{7} \end{bmatrix}$$

$$\begin{bmatrix} 1 & 0 & 0 & | & \frac{7}{18} & \frac{1}{6} & \frac{1}{18} & | & 2 \\ 0 & 1 & 0 & | & -\frac{1}{36} & -\frac{1}{12} & \frac{5}{36} & | & 0 \\ 0 & 0 & 1 & | & -\frac{23}{36} & \frac{1}{12} & \frac{7}{36} & | & -4 \end{bmatrix}$$

thus, reading directly from the tableau, $x = A^{-1}c$

$$\begin{bmatrix} x_1 \\ x_2 \\ x_3 \end{bmatrix} = \begin{bmatrix} 2 \\ 0 \\ -4 \end{bmatrix}$$

or, using the inverse matrix,

$$\begin{bmatrix} x_1 \\ x_2 \\ x_3 \end{bmatrix} = \begin{bmatrix} \frac{7}{18} & \frac{1}{6} & \frac{1}{18} \\ -\frac{1}{36} & -\frac{1}{12} & \frac{5}{36} \\ -\frac{23}{36} & \frac{1}{12} & \frac{7}{36} \end{bmatrix} \begin{bmatrix} 6 \\ -2 \\ 0 \end{bmatrix} = \begin{bmatrix} 2 \\ 0 \\ -4 \end{bmatrix}$$

Using Cramer's rule,

$$|\mathbf{A}| = \begin{vmatrix} 1 & 1 & -1 \\ 3 & -4 & 2 \\ 2 & 5 & 1 \end{vmatrix} = -4 + 4 - 15 - (8 + 10 + 3) = -36$$

$$x_1 = \frac{\begin{vmatrix} 6 & 1 & -1 \\ -2 & -4 & 2 \\ 0 & 5 & 1 \end{vmatrix}}{-36} = \frac{-24 + 0 + 10 - (0 + 60 - 2)}{-36} = \frac{-72}{-36} = 2$$

$$x_2 = \frac{\begin{vmatrix} 1 & 6 & -1 \\ 3 & -2 & 2 \\ 2 & 0 & 1 \end{vmatrix}}{-36} = \frac{-2 + 24 + 0 - (4 + 0 + 18)}{-36} = 0$$

$$x_3 = \frac{\begin{vmatrix} 1 & 1 & 6 \\ 3 & -4 & -2 \\ 2 & 5 & 0 \end{vmatrix}}{-36} = \frac{0 - 4 + 90 - (-48 - 10 + 0)}{-36} = \frac{144}{-36} = -4$$

PROBLEMS

For each of the following sets of simultaneous linear equations, determine whether there is a unique solution and obtain the solution if there is one.

1. $x + 2y = 1$
   $3x + 4y = 2$

2. $x + y - 2z = 5$
   $2x - 4y + 3z = 6$
   $3x - 3y + z = 11$

3. $x_1 + x_2 + x_3 = 3$
   $2x_1 - x_2 - x_3 = 0$
   $3x_1 + 4x_2 + x_3 = 8$

4. $3x - y + 2z = -2$
   $x + y + z = 5$
   $2x - 2y + z = 3$

5. $x - 5y + 6z = 7$
   $3x + 3y - z = 8$
   $2x + 8y - 7z = 1$

6. $x_1 - 3x_2 = -2$
   $2x_1 + 7x_2 = 3$

7. $x_1 - 4x_2 = -1$
   $3x_1 - 2x_2 - x_3 = 0$
   $x_1 + x_3 = 3$

8. $x_1 + x_2 + x_3 = 9$
   $3x_1 + 2x_3 = 17$
   $x_2 + x_3 = 10$

9. $3x - y = 0$
   $2x + 4y = -14$

10. $3x_1 - 4x_2 = -3$
    $6x_1 + x_2 = 3$

11. $4x_1 - 5x_2 - 7x_3 = 15$
    $3x_1 + 2x_2 - 6x_3 = 8$
    $x_1 - 7x_2 - x_3 = 6$

12. $5x_1 - 2x_2 + x_3 = 12$
    $2x_1 + 2x_2 - 3x_3 = 7$
    $x_1 - 6x_2 + 7x_3 = -2$

13. $2x_1 + 3x_2 + x_3 = 0$
    $4x_1 - 8x_2 - 6x_3 = 2$
    $6x_1 + x_2 - x_3 = 0$

14. $x_1 + 5x_2 - 4x_3 = 0$
    $3x_1 - x_2 + 4x_3 = -4$
    $2x_1 + 3x_2 - 8x_3 = 0$

15. $3x_1 - 3x_2 + 4x_3 = -18$
    $4x_1 - 4x_2 + 4x_3 = -24$
    $2x_1 - 2x_2 + 4x_3 = 6$

16. $x_1 + x_2 + 6x_3 = -2$
    $3x_1 + 2x_2 + x_3 = 0$
    $2x_1 + x_2 + 5x_3 = 2$

17. $x_1 + 2x_2 = 0$
    $x_1 + x_2 + x_3 = 2$
    $2x_1 + 2x_2 + 3x_3 = 7$

18. $x_1 + x_2 + x_3 = 4$
    $2x_1 + 3x_2 + 2x_3 = 5$
    $3x_1 + 4x_2 - 3x_3 = -3$

Answers to Odd-Numbered Problems

1. $x = 0$, $y = \frac{1}{2}$
3. $x_1 = 1$, $x_2 = 1$, $x_3 = 1$
5. linearly dependent, no unique solution
7. $x_1 = 1$, $x_2 = \frac{1}{2}$, $x_3 = 2$
9. $x = -1$, $y = -3$

11. inconsistent, no solution
13. $x_1 = -\frac{1}{2}$, $x_2 = 1$, $x_3 = -2$
15. inconsistent, no solution
17. $x_1 = -2$, $x_2 = 1$, $x_3 = 3$

7.10 Characteristic Roots and Vectors of a Matrix

The characteristic roots and vectors of an $n \times n$ matrix A are obtained by solving the equation

$$Ax = \lambda x$$

for a scalar λ and a vector $x \neq 0$. The scalar λ is a *characteristic root* of A, and x is a *characteristic vector* of A. Characteristic roots and vectors are also referred to as *latent roots* and *vectors* or *eigenvalues* and *eigenvectors*.

DETERMINING CHARACTERISTIC ROOTS

The equation $Ax = \lambda x$ or $[A - \lambda I]x = 0$ has a nontrivial solution, $x \neq 0$, if and only if $[A - \lambda I]$ is singular, that is, if and only if

$$|A - \lambda I| = 0$$

this determinant is an nth-degree polynomial in λ, and thus A has n characteristic roots, $\lambda_1, \lambda_2, \ldots, \lambda_n$, not necessarily all distinct.

Consider the general 2×2 matrix

$$A = \begin{bmatrix} a_{11} & a_{12} \\ a_{21} & a_{22} \end{bmatrix}$$

Then $Ax = \lambda x$ or $[A - \lambda I]x = 0$ can be written

$$(a_{11} - \lambda)x_1 + a_{12}x_2 = 0$$

$$a_{21}x_1 + (a_{22} - \lambda)x_2 = 0$$

which has a nontrivial solution, $x \neq 0$, if and only if $|A - \lambda I| = 0$; that is,

$$\begin{vmatrix} a_{11} - \lambda & a_{12} \\ a_{21} & a_{22} - \lambda \end{vmatrix} = 0$$

$$(a_{11} - \lambda)(a_{22} - \lambda) - a_{12}^2 = 0$$

$$\lambda^2 - (a_{11} + a_{22})\lambda + (a_{11}a_{22} - a_{12}a_{21}) = 0$$

which has the solution

$$\lambda_1 = \tfrac{1}{2}[(a_{11} + a_{22}) + \sqrt{(a_{11} + a_{22})^2 - 4(a_{11}a_{22} - a_{12}a_{21})}]$$

$$\lambda_2 = \tfrac{1}{2}[(a_{11} + a_{22}) - \sqrt{(a_{11} + a_{22})^2 - 4(a_{11}a_{22} - a_{12}a_{21})}]$$

For the special case of a symmetric matrix, $a_{12} = a_{21}$, the solution is

$$\lambda_1 = \tfrac{1}{2}[(a_{11} + a_{22}) + \sqrt{(a_{11} - a_{22})^2 + 4a_{12}^2}]$$

$$\lambda_2 = \tfrac{1}{2}[(a_{11} + a_{22}) - \sqrt{(a_{11} - a_{22})^2 + 4a_{12}^2}]$$

Note that the characteristic roots of a symmetric matrix are always real, since $(a_{11} - a_{22})^2 + 4a_{12}^2$ is always nonnegative.

EXAMPLE

Find the characteristic roots of the matrix

$$A = \begin{bmatrix} 10 & 3 \\ 3 & 2 \end{bmatrix}$$

A is a symmetric matrix, and its characteristic roots are given by

$$\lambda = \tfrac{1}{2}[(a_{11} + a_{22})^2 \pm \sqrt{(a_{11} - a_{22})^2 + 4a_{12}^2}]$$

$$= \tfrac{1}{2}[12 \pm \sqrt{64 + 36}]$$

$$= 11, 1$$

PROPERTIES OF CHARACTERISTIC ROOTS

Characteristic roots have the following properties:

1. The characteristic roots of a real symmetric matrix are all real.
2. The product of the characteristic roots of a matrix A is equal to $|A|$; that is, $\prod_{i=1}^{n} \lambda_i = |A|$.

3. The sum of the characteristic roots of a matrix A is equal to the trace of A; that is, $\sum_{i=1}^{n} \lambda_i = \text{tr } (A)$.
4. The characteristic roots of a diagonal matrix are its diagonal elements. Note that in the preceding example, $\prod_{i=1}^{2} \lambda_i = 11 = |A|$ and $\sum_{i=1}^{2} \lambda_i = 12 = \text{tr } (A)$.

DETERMINING CHARACTERISTIC VECTORS

Associated with every characteristic root λ_i of A is a characteristic vector, x_i, which satisfies the homogeneous system of equations

$$[A - \lambda_i I]x_i = 0$$

By definition of the characteristic roots, $|A - \lambda I| = 0$, and a nontrivial solution for x_i always exists. However, the elements of x_i are determined only up to a scale factor, since if x_i satisfies $[A - \lambda_i I]x_i = 0$, so also does kx_i, where k is an arbitrary constant. The characteristic vectors are frequently normalized so that $x_i' x_i = 1$ for all i.

EXAMPLE

For the matrix A given in the example above, the characteristic roots are $\lambda_1 = 11$ and $\lambda_2 = 1$. The corresponding characteristic vectors can be obtained as follows.

For $\lambda_1 = 11$,

$$[A - \lambda_1 I]x_1 = \left[\begin{bmatrix} 10 & 3 \\ 3 & 2 \end{bmatrix} - \begin{bmatrix} 11 & 0 \\ 0 & 11 \end{bmatrix} \right] \begin{bmatrix} x_{11} \\ x_{12} \end{bmatrix} = \begin{bmatrix} 0 \\ 0 \end{bmatrix}$$

$$-x_{11} + 3x_{12} = 0$$

$$3x_{11} - 9x_{12} = 0$$

$$x_{11} = 3x_{12}$$

Normalizing so that $x_1' x_1 = 1$,

$$x_{11}^2 + x_{12}^2 = 1$$

$$9x_{12}^2 + x_{12}^2 = 1$$

$$x_{12} = \frac{1}{\sqrt{10}}$$

$$x_{11} = \frac{3}{\sqrt{10}}$$

$$x_1' = \left[\frac{3}{\sqrt{10}}, \frac{1}{\sqrt{10}} \right]$$

For $\lambda_2 = 1$,

$$[A - \lambda I]x_2 = \left[\begin{bmatrix} 10 & 3 \\ 3 & 2 \end{bmatrix} - \begin{bmatrix} 1 & 0 \\ 0 & 1 \end{bmatrix} \right] \begin{bmatrix} x_{21} \\ x_{22} \end{bmatrix} = \begin{bmatrix} 0 \\ 0 \end{bmatrix}$$

$$9x_{21} + 3x_{22} = 0$$

$$3x_{21} + x_{22} = 0$$

$$x_{22} = -3x_{21}$$

Normalizing so that $x_2' x_2 = 1$,

$$x_{21}^2 + x_{22}^2 = 1$$

$$x_{21}^2 + 9x_{21}^2 = 1$$

$$x_{21} = \frac{1}{\sqrt{10}}$$

$$x_{22} = -\frac{3}{\sqrt{10}}$$

$$x_2' = \left[\frac{1}{\sqrt{10}}, \quad \frac{-3}{\sqrt{10}} \right]$$

Note that $x_1' x_2 = x_2' x_1 = 0$. Thus x_1 and x_2 are *orthogonal* vectors. A set of normalized orthogonal vectors is an *orthonormal* set. Since x_1 and x_2 are normalized, they are an orthonormal set.

PROPERTIES OF CHARACTERISTIC VECTORS

Characteristic vectors have the following properties:
1. The characteristic vectors of a real symmetric matrix are orthogonal.
2. If a characteristic root has multiplicity k, that is, if it is repeated k times, there are k orthogonal vectors corresponding to this root.

EXAMPLE

Determine the characteristic roots and vectors of the matrix

$$A = \begin{bmatrix} 2 & 1 & 1 \\ 1 & 2 & 1 \\ 1 & 1 & 2 \end{bmatrix}$$

For the characteristic vectors to be nontrivial, $|A - \lambda I| = 0$; that is,

$$\begin{vmatrix} 2 - \lambda & 1 & 1 \\ 1 & 2 - \lambda & 1 \\ 1 & 1 & 2 - \lambda \end{vmatrix} = 8 - 12\lambda + 6\lambda^2 - \lambda^3 + 2 - 3(2 - \lambda) = 0$$

$$\lambda^3 - 6\lambda^2 + 9\lambda - 4 = 0$$

$$\lambda = 4, 1, 1$$

For $\lambda = 4$, the corresponding characteristic vector is the solution of the simultaneous linear equations

$$[A - \lambda I]x_1 = 0$$

$$\begin{bmatrix} -2 & 1 & 1 \\ 1 & -2 & 1 \\ 1 & 1 & -2 \end{bmatrix} \begin{bmatrix} x_{11} \\ x_{12} \\ x_{13} \end{bmatrix} = \begin{bmatrix} 0 \\ 0 \\ 0 \end{bmatrix}$$

$$-2x_{11} + x_{12} + x_{13} = 0$$

$$x_{11} - 2x_{12} + x_{13} = 0$$

$$x_{11} + x_{12} - 2x_{13} = 0$$

so

$$x_{11} = x_{12} = x_{13}$$

Normalizing so that $x_1' x_1 = 1$,

$$x_{11}^2 + x_{12}^2 + x_{13}^2 = 1$$

$$x_{11} = x_{12} = x_{13} = \frac{1}{\sqrt{3}}$$

and

$$x_1' = \left[\frac{1}{\sqrt{3}}, \frac{1}{\sqrt{3}}, \frac{1}{\sqrt{3}} \right]$$

For $\lambda = 1$, the corresponding characteristic vector is the solution of the simultaneous linear equations

$$[A - \lambda I]x_2 = 0$$

$$\begin{bmatrix} 1 & 1 & 1 \\ 1 & 1 & 1 \\ 1 & 1 & 1 \end{bmatrix} \begin{bmatrix} x_{21} \\ x_{22} \\ x_{23} \end{bmatrix} = \begin{bmatrix} 0 \\ 0 \\ 0 \end{bmatrix}$$

$$x_{21} + x_{22} + x_{23} = 0$$

which has general solution

$$[a, b, -a - b]$$

where a and b can be chosen to generate two linearly independent characteristic vectors, since $\lambda = 1$ occurs twice. Note that any choice of a and b will give a vector orthogonal to the first characteristic vector $(1, 1, 1)$.

If the vectors are normalized,

$$a^2 + b^2 + a^2 + 2ab + b^2 = 1$$

$$a^2 + ab + (b^2 - \tfrac{1}{2}) = 0$$

$$a = \frac{\sqrt{-b \pm b^2 - 4(b^2 - \tfrac{1}{2})}}{2}$$

$$= \frac{-b \pm \sqrt{2 - 3b^2}}{2}$$

If, for example, $b = 0$, then $a = \pm \dfrac{\sqrt{2}}{2}$ and

$$x_2' = \left[\frac{\sqrt{2}}{2}, 0, -\frac{\sqrt{2}}{2} \right]$$

$$x_3' = \left[-\frac{\sqrt{2}}{2}, 0, \frac{\sqrt{2}}{2} \right]$$

Note that the properties of characteristic roots and vectors given above are satisfied by the characteristic roots $\lambda_1 = 4$, $\lambda_2 = \lambda_3 = 1$ and the corresponding characteristic vectors

$$x_1' = \left[\frac{1}{\sqrt{3}}, \frac{1}{\sqrt{3}}, \frac{1}{\sqrt{3}} \right], \qquad x_2' = \left[\frac{\sqrt{2}}{2}, 0, -\frac{\sqrt{2}}{2} \right], \qquad x_3' = \left[-\frac{\sqrt{2}}{2}, 0, \frac{\sqrt{2}}{2} \right]$$

$$\prod_{i=1}^{3} \lambda_i = 4 = |A|, \text{ since } |A| = 8 + 1 + 1 - (2 + 2 + 2) = 4$$

$$\sum_{i=1}^{3} \lambda_i = 6 = \text{tr}(a), \text{ since tr}(A) = 2 + 2 + 2 = 6$$

$$x_i' x_j = \begin{cases} 1 & \text{if } i = j = 1, 2, 3 \\ 0 & \text{if } i, j = 1, 2, 3 \text{ and } i \neq j \end{cases}$$

PROBLEMS

For each of the following matrices, determine the characteristic roots and vectors and verify that they have the properties discussed.

1. $\begin{bmatrix} 5 & -2 \\ -2 & 2 \end{bmatrix}$

2. $\begin{bmatrix} 4 & 3 \\ 3 & 4 \end{bmatrix}$

3. $\begin{bmatrix} 3 & 0 & 0 \\ 0 & 2 & 0 \\ 0 & 0 & -2 \end{bmatrix}$

4. $\begin{bmatrix} -1 & 0 & 0 \\ 0 & -2 & 0 \\ 0 & 0 & 3 \end{bmatrix}$

5. $\begin{bmatrix} 1 & 2 & 2 \\ 2 & 1 & 2 \\ 2 & 2 & 1 \end{bmatrix}$

6. $\begin{bmatrix} 10 & 4 \\ 4 & 4 \end{bmatrix}$

Answers to Odd-Numbered Problems

1. $\lambda_1 = 6, \lambda_2 = 1$

$$x_1' = \left[\frac{-2}{\sqrt{5}}, \frac{1}{\sqrt{5}}\right]$$

$$x_2' = \left[\frac{1}{\sqrt{5}}, \frac{2}{\sqrt{5}}\right]$$

3. $\lambda_1 = 3, \lambda_2 = 2, \lambda_3 = -2$

$x_1' = [1, 0, 0]$

$x_2' = [0, 1, 0]$

$x_3' = [0, 0, 1]$

5. $\lambda_1 = 5, \lambda_2 = \lambda_3 = -1$

$$x_1' = \left[\frac{1}{\sqrt{3}}, \frac{1}{\sqrt{3}}, \frac{1}{\sqrt{3}}\right]$$

$$x_2' = \left[\frac{\sqrt{2}}{2}, 0, -\frac{\sqrt{2}}{2}\right]$$

$$x_3' = \left[-\frac{\sqrt{2}}{2}, 0, \frac{\sqrt{2}}{2}\right]$$

7.11 Vector Differentiation

In some maximization and minimization problems, expressions involving vectors and matrices must be differentiated. The derivatives of simple expressions involving vectors and matrices can be obtained directly from the definitions. The vector derivatives of linear functions, quadratic forms, and bilinear forms are defined and illustrated in this section. Second- and higher-order vector derivatives are not discussed explicitly, but can be obtained by successive differentiation in the usual manner.

VECTOR DIFFERENTIATION OF A LINEAR FUNCTION

An expression of the form $\mathbf{a}'\mathbf{x}$ where $\mathbf{a}$ is $n \times 1$ and $\mathbf{x}$ is $n \times 1$ is a *linear function*. For the linear function

$$\mathbf{a}'\mathbf{x} = [a_1, a_2, \ldots, a_n] \begin{bmatrix} x_1 \\ x_2 \\ \vdots \\ x_n \end{bmatrix}$$

$$= a_1 x_1 + a_2 x_2 + \cdots + a_n x_n$$

the partial derivatives of $\mathbf{a}'\mathbf{x}$ with respect to the scalar x_i, $i = 1, 2, \ldots, n$, are

$$\frac{\partial(\mathbf{a}'\mathbf{x})}{\partial x_1} = a_1$$

$$\frac{\partial(\mathbf{a}'\mathbf{x})}{\partial x_2} = a_2$$

$$\vdots$$

$$\frac{\partial(\mathbf{a}'\mathbf{x})}{\partial x_n} = a_n$$

that is, the partial derivatives are the elements of the vector $\mathbf{a}$. Thus if the n partial derivatives are arranged as a vector $\mathbf{a}$, the process of vector differentiation is defined by

$$\frac{\partial(\mathbf{a}'\mathbf{x})}{\partial \mathbf{x}} = \mathbf{a}$$

where $\dfrac{\partial(\mathbf{a}'\mathbf{x})}{\partial \mathbf{x}}$ indicates the operation of differentiating $\mathbf{a}'\mathbf{x}$ with respect to the elements of the vector $\mathbf{x}$.

EXAMPLE

If $\mathbf{a} = \begin{bmatrix} 2a \\ -a \\ 3a \\ a \end{bmatrix}$ and $\mathbf{x} = \begin{bmatrix} x_1 \\ x_2 \\ x_? \\ x_4 \end{bmatrix}$, then

$$\mathbf{a}'\mathbf{x} = 2ax_1 - ax_2 + 3ax_3 + ax_4$$

and

$$\frac{\partial}{\partial x_1}(\mathbf{a}'\mathbf{x}) = 2a$$

$$\frac{\partial}{\partial x_2}(\mathbf{a}'\mathbf{x}) = -a$$

$$\frac{\partial}{\partial x_3}(\mathbf{a}'\mathbf{x}) = 3a$$

$$\frac{\partial}{\partial x_4}(\mathbf{a}'\mathbf{x}) = a$$

Thus

$$\frac{\partial}{\partial \mathbf{x}}(\mathbf{a}'\mathbf{x}) = \begin{bmatrix} 2a \\ -a \\ 3a \\ a \end{bmatrix} = \mathbf{a}$$

Vector Differentiation of a Vector of Functions

If $\mathbf{y}$ denotes an n-dimensional column vector each element of which is a function of the m elements of $\mathbf{x}$, that is, if

$$y_i = f_i(x_1, x_2, \ldots, x_m) \qquad i = 1, 2, \ldots, n$$

then each y_i can be differentiated partially with respect to each x_j and these partial derivatives can be arranged in an $m \times n$ matrix as follows:

$$\frac{\partial \mathbf{y}}{\partial \mathbf{x}} = \begin{bmatrix} \dfrac{\partial y_1}{\partial x_1} & \dfrac{\partial y_2}{\partial x_1} & \cdots & \dfrac{\partial y_n}{\partial x_1} \\[2ex] \dfrac{\partial y_1}{\partial x_2} & \dfrac{\partial y_2}{\partial x_2} & \cdots & \dfrac{\partial y_n}{\partial x_2} \\[2ex] \vdots & \vdots & & \vdots \\[2ex] \dfrac{\partial y_1}{\partial x_m} & \dfrac{\partial y_2}{\partial x_m} & \cdots & \dfrac{\partial y_n}{\partial x_m} \end{bmatrix}$$

EXAMPLE

If

$$\mathbf{y} = \begin{bmatrix} x_1^2 + 2x_2^2 - 3x_1 x_3 \\ 3x_1 x_2^2 - x_2^2 + 4x_2 x_3^2 \end{bmatrix}$$

then

$$\frac{\partial \mathbf{y}}{\partial \mathbf{x}} = \begin{bmatrix} 2x_1 - 3x_3 & 3x_2^2 \\ 4x_2 & 6x_1 x_2 - 2x_2 + 4x_3^2 \\ -3x_1 & 8x_2 x_3 \end{bmatrix}$$

VECTOR DIFFERENTIATION OF A QUADRATIC FORM

An expression of the form $\mathbf{x}'\mathbf{A}\mathbf{x}$, where $\mathbf{A}$ is an $n \times n$ symmetric matrix, is a *quadratic form*. The quadratic form $\mathbf{x}'\mathbf{A}\mathbf{x}$ can be expanded as follows

$$\mathbf{x}'\mathbf{A}\mathbf{x} = [x_1, x_2, \ldots, x_n] \begin{bmatrix} a_{11} & a_{12} & \cdots & a_{1n} \\ a_{12} & a_{22} & \cdots & a_{2n} \\ \vdots & \vdots & & \vdots \\ a_{1n} & a_{2n} & \cdots & a_{nn} \end{bmatrix} \begin{bmatrix} x_1 \\ x_2 \\ \vdots \\ x_n \end{bmatrix}$$

$$= a_{11} x_1^2 + 2a_{12} x_1 x_2 + 2a_{13} x_1 x_3 + \cdots + 2a_{1n} x_1 x_n$$
$$+ a_{22} x_2^2 + 2a_{23} x_2 x_3 + \cdots + 2a_{2n} x_{2n}$$
$$+ \quad \cdot \quad \cdot \quad \cdot$$
$$\cdot$$
$$\cdot$$
$$\cdot$$
$$+ a_{nn} x_n^2$$

Taking partial derivatives with respect to the elements of $\mathbf{x}$,

$$\frac{\partial}{\partial x_1}(\mathbf{x}'\mathbf{A}\mathbf{x}) = 2(a_{11}x_1 + a_{12}x_2 + a_{13}x_3 + \cdots + a_{1n}x_n)$$

$$\frac{\partial}{\partial x_2}(\mathbf{x}'\mathbf{A}\mathbf{x}) = 2(a_{12}x_1 + a_{22}x_2 + a_{23}x_3 + \cdots + a_{2n}x_n)$$

$$\vdots \qquad\qquad\qquad \vdots$$

$$\frac{\partial}{\partial x_n}(\mathbf{x}'\mathbf{A}\mathbf{x}) = 2(a_{1n}x_1 + a_{2n}x_2 + a_{3n}x_3 + \cdots + a_{nn}x_n)$$

Apart from the factor 2, the right-hand side of this set of equations contains the elements of $\mathbf{A}\mathbf{x}$, which is an n-dimensional column vector; alternatively, the right-hand side contains the elements of $\mathbf{x}'\mathbf{A}$, which is an n-dimensional row vector. Thus

$$\frac{\partial}{\partial \mathbf{x}}(\mathbf{x}'\mathbf{A}\mathbf{x}) = 2\mathbf{A}\mathbf{x}$$

or

$$\frac{\partial}{\partial \mathbf{x}}(\mathbf{x}'\mathbf{A}\mathbf{x}) = 2\mathbf{x}'\mathbf{A}$$

In practice, the choice between these two forms usually depends on the context in which differentiation occurs, since matrices can be equated only if they are of the same order; specifically, a row vector can be set equal to another row vector having the same number of elements but cannot be set equal to a column vector.

EXAMPLE

If $\mathbf{x} = \begin{bmatrix} x_1 \\ x_2 \\ x_3 \end{bmatrix}$ and $\mathbf{A} = \begin{bmatrix} 3 & 1 & -2 \\ 1 & 0 & 3 \\ -2 & 3 & 2 \end{bmatrix}$, then

$$\mathbf{x}'\mathbf{A}\mathbf{x} = [x_1, x_2, x_3] \begin{bmatrix} 3 & 1 & -2 \\ 1 & 0 & 3 \\ -2 & 3 & 2 \end{bmatrix} \begin{bmatrix} x_1 \\ x_2 \\ x_3 \end{bmatrix}$$

$$= [3x_1 + x_2 - 2x_3, \quad x_1 + 3x_3, \quad -2x_1 + 3x_2 + 2x_3] \begin{bmatrix} x_1 \\ x_2 \\ x_3 \end{bmatrix}$$

$$= 3x_1^2 + x_1 x_2 - 2x_1 x_3 + x_1 x_2 + 3x_2 x_3 - 2x_1 x_3 + 3x_2 x_3 + 2x_3^2$$

$$= 3x_1^2 + 2x_3^2 + 2x_1 x_2 - 4x_1 x_3 + 6x_2 x_3$$

and

$$\frac{\partial}{\partial x_1}(\mathbf{x}'\mathbf{A}\mathbf{x}) = 6x_1 + 2x_2 - 4x_3$$

$$\frac{\partial}{\partial x_2}(\mathbf{x}'\mathbf{A}\mathbf{x}) = 2x_1 + 6x_3$$

$$\frac{\partial}{\partial x_3}(\mathbf{x}'\mathbf{A}\mathbf{x}) = 4x_3 - 4x_1 + 6x_2$$

Thus

$$\frac{\partial}{\partial \mathbf{x}}(\mathbf{x}'\mathbf{A}\mathbf{x}) = 2\begin{bmatrix} 3x_1 + x_2 - 2x_3 \\ x_1 + 3x_3 \\ -2x_1 + 3x_2 + 2x_3 \end{bmatrix} = 2\mathbf{A}\mathbf{x}$$

or

$$\frac{\partial}{\partial \mathbf{x}}(\mathbf{x}'\mathbf{A}\mathbf{x}) = 2[3x_1 + x_2 - 2x_3, \quad x_1 + 3x_3, \quad -2x_1 + 3x_2 + 2x_3] = 2\mathbf{x}'\mathbf{A}$$

VECTOR DIFFERENTIATION OF A BILINEAR FORM

An expression of the form $\mathbf{x}'\mathbf{B}\mathbf{z}$, where $\mathbf{x}'$ is $1 \times m$, $\mathbf{B}$ is $m \times n$ and $\mathbf{z}$ is $n \times 1$, is a *bilinear form*. The following derivatives for a bilinear form can be verified using the procedures above.

$$\frac{\partial}{\partial \mathbf{x}}(\mathbf{x}'\mathbf{B}\mathbf{z}) = \mathbf{B}\mathbf{z}$$

$$\frac{\partial}{\partial \mathbf{z}}(\mathbf{x}'\mathbf{B}\mathbf{z}) = \mathbf{B}'\mathbf{x}$$

EXAMPLE

If

$$x = \begin{bmatrix} x_1 \\ x_2 \\ x_3 \end{bmatrix} \qquad B = \begin{bmatrix} 2b_1 & b_1 + b_2 \\ b_2 + 2b_3 & 3b_2 \\ b_1 + b_3 & 4b_3{}^2 \end{bmatrix} \qquad z = \begin{bmatrix} z_1 \\ z_2 \end{bmatrix}$$

then

$$\mathbf{x}'\mathbf{B}\mathbf{z} = [x_1, x_2, x_3]\begin{bmatrix} 2b_1 & b_1 + b_2 \\ b_2 + 2b_3 & 3b_2 \\ b_1 + b_3 & 4b_3^2 \end{bmatrix}\begin{bmatrix} z_1 \\ z_2 \end{bmatrix}$$

$$= [2b_1 x_1 + b_2 x_2 + 2b_3 x_2 + b_1 x_3 + b_3 x_3, \quad b_1 x_1 + b_2 x_1 + 3b_2 x_2 + 4b_3^2 x_3]\begin{bmatrix} z_1 \\ z_2 \end{bmatrix}$$

$$= 2b_1 x_1 z_1 + b_2 x_2 z_1 + 2b_3 x_2 z_1 + b_1 x_3 z_1 + b_3 x_3 z_1 + b_1 x_1 z_2$$
$$+ b_2 x_1 z_2 + 3b_2 x_2 z_2 + 4b_3^2 x_3 z_2$$

and

$$\frac{\partial}{\partial x_1}(\mathbf{x}'\mathbf{B}\mathbf{z}) = 2b_1 z_1 + b_1 z_2 + b_2 z_2$$

$$\frac{\partial}{\partial x_2}(\mathbf{x}'\mathbf{B}\mathbf{z}) = b_2 z_1 + 2b_3 z_1 + 3b_2 z_2$$

$$\frac{\partial}{\partial x_3}(\mathbf{x}'\mathbf{B}\mathbf{z}) = b_1 z_1 + b_3 z_1 + 4b_3^2 z_2$$

Thus

$$\frac{\partial}{\partial \mathbf{x}}(\mathbf{x}'\mathbf{B}\mathbf{z}) = \begin{bmatrix} 2b_1 z_1 + b_1 z_2 + b_2 z_2 \\ b_2 z_1 + 2b_3 z_1 + 3b_2 z_2 \\ b_1 z_1 + b_3 z_1 + 4b_3^2 z_2 \end{bmatrix} = \mathbf{B}\mathbf{z}$$

and

$$\frac{\partial}{\partial z_1}(\mathbf{x}'\mathbf{Bz}) = 2b_1 x_1 + b_2 x_2 + 2b_3 x_2 + b_1 x_3 + b_3 x_3$$

$$\frac{\partial}{\partial z_2}(\mathbf{x}'\mathbf{Bz}) = b_1 x_1 + b_2 x_1 + 3b_2 x_2 + 4b_3^2 x_3$$

Thus

$$\frac{\partial}{\partial \mathbf{z}}(\mathbf{x}'\mathbf{Bz}) = \begin{bmatrix} 2b_1 x_1 + b_2 x_2 + 2b_3 x_2 + b_1 x_3 + b_3 x_3 \\ b_1 x_1 + b_2 x_1 + 3b_2 x_2 + 4b_3^2 x_3 \end{bmatrix}$$

$$= \begin{bmatrix} 2b_1 & b_2 + 2b_3 & b_1 + b_3 \\ b_1 + b_2 & 3b_2 & 4b_3^2 \end{bmatrix} \begin{bmatrix} x_1 \\ x_2 \\ x_3 \end{bmatrix}$$

$$= \mathbf{B}'\mathbf{x}$$

APPLICATIONS OF VECTOR DIFFERENTIATION IN MAXIMIZATION AND MINIMIZATION

Vector differentiation is used in solving many problems involving maximization and minimization. In particular, the derivations of most of the estimators in multivariate analysis involve vector differentiation. As an example of these applications, the derivation of least squares multivariate regression estimators is discussed in this section.

In multivariate regression analysis, the model involves the assumption of a linear relationship between a predicted variable y and k, explanatory variables $x_1, x_2, \ldots, x_k$, and a disturbance term u. For a sample of n observations on y and the x's,

$$y_i = \beta_0 + \beta_1 x_{1i} + \beta_2 x_{2i} + \cdots + \beta_k x_{ki} + u_i \qquad i = 1, 2, \ldots, n$$

and the n equations can be written in matrix notation as

$$\mathbf{y} = \mathbf{x}\boldsymbol{\beta} + \mathbf{u}$$

where

$$\mathbf{y} = \begin{bmatrix} y_1 \\ y_2 \\ \vdots \\ y_n \end{bmatrix} \qquad \mathbf{x} = \begin{bmatrix} 1 & x_{21} & \cdots & x_{k1} \\ 1 & x_{22} & \cdots & x_{k2} \\ \vdots & \vdots & & \\ 1 & x_{2n} & \cdots & x_{kn} \end{bmatrix}$$

$$\boldsymbol{\beta} = \begin{bmatrix} \beta_1 \\ \beta_2 \\ \vdots \\ \beta_k \end{bmatrix} \qquad \mathbf{u} = \begin{bmatrix} u_1 \\ u_2 \\ \vdots \\ u_n \end{bmatrix}$$

The intercept β_0 is represented by the column of ones in the $\mathbf{x}$ matrix. As a result of the convention of denoting the ith observation on the kth variable by x_{ki}, the subscripts in the $\mathbf{x}$ matrix are the reverse of the usual pattern, which indicates the row by the first subscript and the column by the second subscript.

The problem is to obtain estimates of the β's. These estimates are customarily obtained using the least squares criterion. Let

$$\hat{\boldsymbol{\beta}} = \begin{bmatrix} \hat{\beta}_1 \\ \hat{\beta}_2 \\ \vdots \\ \hat{\beta}_k \end{bmatrix}$$

denote a vector of estimates of $\boldsymbol{\beta}$. Then $\mathbf{y} = \mathbf{x}\hat{\boldsymbol{\beta}} + e$ where e denotes the column vector of n residuals $(\mathbf{y} - \mathbf{x}\hat{\boldsymbol{\beta}})$. The least squares criterion requires that the sum of squared residuals is minimized.

$$\sum_{i=1}^{n} e_i^2 = e'e$$

$$= (\mathbf{y} - \mathbf{x}\hat{\boldsymbol{\beta}})'(\mathbf{y} - \mathbf{x}\hat{\boldsymbol{\beta}})$$

$$= \mathbf{y}'\mathbf{y} - 2\hat{\boldsymbol{\beta}}'\mathbf{x}'\mathbf{y} + \hat{\boldsymbol{\beta}}'\mathbf{x}'\mathbf{x}\hat{\boldsymbol{\beta}}$$

Note that $(\mathbf{y} - \mathbf{x}\hat{\boldsymbol{\beta}})' = \mathbf{y}' - \hat{\boldsymbol{\beta}}'\mathbf{x}'$ and $\hat{\boldsymbol{\beta}}'\mathbf{x}'\mathbf{y}$ is a scalar and thus equal to its transpose $\mathbf{y}'\mathbf{x}\hat{\boldsymbol{\beta}}$. To obtain the estimates $\hat{\boldsymbol{\beta}}$ which minimize the sum of squared residuals, differentiate $e'e$ with respect to $\hat{\boldsymbol{\beta}}$,

$$\frac{\partial}{\partial\hat{\boldsymbol{\beta}}}(e'e) = -2\mathbf{x}'\mathbf{y} + \mathbf{x}'\mathbf{x}\hat{\boldsymbol{\beta}} + (\hat{\boldsymbol{\beta}}'\mathbf{x}'\mathbf{x})'$$

$$= -2\mathbf{x}'\mathbf{y} + 2\mathbf{x}'\mathbf{x}\hat{\boldsymbol{\beta}}$$

If $\dfrac{\partial}{\partial\hat{\boldsymbol{\beta}}}(e'e) = 0$.

$$\mathbf{x}'\mathbf{x}\hat{\boldsymbol{\beta}} = \mathbf{x}'\mathbf{y}$$

and

$$\hat{\boldsymbol{\beta}} = (\mathbf{x}'\mathbf{x})^{-1}\mathbf{x}'\mathbf{y}$$

Alternatively,

$$\frac{\partial}{\partial\hat{\boldsymbol{\beta}}}(e'e) = -2\mathbf{y}'\mathbf{x} + 2\hat{\boldsymbol{\beta}}'\mathbf{x}'\mathbf{x}$$

If $\dfrac{\partial}{\partial\hat{\boldsymbol{\beta}}}(e'e) = 0$,

$$\hat{\boldsymbol{\beta}}'\mathbf{x}'\mathbf{x} = \mathbf{y}'\mathbf{x}$$

$$\hat{\boldsymbol{\beta}}' = \mathbf{y}'\mathbf{x}[\mathbf{x}'\mathbf{x}]^{-1}$$

and

$$\hat{\boldsymbol{\beta}} = [\mathbf{x}'\mathbf{x}]^{-1}\mathbf{x}'\mathbf{y}$$

is the vector of least squares estimates for the regression coefficients.

NOTE: To show that $\hat{\boldsymbol{\beta}} = [\mathbf{x}'\mathbf{x}]^{-1}\mathbf{x}'\mathbf{y}$ is a minimizing solution, the second derivative must be considered.

$$\frac{\partial^2}{\partial\hat{\boldsymbol{\beta}}^2}[e'e] = \frac{\partial}{\partial\hat{\boldsymbol{\beta}}}[-2\mathbf{x}'\mathbf{y} + 2\mathbf{x}'\mathbf{x}\hat{\boldsymbol{\beta}}]$$

$$= 2\mathbf{x}'\mathbf{x}$$

Thus the second order condition for minimization requires that $\mathbf{x}'\mathbf{x}$ is positive definite, that is, that $\mathbf{y}'[\mathbf{x}'\mathbf{x}]\mathbf{y}' > 0$ for all $y > 0$. In practical examples, $\mathbf{x}'\mathbf{x}$ is positive definite.

EXAMPLE

If $\mathbf{x} = \begin{bmatrix} 1 & -1 \\ 1 & 0 \\ 1 & 1 \\ 1 & -2 \end{bmatrix}$ $\quad \mathbf{y} = \begin{bmatrix} 5 \\ 3 \\ -2 \\ 8 \end{bmatrix}$

find the least squares estimates $\hat{\boldsymbol{\beta}}$ for the regression equation $\mathbf{y} = \mathbf{x}\boldsymbol{\beta} + \mathbf{u}$.

$$\mathbf{x}'\mathbf{x} = \begin{bmatrix} 1 & 1 & 1 & 1 \\ -1 & 0 & 1 & -2 \end{bmatrix} \begin{bmatrix} 1 & -1 \\ 1 & 0 \\ 1 & 1 \\ 1 & -2 \end{bmatrix}$$

$$= \begin{bmatrix} 4 & -2 \\ -2 & 6 \end{bmatrix}$$

$$|\mathbf{x}'\mathbf{x}| = 24 - 4 = 20$$

$$[\mathbf{x}'\mathbf{x}]^{-1} = \begin{bmatrix} \frac{3}{10} & \frac{1}{10} \\ \frac{1}{10} & \frac{1}{5} \end{bmatrix}$$

and

$$\hat{\boldsymbol{\beta}} = [\mathbf{x}'\mathbf{x}]^{-1}\mathbf{x}'\mathbf{y} = \begin{bmatrix} \frac{3}{10} & \frac{1}{10} \\ \frac{1}{10} & \frac{1}{5} \end{bmatrix} \begin{bmatrix} 1 & 1 & 1 & 1 \\ -1 & 0 & 1 & -2 \end{bmatrix} \begin{bmatrix} 5 \\ 3 \\ -2 \\ 8 \end{bmatrix}$$

$$= \begin{bmatrix} \frac{19}{10} \\ -\frac{16}{5} \end{bmatrix}$$

Thus the estimated regression equation is $\hat{y} = \frac{19}{10} - \frac{16}{5}x$.

PROBLEMS

1. If $\mathbf{b} = \begin{bmatrix} 3 \\ -2 \\ 1 \end{bmatrix}$ and $\mathbf{x} = \begin{bmatrix} x_1 \\ x_2 \\ x_3 \end{bmatrix}$, find $\dfrac{\partial}{\partial \mathbf{x}}[\mathbf{b}'\mathbf{x}]$.

2. If $\mathbf{c} = \begin{bmatrix} -c \\ 0 \\ 2c \\ -3c \end{bmatrix}$ and $\mathbf{y} = \begin{bmatrix} y_1 \\ y_2 \\ y_3 \\ y_4 \end{bmatrix}$, find $\dfrac{\partial}{\partial \mathbf{y}}[\mathbf{c}'\mathbf{y}]$.

3. If $\mathbf{c} = \begin{bmatrix} c^2 + 1 \\ 3c \\ 4c - 5 \\ c^3 \end{bmatrix}$ and $\mathbf{x} = \begin{bmatrix} x_1 \\ x_2 \\ x_3 \\ x_4 \end{bmatrix}$, find $\dfrac{\partial}{\partial \mathbf{x}}(\mathbf{c}'\mathbf{x})$.

4. If $\mathbf{y} = \begin{bmatrix} 2x_1^2 - 3x_2 x_3 \\ x_1 - 4x_1 x_2 x_3 \\ x_1^2 - 2x_2 + x_3 \end{bmatrix}$, find $\dfrac{\partial \mathbf{y}}{\partial \mathbf{x}}$.

5. If $\mathbf{y} = \begin{bmatrix} x_1^2 + 3x_2 \\ 2x_1 x_2 - x_2 \\ 2x_1 + x_1 x_2 - 3x_2^2 \\ 3x_1^2 - x_1^2 x_2 - x_2^3 \end{bmatrix}$, find $\dfrac{\partial \mathbf{y}}{\partial \mathbf{x}}$.

6. If $\mathbf{x} = \begin{bmatrix} x_1 \\ x_2 \end{bmatrix}$, $\mathbf{B} = \begin{bmatrix} 3 + b_1 & b_1 + 2b_2 & 4b_2^2 \\ b_2^2 & 4b_1 & b_1 b_2 \end{bmatrix}$

and $\mathbf{y} = \begin{bmatrix} y_1 \\ y_2 \\ y_3 \end{bmatrix}$, find $\dfrac{\partial}{\partial \mathbf{x}}[\mathbf{x}'\mathbf{By}]$ and $\dfrac{\partial}{\partial \mathbf{y}}[\mathbf{x}'\mathbf{By}]$.

7. If $\mathbf{x} = \begin{bmatrix} x_1 \\ x_2 \\ x_3 \end{bmatrix}$, $\mathbf{A} = \begin{bmatrix} 3 & 0 & -1 \\ 2 & 1 & 4 \\ -1 & 0 & 3 \end{bmatrix}$

and $\mathbf{y} = \begin{bmatrix} y_1 \\ y_2 \\ y_3 \end{bmatrix}$, find $\dfrac{\partial}{\partial \mathbf{x}}[\mathbf{x}'\mathbf{Ay}]$ and $\dfrac{\partial}{\partial \mathbf{y}}[\mathbf{x}'\mathbf{Ay}]$.

8. If $\mathbf{x} = \begin{bmatrix} 1 & -1 \\ 1 & 1 \\ 1 & 2 \end{bmatrix}$ and $\mathbf{y} = \begin{bmatrix} -3 \\ 5 \\ 11 \end{bmatrix}$,

find the least squares estimate $\hat{\boldsymbol{\beta}}$ for the regression $\mathbf{y} = \mathbf{x}\boldsymbol{\beta} + \mathbf{u}$.

Answers to Odd-Numbered Problems

1. $\begin{bmatrix} 3 \\ -2 \\ 1 \end{bmatrix}$

3. $\begin{bmatrix} c^2 + 1 \\ 3c \\ 4c - 5 \\ c^3 \end{bmatrix}$

5. $\begin{bmatrix} 2x_1 & 2x_2 & 2 + x_2 & 6x_1 - 2x_1 x_2 \\ 3 & 2x_1 - 1 & x_1 - 6x_2 & -x_1 - 3x_2^2 \end{bmatrix}$

7. $\begin{bmatrix} 3y_1 - y_3 \\ 2y_1 + y_2 + 4y_3 \\ -y_1 + 3y_3 \end{bmatrix}$, $\begin{bmatrix} 3x_1 + 2x_2 - x_3 \\ x_2 \\ -x_1 + 4x_2 + 3x_3 \end{bmatrix}$

Applications of Matrix Algebra

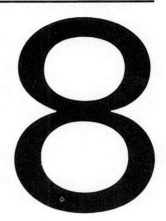

8.1 Introduction

Matrix algebra is widely used both in theoretical analyses and in applications involving manipulation of large data sets. In this chapter the use of matrix algebra is illustrated in determining maxima and minima of functions of n variables and in input-output analysis, linear programming, game theory, and Markov processes.

8.2 Maxima and Minima of Functions of n Variables

The necessary and sufficient conditions for a point to be a maximum or minimum of a function of two variables are discussed in previous sections. These results are a special case ($n = 2$) of the conditions for a maximum or minimum of a function of n variables; the general results are given below in matrix notation. Unconstrained maximization and minimization and constrained maximization and minimization using Lagrange multipliers and the Kuhn-Tucker conditions are discussed and illustrated.

UNCONSTRAINED MAXIMA AND MINIMA

Consider a function of n variables $f(x_1, x_2, \ldots, x_n)$ at a point $x^* = (x_1^*, x_2^*, \ldots, x_n^*)$ such that the n partial derivatives are zero:

$$\frac{\partial f}{\partial x_1}\bigg|_{x^*} = 0 \qquad \frac{\partial f}{\partial x_2}\bigg|_{x^*} = 0, \qquad \ldots, \qquad \frac{\partial f}{\partial x_n}\bigg|_{x^*} = 0$$

Define the determinant Δ_n of second-order partial derivatives

$$\Delta_n = \begin{vmatrix} \dfrac{\partial^2 f}{\partial x_1^2} & \dfrac{\partial^2 f}{\partial x_1\,\partial x_2} & \cdots & \dfrac{\partial^2 f}{\partial x_1\,\partial x_n} \\[2mm] \dfrac{\partial^2 f}{\partial x_2\,\partial x_1} & \dfrac{\partial^2 f}{\partial x_2^2} & \cdots & \dfrac{\partial^2 f}{\partial x_2\,\partial x_n} \\[2mm] \vdots & \vdots & & \vdots \\[2mm] \dfrac{\partial^2 f}{\partial x_n\,\partial x_1} & \dfrac{\partial^2 f}{\partial x_n\,\partial x_2} & \cdots & \dfrac{\partial^2 f}{\partial x_n^2} \end{vmatrix}$$

sometimes referred to as a *Hessian determinant*.

The *principal minors* of Δ_n are

$$\Delta_1 = \frac{\partial^2 f}{\partial x_1^2}$$

$$\Delta_2 = \begin{vmatrix} \dfrac{\partial^2 f}{\partial x_1^2} & \dfrac{\partial^2 f}{\partial x_1\,\partial x_2} \\[3mm] \dfrac{\partial^2 f}{\partial x_2\,\partial x_1} & \dfrac{\partial^2 f}{\partial x_2^2} \end{vmatrix}$$

$$\Delta_3 = \begin{vmatrix} \dfrac{\partial^2 f}{\partial x_1^2} & \dfrac{\partial^2 f}{\partial x_1\,\partial x_2} & \dfrac{\partial^2 f}{\partial x_1\,\partial x_3} \\[3mm] \dfrac{\partial^2 f}{\partial x_2\,\partial x_1} & \dfrac{\partial^2 f}{\partial x_2^2} & \dfrac{\partial^2 f}{\partial x_2\,\partial x_3} \\[3mm] \dfrac{\partial^2 f}{\partial x_3\,\partial x_1} & \dfrac{\partial^2 f}{\partial x_3\,\partial x_2} & \dfrac{\partial^2 f}{\partial x_3^2} \end{vmatrix}$$

$$\vdots$$

$$\Delta_n$$

The stationary point $x^* = (x_1^*, x_2^*, \ldots, x_n^*)$ is a

Local maximum if $\Delta_1 < 0$, $\Delta_2 > 0$, $\Delta_3 < 0$, …

Local minimum if $\Delta_1 > 0$, $\Delta_2 > 0$, $\Delta_3 > 0$, …

If neither of these conditions holds, the function must be examined in the region of the stationary point. Note that the conditions given previously for maxima and minima of a function of two variables are a special case of those given above for n variables.

EXAMPLE

Determine the maxima or minima (if any) of the function

$$f(x_1, x_2, x_3) = x_1^2 + 2x_2^2 + x_3^2 + x_1 x_2 - 2x_3 - 7x_1 + 12$$

$$\frac{\partial f}{\partial x_1} = 2x_1 + x_2 - 7$$

$$\frac{\partial f}{\partial x_2} = 4x_2 + x_1$$

$$\frac{\partial f}{\partial x_3} = 2x_3 - 2$$

If $\dfrac{\partial f}{\partial x_1} = 0$, $\dfrac{\partial f}{\partial x_2} = 0$, $\dfrac{\partial f}{\partial x_3} = 0$, then

$$2x_1 + x_2 = 7$$

$$x_1 + 4x_2 = 0$$

$$2x_3 = 2$$

Thus

$$x_2 = -1$$

$$x_1 = 4$$

$$x_3 = 1$$

$$\frac{\partial^2 f}{\partial x_1^2} = 2 \qquad \frac{\partial^2 f}{\partial x_1\, \partial x_2} = 1 \qquad \frac{\partial^2 f}{\partial x_1\, \partial x_3} = 0$$

$$\frac{\partial^2 f}{\partial x_2^2} = 4 \qquad \frac{\partial^2 f}{\partial x_2\, \partial x_3} = 0$$

$$\frac{\partial^2 f}{\partial x_3^2} = 2$$

$$\Delta_1 = 2$$

$$\Delta_2 = \begin{vmatrix} 2 & 1 \\ 1 & 4 \end{vmatrix} = 8 - 1 = 7$$

$$\Delta_3 = \begin{vmatrix} 2 & 1 & 0 \\ 1 & 4 & 0 \\ 0 & 0 & 2 \end{vmatrix} = 16 + 0 + 0 - (0 + 0 + 2) = 14$$

$\Delta_1 > 0$, $\Delta_2 > 0$, $\Delta_3 > 0$, so the point $(4, -1, 1)$ is a local minimum of the function $f(x_1, x_2, x_3) = x_1^2 + 2x_2^2 + x_3^2 + x_1 x_2 - 2x_3 - 7x_1 + 12$.

EXAMPLE

Determine the maxima and minima (if any) of the function

$$f(x, y, z) = e^{-x^2 - y^2 - z^2 + 2y + xz}$$

$$\frac{\partial f}{\partial x} = (-2x + z)e^{-x^2 - y^2 - z^2 + 2y + xz}$$

$$\frac{\partial f}{\partial y} = (-2y + 2)e^{-x^2 - y^2 - z^2 + 2y + xz}$$

$$\frac{\partial f}{\partial z} = (-2z + x)e^{-x^2 - y^2 - z^2 + 2y + xz}$$

If $\dfrac{\partial f}{\partial x} = 0$, $\dfrac{\partial f}{\partial y} = 0$, $\dfrac{\partial f}{\partial z} = 0$, then

$$-2x + z = 0$$

$$2y = 2$$

$$x - 2z = 0$$

Thus

$$x = z = 0$$

$$y = 1$$

$$\frac{\partial^2 f}{\partial x^2} = [(-2x + z)^2 - 2]e^{-x^2 - y^2 - z^2 + 2y + xz} \qquad \left.\frac{\partial^2 f}{\partial x^2}\right|_{(0,\, 1,\, 0)} = -2e$$

$$\frac{\partial^2 f}{\partial x\, \partial y} = (-2x + z)(-2y + 2)e^{-x^2 - y^2 - z^2 + 2y + xz} \qquad \left.\frac{\partial^2 f}{\partial x\, \partial y}\right|_{(0,\, 1,\, 0)} = 0$$

$$\frac{\partial^2 f}{\partial x\,\partial z} = [(2x + z)(-2z + x) + 1]e^{-x^2 - y^2 - z^2 + 2y + xz}$$

$$\left.\frac{\partial^2 f}{\partial x\,\partial z}\right|_{(0,\,1,\,0)} = e$$

$$\frac{\partial^2 f}{\partial y^2} = [(-2y + 2)^2 - 2]e^{-x^2 - y^2 - z^2 + 2y + xz}$$

$$\left.\frac{\partial^2 f}{\partial y^2}\right|_{(0,\,1,\,0)} = -2e$$

$$\frac{\partial^2 f}{\partial y\,\partial z} = (-2y + 2)(-2z + x)e^{-x^2 - y^2 - z^2 + 2y + xz}$$

$$\left.\frac{\partial^2 f}{\partial y\,\partial z}\right|_{(0,\,1,\,0)} = 0$$

$$\frac{\partial^2 f}{\partial z^2} = [(-2z + x)^2 - 2]e^{-x^2 - y^2 - z^2 + 2y + xz}$$

$$\left.\frac{\partial^2 f}{\partial z^2}\right|_{(0,\,1,\,0)} = -2e$$

$$\Delta_1 = -2e$$

$$\Delta_2 = \begin{vmatrix} -2e & 0 \\ 0 & -2e \end{vmatrix} = 4e$$

$$\Delta_3 = \begin{vmatrix} -2e & 0 & e \\ 0 & -2e & 0 \\ e & 0 & -2e \end{vmatrix} = -8e^3 + 2e^3 = -6e^3$$

$\Delta_1 < 0$, $\Delta_2 > 0$, $\Delta_3 < 0$, so the point $(0, 1, 0)$ is a local maximum of the function $f(x, y, z) = e^{-x^2 - y^2 - z^2 + 2y + xz}$.

EXAMPLE

Total profit is equal to total revenue minus total cost. In a perfectly competitive market, total revenue is equal to the product of the number of units sold and the fixed unit price; thus

$$P = pq - C$$

where P is profit, p is price per unit, q is quantity sold, and C is total cost. If the production function is

$$q = f(x_1, x_2)$$

where x_1 and x_2 are the variable inputs, and the cost function is

$$C = p_1 x_1 + p_2 x_2 + b$$

where p_1 and p_2 are the unit prices of x_1 and x_2, respectively, and b is the cost of the fixed inputs, then

$$P = pf(x_1, x_2) - p_1 x_1 - p_2 x_2 - b$$

Profit is thus a function of x_1 and x_2 and is maximized with respect to these variables as follows.

$$\frac{\partial P}{\partial x_1} = pf_1 - p_1 = 0$$

$$\frac{\partial P}{\partial x_2} = pf_2 - p_2 = 0$$

or

$$pf_1 = p_1$$

$$pf_2 = p_2$$

Since f_1 and f_2 are the marginal products of the two inputs, pf_1 and pf_2 are the values of these marginal products, that is, the rates at which revenue would increase with increase of the respective inputs. Thus the first-order conditions for profit maximization require that each input be increased until the value of its marginal product equals its price. Note that the maximum profit-input combination lies on the expansion path since the conditions $pf_1 = p_1$ and $pf_2 = p_2$ are a special case of the condition $f_1/f_2 = p_1/p_2$.

Second-order conditions require that the principal minors of the Hessian determinant

$$\begin{vmatrix} \dfrac{\partial^2 P}{\partial x_1^2} & \dfrac{\partial^2 P}{\partial x_1\,\partial x_2} \\[2ex] \dfrac{\partial^2 P}{\partial x_2\,\partial x_1} & \dfrac{\partial^2 P}{\partial x_2^2} \end{vmatrix}$$

alternate in sign. That is, for a maximum it is required that

$$\frac{\partial^2 P}{\partial x_1^2} < 0$$

$$\begin{vmatrix} \dfrac{\partial^2 P}{\partial x_1^2} & \dfrac{\partial^2 P}{\partial x_1\,\partial x_2} \\[2ex] \dfrac{\partial^2 P}{\partial x_2\,\partial x_1} & \dfrac{\partial^2 P}{\partial x_2^2} \end{vmatrix} > 0$$

Expanding the determinant, the second condition is

$$\left(\frac{\partial^2 P}{\partial x_1^2}\right)\left(\frac{\partial^2 P}{\partial x_2^2}\right) - \left(\frac{\partial^2 P}{\partial x_1 \partial x_2}\right)^2 > 0$$

Since $\dfrac{\partial^2 P}{\partial x_1^2} < 0$ (first condition) and $\left(\dfrac{\partial^2 P}{\partial x_1 \partial x_2}\right)^2 > 0$, the second condition requires that

$$\frac{\partial^2 P}{\partial x_2^2} < 0$$

The second-order partials can be evaluated as follows:

$$\frac{\partial^2 P}{\partial x_1^2} = pf_{11} < 0$$

$$\frac{\partial^2 P}{\partial x_2^2} = pf_{22} < 0$$

and, since $p > 0$, the second-order conditions for maximization require that

$$f_{11} < 0$$
$$f_{22} < 0$$

Thus the second-order conditions for maximization require that both marginal products be decreasing. This is reasonable, since the price of a variable is constant under free competition and thus, if the marginal product of a variable were increasing, profit could be increased by increasing the quantity of the variable.

PROBLEMS

1. Determine the values of x_1, x_2, and x_3 (if any) that maximize or minimize the function
$$f(x_1, x_2, x_3) = x_1 x_2 + 10x_1 - x_1^2 - x_2^2 - x_3^2.$$

2. Determine the values of x, y, and z (if any) that maximize or minimize the function
$$f(x, y, z) = e^{4x^2 + 2y^2 + z^2 - 5xy - 4z}.$$

3. Determine the values of x, y, and z (if any) that maximize or minimize the function
$$f(x, y, z) = e^{-x^2 - 2y^2 - z^2 - 2xy}.$$

4. Determine the values of x_1, x_2, and x_3 (if any) that maximize or minimize the function

$$f(x_1, x_2, x_3) = x_1^2 + x_2^2 + 7x_3^2 - x_1 x_2.$$

Answers to Odd-Numbered Problems

1. $x_1 = \frac{20}{3}$, $x_2 = \frac{10}{3}$, $x_3 = 0$ (maximize)
3. $x = y = z = 0$ (maximize)

LAGRANGE MULTIPLIERS

Consider a function of n variables $f(x_1, x_2, \ldots, x_n)$ subject to the constraint $g(x_1, x_2, \ldots, x_n) = 0$ at a point $x^* = (x_1^*, x_2^*, \ldots, x_n^*)$ which satisfies the $n + 1$ equations

$$\frac{\partial f}{\partial x_1} - \lambda \frac{\partial g}{\partial x_1} = 0$$

$$\frac{\partial f}{\partial x_2} - \lambda \frac{\partial g}{\partial x_2} = 0$$

$$\vdots$$

$$\frac{\partial f}{\partial x_n} - \lambda \frac{\partial g}{\partial x_n} = 0$$

$$g = 0$$

Note that for $x^* = (x_1^*, x_2^*, \ldots, x_n^*)$, $\lambda = (f_{x_i}/g_{x_i})$, $i = 1, 2, \ldots, n$. Define the determinant

$$\Delta_{n+1} = \begin{vmatrix} 0 & g_{x_1} & g_{x_2} & \cdots & g_{x_n} \\ g_{x_1} & f_{x_1 x_1} - \lambda g_{x_1 x_1} & f_{x_1 x_2} - \lambda g_{x_1 x_2} & \cdots & f_{x_1 x_n} - \lambda g_{x_1 x_n} \\ g_{x_2} & f_{x_2 x_1} - \lambda g_{x_2 x_1} & f_{x_2 x_2} - \lambda g_{x_2 x_2} & \cdots & f_{x_2 x_n} - \lambda g_{x_2 x_n} \\ \vdots & \vdots & \vdots & & \vdots \\ g_{x_n} & f_{x_n x_1} - \lambda g_{x_n x_1} & f_{x_n x_2} - \lambda g_{x_n x_2} & \cdots & f_{x_n x_n} - \lambda g_{x_n x_n} \end{vmatrix}$$

sometimes referred to as a *bordered Hessian determinant*. In order to determine whether $x^* = (x_1^*, x_2^*, \ldots, x_n^*)$ is a maximum or minimum, the $n - 1$ principal minors of Δ_{n+1}: $\Delta_3, \Delta_4, \ldots, \Delta_{n+1}$, must be evaluated for $x^* = (x_1^*, x_2^*, \ldots, x_n^*)$. Note that Δ_i consists of the first i rows and i columns of Δ_{n+1}. The point $x^* = (x_1^*, x_2^*, \ldots, x_n^*)$ is a

Local (constrained) maximum if $\Delta_3 > 0$, $\Delta_4 < 0$, $\Delta_5 > 0$, $\ldots$

Local (constrained) minimum if $\Delta_3 < 0$, $\Delta_4 < 0$, $\Delta_5 < 0$, $\ldots$

If neither of these conditions holds, the function must be examined in the region of the stationary point. Note that the conditions given previously for constrained maxima and minima of a function of two variables are a special case of those given above for n variables.

EXAMPLE

Determine the minimum of the function

$$f(x_1, x_2, x_3) = x_1 x_2 + x_1 x_3 + x_2 x_3 \qquad \text{if } x_1 x_2 x_3 = 125.$$

$$F(x_1, x_2, x_3, \lambda) = x_1 x_2 + x_1 x_3 + x_2 x_3 - \lambda(x_1 x_2 x_3 - 125)$$

$$\frac{\partial F}{\partial x_1} = x_2 + x_3 - \lambda x_2 x_3$$

$$\frac{\partial F}{\partial x_2} = x_1 + x_3 - \lambda x_1 x_3$$

$$\frac{\partial F}{\partial x_3} = x_1 + x_2 - \lambda x_1 x_2$$

$$\frac{\partial F}{\partial \lambda} = -(x_1 x_2 x_3 - 125)$$

If $\dfrac{\partial F}{\partial x_1} = 0, \ \dfrac{\partial F}{\partial x_2} = 0, \ \dfrac{\partial F}{\partial x_3} = 0, \ \dfrac{\partial F}{\partial \lambda} = 0$, then

$$x_1 = x_2 = x_3 = \sqrt[3]{125} = 5 \qquad \lambda = \tfrac{2}{5}$$

$$f_{x_1 x_1} = 0 \qquad\qquad f_{x_2 x_2} = 0 \qquad\qquad f_{x_3 x_3} = 0$$

$$f_{x_1 x_2} = 1 \qquad\qquad f_{x_1 x_3} = 1 \qquad\qquad f_{x_2 x_3} = 1$$

$$g_{x_1} = x_2 x_3 = 25 \qquad g_{x_2} = x_1 x_3 = 25 \qquad g_{x_3} = x_1 x_2 = 25$$

$$g_{x_1 x_1} = 0 \qquad\qquad g_{x_2 x_2} = 0 \qquad\qquad g_{x_3 x_3} = 0$$

$$g_{x_1 x_2} = x_3 = 5 \qquad\quad g_{x_1 x_3} = x_2 = 5 \qquad\quad g_{x_2 x_3} = x_1 = 5$$

$$\Delta_3 = \begin{vmatrix} 0 & 25 & 25 \\ 25 & 0 & -1 \\ 25 & -1 & 0 \end{vmatrix} = 0 - 625 - 625 - (0 + 0 + 0) = -1250$$

$$\Delta_4 = \begin{vmatrix} 0 & 25 & 25 & 25 \\ 25 & 0 & -1 & -1 \\ 25 & -1 & 0 & -1 \\ 25 & -1 & -1 & 0 \end{vmatrix}$$

$$= 0 - 25 \begin{vmatrix} 25 & -1 & -1 \\ 25 & 0 & -1 \\ 25 & -1 & 0 \end{vmatrix} + 25 \begin{vmatrix} 25 & 0 & -1 \\ 25 & -1 & -1 \\ 25 & -1 & 0 \end{vmatrix} - 25 \begin{vmatrix} 25 & 0 & -1 \\ 25 & -1 & 0 \\ 25 & -1 & -1 \end{vmatrix}$$

$$= 0 - 25[0 + 25 + 25 - (0 + 25 + 0)] + 25[0 + 0 + 25 - (25 + 25 + 0)]$$
$$- 25[25 + 0 + 25 - (25 + 0 + 0)]$$

$$= 0 - 625 - 625 - 625 = -1875$$

$\Delta_3 < 0, \ \Delta_4 < 0$, so the point $(5, 5, 5)$ is a local minimum of the function $f(x_1, x_2, x_3) = x_1 x_2 + x_1 x_3 + x_2 x_3$ subject to $x_1 x_2 x_3 = 125$.

EXAMPLE

Determine the maximum of the function

$$f(x, y, z) = -x^2 - 2y^2 - z^2 + xy + z \qquad \text{if } x + y + z = 35.$$

$$F(x, y, z, \lambda) = -x^2 - 2y^2 - z^2 + xy + z - \lambda(x + y + z - 35)$$

$$\frac{\partial F}{\partial x} = -2x + y - \lambda$$

$$\frac{\partial F}{\partial y} = -4y + x - \lambda$$

$$\frac{\partial F}{\partial z} = -2z + 1 - \lambda$$

$$\frac{\partial F}{\partial \lambda} = -(x + y + z - 35)$$

If $\dfrac{\partial F}{\partial x} = 0$, $\dfrac{\partial F}{\partial y} = 0$, $\dfrac{\partial F}{\partial z} = 0$, $\dfrac{\partial F}{\partial \lambda} = 0$, then

$$-2x + y = \lambda$$

$$-4y + x = \lambda$$

$$-2z + 1 = \lambda$$

From the first and second equations,

$$3x = 5y$$

$$x = \tfrac{5}{3}y$$

From the first and third equations,

$$-2z + 1 = y - \tfrac{10}{3}y = -\tfrac{7}{3}y$$

$$z = \frac{1 + \tfrac{7}{3}y}{2} = \frac{3 + 7y}{6}$$

Substituting for x and z in the constraint equation $x + y = z = 35$,

$$\frac{5y}{3} + y + \frac{3 + 7y}{6} = 35$$

$$10y + 6y + 3 + 7y = 210$$

$$23y = 207$$

$$y = 9$$

$$x = \frac{5y}{3} = 15$$

$$z = \frac{3 + 7y}{6} = 11$$

$$\lambda = -2x + y = -21$$

$f_{xx} = -2$ $\qquad f_{yy} = -4$ $\qquad f_{zz} = -2$

$f_{xy} = 1$ $\qquad f_{xz} = 0$ $\qquad f_{yz} = 0$

$g_x = 1$ $\qquad g_y = 1$ $\qquad g_z = 1$

$g_{xx} = 0$ $\qquad g_{yy} = 0$ $\qquad g_{zz} = 0$

$g_{xy} = 0$ $\qquad g_{xz} = 0$ $\qquad g_{yz} = 0$

$$\Delta_3 = \begin{vmatrix} 0 & 1 & 1 \\ 1 & -2 & 1 \\ 1 & 1 & -4 \end{vmatrix} = (0 + 1 + 1) - (-2 + 0 - 4) = 8$$

$$\Delta_4 = \begin{vmatrix} 0 & 1 & 1 & 1 \\ 1 & -2 & 1 & 0 \\ 1 & 1 & -4 & 0 \\ 1 & 0 & 0 & -2 \end{vmatrix}$$

$$= 0 - \begin{vmatrix} 1 & 1 & 0 \\ 1 & -4 & 0 \\ 1 & 0 & -2 \end{vmatrix} + \begin{vmatrix} 1 & -2 & 0 \\ 1 & 1 & 0 \\ 1 & 0 & -2 \end{vmatrix} - \begin{vmatrix} 1 & -2 & 1 \\ 1 & 1 & -4 \\ 1 & 0 & 0 \end{vmatrix}$$

$$= 0 - [8 + 0 + 0 - (0 + 0 - 2)] + [-2 + 0 + 0 - (0 + 0 + 4)]$$
$$- [0 + 8 + 0 - (1 - 0 + 0)]$$

$$= 0 - 10 - 6 - 7 = -23$$

$\Delta_3 > 0$, $\Delta_4 < 0$, so the point (15, 9, 11) is a local maximum of the function $f(x, y, z) = -x^2 - 2y^2 - z^2 + xy + z$ subject to $x + y + z = 35$.

EXAMPLE

When utility analysis is generalized to the case of n commodities, the utility function is given by

$$U = f(q_1, q_2, \ldots, q_n)$$

where $q_1, q_2, \ldots, q_n$ are the quantities of the n commodities, and the budget constraint is given by

$$y - \sum_{i=1}^{n} p_i q_i = 0$$

where $p_1, p_2, \ldots, p_n$ are the unit prices of the n commodities. Then the function to be maximized is

$$F = f(q_1, q_2, \ldots, q_n) - \lambda \left(y - \sum_{i=1}^{n} p_i q_i \right)$$

and, for maximization,

$$\frac{\partial F}{\partial q_i} = f_i + \lambda p_i = 0 \qquad i = 1, 2, \ldots, n$$

$$\frac{\partial F}{\partial \lambda} = -\left(y - \sum_{i=1}^{n} p_i q_i \right) = 0$$

The demand curves for the n commodities can be obtained by solving for the q's. The conditions

$$\frac{\partial F}{\partial q_i} = f_i + \lambda p_i = 0 \qquad i = 1, 2, \ldots, n$$

can be written as

$$-\frac{\partial q_i}{\partial q_j} = \frac{p_j}{p_i} \qquad \text{for all } i \text{ and } j$$

That is, the rate of substitution of commodity i for commodity j must equal the price ratio p_j/p_i. The second-order conditions for maximization require that the principal minors of the bordered Hessian determinant must alternate in sign; that is,

$$\begin{bmatrix} 0 & -p_1 & -p_2 \\ -p_1 & f_{11} & f_{12} \\ -p_2 & f_{21} & f_{22} \end{bmatrix} > 0 \qquad \begin{vmatrix} 0 & -p_1 & -p_2 & -p_3 \\ -p_1 & f_{11} & f_{12} & f_{13} \\ -p_2 & f_{21} & f_{22} & f_{23} \\ -p_3 & f_{31} & f_{32} & f_{33} \end{vmatrix} < 0$$

$$\cdots (-1)^n \begin{vmatrix} 0 & -p_1 & -p_2 & \cdots & -p_n \\ -p_1 & f_{11} & f_{12} & \cdots & f_{1n} \\ -p_2 & f_{21} & f_{22} & \cdots & f_{2n} \\ \vdots & \vdots & \vdots & & \vdots \\ -p_n & f_{n1} & f_{n2} & \cdots & f_{nn} \end{vmatrix} > 0$$

KUHN-TUCKER CONDITIONS

Consider a function of n variables $f(x_1, x_2, \ldots, x_n)$ subject to the constraint $g(x_1, x_2, \ldots, x_n) \leq 0$. A point $x^* = (x_1^*, x_2^*, \ldots, x_n^*)$ is a local maximum of $f(x_1, x_2, \ldots, x_n)$ subject to $g(x_1, x_2, \ldots, x_n)$ only if there exists a nonnegative λ such that λ and $(x_1^*, x_2^*, \ldots, x_n^*)$ satisfy the Kuhn-Tucker conditions:

$$h_i = \frac{\partial f}{\partial x_i} - \lambda \frac{\partial g}{\partial x_i} = 0 \qquad i = 1, 2, \ldots, n$$

$$\lambda g(x_1, x_2, \ldots, x_n) = 0$$

$$g(x_1, x_2, \ldots, x_n) \leq 0$$

These conditions are also sufficient if $f(x_1, x_2, \ldots, x_n)$ is concave and $g(x_1, x_2, \ldots, x_n)$ is convex. Since a maximum point of $f(x_1, x_2, \ldots, x_n)$ is a minimum point of $-f(x_1, x_2, \ldots, x_n)$, this result is also applicable when a convex function is minimized over a convex set.

NOTE: A function $f(x_1, x_2, \ldots, x_n)$ is convex in a region if for any two points $(\tilde{x}_1, \tilde{x}_2, \ldots, \tilde{x}_n)$ and $(\bar{x}_1, \bar{x}_2, \ldots, \bar{x}_n)$,

$$f[(1-t)\tilde{x}_1 + t\bar{x}_1, \ldots, (1-t)\tilde{x}_n + t\bar{x}_n]$$

$$\leq (1-t)f(\tilde{x}_1, \tilde{x}_2, \ldots, \tilde{x}_n) + tf(\bar{x}_1, \bar{x}_2, \ldots, \bar{x}_n)$$

The function is strictly convex if $\leq$ can be replaced by $<$; the function is concave if $\leq$ can be replaced by $\geq$ and strictly concave if $\leq$ can be replaced by $>$.

The method of Lagrange multipliers can be modified to determine the maximum or minimum of a function of n variables subject to one inequality constraint in a manner similar to the modification for a function of two variables subject to one inequality constraint. Assume that the inequality constraint holds as an equality constraint and obtain the maximum (or minimum) using the method of Lagrange multipliers. Then, if $\lambda > 0$, this maximum (or minimum) is also the maximum (or minimum) subject to the inequality constraint; if $\lambda \leq 0$, the maximum (or minimum) determined without regard to the constraint satisfies the constraint and is thus also the constrained maximum (or minimum).

EXAMPLE

Find the minimum of $f(x_1, x_2, x_3) = x_1 x_2 + x_1 x_3 + x_2 x_3$ subject to the constraint $x_1 x_2 x_3 \geq 125$.

Assuming the inequality constraint to hold as an equality constraint, $\lambda = \frac{2}{5}$ (see page 641). Since $\lambda > 0$, the minimum $(5, 5, 5)$ assuming the equality constraint is also the minimum assuming the inequality constraint.

Alternatively, using the Kuhn-Tucker conditions,

$$\frac{\partial f}{\partial x_1} - \lambda \frac{\partial g}{\partial x_1} = x_2 + x_3 - \lambda x_2 x_3 = 0$$

$$\frac{\partial f}{\partial x_2} - \lambda \frac{\partial g}{\partial x_2} = x_1 + x_3 - \lambda x_1 x_3 = 0$$

$$\frac{\partial f}{\partial x_3} - \lambda \frac{\partial g}{\partial x_3} = x_1 + x_2 - \lambda x_1 x_2 = 0$$

$$\lambda(x_1 x_2 x_3 - 125) = 0$$

$$x_1 x_2 x_3 \geq 125$$

Either $\lambda = 0$ or $x_1 x_2 x_3 - 125 = 0$. If $\lambda = 0$,

$$x_2 + x_3 = 0$$

$$x_1 + x_3 = 0$$

$$x_1 + x_2 = 0$$

and $x_1 = x_2 = x_3 = 0$; but then $x_1 x_2 x_3 \geq 125$ is not satisfied. If $x_1 x_2 x_3 - 125 = 0$,

$$\frac{x_2 + x_3}{x_2 x_3} = \frac{x_1 + x_3}{x_1 x_3} = \frac{x_1 + x_2}{x_1 x_2}$$

and $x_1 = x_2 = x_3 = 5$; this solution satisfies the Kuhn-Tucker conditions. Thus, as above, the minimum of $f(x_1, x_2, x_3) = x_1 x_2 + x_1 x_3 + x_2 x_3$ subject to $x_1 x_3 x_3 \geq 25$ is $x_1 = x_2 = x_3 = 5$.

EXAMPLE

Find the maximum of $f(x, y, z) = -x^2 - 2y^2 - z^2 + xy + z$ subject to the constraint $x + y + z \leq 35$.

Assuming the inequality constraint to hold as an equality constraint, $\lambda = -21$ (see page 642). Since $\lambda = 0$, the unconstrained maximum is also the maximum subject to the unequality constraint.

$$\frac{\partial f}{\partial x} = -2x + y \qquad \frac{\partial^2 f}{\partial x^2} = -2 \qquad \frac{\partial^2 f}{\partial x \, \partial y} = 1$$

$$\frac{\partial f}{\partial y} = -4y + x \qquad \frac{\partial^2 f}{\partial y^2} = -4 \qquad \frac{\partial^2 f}{\partial x \, \partial z} = 0$$

$$\frac{\partial f}{\partial z} = -2z + 1 \qquad \frac{\partial^2 f}{\partial z^2} = -2 \qquad \frac{\partial^2 f}{\partial y \, \partial z} = 0$$

If $\dfrac{\partial f}{\partial x} = 0$, $\dfrac{\partial f}{\partial y} = 0$, $\dfrac{\partial f}{\partial z} = 0$, then

$$2x - y = 0$$

$$x - 4y = 0$$

$$2z = 1$$

and thus

$$x = y = 0$$

$$z = \tfrac{1}{2}$$

$$\Delta_1 = -2$$

$$\Delta_2 = \begin{vmatrix} -2 & 1 \\ 1 & -4 \end{vmatrix} = 8 - 1 = 7$$

$$\Delta_3 = \begin{vmatrix} -2 & 1 & 0 \\ 1 & -4 & 0 \\ 0 & 0 & -2 \end{vmatrix} = -16 + 0 + 0 - (0 + 0 - 2) = -14$$

$\Delta_1 < 0$, $\Delta_2 > 0$, $\Delta_3 < 0$ so the point $(0, 0, \tfrac{1}{2})$ is a maximum.
Alternatively, using the Kuhn-Tucker conditions,

$$\frac{\partial f}{\partial x} - \lambda \frac{\partial g}{\partial x} = -2x + y - \lambda = 0$$

$$\frac{\partial f}{\partial y} - \lambda \frac{\partial g}{\partial y} = -4y + x - \lambda = 0$$

$$\frac{\partial f}{\partial z} - \lambda \frac{\partial g}{\partial z} = -2z + 1 - \lambda = 0$$

$$\lambda(x + y + z - 35) = 0 \qquad x + y + z \le 35$$

Either $\lambda = 0$ or $x + y + z - 35 = 0$. If $\lambda = 0$,

$$x = y = 0 \qquad z = \tfrac{1}{2}$$

$x + y + z \le 35$ is satisfied, and $f(0, 0, \tfrac{1}{2}) = \tfrac{1}{4}$. If $x + y + z = 35$, solving the first three equations,

$$-2x + y - \lambda = 0$$

$$x - 4y - \lambda = 0$$

$$2z + \lambda = 1$$

From the first two equations,

$$3x - 5y = 0$$

and from the second two equations,

$$x - 4y + 2z = 1$$

and, since $x + y + z = 35$, $z = 35 - x - y$ and

$$x - 4y + 2(35 - x - y) = 1$$

$$x + 6y = 69$$

$$3x - 5y = 0$$

$$23y = 207$$

$$y = 9$$

$$x = 15$$

$$z = 11$$

The solution $x = 15$, $y = 9$, $z = 11$ satisfies $-2x + y - \lambda = 0$, $x - 4y - \lambda = 0$ and $2z + \lambda = 1$ if $\lambda = -21$. $f(1, 9, 11) = -362$, which is less than $f(0, 0, \tfrac{1}{2})$. Thus, as above, the maximum of $f(x, y, z) = -x^2 - 2y^2 - z^2 + xy + z$ subject to the constraint $x + y + z \le 35$ is $x = y = 0$, $z = \tfrac{1}{2}$.

PROBLEMS

1. Determine the values of x_1, x_2, and x_3 that minimize the function

$$f(x_1, x_2, x_3) = x_1^2 + 4x_2^2 + x_3^2 - 4x_1 x_2 - 6x_3$$

subject to the constraint $x_1 + x_2 + x_3 = 15$.

2. Determine the values of x_1, x_2, and x_3 that maximize the function

$$f(x_1, x_2, x_3) = 6x_1 x_2 + 4x_2 x_3 + 6x_2 - 3x_3^2 - x_2^2$$

subject to the constraint $x_1 + 2x_2 + x_3 = 75$.

3. Determine the values of x_1, x_2, and x_3 that minimize the function

$$f(x_1, x_2, x_3) = x_1^2 + x_2^2 + x_3^2 + x_1 x_2 x_3$$

subject to the constraint $x_1 x_2 x_3 = 1000$.

4. Determine the values of x_1, x_2, and x_3 that minimize the function

$$f(x_1, x_2, x_3) = 5x_1^2 + 10x_2^2 + x_3^2 - 4x_1 x_2 - 2x_1 x_3 - 36x_2$$

subject to the constraint $x_1 + x_2 + x_3 = 3$.

5. Determine the values of x_1, x_2, and x_3 that minimize the function

$$f(x_1, x_2, x_3) = x_1^2 + 4x_2^2 + x_3^2 - 4x_1 x_2 - 6x_3$$

subject to the constraint $x_1 + x_2 + x_3 \geq 15$ (see Problem 1).

6. Determine the values of x_1, x_2, and x_3 that maximize the function

$$f(x_1, x_2, x_3) = 6x_1 x_2 + 4x_2 x_3 + 6x_2 - 3x_3^2 - x_2^2$$

subject to the constraint $x_1 + 2x_2 + x_3 \leq 75$ (see Problem 2).

7. Determine the values of x_1, x_2, and x_3 that minimize the function

$$f(x_1, x_2, x_3) = x_1^2 + x_2^2 + x_3^2 + x_1 x_2 x_3$$

subject to the constraint $x_1 x_2 x_3 \geq 1000$ (see Problem 3).

8. Determine the values of x_1, x_2, and x_3 that minimize the function

$$f(x_1, x_2, x_3) = 5x_1^2 + 10x_2^2 + x_3^2 - 4x_1 x_2 - 2x_1 x_3 - 36x_2$$

subject to the constraint $x_1 + x_2 + x_3 \geq 3$ (see Problem 4).

Answers to Odd-Numbered Problems

1. $x_1 = 8$, $x_2 = 4$, $x_3 = 3$ 5. $x_1 = 8$, $x_2 = 4$, $x_3 = 3$
3. $x_1 = x_2 = x_3 = 10$ 7. $x_1 = x_2 = x_3 = 10$

8.3 Input-Output Analysis

Input-output analysis traces the flow of production for the purpose of studying the effects of a change in the demand for final goods on production of primary, intermediate, and finished goods. The primary purpose of input-output analysis is to calculate the output levels in various industries that would be required by particular levels of final goods demand. Input-output analysis can also be applied in studying sectors of the economy, either using a closed model where the output for a sector is equal to the sum of its inputs in the other sectors or using an open model which includes final demand in addition to demands from other sectors.

Assume that an economy is divided into n industries and that each industry produces only one type of output. Industries are usually related in the sense that each

Table 8.1

Producer	User 1	2 $\cdots$ n	Final demand	Total output
1	b_{11}	$b_{12} \cdots b_{1n}$	h_1	x_1
2	b_{21}	$b_{22} \cdots b_{2n}$	h_2	x_2
$\vdots$	$\vdots$	$\vdots \qquad \vdots$	$\vdots$	$\vdots$
n	b_{n1}	$b_{n2} \cdots b_{nn}$	h_n	x_n

must use some of the others' products in order to operate. In addition, an economy must usually produce some finished products for final demand. Input-output analysis determines the production of each of the industries if final demand changes, assuming the structure of the economy does not change.

It is convenient to tabulate the data for input-output analysis as shown in Table 8.1, where b_{ij} is the dollar amount of the products of industry i used by industry j, h_i is the final demand for the products of industry i, and $x_i = \sum_{j=1}^{n} b_{ij} + h_i$ is the total output of industry i.

The structure of the economy can be described by the technological matrix

$$\mathbf{A} = (a_{ij})$$

where $a_{ij} = (b_{ij}/x_j) =$ dollar value of the output of industry i that industry j must purchase to produce one dollar's worth of its own products. Note that this definition of a_{ij} assumes that the purchases of intermediate products of an industry are proportional to the level of output of the industry. This assumption of constant proportionality between inputs and outputs is customary for input-output analysis.

The ith industry must produce outputs

$$a_{i1} x_1 + a_{i2} x_2 + \cdots + a_{in} x_n \qquad \text{for } i = 1, 2, \ldots, n$$

in order to supply the needs of all other industries. The interindustry demand vector can thus be written $\mathbf{AX}$, where

$$\mathbf{A} = \begin{bmatrix} a_{11} & a_{12} & \cdots & a_{1n} \\ a_{21} & a_{22} & \cdots & a_{2n} \\ \vdots & \vdots & & \vdots \\ a_{n1} & a_{n2} & \cdots & a_{nn} \end{bmatrix} \qquad \text{and} \qquad \mathbf{X} = \begin{bmatrix} x_1 \\ x_2 \\ \vdots \\ x_n \end{bmatrix}$$

the production of the economy must be adjusted to meet both interindustry needs and final demand. If the final demand vector is

$$\mathbf{H} = \begin{bmatrix} h_1 \\ h_2 \\ \vdots \\ h_n \end{bmatrix} \qquad h_i \geq 0 \qquad i = 1, 2, \ldots, n$$

this requirement can be written

$$\mathbf{X} = \mathbf{AX} + \mathbf{H}$$

Thus

$$[\mathbf{I} - \mathbf{A}]\mathbf{X} = \mathbf{H}$$

and

$$\mathbf{X} = [\mathbf{I} - \mathbf{A}]^{-1}\mathbf{H}$$

the matrix $\mathbf{I} - \mathbf{A}$ is known as the *Leontief matrix*.

There are a number of mathematical and practical problems associated with input-output analysis. For example, the technological matrix must be such that each of the x_i's is nonnegative; otherwise, the solution is not economically meaningful. There are also problems concerning industry classification and stability of the technological matrix.

Given a set of positive final demands, consider the problem of determining the conditions under which there is a unique set of positive production levels consistent with the set of final demands. First, since $[\mathbf{I} - \mathbf{A}]^{-1}$ must exist, $|\mathbf{I} - \mathbf{A}|$ must be nonzero. In addition, each element of $[\mathbf{I} - \mathbf{A}]^{-1}$ must be nonnegative, since otherwise an increase in final demand would result in a decrease in production at some point in the production process. It can be shown that, in order for positive gross-output levels to be associated with any given set of positive demands, the following conditions are required

$$1 > a_{ij} \geq 0 \qquad \text{all } i \text{ and } j$$

$$|\mathbf{I} - \mathbf{A}| > 0$$

Since any k-industry subset of the n industries must be able to satisfy interindustry demands with some surplus to satisfy demands external to the k industries, all principal minors of the n industry Leontief determinant

$$|\mathbf{I} - \mathbf{A}| = \begin{vmatrix} 1 - a_{11} & -a_{12} & \cdots & -a_{1n} \\ -a_{21} & 1 - a_{22} & \cdots & -a_{2n} \\ \vdots & \vdots & & \vdots \\ -a_{n1} & -a_{n2} & \cdots & 1 - a_{nn} \end{vmatrix}$$

must be positive.

EXAMPLE

Consider a very simple hypothetical economy of two industries, A and B, represented in Table 8.2, where data are in millions of dollars of products.

Determine the output vector of the economy if final demand changes to 200 for A and 100 for B.

$$\mathbf{A} = \begin{bmatrix} \frac{1}{2} & \frac{7}{16} \\ \frac{8}{25} & \frac{9}{20} \end{bmatrix}$$

$$\mathbf{I} - \mathbf{A} = \begin{bmatrix} \frac{1}{2} & -\frac{7}{16} \\ -\frac{8}{25} & \frac{11}{20} \end{bmatrix}$$

$$[\mathbf{I} - \mathbf{A}]^{-1} = \frac{200}{27} \begin{bmatrix} \frac{11}{20} & \frac{7}{16} \\ \frac{8}{25} & \frac{1}{2} \end{bmatrix}$$

NOTE: $|\mathbf{I} - \mathbf{A}| = \frac{1}{2} \cdot \frac{11}{20} - \frac{7}{16} \cdot \frac{8}{25} = \frac{27}{200}$.
As must be the case,

$$\mathbf{X} = [\mathbf{I} - \mathbf{A}]^{-1}\mathbf{H} = \frac{200}{27} \begin{bmatrix} \frac{11}{20} & \frac{7}{16} \\ \frac{8}{25} & \frac{1}{2} \end{bmatrix} \begin{bmatrix} 150 \\ 120 \end{bmatrix} = \begin{bmatrix} 1000 \\ 800 \end{bmatrix}$$

Table 8.2

| Producer | User | | Final demand | Total output |
	A	B		
A	500	350	150	1000
B	320	360	120	800

And, if $\mathbf{H} = \begin{pmatrix} 200 \\ 100 \end{pmatrix}$, then

$$\mathbf{X} = [\mathbf{I} - \mathbf{A}]^{-1}\mathbf{H} = \tfrac{200}{27}\begin{bmatrix} \tfrac{11}{20} & \tfrac{7}{16} \\ \tfrac{8}{25} & \tfrac{1}{2} \end{bmatrix}\begin{bmatrix} 200 \\ 100 \end{bmatrix} = \begin{bmatrix} 1138\tfrac{8}{9} \\ 844\tfrac{4}{9} \end{bmatrix}$$

That is, industry A must have an output of $1138\tfrac{8}{9}$ and industry B must have an output of $844\tfrac{4}{9}$, where output is given in millions of dollars of products.

EXAMPLE

Consider a very simple hypothetical economy of three industries, A, B, and C, represented in Table 8.3, where data are in millions of dollars of products.

Determine the output vector of the economy if final demand changes to:

(a) 50 for A, 10 for B, and 100 for C
(b) 100 for A, 20 for B, and 60 for C
(c) 80 for A, 100 for B, and 120 for C.

$$\mathbf{A} = \begin{bmatrix} \tfrac{1}{6} & \tfrac{1}{4} & \tfrac{1}{4} \\ \tfrac{1}{4} & \tfrac{1}{4} & \tfrac{1}{3} \\ \tfrac{1}{2} & \tfrac{1}{3} & \tfrac{1}{3} \end{bmatrix}$$

$$[\mathbf{I} - \mathbf{A}] = \begin{bmatrix} \tfrac{5}{6} & -\tfrac{1}{4} & -\tfrac{1}{4} \\ -\tfrac{1}{4} & \tfrac{3}{4} & -\tfrac{1}{3} \\ -\tfrac{1}{2} & -\tfrac{1}{3} & \tfrac{2}{3} \end{bmatrix}$$

$$[\mathbf{I} - \mathbf{A}]^{-1} = \tfrac{864}{109}\begin{bmatrix} \tfrac{7}{18} & \tfrac{1}{4} & \tfrac{13}{48} \\ \tfrac{1}{3} & \tfrac{31}{72} & \tfrac{49}{144} \\ \tfrac{11}{24} & \tfrac{29}{72} & \tfrac{9}{16} \end{bmatrix}$$

NOTE: $\quad |\mathbf{I} - \mathbf{A}| = \tfrac{5}{6}\cdot\tfrac{3}{4}\cdot\tfrac{2}{3} - \tfrac{1}{4}\cdot\tfrac{1}{3}\cdot\tfrac{1}{2} - \tfrac{1}{4}\cdot\tfrac{1}{3}\cdot\tfrac{1}{4}$

$$- \left(\tfrac{1}{4}\cdot\tfrac{3}{4}\cdot\tfrac{1}{2} + \tfrac{1}{3}\cdot\tfrac{1}{3}\cdot\tfrac{5}{6} + \tfrac{2}{3}\cdot\tfrac{1}{4}\cdot\tfrac{1}{4} \right)$$

$$= \tfrac{109}{864}$$

$c_{11} = (-1)^{1+1}\begin{vmatrix} \tfrac{3}{4} & -\tfrac{1}{3} \\ -\tfrac{1}{3} & \tfrac{2}{3} \end{vmatrix} = \tfrac{7}{18}$
$\qquad c_{23} = (-1)^{2+3}\begin{vmatrix} \tfrac{5}{6} & -\tfrac{1}{4} \\ -\tfrac{1}{2} & -\tfrac{1}{3} \end{vmatrix} = \tfrac{29}{72}$

$c_{12} = (-1)^{1+2}\begin{vmatrix} -\tfrac{1}{4} & -\tfrac{1}{3} \\ -\tfrac{1}{2} & \tfrac{2}{3} \end{vmatrix} = \tfrac{1}{3}$
$\qquad c_{31} = (-1)^{3+1}\begin{vmatrix} -\tfrac{1}{4} & -\tfrac{1}{4} \\ \tfrac{3}{4} & -\tfrac{1}{3} \end{vmatrix} = \tfrac{13}{48}$

$c_{13} = (-1)^{1+3}\begin{vmatrix} -\tfrac{1}{4} & \tfrac{3}{4} \\ -\tfrac{1}{2} & -\tfrac{1}{3} \end{vmatrix} = \tfrac{11}{24}$
$\qquad c_{32} = (-1)^{3+2}\begin{vmatrix} \tfrac{5}{6} & -\tfrac{1}{4} \\ -\tfrac{1}{4} & -\tfrac{1}{3} \end{vmatrix} = \tfrac{49}{144}$

$c_{21} = (-1)^{2+1}\begin{vmatrix} -\tfrac{1}{4} & -\tfrac{1}{4} \\ -\tfrac{1}{3} & \tfrac{2}{3} \end{vmatrix} = \tfrac{1}{4}$
$\qquad c_{33} = (-1)^{3+3}\begin{vmatrix} \tfrac{5}{6} & -\tfrac{1}{4} \\ -\tfrac{1}{4} & \tfrac{3}{4} \end{vmatrix} = \tfrac{9}{16}$

$c_{22} = (-1)^{2+2}\begin{vmatrix} \tfrac{5}{6} & -\tfrac{1}{4} \\ -\tfrac{1}{2} & \tfrac{2}{3} \end{vmatrix} = \tfrac{31}{72}$

Table 8.3

Producer	User			Final demand	Total output
	A	B	C		
A	90	150	225	75	540
B	135	150	300	15	600
C	270	200	300	130	900

As must be the case,

$$\mathbf{X} = [\mathbf{I} - \mathbf{A}]^{-1}\mathbf{H} = \tfrac{864}{109} \begin{bmatrix} \frac{7}{18} & \frac{1}{4} & \frac{13}{48} \\ \frac{1}{3} & \frac{31}{72} & \frac{49}{144} \\ \frac{11}{24} & \frac{29}{72} & \frac{9}{16} \end{bmatrix} \begin{bmatrix} 75 \\ 15 \\ 130 \end{bmatrix} = \begin{bmatrix} 540 \\ 600 \\ 900 \end{bmatrix}$$

(a) If $\mathbf{H} = \begin{bmatrix} 50 \\ 10 \\ 100 \end{bmatrix}$,

$$\mathbf{X} = [\mathbf{I} - \mathbf{A}]^{-1}\mathbf{H} = \tfrac{864}{109} \begin{bmatrix} \frac{7}{18} & \frac{1}{4} & \frac{13}{48} \\ \frac{1}{3} & \frac{31}{72} & \frac{49}{144} \\ \frac{11}{24} & \frac{29}{72} & \frac{9}{16} \end{bmatrix} \begin{bmatrix} 50 \\ 10 \\ 100 \end{bmatrix}$$

$$= \begin{bmatrix} 388.62 \\ 435.96 \\ 659.45 \end{bmatrix}$$

(b) If $\mathbf{H} = \begin{bmatrix} 100 \\ 20 \\ 60 \end{bmatrix}$,

$$\mathbf{X} = [\mathbf{I} - \mathbf{A}]^{-1}\mathbf{H} = \tfrac{864}{109} \begin{bmatrix} \frac{7}{18} & \frac{1}{4} & \frac{13}{48} \\ \frac{1}{3} & \frac{31}{72} & \frac{49}{144} \\ \frac{11}{24} & \frac{29}{72} & \frac{9}{16} \end{bmatrix} \begin{bmatrix} 100 \\ 20 \\ 60 \end{bmatrix}$$

$$= \begin{bmatrix} 476.70 \\ 494.31 \\ 694.68 \end{bmatrix}$$

(c) If $\mathbf{H} = \begin{bmatrix} 80 \\ 100 \\ 120 \end{bmatrix}$,

$$\mathbf{X} = [\mathbf{I} - \mathbf{A}]^{-1}\mathbf{H} = \tfrac{864}{109} \begin{bmatrix} \frac{7}{18} & \frac{1}{4} & \frac{13}{48} \\ \frac{1}{3} & \frac{31}{72} & \frac{49}{144} \\ \frac{11}{24} & \frac{29}{72} & \frac{9}{16} \end{bmatrix} \begin{bmatrix} 80 \\ 100 \\ 120 \end{bmatrix}$$

$$= \begin{bmatrix} 702.39 \\ 876.33 \\ 1144.95 \end{bmatrix}$$

PROBLEMS

1. A simple hypothetical economy of three industries, A, B, and C, is represented in the following table (data are in millions of dollars of products):

Producer	User			Final demand	Total output
	A	B	C		
A	80	100	100	40	320
B	80	200	60	60	400
C	80	100	100	20	300

Determine the output vector for the economy if the final demand changes to a. 120 for A, 40 for B, and 10 for C; b. 60 for A, 60 for B, and 60 for C.
2. A simple hypothetical economy of two industries, A and B, is represented in the following table (data are in tens of millions of dollars of products):

Producer	User A	B	Final demand	Total output
A	14	6	8	28
B	7	18	11	36

Determine the output vector for the economy if the final demand changes to a. 16 for A and 3 for B; b. 2 for A and 4 for B.

3. A simple hypothetical economy of two industries, A and B, is represented in the following table (data are in millions of dollars of products):

Producer	User A	B	Final demand	Total output
A	150	240	210	600
B	200	120	160	480

Determine the output vector for the economy if the final demand changes to a. 100 for A and 200 for B; b. 50 for A and 60 for B.

4. A simple hypothetical economy of three industries, A, B, and C, is represented in the following table (data are in tens of millions of dollars of products):

Producer	User A	B	C	Final demand	Total output
A	5	4	3	3	15
B	3	10	6	1	20
C	3	4	4	1	12

Determine the output vector for the economy if the final demand changes to a. 1 for A, 2 for B, and 10 for C; b. 2 for A, 3 for B, and 2 for C.

Answers to Odd-Numbered Problems

1. a. 481.74 for A, 469.57 for B, and 371.74 for C
   b. 469.57 for A, 542.61 for B, and 469.57 for C
3. a. 442.11 for A and 463.16 for B
   b. 170.53 for A and 155.79 for B

8.4 Linear Programming

Many problems in business and economics are concerned essentially with the allocation of limited resources—money, personnel, materials, machines, space, time—in
order to maximize some measure of performance or minimize some measure of cost.
The mathematical techniques for determining such allocations are referred to as
mathematical programming; the special case, as in the example below, in which the
measure of performance or cost is a linear function and the restrictions on the
availability or utilization of resources are expressed as linear equations or inequalities is reffered to as *linear programming*.

Consider, for example, the manufacture of several products which require use of the same personnel and raw materials. Suppose the numbers of units of n products manufactured by a firm are denoted, respectively, q_1, q_2, ..., q_n, and that these products are sold at unit profits p_1, p_2, ..., p_n, respectively. Then total profit is given by

$$P = p_1 q_1 + p_2 q_2 + \cdots + p_n q_n = \sum_{j=1}^{n} p_j q_j$$

If manufacturing the n products requires the use of m types of personnel and raw materials, then linear constraints on production can be written

$$
\begin{aligned}
a_{11} q_1 + a_{12} q_2 + \cdots + a_{1n} q_n &\leq b_1 \\
a_{21} q_1 + a_{22} q_2 + \cdots + a_{2n} q_n &\leq b_2 \\
&\vdots \\
a_{m1} q_1 + a_{m2} q_2 + \cdots + a_{mn} q_n &\leq b_m
\end{aligned}
$$

where a_{ij} is the amount of personnel or material of type i required to manufacture one unit of product j and b_i is the total amount of personnel or material of type i that is available.

Note that the profit and constraint equations in this example are linear. Linearity of the profit function seems intuitively reasonable, at least for ranges of q_i which are not too large. However, in some situations, quantity discounts or elasticity of demand, for example, might result in a nonlinear profit function. Similarly, the constraint function may be nonlinear if, for example, one or more of the production functions is nonlinear in the relevant range, that is, if the amount of a resource required per unit of product manufactured is not constant for various quantities of the product.

In this example, profit to the firm is maximized subject to the m constraints on the available resources; that is, the problem is to obtain

$$\max P = \sum_{j=1}^{n} p_j q_j$$

subject to the resource allocation constraints

$$\sum_{j=1}^{n} a_{ij} q_j \leq b_i \qquad \text{for } i = 1, 2, \ldots, m$$

From an economic viewpoint, the problem is to allocate the available limited resources in a manner that maximizes total profit to the firm.

More generally, the linear programming problem involves maximizing or minimizing a linear function of several *primary variables*, referred to as an *objective function*, subject to a set of linear equalities or inequalities referred to as *constraints*. None of the variables may be negative. (Note, however, that a negative variable may be written as the difference of two positive variables.)

Mathematically, the linear programming problem for maximization is written:

Maximize an objective function $Z = c_1 X_1 + c_2 X_2 + \cdots + c_n X_n$

subject to the constraints

$$
\begin{aligned}
a_{11} X_1 + a_{12} X_2 + \cdots + a_{1n} X_n &\leq b_1 \\
a_{21} X_1 + a_{22} X_2 + \cdots + a_{2n} X_n &\leq b_2 \\
&\vdots \\
a_{m1} X_1 + a_{m2} X_2 + \cdots + a_{mn} X_n &\leq b_m \\
X_j \geq 0 \qquad j &= 1, 2, \ldots, n
\end{aligned}
$$

This may be written more compactly as

$$\text{Maximize } Z = \sum_{j=1}^{n} c_j X_j$$

$$\text{subject to } \sum_{j=1}^{n} a_{ij} X_j \leq b_i \qquad \text{for } i = 1, 2, \ldots, m$$

$$X_j \geq 0 \qquad \text{for } j = 1, 2, \ldots, n$$

and, in matrix notation, as

Maximize $\mathbf{Z} = \mathbf{CX}$

subject to $\mathbf{AX} \leq \mathbf{B}, \mathbf{X} \geq \mathbf{O}$, where

$$\mathbf{C} = (c_1, c_2, \ldots, c_n)$$

$$\mathbf{X} = \begin{bmatrix} x_1 \\ x_2 \\ \vdots \\ x_n \end{bmatrix}$$

$$\mathbf{A} = \begin{bmatrix} a_{11} & a_{12} & \cdots & a_{1n} \\ a_{21} & a_{22} & \cdots & a_{2n} \\ \vdots & \vdots & & \vdots \\ a_{m1} & a_{m2} & \cdots & a_{mn} \end{bmatrix}$$

$$\mathbf{B} = \begin{bmatrix} b_1 \\ b_2 \\ \vdots \\ b_m \end{bmatrix}$$

Similarly, a linear programming problem involving minimization may be stated in matrix notation as

Minimize $\mathbf{Z} = \mathbf{CX}$

subject to $\mathbf{AX} \geq \mathbf{B}, \mathbf{X} \geq 0$. These formulations are referred to as the standard forms for the problems of linear maximization and minimization, respectively, because the constraint inequalities are all expressed in the form $\leq$ for the maximization problem and in the form $\geq$ for the minimization problem. In order to write a problem in standard form, it may be necessary to reverse the direction of an inequality by multiplying by a negative one. For example,

$$a_{11} x_1 + a_{12} x_2 \leq b$$

can be written

$$-a_{11} x_1 - a_{12} x_2 \geq -b$$

Although the standard form is frequently convenient, it is not necessary for the solution of a linear programming problem. However, the standard form is necessary for obtaining the dual, as discussed later in this section.

It can be shown that when there are m constraints in a linear programming problem, there are at most m variables or allocations in its solution. Various methods are available for determining which combination of m of the X_j's maximizes or minimizes the objective function Z. Linear programming problems involving no more than two primary variables can be solved geometrically; although algebraic solution is usually more efficient, even for these problems, geometric solution is intuitively appealing and helps develop a basic understanding which is applicable to more complicated problems. For this reason, geometric solution is discussed in the following section prior to discussion of algebraic solution. There are several algebraic methods for solving linear programming problems; for more complicated problems, involving many variables and many constraints, the *simplex method* is the most efficient of these methods. The simplex method is an iterative computational routine, based on matrix algebra, which develops successively better solutions until the optimal solution is obtained. Most computer packages include a program for simplex solution of linear programming problems. Simplex solution is discussed and illustrated in this section. The interpretation of the dual of a linear programming problem is also considered.

GEOMETRIC SOLUTION

Linear programming problems involving two primary variables are solved geometrically by graphing the inequality constraints as equalities and thus determining a polygon of feasible solutions. A solution is said to be *feasible* if it satisfies all the constraints of a linear programming problem. Once the polygon of feasible solutions has been obtained, the next step is to determine which feasible solution optimizes (maximizes or minimizes) the objective function and is thus the solution of the problem. The following theorem is used to reduce the number of feasible solutions which must be checked.

THEOREM: If there is a unique solution which maximizes or minimizes a linear objective function, then that solution must correspond to a vertex (or corner) of the polygon of feasible solutions; if there is more than one solution, at least two of the solutions must correspond to adjacent vertices of the polygon of feasible solutions.

Thus, in order to determine the optimal solution, the value of the objective function need be computed only for solutions corresponding to vertices of the polygon of feasible solutions. (In some cases certain of these solutions are clearly inferior to others and the corresponding values of the objective function need not be computed.)

EXAMPLE

A manufacturer produces bicycles and motor scooters, each of which must be processed through two machine centers. Machine center 1 has a maximum of 120 hours available and machine center 2 has a maximum of 180 hours available. Manufacturing a bicycle requires 6 hours in machine center 1 and 3 hours in machine center 2; manufacturing a motor scooter requires 4 hours in machine center 1 and 10 hours in machine center 2. If profit is \$45 for a bicycle and \$55 for a motor scooter, determine the number of bicycles and the number of motor scooters that should be manufactured in order to maximize profit.

If X_1 = number of bicycles and X_2 = number of motor scooters, the problem can be stated as follows:

Maximize $Z = 45X_1 + 55X_2$

subject to $6X_1 + 4X_2 \leq 120$, $3X_1 + 10X_2 \leq 180$, and $X_1, X_2 \geq 0$. The polygon of feasible solutions is obtained by graphing the equations

$$6X_1 + 4X_2 = 120$$

$$3X_1 + 10X_2 = 180$$

$$X_1 = 0$$

$$X_2 = 0$$

Figure 8.1

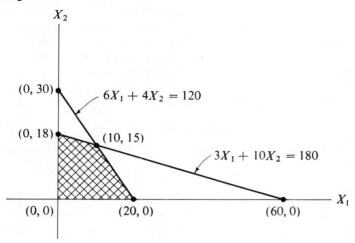

Any point lying within or on the edge of the shaded polygon in Figure 8.1 corresponds to a pair of values X_1 and X_2 which satisfy the constraints of the problem and thus are a feasible solution. The optimal solution corresponds to one of the vertices of the polygon; the objective function thus must be evaluated for the solutions $(0, 0)$, $(0, 18)$, $(10, 15)$, and $(20, 0)$.

Solution	$Z = 45X_1 + 55X_2$
(0, 18)	$ 990
(10, 15)	$1275
(20, 0)	$ 900

Since $(0, 0)$ is clearly inferior to $(0, 18)$, it need not be considered. Thus the optimal solution is $(10, 15)$; that is, manufacture 10 bicycles and 15 motor scooters.

EXAMPLE

A company produces two commodities in quantities X_1 and X_2, respectively, and wishes to minimize Cost $= 2X_1 + 10X_2$ subject to the constraints

$$2X_1 + X_2 \leq 6$$

$$5X_1 + 4X_2 \geq 20$$

$$X_1, X_2 \geq 0$$

Determine the optimal quantities of each commodity to be produced and the associated cost.
  The polygon of feasible solutions is obtained by graphing the equations

$$2X_1 + X_2 = 6$$

$$5X_1 + 4X_2 = 20$$

$$X_1 = 0$$

$$X_2 = 0$$

Figure 8.2

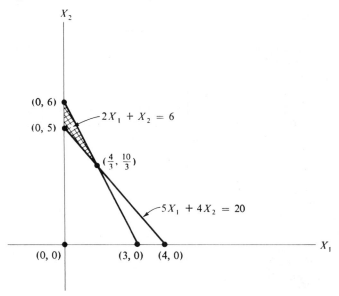

Any point lying in or on the edge of the shaded polygon in Figure 8.2 corresponds to a feasible solution. The optimal solution is one of the vertices $(0, 5)$, $(0, 6)$, and $(\frac{4}{3}, \frac{10}{3})$.

Solution	$Z = 2X_1 + 10X_2$
$(0, \ 5)$	\$50
$(\frac{4}{3}, \frac{10}{3})$	\$36

Note that $(0, 6)$ need not be evaluated, since clearly it is associated with a higher cost than $(0, 5)$. The optimal solution is $(\frac{4}{3}, \frac{10}{3})$; that is, produce $\frac{4}{3}$ units of the first commodity and $\frac{10}{3}$ units of the second commodity. The associated cost is \$36.

Note that the constraints determine the polygon of feasible solutions. The objective function is used in determining which of these feasible solutions is optimal. It is possible to write sets of constraints for which there is no feasible solution. For example, there is no set of values for X_1 and X_2 which satisfies the constraints

$$2X_1 + X_2 \le 6$$

$$5X_1 + 4X_2 \ge 40$$

(See Figure 8.3.)

There are also some sets of constraints for which the polygon of feasible solutions is not bounded. For example, if the inequality sign of the first constraint above is reversed and the second constraint is unchanged,

$$2X_1 + X_2 \ge 6$$

$$5X_1 + 4X_2 \ge 40$$

the polygon of feasible solutions is unbounded. (See Figure 8.4.) In this case, the linear programming problem has a solution if it involves minimization, but not if it involves maximization.

THE SIMPLEX METHOD

The simplex method solves linear programming problems by obtaining a feasible solution and, by an iterative procedure, improving this solution until the optimal solution is obtained. The computational routine for the simplex method is based on matrix algebra and consists essentially of obtaining an inverse matrix in order to solve a set of simultaneous linear equations.

For simplex solution it is necessary to write the constraint inequalities as equalities (that is, equations) by adding positive variables, referred to as *slack variables*, to the left-hand side of the inequalities. For a maximization problem written in standard form, one slack variable is added to the left-hand side of each inequality. If the

Figure 8.3

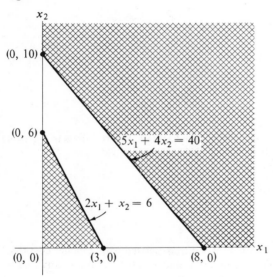

Figure 8.4

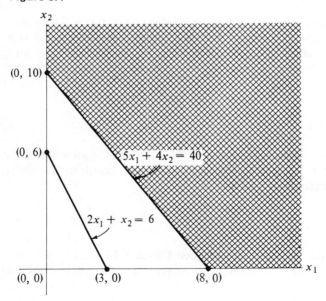

slack variable added to the ith equation is denoted by X_{n+i}, the problem can be rewritten as follows:

Maximize $Z = c_1 X_1 + c_2 X_2 + \cdots + c_n X_n$

subject to

$$a_{11} X_1 + a_{12} X_2 + \cdots + a_{1n} X_n + X_{n+1} = b_1$$
$$a_{21} X_1 + a_{22} X_2 + \cdots + a_{2n} X_n + X_{n+2} = b_2$$
$$\vdots$$
$$a_{m1} X_1 + a_{m2} X_2 + \cdots + a_{mn} X_n + X_{n+m} = b_m$$
$$X_j \geq 0 \qquad j = 1, 2, \ldots, n + m$$

In this problem there are n primary variables and m constraints. The addition of slack variables results in m equations involving $m + n$ unknowns. Note that the slack variables are omitted from the objective function or, equivalently, are given a value of zero in the objective function.

If an inequality is of the form $\geq$, a positive slack variable is subtracted from the left-hand side of the inequality; this slack variable is given a value of zero in the objective function. In order to obtain a feasible solution, an artificial variable is added to the left-hand side of the inequality; this artificial variable is given a value of $-M$ in the objective function for a maximization problem and a value of $+M$ in the objective function for a minimization problem, where M is very large in absolute value. The artificial variable is thus assigned a value in the objective function that precludes its appearance in the final solution. For example, if an inequality is of the form

$$a_{11} X_1 + a_{12} X_2 + \cdots + a_{1n} X_n \geq b_1$$

a slack variable X_{n+1} is subtracted from and an artificial variable X_{n+2} is added to the left-hand side

$$a_{11} X_1 + a_{12} X_2 + \cdots + a_{1n} X_n - X_{n+1} + X_{n+2} = b_1$$

where the value of X_{n+1} in the objective function is zero and the value of X_{n+2} in the objective function is $-M$ for maximization and $+M$ for minimization.

For convenience, the data are arranged in a simplex tableau which is used in performing the computational routine. The initial tableau for the maximization problem stated above is of the form shown in Table 8.4. In the simplex method, two

Table 8.4

Profits per unit
| Variables in the solution
| | Quantities of the variables
| | | in the solution
↓ ↓ ↓

C_j	Variables allocated	Quantity	C_1 X_1	C_2 X_2	$\cdots$	C_n X_n	0 X_{n+1}	0 X_{n+2}	$\cdots$	0 X_{n+m}
0	X_{n+1}	b_1	a_{11}	a_{12}	$\cdots$	a_{1n}	1	0	$\cdots$	0
0	X_{n+2}	b_2	a_{21}	a_{22}	$\cdots$	a_{2n}	0	1	$\cdots$	0
$\vdots$	$\vdots$	$\vdots$	$\vdots$	$\vdots$		$\vdots$	$\vdots$	$\vdots$		$\vdots$
0	X_{n+m}	b_m	a_{m1}	a_{m2}	$\cdots$	a_{mn}	0	0	$\cdots$	1

$\mathbf{A}_{m \times n}$ (body matrix) $\mathbf{I}_{m \times m}$ (identity matrix)

rows are usually included in addition to the rows representing the constraints: these are the Z_j row, representing the total profit from the solution, and the $C_j - Z_j$ row, representing the net profit from adding one unit of a variable.

The simplex method consists of the following basic steps, which are illustrated in detail in the examples:

1. Add the necessary slack and artificial variables to convert inequalities to equalities.
2. Arrange the data in a simplex tableau.
3. Determine a feasible solution from the simplex tableau.
4. Check the solution for optimality.
5. If the solution is not optimal, determine from the tableau the entering variable and the departing variable for the next solution.
6. Compute the entries for the revised tableau.
7. Check the solution of the revised tableau for optimality.
8. Repeat this procedure (steps 5 through 7) until the optimal solution is obtained.

Consider the problem of the manufacturer of bicycles and motor scooters (see page 655). Adding the slack variables X_3 and X_4, the linear programming problem can be stated as follows:

Maximize $Z = 45X_1 + 55X_2$

subject to

$$6X_1 + 4X_2 + X_3 = 120$$

$$3X_1 + 10X_2 + X_4 = 180$$

$$X_1, X_2, X_3, X_4 \geq 0$$

With the necessary slack variables included, the data are arranged in a simplex tableau, and an initial feasible solution is indicated in the tableau (steps 1 through 3). The initial simplex tableau is shown in Table 8.5.

Note the following characteristics of the initial simplex tableau:

a. Any unknown that occurs in one equation occurs (implicitly at least) in all equations; the unknowns that do not appear explicitly in an equation are considered to have zero coefficients in that equation. Thus the zeros in the X_4 column of the first

Table 8.5

			C_j: $45	$55	$0	$0
C_j	Variables allocated	Quantity	X_1	X_2	X_3	X_4
$0	X_3	120	6	4	1	0
$0	X_4	180	3	10	0	1
	Z_j	$0	$0	$0	$0	$0
	$C_j - Z_j$		$45	$55	$0	$0

↑
Optimal column

row and the X_3 column of the second row correspond to the zeros in the equations

$$6X_1 + 4X_2 + X_3 + 0X_4 = 120$$
$$3X_1 + 10X_2 + 0X_3 + X_4 = 180$$

b. The initial tableau is constructed for the solution having zero profit. The objective function can be written

$$Z = 45X_1 + 55X_2 + 0X_3 + 0X_4$$

If $X_3 = 120$ and $X_4 = 180$, then $X_1 = X_2 = 0$ and Z is also zero. This solution is obviously not optimal, but provides a convenient initial feasible solution. The solution is then checked for optimality and systematically improved until optimality is attained.

Step 4. Check for optimality: The $C_j - Z_j$ row gives the net profit from adding one unit of a variable. For a maximization problem, the presence of at least one positive number in the $C_j - Z_j$ row indicates that profit can be improved; absence of positive numbers in the $C_j - Z_j$ row indicates that profit cannot be improved, that is, the optimal solution has been obtained. For a minimization problem, the presence of at least one negative number in the $C_j - Z_j$ row indicates that cost can be decreased; absence of negative numbers in the $C_j - Z_j$ row indicates that cost cannot be decreased, that is, the optimal solution has been obtained. In this example, there are positive numbers in the $C_j - Z_j$ row of the initial tableau, so the corresponding solution is not optimal.

Step 5. Entering and departing variables: The largest contribution to profit per unit ($55) is made by variable X_2, so it is the entering or replacing variable. To determine the departing variable, the quantities of X_3 and X_4 in the initial tableau are divided respectively by their corresponding entries in the optimal column:

$$X_3 \text{ row:} \quad \frac{120 \text{ hours available}}{4 \text{ hours per unit}} = 30 \text{ units of } X_2$$

$$X_4 \text{ row:} \quad \frac{180 \text{ hours available}}{10 \text{ hours per unit}} = 18 \text{ units of } X_2$$

The variable corresponding to the smaller positive ratio is the departing or replaced variable; thus X_4 is the replaced variable in the example. (Note that 18 is the largest number of units of X_2 than can be added without violating the constraints.)

Step 6. Recompute the simplex tableau: The X_2 row of the revised tableau is computed by dividing each number in the replaced row X_4 by the element in the optimal column of the replaced row, which is 10 in this example (Table 8.6).

The entries in the X_2 row are

$$18 \qquad \tfrac{3}{10} \qquad 1 \qquad 0 \qquad \tfrac{1}{10}$$

All the remaining rows corresponding to variables in the tableau are computed using the formula

$$\begin{pmatrix} \text{element in} \\ \text{new row} \end{pmatrix} = \begin{pmatrix} \text{element in} \\ \text{old row} \end{pmatrix} - \begin{pmatrix} \text{element of old row} \\ \text{in the optimal} \\ \text{column} \end{pmatrix} \times \begin{pmatrix} \text{corresponding} \\ \text{element in} \\ \text{replacing row} \end{pmatrix}$$

Table 8.6

C_j	Variables allocated	Quantity	C_j: $45 X_1	$55 X_2	$0 X_3	$0 X_4
$0	X_3	48	$\frac{24}{5}$	0	1	$-\frac{2}{5}$
$55	X_2	18	$\frac{3}{10}$	1	0	$\frac{1}{10}$
	Z_j	$990	$\frac{33}{2}$	$55	$0	$\frac{11}{2}$
	$C_j - Z_j$		$\frac{57}{2}$	$0	$0	$-\frac{11}{2}$

$\uparrow$

In this example, the only remaining variable row is X_3; its entries in the revised tableau are

$$120 - (4 \times 18) = 48$$
$$6 - (4 \times \tfrac{3}{10}) = \tfrac{24}{5}$$
$$4 - (4 \times 1) = 0$$
$$1 - (4 \times 0) = 1$$
$$0 - (4 \times \tfrac{1}{10}) = -\tfrac{2}{5}$$

Z_j is the total profit for the solution and equals $0 \cdot 48 + 55 \cdot 18 = 990$

$$\left.\begin{aligned}
Z_j \text{ for } X_1 &= (0)(\tfrac{24}{5}) + (55)(\tfrac{3}{10}) = \tfrac{33}{2}\\
Z_j \text{ for } X_2 &= (0)(0) + (55)(1) = 55\\
Z_j \text{ for } X_3 &= (0)(1) + (55)(0) = 0\\
Z_j \text{ for } X_4 &= (0)(-\tfrac{2}{5}) + (55)(\tfrac{1}{10}) = \tfrac{11}{2}
\end{aligned}\right\}
\begin{aligned}
&\text{profit given up by adding}\\
&\text{one unit of the variable}
\end{aligned}$$

The $C_j - Z_j$ row gives the net profit per unit (profit per unit minus profit given up by adding one unit). The positive entry $\$\frac{57}{2}$ in the revised tableau indicates that the solution can be improved by the inclusion of variable X_1. Checking to see which variable is to be omitted (although it is obviously X_3 in this example),

$$X_3: \frac{48}{\frac{24}{5}} = 10$$

$$X_2: \frac{18}{\frac{3}{10}} = 60$$

The smallest positive ratio corresponds to X_3, and X_3 is thus the departing variable. The simplex tableau is recomputed the same way as in the preceding stage (see Table 8.7). The absence of positive entries in the $C_j - Z_j$ row indicates that the optimal solution has been obtained: Manufacture 10 bicycles and 15 motor scooters, as was also determined above using the geometric method.

Note the following characteristics of the simplex tableau:

a. Slack and artificial variables are included in the constraint equations as follows: If an inequality constraint is of the form $\leq$, a slack variable is added and is given a value of zero in the objective function for both maximization and minimization problems. If an inequality constraint is of the form $\geq$, a slack variable is subtracted and is given a value of zero in the objective function for both maximization

Table 8.7

C_j	Variables allocated	Quantity	C_j: $45 X_1	$55 X_2	$0 X_3	$0 X_4
$45	X_1	10	1	0	$\frac{5}{24}$	$-\frac{1}{12}$
$55	X_2	15	0	1	$-\frac{1}{16}$	$\frac{1}{8}$
	Z_j	$1275	$45	$55	$\frac{95}{16}$	$\frac{25}{8}$
	$C_j - Z_j$		$0	$0	$-\frac{95}{16}$	$-\frac{25}{8}$

and minimization problems; in addition, an artificial variable is added and is given a value in the objective function of $-M$ for maximization problems and $+M$ for minimization problems.

b. The elements of the body and identity matrices of the simplex tableau represent marginal rates of substitution between the variables in the solution and the variables heading the columns. For example, in Table 8.6, X_3 must be decreased by $\frac{24}{5}$ units if 1 unit of X_1 is added; X_3 must be increased by $\frac{2}{5}$ units if 1 unit of X_4 is added, and so forth. Note that a variable always has a marginal rate of substitution of 1 with itself and a marginal rate of substitution of 0 with a variable with which it is not substitutable.

c. The body matrix of the initial tableau has become an identity matrix in the final tableau; the identity matrix of the initial tableau has become the inverse of the initial body matrix in the final tableau.

d. In the final tableau, the $C_j - Z_j$ row consists of zero or negative numbers for a maximization problem and of zero or positive numbers for a minimization problem.

EXAMPLE

Consider the problem of cost minimization discussed above (see page 656). Adding the slack variables X_3 and X_4 and the artificial variable X_5, the linear programming problem can be stated as follows.

Minimize $Z = 2X_1 + 10X_2$ subject to

$$2X_1 + X_2 \leq 6$$
$$5X_1 + 4X_2 \geq 20$$
$$X_1, X_2 \geq 0$$

Adding slack and artifical variables, the problem can be written

Minimize $Z = 2X_1 + 10X_2 + MX_5$

subject to

$$2X_1 + X_2 + X_3 = 6$$
$$5X_1 + 4X_2 - X_4 + X_5 = 20$$
$$X_1, X_2, X_3, X_4, X_5 \geq 0$$

The initial simplex tableau is shown in Table 8.8.

Table 8.8

C_j	Variables allocated	Quantity	C_j: $2 X_1	$10 X_2	$0 X_3	$0 X_4	$M X_5
$0	X_3	6	2	1	1	0	0
$M	X_5	20	5	4	0	−1	1
	Z_j	$20M	$5M	$4M	$0	$ − M	$M
	$C_j − Z_j$		$(2 − 5M)	$(10 − 4M)	$0	$M	$0

$$\uparrow$$
Optimal column

The variable to enter at the next step is X_1 and the variable to be replaced is X_3 since

$X_3: \frac{6}{2} = 3$

$X_5: \frac{20}{5} = 4$

The revised simplex tableau is shown in Table 8.9.

Table 8.9

C_j	Variables allocated	Quantity	C_j: $2 X_1	$10 X_2	$0 X_3	$0 X_4	$M X_5
$2	X_1	3	1	$\frac{1}{2}$	$\frac{1}{2}$	0	0
$M	X_5	5	0	$\frac{3}{2}$	$-\frac{5}{2}$	−1	1
	Z_j	$(6 + 5M)	$2	$(1 + 3M/2)	$(1 − 5M/2)	$ − M	$M
	$C_j − Z_j$		$0	$(9 − 3M/2)	$(−1 + 5M/2)	$M	$0

$$\uparrow$$
Optimal column

The variable to enter at the next step is X_2 and the variable to be replaced is X_5 since

$$X_1: \frac{3}{\frac{1}{2}} = 6$$

$$X_5: \frac{5}{\frac{3}{2}} = \frac{10}{3}$$

Table 8.10

C_j	Variables allocated	Quantity	C_j: $2 X_1	$10 X_2	$0 X_3	$0 X_4	$M X_5
$2	X_1	$\frac{4}{3}$	1	0	$\frac{4}{3}$	$\frac{1}{3}$	$-\frac{1}{3}$
$10	X_2	$\frac{10}{3}$	0	1	$-\frac{5}{3}$	$-\frac{2}{3}$	$\frac{2}{3}$
	Z_j	$36	$2	$10	$ − 14	$ − 6	$6
	$C_j − Z_j$		$0	$0	$14	$6	$(M − 6)

The revised simplex tableau is shown in Table 8.10. The absence of negative entries in the $C_j - Z_j$ row indicates that the optimal solution has been obtained: manufacture $\frac{4}{3}$ units of the first commodity and $\frac{10}{3}$ units of the second commodity at a total cost of \$36, as was also determined above by the graphical method.

There are several variations of the standard simplex method, although none differs substantially from the version discussed above. In addition, there are some linear programming problems in which the coefficients in the constraints have particular forms and special cases of the simplex method, which require less computation, can be used. It should be noted that the simplex method must be modified if the solution variables are required to be integer-valued; this modification is referred to as integer programming.

THE DUAL OF A LINEAR PROGRAMMING PROBLEM

Corresponding to every linear programming problem is a second linear programming problem referred to as the *dual*. When the initial or *primal* problem involves maximization (minimization) of an objective function, the dual problem involves minimization (maximization) of an objective function. The number of variables in the dual problem is equal to the number of constraints in the primal problem and the number of constraints in the dual problem is equal to the number of variables in the primal problem.

For the linear programming problem stated above (page 653), the dual can be stated as follows:

Minimize $Z_{\text{dual}} = b_1 Y_1 + b_2 Y_2 + \cdots + b_m Y_m$

subject to

$$a_{11} Y_1 + a_{21} Y_2 + \cdots + a_{m1} Y_1 \geq c_1$$
$$a_{12} Y_1 + a_{22} Y_2 + \cdots + a_{m2} Y_m \geq c_2$$
$$\vdots$$
$$a_{1n} Y_1 + a_{2n} Y_2 + \cdots + a_{mn} Y_m \geq c_m$$
$$Y_j \geq 0 \qquad j = 1, 2, \ldots, m$$

Thus if a linear programming problem, written in standard form, is

Maximize **CX**

subject to

$$\mathbf{AX} \leq \mathbf{B}$$
$$\mathbf{X} \geq \mathbf{0}$$

then its dual, written in standard form, is

Minimize **BY**

subject to

$$\mathbf{A'Y} \geq \mathbf{C}$$
$$\mathbf{Y} \geq \mathbf{0}$$

and, similarly, if a linear programming problem, written in standard form, is

Minimize **CX**

subject to

AX $\geq$ **B**

X $\geq$ **0**

then its dual, written in standard form, is

Maximize **BY**

subject to

A′Y $\leq$ **C**

Y $\geq$ **0**

The correspondence between the primal and dual problems can be summarized as follows:

1. The constants in the constraints of the primal are the coefficients in the objective function of the dual.

2. The coefficients in the objective function of the primal are the constants in the constraints of the dual.

3. The inequality signs in the constraints of the primal and dual are reversed.

4. The matrices of coefficients in the constraints of the primal and dual are transposes of each other; for example, the ith row of coefficients in the constraints of the primal is the ith column of coefficients in the constraints of the dual.

Note that the dual of the dual problem is the primal problem.

EXAMPLE

Write the dual of each of the following linear programming problems.

(a) Min $5X_1 + 9X_2$

subject to

$3X_1 + 2X_2 \leq 6$

$5X_1 + X_2 \geq 10$

$X_1 + 10X_2 \geq 9$

$X_1 \geq 0 \qquad X_2 \geq 0$

Writing the problem in standard form,

Min $5X_1 + 9X_2$

subject to

$-3X_1 - 2X_2 \geq -6$

$5X_1 + X_2 \geq 10$

$X_1 + 10X_2 \geq 9$

$X_1 \geq 0 \qquad X_2 \geq 0$

and its dual is

Max $-6Y_1 + 10Y_2 + 9Y_3$

subject to

$$-3Y_1 + 5Y_2 + Y_3 \le 5$$
$$-2Y_1 + Y_2 + 10Y_3 \le 9$$
$$Y_1 \ge 0 \qquad Y_2 \ge 0 \qquad Y_3 \ge 0$$

(b) Max $X_1 + 9X_2 + 15X_3$

subject to

$$3X_1 + 2X_2 \ge 11$$
$$X_1 + X_2 + X_3 \ge 15$$
$$8X_2 + 7X_3 \le 25$$
$$X_1 \ge 0 \qquad X_2 \ge 0 \qquad X_3 \ge 0$$

Writing the problem in standard form,

Max $X_1 + 9X_2 + 15X_3$

subject to

$$-3X_1 - 2X_2 \le -11$$
$$-X_1 - X_2 - X_3 \le -15$$
$$8X_2 + 7X_3 \le 25$$
$$X_1 \ge 0 \qquad X_2 \ge 0 \qquad X_3 \ge 0$$

and its dual is

Min $-11Y_1 - 15Y_2 + 25Y_3$

subject to

$$-3Y_1 - Y_2 \ge 1$$
$$-2Y_1 - Y_2 + 8Y_3 \ge 9$$
$$-Y_2 + 7Y_3 \ge 15$$
$$Y_1 \ge 0 \qquad Y_2 \ge 0 \qquad Y_3 \ge 0$$

The solution of the dual problem also provides the solution of the primal problem, and in some cases it may be more convenient to solve the dual. The number of iterations required for simplex solution depends in part on the number of rows of variables in the simplex tableau; thus, if $m < n$, solution of the dual problem usually requires less computation and is therefore preferable.

The correspondence between the primal and dual solutions can be summarized as follows:

1. The value of the objective function is the same for the primal and dual solutions.

2. The criteria for the primary variables of the primal are the solutions for the slack variables of the dual.

3. The criteria for the slack variables of the primal are the solutions for the primary variables of the dual.

668 / Applications of Matrix Algebra

4. The solutions for the primary variables of the primal are the negative values of the criteria for the slack variables of the dual.

5. The solutions for the slack variables of the primal are the negative values of the criteria for the primary variables of the dual.

EXAMPLE

For the maximization problem on page 655,

$$\text{Max } Z = 45X_1 + 55X_2$$

subject to

$$6X_1 + 4X_2 \leq 120$$
$$3X_1 + 10X_2 \leq 180$$
$$X_1, X_2 \geq 0$$

the dual is given by

$$\text{Min } 120Y_1 + 180Y_2$$

subject to

$$6Y_1 + 3Y_2 \geq 45$$
$$4Y_1 + 10Y_2 \geq 55$$
$$Y_1, Y_2 \geq 0$$

With slack and artificial variables, the dual problem is

$$\text{Min } 120Y_1 + 180Y_2 + MY_4 + MY_6$$

subject to

$$6Y_1 + 3Y_2 - Y_3 + Y_4 = 45$$
$$4Y_1 + 10Y_2 - Y_5 + Y_6 = 55$$
$$Y_1, Y_2, Y_3, Y_4, Y_5, Y_6 \geq 0$$

The final tableau of the simplex solution of the dual is given in Table 8.11. Note the correspondence between Tables 8.7 and 8.11 with respect to the properties listed above.

Table 8.11

C_j	Variables allocated	Quantity	C_j: $120	$180	$0	$M	$0	$M
			Y_1	Y_2	Y_3	Y_4	Y_5	Y_6
$120	Y_1	$\frac{95}{16}$	1	0	$-\frac{5}{24}$	$\frac{5}{24}$	$\frac{1}{16}$	$-\frac{1}{16}$
$180	Y_2	$\frac{25}{8}$	0	1	$\frac{1}{12}$	$-\frac{1}{12}$	$-\frac{1}{8}$	$\frac{1}{8}$
	Z_j	$1275	$120	$180	$ - 10	$10	$ - 15	$15
	$C_j - Z_j$		$0	$0	$10	$(M - 10)	$15	$(M - 15)

EXAMPLE

For the minimization problem on page 656,

$$\text{Min } 2X_1 + 10X_2$$

subject to

$$2X_1 + X_2 \leq 6$$
$$5X_1 + 4X_2 \geq 20$$
$$X_1, X_2 \geq 0$$

the dual is given by

$$\text{Max } -6Y_1 + 20Y_2$$

subject to

$$-2Y_1 + 5Y_2 \leq 2$$
$$-Y_1 + 4Y_2 \leq 10$$
$$Y_1, Y_2 \geq 0$$

With slack and artificial variables, the dual problem is

$$\text{Max } -6Y_1 + 20Y_2$$

subject to

$$-2Y_1 + 5Y_2 + Y_3 = 2$$
$$-Y_1 + 4Y_2 + Y_4 = 10$$
$$Y_1, Y_2, Y_3, Y_4 \geq 0$$

The final tableau of the simplex solution of the dual is given in Table 8.12. Note the correspondence between Tables 8.10 and 8.12 with respect to the properties listed above.

Table 8.12

C_j	Variables allocated	Quantity	C_j: $\$-6$ Y_1	$\$20$ Y_2	$\$0$ Y_3	$\$0$ Y_4
$\$20$	Y_2	6	0	1	$-\frac{1}{3}$	$\frac{2}{3}$
$\$-6$	Y_1	14	1	0	$-\frac{4}{3}$	$\frac{5}{3}$
	Z_j	$\$36$	$\$-6$	$\$20$	$\$\frac{4}{3}$	$\$\frac{10}{3}$
	$C_j - Z_j$		$\$0$	$\$0$	$\$-\frac{4}{3}$	$\$-\frac{10}{3}$

Thus the dual problem is completely symmetric to the primal problem and the solution of one problem provides the solution of the other problem. Since the number of iterations required for simplex solution depends in part on the number of rows in the simplex tableau, the dual can provide a simpler computational problem than the primal when the simplex tableau of the dual has fewer rows than the simplex tableau of the primal.

The solution of the dual problem provides *implicit, imputed, artifical,* or *shadow prices* or *values.* These values have important economic interpretations in some applications of linear programming, for example, in analyzing optimal allocation of resources.

Consider the example at the beginning of this section. The primal problem involves determining the profit-maximizing output levels for each of the firm's several products with output and, therefore, profit limited by availability of resources. Since profit cannot be earned without using resources, the resources have value to the firm. One approach to determining the value of the resources would be to calculate their cost, taking account of labor rates, overhead allocations, depreciation, maintenance charges, and so on. Alternatively, recognizing that profit depends on resources, a certain portion of the firm's profit can be *imputed* to each resource. The solution of the dual problem involves determining these *imputed values* of the resources.

In the dual formulation of the example, an artifical accounting price or value is imputed to each resource in such a way that the total value of the resources used is equal to the total profit. Note that the imputed value of a resource is not equal to its cost but is based on the fact that resources are used to generate profit to the firm.

The variables in the dual problem are the imputed values of the resources. The imputed value of a resource is equal to its marginal value, that is, to the change in the objective function of the primal that results from using an additional unit of the resource. The imputed value of a resource represents its value in generating profit. For a particular set of variables in the primal problem, the marginal value and, thus, the imputed value of each resource is constant.

In order to maximize profits, resources must be allocated to the most profitable combination of products. This requires utilization of resources so that the marginal value of additional units is minimized. If this were not the case, additional units of a resource would have greater value than those already used, which would imply nonoptimal allocation of resources. Thus the objective of the dual problem is to allocate resources so that the total imputed value of the resources is minimized.

The left side of the jth constraint in the dual gives the value to the firm of the resources required for the manufacture of the jth product. The constraints show that the value to the firm from allocating the resources to manufacture one unit of a product must at least equal the contribution margin from that product. If the value to the firm from using the resources to manufacture the product exactly equals the contribution to profit resulting from the sale of that product, the product is included in the optimal tableau of the primal solution.

Another possibility regarding a constraint is that the value of the resources required to produce one unit of product exceeds the contribution margin of the product. In this case, the firm can more profitably employ the resources in manufacturing one or more other products. If this is so, the surplus variable associated with the constraint is included as a variable in the optimal tableau of the dual solution. Thus the $C_j - Z_j$ entry for the surplus variable is zero. This $C_j - Z_j$ value is equal to the value of the corresponding primal variable, so that variable is zero.

Since the solution of the dual problem provides the imputed or marginal values of the resources, it is useful in analyzing their profit contributions and in considering possible changes in resource limitations. The effects of changes in the objective function or constraints are frequently studied in the context of sensitivity analysis, as discussed in the following section.

SENSITIVITY ANALYSIS

In the discussion of linear programming in the preceding sections, the parameters of a linear programming problem are assumed to be known and fixed. For example, the contribution margin for each product and the number of available units of each resource are assumed to be known. These assumptions may not be realistic in practice.

For example, contribution margin depends on allocation of fixed costs, on costs of material and labor, and on price of the product, all of which are subject to change. The sensitivity of the optimal solution to changes in the contribution margins of the products is important to the decision maker. This sensitivity is measured by the range over which the contribution margin can vary without resulting in a change in the optimal solution. The decision maker knows that if the contribution margin stays within this range, the optimal solution will not change; conversely, if the contribution margin changes sufficiently to fall outside the range, the optimal solution will change.

Sensitivity analysis is also used to determine the effects of changes in the right-hand or left-hand side of the constraint equations. Concerning the right-hand side of the constraint equations, various factors can result in changes in availability of resources. For example, breakdowns, strikes, shipping delays, defects, and so forth, can alter resource availability and thus affect the optimal solution. Similarly, concerning the left-hand side of the constraint equations, changes in the products or constraints can affect the optimal solution. Sensitivity analysis can be used to determine the effect of adding a new product, adding a new constraint, or changing the coefficients in one or more of the constraint equations.

In general, sensitivity analysis consists of adding a variable to the parameter under consideration and then determining the values of the variable for which the optimal solution is not changed. For example, the sensitivity of the optimal solution to changes in the coefficients of the objective function is determined by adding a variable Δ_j to the objective function coefficient c_j. The values of Δ_j for which the optimal solution does not change, that is, for which $C_j - Z_j$ remains nonpositive for a maximization problem or nonnegative for a minimization problem, are then determined. Thus sensitivity of the optimal solution to changes in the coefficient c_j of the objective function is determined by obtaining the values of Δ_j for which the optimal solution does not change. Sensitivity of the optimal solution to changes in other parameters is determined in a similar manner.

Sensitivity analysis, applied to either the primal, the dual, or both, is an important aspect of many applications of linear programming. One of the major objections to linear programming is the strictness of its formulation and assumptions. Sensitivity analysis provides at least a partial response to this objection.

PROBLEMS

1. A company manufactures two types of novelty souvenirs made of plywood. Souvenirs of type A require 5 minutes each for cutting and 10 minutes each for assembling; souvenirs of type B require 8 minutes each for cutting and 8 minutes each for assembling. There are 3 hours and 20 minutes available for cutting and 4 hours available for assembling. The profit is 50¢ for each type A souvenir and 60¢ for each type B souvenir. How many souvenirs of each type should the company manufacture in order to maximize profit?

2. Determine the values of x and y that maximize the function

$$f(x, y) = 0.4x + 0.9y$$

subject to the constraints

$$5x + 3y \leq 30 \qquad 7x + 2y \leq 28 \qquad x \geq 0 \qquad y \geq 0$$

3. Determine the values of x_1 and x_2 that maximize the function

$$f(x, x_2) = 3x_1 + 5x_2$$

subject to the constraints

$$x_1 + 2x_2 \le 10 \qquad 3x_1 + x_2 \le 10 \qquad x_1 \ge 0 \qquad x_2 \ge 0$$

4. Determine the values of x_1 and x_2 that maximize the function

$$f(x_1, x_2) = 3x_1 + 6x_2$$

subject to the constraints

$$2x_1 + 5x_2 \le 20 \qquad 2x_1 + 2x_2 \le 10 \qquad x_1 \ge 0 \qquad x_2 \ge 0$$

5. Determine the values of x and y that maximize the function

$$f(x, y) = 3x + 2y$$

subject to the constraints

$$x + y \le 7 \qquad 2x + 3y \le 16 \qquad x \ge 0 \qquad y \ge 0$$

6. A manufacturer of a line of hair shampoos is planning a production run for products A (for dry hair) and B (for oily hair). There are sufficient ingredients on hand for 60,000 bottles of each shampoo but there are only 60,000 bottles into which either shampoo can be put. It takes 4 hours to prepare enough shampoo to fill 1000 bottles of shampoo A and 3 hours to prepare enough shampoo to fill 1000 bottles of shampoo B; there are 200 hours available for preparation. Profit is 9 cents a bottle for shampoo A and 7 cents a bottle for shampoo B. How should production be scheduled to maximize profit?

7. The Tr-Ply Company manufactures two types of heavy-duty wood crates. The profit on each crate of type 1 is $9 and the profit on each crate of type 2 is $12. Each crate must go through two production lines; a total of 10 hours are available on production line A and a total of 12 hours are available on production line B. Each crate of type 1 requires 2 hours on line A and 4 hours on line B. Each crate of type 2 requires 5 hours on line A and 3 hours on line B. Determine the number of crates of each type that should be produced in order to maximize the associated profit.

8. The UP-DOWN Ladder Company can manufacture three types of ladders; profit is $5 per ladder of type 1, $7 per ladder of type 2, and $8 per ladder of type 3. Each ladder must be processed through three centers according to the following requirements:

	Center 1 (min)	Center 2 (min)	Center 3 (min)
Type 1	4	5	6
Type 2	5	7	9
Type 3	6	7	7
Total available	80	100	120

In order to maximize profit, determine the number of ladders of each type that should be manufactured.

9. The Capsize Yachting Company produces two models of racing boats. Their profit is $520 for Model 1 and $450 for Model 2. Model 1 requires 40 hours for cutting and assembling and 24 hours for finishing. Model 2 requires 25 hours for cutting and assembling and 30 hours for finishing. There are 400 hours available for cutting and assembling and 360 hours available for finishing. Determine the optimal number of each model for the company to produce and the resulting profit.

10. The Duoply Company can make three products; their profit is $10 per unit for Product 1, $14 per unit for Product 2, and $15 per unit for Product 3. Each of these products is manufactured using three raw materials according to the following requirements:

	Material 1	Material 2	Material 3
Product 1	3 lb/unit	4 lb/unit	5 lb/unit
Product 2	5 lb/unit	7 lb/unit	7 lb/unit
Product 3	4 lb/unit	8 lb/unit	6 lb/unit
Total lb available	220	280	320

Determine the optimal product mix.

11. College Publishers, Inc., plans to use one section of its plant to produce two textbooks. The profit is $2 for Textbook 1 and $3 for Textbook 2. Textbook 1 requires 4 hours for printing and 6 hours for binding. Textbook 2 requires 5 hours for printing and 3 hours for binding. There are 200 hours available for printing and 210 hours available for binding. Determine the optimal number of each textbook for the publishers to produce and their resulting profit.

12. Obtain the solution for the following linear programming problem.

Maximize $6X_1 + 3X_2$

subject to

$$4X_1 + X_2 \leq 12$$

$$2X_1 + 2X_2 \leq 10$$

$$2X_1 + 4X_2 \geq 8$$

$$X_1, X_2 \geq 0$$

13. Obtain the solution for the following linear programming problem.

Minimize $12X_1 - 5X_2$

subject to

$$X_1 - 2X_2 \geq 3$$

$$X_1 - X_2 \geq 4$$

$$X_1 \geq 1$$

$$X_1, X_2 \geq 0$$

Write the duals of the following linear programming problems.

14. Max $X_1 + X_2 + 5X_3$

subject to $4X_1 + 3X_2 + X_3 \leq 10$

$$2X_1 + 10X_2 + 3X_3 \geq 15$$

$$X_1, X_2, X_3 \geq 0$$

15. Min $3X_1 + 5X_2 + X_3$

subject to $X_1 + X_2 + X_3 \geq 6$

$$3X_1 + 8X_2 + 9X_3 \leq 50$$

$$6X_1 + 7X_3 \geq 12$$

$$12X_2 + 4X_3 \geq 15$$

$$X_1, X_2, X_3 \geq 0$$

16. Max $5X_1 - 6X_2 + 10X_3$

    subject to $X_1 + X_2 + X_3 \geq 15$
    $$2X_1 + 3X_2 + 4X_3 \leq 35$$
    $$3X_1 - 4X_2 + 6X_3 \leq 30$$
    $$X_1 - X_2 \geq 0$$
    $$X_1, X_2, X_3 \geq 0$$

17. Min $2X_1 + 10X_2$

    subject to $X_1 + X_2 + X_3 \geq 5$
    $$3X_1 - 2X_2 + 6X_3 \leq 20$$
    $$X_2 + 3X_3 \geq 10$$
    $$X_1, X_2, X_3 \geq 0$$

18. Max $8X_1 - 3X_2$

    subject to $9X_1 + 2X_2 \leq 20$
    $$10X_1 + 3X_2 \leq 32$$
    $$X_1, X_2 \geq 0$$

19. Max $5X_1 + 3X_2 + 14X_3$

    subject to $2X_1 + X_2 + 3X_3 \leq 14$
    $$X_1 + 3X_2 + 2X_3 \leq 15$$
    $$X_1 + X_2 + X_3 \geq 8$$
    $$X_1, X_2, X_3 \geq 0$$

20. Min $6X_1 - 3X_2 + 4X_3$

    subject to $3X_1 + 6X_2 + 2X_3 \leq 30$
    $$5X_1 + X_2 + 6X_3 \geq 25$$
    $$X_1, X_2, X_3 \geq 0$$

Answers to Odd-Numbered Problems

1. 8 type A and 20 type B
3. $x_1 = 2, x_2 = 4$
5. $x = 7, y = 0$
7. $\frac{15}{7}$ type 1, $\frac{8}{7}$ type 2, profit \$33
9. 5 Model 1, 8 Model 2, profit \$6200
11. 0 Textbook 1, 40 Textbook 2, profit \$120
13. $X_1 = 4, X_2 = 0$, min $= 48$
15. Max $6Y_1 - 50Y_2 + 12Y_3 + 15Y_4$

    subject to $Y_1 - 3Y_2 + 6Y_3 \leq 3$
    $$Y_1 - 8Y_2 + 12Y_4 \leq 5$$
    $$Y_1 - 9Y_2 + 7Y_3 + 4Y_4 \leq 1$$
    $$Y_1, Y_2, Y_3, Y_4 \geq 0$$

17. Max $5Y_1 - 20Y_2 + 10Y_3$

    subject to $Y_1 - 3Y_2 \leq 2$
    $$Y_1 + 2Y_2 + Y_3 \leq 10$$
    $$Y_1 - 6Y_2 + 3Y_3 \leq 0$$
    $$Y_1, Y_2, Y_3 \geq 0$$

19. Min $14Y_1 + 15Y_2 - 8Y_3$

    subject to $2Y_1 + Y_2 - Y_3 \geq 5$
    $$Y_1 + 3Y_2 - Y_3 \geq 3$$
    $$3Y_1 + 2Y_2 - Y_3 \geq 14$$
    $$Y_1, Y_2, Y_3 \geq 0$$

8.5 Game Theory

Game theory was developed for the purpose of analyzing competitive situations involving conflicting interests. In game theory, there are assumed to be two or more persons with different objectives, each of whose action influences, but does not completely determine, the outcome of the game; furthermore, each person is assumed to know his opponent's objectives. Game theory provides solutions to such games, assuming that each of the players wishes to maximize his minimum expected profit or, equivalently, minimize his maximum expected loss. This criterion, which is based on a somewhat conservative view of the problem, is referred to as the *minimax* or *maximin criterion.* It is the basis for the *theory of games of strategy*, originally developed by John von Neumann and Oskar Morgenstern and subsequently applied in various areas.

Note that the theory of games assumes a particular type of situation that involves maximizing the expected value of a decision made under uncertainty. Some decisions made under uncertainty involve only one person making a decision; the events which, with the decision, influence the result are thought of as being controlled by some random nonrational device. Unless they are reformulated, these decision problems do not involve games of strategy, since the decision maker does not have a rational opponent. However, a minimax or game theory solution may be appropriate even for these decision problems if the decision maker wishes to protect himself against the worst possible occurrence, even though it results from a random event rather than from the decision of a rational opponent.

Most recreational games such as tick-tack-toe, checkers, backgammon, chess, poker, bridge, and other card games can be analyzed as games of strategy. As usually formulated, gambling games such as dice and roulette are not games of strategy, since a person playing one of these games is "playing against the odds," not against a rational opponent.

The applications of game theory are not limited to parlor games but include competitive situations in economics, business, warfare, and social behavior. There are several fundamental characteristics by which games are classified for solution. The most important of these are the number of persons, the nature of the payoff, and the number of available strategies. These characteristics are discussed and methods of solving games are then considered.

Number of Persons

Games are classified according to the number of distinct sets of interests or objectives present in the game. From the game theory point of view, the number of persons in the game is not necessarily the same as the number of people playing the game—that is, if two or more players form a coalition in which they agree to pool their winnings or losses, game-theory analysis treats them as a single person.

Most of the work done thus far in game theory deals with two-person games and the discussion in the following sections is confined to this case. In general, analysis of games involving more than two persons is quite difficult. Note that many situations that are not strictly two-person games may be analyzed as though they were—for example, the interests in a game of cards can be considered as "his" and "everybody else's."

The Payoff

Games are also classified with respect to the nature of the payoff, that is, what happens at the end of the game. The distinction in this respect is between zero-sum games and nonzero-sum games. If the sum of the payoffs to all players of a game is zero, counting winnings as positive and losses as negative, then the game is *zero-sum*; otherwise, it is *nonzero-sum*. In a zero-sum game, anything won by one player is lost by another player, and vice versa. The importance of this distinction lies in the fact that a zero-sum game is a closed system and a nonzero-sum game is not. Almost all parlor games are zero-sum, and many other situations can be analyzed as zero-sum games. Most of the work in game theory has concerned zero-sum games and the discussion in the following sections is confined to such games. Note that a nonzero-sum game may be made zero-sum by adding a fictitious player, say Nature, but this necessitates a more difficult analysis, especially if the original game was a two-person game.

Strategies

In game theory, a strategy for a particular player is a plan which specifies his action for every possible action of his opponent, that is, a strategy is a complete plan for playing the game, without any connotation of skillfulness on the part of the player. In a game completely amenable to analysis, it is possible, at least conceptually, to foresee all eventualities and thus to catalogue all possible strategies. Games are classified according to the number of strategies available to each player: if player 1 has m possible strategies and player 2 has n possible strategies and they are the only players, then the game is $m \times n$, that is, m by n. The important distinction in classifying games on the basis of strategies is between finite games and infinite games. If the greatest number of strategies available to any player is finite, then the game is *finite*; if at least one player has an infinite number of available strategies, then the game is *infinite*. The theory of infinite games is very difficult and is not discussed in the following sections. For the analysis of finite games, it is convenient to distinguish three cases: those in which the player having the least number of strategies has two, three, or more than three.

In summary, the discussion in following sections will generally concern finite, zero-sum, two-person games.

The Game Matrix

A problem is usually set up for game-theory analysis in the form of a game matrix. A *game matrix* or *payoff matrix* is a rectangular array of the payoffs, where the rows represent the strategies of one player and the columns represent the strategies of the other player; thus an $m \times n$ game is represented by an $m \times n$ game matrix. It is conventional to write the payoffs from the point of view of the player whose strategies are associated with the rows of the matrix; in a zero-sum game, the payoffs for the other player are then given by the negative of this matrix.

Game theory thus assumes that the strategies available to each player can be enumerated and that the corresponding payoffs can be expressed in meaningful, although not necessarily monetary, units. This information is sufficient for solution of the game—that is, for determining which choice of strategies each player should make—assuming that each player wishes to maximize his minimum expected profit or minimize his maximum expected loss. The minimax theorem, the key result of the theory of games, states that such a minimax solution exists for every finite, zero-sum, two-person game. Note that minimax is not the only possible criterion for solving a game matrix and that its use leads to a conservative theory, since the opponent is assumed to be skillful and to use his best strategy.

The *value* of a game is the expected or average payoff per play over a long series of plays, assuming that both players consistently use their optimum strategies. It is

Table 8.13

Player Y

	1	2	$\cdots$	n	
1	a_{11}	a_{12}	$\cdots$	a_{1n}	$\min_{j} a_{1j}$
2	a_{21}	a_{22}	$\cdots$	a_{2n}	$\min_{j} a_{2j}$
$\vdots$	$\vdots$	$\vdots$	a_{ij}	$\vdots$	$\vdots$ $\max_{i} \min_{j} a_{ij}$
m	a_{m1}	a_{m2}	$\cdots$	a_{mn}	$\min_{j} a_{mj}$

Player X (left of rows)

$$\max_{i} a_{i1} \qquad \max_{i} a_{i2} \qquad \cdots \qquad \max_{i} a_{in}$$

$$\min_{j} \max_{i} a_{ij}$$

conventional to regard value from the point of view of the player whose strategies correspond to the rows of the payoff matrix. A game is said to be *fair* if its value is zero; in a fair game neither player has an advantage. In a game that is not fair, one player will win from the other in the long run if both play their optimum strategies; if the value of the game is positive, the row player has the advantage; if the value of the game is negative, the column player has the advantage.

Saddle Points

If a game matrix contains an entry that is simultaneously a maximum of row minima and a minimum of column maxima, this minimax entry is said to be a *saddle point* of the game and the game is said to be *strictly determined*. In this case, according to the minimax criterion of game theory, the *optimum strategies* for the respective players are represented by the row and column whose intersection is the saddle point. The value of a strictly determined game is the value of its saddle point.

The first step in the solution of a matrix game is to check for a saddle point; if one is found, the game is solved; if not, further analysis is necessary. Checking for a saddle point is usually done by writing the row minimum beside each row and the column maximum at the bottom of each column. The maximum of the minima and the minimum of the maxima are then determined and, if they are equal, a saddle point has been found. A saddle point can also be determined by checking for an entry which is simultaneously the minimum of the row in which it occurs and the maximum of the column in which it occurs (see Table 8.13).

EXAMPLE

Check the following games for saddle points.

(a)

12	2	25	-10	-10
16	③	4	10	3
-2	-1	26	0	-2
14	-4	8	6	-4

max min = 3

$$16 \qquad 3 \qquad 26 \qquad 10$$

min max = 3

There is a saddle point at the intersection of the second row (player X's optimum strategy) and the second column (player Y's optimum strategy); the value of the game is 3.

(b)

−15	22	10	8	6	−14	−8	−15	
−3	4	−6	0	−4	22	−10	−10	max min = −6
−2	3	4	10	−1	0	−6	−6	
−2	22	10	10	6	22	−6		

min max = −6

There is a saddle point at the intersection of the third row (player X's optimum strategy) and the seventh column (player Y's optimum strategy); the value of the game is −6.

(c)

−3	2	4	−3	
6	1	3	1	
3	10	12	3	max min = 3
5	0	−2	−2	
0	−4	6	−4	
6	10	12		

min max = 6

There is no saddle point.

(d)

2	0	6	−4	8	10	25	−10	12	14	−10	max min = −10
−14	−2	0	14	9	12	15	0	−10	−3	−14	
2	0	6	14	9	12	25	0	12	14		

min max = 0

There is no saddle point.

SOLUTION OF TWO-PERSON, TWO-STRATEGY GAMES

The basic concepts of game-theory analysis discussed above are illustrated in the following sections for zero-sum two-person, two-strategy games, that is, for games in which at least one of the two players has only two strategies. By convention, the strategies for player X are listed and indexed in a column along the left edge of the game matrix and the strategies for player Y are listed and indexed in a row along the top edge. The payoffs are to player X, that is, a positive number indicates a payoff from player Y to player X and a negative number indicates a payoff from player X to player Y.

2×2 Games

The most easily analyzed two-strategy games are 2×2, that is, games in which each player has only two possible strategies. Solution of 2×2 subgames is also frequently necessary as a step in the solution of larger ($2 \times n$ or $m \times 2$) two-strategy games.

The existence or nonexistence of a saddle point is easily determined for a 2×2 game, either by the methods discussed above or by using the following theorem.

THEOREM: The 2×2 matrix game

$$G = \begin{array}{|c|c|} \hline a & b \\ \hline c & d \\ \hline \end{array}$$

is nonstrictly determined if and only if one of the following two conditions is satisfied:

1. $a < b$, $a < c$, $d < b$, and $d < c$.
2. $a > b$, $a > c$, $d > b$, and $d > c$.

That is, a 2×2 matrix game is nonstrictly determined if and only if each of the two entries on one diagonal of the matrix is greater than each of the two entries on the other diagonal.

EXAMPLE

The game

Player Y

$$\begin{array}{cc} & \begin{array}{cc} 1 & 2 \end{array} \\ \text{Player } X \quad \begin{array}{c} 1 \\ 2 \end{array} & \begin{array}{|c|c|} \hline ⓪ & 1 \\ \hline -3 & 10 \\ \hline \end{array} \end{array}$$

is strictly determined and fair. Player X's optimum strategy is 1; player Y's optimum strategy is 1.

EXAMPLE

The game

Player Y

$$\begin{array}{cc} & \begin{array}{cc} 1 & 2 \end{array} \\ \text{Player } X \quad \begin{array}{c} 1 \\ 2 \end{array} & \begin{array}{|c|c|} \hline 5 & ② \\ \hline -7 & -4 \\ \hline \end{array} \end{array}$$

is strictly determined, but not fair (its value is 2). Player X's optimum strategy is 1; player Y's optimum strategy is 2.

EXAMPLE

The game

Player Y

$$\begin{array}{cc} & \begin{array}{cc} 1 & 2 \end{array} \\ \text{Player } X \quad \begin{array}{c} 1 \\ 2 \end{array} & \begin{array}{|c|c|} \hline 0 & 1 \\ \hline 2 & 0 \\ \hline \end{array} \end{array}$$

is not strictly determined.

In a nonstrictly determined game, there is no clearly optimum strategy for either player to use consistently and, furthermore, consistent use of any particular strategy by either player can be capitalized on by the other player. There is thus an important difference between strictly determined and nonstrictly determined games: In a strictly determined game there is an optimum strategy for each player and no "security measures" are necessary; in a nonstrictly determined game, optimal play involves preventing the opponent from knowing what strategy is to be used on a given play. This is accomplished by selecting the strategy to be used for each play at random, according to probabilities that can be computed from the game matrix. Such a strategy, which consists of a probability mixture of more than one (pure) strategy, is called a *mixed strategy*.

The solution of a 2×2 nonstrictly determined game consists of a pair of probabilities p_1 and $p_2 = 1 - p_1$ with which player X selects at random his strategies 1 and 2, respectively, and a pair of probabilities q_1 and $q_2 = 1 - q_1$ with which player Y selects at random his strategies 1 and 2, respectively. These probabilities provide the optimum mixed strategies, that is, the strategies by which each player, respectively, can maximize his minimum expected profits or minimize his maximum expected losses against optimal play by the other player.

The value of p_1 can be obtained by equating the two possible expected payoffs for player X and solving for p_1, since for any other p_1 one of the two expected payoffs is less than the other and thus the minimax criterion is violated. Similarly, q_1 can be obtained by equating the two possible expected payoffs for player Y and solving.

If

$$G = \begin{array}{|c|c|} \hline a & b \\ \hline c & d \\ \hline \end{array}$$

represents the game matrix, then the expected payoff to player X if player Y uses strategy 1 is

$$ap_1 + c(1 - p_1)$$

and if player Y uses strategy 2 is

$$bp_1 + d(1 - p_1)$$

Thus, equating the expected payoffs,

$$ap_1 + c(1 - p_1) = bp_1 + d(1 - p_1)$$

$$p_1(a - b - c + d) = d - c$$

$$p_1 = \frac{d - c}{a - b - c + d}$$

$$p_2 = 1 - p_1 = \frac{a - b}{a - b - c + d}$$

Similarly, equating the (negative) expected payoffs to player Y,

$$aq_1 + b(1 - q_1) = cq_1 + d(1 - q_1)$$

$$q_1(a - b - c + d) = d - b$$

$$q_1 = \frac{d - b}{a - b - c + d}$$

$$q_2 = 1 - q_1 = \frac{a - c}{a - b - c + d}$$

The value of a game has the same meaning for strictly and nonstrictly determined games: The value of a game is the payoff that a player can expect to obtain per play; on the average, a player cannot win more than the value of a game unless his opponent plays poorly, nor can he win less than the value of a game unless he plays poorly.

The value of the game

$$G = \begin{array}{|c|c|} \hline a & b \\ \hline c & d \\ \hline \end{array}$$

(to player X) is

$$v = ap_1 + c(1 - p_1) = bp_1 + d(1 - p_1)$$
$$= -[aq_1 + b(1 - q_1)] = -[cq_1 + d(1 - q_1)]$$
$$= \frac{ad - bc}{a - b - c + d}$$

The negative of this quantity is the payoff to player Y.

EXAMPLE

The game $\begin{array}{|c|c|} \hline 2 & 0 \\ \hline 0 & 2 \\ \hline \end{array}$ is nonstrictly determined. The optimal mixed strategies are

$p_1 = \frac{2}{4} = \frac{1}{2}$

$p_2 = \frac{2}{4} = \frac{1}{2}$

$q_1 = \frac{2}{4} = \frac{1}{2}$

$q_2 = \frac{2}{4} = \frac{1}{2}$

and the value is $\frac{4}{4} = 1$; the game is biased in favor of player X.

EXAMPLE

The game $\begin{array}{|c|c|} \hline -1 & 0 \\ \hline 0 & -2 \\ \hline \end{array}$ is nonstrictly determined. The optimal mixed strategies are

$p_1 = \frac{-2}{-3} = \frac{2}{3}$

$p_2 = \frac{-1}{-3} = \frac{1}{3}$

$q_1 = \frac{-2}{-3} = \frac{2}{3}$

$q_2 = \frac{-1}{-3} = \frac{1}{3}$

and the value is $v = \frac{-2}{-3} = -\frac{2}{3}$; the game is biased in favor of player Y.

EXAMPLE

The game
7	−6
5	8

is nonstrictly determined. The optimal mixed strategies are

$p_1 = \frac{3}{16}$

$p_2 = \frac{13}{16}$

$q_1 = \frac{14}{16} = \frac{7}{8}$

$q_2 = \frac{2}{16} = \frac{1}{8}$

and the value is $v = \frac{86}{16} = 5\frac{3}{8}$; the game is biased in favor of player X.

EXAMPLE

The game
10	−30
−10	20

is nonstrictly determined. The optimal mixed strategies are

$p_1 = \frac{30}{70} = \frac{3}{7}$

$p_2 = \frac{40}{70} = \frac{4}{7}$

$q_1 = \frac{50}{70} = \frac{5}{7}$

$q_2 = \frac{20}{70} = \frac{2}{7}$

and the value is $v = -\frac{100}{70} = -1\frac{3}{7}$; the game is biased in favor of player Y.

The play of a game, that is, the optimum strategy, is not affected by adding a constant to all payoffs or by multiplying all payoffs by a positive constant. The value of the game is affected by the same transformation as that applied to the payoffs of the game matrix.

EXAMPLE

For each of the games

$G_1 =$
8	1
4	6

$G_2 =$
11	4
7	9

$G_3 =$
16	2
8	12

$p_1 = \frac{2}{9}, p_2 = \frac{7}{9}, q_1 = \frac{5}{9}, q_2 = \frac{4}{9}$. Note that $G_2 = G_1 + 3$; the value of G_1 is $4\frac{8}{9}$ and the value of G_2 is $7\frac{8}{9}$. $G_3 = 2G_1$; the value of G_1 is $4\frac{8}{9}$ and the value of G_3 is $9\frac{7}{9}$.

Solution of 2×2 Games by Matrix Algebra

The optimum strategies and the value of a nonstrictly determined 2×2 game can be obtained using matrix algebra as follows: If the payoff matrix is represented by

$$\mathbf{A} = \begin{bmatrix} a_{11} & a_{12} \\ a_{21} & a_{22} \end{bmatrix}$$

then X's optimal strategies are given by

$$[p_1, p_2] = \frac{[1, 1][\text{adj A}]}{[1, 1][\text{adj A}]\begin{bmatrix} 1 \\ 1 \end{bmatrix}}$$

Y's optimal strategies are given by

$$[q_1, q_2] = \frac{[1, 1][\text{adj A}]'}{[1, 1][\text{adj A}]\begin{bmatrix} 1 \\ 1 \end{bmatrix}}$$

and the value of the game is given by

$$v = \frac{|\text{A}|}{[1, 1][\text{adj A}]\begin{bmatrix} 1 \\ 1 \end{bmatrix}}$$

Alternatively, the value of the game is given by

$$v = [p_1, p_2]\begin{bmatrix} a_{11} & a_{12} \\ a_{12} & a_{22} \end{bmatrix}\begin{bmatrix} q_1 \\ q_2 \end{bmatrix}$$

The examples on pages 681 and 682 can be used to illustrate this method of solution.

EXAMPLE

The game $\begin{array}{|c|c|} \hline 2 & 0 \\ \hline 0 & 2 \\ \hline \end{array}$ is nonstrictly determined.

$$[p_1, p_2] = \frac{[1, 1][\text{adj A}]}{[1, 1][\text{adj A}]\begin{bmatrix} 1 \\ 1 \end{bmatrix}}$$

$$= \frac{[1, 1]\begin{bmatrix} 2 & 0 \\ 0 & 2 \end{bmatrix}}{[1, 1]\begin{bmatrix} 2 & 0 \\ 0 & 2 \end{bmatrix}\begin{bmatrix} 1 \\ 1 \end{bmatrix}} = \frac{[2, 2]}{4} = \begin{bmatrix} \dfrac{1}{2}, \dfrac{1}{2} \end{bmatrix}$$

$$[q_1, q_2] = \frac{[1, 1][\text{adj A}]'}{[1, 1][\text{adj A}]\begin{bmatrix} 1 \\ 1 \end{bmatrix}}$$

$$= \frac{[1, 1]\begin{bmatrix} 2 & 0 \\ 0 & 2 \end{bmatrix}}{[1, 1]\begin{bmatrix} 2 & 0 \\ 0 & 2 \end{bmatrix}\begin{bmatrix} 1 \\ 1 \end{bmatrix}} = \frac{[2, 2]}{4} = \begin{bmatrix} \dfrac{1}{2}, \dfrac{1}{2} \end{bmatrix}$$

$$v = \frac{|\text{A}|}{[1, 1][\text{adj A}]\begin{bmatrix} 1 \\ 1 \end{bmatrix}}$$

$$= \frac{4}{4} = 1$$

Alternatively,

$$v = [p_1, p_2] \begin{bmatrix} a_{11} & a_{12} \\ a_{21} & a_{22} \end{bmatrix} \begin{bmatrix} q_1 \\ q_2 \end{bmatrix}$$

$$= [\tfrac{1}{2}, \tfrac{1}{2}] \begin{bmatrix} 2 & 0 \\ 0 & 2 \end{bmatrix} \begin{bmatrix} \tfrac{1}{2} \\ \tfrac{1}{2} \end{bmatrix}$$

$$= [1, 1] \begin{bmatrix} \tfrac{1}{2} \\ \tfrac{1}{2} \end{bmatrix}$$

$$= 1$$

(as obtained above using algebraic methods).

EXAMPLE

The game $\begin{array}{|c|c|} \hline -1 & 0 \\ \hline 0 & -2 \\ \hline \end{array}$ is nonstrictly determined.

$$[p_1, p_2] = \frac{[1, 1][\text{adj } A]}{[1, 1][\text{adj } A] \begin{bmatrix} 1 \\ 1 \end{bmatrix}}$$

$$= \frac{[1, 1] \begin{bmatrix} -2 & 0 \\ 0 & -1 \end{bmatrix}}{[1, 1] \begin{bmatrix} -2 & 0 \\ 0 & -1 \end{bmatrix} \begin{bmatrix} 1 \\ 1 \end{bmatrix}} = \frac{[-2, -1]}{-3} = \begin{bmatrix} 2 & 1 \\ 3 & 3 \end{bmatrix}$$

$$[q_1, q_2] = \frac{[1, 1][\text{adj } A]'}{[1, 1][\text{adj } A] \begin{bmatrix} 1 \\ 1 \end{bmatrix}}$$

$$= \frac{[1, 1] \begin{bmatrix} -2 & 0 \\ 0 & -1 \end{bmatrix}}{[1, 1] \begin{bmatrix} -2 & 0 \\ 0 & -1 \end{bmatrix} \begin{bmatrix} 1 \\ 1 \end{bmatrix}} = \frac{[-2, -1]}{-3} = \begin{bmatrix} 2 & 1 \\ 3 & 3 \end{bmatrix}$$

$$v = \frac{|A|}{[1, 1][\text{adj } A] \begin{bmatrix} 1 \\ 1 \end{bmatrix}}$$

$$= \frac{2}{-3} = -\frac{2}{3}$$

Alternatively,

$$v = [p_1, p_2] \begin{bmatrix} a_{11} & a_{12} \\ a_{21} & a_{22} \end{bmatrix} \begin{bmatrix} q_1 \\ q_2 \end{bmatrix}$$

$$= [\tfrac{2}{3}, \tfrac{1}{3}] \begin{bmatrix} -1 & 0 \\ 0 & -2 \end{bmatrix} \begin{bmatrix} \tfrac{2}{3} \\ \tfrac{1}{3} \end{bmatrix}$$

$$= [-\tfrac{2}{3}, -\tfrac{2}{3}] \begin{bmatrix} \tfrac{2}{3} \\ \tfrac{1}{3} \end{bmatrix}$$

$$= -\tfrac{2}{3}$$

(as obtained above using algebraic methods).

EXAMPLE

The game
7	−6
5	8
is nonstrictly determined.

$$[p_1, p_2] = \frac{[1, 1][\text{adj } A]}{[1, 1][\text{adj } A]\begin{bmatrix}1\\1\end{bmatrix}}$$

$$= \frac{[1, 1]\begin{bmatrix}8 & 6\\-5 & 7\end{bmatrix}}{[1, 1]\begin{bmatrix}8 & 6\\-5 & 7\end{bmatrix}\begin{bmatrix}1\\1\end{bmatrix}} = \frac{[3, 13]}{16} = \begin{bmatrix}\frac{3}{16}, \frac{13}{16}\end{bmatrix}$$

$$[q_1, q_2] = \frac{[1, 1][\text{adj } A]'}{[1, 1][\text{adj } A]\begin{bmatrix}1\\1\end{bmatrix}}$$

$$\frac{[1, 1]\begin{bmatrix}8 & -5\\6 & 7\end{bmatrix}}{[1, 1]\begin{bmatrix}8 & 6\\-5 & 7\end{bmatrix}\begin{bmatrix}1\\1\end{bmatrix}} = \frac{[14, 2]}{16} = \begin{bmatrix}\frac{7}{8}, \frac{1}{8}\end{bmatrix}$$

$$v = \frac{|A|}{[1, 1][\text{adj } A]\begin{bmatrix}1\\1\end{bmatrix}}$$

$$= \frac{86}{16} = \frac{43}{8}$$

Alternatively,

$$v = [p_1, p_2]\begin{bmatrix}a_{11} & a_{12}\\a_{21} & a_{22}\end{bmatrix}\begin{bmatrix}q_1\\q_2\end{bmatrix}$$

$$= [\tfrac{3}{16}, \tfrac{13}{16}]\begin{bmatrix}7 & -6\\5 & 8\end{bmatrix}\begin{bmatrix}\frac{7}{8}\\\frac{1}{8}\end{bmatrix}$$

$$= [\tfrac{43}{8}, \tfrac{43}{8}]\begin{bmatrix}\frac{7}{8}\\\frac{1}{8}\end{bmatrix}$$

$$= \tfrac{43}{8}$$

(as obtained above using algebraic methods).

EXAMPLE

The game
10	−30
−10	20
is nonstrictly determined.

$$[p_1, p_2] = \frac{[1, 1][\text{adj } A]}{[1, 1][\text{adj } A]\begin{bmatrix}1\\1\end{bmatrix}}$$

$$= \frac{[1, 1]\begin{bmatrix}20 & 30\\10 & 10\end{bmatrix}}{[1, 1]\begin{bmatrix}20 & 30\\10 & 10\end{bmatrix}\begin{bmatrix}1\\1\end{bmatrix}} = \frac{[30, 40]}{70} = \begin{bmatrix}\frac{3}{7}, \frac{4}{7}\end{bmatrix}$$

$$[q_1, q_2] = \frac{[1, 1][\text{adj } \mathbf{A}]'}{[1, 1][\text{adj } \mathbf{A}]\begin{bmatrix} 1 \\ 1 \end{bmatrix}}$$

$$= \frac{[1, 1]\begin{bmatrix} 20 & 10 \\ 30 & 10 \end{bmatrix}}{[1, 1]\begin{bmatrix} 20 & 30 \\ 10 & 10 \end{bmatrix}\begin{bmatrix} 1 \\ 1 \end{bmatrix}} = \frac{[50, 20]}{70} = \begin{bmatrix} \frac{5}{7}, \frac{2}{7} \end{bmatrix}$$

$$v = \frac{|\mathbf{A}|}{[1, 1][\text{adj } \mathbf{A}]\begin{bmatrix} 1 \\ 1 \end{bmatrix}}$$

$$= \frac{-100}{70} = -\frac{10}{7}$$

Alternatively,

$$v = [p_1, p_2]\begin{bmatrix} a_{11} & a_{12} \\ a_{21} & a_{22} \end{bmatrix}\begin{bmatrix} q_1 \\ q_2 \end{bmatrix}$$

$$= [\tfrac{3}{7}, \tfrac{4}{7}]\begin{bmatrix} 10 & -30 \\ -10 & 20 \end{bmatrix}\begin{bmatrix} \frac{5}{7} \\ \frac{2}{7} \end{bmatrix}$$

$$= [-\tfrac{10}{7}, -\tfrac{10}{7}]\begin{bmatrix} \frac{5}{7} \\ \frac{2}{7} \end{bmatrix}$$

$$= -\tfrac{10}{7}$$

(as obtained above using algebraic methods).

$2 \times n$ Games and $m \times 2$ Games

In $2 \times n$ games and $m \times 2$ games, one player has two strategies and the other player has more than two strategies; the solution of a $2 \times n$ game or an $m \times 2$ game can be reduced to the solution of a 2×2 subgame.

As in the solution of 2×2 games, the first step is to check for a saddle point if one exists; the optimum (pure) strategies and the value of the game are thus determined.

EXAMPLE

The game

4	4
5	3
6	⑤
1	3
5	4

has a saddle point at the intersection of the third row (player X's optimal strategy) and the second column (player Y's optimal strategy); the value of the game is 5.

EXAMPLE

The game

1	7	⓪	3
4	8	-1	6

has a saddle point at the intersection of the first row (player X's optimal strategy) and the third column (player Y's optimal strategy); the value of the game is zero.

Dominance

In an $m \times n$ matrix game, row i is said to *majorize* or to *dominate* row h if every entry in row i is as large or larger than the corresponding entry in row h. Similarly, column j is said to *minorize* or to *dominate* column k if every entry in column j is as small as or smaller than the corresponding entry in column k. Note that any dominated (majorized) row or dominated (minorized) column can be omitted from the matrix game without affecting its solution, since such strategies are clearly not optimal. If a $2 \times n$ or an $m \times 2$ game does not have a saddle point, that is, is not strictly determined, all majorized rows and minorized columns should be eliminated as the next step in the solution.

The solution of a $2 \times n$ game consists of probabilities p_1 and $p_2 = 1 - p_1$ with which player X selects, at random, his strategies 1 and 2, respectively, and probabilities $q_1, q_2, \ldots, q_n$, where $\sum_{i=1}^{n} q_i = 1$, with which player Y selects, at random, his strategies $1, 2, \ldots, n$, respectively. Similarly, the solution of an $m \times 2$ game consists of probabilities $p_1, p_2, \ldots, p_m$, where $\sum_{i=1}^{m} p_i = 1$, for player X and probabilities q_1 and $q_2 = 1 - q_1$ for player Y.

EXAMPLE

The game

2	5
4	3
3	6
5	4
4	4

has no saddle point. However, row 3 dominates row 1 and row 4 dominates rows 2 and 5. Thus the game is reduced, for calculation, to the subgame

3	6
5	4

EXAMPLE

The game

−6	−1	1	4	7	4	3
7	−2	6	3	−2	−5	7

has no saddle point. However, columns 3, 4, 5, and 7 are dominated by column 2. Thus the game is reduced, for calculation, to the subgame

−6	−1	4
7	−2	−5

After dominance has been used to reduce a $2 \times n$ or an $m \times 2$ game for calculation, all possible 2×2 games that can be derived from the matrix of this reduced game can be solved. The value of the original game is the value of one of these

688 / Applications of Matrix Algebra

derived 2×2 games and the optimal strategies of the original game are those of that derived 2×2 game, extended for one player by the addition of zeros. Which of the derived games provides the solution of the original game can be determined either by trial and error or graphically.

The trial-and-error procedure consists of solving the derived 2×2 games until one is found for which the two-strategy player does at least as well (usually better) against all his opponent's other strategies as he does against the pair appearing in the 2×2 subgame. When such a game is found, its solution provides the solution of the original game.

EXAMPLE

In the first example above, only one 2×2 subgame remained

3	6
5	4

Its solution is $p_1 = \frac{1}{4}$, $p_2 = \frac{3}{4}$; $q_1 = \frac{1}{2}$, $q_2 = \frac{1}{2}$; and the solution of the 5×2 game is thus $p_1 = 0$, $p_2 = 0$, $p_3 = \frac{1}{4}$, $p_4 = \frac{3}{4}$, $p_5 = 0$; $q_1 = \frac{1}{2}$, $q_2 = \frac{1}{2}$. For both the subgame and the original game, $v = \frac{9}{2}$.

EXAMPLE

In the second example above, a 2×3 subgame remained

-6	-1	4
7	-2	-5

and thus there are three 2×2 games for possible solution. The first of these 2×2 games,

-6	-1
7	-2

has the solution $p_1 = \frac{9}{14}$, $p_2 = \frac{5}{14}$; $q_1 = \frac{1}{14}$, $q_2 = \frac{13}{14}$; its value is $-\frac{19}{14}$.

Against the other remaining strategy of player Y, column 3 of the reduced game, $p_1 = \frac{9}{14}$, $p_2 = \frac{5}{14}$ has the value

$$\tfrac{9}{14}(4) + \tfrac{5}{14}(-5) = \tfrac{11}{14}$$

which is greater than $-\frac{19}{14}$, so the solution of this 2×2 game extended is the solution of the original game:

$$p_1 = \tfrac{9}{14} \qquad p_2 = \tfrac{5}{14}$$

$$q_1 = \tfrac{1}{14} \qquad q_2 = \tfrac{13}{14} \qquad q_3 = q_4 = q_5 = q_6 = q_7 = 0$$

NOTE: The 2×2 game

-1	4
-2	-5

has a saddle point; thus $p_1 = 1$, $p_2 = 0$, and the value of the game is -1. Against the other remaining strategy of player Y, column 1 of the reduced game, $p_1 = 1$, $p_2 = 0$ has the value -6, which is *not* greater than -1, so the solution of this game is *not* the solution of the original game. The 2×2 game

-6	4
7	-5

has the solution $p_1 = \frac{6}{11}$, $p_2 = \frac{5}{11}$, and the value of the game is $-\frac{1}{11}$. Against the other remaining strategy of player Y, column 2 of the reduced game, $p_1 = \frac{6}{11}$, $p_2 = \frac{5}{11}$ has value $-\frac{16}{11}$, which is *not* greater than $-\frac{1}{11}$, so the solution of this game is *not* the solution of the original game.

Graphical Solution

Graphically, the 2×2 game whose solution is the solution of a $2 \times n$ game is determined as follows. Plot the pairs of payoffs of the n strategies of player Y on two vertical axes and connect the pairs of points by straight lines; locate the highest point on the line segments that form the lower boundary of the graph. The lines that intersect at this point identify the strategies player Y should use in his optimum strategy. Note that it may be possible to reduce a game by dominance before obtaining the solution by graphical analysis.

EXAMPLE

In the game

2	−2	3	7	6
6	5	1	4	0

column 5 dominates column 4 and column 2 dominates column 1. The 2×3 game to be solved is

−2	3	6
5	1	0

which can be solved by solving the 2×2 game

−2	3
5	1

(See Figure 8.5.)

Figure 8.5

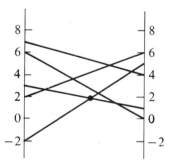

The solution of this 2×2 subgame is $p_1 = \frac{4}{9}$, $p_2 = \frac{5}{9}$; $q_1 = \frac{2}{9}$, $q_2 = \frac{7}{9}$; its value is $\frac{17}{9}$. Thus the solution of the original game is $p_1 = \frac{4}{9}$, $p_2 = \frac{5}{9}$; $q_1 = 0$, $q_2 = \frac{2}{9}$, $q_3 = \frac{7}{9}$, $q_4 = 0$, $q_5 = 0$; its value is $\frac{17}{9}$.

The payoffs corresponding to all five of player Y's strategies are plotted in Figure 8.5, although the first and fourth strategies could be eliminated by dominance. Note that the line corresponding to the payoffs for the first strategy lies entirely above the line corresponding to the payoffs for the second strategy, which dominates it. Similarly, the line corresponding to the payoffs for the fourth strategy lies entirely above the line corresponding to the payoffs for the fifth strategy, which dominates it.

Similarly, for an $m \times 2$ game, the payoffs of the m strategies of player X are plotted and the lines that intersect at the lowest point on the line segments that form the upper boundary of the figure identify the strategies player X should use in his optimum strategy.

EXAMPLE

In the game

−3	6
6	3
8	−2

no strategy is dominated; the 2×2 game to be solved is (see Figure 8.6)

−3	6
6	3

The solution of this 2×2 subgame is $p_1 = \frac{1}{4}$, $p_2 = \frac{3}{4}$; $q_1 = \frac{1}{4}$, $q_2 = \frac{3}{4}$; its value is $\frac{15}{4}$. Thus the solution of the original game is $p_1 = \frac{1}{4}$, $p_2 = \frac{3}{4}$, $p_3 = 0$; $q_1 = \frac{1}{4}$, $q_2 = \frac{3}{4}$; its value is $\frac{15}{4}$.

Figure 8.6

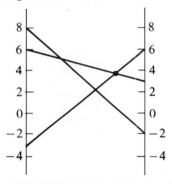

EXAMPLE

An automobile manufacturer has five proposed designs for next year's new cars. Which of these is likely to sell best depends largely on whether his competitor's standard model is excellent, good, fair, or poor. If the model is excellent, his net profit (millions of dollars) will be 100, 150, 50, 125, and 90, respectively; if the model is good, his profit will be 80, 55, 55, 60, and 70, respectively; if the model is fair, his profit will be 150, 100, 100, 100, and 125, respectively; if the model is poor, his profit will be 50, 80, 25, 80, and 75, respectively. What design should he choose in order to maximize his minimum expected profit?

Competitor's model

		Excellent	Good	Fair	Poor
	1	100	80	150	50
	2	150	55	100	80
Design	3	50	55	100	25
	4	125	60	100	80
	5	90	70	125	75

Figure 8.7

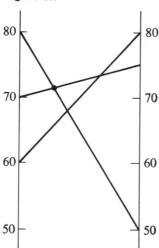

The first and third columns are dominated by the fifth column; the third row is then dominated by the first row, and the second row is dominated by the fourth row. The 2 × 2 game to be solved is (see Figure 8.7)

80	50
70	75

The solution of this 2 × 2 subgame is $p_1 = \frac{1}{7}$, $p_2 = \frac{6}{7}$ and $q_1 = \frac{5}{7}$, $q_2 = \frac{2}{7}$. Thus the manufacturer should produce model 1 with probability $\frac{1}{7}$ and model 5 with probability $\frac{6}{7}$; his competitor should produce a good model with probability $\frac{5}{7}$ and a poor model with probability $\frac{2}{7}$; the value is $\frac{500}{7} = 71\frac{3}{7}$. Note that the payoffs in this problem are all positive and the competitor must therefore have some external reason (such as trying to enter the market) for manufacturing at an inevitable loss. This is assuming that the matrix literally represents net profits and not some type of additional revenue.

EXAMPLE

The Defense Department plans to award a contract for a new missile range at one of two locations, A or B. A real estate speculator intends to invest $5000 in land—all at location A, all at location B, or half at each location. If he buys at location A, the land will be worth $10,000 if the missile range is built there, but $3000 if it is built at location B. If he buys at location B, the land will be worth $4000 if the missile range is built at location A and $8000 if it is built at location B. If he buys at both locations, the land will be worth $6000 if the missile range is built at location A and $5000 if it is built at location B. In order to maximize his minimum expected profits, what should the speculator do?

		Missile range	
		A	B
Investment	A	10,000	3,000
	B	4,000	8,000
	A and B	6,000	5,000

Figure 8.8

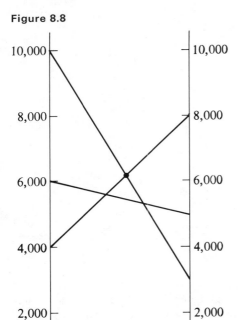

No strategy is dominated; the 2 × 2 subgame to be solved is (see Figure 8.8)

10,000	3,000
4,000	8,000

The solution of this 2 × 2 subgame is $p_1 = \frac{4}{11}$, $p_2 = \frac{7}{11}$. Thus the speculator should invest his money in property A with probability $\frac{4}{11}$ and property B with probability $\frac{7}{11}$; the value is $6181.82. If the Defense Department is considered to be somehow plotting against the speculator, it should choose location A with probability $\frac{5}{11}$ and location B with probability $\frac{6}{11}$. Alternatively, the speculator can be considered to be choosing in order to protect himself against the worst possible occurrence, whether that occurrence is in fact random or is the result of Defense Department strategy against him.

SOLUTION OF LARGER GAMES

For 3 × 3 and larger games, if there is no saddle point and the original game cannot be reduced to a smaller game by dominance, linear programming provides the most efficient method of solution. As discussed in Section 8.4, linear programming is concerned with the problem of maximizing or minimizing a linear function whose variables are restricted to values satisfying a system of linear constraints. A matrix game can be expressed as a problem of this type, since each player is concerned with maximizing the value of the game to himself but is subject to the constraints imposed by the payoff matrix.

If, as above, the payoff matrix is represented by

$$
\mathbf{A} = \begin{bmatrix} a_{11} & a_{12} & \cdots & a_{1n} \\ a_{21} & a_{22} & \cdots & a_{2n} \\ \vdots & \vdots & & \vdots \\ a_{m1} & a_{m2} & \cdots & a_{mn} \end{bmatrix}
$$

and Y's optimal strategies are represented by $(q_1, q_2, \ldots, q_n)$, the inequalities which express the expectations of Y are given by

$$a_{11}q_1 + a_{12}q_2 + \cdots + a_{1n}q_n \le v$$
$$a_{21}q_1 + a_{22}q_2 + \cdots + a_{2n}q_n \le v$$
$$\vdots$$
$$a_{m1}q_1 + a_{m2}q_2 + \cdots + a_{mn}q_n \le v$$
$$q_1 + q_2 + \cdots + q_n = 1$$

Substituting $\bar{q}_i = q_i/v$,

$$a_{11}\bar{q}_1 + a_{12}\bar{q}_2 + \cdots + a_{1n}\bar{q}_n \le 1$$
$$a_{21}\bar{q}_1 + a_{22}\bar{q}_2 + \cdots + a_{2}\bar{q}_n \le 1$$
$$\vdots$$
$$a_{m1}\bar{q}_1 + a_{m2}\bar{q}_2 + \cdots + a_{mn}\bar{q}_n \le 1$$
$$\bar{q}_1 + \bar{q}_2 + \cdots + \bar{q}_n = \frac{1}{v}$$

Player Y's objective is to minimize v or, equivalently, maximize $1/v$. Thus the solution of the matrix game can be written as a linear programming problem as follows:

Maximize $\bar{q}_1 + \bar{q}_2 + \cdots + \bar{q}_n$

subject to

$$a_{11}\bar{q}_1 + a_{12}\bar{q}_2 + \cdots + a_{1n}\bar{q}_n \le 1$$
$$a_{21}\bar{q}_1 + a_{22}\bar{q}_2 + \cdots + a_{2n}\bar{q}_n \le 1$$
$$\vdots$$
$$a_{m1}\bar{q}_1 + a_{m2}\bar{q}_2 + \cdots + a_{mn}\bar{q}_n \le 1$$

$$\bar{q}_1 + \bar{q}_2 + \cdots + \bar{q}_n = \frac{1}{v}$$

or, more concisely,

Maximize $\displaystyle\sum_{i=1}^{n} \bar{q}_i$

subject to

$$\sum_{j=1}^{n} a_{ij}\bar{q}_j \le 1 \qquad \text{for } i = 1, 2, \ldots, m$$

$$\sum_{j=1}^{n} \bar{q}_j = \frac{1}{v}$$

PROBLEMS

Using the minimax criterion, find the optimal strategies for the players of each of the following matrix games.

1.

8	10	13	16	9
10	12	6	15	10
16	18	9	13	25
4	9	18	20	6

2.

5	8	7
−1	−3	10
2	12	−6

3.
10	8	6	2
15	12	2	4
-4	6	-3	1
12	-2	8	-6
16	13	7	12

5.
15	-20	-12	3
4	2	-10	-6
20	-18	-15	-8
-12	8	-10	6
10	9	-11	4

4.
14	3	5	8	4
-3	-1	6	-2	5
2	12	10	13	16

6.
3	10	20	18	0
-9	-8	46	10	4
2	0	17	18	0
-1	1	13	5	3

Find the optimal strategies for the players of each of the following matrix games using the minimax criterion and determine the value of each game.

7.
7	-1	7
10	-2	-5
9	5	6

13.
4	6
9	5
3	1
7	8
10	2

8.
3	5	2	1
0	4	8	3
2	7	14	9

14.
6	-10	12	25	0	5	3	-2
2	-8	4	-6	-7	9	4	10

9.
5	4	-2	1
7	-6	3	6
12	8	10	9
6	18	-9	14

15.
0	2
1	3
-1	0
2	0

10.
3	-10	-5
2	-4	-3
4	-5	-2
-6	-4	0
10	-8	1

16.
9	-5	7	1	-3
-10	4	-8	-6	2

11.
12	-10	8	-6	7	-11
18	2	-3	-4	8	10
5	-3	14	0	-10	-12
3	12	16	1	8	2
-15	16	12	-2	9	-9

12.
10	8	11	-2
14	6	-5	5
9	7	5	-4
15	4	-3	3

17. A contractor is going to build a large number of houses for a housing development. Four types of houses have been discussed: colonial, ranch, split-level, and contemporary; the

development committee will choose two of these types for the contractor to construct. The contractor has the opportunity to buy materials in carload lots, thus saving considerable money, but he must order in advance of the committee's decision and can order only one type of material. If the committee chooses colonial and ranch, the contractor will make an (extra) profit (in thousands of dollars) of 125, 120, 60, and 50 if he orders colonial, ranch, split-level, and contemporary materials, respectively. If the committee chooses colonial and split-level, he will make 90, 40, 80, 75, respectively; if the committee chooses colonial and contemporary, he will make 150, 30, 75, 100, respectively; if the committee chooses ranch and split level, he will make 70, 70, 75, 65, respectively; if the committee chooses ranch and contemporary, he will make 90, 80, 80, 120, respectively; if the committee chooses split-level and contemporary, he will make 80, 40, 130, and 80, respectively. How should the contractor order to maximize his minimum expected extra profit?

18. A plant manager must set up his reactors to produce a certain type of polythene using process 1, 2, 3, 4, or 5. Unfortunately, the chemical raw material varies in nitrogen content and may contain 3, 4, 5, or 6% nitrogen. The nitrogen content affects the relative efficiency of the five processes. With 3% nitrogen, the five processes have an output of 50, 45, 60, 50, and 30 tons, respectively. With 4% nitrogen, the outputs are 60, 70, 75, 90, and 60 tons, respectively; with 5% nitrogen, the outputs are 30, 55, 60, 45, and 70 tons, respectively; with 6% nitrogen, the outputs are 45, 80, 80, 65, and 85 tons, respectively. Testing for nitrogen content is too expensive to be practical. What process should the plant manager use to maximize the minimum expected output?

19. A firm builds construction machinery whose performance depends on the reliability of a gasoline motor. The firm can buy an expensive motor, fully guaranteed including replacement costs, for $500; the firm can also buy a moderately expensive motor for $400, guaranteed for half its cost and the cost of replacement, so that a failure means the firm pays $600 for the motor; or the firm can buy a cheaper motor for $300; if it buys this cheaper motor it can either guarantee replacement for a total cost of $700, or it can pay $50 to have the motor examined before installation, so total cost, if the motor is defective, is $650. To minimize maximum expected costs, what should the firm do?

20. Mr. Smith and Mr. Jones each have a small hothouse in which they grow plants to sell. Each of them grows either tomatoes, flowers, or strawberries in any particular year but they are very secretive about their plans. If Mr. Smith grows tomatoes, his profit is $100 if Mr. Jones grows tomatoes, $150 if Mr. Jones grows strawberries, and $200 if Mr. Jones grows flowers. If Mr. Smith grows strawberries, his profit is $180, $125, $200 if Mr. Jones grows tomatoes, strawberries, flowers, respectively. If Mr. Smith grows flowers, his profit is $140, $125, $100 if Mr. Jones grows tomatoes, strawberries, flowers, respectively. To maximize his minimum expected profit, what should Mr. Smith grow?

21. Mr. Reno has decided to bet $5 on a basketball game between Anglewood and Barleyville. Mr. Las and Mr. Vegas have each offered Mr. Reno a bet. Mr. Las wants to bet on Barleyville and is willing to pay Mr. Reno $10 if Anglewood wins and collect $5 if Barleyville wins. Mr. Vegas wants to bet on Anglewood and is willing to pay Mr. Reno $4 if Barleyville wins and collect $5 if Anglewood wins. If he wants to maximize his minimum expected winnings, what should Mr. Reno do?

22. Casey has a concession at the Yankee Stadium for the sale of sunglasses and umbrellas. He has observed that he can sell about 500 umbrellas when it rains, and about 100 when it is sunny; and in the latter case he can also dispose of 1000 sunglasses. Umbrellas cost $0.50 and sell for $1.00; sunglasses cost $0.20 and sell for $0.50. He is willing to invest $250 in the project. Assuming that everything that isn't sold is a total loss, what should he purchase to maximize his minimum expected profit?

23. Mr. Hilton Conrad is faced with the following decision: The State Medical Society would like to use his hotel for their annual convention; they would essentially take over all facilities of the hotel (so business from other sources would be negligible) and would pay $20,000 for this privilege. Ordinarily the hotel would do $10,000 business during the time the convention would be in session; however, there is a chance that the World Series will be played in the city at that time and, in this event, the hotel would do $50,000 business. Should Mr. Hilton Conrad accept or decline the Medical Society's offer in order to maximize his minimum expected business?

24. An investor has a choice of buying one of three stocks: A, B, or C. The outcome of his purchase depends on whether a particular company executes a merger, divests itself of a subsidiary, or maintains the status quo. In case of a merger, stock A results in a gain of 20, stock B in a loss of 25, and stock C in a gain of 12. In case of divesting, stock A results in a loss of 5, stock B in a loss of 10, and stock C in a loss of 12. If the status quo is maintained, stock A results in a gain of 5, stock B in a gain of 30, and stock C in a loss of 4 (amounts are in thousands of dollars). a. In order to maximize his minimum expected gains, what stock should the investor buy? b. If divesting were impossible, but the gains and losses from the other possibilities were unchanged, what stock should he buy to maximize his minimum expected gains?

25. A commuter must decide what to do about buying insurance for his car. He will definitely carry liability insurance, but the car is rather old and he is not sure whether collision insurance is worthwhile. He can either carry no collision insurance, buy a $50 deductible policy for $60, or buy a full-coverage policy for $70. The commuter drives this car only to and from work and he thinks one of three things will happen during the year: He will have no accident, he will have one minor accident not exceeding $50 damage, or he will have one more serious accident not exceeding $250 damage (the car is worth only about $400 so this is not unreasonable optimism). The commuter realizes he could possibly have more than one accident during the year, but on the basis of his past experience he is willing to assume that he won't. What should he do to minimize his maximum expected cost?

26. In the summer Mr. Smith is considering the winter coal problem. During a normal winter, it takes about 15 tons of coal to heat his shop, but he has observed extremes where as little as 10 tons or as much as 20 tons were used. The price per ton seems to fluctuate with the weather, being $10, $15, and $20 a ton during mild, normal, and severe winters, respectively. He can buy now at $10 a ton. Mr. Smith considers three possible alternatives: to buy 10, 15, or 20 tons now and the rest, if any additional is needed, later. Assuming that all coal not used is a total loss (Mr. Smith plans to sell the shop in the spring), what should he do to minimize his maximum expected cost?

27. A student must decide how to study for a final exam in history. He studies differently for true-false, multiple-choice, and essay exams, and he doesn't know which type this exam will be. The student thinks that if he studies for a true-false test, he will score 85 on a true-false test, 80 on a multiple-choice test, and 75 on an essay test. If he studies for a multiple-choice test, he expects to score 85 on a true-false test, 90 on a multiple-choice test, and 85 on an essay test. If he studies for an essay test, he expects to score 80 on a true-false test, 90 on a multiple-choice test, and 90 on an essay test. To maximize his minimum expected score, for what type of test should the student study?

28. A service station must have its service and parking area plowed after every heavy snowfall. The manager can pay $10 every time the area needs plowing; he can buy a contract for $50, which provides plowing for up to and including six snowfalls, with a cost of $6 for each additional plowing; or he can buy a contract for $60, which provides plowing as many times as it is needed. What should the manager do to minimize his maximum expected cost of plowing if he is willing to assume (based on past records) that there will be between 3 and 8 (inclusive) snowfalls during the winter?

Answers to Odd-Numbered Problems

1. $p_1 = p_2 = 0$, $p_3 = \frac{2}{3}$, $p_4 = \frac{1}{3}$
   $q_1 = \frac{3}{7}$, $q_2 = 0$, $q_3 = \frac{4}{7}$, $q_4 = q_5 = 0$
3. $p_1 = p_2 = p_3 = 0$, $p_4 = \frac{5}{19}$, $p_5 = \frac{14}{19}$
   $q_1 = q_2 = 0$, $q_3 = \frac{18}{19}$, $q_4 = \frac{1}{19}$
5. $p_1 = 0$, $p_2 = 1$, $p_3 = p_4 = p_5 = 0$
   $q_1 = q_2 = 0$, $q_3 = 1$, $q_4 = 0$
7. $p_1 = p_2 = 0$, $p_3 = 1$
   $q_1 = 0$, $q_2 = 1$, $q_3 = 0$
   $v = 5$

9. $p_1 = p_2 = 0$, $p_3 = \frac{27}{29}$, $p_4 = \frac{2}{29}$
   $q_1 = 0$, $q_2 = \frac{19}{29}$, $q_3 = \frac{10}{29}$, $q_4 = 0$
   $v = \frac{252}{29}$

11. $p_1 = p_2 = p_3 = 0$, $p_4 = 1$, $p_5 = 0$
    $q_1 = q_2 = q_3 = 0$, $q_4 = 1$, $q_5 = q_6 = 0$
    $v = 1$

13. $p_1 = 0$, $p_2 = \frac{1}{5}$, $p_3 = 0$, $p_4 = \frac{4}{5}$, $p_5 = 0$
    $q_1 = \frac{3}{5}$, $q_2 = \frac{2}{5}$
    $v = \frac{37}{5}$

15. $p_1 = 0$, $p_2 = \frac{1}{2}$, $p_3 = 0$, $p_4 = \frac{1}{2}$
    $q_1 = \frac{3}{4}$, $q_2 = \frac{1}{4}$
    $v = \frac{3}{2}$

17. buy for colonial with probability $\frac{3}{14}$ and for split-level with probability $\frac{11}{14}$
19. buy expensive motor
21. bet Las with probability $\frac{3}{8}$ and Vegas with probability $\frac{5}{8}$
23. accept offer of a convention
25. buy full coverage
27. study for multiple-choice test

8.6 First-Order Markov Processes

Sequences of observations or experimental outcomes are sometimes considered to be independent; that is, the probability of observing any particular outcome is assumed to be constant over the sequence. The simplest generalization of this model permits the probability of the outcome for any experiment or observation to depend on the outcome of the immediately preceding observation, but not on the outcomes of other prior observations. A process or sequence of this type is said to be a *first-order Markov chain process*, *first-order Markov chain*, or *first-order Markov process*. First-order Markov processes and their steady or equilibrium states are defined and illustrated in this section.

DEFINITION OF A FIRST-ORDER MARKOV PROCESS

Suppose that each of a sequence of experiments or observations has one of a finite number of possible outcomes $a_1, a_2, \ldots, a_r$. The probability of outcome a_j for any given experiment or observation depends on at most the outcome of the immediately preceding observation. These probabilities are denoted by p_{ij}, $i = 1, 2, \ldots, r$ and $j = 1, 2, \ldots, r$, where p_{ij} represents the probability of outcome a_j for any particular observation given that outcome a_i occurred for the immediately preceding observation. The outcomes $a_1, a_2, \ldots, a_r$ are called *states* and the p_{ij} are called *transition probabilities* of a first-order Markov chain. If it is assumed that the process begins in some particular state, the probabilities of various sequences of observations can be calculated. Thus a first-order Markov chain is specified by defining its possible states, specifying the initial probability distribution for these states, and specifying the transition matrix.

The transition probabilities can be summarized in a square matrix. For a Markov process with states $a_1, a_2, \ldots, a_r$, the matrix of transition probabilities is

$$\mathbf{P} = \{p_{ij}\} = \begin{bmatrix} p_{11} & p_{12} & \cdots & p_{1r} \\ p_{21} & p_{22} & \cdots & p_{2r} \\ \vdots & \vdots & & \vdots \\ p_{r1} & p_{r2} & \cdots & p_{rr} \end{bmatrix}$$

Note that the sum of the elements in each row of the matrix $\mathbf{P}$ is 1, since the elements of the ith row represent the probabilities for all possible transitions when the process is in state a_i. That is,

$$\sum_{j=1}^{r} p_{ij} = 1 \qquad \text{for } i = 1, 2, \ldots, r$$

Thus if the probability distribution of the states on trial n is $[p_1, p_2, \ldots, p_r]$, the probability distribution of the states on trial $n + 1$ is

$$[p_1, p_2, \ldots, p_r]\begin{bmatrix} p_{11} & p_{12} & \cdots & p_{1r} \\ p_{21} & p_{22} & \cdots & p_{2r} \\ \vdots & \vdots & & \vdots \\ p_{r1} & p_{r2} & \cdots & p_{rr} \end{bmatrix} = \left[\sum_{i=1}^{r} p_i p_{i1}, \sum_{i=1}^{r} p_i p_{i2}, \ldots, \sum_{i=1}^{r} p_i p_{ir} \right]$$

STEADY STATE OR EQUILIBRIUM

The probability distribution of the outcomes for the nth observation of a first-order Markov process is the product of the initial probability vector and the nth power of the transition matrix. This can be shown by extending the arguments of the previous section. If the vector of initial probabilities is denoted by p_0 and the vector of probabilities at step n is denoted by p_n, then $\mathbf{p}_1 = \mathbf{p}_0 \mathbf{P}$, $\mathbf{p}_2 = \mathbf{p}_1 \mathbf{P} = \mathbf{p}_0 \mathbf{P}^2$, $\mathbf{p}_3 = \mathbf{p}_2 \mathbf{P} = \mathbf{p}_0 \mathbf{P}^3, \ldots, \mathbf{p}_n = \mathbf{p}_0 \mathbf{P}^n$. Under rather nonrestrictive mathematical assumptions, it can be shown that a first-order Markov process approaches a steady state or equilibrium as the number of observations increases, that is, as n approaches infinity.

By definition, when a first-order Markov process is in equilibrium, the probability of each possible state or outcome is constant from observation to observation. The first-order Markov processes used to describe situations in business and economics almost invariably fulfill the mathematical assumptions for equilibrium; the probability distribution of the states in equilibrium is frequently the most interesting property of these processes.

It can be shown that if a first-order Markov chain approaches a steady or equilibrium state as the number of observations or transitions approaches infinity, the stationary (equilibrium) probability distribution of its states is unique and depends only on the transition matrix and not on the initial probability distribution of the states. Any particular Markov chain is, of course, in one particular state for any given observation. The physical and computational significance of stationarity thus becomes apparent only if a number of Markov processes are in the same equilibrium state simultaneously. In this case if there are N such processes and p_i is the equilibrium probability of state i, $p_i N$ of the processes are expected to be in state i for any given observation. Thus, if N is large, a state of macroscopic equilibrium is maintained by a large number of transitions in opposite directions. Most statistical equilibria in physics are of this kind.

Computationally, the stationary probability distribution $[p_1, p_2, \ldots, p_r]$ of the states of a Markov chain is obtained by solving the equations given in matrix form by

$$[p_1, p_2, \ldots, p_r]\begin{bmatrix} p_{11} & p_{12} & \cdots & p_{1r} \\ p_{21} & p_{22} & \cdots & p_{2r} \\ \vdots & \vdots & & \vdots \\ p_{r1} & p_{r2} & \cdots & p_{rr} \end{bmatrix} = [p_1, p_2, \ldots, p_r]$$

where p_i is the probability of being in state i, $i = 1, \ldots, r$ and $\sum_{i=1}^{r} p_i = 1$. This involves solution of the r independent linear equations

$$\sum_{i=1}^{r} p_i p_{ij} = p_j \qquad \text{for } j = 1, 2, \ldots, r \quad (r - 1 \text{ of which are independent})$$

$$\sum_{i=1}^{r} p_i = 1$$

Note that these equations actually define equilibrium: If $[p_1, p_2, \ldots, p_r]$ is the probability distribution of the states for a given observation, the product

$$[p_1, p_2, \ldots, p_r] \begin{bmatrix} p_{11} & p_{12} & \cdots & p_{1r} \\ p_{21} & p_{22} & \cdots & p_{2r} \\ \vdots & \vdots & & \vdots \\ p_{r1} & p_{r2} & \cdots & p_{rr} \end{bmatrix}$$

gives the probability distribution of the states for the next observation. If that distribution is also $[p_1, p_2, \ldots, p_r]$, the same as for the preceding observation, the system is in equilibrium.

EXAMPLE

Suppose that, on September 1, of the subscribers in a fixed area, the Herald has $\frac{1}{2}$, the Tribune has $\frac{1}{4}$, and the Gazette has $\frac{1}{4}$. During the month of September, the Herald retains $\frac{7}{8}$ of its subscribers and loses $\frac{1}{8}$ of them to the Tribune; the Tribune retains $\frac{1}{12}$ of its subscribers and loses $\frac{3}{4}$ of them to the Herald and $\frac{1}{6}$ of them to the Gazette; the Gazette retains $\frac{1}{3}$ of its subscribers and loses $\frac{1}{2}$ of them to the Herald and $\frac{1}{6}$ of them to the Tribune. Assume there are no new subscribers and that no one quits subscribing.

(a) What proportion of the subscribers does each paper have on October 1?
(b) If the same pattern of gains and losses continues for October, what proportion of the subscribers does each paper have on November 1?
(c) If the same pattern of gains and losses continues each month, what proportion of the subscribers will each paper have in the long run (that is, in equilibrium)?

The transition matrix is

$$\begin{array}{c} \\ \text{Herald} \\ \text{Tribune} \\ \text{Gazette} \end{array} \begin{array}{ccc} \text{Herald} & \text{Tribune} & \text{Gazette} \\ \begin{bmatrix} \frac{7}{8} & \frac{1}{8} & 0 \\ \frac{3}{4} & \frac{1}{12} & \frac{1}{6} \\ \frac{1}{2} & \frac{1}{6} & \frac{1}{3} \end{bmatrix} \end{array}$$

(a)

$$[\tfrac{1}{2}, \tfrac{1}{4}, \tfrac{1}{4}] \begin{bmatrix} \frac{7}{8} & \frac{1}{8} & 0 \\ \frac{3}{4} & \frac{1}{12} & \frac{1}{6} \\ \frac{1}{2} & \frac{1}{6} & \frac{1}{3} \end{bmatrix} = [\tfrac{3}{4}, \tfrac{1}{8}, \tfrac{1}{8}]$$

Thus on October 1, of the subscribers, the Herald has $\frac{3}{4}$, the Tribune has $\frac{1}{8}$, and the Gazette has $\frac{1}{8}$.

(b)

$$[\tfrac{3}{4}, \tfrac{1}{8}, \tfrac{1}{8}] \begin{bmatrix} \frac{7}{8} & \frac{1}{8} & 0 \\ \frac{3}{4} & \frac{1}{12} & \frac{1}{6} \\ \frac{1}{2} & \frac{1}{6} & \frac{1}{3} \end{bmatrix} = [\tfrac{13}{16}, \tfrac{1}{8}, \tfrac{1}{16}]$$

Thus on November 1, of the subscribers, the Herald has $\frac{13}{16}$, the Tribune has $\frac{1}{8}$, and the Gazette has $\frac{1}{16}$.

(c)

$$[p_1, p_2, p_3] \begin{bmatrix} \frac{7}{8} & \frac{1}{8} & 0 \\ \frac{3}{4} & \frac{1}{12} & \frac{1}{6} \\ \frac{1}{2} & \frac{1}{6} & \frac{1}{3} \end{bmatrix} = [p_1, p_2, p_3]$$

$$\tfrac{7}{8}p_1 + \tfrac{3}{4}p_2 + \tfrac{1}{2}p_3 = p_1$$

$$\tfrac{1}{8}p_1 + \tfrac{1}{12}p_2 + \tfrac{1}{6}p_3 = p_2$$

$$\tfrac{1}{6}p_2 + \tfrac{1}{3}p_3 = p_3$$

$$p_1 + p_2 + p_3 = 1$$

Multiplying the first equation by 8, the second equation by 24, and the third equation by 6,

$$-p_1 + 6p_2 + 4p_3 = 0$$

$$3p_1 - 22p_2 + 4p_3 = 0$$

$$p_2 - 4p_3 = 0$$

$$p_1 + p_2 + p_3 = 1$$

Solving the first, third, and fourth equations simultaneously (any three of the four equations are independent),

$$\begin{bmatrix} 1 & 1 & 1 & | & 1 \\ 0 & 1 & -4 & | & 0 \\ -1 & 6 & 4 & | & 0 \end{bmatrix}$$

$$\begin{bmatrix} 1 & 1 & 1 & | & 1 \\ 0 & 1 & -4 & | & 0 \\ 0 & 7 & 5 & | & 1 \end{bmatrix}$$

$$\begin{bmatrix} 1 & 0 & 5 & | & 1 \\ 0 & 1 & -4 & | & 0 \\ 0 & 0 & 33 & | & 1 \end{bmatrix}$$

$$\begin{bmatrix} 1 & 0 & 0 & | & \frac{28}{33} \\ 0 & 1 & 0 & | & \frac{4}{33} \\ 0 & 0 & 1 & | & \frac{1}{33} \end{bmatrix}$$

Thus in the long run, of the subscribers, the Herald will have $\frac{28}{33}$, the Tribune will have $\frac{4}{33}$, and the Gazette will have $\frac{1}{33}$.

EXAMPLE

In the community of Gardenville, each year 5 percent of the residents in the city proper move to the suburbs and 2 percent of the people in the suburbs move to the city. Assuming that the total number of people in the community remains constant, determine the long-run proportions of city and suburban residents.

The transition matrix is

	City	Suburbs
City	0.95	0.05
Suburbs	0.02	0.98

and the equilibrium probabilities are determined by

$$[p_1, p_2]\begin{bmatrix} 0.95 & 0.05 \\ 0.02 & 0.98 \end{bmatrix} = [p_1, p_2]$$

$$0.95p_1 + 0.02p_2 = p_1$$

$$0.05p_1 + 0.98p_2 = p_2$$

$$p_1 + p_2 = 1$$

Multiplying the first two equations by 100,

$$-5p_1 + 2p_2 = 0$$

$$5p_1 - 2p_2 = 0$$

$$p_1 + p_2 = 1$$

Solving the first and third equations simultaneously (any two of the three equations are independent),

$$\begin{bmatrix} 1 & 1 & | & 1 \\ -5 & 2 & | & 0 \end{bmatrix}$$

$$\begin{bmatrix} 1 & 1 & | & 1 \\ 0 & 7 & | & 5 \end{bmatrix}$$

$$\begin{bmatrix} 1 & 1 & | & 1 \\ 0 & 1 & | & \frac{5}{7} \end{bmatrix}$$

$$\begin{bmatrix} 1 & 0 & | & \frac{2}{7} \\ 0 & 1 & | & \frac{5}{7} \end{bmatrix}$$

Thus, eventually, of the people in the community, $\frac{2}{7}$ will be city residents and $\frac{5}{7}$ will be residents of the suburbs. Note that in this equilibrium state $0.05 \times \frac{2}{7} = \frac{1}{70}$ of the people move each year from the city to the suburbs and $0.02 \times \frac{5}{7} = \frac{1}{70}$ of the people move each year from the suburbs to the city—the numbers of city and suburban residents thus are unchanged or stable.

EXAMPLE

A broker is studying the price movements of various stocks on the market and is particularly interested in a company called Astronaut Instruments. He has observed that if this stock goes up on a given day, then the next day it has a 50 : 50 chance of going up again, a $\frac{1}{3}$ chance of staying the same price, and a $\frac{1}{6}$ chance of going down. If the stock stays the same on a given day, then it is equally likely to go up, stay the same, or go down the next day. If the stock goes down on a given day, then the next day it has a 50 : 50 chance of going down again, a $\frac{1}{3}$ chance of staying the same price, and a $\frac{1}{6}$ chance of going up. What proportion of the time (in the long run) does the stock go up, stay the same, and go down?

The transition matrix is

	Up	Same	Down
Up	$\frac{1}{2}$	$\frac{1}{3}$	$\frac{1}{6}$
Same	$\frac{1}{3}$	$\frac{1}{3}$	$\frac{1}{3}$
Down	$\frac{1}{6}$	$\frac{1}{3}$	$\frac{1}{2}$

and the equilibrium probabilities are determined by

$$[p_1, p_2, p_3] \begin{bmatrix} \frac{1}{2} & \frac{1}{3} & \frac{1}{6} \\ \frac{1}{3} & \frac{1}{3} & \frac{1}{3} \\ \frac{1}{6} & \frac{1}{3} & \frac{1}{2} \end{bmatrix} = [p_1, p_2, p_3]$$

$$\tfrac{1}{2}p_1 + \tfrac{1}{3}p_2 + \tfrac{1}{6}p_3 = p_1$$

$$\tfrac{1}{3}p_1 + \tfrac{1}{3}p_2 + \tfrac{1}{3}p_3 = p_2$$

$$\tfrac{1}{6}p_1 + \tfrac{1}{3}p_2 + \tfrac{1}{2}p_3 = p_3$$

$$p_1 + p_2 + p_3 = 1$$

Multiplying the first equation by 6, the second equation by 3, and the third equation by 6,

$$-3p_1 + 2p_2 + p_3 = 0$$

$$p_1 - 2p_2 + p_3 = 0$$

$$p_1 + 2p_2 - 3p_3 = 0$$

$$p_1 + p_2 + p_3 = 1$$

Solving the second, third, and fourth equations simultaneously (any three of the four equations are independent),

$$\begin{bmatrix} 1 & 1 & 1 & | & 1 \\ 1 & 2 & -3 & | & 0 \\ 1 & -2 & 1 & | & 0 \end{bmatrix}$$

$$\begin{bmatrix} 1 & 1 & 1 & | & 1 \\ 0 & 1 & -4 & | & -1 \\ 0 & -3 & 0 & | & -1 \end{bmatrix}$$

$$\begin{bmatrix} 1 & 0 & 5 & | & 2 \\ 0 & 1 & -4 & | & -1 \\ 0 & 0 & -12 & | & -4 \end{bmatrix}$$

$$\begin{bmatrix} 1 & 0 & 0 & | & \frac{1}{3} \\ 0 & 1 & 0 & | & \frac{1}{3} \\ 0 & 0 & 1 & | & \frac{1}{3} \end{bmatrix}$$

Thus, in the long run, the stock goes up $\frac{1}{3}$ of the time, stays the same $\frac{1}{3}$ of the time, and goes down $\frac{1}{3}$ of the time.

PROBLEMS

1. A country has a three-party political system and the results of elections follow a definite pattern: If a party wins an election, its chance of winning the next election are 50 : 50 and if it loses the next election, each of the other two parties has a 50 : 50 chance of winning. What proportion of the elections does each party win over a long period of time?

2. A trucking company offers its drivers three approved routes between two cities: over the Mystic Bridge, on the Interstate Parkway, and on Route 1. If a trucker goes on the Mystic Bridge, the chance of his getting into a traffic jam is $\frac{1}{3}$; if he does get in a traffic jam, the next day he takes the Interstate Parkway with probability $\frac{2}{3}$ and Route 1 with probability $\frac{1}{3}$; if he doesn't get in a traffic jam, the next day he takes the Mystic Bridge again with probability $\frac{1}{2}$, the Interstate Parkway with probability $\frac{1}{6}$, and Route 1 with probability $\frac{1}{3}$. If he takes the Interstate Parkway the chance of his getting into a traffic jam is $\frac{1}{2}$; if he does get in a traffic jam, the next day he takes the Mystic Bridge; if he doesn't get in a traffic jam, the next day he takes the Mystic Bridge, the Interstate Parkway, and Route 1 with

equal probability. If he takes Route 1, the trucker is invariably late, so he never takes Route 1 two days in a row and the next day he takes the Mystic Bridge with probability $\frac{1}{3}$ and the Interstate Parkway with probability $\frac{2}{3}$. What proportion of the time does the trucker go on the Mystic Bridge, the Interstate Parkway, and Route 1, respectively?

3. Every year the Smith family goes on a vacation—a camping trip (preferred by the children), a visit to the city (preferred by Mrs. Smith), or a winter vacation (preferred by Mr. Smith). They never take the same kind of vacation 2 years in a row. Each year they flip a coin to decide which of the two types of vacation they did not take the previous year they will take that year. What proportion of the time do the Smiths go on a camping trip, visit the city, and take a winter vacation, respectively?

4. A mechanic has a very unreliable automobile. Every morning he goes out to the garage hoping to start it; some days it starts by itself, some days it starts if he gets a push from a neighbor, other days no amount of pushing is effective and the service station must be called. If it starts one day, the chances are $\frac{1}{2}$ it will start, $\frac{1}{3}$ it must be pushed, and $\frac{1}{6}$ the service station must be called the next day. If it is pushed one day, the chances are $\frac{1}{3}$ it will start and $\frac{2}{3}$ the service station must be called the next day (it is never pushed 2 days in a row). If the service station is called one day, the chances are $\frac{5}{6}$ it will start and $\frac{1}{6}$ it must be pushed the next day (the service station is never needed 2 days in a row). In the long run, what proportion of the days will the auto start, be pushed, and need the service station, respectively?

5. The students of Professor Geology never know what's going to happen in class; the professor may give them a surprise quiz, take them on a field trip, discuss the daily assignment, or deliver a lecture. If he gives a quiz one day, the next day there is always a field trip. If there is a field trip one day, there is never a quiz or a field trip the next day, but discussing the assignment and a lecture are equally likely. If he discusses the assignment one day, there is $\frac{1}{4}$ chance of a quiz, $\frac{1}{4}$ chance of a field trip, $\frac{1}{6}$ chance of discussing the assignment, and $\frac{1}{3}$ chance of a lecture the next day. If he lectures one day, there is $\frac{1}{4}$ chance of a quiz, $\frac{1}{8}$ chance of a field trip, $\frac{1}{8}$ chance of discussing the assignment, and $\frac{1}{2}$ chance of a lecture the next day. One of the students has calculated that they can expect quizzes $\frac{43}{287}$ of the days, field trips $\frac{72}{287}$ of the days, discussion of the assignment $\frac{60}{287}$ of the days, and lectures $\frac{112}{287}$ of the days. Is he correct?

6. Mr. S (who prefers steak), Mr. C (who prefers chicken), and Mr. H (who prefers ham) are invited frequently to the home of a friend who serves only these three entrees. They have decided to bet before each dinner engagement on which entree will be served. Suppose that if the hostess serves steak on one occasion, she never serves it next time; she tosses a fair coin and serves chicken if it comes up heads and ham if it comes up tails. If she serves chicken on one occasion, then the next time she tosses two dice and serves chicken if the dice come up the same; if the dice come up different on the first toss, she tosses them again and serves steak if they come up the same and ham otherwise. If she serves ham on one occasion, then the next time she draws a card randomly from a deck and serves chicken if it is a diamond and steak otherwise. If each man always bets on his preference, what proportion of the time, in the long run, will each win?

7. Every summer the Stormy Lakes Yachting Association must decide whether to hold its annual regatta in June, July, or August. If the regatta is in June, the probability of good weather is $\frac{3}{4}$; if there is good weather, the next year the regatta will be held in June with probability $\frac{2}{3}$, in July with probability $\frac{1}{6}$, and in August with probability $\frac{1}{6}$; if there is bad weather, the next year the regatta will be held in July and August with equal probabilities. If the regatta is in July, good and bad weather are equally probable; if there is good weather, the next year the regatta will be held in July; if there is bad weather, the regatta will be held in August with probability $\frac{2}{3}$ and in June with probability $\frac{1}{3}$. If the regatta is in August, the probability of good weather is $\frac{2}{5}$; if there is good weather, the next year the regatta will be held in July and August with equal probabilities; if there is bad weather, the regatta will be held in June with probability $\frac{1}{3}$ and in July with probability $\frac{2}{3}$. What proportion of the time is the regatta held in June, July, and August, respectively?

8. A scientific book club has three mailing lists: a selected list consisting of members of 3 years or more of active membership, a membership list consisting of current members, and

an augmented list consisting of current members and others who have shown interest in the club's activities in the past. For each new publication, it must be decided which list to use for mailing the sales literature. If after the preceding mailing there were too few copies ordered, the secretary uses the member list with probability $\frac{1}{4}$ and the augmented list with probability $\frac{3}{4}$; if after the preceding mailing there was a satisfactory response, the secretary uses the member list and the augmented list with equal probability; if after the preceding mailing, the publication was oversold, the secretary uses the selected list with probability $\frac{1}{3}$ and the member list with probability $\frac{2}{3}$. If the selected list is used, there are too few sold or a satisfactory number sold with equal probability; if the member list is used, there are too few sold with probability $\frac{1}{4}$ and an adequate sale with probability $\frac{3}{4}$; if the augmented list is used, there is an adequate sale with probability $\frac{1}{3}$ and an oversale with probability $\frac{2}{3}$. What proportion of the time are the sales too small, adequate, and an oversale, respectively?

9. A housewife always buys one of three brands of detergent: A, B, or C. Which brand she buys depends partly on which, if any, of the three companies are having a promotional campaign (free combs, plastic roses, etc.). The companies time these campaigns at random, paying no attention to whether the competition is running one at the same time. Company A runs a campaign $\frac{1}{2}$ of the time, company B runs a campaign $\frac{1}{3}$ of the time, and company C runs a campaign $\frac{1}{3}$ of the time. If the housewife buys brand A one time, the next time she buys brand A if brand A is running a campaign or if none of the brands is running a campaign, she buys brand B if brand B is running a campaign but brand A is not, and she buys brand C if brand C is running the only campaign at the time. If she buys brand B one time, the next time she buys brand A if it is running the only campaign at the time and brand B otherwise. If she buys brand C one time, the next time she buys brand A if it is running the only campaign at the time, brand C if it is running a campaign and B is not, and brand B otherwise. What proportion of the time does the housewife buy brands A, B, and C, respectively?

HELPFUL HINT: From $P(A) = \frac{1}{2}$, $P(B) = \frac{1}{3}$, $P(C) = \frac{1}{3}$ given above, the following probabilities can be obtained with a little arithmetic:

$P(A \text{ only}) = \frac{2}{9}$ $P(A \text{ and } C, \text{ not } B) = \frac{1}{9}$

$P(B \text{ only}) = \frac{1}{9}$ $P(B \text{ and } C, \text{ not } A) = \frac{1}{18}$

$P(C \text{ only}) = \frac{1}{9}$ $P(A, B \text{ and } C) = \frac{1}{18}$

$P(A \text{ and } B, \text{ not } C) = \frac{1}{9}$ $P(\text{no campaign}) = \frac{2}{9}$

10. Computeronics Corporation orders 2-foot lengths of wire for use in its experimental models from a supplier who claims that the wire has a specified strength desired by the Computeronics engineers. Each shipment is classified by the engineers who use it as satisfactory in strength (no report is made to the supplier), below standard (the supplier is notified by letter that the shipment was not as claimed), or unacceptable (the shipment is returned and a replacement which has been subjected to a 100% test is sent by the supplier in accordance with the guarantee). The classification depends upon the extent to which a shipment fulfills or fails to fulfill the supplier's claim regarding strength. The engineers have observed that if a shipment is classified as satisfactory, the next shipment is satisfactory $\frac{4}{5}$ of the time, below standard $\frac{3}{20}$ of the time, and unacceptable $\frac{1}{20}$ of the time; if a shipment is classified as below standard, the next shipment is satisfactory $\frac{19}{20}$ of the time, below standard $\frac{1}{20}$ of the time, and never unacceptable. What proportion of the shipments is satisfactory, below standard, and unacceptable in the long run, respectively?

Answers to Odd-Numbered Problems

1. $\frac{1}{3}, \frac{1}{3}, \frac{1}{3}$

3. $\frac{1}{3}, \frac{1}{3}, \frac{1}{3}$

5. yes

7. $\frac{24}{91}, \frac{42}{91}, \frac{25}{91}$

9. $\frac{4}{9}, \frac{31}{63}, \frac{4}{63}$

Tables

Exponential Functions

x	e^x	e^{-x}	x	e^x	e^{-x}
0.00	1.000	1.000	3.00	20.086	0.050
0.10	1.105	0.905	3.10	22.198	0.045
0.20	1.221	0.819	3.20	24.533	0.041
0.30	1.350	0.741	3.30	27.113	0.037
0.40	1.492	0.670	3.40	29.964	0.033
0.50	1.649	0.607	3.50	33.115	0.030
0.60	1.822	0.549	3.60	36.598	0.027
0.70	2.014	0.497	3.70	40.447	0.025
0.80	2.226	0.449	3.80	44.701	0.022
0.90	2.460	0.407	3.90	49.402	0.020
1.00	2.718	0.368	4.00	54.598	0.018
1.10	3.004	0.333	4.10	60.340	0.017
1.20	3.320	0.301	4.20	66.686	0.015
1.30	3.669	0.273	4.30	73.700	0.014
1.40	4.055	0.247	4.40	81.451	0.012
1.50	4.482	0.223	4.50	90.017	0.011
1.60	4.953	0.202	4.60	99.484	0.010
1.70	5.474	0.183	4.70	109.95	0.009
1.80	6.050	0.165	4.80	121.51	0.008
1.90	6.686	0.150	4.90	134.29	0.007
2.00	7.389	0.135	5.00	148.41	0.007
2.10	8.166	0.122	5.10	164.02	0.006
2.20	9.025	0.111	5.20	181.27	0.006
2.30	9.974	0.100	5.30	200.34	0.005
2.40	11.023	0.091	5.40	221.41	0.005
2.50	12.182	0.082	5.50	244.69	0.004
2.60	13.464	0.074	5.60	270.43	0.004
2.70	14.880	0.067	5.70	298.87	0.003
2.80	16.445	0.061	5.80	330.30	0.003
2.90	18.174	0.055	5.90	365.04	0.003
3.00	20.086	0.050	6.00	403.43	0.002

Common Logarithms

N	0	1	2	3	4	5	6	7	8	9
10	0000	0043	0086	0128	0170	0212	0253	0294	0334	0374
11	0414	0453	0492	0531	0569	0607	0645	0682	0719	0755
12	0792	0828	0864	0899	0934	0969	1004	1038	1072	1106
13	1139	1173	1206	1239	1271	1303	1335	1367	1399	1430
14	1461	1492	1523	1553	1584	1614	1644	1673	1703	1732
15	1761	1790	1818	1847	1875	1903	1931	1959	1987	2014
16	2041	2068	2095	2122	2148	2175	2201	2227	2253	2279
17	2304	2330	2355	2380	2405	2430	2455	2480	2504	2529
18	2553	2577	2601	2625	2648	2672	2695	2718	2742	2765
19	2788	2810	2833	2856	2878	2900	2923	2945	2967	2989
20	3010	3032	3054	3075	3096	3118	3139	3160	3181	3201
21	3222	3243	3263	3284	3304	3324	3345	3365	3385	3404
22	3424	3444	3464	3483	3502	3522	3541	3560	3579	3598
23	3617	3636	3655	3674	3692	3711	3729	3747	3766	3784
24	3802	3820	3838	3856	3874	3892	3909	3927	3945	3962
25	3979	3997	4014	4031	4048	4065	4082	4099	4116	4133
26	4150	4166	4183	4200	4216	4232	4249	4265	4281	4298
27	4314	4330	4346	4362	4378	4393	4409	4425	4440	4456
28	4472	4487	4502	4518	4533	4548	4564	4579	4594	4609
29	4624	4639	4654	4669	4683	4698	4713	4728	4742	4757
30	4771	4786	4800	4814	4829	4843	4857	4871	4886	4900
31	4914	4928	4942	4955	4969	4983	4997	5011	5024	5038
32	5051	5065	5079	5092	5105	5119	5132	5145	5159	5172
33	5185	5198	5211	5224	5237	5250	5263	5276	5289	5302
34	5315	5328	5340	5353	5366	5378	5391	5403	5416	5428
35	5441	5453	5465	5478	5490	5502	5514	5527	5539	5551
36	5563	5575	5587	5599	5611	5623	5635	5647	5658	5670
37	5682	5694	5705	5717	5729	5740	5752	5763	5775	5786
38	5798	5809	5821	5832	5843	5855	5866	5877	5888	5899
39	5911	5922	5933	5944	5955	5966	5977	5988	5999	6010
40	6021	6031	6042	6053	6064	6075	6085	6096	6107	6117
41	6128	6138	6149	6160	6170	6180	6191	6201	6212	6222
42	6232	6243	6253	6263	6274	6284	6294	6304	6314	6325
43	6335	6345	6355	6365	6375	6385	6395	6405	6415	6425
44	6435	6444	6454	6464	6474	6484	6493	6503	6513	6522
45	6532	6542	6551	6561	6571	6580	6590	6599	6609	6618
46	6628	6637	6646	6656	6665	6675	6684	6693	6702	6712
47	6721	6730	6739	6749	6758	6767	6776	6785	6694	6803
48	6812	6821	6830	6839	6848	6857	6866	6875	6884	6893
49	6902	6911	6920	6928	6937	6946	6955	6964	6972	6981
50	6990	6998	7007	7016	7024	7033	7042	7050	7059	7067
51	7076	7084	7093	7101	7110	7118	7126	7135	7143	7152
52	7160	7168	7177	7185	7193	7202	7210	7218	7226	7235
53	7243	7251	7259	7267	7275	7284	7292	7300	7308	7316
54	7324	7332	7340	7348	7356	7364	7372	7380	7388	7396

Common Logarithms

N	0	1	2	3	4	5	6	7	8	9
55	7404	7412	7419	7427	7435	7443	7451	7459	7466	7474
56	7482	7490	7497	7505	7513	7520	7528	7536	7543	7551
57	7559	7566	7574	7582	7589	7597	7604	7612	7619	7627
58	7634	7642	7649	7657	7664	7672	7679	7686	7694	7701
59	7709	7716	7723	7731	7738	7745	7752	7760	7767	7774
60	7782	7789	7796	7803	7810	7818	7825	7832	7839	7846
61	7853	7860	7868	7875	7882	7889	7896	7903	7910	7917
62	7924	7931	7938	7945	7952	7959	7966	7973	7980	7987
63	7993	8000	8007	8014	8021	8028	8035	8041	8048	8055
64	8062	8069	8075	8082	8089	8096	8102	8109	8116	8122
65	8129	8136	8142	8149	8156	8162	8169	8176	8182	8189
66	8195	8202	8209	8215	8222	8228	8235	8241	8248	8254
67	8261	8267	8274	8280	8287	8293	8299	8306	8312	8319
68	8325	8331	8338	8344	8351	8357	8363	8370	8376	8382
69	8388	8395	8401	8407	8414	8420	8426	8432	8439	8445
70	8451	8457	8463	8470	8476	8482	8488	8494	8500	8506
71	8513	8519	8525	8531	8537	8543	8549	8555	8561	8567
72	8573	8579	8585	8591	8597	8603	8609	8615	8621	8627
73	8633	8639	8645	8651	8657	8663	8669	8675	8681	8686
74	8692	8698	8704	8710	8716	8722	8727	8733	8739	8745
75	8751	8756	8762	8768	8774	8779	8785	8791	8797	8802
76	8808	8814	8820	8825	8831	8837	8842	8848	8854	8859
77	8865	8871	8876	8882	8887	8893	8899	8904	8910	8915
78	8921	8927	8932	8938	8943	8949	8954	8960	8965	8971
79	8976	8982	8987	8993	8998	9004	9009	9015	9020	9025
80	9031	9036	9042	9047	9053	9058	9063	9069	9074	9079
81	9085	9090	9096	9101	9106	9112	9117	9122	9128	9133
82	9138	9143	9149	9154	9159	9165	9170	9175	9180	9186
83	9191	9196	9201	9206	9212	9217	9222	9227	9232	9238
84	9243	9248	9253	9258	9263	9269	9274	9279	9284	9289
85	9294	9299	9304	9309	9315	9320	9325	9330	9335	9340
86	9345	9350	9355	9360	9365	9370	9375	9380	9385	9390
87	9395	9400	9405	9410	9415	9420	9425	9430	9435	9440
88	9445	9450	9455	9460	9465	9469	9474	9479	9484	9489
89	9494	9499	9504	9509	9513	9518	9523	9528	9533	9538
90	9542	9547	9552	9557	9562	9566	9571	9576	9581	9586
91	9590	9595	9600	9605	9609	9614	9619	9624	9628	9633
92	9638	9643	9647	9652	9657	9661	9666	9671	9675	9680
93	9685	9689	9694	9699	9703	9708	9713	9717	9722	9727
94	9731	9736	9741	9745	9750	9754	9759	9763	9768	9773
95	9777	9782	9786	9791	9795	9800	9805	9809	9814	9818
96	9823	9827	9832	9836	9841	9845	9850	9854	9859	9863
97	9868	9872	9877	9881	9886	9890	9894	9899	9903	9908
98	9912	9917	9921	9926	9930	9934	9939	9943	9948	9952
99	9956	9961	9965	9969	9974	9978	9983	9987	9991	9996

Selected References

Almon, Clopper. *Matrix Methods in Economics*. Reading, MA: Addison-Wesley, 1967.

Aubin, Jean-Pierre. *Mathematical Methods of Game and Economic Theory*. New York: North Holland, 1979.

Baumol, William J. *Economic Theory and Operations Analysis*. Englewood Cliffs, NJ: Prentice-Hall, 1961.

Bellman, Richard E. *Introduction to Matrix Analysis*. New York: McGraw-Hill, 1970.

Bentley, Donald L. and Kenneth L. Cooke. *Linear Algebra and Differential Equations*. New York: Holt, Rinehart and Winston, 1973.

Billingsley, Patrick. *Statistical Inference for Markov Processes*. Chicago: University of Chicago Press, 1961.

Birkoff, Garrett and Gian-Carlo Ruta. *Ordinary Differential Equations*. New York: Wiley, 1978.

Brinkman, Heinrich W. *Linear Algebra and Analytic Geometry*. Reading, MA: Addison-Wesley, 1971.

Buck, Robert C. *Advanced Calculus* (3rd ed.). New York: McGraw-Hill, 1978.

Buck, Robert C. *Introduction to Differential Equations*. Boston: Houghton Mifflin, 1976.

Chiang, Alpha C. *Fundamental Methods of Mathematical Economics*. New York: McGraw-Hill, 1974.

Childress, Robert L. *Mathematics for Managerial Decisions*. Englewood Cliffs, NJ: Prentice-Hall, 1974.

Childress, Robert L. *Sets, Matrices and Linear Programming*. Englewood Cliffs, NJ: Prentice-Hall, 1974.

Chorlton, Frank. *Ordinary Differential and Difference Equations; Theory and Applications*. New York: Van Nostrand, 1965.

Derman, Cyrus. *Finite State Markovian Decision Processes*. New York: Academic Press, 1970.

Flanders, Harley and Justin J. Price. *Calculus with Analytic Geometry*. New York: Academic Press, 1978.

Franklin, Jose N. *Methods of Mathematical Economics: Linear and Nonlinear Programming: Fixed Points Theorems*. New York: Springer-Verlag, 1980.

Freedman, David. *Markov Chains*. San Francisco: Holden-Day, 1971.

Fryer, Michael J. *An Introduction to Linear Programming and Matrix Game Theory*. New York: Wiley, 1978.

Fuller, Gordon and Robert M. Parker. *Analytic Geometry and Calculus*. New York: Van Nostrand, 1964.

Gass, Saul I. *Linear Programming: Methods and Applications* (4th ed.). New York: McGraw-Hill, 1975.

Goldberg, Samuel. *Introduction to Difference Equations with Illustrative Examples from Economics, Psychology and Sociology*. New York: Wiley, 1958.

Henderson, John M. and Richard E. Quandt. *Microeconomic Theory, A Mathematical Approach* (2nd ed.). New York: McGraw-Hill, 1971.

Hildebrand, Francis B. *Advanced Calculus for Applications* (2nd ed.). Englewood Cliffs, NJ: Prentice-Hall, 1976.

Isaacson, Dean L. *Markov Chains, Theory and Applications*. New York: Wiley, 1976.

Jolley, L. B. W. *Summation of Series* (2nd ed.). New York: Dover, 1961.

Kaplan, William. *Advanced Calculus* (2nd ed.). Reading, MA: Addison-Wesley, 1973.

Leighton, Walter. *An Introduction to the Theory of Ordinary Differential Equations*. Belmont, CA: Wadsworth, 1976.

Levin, Richard I. and Robert B. Des Jardins. *Theory of Games and Strategies*. Scranton, PA: International Textbook, 1970.

Miller, Kenneth S. *An Introduction to the Calculus of Finite Differences and Difference Equations*. New York: Holt Rinehart and Winston, 1960.

O'Neil, Peter V. *Advanced Calculus, Pure and Applied*. New York: Macmillan, 1975.

Perlis, Sam. *Theory of Matrices*. Cambridge, MA: Addison-Wesley, 1952.

Rorres, Chris and Howard Anton. *Applications of Linear Algebra* (2nd ed.). New York: Wiley, 1979.

Ross, Shepley L. *Introduction to Ordinary Differential Equations* (3rd ed.). New York: Wiley, 1980.

Rothenberg, Ronald I. *Linear Programming*, New York: North Holland, 1979.

Sasaki, Kyohei. *Introduction to Finite Mathematics and Linear Programming*. Belmont, CA: Wadsworth, 1970.

Schkade, Lawrence L. *Vectors and Matrices*. Columbus, OH: Merrill, 1967.

Schwartz, Abraham. *Calculus and Analytic Geometry* (2nd ed.). New York: Holt, Rinehart and Winston, 1967.

Taylor, Angus E. *Calculus with Analytic Geometry*. Englewood Cliffs, NJ: Prentice-Hall, 1959.

Thie, Paul R. *An Introduction to Linear Programming and Game Theory*. New York: Wiley, 1979.

Thomas, George B., Jr. *Calculus and Analytic Geometry* (5th ed.). Reading, MA: Addison-Wesley, 1972.

Thompson, Gerald E. *Linear Programming: An Elementary Introduction*. New York: Macmillan, 1971.

Thrall, Robert M. and Leonard Tornhein. *Vector Spaces and Matrices*. New York: Dover, 1970.

Tierney, John A. *Differential Equations*. Boston: Allyn & Bacon, 1979.

von Neumann, John and Oscar Morgenstern. *Theory of Games and Economic Behavior* (3rd ed.). Princeton, NJ: Princeton University Press, 1953.

Wonnacott, Thomas H. *Calculus: An Applied Approach*. New York: Wiley, 1977.

Zionts, Stanley. *Linear and Integer Programming*. Englewood Cliffs, NJ: Prentice-Hall, 1974.

Index

STANDARD FORMS FOR INTEGRATION

$$\int dx = x + C.$$

$$\int K\, dx = K \int dx, \text{ where } K \text{ is any constant}$$

$$\int [du + dv] = \int du + \int dv$$

$$\int x^n\, dx = \frac{x^{n+1}}{n+1} + C, n \neq -1.$$

$$\int u^n\, du = \frac{u^{n+1}}{n+1} + C, n \neq -1.$$

$$\int \frac{1}{u}\, du = \ln u + C$$

$$\int e^u\, du = e^u + C.$$

$$\int a^u\, du = \frac{a^u}{\ln a} + C.$$

$$\int \sin u\, du = -\cos u + C.$$

$$\int \cos u\, du = \sin u + C.$$

$$\int \sec^2 u\, du = \tan u + C.$$

$$\int ue^u\, du = e^u(u - 1) + C.$$

$$\int \ln u\, du = u \ln u - u + C.$$

$$\int u^n \ln u\, du = u^{n+1}\left[\frac{\ln u}{n+1} - \frac{1}{(n+1)^2}\right] + C.$$